DATE DUE

DEMCO 38-296

INTERNATIONAL ENCYCLOPEDIA OF PUBLIC POLICY AND ADMINISTRATION

INTERNATIONAL ENCYCLOPEDIA OF PUBLIC POLICY AND ADMINISTRATION

Jay M. Shafritz

EDITOR IN CHIEF

Volume 4: R-Z

Westview Press

A Member of the Perseus Books Group

Copyright © 1998 by Westview Press, A Member of the Perseus Books Group

Published in 1998 in the United States of America by Westview Press, 5500 Central Avenue, Boulder, Colorado 80301-2877, and in the United Kingdom by Westview Press, 12 Hid's Copse Road, Cumnor Hill, Oxford OX2 9JJ

Library of Congress Cataloging-in-Publication Data

The international encyclopedia of public policy and administration /
   Jay M. Shafritz, editor in chief.
       p.   cm.
     Includes bibliographical references (p.   ) and index.
     Contents: v. 1. A-C – v. 2. D-K – v. 3. L-Q – v. 4. R-Z, index.
     ISBN 0-8133-9973-4 (vol. 1 : hardcover : alk. paper). – ISBN
0-8133-9974-2 (vol. 2 : hardcover : alk. paper). – ISBN
0-8133-9975-0 (vol. 3 : hardcover : alk. paper). – ISBN
0-8133-9976-9 (vol. 4 : hardcover : alk. paper)
     1. Public policy–Encyclopedias.   2. Public administration–
Encyclopedias.   I. Shafritz, Jay M.
H97.I574   1998
351'.03–dc21   97-34169
                                                                          CIP

The paper used in this publication meets the requirements of the American National Standard for Permanence of Paper for Printed Library Materials Z39.48-1984.

10   9   8   7   6   5   4   3

R

RAINY DAY FUND. A sum of money set aside by a government during normal times, to be drawn down during periods of fiscal stress.

Rationale and Operation

Rainy day funds are primarily a tool of state government finance, because most states are prevented from using deficit finance. Thus, in order to deal with unanticipated downturns in state revenues, states can build up a surplus of funds during normal times that can be drawn down when revenue growth declines.

The legal prohibitions on deficit finance vary in their details from state to state, but most states can simply build up a surplus of general revenues in one year that can then be spent in later years. Alternatively, they can set up explicit rainy day funds to be used to alleviate fiscal stress caused by recessions or other problems. Surplus balances built up in general revenues, outside of explicit rainy day funds, can be used to mitigate fiscal stress, but three factors work against a state's building up general revenues. First, a legislature has many pressures to spend money, making it difficult for a state to build up revenues to begin with and making the revenues it does build vulnerable to being drawn down in later years, whether or not the state faces any fiscal problems. Second, a state's prudent accumulation of general revenues may signal its taxpayers that taxes can be cut. (One of the factors leading to the passage of California's Proposition 13 in 1978 was the large balance of general revenue funds held by the state.) Third, many states have constitutional requirements limiting the amount by which general revenues can accumulate. Thus, states have an incentive to set up explicit rainy day funds, which are built up during normal years and drawn down when states experience fiscal stress.

The establishment of explicit rainy day funds is a relatively recent development in the United States, prompted in large part by fiscal crises that the states suffered during the 1982 and 1991 recessions. In 1982 only 12 states had rainy day funds, but the number increased to 44 states by 1994.

The provisions of these funds vary significantly from state to state. Some states require that money be deposited into their funds, but others have no requirement. Certain contingencies need to occur in some states before money can be withdrawn. Other states allow withdrawal of funds at any time, subject only to majority approval of the legislature. Some states have capped the amount that can be placed in their rainy day fund, and others have not.

The evidence suggests that, on one hand, states have been relatively prudent in not withdrawing rainy day funds until fiscal problems pushed them to do so, meaning that explicit withdrawal requirements have had little effect on the performance of the funds. On the other hand, states without an explicit requirement that money be deposited into their rainy day funds have been lax about building their funds up, so they have found themselves more underfunded than have states with explicit rainy day deposit requirements.

Fiscal Stress and Rainy Day Funds

During the 1950s and 1960s state government budgets grew much faster than in the 1970s and 1980s, partly because states expanded their tax bases and partly because they increased tax rates on the bases they already taxed. Because of more rapidly growing revenues before the 1970s, states did not suffer widespread fiscal problems until the early 1970s. State fiscal problems during the 1970s might have been viewed as being a part of recessions and slow growth at the national level, but hindsight has shown that states have had significantly more severe fiscal problems in the 1970s and after, when compared to earlier decades. By the 1970s, state taxes had already risen significantly, and taxpayer resistance to new increases was beginning to grow. During the recessions of 1982 and 1991, many states ran into significant fiscal problems because their spending commitments exceeded their revenue growth during those recessions. It was in response to these fiscal crises during recessionary periods that many states established rainy day funds.

Even though states can set aside general revenues during good years and use those surplus general revenues to augment expenditures during recessions, explicit rainy day funds offer a number of advantages. First, because the money is set aside for budget stabilization purposes, it is insulated to a degree from demands for additional expenditures. There will always be a greater demand for government expenditures than there will be revenues to fund those expenditures, and an explicit rainy day fund helps to enforce the fiscal discipline to save during good years in order to help smooth expenditures over the business cycle. Second, a surplus of general revenue funds can lead to a call for lower taxes, which would defeat the purpose of setting the money aside as general revenue surpluses. Third, some states have explicit provisions to prevent the accumulation of excess general revenues, which in some cases require at least a partial refund of tax collections that exceed expenditures.

The cyclical nature of tax revenues is not the only reason states might want to set aside rainy day funds. Revenues might also be desired in the event of a bad revenue forecast, or as a result of changes in federal tax laws that adversely affect state revenue collections. (The use of rainy day funds to offset changes in federal tax law is explicitly provided for in the regulations governing Virginia's rainy day fund.) In addition, rainy day funds might also be used to cover unanticipated expenditures, such as disaster relief. A number of states have established separate disaster relief funds in addition to their rainy day funds.

Operation of the Funds

Because rainy day funds are the creation of state governments, every state's rainy day fund has different provisions. In most states, rainy day fund balances can be accessed by simple legislative approval–which leaves open the threat that the funds will routinely be raided to augment state budgets when the legislature wants to increase expenditures. Other states have some type of trigger mechanism, such as a specified shortfall in revenues, that keeps funds from being allocated except for those clearly specified contingencies. In practice, the lack of constraints on withdrawals does not appear to have been a problem, and states that allow funds to be accessed with legislative approval have not had any worse experiences with their funds than states with clearly defined triggers.

Some states have legal requirements mandating the amount of money that must be deposited into their rainy day funds, but others make deposits into their funds by appropriation rather than by a rigid requirement that money be added. States without deposit requirements have found that their rainy day funds are consistently smaller than states that mandate requirements, and at the extreme, some states have created rainy day funds but do not have any money in them. It appears that unless states have a legal requirement that deposits of a specific amount be made into a rainy day fund, their legislatures do not have the fiscal discipline to make deposits. (For example, 38 states had established rainy day funds by 1989, but only 29 of those states had positive balances in the funds.) To be effective, the simple creation of a rainy day fund is not enough. A state must also have some legally mandated schedule for contributing to the fund if the fund is to work as it is designed to.

Some states have chosen to cap their rainy day funds so that they cannot grow beyond the specified limits. The most common upper limit is either 5 or 10 percent of the state's annual budget. Many states have no cap, however. The rationale for a ceiling, though, is to prevent states from accumulating unnecessarily large amounts of surplus funds. Typically, rainy day fund provisions call for tax cuts and refunds to taxpayers if the rainy day fund exceeds its maximum specified size. States with ceilings on their rainy day funds tend to have smaller funds than states without

ceilings, although states rarely fill the fund completely. A cap may have the effect of reducing deposits into a fund because it creates a concern among legislators that taxes will have to be cut if the cap is reached.

The Optimal Size of Rainy Day Funds

How large of a rainy day fund should a state create? The answer depends upon the goals the state hopes to achieve by having the fund. One way to analyze the question is to assume that a state wants a rainy day fund large enough to eliminate completely any fiscal stress due to a recession. (The absence of fiscal stress can be defined as expenditure growth remaining at its long-run trend-level, without tax increases.) Some calculations from the 1991 recession show that to maintain trend expenditure growth without increasing taxes, the typical state would have to have a rainy day fund equal to 34 percent of its annual budget. No state has ever come close to having this much in surplus funds, and, as already noted, some states have capped their rainy day funds at levels as low as 5 or 10 percent of their expenditures. During a normal recession, rainy day funds of this magnitude would be inadequate to avoid fiscal stress.

Other goals may be more appropriate than the maintaining of trend expenditure growth without tax increases to avoid fiscal stress. A simple elimination of fiscal stress by this measure might actually understate the amount of fiscal stress, because many categories of state expenditures tend to be countercyclical. In order to meet countercyclical demands for state government services, states might want to increase their expenditure growth during recessions, and, in this case, even larger rainy day funds would be appropriate. Alternatively, a reduction in public sector expenditure growth might seem appropriate at a time when private sector growth is slowing. Thus, rainy day funds might be viewed more as a buffer to guard against larger-than-expected revenue declines rather than as a source of revenues intended to make up the entire amount of revenue shortfalls. Viewed in this way, a rainy day fund equal to 5 or 10 percent of a state's budget is probably reasonable.

Although a cushion of 5 or 10 percent might at first seem substantial, recessions often last more than one year, so disbursements from rainy day funds must be spread over several years to eliminate completely any recessionary impact. In the recession of the years 1990–1991, revenues started declining in 1989, before the official onset of the recession. Even though most states were able to cope through 1989 and even 1990, by 1991 they experienced widespread fiscal crises, clearly indicating that the balances they had set aside prior to the recession were insufficient to mitigate the recession's impacts.

The Effectiveness of Rainy Day Funds

Studies examining the effectiveness of rainy day funds show that they are effective in reducing fiscal stress, but they do not come close to eliminating fiscal stress. Even under the best of circumstances, states with rainy day funds may still have to reduce their expenditures or increase taxes. Simply creating a rainy day fund has no effect, but it has been shown that states with rainy day funds that have deposit requirements are less adversely affected by recessions than states with no funds or with funds that do not have deposit requirements. Thus the creation of a deposit requirement is crucial to a rainy day fund's effectiveness. Furthermore, the greater the fund's balance, the more effective the fund is at reducing fiscal stress due to recessions, as would be expected.

Looking at the 1990–1991 recession, one can see that there was a close correlation between the level of surplus balances that states had going into the recession and the severity with which states were impacted by the downturn. Thus, states that by this measure were more in need of surplus balances tended to be the ones that had them. However, the level of balances they had was not sufficient to mitigate the severity of the recession. Furthermore, when states are negatively impacted by recessions, those with rainy day funds are more likely to meet their budgetary shortfalls with expenditure reductions rather than with tax increases. This is, perhaps, because voters believe that the rainy day fund was established to prevent the necessity for tax increases during recessions. Thus, state budgets are likely to be most severely impacted by recessions in states that have rainy day funds but that have failed to contribute to them, because tax increases are less likely. Ironically, the establishment of a rainy day fund without contributing to the fund once it is established is likely to reduce the amount of revenue available to a state during recessions.

Conclusion

Rainy day funds are established to reduce the negative impact of cyclical downturns on state government budgets. Well-designed rainy day funds have been able to mitigate some of the negative impacts of fiscal stress, but no rainy day fund has been large enough to eliminate completely the fiscal stress that results from recessions. An examination of the actual performance of rainy day funds shows that the mere creation of a rainy day fund will not help a state cope with a recession, and may actually hurt, because states with rainy day funds are less likely to increase taxes. The key to establishing an effective rainy day fund is to have a legal requirement that money actually be contributed to the fund.

The creation of a cap on the amount that can be deposited to a rainy day fund also limits its ability to mitigate the adverse effects of a recession. Legal requirements limiting when money can be withdrawn from rainy day funds do not seem to be necessary, however. One might be concerned that legislatures would raid a rainy day fund prematurely unless specific criteria for withdrawing funds were established, but in practice this has not been a problem, and states without explicit criteria seem to benefit as much from their rainy day funds as those with such criteria.

A rainy day fund large enough to completely eliminate any negative fiscal impact from a recession like the 1990–1991 recession would have to be about one-third the size of a state's annual budget. No state has ever had a rainy day fund anywhere near this large, and many cap their funds at much lower levels. Thus, as they are currently constituted, rainy day funds will not be able to smooth state government expenditures completely over the business cycle. However, in many states they are large enough to provide a cushion going into a recession so that they have some extra time to adjust their expenditures to a reduction in the growth of their revenue streams.

RANDALL G. HOLCOMBE

BIBLIOGRAPHY

Bryan, Tom, and Dick Howard, 1979. "Michigan's Budget and Economic Stabilization Fund." *Innovations,* Council of State Governments (May): 1–11.

Crider, Robert A., 1978. *The Impact of Recession on State and Local Finance.* Urban and Regional Development Series No. 6. Columbus, Ohio: Academy for Contemporary Problems.

Elder, Harold W., 1992. "Exploring the Tax Revolt: An Analysis of the Effects of State Tax and Expenditure Limitation Laws." *Public Finance Quarterly,* vol. 20, no. 1 (January): 47–63.

Gold, Steven D., 1983. *Preparing for the Next Recession: Rainy Day Funds and Other Tools for the States.* Legislative Finance Paper No. 41. Denver: National Conference of State Legislatures.

Gramlich, Edward M., 1991. "The 1991 State and Local Fiscal Crises." *Brookings Papers on Economic Activity,* vol. 2: 249–287.

Macsherry, Cathy Daicoff, 1986. "Assessing Revenue-raising Ability: A Private-sector View of Changes." In H. Clyde Reeves, ed., *Measuring Fiscal Capacity.* Boston: Oelgeschlager, Gunn & Hain, in association with the Lincoln Institute of Land Policy.

Mattoon, Richard H., and William A. Testa, 1992. "State and Local Governments' Reaction to Recession." *Economic Perspectives,* Federal Reserve Bank of Chicago, vol. 16, no. 2 (March-April): 19–27.

Vasche, Jon David, and Brad Williams, 1987. "Optimal Government Budgeting Contingency Reserve Funds." *Public Budgeting and Finance,* vol. 7, no. 1 (Spring): 66–82.

Vogel, Robert C., and Robert P. Trost, 1979. "The Response of State Government Receipts to Economic Fluctuations and the Allocation of Counter-Cyclical Revenue Sharing Grants." *Review of Economics and Statistics,* vol. 61, no. 3 (August): 389–400.

RATIONALITY IN PUBLIC ADMINISTRATION.

Rationality is a behavioral consistency with decision rules designed to maximize goal accomplishment.

Rationality in the organizational context is relatively new, given that large organizations are a twentieth-century phenomenon. Rationality may have been implicit in the rules of logic or in the exhortations to efficiency found in scientific management, but a clear reference to rationality only began developing in the 1940s.

The theory of games (Von Neuman and Morgenstern 1944) introduced rational decision strategies, but it was Herbert Simon (1955, 1957) who receives the most credit, along with a Nobel Prize, for introducing "rationality" into the organizational lexicon.

Rationality is both a relevant and a ubiquitous phenomenon in organizational and other social contexts. "All of the social sciences, in one way or another, have to deal with what is rational behavior and how it comes about. My whole career has depended on that fact" (Simon 1993, p. 395). In the behavioral sciences, conscious choice or decisions have been a key focus. "In some ways we can describe decision-making as the most common human activity. Almost everything we do involves decisions" (Watson and Buede 1989, p. 9).

Despite this half-century search by Simon and others for more "rational" approaches to decisionmaking, public administration has often offered only short shrift, if not open scorn, to the benefits of rationality for public decisions. Some of this scorn may result from the political training encountered by most public administration scholars. A rather bogus "straw man" is typically constructed to support other decision strategies. "Comprehensive" is added to rationality in support of these constructions, which typically observe that "according to the rational-comprehensive model, in considering the potential means to the objectives, the public administrator is required to try to project *all* the consequences of each of the means on all the various areas of governmental concern" (Rosenbloom 1993, p. 325). Since it is obvious that no administrator could possibly accomplish all the required steps for rational and comprehensive decisions, rationality in public organizations is often quickly eliminated as a competing decision strategy in a complex and politically contentious organizational world.

Before accepting such swift elimination, however, one should examine more carefully the many meanings, or shades of meaning, of rationality in organization decision. Precisely, how has the concept evolved? What are the conceptual facets or nuances? Equally important, how is rationality limited in organizations, beyond, perhaps, the often-noted failures of comprehensiveness? Correspondingly, what contributions might rational decisions make in the complex and political organizational world of public administration? What is the future of public administration

decisionmaking; will it be more or less rational? How can public organizations become more rational?

Theoretical Bases of Rationality

Instead of being the one "impossible dream" of organization decisions, rationality has many facets. First, modern definitions of rational decisions are much less demanding than the comprehensive straw men that are so easily "blown away" in some fields. Simon now symbolizes this simpler approach, after having studied the concept for fifty years.

> I don't mean anything very complicated by rational. Behavior is rational, and the decisions leading up to behavior are rational if it turns out that the behavior prescribed is well adapted to its goals—whatever those goals might be. Rationality is the set of skills or aptitudes we use to see if we can get from here to there—to find courses of action that will lead to the accomplishment of our goals. (1993, p. 393)

Others have used simple definitions of rationality, as well. Rational decisionmaking "involves . . . nothing but consistent preferences and (to anticipate) consistent plans" (Elster 1983, p. 10). "We will say that we are rational when, having adopted rules which our statements or actions should conform to, we act in a way that is consistent with them" (Watson and Buede 1989, p. 12).

In all of these definitions, there are two major components, although some clearly emphasize only one. These components of rationality are goal- or ends-based rationality and process- or means-based rationality. The difference is simply answered by one of the following two questions. First, did we maximize our level of goal accomplishment? Or, second (disregarding the end result), did we follow a carefully established set of decision rules? In reality, it is nearly impossible to separate goals-based from process-based rationality. The definition offered previously includes both, but both definitional dimensions deserve some specific consideration here.

Goals- or Ends-Based Rationality

With ends-based rationality, one defines the quality of a decision by how well it achieves its ultimate objectives. Ends-based rationality is thus more descriptive than prescriptive. It follows rules of logic. Although it is somewhat technical, in one ends-based approach, rationality is defined as the "dependent variable of a decision-making process," reflecting "the extent to which the expected value of decision error has been effectively minimized" (Sutherland 1977, p. 47).

In this domain of rationality, once the goals are determined, the administrator follows rules of logic to "optimize" the decision outcome. "We argue that rationality has a lot to do with consistency. If I assert that A implies B, and also that B implies C, then I will presumably assert that A implies C. We say that it is irrational to do otherwise. . . . We are . . . making an inference according to a principle of logic, namely that implication should be transitive" (Watson and Buede 1989, p. 12). Thus, once the goal is established, logical decision rules should prevail to maximize the choice.

Simon has defined this domain as "economic rationality." "You decide what is rational by looking at the action taken. Does it in fact achieve the goals? How does the administrator know which choice will achieve this end? You all know what the answer is. You choose the one with the greatest utility" (Simon 1993, pp. 395–396). Obviously, the greatest unanswered question with ends-based rationality involves determining just what the goals are.

Toward this end, James March (1988) offered a variety of alternative rationalities. Among these are "game rationality," in which individuals interact with other individuals or social institutions based on their calculations of self-interest. Another type is "adaptive rationality," which emphasizes the learning occurring when individuals and institutions make repetitive decisions. Other types of rationality include: political rationality, social rationality, economic rationality, organizational rationality, and the like. The point is that rational decisions involve choosing the alternative that will optimize whatever goal the individual or organization is seeking to accomplish. The question is Are humans able, conceptually, to gather and to analyze all the information required to accomplish that task?

Process- or Means-Based Rationality?

Process-based rationality requires following systematic steps to make rational decisions. It is assumed that following these steps will accomplish the most optimal outcome, but the emphasis is on procedure. This type of rationality may be implied from the antipolitical emphasis on efficiency of earlier administrative scientists, such as Gulick and Urwick. Process-based rationality is more prescriptive; it emphasizes how administrators should make decisions, putting less emphasis on the decision outcomes.

Works abound with guidance on rational ways to make decisions. They usually include specific steps, such as, formulate the approach to analysis, collect data, build a model, process the decision, run a sensitivity analysis, and evaluate the outcomes (Nutt 1989). These models stress a systematic approach to decisionmaking. Simon (1993) gives reference to this as psychological rationality.

March (1988) has observed that rationality involves two kinds of guesses: guesses about future consequences of current actions and guesses about future preferences. He further observed that "models of rational choice seem

obviously appropriate as guides to intelligent action, but more problematic for predicting behavior. In practice, the converse seems closer to the truth" (March 1988, p. 267). Apparently, March now believes that people often behave more rationally than he first presumed.

The Reality of Public Decisions: The Limits of Rationality

Even though rationality would appear to be a "guide to intelligent action," there are many limitations that have received abundant attention by scholars for several years. First, rational choice is a normative concept. It is an approach adopted largely in the Western world. There are other competing approaches, such as randomization and intuition. With randomization, one might simply toss a coin to achieve a decision that is objective and fair. This approach is used in many athletic contests and with scientific sampling. If our rational goal is to be fair, randomization works well when each alternative has an equal claim on the outcome. Intuition, alternately, involves choice. Decisionmakers are urged to trust their feelings or "gut instincts." A primary assumption here is that administrative decisionmakers have a wealth of background information and learning that guides a decision process better than the gathering and analyzing of new data.

Both of these decision models imply that the inherent limitations of rational decisions are too great to overcome. To assess these limitations, the principal problems inherent in complex, administrative decisions should be considered. The four principal problems are (1) complexity, (2) uncertainty, (3) conflicting objectives, and (4) multiple decisionmakers (Watson and Buede 1989, p. 11). These problems have given rise to two prominent schools of decision thought and practice. In the face of complex and uncertain choices, some have proposed incrementalism as a decision strategy. Correspondingly, decisions in a political milieu with conflicting objectives and multiple decisionmakers have led others to propose, perhaps with assignation, a pluralist approach.

Incrementalism and Bounded Rationality

An incremental approach naturally follows from perceived limitations in rationality. "Critics of the rational-comprehensive model of decision making argue that it is unrealistic" (Rosenbloom 1993, p. 331). Inherent in these criticisms is that the ability to gather information pales in comparison to the enormous complexity and uncertainty of the decisions. "The capacity of the human mind for formulating and solving complex problems is very small compared with the size of the problems whose solution is required for objectively rational behavior in the real world" (Simon 1957, p. 198). Therefore, incrementalists argue, the administrator is well advised simply to make decisions on a very limited basis—"successive limited approximations" (Lindblom 1959). An apt metaphor might be how people proceed when a strange building goes suddenly dark. They proceed very slowly and with considerable caution.

One leading decision theorist has expounded on the specific informational limitations that might justify that decisionmaking approach. Anthony Downs (1966) noted that (1) decisionmakers are limited in their human capacity for processing information, (2) they are limited by the time available for those decisions, (3) administrative decisionmakers are limited by the number of activities that draw their attention away from focusing on any one problem, (4) the amount of information initially available is only a small fraction of what is needed, (5) the cost of procuring additional data rises rapidly as it is increasingly needed, and (6) some information cannot be gathered at all (p. 75). In these cases, the smallest adjustment possible defines, for incrementalists, the appropriate range of decision outcomes. Of course, a major criticism of the incremental approach is its conservatism, since long-range goals are often avoided.

With the informational limits of humans in mind, both Simon and Etzioni have offered solutions. Simon recognized the human computational limitations. He proposed the adoption of sensible decision procedures that focused on making decisions when information was sufficient for a satisfactory solution. "As a short-hand label for such procedures, [Simon] coined the term 'satisficing'" (March 1988, p. 270). Satisficing (a combination of "satisfy" and "suffice") requires the administrator to gather only a sufficient amount of information to reach a satisfactory conclusion. Simon defines the utility of satisficing when he says,

> The question is not how the search (for information) is carried out, but how it is decided when to terminate it—that is, the amount of search. . . . In an optimizing model, the correct point of termination is found by equating the marginal cost of search with the (expected) marginal improvement in the set of alternatives. In a satisficing model, search terminates when the best offer exceeds an aspiration level that itself adjusts gradually to the value of the offers received so far. . . . [The] search becomes another factor of production. . . . Information gathering is not a free activity, and . . . unlimited amounts of it are not available (Simon 1978, p. 10).

Hence, given the inability of public administrators to be perfectly rational in terms of goal accomplishment—their inability to gather all the information required for total comprehensiveness—they should adopt a decision rule that allows them to stop searching when an alternative has been found that satisfies a reasonable aspiration level for goal ac-

complishment. In this sense, Simon's focus is on moderating decision goals and outcomes.

Even such a simple compromise, however, is not without critics. Jon Elster has argued that the reality of bounded rationality is both its main strength and its main weakness. It is important to understand that people should and usually do discontinue searching when they are happy that a particular answer is good enough, but "there is to my knowledge no robust explanation of why people have the aspiration levels they do. . . . The theory describes behaviour, but does not really explain it" (Elster 1989, p. 29) He concludes that the rational choice hypothesis is simpler, more general, and more powerful than bounded rationality, that is, people are guided by their aspiration levels. Elster has further observed that determining when the marginal utility of additional information no longer justifies the continued search for it involves an extremely rational choice. Thus, although some might argue that public decisions are not rational when they are insufficiently comprehensive, Elster argues the opposite. Being totally comprehensive is, itself, irrational.

Etzioni (1967) has proposed a mixed-scanning approach in which small decisions are handled incrementally and larger decisions confront a more rational process. More specifically, long-range goals and objectives would deserve more rational and comprehensive scrutiny, but decisions that are consistent with goals and have little effect on them could cause the decisionmaker to avoid a tedious and detailed analysis. According to Etzioni,

> Each of the two elements in mixed-scanning [thus] helps to reduce the effects of the particular shortcomings of the other; incrementalism reduces the unrealistic aspects of rationalism by limiting the details required in fundamental decisions, and . . . rationalism helps to overcome the conservative slant of incrementalism by exploring longer-run alternatives (1967, p. 390).

Pluralistic Garbage Cans

Pluralism is a concept that was developing about the same time as rationality. It describes, fairly accurately, most democratic political processes, both in the United States and abroad. As a decision model, pluralism meets the twin challenges of conflicting objectives and multiple decisionmakers. Strict rational choice might define the public interest in goal-based terms—what decision or policy is best for the community in terms of achieving its ends? Pluralism, however, defines the public interest in process terms as decisions that emerge victorious, if you will, from the conflicts between competing interests. Hence, the "best" policies on civil rights or the environment results from the interaction of opposing sides. Pluralism may be more descriptive of domestic policy, since competing groups play a smaller role in military strategy.

Some might argue that pluralistic decisions are themselves rational in a politically contentious world. Indeed, Aaron Wildavsky highlighted political versus economic rationality when he said, " I have sought to emphasize the economic rationality, however laudible in its own sphere, ought not to swallow up political rationality" (1966, p. 310). Moreover, current concepts and practices, such as strategic planning and Total Quality Management, include pluralistic components with their respective emphases on stakeholders and customers. Although that may well be useful in some decision arenas, Kemeny (cited in Morgan and Henrion 1990, p. 30) counters by asking if any rational person would fly in an airplane designed by Congress, "with each committee designing one component of it and an eleventh-hour conference committee deciding how the various pieces should be put together?" Even though Congress does not design airplanes (some Defense Department procurement officials may disagree), it does make major decisions about public policy in much the same way.

An extension, or perhaps a distortion, of pluralism is the garbage can model of organization described by Michael Cohen, James March, and Johan Olsen as "organized anarchies" (1972). There are three principle components to the garbage can model. First, the organization has a variety of inconsistent and ill-defined preferences (conflicting objectives). Second, even its own members fail to understand, and may even reject, its decision rules and processes (unclear decision technology). Finally, there is fluid participation in which there is a variety of time and effort contributed by group members. There are often loose boundaries as to who can participate (multiple decisionmakers) (Cohen, March, and Olsen 1972, p. 1). Cohen, March, and Olsen focused specifically on academic institutions as organized anarchies, but there are many relevant cases in other government settings. A wide lattitude in decision procedures invites lobbying and other forms of influence peddling, which gives rise to questions, not only of rationality but also sometimes of ethical and criminal behavior, as well.

The Benefits of Rationality: The Other Side of Public Decisions

With all the limits of rational decisions, one should wonder if the attempt is worth the effort. Why should public administrators consider rational decision approaches? "Rationality is defined in terms of adherence to a set of rules; there is no reason why a decision-maker ought to abide by the rules of decision theory, or indeed any rules for that matter!" (Watson and Buede, 1989, p. 52). Perhaps, a partial answer to the question lies with acknowledging human limitations in decisionmaking. Humans are not only limited by information deficiencies, but these deficiencies often encourage a greater use of biases and heuristics in decisionmaking.

Heuristics are a source of limits on decisionmaking. They include "rules of thumb" adopted by decisionmakers, as well as subconscious judgment routines that limit optimal outcomes. An early study of heuristics looked at how humans handled the most elementary principle of probability, the conjunction rule. Subjects were presented personality sketches and asked to determine the more probable outcome. For example,

> Linda is 31 years old, single, outspoken, and very bright. She majored in philosophy. As a student, she was deeply concerned with issues of discrimination and social justice, and also participated in anti-nuclear demonstrations. Which is more probable: A. Linda is a bank teller; B. Linda is a bank teller who is active in the feminist movement? (Kahneman and Tversky 1982, p. 126)

The researchers found that in a large sample of "statistically naive" undergraduates, 86 percent picked the second statement to be more probable, but only 50 percent of a sample of psychology graduate students, presumedly less naive, picked B. It might be added that Daniel Kahneman and Amos Tversky also asked their respondents generally if "the probability of X is always greater than the probability of X and Y," and although 81 percent of their respondents endorsed the principle in theory, most of them had obviously been unable to apply the conjunction rule in practice.

What this implies is that humans are not logical processors of information. Kahneman and Tversky identified three primary heuristics: (1) availability, (2) representativeness, and (3) anchoring and adjustment. The availability heuristic is based on the notion that searchers for decision information simply use information that is readily available—they perform little, if any, searching. Eighty-six percent of one group of respondents replied that more people died each year from motor vehicle accidents than from stomach cancer when, in actuality, over twice as many people died from stomach cancer that year in the United States. It was also found that two typical newspapers had published 137 reports on motor vehicle deaths during the year, but only one on a death due to stomach cancer (Russo and Schoemaker 1989, p. 83). Thus, the availability of information may have given a false perception of reality.

The representative heuristic stems from the fact that humans are not governed by information derived from a representative sample of their experiences; instead, they remember only certain aspects or examples from their situations. Vivid examples dominate our consciousness; we are affected by selective perception and recall (Nutt 1989).

Finally, humans alter current "reality" to conform with the past. They are likely to interpret new events to be consistent with long-held perceptions and beliefs. In sum, humans, left to their own devices, are not good data handlers, which is probably why research methods courses are required for most master's level education of managers and administrators. Of course, a related question may be Are good researchers more successful decisionmakers than people with no methods training?

Even the framing of decisions or choices affects their outcome. Survey researchers have known that the number of alternatives affects choice. Since people avoid extremes, the use of a three-point scale generates a different distribution than does a five-point scale. Moreover, the wording of alternatives, even though they present the same alternatives, can significantly affect the result.

Barbara McNeil, Stephen Pauker, and Amos Tversky (1988) surveyed 390 postgraduate students at Brigham and Women's Hospital and Harvard Medical School and 402 medical and science students at the Hebrew University in Jeruselem, Israel. The subjects were asked to prescribe radiation or surgery for lung cancer. The problem was framed by information stated either in terms of *survival* (100% will live through treatment, 77% will live beyond the first year, and 22% will be alive at the end of five years) or *mortality* (0% will die during treatment, 23% will die by the end of the first year, and 78% will have died by the end of five years), or in a mixed mode. The percentages for both the American and Israeli groups was very similar. Although the outcomes of the frames are identical, 18 percent of the subjects favored radiation over surgery when the information was presented in the survival mode, 47 percent favored radiation when it was presented in the mortality mode, and 40 percent favored radiation when it was presented in the mixed mode. (The prospect of dying seems to have more impact than the prospect of surviving.) Overall, the choice of radiation treatment versus surgery was over 2.5 times greater when the likely outcome was stated in terms of mortality, rather than in terms of survival. And, in this case, the judgments were not rendered by "naive" subjects.

Biases and values have an obvious affect on decision outcomes. In politics, certain outcomes are desired because of who wins and who loses. Blatant political interference in policymaking has been the subject of popular as well as professional periodicals in public administration, and it may thrive in a garbage can situation. Moreover, in a political world, decisions are often made to be consistent with a particular political philosophy. Hence, policies may be labeled as "liberal" and "conservative," and generate support for mere ideological reasons. But, many biases are found in much more subtle ways.

Paul Nutt (1989) has labeled "unconscious preferences" as preferences that are derived from personal management styles. Based on the Myers-Briggs typology, he

has categorized information-gathering styles as systematic, speculative, judicial, and heuristic. The resultingly different decision styles are characterized as procedural, evaluative, ordered, intellectual, political, mediator, and so on. The point is, decisionmaker personalities may greatly influence their decision styles, and thus, their decision outcomes.

Many biases accrue from normal human frailties. Irving L. Janis (1989) has identified several of the personal biases resulting from "affiliative" decision rules. Among these, virtually self-explanatory rules are avoid punishment and one-upmanship, follow the party line and preserve group harmony (or the "group think" concept, which made that author famous). Of course, some of these affiliative rules can be applied in the political ways discussed previously. In sum, decisionmakers lean toward alternatives that accrue to their narrowly conceived self-interests. Although their biases may be concealed, greater weight is placed on alternatives that give greater credit and support to the particular decisionmaker.

Nutt (1989) has provided an excellent summary of human limitations in decisionmaking. These limitations involve steps to simplify and reduce effort in the processing of information, including heuristics, a reluctance to adjust preliminary judgments, and the affect of vivid information or of illusory associations often mistaken as causal. Second, errors in judgment occur from biases and values found in decisionmaking styles and those revolving around wishful thinking about outcomes. Third, decisionmakers often resist learning from their own experiences. More often than not, no particular process is established to evaluate previous decisions, and biased hindsight often leads decisionmakers to place the most favorable light on their past accomplishments.

Overall, even with good information, there is reason to question how decisionmakers will process it. Left to unfettered discretion, decisions by well-meaning administrators will likely become victims of personal bias or faulty decision rules that flaw decision outcomes.

Recommendations for Improving Rationality in Decisionmaking

In its brief history, rationality has been both praised and criticized. The primary criticism stems from a person's inability to gather all the information necessary for his or her decision to be both rational and comprehensive. Two competing schools have formed around decision problems. *Incrementalism* focuses on complexity and uncertainty of public decisions, and *pluralism* centers on the conflicting values and multiple decisionmakers characteristic of most public settings. In the face of these competing ideas, however, public decisionmakers have been found lacking in the ability to process the limited information available to them. They are often biased or, in the absence of guidance, they adopt simplistic decision rules, such as heuristics, to guide the process, but these "rules of thumb" often misinform decisionmakers. Five points are offered to enhance public decisions through rationality.

Decision Rules

Stephen Watson and Dennis Buede (1989) offer advice on improving decisions through rationality. "To be rational in decision-making, therefore, we will need to construct a set of rules that we will wish to adopt in determining what to do in complex decision situations" (p. 12). They offer four properties needed to inform those rules: (1) There needs to be a clear set of decision rules; (2) the rules must address the values of problem-owners; (3) the rules must state what is rational in the face of uncertainty; and (4) the rules must steer decision-makers through complex problems (Watson and Buede 1989, p. 17).

Multicriteria Decision Models (MCDMs)

The decision rules should be sufficient to deal with uncertainty, complexity, conflicting objectives, and multiple decisionmakers. One likely approach is with multicriteria decision models (Keeney and Raiffa 1976). MCDMs have been used extensively in Europe, and they are increasingly being used in the United States. There should be a necessary balance between the power of the model and its simplicity. A general rule is that the model should be as simple as possible, including all the necessary components, but it should be no simpler.

Technology

The increasing power and use of computer technology has made information processing, especially in complex settings, more feasible. Each year, new information and more powerful decision models are developed. In some cases, the simplicity of decision models makes them politically powerful—especially with untrained decisionmakers. Using computers to aid decisions will become increasingly prevalent as those models are enhanced (Nagel 1987).

Training

"The basic reason for the lack of rationality in the administration of complex enterprise is the lack of properly qualified administrators" (Sutherland 1977, p. 24). It is important to train administrative decisionmakers in the use (and make them aware of the possible abuse) of computer-aided decision techniques. Inappropriate uses of MCDMs, however, often generate incorrect conclusions, especially when they are employed by untrained decisionmakers (Teasley 1989 and 1994).

Professionalism

Professionalism refers to the continued development of, in this case, public administrators. Thus, with regard to training, professional public decisionmakers should be keenly aware and interested in improving the process. In addition, for professional administrators to be effective, they must make decisions that accomplish goals in a rational manner. Following the "rational" decision guidelines suggested here can make them more effective with other decisionmakers in a pluralistic political world. It is, therefore, not an exaggeration to believe that professionalism and rationality in public administration will experience parallel and complimentary developments during the twenty-first century.

C. E. TEASLEY III

BIBLIOGRAPHY

Cohen, Michael D., James G. March, and Johan P. Olsen, 1972. "A Garbage Can Model of Organizational Choice." *Administrative Science Quarterly*, vol. 17 (March): 1–25.

Downs, Anthony, 1966. *Inside Bureaucracy*. Boston: Little, Brown.

Elster, Jon, 1983. *Sour Grapes: Studies in the Subversion of Rationality*, Cambridge, England: Cambridge University Press.

———, 1989. *Solomonic Judgements: Studies in the Limitations of Rationality*. Cambridge, England: Cambridge University Press.

Etzioni, Amitai, 1967. "Mixed Scanning: A 'Third' Approach to Decision Making." *Public Administration Review*, 27: 385–92.

Janis, Irving L., 1989. *Crucial Decisions*. New York: Free Press.

Kahneman, Daniel, and Amos Tversky, 1982. "On the Study of Statistical Intuitions." *Cognition*, vol. 11: 123–141.

Keeney, Ralph, and Howard Raiffa, 1976. *Decisions with Multiple Objectives*. New York: Wiley.

Lindblom, Charles E., 1959. "The Science of 'Muddling-Through.' " *Public Administration Review* 19:79–88.

March, James G., 1988. *Decisions and Organizations*. New York: Basil Blackwell.

McNeil, Barbara J., Stephen G. Pauker, and Amos Tversky, 1988. "On the Framing of Medication Decisions." In David E. Bell, Howard Raiffa, and Amos Tversky, eds., *Decision Making: Descriptive, Normative, and Prescriptive Interactions*. New York: Praeger.

Morgan, M. Granger, and Max Henrion, 1990. *Uncertainty: A Guide to Dealing with Uncertainty in Quantitative Risk and Policy Analysis*. Cambridge, England: Cambridge University Press.

Nagel, Stuart S., 1987. "Evaluation Analysis with Microcomputers." *Public Productivity Review*, vol. 10: 67–82.

Nutt, Paul C., 1989. *Making Tough Decisions: Tactics for Improving Managerial Decision Making*. San Francisco: Jossey-Bass.

Rosenbloom, David H., 1993. *Public Administration: Understanding Management, Politics, and Law in the Public Sector*. 3d ed. New York: McGraw-Hill.

Russo, Edward J., and Paul J. H. Schoemaker, 1989. *Decision Traps: Ten Barriers to Brilliant Decision-Making and How to Overcome Them*. New York: Doubleday.

Simon, Herbert A., 1955. "A Behavioral Model of Rational Choice." *Quarterly Journal of Economics*, vol. 69: 99–118.

———, 1957. *Models of Man*. New York: John Wiley and Sons.

———, 1978. "Rationality as Process and as Product of Thought." *American Economic Review*, vol. 68: 1–16.

———, 1993. "Decision Making: Rational, Nonrational, and Irrational." *Educational Administration Quarterly*, vol. 29 (August): 392–411.

Sutherland, John W., 1977. *Administrative Decision-Making: Extending the Bounds of Rationality.* New York: Van Nostrand Reinhold.

Teasley III, C. E., 1989. "Some Subtle and Some Not-So-Subtle Ways Analysts Can Determine Computer Assisted Outcomes." *Journal of Management Science and Policy Analysis* (Winter): 163–172.

———, 1994. "A Bridge Over Troubled Waters: The Limits of Judgement in Decision Making." *Public Productivity and Management Review,* vol. 17, forthcoming.

Von Neuman, John, and Oskar Morgenstern, 1944. *The Theory of Games and Economic Behavior.* New York: John Wiley.

Watson, Stephen R., and Dennis M. Buede, 1989. *Decision Synthesis: The Principles and Practice of Decision Analysis.* Cambridge, England: Cambridge University Press.

Wildavsky, Aaron, 1966. "The Political Economy of Efficiency: Cost-Benefit Analysis, Systems Analysis, and Program Budgeting." *Public Administration Review* 26: 292–310.

RECOMMENDATION.

An act that is not legally binding but that has been adopted by the institutions of the European Union, often to complement existing European Economic Community (EEC) legislation, to float ideas, or to offer guidelines regarding the interpretation of national provisions adopted. Though recommendations cannot create rights for individuals that must be protected and upheld by national courts, they do have some legal significance, however variable.

On the question of whether the Court of Justice has jurisdiction to give rulings on the interpretation of nonbinding acts such as recommendations, the Court has concluded that it has jurisdiction by virtue of the fact that article 177 of the European Economic Community Treaty, which defines areas in which the Court may make rulings, does not explicitly exclude recommendations.

Opinions under the EEC are similar to recommendations to the extent that they are not legally binding. They offer guidelines and advice that national authorities may follow.

Recommendations under the treaty establishing European Coal and Steel Community, signed in Paris in 1951, are equivalent to directives under the treaty signed in Rome in 1957, which established the European Economic Community in 1958.

MARGARET MARY MALONE

BIBLIOGRAPHY

Hartley, T. C., 1989. *The Foundations of European Community Law.* 2d ed. London: Clarendon Press.

Lasok, D., and J. W. Bridge, 1987. *Law and Institutions of the European Communities.* 4th ed. London: Butterworths.

Nugent, Neill, 1991. *The Government and Politics of the European Community.* 2d ed. London: Macmillan.

Parry, Anthony, and James Dinnage, 1981. *EEC Law.* 2d ed. London: Sweet and Maxwell.

Wyatt, D., and A. Dashwood, 1987. *The Substantive Law of the EC.* 2d ed. London: Sweet and Maxwell.

RECONCILIATION.

A procedure used by the U.S. Congress as part of its budget process to lower the deficit by reducing entitlement spending and, usually, increasing taxes. Beginning with instructions in the budget resolution, reconciliation incorporates a complex series of legislative activities, culminating in a comprehensive bill, changing entitlement programs and tax law.

Budget reconciliation refers to specific budget-related procedures undertaken by congressional committees, and by the full House and Senate when reconciliation instructions are included in the congressional budget resolution. These instructions indicate by committee or federal program the amount of deficit reduction, or budgetary savings, to be achieved over a given period of years. The savings are to be realized as a result of changes to revenue and entitlement legislation initiated by the committees with jurisdiction over revenues and the entitlement programs targeted in the budget resolution. These committees are required to submit new legislation to the budget committees of the House and Senate to reduce spending or increase revenues by the amounts stipulated in the budget resolution.

The budget committees, in turn, package the changes into a single reconciliation bill, usually referred to as an omnibus budget reconciliation bill, and report it to their respective chambers for further action. On the floor of the House and Senate, reconciliation bills are subject to debate and amendment within a relatively strict set of procedural rules designed to expedite passage and insure that the overall deficit reduction goals of the bill are met.

Because they usually cover multiple years and incorporate enormous amounts of spending and revenue changes affecting a range of programs, budget reconciliation bills are typically among the most far-reaching and controversial budget bills passed in any Congress. As entitlement spending became the largest and fastest growing portion of the U.S. federal budget and Congress experienced increasing pressure to reduce the deficit, reconciliation bills became critical to congressional budgeting in the 1980s and 1990s.

Reconciliation as Originally Conceived

Reconciliation derives from the Congressional Budget Act of 1974 (CBA). When Congress attempted to employ reconciliation in the years immediately after passage of the CBA, its purpose was distinctly different from the objectives it has served since 1980. Congress originally attempted to use reconciliation to resolve differences be-

tween budget resolutions when more than one resolution was passed in a given year. During this period, the practice was to pass a tentative resolution early in the year setting total spending and revenue levels and the resulting deficit and debt figures. This resolution was subject to change as spending and revenue decisions were made during the year.

A second resolution, which was to be completed by September 15, near the end of the fiscal year, was the final, or binding, budget resolution. In its original form, reconciliation was to be used in conjunction with this second resolution. It would reconcile the differences between the budget aggregates in the second, or binding, budget resolution and the spending and revenue bills Congress passed since it approved the first, or tentative, budget resolution. This approach assumed that reconciliation could be used to adjust all types of federal spending.

Because the budget resolution triggering reconciliation was considered so late in the fiscal year and because the procedures for producing the savings implied by reconciliation were faulty, this approach to reconciliation proved unworkable, and was abandoned (Schick 1981, p. 5). Congress shifted to a single binding budget resolution, to be adopted early in the fiscal year (the current deadline, though frequently missed, is April 15). Similarly, Congress attempted to address reconciliation earlier in the year by setting a June 15 target for completion of reconciliation legislation. Reconciliation was further adapted by limiting its spending reduction capabilities to a single broad category of spending, referred to as entitlements (see entitlements). These changes, which took effect in the early 1980s, marked the beginning of the employment of reconciliation as a major tool for deficit reduction.

Reconciliation After 1980

Most students of congressional budgeting agree that reconciliation, as we now understand the process, began in 1980, with the development of the fiscal year (FY) 1981–1982 budget (Keith 1981, p. 39). Signaling the beginning of a new and more effective role for reconciliation, Congress shifted reconciliation to the first budget resolution and made relatively minor spending cuts and tax increases that year as part of its budget process. However, reconciliation made its major debut as a tool of deficit reduction the following year.

Reconciliation in 1981 was orchestrated by President Ronald Reagan's budget director, David Stockman, in collaboration with Senator Pete Domenici (R–NM), chairman of the Senate Budget Committee (Miller and Range 1983, pp. 8–13; Tate 1981, p. 1463). Stockman observed that in proposing a sweeping reconciliation bill to implement the President's budget policies in Congress, the White House "wanted something big and new and rolling fast to break down parochial resistance" (Miller and Range 1983, p. 9). In this important year in the evolution of reconciliation, "everything about reconciliation was colossal" (Keith 1981, p. 46). The largest conference committee in congressional history met to iron out differences between the House and Senate versions of reconciliation legislation, producing a final omnibus bill of more than 400 pages (Keith 1981, p. 46).

Reconciliation has subsequently been used in the 1980s and 1990s as the primary procedural means for reducing entitlement spending and raising revenues to lower federal deficits. Though its implementation has varied slightly from year to year and the procedural and political aspects are complex and controversial, the logic of reconciliation is relatively simple.

Reconciliation is the legislative and procedural means by which Congress implements key fiscal policy decisions taken in its budget resolution. Resolutions reflect majority views in Congress regarding spending and revenue totals, as well as the resulting levels of deficits (or surpluses, though none have occurred since passage of the CBA of 1974) and debt. If majorities in Congress agree to lower the deficit by raising revenues or reducing spending for programs referred to as entitlements, that agreement is incorporated into the budget resolution in the form of reconciliation instructions. Because budget resolutions are not laws, and therefore cannot compel changes in fiscal policy, Congress must implement the fiscal policy set out in the resolution by passing the necessary statutory laws. The statutory vehicle for implementing changes in entitlement spending and taxes is reconciliation.

The major exception to this rule is Social Security, the largest, most widely distributed, and most popular entitlement program in the federal budget. By law, Congress is prohibited from using reconciliation to reduce Social Security. It should also be noted that when Congress votes on a budget resolution calling for cuts in entitlement spending or increased taxes to reduce the deficit, it may also approve reductions in other, nonentitlement spending as part of that effort. Those spending cuts, however, are implemented through appropriations bills rather than reconciliation.

Stage One: Reconciliation Instructions

Reconciliation is a two-stage process. It begins with the annual budget resolution, when the decision is made to include entitlement programs and taxes in the congressional deficit reduction policy. Because the budget committees of the House and Senate play a key role in shaping the budget resolution, their decisions regarding the size and scope of the entitlement cuts and tax increases are important. After considering the President's budget request, which may or may not include entitlement cuts and tax increases, the budget committees hold hearings and consult widely within Congress before inserting reconciliation instructions in the budget resolution. Without broad support for such measures–preferably bipartisan congressional support and presidential endorsement–a budget resolution calling for unpopular tax hikes and entitlement cuts may fail.

The reconciliation instructions adopted by the budget committees and approved by the full House and Senate during their deliberations on the budget resolution are written in very general terms. The committees that exercise jurisdiction over the entitlements to be reduced or taxes to be raised are given targets to hit for one year or several years. These targets are expressed as dollars, or as savings to be achieved by the committees named in the instructions. The savings are computed with reference to baselines provided by the Congressional Budget Office. The instructions (and by implication, the budget committees) do not tell the targeted committees how to achieve the indicated savings, only the amounts to be saved by year as part of the overall deficit reduction policy set out in the budget resolution. This preserves for these committees their prerogatives concerning the exact nature of the changes to be made in order to hit their targets.

Once a budget resolution containing reconciliation instructions takes effect, the committees named in those instructions are expected to produce legislation that achieves the savings stipulated in the instructions. Most reconciliation instructions require more than one committee to achieve some savings. The savings can be produced in many ways, depending upon the jurisdiction of the committees named in the instructions. This is true whether the savings are from entitlement program cuts or tax increases. Committees with jurisdiction over both revenues (e.g., user fees) and entitlement programs are even allowed to substitute some tax increases for program cuts, as long as they meet their total savings target. The point in all cases is to adjust current law governing revenues or entitlements in such a manner that spending will be reduced or taxes increased by the targeted amounts.

Stage Two:
Omnibus Reconciliation Legislation

Once the committees required by reconciliation instructions have produced the necessary legislation, their bills are submitted to the appropriate House or Senate Budget Committee. The budget committees compile the separate bills into a single omnibus reconciliation bill and report it to their respective chambers for consideration. As with other major pieces of legislation, the House and Senate produce different versions of reconciliation. Differences between the House-passed and Senate-passed reconciliation bills must be resolved in a conference. Once this is ac-

complished, a single omnibus reconciliation bill can be presented to the President for signature and thus become law.

The Frequency and Scope of
Reconciliation in the 1980s and 1990s

Once reconciliation was adapted for use as a mechanism for reducing entitlement spending and raising taxes as part of the congressional budget process, it became a more or less common part of that process. In 11 of the 15 years between 1980 and 1995, Congress included reconciliation instructions in its budget resolution, and in each of those years omnibus budget reconciliation bills were passed (Keith and Davis 1993, p. 2; Hager 1995). Every reconciliation bill passed by Congress was signed by the President except the original 1995 bill; that bill, the largest reconciliation bill to date, was vetoed by President Bill Clinton (Hager 1995, p. 3286; 1995a, p. 3721).

Though the CBA originally provided for reconciliation bills that covered a single year, Congress has extended the time frame. Reconciliation bills covering three years were the norm in the 1980s, and five-year bills became commonplace in the first half of the 1990s. The 1995 bill, designed to eliminate the deficit by 2002, covered seven years in order to achieve that objective (Hager 1995a, p. 3722).

With two exceptions, every reconciliation bill passed by Congress between 1980 and 1995 included both entitlement spending cuts and tax increases. In terms of their contribution to deficit reduction, the spending cuts and the tax increases in bills incorporating both have been roughly equal over this period (U.S. Senate, Committee on the Budget, n.d., Congressional Budget Office 1993). The first exception was the 1981 reconciliation bill, which included no tax increases. In fact, Congress passed and President Reagan signed separate legislation that year that reduced taxes by an amount larger than the spending cuts in the reconciliation bill (Penner and Abramson 1988, p. 49). In 1995, major tax cuts were actually included in the budget resolution as part of the reconciliation instructions. The ensuing reconciliation bill passed by Congress and vetoed by President Clinton called for US $245 billion in tax cuts (Hager 1995a, p. 3722).

On the floor of the House and Senate, reconciliation bills are considered under special rules intended to increase the likelihood that the savings stipulated in the reconciliation instructions are ultimately achieved. In both the House and the Senate, the rules discourage the attachment of extraneous measures or provisions that would decrease savings, thereby increasing the deficit and defeating the purpose of reconciliation. Time for debate is strictly limited, as are the number and type of amendments that can be offered.

In the Senate, the special rules protect reconciliation against the filibuster. In 1985, the Senate adopted the Byrd rule, named after its principal sponsor, Senator Robert Byrd (D–WV). This rule was later made permanent law by its incorporation within the CBA. The Byrd rule consists of an elaborate system of rules and enforcement mechanisms designed to prevent the attachment of extraneous matter to reconciliation bills. Although extraneous matter is generally understood to refer to items unrelated to the deficit reduction objectives of reconciliation, it must be interpreted within the context of the bill or amendment at issue. Although the Byrd rule spells out criteria defining extraneous matter, its implementation can be contentious. One student of the Byrd rule concluded that "on the whole" it has been used successfully by those opposed to the inclusion of extraneous matter on reconciliation bills (Keith and Davis 1993, p. 8).

Reconciliation Bills
As "Must Pass" Legislation

Reconciliation bills have become "must pass" bills. Such bills are so named because most in Congress assume that the bills must become law within a defined period of time, in order, for example, to keep the government functioning. Reconciliation bills acquire this status for several reasons. First, they incorporate significant savings from program cuts and revenue increases. Without these savings, the deficit reduction goals of the budget resolution cannot be achieved.

Second, they frequently include significant changes to the budget process, added to improve that process or to "lock in" some of the reconciliation savings. For example, Gramm-Rudman-Hollings I (1985), Gramm-Rudman-Hollings II (1987), and the Budget Enforcement Act of 1990 became law as part of reconciliation bills.

Third, Congress frequently includes statutory changes to the federal debt limit on reconciliation bills. Until deficits are completely eliminated, the federal debt will continue to grow, requiring Congress to vote to raise the debt limit. This vote can be less difficult (or simply less visible) if it is made part of a reconciliation bill that purports to reduce the deficit in the future.

These factors, acting in combination, encourage the media to portray reconciliation bills as "the" deficit reduction bill in those years when reconciliation is part of the congressional budget process (Schick 1995, p. 86). This packaging, in turn, makes it easier for members to vote to cut entitlement programs and raise taxes, two positions generally unpopular with voters. One of the procedural tactics associated with reconciliation is to encourage the characterization of reconciliation bills as broad and historic legislation, moving the government toward a more sustainable fiscal policy.

The Effectiveness of Reconciliation

As a tool to assist Congress in reducing the deficit, reconciliation receives mixed reviews. Clearly, it has evolved into a process that can affect broad segments of spending and taxing, affecting many political constituencies and congressional committees. As such, it has been the subject of both praise and blame.

The fact that reconciliation directs committees to make major changes to spending or revenue programs within their jurisdiction was problematic because it challenges the traditional power of those committees to control their agendas. John Gilmour considers reconciliation a "revolutionary tool" that significantly reduces the "virtual veto power committees have had over changes and reductions in entitlement programs" (1990, p. 5). The special protection afforded reconciliation bills to minimize delay and avoid amendments, which might reduce the savings they are to achieve, has alarmed some in Congress. Hence Senator Robert Byrd's reference to reconciliation as a "super, super, colossally super, gag rule" (1994, p. 743).

The new authority to compel spending cuts and raise taxes implicit in reconciliation notwithstanding, the expected savings have not always been realized. Committees, and sometimes congressional leaders, have resisted the trend inherent in reconciliation to give broad authority over other committees to the congressional budget committees. Opposition, grounded in procedural or substantive considerations, is possible because, as Schick has noted, "At all stages, reconciliation depends on the willingness of key congressional participants to make it work" (1990, p. 114).

Given the complexity of the many programs involved in reconciliation, there are many possibilities for budgetary legerdemain with the committee-produced legislation. Some committees have even been able to use reconciliation to expand programs rather than cut them (Schick 1990, p. 116; Meyers 1994, p. 120). For example, of the seven expansions of Medicaid that occurred between 1984 and 1990, six were effected through reconciliation bills (White 1995, p. 60). The *Washington Post* referred to the 1989 reconciliation bill passed by the House as "Wreckonciliation" because of the number and variety of new programs increasing rather than decreasing spending added to that bill (1989, p. A24).

The budget committees have very little power to insure that targeted committees produce their reconciliation bills in a timely manner, or that the bills reported out by the targeted committees actually achieve the savings required in the reconciliation instructions. The budget committees are prohibited by the CBA from making substantive changes to the legislation submitted to them by the targeted committees (Schick 1990; Keith and Davis 1993, p. 55). In the absence of formal penalties for noncompliance, compliance with reconciliation instructions has sometimes been merely symbolic. Congressional leaders, including the budget committee chairs, rely upon the desire of targeted committees to avoid flaunting the policy of Congress as expressed in the budget resolution's reconciliation instructions.

Summary

Reconciliation represents the need for integration within the congressional budget process. Its opposite is the legislative fragmentation, focusing on committee prerogatives, that dominated that process until passage of the CBA in 1974. Integration, however, has not replaced fragmentation; the two countervailing principles continue to coexist in Congress. The evolution of reconciliation reflects this compromise. On one hand, reconciliation defers to the committees targeted in the instructions for specific program cuts and tax increases and minimizes the power of the budget committees to "police" these actions. On the other hand, it has been given extraordinary procedural protections to expedite passage and safeguard budgetary savings.

The fact that reconciliation has been used so frequently since its introduction to congressional budgeting suggests that it serves a valuable purpose. Its association with cutbacks in entitlements pursuant to deficit reduction is particularly important insofar as deficit reduction continues to play a role in national politics. Estimates by the Congressional Budget Office indicate that entitlement spending will continue to increase its already dominant share of federal spending. At the beginning of 1995, this office predicted that total spending would increase by slightly more than US$1 trillion over the next decade, causing deficits to grow. Spending for entitlements accounts for more than 70 percent of this increase (Congressional Budget Office 1995, p. 58).

Reconciliation is simply a means of bringing the political will of the majority to bear on the issue of the deficit and the extent to which entitlement programs will be reduced and taxes increased to reduce it. Its use and evolution will be determined by the many economic and political factors that affect this issue.

RICHARD DOYLE

BIBLIOGRAPHY

Byrd, Robert, 1994. The Senate 1789–1989, Washington, DC: USGPO.

Congressional Budget Office, 1993. *The Economic and Budget Outlook: An Update.* Washington, DC: USGPO.

———, 1995. *The Economic and Budget Outlook: Fiscal Years 1996–2000.* Washington, DC: USGPO.

Gilmour, John, 1990. *Reconcilable Differences, Congress, the Budget Process, and the Deficit.* Berkeley, CA: University of California Press.

Hager, George, 1995. "Reconciliation Now a Major Tool." *Congressional Quarterly,* October 28, p. 2286.

———, 1995a. "Harsh Rhetoric on Budget Spells a Dismal Outlook." *Congressional Quarterly* December 9, pp. 3721–3725.

Keith, Robert, 1981. "Budget Reconciliation in 1981." *Public Budgeting and Finance* (Winter): 37–47.

Keith, Robert, and Edward Davis, 1993. *The Senate's "Byrd Rule" Against Extraneous Matter in Reconciliation Measures.* Washington, DC: Congressional Research Service.

Meyers, Roy T., 1994. *Strategic Budgeting.* Ann Arbor, MI: University of Michigan Press.

Miller, James, and James Range, 1983. "Reconciling an Irreconcilable Budget: The New Politics of the Budget Process." *Harvard Journal of Legislation,* vol. 20, no. 4: 4–30.

Penner, Rudolph, and Alan Abramson, 1988. *Broken Purse Strings, Congressional Budgeting, 1974–1988.* Washington, DC: Urban Institute Press.

Schick, Allen, 1981. *Reconciliation and the Congressional Budget Process.* Washington, DC: AEI.

———, 1990. *The Capacity to Budget.* Washington, DC: Urban Institute Press.

———, 1995. *The Federal Budget, Politics, Policy, Processes.* Washington, DC: Brookings Institution.

Tate, Dale, 1981. "Reconciliation's Long-Term Consequences in Question As Reagan Signs Massive Bill." *Congressional Quarterly* August 15, pp. 1463–1466.

U.S. Senate, Committee on the Budget, n.d. "Summary of Reconciliation Instructions, From Budget Resolution to Public Law, Fiscal Years 1981–1991." Unpublished report.

Washington Post, 1989. Editorial, p. A24.

White, Joseph, 1995. "Budgeting and Health Policymaking." In Thomas Mann and Norman Ornstein, eds., *Intensive Care, How Congress Shapes Health Policy.* Washington, DC: American Enterprise Institute and the Brookings Institution.

RECRUITMENT. A process designed to publicize job openings occurring within an organization and to attract a sufficient number of qualified applicants to fill open positions. Governments throughout the world normally engage in a vast assortment of work activities; therefore, recruitment processes must be developed for an incredibly wide range of public sector job openings.

In the United States there are approximately 17 million public employees working at the national, state, and local levels of government. Approximately one out of six in the total workforce is employed by government. The constant acquisition of human skills to carry on the ever-changing work of governing is a ceaseless task.

Throughout American history, government has adopted a different recruitment philosophy than private industry. Private industry has traditionally engaged in an aggressive, positive, outreaching approach; government has been far more passive and negative in its attitude. Private industry was been more willing to travel to college campuses, publicize their companies in a positive way, interview interested and promising candidates, pay travel expenses of promising candidates for job interviews, minimize the time between interviews and actual job offers,

and, in general, willingly invest organizational resources into the acquisition of new talent. Government has been more interested in a negative approach, stressing the control of political influence in the recruitment and selection processes—"keeping the rascals out" of governmental service. This attitude has been one important legacy of the spoils era.

In the view of some, government has usually been able to attract an ample number of job applicants for most positions and therefore has been more acquiescent in publicizing jobs, visiting college campuses for interviews, and in being unwilling to pay travel expenses for prospective candidates. Although it may take three or four months from the time an applicant hears about a government job until a job offer is actually made, this has been an accepted part of the costs of operating a "merit" system and of minimizing political influence.

For several decades, beginning in the 1960s, the United States government has become more active by targeting their recruitment efforts toward more minorities and women and thereby achieving their affirmative action hiring goals. Merit Principle Number One governing the federal personnel system and made law by the Civil Service Reform Act of 1978 states that "recruitment should be from qualified individuals for appropriate sources in an endeavor to achieve a work force from all segments of society." (Considerable progress was made in the 1990s in achieving a more representative workforce.)

By the 1980s, recruitment efforts seemed to be falling short of achieving desired goals, and the federal government was having trouble filling positions in critical areas. At least three important reasons for this failure were non-competitive pay, insufficient information about federal job opportunities, and a negative image of the federal government.

The Office of Personnel Management (OPM) traditionally has shared recruiting responsibilities with the operating agencies. By the late 1980s and into the 1990s, OPM was taking a series of steps designed to allow operating agencies more freedom in carrying on their recruitment and selection activities. More and more agencies were given "direct hire" authority, more college campus recruiting was encouraged, procedures were put into place allowing immediate job offers to particularly promising scholars—that is, candidates who had particularly high grade-point averages (GPAs) or who had finished in the top 10 percent of their graduating class. As a result of the National Performance Review headed by Vice President Al Gore, OPM has been urged to further streamline the recruitment and selection processes of the federal government by eliminating many of its cumbersome rules and regulations and simplifying the government's often complex application form.

As studies have indicated, the demographics of the federal workforce are rapidly changing. The job needs of the 1990s may not be the job needs of the twenty-first century. Resources at the federal, state, and local levels must be invested into better coordinated and more aggressive recruitment plans if the United States is to meet its future human resource needs.

ROBERT H. ELLIOTT

BIBLIOGRAPHY

Kellough, J. E., 1990. "Integration in the Public Workplace: Determinates of Minority and Female Employment in Federal Agencies." *Public Administration Review,* vol. 50, no. 5: 557–566.
U.S. General Accounting Office, 1990. *Federal Recruiting and Hiring: Making Government Jobs Attractive to Prospective Employees.* Washington, DC: U.S. GPO.
U.S. Merit Systems Protection Board, 1988. *Attracting Quality Graduates to the Federal Government: A View of College Recruiting.* Washington, DC: U.S. GPO.

RED TAPE. Term used to describe official routines, formal processes, and excessive paperwork, which contribute to a lack of responsiveness and delay in action not only in the public sector but in the private sector organizations as well.

"Red tape" is derived from the sixteenth-century practice in Europe of binding official and legal documents in red ribbons. Since that time, it has become a popular way of characterizing government as being ineffective and inefficient. The development of the term in the English language is in large part due to the contributions of nineteenth-century British authors, often satirically. Sydney Smith (1808) used it in relationship to change and reform of the Church of England. Charles Dickens used it in 1857 to describe how a "Public Department of Circumlocution" found ways not to do something. Henry Morford used it in 1864 to illustrate how unproductive procedures used by "Pigeon-Hole Generals" obstructed a campaign on the Potomac. Thomas Carlyle (1841) and Bulwer Lytton (1849) formed adjectives: "red-tape talking machine" and "red-tape minister as a mere official manager of details," respectively. Herbert Spencer (1862) analyzed it as an outcome of evolutionary sociological progress.

The term has developed subtle nuances over time. Red tape has been called a "cult of administrative procedure" (Waldo 1946). Peter Blau and Marshall Meyer (1979) have viewed it as the necessary but misunderstood procedural safeguards that insure equal and impartial treatment in a democracy. Herbert Kaufman (1977) has noted that red tape is our way of limiting public servants' discretion, as well as our way of holding them accountable. R. A. Rosenfeld (1984) has written about red tape as excessive guidelines, forms, or rules that are pointless in regard to decisionmaking. Most recently, The National Performance

Review article (1993) has termed red tape as regulations that do not give managers the power to mold their organizations unlike that enjoyed by private sector managers.

Red Tape and Organizational Size

Citizens, elected officials, candidates, and the media have used "red tape" interchangeably with "bureaucracy," and, according to Roy Francisco and Robert Stone (1956), to refer to ills associated with bigness in government. Some authors have suggested that red tape is more a function of organizational size than organizational or individual behavior (Bretschneider and Bozeman 1995). According to others, increases in organizational size are associated with the development of greater administrative specialization and that, therefore, creates red tape. Other scholars look at and analyze what actually creates red tape. They suggest that the relationship between size and red tape depends more upon whether the organization is in a state of decline or growth than it does simply on size. Growth demands organizational complexity and results in the need to insure standardization, coordination, and control across employees and departments.

There is a tendency for large organizations to create formalized procedures, to have high employee orientation to rules and regulations, and to be characterized by *bureaucratization*—rigid application of regulations and routines, resulting in delays and exasperation. This view has been supported by R. Wintrobe (1982), and the use of red tape colloquially to mean inefficiency has been widely accepted. G. Kingsley and Barry Bozeman (1992) have suggested that there is a tendency for large organizations to be *perceived* as having red tape. Some people have proposed that red tape was, in part, simply a congressional function to give single agencies multiple and contradictory missions.

Red Tape as an Administrative Necessity

Because governmental action is directly or indirectly a function of law, public organizations are never free to act without procedures. Public administration is constrained by enabling legislation, agency mission, actions by others in a democratic system of governance (e.g., the courts, the chief executive, other agencies, the press, and watchdog groups.) As D. P. Warwick (1975) reports, these procedures represent good management and account for positive affects: minimizing uncertainty and maintaining a level of predictability in an organization's internal and external environments.

Pressures to create red tape are both formal and informal, according to J. N. Baldwin (1990), and create an environment in which the public agencies operate that is highly scrutinized by the media, public opinion, political parties, and other public organizations. It is the excessive attention to procedures as a means of control and insurance against criticism and a benchmark for effective performance that results in red tape, according to both Victor Thompson (1961) and J. L. Perry and L. W. Porter (1982).

At the same time, others contend that red tape is perhaps the public's best insurance that all citizens receive equal treatment at the hand of government and that laws are administered fully and fairly. According to Paul Appleby (1970) and Lynella Grant (1995), customer dissatisfaction and the perception of red tape are the direct result of hidden requirements, such as the need to insure thoroughness through duplication and interdepartmental coordination. The insistence for full public accountability in governmental management for every step of public program implementation requires a system that may be perceived as red tape, but that red tape actually ensures "overall system reliability" (Landau 1969).

Delays as a Function of Red Tape

It is when organizations become "overcontrolled" or "undercontrolled" (Bozeman 1993), that red tape results in delays and nonresponsive organizations. In his "rule density" conceptualization, Barry Bozeman agrees with Victor Thompson (1961) and Robert Merton (1940) that there is a distinction between "good organizational rules and procedures gone bad."

Red tape is sometimes created when an organization is characterized by inertia and indifference and when any change in routine is resisted due to the disruptive effects of that change. It has also become associated with nonresponsiveness to customer and citizen requests (CRM Films 1994, National Performance Review 1995). Red tape is nonresponsiveness experienced by businesses dealing with all levels of government (Grant 1995).

Red Tape and Employee Discretion

Red tape creation as an individual organizational behavior has been discussed generally in terms of individual alienation (Gouldner 1954), the impersonalization and organizational opposition, and in terms of "deviations from the bureaucratic ideal" and ways to eliminate those abuses or to "institutionalize dissent" (Weinstein 1979). Many studies attempt to measure red tape by asking employees their perceptions regarding the amount, level, or effects of red tape on the organization (e.g., Buchanan 1975; Baldwin 1990; Rosenfeld 1984; Bozeman and Loveless 1987). Some scholars insist that red tape is necessary to control the information costs that accompany public employee discretion and to coordinate and monitor employee performance. Red tape has been acknowledged as a way to limit public servant discretion by (Kaufman 1977), much akin to checks and balances created by the United States Constitution. In this regard, some also asserted that public agencies were never intended to operate efficiently (Goodsell 1994; Gouldner 1954). Red tape may thus be a system that holds people accountable for the process rather than the results. Red tape is something that government employees want to eliminate.

Red Tape As a Government Phenomenon

H. G. Rainey (1983) and J. N. Baldwin (1990) have found higher levels of formalization and red tape perceived among public managers than among their private counterparts. Higher levels of formalization and procedural routine have been reported in public educational institutions (Holdaway 1975, Chubb and Moe 1990) and in hospitals (Clarkson 1972). These higher levels of formalization have also been reported on in France (Church 1981) and Britain (Craig 1955; Mallalieu 1942). James Burke (1976) has suggested that red tape is created by governmental agencies and individual bureaucrats as an obstacle to reform.

Eliminating red tape is a desire of both public and private sector organizations interested in effectively serving customers and improving processes.

Conclusion

Red tape has become an inevitable aspect of legal requirements and organizational growth, and of the necessity for government to treat citizens fairly and to implement programs fully and equally. It has come to mean organizational inefficiency and ineffectiveness, as well as obstructive employee behavior and customer dissatisfaction. It has been described as both "good" and "bad," "informal" and "formal." It has been analyzed and measured in terms of process complexity, number of forms required, organizational size and age, number of regulations generated, response times, and centralization of responsibility and accountability. A precise definition varies with each individual's perception. After all, one person's red tape is another person's prudent management and proper program implementation.

CHRISTINE GRESHAM GIBBS

BIBLIOGRAPHY

Appleby, Paul H., 1970. *Big Democracy.* New York: Russell and Russell.

Baldwin, J. N., 1990. "Perceptions of Public vs. Private Sector Personnel and Informal Red Tape: Their Impact on Motivation." *American Review of Public Administration* 20 (1): 7–28.

Benveniste, Guy, 1977. *Bureaucracy.* San Francisco: Boyd and Fraser.

Blau, Peter M., and Marshall W. Meyer, 1971. *Bureaucracy in Modern Society.* New York: Random House.

Bozeman, Barry, 1993. "A Theory of Government Red Tape." *Journal of Public Administration Research and Theory,* vol. 3: 273–304.

Bozeman, Barry, and S. Loveless, 1987. "Sector Context and Performance." *Administration and Society,* vol. 19: 197–235.

Bretschneider, Stuart I., and Barry Bozeman, 1995. "Understanding Red Tape and Bureaucratic Delays." Halachmi Arie and Geert Bouckaert, eds., *The Enduring Challenges in Public Management: Surviving and Excelling in a Changing World,* pp. 81–118. San Francisco: Jossey-Bass.

Buchanan, B., 1975. "Red Tape and the Service Ethic: Some Unexpected Differences Between Public and Private Managers." *Administration and Society* 6 (4): 432–444.

Burke, James, 1976. *Paper Tomahawks: From Red Tape to Red Power.* Winnipeg, Manitoba, Canada: Queenston House.

Carlyle, Thomas, 1841. *On Heroes, Hero-Worship, and the Heroic in History.* N.P.

Chubb, J., and T. Moe, 1990. *Politics, Markets, and America's Schools.* Washington, DC: Brookings Institution.

Church, Clive H., 1981. *Revolution and Red Tape.* Oxford, England: Clarendon Press.

Clarkson, K., 1972. "Some Implications of Property Rights in Hospital Management." *Journal of Law and Economics,* vol. 12: 33–42.

Clarkson K., and D. Martin, eds., 1980. *The Economics of Nonproprietary Organizations.* Greenwich, CT: JAI Press.

Craig, John Herbert McCutcheon, 1955. *The History of Red Tape.* London: Macdonald and Evans.

CRM Films, 1994. *The Invisible Man Meets the Dummy, or How to Serve the Customer You Didn't Know You Had Without Getting Wrapped up in Red Tape.* Carlsbad, CA: CRM Films.

David, D., 1977. "Property Rights and Economic Efficiency." *Journal of Law and Economics,* vol. 20: 223–226.

Demsetz, H., 1967. "Toward a Theory of Property Rights." *American Economic Review* 57: 347–359.

Dickens, Charles (from *Little Dorritt, III,* 1857), 1984. In H. L. Mencken, ed., *A New Dictionary of Quotations on Historical Principles from Ancient and Modern Sources.* New York: Knopf.

Francisco, Roy G., and Robert C. Stone, 1956. *Service and Procedure in Bureaucracy.* Minneapolis: University of Minnesota Press.

Goodsell, Charles T., 1994. *The Case for Bureaucracy: A Public Administration Polemic.* New York: Chatham House.

Gouldner, Alvin W., 1954. *Patterns of Industrial Bureaucracy.* New York: Free Press.

Grant, Lynella, 1995. "Four Ways to Cut Red Tape: Hate Dealing with Bureaucrats? Here's How to Make It Easier." *Independent Business,* vol. 6, no. 4 (July-August): 28–20.

Holdaway, E., J. F. Newberry, D. J. Hickson, and R. P. Heron, 1975. "Dimensions of Organizations in Complex Societies: The Educational Sector." *Administrative Sciences Quarterly,* vol. 20: 37–58.

Kaufman, Herbert, 1977. *Red Tape: Its Origins, Uses, and Abuses.* Washington, DC: Brookings Institution.

Kingsley, G., and Barry Bozeman, 1992. "Bureaucratization in Public and Private Organizations: The Impact of Task Structure and External Environment." Paper presented at the April Joint Meeting of the Institute for Management Science/Operations Research Society of America. Orlando, Florida.

Lan, Z., and H. Rainey, 1992. "Goals, Rules and Effectiveness in Public, Private and Hybrid Organizations: More Evidence on Frequent Assertions About Differences." *Journal of Public Administration Research and Theory,* vol. 2: 5–24.

Landau, M., 1969. "Redundancy, Rationality and the Problem of Duplication and Overlap." *Public Administration Review,* vol. 29: 346–358.

Luxheimer, Alvin, 1970. "Red-Faced Over Red Tape." *Compact* (April).

Lytton, Bulwer, 1849. *The Caxtons.* N.P.

Mallalieu, J.P.W., 1942. *Passed to You, Please: Britain's Red Tape Machine at War.* London: V. Gollancz.

Meier, Kenneth J., 1979. *Politics and the Bureaucracy: Policymaking in the Fourth Branch of Government.* North Scictuate, MA: Duxbury Press.

Merton, Robert R., 1940. "Bureaucratic Structure and Personality." *Social Forces,* vol. 17: 560-568.

———, 1952. *Reader in Bureaucracy.* New York: Columbia University Press.

Meyer, Marshall, 1979. *Change in Public Bureaucracies.* London: Cambridge University Press.

Morford, Henry, 1864. *Red Tape and Pigeon-Hole Generals: As Seen from the Ranks During a Campaign in the Army of the Potomac.* New York: Carleton.

Morstein-Marx, Fritz, ed., 1959. *Elements of Public Administration.* Englewood Cliffs, NJ: Prentice-Hall.

National Performance Review, 1993. *From Red Tape to Results: Creating a Government that Works Better and Costs Less.* Washington, DC: GPO.

———, 1995. *Putting Customers First: '95 Standards for Serving the American People.* Washington, DC: GPO.

Perry, J. L., and L. W. Porter, 1982. "Factors Affecting the Context for Motivation in Public Organizations." *Academy of Management Review,* vol. 7: 89-98.

Rainey, H. G., 1983. "Public Agencies and Private Firms: Incentives, Structures, Goals, and Individual Roles." *Administration and Society,* vol. 15: 207-242.

Rosenfeld, R. A., 1984. "An Expansion and Application of Kaufman Model of Red Tape: The Case of Community Development Block Grants." *Western Political Science Quarterly,* vol. 37: 603-620.

Smith, Sydney, 1808. *Peter Plymley Letters.* London.

Spencer, Herbert, [1862] 1876-1896. *The Principles of Sociology* (3 vols). N.P.

Stevens, Richard,1979. "Red Tape: Federal Indian Funding." *Human Organization* (Fall): 283-293.

Thompson, Victor, 1961. *Modern Organizations.* New York: Knopf.

Tourevski, Mark, 1993. *Cutting the Red Tape: How Companies Can Profit in the New Russia.* Toronto: Free Press.

Waldo, D., 1946. "Government by Procedure." F. Morstein-Marx, ed., *Elements of Public Administration.* Englewood Cliffs, NJ: Prentice-Hall.

Warwick. D. P., 1975. *A Theory of Bureaucracy.* Cambridge: Harvard University Press.

Webster's New Twentieth Century Dictionary, Unabridged, 1979. New York: Simon and Schuster.

Weinstein, Deena, 1979. *Bureaucratic Opposition: Challenging Abuses at the Workplace.* New York: Pergamon Press.

Wilson, James Q., 1989. *Bureaucracy: What Government Agencies Do and Why They Do It.* New York: Basic Books.

Wintrobe, R., 1982. "The Optimal Level of Bureaucratization Within a Firm." *Canadian Journal of Economics,* vol. 15: 649-668.

REDUCTION IN FORCE (RIF).

Cutting back or paring down the number of employees within an organization. This reduction often becomes necessary because of austere fiscal times and the subsequent difficulty in balancing governmental budgets. It may also occur within the context of the reevaluation of an agency's mission or a shift in political alignment and power.

Faced with declining budgets, many government agencies must periodically deal with the prospect of a major reduction in force. In addition, the U.S. military continues to be pressured to decrease its size, following the breakup of the Soviet Union and the end of the Cold War.

From an organizational perspective, a successful RIF requires effective leadership and careful planning. A clear picture or vision of what the organization will become and how it will function once the RIF is completed is critically important. A RIF can be accomplished through a variety of strategies, including:

1. up-front job terminations;
2. phased-in layoffs over time;
3. enhanced retirement incentive programs;
4. voluntary separation, with inducements such as severance pay, extended benefits, and job placement assistance;
5. normal attrition, with the implementation of a partial or complete hiring freeze.

Of these strategies, it is better from the standpoint of morale, litigation, and continuing productivity for an organization to reduce its workforce as much as possible through enhanced retirement, voluntary separation, and normal attrition.

Since the late 1980s, enhanced retirement programs have received a great deal of attention. According to the results of a survey conducted by Seymour LaRock (1992), more than 25 percent of the public sector and nonprofit employers responding stated that they offered some kind of early retirement incentive program. The most common plan consisted of crediting the employee with extra years of service and/or age or of providing a monthly supplemental benefit, payable until age 62.

Voluntary separation is also frequently used to accomplish a RIF. However, both voluntary separation and enhanced retirement incentives can lead to the loss of highly valued employees. In the short run, this loss can cause significant upheaval and harm to the organization. One advantage of layoffs, then, is the ability of the agency to select strategically the individuals who will be terminated.

A RIF through normal attrition is the least-painless option for employees, but it is only possible if the agency's reduced workforce timetable coincides with the expected rate of turnover of those leaving under normal conditions, such as regular retirement and the customary level of resignations and terminations. Unfortunately, in difficult fiscal times, the normal rate of attrition is often too slow to accomplish workforce reductions when they are needed.

Layoffs or forced terminations, whether they are immediate or phased-in over time, cause the greatest turmoil and trauma for an agency and its employees. Aside from the impact on the workload and on the scope and quality of service and morale, forced terminations may place public sector unions in an adversarial relationship with the agency. Consequently, it is important that, whenever appropriate, an agency work with any public sector unions that its employees may belong to. Union support should be enlisted to (1) assist in communicating the need for layoffs, and (2) provide advice to the agency in dealing with the human resource (HR) needs of those being terminated and those surviving the layoffs. Since civil service layoffs are usually based on seniority, they tend to have an adverse impact on any recent gains an agency may have made in the area of affirmative action. This is another problem that management needs to be aware of when contemplating layoffs.

Human Resource Considerations and Other RIF Related Problems

It is important that management treat departing employees with dignity and compassion. This will help to overcome morale problems for the laid off as well as the surviving employees. Layoffs can be especially traumatic for employees and their families because they challenge the basic assumption of governmental job security. Accordingly, the personnel or human resources department needs to take an aggressive leadership role in providing support services for everyone affected by the RIF. This, of course, presupposes the support and cooperation of upper-level management.

Past experience suggests that laid-off employees often believe that their terminations were arbitrary or biased. To help dispel these perceptions, management needs clearly to communicate the need and specific criteria for terminations. Once this is done, the agency must be prepared to deal with the emotional trauma many laid-off and surviving employees will experience. Research indicates that trauma runs the gamut, from denial and fear to anger and guilt, emerging at various stages in the RIF process. Supervisors handing out "pink slips" should receive guidance in the form of workshop training and role-playing scenarios to deal with this difficult task wisely and humanely.

If possible, the agency should establish comprehensive job bridging, or a combination of career counseling and out-placement support. According to the research of Helene Liebman and Steve McCarthy (1993), an effective job-bridging program should consist of 7 elements: (1) a functioning career transition center, (2) career counseling with résumé and government employment-form development, (3) motivation workshops, (4) training, (5) continuous evaluation of all career center activities, (6) ongoing management support, and (7) job matching.

With respect to job matching, the career transition center needs to classify a worker's skills, identify outside vacancies, and match appropriate vacancies to the individual worker. Job matching also tends to minimize the sense of failure that comes from applying for jobs for which the employee is not qualified. Successful out-placement is the ultimate and optimum goal of a job-bridging program.

Once the RIF has taken place, there is a need to rebuild the confidence and sense of job security of the retained employees. This may require retraining (including cross-training), in-service education, the implementation of various individual and team-building empowerment techniques, and counseling and other support services for the RIF survivors. The remaining employees should also be given the opportunity to evaluate the RIF experience from their own perspective in an open dialogue with mid- and upper-level management. This discussion may also serve to modify the goals and strategies of future RIFs that the agency may be involved in.

As observed by Daniel Feldman and Carrie Leana (1994) and by Milan Moravec and Elizabeth Branstead (1994), and others, agencies that plan and carry out better practices in managing layoffs demonstrate that it is possible to go through a RIF without the agency incurring undue anguish and dysfunctionalism. Affected organizations should also work cooperatively with other government agencies, unions, client groups, and even the private sector in setting new and realistic expectations of agency performance with a newly streamlined workforce. Finally, whenever possible, a RIF should be seen as an opportunity to revitalize an agency and help assure its future survival while reaffirming its newly examined mission.

GARY D. HELFAND

BIBLIOGRAPHY

Feldman, Daniel C., and Carrie R. Leana, 1994. "Better Practices in Managing Layoffs." *Human Resources Management*, vol. 33 (Summer): 239–260.
LaRock, Seymour, 1992. "Both Private and Public Sector Employees Use Early Retirement Sweetners." *Employee Benefit Plan Review*, vol. 47 (August): 14–20.
Liebman, Helene G., and Steve McCarthy, 1993. "Job Bridging: Downsizing Without RIF." *Public Manager*, vol. 22 (Summer): 25–27.
Moravec, Milan, and Elizabeth Branstead, 1994. *From Downsizing to Recovery: Strategic Transition Options for Organizations and Individuals*. Palo Alto, CA: CPP Books.
Zeller, Michael R., and Michael F. Mooney, 1992. "Legally Reducing Work Forces in a Recessionary Economy." *Human Resources Professional*, vol. 4 (Spring): 14–18.

REENGINEERING. A management approach to change for organizations that revisualizes and redesigns an organization's core work processes to achieve dramatic improvements in organizational performance by significantly decreasing operating and support costs, improving production and service cycle time frames, and increasing customer satisfaction with the product and the service quality and value.

Reengineering, perhaps better termed Business Process Reengineering (BPR), has become the 1990s change management method of choice. Although definitions abound, there is a general understanding that reengineering involves revisualizing and redesigning an organization's core work processes to accomplish very dramatic and rapid improvements. Such redesigns focus primarily on (1) lowering operating and support costs, (2) improving service delivery time and response levels, (3) increasing product and service quality levels, and (4) enhancing employee involvement in reaching organizational goals.

Reengineering as a change strategy assumes that organizations must have lower costs, faster service, more innovative products, and are beyond trading off one facet against the other. Most organizations have used various forms of cutback management to reorganize or realign resources to handle increased workloads or to speed up service response times by reassigning staff or adding more personnel. But to cut costs by increasing levels of productivity by 50 percent, speed up product completion or service delivery (what is referred to as "cycle time") by 75 percent to 100 percent, or create entirely new service features or products for customers goes considerably beyond reorganizing, simplifying, and streamlining work activities. A central premise of reengineering is that the goals are so ambitious that they can only be accomplished by completely rethinking and redesigning the way work is performed and the methods by which outputs are delivered.

Reengineering As a Management Strategy for Change

Most of the methods and techniques used in BPR are not new. In fact, many organizations have used variations of reengineering as part of their strategic or breakthrough planning or quality management efforts. Among the more advanced organizations which have pioneered in quality management, reengineering was an innovation strategy to be applied selectively to redesign processes for breakthroughs while the rest of the organization continued its overall pursuit of continuous incremental improvement.

The term "reengineering" emerged in the early 1990s. Credit is usually given to Boston-based consultant Michael Hammer for his description of the concept in a 1990 *Harvard Business Review* article entitled "Reengineering: Don't Automate; Obliterate." In 1992, Hammer and James Champy coauthored *Reengineering the Corporation,* popularizing the concept.

Hammer and Champy are not the only notables who have developed reengineering as a management concept. James Harrington published *Business Process Improvement* in 1991, which is a comprehensive guidebook to the techniques and methods that organizations can use to modify and redesign their business processes. In 1993, Thomas Davenport published *Process Innovation,* which remains one of the most in-depth studies of reengineering methods. Davenport sees reengineering as a radical strategy for change that must carefully consider complex implementation issues involving the workforce, technology, and organizational culture.

Of course, the reengineering bookshelf has grown demonstrably in even the short span of two to three years. These three works are notable because they were among the first volumes, they were written by major names in the consulting field, and—for purposes here—they nicely illustrate the continuum of change that organizations must address, as follows: Reorganization; Total Quality Management (TQM); Business Process Improvement (BPI); Business Process Reengineering (BPR); minor change; and, finally, major change.

Reengineering is the far point, and, as Hammer and Champy and Davenport have noted, it requires the highest degree of top management commitment because of its high-risk and its ambitious goals. Business Process Improvement (Harrington's term) is more modest: it might involve undertaking major streamlining, removal of major barriers, and reworking delays or problems in core work processes, or BPI may even be accomplished through a redesign of an entire process; but the goals are usually couched in such terms as a 20 percent to 30 percent improvement in cost reduction or productivity enhancement levels. TQM aims for modest but sustainable improvements of 10 percent to 15 percent each year, primarily by reducing revisions and improving reliability.

There are a host of management strategies for change that can be used to achieve reorganization or incremental improvement. The key point of this continuum is that an organization chooses a BPR approach when only "radical change" will do. When major innovation and radical redesign are required, reengineering is the appropriate choice. Davenport would add, however, that reengineering also requires rethinking the *level of innovation* required for organizational-wide culture change and realignment of the organization infrastructure (people, technology, and management systems).

Reengineering is so different from other strategies because it is premised on major levels of top management involvement and commitment. It is a high-risk strategy, by definition, because its assumption is that both *what* the organization is doing and *how* it is doing it *can and must be radically altered.*

Top management involvement requires the complete participation of a firm's managers. (One recent *Harvard Business Review* article estimated that in successful BPR efforts, top managers had to commit 20 to 30 percent of their time personally to champion the efforts to change and to carry them through.) Management must also want the change effort. Unlike other change strategies, reengineering will not be accomplished without the total support of the people at the head of the company.

Relating Reengineering to TQM and Downsizing

What does reengineering have to do with total quality management? Everything; but, unfortunately, there is a growing dispute between TQM and BPR advocates over how organizations should change and whether an organization can sustain a BPR effort without having created a quality management base. This dispute is partly a disagreement among consultants who are looking for market share and partly a difference between the views of quality proponents, who see nothing new in BPR, and those of BPR proponents, who see everything related to TQM as being too old. This conflict is understandable, given that BPR is a highly selective, fast-paced, innovative, top-down-driven change approach and that TQM is just the opposite. TQM emphasizes a broad-based, slow (but sure) cumulative improvement, with a bottom-up approach. The two systems do share all of the important things, however, such as emphases on management by process, concern for customers, extensive use of work teams, and decisions based on performance results data.

Quality management provides an effective foundation for best management practice, and BPR may be used selectively to drive radical change efforts where needed. (And it would be nice to think that BPR advocates would want to learn from the many mistakes made in implementing TQM).

But what is the relationship between reengineering and downsizing? Business Process Reengineering done incorrectly *is* downsizing. When BPR is done correctly, however, the two methods should be totally different.

Typically, a corporation (or a government) reassesses its financial position when it is facing a crunch. It may subsequently announce a series of layoffs or workforce cuts that are needed to meet a financial objective. The organization then sets up some sort of personnel scheme to get people to leave their jobs so it can realize the necessary savings. It then waits for the next crisis. (It is no wonder that downsizing is derisively called "dumbsizing.") If the organization is grossly overstaffed, then the personnel cuts cause no problems in terms of the company coping with a reduced staff. If it is understaffed, however, the organization may experience significant performance problems and may have to rethink its cutback strategy.

When reengineering is used correctly, it is focused on targets selected by the strategic planning process. What is important is to change the way work is done, not just how many are doing it. The redesign effort itself might require more resources (not less) to accomplish. Although the im-

plementation effort might result in significant cuts in the workforce responsible for that process, there are major implications for the firm with regard to retraining and reinvestment in the employees that are retained (what is often called "upskilling") and for rethinking the management of work teams.

In reengineering, the workforce and cost reductions come after the target is selected and the redesign is accomplished. In downsizing, the workforce and cost reductions often are announced before any redesign has been accomplished.

The Heart of the Matter: Managing by Process

There is one area in which quality and reengineering methods agree, and that is the importance of process management. A process is a sequence of related activities that begins with some type of input, has some value added, and results in some type of output. For example, it is a series of actions that begins with a customer need and is done only when customer expectations are satisfied. But managing by process has immense implications for organizations.

Both TQM and BPR advocates recognize that the change that must be made in organizations must be the movement away from a vertical (hierarchical), or functional, management to horizontal, or process, management.

Most organizations manage by functions. Their structure, lines of communication, and their allocation of resources are all vertically aligned. Indeed, functional management even has functional performance criteria in place to insure that the organization meets these specialized goals. The first assumption is that if each function meets its targets, the organization will meet its objectives. The second assumption is that strong functions will define organizational excellence.

Of course, for years management theorists have argued that there is a downside to strong functional management. For example, functional management can be highly competitive, to the point that "turf-protection" is equated to any organizational resistance to change. But functional management is also very risk-aversive. Most managers would recognize the following functional management strategies as prudent steps to insure that the organization has the capability to react and solve any and all problems.

1. *Build in redundancy.* Add extra steps to verify work done by someone else; inspect for quality defects.
2. *Strive for self-containment.* Dedicate extra resources to fix other units' mistakes or to redo work, instead of having to rely on others' inputs.
3. *Inflate work time for tasks.* Add extra time requirements to permit grouping of work tasks to achieve economies

of scale; add lead time to allow for more planning; and create backlogs to allow for economies of scheduling or to discourage work requests.

4. *Increase supervision and lower span of control.* Add extra supervision or create additional layers of supervision and coordination that can be dedicated to firefighting, managing reports, inspection, and coordination between units.

Perhaps the biggest problem with functional management is that firms that use it may too easily lose sight of the customer. With this method, dealing with customers, primarily through handling their complaints, is relegated to some form of customer service unit or to the marketing department. Important information from the customer's perspective about how products and services could be better designed, developed, delivered, and supported is not shared throughout the organization, nor is it systematically developed to guide the growth of new products and services. With functional management, only one part of the organization truly focuses on what is its most significant priority—serving customers.

If the organization were structured more with the customer in mind, it would act horizontally. Indeed, process management is structured horizontally. The company would seek to lower, if not tear down, organizational walls and create work teams that were cross-functional, that would have more direct contact with their customers (and their suppliers), and that would be better able to cooperate with other units. Process management encompasses a very different set of performance criteria.

Most important, process management methods place a premium on cycle time and on choice. *Cycle time* is defined as the real time measurement from start to finish, for the completion or delivery of a product or service. This time period is different than an organization's productivity time, which is how long it takes to do a task. For example, if it takes an organization twenty minutes to process an order, but it waits fifteen days for the financial transaction to clear and another five days to have the order delivered by the postal service, then the total cycle time is over 20 days. (The cycle would actually begin the day the order was sent by the customer.) The organization may be proud of its fast productivity and work accuracy levels, but the customer may view the final product quite differently.

Choice is another critical variable for process management. A utility may pride itself on having a 24-hour response time for its repair service, but the customer who is pinned down at home, having to take a day off from work, waiting for the service person to show up may be considerably less pleased. Given a choice, the customer might prefer getting his or her service fixed within 48 or 72 hours, *if* the utility would guarantee a specific appointment time and arrive within 30 minutes of the time promised. Thus one of the most powerful reasons to adopt process man-

agement is the capability it creates for the company to focus on customers.

Process Management and the End of Supervision?

The use of process management also has major implications for managers and workers. Managing by process means creating a whole new approach for supervision. Process management assumes that the old job of the supervisor (to inspect work, respond to emergencies, and control the work environment) is a non-value-added position (to use the reengineering term). The process management supervisor is a "process owner" who sets team goals, coaches team members, and facilitates team cooperation and organizational communications. The process team itself consists of workers who are rewarded, trained, and developed to work for group goals such as customer satisfaction, problem prevention, lower cost and faster cycle time, and so forth.

Something should be said about the link between process management and participative management. With the latter method the firm tries to empower its employees in order to solve problems and improve performance. Few could argue that more empowerment is important, but process management, especially when accomplished through reengineering, is more than new uses for teamwork. In fact, the cross-functional team envisioned in process management may not at all resemble the self-directed work team of the 1990s. Self-directed work teams manage their work without supervisors, for the most part. Process teams push decisionmaking down to the problem source, but they carefully think through internal and external communication, working in a parallel, not serial, information sharing and developing metrics (work group measurements).

Special attention must also be given to new advances in technology. Greater technology will alter work performed and the ability to monitor and coordinate work, substantially enhancing the abilities of organizations to enlarge unit sizes, reduce direct supervision, and promote cross-functional and cross-organizational communication. Increasingly, decentralized decisionmaking with autonomous work groups and project teams that are supported by information management systems will prevail as dominant organizational structures. This trend toward participative management reduces organizational layers and changes supervision to facilitation and coordination. This requires that organizations reconceptualize the roles of supervisor and employee (through cultural change, education, or process reengineering strategies). However, for any type of work team to be effective, major obstacles must be dealt with that require careful planning, training, and preparation.

There is a distinction between the practice of what is often called "self-declared work teams" and that of "self-directed teams," or process teams. Teams need more than cheerleading from top management. Telling workers that they now have the freedom to go out and meet with customers, solve problems, and schedule their own work is not enough.

Process management lies at the core of what reengineering seeks to change most in bureaucratic organizations. This change goes well beyond the more simplistic goals touted in most management reform movements; that is, less administrative regulation, reduction in hierarchy and regional structures, broader span of control, and systems' streamlining and simplification. Process management offers a very different structure and alignment of work activity, with better customer (and supplier) communication.

Seven Questions for Would-Be Reengineers

Brief answers are provided to seven questions often asked about reengineering. The point is that if management cannot answer these basic questions, they are not ready for reengineering.

Why Is Reengineering Important?

Reengineering assumes that current work organizational systems are outmoded and badly in need of significant change to meet current economic needs and future environmental realities. In addition, reengineering also seeks to take advantage of major information and communication technology advances that make possible vastly different approaches to doing work. (Although it is critical to avoid simply applying technology to existing processes to speed up production times—commonly referred to as "paving the cow path.")

What Does Reengineering Seek to Change?

Reengineering focuses on the organization's key work processes and redesigns organizational management and support systems to fit external, not internal, requirements. The emphasis is on reducing processes; producing work products and services that are value-added from a customer perspective; realigning technology and communications to link suppliers, producers, and customers more directly; creating work teams that are cross-functional; and restructuring administrative support so that it is an enabling, rather than a regulatory activity.

For Whom Is Reengineering Done?

Reengineering focuses on customers, emphasizing "value-addedness" from their perspective as the key to remaining competitive. Some reengineering methods push distinctions between external customers (value-added by definition) and internal customers (where benefits must outweigh costs). Such distinctions help firms to identify waste (defined as working for no one) and subject all internal customers to special scrutiny, such as having units calculate and send bills to "customers" for reports generated or services performed.

Reengineering also emphasizes employees and their roles in resolving problems. This is much more than only training workers to handle customer complaints. Reengineering seeks solutions through process management, by which the workforce is actively engaged in measuring quality and customer satisfaction levels, assessing cycle time and costs, and reviewing customer complaints and market data. Process team members are expected to review these metrics and propose solutions and design changes to meet organizational performance goals.

When Should Reengineering Be Started?

Reengineering should begin after the organization recognizes that to maintain the status quo is unacceptable and that innovative change is more desirable than is improving business as usual.

In the early years of BPR, most organizations pursued reengineering because their survival was threatened. (This is usually called a "burning platform.") One advantage of the burning platform is that employees do not have to be convinced that there is a compelling reason to change or that the pain of change is unavoidable.

There are now numerous organizations that pursue reengineering from a "position of strength"; using the adage that the best time to fix something is when it is not broken. Increasingly, the initiating factor is less relevant; the key lesson learned is not to undertake any change effort unless the organization has prepared for it by laying the foundation, creating and communicating a vision for change, and clearly articulating the change priorities tied to the vision.

How Is Reengineering Accomplished?

Three requirements seem critical for reengineering:

1. *Commitment from top management* is necessary to insure that reengineering is aimed at management's top priorities. This action runs counter to many of the lessons learned in quality management, which argues the case for beginning change by generating small successes. In reengineering there are two slogans that speak to this requirement: "If we are going to fail, then fail over something really important"; and "If we are going to fail, then fail quickly."
2. *Use of good methodologies* is required that compare current state problems and customer limitations with future state requirements and market expectations. Use of good methodologies also means providing redesign models that can be tested to prove how well they work and how easily they can be implemented.

3. *Involve the best experts across functions* in the redesign effort. Reengineering is fast-paced, full-time work. It should not be seen as only another task force meeting to attend or another competing work priority on an already overfilled agenda. If the organization wants a new and radical solution to change it will chose its best people and its most innovative thinkers to be on the redesign team. Above all, the reengineering group must have the resources, time, information, and training if it is to succeed.

Who Does What to Implement Reengineering?

Usually, top management establishes a *steering committee* at a high level to coordinate the overall reengineering efforts. This group has major ongoing responsibilities for coordination and communication. To accomplish the reengineering work itself, some type of high caliber work group or *reengineering team,* consisting of internal and external experts, does the analysis and new design. In addition, there is some type of internal *implementation team* that oversees the conversion and translation of the change effort. Often, the implementation issues are so difficult that organizations will resort to a transition step that creates a conversion and integration team. Such a team plans out the necessary changes in work policies, training, workforce reinvestment, customer, communications, and so on.

How Long Does Reengineering Take?

Fast-track reengineering efforts can produce studies and new proposals in 3 to 6 months and implement changes in 9 to 18 months. Normally, organizations use 6 to 12 months for analysis and redesign, with 12 to 18 months for conversion and complete implementation. An entire reengineering project might span 24 to 30 months in terms of total cycle time. But, since many of the reengineering stages can be done in overlapping and parallel sequence, results can be produced much more quickly.

These long time frames to complete implementation are also balanced with 3-month (or shorter) "deliverables." Deliverables are measurable improvements or milestones that are reached at regular intervals to demonstrate success (or "fast" failure, if that is the case). Implementation plans try to create fast returns up front in the planning process.

Reengineering As Process and Methodology

There is both a process of reengineering and a methodology that are vital to making reengineering change efforts work. The process guides how an organization (1) selects the targets for reengineering; (2) creates and communicates the vision for change; (3) redesigns and validates the new process; (4) transitions from the old ways to the new; and (5) implements and improves the new process.

There are also very distinct methodologies behind BPR that usually involve a linked three-pronged approach, consisting of:

1. *process mapping*: the flowcharting (and cost and cycle time measurement) of how an organization currently delivers services and products as a process (often called a current state analysis) and detailing what technology support is used;
2. *customer or stakeholder assessments*: evaluating customer current needs and market future expectations through focus groups, surveys, and meetings with consumers to determine product and service requirements and needs; and
3. *process visioning*: rethinking how work processes ought to work and generating new models for innovation and radical improvement (often called a future state analysis).

Of course, different organizations will tackle different process reengineering projects in different ways. But unlike quality management, which was often criticized for lack of guidance about how to do TQM and how long it would take to see results, reengineering is very specific about what has to happen. Each of the major phases is discussed in the five sections that follow:

Phase One: Preplanning— Is the Organization Ready?

An organization's decision and commitment to start change through reengineering is not easily achieved. In most organizations, top management is constantly looking for feasible approaches to make change work. The problem is how to lead that process to insure that management's resolve to push through change is not doubted and to insure that change will work as intended.

Skepticism about change runs deep in most managers, especially in mid-level managers and supervisors. Their belief, as more than one manager has remarked, is that change is constant; organizations seem always to be changing. The problem is how to make things better, to translate change into performance improvement.

So, before choosing reengineering as the change strategy, top management has to think through the need to change and the timing of change. Typically, top managers conduct a policy and planning review of where the organization is headed in terms of political environment and organizational culture. If there are unions involved, labor-management relationships must also be assessed.

This review tries to gauge the "window for change" to create a workable schedule to orchestrate the change process. Nothing makes top management look worse than to produce an innovative and bold reengineering effort that sits on the desk waiting for executive review and legislative approval—the reengineering team feels betrayed and the workforce becomes more frustrated over the delays and uncertainty.

Top managers are not going to do the actual redesign; but they do need to insure that certain resources are in place and that preparatory actions have been taken to launch the effort when the time is right. For starters, top managers need to assure the organization that there will be some continuity and that they will see the effort through at least to the transition stage. This assurance may be less of a problem than one might suspect, given the fast time frames for the first three phases of reengineering—preplanning, vision, and redesign.

Part of the appeal of reengineering is that the change is rapid enough that the leadership will actually see something in place before their tenure is up (usually between 18 months and two years).

The organization's other major activity in the preplanning stage is making sure that resources are in place and that players have been selected to drive the change effort. Most organizations use some form of consulting intervention to start, so the most problematical task is to find a reasonable external consultant or a capable internal consultant, or a blend of both.

The services of external consultants with experience and expertise are expensive. Internal consultants, however, may be suspected of not being impartial or may be seen as inexperienced. Obviously, there are no easy ways out of this dilemma, but top management has to choose the project and then balance the needs for facilitation, analysis, and perspective.

Preplanning ends with a go-ahead decision. An announcement has to be made explaining to the organization the importance of the project and the choice of a radical change methodology. Above all, top management needs to communicate to the workforce, customers, suppliers, and all stakeholders that it is aware of the "pain" of change, (even though consultants may disagree over how high that pain threshold really is). The case for change has to be made from the start and recommunicated at every stage in the process of reengineering.

Phase Two: Strategic Planning— Is There a Vision?

Reengineering objectives are set by top management and some form of steering committee. Therefore, the first task is to appoint a top-level working group or committee, which previews and selects core process "targets" for innovation and redesign. This group plays a key role as "process sponsor." It is responsible for creating internal work groups to conduct the process reengineering analysis and make recommendations for redesign and restructuring. If consultants are to be used, they are also managed by the steering committee, which monitors requirements, schedules, and time frames.

The first step in BPR is the selection of projects. Top management and the steering committee are expected to *determine the priority (or sequence) for reengineering,* based on current and future needs. (In fact, some theorists and consultants hold that this selection process should be conducted as a part of a "portfolio," with the list of projects being reevaluated periodically.)

When a project is selected, as the second step, managers and the steering committee *should provide some form of initial "strategic direction,"* what is often called "the business case" or "compelling case for change." This case reviews where the process is going in the organization's future, how important it is, what values and characteristics should define it, what old and new customer groups and expectations are involved, and so forth. It also provides a frank review of current budget realities in terms of workload, operating costs, administrative support, and future budget cuts.

The case for change ends with determining what some call "stretch objectives": How much should this process improve in the future; how good should it seek to be? Can it be the best, or is better-than-average sufficient? (This is what some call "best practice" versus "leading practice.") Should it seek to be so?

The stretch objectives need to be very specific. They should enumerate the quality levels, how much the cycle time should improve, how efficient costs should be, and how satisfied customers (and even employees) should be with the process results.

All in all, BPR requires a vision, but it also requires appropriate methodologies, tools, peoples' competence, planning, and so on.

Of course, the steering committee does not give the go-ahead until it has properly laid the foundation. When commissioning the reengineering team that will redesign the process, the steering committee will insure that some form of basic measurements are in place to set baselines and or benchmarks for change. (In this case, a baseline is some form of current measurement of cost, quality, cycle time, productivity, and customer satisfaction, to be used to make interval comparisons of progress. Benchmarking refers to collecting the same types of information, but comparing it to other organizations with the same process.)

To keep the reengineering effort focused, the steering committee should be assured that the organization has a good understanding of the core business processes and the boundaries for the current redesign effort. To round out the view of processes the organization should provide the committee with preliminary listings of customers and suppliers to be included in the redesign. Clear statements about what the process entails, what resources are used, and what products and services are given to which customers are invaluable to the reengineering team.

Last, and most important, the steering committee completes its strategic planning phase by selecting the redesign team. Depending upon the size and complexity of the processes to be changed, these teams will be made up of 6 to 10 or 12 to 25 individuals chosen for their knowledge and expertise and also for their willingness to function as change agents and innovators. In the next phase, the rules for how a redesign team operates are discussed, but there are two major considerations: First, to the extent possible, reengineering work is full time (or at least the highest priority of the team members' work responsibilities); second, reengineering teams are almost always cross-functional—they require a range of perspectives that cannot be provided by a single unit or function, no matter how narrow the process.

Phase Three: Process Redesign— Is There a Methodology?

Reengineering analysis is usually carried out by some group of individuals chosen specifically to pursue process innovation or reengineering. These teams document, chart, and analyze existing process, explore ideal models or new visions of processes, oversee customer surveys, and redesign core processes or new process innovations. Once a team has been selected and given a process to redesign, it must choose some type of measurement approach.

Process reengineering requires considerable information, both to analyze proposed design changes and to validate that the changes work. In terms of skills (and potential training) reengineering teams should have expertise in the following areas: Process flowcharting, cycle time metrics, defect- and rework-level measurements, resource requirements planning and review, customer satisfaction measurements, and market share and other performance indicators.

In addition, major consideration of the information technology dimensions of process reengineering is vital. Information (and communications) technology plays a pivotal role in determining process cycle time, connectivity, and control, but information management is vital to the redesign effort. Software applications and models can be quite effectively used to track various process metrics, to plan and test prototypes for redesign models, and to validate conversion and implementation efforts. Therefore, reengineering teams may require special training in software applications or modeling and simulations.

Reengineering teams also require supplemental training and preparation. Once selected, the participants should be trained as a team in reengineering methodology, teamwork, decisionmaking, and communication skills. Attention must be paid to the training and education needs of team members over the course of their group effort.

But at the core of the reengineering apple, so to speak, are the methodologies that produce the redesign. Three methodologies were referred to previously: process map-

ping, customer assessments, and process visioning. This review will only outline some of the key steps that a reengineering team might take when it uses these methodologies. There is considerable flexibility in how the team divides up and sequences the work assignments, of course. Some organizations construct three separate subteams and conduct three different inquiries. The teams reassemble, present their findings, and create the new redesign.

Another model is to have the whole team undertake a part of each methodology and then to build a cumulative analysis that creates the new redesign.

Redesign, Step One: Process Mapping— What Is Wrong With It and How Is It Done?

There are a variety of techniques that can be used to review how the organization works, such as activity-based costing and value-added assessments, but most reengineering starts with a basic documentation step called process mapping. Process mapping is little more than horizontal flowcharting—tracking what work activities are performed, by whom, when, and what decisions are made in delivering the final product or service to a customer.

The purpose of mapping is always related to the objective of showing how work gets done in an organization. The vantage point is the customer's; so when work crosses organizational boundaries (commonly referred to as "hand-offs" or "linkage of process") this objective must be clearly identified.

Other factors shown when making process maps include all activities within blocks in sequence as stages, all hand-offs (crossing organizational units), decision points (and especially rejects or rework), suppliers (contractors), if involved, and the final product of service going to the customer.

A major dimension of the process map is its metrics, or completion time and productivity measurements. Each process map should provide data or estimates of the following:

> *quality rate*, the accuracy or reject rates of output;
> *cycle time*, how long the process takes from start to finish;
> *productivity*, how long it takes to accomplish each work task; and
> *cost*, levels of labor and capital used in completing work tasks.

Many reengineering consultants provide a note of caution before starting process mapping. Remember that the purpose is to get a better understanding of the current limitations, problems, and barriers in the process in order to change it. Extensive documentation and complex measurements should be kept to a minimum. The reengineering team will normally map out the key subprocesses, devoting most of its effort to activities that use the most resources or take the longest time to complete.

Redesign, Step Two: Customer/Stakeholder Assessments— What Is Value-Added?

Next is a detailed analysis of how customers and their needs are changing. This can be compiled informally through meetings or visits. But, increasingly, reengineering teams are turning to more formal methods such as customer satisfaction and expectation surveys or focus groups. Whether the analysis is informal or formal, the teams' goal is to produce a detailed assessment of the customer's environment, which can be translated into product and service design and delivery that will exceed customer expectations and future market needs. Sometimes this information can be obtained through face-to-face sessions with customers, asking them to detail their current requirements and then to project their requirements for the future.

Another important technique is to compare the current customer base and project how the base will change in terms of size, demographics, and other vital characteristics (such as use and access to technology).

Reengineering teams must be wary of competing or conflicting interests of different customers and factor this aspect into their customer review. A useful byproduct of the customer assessment can also be new customer service standards and customer satisfaction measurement surveys.

Recently, a new model for customer assessments has emerged that will be of increasing interest to reengineering teams. The model—called "concept engineering" because it tries to impart customer information into initial design stages—uses five core steps of diagnosis, as outlined:

1. *environment scan:* understanding the consumer's environment by surveying market demands and customer expectations from both current customers and noncustomers;
2. *customer requirements:* translating market dynamics to customer needs after analyzing customer base projections and feedback;
3. *operational requirements:* operationalizing customer requirements by creating specific measurements of customer requirements and priorities;
4. *design options:* generating design concepts and design alternatives by brainstorming design ideas and creating design solutions; and
5. *design specifications:* selecting solutions and designs by assessing options, choosing the solution, and listing all specifications for product, service delivery, and feedback.

All this may sound very complicated, but it does illustrate the point that there is more to customer assessment than simply asking the customer questions. Too many times, organizations have learned the hard way that customers often do not know what they want, sometimes they have expectations that are too low, and, even occasionally, they do not trust the organization to use customer feedback constructively.

Redesign, Step Three: Process Visioning— How Should It Work?

Last, but not least, there remains the task of creating the new model. To capture the spirit of this approach the term "clean sheet of paper" is often used. The idea is for the team to think as if it could start over, that is, ignore the current system and design it all over again. This idea may sound attractive, but, as many teams will discover, the jump from "what the system does not do" to "what it needs to do" may be immense.

When a firm is facing the redesign or process visioning phase it may be more useful to begin with a simple description of an ideal model—how this process should meet customer needs and how it should provide a "competitive niche" for the organization. This first link (called the *process vision ideal*) leads to a definition of the internal process steps, resource usage, and performance levels that the organization should commit to in order to make this new process work (called the *process attributes*). A third link incorporates the external attributes, that is, what levels of quality are required to satisfy customer requirements and expectations. But this link also includes a review of values, such as choice and cycle time, and insures that they are fully considered (called the *customer attributes and values*). The new redesign must be supported by technology, resources management, workforce training, and other *renewal processes,* which complete the institutional support part of the reengineering process.

In the final analysis, process visioning requires innovative ideas and creative brainstorming. Often, the team may invite suppliers, customers, and other stakeholders to attend the sessions and help create the new redesign. As tempting as it is to think that the best solutions are just lying out there, waiting to be implemented, this is just not the case. Innovation for new processes is no different than any invention; it requires creative, talented people who have a thorough knowledge of what is required for major change and a commitment to accomplish that change.

Once the redesign has been created and documented, it should be validated and tested. A follow-on step is to provide a flowchart of the new process, specify the desired performance and process metrics, and confirm the technology, workforce, and budget impacts. If possible, the performance of some form of test, or the construction of what is generally called a prototype, is an important step. For example, the firm could work with a limited number of customers and employees and test the new process (simulating the technology if necessary). Top management may then be more receptive to the new design, given the nature of its involvement; and prototyping will help prove the new design to those in the organization whose jobs are going to change and to those who are soon to be called upon to implement the new system and improve upon it.

Phase Four: Conversion— Is There a Transition Strategy?

Assuming acceptance of the new design by management, there remains the task of implementation planning. There must be some sort of organizational hand-off from the steering committee and the reengineering team to the actual unit implementation team that represents "the process owners." The more complex and far-reaching the redesign, the more likely the organization is to create a special team to handle the transition. This group is generally called the conversion team. It plans the transition process by considering, for example, how the organization will get its current work done while it is installing the new process design, and what will happen as the organization makes the process redesign work.

Once the organization initiates and makes a process reengineering decision, it must develop an overlapping implementation and conversion process. Process redesign and innovation, by definition, require major changes in all aspects. This redesign will impact many areas, including converting old policies to new policies, changing work assignments, retraining employees, realigning organizational structures, reconfiguring information technology, and reaffirming customer interfaces and requirements.

Perhaps the most difficult task facing the conversion team is dealing with the redesign's impact on the workforce. No matter how much of an improvement the new redesign is, many people in the workforce will be suspicious and resentful of it. They will want answers to three questions: Will I still have a job? How is my job going to change? Will I be able to do my new job with my current skills?

The conversion team leads what is called the "upskilling" effort to deal with these fears. For starters, there is a workforce planning review—what jobs are needed, where, and with what skill requirements. Then training and development plans must be created for process workers—those who will now require cross-functional training, new technology skills, and other competencies. Finally, if the redesign features self-directed work teams, plans must be laid to convert work groups into work teams by training workers in teamwork, meeting skills, cooperation and coaching, and so on. The transition is completed when all of these

steps are included in a formal implementation plan, which is then passed on to the firm for the last stage of the reengineering process.

Phase Five: Implementation—Is There a Commitment for Real Change?

Organizations must be made aware of the high failure rate of reengineering efforts. Estimates of failure range from 50 to 60 percent.

Perhaps the most critical success factor impacting the future effectiveness of the redesign concerns communications. The effects of reengineering are large; it reorganizes unit structures, realigns technology usage, redesigns workforce roles, and even reshapes organizational culture. Normal lines of communication (effective or ineffective) are by definition uprooted. This dimension is so vital that the entire process of reengineering itself is dependent on enhanced communication before, during, and especially after the conversion and implementation processes. If the organization is going through any level of downsizing, there may be even more resistance from managers and employees and substantial communications problems between them when trying to understand the new process designs.

Understanding the reasons for failure of reengineering should not be too difficult. To begin with, the extensive use of process metrics and activity cost and results data makes it easy to see where the problems are and what is not being accomplished as planned. Therefore, the first rule of planning implementation is to make sure that the redesign has been properly tested and has the necessary metrics to show degree of success or failure.

Nevertheless, even the best redesigns and prototypes have fallen prey to a variety of conversion and change problems that should have been anticipated. Typically, the biggest problem is starting the implementation process too late. The larger the implications of change, the greater is the necessity to form an implementation team that overlaps the redesign phase. In some respects, there is a tendency for organizations to use a conversion or transition stage (phase four) as a way to correct for not having planned the implementation process early enough.

Implementation should also include active roles for administrative support staffs, customer representatives, suppliers, and contractors.

Internal resistance to the new redesign has to be anticipated and not simply reacted to after the plan has been put forward. No matter how much communication occurs, opponents can be expected to be passive before the redesign occurs. Indeed, their arguments gain additional credibility if they can claim they were not consulted.

No matter, there is only one unforgivable failure when confronting inside critics; this is having to admit that the team failed to consider something.

Reengineers should never be taken by surprise by the level of opposition and the emotional strength of criticisms of the redesign. After all, the old organization has huge investments in the old way of doing things. Entire careers were built on the basis of expertise and knowledge of how to make the old system perform (perhaps cope is the better word).

Finally, there is a team approach in process management that may be perceived by many middle managers as threatening to their control and to their primary role in the old organization—mainly that of supervision.

If firms want their engineering efforts to be successful they must have a realistic plan that integrates workforce involvement, upskilling, team development, changing human resources, and budget supporting processes, and they must systematically address how the organizational culture will be transformed. Of course, the key to making BPR work is to communicate, before, during, and after every phase of the reengineering effort.

Summing Up

As powerful as reengineering is as a change methodology, it will not succeed without extensive planning, measurement, analysis, and, above all, talent. If there is one way to convey to everyone in the organization the commitment to change and management's resolve to sustain change through reengineering, it is to assign the organization's best and brightest to the redesign effort. The workforce and future managers will not only take notice of who is leading the change effort but will also understand that this level of investment can only mean that the old ways must finally give way.

The premise of reengineering is that organizations can change in ways and at speeds previously thought impossible. Reengineering can help make that happen if there is a clear vision of the future, a plan to get there, a methodology to accomplish the journey, and a purpose important enough to capture the imagination and best talent of the organization.

ALBERT C. HYDE

REGIME VALUES.   An expression used frequently in public administration literature to denote the fundamental principles of a polity which, ordinarily, should guide administrative behavior. Although the term applies in principle to any polity, de facto it appears almost exclusively in literature focused on the United States. The expression entered the public administration literature in the first edition of this author's *Ethics for Bureaucrats: An Essay on Law and Values.*

When the Watergate scandal turned professional attention to questions of ethics in the mid-1970s, professors of public administration puzzled over how to go about teaching ethics to their students. At least four possible approaches emerged: legal, philosophical, psychological, and socially equitable.

Each approach brought certain problems in its wake. The legal approach was too narrow and too negative. Neither students nor their professors seemed willing to rest content in compliance with conflict-of-interest statutes and financial disclosure regulations. Philosophy was found wanting because few public administration students could be reasonably expected to have the specialized background required to grasp and apply the subtle complexities of philosophical argument. Humanistic psychology held considerable appeal, but proved inadequate because of its failure to address the demands of "role morality" that inevitably arise in the field of professional ethics. That is, professional ethics necessarily deals with the standards suitable for a particular calling—for example, lawyers must not suborn perjury, physicians must get informed consent, and so forth. Psychology quite properly focuses on the well-being of the human person as such and, consequently, raises questions far broader than the relatively narrow concerns of any profession, including public administration.

The "social equity" movement associated with the "New Public Administration" had an enormous impact on the field, but its egalitarian and redistributive thrust was too controversial to serve as a broad-based ethical standard for the entire field of public administration.

The "regime values" method attempted to fill the gap in the ethics literature by arguing that since public servants were often required to take an oath to uphold the Constitution as a condition of employment, that oath should serve as a starting point for their ethical formation. Since American civil servants could be assumed to support the Constitution of the United States, this document could serve as a foundation for a community of moral discourse on just what the Constitution and its traditions might mean concretely for contemporary public administrators. Students were encouraged to examine the richness of the constitutional tradition in order to stimulate their moral imagination. The breadth of this tradition, with its conflicts and contradictions, would safeguard against the collapse of the regime values method into a narrow orthodoxy. Supreme Court decisions with their multiple opinions—opinions of the Court, plurality, concurring and dissenting opinions—were proposed as particularly effective pedagogical devices to encourage informed argument about fundamental principles. To focus the discussions in classrooms and training centers, equality, freedom, and property were designated as examples of salient fundamental values that helped to shape and define the American regime established in 1789. Hence, these values were called "regime values"—regime being considered the most suitable translation of Aristotle's *politeia*. Those who used the expression "regime values" were advised to make clear the Aristotelian origin of the term in order to avoid confusion with the journalistic use of the word, as in "the Clinton regime," "the Bush regime," and so forth.

JOHN A. ROHR

REGION.   A group of countries located in the same geographical area such as, for instance, Western Europe or the Scandinavian countries (Loughlin 1993).

The other meaning of the term "region" refers to territories and governmental structures located beneath the level of the nation-state (Sharpe 1993). Sometimes those regions are wholly contained within the nation-state and sometimes they straddle frontiers. But even in this sense, the term may be defined in very distinct ways. Political science and public administration see regions as territories with their own political or administrative structures beneath the state-level and, most of the time, between national level and local government tiers (Loughlin 1993). Regions, as they are dealt with here, are thus part of a state.

Historical Background

The interwar fascist and Nazi regimes in Europe propagated strong national leadership. In some countries local democracies were destroyed and the first priority of the politicians who emerged from wartime darkness was to root public rights and freedoms in institutions protected by strong constitutions (Norton 1994). Although in Germany, the federal state emerged, in Italy the new Italian Constitution of 1948 (as also, later on, the new Constitution in Spain after Francisco Franco) provided for autonomous regional governments. Although in the late 1940s and early 1960s some regions were already created in Italy with a special status (as will be seen later), the Italian legislation enabling regions in the entire country to exercise their constitutional role was not implemented until the 1970s.

Regionalization in Spain was adopted as the means of providing for the autonomy of so-called autonomous communities.

In Belgium the existence of regions and communities has a slightly different historical background. Here, state reform should provide the answer for the coexistence of different language communities and for managing differences at the political, economic, and social level. These differences explain the will for self-government of Flanders, Wallonia, the Brussels region, and, as will be seen, the German-speaking community in Belgium.

In the 1980s, France established its own form of elected regional government (Norton 1994).

The Regional Concept

One can distinguish more or less three kinds of regionalism in Europe: regionalism that introduces some characteristics of federal-state organization in a unitary state, also called a regional state; regionalism as a newly created tier of local government; and functional regionalism.

Regional State

Regionalism refers to political movements and ideologies that most of the time originate in the regions themselves. Regionalism is primarily concerned with gaining power over the social, economic, political, and cultural affairs of the region. The aim of these movements is usually the establishment of a democratically elected regional assembly with extensive political powers (Loughlin 1993).

The regional state is a quite recent form of state. It is now in expansion in Spain and Italy and has already been more than completed in Belgium. The question is whether this kind of state is here to stay or whether it must be seen only as a transitional form from a unitary state to a federal state. The regional state already has many things in common with a federal state. One important aspect is the consequence that formerly exclusive legislative and government competencies are now divided between the national parliaments and governments on one hand and the regional assemblies and governments on the other hand.

The main characteristics of a regional state are (1) the devolution of legislative competencies: This means that there is a certain category of matters for which the regions themselves can act in a legislative way; (2) the general, direct election of the regional council; (3) the existence of a regional executive board or government, which is politically responsible toward the regional council; and (4) its own fiscal competencies, linked with an allocation system. In this kind of system the residual competencies stay with the national government.

The two most important differences between a regional state and a federal state are, first of all, that there are no two constitutional regulations like in a federal state, and the division of competencies is laid down in the national constitution. And second, the regions are not represented in the Second Chamber.

Belgium, however, can in this case be seen as an exception because the Belgian Senate consists mainly of representatives from the federating entities.

Territorial Decentralization: Regions As the Upper Tier of Local Government

The following criteria are important when talking about territorial decentralization or local government organization:

- the decentralized government has its own corporate personality and its own means, separate from the central government;

- the decentralized authorities possess a degree of self-government, although the legislative power stays with the national parliament. The legislator can intervene to regulate the actions of local government and he or she can delegate some tasks; thereby it is possible for a territorially decentralized body to carry out some tasks for the central government;
- the central government exercises administrative control over decentralized bodies that are financially dependent upon the central government.

Territorial decentralization, like the regional state, is also based on the constitution. It has a political meaning because councils are directly elected, and this allows the inhabitants of a certain region to participate in their region's policy.

Functional Regionalism

In the special form of functional decentralization, a certain specific competence can be given to an independent agency, which the central government will supervise. Functional decentralized bodies also dispose of corporate personality, but functional regionalism is not based on the constitution. These agencies do not have a political character because they generally provide technical or executive tasks. These organizations can have a regional territory—for instance a city region—as a working area or they can coincide with the territory of the local governmental units. It is also possible for them to be created only for a certain specific area.

Cases of Regionalism in Western Europe

To make the theory transparent we give some examples of the different regions in Europe.

Belgium, Spain, and Italy

Belgium. The Belgian Constitution has been changed several times in the past two decades. Driving forces were not only the differences in the use of language but also the emancipation of the Dutch-speaking community, fear of minorization of the Walloon region inside a unitary state, economic differences, political-ideological differences, and the polarization in Brussels (where two language communities live together). The first reforms of the years 1970–1971 laid the basis for the state reform. The following waves of reform (1980, 1988, 1993) transformed the unitary state into a federal one (sui generis). That Belgium is a federal state composed of regions and communities is written down in the Belgian Constitution.

The organization of the state is complex. The regions and communities of which Belgium is composed exist as two different kinds of subnational authorities. As subnational entities they stand at the same level, but they each have their own spheres of competence, and their territories are different.

Many tasks of the national Parliament and government are transferred to the regions and communities, together with the budget and personnel necessary for executing these tasks. The competencies that were left to the federal government are all of those that were not explicitly given to the regions and communities. The most important ones are defense, foreign policy, internal security, social security, and monetary union.

Concerning foreign policy, however, it is important to note that, in principle, the leading competence for external relations is reserved for the federal government (for the king); this competence is exclusively for defense. But for concluding treaties, the federal government (the king) is only competent for those related to federal competencies. The Belgian Constitution explicitly gives the regions and communities the competence to conclude treaties for their own policy areas.

Questions related to the use of language and to cultural identity are community matters (person-related matters). Belgium has three communities, namely the Dutch-speaking community, the French-speaking community, and the German-speaking community. Authority over the use of the territory is regional (territory related matters). Belgium also counts three regions: the Flemish region, the Walloon region, and the Brussels region. Community matters are, for instance, cultural policies, media, education, public health, social welfare (but not social security), integration of migrants, and so on. Regional matters are, for example, urban and spatial planning, environment, housing, economic policy, energy, employment, public works, and local transport.

The three regions and the three communities have their own councils and their own governments. These councils enact "decrees." They stand at the same level as national laws; there is no hierarchy between them. Until recently, only the councils for the German community and for the Brussels region had been directly elected. The other councils were composed of the members of the national Parliament. But at this moment, the other councils are also directly elected for a five-year period.

Spain. The 1978 Spanish Constitution perceives the Spanish nation as a group of nationalities and regions with specific identities, which differ in terms of language, cultural traditions, and symbols of identity (Cuchillo 1993), but it does not challenge "the indissoluble unity of the Spanish nation, common and indivisible fatherland of all Spaniards."

The Spanish Constitution did not explicitly install the seventeen *Comunidades Autónomas,* or autonomous communities, but only provided for certain procedures to make it possible for certain members of the parliament of one province or a group of provinces to start a process of regionalization.

The Constitution did not set out a predetermined map of the regions to be created; in other words, not all the communities in Spain had to become part of a *comunida autónoma*. The creation of a regional government had to take place through a process from below and from the region itself. The level of autonomy that could be reached by the regions ranges from political autonomy, meaning legislative and executive power, to administrative autonomy, implying merely executive powers. That is why the powers transferred to the regions vary widely and why there exist both regions with full autonomy and regions with deferred autonomy. All of these elements had to be laid down in separate statutes; as a consequence there is a wide range of different sorts of autonomous communities. Nevertheless, statutes fall more or less into two categories that reflect two different ways of reaching autonomy: special and general. The first category covers the three historical national minorities, namely the Basque country, Catalonia, and Galicia. Andalucia has been added for political reasons. These four regions have full autonomy statutes, which must be ratified by referendum.

The second category is a transitional category. The autonomous communities in question can, after a five year period, request wider powers to obtain full autonomy. This has already happened on several occasions and means that the Spanish system tends toward greater homogeneity based on full autonomy of the regions (Morata 1992).

The Spanish Constitution lists the powers that are reserved for central government; for instance, those related to foreign affairs; foreign trade; defense; legislation on criminal, private, and commercial law; the monetary system; economic planning; health policy and national health service; and so on.

Powers that may be assumed by all regions are supervision of local government within national regulations; town and country planning and housing within the national basic legislation; public works of regional interest; regional economic development; and so forth (Cuchillo 1993).

The authorities of the regions with full autonomy exist in the form of a regional assembly, or parliament, directly elected by the population; an executive council, or regional government, supported by a majority within the regional parliament; and a president, elected by the regional assembly. The other regions can organize themselves in a different way, but have used the same system with some slight variations. The regions obtain fiscal powers through explicit devolution granted by an Act of Parliament.

Italy. In Italy, centralization was considered to be a product of fascist authoritarianism, and regionalism appeared to be the most effective solution to safeguard a democratic system. The Italian Constitution of 1948 perceives regional and local government as integral parts of a national political system based on law. Article 115 of the Constitution states: "The regions are constituted as autonomous entities with their own powers and functions according to the principles determined in the Constitution" (Norton 1994).

In 1948 and 1963 regions with special status were created for the peripheral areas of Sicily, Sardinia, Trentino/Alto-Adige, Friuli-Venezia Giula, and Val d'Aosta. The statutes of these special regions were promulgated in the form of constitutional laws (Cassese and Torchia 1993). The German-speaking province of Bolzano was given a special autonomous status in 1969. For the five regions with a special status, the Constitution was implemented almost immediately in order to give an answer to the serious ethnic-linguistic or separatist problems of those regions; the creation of the other fifteen regions, however, encountered obstacles for Italy. The difficulties, which delayed the realization of those regions, were mainly due to the political position of the Democrazia Cristiana (the Italian Christian Democratic party). This party thought that regionalization in Italy would allow the north central regions to fall into the hands of the Partito Comunista (the Communist Party). It took until the mid-1970s before all of the other regions were created.

The competencies of the regions can be divided into three areas:

- First of all, there are community and social service matters; that is, health care and welfare, local transport, museums, and a limited role in education (student grants).
- Second, a group of competencies concerns land use policy, comprising urban and regional planning, water supply, and forestry.
- Third, there are the economic issues of a purely regional nature; tourism, agriculture, and so on (Chandler 1993).

The competencies or the range of competencies are not the same for all of the regions. The regions with a special statute have a much wider range of competencies.

The basic internal structure for regional governments in Spain is laid down in the national Constitution. They have three organs: the regional council, the *giuntà*, and the president. The council exercises the legislative and regulatory powers, and the president of the *giuntà* represents the region (Norton 1994). Nevertheless, the regions still often have to cooperate with the national administration.

On one hand, regions are independent for accounting purposes. Ordinary regions have narrow fiscal resources, for example, taxes on concessions of state land and assets, on regional concessions, and on traffic and use of public areas and spaces. The special regions, on the other hand, have wider fiscal resources.

Regions in France

Municipalities, *départements* (counties), and regions share the juridical status of territorial collectivities (*collectivités territoriales*), created in the French Constitution of 1946 and continued in the Constitution of 1958.

In France there are 22 regions, and their core function is to provide a framework to allow local government to act more effectively (Mazey 1993). One may see the regions as a third tier of local government. Regions group two or more *départements*.

Regions in France do not have legislative competence; they have only decentralized administrative competence. A region has no general authority. Its role is more or less complementary; this means coordinating, programming, and organizing social and economic development policy, and providing special wide-area services (Norton 1994). Regions in France are also able to give modest financial aid to other bodies. Tasks of regions are, for instance, regional, economic, social, and cultural development; regional housing policy; financing major road developments; development of local economies and employment; and so on.

In each region there is a deliberative representative assembly, called the regional council. One can also distinguish the regional executive. The president of the regional council is its sole executive. The president also takes the place of some vice-presidents. There exists also an advisory economic and social committee, which represents the interests of the main groups in the area of the region. Representatives of the employers and of the trade unions have a seat on this committee. Another 25 percent of seats are allocated to representatives from a range of organizations "participating in the collective life of the nation" (Norton, 1994).

The principal sources of regional revenue in France are regional taxes and central government grants and loans. After the reforms in 1982, regions were given more responsibilities, for which they receive financial compensation from the state in the form of grants and fiscal transfers.

Functional Regions

In all of the Western European countries functional regions exist, but only the British example is developed here.

First of all, regional economic planning in the United Kingdom falls within this category of functional regions. From 1964 onward there was a system of regional planning institutions consisting of representative councils and boards of civil servants. These institutions were created for each of the eight English regions and one each for Scotland and Wales. Some observers saw those regional bodies as a kind of embryonic regional state (Sharpe 1993) and hoped that this evolution would stimulate regional consciousness. But these regional economic planning institutions only played a minor role.

Another development in the United Kingdom that tried to stimulate regional consciousness was the demand for devolution, which was going in the direction of a regional state; especially in Scotland and Wales. In the late 1970s, attempts were made to create regional elected assemblies in Scotland and Wales, but this was not a success because results from referendums that were required to be held did not meet specific turn-out conditions (Sharpe 1993).

The demand for devolution has faded, although recently devolution has become a political issue again in Scotland.

Another example of functional decentralization in the United Kingdom is the regional bodies of the National Health Service.

The functional regions of other Western European Countries exist as systems of territorial subdivisions in which the different policy sectors—police, fire brigade, social policy, and so forth, are administratively organized.

Europe of the Regions

The slogan "Europe of the Regions" has become part of the political debate concerning the future of Europe. Although the national states defend their autonomy in the face of European and subnational challenges, there is a process of change going on. The European Union and the regions have strengthened their power, and new patterns of institutional links have emerged. Mainly, the regional states are eager for a Europe of the Regions.

At the beginning, regional policy within the European Union was seen only in economic terms, but now also the political role of the regions has come into focus. The European Union is not yet a Europe of the Regions, because the status of the existing regions is different and their role varies from issue to issue and from country to country. Recently, the Committee of the Regions and Local Bodies has been created, and it tries to give local and regional authorities an advisory role in areas of European Community legislation and policies that concern them, including federal states, such as Germany.

CAROLINE MEYERS AND RUDOLF MAES

BIBLIOGRAPHY

Cassese, S., and L. Torchia, 1993. "The Meso Level in Italy." In L. J. Sharpe, ed., *The Rise of Meso Government in Europe*, pp. 91–116. Sage Modern Politics Series, vol. 32. London: Sage Publications.

Chandler, J. A., ed., 1993. *Local Government in Liberal Democracies: An Introductory Survey*. London and New York: Routledge.

Commission of the European Communities, Directorate-General for Regional Policy, 1991. *The Regions in the 1990s: Fourth Periodic Report on the Social and Economic Situation and Development of the Regions of the Community.* Luxembourg, Brussels: Directorate-General.

Cuchillo, M., 1993. "The Autonomous Communities as the Spanish Meso." In L. J. Sharpe, ed., *The Rise of Meso Government in Europe*, pp. 210–246, London: Sage.

Hesse, J.J., ed., 1991. *Local Government and Urban Affairs in International Perspective: Analysis of Twenty Western Industrialised Countries.* Baden-Baden: Nomos.

Loughlin, J., 1993. "Nation, State and Region in Western Europe." In *Europe of the Regions Versus Europe of the Cities: Reader.* Erasmus, PA: Network.

Mazey, S., 1993. "Developments at the French Meso Level: Modernizing the French State." In L. J. Sharpe, ed., *The Rise of Meso Government in Europe*, pp. 61–89. London: Sage.

Morata, F., 1992. "Regions and the European Community: A Comparative Analysis of Four Spanish Regions." *Regional Politics and Policy: An International Journal*, vol. 2, nos. 1–2: 187–216.

Norton, A., 1994. *International Handbook of Local and Regional Government: A Comparative Analysis of Advanced Democracies.* Brookfield, VT: Edward Elgar Limited.

Sharpe, L. J., 1993. "The United Kingdom: The Disjointed Meso." In L. J. Sharpe, ed., *The Rise of Meso Government in Europe*, pp. 247–295. London: Sage.

Ziller, J., 1993, *Administrations Comparées. Les systèmes politico-administratifs de l'Europe des Douze.* Montchrestein: Domat Droit Public.

REGIONAL DEVELOPMENT.

The economic, social, and community growth within parts of a nation.

Regional development became a public policy concern as more and more countries recognized that not all parts of their national economies expanded at the same rate. In some cases, parts (or regions) could have income, social, and community development levels that were well below the national average. Considerable effort has been directed at alleviating the uneven pattern of development within nations. In some countries, too, regional approaches to national development were undertaken in the belief that the overall national pattern would be more efficient and more equitable as a result.

Regional development reflects the interaction of demand and supply factors within a nation. On the supply side, the naturally uneven pattern of resource deposits, agricultural fertility, and general physical characteristics of regions meant that as nations expanded, some parts experienced more economic stimulus than others. More subtle supply forces involved the quality of local infrastructure and the skill and cost of labor; in many cases, regions were unable to supply goods and services at competitive prices, so they did not feel the impact of national economic demand. An important supply side factor has always been transport links, as regions that are well placed on transport

networks have usually been better able to get products to markets and so have attracted more investment and commercial development. In contrast, the isolated region has faced problems in this regard.

On the demand side, development of a region depends upon markets for the products of its firms. This demand provides the underlying industrial and commercial structure of the region, and, in general terms, the broader that base the better the long-term development prospects for the region. In some regions, the industrial structure is made more complex by the location of many component suppliers around a key firm, as in the automobile industry. This contrasts with an agricultural region, where the product is simply shipped out to a market or sent for processing in another region.

These extremes illustrate that the industrial and commercial structure of a region has a critical influence upon its vitality. In this perspective, the process of industrial restructuring in the period from 1970 to 1990 reshaped the pattern of regional development in many nations. Old industrial regions, with crowded infrastructure and old equipment, had problems competing with goods made in new areas. At the same time, many new products came on the national market, and some regions were better able to meet the demand for those products than were others. Regions with a concentration on high technology, for example, have expanded rapidly in the past 20 years.

The patterns of regional development often reflect the patterns of city development, as the latter provide a favorable economic environment for the development of many industries and commercial services. Hence there is usually a clearly defined core region in a nation where income and production are high, and this area corresponds to the largest cities, the major seaports, and the busiest airports. Elsewhere in the country, there are peripheral regions with lower production and lower income. These patterns can change, and the decline of a major industry due to international competition can quickly change a region from core status to that of a periphery.

The policy perspectives on regional development have involved choices between what has come to be called "people prosperity" and "place prosperity." In the former, the objective of policy is to assist the prosperity of people, irrespective of where they live; it is possible that certain targeted programs will be delivered in a few special regions, but, in general, this approach recognizes that people are the ultimate beneficiaries of the development process, and the role of policy is to help people in all regions.

A likely outcome of this approach is the migration of people from areas of low opportunity to areas of high opportunity, assisted in some places by relocation on job search grants, and also by universal education and skill training to allow the workforce to find employment in expanding regions. This approach naturally has the effect of creating more inequality, as people leave peripheral locations and cluster in core areas; because of this move they could eventually overcrowd the core areas and create regional problems of congestion and other matters. The people prosperity approach also faces the difficulty that not all people can move easily. Some could be trapped in a slow-growth region because they lack the skills that are in demand in the core area, or because they cannot sell their houses, or afford housing in the core region.

The alternative approach involves "place prosperity," in which policies are directed at places, in the provision of infrastructure, transport, locally specific training that reflects the needs of the regions' industries, and also considerable effort designed to attract activity from core areas to the peripheral locations. This approach has the greatest political support because it connects the needs of the local community with the resources available from national government. It also unleashes a vigorous battle between regions that are bidding for new investment as a way of stimulating their regional development. At a national level this conflict can lead to wasteful competition infrastructure in the form of industrial land, transport facilities, and power and water supply in anticipation of investment. If the region is unsuccessful in its effort to attract activity, these facilities will be left underutilized.

The issues created in one or another approach to regional development are generally addressed in one of two ways: a top-down approach or a bottom-up approach. The top-down perspective is run by central governments and is often expressed in complex plans for the whole country, which outline the role of particular regions and the level of assistance that each will get. The latter approach usually provides greater assistance in areas of high unemployment. These national approaches also include guidelines that specify the eligibility of areas to receive funding for industrial development. Often, these programs have major components directed at changing the structure of industries, improving regional infrastructure and job training, and encouraging small firm development. In Europe, the European Commission provides a supranational resource allocation mechanism, directing European resources away from the high-income cores to the slower-growth agricultural and industrial peripheries.

The alternative perspective is a bottom-up approach. Here the emphasis in policy development and action is at the level of the individual region, with regional specific organizations designed to facilitate development, promote the region in competition with others, and marshal the local resources and skills of the community to lift the overall level of regional performance. Many of these organizations are funded by national governments, but also attempt to find resources from local sources. This particular approach, like the place prosperity perspective, has become popular as it is better able to incorporate local political opinion and influence. These organizations often stress their region's identity and unique character in promotional brochures, as well as the opportunities for industrial and commercial development. The potential for action in slower-growth regions is limited by the low level of resources many will have, however, so this bottom-up perspective can only hope to be effective if it is funded by the central government. The local focus also leads to an emphasis on community development, as well as the more direct economic aid of traditional regional developmental policy. Actions that will improve community facilities, local transport, and the opportunity for local labor and firms to be active in larger markets all figure in this approach, which has come to be called "local economic development."

Regional development has long been a concern in public policy primarily because the great efforts at national and regional levels have done little to change the distinctive core-periphery pattern of development in most nations over a long period of time. That lack of change reflects strong supply and demand forces that limit the spread of commercial activity and provide special advantages to particular places. There is little sign that these special advantages, and the pattern of development associated with them, will change in the immediate future.

KEVIN O'CONNOR

BIBLIOGRAPHY

Amin, A., and J. B. Goddard, 1986. *Technological Change, Industrial Restructuring and Regional Development*. London: Allen and Unwin.

Eisenchitz, A., and J. Gough, 1993. *The Politics of Local Economic Policy*. London: Macmillan.

Friedman, J., and W. Alonso, eds., 1975. *Regional Policy: Readings in Theory and Applications*. Cambridge, MA: MIT Press.

Stohr, W., 1990. *Global Challenge and Local Response: Initiatives for Economic Regeneration in Contemporary Europe*. London: Mansell.

REGIONALISM. The philosophy inherent in a place, defined by its interdependent shared topography, biota, and socioculture, encompassing a large territorial expanse and a sense of commonweal among its people.

Regionalism includes many applications and interpretations, reflecting the variability of its root word, "region." Terms synonymous with region, based upon the context, include area, district, sector, belt, tract, zone, section, field, realm, and territory. Qualifier adjectives appropriate to the regional policy and planning fields include comprehensive, metropolitan, urban, rural, substate, subnational, and intergovernmental.

Regional policy and planning have concerns more broadly based than those residing in the local communities of interest that underpin the regional community. A regional community has interdependent natural and cultural activities that foster a sense of regional common good and that mark the approximate circumferential boundaries of the region. People engage in these interdependent natural and cultural activities during their normal daily routine when they seek out diversion or sustenance or myriad other activities.

Scholars isolate and study these interdependent activities of the regional community through economics, politics, sociology, and geography, or the many splinter subfields such as cultural geography or sociopsychology. Additional fields of anthropology, history, planning, public policy, and public administration provide other useful frameworks through which to approach and analyze the region.

Scholars in these fields and subfields study aspects such as administrative systems, geologic features, natural topography, language dialects, political boundaries, regional climate, social communities, specialized customs, economic submarkets, cultural unities, and other complex interactions. Differentiation of one regional community from a second neighboring one is based upon distinctions among these various attributes.

The term "regionalism" has been applied well beyond this traditional context in recent years, and the public interchanges the classic regionalism with other more recent terms such as "regionalization of services" and "multicommunity collaboration," which are organizational techniques. The more lax application of the term "regionalism" has caused it to lose some precision and effectiveness. Today, use of regionalism can create great commotion and misunderstanding, particularly in the political arena. Both confusion and emotionalism hinder the development of regionalism as its own distinct discipline, separate from the language borrowed from sociologists or economists or other social scientists. It slows the development of general principles that guide historical interpretation and that permit limited testable projections into the future—often exactly the type of knowledge useful to regional policy development and implementation.

The science of regionalism remains inexact. This lack of exactness in terminology and language remains a handicap to practical and scholarly perusal, and hinders pragmatic and theoretical application of and communication on the subject. Moreover, the development of cyberspace, where Web sites arise that display a common unity of interest among the members, threatens the notion that regional communities of interest must perforce be areal-based and stands to provide additional mysteries to the study of regionalism. If there is cyberspace, there can be cyberregion.

Origin

The use of the region as the geographic unit of the state begins with the multiple causal development of the city

in the millennia following 5000 B.C.E., such that by 1000 B.C.E. there existed a half-dozen spontaneously developed clusters of city-regions flourishing in isolation in various places throughout the Americas, Africa, and Asia. A basic grouping of preconditions formed the path of urban emergence of the city-region in the independently developed global locations—these preconditions being (1) reliable production of a food surplus that permitted (2) a settled society and (3) rituals that slowly begat civilization. The various early city-settlements expressed no specialization at their inception, but they began to move into their own diverse trajectories as they took dominion over their hinterlands to create the first singular attributes of human regionalism as we know it. Writing in *A Theory of Good City Form* (1981), Kevin Lynch, whose preconditions are captured above, proposes these first regions to be characterized as large, dense settlements of heterogeneous people that organize large rural territories around themselves.

Specialization of the regions rapidly followed, as location and natural features emerged to shape their development in a beneficial fashion. Chief among the specializations regions adhered to were strategic military locations, trade route transportation nodes, state administrative districts, economic marketplaces, and religious ceremonial centers. The most advantageous sites pursued multiple specializations. Spreading from the initial half-dozen city-regions, many of the second wave of new city-region settlements were distinguished from the first wave by virtue of being specialized from inception.

The apex of ancient regionalism emerged and flourished in the Greek city-states between 700 and 400 B.C.E. Greek scholar Raphael Sealey has written that Greek settlement characteristics that emerged after the Dark Ages (post 750 B.C.E.) were the city-state or *polis* and the tribal community, or *ethos*. The concept of the regional community, so vital to the sense of the region, was expressed fully in the ancient Greek city-states like Athens and Sparta.

A remarkable interaction between citizens and their "regional place" created a distinctive Athenian sensibility or Spartan quality. Sealey provides much the same preconditions for city-states or regions as did Lynch: a cluster of dwellings, a dependent territory, and a fortified and defensible space, which for Greeks, meant a fortified stronghold on commanding heights—a citadel. To the resident, this created a vivid sense of place that made his or her region distinct and special and that connected all communicants to each other's well-being.

All Greek city-states, as unfettered expressions of their regional community, shared a naturalness of community and connection to the land not evident among the more arbitrary boundaries between ancient empires of the time or between nations and regions of today.

Something as vital and fluid as a regional economy or a regional community cannot be meaningfully defined by a set of political lines drawn arbitrarily across the land-

scape, writes Daniel Kemmis (1995) about the city-state regions of today.

Theory

The theoretical principles behind regionalism vary across the social sciences disciplines. The immensely complex and dynamic interactions within the regions, the confusion regarding terminology, and the lack of a financial and political incentive for their exploration have impeded the development of regionalism into a self-contained discipline or a unified theory. This complex regional reality forces researchers into segmented approaches to the concept and fosters disjointed research approaches.

One instance of specialized regional theory is the application of "central place theory" within urban economics. Central place theory refers to a region's location, size, nature, and the spacing of these clusters of differentiated consumer activity, as defined by Brian J. L. Berry (1967). Central place theory has proved to be a valuable formula for the placement of shopping malls within a region, but it provides no direct insight, for example, into uneven housing opportunities in metropolitan areas.

A further drawback to a unified regionalism theory is the ready availability of oppositional specialized theories. As an example, consider the two distinct theories offered to explain the effect on public goods and services of the decentralized system of government practiced in America's regions. Public choice theorists such as Robert Bish, Elinor Ostrom, and Charles Tiebout have argued that the numerous local governments of a region offer their own public goods and services to create a competitive public marketplace that keeps governmental costs down.

Reformists such as Victor Jones, Robert Wood, and David Rusk have problems with this picture of decentralized regionalism. They have asserted that local government boundaries dissect the natural regional interdependence and activity to create inefficiencies and duplication, among other complaints. These reformists further splinter as a group over what is the best rationale for petitioning public support: appeals based upon regional social equity ("no man is an island") or on local economic self-interest ("all politics is local").

The central dynamic that separates theorists of public choice from those of reform remains the following: Lack of correspondence within a region between the political blueprint and the natural and cultural interdependencies is a source of strength for the region to the public choice theorists and a debilitating handicap for the region to the reformists. Both groups can marshal studies to the defense of their tenets.

Another example of theory and countertheory appears in mainstream urban economics literature. Theorists have elaborated two fundamentally different explanations of suburb-city interaction, according to Todd Swanstrom

(1995). Suburb-city interdependence models posit that suburbs/exurbs are economically dependent upon the central city (Downs 1994; Barnes and Ledebur 1994; Peirce, 1993; Savitch et al. 1993). Therefore, a declining central city will have a markedly negative effect on its surrounding hinterland. Suburb-city independence models state that suburbs/exurbs are new edge cities, economically independent of and even eclipsing central city functions and finances (Garreau 1991; Muller 1981; Fishman 1987). Thus, core cities do not have an economic hold over suburbs, and their health is inconsequential to outer-ring development. The opportunity to build on a consensual foundation for regional theory remains elusive.

Theorists face other fundamental problems on tasks as basic as consistent boundaries for regions in the United States. This happens because there are many types of regions in the United States. Smaller regions can hover at the urbanized area of 50,000 people. Large-scale regions are multiple state entities, such as watersheds, which contain numerous urbanized areas and millions of residents. The U.S. Bureau of the Census provides a common statistical unit.

The Census Bureau's most recent statistical unit for regionalism (1993) is Metropolitan Area (MA), the generic umbrella term covering Consolidated Metropolitan Statistical Areas (CMSA), Primary Metropolitan Statistical Areas (PMSA), and Metropolitan Statistical Areas (MSA). The Census Bureau began an effort at regional definition in 1880 with the tenth Census. In 1900, it first used the term "metropolitan districts," a term that would remain unaltered in the century's first half and receive numerous name and definition changes in the second half.

MA boundaries follow county boundaries outside of New England, or city and town boundaries in New England. All MAs consist of a densely settled population core of 50,000 or more, containing a central city or cities, together with surrounding areas in which a substantial percentage of the workers commute to the core area for work. MAs must have a total population of 100,000 (75,000 in New England) or more, or a central city of 50,000 or more. MAs of one million or higher may be subdivided into PMSAs if population and commuting criteria are met and there is local support for designation. When an area is subdivided into PMSAs, the entire overarching region then becomes the CMSA. All other MAs, that is, those that do not qualify or that do not seek the enlarged designation, are subclassified as MSAs.

The latest recognition of MAs was done in June 1995, based on updated data from the 1990 census. The number of census-defined individual unit MA regions totaled 326. These MAs were subclassified into 253 MSAs and 73 PMSAs, and supraclassified through the PMSA category into 18 CMSAs.

Smaller regions have a separate census category, the Urbanized Area (UA), defined in terms of density rather than the MA jurisdictional- and population-based boundaries. UAs were first defined in 1950 to better separate urban and rural territory and population and housing in the vicinity of larger cities. UAs have one or more central places or cities plus the adjacent densely settled surrounding territory, which together have a minimum of 50,000 persons. This adjacent densely settled territory has a population density of at least 1,000 persons per square mile. Becoming a UA is often the first step toward being recognized later as an MA. The most recent UA listing in 1991 showed 396 UAs.

There are other common ways to demarcate regions. Some researchers and most marketing specialists use aggregates of zip codes to approximate regional boundaries. States have permitted local governments to establish regional councils, another potential unit. The Census Bureau compiled statistics on a regional council basis only once, as the *1977 Census of Governments, Regional Organizations* (United States Bureau of the Census 1978), but continues its quinquennial data series for the statistical Metropolitan Areas and Urbanized Areas. Rarely do any regional council, metropolitan area, zip code delineation, or Urbanized Area Boundaries coincide, again reflecting the complexity of handling information on the concept. During the latter 1990s, federal statistical users were part of a major Census Bureau effort to reevaluate the existing MA and UA units of measure prior to the next governmental census.

Current Practice in the United States

In the federated system of government practiced in the United States, a dense set of interrelations between the national, state, and local divisions of government exists. The permeable nature of the U.S. federal system permits special interests, nonprofit organizations, businesses, and others to engage directly in the influence and implementation of public policy in the region. The result today is a practice of local regionalism that is complex, fragmented, decentralized, and highly personalized to its host region.

The early years of U.S. regionalism paralleled the Greek model in which the boundaries of the regional community matched the boundaries of the governing political apparatus. At the close of the nineteenth century, some visionaries began to notice that U.S. metropolitan regions were starting to outgrow their political boundaries and become Greater Cities. The quandary caused by the emergence of the Greater City came to the attention of Edmund James, who commented in *Annals of the American Academy of Political and Social Science* (1899) that a long time has elapsed in the history of many U.S. great cities after the period when the suburban regions should have been annexed to bring about the adjustment that lay in the wider and larger interests of all.

Creation of a Real City whose political boundaries expanded apace of the outward population sprawl through governmental consolidation or annexation occupied the energies of American reformers for the first two-thirds of the twentieth Century. Reformers had early successes in the creation of the Real City through consolidation and annexation of suburban property, but inhibitory state legislation and the political maturation of suburbs halted the Greater City movement, except in the far West and Southwest.

The emerging professional disciplines of city planning and city administration addressed the special needs of the regional community regardless of the match to political boundaries. By 1925, regional planning bodies were extant in more than a dozen U.S. regions, as inventoried by Theodora Hubbard in April 1925 in *City Planning*. Regional councils, planning bodies where local and elected officials were installed directly on the board of the organization, promoted early access of the public into the regional planning and policy process. Hubbard reported the appearance of the Niagara Frontier Planning Association in Buffalo in 1924 with this board feature, which was designed to increase the implementation chances of regional plans.

The Great Depression and World War II slowed the metropolitan decentralization movement to the suburbs that had begun to grow in the 1920s through streetcar extensions and expanded street routes for automobiles. For the next two decades, the spread of regional planning would be fitful, but, as the war drew to a close and suburbanization reemerged, local citizen groups, chiefly in urban areas, created metropolitan planning commissions. The Advisory Commission on Intergovernmental Relations (ACIR) in its *Substate Regionalism and the Federal System* reported 39 metropolitan planning commissions in 1954.

As early as 1924, policy leaders were proposing a greater involvement of the national government's role in metropolitanism at the local level, arguing that the states of that era were not equipped to meet the challenge. William Anderson (1924) in the *National Civic Review* called for the creation of the National Bureau of Local Government. The federal government provided some early metropolitan planning responsibilities through the Federal Emergency Administration of Public Works in 1933. Coordinated planning among jurisdictions was a test of funding eligibility for this program, and applicants were required to specify whether their area had a regional planning board, whether their application had gone before that board, and what the board's opinion was regarding the application, as reported by the Advisory Commission on Intergovernmental Relations. Some years later, the Housing Act of 1949 had vague requirements for metropolitan planning as a condition of receiving federal assistance.

The first federal program providing for the intergovernmental coordination of planning came in an amendment in 1959 to the Housing Act of 1954, Section 701, with implementation begun in the 1960s. The Section 701 program required the preparation of a comprehensive plan and the establishment of a comprehensive planning process incorporating housing, land use, public facilities, and recreation elements, among others. Metropolitan planning agencies were required as much as feasible to plan for the entire urban area on an interjurisdictional basis. Funds were quadrupled to US $75 million in 1961. Direct eligibility was extended to regional councils of governments in 1965, to local (regionwide) development districts in 1967, and to nonmetropolitan regional economic development districts in 1968.

The other major federal boost to regionalism came with the Intergovernmental Cooperation Act of 1968, Title 5, implemented by Circular A-95. This program enabled many regional agencies to review and comment upon applications for funds to 259 federal programs. The regional agencies were expected to determine the degree to which the applications coordinated with existing areawide policies and plans. Throughout the 1970s the federal government was predisposed to this type of regionalism support. During 1977, three-forths of regional councils' budgets came from the national government, and they dispersed across the United States to reach their organizational highs in the late 1970s, hovering around 670 agencies.

During this decade of the 1970s, a national government federalism research commission, the Advisory Commission on Intergovernmental Relations, sought to standardize terminology and boundaries of federal regional organizations. The acronym UMJO for Umbrella Multi-Jurisdictional Organization was presented in 1973 in ACIR's first volume of their six-volume study of regional councils, but never gained widespread usage. The term "regional council" remains the generic word for these diverse regional agencies. They are voluntary associations of local governments that represent the entire region's interests and coordinate regional comprehensive plans, resources, services, and programs.

The 1980s ushered in an era of reduced national government presence in regionalism. Categorical grant programs that specified regional entities as recipients were eliminated or collapsed into block grant programs under state management, where regionalism might not be a preferred state policy and therefore was deemphasized. The transfer of A-95 to the states through its reformulation as Executive Order 12372, making it a voluntary state program, completed the national deemphasis. Federal funding declined to 45 percent of the regional council budget by 1988.

Through this transition, numerous states did continue their policy support of the regional approach or expanded the reach of regional policy. The timing of federal deemphasis was propitious for a surge in state involvement. States in the 1980s had increased their own professionalism, were managing revenue surpluses, and were supportive of the decentralization process. Regional policy work and state circumstances converged at an advantageous moment.

Numerous states now involve regional councils in state regional policy, sorting along two clusters of activity: ecogrowth policy and administrative policy. Ecogrowth policy encompasses regional issues usually triggered during periods of rapid growth that impact water quality, air quality, land management, solid waste management, wastewater management, land use regulation, wetlands policy, or transportation environmental impacts. The administrative policy usage employs regional councils to streamline governmental procedures, to interface between state services or plans and citizens, and to deliver directly certain service activities, particularly senior services and economic stimulation services.

As early as the 1930s, some states established regional planning processes for sensitive coastal regions. Water shortages and other growth pressures of suburbia prompted a surge among states to provide important planning roles to regional councils during the 1970s.

Georgia provides examples both of regional ecogrowth policy and administrative policy. It pioneered the statewide use of regional councils as administrative intermediaries in the 1960s with the organization of its uniform system of area planning and development commissions, becoming the first state to have a complete multicounty regional district system. A restructuring of the system in 1989 reorganized the commissions into regional development centers and provided additional regional responsibilities to the centers. These duties included review over developments of regional impact, review over developments affecting regionally important resources, mediation of any conflicting projects in local government's plans, and generation of comprehensive regional plans mindful of local plans and consistent with the state's initial plan.

Ten states involve regional councils in ecogrowth policy. These are Florida, Georgia, Idaho, Maine, Minnesota, New Jersey, North Carolina, Oregon, Vermont, and Washington, and many of their policies are covered in a recent book by John DeGrove (1992). Florida legislated regulation of developments of regional impact in 1972, and regional planning councils were provided an active role. A 1985 state act required regional plans that were consistent with a state master plan. In turn, local plans were to maintain consistency with the regional plans. Adequate infrastructure capacity had to be in place, including adequate drainage, recreation, roads, solid waste disposal, water treatment, and wastewater treatment, before regional-impact and local developments could proceed. This concurrency requirement is a strong regulation.

Oregon contains the only elected regional legislators, called councilors, in the United States, sitting as the governing council of Portland's METRO. METRO replaced the more limited Metropolitan Service District, which was preceded by the Columbia Region Association of Governments, and before that, the region's first multicounty planning group, the Metropolitan Planning Commission, from 1957. METRO covers a three-county area and handles the region's urban growth boundary responsibilities, by which most land outside the boundary is protected from development. METRO manages a variety of other services, including the area's convention center, regional solid waste landfills, the library system, the metropolitan zoo, and the recycling program, among other efforts.

Administrative policy states include Florida, Georgia, Kentucky, North Carolina, South Carolina, Tennessee, Texas, and Virginia. Kentucky permits regional councils to provide certain services directly to the consumer and uses regional councils to assist in its own program delivery to local governments, particularly in federally funded services to the elderly and economic development. Federal economic development legislation in 1965 was the impetus to the governor's designation of a statewide system, including directions to state agencies to conform their activities to system boundaries, later statutorily amended.

Texas is another prototypical state in administrative usage of the regional concept. Regional councils in 1969 were promoted to status as political subdivisions of the state, with authority to purchase and sell real property and to perform services under contract to local governments, particularly transportation, wastewater treatment, criminal justice, human services, and job training.

A majority of the 550 or so regional councils across the United States today do not receive ecogrowth or administrative responsibilities from their states. A commonality of all regional councils in the 1990s is a legitimacy based squarely upon the support of their local communities. Regional council policies and activities unfold at the request of their member local governments, providing a national diversity. These specific and often unique policies and projects have supplanted comprehensive regional planning as the basic repertoire of regional councils. One regional council may operate the public cable television station for the area. Another may manage a policy mobile training center for law enforcement officer firearms and other skills practice. For each regional council, the local mix of activities is different.

Regionalism Options

Local governments within regions use many other techniques to achieve coordination of their activities. The techniques of regionalism are classified through a continuum first defined and clarified by Roscoe Martin in 1963. Martin's classification system sorts regionalism tools by the degree of local autonomy remaining to the local jurisdictions, where local governments are suspended between surrendering little or none through use of mutual aid agreements and foregoing all through creation of a unitary metropolitan government.

The Martin classification system has been flexible enough to absorb new practices of regionalism. It remains a valuable base for the expanded current regional techniques list, to which others have made contributions, particularly Patricia Atkins (1995) and David Walker (1995). (See Figure I.) Consider that these techniques intersect one another and are superimposed upon a mighty backdrop of existing federal, state, county, municipal, and perhaps township governments with their own myriad departments and committees, and understand that the rich and chaotic intergovernmental texture of American government is expressed in the region.

The classification list starts with options that require none or very little loss of autonomy for the typical local government. It moves to those requiring greater and greater preemption of localism, such that citizens who opt for choices at the end of the list forgo much local autonomy in exchange for a more focused region.

Another major distinguishing characteristic among the options involves the number of activities conducted within each option. Figure I includes general purpose, delimited purpose, and special purpose usage options. A general purpose (or all-purpose) organization performs most of the general and broad activities of local governments. A delimited purpose agency performs a precise cluster of specified and related activities. A special purpose (or single-purpose) option conducts only one or two specific delegated and related activities.

Local governments in a region will utilize many of these techniques as they discharge their responsibilities to their citizens.

Variations on Political Regionalism in Other Nations

In the United States, political regionalism receives its legitimacy from the consent of those at the local level of government. The vast number of U.S. regional arrangements have their base in the consent of the citizens or elected members of local governments. In other countries, where regionalism may be more directly associated with national policy impulses, local approval may not be so sacrosanct to the creation of regional arrangements.

Canada and the United States have some historic cultural similarities and experienced the same urbanism forces of the nineteenth and twentieth centuries, but Canada has

FIGURE I. DIFFERENT WAYS TO ORGANIZE SERVICES AND GOVERNMENTS FOR CITIZENS

Some of the options for delivering services require very little change for the typical local government. Others are more drastic. This list moves from techniques that require minimal change to those requiring greater change from jurisdictions.

Volunteerism The provision of all or part of a public service through the use of trained and supervised volunteer personnel, employed without pay for a local government.

Informal Agreement An agreement, not backed by law, between two or more units of local government that pledges them to common improvement in a targeted service.

Formal Interlocal Agreement, Joint Powers A legal agreement permitting two or more jurisdictions mutually to plan, finance, and deliver a service for their constituencies.

Interlocal Service Contract A legal agreement permitting one government to supply a specified service for a fee to another government.

Privatization The provision of public services for local governments and their constituency by the private sector.

Multicommunity Partnerships An intergovernmental entity that ranges from loosely connected and informal to formal complex long-term networks, including joint public-private citizen associations, private business-industry alliances with government, and others.

Intersectoral Cooperation Creation of mutually beneficial alliances between government, the nonprofit public sector, and the business sector to best finance and deliver services.

Nonprofit Public Corporation A legal entity used by local governments to own a company jointly and manage it through a board of directors representing the local governments.

Extraterritorial Power A state statute-bestowed grant of power enabling a local government to exercise specific powers or services beyond its legal territorial borders.

Regional Council A voluntary regional organization, regularly convening appointed and elected representatives of area local governments to discuss, study, and adopt multiple-purpose cooperative plans and programs.

Federally Induced Regional Body A single-purpose regional body established or mandated by the national government, as with a metropolitan transportation planning agency.

Local Special Purpose Services District A single-purpose unit legally established to handle one service and not required to follow existing local boundaries.

Transfers of Functions The legal transfer of one or more services from one government to a second deemed more able in resources or area to provide the service.

Annexation An attachment of a portion of unincorporated territory to the contiguous annexing local jurisdiction.

Incorporation A legal process whereby a given community or part of a community is transformed into a legal municipal corporation endowed in law with specific duties, services, rights, and liabilities.

Unified Property Tax Base Sharing A formula that shares a percentage of any new industrial-commercial property development within a region, with that percentage accruing to a general pool, which is then shared regionally by a weighted formula.

Government Equity Fund A voluntary redistribution by a region's local governments based on a complex formula that considers aggregate growth in property values and income and property tax revenues, so that communities not experiencing growth still receive a share of the fund.

Services Consolidation A merging of two services into one delivery mechanism, without changing the underlying local governmental structure.

Reformed Urban County Government The rechartering of a county government to undertake municipal-type services delivery, usually in conjunction with the establishment of an elected county executive.

Regional Special Purpose Services District, Regional Joint District As the local special district, but geographically larger, created to provide a single service to many local jurisdictions.

Regional Special Authority The regional special district, but with stronger and more extensive powers surrounding its specified service.

Regional Delimited Purpose District, Metropolitan Services Authority The regional government, but with responsibilities delimited to a cluster of interrelated services.

Consolidated Government The merger of two or more entire governments into one new unit that replaces them.

Federated Metropolitan Government The incorporation or merger of local governments into one large government containing two tiers, one to handle areawide services and the other, which consists of preexisting local jurisdictional boundaries, to handle local services.

Metropolitan Government, Regional Government The incorporation of a new general-purpose government, encompassing a complete metropolitan area or rural area, which may or may not replace all existing local governments.

crafted an approach to regionalism distinct from that of the United States. A more deferential civility to authority, a more ready acceptance of the collective actions of leadership, a more centralized federal system, and a more pragmatic tolerance of governmental intervention in the private market effected numerous differences, according to Philip Wichern's 1986 analysis. Canadian city leaders continued aggressive annexation long after American efforts faltered, and they were able to institute regional governments in other instances, not through the arduous U.S.

techniques of local politics and referenda but from reforms executed through provincial commissions. Montreal, Toronto, Vancouver, and Winnipeg all instituted regional governments through provincial blessing. Provincial resistance in Alberta to annexation and metropolitan government worked to thwart Edmonton consolidation and to encourage there the fragmentation of political power between suburban local government autonomy and the core city in a pattern more reminiscent of the United States.

In 1994 Australia began the process of delineation of the nation into economic regions by inviting applications from the local level for designation. The Australian guidelines urge areas that have existing regional representative bodies, such as regional organizations of councils or state regional development boards, to develop a broader regional body for the economic delineation. Guidelines urge regions to delineate and market an economic vision that captures the special features of their region, as reported by the Commonwealth of Australia.

By local referendum, the Netherlands permits creation of metropolitan governments or "stadsprovincie." A massive study commission in Rotterdam failed to convince local citizens of the benefits of the proposed metropolitan government, and it was rejected in June 1995. A similar proposal met with defeat at the hands of the citizens of Amsterdam in May 1995. The Amsterdam City Council and neighboring jurisdictions decided to form the Amsterdam City-Province, which called for the subdivision of Amsterdam into thirteen smaller, independent neighborhoods that would join with fourteen existing adjacent municipalities to become *"De Stadsprovincie Amsterdam,"* as explained in the *Referendum Krant: Extra Editie Stadsnieuws* (1995).

Israel regional councils have been shaken by boundary disputes between rural and urban regional councils. Political, economic, and ideological processes have produced severe pressures on their territories and placed the two factions in opposition. According to predictions by E. Razin and S. Hasson (1994) these processes may lead to (1) further fragmentation and contraction of areas managed by rural local government, (2) transformation of rural local governments into entities of a new type, or (3) formation of new forms of urban-rural regional cooperation.

The Kingdom of Saudi Arabia draws its six planning region boundaries along those of centuries-old emirate boundaries, since erased through unification. The planning delineations maintain preexisting political, social, and economic patterns. Each region contains a dominant influential city where sheik leaders and institutions traditionally resided. Regional boundaries are indeterminate zones rather than precise linear indications, but suffice for their task, as noted by Melville Branch (1988) in *Regional Planning*.

South Africa has established its "new regional devolution programme" and chosen nine regions to have some control over education, housing, health, and local security.

They were established to reduce excessive centralization. Economic and traditional considerations influenced boundary demarcation. South African leaders remain under pressure to insure that regionalism does not perpetuate apartheid under another name, according to Garrett Nagle (1994).

Regionalism in China is subject to three strong forces. The first is tension between regions, because rapid and uneven rates of growth within regions have been bolstered by deliberate Chinese policies. The second is the pull of loyalty for the region between the local subgeographical unit, or "difang zhuyi," and the central authority of Beijing national government and the potential threat to Beijing that this represents. The third is the national instability inherent in the process of the succession to Deng Xiaoping. Hong Kong and South China can look to the Shenzhen Special Economic Zone or to Guangdong Province and see emerging autonomy and regional networking independent of Beijing, reported Robert Gage (1995).

A difficult problem immediately confronting regions of the twenty first century will be to remaster regional planning jurisdictions designed for the 1950s and 1960s to be congruent with the more extended and sprawled regional community that now includes Edge Cities and hinterland cybercommuting workers. Two policy choices include the enlargement of the existing regional intergovernmental polity or the creation of still larger regional intergovernmental polities to encompass the twenty-first century's larger regional community of interest. The Province of Ontario chose the latter and created the Office of the Greater Toronto Area to manage this situation in Toronto. The Office of the Greater Toronto Area, a provincial office, is an umbrella to five regional districts, taking in land from exurbia to downtown Toronto. In turn, one of those five regional districts is the original famed METRO Toronto, the original regional umbrella agency for the region, now simply too small to handle regional policy.

Regionalism's large territorial space and interdependent regional community give it a majesty of size and a dignity of place from a shared sense of regional general welfare. The profoundly complex and dynamic interactions within a region forever will enthrall and puzzle the scholars and practitioners from whom it tempts solutions.

PATRICIA S. ATKINS

BIBLIOGRAPHY

Advisory Commission on Intergovernmental Relations, 1973. *Substate Regionalism and the Federal System*, Volume 1, *Regional Decision Making: New Strategies for Substate Districts*. Washington, D.C.: U.S. GPO.

Anderson, William, 1924. "The Federal Government and the Cities." *National Civic Review*. 13: 288–293.

Atkins, Patricia S., 1995. "Techniques of Regional Cooperation in the United States." Paper presented at the American Planning Association 1995 Annual Conference, Toronto.

Barlow, I. M., 1994. *Metropolitan Government.* New York: Routledge.

Barnes, William R., and Larry C. Ledebur, 1994. *Local Economics: The U.S. Common Market of Local Economic Regions.* Washington, D.C.: National League of Cities.

Berry, Brian J. L., 1967. *Geography of Market Centers and Retail Distribution.* Englewood Cliffs, NJ: Prentice-Hall.

Bish, Robert L., 1971. *The Public Economy of Metropolitan Areas.* Chicago: Markham.

Branch, Melville C., 1988. *Regional Planning, Introduction and Explanation.* New York: Praeger.

Cigler, Beverly A., et al., 1994. *Toward an Understanding of Multicommunity Collaboration.* Washington, D.C.: U.S. Department of Agriculture, Economic Research Service, Agriculture and Rural Economy Division.

Commonwealth of Australia, Department of Housing and Regional Development, 1994. *Guidelines for the Regional Development Program: Growth Through Our Regions.* Sydney: Government of Australia Printing Office.

DeGrove, John M., 1992. *Planning and Growth Management in the States.* Cambridge, MA:

Dodge, William R., 1996. *Regional Excellence.* Washington, D.C.: National League of Cities.

Downs, Anthony, 1994. *New Visions for Metropolitan America.* Washington, D.C.: Brookings Institution.

Fishman, Robert, 1987. *Bourgeois Utopias.* New York: Basic Books.

Gage, Robert, 1995. "An Examination of the Questions of Regionalization in China and Their Implications for Hong Kong and the South China Region in the 21st Century." *Journal of Public Policy and Administration* 2: 73–96.

Garreau, Joel, 1991. *Edge City: Life on the New Frontier.* New York: Doubleday.

Hubbard, Theodora Kimball, 1925. "Survey of City and Regional Planning in the United States, 1924." *City Planning* 1: 7–26.

James, Edmund J., 1899. "The Growth of Great Cities in Area and Population," *Annals of the American Academy of Political and Social Science,* 1–30.

Jones, Victor, 1942. *Metropolitan Government.* Chicago: University of Chicago Press.

Kemmis, Daniel, 1995. "The Rebirth of the City-State." *The Regionalist* 1: 43–49.

Lynch, Kevin, 1976. *Managing the Sense of the Region.* Cambridge: MIT Press.

———, 1981. *A Theory of Good City Form.* Cambridge: MIT Press.

Martin, Roscoe C., 1963. *Metropolis in Transition: Local Government Adaptation to Changing Urban Needs.* Washington, D.C.: U.S. GPO, Housing and Home Finance Agency.

Muller, Peter O., 1981. *Contemporary Suburban America.* Englewood Cliffs, NJ: Prentice-Hall.

Nagle, Garrett, 1994. "Challenges for the New South Africa." *Geographical: The Royal Geographical Society Magazine* 56: 45–47.

Nice, David C., 1987. *Federalism: The Politics of Intergovernmental Relations.* New York: St. Martin's Press.

Ostrom, Vincent, Charles M. Tiebout, and Robert Warren, 1983. "The Organization of Government in Metropolitan Areas: A Theoretical Inquiry." *American Political Science Review* 55: 831–842.

Park, Robert B., and R. J. Oakerson, 1989, "Metropolitan Organization and Governance: A Local Public Economy Approach." *Urban Affairs Quarterly* 25: 18–29.

Peirce, Near R., 1993. *Citistates: How Urban America Can Prosper in a Competitive World.* Washington, D.C.: Seven Locks Press.

Razin, E., and S. Hasson, 1994. "Urban/Rural Boundary Conflicts–The Reshaping of Israel's Rural Map." *Journal of Rural Studies* 10: 47–59.

Referendum Krant: Extra Editie Standnieuws, 1995. Amsterdam: The Netherlands.

Rusk, David, 1993. *Cities Without Suburbs.* Washington, D.C.: Woodrow Wilson Center Press.

Savitch, Hank V., et al., 1993. "Ties That Bind: Central Cities, Suburbs, and the Metropolitan Region." *Economic Development Quarterly* 7: 341–358.

Sealey, Raphael, 1976. *A History of the Greek City-States, 700–338 B.C.* Los Angeles: University of California Press.

So, Frank, Irving Hand, and Bruce D. McDowell, 1986. *The Practice of State and Regional Planning.* Chicago: American Planning Association.

Swanstrom, Todd, 1995. "Philosopher in the City: The New Regionalism Debate." *Journal of Urban Affairs* 17: 309–314.

United States Bureau of the Census, 1978. *1977 Census of Governments, Regional Organizations.* Washington, D.C.: U.S. GPO.

Walker, David B., 1995. *The Rebirth of Federalism.* Chatham, NJ: Chatham House Publishers.

Wichern, Philip, 1986. "Metropolitan Reform and the Restructuring of Local Governments in the North American City." In *Power and Place: Canadian Urban Development in the North American Context,* 292–321. edited by Gilbert A. Stelter and Alan F. J. Artibise. Vancouver: University of British Columbia Press.

Wood, Robert, 1958. *Suburbia: Its People and Their Politics.* Boston: Houghton-Mifflin.

REGULATION. A quasi law or rule that is the product of a public agency's rulemaking process. Since the origin of the state, governments have adopted a variety of public policy techniques that are intended to promote the social and economic well-being of rulers, particular interests, or the public, more generally. These techniques have included regulation, subsidies, public ownership, and tax provisions. Regulation has been one of the most favored of these techniques in large part because it shifts many of the costs involved in compliance on the group or sector at which the regulation is directed. For this very reason, regulation has also led to considerable citizen resentment and political controversy.

Regulation can be defined in a variety of ways, but a neutral definition that embraces most of what the term conventionally covers in ordinary parlance is *a state-imposed limitation on the discretion that may be exercised by individuals or organizations, which is supported by the threat of sanction.* Under this definition, motorists are regulated when they are required to halt at stop signs, and automobile manufacturers are regulated when they are compelled to install pollution control equipment in the cars they make. Similarly, regulation includes the German laws that prohibit shops from staying open after certain hours and the laws in every society that prohibit robbery. In each of these cases, the state threatens to impose sanctions for transgressions of the prohibited conduct.

Several conclusions can readily be drawn from this definition. The most obvious is that, first, the purpose of the regulation need not be in the "public interest." Indeed, on one hand, any objective may be a goal of regulation. For example, at one time it was unlawful in Florida for a person to bathe in a bathtub without wearing a bathing suit or some other type of covering apparel. On the other hand, virtually everyone approves of *some* form of regulation that prevents the marketing of pharmaceutical products that have not been adequately tested for safety and efficacy. And, of course, there are many regulations—indeed whole areas—that are the subjects of intensive debate among experts in the field. It similarly follows that, second, the sanctions imposed by a regulation may be inappropriate to alter the conduct at which it is directed. For example, if automobile manufacturers were fined one dollar for each car not equipped with air bags and it cost US $50 to install such devices in each car, the sanction would probably be ineffective.

Third, the direct costs and secondary effects of a regulation may outweigh the benefits. Considered in another way, no one can predict with unerring accuracy how the persons or institutions at which the regulation is directed will modify behavior; the policymakers instituting a regulation may be in for some unpleasant surprises. Consider one of the most dramatic failures in American history. Constitutional Amendment Eighteen declared in 1919 that the manufacture, sale, and transport of alcoholic beverages would be prohibited. Congress and the states enacted regulatory legislation to carry out the prohibition and assigned thousands of agents to enforce it. By 1933 the policy was in shambles, and Amendment Eighteen was repealed. Public behavior was certainly modified, but not in the way Congress and the states intended. Instead of ending the consumption of alcoholic beverages, many people modified their behavior in order to circumvent the prohibition and continue to consume the forbidden product. This historic episode is not an exception to the general rule that people and organizations will often incorporate regulations into their decisionmaking processes in order to circumvent or not comply with them.

A fourth important attribute also follows from the definition. Regulations are usually not self-executing. Instead, some governmental body must obtain information to determine whether a transgression has probably taken place. The difficulty involved in collecting such information can frequently defeat effective enforcement or result in the imposition of exceptionally high costs.

Consider the Florida bathtub regulation previously mentioned. Or consider another Florida statute—now thankfully revoked—that did not allow anyone to crack more than three dishes per day or chip the edges of more

than four cups. It is obvious that information could not easily be collected to enforce these regulatory statutes. Therefore, such regulations would probably not alter behavior. But the connection between the cost of obtaining sufficient information and the enforceability of the regulation is not limited to such examples. Indeed, it plagues some of the most important and contentious public issues today, such as traffic control, abortion, advertising regulation, and civil rights.

Regulation, as one can readily surmise, can cover virtually the entire gamut of governmental activity. But it is conventional to treat such topics as crime, domestic relations, or traffic control separately from the field of regulation. Regulation is conventionally divided into two subfields: economic regulation and social regulation. The former subsumes such topics as natural monopolies, price and entry controls, antitrust, licensing, and network coordination. Social regulation includes such topics as environmental controls, civil rights, wilderness protection, labor regulation, food and drug safety and efficacy, advertising regulation, and the licensing of such occupations as physicians and dentists. One must emphasize, however, that regardless of the categories into which one may divide regulations—and there can be many such typologies—they invariably involve costs and benefits. Simply placing a regulation in this or that category does not obviate the need to attempt an assessment of its probable benefits and costs.

An equally important consideration that follows from the definition is that regulation invariably apportions decisionmaking between the private and public spheres. In contrast, public ownership involves a governmental institution making all of the decisions regarding an activity.

Until the 1980s, for example, most European telephone systems were owned and operated by governmental authorities; there was consequently little need for regulation. In contrast, the U.S. telephone system was privately owned and overwhelmingly dominated by a single private firm. Accordingly, it was regulated by federal and state or local regulatory agencies. When British Telecom was privatized, the government of the United Kingdom created a regulatory authority to supervise its behavior.

The far more important distinction in the contemporary world is between the free market and regulation. Indeed, the arguments that free market advocates make on its behalf raise the issue of why we need regulation at all; in the 1980s, advocacy of the free market and disdain for regulation became an increasingly popular position. The free market argument is still best stated in Adam Smith's words in *The Wealth of Nations:*

> Every individual necessarily labours to render the annual revenue of the society as great as he can. He generally, indeed, neither intends to promote the public interest, nor knows how much he is promoting it. . . . By directing that industry in such a manner as its produce may be of the greatest value, he intends only his own gain, and he is in

this, as in many other cases, led by an invisible hand to promote an end which was no part of his intention.... By pursuing his own interest he frequently promotes that of the society more effectually than when he really intends to promote it (p. 456).

Instances of silly regulations and overregulation have made the view increasingly common in the United States that the regulatory tide needs to be swept back. Although the public generally believes that regulatory policy is the villain, it is more likely that overbearing and insensitive public administration is really their primary complaint. Consider the example of the Occupational Safety and Health Act which, in 1970, created the Occupational Safety and Health Administration (OSHA) to regulate workplace safety and health. Few persons could quarrel with the *broad* need for such regulation, especially in low-skill, highly competitive industries in which employers had strong incentives to engage in cost-cutting at the expense of worker safety. Yet OSHA became a widely criticized agency because of the complexity and absurdity of many of its rules and the burdensome reporting and recordkeeping requirements that it has imposed on many business firms, especially smaller ones.

Even OSHA's chairperson, Robert D. Moran, reported in April 1974 *Nation's Business* that far too many standards are, to paraphrase Winston Churchill, "'riddles wrapped in mysteries inside enigmas.' They don't give the employer even a nebulous suggestion of what he should do to protect his employees" (p. 23). The agency has also been criticized for incompetent inspections and emphasizing trivial, rather than important, matters. Thus, it is not the fundamental notion of regulating workplace safety that many observers are concerned about; it is the public administration of the regulatory statute that actually bothers them. The point is an obvious yet fundamental one, for the swelling tide of complaints about regulation frequently identifies the wrong target—legislation rather than administration.

Most people disapprove of regulatory legislation that does little more than benefit special interests. But regulatory statutes are frequently enacted for reasons that cannot be attributed to special interest lobbying. In general, one can divide legislation in which regulation can be justified into two categories: those that deal with market failure and those that attempt to achieve values that the free market cannot easily attain.

Market failure is defined as the inability of private markets to provide goods at the most desirable (optimal) levels. That is, a situation in which the excess of benefits over costs under the free market use of resources is less than that under an alternative arrangement—such as regulation—is seen as a market failure. The notions of cost and benefit must not be conceived too narrowly. Benefits include not only tangible goods and services but also the many amenities lumped together under "quality of life." Costs include

more than expenditures for goods and services; they also embrace impairments to the quality of life, such as dirty air or ugly physical surroundings. Thus, market failure can justify environmental regulation as well as such traditional regulatory subjects as natural monopoly (electricity, gas, water, etc.). The reckoning of costs and benefits may also embrace lengthy time frames. For example, depleting the ozone layer now may not impose a current cost; instead, the costs may be visited on our grandchildren. Similarly, costs and benefits should not necessarily be calculated within the borders of one country. For example, Edward O. Wilson, the renowned sociobiologist, has pointed out (1992) that the deforestation of the Amazon rain forest may have an enormous worldwide cost in the form of food and pharmaceutical products that will be forever lost as large numbers of species are extinguished.

Free markets usually provide the optimum solutions for two of humanity's paramount values: economic efficiency and liberty. But this list hardly exhausts the values that philosophers and others think are appropriate, and that leads to the second category. Racial fairness is one such value, and civil rights regulation is intended to attain that value. Similarly, although there are many sides to each dispute, such topics as animal cruelty, minimum wage, and aid for the handicapped—to name three diverse areas—illustrate the innumerable values that regulation may be designed to achieve. Whether the statute or administration will, in fact, achieve these values—or, indeed, whether the values are good ones—raise different issues that are outside the scope of this entry.

Regulation thus necessarily involves a mixture of theoretical judgment, value imposition, and prediction. Of course, sometimes one of these factors is more important than the others, but they are all usually present in any regulatory situation. This does not mean that scientific design of regulation is impossible. To the contrary, one can use the findings of economic theory to reject certain regulatory alternatives on that ground.

For example, on one hand, an economist might reject minimum wage regulation on the ground that it would lead to a high rate of unemployment among the working poor, which it is intended to benefit. On the other hand, in a situation in which a proposed course of action involves a trade-off between higher productivity and a cleaner environment, values would ultimately determine the choices made. At other times, a novel course of regulatory action might involve insufficient information and experience upon which to base a highly confident prediction.

The difficulties in evaluating regulation are compounded when we realize that policy decisions are not made only once with respect to a particular policy problem. Instead, regulation frequently involves four levels of decisionmaking.

The first level in the decisionmaking process is usually the legislative level. To illustrate, Congress in 1914 enacted

1945

the Federal Trade Commission Act, charging the newly created agency with the responsibility of declaring unlawful "unfair methods of competition." At the second level, agencies spell out their legislative mandate in more detail, either through a rule or a leading decision. To follow this example, the Federal Trade Commission (FTC) early in its career decided that false and deceptive advertising constituted an unfair method of competition. At the third level of decisionmaking, regulators apply these rules and decisions to a particular situation to ascertain whether it falls inside or outside the prohibition. For example, does the offering of a product at a "special low price" for an extended period of time constitute false and misleading advertising? The final level is the judicial one. Courts will frequently review the decisions and rules made by agencies. Such review, embraced under the rubric of administrative law, can involve not only the procedures undertaken by regulatory administrators but also the substance. For example, courts will not infrequently determine whether a regulatory agency scrupulously followed statutory guidelines.

From the foregoing one can see why regulation is an ongoing process. From the legislative perspective, it is extraordinarily difficult to draft legislation that will cover every situation. It is virtually impossible for legislators, who must look at an enormous body of policy questions during every session of Congress, to develop anything like the expertise in a problem or an industry experienced by those who work with it on a daily basis. Intelligent caution, then, often leads legislators to provide little more than substantive general guidelines in regulatory statutes, leaving wide discretion to agency officials charged with implementing the law. But it is for precisely the reason that unelected regulatory bureaucrats can exercise such extraordinary power over our lives that courts have come to review scrupulously many agency decisions.

Regulatory agencies employ three basic techniques to make policy: informal agreements with interested parties, substantive rulemaking, and adjudication. The first of these can save the extraordinary expenses involved in the latter two techniques. But it is frequently not possible to negotiate a meeting of the minds with the interested parties. Accordingly, the regulatory agency may adopt substantive rulemaking, which resembles the legislative process, or adjudication, which resembles judicial proceedings.

Rulemaking, covering a class of people, is generally to be preferred but is not always available. Both rulemaking and adjudicatory processes have a place in regulation, and most regulatory statutes provide agencies with both procedures. Rulemaking is more applicable to general policy pronouncements than it is to the resolution of factual disputes and the specific principles that arise from such disputes. When adjudicative facts are an issue—who did what, where, when how, why, with what motive or intent—our values dictate that interested parties should have the right to set forth their views. This requires such mechanisms as complaint, notice, answer, hearings, rational decisionmaking, and appeals.

Regulation is often a cumbersome means by which to achieve policy results. It can be costly and time-consuming, and it directs resources that might otherwise be employed in productive activities into uses that do not directly contribute to economic growth. Notwithstanding, the public often demands regulation. In any event, regulation is a widely employed technique in all levels of government in the United States.

Regulation is as old as government, but it has been more common during some periods of history than others. Great spurts of growth in the United States, usually occurring at all levels of government, have been followed by periods of relative dormancy in which few important regulatory statutes were enacted.

In general, the different paces and the substantive thrust of legislation during any particular period are reflections of an underlying public attitude toward the proper role of government. The New Deal (1933–1939) was an intense period of regulatory legislation, largely in response to economic and social problems resulting from the Great Depression that began in 1929. In contrast, the prevailing public philosophy during most of the 1920s—an era of theretofore unprecedented growth and prosperity—saw little need for regulation.

Historians agree that 1887 was a watershed year for regulation. It marked the birth of the Interstate Commerce Commission (ICC), the first independent regulatory commission at the national level. Individual states had begun regulating infrastructure services such as banking, gas, and railroad and streetcar transportation shortly before 1887. These enactments ushered in an era of unprecedented regulatory growth that continued through approximately 1916. In both the earlier years of this period and the later ones—the Progressive Era—states and municipalities also expanded the number of occupations and activities that required licensing and regulation. For example, in 1902 New Jersey began licensing architects, and today they must be licensed in all states.

At the national level, the period from 1887 to 1916 witnessed the creation of the Federal Trade Commission, with jurisdiction over unfair methods of competition, and the Federal Reserve Board (FRB), with jurisdiction over practices of member banks. The first national statutes dealing with monopoly (the Sherman Antitrust Act) and with pure food and drug products (the Food and Drug Act) were enacted in 1890 and 1906, respectively.

Considerable controversy exists among historians as to what accounted for this spurt of intense regulatory activity. One thing is clear: The era witnessed a significant erosion of the principle that unrestricted markets constituted the best method to attain public goals. Regulation became the chosen alternative. In the 1920s, however, the prevailing ideology shifted to one that thought voluntary arrangements between economic units, without government intervention, could better attain goals in most cases. However, no significant statute or agency that came into existence during the period from 1887 to 1916 was dismantled. (In fact, railroad regulation became even more comprehensive.) The only important regulatory additions at the national level in the 1920s were statutes regulating radio transmission, aviation safety, and commodities future trading.

An abrupt change in public philosophy took place during the New Deal, with a host of important new statutes enacted between 1933 and 1939. Confidence in the power of the free market to achieve performance goals was very low in the face of the dismal record of the economic system during the Great Depression. One important statute, the National Industrial Recovery Act (subsequently declared unconstitutional) virtually abolished competition. According to many of the New Dealers, how to stabilize prices and other economic indicators was the principal problem. Regulatory agencies were given an important role in the New Deal plans.

The long list of regulatory agencies created in those relatively few years included the following:

- the Federal Communications Commission (FCC), with jurisdiction over radio and communications common carriers;
- the Securities and Exchange Commission (SEC), with jurisdiction over stock exchanges and new issues of stock;
- the Civil Aeronautics Board (CAB), with jurisdiction over the economic affairs of air carriers;
- a new banking agency–the Federal Deposit Insurance Corporation (FDIC)–as well as the Federal Home Loan Bank Board (FHLBB), with jurisdiction over federally chartered savings and loan associations; and
- the National Labor Relations Board (NLRB), with jurisdiction over collective bargaining disputes and unfair labor practices.

In addition to these new agencies, numerous statutes granted additional regulatory jurisdiction to older agencies. Motor carriers, drugs, natural gas, and price discrimination between competing customers were among the new areas of regulated activity.

During the period following World War II through 1968, the regulatory apparatus in place at the end of the New Deal largely remained intact. Government policymakers established only a few regulatory agencies during this period, including the Atomic Energy Commission (AEC) and the Federal Aviation Administration (FAA), which regulates aviation safety.

The late 1960s marked a sea change. Spurred by the 1966 publication of Ralph Nader's *Unsafe at Any Speed,* which decried the lack of automobile safety, and other critiques of business conduct, Congress enacted numerous new statutes regulating health, safety, and the environment. The new agencies created included

- the Environmental Protection Agency (EPA), with regulatory jurisdiction over air and water quality, toxic substances, and noise levels;
- the Consumer Product Safety Commission (CPSC), whose mission was to reduce product-related injuries to consumers by regulating product design, labeling, and use instructions;
- the Occupational Safety and Health Administration (OSHA), responsible for safety and health conditions in workplaces; and
- the National Highway Traffic Safety Administration (NHTSA), which regulates vehicles in an effort to reduce the number and severity of traffic accidents.

Additional consumer-oriented responsibilities were given to older agencies, and economic regulation expanded rapidly, most notably over the energy industries.

In the mid-1970s a backlash began. The enormous regulatory apparatus was considered by some policymakers and economists to be an impediment to U.S. economic growth as well as a significant source of inflation and declining competitiveness in world markets.

Ronald Reagan's election to the presidency in November 1980 made it official. The impetus to reduce the extent of government regulation became an important part of the new public philosophy, characterized by cries of overregulation and calls for deregulation. By the end of the Reagan presidency, much of the traditional regulatory apparatus had been dismantled or weakened. Economic regulation of air carriers had come to an end (although safety regulation remained intact). Congress and the Interstate Commerce Commission (ICC) combined to deregulate surface transportation, and significant inroads had been made in the energy and communications fields.

The inevitable shift in direction came during the George Bush administration. Cable television was partially reregulated. But, more important, Congress enacted what may be the three most sweeping regulatory enactments in U.S. history. The extraordinarily complex 1990 Clean Air Act amendments were the most comprehensive statutes ever designed to attain ambient air quality standards. Among their most controversial features were mandating enforcement on the states without funding the latter for their efforts. Second, Congress enacted the Americans with Disabilities Act, prohibiting discrimination on the basis of disability in public accommodations, public services, and employment. The most drastic provisions of this badly drafted statute required employers to make "reasonable accommodations" for workers with disabilities and required stores and other facilities to make physical modifications to assist the handicapped. Finally, the Civil Rights Act of 1991 strengthened enforcement under the civil rights laws, provided for compensatory and punitive damages, and expanded the activities embraced within the concept of civil rights.

But by the mid-1990s, the nation once again appears to have been set in the direction of regulatory retreat. Only one prediction is certain: The ebb and flow of regulation will continue into the future.

ALAN STONE

BIBLIOGRAPHY

Breyer, Stephen, 1982. *Regulation and Its Reform*. Cambridge: Harvard University Press.

Cushman, Robert, 1941. *The Independent Regulatory Commissions:* New York: Oxford University Press.

Kahn, Alfred, 1971. *The Economics of Regulation: Principles and Institutions:* 2 vols. New York: John Wiley and Sons.

Kolko, Gabriel, 1963. *The Triumph of Conservatism*. New York: Free Press.

Moran, Robert D., 1974. "Our Job Safety Law Should Say What It Means." *Nation's Business* (April): 23–25.

Peltzman, Sam, 1976. "Toward a More General Theory of Regulation." *Journal of Law and Economics* 19 (August): 211–240.

Posner, Richard, 1974. "Theories of Economic Regulation." *Bell Journal of Economics and Management Science* 5 (Autumn): 335–358.

Smith, Adam, [1776], 1981. *The Wealth of Nations*. Indianapolis, Ind.: Liberty Press.

Stigler, George, 1971. "The Theory of Economic Regulation." *Bell Journal of Economics and Management Science* 2 (Spring): 3–21.

Stone, Alan, 1982. *Regulation and Its Alternatives*. Washington, D.C.: Congressional Quarterly Press.

Swann, Dennis, 1988. *The Retreat of the State: Deregulation and Privatization in the U.K. and U.S.* Ann Arbor: University of Michigan Press.

Vietor, Richard, 1994. *Contrived Competition*. Cambridge: Harvard University Press.

Wilson, Edward O., 1992. *The Diversity of Life*. Cambridge, MA: Belknap Press.

REGULATION (EC).

A form of secondary legislation in the European Union (EU). The institutions of the EU are empowered by Article 189 of the European Economic Community (EEC) Treaty signed in Rome in 1957 to make regulations that "shall have general application." This means that regulations are intended for objectively determined situations and involve legal consequences or categories of persons, viewed in a general and abstract manner.

A regulation is binding in its entirety—it covers legal rights and obligations on those to whom it is addressed. Full observance of its provisions by all member states is required.

Regulations are also directly applicable in all member states and come into legal effect on the date specified in the *Official Journal of the European Communities,* or alterna-

tively, on the twentieth day following their publication. Thus regulations have direct effect and as such create rights for individuals that national courts must protect. A regulation, by implication, prohibits the implementation of any legislation at national level that is incompatible with its provisions.

Regulations are by far the most frequent form of secondary legislation in the European Union. Although some regulations are adopted by the Council of Ministers, most are adopted by the European Commission (EC), which enjoys limited delegated executive powers. Regulations are typically concerned with the detailed and uniform application of policy; they make technical adjustments to existing legislation covering the Common Agricultural Policy of the European Union, in particular. Examples include: Council Regulation (EC) No. 538/95 of 6 March 1995 amending Regulation (EC) No. 519/94 on common rules for imports from certain third countries; Commission Regulation (EC) No. 454/95 of 28 February 1995 laying down detailed rules for intervention on the market in butter and cream; Commission Regulation (EC) No. 540/95 of 10 March 1995 laying down the arrangements for reporting suspected unexpected adverse reactions that are not serious, whether arising in the EEC or in a third country, to medicinal products for human or veterinary use authorized in accordance with the provisions of Council Regulation (EEC) No. 2309/93.

Regulations are known as general decisions under the Paris Treaty signed in 1951, which established the European Coal and Steel Community in 1952.

MARGARET MARY MALONE

BIBLIOGRAPHY

Hartley, T. C., 1989. *The Foundations of European Community Law*. 2d ed. London: Clarendon Press.

Lasok, D., and J. W. Bridge, 1987. *Law and Institutions of the European Communities*. 4th ed. London: Butterworths.

Nugent, Neill, 1991. *The Government and Politics of the European Community*. 2d ed. London: Macmillan.

Parry, Anthony, and James Dinnage, 1981. *EEC Law*. 2d ed. London: Sweet and Maxwell.

Wyatt, D., and A. Dashwood, 1987. *The Substantive Law of the EC*. 2d ed. London: Sweet and Maxwell.

REINVENTING GOVERNMENT.

The theoretical tenets of a public administration policy for process and service improvements to yield an improved government.

Reinventing government may be the most popular paradigm of public administration in the 1990s. David Osborne and Ted Gaebler (1992) in *Reinventing Government* described this popular agenda for a high performance government, and their recommendations for process and service improvements may have greater impact than those contained in a dozen or so comparable efforts over the past century, perhaps because government has never been under such pressure from the public to be more productive, effective, and "unbureaucratic."

The "reinventing government" paradigm is a rather electric synthesis of different approaches. It has ten tenets: (1) government should act as a catalyst—it should "steer" rather than "row"; (2) government should empower rather than serve; (3) government should be competitive; (4) government should be mission-driven rather than rule-driven; (5) government should be results-oriented, and should not base its actions on inputs; (6) it should be customer driven; (7) government should be enterprising; (8) government should anticipate rather than cure social ills; (9) government should be decentralized; and (10) government should be market-oriented (Osborne and Gaebler 1992).

Essentially, Osborne and Gaebler have outlined a cultural and behavioral shift in the management of government away from what they call a bureaucratic government toward an entrepreneurial government. To a large extent *Reinventing Government* attempts to integrate the fair market and privatization literature (Savas 1985, 1987, 1992) with the "excellence in management" literature (Peters and Waterman 1982). According to Osborne and Gaebler,

> most entrepreneurial governments . . . *empower* citizens by pushing control out of the bureaucracy, into the community. They measure the performance of their agencies, focusing not on inputs, but on outcomes. They are driven by their goals—their missions—not by their rules and regulations. They redefine their clients as customers. . . . They prevent problems before they emerge, rather than simply offering services afterward. . . . They decentralize authority, embracing participatory management. . . . They prefer market mechanisms to bureaucratic mechanisms (1992, pp. 19–20).

Osborne and Gaebler's entrepreneurial model is characterized by strong interpersonal skills and a nurtured knowledge and discipline. Reinventing's principles devolve management responsibility to the lowest employee level. At the same time the model advocates accountability to citizens and taxpayers (who are seen as consumers). It is this commitment to both the workforce and the taxpayer that makes reinventing government's organizational and management structure highly pluralistic.

According to Osborne and Gaebler, today's entrepreneurial manager in the public sector must employ strategies that will "return control to those who work down where the rubber meets the road. . . . They [entrepreneurial leaders] use participatory management to decentralize decision making; they encourage teamwork to overcome the rigid barriers that separate people in hierarchical institutions; [and] they create institutional 'champions'" (p. 254).

Osborne and Gaebler's "team" construct is, in large part, from Peter Drucker's *The Age of Discontinuity* (1968). Other writers cited in Osborne and Gaebler's model include Roger Harrison (1972) and Rosabeth Moss Kanter (1983).

The entrepreneurial concept of reinventing government seeks to create a new culture, knowledge, and discipline within the public organization. According to Osborne and Gaebler, the prevailing hierarchical structure of public institutions inhibits the development of such a culture: "While the rest of society has rushed away from hierarchy . . . most governments have held tight to the reins. Their message to employees has not changed: Follow orders. Don't use your heads, don't think for yourself, don't take independent action. . . . This message is enormously destructive. For decades it has cowed public employees, left them docile, passive and bitter." (pp. 253–254).

In a "learning government" managers make a commitment to the "trust and lead" approach, and manage by recognizing employees as "problem solvers and innovators." Gore (1993), and Osborne and Gaebler (1992), however, merely alluded to this culture—"To change the culture of our national bureaucracy . . . toward initiative and empowerment" (Gore 1993, p. 1).

The emphasis in reinventing government is to decentralize and deregulate wherever possible before this new form of thinking can take place. "Ironically in centralized institutions and systems, . . . those at the top must often change the rules before those at the bottom can innovate. Good ideas may bubble up from below, but in centralized systems those ideas are usually ignored. To empower employees to act on their ideas, policy makers must decentralize the locus of decision making" (Osborne and Gaebler 1992, pp. 274–275).

Throughout *Reinventing Government* Osborne and Gaebler argue that the bureaucratic organization is at an important crossroad of change. They suggest that the voting public, elective representatives, and civil servants await eagerly at these crossroads. Reinventing government, according to them "is for those who care about government because they work in government, or work with government, or study government, or simply want their governments to be more effective" (p. xv).

Osborne and Gaebler have described their vision of the new postbureaucratic world: "In today's world, public institutions also need the flexibility to respond to complex and rapidly changing conditions. . . . bureaucratic governments can do none of these things easily. . . . In effect they are captive of sole source, monopoly suppliers: their own employees" (p. 34).

The reinvention agenda was adopted by Vice President Albert Gore (1993) and the National Performance Review (1993) in *Creating a Government that Works Better and Costs Less*. National Performance Review's agenda for national government reform included four major steps and multiple actions at each stage:

Step 1: Cutting red tape
Streamlining the budget process
Decentralizing personnel policy

Streamlining procurement
Reorienting the inspectors general
Eliminating regulatory overkill
Empowering state and local governments

Step 2: Putting customers first
Giving customers a voice and a choice
Making service organizations compete
Creating market dynamics
Using market mechanisms to solve problems

Step 3: Empowering employees to get results
Decentralizing decisionmaking power
Holding all federal employees accountable for results
Giving federal workers the tools they need to do their jobs
Enhancing the quality of work life
Forming a labor-management partnership
Exerting leadership
Step 4: Cutting back to basics
Eliminating what we do not need
Collecting more
Investing in greater productivity
Reengineering programs to cut costs

Under this mandate, the National Institutes of Health (NIH), for example, undertook dozens of detailed, pragmatic initiatives. Some were fully implemented quickly, including the streamlined review processes, and identification of high-risk and high-impact research applications. Others, such as "just-in-time" modular grants and limited electronic submissions were underway as pilot experiments.

Exhibit One: Electronic Research Administration. Both the NIH and the grantee community are burdened by cumbersome communication processes and rely heavily on hard-copy exchange of essential information. The Electronic Research Administration (ERA) initiatives represent a commitment to improve administrative operations through information technologies and reengineering of process. The ultimate goal is to combine more effective investment of federal dollars with more efficient administrative procedures for both the NIH Extramural Program and the awardee community. Pilot projects of streamlined procedures for the exchange of information between the NIH and application organizations and within the NIH have begun.

A key feature of the reeingineering effort is the idea of maintaining the information required for various NIH processes within a client-server in a common files database. This common file is envisioned as the electronic interface between the NIH and the awardee community and the repository for information generated during the life cycle of each ward. The database would be accessible to authorized awardees and NIH staff, who could each review and add information as required. Proposed components of the system include the application shelf, institutional profile, status system (including review dates, scores, and summary statements), notice of grant award, invention reporting, and other required reporting (e.g., women and minorities in clinical research, trainee appointments, and financial reporting). Of these, three are currently in pilot mode: the application shell, invention reporting ("EDISON"), and trainee appointments.

The NIH reinvention activities have been an open process, based on ideas contributed by the extramural research community and NIH staff. NIH views the reinvention approach as an evolving operation that will continue to rely on the valued input of all interested parties.

As much as reinventing government has become a new part of the political-public vocabulary, one must recognize that it is far from a new invention. One line of argument here—decentralization-competition—derives from the public choice school of thought, although as distinguished from public choice, this new current of thought is more pro-government. Emphasis on clients is reminiscent of the pluralist perspective. The reinventing government paradigm calls for more discretion for public administrators, praise for entrepreneurial government, and advocacy of "preventive" rather than "reactive" government. Approaching it this way, it reverses Theodeore Lowi's (1979) logic that "policy without law" is illegitimate. In arguing that the old bureaucratic model must give way to an entrepreneurial approach to public administration, Osborne and Gaebler build from the same tensions that have been resurfacing for decades—bureaucratic control versus individual and group initiative—which have staying power because the problems of bureaucracy are still unsolved and the organizational sciences have not been able to change most organizations—thus bureaucracy is still perceived as violating the public trust.

Nor is reinvention accepted uncritically within the public administration community. James Q. Wilson (1994, p. 668) calls "the near absence of any reference to democratic accountability" the most striking feature of the National Performance (NP) Review's (1993) report, done by the staff of Vice President Al Gore. Instead, the Gore (1993) report emphasizes agency responsiveness to clientele and increased discretion both for managers and employees. The NP report was criticized on the institutionalist grounds of disregarding the public law foundation of public administration and endangering the accountability process in the government (Moe 1994).

One of the main tenets of *Reinventing Government* is the call for competitive government. The authors do not limit competitiveness only to the market or only to private firms that bid for contracts, but call for competitiveness among public and private agencies. Osborne and Gaebler call the renowned guru of privatization, E. S. Savas, "a pragmatic advocate of privatization, rather than an ideologue." (Osborne and Gaebler 1992, p. 343). Based on Savas's (1987) distinction between types of goods (private, toll, common, and collective) and types of service arrangements (government service, government vending, intergovernmental agreement, contracts, franchises, grants, vouchers, market systems, voluntary service, and self-service) and criteria for choosing the best mode of service arrangement, Osborne and Gaebler (1992) propose a framework for tasks that are best suited for different sectors (pp. 347–348). They identify strengths and weaknesses not only for public and private organizations but for third or not-for-profit sector organizations as well. The tasks best suited for the public sector, from their perspective, are policy management, regulation, enforcement of equity, prevention of discrimination, prevention of exploitation, and promotion of social cohesion. The tasks best suited for the private sector include economic and investment tasks, profit generation, and promotion of self-sufficiency. The tasks more appropriate for the third sector are the social tasks–tasks that require volunteer labor and those that generate little profit, and the promotion of individual responsibility, the promotion of community, and the promotion of a commitment to the welfare of others. This typology is, however, a bit abstract and vague, because almost every endeavor the government pursues has multiple goals, and terms such as "economic tasks" are excessively broad.

Public administration is an actively evolving field that tries to adapt to and reflect upon a constantly changing complex web of relationships of interactions between government and society. Stillman (1995) has identified six schools of the "refounding public administration" movement developed since the 1970s: (1) the "reinventors"–an eclectic approach catalyzed by *Reinventing Government;* (2) "the communitarians"–with emphasis on citizenship, family values, and civic participation; (3) the Blacksburg Manifesto (Virginia Polytechnic Institute) "refounders"–who try to extend the meaning of public administration from mere management of public organizations to larger and more legitimate understanding of it as a part of governance; (4) the interpretive theorists and postmodernists–with emphasis on the human condition in a society dominated by organizations; (5) the "tools approach"–with a leading theme that today, with burgeoning of the third (not-for-profit) sector in delivery of public services, there is no one best way of approaching the administration of services even at the federal level; and (6) the new bureaucratic perspectives–with the main emphasis on bureaucratic accountability in a constitutional democracy.

Thus, theoretical frameworks, such as Osborne and Gaebler's, no matter how comprehensive and insightful, will always be incomplete, primarily for two reasons. First, in a democratic society the role of government will always be a matter of heated public debate. And, second, there always will be new developments in the society that the discipline of public administration will try to respond to and incorporate.

VATCHE GABRIELIAN,
MARC HOLZER,
AND PHILIP NUFRIO

BIBLIOGRAPHY

Drucker, Peter, 1968. *The Age of Discontinuity.* New York: Harper Torchbooks.
Gore, Albert, 1993. *From Red Tape to Results: Creating a Government that Works Better and Costs Less.* Report of the *National Performance Review.* 1993. Washington, D.C.: U.S. Government Printing Office.
Hammer, Michael, 1993. *Reengineering the Corporation.* New York: Harper Business.
Harrison, Roger, 1972. "Understanding Your Organization's Character." *Harvard Business Review* (May-June): 119-128.
Lowi, Theodore J., 1979. *The End of Liberalism: The Second Republic of United States.* 2d ed., New York: Norton.
Moe, Ronald C. 1994. "The Reinventing Government Exercise." *Public Administration Review*, vol. 54: 111-122.
Moe, Ronald C. and Robert S., Gilmour, 1995. "Rediscovering Principles of Public Administration: The Neglected Foundation of Public Law." *Public Administration Review.* vol. 55, no. 2: (March/April) 135-145.
Moss-Kanter, Rosabeth, 1983. *The Change Masters.* New York: Harper and Row.
National Commission on the Public Service, 1989. *Rebuilding the Public Service* (Report). Washington, D.C.: National Commission on the Public Service.
National Commission on the State and Local Public Service. (1993). *Hard Truths/Tough Choices: An Agenda for State and Local Reform.* Washington, DC: National Commission on the State and Local Public Service.
National Performance Review, 1993. *Creating a Government that Works Better and Costs Less.* Washington, D.C.: U.S. Government Printing Office.
Osborne, David, and Ted Gaebler, 1992. *Reinventing Government: How the Entrepreneurial Spirit Is Transforming the Public Sector from Schoolhouse to State House, City Hall to Pentagon.* Reading, MA.: Addison-Wesley.
Peters, Tom, and Robert Waterman, 1982. *In Search of Excellence: Lessons from America's Best-Run Companies.* New York: Harper and Row.
Savas, E. S., 1982. *Privatizing the Public Sector: How to Shrink Government.* Chatham, NJ: Chatham House.
———, 1985. "Implementing Privatization." *Urban Resources,* vol. 2, no. 4: 41.
———, 1987. *Privatization: The Key to Better Government.* Chatham, NJ: Chatham House.
———, 1992. Introduction to the Lauder Commission's (New York State Advisory Committee on Privatization) *Privatization for New York: Competing for a Better Future.* Albany: New York Senate Advisory Committee on Privatization.
Stillman, Richard J., II, 1995. "The Refounding Movement in American Public Administration." *Administrative Theory and Praxis,* vol. 17, no. 1: 29–45.
Wilson, James Q., 1994. "Reinventing Public Administration." *PS: Political Science and Politics* (December): 667–673.

RELIGIOUS ORGANIZATIONS. Groups formally established to pursue matters of worship, to provide

pastoral and spiritual care for its members, or to provide service to the larger community. The variety of forms that such organizations take creates problems for the investigator when trying to characterize them, for they include churches, synagogues, welfare and relief associations, advocacy groups, and international societies. Religious organizations are the largest single element of the nonprofit sector. The potential constitutional issues, their impact on the economy, and concerns about government supervision have not slowed their growth in the late twentieth century.

History and Character

Religious organizations have been a part of the human economy since the beginning of recorded history. They represent the earliest form of what we now call the nonprofit organization, dedicated to providing a variety of services to society separate from government and, in more recent times, from private enterprise. From the time of the Diaspora, the synagogue provided a central meeting place for community concerns. The necessity of reading Hebrew created schools. The large Jewish population of Alexandria in Egypt during the Roman Empire built one of the most important libraries in the history of the world. In Christianity, the monastic orders provided schools, libraries, social services, and agricultural support. Following the Islamic Revolution of 632, Moslem schools, universities, and hospices grew up in almost every city of any size throughout the Empire.

For Northern Europeans, the Age of Discovery and the Protestant Reformation combined to bring religiously based communities to colonial outposts. In North America, each colony had its religious foundation. Government in the colonial period comprehended no distinction between church and state. Churches participated as a part of the social order in providing necessary services, including private charity. Only with the dominance of a secular view of government, articulated particularly by Thomas Jefferson and Benjamin Franklin, did this arrangement begin to change. Elective government, market economies, property rights, and a growing secularism led to a growth of benevolent groups. The Great Awakening, an Evangelical revival between 1740 and 1760, brought a spectacular growth of voluntary associations grounded in the religious movement by generating intense debate about popular liberties in the face of entrenched structures.

The Revolutionary War brought disestablishment to most of the colonies, and thereby set off vigorous debates about the rights of popular associations. Jefferson worried that if such groups were left unregulated a new kind of tyranny could be created. In 1792 Virginia acted on this concern to suppress all private charitable corporations, seizing the endowments of the Anglican Church and turning them over to local authorities. Independent groups

were suspect, mainly because the new governments could not figure out how to control them.

As the country grew into the West, private as well as religious organizations were created in many places, and the debate between government and private initiative continued. Tocqueville commented on the way these new Americans formed themselves into groups for all sorts of purposes. Churches were active participants in the Civil War, providing care for individuals and meeting spaces for groups. Church groups founded schools, colleges, and hospitals throughout the American West.

Two developments in the latter part of the nineteenth century saw the expansion of religious involvement in the public economy. The Industrial Revolution and the consequent urbanization of America created a laboring class that was divided by ethnicity and language, and that was ill-equipped to deal with community needs. Parallel to urbanization was the rise of the Social Gospel, in which American Protestantism set out the idea that human beings could be perfected if they followed certain basic moral and spiritual principles. The combined forces energized efforts to provide education for the urban poor—indeed, the first Sunday schools were created to teach literacy via the Bible. A prime example of this movement was Trinity Church, New York City, which managed its many businesses and tenements from its location on Wall Street with an ethical focus rarely seen before or since.

World War I and the Great Depression set back the fervor of religious organization in the United States. The war demonstrated the defectability of humans, and the Depression, because of its international scope, proved to be a far greater affliction than religious groups could possibly address. A further hindrance was the way in which charitable organizations, including religious ones, had too tightly connected themselves to the booming American business community. The Great Depression proved that dependence on business could be fatal. Charitable organizations were the first to be cut from corporate budgets as the economy collapsed.

The explosion of the population into suburban areas after World War II brought a concomitant growth in the churches. Americans were a church- and synagogue-going population through the 1950s and 1960s. Religious edifices blossomed all over the American landscape. The boom economy provided plenty of discretionary income, and a good deal of it went into construction. The period of the Vietnam War, the Civil Rights movement, and the Great Society programs of the 1960s and 1970s saw an enormous increase in religiously based organizations, most of them providing community service programs. Churches and synagogues formed advocacy groups, social welfare agencies, schools, food kitchens, and relief organizations of a dizzying array of types and purposes. Religious groups became major actors in the massive immigration and refugee resettlement programs of the post-Vietnam period. Existing relief groups grew rapidly, and new organizations were formed as churches responded to disasters by providing financial and material relief. In the face of accusations of latent colonialism Protestant groups began pulling back from their missionary efforts in Third World countries.

These groups were succeeded by extensive development programs, funded by members in local congregations. This change can be seen, for example, in the Presiding Bishop's Fund for World Relief of the Episcopal Church, which began in 1938 as a very small effort to assist refugees fleeing from Nazi Germany. By 1980 the fund was spending millions of dollars a year on refugee resettlement and assistance programs, domestic and foreign disaster relief efforts, and both local and overseas development programs. Similar organizations in many other denominations experienced the same type of growth. The National Council of Churches, based in New York, provided some consolidation and coordination of programs, although all member churches retain independent programs and responses.

Since 1980 there has been a decline in church attendance nationwide. As contributions dwindled due to both social and economic factors, church and synagogue social services ebbed as well (Weisbrod 1988). In many cases, religious organizations have taken on a more secular face and now seek not only donations from members but also public donations and government grants for services. Issues that have bedeviled the religious-private-government relationship for generations are coming to the fore as all parts of the economy experience tighter and tighter budgets. Concerns include taxation of religious property and of religious business operations, requirements for reporting funds received and spent, control of church schools, and demands for public accountability. As in the early 1950s when church and philanthropic groups were suspected of subversive activities, the heavily secularized context of the United States today is surfacing a suspicion of motives and a search for appropriate roles for religious organizations.

Constitutional Issues in the United States

A significant question for U.S. public administration is the appropriate relationship between religious organizations and governments. In the U.S. constitutional framework, religious groups are acknowledged participants in American life. The First Amendment to the Constitution states that "Congress shall make no law regarding the establishment of religion, or the free exercise thereof." This language, though deceptively simple, has raised a hornet's nest of complications for U.S. political life. James Madison said that it may not be easy to trace the line of separation between the rights of religion and the civil authority, without avoiding collisions and doubts.

The foundation of church-state theory in U.S. government lies in the colonists' attempts to free themselves from the domination of a single established church, a system then in place in all European governments. As much as some might have wanted their sect established as the state church, the founders realized that choosing one over any others would only lead to further sectarian strife. The logical choice was to free government from ties to institutional religion and guarantee free practice of religious beliefs. Thus, for the first time in human history, a people established a government without calling upon officially sanctioned gods and their state-supported ministers.

In the modern period, people do not have a state confronting a church, or citizens confronting an established church, as was the situation familiar to Madison. Instead, we have religions and governments associating and interacting continually. The line between the essential and unessential has grown fuzzy. In the complex U.S. political and social order, the establishment and free exercise clauses of the Constitution often interfere with each other. For example, does providing state aid to parochial schools violate the establishment clause, or does not providing it violate the free exercise clause? Can governments make grants to religiously based organizations for social services? Can religious property be taxed, even if only on a fee-for-service basis? In reality, the two clauses are so closely intertwined as to make creating reasonable legal tests virtually impossible under the current political and social climate. The primary Supreme Court cases regarding these issues include *Watson* (1871), *Everson* (1947), *Walz* (1970), and *Lemon* (1971).

"Church and state" nowadays denotes a particular tension in U.S. society, rather than a legal philosophy or description of reality. Some believe that the root of the problem lies in the Supreme Court's confusion between churches as institutions and religion as philosophy or theory. This has led some to label the Court's interpretations "incoherent." There is some risk that the Court's confusion has led it to fail to protect religions not associated with Christianity.

The framers intended that there would be no official state religion and, conversely, that the state should not interfere in religious activities. The First Amendment expresses an institutional differentiation, with respectively temporal and spiritual ends for state and religion.

It is a recently popular belief that the separation on institutions intended by the founders means also to separate religious thought from the public sphere. The founders did not believe that religious thought should be eliminated from national life. Neither Jefferson nor Madison thought that separation would lessen the impact of religion. They believed that churches liberated from establishment would have greater moral force. Indeed, the first nation to disestablish religion has become an archetype of public piety. The problem is that legal doctrine on religion seeks to privatize all matters of religious belief, driving discussions farther from the public square. (See Wills 1990 for background.)

The battle lines between accommodationists (those who desire a low wall of separation) and separationists (who prefer a high wall) lie along cultural not legal lines. Religious pluralism in the United States has given rise to suspicion and hostility to religious groups that lie beyond the Judeo-Christian mainstream. In his exploration of the "culture wars" which have confounded modern American politics, James Davison Hunter (1992) has suggested that simply acknowledging the differences between communities may be enough to move people into a potentially resolvable situation. This is what he terms a "principled pluralism and a principled toleration."

In any case, the issues of appropriate roles for religious organizations in U.S. society will be with Americans for a very long time. The administrator needs to be prepared to confront these dilemmas, and to provide leadership toward their resolution.

Nongovernmental Organizations

A nongovernmental organization (NGO) is any nonprofit or voluntary group that works in an international context. Religious organizations and religiously based programs figure prominently among them.

The first voluntary associations to operate outside of their own national context were the missionary movements of the seventeenth and eighteenth centuries. The two most prominent, based in England, were the Society for the Promotion of Christian Knowledge (SPCK) and the Society for the Propagation of the Gospel (SPG). Growing numbers of Protestant churches followed these early leaders with their own missionary programs. Although focused on evangelization, social services were provided through schools, colleges, clinics, and hospitals. Albert Schweitzer's hospital in Africa and Father Damian's care for lepers in Hawaii are prominent examples.

After 1960, as missionaries were withdrawn from Africa and Asia by mainline groups, the programs they had maintained were replaced in many cases by relief and development agencies. These groups worked closely with their home governments (based chiefly in North America and Europe—Japanese corporate foundations were latecomers to this scene) and with host governments, which were not always entirely comfortable with these relatively ungovernable voluntary associations.

Following World War II, then-existing NGOs requested and were granted special status with the new United Nations. Several hundred NGOs were represented in the founding meetings in San Francisco, and there are numerous observer status offices in and around the United Nations and its extended programmatic wings. The Soviets had wanted a greatly reduced role for NGOs, undoubtedly because they represented an alternative to Communist propaganda and doctrine.

NGOs had mixed relations with African and Asian governments in the 1970s, as these newly formed countries struggled to unify power in the new national governments moving out of colonial rule. NGOs represented an alternative to weak government action in developing and state-dominated countries. However, the NGOs usual structure of local control threatened centralized authority. Nonetheless, NGOs remain a basic ingredient of a continuing emergent international society of organizations not under direct state control.

There are over three thousand NGOs operating in the world today, with a primary focus on international affairs, relief, or development. Organizations with religious roots or connections such as Catholic Relief, Save the Children, World Vision, CARE, Oxfam, Heifer Project International, and CROP represent a much longer list. The U.S. Catholic Church, utilizing millions of dollars donated by American members, has been a major player in the old Eastern bloc countries of Europe since the end of the cold war. Jewish organizations and other Christian groups have had energetic presences as well. The great power of these groups is seen in their ability to move money and materials very quickly across international borders. In 1989 alone, grants provided to programs in developing countries by NGOs, most of them with religious ties, amounted to over US $4 billion (Anheier and Cunningham 1994).

Many persons who become involved with secular NGOs do so out of a religious conviction. Often, local religious groups cannot provide a vehicle in which to act out their calling or ministry. Thus, they turn to groups with similar aims, giving to them both money and considerable time and energy.

The connection between state support and religious programs is a continuing concern of both domestic and foreign governments. In both Latin America and Africa, missionaries have been harassed or executed when they were suspected of being agents of a foreign government, typically the United States. The confusion arises because of strong state support of certain programs in European countries, and because of support through grants-in-aid to religious groups in the United States. Even simple intergovernmental and religious NGO cooperation in the midst of a crisis or disaster can be interpreted in other places as collusion. The constitutional issues in the United States are but a part of the larger question of how NGOs, and religious NGOs in particular, fit into U.S. foreign policy and development efforts.

Religious Organizations and Public Administration

The picture drawn here of religious organizations in the United States and elsewhere shows the remarkable complexity of this subsector of the nonprofit domain. Public administration has a part in relating religious organizations to the larger political and social economy of the country. This can be done in two ways. First, it can recognize the power and potential of these groups for the continuing improvement of community life in the United States through their social welfare, educational, and health related efforts. Second, public administration can assist religious organizations to operate more efficiently and effectively. Both of these actions can be taken without compromising either important values or constitutional boundaries.

In the first instance, the potential for improving the public good through the activity of religious organizations is shown by surveys that indicate that one-half of all adult Americans donate three to five hours a week to voluntary organizations. Often, the recipient of this gift of time is a religious organization. Volunteers almost always contribute financially to the program(s) they give time to. The combination of donated time and money is an enormous source of capital for religious organizations. Religious organizations receive 93 percent of their donations from individuals. The remainder comes from foundation grants and government sources. (See Weisbrod 1988 for references and other statistics in this regard.)

It is very difficult to compute the overall capital effect of the tax exemptions given to religious groups in the United States. Again, the amount is substantial, to say the least. The tax break given to religious groups amounts to a significant public subsidy. As public budgets have tightened in recent years legislatures, councils, and commissions have more critically examined these arrangements.

Public administrators can work with religious groups to coordinate effort and make service provision more cost-efficient for the community at large. Simply bringing groups together to discuss programs can be a major contribution to this effort. A good example is the national Voluntary Organizations Active in Disasters (VOAD), with local branches in nearly every state. These associations consist mainly of religious organizations, and the willingness of state disaster coordinators to arrange for their meetings has been very helpful.

Religious groups have been at the forefront of social change in the United States from the civil rights movement through current debates about abortion, capital punishment, and the role of women. Although religious leaders may not be unanimous in their articulation of concerns, they do bring a particular sensitivity to the public square. These leaders can be made active participants in the ongoing discussions that are necessary for U.S. democratic life. The interplay of U.S. religious views has been a major part of the lively social process that has created the United States.

The second contribution that public administration can make to religious organizations is in offering its special expertise in public management. The majority of graduate programs in nonprofit organization management are lo-

cated in public administration schools or programs. A survey of the literature on religious organization management and development shows a dearth of references to popular theories of organizational behavior. Religious nonprofit organizations often hire managers for reasons other than their management ability, and who are thereby ill-equipped in basic management skills and knowledge. Public administration education and practice can provide information and resources in ways that do not violate political or dogmatic boundaries.

The current division between public administration and religious organizations in general is due in part to the lack of awareness in public administration of the diversity and extent of the religious organization sector. For example, one looks in vain in the public administration literature for comprehensive administrative histories that take into account the bureaucratic traditions of churches. Dwight Waldo wrote to *Public Administration Review* in 1988, lamenting the lack of concern for the contributions that religion has made to modern administration. It is a field rich with promise for those who would expand the scope and contributions of this practice.

PETER J. VAN HOOK

BIBLIOGRAPHY

Anheier, Helmut K., and Kusuma Cunningham, 1994. "Internationalization of the Nonprofit Sector." In Robert D. Herman & Assoc., eds., *The Jossey-Bass Handbook of Nonprofit Leadership and Management*. San Francisco: Jossey-Bass.

Bellah, Robert N., et al., 1988. *Habits of the Heart: Individualism and Commitment in American Life*. New York: Harper & Row.

Howard, A. E., 1985. "The Supreme Court and the Serpentine Wall." In Merrill D. Peterson and Robert C. Vaughan, eds., *The Virginia Statute for Religious Freedom: Its Evolution and Consequence in American History*. Cambridge: Cambridge University Press.

Hunter, James Davison, 1992. *Culture Wars: The Struggle to Define America*. New York: Basic Books.

Livezey, Lowell W., 1989. "U.S. Religious Organizations and the International Human Rights Movement." *Human Rights Quarterly*, 11:14–81.

Lockhart, William B., Yale Kamisar, and Jesse H. Choper, 1980. *Constitutional Law: Cases, Comments, Questions*. 5th ed. St. Paul: West.

Wald, Kenneth D., 1992. *Religion and Politics in the United States*. 2d ed. New York: St. Martin's Press.

Weisbrod, Burton A., 1988. *The Nonprofit Economy*. Cambridge: Harvard University Press.

Wills, Garry, 1990. *Under God: Religion and American Politics*. New York: Simon and Schuster.

Yarnold, Barbara M., ed., 1991. *The Role of Religious Organizations in Social Movements*. New York: Praeger.

REORGANIZATION. Refers to any conscious alteration in the structure of government, the process by which it operates, or its responsibilities (Balutis 1984).

There must be a clearly recognizable change in the roles, relationships, and behaviors of a substantial percentage of people in the organizations (Mosher 1967). This does not include changes in programs that do not significantly affect structure. Reorganization is not a simple process, but a multidimensional and multifaceted one. Possibilities for reorganization include: job redesign, redistribution of work among current employees, changing the number of levels or units in the organization, centralizing or decentralizing operations, changing work shifts, consolidating programs and eliminating offices and personnel.

Reorganization ventures have been undertaken by governments of all political persuasions and under a variety of political circumstances. Presidents and presidential candidates frequently undertake plans to reorganize the federal bureaucracy, change its budget procedures, and overhaul its personnel system. Various chief executives have made promises to "restructure," "reform," "reinvent," or "reorganize" government. Similar initiatives have occurred at the state and local levels.

The importance of structure to organizational development is that it is the underlying theory that surrounds reorganization initiatives. It is believed that the manipulation of structural variables is the key to improving how the system operates. This theory is supported by Max Weber, one of the founders of modern sociology. Similarly, the works of Luther Gullick and Lyndall Urwick, scholars of organizational theory, promote reorganizing, span of control, division of labor, and hierarchical control to improve efficiency. The reports of the Grace Commission, the Hoover Commission, and the Brownlow Committee all suggested structural changes for improving the way government works.

Goals and Objectives of Reorganization

Reorganization may have a wide variety of objectives, some that might be stated publicly but others that may remain unstated. One reason commonly expressed to the public for reorganization is the need to deliver services more efficiently. Economy and efficiency were identified as two of the main purposes of the United States federal Reorganization Act of 1939. The way that U.S. government operates is often described as disorganized, cumbersome, wasteful, and ineffective. The remedy for these problems usually includes recommendations for change in the structure or the administrative procedures. The predicted benefits for these changes often include projections of big savings, a decline in red tape, streamlining and simplifying services, and reductions in fraud and abuse, in duplication of services, and in the size of the bureaucracy.

Efficiency as a major goal of reorganization has been touted both on a national and a local level. President Jimmy Carter vowed to "bring the horrible bureaucratic mess under control and restore sound principles of management." President Bill Clinton promised to fix the "broken" government by creating a government that works better and costs less.

At the local level, governors and mayors have also recommended reorganizations before or immediately after taking office. The reorganization efforts of local governments have been promoted as remedies for specific efficiency problems such as the lack of professionalism, fraud, abuse, and corruption. The reorganization efforts of John Lindsay, mayor of New York in the early 1970s, were centered around decentralization of service delivery to make the bureaucracy more accountable. In 1982, Governor Keane promised to overhaul the New Jersey state bureaucracy. His administration's reorganization enterprises (Governor's Management Improvement Program) were designed to reduce high costs, waste, and inefficiency.

The unstated objectives of reorganization efforts include political and cultural motivations. In fact, many modern scholars of organizational theory argue that reorganization is more a political than an administrative or efficiency tool (March and Olsen 1983, p. 281). The argument is made that the chief executive's call for reorganization is often empty rhetoric, with no real intentions to effectuate change. It is suggested that during political campaigns candidates often expound the virtues of reorganization to gain tactical advantage over their competitors (Seyb 1994, p. 725). By touting change, chief executives hope to encourage the public to view their management as different from previous administrations. After all, the public is always attentive to the suggestions and possibilities of change. An administration that declares reorganization efforts, especially at that administration's beginning, often connotates the presence of strong leadership. The public's belief in the possibility of change, however, might be more significant than the implementation of recommendations by public officials.

The public is usually receptive to talk of reorganization. Everyone seems to agree with it in principle. After President Harry S. Truman took office, the need for reorganization and reform was one of the top ten priorities in the White House mail (Seidman 1980, p. 126). It received a higher ranking than the full employment bill, the regulation of prices, and the control of the atomic bomb.

Other political objectives of reorganization endeavors include the desire of the chief administrator to save a program with very little political support. For example, the continual renaming of the foreign aid agency during the Carter administration reflected the administration's need to strengthen congressional support rather than to improve performance.

Effectiveness of Reorganization

What can one say about the effectiveness of reorganization plans or practices? Do they achieve their stated and unstated objectives? Do they improve efficiency and economy? Do they influence public opinion? The verdict is mixed. In terms of its effects on administrative efficiency, some commentators have suggested that, for the most part, there is no evidence that reorganization improves the delivery or reduces the cost of services. Some scholars have argued that in some situations it improves productivity. The New Jersey Governor's Management Improvement Program claimed to have saved state taxpayers approximately US$102 million.

Centralization of services has led to greater uniformity, more agency control over policies and operations, and increased utilization of specialized personnel and equipment. Decentralization of services has brought services closer to the clients, therefore permitting adjustments to suit local needs.

The creation of single-purpose "special districts," in which local governments share responsibilities for a single service, for example sewage and water, has met with some success. The elimination of redundant staff positions has also been suggested as a strong point of reorganization.

The greatest achievement of reorganization seems to be its political value. When chief executives promote reorganization as an attack on bureaucratic inefficiencies, they draw immediate public attention. Their rhetoric stirs up emotions among the public and conveys the message that the newly appointed administrator or president is in charge and is willing to act decisively.

Reorganizations might also stimulate self-inspection on the part of employees and administrators, therefore fulfilling the intentions of reorganization without formal structural change (March and Olsen 1983).

Impact of Reorganization

Reorganizations create concerns from a variety of sources. The concept of reorganization sounds good; however, reactions are different when one is directly affected by the changes. Within the organization, employees worry about how it will affect their status and promotional opportunities. If there is a relocation of office or a change in supervisors, employees might be concerned about expectations. For older workers, the change created by reorganizations can be traumatic. More important, some employees become extremely anxious about the possibilities of losing their jobs.

There is also the discomfort associated with learning new policies and procedures. Employees are often unsure of their new responsibilities. Also, the flow of information from the administrators to the staff is often interrupted because of a lack of proper planning. Training and cross-training of employees might be undesirable because it is a time-consuming process. There might also be apprehensions about the severing of personal friendships, contacts, and alliances that may have developed over the years.

Outside the organization, client groups and other agencies often express concern about reorganization, too. Moreover, the certainty of the policies and procedures of the old organization is replaced by anxieties, uncertainty, and fear of what the new system entails. One problem is that the definition and implementation of the new policies and procedures is often fragmented and unclear. In the interim, clients experience a lack of adequate information and a reduction in the delivery of services.

Reorganization endeavors also affect interest groups. Congress and lobbying groups have been known to resist reorganizations, thus contributing to their lack of success in some situations. March and Olsen (1983) have pointed out that opposition from Congress forced the abandonment of reorganization proposals during the Woodrow Wilson, Harry Truman, Lyndon Johnson, Richard Nixon, and Jimmy Carter administrations. Change is feared. Those who have power resist any suggestions that would alter their status.

Despite the associated problems, there are some legitimate social and political conditions that warrant reorganization. For example, when the population of schoolage children decreases, the needs of the children might be better served if school districts consolidate with other districts. Also, a modernization of technology and equipment within an organization might warrant reorganization of the work processes. And, an increase in the education and experience of employees might require a reorganization of an agency.

In conclusion, it is important to note that reorganization, both in theory and in practice, is a complex process. Implementation is difficult. The short term in office of the chief executive, the inability of the public to focus its attention on the key issues, and the opposition from interest groups have stalled many reorganization initiatives. Moreover, the evaluation of reorganization initiatives is difficult because of the absence of objective standards of measurement and the lack of consensus on the expectations of what results should be achieved. In some instances, reorganization might have administrative benefits. However, its greatest contribution might be its symbolic value of focusing the public on the affairs and operations of government.

PATRICIA MOORE

BIBLIOGRAPHY

Balutis, Alan, 1984. The Reorganization of the Department of Health, Education, and Welfare: "What Happened, Why, and So What?" In *Problems in Administrative Reform,* edited by Robert Miewald, Michael Steinman. Chicago: Nelson-Hall.

Conant, James, 1986. "Reorganization and the Bottom line." *Public Administration Review* 46 (January-February): 48–56.

Downs, George, and Patrick Larkey, 1986. *The Search for Government Efficiency.* Philadelphia: Temple University Press.

March, James, and Johan Olsen, 1983. "Organizing Political Life: What Administrative Reorganization Tells Us About Government." *American Political Science Review,* 77 (June): 281–296.

Mosher, Frederick, 1967. *Governmental Reorganizations: Cases and Commentary.* Inter-University Case Program. New York: Syracuse University.

Rosen, Ellen, 1993. *Improving Public Sector Productivity.* London: Sage.

Savitch, H. V., 1994. "Reorganization in Three Cities: Explaining the Disparities Between Intended Actions and Unanticipated Consequences." *Urban Affairs Quarterly* 29 (June): 565–595.

Seidman, Harold, 1980. *Politics, Position and Power: The Dynamics of Federal Organization.* New York: Oxford University Press.

Seyb, Ron, 1994. "The Death and Rebirth of Reorganization Planning: Symbolic Action, Divided Government, and Orthodox Administrative Theory's Enduring Appeal." *Presidential Studies Quarterly* 24 (Fall): 725–744.

Starling, Grover, 1986. *The Politics of Reorganization–Managing the Public Sector.* Chicago: Dorsey Press.

REPRESENTATIVE BUREAUCRACY.

A diverse civil service that mirrors those it serves in terms of demographic characteristics and that produces policies that are more representative and have more legitimacy than a bureaucracy that is not socially diverse. It is one of a variety of theories that have been offered to suggest how a bureaucracy can be made to be politically responsive to the population at large.

Origin and Development of the Concept

The origin of the term is credited to J. Donald Kingsley (1944), who argued that with the shift in the power of policy formulation from the legislature to the executive branch in the twentieth century, it was becoming all the more important that those involved in administrative policy making be truly representative of social groups in the state. Kingsley wrote that "no group can safely be entrusted with power who do not themselves mirror the dominant forces of society; for they will then act in an irresponsible manner or will be liable to corruption at the hands of the dominant groups" (1944, pp. 282–283).

The focus of Kingsley's analysis was the British Civil Service, which was largely of upper-class and middle-class origin, and therefore in danger of undermining the working-class-oriented policies of the new Labour Party government that came into power after World War II. He argued that only a civil service that was broadly representative in terms of class origins could insure that whichever party was

in power would find at least some administrators willing to carry out its program.

As the movement for equality in employment for minorities and women took hold in the United States, the concept of representative bureaucracy was adapted to suggest that race, ethnicity, and gender are the relevant characteristics for defining the representativeness of the U.S. civil service (see **affirmative action**, **equal employment opportunity**, and **workforce diversity**).

As the bureaucracy came to be recognized as an important institution, particularly following the writings of Max Weber, underrepresented groups were stimulated to try to gain their share of the appointive positions within it. In that sense, a bureaucracy that is representative of various interests in society assures those diverse elements that they not only have equal access to policymaking positions but also that their interests are being given equal consideration.

It also should be noted that the concept of the bureaucracy as a political entity that should represent something is not a new one in the United States. In the early years of the Republic, Thomas Jefferson sought to insure that the percentage of Federalists and Republicans in the government reflected their percentage in the nation as a whole.

The Civil Service (Pendleton) Act in 1883 envisioned geographic representation, calling for civil service jobs to be apportioned among the states and territories and the District of Columbia on the basis of population. In that sense, then, it is not surprising that, at a time when race in particular was becoming a volatile issue in the United States, Kingsley's concept of representative bureaucracy should be intercepted and applied to the importance of minority access to government jobs.

Other Benefits of a Representative Bureaucracy

There are other purposes that a representative bureaucracy is believed to serve. It creates legitimacy for and broad acceptance of governmental policies, presumably because the representatives within the bureaucracy are in a position to encourage support for these policies among the groups they represent. For example, women may be more likely to accept a health policy program that they know women have been involved in designing because it suggests women's health issues may have been given explicit consideration. Moreover, a woman involved in the development of such a policy may be in a better position than a man to urge compliance with the policy among women.

Another argument in favor of a representative bureaucracy is that a diverse workforce brings with it a broader range of skills and creativity, which can lead to the development of more effective and imaginative policies. Those with different cultural backgrounds may provide alternative problem-solving methods or skills outside of those available to a strictly "mainstream group."

Moreover, insuring that all salient groups are represented within the governmental bureaucracy, typically the largest employer in most complex societies (including the United States) and the enforcer of its laws, signals that these groups have equal access to the benefits of this employment and to the social power it brings. If Latinos, for example, were to hold no or very few government jobs, they may begin to wonder whether they have equal opportunity to achieve any of society's benefits. As Samuel Krislov (1967) has argued, "Where there are in theory no barriers, the actual denial of representation in public service becomes even more obviously an affront to dispossessed groups. Such a denial becomes a crude challenge to the loyalty, worth, and power of an unrepresented social group" (pp. 53–54).

Unresolved Issues

Some of the assumptions underlying the concept of representative bureaucracy remain unresolved. For example, as Frederick C. Mosher (1982) has noted, underlying many of the justifications previously outlined for representative bureaucracy is the assumption that "passive" representation translates into "active" representation. Passive representation means simply that members of the various demographic groups in society can be found in the bureaucracy, and active representation suggests that members of those groups actively advocate the interests of those who share their backgrounds. The question is whether it is enough to assume that African Americans from South-Central Los Angeles, for example, working for the Department of Housing and Urban Development (HUD), consciously seek to ensure that HUD's policies reflect the best interests of African Americans living in South-Central Los Angeles, or whether, through the educational process or even by working within an organization, they become socialized into a mold that renders their background irrelevant. Moreover, Frank Thompson (1976) has suggested that even if administrators were able to overcome the effects of socialization and remain loyal to the interests of their community of origin, there are other obstacles standing in the way of their active pursuit of their group's interests. These obstacles can include a lack of power to pursue those interests in their organization, peer pressure, ambiguity about the goals of their community, and formal organizational sanctions against independent behavior and expressions of opinion.

Some scholars have attempted to assess the link between passive and active representation empirically by examining whether, for example, black or white police officers behave any differently toward minority citizens, or whether nonwhite therapists can more easily empathize with nonwhite clients. The results of such analyses, however, have been mixed and have not as yet settled the debate.

Another issue that continues to incite controversy is how to resolve the goal of representative bureaucracy with the objective of a system of hiring and promotion based strictly on merit. Proponents of representative bureaucracy advocate the use of affirmative action programs to insure that minorities and women who have been denied equal access to public sector positions in the past be given special consideration in employment decisions. Opponents of affirmative action argue that the only way to insure that the government workforce is made up of the most qualified and technically competent individuals is to base recruitment on examinations that ignore considerations of race, ethnicity, and gender, even if such exams have the effect of perpetuating the dominance of policy-making positions within the bureaucracy by nonminority men.

Still another unresolved issue is what constitutes a representative bureaucracy and how such representation should be measured. It has already been suggested that whether a given bureaucracy is "representative" has largely been determined based on analysis of the percentage of minorities and women in its workforce, ignoring the question of whether such "passive" representation results in "active" representation. More recently, as the bureaucracy in the United States has become largely representative of the American people as a whole, concern has shifted to whether minorities and women are adequately represented in higher graded positions, where most important decisions are made. At this level, the percentages are not as encouraging. According to J. Edward Kellough (1992), for example, in 1990 women held half of all white-collar (general schedule) jobs in the federal bureaucracy, but only 11 percent of executive positions. Blacks held nearly 17 percent of white-collar jobs but less than 5 percent of executive positions. Thus, the extent and specificity with which full representation should be defined remains unresolved.

Current Status of Representative Bureaucracy in the United States

With the passage of the Civil Service Reform Act (CSRA) of 1978, it became the official policy of the United States, at least for the federal bureaucracy, to achieve a federal workforce reflective of U.S. diversity. The CSRA gave responsibility for achieving this goal to both the Office of Personnel Management (OPM) and the Equal Employment Opportunity Commission (EEOC). OPM is responsible for administering the Federal Equal Employment Opportunity Recruitment Program (FEORP), which requires agencies to conduct affirmative recruitment activities to eliminate the underrepresentation of women and minorities in all occupational categories and at all grade levels. The EEOC was given responsibility for monitoring the success of federal agencies in achieving full representation of minorities and women. To establish the extent to which full representation exists, EEOC requires agencies to compare the representation of various groups with the representation of the same occupations groups in the civilian labor force (CLF). The CLF represents people of working age (16 or over), not employed in the armed forces, who are employed or seeking employment. Thus, although the CSRA gave official credence to the importance of a bureaucracy representative of the nation in terms of race, ethnicity, and gender, in practice in the United States the concept has been defined in terms of a more limited benchmark than one that would compare representation to the population as a whole.

The extent to which efforts to achieve a fully representative workforce have been pursued in the federal bureaucracy remains a political issue, with some administrations giving it more emphasis than others. The Bill Clinton administration has made a deliberate point of promising a government that "looks like America," and there are indications that at least some agency heads are responding by looking for ways to hold individual managers directly accountable for the composition of their work units.

Representative Bureaucracy Outside of the United States

The advantages of including disaffected groups within the bureaucracy has been recognized in countries besides the United States and Britain. Samuel Krislov (1974) has described the experiences of other countries that attempted to enfranchise various segments of society through insuring their access to civil service positions.

In India, for example, positions in the British-created civil service were set aside for qualified members of the "scheduled castes" (also previously known as "untouchables"), although Krislov has suggested that the public service has not been a particularly effective vehicle for banishing the inequities of the caste system, at least in part because to gain privileges reserved for their caste, these people must affirm that they are members of this caste.

In Israel, it was recognized that high degrees of party intervention in the bureaucracy, along with power in the party being largely based on seniority, meant that the composition of the bureaucracy remained unchanged even while the population was undergoing rapid transition with successive waves of immigration. As a result, measures were taken to provide access to underrepresented groups through direct recruiting, with different qualification requirements for different cultural groups.

Similarly, in countries where cultural differences are fueled by language differences, the benefits of government office have been apportioned as a means for keeping the peace. In Belgium, for example, as Krislov (1974) has reported, following a series of Cabinet crises, a number of measures were undertaken to keep the peace between the Flemings and the French-speaking Belgians, including promising parity in governmental and military posts.

Conclusion

Representative bureaucracy is a concept that speaks to the effort to make the federal bureaucracy more responsive to the concerns of the citizenry by demonstrating that politically salient groups have equal access to administrative policymaking positions.

Although on one level, the concept has gained wide acceptance in the United States (as well as other nations) through codification of a policy to achieve a diverse workforce, the operationalization of that policy remains mired in controversy. Unresolved questions include the definition of a "fully representative" bureaucracy, whether such a goal can be reconciled with the desire for a merit system, and whether ascriptive representation really insures that the interests of diverse groups are being served.

As long as politically salient divisions among groups remain in a society, and as long as bureaucracies are viewed as important policymaking institutions, these questions are likely to remain in dispute.

KATHERINE C. NAFF

BIBLIOGRAPHY

Kellough, J. Edward, 1992. "Affirmative Action in Government Employment." *Annals of the American Academy of Political and Social Science,* vol. 523 (September): 117–130.
Kingsley, J. Donald, 1944. *Representative Bureaucracy: An Interpretation of the British Civil Service.* Yellow Springs, OH: Antioch Press.
Krislov, Samuel, 1967. *The Negro in Federal Employment.* Minneapolis: University of Minnesota Press.
———, 1974. *Representative Bureaucracy.* Englewood Cliffs, NJ: Prentice-Hall.
Mosher, Frederick C., 1982. *Democracy and the Public Service.* 2d ed. New York: Oxford University Press.
Thompson, Frank J., 1976. "Minority Groups in Public Bureaucracies: Are Passive and Active Representation Linked?" *Administration and Society,* vol. 8 (August): 201–248.

REPRODUCTIVE RIGHTS POLICY. A government's formal definition, supported in law and set forth in regulation, of its authority over the inception and/or the termination of a woman's pregnancy.

In most Western European and North American countries, the state's interest in regulating reproductive rights focuses on the conditions under which the termination of a pregnancy (or abortion) prior to the fetus's ability to survive independently may occur. Conception, less often a focus for regulation by the state, is more often governed by societal values and religious or tribal law. (Exceptions include contemporary China, where financial incentives are used as inducements to limit conception; Romania, which from 1966 to 1988 set quotas for women to conceive and monitored their progress; and Nazi Germany, whose reproductive policies included forced impregnation of suitable candidates.)

From the pragmatic approach generally attributed to preliterate societies and the permissive views of the early Greeks and Romans, to the more restrictive regimes of the nineteenth and early twentieth centuries, a country's reproductive rights policy generally has reflected social values. Regardless of policy or traditional mores, however, contraception, abortion, and to a lesser extent infanticide are practiced universally in human societies.

In the United States, Britain, Canada, and Australia, the public policy debate over government regulation of reproductive rights is distinguishable from that in other countries in Western Europe, Asia, and Africa because it is defined as a clash of rights—to life, to liberty, and of privacy. In the United States it also entails constitutional guarantees of free speech and the separation of church and state. In most other countries, the discussion is grounded in moral, political, or economic terms, without regard to rights.

Historical Development

Throughout history, reproductive rights policies have been shaped by a number of factors: maternal morbidity in childbirth; quality and availability of medical facilities, of contraceptives, and of methods for terminating a pregnancy; child-spacing needs; a society's wish to conserve resources or augment its workforce; and cultural priorities for dynastic continuity and for addressing improper parentage.

Culture and religion have legitimized and reinforced practices derived from economic or other practical necessities. For example, a limitation on the number of nursing children a nomadic tribe could support at any one time might underlie specific taboos on sexual activity.

Concern with population control and healthy births appears in Plato's *Republic* (370 B.C.E.) and in Aristotle's writings. Although Hippocrates is noted for his opposition to it, abortion was used, in addition to contraception, to address those concerns. Reproductive rights policy in pre-Christian Rome favored propagation among the upper classes, leaving the decision as to how to achieve that to the husband.

Early Christian writings on abortion disagree on the gravity of the act. But the point at which a pregnancy was terminated was pivotal in the characterization of the act as homicide in both civil and church law. Church documents from the first centuries C.E. referred to hominization (when the embryo was formed) as the critical juncture, but there was no consensus as to when that occurred. Papal pronouncements in the sixteenth century alternatively condemned abortion at any stage and recommended lesser penalties prior to hominization. Later, the point of quickening (when the mother first felt fetal movement) was used as the threshold for moral or legal sanctions.

In the nineteenth century, several countries became more involved in the regulation of abortion to protect the public health (many abortifacients were considered to be poisonous). Laws governing pre- and post-quickening terminations and determining upon whom sanctions, if any, should fall, varied, as did their enforcement.

In 1869, the Roman Catholic Church, through the pronouncements of Pope Pius IX, abandoned its distinction between abortion before hominization and after. This was a prelude to the Church's present stand, that all abortion is murder.

In the United States, reproductive rights policy reflected the society's support for individual rights—at least until the second half of the nineteenth century. With the support of the American Medical Association (AMA), founded in 1847, the antiabortion campaign of Dr. Horatio Storer led to the passage in 1873 of a bill amending the federal obscenity statute of 1872. The new legislation, also referred to as the Comstock Law, after Anthony Comstock (1844–1915), a special agent of the Post Office Department charged with the act's enforcement, made it a federal crime to disseminate any information on contraception or abortion in the United States. During this period, Canada also enacted restrictions on the distribution of birth control information or aids.

Twentieth Century

Reproductive rights policy took on increased significance in the twentieth century as governments used the regulation of procreation in service of ideological goals.

Serving Ideology

Russian policy on reproductive rights is a good example. From the beginning of the century, abortion had been common practice due to the primitive medical conditions surrounding pregnancy and birth, as well as the general failure of contraceptive practices. When abortion was legalized by the Soviet government in 1920, Czarist Russia was blamed for creating the conditions that had made abortion inevitable. In this view, as the new regime achieved its goal, there would no longer be a need for abortion; but, in the meantime, legalization would keep women in the workforce. In 1936, Joseph Stalin once more made it illegal to abort a pregnancy. Conception was endorsed as the citizen's duty to naturally augment the country's labor force. Nevertheless, after Stalin's death, abortion was again legalized to combat the public health effects of widespread illegal procedures.

Prior to the breakup of the USSR's satellite bloc in Eastern Europe, its reproductive rights policies mirrored that of the Soviet Union—with the exception of Romania, whose efforts at increasing its population by outlawing abortion and the use of contraceptives (as well as taxing childless women and setting quotas for the others) contributed to the overflowing orphanages whose discovery shocked the world community in 1989. After the fall of Nicolae Ceausescu's government in December 1988, abortion was legalized in Romania again.

Five decades earlier, Nazi Germany's notorious reproductive rights policies (forced impregnation, compulsory abortion, and mandatory sterilization) had gone even further in service of the state—denying any individual rights in order to achieve the goal of a racially pure society. Aryan Germans had a duty to propagate; those determined to be genetically unfit were to be sterilized or their fetuses aborted.

Population Control

Reproductive rights policy in the People's Republic of China generally served the goals set by the Communist leadership for economic growth and population control. After the Great Leap Forward (1958–1962), the population growth rate was judged to be too high; consequently, controls on abortion and contraception were relaxed. As the growth rate continued to accelerate, the government instituted monetary incentives and compulsory termination of a pregnancy to achieve a goal of one child per family. Opposition to the state's policy was based on traditional family values, rather than on any violation of individual rights.

In the 1940s and 1950s, where increasing the population was not a policy goal, several other countries liberalized their reproductive rights laws. Switzerland was among the first. In 1948, Japan enacted the Eugenic Protection Laws, legalizing abortion to restrict the procreation of genetically inferior citizens and to protect the life or health of the mother. In India, as in China, abortion was promoted as a means to control fertility rates.

Opposition to abortion persisted everywhere, but was greatest where religious or tribal influences were strong, as in countries such as Ireland, where the Roman Catholic Church was powerful, or in Pakistan, where conservative Muslim thought prevailed. Opposition to abortion for gender selection—more prevalent since the development of amniocentesis, which can be used to determine the sex of the fetus as well as to detect certain abnormalities—has been mounted by feminists in parts of Asia where it is practiced (in addition to female infanticide).

Great Britain and North America

In Great Britain, improvements in medical procedures encouraged the relaxation of statutes that had criminalized abortion since 1803. In 1929, Parliament passed the Infant Life (Preservation) Act, which recognized exceptions to the prohibition in cases where abortion could save the mother's life. The criteria were ambiguous; consequently, the statute was not uniformly applied. In 1967, Parliament passed the British Abortion Act, legalizing abortion in England, Scotland, and Wales. In Northern Ireland, however, the Offenses Against the Person Act of 1861, outlawing abortion (except as interpreted by the British Court in the 1938 *Bourne* case—to safeguard the health or save the life of the mother), remained in effect.

As in the United States, challenges to Britain's more liberal reproductive rights policies have come from groups asserting rights for the unborn, such as the Society for the Protection of Unborn Children. The debate led to the passage in 1990 of the Human Fertilisation and Embryology Act, which amended the British Abortion Act of 1967, setting 24 weeks as the upper limit for an abortion, but expanding the range of instances when a medical practitioner may terminate a pregnancy.

Following Britain's lead, Canada had liberalized its abortion laws by the late 1960s. In 1988, the Supreme Court of Canada, in *Morgentaler v. Regina*, adopted the reasoning in the U.S. Supreme Court's 1973 ruling in *Roe v. Wade*. Like *Roe*, *Morgentaler* recognized a woman's right to "security of person." Because the decision had the effect of making abortion available upon request, antiabortion groups in Canada continue efforts to enact restrictions.

Reproductive Rights in the United States

As in Western Europe, reproductive decisions in nineteenth century America were made in a relatively permissive legal climate—at least until the vigorous enforcement of the Comstock Law. It was under this statute that the work of birth control activist Margaret Sanger (1883–1966) was blocked. After the Great Depression, birth control as a means to combat poverty steadily gained support, despite the fact that the distribution of information or the use of contraceptives was still illegal in most states.

From the 1940s through the 1960s, the Planned Parenthood Federation of America (PPFA) (founded in 1939 with the merger of the American Birth Control League and the Birth Control Clinical Research Bureau) promoted the integration of family planning into national reproductive rights policy as a means to ameliorate poverty and to foster economic development.

During the period in which Canada and Britain were liberalizing their policies on reproductive rights, several American states—beginning with Colorado in 1967—enacted laws permitting therapeutic abortions (those to protect the life of the mother, in cases of rape or incest, or to prevent the birth of a severely deformed child). Also in 1967, the National Organization for Women (NOW) included control of reproductive rights in the newly promulgated Women's Bill of Rights.

The Court's Role

Advocates for change in reproductive rights policy in the United States were more successful in the Supreme Court than in state legislatures, however. In 1942, the Court in *Skinner v. Oklahoma* (in ruling that compulsory sterilization of certain criminals was unconstitutional) determined that reproduction was a basic right. In 1965, the Court in *Griswald v. Connecticut* held that the use of contraceptives by married couples was legal. The Court reasoned that there was a zone of privacy created in the penumbra of several constitutional guarantees (found in the First, Fifth, Ninth, and Fourteenth Amendments) that the state could not abridge. Seven years later this privacy right was extended to unmarried individuals in *Eisenstadt v. Baird,* which overturned all laws banning the distribution of contraceptives.

In 1973, the U.S. Supreme Court, balancing diverse rights—the woman's the physician's, and the state's—ruled in *Roe v. Wade* and its companion case, *Doe v. Bolton* that, within certain parameters, a woman has a constitutionally protected right to terminate her pregnancy. Constitutional protections were not extended to the unborn. This decision firmly established the U.S. debate as a battle of rights, one that continues unabated into the present.

Also in 1973, the National Association for the Repeal of Abortion Laws became the National Abortion Rights Action League (NARAL). NARAL and Planned Parenthood provided information and support nationally to assist in the establishment of low-cost clinics to complement hospital based services. Many offered a range of reproductive health services. As more hospitals declined to perform abortions, these clinics became more important.

In the same year, the National Conference of Catholic Bishops (NCCB) decreed that, for Catholics, involvement in any phase of abortion would mean excommunication, and the National Right to Life Committee (NRLC) was formed. Both oppose legalized abortion, taking the position that the termination of a fetus prior to viability outside the womb is homicide. In the United States, both groups remain powerful influences in the struggle over reproductive rights policy. The debate is often framed in terms of the right to choose versus the right to life.

In the more than two decades since abortion's legalization in the United States, forceful and effective lobbying by antiabortion groups has resulted in various restrictions on government support for abortion and fetal research in the United States and abroad; has delayed the introduction of RU486 (the "abortion pill" developed in France); and has spawned numerous court challenges, among them, *Rust v. Sullivan,* a 1991 Supreme Court decision upholding the restriction on recipients of federal family planning money from distributing information on abortion (the so-called "gag rule," later lifted in the Bill Clinton administration). In 1992, in *Planned Parenthood v.* *Casey,* the Court upheld Pennsylvania's restrictive abortion statute, which included requirements for informed consent, for a 24-hour waiting period, for parental consent, and for additional reporting and recordkeeping.

Demonstrations in the 1980s by antiabortion groups such as Operation Rescue sought to deny women access to clinics providing reproductive services. Excesses by some demonstrators led to the enactment in 1994 of the Freedom of Access to Clinics Entrances Act. Also since the decision in *Roe v. Wade,* there have been repeated efforts to amend the U.S. Constitution to overturn the ruling. For example, in 1973, amendments extending constitutional protections to the unborn were offered by Senator James Buckley (R–NY) and by Representative Lawrence Hogan (R–MD).

Reproductive Rights in the 1990s

Currently, most countries regulate to some degree the reproductive rights of their citizens—some to control population, others to protect rights, enhance public health, or promote economic growth. Overall, the implementation of reproductive rights policies still varies according to cultural traditions, the role of women in the society, and with the nature of the resistance.

In the majority of industrialized countries, reproductive rights policies facilitate access to contraceptive devices and voluntary sterilization, but regulate the safety and medical environments for abortion more stringently. Some policies are more restrictive than others. For example, to save the mother's life might be the only defense to an early termination of a pregnancy in Ireland (where the Offenses Against the Person Act of 1861 was incorporated into its Constitution in 1983), as well as in conservative Islamic cultures and in many African nations. Other countries, such as Finland, permit abortion for economic and social reasons; Israel does so when the woman's mental or physical health is endangered; and in the Netherlands, abortions are permitted upon request.

If (and as) the political climates in the United States, as well as in Great Britain and Western Europe, become more conservative, the trend toward liberalization of the reproductive rights policy that emerged at the end of World War II could be halted, if not reversed.

MICHELE T. COLE

BIBLIOGRAPHY

Costa, Marie, 1991. *Abortion: A Reference Handbook*. Santa Barbara, CA: ABC-CLIO, Inc.

Gordon, Linda, 1992. "Why Nineteenth-Century Feminists Did Not Support 'Birth Control' and Twentieth-Century Feminists Do: Feminism, Reproduction and the Family." In Barrie Thorne with Marilyn Yalom, eds., *Rethinking the Family: Some Feminist Questions*. Boston: Northeastern University Press.

Lindgren, J. Ralph, and Nadine Taub, 1988. *The Law of Sex Discrimination*. St. Paul, MN: West.

Miller, Patricia G., 1993. *The Worst of Times*. New York: Harper-Collins.

Sachdev, Paul, ed., 1988. *International Handbook on Abortion*. New York: Greenwood Press.

Tribe, Laurence H., 1990. *Abortion: The Clash of Absolutes*. New York: W. W. Norton and Company.

Weddington, Sarah, 1993. *A Question of Choice*. New York: Penguin Books.

REPUBLICANISM.

A body of thought that holds that the advancement of the interests of the people is the principal responsibility of nation-states and that this is properly accomplished through institutions based on direct or indirect popular rule.

Modern versus Ancient Republicanism

The modern Western European countries and the United States are defined as "modern democratic republics." The first republics emerged in the ancient Mediterranean, especially classical Greece and Italy. Our word "republic" comes from the Latin *res publica*, which, literally translated, means "the public things." Thus, the ancients classified societies as republics if state business was essentially public rather than private. In monarchies and small oligarchies, the business of government, indeed, the very workings of society itself, may be considered private. In such societies, decisions are made by an individual or small group for the benefit of that individual or group. Thus, the governing of such a society is essentially little different than the managing of a large estate where many individuals may be involved but all of their behavior is regulated so as to enhance the profit and well-being of the proprietor.

Around the seventh or sixth centuries B.C.E. two Greek cities, Sparta and Athens, seem to have developed the first republican political orders. Although these two regimes differed remarkably from modern republics, such as the United States, and were strikingly different from one another, they each gave a role in government to an assembly of all male citizens and thus recognized a political share in the society that belonged to all of its members. The business of government was recognized as, in some sense, public.

In Sparta, a new constitution was founded, according to ancient sources, by the wise lawgiver Lycurgus, the uncle and regent of one of two Spartan kings. Although there is great confusion about when and even if Lycurgus lived, the Greek philosopher Plutarch (46?–120?), who included his life in his collection of biographies, discounts stories that he preceded the foundation of the Olympic Games (776 B.C.E.) but insists that the reforms that Lycurgus instituted were already ancient by the classical period of the fourth century.

This "constitution," a combination of political institutions, customs, and written policies, which are known as the "Great Rhetra," called for two hereditary kings, descended from separate but related families, who served primarily as military commanders and political figureheads; a council of 30 elders, men over age 60 who could formulate policies and laws; and an assembly of the people, which has to ratify all actions of the kings or elders before they took effect. A smaller council of five citizens between 30 and 60 years of age, the ephors, or overseers, was later added.

The council was elected by the assembly and possessed great powers as the chief judicial court of the government. The constitution pervaded all aspects of public life, prescribing a set education and daily way of life for all citizens, which prepared them for their participation in the public life. This participation was most clearly manifested in the mandatory military service of all able-bodied male citizens. Continuous service was considered the only public pursuit, and therefore the only proper activity for a citizen of the Spartan republic; all men shared in politics in that they all were devoted to the public defense.

Compared to Sparta, Athenian republicanism seems to be more closely related to modern ideas of republicanism. Citizens of Athens in the classical period dictated the direction of public life in the city by direct voting in an assembly in which each individual was granted an equal vote. It was relatively easy to bring a measure to the consideration of the citizen body, to speak for and against proposed measures, and to stand for or hold office. Indeed, many offices were determined by a lot in which all citizens were included, and this random selection illustrates the true sharing of the common business among the citizens.

In Athens a great deal of personal freedom was tolerated for the citizens, but in Sparta only the freedom of the state itself was considered important. Athenian citizens were largely able to choose their own occupations and pursuits, although military service was required when the defense of the state, the guarantor of this freedom, was endangered. Despite this freedom, however, the Athenian republic did not recognize any of the absolute rights associated with modern republicanism. Personal decisions were considered open to review and correction by the ruling assembly. This may be clearly seen in the Athenian trial and execution of Socrates in 399 B.C.E. for his teachings, which were considered dangerous to the fundamental beliefs of the society.

The classical republics were the first societies to promote the rule of the people, but they differed greatly in some respects from their modern counterparts. These societies were small both in number of citizens and land area, which explains the modern practice of translating *politeia*, the Greek word for a regime or society, as "city-state" in modern English.

Limiting the size of the republic was thought to be necessary both for practical and theoretical reasons. Practically, each citizen could only exert influence if the citizen body was small in number and its members close enough in proximity to assemble together to discuss and vote on the public business. As Plato (427?–347 B.C.E.) and Aristotle (384–322 B.C.E.), the two primary political thinkers of antiquity,

claim, having a citizen body that can work together to promote the public good requires that the people are familiar with one another, that they share similar interests and desires, and that they can agree on certain basic opinions, especially those concerning religion and justice. A larger citizen body, or one that was racially or religiously diverse, was thought to be unable to govern itself and to require the "private" management of a powerful king or oligarchy.

Sparta sought to provide these common bonds by giving all of the citizens roughly equal wealth and a single occupation, military service. The "ideal" states described in Plato's *Republic* and Aristotle's *Politics* had similar restrictions on the citizens. Athens, where personal wealth varied widely within the citizen body and many different opinions and occupations were tolerated to some degree, was often thrown into chaos by violent civil conflicts that usually pitted the rich against the poor. The necessity of maintaining small republics was seemingly confirmed later by Rome's inability to maintain anything but a shadow of the republican form after the expansion of its mass and citizenship.

Whereas citizens were treated as political equals in Athens and Sparta, the citizen bodies of each were comparatively small when considering the whole populations of these cities. In Sparta, the helots, who were treated basically as slaves, and the *perioeci*, a noncitizen class of resident artisans and traders, may have outnumbered the citizens by as much as ten to one. This reflected an understanding that citizenship was not a right but a privilege. Indeed, the lack of any belief in "rights" in the modern sense led the classical republics to focus on the duties of citizens and constitutes the great theoretical difference between the ancient and modern conceptions of republicanism.

The modern republic originated in and draws its principles from modern political philosophy. The shift started with Niccolo Machiavelli's (1469–1527) rejection of the classical understanding of virtue and justice. Classical republics had sought through rigid education and carefully prescribed duties to inculcate a certain view of duty in their citizens. However, Machiavelli rejected this standard on the basis that human beings did not, in fact, seek to do what is good per se, but only what is good for themselves. With Machiavelli, self-interest or the desire for self-improvement, not the advancement of transcendant societal interests, was identified as the primary motivator of human beings.

This opinion was shared by Thomas Hobbes (1588–1679) who posited, contrary to Aristotle, that if human beings were primarily individualistic, no government or society, no human association, could be natural, and thus there must have been a state of nature in which each human being acted as an autonomous individual. Societies, according to Thomas Hobbes, are formed by a contract among individuals who seek security from their fellows because in the pre-political state of nature each

person's life is endangered by the self-interested actions of every other person. Persons enter society as equals and seek to maintain their equality insofar as it is consistent with their primacy goal, the preservation of their own existence.

John Locke (1632–1704) followed in the tradition of Hobbes but refused to accept the latter's defense of an absolute monarch as the best solution to the problem posed by the natural pursuit of self-preservation by competitive and self-interested beings. It is Locke's response that represents the true fount of modern republicanism. Locke argued that in the state of nature all people were equal, free, and naturally entitled to enjoy the fruits of their labor, namely their property. Individuals enter into society because although they have a right to these things in the state of nature, their rights are always in danger when there is no power capable of disciplining an individual who harms the rights of another. They seek to make their right secure by providing for a neutral judge who can protect their rights. Thus, as each human being ought to enjoy the same protection within the state, each individual ought to be equal within the state, and a republican government is needed to reflect this equality. The primary purpose of this government must be to protect these natural rights, which are insecure in the state of nature.

Locke proposed a form of republican government that he thought would be most consistent with two principles: It must be derived from consent and it must protect rights. Each of these two key principles feature prominently in the introduction to the American Declaration of Independence. It may be said that the United States separated from Great Britain with the avowed purpose of forming a modern Lockian republic. The Americans made a conscious decision to accept the republican form, the recognition of a key role for the "public," the many, in political life, but they did so while accepting much of Machiavelli and Hobbes' criticism of the ancient republics. In particular they denied the necessity of having a small, homogeneous citizen body devoted to a certain understanding of virtue and called for a republic based upon the rights of each citizen rather than the duties of the citizens to their society. These goals and changes require, according to Locke, a very carefully constructed set of political institutions, which are associated with modern republicanism and may be best seen in the government constructed by the American Constitution.

American Version of the Modern Republic

Drawing on the writings of seventeenth- and eighteenth-century Europeans theorists such as John Locke and the Baron de Montesquieu (1689–1755) and on the British political and common law tradition, the delegates who participated in the Constitutional Convention of 1787 in the United States attempted for the first time in modernity to construct a new national republic based on natural rights principles. For his part, James Madison (1751–1836), "father" of the American Constitution, explored the requisites of a decent and competent republic in what is regarded as the two most significant essays in the *Federalist Papers;* Numbers 10 and 51. Considering the degree to which the American "experiment" in modern republicanism has been imitated, Madison's thoughts on fashioning a defensible republic of rights are worthy of attention.

As monarchies and aristocracies are best when the one sovereign ruler or the ruling class possesses the qualities of character as well as the authority needed for effective governance, so the same is true of modern republics. There are, in short, some conditions that must be met for the modern democratic republic to satisfy the ends with which it is associated. Montesquieu, a French theorist of the eighteenth century, found these conditions well represented in the English republic, with its cultivation of the virtues of a commercial society and its reliance on a system of separated and divided powers.

Several structural arrangements are common to modern republics; among these are separate legislative, executive, and judicial departments. Alexander Hamilton (1755–1804) observed in *Federalist Paper* Number 9 that the system of separated and divided powers represents one of the innovations of the modern science of politics. The delegates at the Constitutional Convention held in Philadelphia in 1787 settled on a single executive who was to be selected by electors who would be chosen by the people. This process of indirect selection was defended as an effective means of combining the principle of popular consent with attention to merit and character. Reliance on a single, rather than plural, executive was defended as advancing both accountability and energy in government. As for the legislative department, the delegates opted to establish a lower house (House of Representatives) whose members would be attuned to local interests as a result of their number, short terms (two years) and likely selection in relatively small electoral districts, and an upper house (Senate) whose members were originally chosen by the state legislatures for six-year terms, and hence were expected to be less given to satisfying the temporary and short-range wishes of the people. The object was to refine or elevate deliberation without sacrificing attention to the preferences of the people and without relying on class or wealth distinctions to insure real checking and balancing within the legislature.

The independent judiciary was the last of the three major departments created by the delegates. A separate national court, the Supreme Court of the United States, was seen to be essential to the protection of national interests in a system that preserved states as important political entities and as an indispensable guard against violations of the Constitution. Though the Constitution only provided for a Supreme Court, an entire lower federal court system was quickly established through legislation. Omitted from

the Constitution in form, but invited through provisions for competitive elections and protection for free speech, press, and assembly, was a system of competitive political parties. Such parties arose almost immediately and have come to be treated as essential political institutions in democratic republics.

If the modern republic is to make good on its commitment to protecting individual liberty and promoting the comfortable preservation of its members, Locke, Montesquieu, and Madison all agreed that it would be essential that the political order contain checks on governmental tyranny. In *Federalist Paper* Number 51, Madison observed that the delegates who attended the Constitutional Convention sought to promote nontyrannical and competent government through a system of separate departments capable of checking one another within a federated republic that distributed power between the national and state governments. They understood that for the system of checks and balances to work each department must have sufficient power to protect itself against encroachments by other departments.

Beyond the possession of a minimum of power to defend themselves by checking the coordinate departments, it is also necessary that each department draw to itself officials who are prepared to use their power to achieve these ends. That is to say, each department must possess real power and the desire or conviction to use that power if the system of checks and balances is to work to promote both nontyrannical and competent government.

From this reasoning, for example, comes the defense of the power of judicial review, as well as the provision for "life tenure" for judges. The power of judicial review permits courts to check unconstitutional action by members of the legislative and executive branches, and "life tenure" facilitates use of this power by giving judicial officials both independence and security. As with all other governmental power, the exercise of judicial review is subject to constraint through the investment of an impeachment power in the legislature and the constitutional amendment process. In addition, the national government as a whole possesses only a portion of all governmental power, the remaining part being left to the states and their localities.

In addition to the conditions needed for the system of checks and balances to work, Madison identified in *Federalist Paper* Number 10 the general social conditions that are required to maintain a decent republic. Above all else, Madison made clear that the constitutional system must be arranged so as to diminish the threat of factious violence, what he calls the distinctive disease of democratic republics. If monarchies must fear the ascent of a foolish or feeble-minded person to the throne, democracies must fear the appearance of factious impulses in the people, specifically the majority of the people. A faction for Madison is any group of persons seeking to advance their interests by threatening or invading the rights of others and, thereby, undermining the common good. Factious majorities make for factious or bad democracies.

The remedy supplied by the American constitutional arrangement takes several forms. For one thing, Madison spoke of the virtues of the extended republic, which can comprehend a larger number and greater diversity of interest groups than a small republic. Since it is unlikely that any one group will contain a majority of the people, exercising political influence will require that groups form coalitions, a process that ordinarily will entail compromise and, hence, should lead to moderate rather than extremist or factious politics.

Another ingredient of the arrangement set out by Madison is the specific encouragement of the pursuit of economic interests and the attendant formation of associations based on economic interests, rather than the pursuit of philosophical or general ideological interests. The republic facilitates this process by providing explicit protection for the citizens' enjoyment of the fruits of their labors. In short, public policies should protect the people in the exercise of their different faculties, and then permit them to enjoy what they have created or produced as a result of their labors. According to Madison, what should result is a society divided into numerous groups whose members are disposed to negotiate and compromise to the end of advancing their economic well-being. What is so special about economic interests is that they are subject to negotiation and division in a way that is not commonly true of religious, philosophical, or ideological interests.

Finally, besides making the case for larger rather than smaller republics, Madison advances the merits of representative rather than direct democracies. In addition to making it possible for the sphere of the political system to be enlarged, since it is not necessary to bring everyone together to make policy, a representative democracy provides an additional check on factious impulses since elected officials are in a position to "check and refine" any dangerous impulses that are not weeded out either when coalitions are created for electoral purposes or for the purpose of lobbying public officials. Effective "checking and refining" by political officials requires government offices to be occupied by persons who are both capable of identifying and prepared to check factious impulses, that is to say, officials who understand what is required to protect rights and promote the common good and possess the fortitude to act on this knowledge.

If a measure of self-discipline and thoughtfulness bred of education and experience are required of public officials for a democratic republic to function well, so also is a measure of each of these qualities required in the larger citizen body. From George Washington's (1732–1799) call for morality in the citizenry in his "Farewell Address" to Thomas Jefferson's (1743–1826) well-known endorsement of a general system of public education, the American founders understood that the formal organizational features of the political system would have to be supported by the right set of mores and skills in the citizenry. A citizen body that feels no compulsion to respect the rights of others or is unwilling to bear sacrifices for the general good or that lacks the ability to sustain the nation in a competitive international system, a matter of special concern to Alexander Hamilton, will not be prepared to support a decent and competent democratic republic.

Not surprisingly, sustaining the vitality of the modern republican state depends in large part on the implementation and administration of public policies that maintain the conditions essential to its well-being. Hence, for example, if Madison was correct when encouraging the formation of interest groups around economic or commercial rather than philosophical interests, then legislation that leads the members of the community to invest their efforts in commercial activities would appear to be preferable to policies that make noneconomic or ideological interests the prime concerns of the citizenry. As Madison understood, the protection of property rights and the opportunity to enjoy the fruits of one's labors are an important incentive to the pursuit of economic interests.

Public policies that are sensitive to the benefits of economic pursuits risk cultivating crass forms of selfishness, however; hence, government policies also should seek to put private interest to work for the public or common good. This requires, among other things, that the members of the republic come to see the convergence between their interests and the interests of the whole. One way to do this, according to the nineteenth-century French theorist Alexis de Tocqueville (1805–1859), is to encourage citizen participation in governance at the local level. That is to say, public policies should provide incentives for citizens to participate in local self-government, thus forcing them to recognize how their interests are bound up with the advancement of the interests of others. By allowing the people to exercise real influence over education in local schools through participation in parent-teacher organizations or over the disposition of criminal cases through participation on juries, they are given reasons to become actively involved in the public domain, where they should come to see how it is in their interest to guard the rights of all others. For example, persons who serve on juries are awakened to the fact that it is in their interest to see that defendants receive fair trials because the jurors themselves may someday be involved in a criminal proceeding. The lesson from Tocqueville in this regard is unambiguous: Involvement in public affairs teaches citizens specific skills and promotes general habits that are productive of vibrant democratic republics.

At the governmental level, policies that insure that the separate departments are equipped and disposed to participate in checking and balancing each other also promote the ends of the modern republic. An executive or judicial department that is too weak or a legislative department whose members seek immediate popularity or are for other reasons incapable of good deliberation will not make the contribution that is needed for the entire political system to work well. Although not set out in any great detail in the American Constitution, the modern republic requires a system of administration that is open to influence by the people and their elected representatives while being sensitive to constitutional principles and the long-term interest of the country. The system of administration should satisfy the principle of government based on consent and contribute to competence in government. In sum, the doctrine of separation of powers with its division of labor is the modern republic's answer to classical statesmanship and the modern state's principal device for making good on its commitment to promote the comfortable preservation of the citizenry.

Challenges to Modern Republicanism

The provocative arguments of Madison and Montesquieu notwithstanding, the modern republic is not without its critics. As early as the seventeenth century, Jean Jacques Rousseau (1712–1778) believed that the assignment of priority to the protection of private rights ultimately would have a disintegrating effect on political communities. He feared that the way of life of the people of modern bourgeois republics could easily come to be selfish and manipulative, not compassionate and cultivated. Life in such orders, for Rousseau, would represent a new form of barbarism that would be in tension with civilization itself. Here is the typical critique of the "left."

From the "right" has come the claim that the modern bourgeois republic is likely to become relativistic and soft. This critique arises from the view that the pursuit of both liberty and equality is likely to cause modern republics to give up on causes and principles that separate and divide people, meaning great principles and causes. The adage "live and let live," which is presumed by theorists of the modern republic to serve the ends both of moderate politics and economic prosperity, is treated by critics such as Friedrich Nietzsche (1844–1900) as a recipe for a type of existence, really mere existence, that provides no nobility for human beings.

The extreme criticisms of both the left and the right are unlikely to disappear for the reason that modern republics, as with all human institutions, will always be imperfect and because the demands of the critics could not be wholly satisfied without altering basic elements of these republics. For their part, the defenders of the modern republic see their critics as being either idealists who seek more than human orders can effectively guarantee, or as unconverted devotees of ways of life rendered anachronistic by the victory of the theory of natural rights that supplies theoretical support for modern republics of the variety represented by contemporary Western European states

and the United States. The success that these states have had in meeting the goal of relatively comfortable preservation for their members within highly multicultural and multiracial communities can be cited by the friends of modern republicanism as evidence of the defensibility of political orders that take seriously the principles of modern natural rights theory.

Despite the recent claims of persons such as Francis Fukuyama (1992) that modern republics are historically determined to be successful, theorists such as Madison would argue that this success has been the product of the judicious blending within modern republicanism of respect for liberty and equality with a pragmatic understanding of the limits of political life. For their part, citizens of modern republics must recognize that they cannot demand more than what is reasonable from government while not demanding less of themselves than what is required if these political orders are to be both decent and competent.

JOSEPH H. LANE, JR.
AND DAVID E. MARION

BIBLIOGRAPHY

Aristotle, 1984. *Politics*. Trans. Carnes Lord. Chicago: University of Chicago Press.
Fukuyama, Francis, 1992. *The End of History and the Last Man*. New York: Free Press.
Hamilton, Alexander, John Jay, and James Madison, 1986. *The Federalist Papers*. New York: New American Library.
Hobbes, Thomas, 1968. *Leviathan*. New York: Penguin Books.
Kaufmann, Walter, ed. and trans. *The Portable Nietzsche*. New York: Penguin Books.
Locke, John, 1988. *Two Treatises on Government*. Cambridge: Cambridge University Press.
Montesquieu, Comte de, 1989. *The Spirit of the Laws*. Trans. Anne Cohler, Basia Carolyn Miller, and Harold Samuel Stone. Cambridge: Cambridge University Press.
Peterson, Merill D., ed., 1975. *The Portable Thomas Jefferson*. New York: Penguin Books.
Rahe, Paul, 1992. *Republics Ancient and Modern*. Chapel Hill: University of North Carolina Press.
Rousseau, Jean-Jacques, 1978. *On the Social Contract*. Ed. Roger D. Masters. New York: St. Martin's Press.
Strauss, Leo, 1953. *Natural Right and History*. Chicago: University of Chicago Press.
Tocqueville, Alexis de, 1969. *Democracy in America*. Ed. J. P. Mayer. New York: Doubleday and Co.

RESOURCE DEPENDENCE THEORY.

A theory of organization(s) that seeks to explain organizational and interorganizational behavior in terms of the critical resources an organization must have in order to survive and function. As an open-systems theory, the resource dependence argument suggests that a given organization will respond to and become dependent on organizations or entities in its environment that control resources that are critical to its operations and over which it has limited control. Such dependence makes the external constraint and control of organizational behavior possible as asymmetrical exchange and power relations are created between organizations. In an attempt to maximize organizational autonomy, organizational leaders use a variety of strategies to manage these external constraints and dependencies. Resource dependence theory thus has as its focus the following: resources; the flow or exchange of resources between organizations; dependencies and power differentials created as a result of unequal resource exchange; the constraining effects dependence has on organizational action; and the efforts by organizational leaders to manage dependence. With its emphasis on resource exchange, resource dependence represents a political economy model of organizational and interorganizational behavior.

Theoretical and Conceptual Roots

Although the unit of analysis associated with resource dependence theory has been the organizational set (Evan 1966), its theoretical and conceptual roots in the social sciences are tied to work done at the individual level of analysis, specifically in attempts to explain social behavior. From the exchange perspective, an individual's behavior becomes externally controlled when others in that person's environment have power over him or her and make requests for behavior based on situations of asymmetric dependence. According to Peter Blau (1964), situations of asymmetric dependence and power are rather unstable. In such relationships, the less powerful actor will often pursue activities that seek to minimize the effects of this power differential.

The notion of power as the antithesis of dependence can be traced to the works of Richard Emerson (1962) and Blau (1964). Using the concept of social exchange to describe power differentials that emerge between individuals, Emerson (1962) suggests that a given social actor 'A' is dependent on actor 'B' to the extent that B controls some resource or performance valued by A, and to the extent that A cannot obtain this resource or behavior from alternative persons. For Emerson, such asymmetric dependence leads to asymmetric power relations between individuals. Hence, power is conceptualized as the antithesis of dependence; to the extent that A is dependent on B, B has power over A.

A third theoretical perspective from the field of social psychology provides an additional backdrop for understanding the development of resource dependence theory. This perspective, known as situationism, represents an attempt to explain individual action (Bowers 1973). Individual action and behavior are not necessarily to be understood in terms of conscious or strategic choice, but as the result of external constraints, demands, and forces over which the individual has little or no control (Bowers 1973). Analyses of individual goals, preferences, and decision-making processes are secondary to the impact of external

constraints in determining human action and behavior. To understand individual behavior, therefore, one must understand the context or environment in which the individual exists.

Considered together, these concepts provide the foundation on which the resource dependence framework has been constructed. Although developed primarily at the individual level of analysis, the logic and rationale associated with each have been used by resource dependence theorists to explain behavior at the organizational level.

Theoretical Components: Past and Present Research

Although several names have been associated with the development of resource dependence theory (Zald 1970; Hasenfeld 1972; Jacobs 1974; Benson 1975; and Pfeffer and Salancik 1978) the work of James Thompson (1967) represents one of the earliest attempts to examine the flow of resources into organizations and the implications of the uncertainty surrounding this flow for organizational-level action and behavior. Speculating on factors that prevent organizations from achieving "complete rationality," Thompson has noted that an organization's need for resources and the subsequent dependence resulting from this need create problems for managers. Because no one organization is self-sufficient, organizations are forced to enter into exchange relations with the other actors, entities, and organizations in their environments. The unequal distribution of valued resources makes the emergence of asymmetric exchange and power relations between organizations inevitable. The cumulative effect of dependence is increased uncertainty for the organization because the move to a more complete rationality is hindered. Thompson (1967) hints at several seminal concepts, which follow, associated with the resource dependence framework, many of which have been further developed and refined by subsequent theorists.

The Scarcity of Organizational Resources and the Need for Interdependence

Resources of various kinds are essential for the continued survival and success of an organization. Yet rarely does an organization possess or control the entire range of resources needed for survival. As a consequence, organizations and the people in them are interdependent with other organizations. These assumptions provide an important basis for understanding and conceptualizing the nature of organizational and interorganizational behavior and activity.

According to Joseph Galaskiewicz and Peter Marsden (1978), organizational resources take a variety of forms; these include raw materials, capital, personnel, information, technology and technological innovations, as well as various services and production operations not performed by the focal organization. Conceived this broadly, resources may be considered as inputs or outputs. The flow of such resources between organizations appears to be both variable and at times unpredictable.

The Necessity of Organizational Negotiation and Exchange

Because no organization is entirely self-sufficient, interorganizational exchange is necessary (Pfeffer and Salancik 1978). In seeking resources, organizations engage in transactions with various organizations in their specific and general environments (Scott 1992). The exchange relationships that exist may be considered multidimensional (Silver 1993). For example, though all organizations enter into exchange relationships, the number of transaction partners varies both across organizations and within a given organization over time. Likewise, the importance of organizational exchange incidents for involved parties varies; some are relatively trivial, but others are critically important (Hall et al. 1977).

Depending on the resource needs of the focal organization and the subsequent exchange balance, the emergent relationship that exists between the focal organization and a resource provider can assume a variety of forms: dependent, reciprocal, or dominant (Silver 1993).

The Emergence of Organizational Dependence

For any given organization, the need for resource acquisition creates dependencies between the organization and other organizations in its environment. Several factors would appear to exacerbate the character of this dependence: the importance of the resource in question to the focal organization, the relative scarcity of the resource, and the degree to which the resource is concentrated in the environment. The most comprehensive explication of these factors (and of resource dependence theory) has been offered by Jeffrey Pfeffer and Gerald Salancik (1978).

Given that interorganizational power differentials grow out of asymmetric economic exchanges between organizations, resource dependencies give rise to political problems that often result in political solutions (Scott 1992). Such power can be used by resource-rich organizations to control the behavior of resource-dependent organizations.

The Presence of External Organizational Constraints

As a result of external dependencies, the choices and actions of the focal organization are somewhat constrained as its managers seek to attend to the demands made by environmental entities that provide resources critical to organizational survival and success. Conceptualizing the effects of external constraints in this fashion is analogous to that described by Robert Kahn et al. (1964) for individuals. Just as individuals in an organization are subject to pres-

sures from those with whom they interact, so organizations are subject to pressures from organizations with whom they are interdependent. Thus, understanding the environmental context of a given organization is of utmost importance in resource dependence theory. It is impossible to understand the structure or behavior of an organization without giving attention to this context. As Pfeffer and Salancik (1978) have noted, "The underlying premise of the external perspective on organizations is that organizational activities and outcomes are accounted for by the context in which the organization is embedded" (p. 39).

The Managing of Dependence

If the formal organization is conceived of as a purposive social form, then the imposition of external constraints brought on by dependence represents a formidable organizational challenge. In response to these constraints, organizational leaders seek to manage and strategically adapt to external dependencies. These attempts at adaptation underscore an important assumption underlying the resource dependence perspective: for organizational leaders, management of the organization's environment is as important as managing the organization itself (Aldrich and Pfeffer 1976).

Attempts by an organization to adapt to and negotiate with the environment are often guided by three overarching principles. First, organizational decisionmakers seek to ensure the continued survival of the organization (Pfeffer and Salancik 1978; Thompson 1967). Given the scarcity and concentration of a particular resource, this means altering the behavior and structure of the organization in such a way so as to make the flow of the resource in question more certain. Second, management often seeks to reduce the effects created by external constraints on internal organizational discretion (Benson 1975). Third, leaders seek to maximize the autonomy and discretion available to them for the larger purpose of enhancing present and future adaptability (Silver 1993). Organizations that are constrained by their environments have limited degrees of freedom with which to address future environmentally induced changes and contingencies.

Considered together, these principles suggest that organizational leaders seek ways to mitigate the disruptive effects of external dependence. Such attempts underscore the implicit view of organizations as entities driven by the need to adapt. This view stands in contrast to more rationally oriented, goal-based views of the organization.

Figure I depicts the general logic and flow associated with resource dependence theory from the perspective of the focal organization. The context of the focal organization is the larger environment in which it exists. The environment represents many things: resources, other organizations, organizational sets and networks, existing and emergent interorganizational exchange relationships, dependence, and uncertainty.

FIGURE I. THE LOGIC OF RESOURCE DEPENDENCE THEORY FROM THE PERSPECTIVE OF THE FOCAL ORGANIZATION

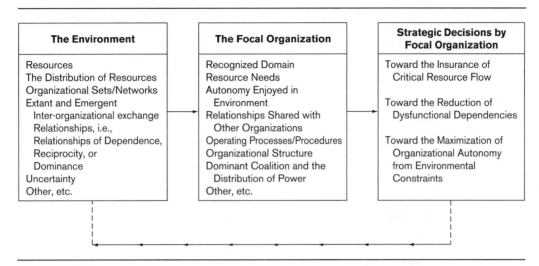

The environment and the elements found therein function to define and constrain the focal organization. An organization's domain, resource flow, autonomy, structure, and internal operating processes and procedures are greatly influenced by environmental dynamics. Strategic decisions are made by organizational leaders to minimize the constraints imposed by the environment. These decisions include attempts to increase the certainty surrounding the flow of critical resources into the organization, reduce dysfunctional relationships of dependence shared with other organizations, and in effect increase organizational autonomy within its environment. Such decisions result in the pursuit of various buffering and bridging activities.

Depending on the level of interorganizational power enjoyed by the focal organization within its environment, the courses of action chosen by organizational decision-makers affect the dynamics and constellation of givens in the environment and the relationships shared by the focal organization with other relevant organizations.

Although the concepts and processes depicted in Figure I are not intended to be an exhaustive representation of resource dependence, the figure does provide an overview of the logic and relationships associated with the theory.

Applications of Resource Dependence Theory

Empirical research in the field has focused primarily on strategies used by organizations to address and negotiate relationships of dependence. The elucidation of these strategies represents one of the major contributions of the resource dependence perspective to the field of organizational theory.

Strategies have been classified into two categories: buffering and bridging. Buffering and bridging function to defend, define, and redefine organizational boundaries (Scott 1992). Each set of strategies represents an attempt by the organization to absorb interdependence and reduce uncertainty. The pursuit of buffering and bridging strategies often leads to structural and personnel changes within the organization. As environmental complexity increases, the organization tends to establish more elaborate and formalized coordination and control structures to ensure the flow of needed resources. Thus, for any given organization, existing organizational processes and structures often reflect environmental complexity as well as past, present, and predicted resource needs.

Buffering strategies involve amplifying and protecting organizational boundaries. In an attempt to reduce the uncertainty that surrounds its technical core and hence maximize productivity, the dependent organization will often seek to buffer this core from the fluctuations brought on by environmental dependence. On the input side, buffering is illustrated by the stockpiling of needed materials and supplies. Stockpiling allows for a consistent, steady flow of inputs into the production process. In effect, it functions to insure a certain degree of autonomy for the organization and its leaders. Other buffering strategies include coding, leveling, forecasting, and adjusting the scale of the organization's technical core.

Bridging involves modifying organizational boundaries through boundary-spanning or boundary-shifting. Because organization leaders seek to reduce the uncertainty surrounding the flow of needed resources, the intent of such strategies is to increase the certainty of resource flow by bridging or linking the organization with exchange partners, competitors, and regulators. Reduced dependence and increased autonomy are the prizes that motivate bridge building.

Although each bridging strategy varies in terms of the strength and stability of the exchange relationship forged, several strategies have been identified and examined in the resource dependence literature (Scott 1992; Pfeffer and Salancik 1978; Thompson 1967). Organizations attempt to reduce dependence either partially through cooperative strategies or more completely through mergers, officer or directorate interlocks or co-optation. Examples of cooperative bridging strategies include joint ventures, contracting, the movement of executives and other personnel across organizations, and resource diversification. Officer and directorate interlocks provide the means whereby two or more organizations can ensure the flow of needed resources between them. Since financial institutions are the dominant actors in the world of interlocking directorates (Mintz and Schwartz 1985), such strategies give organizations a competitive advantage through access to financing, information, and other types of critical resources (Mizruchi and Galaskiewicz 1993).

Resource dependence theory suggests that within any given organizational set, network, or domain, the level of accrued power across representative organizations may in fact be unequal. Even though it is inconceivable to assume that no single organization is all-powerful or powerless, it is reasonable to assume that organizations do find themselves closer to one extreme than the other. Resource dependence provides a useful framework for thinking about these differences.

At one extreme is the captive organization (Thompson 1967), the organization greatly dependent for resources on other organizations in its environment. Limitations to its capacity may be rooted in one or several factors. Among these are: the absence of feasible resource alternatives, the hyper-concentration of needed resources in the environment, and the incapacities of supporting organizations. Given this state of affairs, attempts by captive organizations to alter the environment and remove crippling dependencies often prove unsuccessful. This contrasts sharply, however, with the efforts of the more powerful, resource-rich organization. Due to near-monopolistic control over valued and scarce resources, such organizations are able to achieve an unusual degree of independence from and control over other organizations.

A further contribution of resource dependence theory to the understanding of organizational behavior is found in the description of the choice of adaptive strategies by organizational decisionmakers as a political activity. The distribution of power within an organization is a critical factor in determining the adaptive strategies it pursues. Over time, power accrues to organizational leaders and subunits who prove adept at reducing the constraints, uncertainties, and contingencies that accompany the flow of critical resources. According to resource dependence theory, these individuals determine which adaptive strategies the organization will pursue. Hence, given that internal power

arrangements are central to the decisionmaking process, decisions regarding the management of organizational interdependence are rooted in a political context.

The theory shares a great deal of common ground with other environmentally centered theories. For example, the resource dependence approach shares many features with strategic contingency theory (Lawrence and Lorsch 1967). Both build on Emerson's (1962) formulation of power-dependence relations. Yet whereas the focus of resource dependence is on the organization itself and its relations with other organizations, strategic contingency theory focuses on intraorganizational behavior, specifically, the distribution of power between and among organizational subunits.

Resource dependence theory also shares important features with the population ecology model of organizations (Hannan and Freeman 1977). Like population ecology, resource dependence theorists argue that organizations are externally constrained. Unlike population ecology theory, however, resource dependence emphasizes the conscious and rational attempts by organizational leaders to manage and strategically adapt to their environments—whereas the former stresses selection, the latter emphasizes adaptation.

Difficulties and Limitations Associated with Resource Dependence

Although the resource dependence framework offers a useful set of lenses with which to view organizational and interorganizational behavior, the theory is not without its limitations. Perhaps the most challenging difficulty posed by the theory lies in its inability to delineate fully and clearly the relationship shared between the environment and the organization. Like most open-systems perspectives, the primary focus of resource dependence theory is on the environment. Organizational behavior is seen as somewhat strategic, but resource dependence theory suggests that such behavior is in many ways a function of perceived and potential environmental constraints. It is the environment that functions as the independent variable.

There is a degree of intuitive validity in this assumption, but one is led to question its full validity (Pfeffer and Salancik 1978). Does this represent an accurate description of the relationships shared between the environment and organization? To be sure, environments do constrain and set limits on organizational action. However, it appears equally as valid to conclude that organizations act on and affect the environments in which they exist. Logic would suggest that the relationship shared between the organization and its environment is perhaps more accurately conceptualized as being reciprocal. If this is the case, then the challenge comes in determining when and under what conditions each functions as the dependent and independent variable.

A second set of issues inadequately addressed by resource dependence theorists has as its focus attempts to aggregate individual actions and behavior to the organizational level. The problem is certainly not new to organizational theory, and there is precedent for considering the organization as but the lengthened shadow of one or a handful of individuals (Thompson 1967). Nevertheless, theorists who use this approach shoulder the burden of developing explanations of how complex, interactive microbehaviors within the organization are aggregated to produce organizational-level action. Because organizations vary markedly in size, this aggregation represents no small task. The complexity associated with aggregation would appear to vary directly with organizational size.

Questions regarding the most appropriate unit of analysis represent a third difficulty associated with resource dependence theory. As with other theories seeking to explain interorganizational action and behavior, a variety of options exists. Each presents its own challenges and difficulties. For example, one may choose to focus on the organization, the relationships of the organization, or the resources of the organization. Within each of these three categories, further options are available. For example, if the focus is relationships, will the unit of analysis be a dyadic relationship, a few relationships, or all relationships shared by the organization? If the focus is on resources, will a given study examine a single resource, a small set of critical resources, or all resources needed by the organization to function?

Questions such as these hint at the complexity involved in examining interorganizational relationships from the resource dependence perspective. Whereas the simplest form of interorganizational relationship–the dyad–appears to have received the most attention in empirical research, a more comprehensive understanding of the dynamics of resource dependence among organizations is to be found in examining multiple resources and relationships at both the organizational set and organizational network levels. Since the chosen unit of analysis has implications for statistical and analytical generalizability, questions regarding the most appropriate unit of analysis are significant and as of yet remain unresolved.

In reflecting on the limitations of resource dependence, it should be remembered that this perspective is but one of many that seek to explain organizational action and behavior. Its distinctiveness is found in the attention it gives to resources–resource needs, resource scarcity, and resource exchange among organizations. The emphases given to dependence and the constraints imposed on organizational autonomy as a result of dependence represent its greatest strength. Yet, it is in this strength that a significant limitation can be found. Resource dependence theory assumes that organizational behavior and structures are shaped primarily by materialistic forces. Absent in the literature are discussions regarding the role of rival environmental influences and determinants such as cultural, ideological, and institutional factors and considerations (Scott 1995). Therefore, resource dependence theory must be understood as a partial, middle-range theory of the organization. As such, it offers a unique perspective for understanding and interpreting organizational action and behavior.

BOB L. JOHNSON, JR.

BIBLIOGRAPHY

Aldrich, Howard E., and Jeffrey Pfeffer, 1976. "Environments of Organizations." *Annual Review of Sociology,* vol. 2: 79–105.

Benson, Kenneth J., 1975. "The Interlocking Network as a Political Economy." *Administrative Science Quarterly,* vol. 20 (June): 229–249.

Blau, Peter M., 1964. *Exchange and Power in Social Life.* New York: Wiley.

Bowers, K. S., 1973. "Situationism in Psychology: An Analysis and a Critique." *Psychological Review,* vol. 80: 307–336.

Emerson, Richard M., 1962. "Power-Dependence Relations." *American Sociological Review,* vol. 27 (February): 31–40.

Evan, William, 1966. "The Organization Set: Toward a Theory of Interorganizational Relationships." In James D. Thompson, ed., *Approaches to Organizational Design,* 173–188. Pittsburgh: University of Pittsburgh Press.

Galaskiewicz, Joseph, and Peter J. Marsden, 1978. "Interorganizational Resources Networks: Formal Patterns of Overlap." *Social Science Research,* vol. 7 (June): 89–107.

Hall, Richard H., John P. Clark, Peggy Giordano, Paul Johnson, and Martha Van Roekel, 1977. "Patterns of Interorganizational Relationships." *Administrative Science Quarterly,* vol. 22 (September): 457–474.

Hannan, Michael T., and John Freeman, 1977. "The Population Ecology of Organizations." *American Journal of Sociology,* vol. 82: 929–964.

Hasenfeld, Yeheskel, 1972. "People Processing Organizations: An Exchange Approach." *American Sociological Review,* vol. 37 (June): 256–263.

Jacobs, David, 1974. "Dependency and Vulnerability: An Exchange Approach to the Control of Organizations." *Administrative Science Quarterly,* vol. 19 (March): 45–59.

Kahn Robert L., Donald M. Wolfe, Robert P. Quinn, and J. Diedrick Snoek, 1964. *Organizational Stress: Studies in Role Conflict and Ambiguity.* New York: Wiley.

Lawrence, Paul R., and Jay W. Lorsch, 1967. *Organization and Environment: Managing Differentiation and Integration.* Cambridge, MA: Harvard University Press.

Mintz, Beth, and Michael Schwartz, 1985. *The Power Structure of American Business.* Chicago: University of Chicago Press.

Mizruchi, Mark S., and Joseph Galaskiewicz, 1993. "Networks of Interorganizational Relations." *Sociological Methods and Research,* vol. 22 (August): 46–93.

Pfeffer, Jeffrey, and Gerald R. Salancik, 1978. *The External Control of Organizations: A Resource Dependence Perspective.* New York: Harper & Row.

Scott, W. Richard, 1992. *Organizations: Rational, Natural and Open Systems,* 3d ed. Englewood Cliffs, NJ: Prentice-Hall.

———, 1995. *Institutions and Organizations.* Thousand Oaks, CA: Sage Publications.

Silver, Robin S., 1993. "Conditions of Autonomous Action and Performance." *Administration and Society,* vol. 24 (February): 487–511.

Thompson, James A., 1967. *Organizations in Action.* New York: McGraw-Hill.

Zald, Mayer N., 1970. "Political Economy: A Framework for Comparative Analysis." In Mayer N. Zald, ed., *Power in Organizations*, pp. 221–261. Nashville: Vanderbilt University Press.

RESPONDEAT SUPERIOR.

A legal doctrine used in employment law. It means "let the master answer"—that is, the employer may be liable for the wrongful acts of its employees and a principal may be held accountable for the acts of his or her agents. The doctrine is well suited to preindustrial workplaces in which the employer (master) has a responsibility carefully to select and train apprentices. Its modern applicability rests not so much on policy grounds consistent with the governing principles of tort law as in a deeply rooted sentiment that a business enterprise cannot justly disclaim responsibility for accidents that are characteristic of its activities (*Bushey v. U.S.,* 1968). The reach of respondeat superior depends on whether the harmful activities performed by a servant are inherent in the work performed and/or the working environment. If the harmful activities are reasonably foreseeable under normal working conditions, the employer or principal should be cognizant of the likelihood of the employee or agent's activities occasioning injury or damage to a third party.

As applied to the public sector in the United States, respondeat superior is in tension with the principle of sovereign immunity, which bars suits against the government without its own consent. Federal liability law makes the government responsible for the ordinary torts of its employees, as long as these are work related. However, respondeat superior does not apply to constitutional torts, that is, violations of individuals' constitutional rights (*Federal Deposit Insurance Corporation v. Meyer,* 1994). Federal employees are responsible directly for their constitutional torts. State law regarding ordinary torts varies, but under 42 U.S. Code 1983 (originally the federal Civil Rights Act of 1871) municipalities may face respondeat superior liability for the constitutional torts of their employees. Under *Monell v. New York City Department of Social Services* (1978) a municipality can be sued for money damages for constitutional torts caused by the "execution of a government's policy or custom whether made by its lawyers or those whose edicts or acts may fairly be said to represent official policy" (p. 694). "Official policy" has been defined as "a deliberate choice to follow a course of action . . . made from among various alternatives by the official responsible for establishing final policy with respect to the subject matter in question." (*Pembaur v. City of Cincinnati,* 1986, pp. 483–484). Municipalities can also be held liable for constitutional torts if they fail to train their employees adequately to protect against foreseeable violations of individuals' constitutional rights. For example, in *City of Canton v. Harris* (1989), the U.S. Supreme Court noted that municipal liability could potentially be attached to a city that failed to train its police to provide medical care to those in custody. Municipalities also face potential liability for inadequate care in selecting employees who subsequently violate individuals' constitutional rights (e.g., employing a known sex offender as a security guard or janitor in a public housing project).

HON S. CHAN AND DAVID H. ROSENBLOOM

BIBLIOGRAPHY

Bushey v. U.S., (1968). 398 F.2d 167.

City of Canton v. Harris, (1989). 489 U.S. 378.

Federal Deposit Insurance Corp. v. Meyer, (1994). 127 L. Ed. 2d. 308.

Monell v. New York Department of Social Services, (1978). 436 U.S. 658.

Pembaur v. City of Cincinnati, (1986). 475 U.S. 469.

Walter, Robert, 1992. "Public Employers' Potential Liability from Negligence in Employment Decisions." *Public Administration Review* 52 (5): 491–496.

RETIREMENT.

Cessation of work in one's occupation. As people age, they usually look forward to retiring from their work and devoting their time to other interests. In the U.S. government workforce, retirement may be mandatory or voluntary. Until 1986, when Congress amended the Age Discrimination in Employment Act of 1978, mandatory retirement could be based on age. Thus, typically, age 65 or 70 was used as the mandatory retirement age. Since passage of the 1986 amendments, age cannot be used as the basis for mandatory retirement in most employment. Instead, employees now may be forced to retire based on demonstration that they cannot perform the duties of the position.

Voluntary retirement allows employees to retire when they wish to do so. Normally, there is some minimum number of years an employee has to work in order to receive retirement benefits. Many jurisdictions use a combination of age and number of years of employment with the organization as the basis for determining eligibility for retirement and level of benefits. In cases in which the organization is attempting to reduce payroll costs or institute reductions in force, incentives may be offered to encourage voluntary retirement. Thus, a one-time buyout may occur in which the employee is given a cash payment up front in addition to the normal retirement benefits. In some cases, especially in state and municipal governments in the United States, the formula for figuring pension benefits may be adjusted to the employee's advantage during a specified period of time to encourage retirement.

Another issue is that as the public employees reach retirement age, many of them are retiring early, especially in the federal government, leaving the agencies without the benefit of their experience. This trend is true particularly in the scientific and technical fields.

Early retirement sometimes leads to what is known as double-dipping. In this situation, an employee retires from one public sector job and then goes to work for another while receiving a retirement pension from the first career. Military personnel frequently move into civilian jobs and draw their military pensions. Federal retirees may go to work for state or local governments and draw salaries and qualify for retirement pensions there while drawing federal retirement benefits.

In recent years, employers have developed programs for preretirement planning for their employees. Such plans typically include financial planning, planning for what to do with the new free time, and the psychological and social implications of retirement. As people live longer and longer, retirement planning is a very important consideration.

In many countries, especially socialist states, retirement benefits are not part of the system because everyone in society is guaranteed an income. For many nonsocialist societies, especially in Western Europe, people are provided a pension upon reaching a certain age and employer benefits are not necessary. In the United States, Social Security is a form of such a program, but the benefit normally is not enough to actually live on.

N. JOSEPH CAYER

BIBLIOGRAPHY

Ehrenberg, R., 1980. "Retirement Systems Characteristics and Compensating Differentials in the Public Sector." *Industrial and Labor Relations Review,* vol. 33 (July): 470–483.

Siegel, Sidney R., and Beth Yvonne Rees, 1992. "Preparing the Public Employee for Retirement." *Public Personnel Management,* vol. 21, no. 1 (Spring): 89–100.

Spengler, Joseph J., 1978. *Facing Zero Population Growth: Reactions and Interpretations, Past and Present.* Durham, NC: Duke University Press.

Wolf, James F., Carole M. Neves, Richard T. Greenough, and Bill B. Benton, 1987. "Greying at the Temples: Demographics of a Public Service Occupation." *Public Administration Review* 47 (March-April): 190–198.

REVENUE BUDGETING.

A budget process in which revenue is estimated before the budget process begins and the budget process outcomes are constrained by the revenue estimates provided. Traditionally, this process has been a state and local phenomenon in which there have been legal constraints calling for balanced operating budgets.

Revenue budgeting is a term that is sometimes used to describe the collection of behaviors that decisionmakers exhibit in fiscally constrained jurisdictions: First, they figure out how much revenue they will have to spend, then they decide what needs they can satisfy. Needs always outrun budget dollars, and new needs usually outrun the revenue growth from one year to the next. Consequently, decisionmakers satisfy some needs, while denying resources for others. At the federal level, the ability of the federal government to borrow money to fund growth in needs allows for a different style of budgeting (see incrementalism), one in which needs assessment is done first, revenues are estimated, and the excess of need over revenue is made up by borrowing. This has been the usual federal pattern since the 1930s (see budgeting). Wars, depressions, or great natural disasters have often been the root cause of this pattern, but there has also been an annual cycle to budgeting in which needs are assessed before the revenue decision, and if the need is great enough—or its supporters are intense enough— the need is funded out of borrowing authority when revenues are insufficient. The necessity of guaranteeing national survival is often used to justify this practice.

States and local governments are in a somewhat different position. They do not provide services that guarantee national survival, although they often provide the most immediate services to citizens. They are often constrained by law from operating in a deficit position on their operating budget. They can do short-term borrowing to balance a budget during execution and they can even carry over a deficit to the next fiscal year. They generally have a capital budget for investment purposes, which leaves the annual operating budget free to meet annual service needs. If they get in severe financial trouble, they may be bailed out by a superior level of government; states often provide emergency funds to local governmental units in emergency situations, as does the federal government, particularly in cases of natural disasters.

States can also "lend" themselves money from subordinate units by decreasing shared payments that they would have made to local governments and retaining the increased share for the emerging state need.

Thus, states and local governments can compensate for deficits in certain situations, but they generally are required to propose a balanced operating budget, usually specifying how much revenue there will be to spend in the budget year, before needs are assessed. Naturally, as the budget process proceeds, there is a continuous checking process that casts potential spending against potential tax receipts and tracks changes in the economy that might affect revenues or spending. For example, inflation could drive up tax revenues, but it might also drive up welfare or medical payments that the jurisdiction must pay. This interactive process continues to the end of the budget session, and a typical outcome might see both spending increased and tax revenue structures adjusted to provide for those spending increases.

Characteristics

Revenue budgeting is an approach to the budget decision, rather than a fixed system like zero-based budgeting. What revenue budgeting does is keep the revenue factor foremost in the minds of decisionmakers. At best, it emphasizes most value for least cost; at worst, it simply focuses on cost growth retardation (McCaffery 1981). Since it tends to take the current amount of revenue as a given, revenue budgeting tends to be a retrospective, conservative, and maintenance-oriented approach to the budgeting decision. This method was appropriate for many state and local governments during the 1970s and 1980s and is perhaps the situation the federal government has found itself in the 1990s.

In the 1970s, the characteristics of revenue budgeting included:

- decisionmakers constrained by actual limitations on revenue raising or the perception of limitations;
- inflation driving up the cost of service faster than revenue growth;
- growth in demand for service while capacity appears to shrink;
- budget battles fought around the level of inflation, with many functions being forced to absorb inflation;
- an emphasis by central reviewers on breaking into the base to eliminate old programs;
- fragmented budgets with different pots of money to which different rules apply so that they may be safe from cuts or cuts may not be so severe;
- mandated or entitlement areas in the budget growing faster than discretionary areas;
- finding ways to get functions off the budget base; these include contracting-out and privatizing, but the imperative is not only to find the most efficient provider but also just to get the function off the general tax base;
- end-of-year surpluses or surpluses in minor accounts may become embarrassments as groups use the surplus as a lever to freeze or further reduce general tax capacity and thus also limit future services; and
- budget decisions end up being contested in the courts.

These observations were made about some state and local jurisdictions in the late 1970s. Their continuing familiarity indicates how little the dimensions of the budget struggle has changed.

Decremental Budgeting

In the late 1970s, Dade County, Florida, "invented" a sophisticated revenue budgeting system. Though it looked like a zero-based budgeting system (see zero-based budgeting) in that it called for examining levels of funding at or around the budget base, the most interesting part of the

system was a chart that the departments prepared that indicated what action would be taken to reach each level of service and what the community or citizen response would be to each increment of change. Thus, the chart provided for seven levels of service. Three were below the current level, one was at the current level, and three were above. One of these was the budget bureau recommendation. The columns illustrated for each level what action would be taken, what the impact on program service would be, how the community was expected to react, and what the fiscal effect would be. The fiscal effect column included local revenues and fees, and revenues and grants from other levels of government. This chart enabled decisionmakers to make connections between what service level was to be provided, what its cost would be, and what citizen or community reaction was likely to occur at each level of effort. This chart helped all participants to see what choices were being made in the budget process.

Department administrators had to think about program outcomes; simply being a program advocate was not enough. The format helped the central budget agency identify issues that were likely to be sensitive with the public, and it forced the agencies to indicate where their budgets might be cut. Naturally, departments were not happy about this, but the fiscal situation was bad enough that a sense of fair share provided support for this sort of behavior.

In terms of outcomes, the budget increased from one year to the next, but some programs in the base were eliminated. The process emphasized team building, performance measurement, and a clientele orientation. The system also demanded trust, a great deal of expertise in the budget bureau and in the agencies, and a willingness to work together.

Dade County had developed the system under the threat of a popular initiative, which would have voted in a strict revenue freeze, so its leaders thought it was facing a virtual budget catastrophe. Thus, the appearance of crisis led to a very provocative revenue budgeting system. When popular support for the initiative for a fixed-dollar revenue freeze faded later in the 1980s, some of the elements of Dade County's decremental system began to evaporate as the level of perceived fiscal crisis diminished (Schick 1983). Nonetheless, this is a case of a positive adaptation of a system and its decisionmakers to a fiscal crisis.

JERRY L. McCAFFERY

BIBLIOGRAPHY

McCaffery, Jerry 1981. "Revenue Budgeting: Dade County Tries a Decremental Approach." *Public Administration Review, Special Issue.* "The Impact of Resource Scarcity on Urban Public Finance." vol. 41 (January): 179–188.
Schick, Allen 1983. "Incremental Budgeting in a Decremental Age." *Policy Sciences,* vol. 16: 1–25.

REVENUE DIVERSIFICATION.

Flexibility in the variety, appropriateness, and productivity of local revenue sources for financing adequate services and meeting policymaking responsibilities in a fair, equitable manner.

Local government revenue diversification results from having authority over revenue sources that can be varied in response to new and changing demands for services. Reliance on the extensive use of earmarked sources—whether taxes, charges, or special assessments—and tightly drawn tax bases, reduces fiscal flexibility.

Origins

In the mid-1990s, the property tax accounted for nearly three-quarters of all U.S. local tax revenues, a dependence virtually unchanged since 1980. The use of property taxes varies widely by type of government, however. School districts receive nearly 98 percent of their tax revenues from property taxes, counties receive nearly 74 percent, and municipalities receive roughly 52 percent from that source. There is wide variation among states in the use of local property taxes, with most low-use states in the south and west and high use states tending to be in the north and northeast.

The tax limitation movement of the late 1970s and 1980s, and state and local actions, resulted in a diversification of local revenue bases in general and attempts to make the property tax a better revenue source, for example, through improved assessment practices. Revenue diversification, especially any reduction in the dependence on the local property tax, is important because of the significant role that public finance plays in shaping metropolitan growth patterns. The use of the property tax by multiple jurisdictions in the typically fragmented metropolitan region makes the service delivery system heavily dependent on each community's tax base. Typically, developing communities seek commercial and industrial growth that requires less community services than residential development—to insure the resources necessary for service provision. Competition for tax base resources gives jurisdictions strong financial incentives to try to zone out the poor. Fringe growth often occurs along with disinvestment in the older urban core communities. The revenue bases of those communities shrink, causing service cuts and diminishing their ability to attract growth and development necessary to support even essential services.

Federal disengagement in providing aid to local governments, the tax limitation movement, recessions, deficits, demographic trends, and increasing costs of federal and state mandates have all fueled the trend toward growing fringe areas and a declining inner core in the typical metropolitan region.

The alternatives available to local governments for meeting their responsibilities are difficult: expenditure reduction, thus reducing the level or type of services provided to citizens; increasing tax rates on current sources of revenue, at a time when citizens have expressed dissatisfaction with existing taxes; borrowing, when local debt is already high; finding new sources of revenue, such as new taxes or charges for service, or tax base changes. The latter category generally requires some type of state action.

The state role in empowering local governments for diversifying their revenues is crucial. Four broad options exist for states to increase the revenue flexibility of their local governments. They can (1) change the level or pattern of intergovernmental assistance; (2) alter local tax options; (3) alter user charge or fee use and options; and (4) encourage or mandate a fundamental restructuring of the system of local governance.

The trend in the 1990s has been for states to provide less aid to their local governments, opting instead to target assistance by changing distribution formulas and the conditions of assistance. It is increased local taxing authority through statutory constitutional provision that offers the greatest prospect for achieving local revenue flexibility. Fundamental restructuring of local government is also a major way to increase revenue flexibility, but most difficult to achieve politically.

Tax Authority

A general thrust for tax reform is toward a broader base and lower, less-intrusive rates. County option sales taxes have gained in use, for example, and the major source of untapped local tax revenue is a local option income tax. The states have also made changes that have improved the administration of the property tax. New criteria for defining purely charitable purposes have been developed to limit exemptions from property taxation. Tax increment financing districts can be created to finance public improvements by earmarking part of the regularly assessed property taxes. Circuit-breaker laws can protect the elderly or others from paying more than a set percentage of their income in property taxes.

Nontax revenues are trending toward a greater variety in the types of user charges and fees imposed by local governments for services. This allows a relatively tight link between service provision and payment of the costs of the service. User fees are charged for water, sewage disposal, garbage collection, and recreation, but care must be taken so that low-income persons are not adversely affected by user charge systems.

Increasingly, the costs of supporting fringe growth are perceived to require user fees on a very large scale. Development impact fees are used by communities to have developers help finance public facilities needed to serve new growth and development. Concurrency laws, or "pay-as-you-grow," require that no development can take place unless certain services, for example roads, water, sewer, solid waste, parks and recreation, education, and health, are provided at the same time as the development.

Restructuring Local Government

The greatest likelihood for dramatic change in the local fiscal situation may lie in restructuring local government. This includes: (1) altering relationships among jurisdictions and their revenue bases within a region, for example, by creating special-purpose districts to handle specific service delivery needs (e.g., water and sewer systems); (2) tax base or revenue base sharing among jurisdictions; and (3) transferral of powers among governments (e.g., city-county consolidations; state assumption of policy or poverty-related responsibilities; interlocal agreements; privatization options). All of these options have increased in use and popularity in the 1990s.

Local governments continue to work with the states and other local governments to find alternative revenue sources. Other events, trends, and processes interact with revenue diversification efforts to have an impact on local government revenues. These overlapping factors include new budgeting processes integrated with strategic planning, other productivity improvements that yield cost savings, expenditure reduction efforts, mandate flexibility, financial outcomes from court decisions (e.g., on school financing, prison overcrowding), changes in interest rates; demands for new, often costly, local programs; use of alternative service delivery systems (e.g., functional consolidation of services, contracting-out, and public-private partnerships), among others.

Revenue flexibility does not have to be achieved through additional revenues. Numerous microlevel fiscal processes are important to a local government's general fiscal health. This includes purchasing procedures, use of forecasting and various analytical techniques, broadened investment strategies, innovative financing techniques such as state revolving funds and bond banks to finance local infrastructure, and use of alternative dispute resolution techniques to reduce costs.

Local government revenue systems are undergoing fundamental change. The outcomes for local governments in the 1990s are less influenced by national and state financial aid programs and more directly related to the economic base, political leadership, and management capacity available in specific counties. The states play a pivotal role in that local governments are legally "creatures of the states" who much be empowered to have the authority to gain revenue flexibility through diversification of revenue sources.

BEVERLY A. CIGLER

BIBLIOGRAPHY

Aronson, Richard, and John Hilley, 1986. *Financing State and Local Governments*. Washington, DC: Brookings Institution.

Bland, Robert L., 1989. *A Revenue Guide for Local Government*. Washington, DC: International City Management Association.

Cigler, Beverly A., 1993. "State-Local Relations: A Need for Reinvention?" *Intergovernmental Perspective* 19 (Winter): 15–18.

———, 1993a. "Challenges Facing Fiscal Federalism in the 1990s." *PS: Political Science and Politics*, vol. 26, no. 2 (June):181–186.

———, 1996. "Revenue Diversification Among American Counties." In Donald C. Menzel, ed. *The American County*, University: University of Alabama Press.

Liner, Charles D., 1992. "Alternative Revenue Sources for Local Governments." *Popular Government*, vol. 57, no. 3:22–29.

REVENUE FORECASTING.

The process by which income is projected for a defined period of time (usually 12 months) based on the assumptions the forecaster believes to be most likely at the time the forecast is made.

One of the most challenging tasks in preparing budgets is to accurately forecast revenues. Forecasting any kind of human behavior is difficult; forecasting revenues is even more difficult because of the large number of complex variables and because of the severe consequences if the forecast is wrong.

A forecast that is too optimistic may require severe spending reductions or tax increases later in the budget cycle, after commitments have already been made. A forecast that is too pessimistic may trigger controversy over "hidden" surpluses, or may result in additional unplanned spending that is unsustainable over the long run. In either event, the forecaster's most precious budget resource—credibility with the end user—is undermined.

Fortunately, over recent years scholars have begun to document forecasting practices that help them identify practices that are most likely to produce an accurate forecast. No process can guarantee a good outcome, of course, but use of these practices will substantially increase its likelihood.

What follows are the five practices that are most essential to good revenue forecasting. These are: reasonable economic assumptions; sound estimating techniques; constructive use of alternative forecasts; a system of monitoring, revision, and evaluation; and a clear and complete presentation.

Economic Assumptions

Underlying economic conditions such as inflation, economic growth, and employment have a significant impact on government revenues. Higher economic growth usually means more revenue, lower growth usually means less. Consequently, the expected performance of the economy is the appropriate starting point for a revenue forecast.

Estimates about the condition of the national economy are produced by a variety of sources, including the central governments, business periodicals and individual economists. One of the most commonly used forecast sources in the United States is the Blue Chip indicators, which regularly polls 50 leading economists on a number of key variables such as gross domestic product (GDP), inflation, and employment.

National estimates make it possible to compare the assumptions about the national economy used by forecasters of political subdivisions with those of other experts. Some differences are to be expected, but if the assumptions about the economy used by forecasters are not in the middle range of national forecasts, their assumptions merit detailed scrutiny. State or local forecasters should be able to present strong evidence that explains what they see in the economy that most national economists do not. For example, more recent data may be a plausible explanation. Failure to validate out-of-line assumptions may be evidence of bias or political manipulation.

Although economic conditions in each political subdivision are influenced by the national economy, local economies are likely to behave differently from the national or international economy in important ways. For example, the older industrial states, such as Ohio and Michigan, respond differently to fluctuations in interest or exchange rates than do energy-producing states such as Texas or Wyoming. The technology-based economies of states like Arizona or Massachusetts behave differently from the agriculturally based economies of Kansas or Nebraska.

Forecast users in the largest countries or political subdivisions may turn to a number of independent sources for forecasts about their economies, but not all political units are large enough to have such a wide variety of sources. Some turn to outside experts or a panel of advisers to assist in the difficult task of translating national economic data into locally specific indicators. A 1991 survey by the Federation of Tax Administrators found that 18 of the 50 U.S. states studied used some form of formal review mechanism involving outside economic experts.

Researchers have found that experts and outside advisers do not necessarily lead to more accurate forecasts. However, these outside experts may still be useful as a resource to interpret existing data and to increase user acceptance. The key to the successful use of experts is to insure that their projections are free of bias, intentional or otherwise. This means that the panel should be representative of the important sectors of the local economy and that panel members should feel free to speak frankly. For example, it is unfair to expect the chief economist for a large auto company to make a public prediction of a slump in auto sales when it would severely affect his or her employer's stock. One way to address this problem is to keep individual forecasts confidential, but publish the consensus forecast.

Whatever process is used to determine local and national forecasts, the two forecasts should be consistent. In other words, if the national forecast projects rising interest rates and declining car sales, a local forecast that projects increased employment in automobile manufacturing should be viewed with a high degree of skepticism.

Statistical Techniques

After the economic assumptions are defined, estimating procedures need to be developed for each revenue source, such as the income tax or sales tax. A good data base is the first step to these source estimates. At a minimum this means annual collections totals for each major revenue source (such as sales tax, income tax, etc.) going back at least through two business cycles (eight to ten years) and preferably longer.

In many governments, revenue collections are handled by agencies other than the budget or forecasting agency. In the state of Ohio, for example, the Office of Budget and Management is responsible for the revenue forecasts, but five different state agencies (the Department of Taxation, the Treasurer of State of Ohio, the Ohio Lottery, the Department of Liquor Control, and the Department of Insurance) administer one or more major revenue sources. This puts a premium on the development of a close working relationship between the collecting and forecasting agencies so that the fluctuations caused by processing changes are not incorporated into long-term trend data.

Once the data is collected it needs to be put into usable form. In order to develop an accurate picture of the relationship between a tax source and its growth, discretionary changes (such as rate increase or processing changes) need to be stripped out, so year-to-year growth reflects a comparable base. A record should be kept of these special or one-time events for future reference, however.

Although information collection is an important first step, care needs to be exercised so that information collection does not become an end in itself. In his review of business forecasting practices, Scott Armstrong (1985) points out that forecasters often fall into the trap of chasing the elusive goal of perfect information, when time and resources could have more productively been devoted to analysis and presentation of information already available.

A good database is valuable only insofar as it is useful in forecasting. Usually, some form of statistical technique, or model, is employed to use historical relationships to project future outcomes. The models may be very simple, such as a moving average, or very complex, such as a simultaneous econometric equation that uses several equations.

The problem with simple time series analysis, such as a moving average, is that it assumes that the future will resemble the past—not always a safe assumption in today's economy. Consequently, most forecasters use some form of econometric model that allows more flexibility in the relationships between one or more economic indicators and a revenue source. In their study, Stuart Bretschneider and Wilson Gorr (1987) found that 88 percent of the U.S. forecasters used some sort of econometric model in their forecasts, and that a third of them used more complicated models.

Regardless of how sophisticated an econometric model may be, it still has to capture the relationship between a dependent variable, such as income tax revenue, and an independent variable (or variables), such as personal income. One of the most difficult forecasting tasks is how to quantify this relationship when it is changing over time. Econometric models usually provide a better opportunity to capture this phenomenon than a time series or moving average, but econometric models are by no means foolproof.

Researchers are not in agreement as to which statistical techniques are best under all circumstances. Armstrong (1985) summarizes the available research on technique as follows:

1. More complicated techniques are not necessarily more accurate; however objective techniques, such as simple equations, tend to be more accurate than purely judgmental measures, such as intuition.
2. Estimates based on more than one statistical technique are more likely to be accurate than those that are not based on more than one method.

Alternative Forecasts

Two decades ago, revenue forecasts were generally the exclusive domain of the executive branch, but subsequent years have seen a growth of sophisticated forecasting ability elsewhere, particularly in state legislatures.

Does the existence of an alternative forecast improve accuracy, or does it just add to the confusion and ultimately detract from it? Research suggests that alternative forecasts should be welcomed with open arms. Bretschneider and Gorr (1987) have explained that the U.S. government's separation-of-powers design has been a major force for accurate and realistic accuracy; and they believe that a formal consensus process has improved accuracy even more. This view is consistent with Armstrong's findings that combined forecasts were more likely to be accurate than forecasts that were not combined. In short, two heads are better than one.

The key to the productive use of alternative forecasts is a good working relationship between the forecasting agencies, which facilitates comparisons without compromising the independence of either forecast. If the forecasting agencies can agree in advance on such issues as the starting point for the forecast, definitions of terms, reporting format, and revision schedules, forecast users can concentrate on understanding the substantive differences between the forecasts.

Cooperation, however, should not be allowed to become a substitute for independent analysis. Although it is helpful for both the legislative and executive forecasting agencies to establish some common ground rules, it is essential the two forecasts be arrived at independently.

In Ohio, the recent practice has been for the Legislative Budget Office and the Office of Budget Management to use the economic advisers' national forecast as a starting point, but to develop the remainder of the forecast independently.

Legislators or other review panels need to be prepared to resolve differences in forecasts when they occur. This preparation may involve choosing one forecast over another in its entirety, or splitting the difference between the two. Creating a new forecast that takes the most optimistic components of each is not an acceptable technique.

Monitoring, Revision, and Evaluation

Given the uncertainty inherent in economic behavior, a systematic approach to monitoring, revision, and evaluation is essential to any revenue forecast. The 1985 Public Policy Institute survey of American (1985) states found that revisions of state revenue estimates were very common, but that practices varied greatly among the states. Some states revised monthly, others revised annually. About half of the states revised according to a formula, others on an as-needed basis. Conditions vary from one political unit to another, but some general principles emerge

■ Monitoring (that is, a comparison of actual receipts to forecasted receipts by revenue source) should be done on at least a quarterly basis.

- It is possible to revise too much as well as not enough. Generally, revisions should be done only if a clear trend has developed through three or four months of data. If the budget is prepared on a biennial basis, a mid-biennium revision should be planned.
- Evaluation involves the comparison of the original forecast with actual results, by component. This comparison helps determine which portions of the forecast are working well and which are not.
- A well-managed system should be able to produce a comparison, by revenue source, of the initial forecast and subsequent revisions, with actuals after the budget cycle has ended.
- The margin of error in individual sources is likely to be significantly larger than the error on the estimate as a whole, but the net impact is the most important. An average error of one to two percent should be considered good.

Presentation

The care with which a forecast is presented says a great deal to the user about how well the forecast is put together. A poorly presented forecast may undermine credibility and acceptance just as readily as one that is poorly prepared. A well-presented revenue forecast should specifically address each of the issues named in this entry, clearly laying out the underlying assumptions about the local and national economies. It should show the derivation and explain the methodology behind the revenue estimates for each revenue source. The role of experts and outside advisers should be clearly documented. The forecast should be presented in a format designed to encourage comparison with alternative forecasts. Plans for monitoring, revision, and evaluation should be laid out in advance.

In addition to addressing these fundamental issues, the presentation should include supplemental information to help the user put this information in context. Forecasts presented with many significant digits imply spurious levels of precision. Instead, a good presentation should include upper- and lower-confidence limits. The impact of alternative scenarios should also be discussed. For example, some national and international forecasting firms present their own alternative forecasts based on more optimistic and more pessimistic economic assumptions.

What Forecasting Cannot Do

Up to this point we have examined the elements that go into a good forecast. But it is important to recognize some things that a forecast is not or cannot be, no matter how technically proficient. First, a forecast cannot be expected to be 100 percent precise. Errors occur in information, in technique, in revision, or in interpretation in even the most carefully designed systems. Possible sources of forecast error include errors in underlying assumptions, modeling errors, or estimating errors in individual revenue sources.

Forecasters are particularly poor at predicting turning points in the national and international economy. Leading indicators are one tool available to forecasters to help identify turning points, but experts disagree on how helpful traditional indicators may be in today's uncertain economic environment. In addition, it appears that revenue forecasters tend to underestimate the strength of an economic downturn once it occurs and underestimate a recovery once it begins.

For many years, the conventional forecasting wisdom was to pad the forecast to be deliberately pessimistic as a built-in hedge against bad times. The problem with this approach is that it undermines the credibility of the forecast. An alternative strategy is to build a hedge against uncertainty directly into the budget in the form of a minimum ending balance or a rainy day fund.

Second, a forecast is not a very good substitute for political decisions. What former Ronald Reagan administration budget director David Stockman (1986) described as the "rosy scenario" might provide a means for delaying an unpleasant decision about tax increases or spending cuts, but in the end, a revenue forecast is a prisoner of economic reality. The misuse of a forecast for political purposes undermines credibility, particularly in a period of growing ability of groups outside of government to analyze revenue forecasts. Once credibility is undermined, it is very difficult to restore.

Third, even though the forecast itself should not be a political document, forecasters must always be sensitive to its political implications. Consequently, the best way to keep politics out of forecasting is to keep forecasting out of politics. The six months preceding a state or national election, during which even the seemingly most innocuous fact can spark a major firestorm, are particularly volatile.

Fourth, although objective techniques are important to a good forecast, the forecast cannot be totally devoid of human input or human judgment. Human judgment and experience are helpful when statistical indicators supposedly measuring the same thing seem to contradict one another, when something unprecedented is taking place, or when a statistical model lacks intuitive credibility. When judgment is used in these cases, how that judgment was made and what it means need to be clearly identified in the forecast presentation.

One instance in which judgment may be particularly dangerous is when top management changes the forecast numbers simply because it is unhappy about the potential political consequences of the outcome. Armstrong (1985) suggests that forecasts be developed independent of top management for this reason. However, the high political stakes involved with state revenue forecasts make it essential for forecasters to be sure political leaders have confidence in the forecast *process* before any numbers are produced.

Fifth, is the danger of what Michael Barron and David Targett (1985) have called the "Forecasting Trap," a phenomenon that occurs, when a forecast becomes an end in itself, not just a means to an end. To the degree forecasters withhold or manipulate information to make the forecast look better, they undercut the whole budget process. Recognizing the limits of revenue forecasting frees forecasters and forecast users to concentrate on using a state revenue forecast to do what it does best; that is, provide a reasonable baseline of information upon which to make the political and policy judgments about the allocation of scarce resources.

WILLIAM J. SHKURTI

BIBLIOGRAPHY

Armstrong, J. Scott, 1985. *Long-Range Forecasting: From Crystal Ball to Computer*. New York: John Wiley and Sons.

Bahl, Roger, 1980. "Revenue and Expenditure Forecasting by State and Local Governments." In J. Peterson and C. Spain, eds. *Essays in Public Finance and Financial Management*. Chatham, N.J.: Chatham House Publishers.

Barron, Michael, and David Targett, 1985. *The Manager's Guide to Business Forecasting*. New York: Basel and Blackwell.

Bretschneider, Stuart I., and Wilson L. Gorr, 1987. "State and Local Government Revenue Forecasting." In S. Makridakis and S. Wheelwright, eds., *The Handbook of Forecasting*. 2d ed. New York: John Wiley and Sons.

Federation of Tax Administrators, 1992. "State Revenue Estimating Procedures." *Government Finance Review* (August):38–39.

Public Policy Institute, 1985. "An Analysis of State Revenue Forecasting Systems." Albany Public Policy Institute of New York State.

Shkurti, William J., 1990. "A User's Guide to Revenue Forecasting." *Public Budgeting and Finance* (Spring):79–94.

Stockman, David A., 1986. *The Triumph of Politics: How the Reagan Revolution Failed*. New York: Harper & Row.

REVENUE SHARING. Unconditional fiscal assistance from one government entity to another, as from a federal government to states and localities, or from states to local governments.

In 1972, the U.S. Congress passed the State and Local Fiscal Assistance Act, initiating for the United States an experiment with general revenue-sharing that lasted 14 years. A coalition of liberal and conservative advocates contended that (1) revenue sharing would decentralize government, shifting decisionmaking from Washington to state capitals and local chambers; (2) it would stabilize state and local taxes, decreasing reliance on regressive sales and property taxes and increasing use of the progressive federal income tax; (3) it would equalize resources among the states, between the well off and the poor; (4) it would simplify the grant-in-aid system, since the entire revenue-sharing program could be administered by "20 clerks and a computer," making it possible to eliminate some of the complex categorical grant-in-aid programs; and (5) it would promote modernization of state and local governments and strengthen the authority of generalist state and local decisionmakers (mayors, governors, legislators) against functional administrators aided by categorical grants.

Perhaps equally as important as many of these contentions at the time revenue sharing was debated is that revenue sharing had popular appeal—opinion polls showed the idea of returning federal tax money to state and local governments with "no strings attached" was a popular one.

As passed by Congress, the State and Local Fiscal Assistance Act provided for wide distribution of funds, entitling many of the smallest jurisdictions of local government to federal grants—some for the first time. It provided grants to all states, approximately 39,000 other units of local government, to Native American tribes, and to Alaskan Native villages. The distribution formula was extraordinarily complex, in part because it was a product of political compromise and in part because it had to account for the many different forms of local government found in the states.

The Senate formula included three factors: population, general tax effort (the ratio of total state and local tax revenue to total personal income of the state's residents), and relative income (based on state per capita income in comparison to the nationwide average).

The House bill incorporated a five-factor formula, including population, population times relative income, general tax effort, urbanized population, and a factor to benefit states that imposed income taxes. Unable to reach a compromise, the final legislation incorporated both formulas, with a provision that each state's funds would be determined by the formula that gave it the most, but that the amounts would then be scaled back so that the sum for all the states would not exceed the total amount available for any entitlement period. Within each state, the state government was entitled to one-third of the funds, with two-thirds allocated to local units, according to an even more complex formula.

For the period from 1973 to 1980 (during which revenue-sharing was available to both state and local governments), more than US $6 billion was distributed annually. In 1980, Congress terminated revenue sharing for the states, and the annual amount declined to less than US $5 billion. Along the way, support for the program had begun to weaken, as the federal deficit had grown and as interest groups representing state and local governments had begun to lose their effectiveness. General revenue sharing ended completely in 1986 after President Ronald Reagan failed to support its renewal, and efforts to secure renewal in Congress without his support failed.

Researchers have assessed the effect of revenue sharing using three principal approaches: examination of annual reports of spending that all recipients filed with the U.S. Department of the Treasury; surveys of decisionmakers who participated in allocating revenue-sharing money received by state and local governments; and participant observation of revenue-sharing decisionmaking in small groups of state and local governments. Drawing conclusions from the annual reports was particularly problematic because of fungibility, that is, the ease with which dollars could be shifted from one category to another. A report indicating revenue-sharing money was spent in the category of law enforcement, for example, may mean that police expenditures increased or, instead, may mean that locally raised resources were released to be spent on parks or that the city had cut taxes.

Among the more important conclusions drawn from various revenue-sharing studies were the following: Local governments (especially smaller ones and ones that were well off financially) used revenue sharing for capital expenditures, although this tendency declined as the years passed; for the states, revenue-sharing funds made it easier to increase simultaneously assistance to local governments (especially for education) and to avoid tax increases; and for larger cities (and ones under extreme fiscal pressure) revenue-sharing was used to maintain public programs. There is little evidence that revenue-sharing funds led to major program innovation, and there is little evidence that revenue sharing resulted in state or local tax cuts.

Although there were few "strings" connected to revenue sharing, recipient governments were required to hold public hearings concerning use of the funds and to publish proposed allocations, as steps to increase public participation in decisionmaking. Studies revealed that actual effects of these requirements were minimal. Although some recipients instituted unique processes for deciding how revenue-sharing funds would be spent, many employed the same decisionmaking processes they had used for their general budgets, though technically meeting revenue-sharing requirements. In some cities and states, interest groups competed actively for shares of the new revenue pie.

In comparison to decisionmaking about categorical grants-in-aid, under which both Congress and federal administrators had set out substantive and procedural rules that recipient governments were required to follow, revenue sharing shifted decisionmaking from the federal government to state and local governments. However, because those funds were then spent in hundreds of different program categories in thousands of government units, it was difficult to maintain a sufficiently strong constituency to support its continuation, especially in the face of a rising federal deficit and as it became evident that many state and local governments could financially cope with the loss of revenue-sharing funds.

Revenue Sharing in Other Systems

Revenue sharing is widely employed by U.S. states to provide aid to local governments. In some states it takes the form of providing a portion of a state collected tax (for example, the general sales tax) to city or county governments, either on the basis of where it is collected or on the basis of population. If this revenue is distributed to be used at the discretion of the local decisionmakers, it is a form of revenue-sharing.

Both the Canadian and German federal systems employ revenue sharing as components of their intergovernmental finance structures. The Canadian federal government enters into tax collection agreements with the provinces, under which provincial income taxes are collected by the federal government and distributed to the provinces of origin. The German central government shares a portion of the income tax with the states and cities. In both of these systems, other forms of grants-in-aid are used as well, and general purpose grants with few strings attached play a larger role than they do in the United States.

F. TED HEBERT

BIBLIOGRAPHY

Juster, F. Thomas, ed., 1976. *The Economic and Political Impact of General Revenue-Sharing.* Ann Arbor, MI: Institute for Social Research, University of Michigan.

Marando, Vincent, 1990. "General Revenue-Sharing: Termination and City Response." *State and Local Government Review,* vol. 27, no. 3 (Fall):98–107.

Nathan, Richard P., and Charles F. Adams, Jr., and Associates, 1977. *Revenue-Sharing: The Second Round.* Washington, DC: Brookings Institution.

Nathan, Richard P., Allen D. Manvel, and Susannah E. Calkins, 1975. *Monitoring Revenue-Sharing.* Washington, DC: Brookings Institution.

Reagan, Michael D., and John G. Sanzone, 1981. *The New Federalism.* 2d ed. New York: Oxford University Press.

REVERSE DISCRIMINATION. The notion that equal opportunity efforts, particularly certain forms of affirmative action, have the effect of discriminating against nonminority males (see **affirmative action**). Affirmative action based on numerical goals and timetables for the employment of women and minorities, for example, extends preferences to those groups by favoring their employment until a specified level of representation in the workforce is achieved (see **goals and quotas**). The purpose of such a strategy is to correct the effects of past and current discrimination directed against racial and ethnic minorities and women, but opponents of affirmative action argue that the policy unfairly limits opportunities for nonminority men.

The tendency of some observers to see affirmative action as reverse discrimination may at first glance be understandable. Practices that take race, ethnicity, or gender into account are certainly not neutral. Affirmative action is designed to redistribute opportunity along racial, ethnic, and gender lines from those who have enjoyed historical advantages to those who have suffered discrimination. As a result, nonminority males face competition that they would not have otherwise faced and that they certainly have not faced historically.

The key question, however, is whether the racial, ethnic, and gender distinctions drawn by affirmative action are justifiable. Those who equate affirmative action with reverse discrimination claim that such distinctions cannot be defended. They argue that selection decisions, such as those for employment or college admissions, should be based solely on individual merit without consideration of race, ethnicity, or gender.

The debate over reverse discrimination gained wide attention in the United States in the late 1970s with the Supreme Court decision in *Regents of the University of California v. Bakke* (1978, 438 U.S. 265) The case involved Alan Bakke, a white male who had been refused admission to the medical school at the University of California at Davis although certain minority applicants with poorer academic qualifications were admitted as part of an affirmative action program. Bakke sued, charging that the university had violated the guarantee of equal protection contained in the Constitution's Fourteenth Amendment. The Court issued two separate majority opinions, the first of which indicated that racial quotas contained in the university's affirmative action program were indeed unconstitutional and Bakke should be admitted to the medical school, and the second determining that under certain circumstances an applicant's race could be considered in the admissions process as long as other factors, including qualifications, were also reviewed.

Thus, all race-conscious approaches to affirmative action were not to be rejected. Through a series of subsequent cases, the Court has determined that racial distinctions contained in affirmative action plans by government employers will pass constitutional review if the distinctions serve a compelling governmental interest (such as correcting the effects of past discrimination by the employer) and

no less intrusive means are available to accomplish that interest, that is, the impact on nonminority males is minimized (see *City of Richmond v. J. A. Croson Company,* 1989, 488 U.S. 469).

Constitutional limitations, however, apply only to government programs, and they are not the only source of constraints on affirmative action. Statutory law, such as the Civil Rights Act of 1964 prohibiting discrimination by government or private employers, must also be reconciled with affirmative action programs. This issue was first taken up by the Court in 1979 in *United Steelworkers of America v. Weber* (443 U.S. 616). The case involved an affirmative action plan at the Kaiser Aluminum and Chemical Corporation that reserved for African-Americans 50 percent of the openings in an in-plant craft training program, until the African American proportion of craft workers in the program approximated the proportion of African Americans in the local labor force.

Brian Weber, a white employee denied placement into the training program filed suit alleging that the affirmative action provision violated Title VII of the Civil Rights Act of 1964. The Court held that the prohibition on discrimination contained in Title VII could not be read literally to proscribe all race conscious affirmative action. The Court reasoned that affirmative action could be permitted if it is designed to address a manifest racial imbalance in traditionally segregated job categories, it is constructed as a temporary strategy, and it does not pose an absolute bar to the advancement of white males. In a subsequent case in 1987, the Court applied the standard for race conscious affirmative action set out in the *Weber* decision to affirmative action programs targeting women as well (see *Johnson v. Transportation Agency, Santa Clara County, California,* 1987, 480 U.S. 616).

In confronting the reverse discrimination issue, the Court has attempted to balance society's interest in correcting past and current patterns of discrimination with the interest of nonminority males. Limited preferences designed to benefit minorities and women have been upheld. The Court has reasoned that ethnicity, race, and gender may be taken into consideration in order to overcome the effects of earlier prejudices.

J. EDWARD KELLOUGH

BIBLIOGRAPHY

Epstein, Richard A., 1992. *Forbidden Grounds: The Case Against Employment Discrimination Laws.* Cambridge: Harvard University Press.

Glazer, Nathan, 1978. *Affirmative Discrimination: Ethnic Inequality and Public Policy.* New York: Basic Books.

Greenawalt, R. Kent, 1983. *Discrimination and Reverse Discrimination.* New York: Knopf.

Livingston, John C., 1979. *Fair Game? Inequality and Affirmative Action.* San Francisco: W. H. Freeman and Company.

REVIEWABILITY.   The power of the courts to review and interpret governmental laws and actions to determine their legality and constitutionality. Judicial review is commonly perceived as the most basic remedy available to those who seek relief because they feel that they have been or will be harmed by *illegal* administrative actions (see **judicial review**). (The word illegal is emphasized since the courts cannot provide relief for those who have been hurt by unethical, cruel, insensitive, or blundering administrative acts that are otherwise lawful.)

Seeking relief through the courts, however, appears much easier than it really is. If courts refuse to review a person's plea for review, as they frequently do, the aggrieved person will simply have to learn to live with the agency decision that motivated the appeal.

There are many reasons why a court will not grant review of agency actions, the principal one being that judges usually like to defer to agency discretionary authority and expertise. A great deal of administrative law deals with the more specific and technical justifications cited by the courts for granting or denying petitions for review of administrative decisions, however.

What Is Reviewable?

It is very difficult to answer the question: What is reviewable administrative action? Judges and administrative law scholars have always argued over what should or should not be appropriately considered judicially reviewable agency behavior. Although various legislative and judicial attempts have been made to zero in on what should or should not be subject to review, the painful truth is that the reviewability question has been uncomfortably left unsettled. It would be convenient if one could easily place some agency actions in the reviewable category and others in the unreviewable category, but this simply cannot be done because it is too unclear as to which actions are legitimately reviewable and unreviewable as circumstances change from case to case. The complex and confusing nature of the reviewability question is possibly epitomized best in the intentionally contradictory title of Kim Morris's article, "Judicial Review of Non-reviewable Administrative Action" (Morris 1977, p. 65).

Much of the confusion over the reviewability question exists because the distinction between reviewability and scope of review questions is often not made clear (see scope of review). It is important to understand that the two concepts pose related, but, nevertheless, distinct, legal questions. Reviewability is identified with the basic question: Is the matter within the court's jurisdiction for review, thus, according to administrative law rhetoric, making the dispute available for judicial review? Though a reviewable issue is within the legitimate jurisdiction of the courts (for example, because a statute specifically

provides for review of certain agency decisions), an unreviewable issue is outside the legitimate jurisdiction of the courts (for example, because a statute specifically excludes some action from review, thereby essentially making the decision of agency officials in these unreviewable areas final).

Once a court has answered the necessary questions pertaining to whether the case qualifies or is available for review, then the court can determine how far its legitimate scope in reviewing a reviewable case should extend. For instance, once the court decides that a case pertaining to the use of discretion is within the court's proper jurisdiction for review, then the court can ask: To what depth should our inquiry extend into an agency's use of discretion?

Obviously, courts respond to this question quite differently. Though passive courts are reluctant to review most discretionary agency decisions, active courts like to probe deep into an agency's use of discretion (see **judicial activism/restraint**). Therefore, whether the courts perceive their proper scope of review in narrow or broad terms relates directly to whether they will adopt a passive or active judicial posture.

What determines whether judicial review should be made available to petitioners in administrative law disputes? First, the court must answer *no* to the following basic question: Have applicable statutes prohibited judicial review of the specific administrative action under question? But to the following questions, the court must answer *yes:* Have the relevant statutes explicitly, or at least implicitly, permitted review? Has an eligible party petitioned for review (should the petitioner be given standing to sue)? Has a proper defendant been named in the suit? Is the case ready for review in terms of its timeliness?

The last question implies three important subsidiary questions. Acknowledging that administrative agencies normally have primary jurisdiction, the court must decide whether it should now intervene (assert its jurisdiction) in the dispute (see primary jurisdiction). In seeking relief, has the petitioner exhausted all administrative remedies made available by the agency? (See exhaustion doctrine.) Is the case ripe for review (ready for review in the sense that the legal issues are definitive enough, have evolved enough, and have been presented vividly enough to allow the ruling court to reach a clear decision)? And finally, have proper forms of action (specific and technical legal methods for remedial relief, such as request for an injunction) been followed in filing for review?

A Brief Historical Overview of Reviewability

It should be emphasized that if a court wants to deny petitions for review, all it has to do is answer in the negative just one of the questions previously cited. At one time in U.S. history the courts usually did just that, thereby avoiding having to hear and settle disputes involving administrative agencies.

Until the 1930s, if the legislature was silent on whether agency actions should be reviewed, the courts almost always took the position that the actions should be considered unreviewable. Numerous court decisions substantiate this early judicial tendency to not review. For example, in *Martin v. Mott* (25 U.S. [12 Wheat.] 19 [1827]), the Supreme Court refused to review a question pertaining to the President's discretion in deciding whether circumstances justified using the militia in the public interest. In 1840, in *Decatur v. Paulding* (39 U.S. [14 Pet.] 497), the Court again refused to review an administrative decision. In reference to a dispute over whether a naval officer's widow should receive pension benefits, the Court held that it would be inappropriate for it to step in and decide the matter, especially since Congress did not specifically provide for review in such instances. The Court asserted: "The interference of the Court with the performance of the ordinary duties of the executive departments of the government, would be productive of nothing but mischief; and we are quite satisfied that such a power was never intended to be given to them" (at 516).

In the late 1800s, the Supreme Court in *Hadden v. Merritt* (115 U.S. 25 [1885]), again declined to review an administrative determination. In a case involving a dispute over whether a customs official properly assessed imported items, the Court held that such questions should be resolved by the agency, not the courts.

This common-law perception toward the unreviewability of agency actions continued well into the twentieth century. *Keim v. United States* (177 U.S. 290 [1900]); *Reaves v. Ainsworth* (219 U.S. 296 [1911]); and *Eberlein v. United States* (257 U.S. 82 [1921]), are all cases supportive of the unreviewability stand of the court. Although the courts in more recent times have been reluctant to review agency decisions, they usually refuse review only because statutes specifically prohibit judicial review of the agency actions in question. For example, in *Lynch v. United States* (292 U.S. 571 [1934]), in ruling on the reviewability of pension benefits disputes, the Court held they should be regarded as unreviewable if Congress intends them to be. This decision was based on the argument, however, that pensions are not rights but are really governmental gratuities and, therefore, do not require review: "Pensions, compensation allowances and privileges are gratuities. They involve no agreement of parties; and the grant of them creates no vested right. The benefits conferred by gratuities may be redistributed or withdrawn at any time in the discretion of Congress" (at 577).

But the recent tendency, especially since *Goldberg v. Kelly* (397 U.S. 254 [1970]), for the courts to regard most governmental benefits as rights or "property interests," not privileges, has made the courts more prone to review agency decisions, even though statutes may prohibit review. In *Regents of University of Michigan v. Ewing* (106 S. Ct. 507 [1986]), the Supreme Court, as well as the District Court for the Eastern District of Michigan and the Sixth Circuit Court of Appeals, heard a case because a student claimed that he had a "property interest" in continuing in the six-year "Interflex" program from which he was terminated following four years of a dismal academic performance. Obviously irritated by the fact that this dispute had ever gone to court, the unanimous Supreme Court said: "In view of Ewing's academic record that the Court charitably characterizes as 'unfortunate,' this is a case that never should have been litigated" (at 516).

Several other federal court decisions have conveyed the message that Congress should be entitled to exclude certain agency actions from judicial review if members of Congress believe that it would be appropriate to do so. In *Babcock v. Johnson* (250 U.S. 328 (1919), the Court defended the right of Congress to include a "no-review" clause that prevented servicemen from challenging Treasury Department decisions regarding property lost while on military duty. The Court held: "When the United States creates rights in individuals against itself, it is under no obligation to provide a remedy through the courts" (at 331). In *Tutun v. United States* (270 U.S. 568, 567 [1926]), the Court took the position that the United States, acting through Congress, has the proper authority to "create rights in individuals against itself and provide only an administrative remedy."

In 1958 the Federal District Court for Massachusetts quickly dismissed a veteran's argument that a "no-review" clause, which prohibits the review of Veterans Administration decisions pertaining to veterans' benefits, was unconstitutional. The court simply cited *Babcock, Tutun,* and *Lynch* to substantiate its ruling. Six years later, in *Milliken v. Gleason* (332 F. 2d 122; 1st Cir.; 1964; *cert.* denied, 379 U.S. 1002; 1965), the First Circuit Court of Appeals also relied upon *Babcock, Tutun,* and *Lynch* to support its argument that Congress can make Veterans Administration decisions unreviewable.

In *Southern Ry. Co. v. Seaboard Allied Milling Corp.*, 99 S. Ct. 2388 (1979), however, the Supreme Court ruled that the Interstate Commerce Commission (ICC), if it desired, had statutory authority to refuse to conduct an investigation regarding the appropriateness of rates. Specifically, the unanimous Court held that the ICC's decision not to investigate was not subject to judicial review because Congress had given the ICC unreviewable discretion in this area.

In the 1930s, when the courts started to become more active, they began to review more and more cases prior courts had refused to review. Although the courts' more relaxed position on granting judicial review of agency behavior did not become very noticeable until the days of Franklin D. Roosevelt, courts had demonstrated in the past that they were capable of stepping in and reviewing cases that they believed desperately needed judicial attention.

In fact, in 1902 the Supreme Court, in *American School of Magnetic Healing v. McAnnulty* (187 U.S. 94), handed down a decision that sounds remarkably modern. The case involved a situation in which the postmaster general stopped delivery of mail to a mail order business because he believed that the business was operating under the fraudulent pretense that it could cure sickness through providing proper exercise methods for the "faculty of the brain and mind." The Court granted review, however, because it felt that the postmaster general had exceeded his statutory authority and misused his discretion:

> The facts . . . show that the case is not one which by any construction of those facts is covered or provided for by the statutes under which the Postmaster General has assumed to act, and his determination that those admitted facts do authorize his action is a clear mistake of law, . . . the courts, therefore, must have power in a proper proceeding to grant relief. Otherwise, the individual is left to the absolutely uncontrolled and arbitrary action of a public and administrative officer, whose action is unauthorized by any law and is in violation of the rights of the individual. (at 110).

Although in later cases, such as *Perkins v. Lukens Steel Co.* (310 U.S. 113 [1940]), the wisdom of *McAnnulty* was overruled, the presumption of reviewability established in *McAnnulty* has emerged as the prevailing attitude today, although very recent decisions by the Supreme Court have cast some doubt as to how solid the presumption of reviewability is.

For example, in *Dismuke v. United States* (297 U.S. 167 [1936]), the Supreme Court held that since there did not exist a clear command in relevant statutes to stop the courts from reviewing agency actions pertaining to governmental retirement benefits claims, the courts could review such actions. Of course, this decision represents a complete turnabout from its position nearly a hundred years before in *Decatur*.

In *Shields v. Utah Idaho C.R. Co.* (305 U.S. 177 [1938]), the Supreme Court held that certain administrative actions made unreviewable by Congress can be reviewed anyway. This holding was upheld and strengthened in *Stark v. Wickard* (321 U.S. 288 [1944]), a landmark decision that seemed to inspire future courts to take a much more open position on what administrative action should be considered legitimately reviewable. In *Stark*, the Court argued

that Congress should not have the final word in what is reviewable agency action: "The responsibility of determining the limits of statutory grants of authority . . . is a judicial function . . . Congress established courts to adjudicate cases and controversies as to claims of infringements of individual rights whether by unlawful action of private persons or by the exercise of unauthorized administrative power" (at 309–10).

The Supreme Court in *Bowen v. Michigan Academy of Family Physicians* (106 S. Ct. 2133 [1986]) ruled that certain regulations under the Medicaid program were not barred from judicial review. Justice John Paul Stevens, speaking for the Court, began his decision "with the strong presumption that Congress intends judicial review of administration action" (at 2135). The presumption of reviewability, he said, can be traced back to *Marbury v. Madison* (1 Cranch 137, 163), another case involving judicial review of administrative action, where Chief Justice John Marshall maintained that "the very essence of civil liberty certainly consists in the right of every individual to claim the protection of laws" (at 2136).

Justice Stevens did acknowledge, however, that "Congress can, of course, make exceptions to the historic practice whereby courts review agency action. The presumption of judicial review is, after all, a presumption" and can only be overruled, quoting from *Block v. Community Nutrition Institute* (467 U.S. 340, 349 [1984]), by "'specific language or specific legislative history that is a reliable indicator of congressional intent,' or a specific congressional intent to preclude judicial review that is 'fairly discernible' in the detail of the legislative scheme" (at 2137). In 1994, the Supreme Court in *Thunder Basin Coal Co. v. Reich* (114 S. Ct. 771) also upheld the presumption of reviewability. The Court stressed that Congress can rightfully preclude judicial review when only review by administrative experts would be appropriate. But the Court noted, citing specifically *Michigan Academy of Family Physicians*, that Congress can never " 'prohibit all judicial review,' " particularly when petitioning parties cannot obtain "meaningful review" of legitimate statutory and constitutional due process claims (at 776–781).

The Administrative Procedure Act and Reviewability

By 1946 when the Administrative Procedure Act (APA) was passed, the presumption of reviewability was well established administrative law. The *Stark* decision clearly had a profound impact on the drafting of the APA because the act generally endorses the *Stark* maxim of broad reviewability. Bernard Schwartz once even exclaimed that "the APA codifies the *Stark v. Wickard* principle" (Schwartz 1984, p. 321).

Sections 702 and 704 of the APA uphold the spirit of *Stark*. Section 702 reads: "A person suffering legal wrong because of agency action within the meaning of a relevant statute is entitled to judicial review thereof"; and Section 704 states: "Agency action made reviewable by statute and final agency action for which there is no other adequate remedy in a court are subject to judicial review." If it were not for the two exceptions to review set forth in Section 701, all federal administrative actions would be subject to review. However, Section 701 states that "Chapter 7—Judicial Review" applies "except to the extent that (1) statutes preclude judicial review; or (2) agency action is committed to agency discretion by law." But clearly, Congress, in enacting the legislation, intended for the courts to be able to review agency actions not specifically excluded from review by statutes. Therefore, the APA does establish a presumption of reviewability.

Actually, legislative intent is very clear in regard to the presumption of reviewability when statutes are silent on the availability of review. A House committee stated that "the mere failure to provide specially by statute for judicial review is certainly no evidence of intent to withhold review" (House Judiciary Committee 1946, p. 275).

The cases that uphold the presumption to reviewability under the APA are numerous, but in no decision is the APA's presumption of reviewability better espoused than in *Abbott Laboratories v. Gardner* (387 U.S. 136 [1967]). Justice John Harlan, writing for the majority, upheld the contention asserted in *Rusk v. Cort* (369 U.S. 367, 379–380 [1962]), "that only upon a showing of 'clear and convincing evidence' of a contrary legislative intent should the courts restrict access to judicial review" (at 141). Justice Harlan also maintained, citing *Shaughnessy v. Pedreiro*, 349 U.S. 48, 51 [1954], that the legislative record on the drafting of the APA "manifests a congressional intention that it cover a broad spectrum of administrative actions, and this Court has echoed that theme by noting that the Administrative Procedure Act's 'generous review provision' must be given a 'hospitable' interpretation" (at 140–141).

The general presumption of reviewability as established in *Stark* and *Abbott Laboratories* was emphatically reasserted in *Reno v. Catholic Social Services* (113 S. Ct. 2485 [1993]) and *Thunder Basin Coal Co.* in 1994.

The Reviewability of "Unreviewable" Administrative Actions

Under Section 701(a) (1) (2) of the APA, agency actions are unreviewable if "statutes preclude judicial review" or "agency action is committed to agency discretion by law." But what do these exclusions mean in practice? Does the first exclusion mean that no matter how absurd administrative action may be, as long as it is protected by statute, it cannot be reviewed? Does it mean that administrators

can violate statutory dictates yet remain free from having their actions reviewed? Does the second exclusion mean that administrators can flagrantly abuse their discretionary powers at the expense of claimants, yet feel content that their abusive use of discretion can never be reviewed? Unfortunately, the tendency of the courts has been to answer "yes" to these questions because the courts have been generally reluctant to apply the presumption of reviewability to Section 701 exclusions.

However, the illogic of absolutely precluding judicial review of agency actions under Section 701(a) (1) (2) attracted heated criticisms from the very beginning. Judges and legal scholars have argued that, at times, circumstances justify judicial review of these supposedly unreviewable agency decisionmaking areas.

In 1951 Justice William O. Douglas voiced his opposition to the majority opinion in *United States v. Wunderlich* (342 U.S. 98), in which the Court argued that judicial review of agency action cannot take place even though an administrative determination is shown to be obviously false, as well as having been reached in an arbitrary and capricious manner, if statutory provisions preclude review. In his dissent, Justice Douglas severely criticized the wisdom of any "finality provisions" in statutes that preclude judicial review entirely, regardless of the circumstances.

In response to a specific "finality provision" excluding review of decisions made by contracting officers, Douglas remarked that the majority opinion upholding the validity of the finality provision would have a "devastating effect" and it would tend to make "a tyrant out of every contracting officer" (at 101).

Douglas's dissenting attitude in *Wunderlich* is slowly winning acceptance, but there remains steady judicial resistance. In *Shaughnessy v. Pedreiro* (349 U.S. 48 [1956]), the Court held that statutory provisions barring review of administrative action should not be interpreted so strictly as to preclude review absolutely.

In keeping with the *Shaughnessy* holding, the court held in *Welch v. United States* (446 F. Supp. 75 [D. Comm, 1978]), that a statutory provision that made all military death benefits claims "final and conclusive" (unreviewable), could be reviewed in matters pertaining to questions of law. In *Owens v. Hills* (450 F. Supp. 218 [N.D., Ill., 1978]), the court ruled that a statutory provision that made decisions by the Housing and Urban Development (HUD) secretary "final and conclusive" and "not to be subject to review" should not be applied totally to prohibit judicial review. And in *Ralpho v. Bell* (569 F.2d 607 [1977]), the District of Columbia Circuit Court argued that despite the strong rhetoric precluding judicial review of agency decisions under the Micronesian Claims Act, the "no-review" clause does not preclude judicial intervention to review complaints that the agency has violated either statutory or constitutional mandates. In the district court's view, to preclude absolutely a person's right to seek judicial remedy to correct an agency wrongdoing that has caused the individual harm would cast in doubt how seriously the United States is committed to the promotion of human rights and basic liberties (at 626).

Although clear law has not been established because various courts have not applied Section 701(a) (1) (2) of the APA consistently, it does appear that a strong consensus of judges nonetheless believe that, despite any "absolute" preclusions of judicial review, ultimately these preclusions themselves are scrutinized by the courts, and agency actions are really not final until the courts say they are. As Bernard Schwartz concluded, despite judicial decisions that uphold preclusions to review, there still exists "the strong presumption in our law in favor of judicial review. That presumption normally prevails even in the face of statutory provisions that appear to preclude review" (1994, p. 455).

There have been several recent cases that have upheld the basic presumption of reviewability even in the face of provisions precluding review, although the courts may have upheld the particular preclusion in dispute (*Franklin v. Massachusetts,* 112 S. Ct. 2767 [1993]; *Reno v. Catholic Social Services,* 113 S. Ct. 2485 [1993]; and *Kisser v. Cisneros,* 14 F.2d 615 [1994]).

Probably no court summarizes the situation on the "unreviewability" of agency decisions better than a New York court in *New York City Department of Environmental Protection v. New York Civil Service Commission,* 579 N.E. 2d 1385 (N.Y. 1993), however. In this case, a New York statute made the state's Civil Service Commission's decisions "final and conclusive" and "unreviewable." The court noted that the state legislature has the right to preclude review of agency actions, and it has clearly done so by statute. But citing a prior case, the court responded: "Even where judicial review is proscribed by statute, the courts have the power and the duty to make certain that the administrative official has not acted in excess of the grant of authority given . . . by the statute or in disregard of the standard prescribed by the legislature" (at 1387). The court held that, despite the statutory preclusion of review, the courts still must look to see whether agency actions were "purely arbitrary." The court stressed that despite the explicit preclusion of judicial review of agency actions by statute, "judicial review cannot be completely precluded."

Courts have the responsibility of checking to see whether "the agency has acted illegally, unconstitutionally, or in excess of its jurisdiction" (at 1387). Or, in the succinct words of the District of Columbia Circuit Court, in the U.S. administrative system agency administrators cannot "expect to escape judicial review by hiding behind a finality clause" (*Dart v. United States,* 848 F.2d 217, 224 [D.C. Cir. 1988]).

KENNETH F. WARREN

BIBLIOGRAPHY

House Judiciary Committee, 1946. *Administrative Procedure Act History.* Washington, D.C.: U.S. GPO.
Morris, Kim, 1977. "Judicial Review of Non-Reviewable Administrative Action: Veterans' Administration Benefit Claims." *Administrative Law Review,* vol. 29 (Winter).
Schwartz, Bernard. 1984. *Administrative Law,* 2d ed. Boston: Little, Brown.
———, 1994. "Administrative Law Cases During 1993." *Administrative Law Review,* vol. 46 (Summer).
Warren, Kenneth F., 1996. *Administrative Law in the Political System.* 3d ed Upper Saddle River, N.J.: Prentice-Hall.

REVOLVING FUND.

A sum of money to be loaned for the purpose of financing investment activity, which will be paid back into the fund so future loans can be made in perpetuity.

Theory and Operation

The principle behind revolving fund finance is simple. A fund is established that makes loans for some purpose. The loans are repaid to the revolving fund, and the repayments are loaned again so that loans can continue to be made indefinitely. If interest is paid on the loans, the fund can grow because, over time, more money is being repaid into the revolving fund than was borrowed initially.

Revolving funds have been proposed or used for purposes as diverse as funding projects for environmental protection, for financing merchant ships, and for providing telephone service. The Rural Electrification and Telephone Revolving Fund provides low-interest loans to extend those utilities to people in rural communities, and in 1987 Congress established a State Revolving Fund (SRF) program to finance wastewater treatment. Firms in the private sector have also used revolving funds for purposes such as making borrowing less costly for their customers. In all of these programs, the basic idea is to create a pool of money that can be used in perpetuity for a specific purpose. By establishing a revolving fund, money can be made available indefinitely from a single appropriation. Although the principle is simple, several issues must be addressed to establish a revolving fund, and to insure that it actually works as intended.

The issues behind revolving fund finance might be broken down into four basic areas. The first concerns why the revolving fund should be established at all, rather than just having potential borrowers from the revolving fund enter capital markets to borrow directly. The second issue is what the terms of the loans will be. The terms must be more favorable than borrowing in private capital markets, or there would be no advantage to establishing the revolving fund. The third issue is where the money comes from to establish the revolving fund initially. The fourth issue is whether the terms of the loans made by the revolving fund will allow it to survive in perpetuity, as the revolving fund concept suggests. The resolution of these issues determines how the revolving fund will work. After looking at these issues, it is then worthwhile to evaluate the revolving fund concept for specific applications to see if it can produce the benefits that its creators intend.

Rationale for Revolving Funds

The clearest rationale for revolving fund finance is economies of scale in borrowing. Those who borrow from the revolving fund could enter capital markets directly to take out loans for the projects financed by the revolving fund. There are several costs involved in borrowing in capital markets that might be avoided by a suitably designed revolving fund. First, there are significant costs involved in underwriting a bond issue that might be avoided by using a revolving fund. Second, it is common when borrowing in private capital markets to require that some money be set aside as a reserve to help assure bondholders that the loans will be repaid. This reserve constitutes money that is borrowed but cannot be used for the project for which the money was borrowed. If the revolving fund has less stringent (or no) requirements for reserves, then more of the money can be put to use. Third, small borrowers often must pay higher interest rates because their bonds are viewed as more risky. A revolving fund might be set up by a state to lend money to localities, and if the state has a better credit rating than the localities it lends to, the revolving fund can obtain funds in capital markets at a lower interest rate than those who would borrow from the revolving fund. For all of these reasons, the revolving fund may be able to obtain funds more cheaply than can individual borrowers.

There is another side to each of these arguments, however. The underwriting costs are compensation for the effort of putting together a sound financing package that can reasonably be expected to repay the loan. If underwriters for a bond issue do not do this job, someone administering the revolving fund must do it, to make sure that the money borrowed from the revolving fund actually is repaid. Furthermore, the revolving fund will have similar expenses if it borrows funds and will have administrative expenses that would not be required if borrowers went directly into capital markets. With regard to the expense of maintaining a reserve, this is a safety factor that helps insure repayment. If borrowers from the revolving fund are given lower (or no) reserve requirements, then repayment of the borrowed money is less certain. Furthermore, if the revolving fund borrows money, it will have to set aside a reserve, and if it then loans money and requires its borrowers to have any reserve, the total reserves required for a revolving fund may

exceed those that would be needed for direct borrowing. Finally, the lower interest rate that may be available to the revolving fund reflects a market-determined default risk, and loans made below the market rate shift the default risk onto the revolving fund.

Although savings that could be attributed to revolving funds are probably mostly illusory, revolving funds do provide a method for financing government programs, for standardizing those programs across recipients of revolving fund loans, and for providing some government oversight. At the federal level, there are more than 100 revolving funds, many of them initiated in the 1930s, including the Tennessee Valley Authority (1933), the Federal Housing Administration (1934), and the Commodity Credit Corporation (1938). The federal government has provided funds through the Import-Export Bank for foreign purchasers of American goods to get loans at favorable rates, through the Small Business Administration for small businesses to obtain loans, and has provided money to states to start their own state revolving funds to finance wastewater treatment facilities. These examples show how revolving funds can be used to provide loans to borrowers who might otherwise have limited access to credit markets.

The definition of a revolving fund is sometimes extended to funds that do not receive funds back from those from whom the funds are disbursed. For example, the federal government refers to the Federal Deposit Insurance Corporation as a revolving fund, as well as trust funds administered by the Civil Service Commission for health and retirement benefits. These types of funds in this entry are more closely related to insurance than to the revolving loan activity just described. To consider these types of funds in this entry would broaden the inquiry substantially, so this discussion is limited to funds that actually revolve—that is, funds that lend money and receive the money back in the form of repayments so it can be loaned again.

Terms of the Loans

In order for the revolving fund to provide any benefits to the participants in the revolving fund program, the terms, of the revolving fund loans must be more favorable than the borrowers could obtain through private capital markets. The more favorable the terms, the greater the benefit to recipients of loans. Because the idea of a revolving fund is to provide benefits to the recipients of loans, there is little point in setting up a revolving fund unless the benefits to the recipients provide a substantial enough advantage over direct borrowing to justify the program, so there will be some rationale for making the loan terms as generous as possible.

I have developed a model to calculate the grant equivalence of below-market interest rates for borrowers (Holcombe 1992). Grant equivalence means the amount of money that would have to be provided by an outright grant to provide the same benefit as the lower interest rate from the revolving fund loan. For a 20-year loan, the grant equivalence of a 1 percent reduction in the interest rate is about 7 percent of the value of the loan, for a 2 percent reduction it is about 13 percent of the value of the loan, and a 3 percent reduction is about 20 percent of the value of the loan. An 8 percent reduction (which might be an interest-free loan when the market rate is 8 percent) has a grant equivalence of 51 percent of the value of the loan. For a loan from a revolving fund to provide a substantial benefit to the borrower, the reduction from the market interest rate must be fairly substantial.

From a policy standpoint, it then becomes reasonable to compare setting up a revolving fund with directly subsidizing the activity and having the borrower enter the private capital market. Using the figures in the preceding paragraph, the revolving fund could make a loan at 3 percent below the market rate, or could give the potential borrower the same benefit by providing a cash grant equal to 20 percent of the amount that was to be borrowed. Obviously, the initial benefits could be provided more cheaply by making an outright grant rather than setting up a revolving fund to make loans. However, the revolving fund concept offers the enticement that the money will be paid back, allowing the loans to continue in perpetuity, but when all factors are considered, this enticement may be illusory.

Funding the Fund

A revolving fund needs a source of funds to be established, and with regard to government-operated revolving funds, this means that the money will be raised either through taxation or borrowing. Taxation has the advantage over borrowing that once the money is raised, it need not be paid back. But using tax revenues to make loans rather than direct expenditures has the disadvantage that the impact felt from each tax dollar is significantly less. Using the numbers from the previous section, tax dollars used in a revolving fund making loans 1 percent below market have only 7 percent as much impact as would spending the tax revenues immediately. Interest-free loans, if the market rate is 8 percent, have only half the impact that they would have if the revenues were spent instead of loaned. Using tax revenues to build a revolving fund thus dilutes the immediate impact that could be had if the money were spent directly.

Borrowing money to create a revolving fund almost surely means that the fund's value will erode over time. Repayments into the fund must in turn be used to repay the loans used to finance the revolving fund, but if the revolving fund borrows at market rates and lends at below-market rates, the repayments into the fund are unlikely to be sufficient to repay the fund's initial borrowing. A revolving fund cannot survive in perpetuity if it borrows at the market rate of interest to make loans at below the market rate. The fund will need another source of revenues besides borrowing, and borrowing by the fund will erode the capital value of the fund.

Long-Run Viability of a Revolving Fund

Another factor that must be considered in assessing the long-run viability of a revolving fund is inflation. At 4 percent inflation, for example, the price level will double in less than 20 years, so if a revolving fund is established and makes 20-year loans, repayment of the principal alone will cut the real value of the revolving fund to less than half its initial value in two decades. With a permanent source of revenues, such as when tax revenues are used to start a revolving fund, the interest rate charged to borrowers from a revolving fund must be at least the rate of inflation to retain the real value of the fund. If the revolving fund borrows money, the real value of the revolving fund will decline if the rate of interest at which it loans money is less than the rate at which it borrows, and this almost surely will be the case.

The market rate of interest tends to be about 3 percent above the inflation rate, and this difference may be even narrower for municipal government borrowers that can get lower interest rates because interest payments on their bonds are exempt from federal income taxes. In order for a revolving fund loan to have any substantial value to the borrower, it will probably have to offer an interest rate less than the inflation rate, meaning that the value of the revolving fund will erode over time. If some or all of the money used to seed the revolving fund is borrowed, the erosion will be even more substantial. The concept of setting up a revolving fund that will provide funds into the indefinite future sounds attractive, but there are a number of pitfalls that work against the concept. The nature of revolving funds is such that unless they have a continuing source of revenue in addition to loan repayments, their real value will almost surely decline over time.

Conclusion

Revolving funds are primarily used as an alternative to the direct use of taxation or borrowing in public finance, but they can also be used as a private sector business tool. For example, publishers have set up revolving funds to allow small book stores to borrow money to finance their inventories, and as the money is repaid, it is then made available for new loans. This is a private sector alternative to public institutions like the Import-Export Bank that helps foreign customers of American firms finance their purchases.

Revolving funds can be a way to stretch the impact of a program over a longer period of time, and ideally, in perpetuity, as loan repayments replenish the fund and make money available for new loans. Several factors work to erode the capital value of revolving funds over time, however, including inflation, low-interest loans, and managerial and overhead expenses. Late payments and the possibility of default also can diminish the long-run viability of revolving funds. Although the impact of a program can be stretched by using revolving funds, the immediate impact is lessened if the money is loaned rather than immediately spent. Thus, there is a trade-off between a larger immediate impact and a smaller but long-term impact.

The present value of expenditures from a revolving fund will be the same whether the money is loaned at market rates, used to make low-interest loans, or given away as grants. The establishment of a revolving fund simply affects the timing of the benefits. But the establishment of a revolving fund also means setting up and administering a long-term program, so the rationale for any revolving fund must be that the benefits to the recipients of money from the fund outweigh the administrative costs involved in establishing and running the revolving fund.

RANDALL G. HOLCOMBE

BIBLIOGRAPHY

Blattner, Robert A., and Todd S. Davis, 1990. "The ABCs of SRFs." *Civil Engineering,* vol. 60 (December):54–56.
Comptroller General of the United States, 1977. "Revolving Funds: Full Disclosure Needed for Better Congressional Control." Washington, D.C.: U.S. GPO.
Graham, William D., Paul L. Shinn, and John E. Petersen, 1989. "State Revolving Funds Under Tax Reform." Council of Infrastructure Financing Authorities Monograph No. 2.
Holcombe, Randall G., 1992. "Revolving Fund Finance: The Case of Wastewater Treatment." *Public Budgeting and Finance,* vol. 12, no. 3 (Fall):50–65.
United States Environmental Protection Agency, 1991. "State Revolving Fund (SRF) Final Report to Congress." Washington, D.C.: U.S. GPO.
United States Senate, 1990. "Report to Accompany S.2184, Small Communities Infrastructure Assistance Act of 1990. Washington, D.C.: U.S. GPO.

RIGGS, FRED W. (1917–).

One of the most creative theorists in twentieth century public administration who helped to shape the study of comparative public administration at a time when Western nations were seeking to export their administrative systems to developing countries. Riggs advanced an ecological theory that showed how local conditions fundamentally affect the operation of modern structures, such as bureaus. His "prismatic" theory provided scholars and practitioners with a full-blown alternative to the conventional picture of a modern polity as seen from the West. Throughout his career, he has sought to break down the ethnocentric quality of political and administrative thought, which has been dominated by U.S. writers and the American experience.

Riggs was born in Kuling, China, in 1917. His parents were American missionaries who went to China in 1916 to help local peasants improve their farming methods. American agricultural technologies were not suitable, given conditions prevailing in China at that time. Riggs's father had to develop a new approach in order to promote agricultural improvement, one based on local conditions and tools. The experience strongly impressed the young Riggs and provided much of the inspiration for his later work.

In 1935 Riggs came to the United States to study journalism and political science at the University of Illinois, hoping eventually to become a foreign correspondent. He graduated in 1938, having abandoned his journalistic ambitions for an academic career in international relations. In 1941 he received a master's degree from the Fletcher School of Law and Diplomacy. Following wartime public service assignments, he received a doctorate in political science, with a specialization in international relations, from Columbia University in 1948. His dissertation (published as a book in 1950) dealt with the repeal of the Chinese Exclusion Acts. The dissertation introduced Riggs to the important role played by administrative agencies in shaping public policy.

Although Riggs had not taken any formal coursework in public administration as a graduate student, he found himself increasingly drawn to issues of administrative politics. In 1951 he took a position as assistant to the director of the Public Administration Clearing House in New York, where he explored the challenges of public administration in developing countries. As a visiting professor at Yale University in the years 1955–1956, he team-taught one of the first graduate seminars on comparative public administration. In 1956, in the May issue of the *Annals of the American Academy of Political and Social Science,* he published an article criticizing economic development experts for neglecting the role of public administration in their efforts to modernize newly emerging nations.

In 1956 Riggs joined the faculty of the Government Department at Indiana University. Seeking to further understand public administration from a non-Western point of view, he accepted an appointment as a visiting scholar in Thailand for the following year. Riggs immersed himself in a study of government programs affecting rice, observing the paradoxical nature of public administration at work. He continued his field studies in the years 1958–1959 as a

visiting professor at the Institute of Public Administration in the Philippines. On the return journey to the United States, he stopped at the Indian Institute of Public Administration and delivered several lectures on "The Ecology of Public Administration."

Riggs's ecological theory spread quickly among people studying comparative administration, often through non-Western outlets. An article on a key feature of his prismatic model, "The Bazaar-Canteen Model," appeared in the July-October 1958 issue of the *Philippine Sociological Review,* before his return to the United States. "Prismatic Society and Financial Administration" appeared in the June 1960 issue of *Administrative Science Quarterly.*

The Indian Institute of Public Administration published his lectures in *The Ecology of Public Administration* in 1961. Riggs followed with *Administration in Developing Countries: The Theory of Prismatic Society* (1964) and *Thailand: The Modernization of a Bureaucratic Policy* (1966).

Shortly after his return to the University of Indiana in 1959, Riggs became chair of the newly formed Comparative Administration Group (CAG), an offshoot of the American Society for Public Administration. He held the position from 1960 to 1971. The gathering provided a forum for intellectuals trying to make sense out of the degree to which administration overseas diverged so widely from what was thought to be conventional models. CAG helped to spread the comparative perspective among what had previously been a field of study focused on the American experience. In 1971 Riggs contributed *Frontiers of Development Administration,* which he edited, to the list of CAG-sponsored publications.

To provide more time for writing, Riggs took an appointment as a visiting scholar at the Massachusetts Institute of Technology in 1965. The following year, he worked at the Center for Advanced Study in the Behavioral Sciences at Stanford University. In 1967 he settled at the University of Hawaii, where he remained through his emeritus appointment in 1987.

In seeking to explain the simultaneous modern and traditional features of government in non-Western countries, Riggs drew upon concepts found in structural functional analysis, an approach popular among social scientists at that time. All societies must perform common functions, from rulemaking to providing for the dead. Societies perform these functions through a bewildering array of structures, which differ from country to country. In a traditional society, people rely upon a relatively limited number of structures to perform many functions. To use an analogy from the science of optics, the structures are fused. In industrialized societies, structures are differentiated and specialized. As traditional societies undergo modernization, new structures are superimposed over traditional ones. The old structures, however, do not disappear. The new structures are laid over them.

Riggs employed the analogy of the prism to explain this phenomenon. When fused or white light passes through a prism, it diffracts into its constituent colors. Structures in the prismatic society contain elements of both. Like light trapped in a prism, the structures are simultaneously fused and diffracted. Modern structures such as banks and specialized government bureaus appear in the prismatic society, but they do not operate in the same manner as their counterparts in fully industrialized countries. People in the society cannot rely upon new structures to achieve the level of integration necessary to carry out cooperative affairs. As a consequence, people turn to the traditional structures and values as a means to complete the necessary functions. The old structures and values remain submerged, however, as the secret but effective operational codes. The new structures do not work as intended. They are observed only in a formalistic way, being set aside when real work has to be done.

The prismatic state, Riggs pointed out, was not synonymous with the process of modernization. Modernization implies that a society is moving from a traditional to an industrialized state. Riggs worked hard to discourage the notion that prismatic society could be viewed solely as a temporary phase experienced by developing countries moving between polar extremes. Any society, even an industrialized one, can become prismatic if traditional norms intrude upon modern structures. In the monograph *Prismatic Society Revisited* (1973), Riggs presented the prismatic model as a social trap into which any country could fall. Where contradictory values and institutions coexist in a turbulent society, the characteristics of prismatic polities will tend to emerge.

It is impossible in a prismatic society to describe administrative and economic activities using Western words. Western terminology cannot capture the subtlety of activities so far transformed. The concept of *bureau* in a prismatic society, for example, has an entirely different meaning than in such Western countries as France or the United States. Consequently, Riggs invented a new vocabulary to describe the economic, political, and administrative operations of the prismatic world. This rich and often perplexing vocabulary was one of Riggs's more creative contributions to comparative administrative studies.

Riggs used the word *sala* to characterize government bureaus in a prismatic state. Sala is a Spanish word that describes a room in one's home where business with outsiders is transacted, simultaneously satisfying both personal and official functions. He characterized economic activities as a *bazaar-canteen* in which prices are based on the reciprocal power of the trading partners as well as the more impersonal pressures of supply and demand. In bazaars, prices fluctuate as people strike bargains based on their status, negotiating skill, and ability to deceive. In a canteen, special privileges are institutionalized for a select few such as powerful military and civil officials.

Western interest groups reappear in prismatic societies as *clects,* a combination of the words clique and sect. *Clects* resemble associations in Western countries, but behave like traditional families or clans. Membership is restricted to persons sharing a common religious, racial, or linguistic background. Formal goals are specific but mask the widely diverse functions actually performed.

Prismatic societies exhibit a high degree of *formalism.* Things are not as they appear to be. Modern rules and structures are created, but they do not work as they would in the West. Prismatic societies often suffer under the weight of excessive bureaucracy. Rather than treat super-fluous bureaucracy as an obstacle to the proper functioning of the state, Riggs points out in anthropological fashion that excessive rules actually satisfy local needs. Rules are so complex that official business can be conducted only by suspending them. This enlarges the power and discretion that bureaucrats enjoy and allows them to return to the traditional practices that the new rules disallow. Local officials adopt complex rules confident in the knowledge that they will not be strictly enforced.

Work on the prismatic theory encouraged Riggs to branch out into related fields. Problems encountered with the terminology of the prismatic model led him to examine the whole area of social science communication, where he sought to develop materials that would promote a more consistent and precise vocabulary. His interest in comparative studies drew him to examine why the presidential system of government, so persistent in the United States, broke down so catastrophically in other societies. In characteristic fashion, he returned to ecological explanations, including those arising from the nature of the public bureaucracy. His comparative analysis explained how apparently undemocratic features of the American bureaucracy, like the fondness for forming subsystems, help to preserve the presidential system of government.

This line of inquiry pointed up what many overseas already suspected: American public administration is the product of very unique political and historical circumstances, severely restricting its applicability to other countries. More recently, Riggs has investigated the degree to which democratic institutions and enhanced administrative capabilities can stem the tendency toward violent breakdowns within multicultural nations.

HOWARD E. MCCURDY

BIBLIOGRAPHY

Works by Fred W. Riggs

1956. "Public Administration: A Neglected Factor in Economic Development." *Annals of the American Academy of Political and Social Science* 305 (May): 70–80.

1961. *The Ecology of Public Administration.* Bombay: Asia Publishing House.
1964. *Administration in Developing Countries: The Theory of Prismatic Society.* Boston: Houghton Mifflin.
1966. *Thailand: The Modernization of a Bureaucratic Polity.* Honolulu: East-West Center Press.
1971. ed., *Frontiers of Development Administration.* Durham, NC: Duke University Press.
1973. *Prismatic Society Revisited* Morristown. NJ: General Learning Press.
1976. "The Group and the Movement: Notes on Comparative and Development Administration." *Public Administration Review* 36 (November-December): 648–654.
1994. "Bureaucracy and the Constitution." *Public Administration Review* 54 (January-February): 65–72.
1994a. "Bureaucracy: A Profound Puzzle for Presidentialism." In Ali Farazmand, ed., *Handbook of Bureaucracy.* New York: Marcel Dekker.

Other Works

Ramesh K. Arora, ed., 1992. *Politics and Administration in Changing Societies: Essays in Honour of Professor Fred W. Riggs.* New Delhi: Associated Publishing House.

RIGHT TO DIE. The assertion of the privilege of an ill person, whose prognosis for recovery is nil, to choose (via self or by proxy) the timing and circumstances of his or her own death. Public policy issues associated with the right to die usually address the right to discontinue technological preservation of bodily function by mechanical or pharmacological means. In recent years, the right to ask for medical assistance with suicide when suffering from an incapacitating or terminal illness has come to be considered a right to die issue as well.

These issues have evolved from the concern of citizens about the quality and impact of the circumstances of dying. Where a person lives greatly impacts this issue. The cultural, social, economic, and political context of a nation not only determines the quality of life and of death but also defines the kinds of moral problems that are considered important. This entry will focus on right to die issues in the United States and other developed Western countries.

Questions about the value of human life and definition of death are at the core of public policy that addresses right-to-die issues. Issues of dying and the right to die are discussed and studied in various disciplines including ethics, law, religion, medicine, nursing, psychology, philosophy, and economics. Some philosophers and ethicists have claimed that the concept of "choice of the circumstances of one's death" as a "right" is, in itself, controversial, that is, that to die is not a right. Alan Meisel (1989) has stated that right to die springs from concerns for human dignity, self-determination, and unwanted infringement on bodily integrity. In Western culture, on one hand, the right to make one's own choices about personal matters is held in high regard. On the other hand, individual and collective cultural, religious, and moral views about death and dying differ. Some persons may believe that life must be preserved at all costs and that any act contributing to the onset of death is morally reprehensible. In contrast, others may believe that passive euthanasia or allowing death to occur in hopeless circumstances by withdrawal of drugs and medical equipment is appropriate. Some persons feel that one person (physician or not) cannot be countenanced to kill, even on request, and other individuals may hold the opinion that part of a physician's mission is to assist a dying patient to a peaceful death. The latter is referred to as active euthanasia or physician-assisted suicide. Conflicting social, ethical, and legal pressures will always be a part of policymaking in regard to right-to-die issues.

Historical Aspects

In nations with fully developed provision of medical care, the quality of dying has changed greatly over the past 50 years. Since the early 1940s and the discovery of antibiotics, infectious diseases are a less-common cause of death in persons dying in developed countries. Most deaths are due to chronic disease or accident. In the United States, approximately 2.2 million persons die every year; 85 percent of (U.S.) deaths are related to chronic illness. Persons who have chronic illness and receive modern medical care live much longer than they once did; however, because of increasing disability, they may come to question the quality of their lives and the extension of their sometimes painful or undignified life experience. These circumstances may lead a person to ask a health care provider to prescribe a treatment that brings on or hastens death.

Until the mid-1960s people died when they "ceased to breathe." Then, with the advent of technology to support vital functions such as breathing, the quality and circumstance of dying changed rapidly. In the United States over 80 percent of deaths occur in health care facilities. At this point, with the use of life-preserving equipment and medications, bodily function can be sustained for decades. Policy issues have evolved both from claims for protection of life, in other words, continuation of life-support; and from claims that prolonged maintenance on life-support equipment may prevent a peaceful death, create loss of human dignity, and prolong suffering.

Thus, two factors, (1) the ability of modern medicine to sustain life over long periods of time, and (2) the lengthy debilitative process experienced by many persons who die slowly of chronic illness have brought about radical changes and proposed changes in public policy addressing death and the right to die.

Definition of Death

One focus of the controversy has been "What is death?" In 1968, Clarence Nicks was severely beaten and admitted to a hospital in a comatose state. He had stopped breathing and electrical evaluation of his brain indicated that his brain waves were flat (absence of brain function). His heart was still beating, and he was placed on a respirator to maintain breathing function. He was pronounced dead by one physician, but another disagreed. Nevertheless, his heart was removed and transplanted to another patient. Subsequently, the attorney for those accused of beating Nicks claimed that his clients could not be charged with murder because it was the removal of his heart that killed the patient, not the beating.

Cases such as Nick's have initiated numerous laws and policies to define when death has occurred. Whether the definition of death should be a legal or medical one remains under debate. Currently, most developed countries use guidelines such as those developed in the California Natural Death Act of 1976 and by the President's Commission for the Study of Ethical Problems in Medicine and Biomedical and Behavioral Research in 1981. These guidelines direct that an individual is dead who sustains irreversible cessation of respiratory or circulatory function, or cessation of all functions of the entire brain, including the part of the brain that maintains vital functions (such as breathing), called the brain stem. The use of criteria indicating that the whole brain must be nonfunctioning has been criticized; recently, some ethicists and physicians have suggested that death be defined as loss of higher brain function in the cerebral cortex. This is the part of the brain that provides intellectual power, voluntary movement, perception, awareness, emotions, and personality.

Right to Forgo Treatment

In the United States, right-to-die legislation is part of the body of tort, constitutional, and criminal law that governs the manner in which decisions about medical treatment must be made. Federal and state courts have the duty to protect and preserve human life. Decisions about withdrawal of treatment have been based on the common law right to freedom from unwanted interferences with bodily integrity or peace of mind, or the constitutional right to privacy. The right of the patient or an established proxy to consent to or to refuse medical treatment is considered fundamental and serves as a guide to treatment in most clinical situations.

Most U.S. states have passed laws providing for the establishment of advance directives or living wills or health care power of attorney. These are formal documents describing the individual's preferences for life-sustaining treatment and/or designating who should make such decisions if he or she should become incompetent. In 1990 Congress passed the Patient Self-Determination Act (Omnibus Reconciliation Act) requiring most health care facilities to supply patients with literature describing their rights to refuse treatment and complete advance directives.

Most of the cases that have come to litigation involve patients who cannot speak for themselves and have left no written prior direction. Additionally, many of the cases involving withdrawal of life support concern patients who are in an irreversible deep coma or vegetative state. These patients do not qualify as dead by the whole brain criteria previously noted, but, in most cases, they would be considered dead if the higher brain criteria were employed.

The first legal cases of importance in the United States dealt with the withdrawal of life-supporting equipment or feeding tubes from individuals who were in a vegetative state, having left no clearly written direction regarding their wishes for end-to-life treatment. The first case involved Karen Quinlan, a young woman from New Jersey who sustained irreversible brain damage and was in a vegetative state. In 1976, the New Jersey court drew from prior federal constitutional precedents dealing with reproductive rights and control of one's own body to provide a decision to allow withdrawal of life support equipment from Quinlan based on the right to privacy.

A year later, in the Saikewicz case, and in 1990, in the Cruzan case, state courts laid the groundwork for use of the substituted judgment standard. This standard dictates that those representing the ill person, or surrogate decisionmakers, should make decisions about life support based on what the patient would have wanted if he or she could speak for him- or herself. For example, in the Nancy Cruzan case, judges required that witnesses describe specific clear prior incidence of Cruzan's solemn indication that she would not have desired to continue life in a vegetative state. In ruling on the Cruzan case, the U.S. Supreme Court indicated that the right to refuse treatment was constitutionally protected and the use of artificial nutrition and hydration was no different from other medical interventions.

The factors that influence consideration of the right to die by forgoing life support vary with geographic, economic, religious, social, and political differences. Several examples follow.

In China, the influence of Confucian tradition is strong. According to this tradition, if a daughter or son agrees to an ill or dying parent's refusal of medical treatment, this is a violation of "filial piety" and results in public shame. Legal considerations have not influenced such decisions because, since 1950, the Chinese courts and lawyers have been prohibited from involvement in medical matters based on grounds that they have inadequate medical knowledge (Qui 1987). In Germany, use of respi-

rators and feeding tubes are considered usual treatment, and forgoing medical treatment at the patient's request parallels policy in the United States. Historical factors related to the World War II and heinous war crimes carried out by the Third Reich have effected a very conservative position concerning euthanasia (Koch and Ulshoefer 1987). In Italy, traditionally consistent with Roman Catholic religious teaching, most physicians tend to sustain life at all costs (Mori 1987).

In England, which has been strongly influenced by a socialized medical system, decisions about forgoing life support involve consideration of expected quality of life as well as availability of resources. The physician is under no obligation to institute treatment that is not beneficial to the patient. End-of-life treatment is guided by English common law, which bases acceptability on whatever is common practice in the medical community (Nicholson 1987). In Canada, weighing the burdens of a clinical intervention against the benefits is referred to as the proportionality rule; physicians are not required to administer treatments that are of no benefit to the patient (Roy and Williams 1987).

Physician-Assisted Suicide

Physician-assisted suicide, or active euthanasia, refers to the physician taking active steps to prescribe for a mentally competent dying person, at his or her request, a lethal dosage of drugs to hasten death. The taking of another's life, regardless of motive, is virtually always considered criminal homicide. The modern movement to legally permit actively bringing on death started in England in the 1930s with the formation of the Voluntary Euthanasia Society and in the United States with the Society for the Right to Die (later called Choice in Dying, Inc.) and the National Hemlock Society, based in Eugene, Oregon. Similar societies formed in the Netherlands and Australia in the 1970s.

In the United States, consideration of the right to privacy supports the forgoing of medical treatment in cases of terminal illness, but assisting with suicide is a crime. Since the late 1980s, laws against assisted suicide in the state of Michigan have been challenged by a retired physician, Jack Kevorkian, who at the date of this writing has assisted over 40 ill persons to die. In 1991 in the state of Washington and in 1992 in California, voters rejected (by a 54-to-46 majority in both states) proposed changes in state law to legalize physician-assisted suicide.

Technically, assisted suicide is also illegal in the Netherlands; however, euthanasia guidelines have been established by common consensus. The Dutch Reformed Church does not obstruct the voluntary ending of life when life is intolerable. Established guidelines specify what conditions must be met in order to proceed with active euthanasia; these include intolerable and irreversible pain, clear and convincing evidence of repeated consideration, consultation of two physicians, and implementation by a qualified physician. Adherence to the guidelines are carefully regulated. Sleep is induced, and then the patient is given a paralyzing drug. Within the population of 14.5 to 15 million, approximately 2,000 to 3,000 active euthanasias occur each year in the Netherlands. That number represents 1 to 2 percent of deaths.

In the United States the issue of the acceptability of physician-assisted suicide continues to be openly debated. The outcomes of this debate have included attention to the very difficult situations faced by chronically ill, debilitated persons and reevaluation of the treatment of terminally ill patients, particularly efforts to control pain. Consensus on right-to-die issues is unlikely; individual and group moral, cultural, and religious views vary widely. The rapidity of technological advance has exceeded the ability of society to alter value systems. Change does occur, however, as described in the preceding paragraphs, through dialogue, evolving public policy, and the law.

VALERIE SWIGART

BIBLIOGRAPHY

American Medical Association Council on Ethical and Judicial Affairs, 1992. "Decisions Near the End of Life." *Journal of the American Medical Association*, vol. 267, no. 16:2229–2233.

Berger, Arthur A., and Joyce Berger, 1990. *To Die or Not to Die: Cross-Disciplinary, Cultural and Legal Perspectives on the Right to Choose Death.* New York: Praeger.

Burnell, George, 1993. *Final Choices: To Live or Die in the Age of Medical Technology.* New York: Plenum Press.

California Natural Death Act, 1976. Chapter 1439, Cal. Health and Safety Code, sections 7185–7195.

Cruzan v. Directors, Missouri Department of Health, 1990. 497 U.S. 261.

Cruzan v. Harmon, 1988. 760 Mo. S.W.2d. 408, 411.

Jecker, Nancy, 1994. "Physician-Assisted Death in the Netherlands and United States: Ethical and Cultural Aspects of Health Policy Development." *Journal of the American Geriatrics Society,* vol. 42, no. 6:672–678.

Kamisar, Yale, 1991. "When Is There a Constitutional 'Right to Die'? When Is There No Constitutional Right to Live?" *Georgia Law Review,* vol. 25:11203–11242.

Kass, Leon, 1993. "Is There a Right to Die?" *Hastings Center Report,* vol. 23, no. 1:34–43.

Koch, Hans-George, and Tatjana Ulshoefer, 1987. "Commentary–Biomedical Ethics: A Multinational View." *Hastings Center Report* (June), Special Supplement (hereafter Spec. Sup.):24–25.

Meisel, Alan, 1989. *The Right to Die.* New York: Wiley and Sons.

Mori, Maurizio, 1987. "Commentary–Biomedical Ethics: A Multinational View." *Hastings Center Report* (June), Spec. Sup.: 34–36.

Nicholson, Richard, 1987. "Commentary–Biomedical Ethics: A Multinational View." *Hastings Center Report* (June), Spec. Sup.:23–24.

Omnibus Budget Reconciliation Act of 1990, P.L. 101–508, secs. 4206 and 4751.

President's Commission for the Study of Ethical Problems in Medicine and Biomedical Behavioral Research, 1981. *Report on the Medical Legal and Ethical Issues in the Determination of Death.* Washington, DC: GPO.

———, 1983. *Deciding to Forego Life-Sustaining Treatment.* Washington, DC: GPO.

Qui, Ren-Zong, 1987. "Commentary–Biomedical Ethics: A Multinational View." *Hastings Center Report* (June), Spec. Sup.: 25–26.

Quinlan, 1976. 70 NJ 10, 355 A.2d 647.

Roy, David, and June Williams, 1987. "Commentary-Biomedical Ethics: A Multinational View." *Hastings Center Report,* (June), Spec. Sup.:32–34.

Superintendent of Belchertown vs. Saiekwicz, 1977, 373 Mass. 728, 370 N.E. 2d 417.

Veatch, Robert, 1989. *Death, Dying, and the Biological Revolution: Our Last Quest for Responsibility.* New Haven, CT: Yale University Press.

———, 1993. "The Impending Collapse of the Whole Brian Definition of Death." *Hastings Center Report,* vol. 23, no. 4:18–24.

RIGHT TO PRIVACY. Although not specifically mentioned anywhere in the Constitution, privacy has evolved into a recognized, constitutionally protected right. One of the earliest definitions of privacy comes from Justice Louis Brandeis in his dissenting opinion in the U.S. Supreme Court decision in *Olmstead v. United States* (1928). He referred to the right to privacy as the right to be "left alone" and called it "the most comprehensive of rights and the right most valued by civilized men." In the Supreme Court's decision in *Skinner v. Oklahoma* (1942), a compulsory sterilization law applicable to certain classes of criminals was struck down as an infringement on their fundamental rights of marriage and procreation (not mentioned in the Constitution). This decision was a precursor to future court decisions involving the right to privacy.

One of the earliest articulations of the right to privacy as a constitutionally protected right is in the majority opinion of Justice William Douglas in the U.S. Supreme Court decision in *Griswold v. Connecticut* (1965). In this case, the Court was asked to decide whether the state of Connecticut could criminally prosecute those who used contraceptives or who counseled or assisted others in doing so. The Court held that the law interfered with the *fundamental right to privacy* (here, the intimate relation of husband and wife), which is derived from the First, Fourth, and the Fifth Amendments in the Bill of Rights (in other words, the freedom of association, and the right to be secure against unreasonable searches and seizures). In this decision, the Court said that the fact that the term "privacy" is not specifically mentioned in the Constitution does not mean that privacy is not protected.

After the *Griswold* decision, the Supreme Court expanded upon the right to privacy in two decisions. In *Eisenstad v. Baird* (1972), the right to privacy was expanded to the "right of the individual, married or single, to be free from unwarranted government intrusion into matters so fundamentally affecting a person as the decision whether to beget a child." This decision clearly elevates the right to privacy to a fundamental right that the government can only infringe upon if it has a *compelling* interest and the law is *narrowly* drawn to protect that compelling interest—at least as to matters relating to procreation. The Court's decision in *Roe v. Wade* extended the fundamental right of privacy to encompass a woman's decision whether to terminate a pregnancy.

Although there have been restrictions placed on the right to terminate a pregnancy in cases decided since *Roe versus Wade* (such as requiring parental consent for minors, requiring a waiting period, etc.), the right articulated by *Roe* has been reaffirmed many times over, most recently by the Supreme Court in *Planned Parenthood v. Casey* (1992).

In a more general context, separate from the right to procreation, the Supreme Court has ruled that the right of an individual or corporation to withhold him- or herself and his or her property from public scrutiny exists only to the extent consistent with the law or public policy. In a case in which public policy requires compensation, and if there is no monetary compensation established by law, then courts will grant another type of compensation that will restore the status quo *(Federal Trade Commission v. American Tobacco Company*, 1924). In addition, the less intrusive a governmental intervention is on the right to privacy, the lesser the burden on the government to justify the intrusion. That is, for only minimally intrusive actions, the government only has to show a rational relationship between the intrusion and a governmental interest.

Another aspect of the right to privacy involves the "fair" use of personal information maintained by federal agencies on U.S. citizens. The Privacy Act of 1974 (Public Law 93–57a) was passed to address the need to safeguard individuals' private records in their dealings with the federal government.

The Privacy Act seeks to prevent the misuse of personal information by federal agencies by providing for individual access to this information and to prevent the transfer of personal information records to other federal agencies for nonroutine uses. The act also provides for civil and criminal lawsuits by individuals whose personal records have been used in violation of the Privacy Act.

ROBERT A. CROPF

BIBLIOGRAPHY

Black's Law Dictionary, 1994. ("Right of Privacy" entry.) St. Paul, MN: West.

Shafritz, Jay M., 1985, "Privacy Act of 1974." In *Facts on File Dictionary of Public Administration*. New York: Facts on File.

RIGHT-TO-WORK LAW.   State laws, authorized by Section 14(b) of the Taft-Hartley Act of 1947, that prohibit collective bargaining, contractual provision, and other arrangements from requiring compulsory union membership as a condition of employment (union shop, closed shop, maintenance of membership, agency shop, preferential hiring). The relevant language of Section 14(b) is: "Nothing in this Act shall be construed as authorizing the execution or application of agreements requiring membership in a labor organization as a condition of employment in any state or Territory in which such execution or application is prohibited by state or Territorial law."

This provision was a congressional reaction to a series of strikes in 1946. It affirms the First Amendment right of freedom of association. The reasoning is that unions are private, voluntary organizations in which membership should be the result of conscious choice of the worker. An individual forced by a union security provision to join a labor organization constitutes a violation of free association. It has also been argued that union security measures corrupt the merit principle, since public employees should be hired on the basis of qualification for the job rather than membership in an organization.

Twenty states have adopted the right-to-work provision through statute or constitutional provision, thereby making compulsory union membership illegal. Most are situated in the Sunbelt or Rocky Mountain area, where support for labor unions is weak. Ten are found in states of the old Confederacy. Right-to-work laws may hinder union growth, financial security, and effectiveness through depressing the number of dues-paying members and encouraging free riders, but some studies indicate that these laws merely reflect underlying antiunion sentiment and have little or no effect on union strength.

If a bargaining unit member does join a union in a right-to-work state, he or she must abide by union by-laws, pay dues, and meet other membership requirements, or face expulsion from the union. But he or she cannot be discharged from the job for failure to pay union dues, because Section 14(b) prohibits making employment contingent upon payment of dues or initiation fees.

Under Title VII of the Civil Service Reform Act of 1978, federal employees are effectively granted the right to work. This federal statute does not permit any union security provisions in federal collective bargaining contracts. The twenty right-to-work states are as follows:

Alabama	Nevada
Arizona	North Carolina
Arkansas	North Dakota

Georgia	South Carolina
Idaho	South Dakota
Iowa	Tennessee
Kansas	Texas
Louisiana	Utah
Mississippi	Virginia and
Nebraska	Wyoming.

RICHARD C. KEARNEY

RIPENESS PRINCIPLE. A legal doctrine employed by judges to justify accepting or rejecting cases that are ripe or not ripe for review. *Ripeness* implies what one would think it implies. When a contested agency determination is ripe, it is mature enough to be ready for judicial review (see **judicial review**). Just as apples need to ripen before they are edible, disputes with administrative agencies need to ripen before the courts will hear them. If the court perceives a controversy as green, it will regard the controversy as premature and deny review until it reaches maturity. In this regard, then, the ripeness principle is very much a matter of common sense (*Seafarers International Union v. United States Coast Guard*, 736 F.2d 19 [2d Cir., 1984]).

But when does a challenged agency action become ripe enough for review? Of course, to be ripe, a controversy must satisfy several basic legal tests. That is, a petitioner must have a legitimate justiciable dispute, must have exhausted all available administrative remedies (see **doctrine of exhaustion**), must have satisfied the primary jurisdiction requirements (see **primary jurisdiction**), and must have passed the test for standing. The ripeness test is a broad test that goes beyond specific reviewability tests to discover whether the case is totally ripe.

Because of the general nature of the ripeness principle, it is frequently confused with other more specific tests, particularly with standing and exhaustion tests. Although standing and exhaustion tests ask specific questions, ripeness poses the broad question: What general role should the court play in light of this case? In general, is this the type of controversy that the court should decide? Kenneth C. Davis's classic distinction between exhaustion and ripeness helps to convey the point: "Both the requirements of ripeness and the requirement of exhaustion of administrative remedies are concerned with the timing of judicial review of administrative action, but the ripeness focus is upon the nature of the judicial process—upon the types of functions that courts should perform, and the exhaustion focus is upon the relatively narrow question whether a party should be required to pursue an administrative remedy before going to court" (1977, p. 147).

The ripeness principle also serves a dual purpose, as do the doctrines just discussed. That is, the ripeness principle functions to protect the administrative process from undue interference by the courts, as well as to protect the courts from having to hear controversies that they were not designed to decide. In *Abbott Laboratories v. Gardner* (387 U.S. 136, 148 [1967]), the Supreme Court asserted that the primary purpose of ripeness "is to protect the courts, through avoidance of premature adjudication, from entangling themselves in abstract disagreements over administrative policies, and also to protect the agencies (see **agency**) from judicial interference until an administrative decision has been formalized and its effects felt in a concrete way by the challenging parties."

Davis has written that "the basic principle of ripeness is easy to state: Judicial machinery should be conserved for problems which are real and present or imminent, not squandered on problems which are abstract or hypothetical or remote" (1977, p. 147).

When the courts test for ripeness, they want to discover, essentially, whether an agency action has had an adverse effect on the petitioner. Bernard Schwartz explains: "The tests of ripeness are adverse effect, concreteness, and imminence. Whether an agency act is sufficiently ripe for review depends primarily upon the effect of the act. If an agency act does have adverse effect upon the person or property of private individuals, then it should be reviewable at the instance of such persons. If, on the other hand, it is only a preliminary or procedural measure, which does not of itself have impact upon them, review should be denied" (1991, p. 563).

Employing these tests for ripeness, the Supreme Court in *Thomas v. Union Carbide Agricultural Products Company* (105 S.Ct. 3325 [1985]), decided that the particular dispute in question indeed constituted a case in controversy that could only be resolved by the exercise of judicial powers, as authorized by Article 3 of the Constitution, thus making the case ripe for review (at 3332–3333).

Justice Sandra Day O'Connor, speaking for the Court, concluded that because possible injury could occur to Union Carbide Agricultural Products Company and other pesticide chemical manufacturers because the constitutionality of a certain arbitration scheme used by the Environmental Protection Agency under the Federal Insecticide, Fungicide, and Rodenticide Act was in question, the Court could provide "preventive relief" (at 3333).

As long as all means of appeal have been exhausted, it is not difficult for the courts to determine whether a case is ripe if an administrative agency simply orders a party to act or not to act in a particular manner. It is also easy to see that when a welfare agency makes a final decision to deny a person a welfare benefits claim, the dispute is ripe for review (as long as statutes do not preclude review).

Schwartz has noted that cases are clearly ripe for review when decisions (for example, orders or directives) have an immediate impact upon a particular person's "rights and obligations": "Their adverse effect makes them ripe as soon as they are issued, unless there are further administrative remedies to be exhausted" (Schwartz 1991, p. 563).

Problems emerge in judging whether a case is ripe, however, when contested general agency directives are issued that are not aimed at specific parties. The Supreme Court struggled with this problem in the *Abbott Laboratories* case. When the Food and Drug Administration issued a regulation that required all drug labels to carry particular information, the drug manufacturer brought suit, arguing that the commission had exceeded its authority.

The government argued that the case was not yet ripe for review since the regulation had not been enforced, and, therefore, the impact of the regulation upon the industry was impossible to assess. But the Supreme Court held the government's "preenforcement" argument to be unreasonable because the regulation created an immediate and obvious hardship on the drug manufacturers, thus making the case ripe for review. Specifically, the hardship was that the drug manufacturers had to comply with the directive or risk prosecution and costly penalties for noncompliance.

However, in 1993, a more conservative Supreme Court in *Reno v. Catholic Social Services* (113 S.Ct. 2485) apparently restricted its decision in *Abbott Laboratories* by arguing that a "benefit-conferring" rule by an administrative agency is not ripe for review until the petitioner actually has applied for the benefit and is rejected. Under *Abbott Laboratories,* the benefit-conferring rule could actually be challenged as to its fairness or legality before the challenger actually applied for the benefit. Bernard Schwartz believes that the Supreme Court's ruling on ripeness in *Catholic Social Services* will unfortunately now "require an untold number of plaintiffs to make unnecessary expenditures of time and money before they can obtain decisions on the validity of rules that may directly affect them" (1994, p. 324).

KENNETH F. WARREN

BIBLIOGRAPHY

Davis, Kenneth C., 1977. *Administrative Law: Cases Text-Problems.* St. Paul, MN: West.
Schwartz, Bernard, 1991. *Administrative Law.* 3d ed. Boston: Little, Brown and Co.
———, 1994. "Administrative Law Cases During 1993." *Administrative Law Review,* vol. 46 (Summer).
Warren, Kenneth F., 1996. *Administrative Law in the Political System,* 3d ed. Upper Saddle River, NJ: Prentice-Hall.

RISK ASSESSMENT. An analysis of the impacts of chemicals in the environment on human health.

Risk is the chance that some threat or hazard will be realized. Risk threats involve the probability of human health hazards occurring from environmental exposure to a variety of chemicals that originate primarily from human activity.

The categories of risk and their measurement remain matters of both scientific and political disagreement. Risk assessors analyze the impacts of chemicals in the environment on human health. However, politics decides such questions as: Should there be zero tolerance or is some risk exposure acceptable? What is a significant or minimal level of risk? Was it reasonable regulation by government? How much certainty should be afforded to scientific or objective approaches for measurement of risk?

Risk management is a process aimed at achieving risk reduction, avoidance, or aversion through the use of risk assessment. Health and economic interests must be balanced and scientific conclusions must be weighed against political judgment. The political nature of risk assessment is inherently intertwined with the nature of scientific certainty in assessing acceptable levels of risk. Faced with uncertainty, scientific regulators often attempt to err on the side of safety, thus raising costs to regulated industries and the general public (who pay for regulations). Those who may disagree with the economics of risk regulation attack the objectivity of science and the standards and measurements used to devise regulations.

A scientific approach to risks necessarily attempts to avoid discussion of value positions until there is an objective estimation of the level and type of risk. This avoidance assumes that more subjective decisionmaking may follow in order to decide whether changes should be made in terms of bearing, avoiding, or changing the risk exposure—and who will pay. Many would argue that value-neutral science is a myth, however. Clashes, for example, over the siting of locally unwanted land uses (LULUs) often result from the differing views of the general public and of scientific experts and regulators who are not trusted by the public.

Traditional risk assessment and risk management in regulatory decisionmaking have been highly fragmented and separated. A chemical-by-chemical, risk-by-risk approach complicates the adoption of a comprehensive cross-media (e.g., air, land, water) approach, according to the national Commission on Risk Assessment and Risk Management (1996). In addition, risk assessors have long been cautioned to separate risk assessment from risk management so that there are no adverse consequences from an intrusion of policy considerations into interpretations of scientific information (Wilson 1996). Yet, such strict separation of risk assessment from policy formation may lead to information that is not useful for developing remedies. Objectivity is difficult to maintain in connecting risk assessment to risk management.

The old system is being replaced, however, with a standardized process that allows health hazards to be considered in a broader context. The new framework for developing risk assessment decisions is being promoted by the Commission on Risk Assessment and Risk Management. This framework engages a wide array of stakeholders and addresses the cumulative effects of various problems.

This more-integrated approach to risk assessment and management involves several steps: (1) formulating the problem in broad context; (2) analyzing the risks; (3) defining the options; (4) making sound decisions; (5) taking actions to implement the decisions; and (6) evaluating the effects of any actions taken. The new framework enables regulatory agencies to evaluate risks across media and pollutants to insure that they are treated consistently in all programs. The most dangerous hazards can be identified, and budget resources can be steered toward the greatest threats.

The integrated framework offers a comprehensive approach to environmental and public health problems, instead of a piecemeal, fragmented approach. The flexible framework promotes collaboration, communication, and negotiation in an open process among stakeholders so that public values can influence risk management policies. At any stage, new information can lead to changed conclusions and decisions and a reevaluation of the problem. An agency such as the U.S. Environmental Protection Agency could review hazardous air pollutants in the context of risks from other sources of air pollution, consider future land use at the beginning of a Superfund cleanup, and adopt a watershed management approach to evaluate water sources within a geographical area.

BEVERLY A. CIGLER

BIBLIOGRAPHY

Bushell, George E., Charles Mallory, and Tony K. S. Quon, 1995–1996. "Risk Analysis in a Policy Framework." *Journal of Public Sector Management,* vol. 26 (3): 17–28.
Commission on Risk Assessment and Risk Management, 1996. *Risk Assessment and Risk Management in Regulatory Decision-Making.* Washington, DC: U.S. GPO (draft).
Wilson, James D., 1996. "Connecting Risk Assessment to Risk Management: The Center's Risk Analysis Program," *Center for Risk Management Newsletter,* no. 9 (Winter): 2–4.
Zimmerman, Rae, 1990. *Governmental Management of Chemical Risk: Regulatory Processes for Environmental Health.* Chelsea, MI: Lewis Publishers.

ROOSEVELT, FRANKLIN DELANO (1882–1945).

The thirty-second president of the United States, who was responsible for the creation of the executive office of the President, one of the most important administrative reforms of the twentieth century. Historians generally rank him among the two or three most influential presidents in U.S. history, largely because of his role in forging the modern presidency.

Roosevelt was born at Hyde Park, New York, on January 30, 1882. His father, James Roosevelt, had remarried two years earlier at the age of 51 to the 26-year-old Sara Delano, the daughter of a successful sea merchant. Although he had tried his luck at business ventures, James Roosevelt was in fact a member of America's leisure class, the product of a well-established family fortune. By the time of his marriage, he had retired to his country estate at Hyde Park.

An only child, Franklin led a sheltered life. His parents did not enroll him in an organized school until he was 14. At Harvard University, where he received his undergraduate degree in 1903, he was distinguished more for his extracurricular activities than for his academics. Roosevelt attended Columbia University School of Law for only as long as was necessary to pass the New York bar examination.

In 1910 Democratic leaders persuaded Roosevelt to run for the New York state senate and represent the rural counties around his family's Hudson River estate. This was seen to be an apparently futile effort, but Roosevelt surprised party leaders by defeating the Republican incumbent. After supporting the reform candidacy of Democratic presidential nominee Woodrow Wilson in 1912, Roosevelt received an appointment as assistant secretary of the navy. This was traditionally a management job, and Roosevelt established a reputation as a person who could cut through red tape and bureaucratic procedures to mobilize the U.S. Navy for World War I. Roosevelt held the post for seven years.

From a list of available candidates, Democratic presidential nominee James M. Cox picked the young Roosevelt to run with him on the 1920 national ticket as his party's choice for vice president of the United States. The ticket lost in a Republican landslide. One year later, Roosevelt was stricken with a severe case of poliomyelitis while on vacation at the family retreat at Campobello Island, New Brunswick. Although he survived the disease, he never recovered the use of his legs.

During the 1920s Roosevelt sought to reorganize the Democratic Party in order to convert it into an effective national organization. Although it was not successful, the effort helped to maintain Roosevelt's national standing. In 1928, at the urging of New York governor and Democratic presidential nominee Alfred E. Smith, Roosevelt accepted his party's nomination for governor of New York. Smith went down to defeat, but Roosevelt triumphed by a margin of 26,000 votes.

Franklin Roosevelt, as governor, faced a Republican legislature and a medley of Democratic interests. Administrative reforms, such as the newly enacted executive budget and the governor's appointment powers, had to be maintained with political acumen. As he had done as assistant secretary of the navy, Roosevelt balanced administrative principles with political necessities. He was a popular governor, and he won reelection as governor in 1930 by a huge margin and become the presumptive nominee of his party for the 1932 presidential election.

Roosevelt served as president from 1933 until his death on April 12, 1945. He was the only president in the history of the republic to be elected four times. He forged a majority Democratic Party coalition, directed the creation of emergency agencies to combat the Great Depression, mobilized the nation for World War II, and presided over the grand alliance that won the war.

In the rush to create emergency agencies during Roosevelt's first term, little attention was given to the means by which they would be integrated into the permanent operations of the federal government. In part to correct this deficiency, Roosevelt in early 1936 created the President's Committee on Administrative Management. The committee, led by chairman Louis Brownlow, Luther Gulick, and Charles E. Merriam, with the assistance of a sizable staff, launched an extensive study of the federal executive branch. It urged Roosevelt to consolidate some 100 agencies under a few large departments reporting directly to the President and to expand the White House staff so that the President could effectively act as the general manager of the executive branch.

Consolidation proposals were defeated by Congress, which objected to the new philosophy of executive management on the grounds that it would give the President dictatorial powers.

In 1939, following the recommendations of his committee, Roosevelt established the executive office of the President by executive order. Beginning with the transfer of the Bureau of the Budget from the Treasury Department to the new executive office in 1939, the executive office grew into a vigorous staff organization with over 1,500 permanent and presidential employees. Establishment of the executive office provided the staff support necessary for the President to carry out newly created responsibilities and made possible the modern presidency.

The first test of Roosevelt's new executive office came quickly with the outbreak of World War II. Past history had convinced Roosevelt that he did not want to turn war mobilization over to the War Department, nor did he want Congress to interfere in the creation of every new activity. An inconspicuous clause deliberately inserted in the 1939 reorganization order allowed the President independently to create a whole series of emergency management agencies under the umbrella of the executive office of the President. Roosevelt and the White House staff used this authority to create war agencies and exercise much closer supervision over their activities than was previously possible.

Franklin Roosevelt was thoroughly acquainted with the progressive management theories of his day. (As assistant secretary of the navy he had been obliged to rule against the use of Frederick Taylor's time-and-motion studies in navy shipyards.) A keen student of agency culture and administrative politics, he understood the limits to which management theories could be pushed.

When the Brownlow Committee recommended the merger of all federal loan programs under the Treasury Department, Roosevelt vetoed the move. The "glass-eyed bankers in Treasury," Roosevelt reportedly observed, "will never make a loan to anybody."

Roosevelt favored a moderate degree of confusion in administrative affairs, allowing conflicting jurisdictions and multiheaded agencies where it suited his purposes. A certain amount of administrative confusion promoted competition, guarded against bureaucratic inertia, and helped to maintain the free flow of communication, especially to him. Roosevelt created a large number of wartime mobilization agencies, for example, but refused to give his Office of Emergency Management (part of the executive office of the President) the power centrally to coordinate them. The combination of formal administrative principles with respect for political necessities remains a hallmark of Roosevelt's administrative approach.

HOWARD E. McCURDY

BIBLIOGRAPHY

Brownlow, Louis, 1958. *A Passion for Anonymity.* Chicago: University of Chicago Press.
Burns, James MacGregor, 1956. *Roosevelt: The Lion and the Fox.* New York: Harcourt Brace.
———, 1970. *Roosevelt: The Soldier of Freedom.* New York: Harcourt Brace Jovanovich.

ROYAL COMMISSIONS. Committees appointed by royal warrant to advise on a specified subject in the United Kingdom and in certain commonwealth countries.

In the United Kingdom, royal commissions are set up under prerogative power; in contrast, in other countries the source of power for creating a royal commission is a statute. Although the Queen acts on the advice of her ministers, and royal commissions may differ little in this method of working from other advisory committees appointed by government (with which they are sometimes confused), royal commissions gain considerable prestige and influence from the way in which they are appointed and because they submit their reports directly to the Queen and Parliament, rather than to the government.

In the United Kingdom, the royal warrant is normally countersigned by the home secretary; it contains the commission's terms of reference and its authority to call for witnesses and information. In practice, the terms of reference usually take the form of a request to investigate a problem and to "make recommendations."

In contrast to royal commissions, departmental committees are appointed by the minister concerned with the object of the inquiry; he or she sends letters of appointment to the individual members, and, in the case of the chair, the letter is likely to contain guidance about how the inquiry should be conducted.

Although power to send for "persons and papers" is usually given in the royal warrant, there is no means of enforcing the power if the persons do not choose to attend and the papers are not forthcoming. As with other commissions and committees, there is no general rule about royal commissions sitting in public or in private, or deciding whether, how, and when to publish some or all of the evidence presented to the inquiry.

The prestige and status of a royal commission may evoke greater cooperation than a departmental committee, so it may in practice have greater authority, although it has no greater effective power. The status of an inquiry by royal commission may similarly be an added attraction to persons invited to serve on it. Recommended names for appointment are submitted to the Queen by the prime minister, who is in turn is advised by the relevant departmental minister, following consultation with other departments and the chief whip.

The chair is always appointed as such, and is not elected by the members from among themselves. Sometimes the chair, through being approached first, may influence the choice of other members, but there is no clear rule or convention about this. However, members are always informally approached before being formally appointed.

Members of royal commissions do not usually receive a salary, and, although they have received expenses, it is only recently that they have begun to receive some payment for time spent at meetings. Some may be seconded or given time off with pay by their employers to enable them to serve, but all members must expect to lose out in terms of both leisure and earnings opportunities. In comparison with other types of public service, however, it remains the case that, as H. McD. Clokie and J. William Robinson (1937) have commented: "The publicity, recognition, and influence which are accorded Royal Commissions undoubtedly keep up the supply of those willing and anxious to undertake these advisory duties" (p. 157). The work of royal commissions therefore depends on the willingness of members to serve in a spirit of disinterested public service (which is said to be noticeable even among persons with obvious interests in the outcome of an inquiry).

The selection of persons to serve on a royal commission is often an exercise in compromise seen from various perspectives. Most include people drawn from a variety of backgrounds in the academic world, industry, and public life, though they serve as individuals and not as representatives of organizations or professions.

It is usually at its first meeting that the commission discusses such matters as its terms of reference, how it will obtain evidence, whether it wishes to commission research, what public pronouncements it will make, and its program of meetings.

A significant role may be played by the secretary to a royal commission. Generally he or she, and any supporting staff, are drawn from within the department of government concerned with the subject being investigated; and sometimes he or she has been involved in preliminary work before members meet for the first time; but as secretary to the commission he or she acts under its direction. Almost always it is the secretary who prepares drafts of the report for the commission to discuss and approve; sometimes numerous drafts are prepared when topics of particular sensitivity are under continuing discussion.

Guidance for secretaries originates from a document prepared by Edward Bridges (head of the civil service from 1945 to 1956), based on his unique experience of serving as secretary to three royal commissions. The document he produced was of a basic factual type, covering (1) the advantages and disadvantages of using questionnaires and convening commission conferences, (2) guidance on matters of office routine, (3) hints on reporting verbatim evidence, (4) the importance of the members of the commission meeting informally as well as formally, and (5) managing the demands of the chair. In the United Kingdom the report of a royal commission is always published as a Command Paper, that is "Presented to Parliament by Command of Her Majesty"; departmental committees and other inquiries may report by other means, depending on the nature and status of the inquiry.

In the United Kingdom, royal commissions are now ad hoc, to investigate a particular problem and report (for example, the 1969 [Redcliffe-Maud] Royal Commission on Local Government), or *standing*, which means the commission is permanent and gives regular advice within a particular sphere of activity (for example, the Royal Commission on Environmental Pollution, which was established by royal warrant in 1970 and has published a series of reports on topics selected by it or referred to it by ministers).

In recent years, the number of new royal commissions, which have sometimes been criticized for being slow or being exercises in compromise, has declined in favor of quicker forms of inquiry, which are often of a less-independent nature. Departmental committees, parliamentary select committees, and independent or quasi-independent think tanks, such as institutes for policy research, all contribute to public policy making. The advantages of royal commissions, however, are their relative freedom from party political and interest group pressures, their practice of taking into account a very wide range of viewpoints, and their ability to pursue lines of inquiry in depth, and often in a more open manner which stimulates interest and debate on matters that might otherwise not receive such public interest.

RICHARD A. CHAPMAN

BIBLIOGRAPHY

Cartwright, T. J., 1975. *Royal Commissions and Departmental Committees in Britain.* London: Hodder and Stoughton.
Chapman, Richard A., ed., 1973. *The Role of Commissions in Policy Making.* London: Allen and Unwin.
Clokie H. McD., and J. William Robinson, 1937. *Royal Commissions of Inquiry: The Significance of Investigations in British Politics.* Stanford: Standford University Press.
Rhodes, Gerald, 1975. *Committees of Inquiry.* London: George Allen and Unwin.
Wheare, Kenneth C., 1955. *Government by Committee, An Essay on the British Constitution.* London: Oxford University Press.

RULE.
A binding statement of law or policy issued by an agency of government that establishes future rights, obligations, or procedures.

Rules profoundly influence the conduct and success of public administration in the United States. A good case can be made that rules are the most important products of government agencies. Rules give specific form and meaning to statutory provisions that are often broad, imprecise, and incomplete. In performing this function, rules establish both the benefits one can expect from government and the obligations one bears. Rules, by providing the content of many public programs, also structure their subsequent implementation and administration. In so doing, they channel the expenditure of enormous resources, human and otherwise, in both the public and private sectors. In this way rules are the form of law and public policy that have the most direct, immediate, and profound effect on the performance of public programs, and, ultimately, the quality of life in the United States. Despite concerted efforts over the past two decades to reduce their prominence and impact, rules remain a dominant force in all aspects of U.S. society.

A Definition of Rule

Defining the term "rule" is not a trivial exercise in semantics. On the contrary, when it is determined that an action of the public sector is or will be a rule, the government bears heavy legal obligations to proceed with that action, using certain prescribed techniques. It is important to be quite clear about how one defines what is arguably the most important product of government agencies.

The best starting point in any consideration of the meaning of "rule" is with the authoritative definition of the term found in the Administrative Procedure Act (APA) of 1946 (60 stat. 237; as amended). Its Section 551 (4) states that "rule means the whole or part of an agency statement of general or particular applicability and future effect designed to implement, interpret, or prescribe law or policy." This definition is worthy of careful deconstruction because it, in fact, does contain reference to the most important dimensions of rules.

Agencies As the Sources of Rules
The definition makes it clear that rules are not the products of the major institutions created by the framers in the Constitution. Rules are not written in Congress, by the President, or the courts. Rules are the responsibility of public bureaucracies. Because their authorities and powers are derivative, one generally considers these varied agencies and departments inferior to Congress, the President, and courts. The power to issue rules is, however, a great equalizer. The constitutional branches have recognized the enormous power that agencies can exert through the instrumentality of the rule. These branches struggle mightily with agencies, and with each other, for influence over the content of rules.

Law and Policy As the Proper Subjects of Rules
It is important to note that the Administrative Procedure Act's substantive limits on the contents of rules could not have been written more broadly. This section of the definition confers no independent authority on agencies; all rules must be at least authorized, if not mandated, by congressional legislation. Nevertheless, Congress assumes by the APA that agencies are fully competent to fashion rules in any area of law or policy in which a valid statute exists. A perusal of the *Code of Federal Regulations*, the official compilation of all rules currently in effect, confirms that their substantive range is simply vast.

Implementation, Interpretation, and Prescription: The Functions of Rules
The Administrative Procedure Act established a robust role for rules in the larger political system. Each of these functions is important in its own right, but, taken together, they establish for rules the fullest scope of influence over law and policy. The least influence is felt when rules "implement." This function suggests that rules need add little if any substance to existing law and policy. In this instance, they may provide procedural guidance or minor elaboration on already well-defined terms. When rules "interpret," the role is more substantial. Law and policy may already be well developed and understood, but an effort is required to adapt them to new or unanticipated circumstances. Alter-

natively, statutory terms may be subject to variable interpretations, and effort is needed to give them a more precise, and authoritative, meaning.

The most dramatic power is in evidence when rules "prescribe." In this instance, congressional statutes establish goals and objectives using obscure, vague, or incomplete language. Rules are then needed to give meaning to terms, such as "healthy" or "safe," that would otherwise be subject to widely divergent interpretations. Rules also provide specific requirements that establish how the defined goals are to be achieved. Political scientist Theodore Lowi (1987) has commented extensively, and critically, of the tendency in landmark regulatory status, such as the Clean Air Act and the Occupational Safety and Health Act, to adopt such language and thus greatly increase the importance of rules. It is when rules prescribe that agencies assume the legislative function most fully. Such uses of delegated authority are destined to be controversial.

General and Particular Applicability: Circumstances Affected by Rules

This element of the APA definition parallels that devoted to subject matter, in that it addresses the range of affected parties and circumstances that rules may affect. Similarly, the APA adopts a comprehensive view of applicability by allowing rules to apply to parties and circumstances ranging from individuals to very large groups. The notion of constructing legislative instruments, be they laws or rules, to benefit or harm individual persons, firms, groups, institutions, or units of government is highly suspect. Such acts that confer benefits may bespeak special privilege or corruption; those bringing harm must confront the constitutional prohibition on bills of attainder.

There is no evidence that the APA intended to promote such questionable practices in rules. Instead, the effect of this element of the definition is to avoid confining rules to those circumstances in which broad categories of parties or circumstances are affected. In this sense, the APA definition anticipated the enormous expansion of governmental activity that occurred in subsequent decades. American society and its economy are now swept broadly and penetrated deeply by contemporary law and public policy. Rules must deal with small segments of the population or sectors of the economy in order to fully interpret, implement, or prescribe law and policy.

Future Effect: Rules and the Legislative Function

Legislation attempts to structure the future, to create conditions that improve the quality of life for citizens. The future orientation of legislation is emphasized in the Constitution, most directly in its prohibition of the enactment of ex post facto legislation. With the phrase "future effect"

Congress reinforces the legislative origins, nature, and purposes of rules.

Types of Rules

It should be evident from the foregoing that any attempt to establish a complete and coherent categorization of rules will face daunting obstacles. Nevertheless, there are a variety of approaches that provide some insights, and, taken together, they at least convey the tremendous variety, and volume, of rules.

There are two notable official means of classifying rules. The *Code of Federal Regulations* is organized by titles, each containing a distinct policy area and/or agency of origin and responsibility. The *Code* has 50 such titles and fills hundreds of volumes and thousands of pages. The rules that apply to protection of the environment, for example, can be found in Title 40, while those governing banks and banking are contained in Title 12. Another schema is the three-part categorization of rules found in the Administrative Procedure Act (60 stat. 237; 1946, as amended). The APA, sec. 551, 553, refers to "legislative," "interpretive," and "procedural" rules. These categories correspond roughly to the functions of rules outlined previously. "Legislative" rules are those that prescribe law and policy. The APA adopts this term in recognition that, in these types of rules, agencies are acting clearly as surrogates for Congress. "Interpretive" rules do what the title suggests. "Procedural" rules correspond to one important dimension of the implementation function. These rules establish the internal organization and process of the agency and thus inform the public how the agency intends to manage and administer its statutory obligations.

Although they draw useful distinctions, the APA categories do not capture the rich variety of rules. The categories of the *Code* are very useful in summarizing the substantive range of the content of rules, but are not very helpful in identifying the next level of general functions of rules that flow from their role in interpreting, implementing, and prescribing law. Nor do they suggest the general types of activities and parties that rules affect. To better understand these features it will be helpful to think about three types of rules—those affecting private behavior, rules for those who approach the government, and rules for government itself.

Rules affect private behavior in a number of ways. On occasion, a rule will contain an outright prohibition on certain types of activities. Bans of cyclamates, cigarette and hard liquor advertising on television, and drinking alcohol by airline pilots in the 24 hours prior to takeoff are good examples of this type of rule. More common are rules that set standards or establish limits for a substance, product, or activity. These rules are very common and include such standards as limits on occupational exposures to dangerous chemicals and standards to insure safety of consumer products and levels of purity expected in drinking water. There is an obvious relationship between these types of rules and those that prohibit acts. Behavior of a private party that does not fall within prescribed limits or meet established standards is, in effect, prohibited. Finally, there are many rules that require private parties to collect, maintain, and report information about their activities. These rules are usually adjuncts to others that prohibit or set limits and standards, and they are a primary means by which the government monitors private sector compliance with legal obligations.

Persons, organizations, and firms approach the government to secure benefits to which they are entitled, to sell goods and services, to obtain licenses or other forms of permission to engage in certain types of businesses or activities, or simply to complain about actions of others or the government itself. Rules establish channels for these approaches and set criteria to inform the private parties what they can expect when the government responds. Many of these rules could be classified as the "procedural" rules referred to in the APA. Others that specify eligibility criteria for benefits or licenses are more likely to be "interpretive" or "legislative" rules.

Finally, all the rules for government could be considered variants on the "procedural" category. But, it would be a serious mistake to consider them bureaucratic minutiae. They include agency policies for compliance with landmark laws, such as the National Environmental Policy Act, the Freedom of Information Act, the Privacy Act, sunshine statutes, and many, many others.

Effects of Rules

Rules pervade American life. Any effort to calculate the value of the benefits they produce and the costs they impose confronts major methodological obstacles. More effort has been devoted to measuring and reporting costs than to valuing benefits. Here, the numbers are simply staggering. Recent estimates of the total economic burden of rules related only to regulation have ranged from US $100 billion to $500 billion, according to the Center for the Study of American Business at Washington University (Warren, 1992, p. 2). The effects on particular sectors vary considerably. The Federal Financial Institutions Examination Council estimates that compliance with federal regulation alone constitutes 6 percent to 14 percent of noninterest costs to depository institutions. A 1992 study sponsored by the Air Transport Association estimated the removal of one group of rules affecting major carriers would, over a five-year period, result in over $17 billion in savings and create 127,000 jobs (WEFA Group, 1992, p. 4). Even if one were to control for the normal tendency in affected persons to overestimate the effects, the impact of

rules on the United States is enormous. Any effort to reduce significantly their role in society will have to be equally massive and sustained.

Conclusion

Colin Diver (1989), dean of the University of Pennsylvania Law School, in a paraphrase of Oliver Wendell Holmes, has written that a rule is "the skin of a living policy. . . . It hardens an inchoate normative judgement into the frozen form of words. . . . Its issuance marks the transformation of policy from the private wish to public expectation. . . . The framing of a rule is the climatic act of public policy" (p. 199) The significance of rules as instruments of governance has never been captured better than in these words. They also underscore the profound importance of the process by which rules come into being.

CORNELIUS M. KERWIN

BIBLIOGRAPHY

Diver, Colin, 1989. "Regulatory Precision," in *Making Regulatory Policy*, eds., Keith Hawkins and John Thomas. Pittsburg: University of Pittsburgh Press.
Kerwin, Cornelius M., 1994. Rulemaking: How Government Agencies Write Law and Make Policy. Washington, D.C.: Congressional Quarterly, Inc.
Lowi, Theodore, 1987. "Two Roads to Serfdom." *American University Law Review,* vol. 36: pp. 295–322.
Warren, Mclinda, 1992. *Government Regulation and American Business.* St. Louis: Center for the Study of American Business.
WEFA Group, 1992. The Potential Impact of Selected Airline Tax and Regulatory Changes in the U.S. Economy. Bala Cynwyd, Pa: WEFA Group.

RULEMAKING. The process by which government agencies develop, change, and eliminate rules.

A Simple Definition

The Administrative Procedure Act (APA) (60 stat. 237; 1946, as amended) defines rulemaking as "agency process for formulating, amending, or repealing a rule" [sec. 551(5)]. The definition is deceptive in its appearance of permissiveness. Later in the APA, Congress constrained agency discretion in the exercise of the rulemaking power by establishing in Section 553(3)(c) certain minimal procedural requirements that must be observed unless a given rule is exempted from them. But, these requirements, which are discussed later, are really only the starting point in an exploration of the process by which rules are developed.

In the 50 years since enactment of the APA, the importance of rules in the U.S. system of government increased dramatically to the point at which it has been argued that they are the most important means for articulating law and policy. Not surprisingly, during these same 50 years much attention has been paid to the manner in which agencies create these instruments of government. The constitutional branches–Congress, the President, and the judiciary–have each labored to insure that rulemaking proceeds in a manner consistent with their values and priorities. The result of all of this effort is a process that can be enormously complex, contentious, and expensive. It is essential for readers to appreciate at the outset the significance of rulemaking to the quality of life in the United States. When rulemaking fails so too does the underlying law and policy it seeks to interpret, implement, or prescribe.

Origins and History

The origin of rulemaking can be traced to the first Congress, which enacted laws authorizing the President to regulate various types of commercial activities involving Indian tribes and aspects of international trade. Little if anything is known about how the President proceeded to establish the necessary standards and communicate them to those who needed to know, but it is unlikely that George Washington did it alone, in isolation from those expert in such matters.

From these modest beginnings, rulemaking grew in parallel with the developing national government. The history can be summarized in terms of recognizable periods and eras.

The Evolution of Legal Requirements

The law that pertains to the conduct of rulemaking arises from four distinct sources. Congress enacts legislation that can affect the entire rulemaking process or rules used in a single agency or program. Recent presidents have issued executive orders that establish requirements that must be met by rulemaking agencies under the President's direct managerial control. The agencies themselves have adopted procedural rules that bind them to the use of certain processes and techniques. Finally, court decisions have interpreted and extended requirements established in statutes, executive orders, and agency procedural regulations. In some instances, the judges have created requirements of their own.

The body of law pertaining to the development of rules is enormous. But virtually all of this law relates to one or more of the three fundamental elements of the rulemaking process that were identified in the Administrative Procedure Act–information, participation, and accountability.

Information

The Administrative Procedure Act requires that agencies inform the public through a notice in the *Federal Register* of their intention to promulgate a rule. The act says little else about the type of information to be contained in the notice, allowing the agency to publish actual proposed text or merely a description of what it is intending to do. Subsequent legal developments, including the rules and policies of the *Federal Register* itself, have made the publication of the actual proposed language common practice, and there has been occasional diversification of the vehicle for providing notice in statutes and by rulemaking agencies. But the far more significant legal developments in this area relate to the types of information agencies must develop, and usually disclose, during the process of developing a rule.

Regarding this information, the APA is generally silent except for the general admonition that to survive judicial review rules cannot be "arbitrary or capricious" and, in certain instances, must be based on "substantial evidence." But subsequent statutes, executive orders, and court decisions have, among other things, required certain types of scientific studies, such as risk assessment; the evaluation of economic effects, including paperwork burdens and impacts on small business; and the estimates of implications of rules for state governments and damage to the environment. In some of these instances, the agency is required to disclose the results of these studies in the proposed and final rule. Where such is required, interested and affected parties have access to the Freedom of Information Act once the rule becomes final.

There are two fundamental purposes of the information requirements established in law that are closely related to the other fundamental elements of rulemaking previously identified. The first is to inform the public of the basis, purpose, and implications of rules so that they can better participate in the process. The second is to develop sufficient information so that agencies can be held accountable by Congress, the President, and the courts.

Participation

Participation mandated by the Administrative Procedure Act is confined to the requirement that agencies allow the public to submit written comments on proposed rules. The act does not state what agencies are expected to do with comments they receive. However, laws that have developed since require agencies to respond to significant comments that are received in the preamble of the final rule. As significant, perhaps, individual authorizing statutes and executive orders have diversified the opportunities for participation that agencies are required to offer and have limited the ability of agencies to provide some forms of preferential access to the rulemaking process.

Additional opportunities for participation include public hearings, multiple stages of public comment, cross-examination of agency rulemakers, and the use of consensual processes for the development of rules. Limits on preferential access include prohibitions on ex parte contacts, after publication of a notice of proposed rulemaking, the Federal Advisory Committee Act, and the Government in the Sunshine Act. As is documented later, these legal developments (and a general movement that occurred during the 1960s and 1970s toward more active citizen involvement in governmental decisionmaking), have created a rulemaking process in which public participation is extensive and growing.

Accountability

The APA established the right of judicial review when parties are aggrieved as a result of rulemaking. But the criteria for judicial action set forth in the act appeared to give considerable discretion to agencies over the substance of rules and the process by which they were developed. Over time, however, the courts, through a more expansive interpretation of APA provisions have become deeply involved in reviews of both the substance and the process of rulemaking actions.

Judicial decisions have highly variable effects on rulemaking agencies and include simple ratification of the agency's action, partial or complete invalidation of the rule, and orders to initiate individual or multiple rulemakings, sometimes with mandatory deadlines. Both Congress and the President engage in serious oversight of the rulemaking process. Congress uses its normal oversight powers, including budget, investigations, and approval of appointments. The legislative veto, which allowed Congress to repudiate individual rules, was found to be unconstitutional in 1983, but a new version of it surfaced in the House Republicans' Contract with America. Accountability to the White House is accomplished through agency submissions to the regulatory agenda, and more directly through review of proposed and final rules by the Office of Management and Budget. This review seeks to insure that agencies comply with the regulatory principles that have been articulated in executive orders by every U.S. president since Lyndon Johnson.

An Overview of the Rulemaking Process

The rulemaking process often begins long before a notice of proposed rulemaking appears in the *Federal Register* and often ends long after a final rule is similarly published. Space does not permit a full exploration of the complexities of contemporary rulemaking, but it is important to review several critical stages.

Planning and development activities, sometimes quite extensive, precede the actual drafting of a proposed rule. Rules are initiated in a variety of ways. Some are explicitly mandated in legislation. Others are merely authorized in statutes, leaving it to agencies to set priorities for the types of rules to be developed and the timing of rulemaking actions. In this, they are influenced by legal analyses by offices of general counsel, advice from staffs about the rules that are more important to program implementation or ongoing management, and by recommendations and formal petitions from interested members of the public. The approval of senior political appointees may be required before development of a rule can begin.

Once a rulemaking is initiated, several activities are triggered. Responsibility for development of the rule is assigned to one or more agency staffs. Other resources are assigned to the task. Attorneys will be consulted at the outset regarding what the relevant law directs the agency to accomplish substantively and procedurally. The frequently formidable task of assembling the information on which the rule will be based is undertaken, often with the assistance of multiple offices in the agency, consultants, experts, and members of the public. Draft proposals are circulated internally, and perhaps externally, to test the waters before a formal proposal is actually completed. Consultation with the *Federal Register* may be needed since it has strict guidelines for the publication of both proposed and final rules. Virtually all agencies have a well-developed system for formal review and concurrence by senior officials with proposed and final rules before they are transmitted to the *Register.*

Once the proposal appears, the formal public participation stage begins. As noted previously, participation may be confined to the development of written comments or there may be opportunities for a more direct interaction with responsible agency officials through public hearings or even cross-examination. It is important to recall that this formal stage of participation may be a mere supplement to the more significant participation that occurred informally early in the development of the rule. At some point, however, the public views are collected and reviewed. The agency decides what, if any, changes it will make and prepares responses to the significant comments it has received. These summaries of comments and agency responses appear in a new preamble to what will be the final rule. When the final rule is published the agency may also engage in a number of other activities to publicize the new rule and to insure that those with a need to know are familiar with the requirements it establishes.

For important and controversial rules, publication in the *Federal Register* may not be the end of the rulemaking agency's work. In fact, it may be the beginning of a more difficult stage. Several prominent rulemaking agencies experience high levels of litigation over the rules they write.

For example, virtually all the health rules developed by the Occupational Safety and Health Administration over the past two decades have been challenged in court, and at one time the Environmental Protection Agency estimated that the litigation rate for its most significant rules approached 80 percent (Office of Solid Waste and Emergency Response, 1984, p. 7). But, even when litigation is not an issue, additional work on the final rule may be needed. Errors in rules may require publication of what is known as a "technical correction" Most agencies allow the public to file a "petition for reconsideration" when they believe a wrong or unwise decision has been made.

This brief summary conveys the magnitude of work that an agency faces when it undertakes the development of even a modest rule and shows the challenges faced by contemporary rulemakers.

Issues and Challenges

No process so central to the conduct of contemporary democracy could avoid controversy, and rulemaking certainly has not. What is evident in the criticisms, however, is that they arise from fundamental dilemmas and contradictions in the U.S. political system. Until these conflicts are resolved, it will be impossible to mollify the critics of rulemaking. Nevertheless, it is important to review them briefly.

Volume

The sheer amount of rulemaking is an object of concern and controversy. The number of proposed and final rules at the federal level alone number in the thousands each year. Of course, volume, in itself, does not create a problem. The difficulty arises in terms of institutional capacity in both the public and private sectors. In the private sector, as the number of rules and the requirements they contain continue to grow, the ability of private firms, organizations, and individuals to keep abreast and comply is challenged, sometimes severely. The resources of public agencies who are expected to implement and administer an increasing body of rules are generally not growing. In most instances, exactly the opposite is happening. These agencies share with the private sector serious obstacles to meeting the obligations created by new rules.

Quality

The quality of rules is faulted on two broad grounds. Some have argued that rules are ineffective because they fail to produce the type of programmatic results contemplated in the statutes they are supposed to be implementing. Others argue that rules are inefficient in that they impose requirements that are more expensive than they should be for the benefits they produce.

There are several potential sources of ineffectiveness or inefficiency when it occurs. Agencies may not have adequate information when developing the rule and insufficient resources to fill these gaps. Agency rulemakers may lack the technical expertise to work with good information when it is available. Or, they may have no incentive to make effectiveness and efficiency priorities when they write rules. This lack of incentive can occur when underlying statutes mandate a particular course of action that proves to be ineffective or inefficient but that the agency is required to pursue. It can also occur if those in agencies are under pressure to produce a rule by a certain deadline and on or under budget. This pressure diverts rulemakers from a concern for quality to a concern for simply getting the rule out the door. Finally, both effectiveness and efficiency are at risk when those writing rules are influenced by personal ideology or career concerns that may be at odds with either of these two quality criteria.

Timeliness

It may strike some as odd that, in light of the criticism that there are too many low-quality rules, others would complain that rules take too long to write. Clearly, there are always persons who benefit from the development of rules, but some individuals still decry the time the rulemaking process consumes. There are examples of rules that have taken literally a decade or more to develop. A recent study by the Environmental Protection Agency (Office of Solid Waste and Emergency Response, 1984, p. 19) found that rules took, on average, anywhere from two to four and one-half years to develop, depending on the program area in question.

The reasons for delay in rulemaking are not surprising given what we know about other problematical aspects of the process. Some rules are highly complex, requiring a great deal of information and study. Others are highly controversial, leading to long periods of time during which the agency attempts to resolve the conflict in order to avoid a lawsuit or political ramifications. Still other rules can be affected by shifting priorities within rulemaking agencies, caused by judicial decisions with deadlines, new legislation, unanticipated crises or calamities, by White House initiatives, or by an outpouring of public concern.

There is absolutely no reason to assume that any of these problems connected with rulemaking will grow less severe over the near term. The United States will not solve the fundamental dilemmas that cause people to argue simultaneously that we have too many and too few rules. Sufficient resources will not be made available to produce the kind of information that will dramatically improve the quality of rules. The world and the U.S. political system will not get simpler, sufficiently coherent, or cordial enough to guarantee that the rulemaking priorities of agencies will remain fixed and firm or that the rulemaking process will move with the type of dispatch some would prefer.

Participation in Rulemaking

Because rulemaking is lawmaking, and lawmaking is the pre-eminent constitutional power, participation by the public in the process is critical to the maintenance of U.S. democracy. It is also an absolutely critical source of information for rules. Surveys of interest groups, conducted by the author, shed considerable light on actual patterns of participation in rulemaking and provide reasons to be both encouraged and concerned.

A review of the *Federal Register* for the first half of 1991 revealed that 60 percent of notices of proposed rulemaking produced comment from the public. Although this figure may seem low, taken alone the statistic does not reveal much since there is no control for the relative significance of the rule.

Other data make it plain that interest groups take rulemaking very seriously, with a substantial majority of groups reporting that they consider it as or more important than lobbying Congress, doing grassroots political work, making political contributions, and engaging in litigation. The survey indicates that interest groups, in addition to written comments, use a wide variety of techniques to influence rulemaking, including attending hearings, forming coalitions with other groups, mobilizing at the grassroots level, and making informal contacts with agency officials both before and after the notice of proposed rulemaking. It is interesting to note that the groups rated making informal contacts before the requirement of notice and coalition formation as the most effective means of participation. Most interesting, perhaps, is that the groups found that their participation was effective in getting results. They reported success in influencing rulemaking half or more of the times they get involved. (Kerwin, 1994, Ch. 5)

Though these surveys do not address the critical questions of equity and breadth in participation, they do indicate at least that a segment of the American public is actively involved in the development of rules.

Conclusion

Rulemaking is the source of the most important law in the United States in that it provides the most specific guidance U.S. citizens receive about our rights and obligations. Congress chooses to delegate its power to legislate because of a combination of institutional limitations and political considerations. Rulemaking will continue to occupy its central role in the U.S. political system unless these factors, and the underlying forces that produce them, change in fundamental ways.

CORNELIUS M. KERWIN

BIBLIOGRAPHY

Kerwin, Cornelius M., 1994. Rulemaking: "How Government Agencies Write Law and Make Policy." Washington, D.C.: Congressional Quarterly, Inc.
Office of Solid Waste and Emergency Response, "The Nation's Hazardous Waste Management Program at a Crossroads." Washington, D.C.: CQ Press.

RULE OF LAW. The term that connotes a high democratic principle that places all governmental actions under law and that makes all human behavior subject to law. That a civilized society should be one of laws, not of the whims of those who govern, is a concept that virtually everyone living in democratic societies accepts. Only some intellectuals afflicted with postmodernism, criminals, and persons who conceive that the system of justice is little more than a capitalist device designed to oppress the masses do not accept the principles embraced within the term "rule of law." These fundamental principles are often difficult to apply in practice, and they raise important political issues.

At the simplest level, the rule-of-law concept embraces the idea that laws should be framed in terms of general principles that can be readily applied the same way in individual instances regardless of the specific jurist or administrator. One should be able to state laws as maxims, and they should be applicable to every person in the group on equal terms. Discretion in the application of the principles should be sharply limited. It follows from the foregoing, that the legal principle ranks above the jurist or administrator applying it. In this sense government should be ruled by laws, not by persons. Without such restrictions on the discretion of government, neither liberty nor property is secure because, as John Locke (1960) advised in *Two Treatises of Government,* "Without settled standing laws" and "stated rules of right and property" the arbitrary power of government to do what it pleases makes a mockery of the security of citizens' lives, liberties, and property (p. 359).

The history of the rule-of-law principle and its conflict with the idea that some figures—kings, clerics, the Gestapo, and so on—are above the law highlights its centrality in the continuing struggle for liberty. The fundamental conceptions of the rule-of-law principle are, in the West, as old as its civilization. Plato (1892) in the *Laws* used his principal speaker to assert that when laws are above the magistrates, all the blessings of the gods are bestowed on states, but when the law is subservient, the state will ultimately be ruined. Aristotle (1941) in the *Nicomachean Ethics* and the *Politics* argued that without legal supremacy a man tends to rule for his own benefit and, thus, can readily become a tyrant. During the early Middle Ages, the Germanic tribal notion that the king is bound by the same laws that bind his people survived in conflict with the dominant notion of monarchical supremacy. The two principles would war during the Middle Ages, with the *Magna Carta* (1215) being a clear push in the direction of the rule-of-law principle, which Chapter 39 of that document most forcefully reasserted: "No free man shall be taken or imprisoned, or disseised [dispossessed] or outlawed . . . except by the lawful judgment of his peers or by the law of the land" (p. 327).

Nevertheless, even on its ascendancy in the later Middle Ages, the principle was asserted in a rudimentary form, without elaboration or a major theoretical underpinning. Most important, it was decisively restrained by the theological conception of authority. The theoretical underpinning of a king's authority was that the monarch derived his authority from God. He was therefore required to interpret God's law to guarantee the piety of his subjects. Consequently, the king's discretion was very wide and most certainly not bound by mere humanmade laws. In practice, the monarch's advisers sometimes implored him to obey the laws in order to set a good example for his subjects. Thus, for the rule of law to become paramount, the legal system had to become divorced from theology.

The great breakthrough in England occurred when Edward Coke became chief justice of the Common Pleas in 1606. According to Coke (1986), the common law was the supreme law, and its judges, unfettered by anything other than that legal system, were its sole exponents. This bold claim conflicted with the belief of James I that judges had no more authority than any other administrators of the Crown. Thus, under the doctrine of the royal prerogative, the king could supersede the common law just as he could a policy undertaken by any of his administrators. Shortly thereafter, Coke and the common law judges asserted that the Church and its courts were equally bound by the common law. According to F. W. Maitland (1961), a leading legal historian, Coke was able to assert the authority of the common law judges against both the king and the Church because of the enormous public approval of the common law and its courts that had augmented over the centuries. From the time of Coke forward, the rule of law was on the ascendancy in England, and the royal prerogative was in decline. Gradually–but not without backsliding–other Western nations followed suit.

It remained for Albert V. Dicey (1885), the nineteenth-century English legal scholar, to provide the first comprehensive formulation of the rule-of-law principle in *Introduction to the Study of the Law of the Constitution*. That work provided a coherent framework for modern debates concerning the rule of law. Dicey began by observing that acute foreign observers viewed the supremacy of the law as England's distinguishing characteristic, compared to continental European nations. Yet they were unable to specify precisely what they meant. That is because the rule of law has three distinct but clearly interrelated meanings. First,

no person can be punished or be made to suffer a property or personal loss except for a clear breach of the law. In contrast, virtually every continental executive wielded far more discretionary authority. Whenever there is discretion, Dicey observed, there is room for arbitrariness, noting that this is the case whether the form of government is a republic or a monarchy. He illustrated by noting examples of arbitrariness in both royal and republican France.

The second meaning of the rule of law is that no person is above the law. Moreover, every person, regardless of rank or condition, is subject to the ordinary laws of the nation and can be tried in its usual tribunals. In contrast to England, in other legal systems different classes of people were subject to different systems of law or to no law at all. This discriminatory treatment applied in England, as well, where, until the sixteenth century, nobles and priests could defy the law.

The third meaning of the rule-of-law principle is that the decisions affecting personal liberties result from general principles embodied in a constitution that are enforced by judges. The important point to Dicey was that such ideas as freedom from arbitrary arrest or freedom of conscience stem from the ordinary law of the land and are deeply ingrained, rather than conferred by a legislative act.

Such liberties are grounded in the conception of rights rather than permissions decreed by a legislature. There are several practical consequences that stem from this difference. First, a change in the political composition of the legislature can alter overnight the permissions granted. In contrast, judges have secure tenure and are, in any event, further isolated from the whims of politics than legislators. Second, in periods of emergency liberties have been suspended by legislatures purportedly until the emergency passes. But in fact, such suspensions have lasted beyond the emergency period. The tragic suspension in 1933 of the Weimar Constitution in Germany that led to Adolf Hitler's consolidation of power tragically confirms Dicey's prophetic complaint. In contrast, once again, courts grounded more zealously in the doctrine of rights are concerned above all with protecting those rights, not in short-term problems of public policy. Finally, Dicey concluded that the three conceptions of rule of law are not separate. All should be present for the principle to operate effectively.

Dicey's world was a relatively simple one compared to our own, in which legislatures enact laws on complex topics that Dicey would not have considered in 1885. Now, an enormous administrative apparatus must enforce laws through rules and decisions under legislation that, at best, can only provide guideposts.

One need not even delve into such contemporary areas as safety of pharmaceutical products or environmental controls involving scientific facts and judgments to see the rise of discretionary decisionmaking. Consider the

1914 Federal Trade Commission Act, in which Congress gave up trying to list all of the possible ways in which businesses could unfairly compete with each other. Instead, it created an agency charged with pursuing "unfair methods of competition," with the agency being charged with compiling the list in ongoing fashion through litigation and substantive rulemaking. Finally, one must also note that many judges have been called upon to decide many kinds of cases that they did not have to confront in the nineteenth century. Some judges have clearly become policymakers, endeavoring to produce "better" social outcomes than those to which traditional principles would have led.

This complex, new legal environment has led some of the most important legal theorists to elaborate, in the context of contemporary conditions, on the principles Dicey set forth. Lon Fuller (1977) has provided one of the most important and influential reformulations. Fuller was primarily concerned with discovering the internal moral basis of law. He urged that there must be rules, that the rules must be knowable, and that those administering the rules must observe them. This led Fuller to propose eight requirements to meet the rule of law principle. First, the rules must be general; that is, they must be more general than specific cases and must be clearly applicable to those cases. For example, the prohibition against operating a motor vehicle in excess of 65 miles per hour on a highway is more general than the specific situation of driving a car at 85 miles per hour on the San Diego Freeway.

Second, those who are expected to observe the rule must be provided in advance with notice and information about it. This, of course, does not mean that the authorities must provide each person covered by the rule with personal notice of its contents. Instead, the information must be reasonably available so that persons who might be covered can determine the conduct that falls within the prohibition. (The extreme contrary example is Franz Kafka's [1925] *The Trial,* in which the novel's tension is based on an accused person not knowing what illegal act he committed.) Most people know the conduct that constitutes a crime, tort, or breach of contract without having read the applicable statutes and decisions. They learn the requisite behavior indirectly. Further, in many situations, one is required to learn the rules before one can lawfully engage in an activity. These include such common activities as driving a motor vehicle or operating a restaurant.

The third of Fuller's requirements is prospectivity. That is, the rules must have come into existence before the actions that transgressed them occurred. This requirement obviously follows from the second one. In U.S. practice, however, the Supreme Court modified this principle in *Calder v. Bull* (1798), holding that the constitutional prohibition against ex post facto laws did not apply to civil laws (and, by extension, administrative regulations based on them). Nevertheless, although U.S. practice constitutionally permits retroactivity in noncriminal matters, such ac-

tions are undertaken very infrequently. It is probable that this reluctance stems from the fundamental moral sense that the retroactive application of law is usually wrong.

Fuller's fourth requirement is clarity. Those who are expected to obey the rules must be able to understand them. Obviously, ordinary laypeople need not understand rules that are directed to pharmaceutical manufacturers or electrical engineers. Nevertheless, one of the most common charges leveled against the rules promulgated by U.S. regulatory agencies is that they violate the canon of clarity, especially with respect to the rules with which relatively unsophisticated business persons or small businesses must comply. (For example, the June 1973 Federation of American Scientists' *FAS Newsletter* complained of the Occupational Safety and Health Administration that: "Regulations are voluminous and complex; the language is convoluted beyond recognition except by a scientist or lawyer" [p. 1]). Indeed, it is probable that much of the American public's resentment directed toward bureaucrats and red tape flows from regulators' frequent lack of clarity.

Fuller's fifth element is noncontradictoriness. Those at whom the rule is directed should not expect to obey both one rule *and* a conflicting one. Of course, it is not uncommon for different tribunals, such as federal district courts, to reach contradictory decisions. But, ultimately, a higher court will usually resolve such conflicts. In general, the legal systems in democratic societies have guidelines for this resolution. For example, later statutes prevail over earlier ones, and statutory laws prevail over common laws in conflict with them in the Anglo-American legal system.

The sixth requirement is that persons at whom a rule is directed must be able to conform their behavior to it. At the simplest level, most of us are able to refrain from violating such traditional rules as those proscribing theft. Even when the prohibition is more ambiguous, such as the prohibition against false and misleading advertising, advertisers can conform their behavior by scrutinizing advertising with respect to veracity and the way consumers will interpret the claims. If it appears that the advertisement will probably mislead consumers, it can be modified.

There is one important situation in which government agencies have violated this element in recent times. In environmental regulation, it has become increasingly common for legislators and regulators to impose certain standards on manufacturers that must be met by a certain date. Often, the legislators and regulators are in blissful ignorance about whether it is technologically possible for the manufacturer to comply in the time required. (The rules instituted by California and other states requiring automobile manufacturers economically and technologically to produce viable electric cars by a date that the carmakers say cannot be met illustrates current issues regarding conformity.)

The seventh element, stability—that rules should not change so frequently that they cannot be learned and

followed—provides no difficulty in most democratic nations. Indeed, a traditional complaint is that both legislators and administrators work too slowly. (One is often reminded that it took the Food and Drug Administration 12 years to adopt final standards on the minimum peanut content for peanut butter.)

Finally, Fuller's eighth requirement is congruence. Essentially, this means that the rules actually being enforced must conform to those articulated. The Volstead Act that prohibited the manufacture, sale, and consumption of alcoholic beverages during the 1920s was a notorious example of incongruence.

The administrative apparatuses in most democratic nations have swelled during the twentieth century; therefore, it is apparent that there are many instances in which Fuller's eight requirements have not been fulfilled. The rule of law has become a subject of political controversy. Critics of the strict rule-of-law principle tend to be political liberals (in the twentieth-century sense) who believe in the positive state and, therefore, wide administrative discretion. Without such wide discretion, agencies are often hampered in creatively using their broad missions in such areas as environmental regulation or civil rights enforcement. In contrast, conservatives who place a paramount value on limited state action are bound to laud the rule-of-law principle and point to the dangers to liberty when the principle is compromised or weakened through widespread discretion.

Modern critics of the principle assert that it is not the equivalent of substantive justice. It is entirely possible to fulfill Fuller's eight requirements in regimes that deny human rights, practice racial segregation, or engage in religious persecution. Although conceding the possibility, the defenders of the principle answer that it is only one of several necessary bulwarks of liberty. Without the rule of law, the fulfillment of liberty is less likely. Certainly, civil liberties, free elections, and a number of other safeguards are also necessary to maintain a free society, but the rule of law is certainly one of the most important. Moreover, as legal theorist Margaret Jane Radin (1989) has argued, the rule-of-law principle is two-faced. On one hand it can be used to induce certain behavior, but on the other it can also be used substantively to attain such values as human dignity, fairness, and democracy.

A second tier of criticism comes from those who assert that the strict rule-of-law principle cannot fulfill government's tasks in a modern democratic society. These critics—who are frequently experts in administrative law—offer different arguments. Administrative law expert Kenneth Culp Davis (1972) is a leading spokesperson for this perspective. First, judges traditionally have exercised widespread discretion based on a large number of factors concerning persons and circumstances. Consider sentencing for crime. It is ludicrous to suggest that all factors, including new ones that will arise in future proceedings, can be neatly categorized

in a list, with appropriate weights attached to each one. Life is simply too complex. Judges and administrators, when fashioning a civil decree or order, must frequently consider many novel aspects of a situation that cannot readily be reduced to clear, unambiguous statements made before the specific matters are considered. In the AT&T case in 1984, for example, the decree was fashioned under Section 2 of the Sherman Act, a statute enacted in 1887. When the Sherman Act was framed, no one could have remotely conceived the unique structure and practice of the telephone industry in the last quarter of the twentieth century. To list all the factors and considerations in 1887 that would institute competition in the telephone industry in 1984 would have been impossible. Thus, the statute was ambiguous and discretionary and the best that a judge could have hoped for was guiding principles.

Second, Davis has argued that courts and administrative agencies must change their minds based on facts not previously considered or based on new ways of reasoning about recurring situations, because jurists or administrators are no different than anyone else in any other decisionmaking activity. To err is, unfortunately, human, but the difference between the wise person and the fool is that the former will be sufficiently open-minded to reconsider prior judgments. Consider *Brown v. Board of Education of Topeka,* in which the Supreme Court rejected prior decisions about the constitutionality of segregated facilities, a decision involving wide discretion. Davis has observed that such behavior is not uncommon among judges or administrators, and to demand rigorous inflexibility is foolish.

Third, according to Davis, there are many situations in which statutes contain ambiguous language that may be interpreted in several ways. When judges or administrators then consult the legislative history to receive guidance and reduce the number of possible constructions, they find that the confusion does not disappear; indeed, it may even get worse! The reasons for this are that legislators are often not very clear about the statutes they enact. They are more certain of what they *hope* a statute will accomplish than about the procedures and rules that will accomplish the goals. Additionally, legislation is not infrequently the result of compromise among conflicting groups of legislators and interest groups. When this compromise occurs, as political scientist Theodore J. Lowi observed in *The End of Liberalism* (1969), the legislators may deliberately wrap the statute in ambiguity so that administrators or judges make the detailed decisions. In this way legislators accept the credit for having addressed the problem without engaging in the painful task of determining winners and losers under the statute. Thus, the inherent nature of modern legislation leads to administrative and judicial discretion.

Davis has pointed out a fourth problem in that many decisions have important foreign policy ramifications; therefore, a better policy, when there is uncertain foreign response, is to grant the President and administrators broad authority, rather than to tie their hands in advance. Finally, along similar lines, Davis has mentioned that many desirable public policies require expertise beyond the knowledge of legislatures, which inexorably leads to widespread discretion. Should a legislature, for example, specify the precise information that an aspiring physician should command before being allowed to practice medicine? Clearly, it is better for a group of state-appointed medical boards to ascertain the general guidelines in such matters.

Because of the foregoing reasons, Davis has concluded that the strict rule-of-law principle is impossible to follow in a world in which the public demands legislation on a host of complex and difficult matters. Since discretion is inevitable, the more important task is how to confine discretion through due process and administrative law principles.

In many ways U.S. Supreme Court Justice Antonin Scalia (1989) would agree with Kenneth Culp Davis. But this foremost proponent of the strict rule-of-law principle, having recognized the difficulties Davis has raised, has said that just because some discretion is inevitable, citizens should not throw up their hands and give up all attempts to make our governmental system one of laws, not personal discretion (Scalia 1989). To do so is to abandon such values as uniformity, predictability and, ultimately, justice. "Only by announcing rules do we hedge ourselves in" (Scalia 1989, p. 1179). He has therefore concluded that judges and administrators must do their best to uphold the rule-of-law principle, insofar as it can possibly be done. Justice Scalia has consistently and predictably followed this position while on the Supreme Court; but, of course, many other judges and administrators reject it. The struggle between the rule-of-law principle and discretion goes on!

ALAN STONE

BIBLIOGRAPHY

Aristotle, 1941, "Nicomachean Ethics" in (ed) McKeon, Richard, *Basic Works of Aristotle.* New York: Random House Aristotle, 1941, "Politics" in *Ibid.*

Coke, Edward, 1986. *Institutes of the Laws of England.* Buffalo: W.S. Hein (1797).

Council of the Federation of American Scientists "Statement," *FAS Newsletter* (June) (1973).

Davis, Kenneth Culp, 1972. *Administrative Law Text.* 3d ed., St. Paul, MN: West.

Dicey, A.V., 1885. *Introduction to the Study of the Law of the Constitution.* London: Macmillan, 1952.

Fuller, Lon, 1964. *The Morality of the Law,* Rev. ed.: New Haven: Yale University Press.

Holt, J.C. (1965), *Magna Carta.* Cambridge, Eng.: Cambridge University Press.

Kafka, Franz, 1925. *The Trial,* London: Secker and Warburg Lowi, Theodore J., 1969. *The End of Liberalism.* New York: W.W. Norton.

Locke, John, 1698, *Two Treatises of Government.* New York: Cambridge University Press (1960).

Maitland, Frederic (1961), *The Constitutional History of England.* Cambridge, Eng.: Cambridge University Press (1887).

Mootz, Francis J., III, 1993. "Is the Rule of Law Possible in a Postmodern World?" *Washington Law Review* (April).

Plato, 1892, "The Laws" in (ed) Jowett, B. *The Dialogues of Plato.* London: Macmillan.

Radin, Margaret Jane, 1989. "Reconsidering the Rule of Law." *Boston University Law Review* (July).

Scalia, Antonin, 1989. "The Rule of Law as a Law of Rules." *University of Chicago Law Review* (Fall).

RULE OF THREE, THE.

A procedure commonly found in merit systems wherein the top three names based on qualifications (test scores, experience, education) are certified to the hiring authority as being qualified and eligible for employment. The hiring authority then must choose from among those three names in filling a position. All merit systems must have some procedure enabling the most meritorious candidates' names to be verified and forwarded to those in positions of hiring authority. There are many ways this process can be accomplished; the rule of three is one commonly used variation.

In the United States, the Pendleton Act of 1883 simply indicated that appointments should be made "from among those graded highest." It was understood that Congress, in a separation-of-powers system such as the United States, could not unduly limit the president's powers to appoint and remove executive branch officials. Thus, there had to be some discretion allowed to appointing authorities. Historically, the rule of three was a part of the original but short-lived civil service commission established under the Grant presidential administration. From 1883 until 1888, a "rule of four" was used under an attorney general's opinion before the rule of three was finally adopted. This rule of three was used by many state and local governments when they passed merit system legislation.

The rule of three was an effort to deal with desires for some managerial flexibility and at the same time limit political favoritism. Theoretically, the rule of three was intended to minimize political favoritism by limiting the total number of names certified to hiring officials and by basing those names on qualifications. At the same time, it was expected to give managers in the hiring departments some flexibility by allowing them more than a single name for their choice.

Historically, the rule of three has been favored by unions as a means of limiting the discretion of management; at the same time, it has been criticized by minority groups as being detrimental to the progress of affirmative action programs.

At the state level of government in the United States where some states are not required to use the three, there have been variations in the process of certification, sometimes by using a "rule of the top ten" or by grouping names into various categories based on qualifications. One possible scheme might contain one category consisting of individuals with a range of qualifications listed as "most qualified," a second category range containing individuals with slightly lower qualifications labeled "qualified," and a third group labeled "unqualified." Under typical hiring rules and regulations, all names in the first category must be used before passing down the hiring register to lower level names in category two. Here, the total number of names certified to line authorities would be increased, as would management flexibility. At the same time, merit-based selection would be maintained.

Some of the rationale for certifying a larger group of names to hiring authorities rests with the nature of written testing, which serves as the basis for the order of names on the hiring register. Written tests that are commonly used all have some error of measurement. That is, no written test is a perfect measure of job knowledge. With this in mind, it sometimes seems artificial to contend, as is the case with traditional rule of three systems, that candidate number one, who may have scored 99, is actually a better worker than candidate number two, who scored 98. The error of measurement of most tests would mean that, in actuality, if these two candidates took this test a second time, their two scores might well be reversed. Thus, in categorical certification systems candidates are divided into larger groupings. For instance, all candidates who scored between 99 and 92 on a test might be grouped into the "most qualified" category, with each candidate considered equally qualified, and therefore the entire list of candidates scoring in this range can be certified out to hiring authorities. Candidates scoring between 91 and 83 might be placed into category two. These categorical certification systems have been useful in the implementation of many state and local affirmative action plans because minority candidates have a better chance of being certified out to line officials for possible appointment.

Although there have been various attempts to change the rule of three, and although there have been numerous experiments with other arrangements, this rule has been a constant feature of the American merit system and is still the most commonly used certification method in merit systems at the state and local level.

ROBERT H. ELLIOTT

BIBLIOGRAPHY

"An Act to Regulate and Improve the Civil Service of the United States" (the Pendleton Act), 1883. United States Congress, 22 Stat. 27.

Van Riper, Paul, 1991. "Americanizing a Foreign Invention: The Pendleton Act of 1883." In Frank Thompson, ed. *Classics of Personnel Policy*. Pacific Grove, CA: Brooks/Cole.

RURAL GOVERNANCE.

A style of administration and politics associated with small communities and characterized by informality, generalist rather than specialist roles, overlapping policy-administration tasks, and intimate government-citizen relations.

Rural governance is a style of public organization and behavior that has its roots in the traditions of American small-town and countryside democracy. It is typified by aspects of informal administration, including limited bureaucracy, weak policy-administration distinctions, flexible resource substitution, and extensive citizen voluntarism. Generally, these are the characteristics of small government organizations and their political environments in communities of small size and minimal urbanization.

Over the years, the classic features of rural governance throughout the United States have been nibbled away by urban growth, the expansion of local government programs even in the smallest locales, and the forces of social and political centralization. However, the attributes of rural governance linger on in many places, intermixed with more developed or sophisticated styles of governance. Numerous communities retain a preference for informal organization and their local public agencies are too small to make a thorough transition to bureaucratic and professional government. One continuing manifestation of rural governance is the annual town meeting still used throughout New England.

Small Governments

The features of public organization and operations that define rural governance are products of small size—both of the governments and the communities they serve. Most small communities in turn are "rural" places, the Census Bureau designation for population centers of less than 2,500 population apiece. But popular views and even formal policy as to what is truly "small" or "rural" extend further up the population ladder. Some intergovernmental grant programs, for example, specify 25,000 or 50,000 population as the cutoff for designating an "urban "or "large" community.

Whatever the standard, it is clear that the great majority of the 85,000 units of local government in the United States operate in certifiably small communities. Using 10,000 population as one measure, "small" communities in 1992 were served by the following:

- −87.7 percent (16,918 of 19,279) of all municipal governments, with an aggregate population of 28.1 million persons.
- −93.4 percent (15,569 of 16,656) of all town and township governments, with a combined population of 22.4 million. Similar patterns apply to special districts and school districts. A little more than half of the nation's 14,400 independent school districts enrolled fewer than 1,000 students apiece in 1992, even after sev-

eral decades of extensive consolidation that eliminated thousands of tiny districts. County governments serve larger populations on average than the other local governments, because of their regional jurisdictions, but still a quarter (728 of 3,043) of all counties had less than 10,000 population each in 1992.

As well as serving small populations, the large majority of local governments in the United States are organizationally small, when measured by number of employees, finances, or program activity. Most town and township governments and about one-fifth of all municipalities have no full-time employees at all. They operate through the combined efforts of part-time workers, volunteers, and the donated services of their elected officials. Alan Schenker (1985) refers to these units as "ZEGs," or "Zero Employment Governments."

Public Service Delivery

General-purpose local governments that serve small communities resemble in their programs larger and more urban governments. So the basic service repertoire of municipalities is similar across size categories—including law enforcement, fire protection, streets, sewers, water supply, parks, libraries, land-use regulation, animal and nuisance regulation, and economic promotion. But differences arise within these program areas in the degree of specialized services. Only in larger cities, for example, can police departments afford or justify crime laboratories, separate detective bureaus, and task forces.

Size differences are seen even more sharply in how public services are administered and financed. In theory, small organizations are greatly handicapped by the limitations of scale—in high costs per unit of service, limited and inflexible budgets, and high marginal costs. The marginal cost problem is illustrated by the difficulty a small city may have in expanding police patrols from a part-time to an around-the-clock service that requires at least four shifts. A staff of three officers falls short of full-time service, while four or five is the minimum for permitting it. Adding one or two officers may involve a minor expenditure adjustment in a big city but for a small municipality requires committing a very large part of the budget.

Practically, small governments are able to avoid some of the obstacles of limited scale by operating less expensively. They do so by keeping administrative overhead to a minimum, compensating employees at less than big-city levels, and stretching out the use of equipment.

Informal Administration

At the heart of the rural governance style is a prevailing informality that seems antithetical to formal bureaucracy. Small communities prefer face-to-face relations in the work of their local governments. In place of the universalistic values of expertise and objectivity that undergird bureaucracy, rural governance emphasizes the particularistic value of common sense, community knowledge, and primarily group links. Small-town citizens want to be governed in familiar and accessible ways; they dislike impersonal procedures and officeholder distance. Among the expressions of informal administration are the reluctance to employ professional administrators, policymakers serving in administrative jobs, the flexible mixing of positions and tasks, and extensive citizen voluntarism.

Limited Professionalism

Relatively few small municipalities, counties, and other local governments employ professional chief administrative officers (CAOs). School districts are the exception, since most are led by certified superintendents because of state education code requirements. A natural result of small organizational size and limited resources, restricted use of CAOs also reflects a deep-seated citizen resistance to bureaucracy as limiting popular control. Proposals to make local government more professional by creating CAO positions are controversial in small communities. Usually outsiders, the professional administrators are seen by local traditionalists as representing foreign values. Still, the number of small-city, town, and county governments that adopt CAO arrangements increases steadily, as governing boards and some voters become convinced that the growing complexity of local government demands professional administration.

Even when CAOs are employed by small governments, the tendency is to restrict their authority. In place of full-fledged city managers with the ability to hire and fire department heads, for example, many small cities narrow the discretion of their CAOs in the personnel area. Often they are hired not as "managers," but under other titles—"administrator," "administrative assistant," and so forth—indicating limited powers.

Blurring the Policy-Administration Line

In the absence of a professional central administrator, much of the management task falls on the shoulders of the elected mayor and governing board—the city council, county commission, or town board. Typically, this means a form of collegial administration in which the members of the board divide among themselves, either as committee or individual assignments, the supervision of particular programs or functions—public works, police, finances, and so on. At times, mayors and board members, especially in governments with no or few full-time employees, may take direct part in service delivery operations, such as oiling the streets or driving a snow plow. But the more common practice is to use the administrative assignments to exercise oversight over department heads and other employees.

One consequence of such involvement in management is a blurring of an elected governing board's roles, especially a neglect of its policy role. Often, small-town elected officials prefer tackling the routine details of administering an organization to the more abstract and difficult job of deliberating major issues and planning the community's future. There may be more personal satisfaction and citizen support in keeping to the familiar than in tackling high risk and potentially unpopular projects.

Multiple Jobs

A more positive view of informal administration suggests that small governments can be flexible and inventive in making do without the expertise, sophisticated procedures, and budgets of larger governments. In large part, this means substituting existing resources for more expensive and unavailable ones—such as giving generalist officials some of the work assigned to specialists in larger places. Small governments seldom have separate job descriptions for purchasing agent, risk management officer, or budget director. Rather, these are jobs that are combined together or with other responsibilities. Individual persons handle multiple duties. A small-town CAO will have these responsibilities and more. For governments without CAOs, such administrative duties may be parceled out to elected mayors or governing board members and others.

The key figure in this mixing of duties and positions often is the city or town clerk, whether elected or appointed, because of her central location in the organization's flow of information. In charge of their jurisdictions' records and serving as the only or principal staff to mayors and governing boards, clerks frequently take on other administrative tasks, such as budget preparation and personnel management. Small governments also tap the expertise of outside consultants, especially attorneys and engineers, sometimes relying on them for advice and information that extends beyond their specializations.

The Fire Department and Other Volunteers

Volunteers are another form of resource substitution. Proportionately more so than in larger places, ordinary citizens without official positions are directly involved in service delivery. The classic example of such personal involvement is the volunteer fire department, the standard mode of suppressing fires in small communities. Volunteers also provide many other public services in small towns, working in libraries, serving as police reserves, and constructing public facilities such as parks and sports fields.

Citizen contributions of this sort are an enormously valuable resource in small communities; besides reducing service delivery costs, they also boost community spirit and identity. Voluntarism, however, is not always a "free" good. Questions of liability arise and often there are tensions between volunteer groups and local governments that fund their activities over who actually controls the services they deliver.

The Town Meeting

Rural governance practices are most common in small New England towns and in the Mid-Atlantic and Midwestern townships that are their offspring. Small and relatively homogeneous populations, more evident in the communities served by such governments than by municipal and county organizations, are fertile environments for informal administration. Another aspect of rural governance, the intimate citizen-government connection, is also displayed here—especially in the venerable town meeting that originated in precolonial times. Some towns, especially larger ones, have adopted the limited or representative form of meeting or have their elected councils share some traditional meeting functions. But most New England towns still conduct annual and special town meetings that are open to all registered voters. Despite low voter turnout in many cases, Joseph Zimmerman (1984) found that these are truly deliberative and participatory affairs, with members legislating tax levies, budgets, programs, land-use policies, and organizational changes.

The influence of this New England institution is widespread throughout American government. It serves as a model for citizen participation and government openness elsewhere, so much so that the "town meeting" or "town hall" label now refers generically to collective deliberation in a public setting.

The Survival of Rural Governance

Few local governments and community political systems have not undergone major change in recent decades, as a result of both external and internal pressures. National policy and political developments reach into the smallest and most geographically remote communities. Small municipal and town/township governments were relative latecomers to federalism, but beginning in the late 1960s, they became full participants in national grant and regulatory programs. As well as improving public services, the effect was to expose small governments to more expert and professional techniques in service delivery and in such areas of administration as personnel and fiscal management. The accounting and other requirements of federal and state fiscal aid programs, for example, literally pulled numerous small governments out of the "cigar-box" age of account keeping during this period.

The dynamics of local politics at the same time were impacted by comparable population and cultural changes—including the turnover resulting from a combination of immigration and outmigration, a growing popular taste for good public services, and reduced isolation brought on by national television and the interstate highway system. Small communities as a result became less socially and politically homogeneous. The emphasis on political conformity lessened and it become more acceptable and possible to disagree and compete openly on public matters. Some loss of community identity and loyalty may have been a consequence.

Despite these profound changes, the norms of traditional rural governance still persist, although in reduced strength. They coexist in many small communities with the more modern public-sector techniques introduced by outside forces. Small-town citizens still want informal, familiar, and personal governance, and their elected and appointed officials are only too willing to oblige.

ALVIN D. SOKOLOW

BIBLIOGRAPHY

Schenker, Alan, 1985. "Zero Employment Governments: Survival in the Tiniest Towns." *Small Town,* vol. 16 (September-October): 4–11.

Seroka, Jim, ed., 1986. *Rural Public Administration: Problems and Prospects.* New York: Greenwood.

Sokolow, Alvin D., 1982. "Small Town Government: The Conflict of Administrative Styles." *National Civic Review,* vol. 71 (October): 445–452.

———, 1988. *Back Home: Grassroots Governments and the People They Serve.* Washington, D.C.: National Center for Small Communities.

Sokolow, Alvin D., and Beth Walter Honadle, 1984. "How Rural Local Governments Budget: The Alternatives to Executive Preparation." *Public Administration Review,* vol. 44 (September-October): 373–383.

U.S. Bureau of the Census, 1994 and 1988. *1992 and 1987 Census of Governments.* Washington, D.C.: U.S. Department of Commerce.

Vidich, Arthur J., and Joseph Bensman, 1968. *Small Town in Mass Society: Class, Power and Religion in a Rural Community.* Princeton, NJ: Princeton University Press.

Zimmerman, Joseph F., 1984. "The New England Town Meeting: Pure Democracy in Action?" In *1984 Municipal Year Book.* Washington, D.C.: International City Management Association, 102–106.

S

SALARY EQUITY. The perception among employees that salary or pay is equitable or fair. There are three types of equity: external, internal, and individual. From an employee's viewpoint, external equity is achieved when salary is perceived as equal to the market rate for similar positions in like organizations or governments. Internal equity is achieved when the worth of the position held by an employee is fair compared to the worth of other positions within the organization/government. Individual equity is achieved when levels of performance are rewarded fairly compared to the levels of performance of other employees. Although it is possible to conceptually separate these three types, in practice maintaining equity for one is likely to impact equity concerns for the other two.

Causes of Salary Inequity

If salary is viewed as inequitable, there are several possible causes. If external equity is not present, it may be that the government has adopted a policy that supports wages deliberately set below the market rate; or, alternatively, no market rate policy may exist. In addition, if salaries outside the government have not been surveyed recently, information concerning the market rate may be out of date. Even if up-to-date information has been collected, if pay structures and relevant pay policies for the surveyed organizations are different from those of the surveying government, it may be difficult to interpret the collected data so that the appropriate market rate may be clearly identified.

Even if organizations do identify an accurate market rate, a raise policy that would offer market adjustment raises to existing employees is rarely found. Salary surveys may result in pay range adjustments that favor higher salaries for new hires.

Traditionally, internal equity may become a concern if there is evidence of grade creep. This phenomenon is found when positions are reclassified to a higher pay range without sufficient changes in the nature of the duties and knowledge, skills, and abilities (KSAs) to warrant such an action. When it happens for one position, gradually other employees who hold similar positions elsewhere in the government pressure their supervisors to approve similar upgrades.

Raise policy can contribute to internal inequity. It is often easier politically to approve cost of living allowances (COLAs) rather than provide raises that move the salary of an incumbent further up a pay range. Realizing that pay raises provided to existing employees often do not keep up with increases in market rate, governments tend to also provide the same percentage increases to pay range minimums and maximums as is given to COLAs. The relative position of incumbents' salaries on the pay range does not change.

The greatest potential threat to internal equity is a job evaluation system that is either biased or misused. In measuring a job factor such as job knowledge, if more weight is given to knowledge obtained from work experience rather than formal education, for example, then there may be a built-in bias to the worth allotted to a position. This issue is often raised by those claiming a gender bias in pay equity, since for many supervisory or management positions, males often have more experience and less formal education than women.

Similarly, the weight or importance of each factor is often determined by analyzing the existing wage structure for the government or organization. To the extent that there are biases or inaccuracies in the existing structure, then, the application of a given job evaluation system based upon these is likely to result in inequities.

Furthermore, even using a "bias-free" job evaluation system may still lead to inequity if it is misused. When using a point rating job evaluation system, governments may use inconsistent point spreads in allocating points to each pay range. Additionally, if the points awarded to various factors for each position are not reviewed within each job series (e.g., all secretarial positions) or department as well as for each pay range, the assigned pay range for positions at higher levels in an organization may be incorrect.

Individual equity concerns arise for two primary reasons. First, the manner in which performance is measured may be of low validity. The typical graphic rating performance evaluation system used in government, one which is applied uniformly to all positions, suffers from an overemphasis on personality traits. Also, such systems do not provide sufficient distinction between performance levels for many positions. Typically, employees are rated on a five-point scale from unsatisfactory to excellent, with over 90 percent receiving a satisfactory, above satisfactory, or excellent rating.

Second, there is often an inadequate relationship between levels of performance and the amount of reward received. In many cases, if the raises provided are only in terms of COLAs, there may be no relationship between pay raises and performance levels. Alternatively, if an employee receiving an excellent performance rating is given a raise that is only 0.5 percent higher than an employee who obtains a satisfactory performance rating, for example, individual inequity is likely to be perceived. Furthermore, if the total non-COLA raise package is small, then the total dollar difference allocated to each performance level may further aggravate individual equity problems.

Salary Compression

Salary compression is a condition that reflects all three types of inequities. It can be defined as a perceived inequality between two or more employees concerning the relationship among salary, years of service, and performance levels. Salary compression is most easily seen when the salary of a new hire is the same or only slightly less than that of the more experienced employee performing the same tasks. This inequity occurs primarily because the average raises of incumbents over time are less than the increases in the marketplace salaries.

Pay structure characteristics and raise policies may also aggravate salary compression. If there are no steps in the pay structure, with employees' salaries rising one step annually if performance is at least satisfactory, then the salary of an incumbent will remain the same distance from the minimum salary of the pay range. In many cases, a large percentage of salaries remain within the first quartile of the pay range.

Since COLA raises increase the minimum and maximum of the pay range as well as the employee's salary by the same percentage, they do not serve to move the salary further up the pay range. If a pay-for-performance system does reward different levels of performance but does not significantly discriminate among percentage increases for different levels, then individual inequity may contribute to salary compression (see **pay-for-performance**).

Impact of Salary Inequity

When salary equity is ignored, or efforts to maintain it are not effective, several problems are likely to emerge. First, employee turnover will increase. As salary rates fall behind the market rate, employees will find employment in other organizations or governments at a higher rate of pay. Second, salary compression is likely to increase, as new hires with less experience will be given a salary close to, equal, or even greater than that of incumbents with many more years of experience. Complaints about unfair salaries will be more frequent. Increased pressure for promotion or upgrades will likely occur as well. Overall, morale and productivity are likely to decline, as the highly productive employee who does not feel sufficiently rewarded for high levels of performance compared to a less productive coworker is likely not to continue to perform at the same high level.

Strategies to Maintain Salary Equity

To solve salary inequities and maintain salary equity, several approaches are possible. Periodic salary surveys will help maintain external equity, at least for new hires and recently promoted employees. In choosing which outside or-

ganizations or governments to survey, several factors must be considered, including (1) the similarity in size and like positions, (2) geographical proximity, and (3) the likelihood of competitive employment. Information concerning pay range minimums and maximums must be collected. If possible, average pay data are also helpful. A government does not have to request information on all positions. Salary information for benchmark positions, for instance, one within a secretarial series, could be requested.

If a job evaluation is performed for all positions in the government at approximately the same time salaries from other governments/organizations are surveyed, then any internal inequities can be corrected as well. Using a job analysis to collect up-to-date information concerning the tasks and duties performed by each employee, each job can be reevaluated. Ideally, if a point factor job evaluation system is used, a total number of points can be assigned for each position by adding the points given to each job factor. Coupled with the salary survey information, the pay structure(s) can be revised, allowing each position to be placed on a pay range that is appropriate for internal equity concerns.

Salary compression can be overcome to some extent by ensuring that incumbent salaries are allowed to advance through pay ranges so that over time there is a greater distance between the salary and the minimum of the pay range. There are several policies that can accomplish this goal. First, a pay structure may contain pay ranges that are divided into steps. Traditionally, the salary of an incumbent is raised at least one step per year (assuming minimally satisfactory performance), while the salary of new hires is that of the first step. Second, typical promotional policies often contain a minimally specified pay raise. If there is also a governmental or organizational commitment to a "promote-from-within" policy, the salary of incumbents is likely to be further away from the minimums of pay ranges as they are promoted. Third, a pay-for-performance system that rewards different performance levels with increases in an employee's base pay will result in the salary of the consistently highest performers being placed increasingly further from the minimum of pay ranges.

Maintaining individual equity is a challenging task for any compensation administrator. First, a performance-evaluation, or pay-for-performance, system that validly measures performance levels must be established. In many cases, this may mean discarding the graphic rating performance evaluation system, in which one form is used to evaluate the performance of all employees, and replacing it with a system that describes behaviors linked to performance standards for each separate position. The more tasks are easily measurable, the easier it becomes to create a system that more validly measures performance levels. For more managerial, professional positions, in which tasks are complex and/or not easily measurable, more macromeasures of group or organizational results may be used to measure performance. The performance of a manager who supervises eight employees as they process paperwork may be rated by various work, or output, measures such as the number of claims processed on time.

In any pay-for-performance system, implementation difficulties are common. To ensure that such a system can be successful, there must be a supportive organizational culture, one in which (1) subordinates trust management, (2) objective performance measures are devised as much as possible, and (3) all employees play a significant role in creating and maintaining the system.

WENDELL C. LAWTHER

BIBLIOGRAPHY

Henderson, Richard, 1994. *Compensation Management: Rewarding Performance*, 6th ed. Englewood Cliffs, NJ: Prentice-Hall.
Lawler, E. E., 1981. *Pay and Organization Development.* New York: McGraw Hill.
Lawther, Wendell C., 1989. "Monitoring and Solving Pay Compression." *Personnel*, vol. 66: 84–87.
Snyder, Julie K., Gerald W. McLaughlin, and James R. Montgomery, 1992. "Diagnosing and Dealing with Salary Compression." *Research in Higher Education*, vol. 33: 113–124.
Treiman, Donald J., 1979. *Job Evaluation: An Analytic Review.* Washington, DC: National Academy of Sciences.
Treiman, Donald J., and Heidi I. Hartmann, eds., 1981. *Women, Work, and Wages: Equal Pay for Jobs of Equal Value.* Washington, DC: National Academy Press.
Wallace, Marc J., and Charles H. Fay, 1988. *Compensation Theory and Practice.* Boston, MA: PWS-Kent.

SALES AND CONSUMPTION TAXES.

Taxes applied to transactions that involve the sale of goods or services. A sales tax may have a broad base, as with the general sales tax, or a narrow base, as with excise or selected sales and consumption taxes. Sales taxes may also be applied to the final retail transaction, as is typically the case in the United States, or to intermediate stages in the production and distribution tax, as is the case with the value-added tax used in many other countries.

General Sales Tax

A general sales tax is applied to all transactions at the level at which it is imposed, with the exception of exempted transactions. Today, the general sales tax is the largest single source of state tax revenue. Sales tax rates typically range from 3 to 7.5 percent. The broad base of the general sales tax distinguishes it from selected sales or excise taxes, applied to specific transactions. The general sales tax is typically an *ad valorem* tax, applied to the value of a transac-

tion (a fixed percentage multiplied by the dollar value of the transaction), as opposed to a specific tax that is applied to the number of units sold (so many cents charged per gallon of gasoline sold, for example).

States shifted their revenue bases dramatically during the twentieth century. At its beginning, about half of state revenue came from property taxes and the remainder from selected excise taxes. During the Great Depression of the 1930s, failure to pay property tax and bank foreclosures limited and jeopardized property tax revenues. States began to abandon property taxes to local governments and replaced it with a general sales tax.

The commonly used approach to general sales taxes in the United States is a single-stage tax, applied to only the final retail transaction, as opposed to a multistage tax, applied to every stage in the production and distribution process. General sales taxes also are rarely earmarked for specific purposes, whereas excise taxes and other selected sales taxes often are. Motor fuel taxes, for example, are frequently earmarked for highways and transportation expenditures.

Sales and general consumption taxes are typically productive, generating a large revenue yield, and stable, vacillating less than revenues from other sources, especially income taxes. These characteristics have made sales taxes appealing to state legislatures. Forty-five states and the District of Columbia use the general sales tax. Exceptions are Alaska, Delaware, Montana, New Hampshire, and Oregon.

Thirty-three states also allow municipalities to levy an additional amount of sales tax. In such states, the local tax is collected through the same mechanism as the state sales tax and revenues are subsequently divided between jurisdictions based on location of the business enterprise. Critics of local sales taxes argue that it distorts consumption patterns and hurts businesses in municipalities with a local add-on, as consumers will cross municipal boundaries to avoid paying the tax. The local add-on to sales tax, then, is most effective when the differential between adjacent municipalities is not great, minimizing the incentive to make purchasing decisions based on taxes.

Sales taxes are regressive, having a greater proportionate impact on the poor than on the rich. Although the tax rate applied to a dollar of expenditures is the same for the poor as for the rich, the poor tend to spend a greater proportion of their total income on taxable items than do the rich, resulting in the poor paying a higher proportion of total personal income in sales taxes than those in higher income brackets. To alleviate regressivity, 28 states and the District of Columbia exempt food, which typically constitutes one-third of the tax base; 32 exempt utility bills; and 43 and the District of Columbia exempt prescription drugs. Eight states allow individuals a tax credit on their state personal income tax against sales tax paid; in 3 of the

8 states, the tax credit is for low-income senior citizens; in the other 5 states all low-income persons are eligible regardless of age. Cash refunds are paid to families and individuals that do not make enough income to recover the entire credit.

When calculating sales tax owed by an individual, fractional tax rates will often result in a tax liability that includes a fraction of a cent. These fractions of cents cannot be collected. Some states use brackets that define what the tax due in the bracket should be. These stated rates may follow regular rounding rules. Other states increase any fraction of a cent due to the next cent.

As with income taxes, collection of sales taxes is delegated to businesses. Vendor compliance is crucial to maintenance of sales tax revenues. Some states offer vendors a discount of as much as 5 percent of collections to compensate for the cost of compliance. Other states, such as Minnesota, provide no discounts. Critics contend that sales tax discounts vary by volume of sales, but there is little evidence that either compliance or compliance costs vary similarly. Other major taxes do not provide discounts for compliance either.

Sales and consumption taxes are often evaluated by the criteria of revenue productivity and neutrality. Sales taxes applied to a broad base produce more revenues, a desirable outcome for policymakers. But broad application of the sales tax may undercut attempts to make the general sales tax less regressive, by exempting necessities. Neutrality, or economic efficiency, means that the tax does not interfere with market functioning by distorting consumer preferences from what they would otherwise be. Again, a broad-based tax widely applied introduces the least distortion but is in opposition to exclusions designed to reduce regressivity and increase equity.

Some states exempt certain types of producer purchases from sales tax. Applying the tax to producer purchases as well as retail purchases increases revenue productivity and results in more funds for government. Critics contend, however, that taxes on producer purchases violate neutrality, as some final retail products use more producer goods than do others. The producer-purchase tax becomes embedded in the cost of the final retail product, causing such products to rise in price, and may distort some consumer preferences. States use two general rules for business-purchase exemptions: the component-part, or physical-ingredient, rule and the direct-use rule.

According to the component-part rule, an item is resold and therefore not taxable if it becomes a physical ingredient or component part of a good that is itself being sold. Thus, computer chips sold to a firm producing electronic door openers would be a component part and not taxed. If the good does not become a part of another, such as cement, it is taxed at the retail rate. This rule both yields a larger tax base and is easier to use. The direct-use rule is broader and exempts machinery and equipment used in the production process as well as physical ingredients. An oven used in a bakery or a machine used for stamping metal parts would be excluded under this rule. Typically, goods exempted by one of these two rules receive a certificate of exemption at the time of sale that allows tax collection on that item to be suspended.

In addition to food, utility bills, and prescription drugs that may be exempted from sales taxation to reduce regressivity, six states exempt clothing (Connecticut, Massachusetts, Minnesota, New Jersey, Pennsylvania, and Rhode Island). Although clothing is a necessity, it can also be a luxury. Clothing expenditures tend to be less concentrated among low-income taxpayers than the other items identified here.

To reduce regressivity, some states use a tax credit or rebate instead of a commodity exemption. Hawaii, Idaho, Kansas, New Mexico, South Dakota, Vermont, and Wyoming have chosen this approach. This method more accurately targets low-income taxpayers. Rather than reduce taxes for all purchases of a particular item, as the commodity exemption does, tax credit systems return a fixed sum to taxpayers at the end of the year, usually equal to the estimated payment of sales tax on food purchases by individuals in the lowest-income bracket. If high-income individuals have higher food expenses, they are reimbursed only to the level of consumption by low-income persons, as the rebate does not increase with the dollar value of household food purchases. The rebate approach more effectively reduces regressivity than does the commodity exemption, although it does require that individuals file returns with the state and the state make cash payments to individuals.

In most states, the general sales tax is applied mostly to tangible personal property, and only selectively if at all to purchases of services. Yet plainly, the service sector of the economy is the fastest growing. Among services currently taxed in some states are the lease or rental of tangible personal property, such as motor vehicles, video tapes, and so forth; the rental of transient accommodations (hotel and motel taxes); and some utility services. Only about half of the states tax repairs of tangible property. Most do not tax professional services, such as financial advising, accounting services, legal services, or medical services.

Consumers in high-sales-tax states may try to avoid paying taxes, especially on large purchases such as automobiles, appliances, and electronic equipment, by buying the products in a low-tax state. States are prohibited to tax transactions in interstate commerce to combat such avoidance. States have developed a use tax to replace lost sales tax revenues when consumers buy taxable products out of state and bring them into the state for use. The use of the product is taxed, as opposed to the sale. This tax, however, is difficult to enforce. Automobile use tax can be collected when the consumer registers the car with the state to obtain a license plate and registration. Income-tax audits where taxable items have been deducted as expenses may yield some additional tax revenues. But full implementation and effective enforcement of the use tax remains elusive. Catalog sales and telemarketing present special challenges to enforcement of this tax.

Selected Excise Taxes

Selected excise taxes place differential (usually higher) tax rates on differential commodities. While any specific excise tax may generate income, often the rationale is not revenues, but rather altering some aspect of taxpayer behavior. This violates the criterion of neutrality, but selected sales taxes are typically designed to maximize other criteria. Included are luxury, sumptuary, benefit-base, and regulatory and environmental excise taxes.

Luxury Excise Taxes

The tax criterion most enhanced by luxury taxes is ability-to-pay equity. Luxury taxes are applied to commodities more likely to be bought by the affluent. Federal excise taxes have been applied to jewelry, furs, entertainment, services, yachts, expensive aircraft, and expensive automobiles. Critics contend that the tax distorts consumer and producer choices. The tax is distributed on the basis of preference for the luxury item, which may not reflect those most able to pay. Administrative problems also exist in administering this tax. Merchants may have difficulty in separating out the different ways income was earned. And luxury taxes are not very elastic, so they do not typically experience rapid revenue growth relative to the tax base. These taxes do, however, yield some revenues, even though unlike the general sales tax, they are not typically a large part of the overall governmental revenue base. Luxury taxes have few political opponents except for the lobbyists of the taxed industries and often have popular appeal.

Sumptuary Excise Taxes

Sumptuary excise taxes are implemented to discourage consumption of products considered to be unhealthy or unsafe. Sometimes called "sin taxes," sumptuary excises include taxes on tobacco products and alcohol and are among the oldest taxes in the United States. Product demand for these items is usually inelastic, or price insensitive, so imposing the tax does not actually curb consumption, short of imposing an inhibitive rate. Legislatures rarely impose an extraordinarily high tax rate, however, for doing so would actually diminish tax revenues if the tax were high enough to stop consumption. The most

vocal criticisms of sumptuary taxes originate with producers, not consumers. These taxes are criticized for taking consumer dollars away from more desirable products, since price is inelastic and any moderate increase in the tax rate results in more money allocated to the taxed product rather than an immediate drop in consumption. They are also criticized for falling more heavily on low-income people, who spend greater proportions of their personal income on products on which sumptuary taxes have been levied.

Benefit-Base Excise Taxes

Benefit-base excise taxes have been applied to motor-fuel products. The product tax is an implied tax on highway usage, as high users of gasoline are also heavy users of highways. The tax on gasoline is usually included in the total price at the pump. Some states use motor-fuel taxes specifically for highway construction and maintenance, whereas other states disperse the funds for transportation expenditures that are more broadly defined. In the 1990s, the Russian Mafia in the New York area began scamming governments out of motor-fuel oil taxes. In a multimillion-dollar fraud scheme, the mob set up phony corporations through which the motor-fuels were bought and sold. In the process of the transactions, Mafia members claimed taxes had been paid when they had not. The paper trail proved difficult to track. Learning of the huge profits from the scam, the Italian Mafia began similar scams. Law enforcement and prosecutors attempted to sort out the convoluted commercial transactions in order to secure indictments and prevent future fraud.

Regulatory and Environmental Excise Taxes

Regulatory and environmental excise taxes are applied to alter consumer behavior and prevent socially harmful actions, with revenue collection being secondary to the regulatory impact. These taxes are applied on pollutants or as taxes on excessive resource usage. The taxes that generate revenues for the Superfund for cleanup of toxic wastes are an example, as are taxes applied on automobiles that are not fuel efficient.

Value-Added Taxes

The value-added tax (VAT) is used in about 75 countries, including all of the European Community, New Zealand, Japan, Mexico, and the Canadian central government. VAT provides an alternative method to the general sales tax for taxing consumption. VAT is a multistage tax applied to each stage of production-distribution on the value added to the product at that stage. It does not pyramid into tax being paid on tax, however, as it applies only to the increment added to value and not to value created in earlier stages taxed previously.

Proponents contend the VAT, like the general sales tax, is relatively productive, but unlike the general sales tax, which is added separately on each transaction, is embedded in the price and largely hidden from public view, making it easier to implement. Proponents also contend that VAT is largely self-enforcing, as any intermediate producer who adds value to a product must have at time of sale tax receipts for the whole value created to that point in the production process. Thus, producers themselves have an incentive to collect and enforce tax payments along the production chain. Proponents also argue that the VAT can be easily removed from products sold for export, increasing the competitive advantage of the country in global competition.

Critics contend that hiding the VAT in the product price allows higher tax rates to be applied than U.S. consumers would tolerate with the U.S. sales tax. They argue that like the general sales tax, the heaviest burden would be placed on manufacturing products. Further, the VAT is regressive.

Alleviating the regressivity of the VAT and other general consumption taxes more precisely than the blunt instrument of product exemptions would require changing the tax from an indirect tax on transactions to a direct tax on the consumption of individuals. Proponents of this argue that an individual consumption tax could replace the income tax at federal and state levels, instead of the general sales tax or a VAT. A direct consumption tax would be implemented in a similar fashion as the individual income tax and would require only two additional pieces of individual financial data.

As with the calculation of the income tax, individuals would add up all sources of taxable income, allowable deductions, and so forth. Individuals would also keep data on the value of their savings at the beginning of the tax year and at the end of the tax year. The net change in savings would be used to calculate the dollar value of total individual consumption, the sum on which taxes are due. Total individual consumption would be total income plus the net change in savings. If savings were reduced during the year, the net savings change would be added to income and total consumption would be greater than income, as the taxpayer spent down savings. If savings were increased during the year, the net savings change would be subtracted from income, and total consumption would be less than income, as the taxpayer built up savings. A progressive rate schedule would then be applied to total personal consumption, much as progressive rates are now applied to personal income.

Supporters of this approach argue that it would increase progressivity, would promote work by taxing consumption not income, and would encourage savings. Further, a personal consumption tax would avoid many of the enforcement and implementation problems associated with current sales taxes. Critics contend that calculating net savings changes would be complicated.

MARCIA LYNN WHICKER

BIBLIOGRAPHY

Conlan, Timothy J., Margaret T. Wrightson, and David R. Beam, 1990. *Taxing Choices: The Politics of Tax Reform.* Washington, DC: Brookings Institution.
Mikesell, John L., 1991. *Fiscal Administration.* Belmont, CA: Wadsworth.
Pechman, Joseph A., 1987. *Federal Tax Policy.* 5th ed. Washington, DC: Brookings Institution.
Whicker, Marcia Lynn, and Raymond A. Moore, 1988. *Making America Competitive: Policies for a Global Future.* New York: Praeger.

SCENARIO DEVELOPMENT PLANNING.
The technique of projecting various assumptions and options for organizations about complex future possibilities and probabilities to enable them to minimize risk and uncertainty in the environment.

What Is Scenario Development Planning?

Scenario development planning is a technique used to anticipate and prepare for possibly complex alternative futures. A scenario is a description of a possible or probable future. Scenarios convey projections of the future with various possibilities rather than one single view of how the future might look. Developing scenarios for planning purposes allows an organization to examine several options or risks that might have been overlooked in a plan constructed around a single expectation and to develop strategic responses in advance.

Military and law enforcement agencies have long used scenario development in their planning, but only after World War II did the use of scenario building expand significantly beyond these two areas. With the recognition that environmental changes are often complex and that accurate prediction about an organization's future surroundings are quite difficult, there came a realization that effective planning must do more to incorporate unpredictability. By the 1970s, scenario development planning was used extensively in corporate planning and now has expanded to a wide variety of arenas, including energy, transportation, aerospace, telecommunications, consumer products, banking, and education, and indeed generally throughout the manufacturing and service industries. Interestingly, although it got its start in government, it is not yet widely used in public administration.

The Advantages of Scenario Development Planning

Like the related technique of contingency planning, one of the main advantages of scenario development planning is that it helps an organization avoid surprise, prevent panic, and eliminate the need to scramble for a response. They allow the organization to think about the unthinkable and even to plan for it. Both techniques are particularly useful in preparing for rapid, dramatic, and profound changes in the operating environment by allowing organizations to anticipate problems and opportunities, and to prepare courses of action well in advance (see **contingency planning**).

In addition to its main benefit of allowing decisions to be made in advance and in a more orderly fashion, minimizing the need to scramble for a response, scenario development planning provides other advantages. The scenarios can serve as a guide for monitoring change and allow organizations to rehearse potential futures so that they are able to adapt, rather than simply react, to change. In addition, the sophistication of the scenarios provides for the description of the dynamics of forces and the ways in which they might combine to shape the future.

Scenarios can be developed for any environment that might change from the historical or expected path. They can draw from any field, and it is not uncommon for a scenario to anticipate changes in economic conditions, such as business cycles, market growth, and increases or decreases in inflation or interest rates. Social and political factors, such as demographic changes, elections, wars, unrest, strikes, and cultural phenomena are relevant, as are scientific factors such as weather conditions, climate change, technological advances, disease, and medical breakthroughs. All of these can become part of the plot that is written into a scenario much as a screenplay.

Given the large number of forces in the environment that could affect an organization, an endless number of scenarios could be generated. However, generally a few plots are most relevant in scenarios, and organizations tend to focus on the plots that are most appropriate to them and their missions. At the minimum, this usually results in an optimistic scenario, a pessimistic scenario, and a surprise-free scenario.

Procedures for Scenario Development Planning

There is no one rigid procedure for scenario development planning, and approaches are often tailored to the particular organization's needs, but a generalized approach would probably include the following:

1. *Background preparation*: identification of the organization's mission, objectives, policies, and planning focus. A review of documents that have guided the organization and events that have affected it is conducted, along with a thorough scanning of the organization's environment. The organization's points of vulnerability, or areas in which change could have a significant effect, are identified, or at least estimated, and a choice is made regarding the specific year for which to construct the scenarios.
2. *Critical indicator selection*: identification of driving forces or key variables that have the greatest ability to affect the organization's future environment as well as those that will have make-or-break consequences for the organization.
3. *Secondary variable selection*: identification of other environmental variables that might affect the behavior of the driving forces or key variables.
4. *Scenario writing*: construction of several descriptions of possible futures that show a range of behavior of the driving forces and key variables.
5. *Strategic response generation*: mapping out the best response to each scenario. Usually a moderately but not overly detailed response mapping is best. Scenario development planning can often lead to contingency planning, in which more detailed responses are usually developed since that technique focuses on a more limited range of events.
6. *Evaluation*: each scenario is tested, often through a simulation, to determine its utility and to ensure that it is credible, complete, and realistic.

Whereas most traditional planning techniques focus on one set of assumptions about the future, scenario development planning assumes various possibilities and events that may not normally be considered. However, use of the technique is not without pitfalls. Organizations may inadvertently put so much stock in a scenario that it becomes a self-fulfilling prophecy. But the technique does make it possible for organizations to quickly and strategically position themselves to minimize the effects of negative events and to take advantage of opportunities from positive events.

Scenario development planning raises awareness as to what could happen and incorporates response systems to react successfully. In essence, it allows organizations to effectively cope with uncertainty.

Michael J. Bloom

BIBLIOGRAPHY

Cline, Ray S., 1951. *Washington Command Post: The Operations Division.* War Department, Washington, DC: Office of the Chief of Military History.

Drabek, Thomas E., and Gerard J. Hoetmer, eds., 1991. *Emergency Management: Principles and Practice for Local Government.*

Washington, D.C.: International City Management Association.

Fink, Steven, 1986. *Crisis Management: Planning for the Inevitable.* New York: AMACOM, American Management Association.

Ford, Kristina, with Banes Lopach and Dennis O'Donnell, 1990. *Planning Small Town America: Observations, Sketches, and a Reform Proposal.* Chicago: Planners Press.

Perla, Peter P., 1990. *The Art of Wargaming: A Guide for Professionals and Hobbyists.* Annapolis: Naval Institute Press.

Watson, Mark S., 1950. *Chief of Staff: Prewar Plans and Preparations.* War Department, Washington, DC: United States Army Center of Military History.

SCHENGEN AGREEMENT.

Common title of a convention signed on June 14, 1985, in the Luxembourg village of Schengen between Belgium, France, Germany, Luxembourg, and the Netherlands on the gradual removal of controls at common frontiers, succeeded by the Schengen Implementing Convention, which was adopted and signed at Schengen on June 19, 1990.

Origin and Subsequent History

The 1957 Treaty of Rome establishing the European Economic Community (EEC) was amended in 1986 by virtue of the Single European Act (SEA), which proclaimed a Europe without internal frontiers. An important amendment was the fixing of a deadline (December 31, 1992) for the establishment of an internal market as an area without frontiers in which the free movement of goods, services, and capital is ensured. When the SEA was adopted, the European Community (EC) member states made a political declaration to the effect that the promotion of the free movement of persons would be parallelled by cooperation between the member states with regard to the entry, movement, and residence of nationals of non-EC states and with regard to the combating of terrorism, crime, traffic in drugs and illicit trading in works of art and antiques. Another general declaration that was made in Articles 9 to 13 of the SEA maintained the right for member states to adopt measures for the improvement of their internal security as long as these were compatible with EC legislation.

In anticipation of the December 1992 deadline, EC member states that already had bilateral and multilateral conventions allowing for the free movement of goods, services, and persons started negotiations on a common passport-free agreement. Belgium, the Netherlands, and Luxembourg had already signed the Benelux Treaty on Extradition and Mutual Assistance in Criminal Matters (1962), and France and Germany were signatories to the Convention of Paris (1977) and the Saarbrücken Convention (1984), respectively on police cooperation in the German-French border area and on the easing of controls on individuals at the common border. Given this experience, France, Germany, Belgium, Luxembourg, and the Netherlands decided to advance wider negotiations about the abolition of internal frontier controls.

The main rationale underlying the Schengen negotiations was that the abolition of border controls would have to be compensated by additional measures to prevent a weakening of the internal security of the states involved. This rationale was supported by the presumption that open borders would stimulate the mobility of criminals and criminal activities, and would increase the movement of illegal immigrants. In the wider context of the EC, other member states followed suit when a working program was initiated at the summit of the European Council at Rhodes in 1988 (the Palma document). In this context, the Schengen Agreement has often been called a "laboratory," "test garden," or "blueprint" for future European integration.

The 1985 Schengen Convention set the stage for a number of short-term measures for the relaxation of border controls, such as the introduction of visual checks on EEC citizens by means of a green sticker at the front window of small motorized vehicles. Furthermore, the Schengen parties decided to coordinate the fight against the illegal trade in drugs and to enhance the cooperation between customs and police authorities particularly with regard to serious international crime and illegal immigration. In the long run, the parties would harmonize their visa policies, firearms and ammunition laws, and rules on the registration of travelers in hotels. The practical implementation of these long-term measures formed the basis for the Schengen Implementing Convention. Like its forerunner, this convention had an intergovernmental status but was given more binding force as the parties agreed to the conditions under which internal frontier controls would be abolished.

The Schengen negotiations were undertaken by a central negotiating group consisting of senior officials from the different parties. Four different steering groups developed relevant themes in further detail: (1) police and security (which included working parties on drugs, firearms and ammunition, radio and telecommunications in border areas, and legal expertise on matters such as extradition and legal assistance), (2) movement of people (external border controls, design of a handbook for border officials), (3) transport, and (4) movement of goods (in particular agricultural products with risks and applicable health regulations). There was also a steering group on the Schengen Information System (SIS), which included working parties on data-processing problems and the supplementary information service (SIRENE). Political decisions and mandates were established at the Meeting of Ministers and Secretaries of State. The European Commission had observer status in these meetings.

At their meeting in Paris in June 1989, the five parties failed to reach agreement on issues such as extradition, the harmonization of drug policies, visa policy, and police activities on foreign territory. Remaining obstacles were the harmonization of asylum procedures, the lifting of bank secrecy in Luxembourg, and the location and creation of the Central Schengen Information System. More significant were the macropolitical events in Central and East Europe. German signature of the implementing convention was postponed because the nature of the external frontier and the responsibility for border controls underwent fundamental changes. Negotiations were resumed in March 1990, when other issues had been arranged more tightly: (1) the Schengen parties decided to ratify the Council of Europe Convention of January 28, 1991, for the Protection of Individuals with Regard to the Automatic Processing of Personal Data, to introduce national data protection legislation and to introduce complaint procedures before the SIS could become operational; (2) the provisions on asylum seekers would be explicitly linked with the 1951 Geneva Convention of the United Nations on the status of refugees (amended by the New York protocol of January 31, 1967, hereafter "Geneva Convention"); 3) the bank secrecy employed by Luxembourg would not be abolished but would be enfeebled as a consequence of Luxembourg's signature of the EC Directive on Money Laundering.

The Schengen Implementing Convention was signed on June 19, 1990, with the expectation of the unification between West and East Germany, it being agreed that the external border controls would apply at the borders between East Germany, Poland, and Czechoslovakia. This situation culminated in a readmission agreement between the Schengen states and Poland (concluded on March 29, 1991) concerning the return of illegal aliens to Polish territory.

The convention would come into effect in 1990 after the German unification, and it extended the same rights and obligations to all Germans. The implementation of the Schengen Agreement was postponed a number of times because of political disagreement about the quality of immigration and drug control, technical problems with the establishment of the SIS, and financial-economic implications for airports and certain trade sectors. The Schengen Agreement has been signed by all current member states of the European Union (EU) with the exception of Denmark, Ireland, and the United Kingdom.

Contents of the Agreement

The Schengen Agreement presents an outline of rules and measures effecting the free movement of persons, goods, services, and capital between the states that have signed it.

The Schengen Implementing Convention consists of eight titles. Title I states a number of definitions. "Internal frontiers" are defined as the common land frontiers of the contracting parties, their airports for internal flights and seaports for regular ferry connections originating exclusively from or proceeding exclusively to other ports in the territory of the contracting parties, without calling at ports outside that territory. Title I also defines other concepts, such as "external frontiers," "internal flight," "nonparty state," "alien," "aliens reported for purposes of nonadmission," "frontier crossing point," "frontier control," "carrier," "residence permit," "request for asylum," and "person seeking asylum."

Title II covers a series of measures on the removal of controls at internal frontiers and movement of persons. Chapter 1, Article 2 states that individuals may cross internal frontiers without any controls except when the *ordre public*, or national security, is in danger. In such a situation, an individual Schengen state can decide to reinstate internal frontier controls. Other Title II chapters include measures on the crossing of external frontiers, a common visa policy, conditions of movement of aliens, the issuing of residence permits to aliens, the introduction of carrier liability (sanctions), and the responsibility of contracting parties for asylum seekers.

External frontiers may in principle only be crossed at frontier crossing points. The parties will sanction unauthorized crossing of external frontiers outside these crossing points and fixed opening times. Aliens are allowed to stay in the territory of the contracting parties if they satisfy a number of criteria, such as the possession of a valid document or a valid visa if required (Article 5). Traffic across the external frontiers shall undergo control, such as the verification of travel documents and the search for and prevention of threats to national security and public order (Article 6).

The Schengen states adopted a common visa policy, which effectively means that they have drawn up a common list of "third" countries whose citizens require a visa to enter the Schengen territory (Article 9). A uniform visa valid for all contracting parties is also provided for in the agreement (Articles 10 and 11). Conditions and rules for the consideration of visa applications are laid down in Articles 12 to 17. There is no common visa regime for stays of more than three months (Article 18). Once citizens from third countries ("aliens") have acquired a uniform visa, they can enter the territory of one of the contracting parties and may move freely within the territory of all parties (Article 19). Articles 20 and 21 state conditions of movement for aliens not requiring a visa and for aliens holding a residence permit (Article 21). Article 22 states that an alien who duly enters the territory of a party must register with the authorities (Article 22) and if this person no longer fulfills the conditions, the person must leave the territory of one party immediately (Article 23). If a party considers the issue of a residence permit to an alien reported for the purposes of nonadmission, the party who reported that person has to be consulted (Article 25); this provision is relevant in connection with the use of the SIS (see later). Article 26 introduces a regime of carrier liability conditions (introduced in most Schengen member states before the agreement) to the extent that the carrier taking an alien who is refused entry to the territory of the contracting parties must retake responsibility and return the alien to the nonparty State; the carrier must ensure that the alien posesses the appropriate travel documents before the alien boards an airplane, ship, or vehicle. Carriers can be sanctioned in the event of noncompliance, but these sanctions are subject to conditions under the Geneva Convention. Man smugglers or those who, in pursuance of profit, assist aliens to enter the territory of the contracting parties will be prosecuted and sanctioned (Article 27).

Articles 28 to 38 provide rules for the responsibility for processing asylum requests, which to a large extent is a similar framework to that of the 1990 Convention for determining the member state responsible for examining an asylum application in one of the member states of the European Community (hereafter "Dublin Asylum Convention"). In popular terms, the rules seek to prevent "asylum shopping," which can be defined as the submission of an asylum request in more than one state. In Article 28, the contracting parties reaffirm their obligations under the Geneva Convention. Only one contracting party is responsible for the processing of an asylum request, and this party (usually the country in which the asylum seeker arrives) retains the right to refuse asylum status to the applicant (Article 29). The criteria on which the asylum request is judged may vary from one party to another (Article 33), which implies that the asylum applicant may stand more chance in one than in another Schengen member state; hence, the applicant may select the country where it is most likely to receive asylum status. The party responsible for processing the asylum request is usually the party that has issued a visa or residence permit to the applicant or the visa or residence permit with the longest period of validity (Article 30 provides further criteria to determine this responsibility). The responsible party shall also take back applicants found irregularly in the territory of another party while the asylum procedure continues or after the procedure has been terminated (Articles 33 and 34). Articles 35 and 36 provide rules on the processing of asylum requests by family members of the applicant and on the transfer of applications to other contracting parties for family or cultural reasons. Articles 37 and 38 issue rules on the exchange of legislative, statistical, and strategic information on asylum requests and of personal information on asylum applicants. In the context of similar cooperation between the EU member states, an information center has been established to coordinate these information exchanges, namely the CIREA (Center for Information, Discussion, and Exchange on Asylum).

Title III covers matters related to police and security, and includes compensatory measures in the sphere of police cooperation, drugs, and firearms. The detail of the rules in this title is unprecedented.

Chapter 1 (Articles 39–47) states that the police services in the contracting parties shall assist each other in the prevention and investigation of crime, in accordance with national legislation and within the limits of their competence. Article 39 provides further practical arrangements for the request and use of written information or evidence from another party, the channeling of these requests via national central police units, the regulation of police cooperation in frontier regions, and the conclusion of more complete bilateral agreements between contracting parties that share a common frontier. Article 40 states the conditions for cross-border surveillance: Persons presumed to have taken part in extraditable crimes may be observed in the territory of another contracting party if it has authorized this activity on the basis of a preceding request for mutual assistance (extraditable crimes are assassination, murder, rape, arson, counterfeiting of currency, aggravated theft and receiving, extortion, abduction and taking hostage, trading in human beings, illegal drug trafficking, arms and explosives offenses, destruction by explosives, and illegal transport of toxic and harmful waste). A document with the mandate must be carried by the officers executing the observation; these officers must be able to prove their official capacity at all times; they are allowed to carry their service weapons (but not to use them except in self-defense); and they may not perform house searches, interrogations, or arrests. A report of the operation must be submitted to the party on whose territory the observation took place, and the state from where the officers come gives the required assistance in further inquiries and judicial proceedings. The remainder of Article 40 states specific conditions that apply to the various contracting parties (officers authorized to carry out cross-border surveillance and respective authorities).

Article 41 provides rules on the right of pursuit: If officers of a contracting party pursue a person who has committed or who has participated in an extraditable crime, they may continue the pursuit across a border shared with another contracting party without prior authorization. This applies equally to persons who have escaped while under temporary arrest or those who are serving a period of detention or imprisonment. The officers performing the "hot pursuit" have to apply to the competent authorities as soon as they cross the border. These authorities may request termination of the pursuit, in which case it has to be discontinued, and apprehend the person pursued on request of the pursuing officers. The latter do not have the right of interrogation but can nevertheless question the person pursued until the officers of the other contracting party can establish the person's identity or arrest the person.

The zones or periods starting from the crossing of the frontier are not identical but further specified in the declaration: Germany does not impose any restrictions on the cross-border pursuit of offenders by Dutch, Belgian, French, and Luxembourg police officers, and in most other contracting parties the zone extends to maximally ten kilometers. The "hot pursuit" is subject to a number of conditions, namely that the pursuing officers comply with the law of the contracting party and obey the orders of the competent local authorities, that the pursuit only takes place across land frontiers, that the pursuing officers are easily identifiable, and that they report to the competent local authorities of the contracting party in whose territory the pursuit has taken place. Rules concerning house searches, carrying service weapons, and assistance with further inquiries are identical to those stated concerning cross-border surveillance.

The remainder of Article 41 specifies the officers authorized to perform the pursuit and states that it does not affect—for the contracting parties concerned—Article 27 of the Benelux Treaty of June 27, 1962, on Extradition and Mutual Assistance in Criminal Matters, as amended by the Protocol of May 11, 1974. Articles 42 and 43 provide accountability rules for officers on mission. The remaining articles cover matters such as technical cooperation (telephone, radio, and telex links) and the secondment and exchange of liaison officers.

Chapter 2 (Articles 48–53) supplements the Council of Europe Convention on Mutual Assistance in Criminal Matters and states conditions under which mutual assistance shall also be granted, for example, in proceedings for a pardon and civil actions with criminal proceedings. There are also rules on the admissibility of letters, the sending of procedural documents, and requests for mutual assistance between judicial authorities.

Chapter 3 (Articles 54–58) specifies the application of the *non bis in idem* principle: A person who has been tried for an offense on which a final decision has been given by a contracting party cannot be prosecuted for the same offense in another member state (save some exceptions).

Chapter 4 (Articles 59–66) arranges extradition of persons between the contracting parties and supplements the European Convention in Extradition of September 13, 1957, and—for the Benelux members—Chapter 1 of the Benelux Treaty of June 27, 1962. Article 62 states the conditions of extradition in the event of amnesty, a complaint or an official notice authorizing criminal proceedings. Article 63 provides that the contracting parties undertake to extradite between themselves persons against whom proceedings are brought by the judicial authorities of the requesting party for an extraditable offense (see earlier, Article 50) or persons who are wanted for the carrying out of a penalty or precautionary measure. Reports in the SIS will have the same status as a request for provisional arrest within the meaning of Article 16 of the European Convention on Extradition (Article 64). Extradition may be authorized without a formal extradition procedure provided the wanted person consents (Article 66).

Chapter 5 (Articles 67–69) provides rules for the transfer of the execution of criminal sentences and supplements the Council of Europe Convention of March 21, 1981, on the Transfer of Sentenced Persons between those contracting parties that are parties to that convention.

Chapter 6 contains a declaration of a joint war against drugs in conformity with the 1961 Single Convention on Narcotic Drugs (amended in 1972), the 1971 Convention on Psychotropic Substances, and the 1988 Convention on Illegal Trafficking in Narcotic Drugs and Psychotropic Substances, implying the prevention and punishment of illegal trafficking, export, sale, supply, and delivery in drugs and psychotropic substances. To this purpose, the contracting parties shall establish a permanent working party responsible for examining common problems on the prevention of drug-related crimes (Article 70). Controls at the external frontiers will be strengthened to combat the illegal importation of drugs and psychotropic substances—including cannabis—and the transfer of police and customs personnel released at internal frontiers (Article 71). Controls will also be removed from internal frontiers to the interior of the member states (Article 74). The contracting parties commit themselves to monitor places known to be used for drug-trafficking and to pass legislation to permit the seizure and confiscation of the proceeds of illegal trafficking in drugs and psychotropic substances (Articles 71-74 and 75). According to Article 73, they will also permit controlled deliveries of illegal drugs, which extends police powers. A certificate will be established for exempted substances (drugs used for medical purposes), and procedural rules will be developed for the control of drugs and psychotropic substances subject to more rigorous controls in the territory of one or more parties than in their own territory (Articles 75 and 76).

Chapter 7 (Articles 77–91) contains rules on the adaptation of national laws on firearms and ammunition to the provisions of the Schengen Agreement. Article 78 classifies the relevant firearms, Article 79 lists prohibited firearms and ammunition, and Articles 80 and 81 list those that shall be subject to licensing or a declaration. Articles 82, 83, and 84 provide conditions of licensing and registration, firearms that are excepted, and the keeping of a register. Furthermore, the contracting parties establish a system of obligation and inspection (Article 85) to enact prohibitions and to incorporate provisions (withdrawal of license, seizure of firearms) in their national legislation (Article 86). On the basis of the European Convention of June 28, 1978, on the Control of the Acquisition and Possession of Firearms by Individuals, the contracting parties agree to establish an exchange of information about the purchase of firearms by private individuals and retail arms dealers (Article 91).

Title IV lays down rules for the establishment and use of the Schengen Information System, which is an automated joint information system consisting of a national system in each Schengen member state and a central technical support system (CIS) in Strasbourg. The system will assist law enforcement authorities in frontier controls, customs checks, and inspections within the country and will provide them with reports on objects (stolen motor vehicles or firearms, but also objects wanted as evidence in criminal proceedings), persons wanted for arrest with a view to extradite them, witnesses and suspects summoned to appear before court in connection with criminal proceedings, persons who have to serve a term in jail, aliens reported for nonadmission, missing persons, and persons who are under surveillance. The particulars that may be filed include last name and first name (and aliases), middle initial, physical distinguishing marks, date and place of birth, sex, nationality, indication that the person concerned is armed and/or violent, reason for report and action to be taken by the authorities.

The system used is a "hit/no-hit" system, which means that there are only a limited number of input questions that can result in an answer. If this system is unsuccessful, the national Supplementary Information Service may be addressed to request or report data. In practice, SIRENE will function as a national service responsible for screening requests for actions to be taken (e.g., validation of a warrant for arrest by another contracting party; Article 108). Title IV also provides an elaborate data protection regime for the use of the SIS, such as authorized access of national agencies to the SIS (Article 101), the conditions under which data can be duplicated, modified, added to, rectified, or erased (Articles 102–107), the right of any person to have access to data and the obtainment of correction (Articles 109–110), and the maximum period data may be kept (Articles 112–113). Persons about whom a report is kept may bring an action before the competent court or authority under national law of a contracting party for correction, deletion, information, or compensation (Article 111).

Each contracting party designates a national supervisory authority (Article 114) and a joint supervisory authority shall be established to supervise the technical support function of the SIS, consisting of two representatives of the national supervisory authority (Article 115). The national supervisory authority is usually the national data protection board (i.e., the *Commission Nationale de l'Informatique et des Libertés* in France, the *Registratiekamer* in the Netherlands). Each contracting party enacts national data protection measures minimally equal to the European Convention of the Protection of Individuals with Regard to the Automatic Processing of Personal Data (1981): National data protection legislation is a prerequisite for signature of the Schengen Agreement (Article 117). Each national party is responsible for implementing rules in respect of the national part of the SIS, such as preventing unauthorized persons from gaining access to installations used for processing personal data (Article 118).

The issue of data protection is more explicitly dealt with in Title VI, including noncomputerized files (Article 127), the incorporation of the Recommendation R(87)15 of September 17, 1987, of the Committee of Ministers of the Council of Europe for regulating the use of personal data in connection with the police (Article 129) and the protection of data transmitted by liaison officers (Article 13).

Title V of the Schengen Implementing Convention covers the transport and movement of goods: The Schengen parties commit themselves to avoid unjustified barriers to the movement of goods across their internal frontiers (Article 120). In accordance with community law, the contracting parties waive the inspections and production of plant health certificates (Article 121). They will further consider the abolition of the obligation to produce a license for the export of strategic industrial products and technologies (Article 123). Checks and inspection of goods linked to the movement of travelers at internal frontiers will be maximally reduced (Article 124), and customs authorities will second liaison officers to other Schengen member states.

The implementation of the Schengen Agreement is in the hands of the Executive Committee, which will oversee the proper implementation of the Schengen Convention. Each party shall have one seat in it, usually the responsible minister assisted by one or more experts (Title VII).

The final provisions of the Schengen Implementing Convention (Title VIII) confirm the compatibility of Schengen with the Geneva Convention and with European Community law (Article 134). Article 140 states that every member state of the European Community (or Union) may become a party to the convention, and Article 142 states that if a Europewide convention for the creation of an area without internal frontiers would be established, the Schengen Agreement will be subject to incorporation, replacement, or alteration (see later).

Legal and Political Context

The considerable delay in the implementation of the Schengen Agreement has made it likely that it will be eclipsed by wider developments in the context of the European Union. Substantial parts of the Schengen Agreement have been or will be replaced by intergovernmental conventions that fall within the scope of Justice and Home Affairs Cooperation (Title VI) of the Treaty on European Union (TEU). First, all EU member states participated in the working program of action for the completion of the Internal Market ("Palma Document"), which listed the compensatory measures for the realization of a European Community without internal frontier controls. Second, the Dublin Asylum Convention, which specifically seeks to prevent double applications for asylum in different states, is set up along lines similar to those in the Schengen Implementing Convention (Articles 28–38). Third, Article 100c of the TEU envisages the introduction of a common visa policy, which overrules the one in the Schengen Agreement. Fourth, Title VI, Article K.1(2) of the TEU regards as a matter of common interest "rules governing the crossing by persons of the external borders of the member states and the exercise of controls thereon;" consequently, the draft Convention on the Crossing of the External Frontiers of the Community–delayed because of a conflict between the United Kingdom and Spain over border controls in Gibraltar–makes the Schengen Agreement potentially subject to incorporation, replacement, or alteration (particularly Chapter 2, Articles 3–8 of the Schengen Implementing Convention).

The European Court of Justice may assume jurisdiction in the circumstance of integration of the Schengen Agreement in the former SEA. The elevation of Schengen into the framework of the EU may thus be subject to the procedure laid down in Article K.3.2(c) of the TEU, which states that conventions may be drawn up, which may stipulate that the European Court of Justice shall have jurisdiction to interpret their provisions. Fifth and relatedly, the External Frontiers Convention is associated with the creation of a European Information System (EIS), which will at least be compatible with, or replace, the SIS.

The overlap between Schengen and Title VI of the TEU is not complete because cross-border executive police powers (cross-border surveillance and right of pursuit) provided in the Schengen Implementing Convention are not included in the range of police cooperation activities (Article K.1[9]) of Title VI of the TEU. Operational cross-border policing activities may have to be arranged by means of an additional series of bilateral or multilateral agreements, which can be established through Article K.7 of the TEU.

The provisions of the Schengen Implementing Convention on money laundering (Article 72) and firearms and ammunition (Articles 77–91) are superseded by the EC Council Directive 91/308 on the prevention of the use of the financial system for the purpose of money laundering and the EC Council Directive 91/477, which makes the acquisition and possession of weapons subject to common rules based on a community list of authorized weapons.

The Schengen Implementing Convention has been contentious for a variety of reasons: democratic control, inconsistency with other international conventions, loss of sovereignty, lack of harmonization, and divergence of criminal justice policies. The European Parliament and some of the national parliaments have deplored the "democratic deficit" of the negotiations on the Schengen Agreement. Its intergovernmental nature has been respon-

sible for bypassing parliamentary consultation procedures, and its inclusion of criminal justice matters, which–at the time of the negotiations–were outside the remit of the European Community, meant that the Schengen Agreement could not be subjected to the EC legislative procedures.

The Dutch Council of State criticized the Schengen Agreement for effectively deteriorating the position of refugees, the absence of a substantial asylum policy, insufficient protection of privacy, and the absence of central judicial control. In France, Parliament challenged the Constitutional Court to interpret the impact of Schengen on national sovereignty. In the absence of substantial harmonization of the criminal justice systems of the Schengen member states, it has been feared that divergent policies on drugs, immigration, and internal security would either contribute to the spreading of related problems across the internal frontiers of the Schengen parties or that national policy approaches–for instance, tolerating the personal use of "hard drugs" or allowing the sale of "soft drugs" to foreigners in coffeeshops–would have to be abandoned in favor of a common, more repressive policy. Finally, it has been regretted that the Schengen Agreement fails to establish a supranational jurisdiction or at least does not authorize a court that could either deal with international legal guarantees for individual citizens or with uniform legal definitions aiming at a gradual harmonization of criminal justice norms and legislation in the areas of asylum, visa, and data protection.

Monica G. W. den Boer

BIBLIOGRAPHY

Fijnaut, Cyrille, 1993. "The Schengen Treaties and European Police Cooperation." *European Journal of Crime, Criminal Law, and Criminal Justice*, vol. 1, no. 1: 37–56.

Fijnaut, Cyrille, Jules Stuyk, and Peter Wytinck, eds., 1992. *Schengen: proeftuin voor de Europese Gemeenschap?* Arnhem/Antwerpen: Gouda Quint bv./Kluwer.

d'Haenens, Jules, and Brice de Ruyver, eds., 1992. *Schengen en de Praktijk*. Gent: Mys & Breesch.

Meijers, Henk, et al., 1991. *Schengen: Internationalisation of Central Chapters of the Law on Aliens, Refugees, Privacy, Security, and the Police*. Zwolle/Deventer, W. E. J. Tjeenk Willink/Kluwer Law and Taxation.

Mols, Gerard, ed., 1990. *Dissonanten bij het akkoord van Schengen*. Deventer: Kluwer.

O'Keeffe, David, 1991. "The Schengen Convention: A Suitable Model for European Integration?" *Yearbook on European Law*, vol. 11: 185–219.

d'Oliveira, H. U. Jessurun, 1994. "Expanding External and Shrinking External Borders: Europe's Defence Mechanisms in the Areas of Free Movement, Immigration, and Asylum." In David O'Keeffe and Patrick Twomey, eds., *Legal Issues of the Maastricht Treaty*. London: Chancery, 261–278.

Outrive, Lode van, 1992 (Rapporteur). *Report of the Committee on Civil Liberties and Internal Affairs on the Entry into Force of the Schengen Agreements*. European Parliament Session Documents, A3-0288/92, Brussels.

Pauly, Alexis, ed., 1993. *Les accords de Schengen: Abolition des frontières intérieures ou menace pour les libertés publiques?* Maastricht: European Institute of Public Administration.
———, 1994. *Schengen en panne.* Maastricht: European Institute of Public Administration.
Peek, Jan, 1990. "Schengen: wegwijzer naar een gewijzigd Europa." In G. N. M. Blonk, C. J. C. F. Fijnaut, and E. L. A. M. de Kerf, eds., *Grensverleggende recherche.* Lochem: Van den Brink, 111–129.
"Schengen Convention on Border Controls 1990 France/Germany/Benelux," 1991. *Commercial Laws of Europe,* vol. 14, part 2.
Taschner, H. C., 1990. *Schengen oder die Abschaffung der Personenkontrollen an den Innengrenzen der EG.* Saarbrücken: Universität des Saarlandes.

SCHUMAN, ROBERT (1886–1963).

One of the founding fathers of the European Union and an ardent European federalist. Schuman was born in Luxembourg into a family that had come from Lorraine. He studied in Germany and began his career as a lawyer in Lorraine when this region was in German hands. Under the Treaty of Versailles in 1919, Alsace and Lorraine were returned to France; it was at this point that Schuman became the parliamentary representative for the region. Schuman, who was a Christian Democrat, concentrated on Franco-German issues, which were to remain his chief concern throughout his political career.

Schuman served in the government of Paul Reynaud when France fell to Nazi Germany in 1940, and he briefly supported Philippe Pétain, who replaced Reynaud. Schuman was deported to Germany during World War II, and, following his release, he worked for the French Resistance. After World War II, Schuman resumed his parliamentary career and led his own party in the National Assembly. He served as prime minister on two occasions in 1947–1948 and in 1948, but it is for his term in office as foreign minister from 1948 to 1952 that he is best remembered.

On May 9, 1950, Schuman announced at a press conference in the Salon de l'Horloge at the Quai d'Orsay a proposal to pool French and German production of coal and steel under a new supranational authority. The declaration was made with the prior approval and support of the French and German governments. The Schuman Plan, which was drafted by Jean Monnet, was in effect the birth certificate of the European Community as it led to the European Coal and Steel Community, the first of the three communities. For Schuman and Monnet, both of whom were ardent European federalists, economic integration was a means to an end, namely, the creation of a political union. The Schuman Plan of 1950 clearly envisaged the pooling of French and German coal and steel production as the first concrete foundation of a European federation indispensable to the preservation of peace.

Schuman also played a part in introducing plans for a common defense policy among the member states of the European Coal and Steel Community, namely, the European Defense Community (EDC), which was proposed in 1950 by the French prime minister of the time, René Pleven. The EDC Treaty, whose spiritual father was Jean Monnet, failed to be ratified by the French National Assembly in 1954 as a result of an alliance between the French Gaullists and the Communists. Schuman subsequently resigned from office and played a less active role in French politics thereafter. In 1955, he became president of the European Movement, an umbrella organization comprised of voluntary organizations, societies, and clubs that promote and propagate the idea of European unity and integration. In 1958, Schuman became the first president of the European Parliamentary Assembly, the successor institution of the Parliamentary Assembly of the European Coal and Steel Community.

MARGARET MARY MALONE

BIBLIOGRAPHY

Diebold, W., 1959. *The Schuman Plan.* New York: Council on Foreign Relations.
Milward, A. S., 1984. *The Reconstruction of Western Europe 1945–1951.* London: Methuen.
Monnet, Jean, and Robert Schuman, 1986. *Correspondance 1947–1953.* Lausanne: Fondation Jean Monnet pour l'Europe, Centre de Recherches Européennes.
———, 1989. *Western Europe Since 1945: A Political History,* 4th ed. London: Longman.
Urwin, Derek W., 1991. *The Community of Europe: A History of European Integration Since 1945.* London: Longman.

SCIENCE, TECHNOLOGY, AND PUBLIC POLICY.

A policy and management-oriented area of study born in response to events in the world of practice. Individuals in government who sought to design policy to deal with the new world that emerged in the wake of World War II came to grips with a reality that the existing literature did not describe, much less analyze. As academic scholars sought greater clarity about what was happening, they created a literature, and this literature came to be a field, taught in courses in universities around the country and the world.

The concept of "public policy" sets the field apart from similar academic endeavors—that is, the history, philosophy, or sociology of science and technology. It provides special linkage with the disciplines of political science and public administration. In many universities, an interdisciplinary field called Science and Technology Studies (STS) has emerged, with its own journal and professional association. The specialty of science, technology, and public policy can be conceived as part of STS, but for most adherents, the term "public policy" creates a strong centrifugal pull and special identity. The strength of this identity lies in giving political scientists and public administrationists a special place in the field. The problem lies in the conflict between the need to put some boundaries on the field to make intellectual progress while simultaneously drawing nourishment from the constantly changing agenda of policy problems. Sociologists of science and technology might well be seen as more "basic" in their approach to science and technology studies, with a search for a tight conceptual framework. Political scientists and especially public administrationists, with a greater "applied" bent, have been less concerned with conceptual "rigor" and more with policy "relevance."

A Discipline to the Field?

It would be too much to say there is a discipline, but there is a discipline to the field. There are certain continuing intellectual concerns even as the agenda of those concerns changes with the policy times. What unites those who think, write, and act in the field of science and technology (S&T) policy is interest in the political processes and organizational dynamics through which societal actors shape science and technology policy.

These central concerns can be better elucidated by discussing their evolution over the years. For purposes of this analysis, the three major periods in the intellectual history of science and technology policy are (1) from World War II to the Apollo moon landing in 1969, (2) from Apollo to the fall of the Soviet Union in 1991, and (3) the present post-cold-war period, whose basic character has barely taken form, but which is unmistakably different from what went on before. These can be characterized as eras of optimistic growth, ambivalent consolidation, and post-cold-war transformation of the scientific state. The literature has reflected changes over time.

Optimistic Growth: From World War II to Apollo

Science and technology were major contributors to the allied victory in World War II. The atomic bomb was the most dramatic evidence of revolutionary change wrought by science and technology. Science, technology, and public policy as a field was born as government practitioners and academics analyzed what had occurred and was crystallizing in the post-World War II period.

The report prepared by Vannevar Bush, *Science: The Endless Frontier,* in 1945, became the rationale for government's support of basic research in universities (Bush 1945). It led in 1950 to the establishment of the National Science Foundation as well as general acceptance of the view that support of science was a legitimate governmental responsibility. A second report in 1947 (known as the Steelman Report) discussed governmental organization for

science, an institutional theme that would continue (President's Scientific Research Board 1947).

Science and technology spending increased and became a significant function of government. Although the National Science Foundation and the existing National Institutes of Health grew to become major funders of basic research, the dominant agencies by far in science and technology from 1945 to 1969 were those concerned with the cold war. These were the Defense Department, Atomic Energy Commission, and National Aeronautics and Space Administration. In terms of S&T policy, the major issues that interested analysts were (1) the role of scientists in the policy process and (2) how science and technology were governed.

One of the pioneers of S&T policy study was Don K. Price, who would serve as the first dean of the Kennedy School at Harvard. Reflecting on his experience in the Truman years, when much science and technology policy was created, Price (1954) wrote *Government and Science.* Price not only touched on the increased policy role of scientific advisers but also noted that government accomplished much of its S&T work through contracts with industry and universities. The governance of science was thus different from other policy areas in terms of actors and mechanisms, presenting difficult problems in accountability.

After Sputnik, President Dwight Eisenhower elevated science within government by appointing the first official presidential science adviser as well as a multimember President's Science Advisory Committee mechanism. Much of the enhanced role of scientists concerned advice on weapons. In 1960, the British writer C. P. Snow warned that democracy could be in danger if nontechnical governmental leaders followed the advice of the "wrong" scientists. This theme of scientists and the relation of knowledge and power became a paramount concern in the literature. Along with scientists' roles in broader policy (i.e., defense), a growing interest for analysts was their place in policy-for-science per se, such as spending for research and development (R&D). Scientists were seen as wanting to make decisions about who got what in R&D and then to have that money spent with little democratic control (Price 1965). In short, scientists were being studied as an interest group in a policy process. What students of S&T policy were elucidating were the special characteristics of scientists as political actors, including power that arose from the public perception of their "apolitical" nature.

In the first half of the 1960s, science experienced what would later be called its "golden age" of federal funding. Part of the reason for the golden age was the rise of NASA in the first half of the 1960s. John F. Kennedy's decision to go to the moon provided not only new funds for scientists and engineers, but also (thanks to NASA Administrator James Webb) funds for science and technology policy studies. Many men and women who would write about S&T policy in later years were nurtured in the 1960s by NASA "institutional" grants and fellowships to what Webb hoped would become "space-age universities." Webb himself contributed to the public administration side of S&T policy with his book *Space Age Management* (New York: McGraw Hill, 1969). Up to 1966, the decade was a time of "can-do" optimism, new frontiers, and rising expectations everywhere. The management innovations of NASA were seen as a wave of the future. With the onset of the Great Society of Lyndon Johnson, science and technology were linked in rhetoric and policy: "If we can go to the moon, why can't we . . . ?" (Lambright 1985). The Department of Housing and Urban Development (1965) and the Department of Transportation (1966) were born with a technocratic flavor. Industrialized housing and new mass transit systems seemed poised to remake the urban landscape (Lambright 1976). However, in 1969, even as S&T practice reached a triumphant climax in the Apollo landing, there also crested a wave of opposition to S&T that was bringing the golden age to a halt and that was strongly reflected in the S&T policy literature.

Ambivalent Consolidation: Apollo to 1991

If Apollo marked a high point in S&T practice, Vietnam was for many critics a low point. Television technology, via satellite, brought to living rooms in the late 1960s and early 1970s the horror of war. Chemicals were used to defoliate trees and bombs to kill soldiers. But technology and the rationalistic management practices associated with it were shown to be blunt and clumsy instruments, with the victims of S&T policy in Vietnam often innocent women and children. The university, a research partner of government, was accused by war critics of complicity in the Vietnam war. Along with the "military-industrial complex," the "government-science marriage" was a focus of protest.

It was not just Vietnam that was bringing science and technology into disrepute. Scientists were again coming to the fore as key actors in public policy, this time to sound the alarm about man's destruction of the environment through pesticides and industrial technology (Carson 1962). In 1970, one year after the Apollo landing, it was not the moon that millions of Americans celebrated, but the first Earth Day. In 1971, technology became a victim of the newly powerful environmental activists, when the supersonic transport development project was terminated. Instead of optimism, there was technological pessimism. A group of scientists published a best-selling book, *Limits to Growth*, that encapsulated the new mood in 1972 (Meadows et al. 1972).

Then came the energy crisis in 1973–1974. As the country scrambled for ways out of the energy predicament while simultaneously protecting new environmental values, science and technology spending rebounded. This would be known as the environment and energy decade. For better or worse, the nation again looked to science and technology for "fixes" to problems. However, this was not the 1960s, and there was a new ambivalence about S&T. Technology was widely seen as a double-edged sword. The dilemma was how to give S&T positive direction, and who would determine what was positive. Various writers searched for ways to study an increasingly complex subject matter. Concerns with scientific elites in the policy process were less in evidence in these times. One of the books that appeared in the middle of this decade was *Governing Science and Technology* (Lambright 1976). This book combined political process with institutional analysis. It showed how political forces shaped government agencies and how those agencies in turn influenced the course of science and technology. Bureaucratic power was shown to be key to understanding S&T policy and how various strategies could enhance or diminish this power.

The field of science, technology, and public policy now reflected an uncertainty about S&T. Writers waxed on terms such as "appropriate technology," meaning technology that a "user" could comprehend and manage. "Small" could be "beautiful." Energy conservation, rather than a nuclear reactor, could be the path of our energy future.

One of the themes that emerged from the environmental movement of the 1970s and which continued thereafter was concern for technological risks. Even as the nation advanced technology, it sought to control it. At the beginning of the 1970s, the mood was about how to arrest runaway S&T; by the end of the decade, the attitude of writers was to advance S&T while minimizing negative side effects. An innovation in the practice as well as theory of S&T policy during the 1970s was the establishment of the Office of Technology Assessment (OTA) as a staff arm of Congress. This grew out of congressional-executive conflicts and the seemingly endless number of technical disputes. "Experts" were in conflict, and these disputes were fanned by an increasingly influential media on the nation's agenda. Love Canal and Three-Mile Island became symbols of the new politics of S&T (Mazur 1981). Also in the 1970s and more and more in the 1980s, the science behind regulation became a highly contentious issue. Where did science end and administrative judgment begin? The boundaries were often obscure. Were scientists advising policymakers or were policymakers getting scientists to legitimate decisions made on nonscience grounds? Whatever else, science advising mechanisms continued to be part of the permanent apparatus of government, but scientists in regulation were scientists in conflict with themselves and their administrative clients.

Post-Cold-War Transformation

In the 1980s, S&T policy at the federal level revolved chiefly around national security issues and the question of how much government should intervene in the economy to make America more technically competitive. The biggest federal programs were defense related, particularly Ronald Reagan's StarWars program. These years underlined the one constant in S&T policy over the years—namely, the cold war. But in 1991, the Soviet Union collapsed and with it the rationale cited for much of the spending on S&T. Without question, a new era began, and science, technology, and public policy—its ideas, actors, institutions, and theoretical literature—evolved. Where is it heading?

There are enough national security threats around the world to demand a significant level of S&T military spending. But there are other, newer priorities for R&D and associated regulatory tools. One area is health. The biotechnology and genetic engineering revolutions have just begun. The Human Genome project will allow genes to be better deciphered and possibly altered. AIDS represents a new kind of epidemic and there could be others. Health raises horrendous issues for using, affording, and controlling new technology (Krimsky 1991).

Another priority is economic competition for high technology products. This assumes government becomes a major player in the private enterprise system to help industry compete with Japan and other nations. It entails consciously "picking winners" among technologies and aiding certain industries while letting others decline (Graham 1991).

A third is environment. The global environment—led by issues of ozone depletion, climate change, and biodiversity—became a large concern in the late 1980s and early 1990s. The demanding and expensive issue of environmental cleanup of cold war related nuclear and military bases will be around for a long time. The specter of Chernobyl hangs heavy in the public mind. Given lax environmental safeguards in Eastern Europe and the former USSR, many nuclear power plants could repeat the Chernobyl experience. Ocean pollution is a growing problem. Climate change is the ultimate environmental threat. Certainly, environment is a growing focus for science and technology policy and could be the proverbial "moral equivalent of war" (Vig and Kraft 1994).

The fourth is space. It is indeed an "endless frontier" and will be further explored and utilized in time. The question is how much, how soon? Building giant facilities in space has become a gargantuan international management endeavor. NASA has come on hard times since its glory days, and issues of reinventing NASA as well as other government S&T agencies are of great interest to analysts (McCurdy 1993). President Bush proclaimed as a mission a return to the moon and then on to Mars. Combined with a "mission to planet earth," a program using satellites to monitor global environmental change, space could usefully absorb many of the nation's scientists and engineers and provide excitement for a world that has need for an uplifting vision.

Conclusion

Which area of S&T policy noted here will dominate the agenda in the future? Or will it be some other? What the four mentioned have in common with national security is their global dimension. If there is one certainty in the post–cold-war era, it is that global concepts have taken on new importance. S&T policy in the United States or any other nation is increasingly part of the global context.

Meanwhile, the science, technology, and public policy literature expands, seeking a framework within which to make sense of events seemingly random (Hamlett 1992). As always, the emphasis is on key actors, institutions, and processes of choice and governance. There is no consensus about any one approach, and the problem, as always, has been to keep up with a moving target. Perhaps in the future the political science and public administration approaches will blend more closely with those of S&T studies generally. In the latter, frameworks called "social constructionism" and "actor-network theory" have taken hold (Bijker et al. 1987). The author has sought some synthesis between traditional S&T policy and S&T studies (Lambright 1994).

The S&T policy enterprise is dynamic, important, and chaotic. Nothing moves faster than science and technology, and therefore the quest for boundaries and focus is a difficult one. The terrain changes constantly. But for those engaged, the thrill is in the chase.

W. Henry Lambright

BIBLIOGRAPHY

Bijker, Wiebe E., Thomas P. Hughes, and Trevor J. Pinch, eds. 1987. *The Social Construction of Technological Systems*. Cambridge: MIT Press.

Bush, Vannevar, 1945. *Science: The Endless Frontier*. Washington, DC: Government Printing Office.

Carson, Rachel, 1962. *Silent Spring*. Boston: Houghton Mifflin.

Graham, Otis L., Jr., 1991. *Losing Time: The Industrial Policy Debate*. Cambridge: Harvard University Press.

Hamlett, Patrick W., 1992. *Understanding Technological Politics: A Decision-Making Approach*. Englewood Cliffs, NJ: Prentice-Hall.

Krimsky, Sheldon, 1991. *Biotechnics and Society: The Rise of Industrial Genetics*. New York: Praeger.

Lambright, W. Henry, 1976. *Governing Science and Technology*. New York: Oxford University Press.

———, 1985. *Presidential Management of Science and Technology: The Johnson Presidency*. Austin: University of Texas.

———, 1994. "The Political Construction of Space Satellite Technology." *Science, Technology, & Human Values,* vol. 19, no. 1 (Winter) 47–69.

Lambright, W. Henry, and Dianne Rahm, eds., 1992. *Technology and U.S. Competitiveness.* New York: Greenwood.

Law, John, and Michael Callon, 1992. "The Life and Death of an Aircraft: A Network Analysis of Technical Change." In Wiebe E. Bijker and John Law, eds., *Shaping Technology/Building Society.* Cambridge: MIT Press.

Mazur, Allan, 1981. *The Dynamics of Technical Controversy.* Washington, DC: Communications Press.

McCurdy, Howard, 1993. *Inside NASA.* Baltimore, MD: Johns Hopkins.

Meadows, Donella, et al., 1972. *The Limits to Growth.* New York: Potomac Association.

President's Scientific Research Board, 1947. *Science and Public Policy.* Washington, DC: Government Printing Office.

Price, Don K., 1954. *Government and Science.* New York: New York University.

———, 1965, *The Scientific Estate.* Cambridge, MA: Harvard.

Snow, C. P., 1960. *Science and Government.* Cambridge: Harvard University.

Vig, Norman, and Michael Kraft, 1994. *Environmental Policy in the 1990s.* Durham, NC: Duke University.

SCIENTIFIC MANAGEMENT.

The name given to the Taylor System and related systems of shop management during hearings of the Interstate Commerce Commission on railroad rates in 1910. Other terms covering the same methods of quantified work study and management are "efficiency engineering," "industrial engineering," and, in the European context, "rationalization." All of these terms grew out of applications of the original Taylor system in ever wider contexts and include time and motion studies, the microdivision of labor, forward planning, and a system of strict labor discipline, usually backed by some variant on the piecework wage (see **Taylor Frederick W.**).

The Taylor System itself, however, was not a single method of increasing productivity but was a collection of techniques that tended to be adapted and to evolve over time and depending upon circumstance. And it was not all the work of one man, Frederick Winslow Taylor, although his work was central to the scientific management movement. Associates such as Henry Laurence Gantt, Morris L Cooke, Carl Barth, and Frank and Lillian Gilbreth, among others, made important contributions to Taylorism. What these techniques had in common was a strong bias toward the rational-utilitarian, the quantified, and the mechanistic. They tended to downplay the element of human nature and sought to control the results of the interaction of human beings as precisely as the output of a machine could be controlled. In the first half of the twentieth century, nearly all the formal management that was taught was Scientific Management: the increase of productivity through rational measurement, the elimination of waste and duplication, and the search for the "one best way."

The Popularization of Scientific Management in the United States

Just how did the U.S. government become involved in the christening of a system of machine-shop management? When the Interstate Commerce Commission held hearings to determine whether the Eastern railroads would be allowed to increase freight rates, Louis Brandeis (later a Supreme Court Justice, but then known as "the people's lawyer" and serving without pay on the case) determined that consumer interests could be upheld and rates kept low if it were shown that the railroads were inadequately managed. At that time, efficiency engineers were actively engaged in reorganizing industry, but their newly developing discipline was little known to the general public. Brandeis met with a group of them (including Gantt and Frank Gilbreth, but not Taylor) in Gantt's apartment in New York City, where he arranged for their testimony and they settled on an attractive new name for the methods of rational work study that they advocated.

The spectacular testimony of these industrial engineers, that the railroads, if properly managed, could save "a million dollars a day," brought headlines and set off an efficiency craze that swept the nation. Suddenly every problem, from governmental sloth to personal inadequacy, could be cured by the new methods if properly applied. Experts wrote popular articles, lecturers and training courses multiplied, and fly-by-night charlatans hastened to palm themselves off as efficiency consultants. President William Taft appointed a Commission on Economy and Efficiency to reform government. Housewives were informed how they might have efficient kitchens, and schoolchildren how they might study with greater efficiency. Efficiency was the virtue that could lead to national salvation. This typically American convulsion of popular enthusiasm set Scientific Management forever at the center of popular culture and the "American way."

The Components of Scientific Management

According to Taylor, the "Father of Scientific Management," Scientific Management was nothing less than a "mental revolution." Instinct and superstition, represented by the "rule of thumb," would be banished from the workplace, replaced by the precise quantification and written record keeping of science. There would be fewer mistakes, fewer false starts, and less time for training. What is more, the objective study of work would eliminate any differences between management and labor as to what fair pay ought to be. Scientific Management would reduce conflict, reduce unionization, and reduce the exploitation of labor. Taylor aimed to get rid of "systematic soldiering," the way in which workers concealed productivity and set their own pace at work. The new system, he promised, would bring about the increase of prosperity for both workers and owners, as well as a "diminution of poverty" in the community as a whole.

In *The Principles of Scientific Management,* Taylor (1911) stated that Scientific Management is "no single element," but a combination summarized as

Science, not rule of thumb.

Harmony, not discord.

Cooperation, not individualism.

Maximum output, in place of restricted output.

The development of each man to his greatest efficiency and prosperity.

Yet, in the popular mind, Scientific Management was usually associated not with these generalizations, but with a set of very specific "efficiency" techniques. These techniques did not vanish, as some academics have suggested. A trip to most business schools, to any factory floor, or to the industrial engineering section of the library will show that many of these techniques are still in use today, having formed the foundation of modern management.

Time Study

The use of the stopwatch to time work is the element most commonly associated with Taylorism. Taylor began timing workers in the 1880s during his employment at Midvale Steel, and his development of time study is at the center of Scientific Management's efficiency methods. In popular lore, Taylorism "is" the stopwatch, and Taylor, in a poetic flourish, is said to have died with his watch in his hand.

Taylor's early time-based approach to the measurement of productivity was broadened by the inclusion of motion study, the microanalysis of motions developed by Frank and Lillian Gilbreth based on a unit of analysis called the "therblig" ("Gilbreth" spelled backwards). By examining and measuring the way in the which each part of a job was performed, the "one best way" (an early Scientific Management slogan coined by the Gilbreths) to do the work could be determined and made standard practice throughout an industry, thus increasing efficiency. Time and motion studies are still an important technique in current use. The Gilbreths' extension of this approach into "fatigue studies" (the study of the kinds of motions that tire or overextend the body) underlies much of modern ergometric and man-machine interface studies. The fatigue study approach also opened the way to the experiments of Elton Mayo and thus to the development of the Human Relations School of management.

Standardization

The approach of Scientific Management was to make the best practice standard practice. This included the standardization of tools and equipment for any given job and their provision to the working person by management. It also included the standardization of "acts or movements of workmen for each class of work" once time and motion studies had discovered the "one best way." Special equipment such as the Barth Slide Rule, developed by Taylor's associate Carl G. Barth, allowed for the optimization of technical tasks (in this case, metal cutting) on a standard pattern. The idea of standardization to increase the interchangeability of parts was taken up almost as a crusade by interested manufacturers. Yet, standardization was also seen as far more than a universal means to efficiency within and between industries; the world standardization movement, which still exists, was buoyed up in the time before World War I with the belief that international standardization would bring about world peace.

One of the great innovations of early Scientific Management was making standard practice a matter of written record. Craft skills were analyzed, measured, broken into their component parts, and stored in written form in the new "planning room" advocated by the Scientific Managers. Also kept there were work and wage calculations as well as newly developed forward planning and coordination devices such as flowcharts and Gantt's new planning bar chart, the "Gantt chart," a device not superseded until the development of computerized planning. The new standardized work process also involved giving each worker written instructions about a job. Printed work blanks were another novel element associated with the adoption of Taylorism. Both, once astonishing to contemporary observers, are now common practice. And Scientific Management, by making explicit, recording, and systematizing previously arcane skills, was the first step on the eventual road to automation.

Wage Incentives

From its very beginning, with the publication of Taylor's (1895) "A Piece-Rate System, Being a Step toward Partial Solution of the Labor Problem," Taylorism was tied not only to technology, but to a specific wage incentive plan derived from a narrow view of human nature. For the success of the technical and standardization components of Scientific Management depended upon the idea of a powerful and precise incentive for laborers to work within the strict confines of the system. The incentive or motivator upon which Taylorism relied was the differential piecework wage, set at a "fair" level calculated by time study, with penalties for lagging behind and bonuses for overfulfillment of the work plan.

The most celebrated example of the differential piecework wage in action is given by Taylor in *The Principles of Scientific Management* when Schmidt, the ox-brained pig iron handler (Taylor's characterization), is induced to load 47 tons of pig iron per day, rather than the standard 12 1/2 tons, by being offered US $1.85 a day, rather than US $1.15 a day. (Taylor did not believe in excessive bonuses. He felt that any bonus over 60 percent would be spent on drink.) It was this element of Taylor's system, so perilously close to the classic "speed-up" and without apparent protection against physical overwork, that most excited the enmity of organized labor.

Money incentives were also applied at the managerial or supervisory level, the most well known being the Gantt task-and-bonus system. But behind the money incentives at every level was a sense that there were also spiritual rewards in Scientific Management, most notably, the uplifting virtue of serving scientific rationality instead of backwardness and superstition, as well as the "hearty teaching relationship" that Taylor advocated between supervisor and supervised. Even Schmidt is represented as being dazzled by the offer to make him a "first-class man," although he needs a great deal of coaxing and explaining to make the concept clear to him.

Accounting and Mnemonic Systems

The efficiency savings of Scientific Management could not be demonstrated without a different sort of accounting system, one that could demonstrate the costs of waste and "down time" effectively. Taylor advocated the use of the Taylor Accounting System as part of the Scientific Management reorganization package. According to Charles Wrege and Ronald Greenwood (1991), the Taylor Accounting System adapted the bookkeeping system developed by William Basley, accountant for the New York and Northern Railroad, later obscuring its origins. Also included in the reform package was the Taylor Mnemonic System, designed to label materials in storage, which considerably reduced the search-and-retrieval time for parts and replacements.

Functional Foremanship

Taylor believed that the increasing complexity of technical tasks at the shop level required the division of authority between several specialist foremen. This element of Scientific Management was the one most often discarded by industrialists who adopted other parts of the system. Functional foremanship violates the principle of the "unity of command" and a Bible quotation, "No man can serve two masters," was often pressed into service as the authority on the question. But with the increasing technological complexity of many tasks today, as well as the growth of teams and other forms of divided authority, there has been a reexamination of the once "impractical" functional foremanship as simply ahead of its time.

The Opposition of Labor

No account of Scientific Management would be complete without mentioning the strenuous opposition to the system mounted by organized labor. Early in his career at

Midvale Steel, Taylor received death threats for trying to speed up work, and when he later worked at Bethlehem Steel, the planning room was mysteriously burned. Because Taylor's system replaced scarce craft labor with unskilled labor, he thought it would eliminate the possibility of strikes, since replacements could be easily trained. But Taylor's methods resembled the dreaded "speed-up" in which piecerates could be lowered to drive workers to substandard wages and exhaustion, and strikes followed the system as it spread. Time study men were driven out of plants and work rates successfully concealed from them. The rumor was even spread, both in the United States and overseas, that Schmidt had died of overwork. In vain the real Schmidt, named Henry Knolle, was produced and shown to be living, indeed, to even have outlived Taylor. Labor activists the world over continued to tell the apocryphal tale of the advanced American industrialist who generously built a company cemetery for the laborers he had worked to death under the new efficiency system.

In 1911, strikes against the installation of Scientific Management in the Watertown Arsenal led to an investigation into the Taylor System by a committee of the House of Representatives. Taylor testified in the Capitol, confronting labor leaders in a session so stormy that it appeared as if blows might be struck. When the committee failed to recommend legislation against the Taylor System, legislators in the House passed a rider to attach to all appropriations bills forbidding the use of stopwatch timing in any government installation. But as Taylor had said, Scientific Management was not the stopwatch alone, and it continued to spread.

Over the next few decades, as Scientific Management became standard practice in industry, organized labor gradually accommodated to the changes involved, many of which were in fact improvements, although unions maintained bargaining leverage by shifting from a largely craft basis to an industry wide basis.

Scientific Management Outside of the United States

Frederick Taylor was convinced from the beginning that the principles of Scientific Management would come into general use "throughout the civilized world," and from the first, an active campaign to export Scientific Management was undertaken by its advocates, and many of them traveled abroad for that purpose. At the Paris Exposition of 1900, the Bethlehem Steel Exhibit demonstrated cutting tools made of Taylor-White steel running red-hot at unheard of speeds. The European steel producers were stunned; when they made inquiries about the tool steel, they discovered that running lathes at that speed required the adoption of the techniques of the Taylor System of management. In this way Taylorism began its spread through the heavy industries of Europe.

In France, Scientific Management met with a great deal of enthusiasm from the technical elite. The distinguished metallurgical engineer Henri-Louis Le Chatelier became an early and active advocate of the Taylor System. He was assisted in adapting Scientific Management to French industry by Charles de Fréminville, former chief engineer of the Paris-Orléans Railway, who was converted by a personal meeting with Taylor. The Michelin brothers, on reading Le Chatelier's articles on Taylorism, arranged a meeting with Taylor when he came to Paris, rushing out immediately afterward to buy a stopwatch for their factory at Clermont-Ferrand. By 1913, there were strikes against the Taylorized industries around Paris, but with World War I high productivity became essential, and Scientific Management was extensively adopted in French industry.

Foreign engineers and specialists descended on Taylorized plants in the United States, returning home to spread the system in their native countries. The Germans, despite an active labor movement that called Taylorism "murder-work," were quick to introduce Scientific Management into their industries, and a number of engineers became firm advocates of the system. However, to avoid the social opposition not only to the term "Taylorism" but also to "Scientific Management," they took their cue from the French, who had renamed the method *"l'organisation rationnel du travail,"* and coined the term *"die Rationalisierung"* (rationalization) to cover the campaign for reorganization. The emphasis on production planning blended well with the corporative state traditions of Germany; the great industrialist Walter Rathenau is counted among the number of Scientific Managers, as is Wichard von Moellendorf, author of a corporatist plan for the reconstruction of German industry between the wars. Other nations that showed an interest in early Scientific Management were the Japanese and the British, although labor and other troubles delayed the widespread application of the system in the latter case.

By far the strangest convert to Scientific Management was Vladimir Lenin, who in 1915 read an article by Frank Gilbreth on motion study as a means of increasing national wealth and brought emigré engineers trained in Taylorism back to the newly founded Soviet Union to improve the operations of industry. Under Lenin, the First Five-Year Plan was drawn up on Gantt charts, although the plan itself was not put into effect until Stalin took power. Echoes of a much distorted Taylorism are seen in some of the task and bonus systems of Soviet socialism, as well as in the strange practices of Stakhanovism (a bizarre and heavily publicized "speed-up" in which "labor heroes" performed humanly impossible tasks of overproduction) during the 1930s. Indeed, in the years between the two world wars, the practices of Scientific Management were estab-

lished worldwide in industry, and management historians continue to unearth new examples of the diffusion of the system with some regularity.

Beyond Scientific Management

Scientific Management spread beyond the confines of the industrial establishment and was extended by its admirers to include earlier attempts to apply rational study and reform to work. For example, Lyndall Urwick, an important figure in British Scientific Management as well as one of the developers of the Administrative Management School of public administration, included the early management experiments and advanced practices of the British steam engine manufacturer Boulton and Watt a century before Taylor in his discussion of pioneers of Scientific Management. Likewise, he included the labor studies of Charles Babbage (1792–1871), although the celebrated inventor of the Difference Engine would seem to require no further laurels.

Scientific Management had a powerful impact on government administration, city management, and educational administration and was even the inspiration for the founding of an obscure American political party. For example, its work of seeking out and standardizing the best practice inspired the work of the New York Bureau of Municipal Research, whose director, Frederick A. Cleveland, was a friend of Taylor's. This approach to local government spread as similar bureaus were founded across the country in the teens of this century to improve administrative practice. Scientific Management's method of developing a single measure of production to calculate efficiency was adapted to education by Morris L. Cooke, who as early as 1910 proposed using the "student hour" to reform educational administration. Cooke, an associate of Taylor's, also directly intervened in the organization of the government of the city of Philadelphia, rationalizing its operations and publishing his observations on city management improvement methods in 1918.

The teachings of the Administrative Management School, many of which developed out of the work done in the New York Bureau, formed the basis for the teaching of public administration for many years. In addition, they provided the theoretical background for the work of the President's Committee on Administrative Management, which in 1937 proposed major reforms of the executive branch that included the establishment of the Executive Office of the President. These reforms, put in place for World War II, still undergird the modern Presidency. At the opposite end of the political spectrum were the zany proposals of Technocracy, Incorporated, an obscure political party that rose to visibility during the Great Depression of the 1930s only to be suppressed and reduced to a handful of eccentrics in the decades that followed. Inspired by Scientific Management and the credo of efficiency bringing national happiness, the technocrats proposed to abolish the Constitution and replace it with a "technate" of engineers, who would restore national prosperity by eliminating energy waste and organizing all of national life along efficient assembly-line principles.

In the century since "A Piece-Rate System" first appeared, Scientific Management has worked its way into the fabric of all modern industrial societies, where it is now so common as to go unnoticed by most people. But its results were profound and lasting, encompassing a "second industrial revolution" of mass production and a "white collar revolution" of expanding middle management made possible by higher worker productivity and made necessary by the requirements of coordinating the new, microdivided labor that created that productivity. Even now, when many management texts, stressing teams and nonmaterial incentives, advocate the dismantling of certain outmoded structures of Scientific Management, they justify these changes with arguments rooted in the very methods of productivity measurement and work study first devised and applied by the Scientific Managers at the beginning of the twentieth century.

JUDITH A. MERKLE

BIBLIOGRAPHY

Aitken, A. G. H., 1960. *Taylorism at the Watertown Arsenal: Scientific Management in Action, 1908–1915.* Cambridge, MA: Harvard University Press.
Alford, L. P., 1932. *Henry Lawrence Gantt: Leader in Industry.* New York: Harper and Bros.
Cooke, Morris L., 1918. *Our Cities Awake: Notes on Municipal Activities and Administration.* New York: Doubleday.
Copley, Frank B., 1923. *Frederick W. Taylor: Father of Scientific Management.* New York: Harper and Bros.
Gilbreth, Frank B., 1917. *Applied Motion Study.* New York: Sturgis and Walton.
Gilbreth, Frank B., Jr., and Ernestine Gilbreth Carey, 1948. *Cheaper by the Dozen.* New York: T. Y. Crowell.
Gilbreth, Frank B., and Lillian M. Gilbreth, 1916. *Fatigue Study: The Elimination of Humanity's Greatest Unnecessary Waste.* New York: Sturgis and Walton.
Gulick, Luther, and Lyndall Urwick, eds., 1937. *Papers in the Science of Administration.* New York: Columbia University Press.
Haber, Samuel, 1964. *Efficiency and Uplift: Scientific Management in the Progressive Era, 1890–1920.* Chicago: University of Chicago Press.
Hoxie, R. F., 1921. *Scientific Management and Labor.* New York: D. Appleton.
Mayo, Elton, 1933. *The Human Problems of an Industrial Civilization.* New York: Macmillan.
Merkle, Judith A., 1980. *Management and Ideology: The Legacy of the International Scientific Management Movement.* Berkeley and London: University of California Press.
Nadworny, Milton J., 1955. *Scientific Management and the Unions 1900–1932.* Cambridge, MA: Harvard University Press.
Nelson, Daniel, 1980. *Frederick W. Taylor and the Rise of Scientific Management.* Madison: University of Wisconsin Press.
Taylor, Frederick W., 1895. "A Piece-Rate System, Being a Step Toward Partial Solution of the Labor Problem." Paper no. 647, *Transactions,* American Society of Mechanical Engineers, vol. 16: 856–903.
———, 1967 [1911]. *The Principles of Scientific Management.* New York: W. W. Norton.
———, 1919. *Shop Management.* New York: Harper Bros.
Urwick, Lyndall, 1949. *The Making of Scientific Management.* London: Management Publications Trust.
———, 1956. *The Golden Book of Management.* London: Newman, Neame.
Wrege, Charles D., and Ronald G. Greenwood, 1991. *Frederick W. Taylor: The Father of Scientific Management; Myth and Reality.* Homewood, IL: Business One Irwin.

SCOPE OF REVIEW.

The extent of court inquiry into the merits of challenged administrative action. The scope of judicial review is an important aspect of administrative law. In dealing with the scope of review, it should be noted that where there is an administrative record, the review proceeding is essentially an appellate proceeding, and review is limited to the record made before the administrative agency. Where the agency has heard evidence, the reviewing court's decision is not based upon evidence produced at a trial in court, but upon the evidence presented before the agency. The focal point for review is the administrative record already in existence, not some new record made in the reviewing court. The only evidence that may be considered is evidence that was before the agency. Evidence may not be received by the reviewing court even if it was wrongfully excluded by the agency or is newly discovered evidence. If the court feels that such evidence should be heard, it should remand the case for it to be received before the agency.

When the courts review administrative acts, the overriding consideration is that of deference to the administrative expert. The result has been a theory of review that limits the extent to which the discretion of the expert may be scrutinized by the nonexpert judge. The basic approach was one stated by the Supreme Court a half century ago: "We certainly have neither technical competence nor legal authority to pronounce upon the wisdom of the course taken by the Commission" (*Board of Trade v. United States,* 314 U.S. 534, 548; 1942)

The consequence has been a theory of review by the courts that provides for only limited review where questions of fact are at issue—the theory being that it should be the primary responsibility of the administrative expert to find the facts in a given case. The courts may review administrative adjudications of fact only to determine whether they are supported by substantial evidence. As interpreted by the Supreme Court, substantial evidence means "such relevant evidence as a reasonable mind might accept as adequate to support a conclusion" (*Consolidated Edison Co. v. NLRB,* 305 U.S. 197, 229; 1938)

The so-called substantial evidence rule tests the rationality of administrative determinations of fact; it is a test of the reasonableness, not the rightness, of administrative factual determinations. All that is needed is evidence that a reasonable person would accept as adequate to support the determination. Different terminology is used when facts found in a rulemaking are challenged; in such a case the reviewing court is said to review whether the agency rules are "arbitrary, capricious, or an abuse of discretion." This standard is also essentially one of reasonableness; under it, the agency is given great latitude.

In two early cases (in 1920 and 1932)—those involving so-called constitutional facts and those involving jurisdictional facts—the Supreme Court indicated that the courts might more fully review the administrative determinations and determine their correctness on their own independent judgment. More recently, the Court has receded from these statements and indicated that even determinations upon which constitutional rights and jurisdiction depend are to be reviewed only under the substantial evidence test—that is, the reviewing courts are to determine only the reasonableness, not the rightness, of these administrative determinations.

Mention should also be made of the so-called *Chevron* doctrine (after *Chevron v. Natural Resources Defense Council,* 467 U.S. 837; 1984), which now governs review of administrative interpretations of statutes. Statutory interpretation is, of course, governed primarily by legislative intent: If Congress has clearly said what a statute means, its intent must be followed. The *Chevron* doctrine applies when a statute is ambiguous—that is, its meaning is not made clear in the language or legislative history of the statute. Under *Chevron,* in such a case, the administrative agency, not the reviewing court, has the primary role in giving meaning to the statute. The agency's statutory interpretation is to be upheld if it is reasonable, even if it is not right, in the sense that the court would interpret the statute in the same way. *Chevron* requires the courts to give effect to a reasonable administrative interpretation of a statute unless that interpretation is inconsistent with a clearly expressed congressional intent.

Chevron has been criticized as inconsistent with the very basis of the law of judicial review. From almost the beginning of administrative law in our system, review has focused upon two main questions: that of jurisdiction and that of proper application of the law. The courts have left questions of fact and policy for the administrator, subject only to limited review. Ensuring that agencies remain within the limits of their delegated powers and that they have not misconstrued the law has, on the contrary, been conceived of as a judicial function. Yet, under the *Chevron* doctrine, both statutory construction and the determina-

tion of agency jurisdiction are taken from the reviewing court and vested primarily in the administrator.

However, reference should also be made to an important extension in the scope of review by the Supreme Court of California, which developed a rule of broad review in cases involving fundamental rights. As stated by the California court, its rule is that "if the order or decision of the agency substantially affects a fundamental vested right, the trial court, in determining . . . whether there has been an abuse of discretion because the findings are not . . . supported by the evidence, must exercise its independent judgment on the evidence and find an abuse of discretion if the findings are not supported by the weight of the evidence" (*Strumsky v. San Diego Employees Retirement Assn.,* 520 P. 2d 29, 31 [Cal. 1974]).

The California rule is a direct consequence of the increasing judicial vigilance to protect individual rights and the growing disenchantment with the claims of administrative expertise. The California court has asserted that, when an agency decision affects a fundamental right, full review is appropriate because "abrogation of the right is too important to the individual to relegate it to exclusive administrative extinction." The result is a substantial broadening of the scope of review, which may set a pattern for other courts in coming years.

From a broader point of view, the California approach may be seen as an indication of the changing attitude of many American courts toward an administrator. There has been increasing articulation of judicial doubts about the desirability of the trend toward narrow review of administrative authority. According to a noted opinion by Federal Judge David Bazelon, it is no longer enough for the courts regularly to uphold agency action "with a nod in the direction of the 'substantial evidence' test, and a bow to the mysteries of administrative expertise." A more positive judicial role is demanded by the changing character of administrative litigation. According to Judge Bazelon, "courts are increasingly asked to review administrative litigation that touches on fundamental personal interests in life, health, and liberty. . . . To protect these interests from administrative arbitrariness, it is necessary . . . to insist on strict judicial scrutiny of administrative action." *Environmental Defense Fund v. Ruckelshaus,* 439 F. 2d 584, 597 (D.C.Cir. 1971)

Judge Bazelon asserted that the American system is now at a watershed: "We stand on the threshold of a new era in the history of the long and fruitful collaboration of administrative agencies and reviewing courts" (Ibid.). The expression of judicial doubts about the desirability of the trend toward limited judicial review is most suggestive for the future of American administrative law.

Despite such expressions, the dominant theme in the scope of review is still that of the *Chevron* deference. Under it, there is now limited review not only over administrative determinations of fact, but also over agency interpretations of law. *Chevron* deference assimilates review of questions of statutory interpretation into review of questions of fact. Indeed, according to critics, the *Chevron* doctrine all but does away with the law-fact distinction that has been so basic in American administrative law.

BERNARD SCHWARTZ

BIBLIOGRAPHY

Davis, Kenneth C., and Richard J. Pierce, Jr., 1994. *Administrative Law Treatise*, 3d ed., Vol. 2, Chapter 11. Boston, MA: Little, Brown.
Schwartz, Bernard, 1991. *Administrative Law*, 3d ed., Chapter 10. Boston, MA: Little, Brown.

SECTION 1983.

Major civil rights provision. Section 1983 is the familiar name given to the federal law officially known as the Civil Rights Act of 1871. The official citation is 42 U.S.C. §1983. The text of §1983 provides in pertinent part as follows:

> Every person who, under color of any statute, ordinance, regulation, custom . . . of any State or Territory or the District of Columbia, subjects . . . any citizen of the United States or other person within the jurisdiction thereof to the deprivation of any rights, privileges or immunities secured by the Constitution and laws, shall be liable to the party injured in an action at law, suit in equity or other proper proceeding for redress.

Section 1983 was originally enacted in 1871 during the Reconstruction era following the United States Civil War. The act was intended to provide a remedy to persons—primarily newly freed blacks, union sympathizers, and federal officials—who were suffering the deprivation of their constitutional rights, privileges, and immunities by state government officials' abuse of authority. Because the act specifically targeted state and local officials, especially in the South, who were members of the Ku Klux Klan or who at least were supporters of the Klan, the act became popularly known as the Ku Klux Klan Act. Congress amended §1983 in 1979 by adding the words "District of Columbia" following "State or Territory," thereby affording protection against infringement of federal rights by those acts of Congress applicable solely to the District of Columbia. Prior to the enactment of §1983, state governments and their officials enjoyed immunity from suit for their actions under the doctrine of sovereign immunity. The sovereign immunity doctrine is derived from the principle that the sovereign—a king or queen "subject to no one"—could not be sued without his or her permission.

The protection afforded by §1983 is not limited to United States citizens but is specifically extended to "other persons within the jurisdiction" of the particular state, municipality, or other governmental unit.

Elements of Action

A plaintiff bringing a lawsuit under §1983 must both (1) allege and prove that the defendant violated the plaintiff's "clearly established" constitutional rights and (2) demonstrate that the defendant was then acting under color of state law. The plaintiff may either seek money damages caused by the alleged deprivation or seek to enjoin further deprivations in the future.

Persons Subject to §1983 Liability

The United States and its agencies are immune from suit under §1983, but federal employees such as Alcohol, Tobacco, and Firearms (ATF) agents, Federal Bureau of Investigations (FBI) agents, and immigration officials enjoy only a limited form of immunity, known as qualified immunity. The qualified immunity doctrine provides that a government official may be sued for his or her action taken in an official capacity if the official knows, or should know, that such action will violate another person's federal rights.

Over the years, the U.S. Supreme Court has refined the qualified immunity doctrine to provide that the federal rights alleged to have been violated must have been "clearly established" at the time of the complaint of conduct. A right protected from infringement under §1983 does not need to have been recognized by a prior U.S. Supreme Court decision to be considered "clearly established." The government official is shielded from liability under §1983, however, if the official reasonably believed in good faith that the action would not violate another's "clearly established" federal rights.

The individual states are not considered "persons" for purposes of imposing liability under §1983 and enjoy absolute immunity from actions for money damages by virtue of the Eleventh Amendment to the United States Constitution. State officials—like their federal counterparts—enjoy only qualified immunity for their actions.

Enactment of §1983 did not abrogate the traditional judicial immunity accorded judges, and both federal and state judges enjoy absolute immunity from suits under §1983 for acts performed within their judicial jurisdiction.

The U.S. Supreme Court initially held that municipal corporations were not intended to be "persons" under §1983 but reversed its position in the landmark case *Monell vs. Department of Social Services*, 436 U.S. 658 (1978). While an official's personal liability under §1983 may be established by showing that the official, while acting under color of state law, caused a deprivation of a federal right, municipal liability only arises when the municipality's policy or custom plays a part in the deprivation. A municipality does not otherwise incur liability simply because one of its agents or employees causes a deprivation of another's federal rights.

Particular Actions

Actions for relief under §1983 are nearly always filed in the U.S. District Court in the judicial district in which the alleged violation occurred, but state trial courts have concurrent jurisdiction to hear the cases. The prevailing party in a §1983 case may be awarded reasonable attorneys' fees and court costs incurred in prosecuting or defending the claim, although in practice attorneys' fees are generally only awarded to a successful plaintiff. There is no federal statute of limitations for §1983 claims. The courts look to the statute of limitations of the particular state in which the action is brought for actions against state officials.

A listing of common—but by no means exclusive—examples of actions brought under §1983 include actions brought (1) by prison inmates against prison officials alleging cruel and unusual conditions of confinement in violation of the Eighth Amendment to the U.S. Constitution; the alleged failure to provide adequate medical care; and the alleged failure to protect the inmates from harm by other inmates or staff; (2) by arrested persons against police officers for the use of allegedly excessive force in bringing about an arrest or for unreasonable searches and seizures; and (3) by or on behalf of involuntarily committed mental patients in state mental hospitals against state mental health officials for the alleged failure to protect the mental patients from self-inflicted harm or from harm by other patients or staff. There is a growing sentiment in the mid-1990s that some prisoners have abused the principles underlying §1983 by filing frivolous actions, and state legislatures have begun to react by attempting to place restrictions on the filing of such actions and imposing sanctions in those instances in which the lawsuits are found to be frivolous.

Leo V. Garvin, Jr.

SENIOR EXECUTIVE SERVICE. A term used to describe the upper-level administrators, both politically appointed and competitively selected, in a government's public-service bureaucracy. In the United States, this label was given to the group of upper-level executives in the federal bureaucracy who signed contracts to enter this new entity created by the Civil Service Reform Act of 1978. This elite group of executives drawn from the ranks of GS 16 through Executive Level IV or their equivalents gave up some of their previous civil service protections in terms of job permanence and appeals rights in exchange for opportunities to have greater impact on public policy and for greater potential financial bonuses.

The idea behind the creation of the Senior Executive Service (SES) was based loosely on the model of the British senior executives who are generalists rather than programmatic specialists and who are mobile problem solvers with a governmentwide perspective. The SES was supposed to create a cadre of generalist managers for the American bureaucratic system—a system whose managers had previously been specific, programmatic managers heavily specialized by narrowly tailored classifications.

The service was envisioned to give upper-level political managers more flexibility in working with SESers—most of whom were to be drawn largely from the ranks of the career civil service. Political executives would now have more direct control over the compensation system for these SESers in a newly created pay system containing substantial bonuses for executives who exceeded their performance standards.

The Senior Executive Service in the United States, by general consensus, at least in its initial phases of implementation, was a disappointment. Because the SES is composed of both political executives and career civil servants, there has been a constant friction caused by the intermingling of political and managerial decisionmaking criteria. During the initial years of the SES, career executives complained that they were being subjected to undue political pressures by political executives. During the first three years after the reform, over 40 percent of the original SES membership was gone from the service. Morale within the service was very low. Congress decided to retrench from original promises made regarding the amount of money allocated for bonuses and to lower the percentages of SESers eligible for such bonus awards. As late as 1989, a Merit Systems Protection Board (MSPB) survey of former SESers revealed high levels of dissatisfaction. Inadequate pay was a major contributing factor to this dissatisfaction, but nonmonetary issues, such as improper political interference and arbitrary management actions, also played a role. These former SESers held in low regard the management skills of political appointees in the service.

The pay cap on SES salaries was removed during the Ronald Reagan presidential administration and, by the 1990s, the Federal Pay Reform Act had partially alleviated some of the reasons for monetary dissatisfactions within the SES. Following these actions, morale within the service appeared to be on the upswing. In fact, a 1994 survey of federal employee attitudes revealed that SESers had higher levels of job satisfaction than any other work group surveyed, including blue collar, GS 1-6, GS 7-12, and Gs/GM 13-15. Throughout this survey, the SESers were consistently positive about their jobs.

Although in general it is true that the SES was an early disappointment, it is also true that the federal bureaucracy is composed of a vast array of heterogenous agencies and bureaus, each with their own version of the way in which the SES succeeded or failed in their own environment. The bottom line is that it is still in operation, and morale has improved somewhat from the initial years of its implementation. The concept of a senior executive service has now been well established; it remains to be seen whether the original objectives can ever be attained in a highly charged political environment.

ROBERT H. ELLIOTT

BIBLIOGRAPHY

Ingraham, Patricia W., and Pamela N. Reed, 1990. "The Civil Service Reform Act of 1978: The Promise and the Dilemma." In Steven W. Hays and Richard C. Kearney, eds., *Public Personnel Administration, Problems and Prospects*, 2d ed. Englewood Cliffs, NJ: Prentice-Hall.

Ingraham, Patricia W., and David H. Rosenbloom, 1993. *The Promise and Paradox of Civil Service Reform*. Pittsburgh: University of Pittsburgh Press.

Merit Systems Protection Board (MSPB), 1989. *The Senior Executive Service, Views of Former Federal Executives*. Washington, DC: U.S. Government Printing Office.

———, 1994. *Working for America: An Update*. Washington, DC: U.S. Government Printing Office.

SENIORITY. The length of time an employee serves in an organization or an organizational unit. It is a criterion that gives priority to individuals who are the most senior (i.e., who have the longest continuous service). Seniority is typically used to determine which employees will be promoted, terminated during reductions in force, transferred, assigned to training programs, or given other employment advantages. "Straight seniority" refers to applications in which seniority is the only criterion; "qualified seniority" applies when other factors are also taken under consideration, such as exam scores or performance appraisals; "competitive seniority" determines which employees will secure promotions, desirable shift assignments, or protection from layoffs; "benefit seniority" measures worker entitlement to benefits such as vacation time; "superseniority" applies to shop stewards, union officers, and other union representatives while they are serving in a union post in order to protect those individuals from reductions in force.

The seniority criterion is widely found in contract clauses in the private sector. According to the Bureau of National Affairs, over 90 percent of private-sector collective bargaining contracts contain seniority provisions. In government, seniority may be applied through provisions in the collective bargaining contract or, more commonly, it is implemented through statute or civil service rules. Seniority offers an advantage in personnel decisions because it is both objective and quantifiable. Length of service with the organization or in a particular job or department is a matter of record and some indication of achievement. In jurisdictions where promotional exams are not validated (demonstrably job related), seniority may be a superior indication of merit.

Seniority is sometimes criticized, however, for conflicting with the merit principle in government, restricting management rights, and hampering management flexibility. When used to determine the order of layoffs, seniority can damage affirmative action hiring programs, because last hired becomes first fired, and the last hired are more likely to be members of affirmative action classes. This issue was the subject of a U.S. Supreme Court ruling in the case of *Memphis Firefighters Local Union No. 1784 v. Stotts* (1984). A federal district court had approved two affirmative action plans for improving the percentage of black firefighters in Memphis. However, a fiscal crisis forced the city to lay off a large number of African American firefighters, most of whom had been hired under the plan. The Supreme Court ruled that bona fide seniority systems, such as existed in Memphis under a collective bargaining contract, take precedence over affirmative action consent decrees when layoff are required.

Seniority limits promotion opportunities for less senior, and often younger, employees who may be superior performers. Straight seniority detracts from merit considerations in some instances, but where qualified seniority prevails, little damage is done. For example, in federal employment, seniority may be used as an evaluative criterion only if it is clearly related to the quality of future job performance or to resolve ties between equally qualified workers. Application of seniority in determining vacation time, shift assignments, days off, and similar working conditions presents little threat to the principle of merit.

The use of seniority as a consideration in personnel decisions is long-standing and it predates the growth of public employee unionism. As a decision rule, it is frequently applied by management even in nonunion jurisdictions because it is objectively measured and preferred by employees. It does restrict management authority and flexibility, but it avoids favoritism, invalidated examinations, and biased performance appraisals.

Most seniority provisions specify that resignation, retirement, or discharge cause a loss of all seniority rights. Credit for prior service may be applied when an employee is rehired within a specified time period. Breaks in service for maternity leave, sick leave, union leave, or related reasons do not usually result in loss of seniority. Military leave counts as seniority time under federal law.

RICHARD C. KEARNEY

SEPARATION OF POWERS. A method of organizing constitutional government internally, whereby executive, legislative, and (more recently) judicial functions are separated and placed in different hands. The purpose of this arrangement is to prevent any person or group of persons from exercising unlimited power. Historically, proponents of the separation of powers have agreed with the general thrust of James Madison's argument in *Federalist* No. 47 that "the accumulation of all powers, legislative, executive, and judiciary, in the same hands, whether of one, a few, or many, and whether hereditary, self-appointed, or elective, may justly be pronounced the very definition of tyranny" (p. 3). Underlying this argument is the assumption that human beings are prejudiced by their passions to prefer their private interests to the common good and that, given the opportunity, they will rule in a self-interested fashion that threatens the political liberty of others. It follows that securing political liberty—that is, securing citizens' mastery over their own lives, families, and goods as defined by law—requires that a rule of law limit the opportunities for an arbitrary rule of persons.

The separation of powers has developed to the greatest extent in the United States, where the three governmental functions of making law, executing it, and applying it in particular cases are explicitly distinguished from one another and vested in three different branches of government. This particular version of the separation of powers goes beyond strict separation, however. It tends to equalize, or balance, the three branches by giving each one a share in the functions of the others, a share sufficient to defend itself against the aggrandizing efforts of persons in the other branches.

In this "balancing version," as William B. Gwyn (1965, 1986) labels it, the framers of the U.S. Constitution relied on the self-interest of persons in each branch of government to serve as counterweights to the self-interest of persons in other branches. They wanted "ambition . . . to counteract ambition" (p.337) according to James Madison in *Federalist* No. 51. The well-known system of checks and balances that resulted from the framers' efforts allows each branch to limit the others even in their own spheres. The legislature, for instance, is limited not only by the fact that it cannot enforce the law that it makes, that is, by the separation of powers. In addition, its power to make law is limited by the president's participation in legislation

through the veto power and by the judiciary's power to review the constitutionality of law. This balancing version of the separation of power has been at the core of a debate in the twentieth century over whether, or how severely, the separation of powers paralyzes government.

Although the version of the doctrine that developed in the United States is widely regarded as definitive, Gwyn argues persuasively that it should not be. The balancing version is one of several versions articulated since the mid-seventeenth century when the separation of powers emerged. Further, the balancing version came late in the history of the doctrine and still is not universal. Even in the United States, the need for governmental powers to balance one another has not been the only justification for separating them. The historical context in which the separation of powers developed is essential for understanding the contemporary debate about the separation of powers.

Origin of the Separation of Powers

Although the separation of powers developed in modern times—in seventeenth-century England—it is actually a step in the evolution of constitutional government, or government that is held to be limited by fundamental laws, customs, and institutions that together denote a common good. The earliest understanding of constitutional government centered on the mixed constitution, which is often confused with the separation of powers. The notion of a mixed constitution can be traced from Plato's *Laws* and Aristotle's *Politics* through the writings of Polybius and Cicero to St. Thomas Aquinas in the Middle Ages to the brink of the modern era in Machiavelli's *Discourses*. The mixture discussed by these theorists involves not the three governmental functions discussed by the Federalists, but the three different estates in society—monarchy, nobility, and people. Generally, each of these estates, or classes, was understood to contribute some quality or virtue to the state. The mixed constitution aimed for a balance among estates to preserve virtue in the state and also to ensure the stability of the state by giving each estate sufficient stake in it to deter revolt. In line with this notion that society is a combination of parts, discussions about how to achieve the proper balance of estates in the Constitution related not to any separation or division of governmental powers but to the estates' common participation in the legislative power. In this respect, the English monarchy from which the separation of powers developed resembled a mixed constitution. In Tudor England, the legislative power was shared by the monarch, the House of Commons, and the House of Lords so that no one estate could dominate.

Like the mixed constitution, the separation of powers is intended to preserve political liberty and the rule of law by preventing a despotic concentration of power. The separation of powers differs, however, in being a distinctly modern arrangement that developed in conjunction with the rise of democracy and the demise of the estates that were supposed to balance each other in the mixed regime. In line with its modern democratic perspective, the separation of powers rejects the view of the mixed constitution that society is a combination of parts in favor of the view that society is a whole. The same perspective dictates that the modern doctrine does not relate to the mixture of social estates, but to the way functions of government are blended. It dictates also that the separation of powers cannot be concerned with an equitable, or a virtue-producing, balance among the parts of society. Its goal is much narrower—preventing any group from exercising unlimited power. Still another difference between the separation of powers and the mixed constitution is that the former is a method of organizing government internally, a mechanical device, that might be used in a variety of different types of government to prevent arbitrary rule. The latter, by comparison, is itself a type of government that is specifically republican. Finally, and most important for understanding contemporary discussions, the separation of powers differs from the mixed constitution in that it does not necessarily entail the notion of balancing.

Most scholars agree that the separation of powers doctrine was first articulated in the mid-seventeenth century as a reflection of dissatisfaction with the Long Parliament, which governed England after the overthrow of Charles I. In 1649, the House of Commons abolished the monarchy and the House of Lords. The new unicameral Parliament was criticized widely for taking on executive functions and failing to abide by the laws it had made. Specifically, it was charged with imprisoning political opponents without regard for whether they had violated an actual law and for prolonging the Civil War to benefit members of Parliament who also held military offices. To preserve the common interest against these self-aggrandizing measures of the Long Parliament, Leveller critics such as John Lilburne insisted that those who make law and those who execute it should not be the same persons. The idea was that a separate executive would keep the legislature from violating a rule of law through biased, selective enforcement (*The Picture of the Council of State*, 1649; *England's Birth-Right*, 1645). However, Lilburne did not insist that the separate governmental powers be arranged to balance each other. Since pure republican thinkers such as the Levellers favored legislative supremacy, they conceived the executive strictly as an agent of the legislature. A major point in Gwyn's history of the separation of powers (1965) is that the notion of an executive check, or veto, on the legislative power was anathematic to those who first articulated the need for separating governmental powers.

Gwyn also notes that, in contrast to Lilburne and other strict republicans such as Marchamont Nedham (*The Excellencie of a Free-State*, 1656), some republican thinkers articulated separation-of-powers arguments that were more Cromwellian; that is to say, they favored a strong executive power. These writers—among them John Hall (*Confusion Confounded*, 1654), John Sadler (*The Rights of the Kingdom*, 1649), Isaac Penington the Younger (*A Word for the Commonweal*, 1650, and *The Fundamental Right, Safety, and Liberty of the People*, 1651)—necessarily moved toward the balancing version of the separation-of-powers doctrine without explicitly adopting it. The strong executive became reality in 1653. At that time, Cromwell dissolved Parliament, which had continually resisted measures to strengthen the executive, and proposed a written constitution, the Instrument of Government, which created an independent executive, the Lord Protector, and gave him the power to veto legislation. However, since the Lord Protector was also named as a participant in the legislative power, as the monarch had been, the veto was not understood by republicans of the time as a way for the executive to check the legislature.

Both the Instrument of Government and the second constitution adopted in the period before Charles II's restoration to the throne, the Humble Petition and Advice (1657), looked to the separation of powers rather than to balance of power to promote the common good. The emphasis on executive power in these constitutions, however, led ultimately away from republican government toward constitutional monarchy and, in 1660, to Charles II's restoration to the throne. By that time, the royalist camp, as well as the parliamentary camp, looked to the separation of powers to inhibit arbitrary government.

With the restoration of the monarchy in 1660, republican arguments for separation of powers were eclipsed by the doctrine of mixed monarchy, a form of the old mixed constitution. According to Gwyn, the only prominent voice for the republican, nonbalancing version of the separation of powers between 1660 and the Glorious Revolution of 1688 was John Locke's. In effect, the English mixed monarchy intertwined the republican separation of powers with the old notion of the mixed constitution, in which different estates or classes balance each other in the legislative power. Until this royalist connection was made in the latter part of the seventeenth century, the separation-of-powers doctrine was not associated with an argument for balancing powers.

At its origin, the separation of powers was associated with republican rationales that more or less adhered to the principle of legislative supremacy and did not entail balancing powers against each other. Gwyn identifies four rationales: (1) Unless those who execute law are different from those who make it, lawmakers can enforce laws selectively, as the Long Parliament did. That subverts the rule of law. (2) If executive officials are allowed to serve in the legislature, the legislature will not be able to hold the executive accountable for enforcing the laws. (3) If executive officials are allowed to serve in the legislature, they will form a legislative faction that is contrary to the common interest. (4) Without a separate executive, laws cannot be executed efficiently. A legislative assembly is ill suited for the task. Gwyn labels these arguments, respectively, as the rule of law, accountability, common interest, and efficiency versions of the separation-of-powers doctrine.

Two differences between these early republican versions of the separation of powers and the balancing version are apparent. One difference is that early versions of the doctrine clearly were not intended to function negatively, to inhibit government action, as the balancing version is said to do. The rule of law, accountability, and the common-interest versions imply that the separation of powers has positive, enabling functions. The efficiency argument, in particular, makes clear that the separation of powers can be a vehicle for promoting rather than inhibiting government action.

The other difference between early republican versions of the doctrine and the U.S. version is that seventeenth-century versions all understood the doctrine to refer to executive and legislative powers. No early version of the separation of powers, including John Locke's *Second Treatise of Government* (1690), articulated the need for the separate judicial branch established in the U.S. Constitution. The reason was not that no one recognized the desirability of separating judgment from other functions. That English political thinkers before Charles de Montesquieu did not separate the judicial function from the executive function reflected the fact that the function of executing the law had long been construed broadly to include the judicial function of applying it in particular cases. The argument that the judiciary should be separated from the executive, principally to keep the king from being judge in his own case and imprisoning opponents for political reasons, was recognized in England after the fifteenth century. The legal basis for an independent judiciary began after the Revolution of 1688 when British monarchs, under pressure to stop removing judges for political reasons, began to appoint judges for life or during good behavior. The practice became mandatory with the 1701 Act of Settlement. However, the judiciary was not considered to have a separate function in government until the mid-eighteenth century when Montesquieu recast the doctrine.

In sum, original republican understandings of the separation of powers involved neither a balance of powers nor a separate branch of government for the judiciary. Both of these ideas imply the existence of relatively independent, more or less equal branches of government that have the power to check each other. Such ideas were alien to the English republicans who first articulated the separation-of-powers doctrine, working as they did in the context of the English parliamentary system and adhering to the principle of legislative supremacy.

Emergence of the Balancing Version of the Doctrine

The balancing version of the separation of powers doctrine emerged gradually. Montesquieu's description of the separation of powers in Book XI of *The Spirit of the Laws* (1748) is often cited as authoritative, not because of its originality, but because it was the first to articulate the combination of elements that gradually merged into the modern separation of powers doctrine. Before Montesquieu, other writers such as John Trenchard (*A Short History of Standing Armies in England,* 1698) and Henry Bolingbroke (*The Craftsman,* 1726–1730's) had combined the separation of powers with balanced government. And Montesquieu's model constitution, as Gwyn notes, still fell short of linking balancing to functions of government. Following the English mixed constitution, Montesquieu looked for balance in the proper mixture of estates in the legislature and distinguished that idea conceptually from his argument that different governmental functions should be exercised by different persons. His distinctive contribution was the incorporation of the judiciary as a third element in the separation of powers.

Building on Montesquieu, William Blackstone's *Commentaries on the Laws of England* (1765–1769) strengthened the role of the judiciary and explicitly stated that a balance and interweaving of social elements is needed to maintain the separation of powers. Only with the U.S. Constitution, however, did the balancing process become firmly tied to a balance of governmental functions instead of a balance of estates and the judiciary become established as a separate branch of government.

Louis Fisher points out that although the framers of the U.S. Constitution were influenced by thinkers such as Locke, Montesquieu, and Blackstone, they arguably were influenced more by their own experience. Their comparatively classless form of the separation of powers was an ideological component of the American Revolution and its rejection of the British monarchy. One major innovation made by the framers, then, was an executive responsible to the people, albeit indirectly, through the electoral college. A second innovation, sparked by antipathy to the influence of the king's ministers in Parliament, was the absolute prohibition in Article I, Section 6 of the Constitution against executive officials serving in the legislature. These two changes removed executive ministers as agents of unity between the executive and the legislature. They established a new context for the separation of powers—the presidential system—in which the executive and legislative branches are independent from each other because each is an agent of its own electorate.

A third innovation of the framers was a judiciary more independent than either Montesquieu or Blackstone had imagined and more independent than parliamentary systems can accommodate, given their general adherence to the principle of legislative supremacy. The framers construed the separation of powers to require a judicial branch so independent from the political branches of government that it could formulate its own understanding of the constitution to judge the legality of acts of the legislative and executive branches. The principle of judicial review, expressed by Alexander Hamilton in *Federalist* No. 78, was reinforced by the Supreme Court in *Marbury v. Madison* (1803).

A fourth innovation stemmed from the experience of state legislatures under the Articles of Confederation. A frequently cited example is Thomas Jefferson's description of the Virginia Constitution of 1776 in *Notes on the State of Virginia* (1780–1784), quoted by Madison in *Federalist* No. 48. Jefferson wrote:

> All the powers of government, legislative, executive, and judiciary, result to the legislative body .... An elective despotism was not the government we fought for; but one which should not only be founded on free principles, but in which the powers of government should be so divided and balanced among several bodies of magistracy, as that no one could transcend their legal limits, without being effectually checked and restrained by the others. For this reason that convention, which passed the ordinance of government, laid its foundation on this basis, that the legislative, executive and judiciary departments should be separate and distinct, so that no person should exercise the powers of more than one of them at the same time. But no barrier was provided between these several powers. The judiciary and executive members were left dependent on the legislative, for their subsistence in office. ... If therefore the legislature assumes executive and judiciary powers, no opposition is likely to be made. ... [The legislature has] accordingly, in many instances, decided rights which should have been left to judiciary controversy: and the direction of the executive, during the whole time of their session, is becoming habitual and familiar. (pp. 324–325).

Circumstances such as these led the framers to agree with Jefferson that the separation of powers would not work unless checks and balances were attached to governmental powers. "A mere demarcation on parchment of the constitutional limits of the several departments, is not a sufficient guard against those encroachments which lead to a tyrannical concentration of all the powers of government in the same hands," (p. 326) Madison declared in *Federalist* No. 48. The requisite balancing mechanisms were, as noted, overlapping, or shared, powers. The president shares Congress's power to make law. The Senate shares the president's appointment power. It can be argued that the balancing version of the separation of powers, rec-

ognizing that a "parchment" separation could not be maintained, translated the balance among estates in the mixed constitution to a balance of powers that would be consistent with democracy.

It is important to note, with Gwyn and Ann Stuart Anderson among others, that the framers of the U.S. Constitution were not solely concerned with balancing when they arranged governmental powers. They did not abandon earlier republican rationales for the separation of powers. *Federalist* No. 51, for example, argues that the separation of powers will promote justice, liberty, and the rule of law. It argues further that the arrangement will ensure that government pursues the common interest rather than the interest of a faction. *Federalist* No. 72 shows the framers' concern for the accountability of the executive to the people, and *Federalist* No. 70 shows their concern for efficiency.

Twentieth-Century Developments

The separation of powers in the United States has been widely criticized for fragmenting government, giving too much access and influence to special interests, leading to deadlock between the executive and legislative branches, and—in the Watergate scandal—preventing the efficient removal of a failed president and producing a constitutional crisis. Critics tend to view the separation of powers as an out-of-date system that hinders the people's elected representatives from formulating and implementing coherent policy responses to pressing problems of the twentieth century.

To many, the changes in executive-legislative relations in the United States testify to the inability of the framers' system of balanced powers to operate in contemporary conditions. In response to demands of war and the need to regulate an increasingly complex economy, executive power has expanded at the expense of the legislature, which cannot act with the requisite speed and coherence.

Since the Civil War, the country has moved from an era in which Congress initiated most legislation to an era in which the executive has been labeled "chief legislator." This apparent reversal of constitutional roles has come gradually as a cumbersome and inexpert legislature sought help from the executive. Congress established new agencies inside the executive branch—a Bureau of the Budget in the Treasury Department in 1921, the council of Economic Advisers in 1946, the National Security Council in 1949, the council on Environmental Quality in 1969, the Domestic Council in 1970—and gave the president the means to control them. During the New Deal, when the Brownlow Commission recommended the establishment of the Executive Office of the President to strengthen the executive, Congress agreed. This trend in executive-legislative relations culminated when Franklin Roosevelt's New Deal legislative initiatives set the pattern for modern presidents as chief legislators.

As the executive bureaucracy has grown, so has the influence of interest groups. The famed iron triangles formed by congressional committees, executive agencies, and the clientele groups they have in common have created multiple, extralegal subgovernments. The result of this process, critics say, is that government is neither unified nor accountable to a popular majority.

Struggling to assert its influence in this situation, Congress has searched for ways to benefit from executive unity and expertise without transferring too much of its policy-making power to the executive branch. It often has delegated wide authority to the president to work out the details of legislation, reserving for itself the power to disapprove the president's initiative. The rise of the formal legislative veto, its demise at the hands of the Supreme Court, and its subsequent resurrection as an informal device illustrate the state of the separation of powers in recent U.S. history.

In a well-known example of the legislative veto, Congress tried to create an alternative to dealing with mandatory deportation of certain categories of aliens through private relief bills, as it had done previously. The Immigration and Nationality Act of 1952 gave the attorney general of the United States the power to intervene in and suspend the deportation of aliens unless either house of Congress vetoed the attorney general's decision. The constitutionality of this legislative veto was questioned by Chadha, an East Indian, when the House of Representatives disapproved the attorney general's decision to suspend his deportation. In *INS v. Chadha* (1983), the Supreme Court declared the one-house legislative veto in violation of the constitutional separation of powers, insisting that only a bicameral procedure and presentment of legislation to the president—in other words, only the steps required for new legislation—would satisfy constitutional requirements. From the Court's perspective, anything less would amount to the legislature's participation in an executive function, which would conflict with the framers' intent to "hermetically" seal the branches of government from each other. This strict view of the separation of powers was reaffirmed later in *Bowsher v. Synar* (1986).

Louis Fisher (1991) viewed the Supreme Court's interpretation of the separation of powers in the *Chadha* and *Bowsher* cases as "rigid and impractical" (p. 14).

The conditions that spawned the legislative veto a half century ago have not disappeared. Executive officials still want substantial latitude in administering delegated authority; legislators still insist on maintaining control without having to pass another law. The executive and legislative branches will therefore develop substitutes to serve as the functional equivalent of the legislative veto (p.149).

Fisher's conclusion is supported by the fact that, since *Chadha*, use of the legislative veto has not declined. Because of the practical need for it by both Congress and the president, the legislative veto has simply been redesigned. According to Fisher, most legislative vetoes now relate to a requirement that appropriations committees approve particular agency decisions; these nonstatutory vetoes are not subject to *Chadha* restrictions. They are extralegal but not illegal.

In two later cases, *Morrison v. Olson* (1988) and *Mistretta v. U.S.* (1989), the Supreme Court took a more flexible and pragmatic view of the separation of powers, admitting that the Constitution did not require the branches of government to be completely separate. These decisions revived the Court's view of the previous decade in *U.S. v. Nixon* (1974), another frequently discussed decision that turned on the separation of powers. There, the Court reaffirmed its own power to interpret the law, even when that involved limiting an executive function. The Court rejected Nixon's claim of absolute executive privilege for the Watergate tapes, reasoning that the president's generalized interest in confidential communications could not override the need for evidence in a specific criminal proceeding.

The Supreme Court's erratic interpretation of the separation of powers, combined with the resourcefulness of the executive and legislative branches in accommodating their practical needs, leads Fisher to conclude that "the meaning of separation of powers has for the most part developed outside the courts. The substance of various clauses and provisions in the Constitution are the result of compromises and accommodations worked out by legislative and executive officials" (p. 285).

Contemporary Controversy

Most of the contemporary debate about the constitutional separation of powers in the United States does, in fact, center on the executive-legislative relations that have always been the focus of separation-of-powers arguments. Those who blame the separation of powers for deadlock, inefficiency, and lack of accountability propose reforms that would bring the U.S. government closer to a parliamentary system by connecting the executive and legislative powers. Common reform proposals are that members of the House of Representatives should have longer terms that correspond to the president's term; that national elections should be allowed during the executive's and legislators' terms to resolve deadlock or, better, to deter it; and that members of Congress should be allowed to serve in the cabinet. Advocates of these proposals see them as vehicles for increasing both the government's efficiency and its accountability to the people.

The critics who propose these reforms have been influenced by British journalist Walter Bagehot's description of the British system (*The English Constitution*, 1867) as one in which powers are "fused" rather than separated. Woodrow Wilson (*Congressional Government*, 1885), Henry Hazlitt (*A New Constitution Now*, 1942), Charles Hardin (*Presidential Power and Accountability: Toward a New Constitution*, 1974), and, more recently, the privately organized Committee on the Constitutional System—whose spokespersons include Douglas Dillon and Lloyd Cutler—have adopted this understanding of the parliamentary system and used it to criticize the American system. This "parliamentary critique" of the separation of powers, as Thomas Sargentich dubs it, casts the separation of powers as the root of the American system's problems and looks to the supposed fusion of powers in the English Parliament as the desirable antidote.

There is a disjuncture between the understanding of the separation of powers in the parliamentary critique and the historical development of the doctrine. The former treats the balancing version of the doctrine that has developed in the United States as definitive; the latter testifies that it is not. That Bagehot and his intellectual descendents neglect the parliamentary origin of the separation of powers and take the U.S. version as definitive has several implications for contemporary debate over the supposed shortcomings of the separations of powers.

1. The terms of the parliamentary critique do not make clear that the critique actually addresses the balancing version of the separation of powers, not the generic doctrine. As it is articulated now, the parliamentary critique implies that lawmaking and law-executing powers should be exercised by the same hands, a point with which no republican in the last 300 years would agree. As Gwyn (1965) shows, by taking the balancing process as definitive of the separation of powers, the parliamentary critique loses sight of a founding principle of modern democratic republics, whether they are parliamentary or presidential. It also ignores the purposes other than balancing that the separation of powers might serve—accountability, rule of law in the common interest, and efficiency.

2. The parliamentary critique implies that parliamentary systems, in which executive and legislative branches have some overlapping membership and the executive cannot rule without majority support in the legislature, do not involve a separation of powers, that only presidential systems have a separation of powers. However, as Blackstone and the Federalists agreed, the principle that all three governmental powers should not be concentrated in the same hands does not require complete separation; it requires only enough separation to prevent the unlimited exercise of power, without regard for law and the common interest. Those who imply or argue explicitly that a parliamentary system does not involve such separation forget, as Gwyn (1986) points out, that "the legislative assembly and the government maintain separate existences, and each, through withdrawal of confidence or dissolution, is able to check the actions of the other" (p. 76). Further, to say that parliamentary systems are not compatible with the requisite degree of separation is to imply that they are tyrannical, also a point with which no republican would agree.

3. Admitting the defining principle of the separation of powers to be the prevention of a despotic concentration of powers requires us to admit that either presidential systems or parliamentary systems can meet the requirements of the doctrine. Gwyn (1986) explains that the system that cannot meet its requirements is the assembly system, in which the executive is completely subordinate to the legislative assembly and can be removed by it at any time. As prime examples, Gwyn lists the Long Parliament that inspired seventeenth-century republicans to argue for the separation of powers and the Paris Commune, which impressed Karl Marx and later became part of the constitutional rhetoric of the Soviet regime.

4. If the parliamentary critique is directed strictly at the balancing version of the separation of powers that emerged in the United States, rather than at the doctrine itself, it is, in effect, directed at a key component of the presidential system of government. It amounts to an argument that parliamentary systems are more accountable and more efficient than presidential systems because they are more unified. Defenders of the separation of powers in the U.S. presidential system—Thomas Sargentich, James W. Ceasar, James Q. Wilson, Arthur Schlesinger, Jr.—contest the point, although usually without recognizing that they are defending a particular version of the doctrine rather than the separation of powers itself. Defenders say that the parliamentary critique relies too heavily on the influence of structure and not enough on the factors of social order, which influence any regime. Unity may come more from the latter than the former. If parliamentary systems are necessarily unified, what accounts for differences between the British and Italian systems? Gwyn (1986) challenges the notion that unity between the executive and legislature is a given even in Britain, citing instances in which members of Parliament have been willing to sacrifice party unity when they disagreed with the prime minister's policies.

Defenders of the U.S. system also accuse the parliamentary critique of failing to acknowledge the benefits of the separation of powers, by which they mean the benefits of the balancing version. They believe that this arrangement offers expanded access to government and opens up dialogue and that it encourages the consideration of alternative policies and prevents the dominance of factions. Sargentich criticizes the parliamentary critique's emphasis on unity for tending to increase executive control and having an unrepublican, managerial bias. Finally, to Charles Hardin's claim that a parliamentary system would have handled Watergate more efficiently and prevented it from becoming an extended constitutional crisis, Sargentich responds that the scandal might not have come to light in a parliamentary system.

5. For those who would reform the balancing version of the separation of powers, who believe that parliamentary-type reforms are needed to improve the efficiency and accountability of government in the United States, the work of Matthew Soberg Shugart and John Carey in comparative politics suggests caution. Shugart and Carey (1992) note that "no existing presidential system has ever changed to a parliamentary system, while several have made the reverse move" (p. 3). In 1992, they observed that most new democracies in the previous 20 years have adopted presidential systems, whereas parliamentary systems tended largely to be the choice in former British colonies. However, even some of these countries—Guyana, Nigeria, and Zimbabwe—replaced parliamentary systems with presidential systems. From the perspective of the contemporary debate over the separation of powers, this means that the balancing version of the doctrine is alive and well in political practice.

Further, Shugart and Carey argue, against prevailing opinion in scholarly literature, that presidential systems and the balancing processes they entail are superior to parliamentary systems in their capacity to provide accountability, mutual checks, and an arbiter in cases of political conflict. These arguments, of course, are reminiscent of the original republican arguments for the separation of power, arguments now combined with the balancing argument and adapted to support a presidential system.

WYNNE WALKER MOSKOP

BIBLIOGRAPHY

Blackstone, William, 1769. *Commentaries on the Laws of England,* vol. 4. London.

Fisher, Louis, 1991. *Constitutional Conflicts Between Congress and the President,* 3d ed., rev. Lawrence: University Press of Kansas.

Goldwin, Robert A., and Art Kaufman, eds., 1986. *Separation of Powers–Does It Still Work?* Washington, D.C.: American Enterprise Institute for Public Policy Research.

Gwyn, W. B., 1965. *The Meaning of the Separation of Powers: An Analysis of the Doctrine from Its Origin to the Adoption of the United States Constitution.* The Hague: Martinus Nijhoff.

———, 1986. "The Separation of Powers and Modern Forms of Government," in Robert A. Goldwin and Art Kaufman, eds., *Separation of Powers–Does it Still Work?* 65–89.

Hamilton, Alexander, John Jay, and James Madison, n.d. *The Federalist: A Commentary on the Constitution of the United States.* New York: Modern Library.

Hardin, Charles, 1989. *Constitutional Reform in America: Essays on the Separation of Powers.* Ames: Iowa State University Press.

INS v. Chadha, 1983. 462 U.S. 919.

Locke, John, 1965. *Second Treatise of Government.* In *Two Treatises of Government,* ed. Peter Laslett. New York: New American Library.

Marbury v. Madison, 1803. 1 Cranch 137.

Montesquieu, Charles de, 1977. *The Spirit of the Laws: A Compendium of the First English Edition,* ed. David Wallace Carrithers. Berkeley: University of California Press.

Sargentich, Thomas O., 1993. "The Limits of the Parliamentary Critique of the Separation of Powers." *William and Mary Law Review,* vol. 34 (Spring) 679–739.

Shugart, Matthew Soberg, and John M. Carey, 1992. *Presidents and Assemblies: Constitutional Design and Electoral Dynamics.* New York: Cambridge University Press.

U.S. v. Nixon, 1974. 418 U.S. 683.

SETTLEMENT HOUSES.

Voluntary social service organizations established in poor urban neighborhoods, first in England, then in the United States, to provide coordinated delivery of services. The settlements' original aim was to ameliorate the problems of urban neighborhoods and their residents by bringing educated women and men into relationships with the working poor and the destitute, especially–in the United States–recent immigrants. Ultimately, the settlement movement hoped to make the ethnic poor more like the middle class and to reduce the likelihood of class conflict.

English Roots

The settlement house originated in England. The first, Toynbee Hall in London's East End, was established by Canon Samuel Barnett and Henrietta Barnett in 1884; by 1911, there were 46 settlements in British cities. British settlers, influenced by the ideas of German philosopher Friedrich Hegel and British social critic Thomas Carlyle, believed in the organic unity of all life; they therefore theorized that the interclass hostility caused by economic disparities could be overcome by positive cooperative efforts among people of different classes. Toynbee Hall was named for British historian Arnold Toynbee, a friend of

Samuel Barnett's, who near the end of his life lived in a London slum and worked to bring education and what was referred to as "culture" to manual laborers.

Toynbee Hall pioneered the idea that well-to-do reformers would take up residence in a poor neighborhood in order to get to know residents and help them with their problems. Behind this idea was the theory, which broke with the individualistic thinking of most charity workers of the time, that the difficulties experienced by the poor were not solely due to their own failings but could be traced in large part to social conditions. Toynbee Hall's programmatic emphasis was on education, through picture exhibitions, lectures, and university extension classes. Barnett hoped that the Hall would become a rallying point for neighborhood improvement, and the residents promoted parks, playgrounds, and cleaner streets.

Toynbee Hall and other important British settlements were mostly staffed by male graduates of Oxford and Cambridge Universities, and nearly a quarter of Toynbee Hall's male residents went on to become civil servants. British settlements thus became seen as stepping stones to government jobs, at least for men.

American Settlements

The early U.S. settlements were directly modeled on Toynbee Hall, usually after their founders made personal visits there. Nevertheless, U.S. settlements evolved in distinctive directions. The movement in America was much larger: between 1886, when Stanton Coit started the Neighborhood Guild on New York City's Lower East Side, and 1910, 400 settlement houses were founded, compared to less than 50 in Britain during the same period. In addition, the philosophy of the U.S. settlers was more democratic; they assumed that they would not only teach the poor but learn from them and better understand the nature of urban problems. In the United States, settlers put more emphasis on using the neighborhood as a base from which to organize the poor in order to break the hold of machine politicians on municipal governments. Perhaps the most striking contrast with Britain, however, was the dominance of the U.S. settlement movement by women, particularly educated, unmarried, middle-class women, many of whom spent virtually their entire adult lives as settlement house residents. A majority of the most-famous and influential settlement movement leaders were female, including Jane Addams, Florence Kelley, Julia Lathrop, Grace Abbott, and Sophonisba Breckinridge of Chicago's Hull House, Lillian Wald of New York's Henry Street Settlement, Vida Scudder of College Settlement in New York, Mary McDowell of the University of Chicago Settlement, and Mary Kingsbury Simkovitch of Greenwich House in New York, all of whom became key leaders in campaigns for groundbreaking social policies.

Settlement House Activities

U.S. settlements perpetuated the types of educational programs initiated by Toynbee Hall, including classes in literature, poetry, and music, as well as the more practical arts of housekeeping, child care, and cooking. Numerous lectures were held, as well as debate clubs, concerts, and discussion groups.

In the United States, however, the emphasis on improving neighborhood conditions blossomed into indepth investigation of the root causes of problems and into advocacy for government action. Beginning with efforts to clean up, paint, plant flowers and trees, and otherwise beautify neighborhoods, settlers quickly expanded into lobbying for better garbage collection, safer water supplies, improved schools and recreational facilities, and into research into the conditions of working women and children, tenement housing, unemployment, and the sweatshop system. U.S. settlers aimed not only to provide direct services to individuals, families, and neighborhoods but to invent and institutionalize service capacity on a permanent basis, typically by involving government.

The American settlement houses pioneered the systematic investigation of the living conditions in urban neighborhoods. Hull House residents made a thorough study of their area, documenting and mapping the nationality and the wages of all the residents. *Hull-House Maps and Papers,* published in 1895, was the first "survey," so styled, in social science (see **survey method**). South-End House in Boston made similar studies, published as *City Wilderness* in 1898 and *Americans in Process* in 1902. Other settlement-house studies followed, presenting charts, maps, statistics, and analytic essays on the conditions in their neighborhoods. As a group, the settlers were convinced that knowledge of these conditions, based on factual evidence, would lead government officials and city leaders to act to improve them.

Social Policy Pioneers

U.S. settlement residents were responsible for establishing the first public playground, the first juvenile court—with settlement residents serving as the first probation officers—paid through private donations they raised themselves, the first state government employment bureau, the first city health and sanitation inspections, the first special education classes, and the first public-health nursing service. They collaborated with female labor leaders to pass laws limiting women's and children's working hours and to improve workplace safety. Joining with a national network of women's clubs, their lobbying led in 1912 to the first federal social welfare agency, the Children's Bureau, headed by Julia Lathrop, the first woman to head a federal government entity. This same network of settlement leaders and clubwomen, spearheaded by Children's Bureau leaders, proceeded to win passage of the first piece of federal social service legislation, the Sheppard-Towner Act of 1921, which established state agencies for maternal and child health services and education. Similar lobbying produced mothers' pension programs, the forerunner of the current Aid to Families with Dependent Children, in 40 states by 1920. Several observers, notably Clarke Chambers (1967), credit the settlement-house reformers with setting programmatic examples and maintaining continuity of leadership during the 1920s, a time when interest in social reforms was generally at a low ebb, and by their efforts setting the stage for the New Deal.

Professionalization

American settlement houses were greatly affected by trends in the development of social work as a profession. Growing emphasis on the need for the proper training and credentialing of social workers was at odds with the settlement emphasis on good-hearted, middle-class people establishing relationships with the poor and being able to help them on the strength of that relationship. Social work as a profession began to attract many of those who were also drawn to settlement work, but as professionals they tended to think of neighborhood residents as clients and frequently lived outside the neighborhood. As Judith Trolander (1987) said, "Instead of seeking to do *with* the neighborhood, they sought to do *for* the neighborhood" (p. 39). In addition, the growing interest in social "casework," emphasizing individual problem diagnosis grounded in psychological theory, clashed with the settlers' stress on the societal causes of urban ills.

By the 1950s, settlement houses generally had professional staff members perform duties that once would have been done by volunteer residents, and most of the staff had masters degrees in social work.

Recent History

After World War II, the settlement-house emphasis on bridging class lines came under attack by more radical agents of social change, most notably Saul Alinsky, the Chicago-based community organizer and social theorist, but also labor leaders, civil rights activists, and other sociologists. They criticized the tendency of settlers to speak for neighborhood residents and urged that residents speak for themselves. Interestingly, however, Henry Street Settlement on New York's Lower East Side can be seen as the birthplace of the community action movement that was the centerpiece of the early War on Poverty. In response to gang warfare in the area, Henry Street's Helen Hall and other settlement leaders, in cooperation with the Columbia University School of Social Work, developed a plan for a concerted attack on juvenile delinquency. Mobilization

for Youth, the resulting agency, became the prototype for community action programs, combining community organization, provision of services, and casework under one aegis.

The general effect of the short-lived War on Poverty on the settlement houses was to make them more oriented to seeking federal grant money and to improve their sensitivity to the participation of neighborhood residents in setting settlement policies. Also, as many of the settlement neighborhoods had changed from white ethnic to African American, so too the professional leadership of settlement houses became largely black. This transition occurred during a time of declining government funding for social programs in general and programs in black neighborhoods in particular.

Contemporary settlement houses have lost their original emphasis on establishing a relationship with the neighborhood, a goal that proved too vague to attract government or foundation funding. The result is, as Trolander (1987) argued, that today's settlement is more of a "neighborhood center," a professionally staffed social agency providing specific services to individuals, and therefore difficult to distinguish from other, similar organizations.

CAMILLA STIVERS

BIBLIOGRAPHY

Addams, Jane, 1981[1910]. *Twenty Years at Hull House.* New York: Penguin/Signet.

Chambers, Clarke A., 1967. *Seedtime of Reform: American Social Service and Social Action, 1918–1933.* Ann Arbor: University of Michigan Press/Ann Arbor Paperbacks.

Davis, Allen F., 1967. *Spearheads for Reform: Social Settlements and the Progressive Movement, 1890–1914.* New York: Oxford University Press.

Pacey, Loren M., 1950. *Readings in the Development of Settlement Work.* New York: Association Press.

Sklar, Kathryn Kish, 1985. "Hull House in the 1890s: A Community of Women Reformers." *Signs: Journal of Women in Culture and Society,* vol. 10, no. 4 (Summer) 658–677.

Skocpol, Theda, 1992. *Protecting Soldiers and Mothers: The Political Origins of Social Policy in the United States.* Cambridge, MA: Belknap Press of Harvard University Press.

Trolander, Judith Ann, 1987. *Professionalism and Social Change: From the Settlement House Movement to Neighborhood Centers, 1886 to the Present.* New York: Columbia University Press.

Wald, Lillian, 1915. *The House on Henry Street.* New York: Henry Holt.

SEXUAL HARASSMENT. Any unwelcomed and unsolicited sexually oriented act that has a detrimental impact on employee performance or morale. Sexual harassment can result from the use of offensive language, gestures, and/or sexually suggestive remarks, or it can involve more overt behavior and coercive demands for sexual favors. Sexual harassment constitutes discrimination because it leads to the unequal treatment of employees in the workplace. There are two main types of sexual harassment:

1. Quid Pro Quo: a form of harassment that occurs when an employer or supervisor demands sexual favors from an employee in exchange for a tangible, work-related benefit. This type of sexual harassment is most likely to occur between individuals of unequal rank, position, or power within an organization. It usually involves such work-related benefits as the promise of a job, the receipt of a promotion, or an increase in salary.

2. Hostile Work Environment: a form of harassment that creates a demeaning, intimidating, or abusive environment for an employee. This type of harassment can occur between employees at any level or position, but it often happens between coworkers who are at relatively equal organizational ranks. It can develop anytime sexually oriented language or conduct has a harmful (i.e., abusive or hostile) impact on an employee's working conditions.

Sexual harassment in either form is a major issue for modern-day organizations. The individual victims of sexual harassment can suffer severe economic, social, and psychological side effects; for example, they might lose their jobs, they might not receive the pay or promotion they deserve; they might feel humiliated by their coworkers, and/or they might suffer emotional stress and embarrassment. Sexual harassment also has significant consequences for employers, managers, and other coworkers within an organization. It can have a direct effect on worker productivity and employee morale. And it can lead to disruptive and time-consuming disputes between employees and costly legal settlements for the agency or company. Thus, sexual harassment must be viewed as an organizational, as well as an individual, problem.

One of the main problems, however, is that it is difficult to identify exactly what qualifies as sexual harassment. Some conduct and behavior is relatively easy to pinpoint. For example, most people would agree that sexual harassment has occurred when a supervisor fires an employee who will not submit to sexual demands. In some of its other forms, however, the task of identifying sexual harassment can be much more problematic. Is a sexually permissive joke always considered to be a form of sexual harassment?

The difficulty of defining these less overt forms of sexual harassment lies is their subjective nature. Employees bring to the workplace their own views of what is right and wrong. People's perceptions are shaped by their generational, cultural, educational, political, and religious backgrounds; all of these factors influence the way an individual views the propriety of a given action or comment. Quite simply, what is sexual harassment to one employee

may be little more than a harmless comment, joke, or prank to another employee.

The subjective element involved in defining sexual harassment presents a major dilemma for organizations. How can an organization combat a problem if it cannot even define precisely when, where, and how it exists? This situation is compounded by the fact that the definition of sexual harassment itself has evolved over time.

The Emergence and Evolution of Sexual Harassment as a Major Policy Issue

The contemporary view of discrimination in general, and sexual harassment in particular, represents the product of years of problem redefinition and refinement. Only a few decades ago, discrimination was a common and unquestioned facet of everyday life in public and private organizations. White males dominated the workplace and used their positions of power to thwart the ascendence of other groups. Eventually, women and other minorities were able to penetrate the artificially created employment barriers; however, their work experiences were often unpleasant and even harmful. White males still occupied most positions of power, and they often acted in their own self-interest, creating work environments that were discriminatory, even hostile, to newcomers. Today, such conduct would be deemed "sexual harassment." Yet, it was seen as perfectly normal, acceptable behavior at the time.

Beginning in the 1950s and 1960s, the public's attitude toward issues like sexual harassment began to change. Part of the shift in public sentiment occurred because of interest group pressure. Civil rights advocates drew attention to a variety of forms of social inequity and discrimination across society. Women's groups pointed out the sharp disparities that existed between men and women in the workplace, particularly in terms of earnings, promotions, and positions. These groups helped to stimulate broader concerns about individual rights and liberties across a wide range of issues. They helped produce a climate in which traditional occupational roles and behavior patterns could be questioned. This, in turn, helped set the stage for governmental action on the issue of sexual harassment.

In the U.S. context, all three branches of government have played a vital role in shaping contemporary views of sexual harassment. The legislative branch took the first step in 1964, when it passed Title VII of the Civil Rights Act. This measure explicitly prohibited discriminatory employment practices, including those based on sex. Unfortunately, however, the 1964 Civil Rights Act did not specifically identify sexual harassment as a form of employee discrimination. Consequently, it was some time before the linkage was made between sexual harassment and sexual discrimination.

Early judicial interpretations viewed acts of sexual harassment as isolated, personal matters between individuals (Faley 1982). As a result, the courts were reluctant to identify sexual harassment as sexual discrimination under the Civil Rights Act. In the mid-1970s, however, the courts began to depart from their previous stand. In *Williams v. Saxbe*, a 1976 case involving a federal government worker who suffered retaliation from her male supervisor for refusing his sexual advances, a U.S. District Court held that the victim had an actionable discrimination claim under Title VII of the Civil Rights Act. This case was important in the development of legal theory on sexual harassment because it was the first case to recognize quid pro quo sexual harassment as a form of sexual discrimination in the workplace.

Another important development in the interpretation of sexual harassment situations occurred several years later. In 1980, the Equal Employment Opportunity Commission (EEOC), the federal agency responsible for handling sexual harassment claims, issued its *Final Guidelines on Sexual Harassment in the Workplace*. In the 1980 guidelines (and then later in the amended guidelines of 1984), the EEOC formally recognized two types of sexual harassment: quid pro quo and hostile environment. Moreover, the commission indicated that both types of harassment were actionable under Title VII of the Civil Rights Act. These guidelines presented a relatively clear, straightforward statement about the scope of sexual harassment cases, and they have served as the basis for contemporary policy discussions and interpretations.

The EEOC guidelines have also been referenced in subsequent judicial decisions on sexual harassment. For example, the *Bundy v. Jackson* case (in 1981) provides an excellent illustration of this. The case involved a female corrections worker who was subjected to sexual requests by her supervisors, although she suffered no tangible losses. The appellate court broke from previous judicial decisions and held that sexual harassment could occur even if there were no tangible losses on the part of the person who was harassed. This decision gave further legitimacy to claims of sexual harassment based on the existence of a hostile work environment as defined in the EEOC guidelines. Then, in a landmark 1986 court case, *Meritor Savings Bank, FSB v. Vinson*, the U.S. Supreme Court affirmed the validity of Title VII claims for both quid pro quo and hostile environment forms of sexual harassment. In reaching its decision, the court gave deference to the EEOC's guidelines on sexual harassment. The court also answered, in part, questions about the extent to which employers may be held liable for sexual harassment by their employees. For quid pro quo harassment, the court applied the standard of strict liability, meaning that employers are responsible for the actions of their employees whether or not the employer knew of the sexual harassment (Paul 1994).

Since the mid-1980s, the definition of sexual harassment, as well as the organizational responses to it, have continued to evolve. In the Civil Rights Act of 1991, the U.S. Congress expanded the types of relief available to victims of employment discrimination, including those affected by sexual harassment. Then, two years later, the U.S. Supreme Court relaxed the requirements for hostile environment harassment cases. In *Harris v. Forklift*, the Court ruled that employees only had to show that an abusive or hostile environment existed and not that this situation actually prevented them from performing their jobs.

Today, sexual harassment is an important public-policy issue in the United States, as well as in other contemporary societies. Governmental institutions are trying to clarify the definition of sexual harassment and derive suitable mechanisms to address such situations. Sexual harassment is also an issue that provokes strong feelings among the general public. An excellent example of this occurred in 1991, during Clarence Thomas' senatorial confirmation hearings for his appointment to the U.S. Supreme Court. Millions of citizens followed the television coverage of these hearings, undoubtedly because sexual harassment charges were one of the main topics of discussion. Events such as this clearly demonstrate that sexual harassment is an issue that generates tremendous public interest and concern.

Sexual harassment is a critical issue for both public and private organizations. Although the incidence of sexual harassment does vary from one type of employment setting to another, there is evidence to suggest that the problem occurs just as frequently in public organizations as it does in the private sector (Bayes and Kelly 1994). After all, sexual harassment can occur anywhere employees are working side by side within the same organizational setting. So, public and private managers have a responsibility to maintain an environment that discourages all forms of discriminatory treatment of their employees, including sexual harassment. There is now an added incentive for organizations to be concerned about sexual harassment problems. If sexual harassment does occur in the workplace, the organization is considered to be at fault for letting this kind of behavior or conduct exist. Thus, there are strong incentives for public and private managers to view sexual harassment as a serious organizational issue.

Current Practices

Organizations must establish both proactive and reactive measures to deal successfully with sexual harassment problems. Proactive measures can prevent the behavior and situations that might lead to sexual harassment; reactive procedures allow an organization to address these situations when they do occur. Each of these general approaches is discussed below.

Proactive Measures

Establish a Clear Policy Statement. The first step that an organization can take to prevent sexual harassment is to establish a firm position against its practice. Normally, this is accomplished by creating a clear policy statement prohibiting behavior and conduct that will lead to sexual harassment. This statement usually provides a basic definition of the problem, as well as some indication of the types of situations and behavior that qualify as sexual harassment. This statement serves several important functions: It makes employees aware of the issue; it conveys a clear organizational position against its practice; and it may reduce the organization's potential liability if an employee ever engages in an act of sexual harassment.

Disseminate Information on Sexual Harassment. Managers can compile and distribute a packet of relevant materials pertaining to sexual harassment issues. This information usually explains how individuals can initiate sexual harassment complaints, as well as what documentation they will need to substantiate their charges. In addition, the materials often describe what investigatory and grievance procedures the organization will follow in such cases. This packet of information can be a valuable resource to employees: It identifies all the steps that must be followed in pursuing a sexual harassment case.

Conduct Training and Orientation Sessions on Sexual Harassment. Many public agencies and private businesses hold informational and orientation sessions on sexual harassment. Sometimes, these are done as part of broader training sessions in which a wide variety of personnel and employee issues are discussed. Increasingly, however, the trend is to arrange separate workshops in which the discussion is solely focused on sexual harassment problems. Regardless of which format is followed, these training sessions are used for the following reasons: to heighten employee awareness about sexual harassment; to identify ways of preventing its occurrence; to specify the grievance procedures available to employees who feel they have been sexually harassed; and to delineate the actions that the organization will take against employees who engage in sexual harassment.

Identify a Contact Person or Unit to Handle Sexual Harassment Issues. Some organizations identify a single person who is responsible for handling sexual harassment cases; others give this responsibility to a personnel unit or an employee benefits office. Regardless, these individuals or divisions play a key role: They provide advice and assistance to employees who feel that they are being (or have been) sexually harassed. They also explain organizational policies in this area, instructing employees on how to deal with instances of sexual harassment. In some settings, these personnel also serve as mediators, actually helping to resolve disputes between employees. They can even be important "change agents" within an organization, promoting alternative work arrangements and employee behavior that will diminish the incidence of sexual harassment behavior.

Devise Appropriate Enforcement Procedures. Organizations cannot wait until a sexual harassment complaint has been made and then determine what they will do about it. They must decide on appropriate sanctions and penalties before sexual harassment charges surface. This allows the organization to take prompt action in dealing with complaints, and it also facilitates the implementation of any disciplinary action that might be warranted. The establishment of sanctions and penalties for sexual harassment also serves another purpose: It indicates that the agency will not tolerate sexual harassment and that it will act promptly to rectify the situation and penalize those who engage in such behavior.

Reactive Measures

Develop and Maintain Appropriate Grievance Procedures. Even when organizations take a proactive stance, there is still a need to develop mechanisms and procedures to deal quickly and effectively with instances of sexual harassment when they do occur. However, one of the major problems is that most incidents of sexual harassment still go unreported. Victims of harassment may be unwilling to lodge a grievance because they are afraid of the reactions from coworkers, or because they do not think that the organization will act on their complaint. Consequently, it is imperative that an organization maintain clear and appropriate grievance procedures for sexual harassment charges. Employees must feel that their complaints will be taken seriously, that they will not suffer any reprisals for lodging complaints, and that the harassers will be dealt with in a timely and appropriate manner. In sum, organizations must establish and adhere to grievance procedures that encourage the victims of harassment to come forward with their complaints.

One way managers can encourage employees to report acts of sexual harassment is by incorporating employee preferences and expectations into the organization's grievance procedures. Yet, even the most well-intentioned grievance procedures will fail if they do not adequately meet the needs of victims. Managers can avoid this problem by asking employees with different perspectives and orientations to help formulate the organization's sexual harassment policies and grievance procedures. Doing so will help to ensure that the procedures are truly an effective and viable means of preventing and resolving sexual harassment situations.

Promptly Review and Investigate Sexual Harassment Complaints. Public and private organizations must deal with sexual harassment complaints in an expeditious and thorough manner. It is critical that the victims of sexual harassment not be subjected to further instances of humiliation, abuse, or harm. At the same time, however, organizations must be careful to review all grievances carefully and fully: The rights of all employees, including those who are accused of harassment, must be protected. Unwarranted charges should be quickly dismissed, and all materials presented in such cases should be held in the strictest confidence.

Invoke Appropriate Sanctions and Take Remedial Action. When a sexual harassment complaint is substantiated, organizations must address the situation swiftly and appropriately. Here, managers can take a variety of actions, depending upon the severity of the offense: They can order the harassment to stop immediately; they can impose disciplinary measures on the charged party; they can restore any employee benefits that the complainant lost because of the harassment; and they can institute measures that will alter the overall working environment of their employees.

Public and private managers must establish and maintain work environments that are nondiscriminatory for all their employees. So, when they discover instances where discriminatory practices exist, it is their responsibility to rectify the situation and to take steps to prevent these situations from ever occurring again. It is imperative that managers keep one overriding principle in mind: The harasser, not the harassed, must be disciplined or sanctioned. So, the victims of sexual harassment should not have to change their jobs or positions to avoid unpleasant situations; instead, the harassers should be transferred, relocated, or terminated.

Future Prospects

Sexual harassment is a prominent, albeit controversial, issue in modern, contemporary societies. Managers in both the public and private sectors recognize the importance of the issue, and they have taken steps to try to diminish its occurrence in the workplace. Despite these efforts, however, sexual harassment has not been eliminated. It is extremely difficult to alter the factors—for example, individual attitudes, employee behavior, and organizational environments—that lead to such discriminatory treatment. It is also difficult to anticipate the new challenges and problems that might surface in this area. Dramatic changes are taking place in organizational environments, producing the need for more flexible management frameworks and more fluid personnel systems. Technological developments are occurring so rapidly that traditional office arrangements, information systems, and communication networks are being radically transformed. These transformations will make it difficult for managers to create and maintain work environments that are totally free of sexual harassment situations. Thus, the future holds even more challenges and dilemmas for managers who must ensure that all employees, regardless of their sex, receive equal treatment in the workplace.

JERRELL D. COGGBURN AND SAUNDRA K. SCHNEIDER

BIBLIOGRAPHY

Bayes, Jane, and Rita Mae Kelly, 1994. "Managing Sexual Harassment in Public Employment." In Steven W. Hays and Richard C. Kearney, eds., *Public Personnel Administration: Problems and Perspectives*, 3d ed. Englewood Cliffs, NJ: Prentice-Hall, 217–231.

Faley, Robert H., 1982. "Sexual Harassment: Critical Review of Legal Cases with General Principles and Preventive Measures." *Personnel Psychology*, vol. 35, no. 3 (Autumn) 583–600.

Gutek, Barbara A., 1985. *Sex and the Workplace*. San Francisco, CA: Jossey-Bass.

Kelly, Rita Mae, 1992. "Sexual Harassment in the States." In Mary Ellen Guy, ed., *Women and Men of the States: Public Administrators at the State Level*. Armonk, NY: M. E. Sharpe, 109–124.

Paul, Ellen Frankel, 1994. "Sexual Harassment: A Defining Moment and Its Repercussions." In David A. Rochefort and Robert W. Cobb, eds. *The Politics of Problem Definition*. Lawrence: The University Press of Kansas, 67–97.

Pellicciotti, Joseph M., 1993. *Title VII Liability for Sexual Harassment in the Workplace*, 2d ed. Alexandria, VA: International Personnel Management Association.

SHARED SERVICES. Services jointly provided by two or more local government units. For instance, the New Jersey Interlocal Services Act (the Act) authorizes any local unit of the state (municipality, county, school district, regional authority or district, authority, board, commission of district [with the consent of the creating local unit]) to enter into a contract with any other local unit or units for the joint provision within their several jurisdictions of any service that any party to the agreement is empowered to render within its own jurisdiction. The units may adopt the contract by resolution or ordinance (State of New Jersey Department of Community Affairs, Division of Local Government Services [SNJDCADLGS] 1990).

Shared-services agreements are a result of government's search for ways to keep up existing levels of services or even to maintain fiscal soundness (Lemov 1993). These interlocal agreements can be formal or informal. Whereas informal agreements are usually unwritten verbal arrangements, formal agreements are "arrangements of mutual obligation between governments. . . . In essence, it is a business transaction between public bodies" (Talley 1980). The services eligible for such contracts include

- general government administration;
- health, police, and fire protection;
- code enforcement;

- assessment and collection of taxes;
- financial administration;
- environmental services;
- joint municipal courts;
- youth, senior citizens, welfare, and social services programs.

Police services seem to be one of the services that most municipalities in New Jersey and the nation refuse to share. "Communities view basic police, public works and certain administrative services as the core of the local services structure and are reluctant to share these services" (Somerset Alliance 1994).

Ronald Fundis et al. (1993) reported that, in general, there are four reasons why government units should consider entering into an interlocal agreement to share services:

1. problems do not respect political boundaries (i.e., flood control, water supply);
2. economy of scale, efficiency, cost sharing, and affordability of services or equipment;
3. defensive strategy to prevent state or federal assumption of a local function/activity or to discourage the growth of special purpose districts;
4. interdependence of local units in an area may require or foster cooperation.

Bruce Talley (1980) identified economy of scale as the chief reason to enter into an interlocal agreement. "An economy is not limited solely to a dollar savings—an increased benefit from the same level of expenditure is also an economy." He further argued that jointly acquiring, building, and sharing the cost of a facility represents economy of scale. Likewise, jurisdictions pay a proportionate share of a specialist's expenses, purchase the required level of service as demands change, and eliminate duplication.

Advantages

In the Somerset Alliance for the Future's report (1994) it was stated:

> One of the principal attractions of a bilateral service agreement is that it usually does not require the creation of a separate administrative agency, the cost of which could negate the savings sought by such partnerships. Conversely, where multiple programs or activities are involved (e.g., education, health), potential for savings and operational efficiency increase with additional participants involved in a regional approach.

Interlocal agreements represent opportunities to maximize the use of resources, financial, physical, and human. Since the agreements involve more than one agency, they can all contribute their expertise in the planning and delivery of services.

Moreover, when one of the parties to the agreements is a school district, the agreements represent opportunities to "reinforce the role of municipalities and school districts as responsible administrators and decision-makers" (SNJDCADLGS 1994).

Shared services often lead the communities involved to realize savings. These types of arrangements are especially helpful for small communities because they help those communities cut the cost of providing the services for themselves. In some instances, shared services provide the opportunity for small communities to provide services to their constituencies that could not be provided before.

These types of interlocal agreements also favor the larger municipalities. Their administrative and overhead costs are set off by sharing the cost with smaller communities. This is the case of the town of Lantana, Florida, which entered into interlocal agreements with neighboring towns/cities that could not afford to provide professional fire/rescue, law enforcement, and advanced life support services by themselves (Ford Foundation 1993). In the *Directory of Interlocal Activities*, it was reported that nearly 63 percent of interlocal agreements under evaluation were being considered because of cost-saving reasons (SNJD-CADLGS 1992).

Over a period of four years, the borough of Avalon, New Jersey, has saved nearly US $1 million through an interlocal agreement to collect Avalon's trash during seven winter months. The agreement is with Sea Isle City, which in return can use Avalon's specialized equipment and operators, including a pothole patcher, a sewer tractor truck, and a street sweeper (National Center for Public Productivity 1994). Both communities have benefited; the need to hire an expensive outside contractor for Avalon and the need to buy expensive specialized equipment for Sea Isle City have been eliminated.

Other examples of cost-saving instances include the following: Winnetka, Illinois, reported saving US $50,000 by sharing an attorney; Tigard, Oregon, saved US $20,000 by billing jointly with a water district; Burbank, California, lopped off US $50,000 by finding a partner to keep city traffic lights in good repair (Lemov 1993). Although in many instances there are no savings to municipalities, "most of them [municipalities] can point to a program or a service that they are still providing on a shared basis that might be gone now if they had to keep providing it on their own" (Lemov 1993 p. 26–27).

Examples of Shared Services That Reduce the Cost of Providing the Service

Michael Pagano, from the National League of Cities, sees a continuum in these cost-sharing efforts. "First you try to maintain existing level of service by finding a partner to share in the costs. If that doesn't work, you're looking at eliminating or curtailing the service" (Lemov 1993 p. 26–27). For example:

- Since 1976, in Union County, New Jersey, the municipalities have been sharing the cost of printing tax bills. The county prints the tax bills for all the municipalities for 14 percent of the market cost of each package. This has saved municipalities over US $70,000 annually (International City/County Management Association [ICMA] Doc# 103510).
- For many years, counties and cities and cities and cities in Virginia have been sharing parks and recreational facilities. For example, the town of Orange shares its park with the county that uses it for its high school's major sports events and graduation ceremonies. The county only pays for its use of lighting (Everson 1991). The town manager, Donald Smith, said "the benefits are that lots of kids get to use the park and that the citizens do not have to pay increased taxes to build a new complex." In other parts of Virginia, counties and cities share their park with 50:50 funding from the jurisdictions.
- The cities of Hollowell and Chelsea of Kennebec County, Maine, entered into an interlocal agreement in 1988 to share a code enforcement officer. Both communities needed but could not afford to hire one. So, they decided to share the cost, US $28,000 needed for the salary of a full-time officer (Starn 1991).
- In Maine, three communities–Mapleton, Castle Hill, and Chapman–have been sharing a manager since the late 1960s. The communities also share many other services. According to Michael Starn (1991), the opportunities that sharing personnel offers are being overlooked by municipalities.
- In Norfolk, Virginia, the school board shares the operation of cable television services with the city. While the city supplements funding, the schools provide production personnel, equipment, and programming to operate the government access channels (Fields 1991).
- Upper Deerfield Township, New Jersey, and its school board have cooperated with each other for a long time. The township includes the schools in its snow removal plan, which has resulted in savings for the district. In addition, vehicles and equipment are loaned between the school board and the township. This has eliminated duplication. Also, they have purchased computers of the same make and model in order to be able to have each serve as a backup for the other. This service has resulted in great savings of money and time (SNJDCADLGS 1994b).
- Gollaway Township, New Jersey, and its school board cooperate with each other in a plan where the township crews repair school bus vehicles and the school

district is billed for the parts only (SNJDCADLGS 1994b).
- Six communities in Pennsylvania joined to create the Northern York County Regional Police Department. Through this agreement, the communities save their residents nearly US $500,000 annually (Commonwealth of Pennsylvania, Department of Community Affairs 1992).

In addition to cost-saving, interlocal agreements for the purpose of sharing services often result in upgrading the quality of service delivered.

Examples of Shared Services That Have Improved the Quality of the Service

Talley (1980) stated that "resources can be pooled and services can be distributed uniformly and equitably.... Overall efficiency can be attained by establishing optimum size operating units on a function-by-function basis." For instance:

- Upper Deerfield Township and its school board have experienced increased service by loaning equipment to each other (SNJDCADLGS 1994a).
- Colerain Township, Ohio, which is part of a consolidated central communication center run by Hamilton County, has consolidated with another department within the township and has realized higher quality service. "It is higher quality service to the taxpayer for the dollar spent" (Thompson 1992).
- Three fire departments were "functionally" consolidated in the Portland, Oregon, metropolitan area. The departments were left whole but are allowing interchangeable use of equipment, facilities, and personnel throughout all three. Because of this "functional" consolidation, political boundaries are no longer an issue; "the closest units respond to the emergency.... Unfortunately, jurisdictional boundaries aren't determined based on response time or access" (Thompson 1992).
- The interlocal agreements between the town of Lantana, Florida, and the smaller towns of Hypoluxo, Manalapan, South Palm Beach, and the city of Atlantis not only provide cost benefits but also highly responsive emergency services as measured by response time. These agreements also allow for employees of Lantana "to receive increased training which facilitates greater capacity and ability to respond to emergency situations" (Ford Foundation 1993).

Examples of Shared Services That Have Achieved Distinctive Objectives

Another characteristic advantage of shared service is that moneys from federal and state sources are easier to obtain for development projects involving two or more local governments:

- The executive director of the Land-of-Sky regional council in western North Carolina stated that his "four-county area would never have gotten federal funding for turning the trash-filled French Broad River into an attractive recreation area if the counties hadn't been working together on it" (Shanahan 1991).
- The New Jersey Division of Local Government Services provides funding under the Interlocal Services AID Program depending upon legislative appropriations.

  The Interlocal Services AID Program pays for feasibility studies: (100 percent state-funded) and implementation of joint services with four-year grant based on the following formula:

  1. new service provided jointly: 10 percent of total program cost;
  2. existing service provided jointly: all extraordinary administrative and operating costs of joint project.

  However, capital costs are not eligible for this funding (SNJDCADLGS 1994a).

- Some states, such as Kansas, see interlocal agreements for sharing services as means to avoid the formation of special purpose districts, which are independent entities with authority or potential to assess revenues from users.

Obstacles to Shared Services

In spite of the many advantages associated with sharing services, to many municipalities and agencies the desire to maintain control, pride of ownership, and home rule is more important. Geoff Herman (1991) wrote about the tension between these advantages and the value of control: "The advantages or disadvantages of working independently rather than joining forces with your neighbors are sometimes difficult to compare or compute because an essential tension exists between the value of local control versus the economy of scale efficiencies that are allegedly available to a multi-municipal entity." He also noted a tension between pride of ownership associated with taking initiative on the local level versus those on the regional structure, which are encouraged and supported by the state (Maine).

The Somerset Alliance for the Future (1994) identified the following obstacles: "Fear of loss in a service partnership—uncertainty as to the financial implications of joint service ventures; the impact of shared service agreements on job security or status of municipal employee; and simple inertia."

Another obstacle is residents' attitudes. Talley (1980) stated that "residents may resent a service being provided by a 'distant' government, even though the service is supplied more efficiently and effectively." In addition, Fundis et al. (1993) identified the following as potential barriers:

- historical antagonisms between city-county, county-county governing bodies and residents;
- concern about loss of community or institutional identity;
- complexity of negotiation, which could be overwhelming for communities with limited professional staff;
- public employees unions with differing affiliations, contract dates, and member priorities; this could complicate service consolidation efforts even when no employees will lose their jobs.

The town of Lantana, Florida, had to overcome yet other obstacles when it entered into the previously mentioned interlocal agreement with the other four towns. One of the obstacles was the rapid expansion. "The town had to adapt quickly to extending its services outside its municipal boundaries, i.e., hiring additional personnel, training current and new personnel, procuring additional equipment, etc." (Ford Foundation 1993).

Political obstacles also became evident in Lantana and the other communities. "The idea that the town had the capacity and ability to extend itself in this way presented political obstacles. The success of the idea had to be illustrated to the political bodies in both communities" (Ford Foundation 1993). Talley (1980) also suggested some additional obstacles, including that the new provider's personnel polices may be insensitive to those of the recipient; communication and reporting systems may be less responsive to day-to-day complaints; spillover benefits to jurisdictions outside an agreement may occur without compensation.

The state of New Jersey recognized that "politics is a part of any intergovernmental agreement. [Therefore], citizens' reaction and confidence has to be assessed in all of the participating jurisdictions" (SNJDCADLGS 1994a). In short, the public must be kept informed and involved in any type of negotiation that in any way, shape, or form will have an impact in the way business is conducted in their community.

The New Jersey Division of Local Government Services (1994) strongly encouraged that those who want to enter into an interlocal agreement conduct a feasibility study. One of the purposes of such a study is to determine public reaction and policy issues. The Seattle School District and the City of Seattle can be cited as an excellent example of how to overcome public resistance. In 1990, the city and the school district of Seattle entered into an interlocal agreement overcoming the unthinkable—a levy. In 1989, the Seattle School District worked hand in hand with the City of Seattle to sponsor a citywide Education Summit in which community members identified the most urgent needs of Seattle children. The following fall, voters of Seattle approved a US $60 million, seven-year municipal levy to support the ongoing partnership of the city and the school district in meeting those needs. Hence, this agreement has been called "the Family and Education Levy Interlocal Agreement" (LOGIN Doc# 57537[2]). Obviously, the success of this agreement was dependent upon citizen support. The community, including citizens, school staff, parents, and organizations were made part of the whole process.

PATRIA D. DE LANCER

BIBLIOGRAPHY

Commonwealth of Pennsylvania, 1992. *Intergovernmental Cooperation, Cooperative Solutions for Municipal Problems.* ICMA Doc# 114497.

Everson, Christy, 1991. "Sharing Parks and Recreational Services Is Common Among Local Governments." *Virginia Town and City* (May) 16–17. ICMA Doc# 105393.

Fields, Mary Jo, 1991. "Joint Efforts Enhance Education." *Virginia Town and City* (September) 20 ICMA Doc# 104987.

Ford Foundation, 1993. Local Government Information Network (LOGIN) Doc# 60238.

Fundis, Ronald J., L. V. Gould, D. Hoy, and A. Morin, 1993. "The Interlocal Agreement: A Reference Guide to Joint Delivery of Service." *Kansas Government Journal (ISSN 0222-86d13),* 364–366. NACo.

Herman, Geoff, 1991. "Interlocal Cooperation, Options Which Are Available." *Maine Townsman* (August) 5–10.

League of Kansas Municipalities, 1991. "Intergovernmental Cooperation: An Inventory of Legal Authority in Kansas." *League of Kansas Municipalities Research/Information Bulletin,* vol. 13. NACo.

LOGIN (Local Government Information Network) Doc# 57537 (2).

LOGIN Doc# 76764.

National Association of Counties, 1981. "Union County Interlocal Cooperation System." *Achievement Award Proposal.* ICMA Doc# 103510.

National Center for Public Productivity, 1994. LOGIN Doc# 57305.

New York State, Department of State, 1987. *Local Government Technical Series: Intergovernmental Cooperation.* Albany, NY.

Shanahan, Eileen, 1991. "Going It Jointly: Regional Solutions for Local Problems." *Governing* (August) 70–76.

Somerset Alliance for the Future, 1994. *A Focus on Sharing Services: Summary of Findings and Conclusion.* Somerville, NJ: The Somerset Alliance for the Future.

Starn, Michael, 1991. "Sharing Employees, Idea Should Be Considered First." *Maine Townsman* (January) 10–11. ICMA DOC# 108515.

State of New Jersey Department of Community Affairs, Division of Local Government Services (SNJDCADLGS), 1990. *Interlocal Services: Working Together; A Reference Guide to Joint Delivery of Services.* Trenton, NJ.

———, 1991. *A Directory of Interlocal Activities.* Trenton, NJ.

———, 1992a. *Cooperative Purchasing: A Guide for Local Officials,* 3d ed. Trenton, NJ.

———, 1992b. *Interlocal Services: Working Together; Interlocal Services Agreements: Sample Language for Selected Activities.* Trenton, NJ.

———, 1994a. *Interlocal Services: Working Together; A Guide to Joint Service Feasibility Studies and Interlocal Agreements.* Trenton, NJ.

———, 1994b. *Interlocal Services: Working together; A Guide to School Board Cooperation: An Overlooked Opportunity.* Trenton, NJ.

Talley, Bruce, 1980. "Intergovernmental Cooperation." *The Productivity Improvement Handbook for State and Local Government,* ed. George Wahins, New York: John Wiley & Sons.

Thompson, Stephanie, 1992. "Spotting a Trend: Fire Department Consolidation." *American City & County* (April) 25–30.

Ward, Janet, 1992. "Can Two Live as Cheaply as One?" *American City & County* (February) 30–36.

SIMON, HERBERT ALEXANDER (1916–).

A Nobel Prize winner in economics, Simon's impact on the field of public administration emerges with his classic book *Administrative Behavior* (1947), the paradigm for decisionmaking as bounded rationality.

In his autobiography, *Models of My Life,* Simon (1991) asked, "How does one age, gradually replacing action by reflection?" One may find this question a paradox when discussing the life and contributions of Herbert Simon. The riddle wrapped in the enigma of this quotation is that although it appears Simon is replacing action with reflection, it is suspected that he is merely transforming the action, or taking a well-deserved restful pause, to allow us to view a different perspective of the man who has caused a paradigm shift in the field of public administration. Today, 50 years after *Administrative Behavior,* Simon's theory of bounded rationality, for many, remains the definitive treatise on the decisionmaking process in an organizational context. What makes Simon's work so appealing and seemingly timeless? The answer to this question can be found in the principles of his work, but the origin of the answer is found in Simon as Renaissance Man. His long-lasting appeal may be attributed to Simon's view of the world, which is truly global. Simon's view of public administration was the perspective of political scientist, economist, psychologist, and computer theorist. His advice was scholarly, with form and texture, pragmatic, and profound, yet elegant in its simplicity.

Simon, in his autobiography, also described his life as mazelike, but not in a whimsical or gut-wrenching decision to take one choice or another. His path was a response to the opportunities that have presented themselves along the way in the maze. Comfortingly, we are assured by Simon that his decisions, made in response to opportunities encountered in his maze, were "rational."

Simon was born June 15, 1916, in Milwaukee, Wisconsin. His father was educated in Germany and earned a degree in electrical engineering before emigrating to the United States and settling in Milwaukee in 1903. Simon's mother was a music teacher until she was married in 1910. His older brother, born in 1911, became a lawyer practicing in Wisconsin. An obvious intellect to his classmates, Simon, at an early age, was referred to as a "brain," and he admits that he enjoyed verbal swordsmanship, an attribute that would serve him well. An example of Simon's expertise in this area can be attested to by readers of *Political Science and Politics* (1993) who have read Simon's response to Theodore Lowi's criticism of the state of the discipline of political science.

At age 17, Simon won a scholarship to the University of Chicago. As an undergraduate and graduate student, he pursued a concentration in political science, while being simultaneously preoccupied with economics. His mentor at the University of Chicago's Political Science Department was its chairperson, Charles Merriam. Merriam was the leader of the political science revolutionaries who incorporated behavioralism as the new essential component to political science theory. Simon married Merriam's secretary, also a fellow graduate student, Dorthea Pye.

Simon's first publication was a coauthored work with Charles Ridley, "Measuring Municipal Activities," which was published in the journal *Public Management* in 1938. This publication led to his becoming a staff member for the International City Managers Association (ICMA). The prevalent theory in public administration at this time was "classical organizational theory," as proposed by Leonard White, Luther Gulick, and Lyndall Urwick. Simon felt that Chester Barnard's work *The Functions of the Executive* (1938) offered him a more compatible insight for looking at the manager as a decisionmaker. Originally, Simon planned to do a doctoral thesis on the logic of administration. However, reflections on the behavior of the decisionmaker were the inspiration of his thesis "Administrative Behavior."

Although Simon may have thought that his idea was revolutionary, *Administrative Behavior* did not catch on immediately. However, to paraphrase Victor Hugo, it was an idea whose time had come. Published in 1947, the book *Administrative Behavior* was an updated version of Simon's doctoral thesis that was presented at the University of Chicago in 1942. Dwight Waldo (1948), in his book *The Administrative State*, referred to Simon's *Administrative Behavior* as the "most notable attempt to lay a new conceptual foundation" (p. xvii). The central theme of *Administrative Behavior* is the notion of "bounded rationality." Simon felt that rationality alone does not determine behavior. Instead, behavior is determined by a boundary of irrational and nonrational elements that surround rationality. Rationality now becomes the "area of adaptability to these nonrational elements" (p. 241). Simon sensed that administrative theory must identify the limits of rationality. In this way organizations can be understood in terms of their decision process, that is, if we achieve a bounded rationality and all other factors are equal, then we should make the "rational" decision. It is essentially this work that has carved a niche in public administration for Simon.

From *Administrative Behavior* came the article "The Proverbs of Administration" (1946). In "Proverbs" Simon identified current principles of administration that were illogical and incongruent at their face value.

Simon's framework of bounded rationality was a pluralistic approach to the study of organizations in that it was the manager, as the decisionmaker, who formed the basis for the theory. The next era for Simon occurred with his collaboration with James March in *Organizations*, published in 1958. Aptly titled, *Organizations* brings to light the differences between what is assumed to be the case and what is occurring in organizations. March and Simon's focus then shifted to the institutional framework.

When a new theory becomes the paradigm, it remains so until another theory in the scientific process comes along that changes our perspective. When this new theory is validated it does not become part of the old paradigm, but it creates a new one. Thomas Kuhn (1962), in his book *The Structure of Scientific Revolutions*, stated that the scientific process is not one of accretion or incrementalism; rather, there is a "historical integrity of that science in its own time." *Administrative Behavior* has remained the dominant standard of organizational behavior despite some threats to its bedrock.

Graham Allison's (1971) *Essence of Decision: Explaining the Cuban Missile Crisis* incorporates the principles of *Administrative Behavior* in the Model II type of decisionmaker. Specifically, Allison's Model II, the Organizational Process Model, encompasses Simon's "five characteristic deviations" from rationality: (1) factored problems, where decisionmakers take complex problems and reduce them to their component problems to simplify problemsolving; (2) satisficing, where maximizing is substituted with the choice that is least consequential or "good enough"; (3) search, where organizations seek solutions in a very structured process that limits alternatives; (4) uncertainty avoidance, where basing solutions on projected outcomes or dealing with uncertainty is avoided; and (5) repertories, where algorithms of specific solutions are developed to deal with cyclical and repetitive problems.

Chris Argyris' (1973a) "Some Limits of Rational Man Organizational Theory" incorporated the theories of Simon (as well as March and Allison) to explain and call for more complex and secular models of man in organizations. Argyris' somewhat critical claim that the models of man that exist in organizations omit variables that are central, options that are crucial, and encourage organizational stasis, elicited a critical analysis from Simon. Simon's (1973) article "Organizational Man: Rational *or* Self-Actualizing?" refocused on rationality, the need for power, work motivation, achievement, and upon self-actualization as part of the fabric of the human institution. He cautioned Argyris not to build a design of human institutional behavior around only one concept or factor. Ultimately, Simon believed that there is a delicate balance between human freedom and social constraint—often shifting, but never disassembled. In his (1973b) response, "Organizational Man: Rational *and* Self-Actualizing," Professor Argyris made an interesting point that illustrates the perpetuation of *Administrative Behavior* as the framework of organizations when he said: "Descriptive research of organizations would not have the same impact if all that was available were the rational-man theories" and "what would make people dissatisfied with the incompleteness of the rational-man view if there were no competing theories?" (p. 356).

Notwithstanding Simon's work in the field of public administration, we cannot claim exclusivity. The turns in the maze and the opportunities and circumstances that presented themselves had taken Simon to other fields, both public and private. These endeavors enriched economics, artificial intelligence, and psychology. One large turn in the maze brought Simon and his family to Pittsburgh in 1949. Here Simon would settle and remain in the same house for over 40 years. What motivated Simon to move to Pittsburgh was the initiative to build a Graduate School of Industrial Administration at the Carnegie Institute of Technology. Within a short time, Simon, his colleagues, and the students of the Graduate School of Industrial Administration had created one of the two or three best business schools in the nation. However, the most auspicious of his accomplishments is the Nobel Prize awarded in economic sciences to Simon in 1978.

Simon, in his autobiography, told of the experience of receiving the Nobel Prize in a laconic, almost stoic, manner. In response to a query as to when he thought he might win the prize, he responded, "The day I got it." To the more introspective question of what change it has made in his life, he responded, "No change." Actually, Simon would rather spare one the tedium of a lengthy reply, "as rude as telling the whole truth when someone asks after your health" (Simon 1991, p. 319).

In the years before receiving the Nobel Prize, Simon received many honors such as prestigious invitations to participate in European convocations in economics and receipt of an honorary doctorate in economics from Erasmus University. Simon's theories of economics were centered on showing that "economics has to be concerned with computation—with the processes people actually use to make decisions—and has to describe the nature of these processes" (Simon 1991, p. 324).

Models of Thought, a collection of Simon's papers in psychology published in 1989, seemed to represent another turn in the maze. This turn involved an evolution from cognitive science to cognitive learning. Simon again became the student, exploring new fields in puzzle solving and short-term memory. As far as one can tell, there does not appear to be a time of quiet reflection in the mind of Simon. He is as perpetual as his ideas.

Simon, in his autobiography, admonished us not to look for a comprehensive "Simple Simon," claiming that one does not exist. True, he did acknowledge that there are fragments of a "Simpler" Simon, and if one looks hard enough, he is easier to find and understand. Specifically, in *Administrative Behavior* Simon ends his thesis with a simple analogy:

Organizing a professional school or an R&D department is very much like mixing oil with water: It is easy to describe the intended product, less easy to produce it. And the task is not finished when the goal has been achieved. Left to themselves the oil and water will separate again. So also will the disciplines and the professions. Organizing in these situations is not a once and for all activity. It is a continuing administrative responsibility, vital for the sustained success of the enterprise.

NICHOLAS A. GIANNATASIO

BIBLIOGRAPHY

Allison, Graham T., 1971. *Essence of Decision: Explaining the Cuban Missile Crisis.* Boston: Little, Brown.

Argyris, Chris, 1973a. "Some Limits of Rational Man Organizational Theory." *Public Administration Review* (May-June).

———, 1973b. "Organizational Man: Rational and Self-Actualizing." *Public Administration Review* (July-August).

Barnard, Chester, I., 1938. *The Functions of the Executive.* Cambridge, MA: Harvard University Press.

Kuhn, Thomas S., 1962. *The Structure of Scientific Revolutions,* 2d ed. Chicago: University of Chicago Press.

March, James G., and Johan P. Olsen, 1989. *Rediscovering Institutions: The Organizational Basis of Politics.* New York: Free Press.

March, James G., and Herbert A. Simon, 1958. *Organizations.* New York: Wiley.

Simon, Herbert A., 1946. "The Proverbs of Administration." *Public Administration Review,* vol. 6 (Winter).

———, 1947. *Administrative Behavior: A Study of Decision-Making Processes in Administrative Organization,* 3d ed. New York: Free Press.

———, 1973. "Organizational Man: Rational or Self-Actualizing?" *Public Administration Review* (July-August).

———, 1989. *Models of Thought.* New Haven CT: Yale University Press.

———, 1991. *Models of My Life.* New York: HarperCollins.

———, 1993. "The State of American Political Science: Professor Lowi's View of Our Discipline." *Political Science,* vol. 26 (March).

Waldo, Dwight, 1948. *The Administrative State.* New York: Ronald Press Co.

SINGLE EUROPEAN ACT (OR EUROPEAN ACT).

The 1986 revision of the Treaty of Paris and the Treaties of Rome (establishing the European Communities), which formalized the objective to establish the

European internal market, which reintroduced the use of majority voting in the Council of Ministers and which provided for a larger parliamentary role in decisionmaking through the introduction of the cooperation procedure and the assent procedure.

Origin

The Single European Act was adopted at the European Council meeting in Luxembourg (December 2 and 3, 1985) by the heads of state and government of the member states of the European Community (EC). On February 17, 1986, nine member states signed the Single European Act, followed by Denmark (after a vote in favor in a referendum), Italy, and Greece on February 28, 1986. After ratification by the parliaments of the member states, the Single European Act entered into force on July 1, 1987. The adoption of the Single European Act together with the adoption of the plan to complete the EC's internal market by the end of 1992 proved to be the basis of a new period of "Euro-optimism" and dynamic changes in the process of European integration.

What internal and external factors explain this new period in the process of European integration, which sharply contrasted with the preceding periods of stagnation (during the 1970s) and Crisis (1979–1984), in the European Community?

The institutional crisis within the European Community, which resulted from the need to find unanimity for any decision, made it clear that the European Community could not survive without changes in its decisionmaking procedures. This was evident as decisionmaking had become even more difficult than before after Greece joined the EC in 1981 and as the accession of Spain and Portugal in 1986 was expected to further complicate the search for unanimity. Decisionmaking in a European Community with 12 member states could not be done with procedures used in a community with 6 member states. The enlargement of the European Community with economically less-developed Southern European countries also increased the pressure to boost other policies than the Common Agriculture Policy (such as the regional and social policy).

The economic crisis and the acknowledgment that the European economic and technological developments were lagging behind those in the United States of America and Japan were an external impetus to take new initiatives within the EC framework. The detailed proposals to complete the internal market by the end of 1992 ("1992 project"), submitted in 1985 by the new Commission of the European Community and its President Jacques Delors, constituted a solid basis for such an initiative. This internal market should already have been realized in the preceding decades, being one of the objectives of the original Treaty of Rome of 1957 on the European Economic Community. The growing use of qualitative measures to defend the different national markets, from the economic crisis of the early 1970s on, had undermined the establishment of a genuine internal market.

The member states were aware that under the existing requirement of unanimity, it would be extremely difficult to get an agreement in the Council of Ministers about all of the some 300 decisions needed to complete the internal market. This awareness forced the member states that were reluctant to change the decisionmaking procedures to accept the principle of majority voting for most decisions on the internal market. During the negotiations on the revision in the decisionmaking process, pressure grew to accept also a greater involvement of the directly elected European Parliament.

These internal and external pressures finally resulted in the Single European Act, which included changes in decisionmaking and competences of the European Community. The disappointment of some member states about the rather limited changes, the pressure to complete the internal market with a genuine economic and monetary policy, the changes in Eastern Europe and German unification in 1989–1990, however, resulted in new pressure to revise the EC treaties. This resulted in the Treaty on European Union (or "Treaty of Maastricht") of 1992, which was a more fundamental revision of the treaties than the Single European Act.

Competences of the European Community

The main new provision with regard to the policy of the community is Article 8A, which states that the "Community shall adopt measures with the aim of progressively establishing the internal market over a period expiring on 31 December 1992. . . . The internal market shall comprise an area without internal frontiers in which the free movement of goods, persons, services and capital is ensured." The introduction of majority voting for most measures on the "1992 project" assured that this project had a considerable impact on the economic developments within the European Community.

The Single European Act introduced new chapters within the Treaty of Rome on policy fields that were previously not or only indirectly treated by the European Community. The new chapters concerned the following policy fields: monetary capacity, which brought the European Monetary System within the EC framework; social policy, aimed at encouraging improvements, especially in the working environment, as regards the health and safety of workers; economic and social cohesion, aimed at reducing disparities between the various regions as well as the backwardness of the least-favored regions; research and technological development, aimed at strengthening the scientific and technological basis of European industry and encouraging it to become more competitive at the international level; and environment.

The provisions on these policy fields in practice had less impact than those on the internal market, which was due to three reasons. First, the provisions on these policy fields were less detailed in comparison with those on the internal market. Second, majority voting was allowed in only a limited number of cases for these policy areas. Third, EC action in these policy fields could not be based on a detailed and realistic plan of the commission, such as was the case for the internal market. Nevertheless, the inclusion of these policy fields within the framework of the EC treaties was important as a basis for further developments in the process of European integration. Monetary integration and economic and social cohesion, for instance, became two major policy fields.

Finally, the Single European Act brought the European Political Cooperation (EPC) within the framework of the EC treaties. European Political Cooperation was the intergovernmental process by which member states of the European Community tried to coordinate their foreign policies since the early 1970s. European Political Cooperation, which functioned on a rather informal basis, was codified and institutionalized through its adoption within the EC framework. The new provisions on European Political Cooperation were not included within the original EC treaties through an amendment of these treaties. This means that they are not part of the Single European Act's Title II ("Provisions Amending the Treaties Establishing the European Communities") but of a separate Title III ("Provisions on European Cooperation in the Sphere of Foreign Policy").

This lasting separation through this separate Title III indicated that the member states wanted to maintain the intergovernmental character of European Political Cooperation. This implies that decisions had to be taken by unanimity and that the Ministers of Foreign Affairs retained all power in this policy field, despite the fact that the provisions of Title III also foresaw some involvement of the Commission and the European Parliament. As the mechanisms of European Political Cooperation were not fundamentally improved, its impact in international relations remained rather limited.

The fall of the communist regimes in Eastern Europe and the German unification in 1989–1990 gave a new impetus to adapt EPC, resulting in the establishment of the "Common Foreign and Security Policy" in the Treaty on European Union of February 1992. This Common Foreign and Security Policy replaces the previously existing European Political Cooperation.

Institutional Provisions

The institutional provisions of the Single European Act include three major changes in the decisionmaking of the European Community. It provided a revaluation of the use of majority voting in the council and a strengthening of the role of the European Parliament through the introduction of two new decisionmaking procedures. These changes moved the institutional balance somewhat in favor of the European Parliament and the commission, slightly increased the supranational character of the community system, and allowed for a more effective decisionmaking process.

The Revaluation of the Use of Majority Votes

The first major adaptation in the institutional structure was the revaluation of the use of majority votes. The use of majority voting was foreseen in the original Treaty of Rome but was de facto rejected as a result of the "empty chair policy" of France in 1965 and the "Compromise of Luxembourg" of January 1966.

Voting by qualified majority replaced unanimity in existing treaty provisions with regard to decisions on alterations to the common customs tariff, the freedom to provide services, the free movement of capital, and the common policy on sea and air transport. Qualified majority became required for certain new provisions. The most important field was the internal market, where most of the approximately 300 measures could be taken by a majority vote. Only the measures related to fiscal provisions, free movement of people and the rights and interests of employed persons still had to be taken by unanimity, which explains why decision on these matters were very difficult. Qualified majority was also required for some aspects with regard to social policy, economic and social cohesion, research and technological development, and the environment.

The "Cooperation Procedure"

The Single European Act introduced two new procedures that increased the parliamentary impact on decisionmaking in the European Union: the "cooperation procedure" and the "assent procedure." The influence of the European Parliament was until then very limited because it was only involved through the nonbinding "advice procedure."

The cooperation procedure, which involves two readings, gives the European Parliament the possibility to influence the voting requirements within the council and to make it more difficult for the council to neglect the opinion of the Parliament. The council retains the final say though. The cooperation procedure leaves the commission with a substantial role to play because the Parliament's influence depends on the support of the commission for the views of Parliament.

First, if the European Parliament rejects the decision (or "common position") of the council, the council can only adopt this common position by unanimity. This implies that the European Parliament can block the decision if at least one member state in the Council votes against the common position. Second, if the European Parliament amends the common position and if the commission supports these amendments, only a qualified majority is needed in the council to accept this amended common position. This implies that the common position as amended by the European Parliament can also be accepted by the council if a limited number of member states vote against this amended common position. A member state has in this case no more the ability to block the decision in the council as the unanimity rule does not apply.

The Single European Act foresees the use of the new cooperation procedure in most decisions with regard to the internal market (except for the above-mentioned measures where unanimity remains required) as well as in a limited number of decisions related to social policy, economic and social cohesion, and research and technological development. This means that use of the cooperation procedure remained excluded for a large number of decisions within the European Community, including decisions in important policy fields such as agriculture. A second disadvantage for the European Parliament was that its influence remained largely dependent on the willingness of the commission to support the parliamentary amendments.

The "Assent Procedure"

The second new procedure introduced by the Single European Act is the assent procedure. This procedure implies that the assent of the European Parliament is required before the council may take the decision to adopt, first, association agreements with third countries or groups of third countries and, second, agreements covering the enlargement of the European Community. This new procedure gave the European Parliament the possibility to influence the foreign policy of the European Community. That is, it deferred consideration of proposals for agreements with Turkey because of the human rights situation in Turkey and rejected protocols with Israel because of the situation in the occupied territories. However, this influence remained limited as the Single European Act did not foresee the use of the assent procedure for all international agreements (such as trade agreements). The other disadvantage for the European Parliament was that it was not allowed to be involved in the negotiations on these agreements and could thus only indirectly influence the substance of these agreements.

STEPHAN KEUKELEIRE

BIBLIOGRAPHY

Corbett, Richard, 1989. "Testing the New Procedures: The European Parliament's First Experiences with Its New 'Single European Act' Powers." *Journal of Common Market Studies,* vol. 27, no. 4:359–372.
Dehousse, Renaud, 1989. "1992 and Beyond: The Institutional Dimension of the Internal Market Programme." *Legal Issues of European Integration,* vol. 1:109–126.
Engel, Christian, and Wolfgang Wessels, eds., 1992. *From Luxembourg to Maastricht: Institutional Change in the European Community after the Single European Act.* Bonn: European Union Verlag.
Fitzmaurice, John, 1988. "An Analysis of the European Community's Co-operation Procedure." *Journal of Common Market Studies,* vol. 26:389–400.
Lodge, Juliet, 1986. "The Single European Act: Towards a New Euro-Dynamism?" *Journal of Common Market Studies,* vol. 24:203–223.
———, 1987. "The Single European Act and the New Legislative Cooperation Procedure: A Critical Analysis." *Journal of European Integration,* vol. 11 no. 1:5–28.
Moravcsik, Andrew, 1991. "Negotiating the Single European Act: National Interests and Conventional Statecraft in the European Community." *International Organisation,* vol. 45 no. 1:19–56.
Pryce, Roy, ed., 1989. *The Dynamics of European Union.* London: Routledge.

SMITH, ADAM (1723–1790).

The Scottish moral and economic philosopher considered to be the founding theorist of capitalism. He was born in 1723 in Kirkcaldy, near Edinburgh. An only child, he was raised by his widowed mother, a remarkable woman of modest but independent means. In 1737, Smith entered the University of Glasgow, arguably the finest university in Great Britain, where he was profoundly influenced by his professor of moral philosophy, Francis Hutcheson (1694–1746). He graduated with his M.A. in 1740 and received a fellowship to Balliol College, in Oxford, to prepare for a career in the clergy.

But Oxford, then devoted to perpetuating the orthodoxies of the status quo, was a vast disappointment. Left to himself, Smith read extensively in the classics, where he was particularly influenced by the stoic philosophers. He returned home in 1746, without his degree, to reconsider his future. Soon after, he was invited by some prominent intellectuals in Edinburgh, including his good friend David Hume (1711–1723), to give a series of public lectures, on rhetoric and belle lettres, among other subjects. He prepared thoroughly, and the lectures were a great success, leading to an invitation to join the faculty of the University of Glasgow in 1751. He had found his profession.

Although he started out as the professor of logic, within a year he became the professor of moral philosophy. He was popular with his students, respected by his colleagues, and an active member of the university community. In his usual fashion, he wrote out his lectures with great care. Those were later assembled into his first, and best, book, *The Theory of Moral Sentiments* (1759), which was published to excellent reviews.

His career took another turn in 1764, when the prominent English politician Charles Townshend employed him to tutor his stepson, the young Duke of Buccleuch. Adam Smith and his pupil went to France, where Smith, in addition to tutoring the young duke, began his economic his-

tory. They returned to London in 1766, where Smith left his tutorial duties, with an annual pension of £300 for life.

This independent income allowed him to devote himself full-time to writing *An Inquiry into the Nature and Causes of the Wealth of Nations,* which was published in 1776 to great acclaim. He lived the remainder of his life in Edinburgh, serving as a commissioner of customs for Scotland, a commissioner of salt duties, and an occasional consultant to the Crown. All were responsible positions, which he performed well. He remained a bachelor and devoted his enormous intellectual energies to refining his first book, which he took through six editions. He died on July 17, 1790.

More than any other philosopher, Adam Smith's ideas have shaped the free economies of the modern world. The popular view of Smith has it that he was an early proponent of an economics of self-interest and the survival of the competitively fittest–positions that he explicitly rejected. But this misconception, which took hold in the early nineteenth century, was promulgated by Karl Marx, among others, and survives to this day in some forms of neoclassical economics.

Unfortunately, all of this has directed attention away from his original intentions: His ideal social, economic, and political systems, based upon both stoicism and a revised version of moral sense theory, called for a compassionate society, which would be morally enhancing to a people who would be free. No small part of the problem results from an overemphasis upon his second book, *The Wealth of Nations,* which places more emphasis upon self-interest, to the neglect of his first book, *The Theory of Moral Sentiments,* which places most emphasis upon good character.

The apparent discrepancy between the two books ("Das Adam Smith Problem") has been resolved by scholars such as Alec Macfie and Glenn Morrow, who demonstrated that Smith intended the second book to be interpreted by the moral philosophy laid down in the first book. Smith made his intentions clear in *The Theory of Moral Sentiments,* where he contrasted his ideal (but attainable) society with a lesser society that relied upon self-interest as its governing principle.

Because of our inescapable human interdependence, every individual is "fitted by nature to that situation for which he was made." In other words, we were intended by nature to care for one another, and when all of our social, economic, and political relationships are governed by the innate need, "the society flourishes and is happy" (p. 85). But it takes moral effort to achieve and maintain such a society, and often human beings allow moral sloth to dominate.

The result is a just, but decidedly lesser society, which "subsists among different men, as among different merchants, from a sense of its utility, without any mutual love or affection; and though no man in it should owe any obligation, or be bound in gratitude to any other, it may still be upheld by a mercenary exchange of good offices according to an agreed valuation" (p. 86). Many fine scholars have defended this mercenary conception of Adam Smith's moral philosophy, but he spent most of his effort in *The Theory of Moral Sentiments* explicating the achievable ideal. To cite but one example: "For one man to deprive another unjustly of anything, or unjustly to promote his own advantage to the loss or disadvantage of another, is more contrary to nature than death, than poverty, than pain, than all the misfortunes which can affect him, either in his body, or in his external circumstances" (p. 236). Thus, in order to conform to Smith's original intentions for a principled society, the ideal should be of greatest interest to public administration.

Although Adam Smith is known primarily as an economist, in fact his moral philosophy was much broader gauged. He argued that all social, economic, and political actions should be based upon intentional individual virtue if the ensuing relationships are to benefit humankind. His ideas are quite comprehensive, but the following four categories will provide an overview.

Moral Truth

The conventional wisdom has it that moral truth is a chimera and that all values are the products of their specific cultures. Adam Smith took the opposite tack, arguing not only that moral truth existed but that it was discoverable by all individuals. Such truth is found in our common, innate human nature, and it is expressed in the classic virtues of propriety, prudence, courage, justice, faith, hope, and charity.

Given the fact of our human nature, the purpose of human life is to achieve true happiness through actualizing that moral truth, in the form of the virtues, in all organizations. And, since all organizations–social, economic, and political–will operate upon the common principles of virtue, all of them will be mutually reinforcing, leading to pervasive human flourishing.

Sympathy

The most fundamental concept, upon which all else depends, in the work of Adam Smith is that of "sympathy." He made his intentions clear in the first sentence of *The Theory of Moral Sentiments*: "How selfish soever man may be supposed, there are evidently some principles in his nature, which interest him in the fortune of others, and render their happiness necessary to him, though he derives nothing from it, except the pleasure of seeing it" (p. 9). This desire for the happiness of others comes from an innate human need to love others, or sympathy. This is not sympathy in its narrow, modern sense, which equates it with a compassion for the sorrows of others. For Smith, sympathy was much more complex, having both moral and psychological dimensions.

The moral dimension comes from the fact that all humans are born with the imperative need to love others. That being the case, no individual can become truly happy without exercising sympathy to the fullest extent. While self-interest has a place, it must always be subordinated to sympathy. Thus, and contrary to the neo-utilitarianism of so much of modern economics, he wrote: "And hence it is, that we feel much for others and little for ourselves, that to restrain our selfish, and to indulge our benevolent affections, constitutes the perfection of human nature" (p. 25). The psychological dimension is the individual's inherent capacity imaginatively put himself or herself into the place of another. As Smith put it, we flinch when we see a blow about to land on the back of an unsuspecting other. The key is our imagination: We can imagine ourselves in the same situation and know how the blow would feel upon our backs. In this sense, nature has provided all individuals with a capacity, the imaginativeness of sympathy, to feel how others would feel, in similar situations. Smith is adamant that to be fully human, we must develop those imaginative capacities to the fullest.

When the moral and the physical dimensions of sympathy are combined, we have individuals who are equipped to live in Smith's ideal society. To return to the example of the blow, the psychological dimension of sympathy allows us to feel how the victim will feel, while the moral dimension of love will compel us to go to the aid of the victim. What is more, Adam Smith stated that we are more inclined to be sympathetic with the joy of others than with their sorrow. Thus, he provides the foundation for a society powerfully linked together by our common sympathy for joy, which means that we can achieve a pervasive sense of brotherhood and sisterhood. It is a quite remarkable formulation.

Without sympathy, society degenerates into a sustainable but cold and mercenary web of relationships based upon mutual benefit. It can even descend further to become a war of all against all.

Virtue

Adam Smith argued that "the love of virtue [is] the noblest and the best passion in human nature" (p. 309). Because of that, virtuous thought and action are the necessary conditions for the true happiness of human flourishing: "The philosophers of all the different sects very justly represented virtue; that is, wise, just, firm, and temperate conduct; not only as the most probable, but as the certain and infallible road to happiness even in this life" (p. 282).

He followed both Hutcheson and David Hume in distinguishing between the natural virtues (courage, love, magnanimity) and the artificial virtues (especially justice), the combination of which allows a good society to exist.

Further, virtue permits no duplicity, for our nature demands the reality of virtue as integral to our character: "Man naturally desires, not only to be loved, but to be lovely; or to be that thing which is the natural and proper object of love. . . . He desires, not only praise, but praiseworthiness; or to be that thing which . . . is . . . the natural and proper object of praise" (pp. 113–114). The gambits of public relations had no place in the Smithian world.

To expand on his example, all people seek praise and go to great, even fraudulent, lengths to obtain it. But happiness comes not from the praise, but the self-awareness of praiseworthiness. Thus, the only worthwhile praise is evoked by virtue made manifest in both intention and action. This being the case, anything that inhibits a life of virtue, either internal (the lack of knowledge about natural virtue, the lack of education, and such) or external (the absence of freedom, unjust institutions, and such), offends the natural right of each individual to flourish. With respect to organizational life, every organizational relationship must rest upon virtue.

Furthermore, Smith argued that virtue is not fully realized by simply following the rules: "Virtue is excellence, something uncommonly great and beautiful, which rises far above what is vulgar and ordinary" (p. 25). For instance, if a man collapses at our feet and we go to his aid, there is only minimal virtue on our part—for that is what sympathy obliges us to do. Virtue is best realized by transcending ordinary obligations—thus, to be kind to one's neighbor is worthy, but the attempt to love humankind is best of all.

Smith argued that all organizational life, from the most mundane to the most sublime, must allow for the individual progress of virtue. The enemies of free enterprise often argue that his moral philosophy was "fit only for shopkeepers." To the contrary, his ideal was far more ennobling: Although it is appropriate for an individual to be prudent, the individual should always be striving for a "superior prudence," which "is the best head joined to the best heart. It is the most perfect wisdom combined with the most perfect virtue" (p. 216).

To conclude, Smith believed that it was honorable to strive to the utmost to become great and to become rich. But he always prefaced his ideal with the admonition that those quests must be preceded by "the study of wisdom and the practice of virtue" (p. 62).

Intentionality

Most contemporary theories of capitalism rely heavily upon the notion that the competition of insatiably self-interested producers and consumers in a free market will result in an overall public good: A variant of the argument of the English writer Bernard Mandeville (1670–1733) that "private vices" will, in some mysterious way, cumulatively turn into "public goods." The arbiter in that Darwinian market is supposed to be Adam Smith's "invisible hand." But that misconstrues Smith's conception of the invisible hand. Granted, he believed that the free competition of those interested only in their own utility would achieve a reasonably equitable balance. But for his ideal of free enterprise to work most effectively, it required competitors who brought intentional virtue to every economic transaction.

Moral intentionality is always central to every aspect of Smith's scheme of things. It is not competition that makes the market work most effectively; rather, it is intentionally virtuous competition that produces the optimal condition. When all participants in all economic relationships are intentionally virtuous, the invisible hand will operate as intended and, for that reason, the market emerges as the most effective and equitable arena for the resolution of the problems of distribution that the world has seen. Such virtuous participants, committed to both moral and productive excellence, will provide the highest quality of goods and services, to the benefit of all.

To conclude, the true intentions of Adam Smith have been largely ignored. But, correctly understood, his moral philosophy, which is eminently practical, offers the basis for a generous and humane society. As he wrote: "Though our effectual good officers can very seldom be extended to any wider society than that of our own country; our good-will is circumscribed by no boundary, but may embrace the immensity of the universe. We cannot form the idea of any innocent and sensible being, whose happiness we should not desire, or to whose misery, when distinctly brought home to the imagination, we should not have some degree of aversion" (p. 235).

DAVID KIRKWOOD HART

BIBLIOGRAPHY

Campbell, R. H., and A. S. Skinner, 1982. *Adam Smith*. London: Croom Helm.

Hollander, Samuel, 1973. *The Economics of Adam Smith*. Toronto: University of Toronto Press.

Macfie, Alec Lawrence, 1967. "Adam Smith's *Moral Sentiments* as Foundation for His *Wealth of Nations*." In A. L. Macfie, *The Individual in Society*. London: George Allen & Unwin, 59–81.

Morrow, Glenn R., 1969 [1923]. *The Ethical and Economic Theories of Adam Smith*. Clifton, NJ: Augustus M. Kelley.

Rae, John, 1965 [1895]. *Life of Adam Smith*. New York: Augustus M. Kelley.

Raphael, D. D., 1985. *Adam Smith*. Oxford: Oxford University Press.

Scott, William Robert, 1965 [1937]. *Adam Smith As Student and Professor*. New York: Augustus M. Kelley.

Smith, Adam, 1981 [1776]. *An Inquiry into the Nature and Causes of the Wealth of Nations*, R. H. Campbell and A. S. Skinner. eds. Indianapolis: Liberty Classics.

———, 1982a [1759; 1790]. *The Theory of Moral Sentiments*, D. D. Raphael and A. L. Macfie, eds. Indianapolis: Liberty Classics.

———, 1982b. *Essays on Philosophical Subjects*, W. P. D. Wightman and J. C. Bryce, eds. Indianapolis: Liberty Classics.

———, 1982c. *Lectures on Jurisprudence*, ed. R. L. Meek, D. D. Raphael, and P. G. Stein, Indianapolis: Liberty Classics.

———, 1985. *Lectures on Rhetoric and Belles Lettres*, J. C. Bryce, eds. Indianapolis: Liberty Classics.

Werhane, Patricia H., 1991. *Adam Smith and His Legacy for Modern Capitalism*. New York: Oxford University Press.

SOCIAL DESIGN.

An approach that aims to achieve democratic and participatory decisions that are derived from interaction and dialogue between multiple stakeholders, reflecting critical assumptions and values of the public, so that social problems can be understood and solved.

The Concept of Design

Any attempt to improve the processes of policymaking, decisionmaking, and problemsolving that emphasizes democratic participation and interaction must come to grips with the basic problem of our approach to understanding problems and exploring alternative solutions: The problem of a design perspective. The concept of design is central to the activities of defining the problem, setting the agenda, making decisions, and developing implementation strategies.

Design is an elusive concept: it relates to people carrying out a broad range of activities. Such people are involved in purposeful and creative actions directed toward the accomplishment of a project or goal. West Churchman (1971) said that "design, properly viewed, is an enormous liberation of the intellectual spirit, for it challenges this spirit to an unbounded speculation about possibilities" (p. 5). Design may also be regarded as that process of human interaction through which relevant actors work, sharing ideas and experiences, to define social reality more accurately. Erich Jantsch (1975) described design as "a process of continuous learning through a multitude of interacting feedback relations linking ourselves and the world of our ideas to reality" (p. 100).

Jantsch's description suggests that the actors in a situation can create and recreate the social world through the process of communicating and sharing ideas. In this context, goals and alternatives are socially constructed and socially sustained: design is a continuous, ongoing accomplishment that emerges from the process of social interaction. Conscious, purposeful, creative activities constitute the dynamics of public administration at its best (Jun 1986, p. 83).

Finally, design is a deliberate process, a process that involves a critical consciousness on the part of the actors who are solving a problem in a creative way. The effectiveness of design depends on how well it solves the problem, which itself depends on a process that involves people, who often have different interests and ideas. Design, as applied to the field of public administration, is a framework used to solve problems through interactive processes.

Approaches to Design

A number of different approaches to policy design are possible. For purposes of comparison, four approaches are briefly discussed here: Crisis, rational, incremental, and social designs. Each approach is different, particularly in terms of its emphasis on the values of other people: How the actor integrates them into the processes of policymaking and implementation. The approaches also differ with regard to the policy actor's orientation toward problemsolving and change, with the actor's actions ranging from proactive to reactive.

1. Crisis design has a low appreciation of human values and a reactive orientation to policymaking and problemsolving. When public bureaucracies experience management crises because of an emergency, scarce resources, or budget cuts, managers tend to adopt a crisis design. The crisis orientation stems from, among other factors, rising social demands, budget deficits, tax cuts, confusing policy directions, declining productivity, clientele anger, or a depressed economy. Many government agencies, schools, and prisons offer case studies of crisis management in these days of declining resources. In the face of turbulent changes of increasing magnitude and complexity, many administrators have become reactive and conservative rather than proactive and innovative. Their approach to problemsolving focuses on survival: the maintenance of the system and their jobs from one fiscal year to the next. The crisis orientation underestimates the long-term implications of crisis solutions, because attention is riveted on short-term needs.

   Crisis-oriented administrators emphasize the importance of formalism: rules, regulations, and standard operating procedures. Their decisions tend to be made as part of the exercise of formal authority and power. Decisions affecting many people are made by a few managers; they are made because a crisis situation demands immediate action and response. Problems are dealt with on a short-term basis with an insufficient understanding of underlying causes and long-term potentials. A continued crisis orientation leads to a sharp deterioration in the quality of working life. Organizational members are likely to experience increased job dissatisfaction, alienation, anxiety, and hostility, along with reduced efficiency, productivity, and collaboration among members. Because the implications of survival strategies are not properly analyzed or debated, problems that have seemingly been solved may surface later in new and possibly more awesome forms.

2. After World War II, an increasing concern for administrative efficiency and the application of scientific methods to decisionmaking led to a rejection of the highly politicized and pluralistic process of policy analysis. Rational design assumes the expert's ability to control all relevant aspects of the organizational environment, to render process and behavior objective and predictable. Because the expert attempts to define the problem, goals, and alternatives based on technical knowledge, the expert can argue for a proactive and futuristic solution to the problem.

   Management science and systems analysis, the logic and processes of which have attracted—or entrapped—many policy analysts, is a natural outgrowth of rational design. Rational analysts are committed to searching for knowledge that will facilitate refinement of administrative systems and guidance of human behavior. They perceive public administration as an arena wherein scientific methods should be applied to determine procedures, solve problems, and measure efficiency and productivity and do much else. A major objective of rational design is to explain policy issues objectively and impartially, and to control irrationalities of politics and human behavior as these manifest themselves in organizational action.

   Rational design uses rigorous procedures and techniques to generate knowledge that facilitates planning and decisionmaking; objective indicators are used as bases for problem solving. Rational analysts begin with a set of questions to pose as a guide for their observations and with a set of categories to organize what they observe. Theoretically, the analysts' observations are not influenced by their values, but analysts often do judge the importance of questions and findings in terms of their own beliefs and training. It is difficult for most people, including rational analysts, to be purely objective. This nonobjective interpretation reinforces the analysts' own premises or mindsets with regard to their area of investigation, findings, and applications (Simon 1976; Quade 1975; Allison 1971).

   An example of rational design is supplied by the expert's role in policy analysis; such a person applies appropriate technical knowledge and skills in order to "enlighten decisionmaking." The expert's approach to policy change normally favors the establishment of long-term goals to meet anticipated problems. The choice of goals is likely to reflect professional perspectives and values, with the attitudes and experiences of citizens given little consideration. Rational designers tend to identify the value preferences of society according to their own frames of reference. Problem-solving and change strategies often include such scien-

tific and rational techniques as systems analysis, cost-benefit measurement, and various budgeting techniques. In recent years, rational procedures have been used widely in public policy studies in both theoretical and practical attempts to make policy choices and evaluation.

3. Incremental design utilizes the policy actor's political skills, such as negotiating, bargaining, making trade-offs, co-optation, and personal experience and intuition. It may be argued that rational designers fail to properly weigh the values and power of political actors. Incremental designers do take these considerations into account in order to reach a "satisficing" decision, but they, in turn, fail to fully weigh the available facts and technology when making decisions. The pluralistic nature of American government results from the variety of beliefs and interests in this country. In such a context, the role of public administrators and other policymakers includes a great deal of interaction with groups and individuals as the policymakers bargain and negotiate in order to reach political consensus.

In coping with changes, incremental designers believe it unwise to change too rapidly, because the effects of swift change may prove to be largely unintended. Thus, short-term changes and problemsolving are perceived as desirable; attempts to make long-term changes are considered futile, even hazardous (Lindblom 1965; Braybrooke and Lindblom 1963). In such a context, the role of the expert is minimal. The important part of incremental (or pluralistic) design is not so much who makes the decisions but that participants are engaged in continually persuading other actors so that "mutual adjustments" evolve, and that people realize the diversity of perspectives regarding issues and develop workable accommodations within this diversity. This is the "art of the possible" at work in administrative behavior.

As a strategy for policymaking and change, incremental design is reactive, focusing as it does on change by degree within a context of agreement. The format offers satisficing rather than maximizing decisions, often drawing support from articulate interests that are only marginally affiliated with the issue at hand but participate in the bargaining to repay old debts or gain future favors. This implies that incremental design rests precariously on ad hoc support structures; thus, continuity of policy, expert advice, experimentation, and other values are in jeopardy.

4. A critique of rational and incremental designs offers a framework that leavens rational processes with the political and social skills of the policy actors; they gain these skills through their interactions with the other actors, who have different backgrounds. Social design has a high appreciation of the values of multiple actors in decision and action situations and a proactive stance regarding policymaking and change. It incorporates the values held by rational and incremental design actors and adds other values to offer a much broader framework (Jun 1986, pp. 87–89). Social design is a process in which a policy actor seeks to design an arena in which the many actors and institutions that may be affected by the policy outcome can interact and debate openly to assess the positive and the negative consequences of a proposed policy (Schon and Rein 1994, p. 168).

Social design is based on a set of assumptions that are different from the assumptions of crisis, rational, or incremental designs. First, the design process emphasizes social interaction among policy actors, public managers, experts, politicians, social groups, clients, and citizens associated with specific issues and problems. Through social interaction involving broad participation of these actors, the problem is defined and decision alternatives are formulated. The process of social design assumes that design participants are working to create relevant solutions and the means for implementing them. Purposes and goals are socially constructed: They develop out of human interaction, dialogue, and mutual learning. Political consensus is not the ultimate task: The focus in social design is to understand the meanings of different ideas, experiences, and technical, social, quantitative, and qualitative knowledge, and to develop shared responsibility through decentralization. Expert knowledge is valued and put to use, but experts' ideas are subject to scrutiny and discussion, as is the experiential knowledge and intuitive feelings of other participants.

Social design can be viewed as the most desirable institutional and governance strategy because the process works better when social interaction is designed at the decentralized level of government structure. It is a new "civic governance" model, and it stresses a situational and participatory approach to public problemsolving (John, Halley, and Fosler 1996). According to D. John et al., the civic governance process involves leaders representing nonprofit and business organizations, public agencies, and service providers. Through social interaction and mutual learning, they can design efficient and effective ways of implementing various socioeconomic programs. These include human services to different client groups and enterprise zones, rural development, environmental protection, and sustainable development projects that derive from community-based activism. Citizen participation is particularly important: It enhances the process of civic governance through democratic policymaking.

The social design process involves communicative action among participants: "Because the actors shape the object through their more-or-less organized interactions, they must communicate with one another, sending and receiving messages in the form of words and action"

(Schon and Rein 1994, p. 168). As Habermas (1981; 1990) pointed out, the experiences and ideas of people in social situations can be in some way understood through communicative action. Communication based on the self-conscious reflection of actors aims at mutual understanding and learning as the actors tune in to one another's consciousness and experiences. Habermas argued that communicative actions through speech acts (conversation) lead to mutual understanding and that these actions are the preconditions for the very existence of a social order (1981, p. 50).

In sum, social design is an approach that aims to achieve democratic and participatory decisions that are derived from social interaction and dialogue among multiple actors, reflecting critical human consciousness and values and emphasizing processes in formulating community-based alternatives, goals, and implementation strategies. Dialogue is critical to the development of intersubjective understanding and shared meanings. Through mutual participation and dialogue, the actors discover a new common ground for understanding. They create the opportunity to challenge assumptions, which would otherwise be accepted without question. The social design perspective involves multiple actors directly in the processes of understanding problems and inventing alternatives in a democratic society. In practice, the approach works more effectively at the decentralized local level of government than at the national level. At the local level of government, citizens, for-profit and nonprofit organizations, and government agencies can interact freely without institutional constraints and debate differences in ideas and alternative solutions to problems.

Application of Social Design in Local Problem Solving

The problems faced at the local level are common to all communities. The issues of crime, drug and alcohol abuse, child abuse, the growth versus no-growth debate, health care, and homelessness are obvious examples. These local problems are also national problems. Given that we live in difficult times, when change is occurring at an alarming rate and many serious problems seem to be accelerating even beyond the crisis level, local government is under immense pressure to produce genuinely workable, lasting solutions. Yet, although life-and-death problems continue seemingly out of control, major stumbling blocks to community dialogue, understanding, and action exist, and these stumbling blocks are apparently passively accepted by the populace. People are committed to certain worldviews that create barriers to the development of innovative ideas and approaches.

The application of social design at the local level brings citizens back into the policy arena. Social design offers the possibility for citizens to regain control over policies that affect their community as they attempt to understand problems and work to solve them. Public administrators who are responsible for community services and problem-solving become facilitators as well as service providers, working with citizens and various organizations in the community.

Social design is practiced most commonly in a community policing program that calls for the participation of citizens in the community in solving crime problems. Traditional policing is reactive, rather than proactive. Reactive policing is the 911 emergency telephone system: Operators receive calls from citizens asking for emergency services. The operators then dispatch police officers to handle the citizens', calls for service. Traditional policing is crisis design administration: As crises arise, police officers are alerted and dispatched to devise a solution to the problem.

Community policing is proactive in its attempt to solve community problems by including citizens in the law enforcement process. It is a popular approach to law enforcement in the 1990s, as citizens seek to enhance the image and effectiveness of police agencies by redefining the role of police officers. The police and the citizens use teamwork in order to maintain safety and order in the community. Because community policing requires that different actors work together to solve community problems, police officers become facilitators, identifying problems and arranging services, such as streetlights for a dark alley or counseling for a youth or a household. Police officers need to be familiar with the different city and private agencies in the area, so that they can refer citizens to the proper service agencies. Furthermore, issues of community policing are openly discussed at city council or neighborhood meetings, which involve police officers, politicians, residents, merchants, school administrators, volunteers, and so on. Although community policing is not the solution to all community crime problems, it has made some important progress in raising citizens' consciousness about crime and promoting a sense of personal responsibility among citizens toward their own community.

Other complex social problems, such as homelessness, community health care, elderly services, and AIDS, require greater participation and collaboration among citizens, for-profit and nonprofit organizations, and government agencies. Crisis, rational, and incremental designs are likely to perpetuate inadequacy in solving public problems. Although social design is a slow process, because of the difficulty in achieving consensus, the process could produce original, creative solutions that would be embraced by the citizenry. It offers a new possibility for enhancing democratic governance through participation and dialogue.

JONG S. JUN

BIBLIOGRAPHY

Allison, G.T., 1971. *Essence of Decision: Explaining the Cuban Missile Crisis.* Boston: Little, Brown.

Braybrooke, D., and C. E. Lindblom, 1963. *A Strategy of Decision: Policy Evaluation As a Social Process.* New York: Free Press.

Churchman, W., 1971. *The Design of Inquiring Systems: Basic Concepts and Organization.* New York: Basic Books.

Habermas, J., 1981. *The Theory of Communicative Action: Reason and the Rationalization of Society,* vol. 1, trans. T. McCarthy, Boston: Beacon Press.

———, 1990. *Moral Consciousness and Communicative Action,* trans. C. Lenhardt, and S. W. Nicholsen, Cambridge: MIT Press.

Jantsch, E., 1975. *Design for Evolution.,* New York: Braziller.

John, D., A. Halley, and S. Fosler, 1996. "Remapping Federalism: The Rediscovery of Civic Governance." In J. S. Jun, and D. S. Wright, eds., *Globalization and Decentralization.* Washington, DC: Georgetown University Press.

Jun, J. S., 1986. *Public Administration: Design and Problem Solving.* New York: Macmillan.

Lindblom, C. E., 1965. *The Intelligence of Democracy.* Englewood Cliffs, NJ: Prentice-Hall.

Quade, E. S., 1975. *Analysis for Public Decisions.* New York: Elsevier.

Schon, D. A., and M. Rein, 1994. *Frame Reflection.* New York: Basic Books.

Simon, H. A., 1976. *Administrative Behavior,* 3d ed. New York: Free Press.

SOCIAL EQUITY.

A phrase used in public administration to denote the need or requirement to deliver public services fairly or equitably. It is also used to connote the value fairness in the use of administrative discretion. Social equity is also a phrase that comprehends government programs designed to help minorities, women, the poor, or others who may have limited political power.

The Origins of Social Equity in Public Administration

Social equity is a phrase that emerged in public administration in the late 1960s, associated with the development of the new public administration. Social equity was put forward as the "third pillar" of public administration, with a status equal to efficiency and economy as organizational objectives or rationales. Initially, the social equity argument was put this way:

> Conventional or classic Public Administration seeks to answer either of these questions: (1) How can we offer more or better services with available resources (efficiency)? or (2) How can we maintain our level of services while spending less money (economy)? New Public Administration asks this question: Does this service enhance social equity? (Frederickson 1971a, 1971b)

In some ways the emergence of social equity as one of the purposes of public administration in the late 1960s reflected the political times–what Dwight Waldo (1971) called *Public Administration in a Time of Turbulence.* Issues of poverty, race, gender, and fairness were central to that time, a time that produced the War on Poverty, Affirmative Action, Head Start, and a broad range of mostly federal initiatives to address issues of justice and fairness.

In 1974, the *Public Administration Review* published a symposium on social equity that included the following topics and authors:

Social Equity, Justice, and the Equitable Administration   David K. Hart

Social Equity and Organizational Man: Motivation and Organizational Democracy   Michael M. Harmon

Social Equity and the Public Service   Eugene B. McGregor, Jr.

Social Equity and Social Service Productivity   Stephen R. Chitwood

Social Equity and Fiscal Federalism   David O. Porter and Teddie Wood Porter

Statistical Theory and Equity in the Delivery of Social Services Orion White, Jr., and Bruce L. Gates

In these essays, the Waldo premise that public administration is a form of political theory was generally accepted (Waldo 1984). It was also assumed that a neutral public administration is essentially impossible and probably not desirable. The argument was rather straightforward: Public administration should advocate efficiency, economy, and social equity. It was put this way:

> To say that a service may be well managed and that a service may be efficient and economical, still begs these questions: Well managed for whom? Efficient for whom? Economical for whom? We have generally assumed in public administration a convenient oneness with the public. We have not focused our attention or concern to the issue of variations in social and economic conditions. It is of great convenience, both theoretically and practically, to assume that citizen A is the same as citizen B and that they both receive public services in equal measure. This assumption may be convenient, but it is obviously both illogical and empirically inaccurate (Frederickson 1980).

Social equity began as a challenge to the adequacy of concepts of efficiency and economy as guide for public administration. In time, social equity took on a broader meaning.

> Social equity is a phrase that comprehends an array of value preferences, organizational design preferences, and management style preferences. Social equity emphasizes equality in government services. Social equity emphasizes responsibility for decisions and program implementation for public managers. Social equity emphasizes change in public management. Social equity emphasizes responsiveness to the needs of citizens rather than the needs of public organizations. Social equity emphasizes an approach to the study of and education for public administration that is interdisciplinary, applied, problem solving in character, and sound theoretically (Frederickson 1980).

The primary voice against the social equity theme belonged to Victor Thompson (1975), who wrote that the new public administration, in abandoning neutrality in the pursuit of equity would "steal the popular sovereignty." Social equity advocates replied that neutrality was a popular and convenient myth in public administration and that it would be more honest to admit that we are not neutral and that we advocate for our programs and for efficiency, economy, and equity.

Although the phrase social equity has not become a mainstream concept in public administration, the general issue of social fairness or justice continues to be a subject relevant to the field. In recent years, these topics have taken on greater currency, both in the country and in the field. In 1988, at Minnowbrook II, 20 years after the original new public administration conference at Minnowbrook, social equity again emerged as a theme for the field (*Public Administration Review* 1989).

The Recent Use of the Phrase "Social Equity" in Public Administration

The 50th anniversary issue of the *Public Administration Review* in 1990 included a treatment of social equity (Frederickson 1990). This elaboration was presented as the Compound Theory of Social Equity and included the following categories drawn heavily from Rae et al. (1981):

Simple Individual Equalities

Individual equality consists of one class of equals, and one relationship of equality holds among them. The best examples would be one person—one vote and the price mechanism of the market, which offers a Big Mac or a Whopper at a specific price to whomever wishes to buy it. The Golden Rule and Immanuel Kant's Categorical Imperative are formulas for individual equalities.

Segmented Equality

Any complex society with a division of labor tends to practice segmented equality. Farmers have a different system of taxation than do business owners, and both differ from wage earners. In segmented equality, one assumes that equality exists between the segments. All forms of hierarchy use the concept of segmented equality. All five-star generals are equal to each other as are all privates first-class. Equal pay for equal work is segmented equality. Segmented equality is critically important for public policy and administration because virtually every public service is delivered on a segmented basis and always by segmented hierarchies.

Block Equalities

Both simple individual and segmented equalities are in fact individual equalities. Block equalities, by contrast, call for equality between groups or subclasses. The railroad accommodations for blacks and whites could be separate so long as they were equal in *Plessy v. Ferguson* (1889). *Brown v. Board of Education* (1954) later concluded that separation by race meant inequality; therefore, the U.S. Supreme Court required school services to be based upon simple individual equality rather than block equality, using race to define blocks. The claims for comparable worth systems of pay for women are, interestingly, block egalitarianism mixed with equal pay for equal work, which is segmented equality.

The Domain of Equality

How does one decide what is to be distributed equally? The domain of equality marks off the goods, services, or benefits being distributed. If schools and fire protection are to be provided, why not golf courses or recreational facilities? Domains of equality can be narrowly or broadly defined, and they can have to do with allocations based on a public agency's resources, or they can be based on claims—claimants' demands for equality. Domains of equality constantly shift, aggregate, and disaggregate. Certain domains are largely controlled by the market such as jobs, wages, and investments, whereas others are controlled primarily by government. It is often the case that the governmental domain seeks equality to correct inequalities resulting from the market or from previous governmental policies. Unemployment compensation, Aid to Families with Dependent Children, college tuition grants, and food stamps are all kinds of governmental compensatory inequality to offset other inequalities outside the governmental domain of allocation but within a broader domain of claims. Domains can also be intergenerational, as in the determination of whether present taxpayers or their children pay for the federal debt built up by current deficits (Frederickson 1994).

Equalities of Opportunity

Equalities of opportunity are divided into prospect and means opportunity. Two people have equal opportunity for a job if each has the same probability for attaining the job under conditions of prospect equality of opportunity. Two people have equal opportunity for a job if each has the same talents or qualifications for the job under conditions of means-equal opportunity. Examples of pure prospect equality of opportunity are few, but the draft lottery for the Vietnam War was very close. In means equality of opportunity, equal rules, such as intelligence quotient (I.Q.) tests, Standard Achievement Test (SAT) scores, equal starting and finishing points for foot races, and so forth, define opportunity. "The purpose and effect of these equal means is not equal prospect of success, but legitimately unequal prospects of success." Aristotle's notion that equals should be treated equally would constitute means-based equality of opportunity.

The Value of Equality

The value of equality begins with the concept of lot equality in which shares are identical (similar housing, one vote, etc.) or equal. The advantage of lot equality is that only the individual can judge what pleases or displeases him or her. Lots can also be easily measured and distributed, and they imply nothing about equal well-being. The problem, of course, is that lot equality is insensitive to significant variations in need. To remedy this, Rae et al. suggested a "person equality" in which there is nonarbitrary, rule-based distribution of shares based on nonneutral judgments about individuals' needs. A threatened person may require more protection (and police officials may so decide) merely to make that person equal to the nonthreatened person. The same can be said for the crippled as against the healthy child, the mentally retarded as against the "mentally able" or "mentally healthy" instead: Person-regarding equality is often practiced in public administration to "make the rules humane."

It is clear that any universal scope for equality is both impossible and undesirable. Rather than a simple piece of rhetoric or a slogan, the Compound Theory of Social Equity is a complex of definitions and concepts. Equality, then, changes from one thing to many things—equalities. If public administration is to be inclined toward social equity, at least this level of explication of the subject is anticipated. In the policy process, any justification of policy choices claiming to enhance social equity would need to be analyzed in terms of questions such as these: (1) Is this equality individual, segmented, or block? (2) Is this equality direct or is it means-equal opportunity or prospect-equal opportunity? What forms of social equity can be advanced so as to improve the lot of the least advantaged yet to sustain democratic government and a viable market economy? The Compound Theory of Social Equity would serve as the language of the framework for attempts both in theory and in practice, and it would serve to answer these questions.

H. GEORGE FREDERICKSON

BIBLIOGRAPHY

Brown v. Board of Education, 1954. (1) 3/4/47 U.S. 483.
Frederickson, H. George, 1971a. "Toward a New Public Administration." In Frank Marini, ed., *Toward a New Public Administration.* Scranton, PA: Chandler, 311.
———, 1971b. "Creating Tomorrow's Public Administration." *Public Management,* vol. 53 (November) 2–4.
———, 1980. *New Public Administration.* University: University of Alabama Press, 37.
———, 1990. "Public Administration and Social Equity." *Public Administration Review,* vol. 50 (March-April) 228–237.
———, 1994. "Can Public Officials Correctly Be Said to Have Obligations to Future Generations?" *Public Administration Review,* vol. 54 (September-October) 457–464.
Plessy v. Ferguson, 1889, 163 U.S. 537.
Public Administration Review, 1974. vol. 34 (January-February) 1– 51.
———, 1989. "Minnowbrook II: Changing Epochs of Public Administration." vol. 49 (March-April).
Rae, Douglas, et al., 1981. *Equalities.* Cambridge, MA: Harvard University Press.
Thompson, Victor, 1975. *Without Sympathy or Enthusiasm.* University: University of Alabama Press.
Waldo, Dwight, 1971. *Public Administration in a Time of Turbulence.* Scranton, PA: Chandler.
———, 1984. *The Administrative State.* New York: Holmes & Meier.

SOCIAL INDICATOR.

A measure that quantifies observations of social change.

The purpose of a social indicator is to gather information on conditions within a society. Society's norms, behaviors, attitudes, and symbols represent artifacts that are counted in a systematic way. Social indicators are generally distinguished from economic indicators. Examples of social indicators include population by age and education, birth rates, number of televisions per household, number of farms, and voter turnout, to name a few. Social indicators are commonly used in three general ways: (1) to access the state or condition of a society with respect to societal values and goals, (2) to evaluate specific activities or programs to determine their impact on a society, and (3) to aid policymakers and decisionmakers by providing useful knowledge on societal relationships and tendencies.

Factors that influence the development of social indicators include measurement technology, social observability, and social acceptance. Measurement technology refers to the susceptibility of the phenomenon to accurate measurement, given the current state and resources of statistical science. For example, money is easier to count than societal norms. Social observability refers to whether the social processes involved are organized, consciously or not, to permit such measurement. Legal activities are easier to document than illegal economic transactions. Social acceptance determines what should be measured, and how, and is greatly influenced by the special perspectives and interests of a society's institutions.

Origin and Subsequent History

The basic premise of social indicators—information gathering on a given population in space and time—has historical roots in the foundations of civilization. Ancient texts, such as the Bible document the recording and maintaining of population parameters. Three books of the old Testament (Numbers, Second Samuel, and Ezra) document census taking on the Hebrew nation. The census recorded in Numbers counted male heads of household over the age of 20. A major purpose was to determine the number of men capable of fighting in battle. Taxation was another motivation for census efforts. In the book of Ezra, the census included the counting of livestock, "basins" of gold and silver, the number of males employed in various occupations including priests, servants, and singers, and the priests' garments.

The current meaning of the term social indicators is relatively synonymous with the original historical meaning of the term "statistics." In their early days, both the Statistical Society of London and the American Statistical Association defined statistics as facts that are calculated to illustrate the conditions and prospects of society. The term "statistics" is derived from the Latin phrase *ratio status* and its Italian equivalent *ragiono di stato*. Both may be translated as "state of the nation." These terms were coined in the Middle Ages to refer to the factual study of politics and government, as distinguished from a philosophical approach to an understanding of the state.

Societies vary significantly in the degree in which they institutionalize the recording and maintaining of social indicators. Japan, for example, has a national statistics day. In the United States, the Founding Fathers instituted the production of the country's statistics in Article I, Section 2 of the U.S. Constitution of 1787 by mandating a decennial census.

In the United States, the movement to establish social indicators may be traced to the work of the early twentieth century sociologist William Ogburn. Ogburn was intent on establishing a series of social indicators that would improve methods of extrapolation and correlation as a means of anticipating the future. Ogburn's goal was social planning, and he determined that one needed an accurate "fix" on social patterns in order to do any useful social planning. The benchmark work, largely written by Ogburn, was *Recent Social Trends*. The volume was an outgrowth of the President's Research Committee on Social Trends, which was established by President Hoover in 1929. This tremendous effort was designed to create a "total" picture on the state of society and societal problems.

Ogburn's theory of social problems is still influential. He argued that social problems emerge as manifestations of unequal rates of economic, technical, political, and social change in society. For example, Ogburn and his associates argued that rising divorce rates were due to the fact that the family had fewer economic functions in the industrial age, which weakened personal ties among its members. Ogburn believed that social problems could be corrected if government built a deliberate feedback system in the environment in order to be given the earliest possible detection of impacts that bear on society's goals.

In the late 1930s, the National Resources Planning Board, prompted by Louis Brownlow and Charles Merriam, organized substantial monographic studies on technology, population, and cities. However, further efforts to establish series of social indicators ended with World War II. The next real interest in social measurement and social-trend analysis did not resume until the 1960s with the ris-

ing concern with domestic social problems such as poverty, racial tensions, environmental pollution, and persistent unemployment. During this time, economists began to apply cost-benefit analyses to some of these social problems and to develop techniques for measuring social costs and social benefits. Political scientists, economists, and scholars in public administration began to formulate Program-Planning-Budgeting Systems as a means of analyzing and comparing diverse government programs.

Theoretical Considerations

Early theorists, such as Ogburn, believed that one could simply learn empirical facts and then rationally apply them in order to solve social problems. Subjective phenomena like ideas, values, emotions, and images were either subordinate to material reality or not subject to the scientific method. This resulted in a mechanical, social engineering approach to the use of social indicators during the early century.

Today, it is recognized that "objective science" has ideological and political dimensions. Social indicators are—like the cultural artifacts they document—value laden. Social problems and attempts to quantify them can only be considered "objective facts" if there is consensus about the meaning and significance of those facts.

Scholars also recognize that social indicators do not provide information on a fixed, deterministic reality. Rather, it is like an ever expanding frontier; the wider the scope of knowledge grows, the more numerous become the points of contact with the unknown at its periphery. Establishment of a series of social indicators does not make understanding social change automatic. However, remarkable strides in the knowledge base of the social sciences have depended in part on the increasing precision and scope of measurement technology and the establishment of social indicators.

SUSAN E. DAY

BIBLIOGRAPHY

Bauer, Raymond, 1966. *Social Indicators*. Cambridge: MIT Press.
Bell, Daniel, 1969. "The Idea of a Social Report." *The Public Interest*, vol. 15 (Spring) 72–84.
Ogburn, William F., President's Research Committee on Social Trends, 1933. *Recent Social Trends in the United States*. New York: McGraw-Hill. reprint, New York: Arno Press, 1979.
Smelser, Neil J., and Dean R. Gertein, eds., 1986. *Behavioral and Social Science: Fifty Years of Discovery*. Washington, DC: National Academy Press.

SOCIAL RESPONSIBILITY OF BUSINESS.

The obligation of the managers of a for-profit enterprise to conduct their business in a manner that is consistent with the expectations of society.

Historical Development

The concept of social responsibility of business has a varied history in Western society. During the Middle Ages, feudal estates had both economic and social responsibilities. The latter were in the form of education, health care, welfare, and other social goods, all provided in return for labor and its output from those who worked the land and from tradespeople. This social role diminished, however, with the rise of mercantilist societies, which operated on the basis of economic exchange. Industrialism extended mercantilism through the development of stock companies (multiple owners) and, because of the scale, managers, who were charged with generating profits for the stockholders. While industrialism led to an unprecedented expansion of business activity, markets, and the availability of goods and services to an ever increasing number of people, its diffused and removed ownership led to many social abuses as well. Poor wages, displacement of people with skills no longer needed, and an increasingly transient workforce, which broke down kinship ties, led to increasing government involvement in the provision of social goods.

In the United States, President Franklin Delano Roosevelt's plethora of social programs, known as the New Deal, was the beginning of large-scale government involvement in social issues. This spawned many arguments over the appropriate role of government in a capitalist economy. In many ways, government was in business. Rural electrification came through quasi-governmental organizations as part of the New Deal, not through government contracting with private companies. Thousands of miles of highways and hundreds of parks were built through government programs, not private companies. Yet, to pay for these programs required government indebtedness and taxes to repay that indebtedness. All of this injected government even more into the sphere of business. Many businesspeople felt that such government intervention was inappropriate, although most grudgingly acknowledged that action was needed to stimulate the depressed economy. Thus, a new stimulus appeared for the debate over the appropriate role of government in society, and it teased the edges of the appropriate role business should play.

Current Debate

The current extremes in debate over the social responsibility of business have changed little in the past 60 years. At one extreme is the work of U.S. economist Milton Friedman, who has argued consistently that the only responsibility of managers is to engage in legal business activities that serve to maximize owner (shareholder) wealth. Doing this is socially responsible because profits support employment and lead to the ability of the enterprise and its employees to purchase goods and services. At the same time, the marketplace wields tremendous power; if a business enterprise is engaging in some behavior that is socially irresponsible, consumers will not purchase its goods or services and wage earners will refuse to work for it. As such, the combination of profit maximization and the marketplace contains all the mechanisms necessary to ensure social responsibility.

Others argue that business enterprises have developed to the extent that, except for the smallest enterprises, most operate in multiple markets and can find labor and other resources wherever they exist and move them to wherever they are needed. Additionally, business enterprises are state chartered, suggesting that managers have a responsibility to society as well. Taken together, governments have a right and obligation to impose, and for consumers to expect, social responsibility from business. Examples of this are found in the environmental arena, where laws exist to prevent further environmental destruction and attempt to repair earlier environmental problems. Similarly, consumer protection laws reduce the number of unsafe products available on the market.

Today, many managers believe it is in their best interest, and the best interest of their businesses, to be socially responsible. Common practices that are considered socially responsible include reducing emissions and other industrial wastes below the legal limits, increasing the use of recycling and of recycled materials, and sponsoring particular social causes with monetary contributions and/or labor.

Implications of Practice

Given this move toward social responsibility of business, it is worthwhile returning to Friedman's concern over maximizing shareholder wealth. Early academic studies of the effect of socially responsible actions on firm performance revealed conflicting results. Many recent studies, however, have found positive monetary returns to social responsibility. This is supported by anecdotal evidence from business managers and executives who have placed a high priority on social responsibility in their businesses. Also, recent surveys reported in both *Fortune* and *Inc.* magazines showed that consumers would support a socially responsible firm over one that was not socially responsible and that a vast majority of business owners believe in and support social responsibility and would do so even if it cut into their profits.

Global Variations

Although much of this entry has been devoted to describing social responsibility of business in the United States of America, it is by no means the only nation in which social responsibility of business occurs. In the United Kingdom, for example, many businesses are involved in a variety of social responsibility initiatives. Among these are environmental cleanups and efforts to reduce or eliminate further environmental damage, demonstrating a caring posture toward employees through provision of fitness programs and facilities and extensive health and health education programs, and support of socially responsible causes with financial and human resources. Thus, we find that social responsibility differs little between these two nations. In other parts of the world, however, even Western companies that act socially responsible at home or in other Western nations have done little more than observe the legal minimums in their non-Western operations.

Summary

What is clear to observers of social responsibility of businesses is that it continues to evolve. As an increasing number of companies engage in such actions and provide empirical data to verify its value, others will follow. As with anything, however, the hurdle of social responsibility will be increasingly higher. Additionally, much is yet to be done in this area in developing nations.

MCRAE C. BANKS

BIBLIOGRAPHY

Amba-Rao, Sita C., 1993. "Multinational Corporate Responsibility, Ethics, Interactions, and Third World Governments: An Agenda for the 1990s." *Journal of Business Ethics,* vol. 12 (July) 553–572.

Aupperle, Kenneth, Archie B. Carroll, and John D. Hatfield, 1985. "An Empirical Examination of the Relationship between Corporate Social Responsibility and Profitability." *Academy of Management Journal,* vol. 28 (June) 446–463.

Avishai, Bernard, 1994. "What Is Business's Social Compact?" *Harvard Business Review,* vol. 72 (January-February) 38–48.

Carroll, Archie B., 1977. *Managing Corporate Social Responsibility.* Boston: Little, Brown.

———, 1979. "A Three-Dimensional Conceptual Model of Corporate Performance." *Academy of Management Review,* vol. 4 (October) 497–505.

Davidson, Jacqueline, 1993. "Responsibility Reaps Rewards." *Small Business Reports,* vol. 18 (February) 56–64.

Friedman, Milton, 1962. *Capitalism and Freedom.* Chicago: University of Chicago Press.

———, 1970. "The Social Responsibility of Business Is to Increase Its Profits." *New York Times Magazine,* vol. 32 (September 13) 122–126.

Herremans, Irene, Parporn Akathaporn, and Morris McInnes, 1993. "An Investigation of Corporate Social Responsibility, Reputation and Economic Performance." *Accounting, Organizations, and Society,* vol. 18 (October-November) 587–604.

"Is Social Responsibility a Crock?" 1993. *Inc.,* vol. 15 (May) 15.

Levy, Jean Philippe, 1967. *The Economic Life of the Ancient World.* Chicago: University of Chicago Press.

Martin, Justin, 1994. "Good Citizenship Is Good Business." *Fortune,* vol. 129 (March 21) 15–16.

McGuire, Jean, A. Sundgren, and Thomas Schneeweis, 1988. "Corporate Social Responsibility and Firm Financial Performance." *Academy of Management Journal,* vol. 31 (December) 854–872.

Owen, Crystal L., and Robert F. Scherer, 1993. "Social Responsibility and Market Share." *Review of Business,* vol. 15 (Summer-Fall) 11–16.

Spragins, Ellyn E., 1993. "Making Good." *Inc.,* vol. 15 (May) 114–122.

Summerfield, Baldwin, 1968. *Business in the Middle Ages.* New York: Henry Holt.

Vyakarnam, Shailendra, 1992. "Social Responsibility: What Leading Companies Do." *Long Range Planning,* vol. 25 (October) 59–67.

Walton, Clarence C., 1967. *Corporate Social Responsibilities.* Belmont, CA: Wadsworth.

Wood, Donna J., 1990. *Business and Society.* Glenview, IL: Scott, Foresman/Little, Brown Higher Education.

SOCIAL SECURITY SYSTEMS (U.S.).

Federally mandated programs that are intended to function as safety nets for the elderly, poor, and disabled citizens of the United States. The system provides those individuals who qualify for assistance with old-age pensions, health insurance, disability compensation, and food stamps.

History and Brief Overview

The philosophy underlying the formation and evolution of the U.S. Social Security system occurred at about the time of the Industrial Revolution. The transformation of agriculturally based, rural societies into industrialized, urbanized societies significantly altered the social and economic structure of the time. Many citizens found themselves working for, and relying on, others for their wages when in the past many families functioned as fairly self-contained units. Although on the positive side, working for others resulted in less dependence on the whims of nature and more economic stability, on the negative side, the move toward urbanization helped to destabilized the extended family structure common during the earlier agrarian-based society. As a result of this familial destabilization, economic difficulties facing the elderly and disabled increased. These increased economic problems fostered the belief among some nations that society had a responsibility to protect its citizens economically. Chancellor Otto von Bismarck of Germany established the world's first insurance programs, health (sickness) insurance, and worker's compensation programs. These programs began in 1883 and were supported by mandatory contributions from workers and employers; by 1889, an old-age insurance program was added. Other countries eventually followed Germany's lead and established social security systems of their own. Most democratic nations have now established some form of social security system. These systems have been generally designed as tools aimed at alleviating the social and economic hardships caused by unemployment, disability, and old age. The systems usually strive to provide the recipient with medical and other essential services. Opponents of the social security systems argue that their benefits could be supplied by the private sector. However, the ideas underlying government involvement in delivering social services were supported by economist John Keynes's (1935) argument that it was not possible for a free-market economy to maintain full employment.

The United States did not enact a national social security system until 1935. The Social Security Act of 1935 was passed by President Franklin D. Roosevelt and was designed to provide pensions for most retired commercial and industrial workers aged 65 years or more. At the same time, the act also helped establish an unemployment insurance system funded and maintained jointly by the states and the federal government.

The Social Security Act of 1935 strove to accomplish two goals. One was to create a safety net for retirees, and the other was to convince the public to support the creation of one of the first compulsory national social programs in the United States. One of the act's major objectives was to create a system in which retired workers could receive at least as much in retirement benefits as they had contributed to the system during their working life. This objective was necessary if the citizens of the United States were going to support the institutionalization of the new Social Security System. One of the philosophical reasons for the existence of this objective was a desire by public policymakers to establish a system of social equity, or adequacy, to ensure that no retired worker in the United States would suffer. This attempt at promoting social adequacy was achieved through the weighted benefit formula. Amendments to the Social Security Act in 1939 supported the nation's commitment to the working poor and were crafted to meet the needs of elderly individuals who were not adequately covered by the states' various old-age assistance programs. These later amendments further weakened the principle of a fair rate of return by calculating retiree benefits based on average earnings over a shorter period of time than the original formula for calculating earnings specified.

The old-age, survivors, disability, and hospital insurance program (OASDI) is administered by, and the principal responsibility of, the Social Security Administration (SSA). In 1946, the SSA replaced the original Social Security Board and became an agency within the newly formed U.S. Department of Health, Education, and Welfare (HEW) in 1953. HEW was reorganized in 1979 and was renamed the Department of Health and Human Services (DHHS). SSA remained as a subsidiary agency within the DHHS until March 1995. In mid-August 1994, President Bill Clinton signed H.R. 4277 into law. Entitled the Social Security Administration Independence Act of 1994, the act legislated into existence the SSA as an independent agency. The purpose behind this change in the agency's organiza-

tional status was an attempt to insulate it from party politics. The SSA is now headed by a commissioner and a deputy commissioner appointed by the president and confirmed by the Senate. These individuals serve six-year terms. The act also has created a 12-person advisory board, which is also appointed by the president. The board has 12 members plus the board chairperson. The board advises the commissioner on policy issues affecting the agency. The new, independent SSA will continue to administer OASDI and the Supplemental Social Security programs. By 1974, SSA had established the federal Supplemental Security Income (SSI) program as defined in Title XVI of the Social Security Act. Applications for SSI are handled by local Social Security offices. The program took over responsibility from state programs for providing aid to the indigent blind, disabled, and elderly. The programs cover about 95 percent of the workers in the United States today and include nearly all private-industry and most public workers.

Several programs that were established in the original 1935 act are handled by agencies other than the SSA, although the intended focus of these programs means that many recipients receive assistance through several programs at once. The 1935 act established the unemployment insurance program in the United States, which is administered by the U.S. Department of Labor. Aid to Families with Dependent Children (AFDC), also established by the Social Security Act in 1935, is the largest cash assistance program serving needy families with children. AFDC has two goals, to assist families with dependent children who have immediate financial needs and to help these families become self-sufficient. AFDC is funded by both the federal and state governments. The programs are administered by the states under discretionary guidelines established by the federal government. Each state establishes its own guidelines as to the amount required by a particular size family in order to live and then develops its own assistance payment level. The federal government monitors state administration with quality control, audit, and compliance reviews. A later legislative modification (1957) in the original 1935 act established the national Disability Insurance (DI) Program, which is handled by SSA. The program established a separate fund from which to provide cash benefits to employees over age 50 who became permanently and totally disabled. In 1960, the employee age limit was removed.

In 1965, legislative amendments to the original act mandated the establishment of the Medicare and Medicaid programs. Medicare provides certain medical benefits for individuals over 65, those with end-stage renal disease and certain other specified disabilities. As of 1995, over 37 million people were covered under the Medicare program. Medicare funds are divided into two parts. Part A is the standard insurance provided to the elderly and primarily pays for the cost of inpatient care. Part B is optional, requires a copayment and helps to pay the costs of outpatient treatments. A separate fund was created to finance Medicare. Medicare is administered by an agency under SSA called the Health Care Financing Administration (HCFA). HCFA has eight regional agencies, which oversee the program and ensure that regulations are obeyed.

Payments to health care providers are not made by HCFA but by intermediaries and carriers. Part A payers are called fiscal intermediaries and are private organizations such as Blue Cross/Blue Shield associations or a commercial insurer. Carriers, or Part B payers, may also be insurance agencies.

HCFA contracts with both state agencies and with fiscal intermediaries to assist HCFA in administering the hospital insurance plan, or Part A. The state agencies examine health care providers to ascertain if they meet the requirements set forth for participation as a hospital, skilled nursing facility, home health agency, or hospice. The state agencies also assist institutions to meet the requirements for participation. As noted previously, the private organizations or fiscal intermediaries oversee the reimbursement portion of Part A. They do this by

1. determining the actual hospital insurance benefits payable to the health care provider agency;
2. having determined the amount of the payment, then actually paying the benefits to the provider using funds advanced to them from the federal government;
3. assisting health care providers in maintaining and establishing the needed fiscal records;
4. acting as a communication channel in areas relating to the hospital insurance protection; and
5. auditing the fiscal and medical records of the health care providers to assure that the benefits paid are correct.

The Medicaid program, created at the same time as Medicare, provides medical benefits for certain categories of the needy poor. These categories can include children and their caretakers, the elderly, and the disabled. Medicaid has become one of the primary payers for nursing home care among the elderly. There were 25 million Medicaid recipients in 1990.

Additional programs that impact on the social welfare of the United States include the food stamp program, which is administered by state public assistance offices and is sponsored by the U.S. Department of Agriculture. The program is designed to provide food stamps, which can be exchanged for groceries at participating vendors for people with low incomes. Social Security offices may take food stamp applications from persons who are receiving, or applying for, SSI if the applicants have another family member who is also receiving or applying for SSI.

In order for all of the various social programs covered under the social security system in the United States to be successful, the government must collect personal income

and employment data. The threat of a violation of individual privacy is a valid danger when this type of data is all collected under one agency. A federal sting conducted in the early 1990s uncovered the fact that private information brokers have bribed SSA employees to perform computer searches of thousands of people's records. The brokers paid the employees US $25 for each individual's earnings history.

Benefits and Coverage

The Social Security Act of 1935 provided retirement benefits only to retired workers. However, by 1939 the first of many legislative changes to the original act provided benefits for survivors and dependents. During the 1950s, government workers, members of the military, domestic workers, many farmworkers, and self-employed workers were legislated into the system. The age at which one could retire, 65, and how benefits would be apportioned was also changed. Women became eligible for reduced benefits at the age of 62 in 1956, and by 1961, men were also given the option of retiring at age 62 with a reduced level of benefits. OASDI now covers about 95 percent of the workers in the United States and pays retirement benefits to the retirees and, under certain conditions, to their dependents as well. The fund pays a small death benefit to eligible survivors and provides survivors' benefits to eligible dependents. As of December 1991, US $920 million dollars in benefits had been distributed to children in need under the OASDI program.

The Disability Insurance fund provides benefits to employees with severe physical or mental conditions that last at least one year or which will result in death. A six-month waiting time is necessary before the disabled workers can collect benefits. As with retired workers receiving OASDI benefits, disabled workers must also have worked in covered employment for a specified time period. As with OASDI, disabled workers and their dependents are eligible for Medicare benefits under certain conditions. The Social Security Administration Independence Act of 1994 set limits on the disability benefits available for individuals who have become addicted to drugs or alcohol. These individuals will find their OASDI and SSI benefits terminated after they have received three years of treatment.

Medicare, Part A, will pay the costs of hospital care, certain skilled nursing facility care costs for up to 100 days, and home health or hospice services for retired workers or disabled individuals covered by the national Disability Insurance fund. Medicare provides health care coverage to workers and their dependents who suffer from chronic, end-stage renal disease. Part A insurance is provided free to all eligible recipients and may be purchased by those not eligible for coverage. Originally, Part A paid health care providers for their services based on a retrospective model. Under this model, providers billed Medicare once services had been performed, and Medicare paid what it felt to be a fair and reasonable fee for these services. Under this model, spending per person for health care under Medicare rose from US $648 in 1967 to an estimated US $3,079 in 1993. In an attempt to curb costs, a new approach to paying for Part A reimbursement was initiated in 1983. This approach was phased in over several years and is called a prospective payment system (PPS). PPS is based on a system of payment derived from Diagnostic Related Groups (DRGs). DRGs cover all costs for the care of an individual based on an assessment of what the average cost for a specific diagnosis should be; the hospital is then paid this amount. Under PPS, hospitals that can care for ill Medicare recipients more efficiently can make more money. As a result of this cost-paying shift, the number of days spent in a hospital by Medicare patients has dropped from about 10.8 to 8.8. However, the cost of Medicare reimbursement has still continued to grow due to the increasing numbers of elderly and ill utilizing the program and due to the fact that more hospitals are offering services not covered by the PPS. Outpatient, or Part B, services have grown three times as fast as Part A services since the implementation of PPS.

Part B pays for doctors' visits, certain outpatient services, and other miscellaneous services. Part B is optional for all individuals who qualify for Part A. Part B recipients pay a small monthly charge for the option, which is withdrawn from their social security check, and they also may make a small copayment for some of the services provided. Many of the services continue to be reimbursed using a retrospective system based on fair and reasonable charges. Physician services, however, are being reimbursed using a system for calculating payment based on a formula entitled Resource Based Relative Value Scale (RBRVS). This scale uses three factors to calculate each physician's reimbursement rate: (1) how much time and what work they do; (2) how expensive it is for them to maintain their practice (this may vary by region); and (3) the cost of malpractice insurance for each particular specialty. An outcome of RBRVS is that specialists are being reimbursed at a lower rate than before the scale was enacted, whereas generalists are being reimbursed at a higher rate. About 97 percent of Part A recipients also choose to take advantage of the Part B option.

The Medicaid program was designed to be run jointly by the states and the federal government. It was to provide a safety net for indigent mothers and their children, and indigent elderly, blind, and disabled individuals who qualified for SSI. States may limit the number of SSI recipients eligible for Medicaid by applying more restrictive eligibility standards than those in use by the current SSI program as long as those standards are not more restrictive than the standards used in the SSI programs prior to 1972.

Congress mandated that Medicaid, as administered by the states, provide at least a basic package. Medicaid recipients must receive the following services: inpatient and outpatient hospital services, rural health clinic services, laboratory and X-ray services, nursing facility services, home health care services for individuals age 21 or older, family planning services and supplies, early and periodic screening, diagnosis and treatment for individuals under age 21, certified midwife services, physician services, certified pediatric and family nurse practitioner services, and federally qualified health ambulatory and health center services. In addition, there are many other services that a state may choose to provide, such as prescription drugs. For the medically needy, states have considerably more discretion in the types of services they provide. States may, and often do, provide more services than are mandated by Congress. Each state administers its own Medicaid program and has developed its own reimbursement structure.

In 1972, mandatory nursing home care coverage was added to the package. Medicaid pays for about 44 percent of total nursing home income and accounts for 65 percent of the nursing home days. About 75 percent of Medicaid payments are used to provide care for the elderly, blind, and disabled who represent only about 28 percent of the Medicaid recipients. The reimbursement systems used by the various states often provide such low payments that private hospitals and many physicians refuse to care for Medicaid recipients.

Supplementary Medicare Insurance (SMI) is another option offered to certain classes of retirees and the disabled and is financed by participants' premiums and from federal tax revenues. SMI helps pay the costs of physicians' services and other specified services not covered by Medicare and OASDI. Medicare and OASDI benefits are financed by the Federal Insurance Contributions Act (FICA) tax, a payroll tax, which has increased from 2 percent at the program's inception to 15.3 percent in 1995. The taxable earnings base, or the maximum amount of earnings that can be taxed, in 1993, was US $57,600 for OASDI and US $135,000 for Medicare. Retirement benefits are usually calculated on average indexed earnings over 35 years. The formula used to calculate benefits is weighted heavily in favor of low-income workers, assuring them of a higher percentage of preretirement earnings than high-wage workers. Workers with dependent spouses receive additional benefits, regardless of the spouse's work history. Retirees may collect full retirement benefits once they reach age 65. Workers aged 65 to 69 may also collect full retirement benefits if their annual salary does not go over a specified amount—in 1993 that amount was US $10,560. Once the worker has reached the age of 70, the individual is eligible for full retirement benefits, and earnings do not enter into the computation. Workers who delay claiming benefits upon reaching age 65 will receive higher benefits when they do retire. The difference in the amount received depends on what age the worker finally claims benefits. Retirees who apply for benefits at 62 will have their benefits reduced by 20 percent from the amount they would have received if they had waited until they were 65. Current discussions under way at the federal level strongly suggest that the age at which one can claim retirement benefits will increase in the coming years. Also, in an attempt to lessen the drain on the OASDI fund, workers may be offered the option of investing 2 percent of their FICA tax monies in retirement accounts, thereby reducing the amount of benefits they are eligible for by a like amount when they retire. In 1993, beneficiaries aged 62 to 64 lost US $1 in benefits for every US $2 in income that they earned over US $7,680, whereas those aged 65 to 69 lost US $1 in benefits for every US $3 in income that they earned over US $10,560. Some individuals and couples whose incomes exceed US $34,000 pay federal income tax on as much as 85 percent of their benefits. However, supporters of the Republicans' 1995 tax cuts support the elimination of all, or part, of the tax on income for those individuals.

As seen in the previous discussion, the United States's social security system provides citizens with a number of different services. These services are intended to promote social equity, social adequacy, and the existence of a safety net for all citizens. These intentions should assure that no citizen suffers unduly from the effects of poverty. However, the sheer size of the system and the economic pressures facing it raise the possibility for failure of the safety net.

ROE ROBERTS

BIBLIOGRAPHY

Betts, Mitch, 1992. "Personal Data More Public Than You Think." *Computerworld,* vol. 26, no. 10 (March) 1, 14.
Rubin, Irene, 1994. "Early Budget Reformers: Democracy, Efficiency, and Budget Reforms." *American Review of Public Administration,* vol. 24, no. 3 (September) 229–252.
Social Security Administration, 1991. *Social Security Bulletin.* DHHS, vol. 55, no. 1 (Winter).
———, 1993. *Social Security Bulletin.* DHHS, vol. 56, no. 4 (Winter).
———, 1995. *Social Security Handbook.*
"Social Security to Become Independent Agency in 1995," 1994. *Employee Benefit Plan Review,* vol. 49, no. 3 (September).

SOCIAL SERVICES.

A term that represents a varying group of programs aimed at helping individuals maintain normalcy of family life and at creating opportunities for them to achieve self-sufficiency. Social services is an American tradition that has been shaped over the years by government policy and the practices of nonprofit-sector organizations.

Roots of Social Services

Most social services focus on supporting individuals who are described as being poor and needy because they are without adequate housing, clothing, or food. Social services in the United States has its roots in religious doctrines and ideology and from practices of ancient societies. For example, the Babylonians' Code of Hammurabi directed community members to support persons who were poor, orphans, and widows. In the pre-Christian Egyptian era, it was believed that the gods rewarded good deeds—such as assisting the poor and needy—with a restful afterlife. The Book of Deuteronomy from the Old Testament commands tithing that could be satisfied not just with money but also by sharing crops with hungry children and widows. The Christian notion of helping and sharing with those who are less fortunate surfaces in the scriptures of Matthew.

Responding to community needs and providing food and shelter to individuals had its advocates, but it also had its detractors. The existence and conditions of poverty in England adversely impacted the concept of helping others in need. With the breakup of the feudal system, social instability caused by vast unemployment and vagrancy plagued municipalities, which responded with ordinances to control begging and to emphasize the importance of working. Despite local lawmaking, townships were unable to control the begging behavior of indigent and able-bodied poor. Consequently, the Parliament responded by establishing the Elizabethan Poor Law of 1601.

The principle behind the poor laws was a fundamental belief that individuals should work and take active responsibility for fulfilling the needs of their families. If a person was unable to care for self and family, then the relatives were to assume responsibility. Last, the community was obliged to assure that individuals did not starve, but the assistance that local governments provided was sometimes very harsh. To discourage vagrancy and begging, homeless individuals were sometimes placed in "poorhouses" or "almshouses."

Personal beliefs of early colonists about poverty and work ethics hardly differed from their English customs and roots. They advanced the concept and principles of the poor laws in the colonies and later in the states. Poor laws became guiding principles for Puritan ideology, setting a tone for the eventual development of a vast system of welfare. Welfare practices in the colonies were supported by local government funds, laying a foundation for response to the needs of the poor but not necessarily a compassionate response. Individuals facing poverty were often thought to be in disfavor with God, who was punishing them.

After the Revolutionary War, the federal government joined in the support of welfare practices, which broadened to include programs such as pensions for veterans of the war.

By the early to mid-nineteenth century, the need for welfare services accelerated in the United States when vast numbers of English migrated to the United States, followed by other poor Europeans. The English were escaping from the harsh views of poverty characterized by Prime Minister Benjamin Disraeli's view that it was a crime to be poor in England and the Poor Law Reform bill of 1834.

America's divergent views of people in poverty were consistent with the sharply contrasting views found in England and Europe. The two contrasting views of poverty are well represented by the expressions of statesman Benjamin Franklin and poet Ralph Waldo Emerson. Franklin stated, "I think the best way of doing good to the poor, is, not making them easy in poverty, but leading or driving them out of it." In contrast, Emerson stated, "Write a sermon on Blessed Poverty. Who have done all the good in the world? Poor men. 'Poverty is a good hated by all men.'"

Early responses to social problems in America were representative of society's values and laissez-faire doctrine of free market, limited government interference, and individualism. Rising urban poverty and social unrest provoked by the economic depression of the 1870s drew attention to the inadequacies of charitable assistance efforts and provided the impetus for creating change through volunteer social service efforts. The early phases of the Charity Organization movement, for example, held to the notion that poverty and dependence on others for assistance were evidence of an individual's ill character. Charity Organization volunteers, known as friendly visitors, gained access to indigent people by providing them with financial assistance. Once inside a person's residence, they also provided literature and advice about finding work and building moral character.

Perceptions about the causes of poverty began to shift when poverty increased after several years of economic depression and working for low wages did not alter impoverishment. Although there was not a sweeping change of opinion, more people started to recognize that social and economic conditions might be important attributes of poverty. No longer was an individual's moral fiber alone seen as the root of poverty. Natural disasters, government policies, unfavorable business practices, and industrialization led to a new brand of poor. Among urban workers, rural farmers, and religious individuals were individuals who, despite personal industry, could not escape the impersonal cruelties of poverty.

The Charity Organization Society also began to recognize that the causes of poverty were quite complex. Over time, they expanded their social services into major cities throughout America. By the turn of the century, their social welfare efforts were highly regarded services, especially in comparison with government-run programs. The Charity Organization Society founded the first training school to prepare individuals for employment in social welfare agencies. It was known as the New York School of Philanthropy, now the Columbia University School of Social Work.

The settlement house was one of the most important social welfare movements in the late 1880s. The first settlement house, Toynbee Hall, was founded in London, England, in 1884 by a group of Oxford University students. Its primary purpose was to improve living conditions and strengthen neighborhoods. Two years later, the first settlement house in the United States, University Settlement, was founded in New York City. In 1889, after visiting Toynbee Hall in London, Jane Addams established a Chicago settlement house with the support of her friend Ellen Gates Starr. Hull House was to become symbolic of Addams' reputation and life-long dedication to improving the living conditions of poor and needy individuals. Her efforts led to her receiving the Nobel Peace Award in 1931.

Settlement houses had a variety of social service programs delivered by volunteers and professionals, including on-site child care, medical exams, and legal advice. As a neighborhood center, the settlement house provided social, recreational, and educational activities for its members. Some settlement houses also encouraged political activism to promote social reform, such as civil rights and child welfare rights.

Another form of social services that was community centered was the mutual aid organization. As large numbers of Europeans immigrated to the United States, many were confronted with prejudice and ill treatment. To protect their communities, ethnic groups formed private, non-profit mutual aid societies. These organizations preserved cultural traditions and customs; supported religious celebrations; provided comfort during crisis, illness, and death; and were centers for events such as weddings and recreational activities.

Mutual assistance groups are still used by various ethnic and religious groups, but they may be promoting a form of ethnic isolationism and a vast duplication of social services. Jewish Family Services, Catholic Charities, Lutheran Social Services, and other similar service organizations associated with specific ethnic groups or religious sects are examples of groups that provide duplicative social services in local communities. Many consumers prefer to receive social services from organizations in which they share an ethnic bond or religious affiliation.

Widespread immigration to the United States and the ten-year Great Depression that followed the stock market crash of October 23, 1929, created a demand among citizens for government relief programs. Recognizing that private, nonprofit social service agencies could not respond to the thousands of individuals who lost their jobs, homes, and savings, the electorate signaled their desire for government involvement by electing Franklin D. Roosevelt to the office of president. Once elected, Roosevelt and Congress passed New Deal legislation to create work relief programs, such as the Federal Emergency Relief Administration (FERA), Civilian Conservation Corps (CCC), Public

Works Administration (PWA), and Works Project Administration (WPA).

The concern that individuals would become permanently dependent on government-sponsored work relief programs impelled Roosevelt to foster the idea of a self-help oriented substitute program. The Social Security Act of 1935 established two self-funded insurance programs with monies from a tax levied on workers. These funds would assist workers during periods of unemployment or after retirement. With benefits paid out at a rate higher than that at which individuals contributed, the Social Security program did not achieve its goal of ending government provision of welfare. Instead, federally funded social services programs flourished. The act also required the federal government to provide funding to states that participated in various welfare programs. Assistance programs that targeted dependent children and the blind, aging, or unemployed became the bedrock of social service programs. Deductions from wage earners' paychecks were pooled to pay for certain social services that might or might not benefit the wage earner. Consequently, as a result of income deductions, all individual workers and their families became significantly intertwined in national and local social service policies.

Issues surrounding social service programs waned during World War II and up to the 1960s. Influenced by a book authored by Michael Harrington, entitled *The Other America*, President John F. Kennedy sought new antipoverty legislation, which included the food stamp program for individuals with incomes below a defined poverty level. As successor to Kennedy, President Lyndon B. Johnson continued with a "War on Poverty," which he thought necessary to achieve a "Great Society." Legislation was passed to develop job training (the Job Corps), Medicare and Medicaid, and Head Start. In addition, Johnson advocated for the Voting Rights Act and civil rights legislation to ban racial discrimination.

The Role of the Nonprofit Sector

Historically, the relationship between the nonprofit sector and government has been one of sharing a common purpose: Promoting the interest of the general public. A prevailing economic theory suggests that nonprofit organizations derive from market failure: When the for-profit sector does not address consumer needs and government does not respond, then opportunities exist for nonprofit organizations to fill the void. Opportunities also exist when government chooses to pay private, nonprofit-sector organizations to deliver services in lieu of government services.

Since the formation of the United States, individuals have always voluntarily come together in their community for the purpose of helping the less fortunate. Forming human ties to solve problems has been a precursor to the formation of nonprofit organizations. Since the mid-1960s, nonprofit organizations have proliferated and become more involved in the delivery of social services, except for cash assistance programs.

Since the onset of the War on Poverty and Great Society programs, many nonprofit organizations have developed a form of resource dependency on government for funding to support service delivery. In fact, the number of nonprofit organizations has grown from approximately 300,000 in the mid-1960s to approximately 800,000 in the mid-1970s and to approximately 1 million by the mid-1980s. During these periods, nonprofit organizations involved in human service delivery were funded at higher rates by government grants and contracts than through contributions from the private sector.

The dependence on government for funds became a critical issue during the Reagan administration. In 1981, Ronald Reagan assumed the Presidency with a theme of giving the government back to the people. His approach included cutting federal support to many social service and community development programs and proposed the consolidation of 12 federally funded social service programs into one block grant for each state. The White House placed greater expectations of decisionmaking and financial support for social services on to state and local governments, private philanthropy, volunteerism, and nonprofit organizations.

The theory behind the White House initiative was that tax incentives combined with local government support and private giving would fill the financing void left from cuts in federal funding. In addition, the Reagan administration believed that nonprofit organizations would replace government-supported social service delivery and shape the services to fit local needs. Social service funding was reduced, but Congress did not agree to consolidate several of the social service programs in the Reagan block grant plan. In the final analysis, there was neither evidence that private philanthropy, corporate contributions, and individual giving replaced the federal government's share of funding cuts, nor did the private sector have the capacity to support nonprofit organizations at the level necessary to replace reduced federal funding. Consequently, it has been estimated that social service programs lost more than 20 percent of their federal funding.

The central idea that the private nonprofit sector has the capability of managing, leading, or assuming the major responsibility for social service programs was furthered under the Bush administration in the early 1990s. Volunteerism and private, nonprofit-sector accomplishments were rewarded with President Bush's One Thousand Points of Light Award. The idea was to encourage competition for recognition among charitable provider organizations by their ability to do more with less. Many nonprofits believed that recognition by the Bush White House would make them more attractive to private and corporate donors.

Fourteen years after the introduction of "Reaganomics," a term for the reordering of government responsibility with proposals to consolidate categorical grant programs into block grants, many welfare reform ideas have reemerged. In 1995, for example, House Speaker Newt Gingrich advanced ideas once advocated by former President Reagan. According to Gingrich and the Republican Party's reform efforts, known as the Contract with America, government cannot afford to continue funding its many social programs, and private nonprofit organizations should assume the financial burdens for continuing social service programs. The idea that, if government eliminates or reduces funding support, charitable organizations will attract more private funding did not work in the early 1980s, and there is no evidence that taxpayers will respond by increasing their charitable contributions in the mid-1990s.

Currently, there are plans to reduce government involvement in social programs by more than US $70 billion. This amount represents approximately one-half of the annual contributions that are currently made by the private sector to nonprofit-sector organizations. In addition to maintaining its current level of financial support, the nonprofit sector would be required to attract an annual total of approximately US $200 billion. In other words, if responsibility for funding social programs was assumed by private nonprofit organizations, then an additional 30 percent (a minimum of approximately US $70 billion) would need to be raised to offset the first year of projected government reductions in funds.

The problem of replacing government funding is exacerbated by the fact that nonprofit organizations already subsidize the payments they receive to deliver social programs in lieu of a comprehensive government direct service delivery system. Therefore, if government reduces the number of grants and contracts and lowers the amount of each award, then nonprofit human service organizations might be forced to reduce the scope of their programs and services, especially if they could not mount a successful fund-raising campaign to supplant government funding cuts.

The nonprofit sector's role in the delivery of social services will be one of increasing demand, influenced by an aging population, divorce and family breakup, absence of affordable day care, rising costs of medical care, and increasing poverty. The expectation that social services will be available through the private nonprofit sector springs from a tradition of being responsive to the needs of individuals in society. However, in the wake of new welfare reform efforts, it is doubtful that the nonprofit sector will be able to secure enough private funding to appropriately respond to the rising demands for social services.

STEPHEN R. BLOCK

BIBLIOGRAPHY

Bernstein, Irving, 1985. *A Caring Society: The New Deal, the Worker, and the Great Depression.* Boston: Houghton Mifflin.

Harrington, Michael, 1962. *The Other America: Poverty in the United States.* New York: Macmillan.

Katz, Michael B., 1986. *In the Shadow of the Poorhouse: A Social History of Welfare in America.* New York: Basic Books.

Kramer, Ralph M., 1981. *Voluntary Agencies in the Welfare State.* Berkeley: University of California Press.

———, 1987. "Voluntary Agencies and the Personal Social Services." In Walter W. Powell, ed., *The Nonprofit Sector: A Research Handbook.* New Haven, CT: Yale University Press, 240–257.

Mead, Lawrence, M., 1992. *The New Politics of Poverty.* New York: Basic Books.

O'Neill, Michael, 1989. *The Third America.* San Francisco, CA: Jossey-Bass.

Palmer, John L., and Isabel V. Sawhill, eds., 1982. *The Reagan Experiment.* Washington, DC: Urban Institute.

Weiss, Ann E., 1990. *Welfare: Helping Hand or Trap?* Hillside, NJ: Enslow Publishers.

Whitman, David, et al., 1995. "Welfare: The Myth of Reform." *U.S. News & World Report* (January 16) 30–33, 35–39.

SOCIAL WELFARE ORGANIZATION.

A civic league or other organization that is organized and operated primarily to advance social welfare. It accomplishes this by promoting the common good and general welfare of a community and by bringing about civic betterments and social improvements.

Although it can be a membership organization, the benefits that it provides should extend beyond its members. For example, the Internal Revenue Service (IRS) concluded that a nonprofit organization that rebroadcast TV signals in an area of poor reception qualified as a social welfare organization because its primary purpose was to promote the general welfare of the community rather than simply benefit the organization's members. In addition, courts have held that organizations established to maintain common areas, such as roadways, parks, sidewalks, and streetlights, qualify as social welfare organizations. By comparison, a homeowners association that maintains a building of condominiums will not qualify as a social welfare organization because its benefits are limited to its members. An example of a social welfare organization is the American Association of Retired Persons (AARP).

Social welfare organizations usually have similar objectives to charitable organizations (see **charitable organization** and **tax-exempt organization**). Although both social welfare organizations and charitable organizations are tax-exempt in the United States, a social welfare organization operates under a disadvantage concerning contributions from donors. Contributors to a social welfare organization cannot claim tax deductions for their contributions, whereas contributors to a charity can. Consequently, most organizations prefer to qualify as a charitable organization under §501(c)(3) of the Internal Revenue Code rather than a social welfare organization under §501(c)(4).

Probably the most common reason that people establish a §501(c)(4) social welfare organization is to engage in activities that cannot be done by a charitable organization. A charity may establish a separate social welfare organization for the principal purpose of engaging in substantial amounts of lobbying for causes that the charity supports. The IRS usually permits this arrangement provided that the two organizations are separately incorporated and maintain separate financial records, and provided that the charity does not make payments for lobbying to the social welfare organization.

CHRISTOPHER HOYT

SOCIAL-POLITICAL GOVERNANCE. New patterns of interaction between government and society.

In many countries, the main tendency in recent years has been to shift the balance between government and society away from the public sector and more toward the private sector. Partly, this added up to privatization and sometimes to deregulation. But there are also efforts to shift the balance toward a sharing of tasks and responsibilities, toward doing things together instead of doing them alone (either by the state or by the market). New patterns of interaction between government and society can be observed in areas such as social welfare, environmental protection, education, physical planning, and urban revitalization. These new patterns are apparently aimed at discovering other ways of coping with new problems or of creating new opportunities for governing. Examples show experiments with coregulation, costeering, coproduction, cooperative management, and public-private partnerships on national, regional, and local levels. These examples can be regarded as concrete, often new, ways of governing on the borderline between government and society, as nontraditional mixtures of the public and private sectors.

More generally, there are many indications that the governing capacity of political/administrative systems either has crossed the threshold of the law of diminishing returns or is quite close to such a boundary. In those situations, actors, either as parts of governing systems or separately or in a combination, not only try to reduce the need for governing (let problems solve themselves) but also rephrase their capacities (let others help). Such changes do not take place in a vacuum. They may be the expression of a change in preference of ways of governance. One could say that they have to do with efforts to deal with matters of governability. In other words, the discussion about new patterns of interaction between government and society takes place on two analytically distinguishable levels. On a concrete governing level, there is the search for new models of governing in terms of different forms of coarrangements.

But one can also observe changes in terms of patterns of governance: Broader and maybe more pervasive efforts to come to grips with more fundamental developments and structural characteristics of the societies we live in. These are what we would like to call changes taking place on the governance level (or even "metagovernance level"). In the conceptualization, new patterns of governing and governance, concepts such as "dynamics," "complexity," and "diversity" of modern societies, play a major role. These concepts are an important tool in trying to understand the purpose of the changes at the governing and the governance level.

In terms of working definitions, governing can be considered as all those activities of social, political, and administrative actors that can be seen as purposeful efforts to guide, steer, control, or manage (sectors or facets of) societies. Social-political forms of governing are forms in which public or private actors do not act separately but in conjunction, together, in combination, that is to say, in coarrangements. The interactive aspects of these forms are quite important. "Governance" can be seen as the patterns that emerge from governing activities of social, political, and administrative actors. These patterns form the "emerging" outcome as well as a more abstract (higher level) framework for day-to-day efforts at governing. Modes of social-political governance should be considered as the source, but also as an outcome of new forms of public and private interaction.

Sectors of societies (social welfare, environmental protection) or intersectoral problem areas (urban revitalization) can be considered to be appropriate empirical levels to study and analyze these new forms of social-political governing and governance.

Interactive social-political governance means creating the social-political conditions for the development of new models of interactive governing in terms of comanagement, costeering and coguidance. Social-political governance and governing are not primarily looked upon as acts of governments, but as more or less continuous processes of interaction between social actors, groups and forces, and public or semipublic organizations, institutions, or authorities. There is a division of labor between them, which may shift during the interaction. This is their strength, yet also their weakness. The possibilities and limitations of the interactional qualities of these forms of social-political governing and governance may become apparent in those new ways of governing and governance.

In a theoretical perspective governance contains elements of systems theory, of theories of interorganizational networks, of theories of public administration and public management, of communication theory, and of theories of the state and civil society. In trying to come to grips with these new tendencies, there is not (yet) the pretension of a new theory.

Where the emphasis is not on the unilateral, but on the bilateral or even multilateral, aspects of these models of governing, this not only means that the boundaries between state and society change, but also that the boundaries themselves change in character. One could say they move and become more permeable. Where government begins and society ends, or the other way around, becomes more diffuse. The borderline between public and private responsibilities itself becomes the object of interaction. These multilateral interactions are often based on the recognition of mutual (inter)dependencies. No single actor, public or private, has all knowledge and information required to solve complex, dynamic, and diversified problems; no actor has sufficient overview to make the application of needed instruments effective; no single actor has sufficient action potential to dominate unilaterally in a particular governing model. These are basically matters of the relation between (meta) governance and governing.

Social-political governing can be conceptualized as a collection of rather specific models of interaction between the public and private sector in terms of comanaging, costeering, coguiding of actors (individuals, authorities, organizations) with public as well as with private responsibilities. The interest is not primarily in these actors themselves, but in their governing activities in conjunction with each other. This makes the "who" somewhat less tangible, but it can be expected to gain in terms of insights in the more systemic aspects of such sectors and the way they are governed. How do interactions develop, what kinds of forces do they express? How are interdependencies translated into decision processes? What kinds of positive and negative feedback processes and loops can be determined?

Such interactive forms of governing cannot be explained from an "official policies" point of view. It might be exactly dissatisfaction with or ineffectiveness of approaches such as "the administrative politics of policies" that lead to the search for other—more interactive—governing models. Social-political governing must be seen as a continuous process of interaction between public and non-public actors. The division of labor between them and the sharing of responsibilities are all part of the same process. Their connection (probably based on perceptions of mutual dependencies) seems to be their essence. In other words, structure, process, and substance, interrelated in dealing with complex, dynamic, and diverse problem situations and the creation of new ways for solutions, are their specific characteristics.

More traditional policy models or arrangements such as neocorporatist seem to be either too government oriented or too limited in scope. And more recent conceptualizations such as policy networks speak about interactions, but little about how these interactions are being governed. Self-organization is often preconceived. Governance conceptualizations are more in line with theoretical

efforts as developed by the "Bielefeld" Project (Kaufmann et al. 1986), which itself builds on earlier work by Robert Dahl and Charls Lindblom, Amitai Etzioni, Karl Deutsch, and others.

It seems as if in these new developments, more basic characteristics of modern societies are finally beginning to emerge, that is, the growing complexity, dynamics, and diversity of our societies, as caused by social, technological and scientific developments.

It might be possible that many governing systems under such pressures realize that new conceptions of governance are needed. So far, these developments in governmental behavior have been taken mainly for granted or just considered to be nasty and difficult. Why not take them seriously and put them in the center of new ways of thinking about how to cogovern, costeer, comanage, cocontrol, and use them?

JAN KOOIMAN

BIBLIOGRAPHY

Dahl, R. A., and C. E. Lindblom, 1953. *Politics, Economics, and Welfare.* New York: Harper & Row.
Deutsch, K., 1963. *Nerves of Government.* New York: Free Press.
Etzioni, A., 1986. *Active Society.* New York: Free Press.
Kaufmann, F. X., G. Majone, and V. Ostrom, 1986. *Guidance, Control, and Evaluation in the Public Sector.* New York: de Gruyter.
Kooiman, J., ed., 1993. *Modern Governance: New Government-Society Interactions.* London: Sage.

SOLICITATION OF GIFTS.

The process of asking for financial contributions and other kinds of support.

For nonprofits who depend upon contributed resources to accomplish their missions, this is the most essential of tasks. Historically, the pattern was set by the clergy, who took the burden of raising the funds necessary to support their ministries and churches by going to the most wealthy, directly asking for gifts. The truly poor begged for their own alms.

With modern technology, systems and people whose tasks were to elicit funds became more pervasive. The first professional fund-raisers extrapolated themselves by enlisting and training volunteers to do the asking, sometimes by rally, sometimes face to face.

Community funds more than a century ago began to see the wisdom of engaging the corporation as ally in organizing workplace solicitations. The cause was all-important in crusades that raised prodigious sums for war relief, setting the stage for future campaigns that relied more on numbers than on sophistication.

Pioneers in professional solicitation such as George Brakely and Harold Seymour began to identify those human traits that led to scientific and artful solicitation of individuals, while the realities and theories of philanthropy that guided the establishment of foundation and corporate giving were still being discovered, as much by those entities themselves as by practitioners.

Current practice dictates that the key to successful solicitation is still the individual donor and that understanding the motivation of generous Americans to contribute to charity is the most reliable guide. Seymour's recitations of human aspirations, basic motivations, and indeed what "people tend to do" is required reading for every beginner and a good refresher for seasoned veterans in the solicitation processes.

In his *Designs for Fund-Raising*, published in 1966, Seymour outlined the following traits that guide the charitable behaviors of Americans. They tend to

- follow leaders who have their confidence—it is the leader who can often motivate giving;
- strive for measurable and praiseworthy attainment—people need a way to win, and it is individual objective and the overall goals that give it to them;
- seek or achieve unity through group action—this is the multiplication principle of fund-raising;
- act only under the pressure of imminent deadlines;
- relish earned reward and recognition;
- repeat pleasurable experiences and avoid the unpleasant;
- conceal unpraiseworthy attitudes—which is why polls and surveys must be taken with some reservations;
- lose their sense of community with mobility and greater numbers—this makes organizing for personal solicitation so much more difficult.

In the same book, Seymour noted some of the basic characteristics of giving, and here is what he found:

- Giving begets giving—the best prospects for gifts are always those who have already given.
- Giving is primarily responsive—seldom do people give without being directly asked to do so.
- Giving is prompted emotionally, then rationalized—it is the heart that leads the way.
- Giving tends to favor round numbers—people may be tempted to buy things with a break at the point where a penny keeps it under a certain level, but giving is motivated in 100s, 1,000s, and so on.
- Giving tends to follow old habit patterns—this is the reason that upgrading annual gifts is a most difficult task.
- Giving is seldom prompted by tax considerations—these may affect the how, but seldom the what.
- Giving tends to prosper commensurately with challenge—this is evidenced by the lack of effect on giving by economic trends.
- Giving is commensurate with the level of involvement of the donor.

Recent studies and campaigns seem to indicate that there are some differences between the way men and women do philanthropy and solicitation. The model for males is generally competitive, and the model for females involves relationship building. A review of the Campaign for Wellesley, which concluded with a total of US $173 million against their US $150 million goal revealed that women were not responsive to the challenge of giving by their peers. The decision process took longer. They wanted to be involved first and give later. The necessity of being solicited by another woman who was viewed as a "peer" did not seem to matter as much as it did for men. The Wellesley Campaign also revealed that women did not seem to require the same sort of recognition for their giving that men's efforts usually entail. This is an area of intensive study by many of the leading nonprofits who count women as significant members of their constituency. Several are establishing women's study groups to engage them in the process of establishing their own fund-raising agendas.

The solicitation of gifts occurs under many formats. Essentially, there are three ways to ask for a gift—through the mail, by phone, and by face-to-face solicitation. A good guide is that the greater the level of gift sought, the greater the degree of personalization required in the solicitation.

Gift solicitation may involve one or more of the following methodologies:

- direct mail—letters, brochures, coupons;
- telephone solicitations—phone-a-thons;
- media solicitation via telethons or radio-a-thons or print with response mechanisms in newspapers or magazines;
- special events—walk-a-thons, bowl-a-thons, auctions, dances, sales in which solicitations may be for pledges or tickets;
- product sales—Girl Scout cookies, for example;
- corporate appeals—done by phone, mail, and face to face, again may be done for outright gifts pledges or gifts in kind;
- foundation grant proposals or applications—seeking a variety of types of support for projects, programs, or ongoing support;
- government funds—sought by a grant application process;
- venture funds—sought from corporations to market products and nonprofits;
- clubs, associations, and church groups are often solicited for funds by nonprofits.

Conventional wisdom surrounding the solicitation process suggests a consistent pattern of thorough preparation is necessary prior to the actual asking for the gift. The purpose behind the preparation is to give the solicitor the optimum chance for success. This is especially inviolate in seeking major gifts from individuals, corporations, and foundations. Essentially, such preparation usually would include the following:

- prospect identification–identifying the most likely sources of funds for the purposes intended;
- prospect research–analyzing the past behavior and interests of the prospect to pinpoint areas of interest and commonality between the prospect and the nonprofit–perhaps in the specific objective that will be the subject of the ultimate solicitation;
- introduction–acquainting the prospect with the nonprofit or, if already acquainted, to the specific purpose or campaign;
- informing–providing the prospect with as much information as is feasible regarding the details of the campaign, project, or community benefit;
- cultivation–involving the prospect directly in the work of the nonprofit and, specifically, in the campaign or project for which the funds are sought. Orchestrating activities that will increase the prospect's feelings of ownership in the organization.
- asking–the culmination of all the development process when the prospect is specifically presented the opportunity to invest in the project. The most effective method is the personal, face-to-face solicitation. However, since it takes the greatest amount of time and skill, this approach should be reserved for major gift prospects with other solicitation techniques used at lower giving levels.

ROBERT W. BUCHANAN AND WILLIAM BERGOSH

BIBLIOGRAPHY

Seymour, H. J., 1966. *Designs for Fund-Raising.* Rockville, MD: Taft Group.

SOLID WASTE ADMINISTRATION. Man-

aging the collection, processing, and disposal of waste products (not including liquid wastes and hazardous wastes). Solid waste services may be provided by public, nonprofit or private, for-profit organizations, or by partnerships involving two or more of these kinds of organizations.

Human use of the earth's resources has always involved the generation of waste products, but solid waste administration is largely a function of urban and industrial life–dense populations inhabiting limited space and engaged in the production and sale of goods and services. Initially, families or individuals managed their own solid waste, but as people crowded into cities their methods caused problems. In both African and Roman ancient

cities, there is evidence that people simply disposed of their solid waste where they lived, on their floors and in their streets. They lived among their waste products and built new streets and houses on top of them. Over time, city dwellers around the world developed ways of removing their waste from their immediate surroundings–through drainage systems, cesspools, sewage systems, scavenger and collection services, and dump sites located outside city limits.

Generally speaking, it was not until the industrial revolution that people made significant changes in their solid waste management practices. Two factors fed a rapid rise in waste generation: industrial urbanization and increases in the affluence of urban residents. Eventually, the magnitude of the problem led people to seek new ways of dealing with it, and the industrial revolution gave rise to a "service revolution." People began to look to municipalities to provide services (including solid waste management) that would improve their quality of life. In England, sanitation services were promoted by the Poor Law Commission's 1842 finding that a filthy environment promoted the spread of communicable diseases. As the connection between filth and disease gained acceptance, the demand for sanitation services in cities increased.

But sanitation services dealt only with the most immediate inconveniences associated with "the garbage problem." This stage of modern solid waste services administration focused on removal of refuse from highly populated areas, and for most people, it was a matter of "out of sight, out of mind." Garbage collectors, scavengers, and recyclers gathered urban waste. Recyclable materials were sometimes separated for reuse. Burnable materials were sometimes sent to incinerators, some of which were used to generate steam or electricity to provide an energy resource. But all of the solid waste that was not reused was dumped either on land or into water.

In the late nineteenth and early twentieth century, the responsibility for solid waste management was most often laid at the door of local government. Whether the services were provided by public or private agencies was a matter of local option, and the dispute over which approach was better was a matter of much discussion. Partly as a function of Progressive Reform efforts, in the late 1800s contracting with private solid waste handlers came under attack as an unreliable, inefficient, uneconomical, and health-threatening approach. Municipal solid waste management departments, however, also had their problems–most notably political interference, both overt and covert.

Increasing public control over solid waste management was followed by increasing public awareness and increasing public complaints. Newspapers, magazines, and professional journals began to address the garbage problem. Citizens groups and civic organizations began to pressure for improved solid waste services and to criticize unsanitary utilization and disposal practices. Often dominated by women, civic reform organizations promoted "municipal housekeeping." Believing there was a connection between cleanliness and moral rectitude, they promoted municipal sanitation as part of the City Beautiful civic improvement approach to improving the quality of urban life.

Because early sanitation efforts had been supported by the filth theory of disease (recognition of a connection between filth and disease), responsibility had often been placed on municipal health departments. As the filth theory became overshadowed by the germ theory of disease, municipalities began to turn to municipal and sanitary engineers to manage solid waste. Because engineering solutions to waste problems worked better with centralized and long-term administrative control, the engineers tended to promote direct municipal control over solid waste management.

Most of the technological solutions offered by the engineers were pioneered in Europe. One of the answers that they promoted was burning waste at high temperatures. Another was the "reduction process," which extracted oils and other by-products through compressing municipal waste. Experience, however, showed that there was no single, final answer. Equipment that worked in Europe could not be applied elsewhere without careful adaptation to local conditions.

In the next stage of modern solid waste administration, removing refuse from populated areas remained a common feature, but people began to be more concerned about where and how the waste was being disposed. Dumping waste into bodies of water had been widely condemned since the beginning of the twentieth century, but it remained a relatively common practice even in the advanced countries of the world in the second half of that century. Dumping waste on land also began to be criticized, largely because of the nuisance factors associated with it—rats, cockroaches, wind spreading lightweight materials beyond the boundaries of the dump, and smoke from fires in the dumps. Consequently, landfills, the use of waste to fill ravines, to level roads, or to "reclaim" marshlands and coastal land, became a popular method of disposal. The "sanitary landfill," one where the waste is covered by dirt each day to prevent fires and refugee materials, became a primary method of disposal in the United States in the 1920s.

Utilizing waste instead of simply disposing of it also gained some adherents. Because it was based on seeing "waste as wealth," reuse and recycling in the first half of the twentieth century was generally driven by economic incentives rather than by environmental sensitivity. Ironically, it may have been because waste was evidence of wealth that the "throwaway" culture of the middle and late twentieth century developed in the United States—to be able to throw away materials was a demonstration of one's affluence.

Whatever the causes may have been, the United States became the most wasteful society in the world. Fortunately, in the latter third of the twentieth century that nation also became aware of the damage it was doing to the ecology. As part of the developing environmental movement's impact on people's awareness of air and water pollution, solid waste began to be seen as the "third pollution." Joining air and water pollution, land pollution became a national concern largely because of its contribution to people's exposure to a growing number of identified and suspected cancer-causing agents.

Increased awareness of environmental problems in the United States occasioned increased demands on the federal government to deal with those problems. As a consequence, that nation's era of local governmental control over solid waste management came to a close. Both environmentalists and business interests pressed for a nationwide approach to regulating solid waste management: environmentalists because ecological problems do not recognize political boundaries; businesses because a national regulation regime means that they do not have to deal with 50 varieties of regulations.

Imposing its preferred solid waste management standards on state and local governments through a form of action that has been labeled "partial preemption," the U.S. Congress (mostly through the Resource Conservation and Recovery Act) and the Environmental Protection Agency have established guidelines that serve as minimum criteria for state action. States have been pressured into developing state solid waste management plans that meet federal criteria, and local governments have been instructed by states to develop plans that fit within the standards and guidelines of the state plans.

Providing a further impetus for federalization of solid waste management, the U.S. Supreme Court made a string of decisions that restricted the potential for local or state control. In 1978, the court ruled in *Philadelphia v. New Jersey* that garbage was to be treated like any other commodity under the U.S. Constitution's interstate commerce clause. In related cases in the 1990s, the court further ruled that the interstate commerce clause does not allow local and state governments to prohibit transportation of solid waste into or out of their jurisdictions or to charge more for disposal of waste generated outside of their jurisdictions.

Another, more subtle, but very powerful force that increased the need for national regulation of solid waste management was the increasing size and reach of private-sector solid waste management organizations and operations. Because more stringent environmental standards significantly increased the per volume unit cost of landfills, economies of scale led to development of large regional landfills that exceeded the financial and legal reach of local governments. Operating within those standards requires considerable and very specialized expertise, so governments often must contract with private companies to provide the needed experts.

Increasing dependency upon private companies meant that governments had less leverage in enforcing regulations on those same companies. As the twentieth century came to a close, solid waste management continued to be conducted by public, private, and/or nonprofit organizations. But as is true in many public-service administration areas, the trend was toward placing management of daily operations in the hands of private or nonprofit contractors.

Finally, in the twenty-first century, it will become increasingly necessary for solid waste management to attend not only to reuse, recycling, reduction, and disposal issues, but also to measures that avoid the generation of waste. European nations have progressed farther in this direction than most of the rest of the world, but as industrial development spreads, the need to forestall waste generation will escalate dramatically.

LARRY S. LUTON

BIBLIOGRAPHY

Blumberg, Louis, and Robert Gottlieb, 1989. *War on Waste: Can America Win Its Battle with Garbage?* Washington, DC: Island Press.
Luton, Larry S., 1996. *The Politics of Garbage: A Community Perspective on Solid Waste Policy-Making.* Pittsburgh: University of Pittsburgh Press.
Melosi, Martin V., 1981. *Garbage in the Cities: Refuse, Reform, and the Environment, 1880–1980.* Chicago, IL: Dorsey Press.
Rathje, William, and Cullen Murphy, 1992. *Rubbish! The Archeology of Garbage.* New York: HarperCollins.
Small, William E., 1970. *Third Pollution: The National Problem of Solid Waste Disposal.* New York: Praeger.

SOVEREIGN IMMUNITY. Exemption from being sued without consent, conferred upon the state, its government or agencies. This immunity is also granted to foreign states and their instrumentalities; but the extent of immunity protection and the range of protected entities have changed over time at the domestic and the international levels.

Domestic Sovereign Immunity

For nearly two centuries, U.S. courts used sovereign immunity to prevent liability suits against the federal and state governments. This practice, interestingly, was not initiated by legislative enactment but was simply inherited from English common law.

Sovereignty was a well-established concept, first developed by the French political theorist Jean Bodin in 1576 as a principle of internal order. A state must have a ruler enjoying unquestioned authority. However, the king's sovereignty in Bodin's thought was not arbitrary or unlimited. It was circumscribed by the rule of reason (understood at the time as a part of divine law) and by what we would call today constitutional law. It was later made absolute by the actual development of monarchical supremacy and theoretical reformulation by Thomas Hobbes, the English philosopher, in 1651. The king became unchallengeable, literally above the law.

Of course, it is ironic that the U.S. legal system readily accepted the judicial doctrine of sovereign immunity despite the dominant concern of keeping governmental power in check under the rule of law. Sovereign immunity is a formula for evading accountability. Government agencies are thus protected from legitimate civil damage claims, and the persons hurt by government action, even when blatantly malicious, are deprived of their judicial means of redress. How can such an unjust doctrine be defended in a rule of law system when, as Kenneth Warren (1996) emphasized, it places the government above the law (p. 465)? This reveals a fundamental clash between two concerns: the rights of individuals to be protected by the rule of law and the pragmatic need to govern with reasonable expeditiousness and efficacy.

It has been argued that the government and its agencies must be protected from the threat of liability suits so that they may remain effective. Lawsuits have a disruptive effect and may lead to excessive caution. Government agencies must be allowed to function even at the cost of letting some private individuals suffer injustice (see **absolute immunity**). The state's interest must come before private interest.

Democratic thought endeavored to balance the need to govern and the rights of the governed. Progressively, pressure mounted to curb sovereign immunity and its tendency to protect irresponsible administrative performance and to endanger the constitutional due-process rights of private individuals. As the Supreme Court put it in *U.S. v. Lee* (1882), "courts of justice are established, not only to decide upon controverted rights of the citizens as against each other, but also upon rights in controversy between them and the government" (106 U.S. 196). There was a need to restore this important function.

Remedial action began in the form of legislation to curtail sovereign immunity under specific circumstances, for example, with the Tucker Act of 1855 conferring jurisdiction on United States District Courts to hear claims against the United States involving contracts, and the Federal Tort Claims Act of 1946, which allowed, under certain circumstances, suits against the U.S. government for tortious acts committed by its officials. The act, however, preserves governmental immunity with respect to international torts and with respect to acts or omissions that fall within the discretionary function of any federal agency or employee. In 1976, Congress amended Sections 702 and 703 of the Administrative Procedure Act for the purpose of allowing the U.S. government to be sued for relief other than money damages (with some qualifications).

Much has also happened at the state and local levels. In the last three decades, statutes have been enacted providing for waivers of sovereign immunity, some fairly cautious as in Utah and California, others comprehensive as in Washington or New York, the latter specifying, for instance, that "the state hereby waives its immunity from liability . . . and consents to have the same determined in accordance with the same rules of law as applied to actions . . . against individuals or corporations" (N.Y. Court of Claims Act, Section 8).

Even more significant during this period is the "judicial attack on sovereign immunity," as Bernard Schwartz put it (p. 573). The landmark case is *Muskopf v. Corning Hospital District* (359 P.2d 458, 460, Cal. 1961), in which the California court declared that "the rule of governmental immunity from tort liability . . . must be discarded as mistaken and unjust." Sovereign immunity in tort "is an anachronism, without rational basis, and has existed only by the force of inertia." In increasing numbers and to varying extents, state courts have abandoned the doctrine of sovereign immunity from tort liability.

In 1978, the U.S. Supreme Court held in *Monell v. Department of Social Services of New York* that local governments can be sued directly under the Civil Rights Act of 1871, Section 1983, for monetary and other specified types of relief, under stated circumstances, thus reversing its position on the issue. The Eleventh Amendment to the U.S. Constitution, however, grants to states sovereign immunity from certain suits in federal courts.

Another kind of immunity came to supplement and in some cases to replace, sovereign immunity, namely, public officer (or official) immunity, the result of a reversal of the common law doctrine of personal liability of government personnel for their acts even if performed in the course of their official functions (see **official immunity**). Judges had always been granted immunity as an exception to the strict common law rule of officer liability for the sake of ensuring their unimpeded freedom of decision and protecting them from any apprehension of personal consequences. The Supreme Court in *Spalding v. Vilas* (1896) extended this privilege to heads of executive departments using a similar rationale: In exercising their functions, they should not fear the possibility of a civil suit for damages. Furthermore, in 1949, the court in *Larson v. Domestic and Foreign Commerce Corp.* ruled that suits against public officials should in most cases be disallowed because they are protected by the government's sovereign immunity. A suit against a government officer is essentially a suit against the government over which the court, in the absence of consent, has no jurisdiction. Official immunity was thus presented as an offshoot of sovereign immunity. In 1959, the Supreme Court in *Barr v. Matteo* extended absolute immunity to virtually all administrative officials.

It is not surprising that absolute official immunity came to be attacked for the same reasons given with regard to the sovereign immunity of governmental agencies. Public officials should not be above the law. At a time when administrative institutions play such a pervasive role in society, citizens need some protection from public officials, particularly when the latter are acting maliciously or in bad faith. The courts eventually retreated and a more equitable doctrine emerged (see **qualified immunity**).

The British administrative law system has moved away from sovereign immunity sooner and more thoroughly than the United States. The liability of the British government to ordinary civil actions is now substantially comparable to that of an ordinary litigant (although Parliament remains absolutely sovereign; except for European Union law, it is beyond legal control). Government liability was formally established by the Crown Proceedings Act of 1947. But, long before that, it was admitted that the government should accept ordinary civil liability, and effective procedures were devised to bring cases before the courts and to avoid injustice. In tort, the British government and its officers can still sometimes remain outside the law for acts performed abroad; but there is pressure to keep this area as narrow as possible. It is interesting to note that developments in the European Union and decisions by the European Court have opened up a wide new area of government liability. Breach of European Union obligations may make a national government belonging to this legal framework liable to pay compensation or damages.

The French administrative law system began abandoning sovereign immunity following the Revolution (1789). But it was in 1873, with the Blanco Case, that the general principle of state liability was established beyond question. The French system has become perhaps the most important model for administrative jurisprudence in the modern world having influenced not only countries once in its own widespread colonial establishment, but also continental Europe and a large number of countries that simply opted for something akin to the French judicial institutions.

Foreign Sovereign Immunity

The doctrine of sovereign immunity still provides extensive protection to a large number of foreign entities: sovereign states, heads of state, governments, high government officials, state property, state instrumentalities, armed forces, and various classes of diplomatic personnel. Originally, under customary international law, these entities enjoyed sovereign immunity regardless of the nature of their activities, even when fraudulent or malicious. This doctrine was based on the notion that all states are equal and absolutely sovereign. No state could therefore exercise authority over any other state without its consent.

The classic formulation of this doctrine was given by Chief Justice John Marshall in *The Schooner Exchange v. McFaddon* (1812).

> One sovereign being in no respect amenable to another; and being bound by obligations of the highest character not to degrade the dignity of his nation, by placing himself or its sovereign rights within the jurisdiction of another, can be supposed to enter a foreign territory only . . . in the confidence that the immunities belonging to his independent sovereign station, though not expressly stipulated, are reserved by implication, and shall be extended to him" (11 U.S. 116).

In this case, even if the vessel had in fact been wrongfully appropriated from its American owners (as they contended), being now in the hands of a foreign state and a unit of its navy, the court ruled that the vessel was entitled to sovereign immunity.

Foreign armed forces remain, to this day, protected by the doctrine of sovereign immunity when they are peaceably received by a foreign state, for instance, warships visiting a foreign port. The Panama Supreme Court stated in the Schwartzfiger Case (1925) that "it is a principle of international law that the armed forces of one state, when crossing the territory of another friendly country, with the acquiescence of the latter, is not subject to the jurisdiction of the territorial sovereign but to that of the officers and superior authorities of its own command" (24 Panama, Registro Judicial, 772). Neither the armed force concerned, nor the state of the force may be sued in the courts of the host state without its consent.

Following World War II, however, many military units were stationed abroad for indefinite periods of time under the provisions of a number of collective defense arrangements, such as The North Atlantic Treaty Organization (NATO). Troops stationed abroad tend to generate local friction (culture clashes, damage caused by members of the force, etc.), inevitably made worse by the sovereign immunity of the units concerned. To alleviate the problem, states involved negotiated status of forces agreements modifying the immunity of the foreign force. In the absence of such an agreement, sovereign immunity remains absolute.

Foreign state property is similarly protected by sovereign immunity, but this is now subject to significant qualifications. In the 1920s, a large-scale expansion of state commercial activity by means of state enterprises of all kinds brought sovereign immunity under sharp attack. When a state concern conducts business operations with private corporations, is it fair to protect it from court action when its private counterparts can be sued under similar circumstances? Numerous decisions in national courts and national statutes soon began to reject this kind of immunity. Today, states, their property and instrumentalities are no longer protected by international law when engaged in commerce as ordinary entrepreneurs. However, it must be acknowledged that there is a grey area in which the commercial and public character of some institutions are intertwined. In *Dunlap v. Banco Central del Ecuador* (Sup. Ct., New York County, 1943), immunity was granted because of public functions in procurement of coins for the national currency, although the Ecuadorean government had only five-elevenths ownership in the corporation.

Diplomatic representatives, from the time of classical antiquity, have enjoyed immunity. This privilege was rooted in the status of the sovereign state they represented, and, undoubtedly there was also an element of practicality since inviolability enabled them to carry out their mission. The object of which was frequently politically sensitive. For the greater part of its history, diplomatic immunity was governed by customary international law; however, the dramatic changes taking place in world affairs following World War II led to revision by means of several conventions negotiated under the auspices of the United Nations (UN). To a large extent, diplomatic institutions remain under the protection of sovereign immunity. The premises of diplomatic missions, their furnishings, archives, documents, official correspondence, are all inviolable; so are the private residences of diplomatic agents and the members of their families forming part of their households. Members of diplomatic missions, however, are now divided into several categories, with a gradation of immunity. Members having diplomatic rank enjoy extensive immunity, including protection from civil and administrative jurisdiction except in cases involving private immovable property not used for the purposes of the mission; matters of succession in which the diplomat is not acting for the sending state; or, finally, commercial activity outside the diplomat's official functions. These are new but rather circumscribed restrictions. Other categories of diplomatic personnel, including UN officials such as the UN secretary general, enjoy similar protection, but qualified in some respects; for example, their immunity does not extend to acts performed outside their official functions.

International law has thus moved away from unqualified sovereign immunity; but it must be noted that diplomatic institutions still enjoy the bulk of their traditional privileges, and the other categories of foreign immunity, such as armed forces and governments, remain extensively protected. The trend is toward a more functional approach in the development of international immunity law. New restrictions could be devised for the application of foreign sovereign immunity without any risk of disrupting the fabric of international relations. But most nation-states remain attached to their often far-fetched notions of sovereignty—a self-defeating proposition in an increasingly interdependent global society. National pride and parochialism, as well as mutual distrust and antagonism are likely to prevent for the foreseeable future a substantial curtailment of sovereign immunity comparable to what has been achieved with regard to domestic institutions.

JEAN-ROBERT LEGUEY-FEILLEUX

BIBLIOGRAPHY

Brown, L. Neville, and John S. Bell, 1993. *French Administrative Law,* 4th ed. Oxford: Clarendon Press.

David, Kenneth Culp, and Richard J. Pierce, Jr., 1994. *Administrative Law Treatise,* 3d ed. Boston: Little, Brown.

Dellapenna, J. W., 1992. "Foreign State Immunity in Europe." *New York International Law Review,* vol. 5 (Summer) 51–62.

Donoghue, J. E., 1992. "Taking the 'Sovereign' out of the Foreign Sovereign Immunities Act: A Functional Approach to the Commercial Activity Exception." *Yale Journal of International Law,* vol. 17 (Summer) 489–538.

Greener, G. J., 1992. "The Commercial Exception to Foreign Sovereign Immunity: To Be Immune or Not to Be Immune? That Is the Question?" *Loyola of Los Angeles International and Comparative Law Journal,* vol. 1 (December) 173–202.

Henkin, Louis, Richard Crawford Pugh, Oscar Schachter, and Hans Smit, 1993. *International Law,* 3d ed. St. Paul, MN: West Publishing.

Krent, H. J., 1992. "Reconceptualizing Sovereign Immunity." *Vanderbilt Law Review,* vol. 4 (November) 1529–1580.

Schwartz, Bernard, 1994. *Administrative Law,* 4th ed. Boston: Little, Brown.

Wade, Sir William, and Christopher Forsyth, 1994. *[English] Administrative Law.* Oxford: Clarendon Press.

Warren, Kenneth F., 1996. *Administrative Law in the Political System,* 3d ed. Upper Saddle River, NJ: Prentice-Hall.

SPACE POLICY.

The course of actions taken by a society on whether and how to carry out activities in outer space. There is no legal definition of outer space. It is understood that outer space begins when the atmosphere of the Earth is too thin to affect significantly objects moving through it. Authorities vary in what they consider the beginning of outer space, ranging from 50 to 100 miles above the Earth to the solar system and beyond. A myriad of activities may be carried out in outer space (hereafter referred to as "space"). These include (1) space travel by humans for exploration, scientific studies, and construction and repair of spacecraft in orbit, (2) scientific studies by automated spacecraft of the Moon, the planets, the sun, other stars and interstellar space, as well as of the Earth viewed from space, (3) military applications, including monitoring of actions that could destabilize peace, (4) commercial applications, including communications by satellite and remote sensing of the Earth as an aid to agriculture, mining, transportation, and construction, among other activities, as well as other purposes, such as processing of materials in space to develop new products.

Space policy is concerned with whether and to what extent these activities should be carried out and the priority which one activity should have over another, given the limited resources that nations are willing to devote to space activities, as well as public-private relations in carrying out space activities.

This entry is concerned primarily with policy for civilian space activities. Since military space activities affect civil space policy, this entry refers to those military space activities or proposals that have an impact on civil space policy. No attempt is made to provide a comprehensive discussion of military space matters.

The end of the Cold War, huge national budget deficits, and the growing importance of space commerce have caused major changes in the political and economic context of space activities. Cooperation between the United States, Russia, and the Ukraine has replaced the rivalry of past decades and joint ventures among the United States, Canada, as well as European and Asian partners are becoming commonplace. Rapid advances in the technologies for satellite communications and remote sensing of the Earth from space are driving new commercial ventures. Concerns over the environment and global change, especially desertification, air and water pollution, crop disease, and the need for earlier warning of natural disasters have made space-based global monitoring a major focus.

Space policy is also concerned with the general objectives and specific goals that a society sets for itself in space activities. Should the prime objective be scientific, military, political, or commercial? Should specific goals include a large, crewed space station, a system of satellites to monitor the Earth's environment, human exploration of Mars, eventual achievement of human space settlement, a solar power satellite to beam energy to the Earth for use in homes and factories, or scientific missions for robotic spacecraft?

The most significant issues in space policy are the following: (1) What is the rationale for space flight? Should societies invest in space activities in view of other pressing needs? (2) If space activities are undertaken, what should be the balance between human (crewed) space flight and space flight by robotic (automated) spacecraft? (3) To what extent should military considerations influence civil space activities? (4) To what extent should space activities be carried out by individual nations or through international cooperation? (5) What is the impact of the changing relations between the public and private sectors? What space activities should be carried out by government and what activities by private enterprise? For each of these issues, fiscal stringency tends to rule out for the near term extremely expensive courses of action and impels policymakers to favor actions that involve expense sharing, such as joint civil-military projects and projects carried out by alliances of several nations.

Several nations and international and regional organizations build, launch, or operate space vehicles. The major spacefaring powers (see Tables I and II) are the United States, for which the National Aeronautics and Space Ad-

TABLE I. SUCCESSFUL LAUNCHES

	1990	91	92	93	94
Russia/CIS	75*	59*	54	47	48
USA	27	18	28	23	26
European Space Agency (ESA)	5	8	7	7	6
China	5	1	3	1	5
Japan	3	2	1	1	2
India	-	-	1	-	2
Israel	-	1	-	-	-

*Soviet Union

Note: Successful launches for the period 1957–1989 were as follows:
Soviet Union–2,180, USA–905, E.S.A.–30, China–23, Japan–38, India–3, Israel–1. Some launches placed two or more satellites in orbit.

SOURCE: Congressional Research Service.

TABLE II. ESTIMATED CIVIL SPACE EXPENDITURES FOR 1994

(in Millions of U.S. Dollars)	
USA	14,084*
Japan	2,102
ESA	3,594
China	180***
Russia/CIS	535**
India	300
Israel	6****

*NASA–13,584; other U.S. civil agencies–500.

**Expenditures totaled approximately $1 billion, including foreign participation. Because of steep inflation and deep discount of the ruble, this amount represents far more domestic purchasing power than its dollar equivalent in other space faring nations. The Soviet Union budget for civil space activities in 1990, according to Roger Bonnet and Vittorio Manno (1994) was US $5.23 billion (p. 68).

***1994 expenditure (latest available figure). Based on recent descriptions of the Chinese space program, it is estimated that expenditures for 1996 were substantially higher than in 1994.

****1994 expenditure (latest available figure). This figure does not include unspecified money for special projects such as satellite development. Based on recent descriptions of the Israeli space program, it is estimated that expenditures for 1996 were substantially higher than in 1994.

SOURCES: Ojalehto and Hertzfeld, 1997; *Space News*, and Congressional Research Service.

ministration (NASA) conducts nearly all civil space activity; Russia/Commonwealth of Independent States (CIS), for which the Russian Space Agency conducts most civil space programs (CIS is made up of former Soviet republics, which are now independent countries. These countries, through CIS, cooperate in space activities. Although Russia carries out most space activities, other CIS countries, particularly the Ukraine and Kazakhstan, conduct important space activities. One of the former Soviet launch sites is located in Kazakhstan, and the Ukraine produces rockets and spacecraft components.); the European Space Agency (ESA) composed of 14 nations of which France and Germany are the main financial contributors (the other members are Austria, Belgium, Denmark, Finland, Ireland, Italy, the Netherlands, Norway, Spain, Sweden, Switzerland, and the United Kingdom), as well as

Japan, China, and India. Israel builds, launches and operates its own satellites. Brazil builds satellites and is expected to launch a satellite in the near future. Several nations own and operate satellites but do not build and launch them. These nations include Indonesia and Mexico. Other nations are emerging as active space participants including Pakistan, South Korea, and Taiwan. Most of the members of ESA also have national space programs.

There are three global international organizations that own and operate fleets of communications satellites: INTELSAT, with 142 member nations, provides worldwide satellite communications for fixed receiving stations; INMARSAT, composed of 80 nations, provides maritime and land-based mobile communications; and Intersputnik, composed of 22 nations, provides satellite communication to many countries of the world. Several regional communications satellite organizations exist, including Arabsat, Asiasat, Eutelsat.

The United Nations Committee for the Peaceful Uses of Outer Space seeks to promote agreements to benefit the world's people and to reduce aggressive uses of space. Under the committee's auspices, several important treaties have been adopted by the United Nations, having been ratified by a sufficient number of nations to go into effect. These are as follows:

1. Treaty on Principles Governing the Activities of States in the Exploration and Use of Outer Space, including the Moon and Other Celestial Bodies (1967). This treaty declares that outer space, including the Moon and other celestial bodies, is not subject to national appropriation and that nuclear weapons or any other kinds of weapons of mass destruction shall not be placed in orbit or on celestial bodies.
2. Agreement on the Rescue of Astronauts, the Return of Astronauts, and the Return of Objects Launched into Outer Space (1968).
3. Convention on International Liability for Damage Caused by Space Objects (1972).
4. Convention on Registration of Objects Launched into Outer Space (1975).
   These treaties have been ratified by all major spacefaring nations.
5. Agreement Governing the Activities of States on the Moon and Other Celestial Bodies (1979). This agreement, in addition to affirming that the Moon and its natural resources are not subject to national appropriation, states that the Moon and its natural resources are the common heritage of mankind and that an international regime would be established to govern the exploitation of the natural resources of the Moon. Third-world and some other countries proposed this treaty as a way to ensure that benefits derived from the Moon would not be monopolized by private exploitation by citizens and corporations of technically

advanced nations. The international regime would regulate mining and other activities related to development of natural resources. The United States and other major space faring powers have not ratified this agreement. Opponents in the United States believe that the international regime would expropriate so much of the wealth that private investment might be thwarted or that a moratorium on space mining would be declared. Although this agreement has not been ratified by the major space powers, it has been ratified by a sufficient number of nations to be in effect.

The International Telecommunications Union (ITU), a specialized United Nations agency, assigns orbital locations and frequencies for communications satellites. Other UN agencies, particularly those concerned with development, endeavor to utilize the applications of space technology, especially in remote sensing, for aiding agriculture and regional planning.

Developing countries which do not engage in space activities, also have an important stake in space policy. They argue that since space and celestial bodies belong to all of the Earth's inhabitants, rather than to individual nations, benefits derived from space should be available to all nations on an equitable basis and not only to the industrialized nations that have dominated space activities. This point of view has led to discussions in the United Nations to grant future access to benefits to developing countries even though they are not yet prepared to engage in space activities.

Numerous private firms are engaged in space commerce, ranging from building launch vehicles and satellites to operation of satellites for communications and remote sensing, as well as providing various space-related services.

Origin and Subsequent History

The beginning of space policy coincided with the launch of *Sputnik* by the Soviet Union on October 4, 1957. This was the first artificial satellite to orbit the Earth. The world was startled by this feat. In the United States, the reaction was immediate and strong. In the context of the Cold War, the capability of the Soviets to loft a satellite weighing 90 kg (almost 200 pounds) was seen by many leaders in the United States as proof of the technological prowess of the Soviets. The successful launch on November 3, 1957, of *Sputnik II,* which weighed 504 kg (1,120 pounds) and carried a live dog, followed on May 15, 1958, by *Sputnik III,* which weighed 1,364 kg (over 3,000 pounds), made it clear that the Soviets had the rocket power and guidance knowledge to threaten the United States with intercontinental ballistic missiles equipped with nuclear warheads. Although the United States had launched its first two satellites in early 1958, each weighed less than 20 pounds. Space policy quickly had become entwined with foreign policy and military policy. Competition in space between the world's two superpowers was to remain the dominant theme in space policy until the collapse of the Soviet Union in 1991.

In a sense, the origins of space policy may be traced to the mid-1950s when the United States and the Soviet Union showed interest in using missile technology to launch satellites for military purposes, such as reconnaissance. In 1955, both nations announced intentions to launch scientific satellites as part of the International Geophysical Year (IGY, July 1957 to December 1958). President Dwight D. Eisenhower, wishing to emphasize that the United States would use space for peaceful purposes, directed that a rocket not based on missile technology–*Vanguard*–would launch the U.S. satellite for the IGY. When the first attempt to launch *Vanguard* in December 1957 failed, Eisenhower allowed the army to use its missile technology to place *Explorer I* in orbit in January 1958. The second *Vanguard* launching attempt succeeded in March 1958.

President Eisenhower, who was in office when the *Sputniks* were launched, refused to enter a full-fledged space race with the Soviets. He viewed the U.S. civil space program primarily as a scientific endeavor and also was concerned with the military potential of space, especially reconnaissance satellites. Eisenhower in 1960 rejected a NASA proposal for a human expedition to the Moon as too expensive. Human exploration should be carried out at a measured pace, according to his views, as funds allowed. President John F. Kennedy, however, intensified the rivalry by challenging the United States in May 1961 to send a man to the Moon and return him safely to Earth by the end of the decade. Kennedy's call was triggered by another Soviet feat. On April 12, 1961, the Soviets placed the first human, Yuri Gagarin, in orbit and returned him safely to Earth. Another factor was a need to shore up the prestige of the United States following the abortive, disastrous Bay of Pigs invasion of Cuba later in April by a group of Cuban exiles trained and financed by the United States.

Kennedy's challenge resulted in the Apollo program and set off a major debate as to whether the lion's share of NASA funds should be devoted to human space flight at the expense of robotic science missions. This controversy continues today.

NASA was led from 1961 to 1968 by James Webb. A dynamic administrator, Webb developed NASA's capacity to manage very large programs, integrating the efforts of government, industry, and universities. He resisted pressures to devote nearly all of NASA's resources to the Apollo project, insisting on a balance among human flight, science, and applications (see **Webb, James A.**).

Human space flight has been given priority for the resources of the U.S. civil space program, with from one-half to two-thirds of the total NASA budget going for expenses related to human space flight. Nevertheless, the science and applications programs in NASA have been vigorous, with many impressive missions to the planets and major accomplishments in astronomy as well as technological breakthroughs in communications and weather and Earth-monitoring satellites. Space science historically has received approximately 20 percent of the total NASA budget, due mainly to the efforts of the scientific community and its advocates in Congress. Although a minor share of the civil space budget, the amount provided annually for space science in the NASA budgets has been roughly equal to the total provided yearly for all physical science disciplines in the U.S. National Science Foundation budgets.

Currently, space science funding is under great pressure due to the drive to balance the U.S. budget and reduce the deficit and the costs of the U.S. space shuttle and the international space station. In 1996, space science received approximately 14 percent of the NASA budget. It is expected that the NASA budget will be level or cut significantly in the next seveal years.

Throughout the 1960s, 1970s, and 1980s, the military dimensions of space activity expanded rapidly in both the United States and the Soviet Union. In the United States, civil and military programs are largely separate from each other. The separation was established in the National Aeronautics and Space Act of 1958, which created NASA. President Eisenhower was a strong advocate for an independent civil space agency. This was consistent with his fear that the United States could be dominated by a "military industrial complex." Since 1981, U.S. military spending for space has matched or exceeded that for civil space activity.

In the Soviet Union, no distinction was made between civil and military space programs until 1985 with many projects such as launch vehicle development, Earth observing, and communications satellites geared to both civil and military aims. The Soviet space science program was vigorous throughout the 1960s, 1970s, and 1980s, especially in exploration of Venus, Mars, and the Moon.

During the 1960s, there was a space race between the United States and the Soviets, especially in human flight. The United States clearly won the race when on July 20, 1969, U.S. astronauts Neil Armstrong and Edwin "Buzz" Aldrin landed on the moon. Although the Soviets failed to match this accomplishment, they scored many firsts for robotic exploration and began a series of flights in 1971 that placed cosmonauts in orbit aboard space stations. The most recent space station, *Mir*, was launched in 1986. *Mir* was still operating as of mid-1997, although it has had serious operational problems. *Mir* has completed more than 60,000 orbits, with over 50 cosmonauts and researchers having been on board. More than 40 extra vehicular activities (EVA) or space walks have been carried out from *Mir*. In March 1995, *Mir* Cosmonaut Valery Polyakov established the world record for human endurance in orbit–437

days and 18 hours. As a result of these efforts, the Russian/CIS space program, which succeeded the Soviet space effort, has far more experience in long-duration flight and associated life sciences than the United States.

The Russian/CIS space effort has continued most of the Soviet space plans and maintains a broad range of space activities, despite severe financial problems. In 1996, 25 successful launches were carried out by the Russian/CIS space program.

Following the exhilaration of the lunar landing, the U.S. civil space program lost momentum. Even before the Moon landing, funding for NASA had been cut due to competing fiscal demands of the Vietnam War and measures to alleviate domestic poverty. By the mid-1970s, the NASA budget in real dollar terms had been cut in half compared to its zenith of the mid-1960s. U.S. astronauts made additional landings on the Moon until 1972, after which Apollo was cancelled. A U.S. space station, *Skylab*, launched in 1973, hosted crews in 1973 and 1974 and remained in orbit until 1979. Astronauts conducted many experiments in this orbital workshop.

In 1969, a Space Task Group chaired by U.S. Vice President Spiro Agnew presented options for future bold undertakings, starting with a reusable launch vehicle and a permanently occupied space station and leading to human missions to Mars. The White House and many members of Congress dismissed the station and manned exploration possibilities as much too ambitious and expensive. NASA was then forced to choose among the options, settling on the space shuttle, which would launch satellites and conduct science and engineering experiments in space. (The shuttle is a reusable vehicle for taking people and cargo into space. It takes off like a rocket and lands like an airplane.) President Richard Nixon approved the shuttle in 1972 with one of the considerations for this action being the jobs that would be generated in California, a crucial state in the upcoming presidential election. To get approval, however, NASA had to strike bargains with both the Office of Management and Budget and the military; NASA agreed to develop the shuttle system at half the originally estimated cost and to make changes in payload size and weight and cross-range capabilities desired by the Department of Defense. Also, the shuttle had to be "cost beneficial" by launching often–25 or more times a year–to get enough launch business to pay for itself. To make this possible, the United States would phase out expendable launch vehicles (ELVs), leaving the shuttle as the sole launcher for civil, military, and commercial payloads.

It was soon evident that the shuttle could not live up to these promises. Technical problems plagued the project while cost overruns forced NASA to skimp on design and testing procedures which could add margins of safety. Due to loss of national interest in expanded space activities, NASA budgets were reduced. This cutback combined with high shuttle costs led to fiscal conditions that could not accommodate all planned activities. NASA scaled back plans for space science missions causing renewed criticism of the priority given to human flight. James Van Allen, the famed discoverer of the radiation belts that bear his name, termed this situation "the slaughter of the innocents." (Van Allen 1986, p. 37)

The shuttle flew successfully from 1981 to 1985 although postflight reviews indicated problems with the shuttle rocket booster seals, or "O-rings." On the eve of the *Challenger* space shuttle flight scheduled for January 28, 1986, NASA officials and officials of Morton-Thiokol Company, the shuttle rocket booster contractor, ignored the warnings of engineering experts from Morton-Thiokol not to launch the *Challenger* in cold weather due to a problem with the O-rings. The *Challenger* explosion killed all seven crew members, shattered NASA's reputation for technical and managerial excellence, and caused a nearly three-year hiatus in shuttle flights.

The investigation of the *Challenger* disaster concluded that while the failure of the O-rings was the immediate cause of the accident, serious management failures contributed to the conditions that led to technological failure. The Rogers Commission (named after its chair, former Secretary of State William Rogers) found that NASA's "dual" reporting chains for shuttle program management and for launch decisionmaking allowed officials to avoid communicating vital information about dangerous conditions in the Shuttle's booster engines to top echelons of NASA and that NASA management had neglected the agency's safety program. (For a discussion of accountability for the *Challenger* disaster, see Romzek and Dubnick 1987).

The 1980s were an active period for both the U.S. and Soviet space programs. In addition, ESA drafted ambitious plans, designed to make the Europeans less dependent on the United States, especially in launching capabilities. Significant activities marked the space programs of China and Japan. Both civil and military space programs accelerated in the United States. In 1984, President Ronald Reagan authorized the development of a permanently occupied space station in partnership with Canada, ESA and Japan. President Reagan in 1983 announced that the United States would develop a system to intercept enemy missiles, called the Strategic Defense Initiative (SDI). Since some concepts of SDI included space-based defenses, SDI also became known as "Star Wars." The announcement drew criticism from the Soviets, who claimed that the system could also be used for aggressive acts, and from critics in the United States, who said that SDI would destabilize peace and would be prohibitively expensive. Many scientists claimed that SDI would not work.

The Reagan administration also advocated rapid commercialization of space activities, particularly of the U.S. land remote-sensing satellites, Landsat. Reagan also continued the earlier policy whereby the space shuttle would launch commercial satellites. Accordingly, all U.S. payloads, civil, commercial, and military, would be launched by the shuttle, with U.S. expendable launchers phased out. Meanwhile, ESA was developing the *Ariane* launch vehicle, which was capable of launching large and medium satellites to geosynchronous orbit. *Ariane* began to capture significant market share for launches. *Ariane's* business increased as a result of the discontinuing of commercial launches on the shuttle after the 1986 *Challenger* explosion. For the past decade, *Ariane* has dominated the market for launches of medium and large communications satellites. Currently, competitors are increasing their market share, challenging *Ariane's* lead.

The 1990s have witnessed a scaling back of plans for space programs worldwide. The growing budget deficit in the United States has put pressure on NASA. The collapse of the Soviet Union in 1991 led to a reduction of space activities in the former Soviet republics, although the Russian/CIS space program remains surprisingly vigorous despite serious financial problems. ESA has had to give up its plans for autonomy due to serious economic problems in Europe. China and Japan have continued their space efforts, with little or no cutbacks. India's space program has retained its momentum. Israel continues to engage in vigorous space activities.

In December 1990, a presidential committee, chaired by Norman Augustine, chief executive officer of the large aerospace firm Martin Marietta (now Lockheed-Martin), recommended that NASA give more emphasis to science, gradually phase out the space shuttle in favor of an advanced expendable launcher, and move forward on a system of satellites to study the Earth's environment called "Mission to Planet Earth." More smaller science missions were also recommended. The space station program was also endorsed. Administrative and organizational changes to strengthen NASA headquarters and reduce overlap among NASA field centers were recommended. The committee, realizing that its prescriptions would be costly, assumed an annual 10 percent increase in the NASA budget.

But fiscal realities soon made it clear that NASA would have to reduce spending. In 1992, President George Bush appointed Daniel Goldin, an aerospace executive, to head NASA, and President Bill Clinton, upon taking office, retained him. Goldin seeks to remake NASA. Science missions must be smaller, faster, and cheaper, and staff and facilities must be trimmed. Accordingly, NASA has cancelled or reduced major projects. The space station has survived in reduced form and Russia became a partner in the project. In 1995, Goldin and many congressional critics called for a major restructuring of NASA, including consideration of privatizing some of its major activities and field centers.

Leadership and Space Policy

The critical element in shaping space policy has been national leadership. President Eisenhower (1953–1961) presided over the creation of NASA, insisting that a civilian agency, independent of the military, lead all non-defense space efforts. He favored a cautious, step-by-step program. President Kennedy (1961–1963) was a strong proponent of a vigorous civil space effort. Kennedy launched the Apollo program for a human Moon landing. President Lyndon B. Johnson (1963–1969) was also a strong supporter, but scaled back NASA due to fiscal constraints caused by the costs of the Vietnam war and domestic antipoverty programs. President Nixon (1969–1974) authorized the space shuttle but did little to assure that the program received adequate funding. President Gerald Ford (1974–1977) essentially continued Nixon's stewardship. President Jimmy Carter (1977–1981) called for a moderate program, emphasizing applications, such as remote sensing. President Reagan (1981–1989) authorized the international space station project and the Strategic Defense Initiative (SDI). President Bush (1989–1993) endorsed a human return to the Moon and human missions to Mars and an environmental Earth-monitoring program (Mission to Planet Earth) but did not press for the funds or the political priority needed to implement the exploration proposals. President Clinton (1993–present), reacting to large cost overruns in the space station program, scaled it back and made Russia one of the partners.

Soviet premiers have been strong advocates of space efforts, both military and scientific, as has President Boris Yeltsin of Russia, despite severe fiscal problems.

European leaders, especially those of France, Germany, and Italy, have been strong advocates for their national space activities, as well as for the ESA programs. However, the United Kingdom has deemphasized space as a national priority. Recently, European leaders, especially in France and Germany, have raised concerns over the extent and cost of ESA programs, particularly ESA participation in the International Space Station. The European Union has shown interest in shaping some aspects of space policy, positioning itself as a rival to ESA in this regard.

Japan's leaders have supported that nation's comprehensive space programs consistently. Leaders of China have been strong supporters of space development, especially for launch vehicles. India's leaders have championed a broad space effort. Israel continues a strong space program.

Analyses of Policy Issues

This section provides brief analysis of the five policy issues identified at the beginning of this entry. Space policy is closely intertwined with other policy areas, particularly foreign policy, military policy, science and technology policy, and economic policy. For example, the Apollo decision dealt with foreign policy and the U.S. national interest. (For a discussion of the foreign policy and national interest issues in the Apollo decision, see Logsdon 1970.) Budgetary and military considerations influenced decisions on the design and utilization of the space shuttle. The International Space Station program involves a potential conflict between space policy and foreign policy. (This conflict is identified and discussed in Smith 1994, pp. 10, 11, 126, 127.) The Clinton administration included Russia as a full space station partner in part to achieve the foreign policy objective of controlling dissemination of ballistic missile technology. The United States made it clear that unless Russia modified an agreement with India for sale of rocket engine technology so that sensitive technology would not be transferred, Russia would not become a partner in the space station, nor would it be allowed to compete for commercial launch services. Russia agreed to this condition and the United States agreed to pay Russia US $400 million for space cooperation, the same amount that Russia said it would lose by modifying its agreement with India. But partnership with Russia could jeopardize the station program by making station construction and operations dependent on Russian spacecraft, hardware, and supply flights at a time when there is severe political and fiscal instability in that nation.

Should a Society Invest in Space Activities?

This question has been debated since the beginning of the space age. During the first three decades of space activity, the excitement generated by space feats and the competition between the United States and the Soviets provided impetus for proponents of new space projects. Their arguments include the value of space exploration to increasing human knowledge and to pave the way for space settlements, the exhilaration of the human spirit that comes with great accomplishments, the pride and prestige a society can gain by demonstrating technological leadership, and the practical benefits realized from satellite applications.

Those against continuing significant investments in space activity argue that, with the Cold War over, the major reasons for space flight–gaining technological, military, and propaganda advantage over a rival power–no longer exist. With fiscal resources stretched to the limit, societies should call a halt to expensive new space projects, they argue.

Balance Between Human Space Flight and Robotic Missions

Although the first spacecraft did not carry crews, human spaceflight has been the major factor in stimulating public and political support for space programs. But there has also been a keen interest in robotic science missions, especially those to the planets.

Proponents of crewed flights argue that there is no substitute for human presence and judgment in space; they point to the unique views that astronauts and cosmonauts bring to their impressions of Earth as seen from space. In addition, humans have successfully repaired satellites in orbit and are providing invaluable experience in life sciences. Also they provide positive role models for youth and generate interest in careers in science and technology. The expectation that eventually people will move off Earth to inhabit the Moon, asteroids, and perhaps even Mars or Venus (if the environment of these planets could be made more Earth-like) underpins much of the interest among some of the advocates in pursuing human space flight (for a discussion of such expectations, see Sagan 1994).

Those who would give significantly less emphasis to human missions argue that robotic flights account for nearly all of the "real" benefits from space activities. They point to communications, weather and remote-sensing satellites, and to knowledge gained from automated missions to the planets, as well as astrophysics missions such as the Hubble Space Telescope. They argue that all this has been accomplished at a fraction of the cost of human space flight. Why expose people to great risks on very expensive missions that societies can ill afford?

Impact of Military Activities on Civil Space Policy

Military space activities have always been significant in nearly all spacefaring nations and have had considerable influence on civil space policy. With the end of the Cold War, the role of military space has been called into question. Those who argue for strong military programs point out that since many nations have the capacity to launch missile attacks, there is a need for systems to detect, intercept, and destroy hostile missiles and to continually update military observation and communications satellites. They point to the vital role that satellites played in the 1991 Persian Gulf War. In addition, they argue that since many military and civil space activities are similar (launches, communications, weather predictions, Earth observations and navigation), programs should be jointly conducted. Since the military has vast experience in conducting large-scale technological programs, it should have a major role in setting policy and managing such joint efforts, they argue.

Those who want to limit military influences on civil space fear that space would become irreversibly militarized if the armed services are permitted to help determine civil policy and management. This could increase world tensions, negate the positive influences of international cooperation, and give new impetus to developing weapons that could be deployed in space. From their point of view, military space capabilities for surveillance, reconnaissance, and communications would best be utilized for enhancing post–Cold War security through multilateral cooperation among nations already possessing military space programs or planning to develop them.

International Cooperation

Many large-scale space activities and even smaller projects are carried out by cooperative efforts of several nations. The arguments for such arrangements are that cooperation takes advantage of multiple national capabilities, reduces costs through burden sharing, and increases scientific interchange and international understanding.

Those who argue for greater emphasis on national projects say that a nation should not become dependent on others and that cooperation inevitably leads to sharing sensitive military or proprietary technology. In addition, opponents point out that cooperation may lead to greater costs and delays since accommodations in design and operations must be made to satisfy the needs of the various partners. They also point out that managing international projects is highly complex, calling for major commitments of expertise and resources by the nations leading international efforts.

Experience with the International Space Station indicates that both sides have points supporting their positions. Cooperation has led to a spirit of joint enterprise but in some instances has caused increased costs and friction among the partners over design, operational, and administrative issues. For example, a study by the U.S. General Accounting Office concluded that U.S.-Russian cooperation on the space station would increase some project costs.

Public-Private

Political trends in nearly all spacefaring nations favor a greater role for the private sector in activities formerly carried out by government. This tendency has become important in space activities, especially with the ascendancy of the Republican party in the U.S. Congress, the push for a market economy in Russia, and actions to privatize government activities in Europe and Asia. Proponents of greater private roles argue that firms can carry out many space activities more efficiently and effectively than governments. Further, private participation would lift cost burdens from national budgets, stimulate economies, and promote competition, they argue.

Those calling for caution argue that space is so closely related to foreign policy and military issues that to allow the private sector to be a major player in determining the nature and extent of space activities would abdicate government's proper role in safeguarding national security and economic well-being. Further, they point out that breakthroughs in space technology have resulted from government research and development programs considered too risky by the private sector. This was the case for satellite communications, weather and remote-sensing satellites, and launch vehicles. In addition, they question whether privatization would actually save money in view of experience with cost overruns by contractors for aerospace projects.

Administrative Considerations

Administration of space activities is crucial for achieving efficient and cost-effective space missions. The major administrative elements for space programs are (1) planning for goals that can gain political and public support; (2) budgeting that supports plans and programs in both the near and long terms; (3) organizational structure that strikes a balance between centralization and decentralization (headquarters-field relationships) and among structure by place, purpose, or clientele. Most space agencies such as NASA or ESA are organized by "space as a place," that is, the activities carried out in space essentially define the agency's reason for existence. A space agency may also be part of a "purpose" department such as one promoting commerce or a department of science. Other arrangements that have been suggested to facilitate fund-raising for capital expenditures are government corporations or authorities or public-private partnerships; (4) organizational cul-

ture that motivates staff to achieve the specific as well as generalized goals of the organization (for a discussion of organizational culture in NASA, see McCurdy 1993); (5) organizational communication that effectively informs administrators and technical personnel at all organizational levels and nationals of different countries in international projects; (6) funding cycles appropriate to long lead times and complexity of space programs such as multiyear funding; (7) personnel systems–for recruiting and retaining highly qualified staff in contrast to the inflexibility of civil service systems; (8) procurement systems–emphasizing the need for competitive contracting; (9) public relations to garner public support and understanding.

In view of the current trends in space policy and the need to reduce space program costs, the most significant issues in administration of space activities are as follows: (1) What institutional arrangements would facilitate cooperative relationships among nations for joint space projects and for confidence building among nations that space would not be used for aggression? (2) What organizational structure would be best for assuring that space science is protected from pressures to devote nearly all of the resources of a space program to human space flight?

MAJOR EVENTS SHAPING SPACE POLICY

October 1957	Soviet Union launches the world's first artificial satellite, *Sputnik I*.
April 1961	Soviet Union places the first human in orbit (Yuri Gagarin) and returns him to Earth safely.
May 1961	President John F. Kennedy announces the goal of landing a U.S. astronaut on the Moon and returning him safely within the decade–Project Apollo.
June 1963	First woman to fly in space, Valentina Tereshovka, carried aloft on Soviet three-day mission.
July 1969	U.S. astronauts Neil Armstrong and Edwin E. "Buzz" Aldrin land on the Moon. A third astronaut, Michael Collins, orbits the moon in Apollo capsule. United States wins race to the Moon with Soviets.
April 1971	Soviets launch first in a series of space stations.
January 1972	President Richard Nixon authorizes development of U.S. space shuttle.
May 1973	United States launches space station, *Skylab*.
March 1983	President Ronald Reagan announces U.S. plans for a Strategic Defense Initiative (SDI, also known as "Star Wars").
January 1984	President Ronald Reagan authorizes development of U.S. space station with international partners.
January 1986	Space shuttle *Challenger* explodes, killing all seven crew members.
December 1991	Collapse of the Soviet Union–end of Cold War.
1982–1993	Europe takes lead in commercial space launches with *Ariane* launch vehicle capturing the largest share of the market for medium and heavy satellite launches. French "Spot," remote-sensing satellite, captures significant market share for commercial remote-sensing data.
1993	President Bill Clinton creates Ballistic Missile Defense Organization to replace SDI and scales back antimissile defense program.
1993	President Bill Clinton orders yet another redesign of space station to reduce cost and scope. Invites Russians to become partner in space-station program.
February 1994	First Russian cosmonaut ever launched on a U.S. spacecraft: Sergei Krikalev flies on U.S. space shuttle.
February 1995	Space shuttle and Russian *Mir* space station rendezvous in space in first practice session for joint U.S.-Russian assembly of space station in orbit.
March 1995	Norman Thagard becomes first U.S. astronaut to ride on Russian rocket on flight to dock with *Mir* space station.
March 1995	*Mir* cosmonaut Valery Polyakov sets world record 437 days and 18 hours in orbit.
September 1996	U.S. astronaut Sharon Lucid sets a world endurance record for women in space–188 days aboard *Mir*.

(3) What measures can be taken to reduce the cost of space flight while maintaining quality and safety? (4) What institutional arrangements would best facilitate joint civil-military projects while ensuring the independence of civil space programs?

Future Prospects

The latter half of the 1990s and the early years of the twenty-first century will witness a vastly different picture of space activity. National and international cooperative space efforts will be constrained by factors of cost and relevance. The huge budget deficits of the large space-faring nations make it clear that the focus will be on cost-effectiveness. For robotic missions, this means smaller spacecraft, which can be planned and flown at a fast pace–3 to 5 years from early plans to launch–as contrasted to 10 to 20 years for large-scale missions conceived in the 1970s and 1980s. Those missions that must be large and complex, such as human exploration of Mars, will be international so that costs may be spread over the treasuries of many nations. In both types of endeavors–the smaller, faster, cheaper missions and the large, international ones–administration will be as crucial as science and technology to ensuring success. The special interests of groups, leaders, and nations will have to be reconciled and coordinated.

Commercial activity will intensify, particularly for satellites that enable personal communications systems, such as hand-held worldwide telephones–which will provide cheap, wireless communications to billions of people in China, India, and parts of Asia and Africa who have never even picked up a telephone.

Value-added companies will offer a plethora of services and information products that will translate satellite images into inexpensive and highly useful data for farmers, mineral explorers, and urban and regional planners. Traffic on land and sea will be guided, monitored, and controlled from space.

Space may also play a decisive role in warfare and hopefully in its prevention. The sad recent history of regional conflicts shows that the end of the Cold War does not mean the end of armed bloodshed. The Gulf War of 1991 clearly demonstrated that reconnaissance satellites can change the course of battle; but they can also facilitate confidence building among nations.

In the new context of accelerated space activities in all areas–science, exploration, commercial and military–it will be essential to have more international cooperation and better international organization both to achieve the benefits of space technology and to prevent harmful impacts. Space activities can and should be carried out for peaceful purposes and the benefit of humanity. Policy and administration should be shaped to achieve these ends.

ARTHUR L. LEVINE

BIBLIOGRAPHY

Bonnet, Roger M., and Vittorio Manno, 1994. *International Cooperation in Space: The Example of the European Space Agency.* Cambridge, MA: Harvard University Press.

Boutros-Ghali, Boutrous, 1994. "International Cooperation in Space for Security Enhancement." *Space Policy,* vol. 10 (November) 265–276.

Burrows, William E., 1986. *Deep Black: Space Espionage and National Security.* New York: Random House.

Byerly, Radford, ed., 1988. *Space Policy Reconsidered.* Boulder, CO: Westview.

———, 1992. *Space Policy Alternatives.* Boulder; CO: Westview.

Galloway, Eilene, 1983. "Law and Security in Outer Space: The Role of Congress in Space Law and Policy." *Journal of Space Law,* vol. 2 (Spring and Fall) 50.

Lambright, W. Henry, 1994. "Administrative Entrepreneurship and Space Technology: The Ups and Downs of 'Mission to Planet Earth'." *Public Administration Review,* vol. 54 (March-April) 97–104.

Levine, Arnold, 1982. *Managing NASA in the Apollo Era.* Washington, DC: NASA.

———, 1975. *The Future of the U.S. Space Program.* New York: Praeger.

———, ed. 1992. "Symposium: The Future of the U.S. Space Program: A Public Administration Critique." *Public Administration Review,* vol. 52 (March-April) 183–203.

Logsdon, John M., 1970. *The Decision to Go to the Moon: Project Apollo and the National Interest.* Cambridge: MIT Press.

———, 1986. "The Space Shuttle Program: A Policy Failure," *Science* 232: (May 30) 1099–1105.

Mack, Pamela, 1990. *Viewing the Earth: The Social Construction of the Landsat Satellite.* Cambridge: MIT Press.

McCurdy, Howard E., 1990. *The Space Station Decision: Incremental Politics and Technological Choice.* Baltimore, MD: Johns Hopkins University Press.

———, 1993. *Inside NASA: High Technology and Organizational Change.* Baltimore, MD: Johns Hopkins University Press.

McDougal, Walter, 1985. *The Heavens and the Earth: A Political History of the Space Age.* New York: Basic Books.

Murray, Bruce, 1989. *Journey into Space: The First Three Decades.* New York: Norton.

Ojalehto, George and Henry Hertzfeld, 1997. "Review of Space Program Budgets." *Aerospace America.* Forthcoming in 1997. (Advance copy furnished to author)

Report of the Presidential Commission on the Space Shuttle Challenger *Accident,* 1986. Washington, DC: U.S. Government Printing Office.

Romzek, Barbara S., and Melvin J. Dubnick, 1987. "Accountability in the Public Sector: Lessons from the *Challenger* Tragedy." *Public Administration Review,* vol. 47 (May-June) 227–238.

Sagan, Carl, 1994. *Pale Blue Dot: A Vision of the Human Future in Space.* New York: Random House.

Smith, Marcia S., 1994. *Space Activities of the United States, CIS, and Other Launching Countries/Organizations: 1957–1993* (CRS Report for Congress 94-347 SPR). Washington, DC: Congressional Research Service, Library of Congress.

———, 1995. *Space Activities of the Untied States, CIS, Other Launching Countries/organizations: 1957–1994* (CSR Report for Congress 95.873 SPR) Washington, D.C.: Congressional Research Services, Library of Congress.

Van Allen, James A., 1986. "Space Science, Technology and the Space Station." *Scientific American,* vol. 254, no. 1 (January)

Webb, James E., 1969. *Space Age Management.* New York: Columbia University Press.

SPECIAL DISTRICTS.
Distinct units of government, created to provide specific services to citizens.

Background

A wide variety of government entities can fall under the heading of special district because this definition is so broad. In fact, differences in definition have directly contributed to one of the major controversies surrounding special districts: How many are there? The U.S. Census Bureau (1994) called special districts "independent, special-purpose governmental units (other than school district governments) that exist as separate entities with substantial administrative and fiscal independence from general-purpose local governments" (p. 23). Many authors have tried to define special districts by what they are not. The Office of the California State Controller (1994), for example, defined them as "legally constituted governmental entities . . . that are neither cities, counties, redevelopment agencies or schools" (p. 2).

The following discussion will exclude strictly financial devices such as redevelopment agencies and benefit assessment districts. Because they are so numerous and have a unique status in law, the convention of excluding school districts from this analysis of special districts will also be observed.

Special districts can be formed to deliver a vast variety of services. Common examples of special districts include those formed for water, fire, road maintenance, mosquito abatement, electricity, airports, and sanitation. Special districts can range in size from a few acres in a city to thousands of square miles, crossing county and even state lines. Special districts can have the same governing powers as other local governments. They can contract, employ workers, and buy real property. Some can issue debt and some can charge fees for services. By virtue of their flexibility, in theory at least, special districts can localize the costs and benefits of specific public services. There are three important characteristics that help differentiate between the many types of special districts: whether they are dependent or independent; whether they are enterprise or nonenterprise funding based; and whether they are single-purpose or multipurpose.

An independent, or autonomous, special district is a self-governing entity, operating under a locally elected board of directors. An independent district will typically be created when residents or landowners want either increased service levels or entirely new services. The residents can form a special district to provide the services they desire and tax themselves, through this device, to pay for the services. In most states, an independent special district can determine its own budget. It can levy taxes and collect charges without the review of other governments. In many cases, it can issue debt.

In contrast, dependent special districts are governments created by governments. They are usually governed by a city council or, more often, a county board of supervisors. In the latter case, the dependent district is typically administered by a board of commissioners, appointed by the governing body to oversee the day-to-day administration of the district. The commission also advises the governing body on such issues as personnel or budget matters. However, the governing body ultimately controls the administrative and financial capabilities of the dependent district.

Governments can create dependent districts for a variety of reasons. A dependent district can allow a county to earmark funds for services that are provided to a specific community. It can remove some revenues and expenses from the county's general operating budget. It can provide a city with the means of controlling services that are provided to areas beyond the city limits. A special form of dependent district called a Joint Powers Agreement, or Joint Powers Authority (JPA), can allow two or more governments to coproduce a service while retaining greater control than simple public-sector contracting would allow. JPAs can also be used to combine assets so that governments can secure better funding at more attractive rates.

Special districts can also be enterprise, nonenterprise, or both, depending upon their methods of financing. Broadly speaking, enterprise districts are typically able to charge fees for some or all of their activities. While nonenterprise districts may charge for some services, these charges are usually not a large percentage of their annual revenues. Function often helps to determine the appropriate classification. Sewage, garbage, and water are examples of enterprise services where a fee can be imposed directly upon the end user. Libraries, police, and fire protection are common examples of nonenterprise activities. It is also not unusual to find districts that are predominantly user-fee financed but which also receive funds from taxes and grants. Generally, if a district receives the preponderance of funds from fees, it is considered an enterprise district.

Public authorities are a common subset of the enterprise district classification. An authority is distinguished by its ability to issue revenue bonds to fund public projects. The bonds are then repaid by user fees once the project is complete. Port authorities, toll roads, and canals are common examples.

The difference between single-purpose and multipurpose districts is not as clear as the terms might indicate. A district that is only concerned with one function, say street lighting, is a single-purpose agency. A district that provides at least two distinct services, for example sewage treatment and parks management, is multipurpose. Between these two ends of the spectrum are special districts that engage in a number of related activities. Fire districts, for example, now commonly provide emergency medical response and hazardous materials services in addition to fire suppression. Water districts may provide watershed management, flood control, and fire flow capability in addition to water delivery. If a district is not providing all of the services outlined in its enabling legislation, those services are considered to be latent powers.

In addition to administrative, fiscal, and service distinctions, special districts can also be categorized on a geographic basis. The existence of multicounty and, in some cases, multistate special districts, create great opportunities for addressing regional service needs and create important political issues in terms of intergovernmental relations.

History

Robert Smith (1974) contended that special districts in the United Kingdom can be traced back 500 years to turnpike trusts. The American experience with public authorities is as old as the nation. George Washington's secretary of the Treasury favored "mixed corporations" for the financing of banks, canals, turnpikes, and bridges. He encouraged the use of such devices by both the national government and the states.

In the nineteenth century, America employed a number of special transportation districts for toll roads and canals. In 1887, the first two irrigation districts were created in California under the Wright Act. Within eight years, those 2 had grown to 49. Spokane, Washington, issued a bond in 1897 to pay for the extension of its water system. An authority scheme, the bond was to be repaid from water fees.

It was the impact of the Depression upon the local tax base that brought about rapid growth in the use of special districts. States employed them as a means of evading debt limitations, thus enabling states to participate in national public works projects. During World War II, a scarcity of materials slowed the growth of districts, but postwar development pressures stimulated the expansion of special governments.

It was at this time that scholars began to be concerned about the problems associated with the use of special districts. In 1957, John Bollens authored the first extensive treatment of the subject in his book *Special District Government in the United States.*

In the 1960s, efforts were undertaken by a variety of states to control the formation of new governments. In concert with a recommendation from the Advisory Commission on Intergovernmental Relations (ACIR) (1964), Texas, Nevada, and California began replacing restrictions on the procedure. In many instances, formal "boundary commissions" were created to rule on both the advisability of new government formations and changes in the responsibilities of existing governments. Research, however, has revealed that because these boundary commissions are typically controlled by existing general governments (counties and cities), they are less likely to approve the creation of

TABLE I. SPECIAL DISTRICT GROWTH

	Number	Compounded Yearly Percentage Change
1952	12,340	–
1967	21,264	3.7
1977	25,962	2.0
1987	29,532	1.3
1992	31,555	1.3

SOURCE: U.S. Bureau of Census, 1994, Table 5.

new governments, which may compete with them for public resources (DiLorenzo 1981).

Characteristics of Special Districts

Growth

Since the U.S. Census Bureau specified that special districts exist as separate entities, most of the national data available on the subject pertains only to independent special districts. With that caveat, Table I shows the growth of special districts from 1952 to 1992.

As can be seen, the number of independent special districts nationally grew rapidly between 1952 and 1967. Since that time, the growth rate has fallen and now has apparently stabilized at about 1.3 percent per year, or one-third of the earlier rate.

Principal Types of Special Districts

Although there are a large number of different types of special districts, most of them fall into three service provision categories: fire protection (18.1 percent), housing and community development (12.0 percent), and water (11.4). Over 40 percent of the single-function independent districts fall into one of these categories. Of multifunction districts, 53 percent provide both water and sewage.

As Table II illustrates, special districts are financed in a variety of ways.

A number of conclusions can be drawn from the data in Table II. Particularly noteworthy is that fact that even districts commonly thought of as purely enterprise do not rely exclusively upon user fees for revenue. Conversely, districts such as fire protection, which are classified as nonenterprise governments, receive some income from nontax sources. To the extent that user charges are feasible, they are implemented by both single- and multi-function districts.

In many cases, special districts can also make use of special assessments to provide income. A special assessment is typically levied on property owners to finance capital improvements. In some states, however, such as California, certain districts can make use of special assessments for purely service provisions. The rationale for these special assessments is that the public capital increases property value of the households or businesses within the dis-

TABLE II. SPECIAL DISTRICT FINANCE—1992

	Number	Uses Property Tax	Uses Other Tax	Uses Special Assignments	Uses User Charges	Uses Grants
Single-Function Totals	29036	13489	1071	4905	8526	11226
Libraries	1043	932	154	68	230	626
Hospitals	737	426	45	65	301	256
Health	584	367	22	65	202	143
Transportation	1306	501	120	202	326	522
Fire Protection	5260	4552	111	611	486	1138
Drain and Flood	2709	620	59	1189	85	242
Irrigation	792	488	21	391	198	124
Soil and Water	2428	202	67	291	831	2026
Parks and Rec.	1156	964	57	202	421	557
Housing and Community Development	3470	155	43	87	825	2810
Sewage and Solid Waste Management	2105	752	74	633	1261	874
Water	3302	1475	99	644	2260	861
Other	4144	2055	199	457	1100	1047
Multiple-Function Totals	2519	1462	103	797	1271	846
Natural Resources and Water	131	82	7	58	47	69
Sewage and Water	1344	710	46	328	761	369
Other	1044	670	50	411	463	408

SOURCE: U.S. Bureau of Census, 1994, Table 19.

trict, and, therefore, those who benefit should pay directly for the improvements. Thus, special assessments are very similar to user fees in both economic effects and justification.

Political and Economic Arguments Concerning Special Districts

Several specific issues arise in any discussion of special districts. In particular, these issues concern the number of special districts, special district responsiveness, special district economics, and special district behaviors. Often these issues are addressed in the context of special district consolidation.

The Numbers

Because they are so plentiful, special districts are often the subject of reformers who want to reduce the amount of government in citizen's lives. There is a tendency to con-

fuse the concept of many governments with the problem of too much government. However, experts ranging from Vincent Ostrom et al. (1988) to the Advisory Commission on Intergovernmental Relations (1987) have argued that multiple providers of public services are important to citizens for a variety of reasons.

Special-purpose governments allow citizens to define a community of interest. By creating a government that provides a specific service and by establishing boundaries that include only those citizens who wish to receive that service, a close relationship can be established between taxes paid and benefits received.

Moreover, special districts enable citizens to express their preferences with far greater precision than general governments. Voters can mark their ballots, for example, to show their satisfaction with water services and discontent with fire protection. With a general government, citizens must average their preferences and compromise their voting choices.

Responsiveness

It is sometimes argued that special districts are unaccountable to voters. Dependent districts and joint powers agreements are particularly vulnerable to this criticism. The day-to-day administration of dependent special districts is often left to appointed commissioners. Although the members of a board of supervisors or a city council serve as the ultimate board of directors for dependent districts, they are elected as officials of a general government, not as directors. Often they serve on the boards of many dependent districts and are thus unable to focus their energies fully on the concerns of any one district. A final consideration is that in those general governments that are not elected at-large, it is probable that the majority of the supervisors or council members sitting on the board of a dependent district neither live in the district, nor were they elected by the citizens of that district. In the special case of joint powers agreements, a substantial number of the board members will necessarily be appointed from governments that are totally unaccountable to large numbers of the district's citizens. For all of these reasons, the U.S. Bureau of Census may be quite correct in excluding dependent districts and JPAs from their count of special district governments.

In the case of independent districts, low voter turnout, limited media coverage, and little citizen attendance at district board meetings are sometimes cited as evidence that districts have no public responsibility. However, officials in these governments stand for election just as officials in cities and counties do. Their board meetings are as open to the press and public as those of general governments. When a citizen wishes to interact with an independent special district, that government is as accessible, or more so, than cities or counties, which often require additional layers of bureaucracy to coordinate their many activities.

Moreover, Robert Hawkins, Jr. (1976), ACIR (1987), and Paul Teske et al. (1993) all found that many citizens are aware of the numerous governments that affect them, that efficiency and responsiveness are augmented by special districts, and that the multiplicity of special districts increases sensitivity to diverse citizen preferences. This is consistent with Charles Tiebout's (1956) argument that if there is a multiplicity of governments from which a citizen can choose, there is likely to be a better match between citizen preferences and local government services.

Paul Downing and Thomas DiLorenzo (1987) cite a study of the Swedish experience after the number of governments was decreased by 80 percent. The study found that voter participation in local elections declined and local elected officials differed more markedly from their constituents in terms of income, social status, and education. Moreover, resistance to spending decreased, and officials tended to follow their own beliefs rather than doing what their constituents wanted.

Economics

One the most popular arguments against special districts is that they tend to be too small to take advantage of economies of scale. These might be, for example, economies that could occur because of quantity discounts, elimination of unnecessary levels of management, and a reduction in duplication of effort that resulted from having the staffs of several districts doing the same work. In some cases this may be true, especially for small organizations. William Fox (1980) has found scale economies for elementary schools up to 300 students, for fire districts up to 10,000 residents, and for refuse collection up to 20,000 inhabitants. However, once these numbers are surpassed, diseconomies of scale tend to occur. In particular, additional transportation costs, capital expenditures, and administrative inefficiencies begin to take place. Further, when districts are consolidated or taken over by larger jurisdictions, the costs of blending the two organizations must be considered. Salary levels for comparable work are almost always increased to match those of employees in the higher-paid organization. Equipment and facility standards are almost always set at the highest levels among the predecessor organizations.

Sources of funding have also become a sensitive issue in the special district debate. Although the ability of nonenterprise districts to impose fees, such as library fines or inspection charges, is generally accepted, the use of property taxes by enterprise districts is occasionally challenged. In states where voters have imposed limitations on the ability of governments to raise taxes, the failure of many enterprise districts to become "fully self-funding" has become the subject of some debate.

In most cases, these enterprise districts were created under enabling legislation that permitted them to diversify their income stream. This power was typically granted in recognition that certain services create externalities that are not fully captured in the transaction between vendor and customer. A port district, for example, may provide economic benefits to a community far beyond the fees it can charge for berthing and recreational use. The hydrant system installed by a water district is used by a fire department without regard to whether the water is poured on the home of a water district customer or noncustomer. A sanitary district cannot always fully recover the costs of installing and maintaining a sewer system in the fees paid by future customers when they ultimately "hook up" to the system.

Thus, there are often appropriate reasons for allowing enterprise districts to participate in communitywide revenue systems. Nonetheless, in states where voters have placed strict controls on the tax system, the equity arguments that once justified tax revenues for enterprise districts are increasingly being ignored.

Behavior

It is often assumed that if numerous small districts are consolidated, the larger successor units of government will continue to behave as did their predecessor organizations. Savings and efficiencies that might be identified in the first year of a merger are projected far into the future. Organization theory and research do not support such assumptions. On the contrary, larger organizations, with greater resources and responsibilities, will tend to identify options that were not available to their predecessor organizations and will often require greater resources than would several small organizations.

Closely allied with the behavior patterns of large organizations is the fiscal behavior of organizations with reduced competition. Evidence exists that larger governments do exhibit monopolistic tendencies and citizens do benefit from competition among governments. William Niskanen (1975) found that the monopoly power of consolidated public agencies will tend to have higher production costs, be less responsive to median voters, and spend more than they would have if the same service level were maintained by a multitude of providers.

John Shannon's (1991) "convoy analogy" for states might also be used to describe the benefits of multiple special districts. He suggested that, if a jurisdiction successfully pioneers a new way of delivering services, word will spread to other jurisdictions and, ultimately, the new way will become the base level. Other jurisdictions are forced by a "catchup" imperative to keep their service levels close to those of their neighbors. The same general argument also applies to the finance system. If a jurisdiction raised its taxes too high in relation to its competitors, economic development would stagnate and citizen welfare would fall. Just like a convoy of governments sailing during wartime, no district can move too far ahead in terms of taxes without facing risks of tax evasion, tax revolt, or declining economic development. Moreover, no government can afford to fall too far behind, in terms of service provision, since it will lose economic development to the higher-service governments.

Conclusion

It is now generally believed that special districts play an important role in our system of government. Properly configured, they provide increased responsiveness to citizens, appropriate economic efficiency characteristics, and reflect a pressure to behave competitively.

STEPHEN P. MORGAN AND JEFFREY I. CHAPMAN

BIBLIOGRAPHY

Advisory Commission on Intergovernmental Relations, 1964. *The Problem of Special Districts in American Government.* Washington, DC: Government Printing Office.
———, 1987. *The Organization of Local Public Economies.* Washington, DC: Government Printing Office.
Bollens, John C., 1957. *Special District Government in the United States.* Berkeley: University of California Press.
DiLorenzo, Thomas J., 1981. "Special Districts and Local Public Services." *Public Finance Quarterly,* vol. 9, no. 3 (July) 353–367.
Downing, Paul B., and Thomas J. DiLorenzo, 1987. "User Charges and Special Districts." In J. Richard Aronson and Eli Shwatz, eds., *Management Policies in Local Government Finance.* Washington, DC: International City Management Association.
Fox, William F., 1980. "Size Economies in Local Government Services: A Review." Economics, Statistics, and Cooperatives Service, U.S. Department of Agriculture, Rural Development Research Report, No. 22.
Hawkins, Robert B., Jr., 1976. *Self Government by District.* Stanford, CA: Hoover Institution Press.
Niskanen, William A., 1975. "Bureaucrats and Politicians." *The Journal of Law and Economics,* vol. 18, no. 3 (December) 617–643.
Office of the State Controller, 1994. *Annual Report 1991–92 Financial Transactions Concerning Special Districts of California.* Sacramento, CA: Office of the State Controller.
Ostrom, Vincent, Robert Bish, and Elinor Ostrom, 1988. *Local Government in the United States.* San Francisco, CA: Institute for Contemporary Studies.
Shannon, John, 1991. "Federalism's 'Invisible Regulator'—Interjurisdictional Competition." In Daphne A. Kenyon and John Kincaid, eds., *Competition among States and Local Governments.* Washington, DC: Urban Institute Press.
Smith, Robert G., 1974. *Ad Hoc Governments: Special Purpose Transportation Authorities in Britain and the United States.* Beverly Hills, CA: Sage.
Teske, Paul, Mark Schneider, Michael Mintron, and Samuel Best, 1993. "Establishing the Micro Foundations of a Macro Theory: Information, Movers, and the Competitive Local Market for Public Goods." *American Political Science Review,* vol. 87, no. 3 (September) 702–713.
Tiebout, Charles M., 1956. "A Pure Theory of Local Expenditures." *Journal of Political Economy* (October) 416–424.
U.S. Department of Commerce, Economics, and Statistics Administration, Bureau of the Census, 1994. *1992 Census of Governments, Volume 1: Government Organization Number 1: Government Organization.* Washington, DC: U.S. Government Printing Office.

SPECIAL RELATIONSHIP.

The cultural, linguistic, military, intelligence, and nostalgic relations between the United Kingdom and the United States that have emerged since World War II.

The term "special relationship" is widely used by politicians and academics alike but is rarely defined in a precise way. The Oxford Dictionary suggests that the word "special" refers to something that is "exceptional," "uncommon," "peculiar to one thing," or "additional to the ordinary." Used to describe relations between two states, the term suggests a relationship that is "different in kind" from those that each has with other states. It implies that each regards the other as its most important ally. More than this, however, it also implies a partnership that is unique and distinctive and that, in Arthur Campbell Turner's (1971) words, stands out from the ordinary "run of the mill" international political relationships between states (p. 5).

Defined in these terms, the concept of a "special relationship" suggests that there is such a thing as a "standard," or "normal," relationship between sovereign states to which most relationships between pairs of states conform. It suggests that in contrast to these "normal" relationships, curious and particular as they might be, there can be relationships between states that are so intimate and extraordinary that they deserve the label "special" as a distinctive form of classification to highlight their unique features.

Origins

The term is usually (but not exclusively) used to refer to the relationship between the United States and Britain. Its first use to describe this relationship appears to have been in Winston Churchill's famous speech at Westminster College, Fulton, Missouri, on March 5, 1946. In this speech, which is better known for the former British prime minister's comments about an "iron curtain" descending across Europe, Churchill spoke about the vital importance of the unprecedented wartime partnership and the need to continue close cooperation in the postwar period as the Cold War gathered momentum. Churchill said:

> Neither the sure prevention of war, nor the continuous rise of world organization will be gained without what I have called the fraternal association of the English-speaking peoples. This means a *special relationship* between the British Commonwealth and Empire and the United States. . . . Fraternal association requires not only the growing friendship and mutual understanding between our two vast but kindred systems of society, but the continuance of the intimate relationship between our military advisers, leading to common study of potential dangers, the similarity of weapons and manuals of instructions, and to the interchange of officers and cadets at technical colleges. It should carry with it the continuance of the present facilities for mutual security by the joint use of all Naval and Air Force bases in the possession of either country all over the world. (in James 1974, p. 7289)

It was the repeated and emphatic use of the term "special relationship" in the Fulton speech that launched it effectively on the world and from that day on secured its wide circulation. It also linked the term firmly to the relationship between Britain and the United States.

A Brief History of the Anglo-American "Special Relationship"

Although the roots of the "special relationship" can be traced back to the origins of the United States, it was only during World War II, as the Fulton speech implies, that a partnership was developed between the two countries, which became so close, intimate, and informal in such a wide spectrum of political, economic, and especially military fields that terms like "exceptional," "unique," or "different from the ordinary" can be applied. It was during this period that the two countries became so intertwined with each other that traditional state sovereignty was eroded and a common Anglo-Saxon identity purpose was developed in their joint war effort against the Axis powers.

In the early stages of war, before Pearl Harbor, what became known as a common-law alliance was established between the two countries. During this period a "gradual mixing-up process" took place with close cooperation involving such things as the exchange of destroyers-for-bases, the sharing of information about atomic energy, joint staff talks, and the beginnings of intelligence collaboration—all of which laid the foundations for the "full marriage," which followed. This involved the formation of a joint war machine after the American entry into the war. This was initiated at the Arcadia Conference in December 1941 with the adoption by the United States of a "Germany-first" strategy and was followed by the creation of a range of combined boards that played a crucial role in the direction and coordination of the joint war effort over the following four years. The war against Germany and Japan, and the two specific areas of Anglo-American cooperation in the fields of atomic energy (the Manhattan Project) and intelligence, all in different ways highlighted the extraordinary degree of collaboration that was achieved. This was summed up in General George Marshall's claim that Anglo-American combined planning between 1941 and 1945 represented "the most complete unification of military effort ever achieved by two allied states" in the history of warfare (Marshall 1945, p. 24).

In the immediate postwar period, however, the intimacy of the Anglo-American wartime relationship was eroded by disputes over a range of issues. These included the abrupt cancellation of lend-lease arrangements, loan negotiations, Palestine, and atomic energy. In the latter case, despite wartime agreements to the contrary, the Truman administration passed the McMahon Act in 1946, cutting Britain off from access to atomic secrets. The result was a British decision to develop an independent nuclear capability in January 1947 and a determination to reestablish the atomic energy partnership in the longer term.

By the late 1940s, the creation of the North Atlantic Treaty Organization (NATO) reflected the restoration of close ties between the two countries, which were being developed as a result of the onset of the Cold War. The war in Korea between 1950 and 1953 further highlighted the military partnership being forged to contain communism. For Britain, the "special relationship" had become the central theme in foreign and defense policy, which necessitated military support for the United States, even though vital British interests were not directly at stake. This perceived need to support the United States at times of international crisis reflected an important dimension of the "special relationship" that was to recur throughout the Cold War era and beyond.

By 1956, despite periodic difficulties, both countries were working in close alliance in a wide range of diplomatic, military, and economic fields. The Suez crisis, however, brought a major disagreement, which shook the bilateral alliance to its foundations. Significantly, instead of fundamentally undermining the "special relationship," Suez reinforced the close ties between the two countries. At a series of summit meetings between Dwight Eisenhower and Harold Macmillan in Bermuda and Washington, a wide range of agreements were signed providing Britain with Thor missiles (under dual-key control), opening up strategic planning between the two air forces and, most important of all, repealing the McMahon Act. Under the Atomic Energy Agreement of 1958, Britain was given access to American nuclear secrets. From this time onward, a new nuclear partnership was developed, which, together with close intelligence links, became the core of the "special relationship" between the two countries. This was reflected in the decision to sell Britain Skybolt missiles when the Macmillan government was forced to cancel its Blue Streak Project in 1960; subsequently, when Skybolt was cancelled, the Kennedy administration agreed at the Nassau Conference in December 1962 to provide Polaris missiles.

Just as the "special relationship" was being firmly established in the 1960s, however, problems began to arise. The Wilson government refused to provide military support for the United States in Vietnam and a major defense review between 1964 and 1968 culminated in the withdrawal of British forces from east of Suez. The result was a distrust of Britain in Washington and an erosion of the worldwide military partnership that had characterized the 1950s. This cooling of the relationship was reflected in the Wilson government's decision to use the term "the close relationship" rather than "the special relationship." This downgrading of the relationship was reciprocated by the Johnson administration, which was becoming more and more preoccupied by the debilitating war in Indo-China.

The difficulties of the mid and late 1960s were continued into the next decade. The new Conservative government under Edward Heath was determined to chart a new course for Britain in Europe. For Heath, Europe and the "special relationship" were competing themes in British foreign policy. If Britain wanted to play a role in Europe, as Heath believed it must, then the "special relationship"

would have to be given less emphasis. To reflect this, the prime minister coined the phrase "the natural relationship" to describe the contemporary shift in priorities. Heath's new initiative paid off, and in 1973 Britain finally joined the European Community.

At the same time that Britain was charting a new course in Europe, the era of détente had opened up the opportunity for the Nixon administration to negotiate a wide range of agreements with the Soviet Union. From Washington's perspective, Britain was a country in decline with less to offer the United States than in the past. The key preoccupations of foreign and defense policy increasingly centered on the withdrawal from Vietnam and arms control negotiation with the Soviet Union designed to reduce the risks of nuclear war.

Nevertheless, those who wrote off the "special relationship" in the 1970s did so prematurely. By the end of the decade, East-West relations were deteriorating and a new, more Atlanticist, prime minister took office in Britain. Margaret Thatcher was determined to reverse the decline in British power and was much less sympathetic than the previous Conservative government under Heath (1970–1974) to the European ideal. With the Soviet intervention in Afghanistan and a much more "hawkish" president, Ronald Reagan, in the White House, Thatcher embarked on a restoration of the "special relationship." This was reflected in the 1980 agreement to purchase Trident missiles from the United States, support for U.S. policy to station Cruise missiles in Britain (and Western Europe), close secret collaboration in weapons and intelligence during the Falklands War, and the American use of British bases to attack Libya in 1986 in response to Colonel Mùammar Gadhafi's support for international terrorism. During the 1980s, as a whole, both the United States and Britain showed once again all the signs of regarding each other as the most important ally.

The Post–Cold War "Special Relationship"

With the collapse of the Warsaw Pact and the subsequent collapse of the Soviet Union, one of the main reasons for the close diplomatic and military ties between the two countries came to an end. Britain still retained the intimate nuclear and intelligence ties of the Cold War era and continued to support American military operations, such as those in the Gulf in 1990–1991 and 1994. At the same time, the disappearance of the perceived threat from the Soviet Union created greater opportunities for significant divergences of interest to emerge. Friction, for example, soon emerged between the Major and Clinton governments over alleged Conservative Party meddling in the U.S. election in favor of President George Bush, over the decision by the American government to supply Gerry Adams, the Sinn Fein leader, with a visa to visit the United States, and over Bosnia.

While the United States became preoccupied with domestic affairs and was more inclined to focus on the Pacific region and Latin America than Europe, Britain began a new attempt to forge closer links with its European allies. Greater support than in the past was shown for the development of a "European Defense and Security Identity," centering on the European Union and the Western European Union (WEU). In the early 1990s, Britain and France also established a permanent forum to discuss a wide range of issues associated with nuclear weapons that had hitherto been one of the key features of the "special relationship." The result was a growing consensus in the mid-1990s that Anglo-American relations were at an important crossroads. Whether the "special relationship" between the two countries continued to exist was increasingly a matter of some dispute. With the election of Tony Blair in May 1997 as British Prime Minister this debate moderated in the light of his political closeness to President Clinton.

The Main Characteristics of the "Special Relationship"

An analysis of Anglo-American relations from World War II onward suggests that there were four main elements that made the relationship "special." These were the personal relations of government leaders, informality, preferential treatment, and the importance of the relationship.

Personal Relationships

It seems apparent that Anglo-American relations have been closest during periods when the leaders of both countries have achieved a personal rapport with each other. This was the case during World War II when Churchill and Franklin D. Roosevelt entered into close correspondence on the conduct of the joint war effort. Later, in the 1950s, Macmillan was able to restore the "special relationship" after the trauma of the Suez crisis due to his close personal friendship with Eisenhower, which went back to World War II. Despite the difference in age, Macmillan was also able to forge a very close relationship with John F. Kennedy in the early 1960s. Both men appear to have had a genuine respect and affection for each other, which had an important impact on the relationship between the two states. The importance of personal friendship can also be seen in the relationship between Thatcher and Reagan during the 1980s. They were compatible in ideological terms, but there also appears to have been some personal chemistry that bound the two leaders together.

In each of these periods, although Anglo-American relations were characterized by a wide range of working relationships at different levels (which were themselves affected by close personal relations), the friendships of the leaders of both countries helped to set the tone for the relationship as a whole. Difficulties encountered in negotiations between officials (such as those stemming from the U.S. cancellation of Skybolt) were often overcome by talks at the highest level of government.

Informality

Although formal arrangements and binding agreements have been an important part of Anglo-American diplomacy, the relationship has also been characterized by an unusual degree of informality. There has been a preponderance of "gentlemen's agreements," "secret unwritten arrangements," and "memoranda of understanding," which have reflected the close personal working relationships that have been established. Henry Kissinger notes in his memoirs that this method of conducting government business was very much the hallmark of the "special relationship."

He points out that "the ease and informality of the Anglo-American partnership has been a source of wonder and no little resentment—to third countries. Our post-war diplomatic history is littered with Anglo-American 'arrangements' and 'understandings,' sometimes on crucial issues, never put into formal documents" (Kissinger 1979, p. 90). The unusual nature of this informality was reflected in the decision by the Attlee government in 1948 to allow American strategic bombers to be based in Britain without any formal agreement being signed. The commander of the American Air Forces in Britain commented at the time: "Never before in history has one first-class power gone into another first-class power's country without an agreement. We were just told to come over and 'we will be pleased to have you.'" (The World Today 1960, p. 320).

Preferential Treatment

The fact that many of these "arrangements" have not gone through the normal process of constitutional scrutiny has resulted in another characteristic of the "special relationship": the preferential treatment of one ally as compared with other allies. This has been particularly evident in the intelligence field, with secret exchanges of intelligence information and the joint use of facilities. It has also been evident in the nuclear field, with the informal exchanges between scientists in the early and mid-1950s and the wide range of cooperation that followed the repeal of the McMahon Act in 1958. The 1958 Atomic Energy Agreement was particularly important as a piece of enabling legislation that provided the American authorities with discretion to give Britain the blueprints of thermonuclear warheads, as well as other information, components, and materials associated with the development of nuclear weapons. Although the United States aided the French nuclear program in the 1970s, Franco-American nuclear relations were never as continuous and far-reaching as those established with Britain.

Importance

The Anglo-American nuclear partnership highlights another characteristic of the "special relationship": the importance of the ties between both countries. Britain has had a wide range of close relationships with many states during World War II and after. These have included relations with Canada, Australia, New Zealand and other Commonwealth states, and more recently with some of its European allies. Similarly, the United States has had close ties with Canada, Israel, Japan, Germany, and various Latin American states. But for much of the period from 1945 to the mid-1960s, there was little talk of these relationships being "special." The term was reserved for the relationship with Britain, which was regarded as the most important U.S. ally.

The argument that the United States has invariably regarded Britain as its closest and most important ally, however, needs some qualification. From the mid-1960s, when Britain faced growing economic difficulties and subsequently withdrew its forces from east of Suez, the relationship with Britain appears to have become relatively less "special" to the United States. This trend was partially reversed in the 1980s under Thatcher and Reagan but continued post-1989 when the Cold War ended. For the United States, Britain has been viewed increasingly as part of Europe rather than an important major actor in international politics deserving of "special" treatment. Linked to this qualification is the argument that, because the United States is a superpower with global responsibilities, it has acquired a series of "special relationships" with a number of its allies, reflecting the importance of these countries to the United States in particular ways. Thus, Germany, Israel, Canada, and even the Soviet Union/Russia are sometimes said to have a "special relationship" with the United States. This said, the use of the term "*the* special relationship" is still normally confined to the partnership between Britain and the United States.

Theoretical Issues

In the literature on the "special relationship" between Britain and the United States, there is a major disagreement over what it is that makes the relationship "special." For some writers, the Anglo-American alliance does not fit into normal alliance theory. According to writers like Dawson and Rosencrance (1966), although the mutuality of interests are an important part of the "special relationship," this is not sufficient in itself to explain the extraordinary quality of the relationship. They point to the Suez crisis and its aftermath to illustrate the unusual partnership between the two countries. In terms of conventional alliance theory, they argued, "Suez should have been the end of the US-British tie; in fact, it was the amphitheatre of its rebirth" (p. 51). The fact that Anglo-American relations survived

Suez—and indeed flourished in the late 1950s and early 1960s—is, in their view, because of the common history, tradition, and affinity of the two countries. It is this, they argued, that makes Anglo-American relations "special."

The idea that the close nature of the alliance stems from sentimental attachments, cultural affinities, historical traditions, similar institutions, and a common language is widely shared by writers on Anglo-American relations. Denis Brogan (1964) is one commentator who has written that "the linguistic and cultural relationship between England and America is not paralleled in any other pair of relationships" (p. 71). In similar vein, Turner (1971) has argued that "the foundation of the special relationship between Britain and the United States is demographic, the basic fact is that to a considerable extent the population of the United States derives from British sources. . . . The common language is the basic thread of Anglo-American communion, the basis of the Anglo-American community" (p. 24). Even one of the more outspoken critics of the "special relationship" in the United States, George Ball (1968), has argued that "to an exceptional degree we look out on the world through similarly refracted mental spectacles. We speak variant patois of Shakespeare and Norman Mailer, our institutions spring from the same instincts and traditions, and we share the same heritage of law and custom, philosophy and pragmatic Weltanschauung. . . . Starting from similar premises in the same intellectual tradition, we recognise common allusions, share many common prejudices, and can commune on a basis of confidence" (p. 91).

This interpretation of the roots of the "special relationship" is not shared by all writers on the subject. Some observers argue that the intimacy, vitality, and comprehensiveness well beyond the norm that characterize Anglo-American relations are the product, like all alliances, of pragmatic calculations of national interest, and nothing more. David Dimbleby and David Reynolds (1988) have described the partnership as a "hard-headed relationship" in which common language and culture are mere "emollients" (p. 331). According to this view, both states came together and entered into a wide range of formal and informal arrangements because it suited their interests in both peace and war. Much the same argument was contained in an analysis of the "special relationship" by Raymond Seitz when he stepped down as the U.S. ambassador in Britain in 1994. Seitz observed that the foreign policy of all states, in the first instance, was based "on its foreign interests, both security and economic, and less on its genetics." (*The Economist*, November 3, 1994)

A variant of this "realist" interpretation of the special relationship is the argument that the term "special relationship" is a myth or rhetorical device used, particularly by the British, to reinforce political and strategic interests. A. Singh (1993) has argued, for example, that the term has acquired "spiritual" and "fraternal" overtones as part of a deliberate attempt by successive British governments to cushion the decline of Britain's global status on the world stage after 1945. According to this view, the British have consciously emphasized the sentimental and linguistic affinities between the two countries in order to harness and steer U.S. policy in a direction that will reinforce its own interests. This reflects, according to Christopher Hitchens (1990), the perceived "superior wisdom" and greater international experience of the British compared with the United States. Macmillan's reference to the alliance between the two countries as akin to the Greeks and Romans is, according to Hitchens, an illustration of the way the British have attempted to manipulate the "special relationship" for their own ends.

Whether history, language, sentiment, or common interests are at the root of the "special relationship" is perhaps not a particularly productive argument; and neither is the critique that suggests that it is simply a device to secure the interests of one of the parties. Sentiment and interest have both played their part. The exceptional nature of the relationship is a product of a particular mix of factors rather than any one on its own. A common outlook toward the world and common values that derive from history and culture have helped to produce what one writer describes as "a shared capacity to see the elements of common interest, in whatever international storms the times may bring" (Bell 1964, p. 119). Thus political calculation, and no doubt manipulation, have often provided the compelling impetus for cooperation, whereas a common history and culture have contributed to the interpretation of state interests and provided an added dimension of warmth and intimacy, which has helped to cement the alliance between the two countries.

JOHN BAYLIS

NOTE:

The author would like to thank Kerry Longhurst for assistance with this entry.

BIBLIOGRAPHY

Ball, G. W., 1968. *The Discipline of Power.* London: Bodley Head.
Bartlett, C. J., 1992. *The Special Relationship: A Political History of Anglo-American Relations since 1945.* New York: Longmans.
Baylis, J., 1984. *Anglo-American Defence Relations 1939–1984: The Special Relationship.* London: Macmillan.
Bell, C., 1964. *The Debatable Alliance: An Essay in Anglo-American Relations.* London: Oxford University Press.
Brogan, D., 1964. *American Aspects.* New York: Harper & Row.
Dawson, R., and R. Rosencrance, 1966. "Theory and Reality in the Anglo-American Alliance." *World Politics,* vol. 19, no. 1 (October).
Dimbleby, D., and D. Reynolds, 1988. *An Ocean Apart.* London: BBC Books.
Hitchens, C., 1990. *Blood, Class, and Nostalgia: Anglo-American Ironies.* London: Chatto and Windus.
James, R. R., ed., 1974. Winston S. Churchill, *His Complete Speeches (1897–1963).* London: Chelsea House.

Kissinger, H. A., 1979. *The White House Years.* London: Weidenfeld and Nicholson.
Marshall, G. C., 1943–1945. *The Winning of the War in Europe and the Pacific.* Biennial Report of the Chief of Staff of the U.S. Army, July, 1943 to June 30, 1945, to Secretary of War.
"Notes of the Month," 1960. *The World Today,* vol. 16, no. 8 (August).
Singh, A. I., 1993. *The Limits of British Influence: South Asia and the Anglo-American Relationship, 1947-65.* London: Pinter.
Turner, A. C., 1971. *The Unique Partnership, Britain and the United States.* New York: Pegasus.
Watt, D. C., 1984. *Succeeding John Bull: America in Britain in Britain's Place 1900–1975.* Cambridge: Cambridge University Press.

SPEED-UPS AND SLOW-DOWNS.
It is not unusual for companies to implement labor-intensive productivity programs. In response, however, employee unions have orchestrated slow-downs that eventually hurt these companies' earnings.

Introduction

Faced with declining resources and increasing demands for goods and services, some public-sector agencies have instituted programs to speed up output. Speed-ups involve intensifying labor and excessive effort to increase output (Prokopenko 1937, pp. 3–4). Due to budget cuts and layoffs, agencies are seldom provided with sufficient resources to serve their clientele. Despite this shortcoming, these agencies are still required to fulfill their mandates, so employees are then put under pressure to increase output. One unwanted outcome from speed-ups is a work slow-down. A slow-down involves staying on the job, meeting minimum job requirements, being paid and "battling the company from within" through adherence to rules (Kotlowitz 1987, pp. 1, 8).

Slow-downs have become very useful weapons for unions involved in disputes with management. Before the mid-1980s, slow-downs, also called working sit-downs, were thought to be spontaneous reactions by workers. Now, they are used systematically to force management to concede to workers' demands. This strategy, according to Anthony McKeown, a management consultant, has tipped the scales in favor of unions. Speed-ups and slow-downs occur in most organizations. Despite this, public administration literature dealing with this issue is limited, and when dealt with, it is handled perfunctorily; the topic seems insignificant in public-sector management. In contrast, private-sector literature addresses the issue and provides several examples of organizations that have made speed-ups part of their operations.

Before proceeding, it is important to draw a distinction between speed-up and productivity. Productivity is the "efficient use of resources—labour, capital, land, materials, energy, information—in the production of various goods and services" (Prokopenko 1987, p. 3). Time is an important element in productivity improvement because the shorter time taken, the more productive the system is considered. In contrast, speed-ups are considered as labor-intense productivity, which is achieved through excessive effort—working harder (Prokopenko 1987, pp. 3–4).

Speed-Ups: The Beginning

There are several factors indicating that speed-ups began in the late eighteenth century. In 1813, Robert Owen addressed the superintendents of manufactories and said that "managers should pay as much attention to their vital machines (employees) as to their inanimate machines" (Shafritz and Ott 1992, p. 11). During the eighteenth century, Adam Smith indicated that the factory was appropriate for mass production. One hundred years later, Frederick Taylor articulated that workers could be much more productive through scientifically designed work, which would increase the speed of machine-shop production. His premise was that there was "one best way" to accomplish any task. In short, Taylor's scientific management sought to "increase output by discovering the fastest, most efficient, and least fatiguing production methods" (Shafritz and Ott 1992, p. 30). The idea that work could be sped up may have emerged from the notion that workers should be considered as machines.

Intensifying employees' work is not a new phenomenon. Although it is difficult to discern exactly when it was first used, evidence points to the factory system, which was introduced during industrialization. The Industrial Revolution facilitated the development of the factory system, which was responsible for a tremendous increase in productivity. Population growth and urbanization required the production of more goods and services. Subsequently, workers were trained to do jobs along with machines, which increasingly determined the speed of work. To ensure that workers maintained speed-ups, they were chained to their machines to keep the pace set by the machines (Harrison et al. 1985, pp. 542–546).

The use of speed-ups during the classical period may be justified by the prevailing management thought that did not view workers as individuals. Instead, they were considered as "interchangeable parts in an industrial machine whose parts were made of flesh only when it was impractical to make them of steel" (Shafritz and Ott 1992, p. 27). The prevailing philosophy was that any organization's output could be increased through proper planning, control of jobs and employees, and organization. Therefore, the focus was placed on the technical aspects of work and the physical environment. Speed-ups then were a reflection of societal values and the conditions of the times. The classical approaches gained popularity during industrialization and dominated the field until the late 1930s (Donnelly et al. 1987, p. 280).

Another justification for speeding up production was articulated by Taylor. He espoused that if workers were to double their output, contrary to the belief that some would lose their jobs, more work opportunities would result. He stated, "All you have to do is to bring wealth into this world and the world uses it. . . . The one great thing that marks the improvement of this world is measured by the enormous increase in outputs of the individuals of this world" (Shafritz and Ott 1992, pp. 69–70).

Scientific management implicitly gave management the view that workers were machines that could be tuned to peak efficiency. Their responsibility then was to determine through experiment what the most efficient methods were and plan jobs to take advantage of the techniques (Denhardt 1984, p. 53). Even classically designed organizations with high complexity, high formalization, and high centralization were used consistently to control workers. These organizations' primary focus was to maximize the use of resources during the production process. The bureaucracy itself with its clear division of labor, well-defined and routine jobs, and a system for measuring output was geared toward speeding up output (Donnelly et al. 1987, pp. 180–181).

Neoclassical Period

Although neoclassical theorists were unhappy with the simplistic approach of the classical school, their main focus was also on the efficient use of resources. Beginning with the Hawthorne studies, employees were recognized as unique and multifaceted and part of groups that could dictate the level of output in the workplace. They could determine the success or failure of an organization. In fact, these work groups not only satisfy their members' needs but exert tremendous control and influence over their performance and behavior. The goal then for management was to create a social environment that would be conducive to proper work relationships. The information gleaned from studies during the period gave management a deeper understanding of what motivated their employees, thereby allowing them to capitalize on their employees. For example, management was to create an atmosphere of cooperation and to institute programs that motivate the workers. According to Herbert L. Petri (1981, p. 4), a motivated person can work harder at a sustained pace. Goals, persistence, and effort, he articulated, were important components of motivation. Implicit in these statements is that motivating workers could be the key to speeding up production.

Systems Approach

The conceptual framework for this perspective was provided by neoclassical theorists. During the 1960s, systems theorists made computers, information technology, and control systems the center of their approach. This approach spawned a debate, as some theorists envisaged a clash between individual freedoms in organizations and technology-based confinement, and domination by computers. In response to the debate, Norbert Wiener stated:

> Render unto man the things which are man's and unto the computer the things which are the computer's. This would seem the intelligent policy to adopt when we employ men and computers together in common undertakings. It is a policy as far removed from that of the gadget worshipper as it is from the man who sees only blasphemy and the degradation of man in the use of any mechanical adjuvants whatever the thoughts. [An adjuvant is defined as something that serves to help or assist.] (in Shafritz and Ott 1992, p. 265)

This quotation indicates that the aim of system theorists was for computers to complement workers in achieving the organization's goals and not to be used as a form of domination.

The debate eventually subsided and by the 1980s information technology was playing an important role in the workplace. Along with enhancing the decisionmaking processes, the systems were being used by management to monitor and control workers. Speed-ups were not abandoned with the introduction of new technology; in fact, the technology provided creative methods to intensify labor.

"I measure everything that moves" is how one bank official described a criterion used to assess his employees' productivity (in Marx and Sherizen 1986, p. 66.) In the United States, managers were increasingly pressured to improve productivity. Subsequently, certain techniques and intrusions that would have been rejected in the past became acceptable methods. Monitoring devices were introduced to check the number of errors and the speed at which employees were working and compared their speed to other employees. One program even displayed messages on the terminal that informed employees, "You are not working as fast as the person next to you." Another program entitled Subliminal Suggestions and Self-Hypnosis allowed management to send messages, such as "work faster." The messages would pass so quickly in front of the workers' eyes that they could not consciously detect them (Marx and Sherizen 1986, pp. 62–72).

Besides the monitoring systems, several others have been instituted to control the costs of production and operations. Just-in-time (JIT) and total quality control (TQC) are two methods used by organizations to gain a strategic advantage over their competitors. However, several scholars argue that they are also used to intensify workers' jobs.

The just-in-time method was introduced with the promise that it would help organizations deliver quality products in the required time. Its purpose is to reduce costs in the production process, which in turn will improve the organization's productivity. JIT eliminates time wasted in long procedures for setting up jobs, and an essential feature is its comprehensive production control system based on the planning of materials control. JIT requires a management team that will fully exploit a production control system. When the system is fully functional, tremendous gains can be obtained. For example, a Hewlett-Packard Plant's JIT system reduced process time for a product from 17 days to 30 hours (Wyles 1986, pp. 35–37). Total quality control is another method designed to increase organizational productivity through the production of a timely, affordable, quality product. TQC is a productivity improvement technique that can improve productivity and increase quality.

Without disputing the productivity gains that can accrue with the JIT/TQC systems, Graham Sewell and Barry Wilkinson (1992), after an examination of places where the systems were implemented, argued that they facilitate surveillance, instill discipline, and enhance central control (p. 271). The authors developed a theoretical framework from Foucault's conception of power/knowledge from his text *Discipline & Punish* and analyzed the mechanisms of surveillance and control in the workplace. Briefly, they argued that JIT/TQC is enhanced by two complementary disciplinary forces: (1) discipline through scrutiny in quality circles, for example, and (2) a disciplinary force derived from the use of powerful management information systems that facilitate surveillance. The outcome is an efficient disciplinary system that facilitates minute control (pp. 271–289).

The JIT/TQC system makes the labor force more visible. It prevents idle time by allowing management to measure targets daily instead of monthly. This made the workers feel that they "were under the gun all the time" (p. 279). The system also had conditions to guarantee speed-ups. First, the TQC component sped up the identification and correction of faults.

Second, the company measured the productivity and quality performance of individuals and teams from all branches throughout the world and used the highest gains as the standard for all the plants. Besides the strong discipline and surveillance guaranteed by the system, it also ensured that individuals and teams were constantly speeding up production to comply with the company's ever changing standards (p. 285).

During the late 1980s, several organizations in both the private and public sectors embraced a team concept, comprising a just-in-time inventory system and a systematic speed-up, which had given General Motors a high increase in labor productivity. After an examination, Mike Parker and Jane Slaughter (1988, pp. 37–44) determined that the system, which they referred to as "management by stress," focused on speeding up production and was driven and regulated by stress. During the assembly process, the speed of the line was increased, making it difficult for employees to keep up. The employees then had the option to stop the assembly line, where they were identified immediately as failing to maintain the speed. To minimize this problem, some workers used their breaks or came early to build stock or get ready. To highlight the trauma, the authors explained the experience of a female worker.

> She had a hard time one day and pulled the stop cord several times. The next day management focused attention on her. Several management officials observed, and they set up a video camera to record her work. She found herself working further into the hole. She worked into the hole too far and fell off the end of the [two-foot] platform and injured her ankle. They told her it was her fault—she didn't pull the stop cord when she fell behind (Parker and Slaughter 1988, p. 42).

The authors indicated that management viewed workers as cogs in the system, one they saw as an intensification of Taylorism. Despite the productivity gains achieved, they concluded that it was "at great cost to the humane work environment" (Parker and Slaughter 1988, p. 44). It seems that several companies, such as the one where information is flashed across the screen, are forcing speed-ups not simply by stress but by deception and manipulation of mental processes.

Speed-Ups: The Disadvantages

There are several views about the use of speed-ups to achieve productivity gains. Unlike "management by stress," workers cannot be removed because they are unable to maintain intense speed to meet demands. Besides resistance from unions, there are several other problems that can emerge.

First, although speed-ups might increase productivity in the short run, the gains might be minimal. Further, they will not be maintained over long periods due to the physical limitations of employees (Prokopenko 1987, pp. 3–4).

Second, speed-ups may require employees to work long hard hours under pressure to meet deadlines. This increased pressure for higher level of performance may cause psychological stress, which ultimately will impact negatively on productivity (Luthans 1985, p. 136).

Third, the constant demands made by supervisors can cause adversarial relationships in the workplace. These conflicts between supervisors and employees can result in low morale, absenteeism, and high turnover. Also, employees may retaliate through sabotage, deception, disruptions, and even violence.

Fourth, one important aspect of productivity is "doing the right things better" (Prokopenko 1987, p. 9). It also involves achieving a higher output and increasing or maintaining quality. With speed-ups, although output might increase, there is no consideration for quality, which can lead to the production of inferior products.

Along with the previously mentioned problems, speed-ups can result in the slowing down of production. Because of the constant pressure placed on employees, the relationship with the union may become adversarial. This may lead to strikes or work to rule, which can be disastrous for the organization. Slow-downs could also occur in response to speed-ups when workers are increasingly pressured, which might make the environment intolerable. However, there are some problems inherent in slow-downs that may occur when unions fail to control their members. Further, slow-downs have had limited effect in companies that are automated. Despite the limitations, during the 1980s, they were used successfully (Kotlowitz 1987, pp. 1, 8).

Slow-Downs: The Disadvantages

A. Kotlowitz (1987) espoused that slow-downs have not been very effective in fully automated organizations and that several problems emerge when they are used. First, some unions have been unable to prevent their members from damaging company property and committing acts of sabotage. Second, some employees do not comply with the unions' policies and instead idle or "rivet air" to appear to be working. These employees when detected have been fired to the dismay of the unions (pp. 1, 8).

Conclusion

It would be erroneous to argue that speed-ups should be removed from management's repertoire of strategic moves. There are times when they might be necessary to help an organization deliver its products timely or even boost productivity. In such situations, however, management should make it clear to employees why speed-ups are necessary.

The workplace continues to be revolutionized with the implementation of different information technologies, which are vital to an organization's performance. However, some firms have not achieved the gains they had envisaged. Research has now identified management as the source of the problems (Shani and Sena 1994, pp. 247–270). This does not come as a surprise when the new technologies are being misused by companies bent on surveilling and controlling their workforce, a trend referred to as an "electronic panopticon" (Sewell and Wilkinson 1992, p. 250). Speed-ups and slow-downs will continue to be a part of organizations, particularly those that are under pressure to increase their productivity. However, management should realize that workers will eventually retaliate whenever their work tasks are intensified. Managers must remember that productivity is achieved through intelligent work, and the key to success, according to Peter Drucker, is knowledge, not sweat (in Sewell and Wilkinson 1992, p. 245).

KEITH CARRINGTON

BIBLIGRAPHY

Denhardt, R., 1984. *Theories of Public Organization.* Belmont, CA: Brooks/Cole.

Donnelly, J. H., Jr., J. L. Gibson, and J. M. Ivancevich, 1987. *Fundamentals of Management,* 6th ed. Plano, TX: Business Publications.

Harrison, J. B., R. E. Sullivan, and D. Sherman, 1985. *A Short History of Western Civilization.* Volume 2. Since 1600, 6th ed. New York: Alfred A. Knopf.

Kotlowitz, A., 1987. "Labor's Shift: Finding Strikes Harder to Win, More Unions Turn to Slowdowns." *Wall Street Journal,* 1, 8.

Luthans, F., 1985. *Organizational Behavior,* 4th ed. New York: McGraw-Hill.

Marx, G. T., and S. Sherizen, 1986. "Monitoring on the Job: How to Protect Privacy as Well as Property." *Technology Review* (November-December) 62–72.

Parker, M., and Jane. Slaughter, 1988. "Management by Stress." *Technology Review* (October) 37–44.

Petri, H. L., 1981. *Motivation: Theory and Research.* Belmont, CA: Wadsworth.

Prokopenko, J., 1987. *Productivity Management: A Practical Handbook.* Geneva, Switzerland: International Labour Office.

Sewell, G., and B. Wilkinson, 1992. "'Someone to Watch over Me': Surveillance, Discipline, and the Just-in-Time Labour Process." *Sociology,* vol. 26, no. 2: 271–289.

Shafritz J. M., and J. S. Ott, 1992. *Classics of Organization Theory,* 3d ed. Blemont, CA: Brooks/Cole.

Shani, A. B., and J. A. Sena, 1994. "Information Technology and the Integration of Change: Sociotechnical System Approach." *Journal of Applied Behavioral Science,* vol. 30, no. 2: 247–270.

Webster, F., and K. Robins, 1993. "'I'll Be Watching You': Comment on Sewell and Wilkinson." *Sociology,* vol. 27, no. 2: 243–252.

Wyles, C., 1986. "Computers: Think Big, but Start Small." *Works Management* (February) 35–37.

SPOILS SYSTEM.

A process whereby rewards in the form of government jobs or other types of preferential treatment are given by successful candidates for public office in exchange for partisan support during the political campaign. It is not at all uncommon to find this spoilslike practice in governmental systems throughout the world. Monarchies, oligarchies, and democracies alike have historically found it convenient to use positions in the public service as rewards for loyal followers and supporters.

In the United States, this system is based on the philosophy of "to the victor belong the spoils," a phrase first used by Senator William Marcy of New York, but widely associated with President Andrew Jackson. President Jackson certainly endorsed this philosophy based on his belief that men of average intelligence should be able to perform government jobs (a distinct anti-elitism attitude) and on the belief that rapid rotation in office for public servants was, in the end, a positive rather than a negative factor.

Under the spoils system, public servants' job tenure at the national, state, and local levels of government was based on having supported the winning political candidate at the last election. Under this system, political loyalty was a crucial factor in filling public-sector jobs.

During the years when spoils politics was widely used in the United States (1830s to 1880s), political parties thrived by exchanging political favors for party loyalty, support, and service. The spoils system also served to bring previously excluded groups such as immigrants and small property owners into the political process. This system served to enhance the political responsiveness of public-sector bureaucracies to elected leadership since the public servants' livelihood was directly related to the success of their candidate.

Spoils, however, also had a very disturbing side. A negative image was created for government service since the general public started to associate government jobs as being based on "who" you know rather than "what" you know. Since loyalty was sometimes heavily preferred to competence and knowledge in the selection process, government employees were sometimes perceived as less competent than their private-sector counterparts. Moral arguments were raised about the propriety, in a political system based on mass participation in free and open elections, of trading a vote on election day for a job or other government favor. Over time, corruption became associated with the buying and selling of government jobs, and, finally, the spoils system was charged with spawning the ultimate in evil–the murder of a president. When President James Garfield was assassinated by a disappointed office seeker named Charles Guiteau, the motivation was spoils based.

Throughout the history of the United States, the spoils system has played a significant role in public-service employment. The necessity for the criteria of political loyalty for some public servants has been recognized over the years by setting aside a number of government jobs that are "exempt" from the merit systems now so commonly found. The numbers of spoils-type positions have declined since their zenith in the 1860s and 1870s to the point today where roughly 90 percent of federal government employees are hired through well-established, merit-based procedures and criteria. The courts have also been active in narrowing the types of positions that can be governed under strictly patronage-type criteria in cases such as *Elrod v. Burns, Branti v. Finkel,* and *Rutan v. Republican Party of Illinois.*

In the Elrod case, the Supreme Court decided that the wholesale dismissal of large numbers of Chicago public servants based on political party affiliation was unjustified and a violation of their First Amendment rights since the dismissals could serve to severely restrict freedom of political belief. The court acknowledged that First Amendment freedom under the U.S. Constitution was not an absolute freedom, but they felt it should only be constrained by the government upon the showing of a legitimate governmental interest in doing so. This interest, the court concluded, should be one of vital importance, and the burden of

showing its importance should be carried by the government. In this case, the rationales advanced by the government for the partisan firings were not accepted as of vital enough consequence to warrant all dismissals, and the court felt dismissals should be limited to employees working in what might be called "policymaking" positions.

In two subsequent cases, *Branti v. Finkel* and *Rutan v. the Republican Party of Illinois,* the court further clarified the issue of the legitimacy of patronage-based personnel actions. In *Branti* the court better defined policymaking positions where "party affiliation is an appropriate requirement for the effective performance of the public office involved." In this case, the Court prevented the patronage-based dismissals of county assistant public defenders since they concluded that their jobs were based in the interests of their clients and not based on partisan political interests. In the 1990 Rutan case, the Court expanded the First Amendment protections to personnel actions other than dismissals. As a result of this decision, patronage-based personnel actions such as transfers, layoffs, recalls, and promotions must meet the same standards as the court laid down in *Elrod* and clarified in *Branti.*

Today then, in the American system, patronage-based personnel actions must take into consideration public-employee protections under the First Amendment. Gone are the days when the philosophy of "to the victor belong the spoils" dominated the hiring and firing of public servants. The advent of merit systems with their protections for merit-system employees and the three court decisions discussed above have severely limited the powers of elected officials to use public-service jobs as a means of political reward or to eliminate individuals from those jobs as a means of political punishment. Today, only employees whose jobs are truly policymaking in nature, a small percentage of public-service employment, are subject to partisan-based dismissals.

ROBERT H. ELLIOTT

BIBLIOGRAPHY

Cayer, N. Joseph, 1989. *Public Personnel Administration in the United States,* 2d. ed. New York: St. Martin's.
Rabin, Jack, Thomas Vocino, W. Bartley Hildreth, and Gerald Miller, eds., 1995. *Handbook of Public Personnel Administration.* New York: Marcel Dekker.
Van Riper, Paul, 1958. *History of the United States Civil Service.* Evanston, IL: Row, Peterson.

STAATS, ELMER B. (1914–). Comptroller General of the United States from 1966 to 1981. He was appointed to this position by President Lyndon B. Johnson after having served as deputy director of the Budget under Presidents Harry S. Truman, Dwight Eisenhower, John F. Kennedy, and Lyndon Johnson.

Elmer Staats was born on June 6, 1914 in Richfield, Kansas, a small prairie town in the southwest corner of the state, located on the North Fork of the Cimarron River near the Colorado state line. He received his undergraduate degree from McPherson College in 1935 and his master of arts the following year from the University of Kansas. Three years later, he earned his Ph.D. in economics and government from the University of Minnesota.

In 1939, he was hired as a staff member of the Bureau of the Budget (now the Office of Management and Budget), where over the next 11 years he rose to become the deputy director. During the World War II period, Staats was responsible for organization, coordination, financing, and management of the principal civilian war agencies.

In 1953, he worked in Chicago in private industry, but, within a year, returned to Washington to become executive director of the Operations Coordinating Board of the National Security Council. He returned to the Bureau of the Budget in 1958 as an assistant director and, in 1959, was appointed deputy director, a position he held until early 1966, when President Johnson selected him as comptroller general. Following Senate confirmation, he was sworn into office on March 8, 1966.

During his 15-year tenure as comptroller general, Staats brought about significant organizational changes within the General Accounting Office (GAO). By the time he retired in 1981, there were 11 divisions and numerous staff offices, 15 regional offices, and 3 overseas offices. Administrative staffing had increased to include three assistant comptrollers general (for Administration, Program Evaluation, and Policy and Program Planning), as well as the position of deputy comptroller general.

Staats was widely known in Congress and entered his term well prepared for the many challenges that lay ahead. The first issue Staats dealt with was the issue of defense contract audits. He placed special emphasis on the implementation of the Truth in Negotiations Act. By placing importance on the internal audit work of the Defense Contract Audit Agency, in conjunction with the Truth in Negotiations Act, he felt GAO could be less involved with detailed audits of defense contracts. An important development related to contract audits was the creation of the Cost Accounting Standards Board (CASB) in 1971. Staats, the comptroller general, was chairman and appointed four other members.

The GAO began a large-scale evaluation of government poverty programs in the late 1960s. Their findings revealed some progress in most programs, but management and administrative improvements were needed.

In 1972, GAO published the *Standards for Audit of Government Organizations, Programs, Activities, and Functions,* or Yellow Book, for application of government audits at all levels. GAO also became involved in the International Organization of Supreme Audit Institutions (INTOSAI). In 1968, Staats attended the 6th International

Congress of INTOSAI in Tokyo, GAO's first participation. In 1971, at the INTOSAI Montreal Congress, Staats led a discussion on management, or operational, auditing. GAO supported publication of INTOSAI's quarterly journal and assumed responsibility for editing and publishing it in five languages. Staats also began GAO's International Auditor Fellowship Program providing GAO training to INTO-SAI's member nations.

New legislation in the early 1970s greatly affected the GAO workload. First was the Presidential Election Campaign Act, which provided for a checkoff procedure on tax forms that allocates US $1.00 to a political party to help finance presidential campaigns. The comptroller general audited candidate expense reports and certified payments to candidates for president and vice president, commencing in 1976.

Another law was the Federal Campaign Act in 1972 that required GAO to issue regulations on spending limits of the media by or for candidates for federal offices. The comptroller general was designated as supervisory officer for presidential and vice presidential campaigns and national convention financing. The comptroller general was to develop regulations and forms for use by candidates and audit expenditure and contribution accounts.

GAO opposed these laws, favoring the creation of a nonpartisan commission but set about to quickly undertake the unwanted duties. The Office of Federal Elections (OFE) was created. This commission developed regulations for finance committees as well as candidates. Committee reports were audited and questionable campaign practices were investigated. The presidential election of 1972 was a major task. One audit report covered campaign contributions to Richard Nixon, monies allegedly spent to support the Watergate burglary. This information was referred to the Department of Justice.

In October 1974, a new Federal Elections Commission (FEC) was established by Congress, which transferred the workload from the comptroller general as administrator of the Presidential Election Campaign Fund and supervisory officer for campaigns. When the FEC began, the OFE ended.

Other new investigations by GAO included reviews of major weapon system acquisitions, consumer protection (food plant sanitation, marketing ineffective vaccines, etc.), and, based on the National Environmental Policy Act and the Clean Air Act, problems of air and water pollution and hazards from pesticides. Even the Federal Bureau of Investigation (FBI) failed to escape GAO's audits. In 1974, GAO began to investigate FBI programs, including the domestic intelligence operations.

GAO audited the Internal Revenue Services (IRS), with reports on tax administration and repetitive taxpayer audits, among others. The banking system was examined with reports of the Federal Reserve System and the Federal Deposit Insurance Corporation. GAO also began auditing international organizations in which the United States participated, such as the United Nations and the World Bank.

Following the Arab-Israeli War of 1973, energy issues were prime requests, such as reports on the Three Mile Island accident, commercializing of solar energy, and Tennessee Valley Authority operations. Economic issues came to the forefront by the mid-1970s, with GAO issuing reports on the New York City fiscal crisis, the competitive nature of international markets, and the national balance of payments.

GAO testimony before congressional committees increased significantly during Staats's tenure. In his first five years as comptroller general, GAO testified an average of 30 times per year; during his last five years, the average was 156 times per year. Financial benefits due to GAO work also increased; from US $1 billion in Staats' first five years to US $16.4 billion between 1976 and 1980.

After retirement on March 4, 1981, following his 15-year tenure as comptroller general, Staats served with various government management organizations, such as the National Academy of Public Administration and the National Commission on the Public Service. He also has served on the Board of Directors of several nonprofit organizations and corporations. He was a founding member in 1939, as well as national president in 1967, of the American Society for Public Administration.

Staats was a member of the Governmental Accounting Standards Board from 1984 to 1990, at which time he was appointed as the first chairman of the Federal Accounting Standards Advisory Board. This board was established by the comptroller general, the treasurer, and the director of the Office of Management and Budget (hereafter referred to as the principals) in response to the requirements of the Chief Financial Officers Act in 1990. The board is responsible for making recommendations to the principals on accounting standards to apply to the federal government.

Eight universities have awarded Staats with honorary degrees. He is also the recipient of numerous other awards, including election to the Accounting Hall of Fame in 1981.

Staats was married in 1940 and had three children. He resides in Washington, D.C., where he is a member of the Cosmos and Chevy Chase Clubs and the Metropolitan Memorial United Methodist Church.

JESSE W. HUGHES

BIBLIOGRAPHY

Trask, Roger R., 1991. *GAO History 1921–1991*. Washington, DC: General Accounting Office.

STAFFING. That process of human resource management that includes both human resource planning

(discussed as a separate term), recruitment (also discussed separately), and selection. Selection–either initial to the organization or selection for some higher-level position–may be composed of a large number of steps with each step designed to narrow the number of eligible candidates until one candidate emerges; or selection may be a simple process of choosing from any number of candidates meeting basic minimum qualifications for a position.

Historically, staffing governmental positions throughout the world has been the end result of any number of competing and oftentimes conflicting national values. In the United States, the elitism of our earliest period of American history was followed by the spoils system generally associated with President Andrew Jackson. This spoils era gradually gave way to the Pendleton Act of 1883 and more merit-based staffing decisions. In more recent years, values such as scientific management and achieving a more representative bureaucracy through affirmative action programs have been added to earlier staffing considerations. Public employment and the nature of the public workforce have always been a reflection of changing societal values at different points in time.

Common selection devices historically used in public-sector selection processes include evaluations of minimum qualifications as determined through answers given on a job application form, a written test designed to measure basic knowledge, skills, or abilities needed to perform the position, a performance test designed to allow the candidate to demonstrate through some job simulation the ability to perform certain job tasks (typing tests, machinery operating tests), a training and experience evaluation, oral interviews between a candidate or candidates and a single hiring official or a panel of interviewers, reference checks, and probationary periods.

Under Title VII of the Civil Rights Act of 1964 with its various amendments added over the decades, American employers must be able to demonstrate, if challenged, that all selection devices are related to actual job duties. In a number of Supreme Court cases dating back to the 1970s (*Griggs v. Duke Power Company, Albemerle Paper Company v. Moody,* and *Washington v. Davis*), the courts have made it clear that where a selection device results in a disproportionate screening out of members of protected groups, employers have a responsibility to demonstrate the job relatedness of these screening devices when they are legally challenged.

In recent years, staffing procedures used in American federal employment have been criticized for being unnecessarily time consuming and complicated. Federal managers have complained that they have too little control over the selection process since much of it is heavily centralized through the Office of Personnel Management (OPM). In response to some of these criticisms, OPM has started to decentralize many selection procedures, allowing departments to become more actively involved in making

selection decisions. Departments are slowly being allowed to give their own tests and make their own staffing decisions. Federal recruiters have sometimes been given authority to make on-sight job offers to candidates on college campuses if those candidates meet certain previously determined criteria. The lengthy and complicated federal job application form is being abolished and simpler application procedures are being instituted. Efforts are all being directed toward shortening the lengthy application process and decentralizing the entire selection system. OPM's new role appears to be one of adviser and facilitator for line management, but not one as the most powerful actor in the staffing process.

ROBERT H. ELLIOTT

BIBLIOGRAPHY

Mosher, Frederick C., 1968. *Democracy and the Public Service.* New York: Oxford University Press.
U.S. General Accounting Office, 1990. *Federal Recruiting and Hiring, Making Government Jobs Attractive to Prospective Employees.* Washington, DC: U.S. Government Printing Office.
U.S. Merit Systems Protection Board, 1990. *Attracting and Selecting Quality Applicants for Federal Employment.* Washington, DC: U.S. Government Printing Office.

STAKEHOLDER. An individual or group who has a "stake," or interest, in an organization–sometimes referred to as an influencer, claimant, public, or constituency. More formally, "stakeholder" has been defined as "any group or individual who can affect or is affected by the achievement of an organization's purpose" (Freeman 1984, p. 53). Whereas Freeman applies the term to business organizations, others have analyzed stakeholders in government and the nonprofit sector. In the business setting, stakeholders can include owners, suppliers, employees, customers, competitors, governments, media, financial institutions, and critics. In government, stakeholders might encompass elected officials (legislators, chief executives, heads of administrative agencies), appointed officials (civil servants, bureau chiefs, department heads), members of interest groups (business, professional, labor advocacy), opinion leaders, political parties, and individual citizens. In nonprofit organizations, such as hospitals, stakeholders might be internal to the organization (e.g., employees), "spanners" on the boundary of the organization and its environment (e.g., governing board), or external to the facility (e.g., government and other health care enterprises). Stakeholder management assumes that the survival and prosperity of an organization is dependent on the degree to which it meets the needs of these key stakeholders and that an organization's strategy will succeed only if it satisfies major stakeholders.

The word "stakeholder" was originally coined by the Stanford Research Institute (SRI) in 1963. Building on the work of planners at Lockheed, stakeholder analysis became an important element in the SRI corporate planning process. While SRI researchers and consultants continued to develop the stakeholder idea in the 1960s and early 1970s, few outside this group applied the concept. By the mid-1970s, interest in stakeholder analysis increased as scholarly and professional writing on strategic planning, systems theory, corporate social responsibility, and organizational theory further developed or refined the stakeholder concept and confirmed its relevance to strategic management. The late 1970s brought the recognition that strategic management processes had to factor in the nontraditional business concerns of government, special interest groups, and other constituencies, leading to "a stakeholder project" undertaken by the Applied Research Center at the Wharton School in 1977, which sought to explore the stakeholder concept as management theory, as a process used in strategic management, and as a framework for analysis. These developments are traced in detail in the literature (Freeman 1984; Freeman and Reed 1983).

Stakeholder Analysis

Stakeholder analysis is a powerful tool that is useful to public, nonprofit and private-sector managers, especially those who operate in a highly political environment, because it takes into account the organization's relationship with specific stakeholder groups as the organization clarifies its mission, formulates its strategy, and conducts its operations. This approach helps managers determine the groups that are likely to affect their organization's operations, what their interests are, the criteria they use to judge the organization's performance, how and when to act toward them, and how to allocate resources for stakeholder management. The key steps in stakeholder management include (1) identification of the stakeholders, (2) construction of a stakeholder map of these individuals and groups, (3) assessment of how well the organization is meeting the needs of stakeholders, and (4) readjusting the organization's priorities to bring it in sync with stakeholder interests.

Stakeholder identification involves specification of the groups, their interests, and their bases of power. Construction of the list of individuals and groups as stakeholders—whether internal or external, hostile or friendly to the organization's purpose—is determined by their potential to "affect and be affected by" the organization's operations. Key questions to ask in completing a stakeholder analysis include the following: Who are stakeholders? What are the goals, expectations, or interests of each stakeholder? To what extent does the status quo meet the goals, expectations, or interests of each stakeholder? How important is

each stakeholder to the organization's success? How can each stakeholder influence the organization's efforts? What is needed from each stakeholder to accomplish the organization's objectives? John Bryson and Barbara Crosby (1992) provide detailed examples of group process methods (e.g., the "snow card" techniques) that have been used successfully in answering these key questions by public-sector organizations seeking policy change. Another consideration in stakeholder analysis is the categorization of individuals and groups based on the scope of their concerns—single issue vs. multiple issue, economic or social interests, concrete or symbolic interests, local, state, national, or international interests (Wood 1994). Following specification of stakeholder interests, the relations between particular groups and the organization can be "mapped."

Stakeholder Mapping

Stakeholder mapping entails assessing the direction, strength, and immediacy of the effect of the stakeholder group on the organization as well as an assessment of the probability that the organization can deal with the demands of the stakeholder group. It is possible to use matrix formats in assessing these factors for each stakeholder group; in some instances, numerical rating and weighting schemes may be employed. Stakeholder maps also identify the linkages among stakeholder groups (e.g., coalitions) and track the changing relations sequentially among groups over time. Stakeholder analysis provides a picture of the key stakeholders and their likely impact on the organization, which can then be used to fashion effective stakeholder management processes.

A typology of stakeholder interests and power has been developed by Edward Freeman and David Reed (1983) with interests categorized as (1) equity (or ownership), (2) economic (involving money or resources), and (3) influence (where symbolic stakes or values rather than material or financial stakes are involved). Power is categorized as (1) formal (or voting), (2) economic, and (3) political power. Knowledge of the stakes and power bases enables stakeholder managers to determine how well their organization is addressing multiple constituencies, devising and applying tailored strategies, and allocating resources to satisfy diverse claimants (Wood 1994).

Bryson and Crosby (1992) as well as Paul Nutt and Robert Backoff (1992) build on Freeman's (1984) work to show how different organizational strategies are needed to deal with particular stakeholders based on the importance of the stakeholders and their stand on the particular issue in question. They suggest use of a two-by-two matrix where one dimension depicts the stakeholder's importance regarding the issue in question and the other dimension indicates the support or opposition of the stakeholder to the organization's position on the issue. These authors propose specific tactics that can be used to deal with various categories of stakeholders, including those that reinforce support (e.g., information dissemination, co-optation, trial balloons, persuasion), lessen antagonism (e.g., blocking coalition formation, developing counterarguments, negotiating, working with neutral stakeholders), and prevent "problematics" from becoming antagonists (e.g., targeting, modifying proposals, preparing defensive tactics). These authors encourage those advocating change to think in stakeholder terms when formulating, adopting, or implementing proposals.

The literature contains numerous examples of the application of stakeholder analysis to public, nonprofit and private-sector issues. In a public-sector example, Nancy Roberts and Paula King (1989) illustrate the usefulness of stakeholder management by showing how a state commissioner of education used its principles to make change in the statewide educational system. The commissioner began with a stakeholder audit, which identified the key actors, including their interests, past behavior, power resources, the effectiveness of past strategies in dealing with them, new strategies required to deal with them, and the effectiveness of these new strategies. The stakeholder map that emerged from this analysis identified two broad coalitions—one supporting her plan and one supporting an alternative. An assessment of current and needed new strategies suggested that a "bridging strategy" with the commissioner as the key "change agent" was appropriate and subsequent evaluation indicated that this approach was effective in bringing the two opposing groups together. The authors conclude with suggestions about important considerations to keep in mind when conducting stakeholder audits.

Other researchers have focused more on the managerial advantages that stakeholder analysis offers to nonprofit organizations. For example, scholars recently sought to identify those groups that make a difference to hospital administrators and how knowledge of such groups can guide strategic decisionmaking regarding formulation of alternative action plans. Awareness of these groups allows administrators to anticipate the likely reactions of key stakeholders and to think strategically about ways to gain stakeholder acceptance of such plans (Fottler et al. 1989). Similarly, other studies have focused on the appropriate action steps required to effectively negotiate with hospital stakeholders (Blair, Savage, and Whitehead 1989).

Stakeholder analysis and management is perhaps most common in private-sector organizations where this approach has been used to better understand social issues management, to see if particular types of stakeholder management devices are associated with various organizational characteristics, to examine the ways firms manage multiple stakeholder relationships (e.g., research on public affairs management, corporate social planning, and social problemsolving), to increase awareness of stakeholder management processes by research using theoretical approaches

from unrelated theoretical traditions (e.g., agent-principle relations, boundary spanning, agency theory, corporate social responsiveness, corporate ethics and strategy), and research on management of specific stakeholder relations (e.g., in corporate philanthropy, community relations, international settings, and business-government relations). For a summary of this literature see Donna Wood (1991) and Freeman (1984).

Stakeholder analysis has made a contribution to strategic planning by expanding the focus of traditional private-sector models of strategy, which center exclusively on economic actors, to include a broader focus that integrates economic, political, social, technological, and ecological concerns. Bryson and William Roering (1987) contended that the mission and values of an organization–key components of strategic planning–should be developed with consideration given to each stakeholder group so that it can "differentiate its responses well enough to satisfy its key stakeholders" (p. 16). These authors cite case study examples from business as well as local government where stakeholder analyses are a useful adjunct to a strategic planning endeavor.

Stakeholder analysis has also contributed to program evaluation and studies of organizational effectiveness. Researchers have proposed a "multiple-constituency" approach for the purpose of assessing organizational effectiveness based on the assumption that an organization's diverse constituencies will arrive at different assessments of an enterprise's effectiveness (Connolly, Conlon, and Deutsch 1980). For example, stakeholder analysis has been used to assess human resource (HR) effectiveness by focusing on the value of the services of an HR, or personnel, department, as perceived by its users (Ulrich 1989). Similarly, survey data were used from five stakeholder groups to evaluate municipal police services (Deutsch and Malmborg 1986).

Strengths and Weaknesses

The stakeholder approach has both strengths and weaknesses. Among its strong points are its focus on competing claimants—supportive and antagonistic, internal and external—and the imperative to meet the needs of key stakeholders to ensure organizational survival, its use of stakeholder analysis to build a list of important stakeholders and to examine the criteria used by the actors in judging an organization's performance, and its potential to be used in conjunction with other approaches to strategic planning and management. The weaknesses of this approach are the lack of criteria to use in assessing these competing claims and the need for additional guidance on the ways to tailor strategies in order to address the interests of multiple constituencies (see Bryson and Roering 1987).

JONATHAN P. WEST

BIBLIOGRAPHY

Blair, John D., Grant T. Savage, and Carlton J. Whitehead, 1989. "A Strategic Approach for Negotiating with Hospital Stakeholders." *Health Care Management Review*, vol. 14, no. 1: 13–23.

Bryson, John M., and Barbara Crosby, 1992. *Leadership for the Common Good*. San Francisco, CA: Jossey-Bass.

Bryson, John M. and William D. Roering, 1987. "Applying Private-Sector Strategic Planning in the Public Sector." *APA Journal* (Winter) 9–22.

Connolly, Terry, Edward J. Conlon, and Stuart Jay Deutsch, 1980. "Organizational Effectiveness: A Multiple Constituency Approach." *The Academy of Management*, vol. 5, no. 2: 211–217.

Deutsch, Stuart Jay, and Charles J. Malmborg, 1986. "A Study on the Consistency of Stakeholder Preferences for Different Types of Information in Evaluating Police Services." *Evaluation and Program Planning*, vol. 9, no. 1: 13–24.

Fottler, Myron D., John D. Blair, Michael D. Laus, and Grant T. Savage, 1989. "Assessing Key Stakeholders: Who Matters to Hospitals and Why?" *Hospital & Health Services Administration*, vol. 34, no. 4 (Winter) 525–546.

Freeman, R. Edward, 1984. *Strategic Management: A Stakeholder Approach*. Boston, MA: Pitman.

———, and David L. Reed, 1983. "Stockholders and Stakeholders: A New Perspective on Corporate Governance." *California Management Review*, vol. 25, no. 3 (Spring) 88–106.

Gray, Barbara, and Donna J. Wood, 1991. "Collaborative Alliances: Moving from Practice to Theory." *Journal of Applied Behavioral Science*, vol. 27, no. 1 (March) 3–22.

Mitroff, Ian I., 1983. *Stakeholders of the Organizational Mind*. San Francisco, CA: Jossey-Bass.

Nutt, Paul C., and Robert W. Backoff, 1992. *Strategic Management of Public and Third Sector Organizations: A Handbook for Leaders*. San Francisco, CA: Jossey-Bass.

Roberts, Nancy C., and Raymond Trevor Bradley, 1991. "Stakeholder Collaboration and Innovation: A Study of Public Policy Initiation at the State Level." *Journal of Applied Behavioral Science*. vol. 27, no. 2 (June) 209–227.

Roberts, Nancy C. and Paula J. King, 1989. "The Stakeholder Audit Goes Public." *Organizational Dynamics*, vol. 17, no. 3 (Winter) 63–79.

Ulrich, Dave, 1989. "Assessing Human Resource Effectiveness: Stakeholder, Utility, and Relationship Approaches." *Human Resource Planning*. vol. 12, no. 4: 301–315.

Wood, Donna, 1991. "Corporate Social Performance Revisited." *The Academy of Management Review*, vol. 16, no. 4 (October) 691–718.

———, 1994. *Business and Society*. New York: HarperCollins.

STANDARDS OF CONDUCT. Ethical guidelines for behavior that prescribe how someone ought to act. A "standard" is most commonly thought of as a rule, value, or principle, sanctioned by an authority, that is used as a basis in making a judgement. In this case, the term "standard of conduct" has an ethical connotation because it offers a moral imperative as to how one should act in relationship to others. The Ten Commandments in Judeo-Christian belief or the Eight-fold Path in Buddhism reflect examples of religious standards of conduct, but the term has relevance in a variety of other contexts as well.

From the viewpoint of public administration, a standard of conduct presumes a public manager behaves according to a defined role with an accompanying set of responsibilities. Standards of conduct provide the basis for how an administrator should act in fulfilling these responsibilities. Often standards are put in the form of moral principles, such as the five outlined in the Code of Ethics for the American Society for Public Administration (1994): (1) serve the public interest, (2) respect the Constitution and the law, (3) demonstrate personal integrity, (4) promote ethical organizations, and (5) strive for professional excellence. In other instances, they may be put in the form of exhortations or prohibitions. For example, the 1980 Code of Ethics for Government Service in the United States admonishes public employees to adhere to nine standards of conduct, such as, "Put loyalty to the highest moral principles and to country above loyalty to persons, party, or Government department" and "Make no private promises of any kind binding upon duties of office, since a government employee has no private word which can be binding on public duty."

Sometimes values, principles, and rules are combined into one specific standard of conduct, such as one taken from the International City Managers' Association Code of Ethics: "Professional Respect. Members seeking a management position should show professional respect for persons formally holding the position or for others who might be applying for the same position. Professional respect does not preclude honest differences of opinion; it does preclude attacking a person's motives or integrity in order to be appointed to a position."

In this case, the principle of "professional respect" is emphasized with an ethical rule that provides a guideline for conduct. Embedded within the standard are a cluster of implied values such as respect, honesty, and freedom of opinion. Taken altogether, this standard of conduct clearly delineates the boundaries of appropriate conduct as it applies to a specific aspect of professionalism.

Standards of conduct emanating from the administrative role reflect two kinds of responsibility. One type of responsibility could be thought of as "objective" in that expectations for behavior are imposed from external authorities such as one's organization, the law that one is obliged to implement, one's profession, and the citizenry. Objective responsibilities obligate the public official to complete certain tasks and be accountable to external authorities for the way in which they are accomplished. Standards of conduct prescribe ethical guidelines for how one is to behave in fulfilling these objective responsibilities. For instance, a federal agency may require its public employees to respect and protect privileged information by upholding confidentiality within the organization, or a professional association may promote the principle of respect for the law by exhorting its members to prevent all forms of mismanagement of public funds by establishing and maintaining strong fiscal and management controls

and by supporting audits and investigative activities. In each case, an external authority is determining what constitutes acceptable ethical behavior.

However, a second kind of responsibility affecting administrative standards of conduct could be termed "subjective" because it reveals an individual manager's idealized value system, the core of which springs from one's feelings and beliefs based on personal experience and professional development. In other words, one's idealized value system becomes the foundation for internal standards of conduct. In this regard, public administrators become their own authority for establishing a set of standards by which to conduct themselves. For instance, if public servants believe in fairness, this may lead them to act with impartiality and consistency in their provision of service to all citizens, or if commitment is a strong personal value, the public servant may strive to administer the public's business in the most competent manner possible. The emphasis here is on the formation of the standard from within the personal framework of the administrator.

Thus, the role of a public official is informed by both objective and subjective responsibilities that give rise to a plethora of standards. Sometimes internal standards of conduct are congruent with external standards of conduct. As an illustration, from a personal and professional perspective a city manager may consider honesty to be a core value. This would resonate with numerous standards of conduct found in the International City Management Association Code of Ethics (1987) such as its guideline regarding credentials: "An application for employment should be complete and accurate as to all pertinent details of education, and personal history. Members should recognize that both omissions and inaccuracies must be avoided." In this case, both objective and subjective responsibilities lead the public administrator to uphold mutually compatible standards of conduct.

However, the variety of authorities that the public manager must serve in fulfilling both kinds of responsibilities can lead to ethical dilemmas involving contending standards of conduct. As a case in point, the fourth principle of the Code of Ethics for the American Society for Public Administration encourages its members to "promote ethical organizations." Among a number of guidelines, one advocates that public officials "subordinate institutional loyalties to the public good." This may clash with the organizational expectation that public employees comply with the directives of their superiors. In this instance, dissension exists between a professional and an organizational standard of conduct.

This example highlights the major strength and weakness of standards of conduct. On the one hand, their primary benefit is that they provide ethical rules of thumb by which the public administrator can discern the boundaries of appropriate behavior. On the other hand, their major liability is that they are limited in instructing managers as to what specific courses of action should be taken in particular situations. In short, adhering to standards of conduct does not ensure that a public official will act ethically, but they can provide useful parameters for responsible administrative action by public servants.

APRIL HEJKA-EKINS

BIBLIOGRAPHY

American Society for Public Administration, 1994. "Code of Ethics." Washington, DC: American Society for Public Administration.

"Code of Ethics for Government Service," 1980. Public Law 96–303, Washington, DC: United States Congress.

Cooper, Terry L., 1990. *The Responsible Administrator: An Approach to Ethics for the Administrative Role*, 3d ed. San Francisco, CA: Jossey-Bass.

International City Management Association, 1987. "Code of Ethics with Guidelines." Washington, DC: ICMA.

Mertins, Herman, Jr., Frances Burke, Robert W. Kweit, and Gerald M. Pops, 1994. "Applying Professional Standards and Ethics in the Nineties: A Workbook and Study Guide with Cases for Public Administrators." Washington, DC: American Society for Public Administration.

Richter, William L., Frances Burke, and Jameson W. Doig, eds., 1990. *Combating Corruption/Encouraging Ethics: A Sourcebook for Public Service Ethics*. Washington, DC: American Society for Public Administration.

STANDING. The legal right to sue another party in court. In the context of administrative law, fundamental standing law holds that those who are harmed by administrative action should have the opportunity to challenge the legality of the action in court, as long as the action is legitimately reviewable agency action on other grounds. The standing issue essentially asks that the court answer the vital question, Should the petitioner have the right to "stand" before the court and argue his/her case? Should the person be given the right to be heard by a court? Or, as Justice William Brennan put it so simply in *Association of Data Processing Organizaions v. Camp*, 397 U.S. 150, 169 fn. 2 (1970), the standing issue addresses the question of "whether the *particular* plaintiff then requesting review may have it".

Although the basic standing issue is a very simple one, the importance of the question of standing should not be underestimated. The doctrine of standing poses a prerequisite question. That is, will the court let a person have standing so that the person can have the opportunity to argue the case on the basis of its merits? Standing must be obtained before the petitioner's dispute will be allowed to continue. Many times, especially in administrative law cases, petitioners fail to pass the entryway standing test and are thereby prevented from presenting a possibly solid case before the court on the basis of the merits. Actually, it has been argued that the courts sometimes unreasonably deny standing to petitioners so that they can avoid having to reach an unwanted decision (a possible example might be a decision that a court feels will create too much social unrest) based upon solid evidence and sound legal arguments.

Since the late 1960s, the courts have become in general more lenient in granting standing. Whereas at one time the courts interpreted injury in very narrow terms, thus precluding the possibility that many would obtain standing before the court, broad judicial interpretations of what constitutes a litigious injury have recently eroded many of the traditional barriers preventing parties from obtaining standing to sue. The relaxation of standing requirements since the mid-1970s has been largely responsible for a new flood of cases in such citizen-consumer areas as consumer, environmental, and housing law. This development is one of the chief reasons that administrative law has become so important to the study of public administration and public policy in recent years.

What tests must a petitioner pass in order to receive standing? The most basic standing requirement that must be satisfied is a constitutional one. That is, in Article 3, Section 2, the Constitution requires that our federal courts can decide only cases of controversy between parties. This means that a genuine dispute must exit, with the court being placed in a position to provide a judicial remedy (relief) to a legally injured party (one who has suffered an "injury of fact") (*Lujan v. Defenders of Wildlife*, 112 S.Ct. 2130, 1992). This constitutional requirement is designed to prevent abstract nonsense suits or to guard against what Justice Oliver Wendell Holmes referred to, in *Giles v. Harris*, 189 U.S. 475, 486 (1903), as "in the air" controversies.

But what constitutes a cognizable (judicially recognizable) injury? In virtually all cases until the late 1960s, the courts would perceive an injury only as an instance in which one party suffers a direct monetary loss as a result of another's actions. Thus, parties went to court to sue for financial settlements to redress wrongs committed against them. For example, a private company, injured economically by a governmental agency, could sue for financial compensation to cover its losses. Even under this narrow interpretation of standing law, petitioners frequently failed to obtain standing because they could not demonstrate to a court that their financial loss is or would be different from what others in a group would suffer. In *Perkins v. Lukens Steel Co.*, 310 U.S. 113 (1940), the Supreme Court held: "Respondents, to have standing in court, must show an injury or threat to a particular right of their own, as distinguished from the public's interest in the administration of law" (at 125). In an earlier suit by a taxpayer challenging the right of the government to spend his tax dollars on a federal program he opposed, the Court ruled that he was not entitled to standing because he could only show that he is suffering in an indefinite way in common with other taxpayers (*Frothingham v. Mellon*, 262, U.S. 477, 1923). Be-

cause of the consequences of ruling otherwise, standing principle as it applies to taxpayers in Frothingham has never been reversed. In 1984, the Supreme Court, for example, in *Valley Forge ETC v. Americans United, ETC.* 102 S.Ct. 752, upheld the Frothingham rule by refusing to grant standing to the respondents, Americans United for Separation of Church and State *et al.*, who tried to prevent the secretary of Health, Education, and Welfare from giving surplus government property to a religious organization. The Court argued that the respondents lacked standing as taxpayers because they could not show that they had or would suffer any personal injury any different from any other taxpayer. Quoting from Frothingham, the Court said: "The party who invokes the power [of judicial review] must be able to show not only that the statute is invalid but that he has sustained or is immediately in danger of sustaining some direct injury as the result of its enforcement, and not merely that he suffers in some indefinite way in common with people generally" (at 761).

Pressures placed on the courts since the mid-1970s by citizen, consumer, and legal action groups have been quite successful in softening standing requirements. The liberalization of standing law is probably best conveyed in a series of public housing opportunity cases during the 1970s, although this liberalization trend can be seen in a host of cases in other public policy areas. In *Warth v. Seldin*, 422 U.S. 490 (1975), the Supreme Court, in a 5-4 decision, denied standing to petitioners challenging a zoning ordinance that they believed discriminated against low- and moderate-income persons, thus depriving them of affordable housing opportunities in Penfield, a relatively affluent white suburban community near Rochester, New York. Although the Court's majority denied standing to the petitioners on the technical grounds that they were third parties (not the low- and moderate-income persons themselves) and, therefore, could not establish a direct, particularized, and "cognizable interest" in the zoned property in question, the majority did imply that parties with a direct stake in the zoning ordinance who could show that they have a "substantial probability" of being harmed by the ordinance's enforcement could obtain standing. The Warth decision, although generally perceived as a somewhat conservative decision on standing, nevertheless remains a relatively modern standing case because the Court did at least recognize that standing could be granted to a petitioner on the basis of (1) a claimed non-economic injury, (2) a substantial probability that the party will be injured by a governmental action, and (3) a denied statutory entitlement.

In *Resident Advisory Bd. v. Rizzo*, 425 F.Supp. 987 (E.D., Pa., 1976), Judge Broderick, building on Warth, ruled that those being denied housing opportunities were entitled to standing because they could both demonstrate an actual injury and show how the Court could provide remedial measures. Regarding the Resident Advisory Board (RAB), which claimed to be composed of and representing

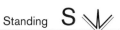

lower-income residents eligible to live in the proposed Whitman public housing project, the Court held:

> RAB is a proper plaintiff with standing to represent its members. Although there is no allegation that RAB was injured as an organization by the termination of the Whitman project, it is clear that RAB has established actual injury to its members. . . . Clearly, if RAB's claims are legally cognizable, its members have been injured by the failure to build the Whitman project. Those RAB members who live in racially impacted areas of the City of Philadelphia are obviously harmed by the failure to build a scheduled housing project in a non-racially impacted area. Those on the waiting list, which is predominantly Black, have lost the opportunity to live in public housing in a Whitman area. Further, the complaint in this case seeks only declaratory and injunctive relief which is prospective in nature and any remedy granted can reasonably be expected to inure to the benefit of those members of the association who have been actually injured. (at 1012)

In *Village of Arlington Heights v. Metropolitan Housing Corp.*, 429 U.S. 252 (1977), the Supreme Court itself cast doubt on the conservative interpretation of Warth by ruling that the Metropolitan Housing Development Corporation (MHDC), a nonprofit organization wishing to build a housing project for lower-income persons, should be given standing on both economic and noneconomic grounds. The Court also emphasized that the MHDC should be given standing because it would likely benefit from a favorable court ruling. In addition, the Court stressed that "it has long been clear that economic injury is not the only kind of injury that can support a plaintiff's standing" (at 262).

In *Duke Power Co. v. Carolina Environmental Study Group*, 438 U.S. 59, a nonhousing case in 1978, the Supreme Court took a bold step toward eliminating several confusing standing requirements. In reviewing previous standing cases, it concluded: "We . . . cannot accept the contention that, outside the context of taxpayers' suits, a litigant must demonstrate anything more than injury in fact and a substantial likelihood that the judicial relief requested will prevent or redress the claimed injury to satisfy the 'use and controversy' requirement of Act III." In many respects, the liberalization of standing law since the late 1960s threw standing law into terrible confusion. Some standing tests were kept, others tossed aside, while still new ones were invented. The confusion over what standing tests should apply under particular circumstances caused many to call for the virtual abandonment of standing requirements. In the future we can expect, as they already do in the states, that courts will grant standing almost routinely, as long as the plaintiffs can pass the simplest standing test of showing only a fairly reasonable causal connection between an injury or likely future injury and the defendant's action. In fact, in *Clarke v. Securities Industry Assn.*, 107 S.Ct. 750 (1987), the Supreme Court applied a simple "zone of interest" test to determine whether standing should be granted. The Court explained that

> the zone of interest test is a guide for deciding whether, in view of Congress' evident intent to make agency action presumptively reviewable, a particular plaintiff should be heard to complain of a particular agency decision. In cases where the plaintiff is not itself the subject of the contested regulatory action, the test denies a right of review if the plaintiff's interest are so marginally related to or inconsistent with the purposes implicit in the statute that it cannot reasonably be assumed that Congress intended to permit the suit. The test is not meant to be especially demanding. (at 757)

In this case, standing was granted because the Court found that "the interest respondent asserts has a plausible relationship to the policies underlying Sections 36 and 81 of the National Bank Act" (at 759).

Unquestionably, it is fairly easy today for parties to obtain standing, yet recent decisions demonstrate that courts are still quick to deny standing if basic standing prerequisites are not satisfied. For example, in *Branton v. FCC*, 993 F.2d 906 (D.C. Cir. 1993), the court denied standing to a listener of a radio broadcast where variations of the "f-word" were aired ten times. After the Federal Communications Commission failed to act upon the listener's complaint, he filed suit in federal court. However, the court held that he lacked standing because no request for damages or other relief for the "marginal" harm was sought, but instead he wanted sanctions imposed against the radio station "in the hope of influencing another's future behavior" (at 909). In *Renne v. Geary*, 111 S.Ct. 2331 (1991), the Supreme Court, although it based its decision on ripeness grounds, argued that it is very questionable whether standing can be given to individual members of a committee because their third-party status does not allow them to sue on behalf of the whole committee. In another case, *INS v. Legalization Assistance Project*, 114 S.Ct. 422 (1993), the high court failed to give standing to Legalization Assistance Project, a legal help organization, which had challenged an INS regulation that placed a limited amnesty on immigrants who had entered the United States illegally. The court argued that Congress intended standing to be given to parties actually suffering from the illegal wrongs committed by the administrative agency or are "within the 'zone of interests' protected by statute, not by third parties outside the 'zone of interests'" (at 423–424).

In sum, despite some grey areas in standing law, Justice Scalia in *Defenders of Wildlife* did an admirable job summarizing the basic elements of standing. He wrote:

Over the years, our cases have established that the irreducible constitutional minimum of standing contains three elements: First, the plaintiff must have suffered an "injury in fact"—an invasion of a legally-protected interest which is (a) concrete and particularized . . . ; and (b) "actual or imminent," not "conjectural" or "hypothetical." Second, there must be a causal connection between the injury and the conduct complained of—the injury has to be "fairly . . . trace(able) to the challenged action of the defendant, and not . . . the result (of) the independent action of some third party not before the court". . . . Third, it must be "likely," as opposed to merely "speculative," that the injury will be "redressed by a favorable decision."

By particularized, Scalia said, "we mean that the injury must affect the plaintiff in a personal and individual way" (at 2136).

KENNETH F. WARREN

BIBLIOGRAPHY

Davis, Kenneth C., and Richard J. Pierce, Jr., 1994. *Administrative Law Treatise*, 3d ed., vol. 3. Boston: Little, Brown, Chap. 16.
Schwartz, Bernard, 1994. *Administrative Law: A Casebook*, 4th ed. Boston: Little, Brown, 721–745.
Warren, Kenneth F., 1996. *Administrative Law in the Political System*, 3d ed. Upper Saddle River, NJ: Prentice-Hall, 426–442.

STATE GOVERNMENT. Political communities, organized on a regional basis, which are subnational units of government in federal systems.

The sovereignty of state governments is typically recognized in a national constitution as well as a constitution of their own. They have a full range of political institutions including legislature, executive, and judiciary, and a head of government usually called a governor.

State governments provide services that are close to the people and vital to the life of local communities including education, health, law and order, roads, transport, some welfare, culture, recreation and parks, and forests. They provide support for industry and regulate other business activities, particularly in relation to consumer standards. State governments have legal authority over local governments including counties, cities, towns, shires, school and health districts. Their responsibilities also typically include provision or regulation of public utilities and infrastructure including electricity, gas, harbors, land, and housing.

States and their governments have existed in various forms from ancient times whenever societies have adopted federal forms of government. In their modern form, they began to appear in Europe from the end of the Middle Ages as confederal, and then federal, governments began to emerge. The most significant development of the modern era was the establishment of a union of states, the United States of America, in the Constitution of September 17, 1787, although independent powers for the state governments had occurred earlier after the Declaration of Independence in 1776 as each former British colony called itself a state to assert its sovereignty or independence.

America has proved to be the dominant model for the subsequent creation of federations around the world. The common pattern has been for preexisting colonies to give up voluntarily some of their powers to form a nation and so share sovereignty with the new national government. Strictly speaking the colonial governments become state governments at the same moment that the nation is formed. In most cases, the states continue to operate under their own constitution as well as the federal constitution.

The relationship between state governments and other levels of government in a federation is usually spelled out in the national constitution. In America, the national government has obligations toward the states. It must respect their territory and not break them up without their consent, protect them against invasion and insurrection, and guarantee that they have a republican form of government. The U.S. Constitution also prevents state governments from interfering in foreign relations or making compacts among themselves and discriminating against interstate commerce. States cannot tax imports or exports or issue paper money. They have constitutional obligations to each other as well, must give "full faith and credit" to the legal processes of other states, and must not discriminate against citizens of other states.

So state governments exist wherever federal governments have come into being including, in particular, countries with large land masses or multicultural societies that desire union but not unity. Some of the better known state governments include those of the United States of America, Canada (provinces), India (states), Australia (states), Germany (Länder), Switzerland (cantons), Malaysia (states). State governments like the states from which they are derived may vary enormously in size of population and area to be served.

New states and their governments have also been created after federation, through constitutional mechanisms provided for the purpose, as witnessed by the growth in the number of American states from the original 13 to the present 50, or the Canadian provinces—4 at federation in 1867 and 10 today.

The concept of state governments rests on a theoretical base that includes the evolution of popular sovereignty and notions of democracy, although state governments have existed in federal systems that have been totalitarian in nature, where their autonomy has been subject to the centralized influence of dictatorships or political parties, as in the former Soviet Union and Yugoslavia.

In democratic federations, the identity of state governments is seen most clearly in the so-called theory, or model, of coordinate, or "layer cake," federalism (Wheare 1963) where each layer, national/state/local, has its own clearly defined and independent functions and revenue sources. But in practice, this model has seldom, if ever, existed, and new theories have been introduced such as "organic" (Sawer 1976), or "marble cake" (Grodzins 1967) federalism to explain the mixture of levels of government in the delivery of many public services. State governments are thus seen nowadays in a new role, as partners, sharing the functions of government like education, health, and transport with other levels of government. These arrangements, and the extent of power sharing involved, depend to some extent on the political whim of the regimes in office at both levels and can change appreciably over time.

Finance

The sources of finance for state governments are many and varied. The taxation they can levy is generally laid out in the national constitution. In most federations, including the United States, state governments are not allowed to levy import or export taxes as these powers are kept for the national government. In the United States, the main state taxes are personal income tax, company tax, sales tax, taxes on alcohol, tobacco, and motor vehicles, taxes on the use of natural resources, inheritance and gift taxes, other business taxes, various forms of land tax, gambling taxes, and fees of varying kinds on the delivery of business and personal services including utilities, electricity, water, and gas.

American states are also heavily dependent on grants from the federal government, which may have conditions attached to them and be designated for particular purposes. Local governments rely heavily on property taxes as their own main source of revenue, but they receive substantial grants from the state governments and the federal government, often linked to their guaranteeing to provide services of a certain standard. Most American states have debt limitations built into their constitutions, and they also control the indebtedness of local governments.

State governments have traditionally faced a degree of uncertainty regarding their financial situation, particularly as they are fairly dependent on federal transfers, which can vary from one political regime to another, and because their tax base is affected significantly by changes in the economy. Combined with a steady demand for the services they provide, such as education, health, and law and order, which are expensive to maintain but do not generate a great deal of revenue, this makes their financial situation unpredictable and more difficult to manage. In most federations, the expenditure of state governments is quite inflexible as it has a high wages-and-salaries component as

well as debt charges. State governments employ most of the government bureaucrats in federal systems because of the labor-intensive nature of their functions.

State governments in federations other than the United States face a similar revenue situation although the mixture of their taxes is often not as broad ranging and the level of dependence on federal transfers can be higher. In Canada, some provincial taxes have been "piggybacked" onto federal taxes, and others have been expressed as a percentage of the federal tax rate. From time to time, there has also been experimentation by some outlying provinces with notable reductions in certain taxes on business activity in an endeavor to attract investment and company headquarters. In Germany, Länder governments share certain taxes with the federal and local governments. As provided in the Basic Law (the German constitution), the percentage share going to each level is determined periodically after a review of the needs of each level of government in relation to their revenue forecasts. The rates of other state taxes in Germany are also set in a similar collaborative manner, the arrangements being finally endorsed by the federal Parliament, which incorporates an upper house, the Bundesrat, which is comprised of delegates appointed by the Länder governments and whose powers cover all aspects of federal/Länder relations.

A significant contrast is provided by Australia, where the federal government took over state income taxing powers during World War II and has retained them ever since. The federal government reimburses the states with transfers, in lieu of their taxing powers, sometimes on a formulas basis but more recently on more ad hoc annual arrangements. The state governments could reenter income taxing but would have to do so unanimously. Through decisions of the Australian High Court, the state governments have also been excluded from levying excise taxes interpreted basically as wholesale taxes. The overall result is that Australian states are heavily dependent on federal transfers, which make up over half their income. They raise less than 20 percent of all the government revenue in Australia yet are responsible for about half of all the nation's public expenditure. Their indebtedness is protected to some extent by nationally coordinated borrowing through the Australian Loan Council, with the federal government guaranteeing most of their borrowings, although they are still subject to the vagaries of the market for the terms of the credit including the interest rates they must pay.

In some federations, an equalization process is introduced to endeavor to give all state governments the capacity to provide services of a comparable standard. Such schemes operate in Canada, Australia, Germany, and India and are becoming more common.

A state government's financial program is laid out in a budget presented by the executive to the legislature for approval, generally once a year. The outcomes of the previous year's budget are also audited and the resulting report is tabled for scrutiny and debate in the legislature so that the performance of the government can be evaluated.

Machinery of Government

The machinery and processes for state government are contained primarily in state constitutions. In the United States, state constitutions typically also include a Bill of Rights. The constitutions can be amended in several differing ways: by putting a proposal directly to the people, by a vote in the state legislature generally requiring a two-thirds or larger majority, or by creating a constitutional convention to adopt amendments subject to ratification by the people. In other federations, amendments to state constitutions are carried out primarily by a vote in the legislature.

In the American states, the executive branch is headed by a governor elected directly by the people, responsible, under the state constitution, for seeing that the laws are faithfully executed. Many other senior officials in the executive in top public-service positions are elected, but some are appointed. Commonly elected officials are secretary of state, treasurer, auditor and attorney general.

The governor has the power to summon the legislature, may veto bills, and oversees the preparation of the state budget. The power of governors has steadily increased, and most serve four-year terms.

All of the American state legislatures (except Nebraska) are bicameral (two-house). Every upper house is known as the Senate and most of the lower houses are called Houses of Representatives. Senators in most states serve four-year terms; most lower-house members serve two-year terms. Most state legislatures meet annually, but some only biennially; a great deal of their work takes place in committees that meet more regularly. State legislatures pass laws, levy taxes, and appropriate expenditure for state departments, agencies, boards, and commissions.

State courts handle the vast majority of criminal and civil cases in the United States. They are headed by a Supreme Court, which typically has seven judges. In the majority of states, the Supreme Court judges are elected by the people, but in some, the governor makes the initial appointment, which is later approved by voters. The typical term of appointment for Supreme Court judges is eight to ten years, and some have an age limit of 70 years. Several trial court judges serve between four- and eight-year terms.

State government practice can vary significantly from the American model in other federations. In constitutional monarchies like Canada and Australia, the state governors are appointed by the Crown on the recommendation of the premier, and their powers include appointment and termination of a government and the summoning of Parliament (legislature). Most of their other powers are exercised by convention rather than by formal rules. It would only be in an exceptionally rare circumstance that a governor would veto a piece of legislation that had the support of the government. However, effective power rests with the elected leader of the government generally called the premier as the person who can command a majority on the floor of the Parliament. The executive in this system consists of the governor (but only in a formal sense) and the cabinet ministers and their officials, all of whom are appointed by the government. Canadian provincial legislatures are all unicameral and elected for a maximum of five years; five of the six Australian state parliaments are bicameral with most having a four-year term.

State legislatures in Canada, Australia, and most federations meet for a number of sessions each year to debate and pass laws, and approve the annual budget.

State courts in other federations have similar functions to those of American states, but the judges are generally appointed rather than elected. In all federations, there are appeals from most decisions of the state courts to the federal Supreme, or High, Court.

State governments remain an extremely important element of federal systems employing the majority of a nation's public servants, spending most of the public expenditure, and being responsible for the bulk of government service delivery. However, their powers and sovereignty are being challenged by the impact of globalization, nation building, and revolutions in information and transport technology, which have produced centripetal forces that strengthen the powers of the national governments.

KENNETH WILTSHIRE

BIBLIOGRAPHY

Bellamy, David J., Jon H. Pammett, and Donald C. Rowat, eds., 1976. *The Provincial Political Systems.* Toronto: Methuen.

Council of State Governments, 1994. *The Book of States.* Lexington, KY.

Davis S. Rufus, 1978. *The Federal Principle.* Berkeley: University of California Press.

Elazar, Daniel J., 1966. *American Federalism: A View from the States.* New York: Cromwell.

"Federalism and Intergovernmental Relations in West Germany: A Fortieth Year Appraisal," 1989. *PUBLIUS,* vol. 19, no. 4 (Fall).

Galston, William A. and Geoffrey Tibbetts, 1994. "Reinventing Federalism: The Clinton/Gore Program for a New Partnership among the Federal, State, Local, and Tribal Governments." *PUBLIUS,* vol. 24, no. 3 (Summer).

Grodzins, Morton, 1967. "The Federal System." In Aaron Wildavsky, ed., *American Federalism in Perspective.* Boston: Little, Brown.

Lumb, R. D., 1991. *The Constitutions of the Australian States.* St. Lucia: University of Queensland Press.

Mathews, R. L., 1980. *Federalism in Australia and the Federal Republic of Germany.* Canberra: ANU Press.

PUBLIUS, vol. 21, no. 1 (Winter 1991).

PUBLIUS, vol. 23, no. 2 (Spring 1993).

Sawer, Geoffrey, 1976. *Modern Federalism.* London: Pitman.

Smiley, D. V., 1987. *The Federal Condition in Canada.* Toronto: McGraw-Hill Ryerson.

Wheare, K. C., 1963. *Federal Government*. London: O.U.P.
Wildavsky, Aaron, ed., 1967. *American Federalism in Perspective*. Boston: Little, Brown.

STATE REINVENTION.

The restructuring, reorganization, and downsizing of state governments in the 1990s.

In the 1980s, state government was increasingly called upon to assume more responsibilities in the U.S. federal system, but questions were raised about state managerial, fiscal, and political capabilities. By the mid-1980s, Ann Bowman and Richard Kearney argued that there was a resurgence of the states, that is, that state governments were more capable of meeting policy challenges and being full partners in American federalism. In fact, trends that began in the 1960s had positive effects on state administrative and policy capability. State legislatures were more professional and deliberative than in the past. Beginning in the 1970s, state legislatures adopted an array of oversight techniques: auditing, evaluation units, administrative rule review, sunset laws, and appropriation of federal funds. Governors began to tackle important, critical issues that arise from changing economic, demographic, and social conditions and showed increased interest in developing a manageable, up-to-date executive branch structure to define major problems and solutions to address them as well as implement programs and policies. State bureaucracies became more professionalized, as did the administration of justice and the courts. Finally, important Supreme Court decisions made it possible for the states to assume a more important role in the political system.

Fueled by prosperity during the 1980s, may states grew rapidly as they began new and costly programs—in education, health, economic development, corrections, and the environment. The states' resurgence was stalled in the early 1990s when many states suffered budget problems. By the mid-1990s, however, the states were in strong financial shape (but that could change, depending on the extent of national aid cuts, a recession, whether the states will build surpluses and rainy day funds or give tax breaks, etc.) By 1994, the national economy was doing well, with positive effects on state budgets; the 1994 national congressional elections led to a conservative U.S. Congress keen on devolving more responsibilities to the states; and many states elected conservative state legislators and governors (mostly Republican).

Commissions on effectiveness and economy as well as management improvement productivity were created between the mid-1980s and early 1990s (e.g., in South Carolina, Texas, Washington, Virginia, and Connecticut). Many states began to restructure their operations, ranging from full-scale restructuring to more limited reorganizations and downsizing efforts. The conservative shift that occurred with the 1994 elections fueled another round of study commissions, along with efforts to "reinvent" the states in more fundamental ways. Attention began to focus more directly on the role that states—and all of government—should play, including which level of government should do what and how. Privatizing options became of greater interest across the political system.

Following the pattern of previous state study and reorganization commissions, the units that emerged in the mid-1990s were organized early in the new gubernatorial administrations, often fueled by interest in the legislatures, and their work proceeded quickly. Through history, these commissions have been budget driven, that is, justified to avoid tax increases and/or to set priorities to achieve major goals. Although these objectives still hold, many of the current reorganizations, downsizings, and restructuring efforts are explicitly guided by perspectives about the proper role of government relative to the private sector.

A good example of a reinvention commission's work is that of South Carolina. Six types of analysis were performed: (1) functional—across agencies' missions, policy objectives, enabling legislation, and major programs; (2) program—comparing all agency programs within a functional grouping (e.g., law enforcement) in order to uncover any duplication or similarity; (3) administrative—functions of agencies within a functional grouping (e.g., budget and finance, information resource management, purchasing) compared to provide an indication of the amount of resources being utilized and potential areas for saving; (4) accountability—assessing the level of agency accountability to the governor; (5) efficiency and effectiveness—assessing the extent to which and how agencies measure their programs; and (6) organizational/management (that is, management's span of control and the potential limits in effectiveness within the existing organizational structure).

Results of the South Carolina Commission and other commissions include increased revenues; cost savings; cost avoidance, that is, reductions of future costs; improved productivity, management, and accountability; and improved services. The aim is to eliminate layers of management in the state executive branch, to consolidate functions and offices, to simplify work processes and reduce administrative controls that are not cost-beneficial; to improve productivity through the use of new technology and more efficient and effective procedures, and to eliminate lower-priority or unnecessary activities.

Current concerns affect governmentwide operations, expenditures, and management. The task forces cover the gamut of state concerns about accountability, responsiveness, productivity, efficiency, effectiveness, and equity. Major multiagency or crosscutting issues are examined. Collectively, these activities have the potential to change both what government does and how it operates.

Executive branch agencies are being abolished and reorganized, sometimes with responsibilities transferred to other units or regions in a state. Efforts are made to reassign service delivery responsibilities to the appropriate level of government. The private sector and consultants are increasingly used for service delivery and management functions. Reporting and administrative regulations are changing, with an array of new methods and procedures for doing routine state agency activities. A litany of well-known productivity approaches have been introduced in state agencies beyond training, merit pay, and employee reward systems. Examples include total quality management, management-by-objectives, quality circles, gain sharing, and organizational design methods.

BEVERLY A. CIGLER

BIBLIOGRAPHY

Behn, Robert D., ed., 1991. *Governors on Governing.* National Governors' Association, Washington, D.C., and Lanham, MD: University Press of America.

Bowman, Ann O'M., and Richard C. Kearney, 1986. *The Resurgence of the States.* Englewood Cliffs, NJ: Prentice-Hall.

Cigler, Beverly A., 1993. "Professionalizing the American States in the 1990s." *International Journal of Public Administration,* vol. 16, no. 12 (Fall): 1965–2000.

Conant, James K., 1986. "Reorganization and the Bottom Line." *Public Administration Review* vol. 46 (January-February): 48-56.

———, 1988. "In the Shadow of Wilson and Brownlow: Executive Branch Reorganization in the States, 1965–1987." *Public Administration Review,* vol. 47 (September-October): 892–902.

Nathan, Richard P., and Fred C. Doolittle, 1987. *Reagan and the States.* Princeton, NJ: Princeton University Press.

National Governors' Association, 1991. "Reorganizations and Efficiency Commissions: Long-Term Strategies for Management Improvement." Washington, D.C., National Governors' Association, Office of State Services.

Osborne, David, 1988. *Laboratories of Democracy.* Boston, MA: Harvard Business School Press.

Osborne, David, and Ted Gaebler, 1992. *Reinventing Government: How the Entrepreneurial Spirit Is Transforming the Public Sector.* Reading, MA: Addison-Wesley.

U.S. Advisory Commission on Intergovernmental Relations, 1985. *The Question of State Capability.* Washington, DC: U.S. Government Printing Office.

Van Horn, Karl E., ed., 1989. *The State of the States.* Washington, DC: Congressional Quarterly.

STATE-LOCAL RELATIONS.

The pattern of interaction between state governments and their local governments in the United States, which includes legal, fiscal, and programmatic dimensions and which varies in the mix of state control and local discretion.

The state-local relationship in the United States system of government is much more of a unitary than federal arrangement. It lacks the tradition of separate and coequal sovereignties that characterizes the national-state relationship. Through constitutional, legislative, and administrative processes, the states create the local entities and maintain continuing control over their organization, powers, finances, and programs. Indeed, viewing the relationship from a national constitutional perspective, a sense of distinct state and local spheres is frequently absent. The U.S. Constitution makes no mention whatsoever of local government, allowing the federal courts over the years to treat the local entities as extensions or components of state government. When the Supreme Court rules on a federal question, the understanding is that references to "states" encompass local governments as well.

In practice, however, there is considerable give and take in the state-local relationship. The respective roles and powers of state and local governments vary greatly from one policy or program area to another, from one state to another, and over time in individual states. To understand both commonalities and variations, we must distinguish between ultimate state legal authority over all local governments and the everyday development of policy, exercise of intergovernmental political influence, and administration of programs.

The central and never completely resolved issue in the relationship is how much flexibility or discretion local governments exercise in operating within their state constitutional frameworks. At times local governments perform as relatively autonomous community institutions, at other times they seem to serve primarily as administrative arms of their states. Legislators, courts, administrators, and statewide electorates are continually changing the specific terms of the relationship.

How Much Home Rule?

The major instruments for the creation and control of local governments are state constitutions and state legislatures. Constitutions generally identify the major varieties of local government possible in a state—including municipalities, counties, towns or townships, special districts, school districts. They also define local powers, usually broadly and with some restrictions. To fill in the details, the constitutions give the legislatures considerable control over organization, powers, and procedures—leading to elaborate local government codes in the statutes of each state.

The degree of home rule granted to local governments, a measure of flexibility or independence from state prescribed frameworks, is a defining characteristic of these constitutional and statutory provisions. In its most restricted meaning, the concept of home rule refers to the scope of power granted or allowed by a state—often classified as either "structural" (form of government and other organizational matters) or "functional" (programs). In its more comprehensive meaning, the concept implies extensive autonomy or self-governance on the part of communities and their citizens–suggesting dimensions of local political will and leadership as well as formal power.

It is the structural dimension that draws the most attention, since aspects of organization are more easily measured or analyzed than the extensive range of local service and other functions. Structural home rule is clearly present when communities can write their own city or county charters, thus opting for organizational features other than those permitted general law governments. Such discretion, for example, extends to the overall form of government (manager, mayor-council, etc.), the division of power between offices, governing board sizes, electoral arrangements, boundary changes, and the formation of new governments.

In the functional area, constitutions usually grant local governments two major types of power. "Corporate" powers cover public works activities and other service delivery functions, while "police" powers involve the ability of local governments to regulate private behavior–including enacting and enforcing traffic and other law enforcement ordinances, protecting public health, establishing building codes, and controlling land use. Constitutions also empower localities with revenue powers and restrict their application, covering forms of taxation, rate or yield limits, and the ability to incur debt.

Different forms of local government in individual states are blessed by varying degrees of structural and procedural home rule. Municipal governments generally have more access to home rule powers than counties, and both forms in most states are granted more flexibility than the limited purpose school districts and special districts.

Over the years, the states have become more generous in the latitude allowed their local governments. They have moved away from "Dillon's rule," the prevailing legal principle in state-local relations for many years. John Dillon was an Iowa judge, whose decisions in a pair of 1868 cases defined local government authority as confined only to the powers expressly granted by state legislatures, an interpretation that was widely applied. The actions expanding local authority in recent decades have included a shift from enumerated to general grants of power in constitutions, the abandonment of legislating for individual governments ("special act") or population-based categories ("classification") in favor of one category of "general law" municipalities or counties, added options for general law units, and increased chartermaking opportunities.

Judicial interpretations also play a role in this expansion trend, rejecting many efforts from taxpayer and other interests to narrowly construe local government authority. They have steadily enlarged the meaning of the police power in local hands, for example, to confirm the constitutionality of regulations over land use and development in the community interest. However, state and federal courts have also placed tight boundaries around some areas of local government activity, especially actions seen as violations of the First Amendment and property use regulations that come in conflict with the "takings" provision of the Fifth Amendment.

The Legislative Arena

In other than basic constitutional terms, the state-local relationship is a fluid one. Nowhere is this more apparent than in each state's annual or biennial legislative sessions, where local government issues compose a larger portion of the bill load. Summarizing from the surveys of state-local relations published in the annual *Municipal Year Book,* the most prolific topics include K–12 education, public employees, local revenue powers, social services, and transportation.

Mandates passed by legislatures are an ongoing concern for local governments, both because of their restrictive nature and their compliance costs. Although most states have formal policies against unfunded mandates, and some even call for reimbursing local governments, such requirements are often easy to waive or ignore by legislatures and administrative departments. Many of the mandates are actually pass-throughs from federal programs in such areas as water quality and welfare administration, in which state governments have little choice but to apply the regulations to local agencies. An intriguing trend over the years is how local officials have come to accept state and federal requirements as a normal part of their operational environment. Indeed, some mandates are seen by many as having a beneficial effect on public services and community conditions, including certain types of civil rights, environmental protection, employment and other requirements. According to a benign concept of mandates, they push local governments in desirable directions that they would not initiate on their own because of the essentially conservative nature of local political systems. Furthermore, mandates are a way of using the extensive mechanisms of local government to carry out state and national standards that ensure access and fairness in the distribution of public services. A more grassroots-oriented concept, however, emphasizes the negative impacts of mandates on community values and autonomy.

Local governments often feel besieged and outgunned in legislative sessions. One reason is that state legislatures and governors, in dealing with local government matters, are more often guided by their perceptions of the greater interest of state government than by a sympathetic understanding of the particular needs of local governments. Then too they are frequently challenged by private interests attempting to circumvent local authority. Unhappy with their treatment at the hands of local government, various organizations seek corrective action from a more powerful and possibly more receptive institution–the legislature. Included are public employee organizations that seek to change the personnel rules, business groups that want to avoid or reduce local regulations (rent control and tobacco ordinances are frequent targets), taxpayers' associations that desire revenue reductions, and property rights groups angry at the exercise of local land-use powers. The more successful of these interests are contributors to political campaigns or those who manage to strike the appropriate ideological chords with legislators.

Local governments do not lack significant political resources. The major types are organized in every state as membership associations to represent their interests in the legislature and before executive agencies, with full-time lobbying and support staffs and usually with offices in the capital city, as well as municipal leagues and county associations. Among the major legislative players in most states, the represented groups include school boards, special districts and authorities of different kinds, and individual types of local officials such as sheriffs, treasurers, and other elected county officers. Local government associations sometimes are accused of being "special pleaders," a charge they counter by pointing to the public responsibilities of their members and their partnership with state government. At the same time, they are disadvantaged in the legislative wars by not being able to spend money on political campaigns from their members' treasuries.

More broadly, local governments enjoy a small amount of inherent protection from unwanted legislative actions in the political structure of state government. The prior local office-holding experiences of many state legislators, and even some governors and other statewide elected officers, give them some understanding of local government problems. To retain their positions or advance to higher offices, state politicians also nurture the continuing support of local government officials and allied community leaders. Because of their great popularity and personal political organizations, some local government officials—notably elected sheriffs in many rural counties—are key campaign resources for legislators and other state office candidates.

Fiscal Relationships

The finances of local governments are greatly affected by two different kinds of state government actions—changes in state fiscal aid to localities (including the funding of mandates) and decisions that expand or contract local revenue authority. They have different implications, since increasing amounts of aid make local governments more dependent on state resources whereas the enlargement of local discretion over taxes and other revenues contributes to local autonomy. With funds for K–12 education and welfare programs in the lead, local aid payments total more than half of state budgets in the United States. The levels of aid are vulnerable to annual fluctuations in state budgetary conditions and compete with direct state spending

priorities. The exceptions include programs that have prescribed minimum payments or other constitutional protections, such as K–12 and local streets and roads in some states. In considering the adequacy of their aid payments, local officials usually complain that the states are less generous with them fiscally than with programmatic and structural discretion, and ask for revenue authority commensurate with their service responsibilities.

In states that provide for the initiative and referendum, local revenue authority is subject to electoral decisions as well as state constitutions, legislatures, and courts. California's well-known Proposition 13 of 1978 helped to stimulate a wave of tax cutting through the ballot box in other states. The major but not exclusive target has been the property tax, once the dominant revenue source for most local governments with K–12 school districts.

Administrative and Programmatic Relationships

State governments have the unquestioned ability to take over entire local governments or individual offices. In extraordinary situations, they have exercised this degree of control. Conditions that can lead to substitute state administration include extreme fiscal stress verging on bankruptcy or a breakdown in a vital function affecting a community's safety or public health. The few cases in recent decades include the replacement of administrators and the bypassing of elected governing boards in school districts in California and Kentucky and law enforcement authorities in several other states.

The much more normal relationship between state and local administrators, however, is a collegial one. Often they have educational and technical backgrounds in the same specialties and they share professional goals. So, close cooperation relating to service delivery is the standard between comparable departments in state and local governments—such as state transportation agencies and city and county public works departments, state health agencies and local public health officers, and state departments of education and K–12 districts. In this way, state administrators become sensitive to local conditions; intergovernmental problems are negotiated rather than arbitrarily resolved, and the impacts of mandates are softened. Still, while seldom reaching the level of contentiousness found in legislative proceedings, the tension level does rise at times in administrative relationships, especially when money and regulations are at issue.

Among the large number of public service programs that involve the joint participation of states and their local governments, respective roles vary widely. State governments are especially dominant in funding, setting the policy direction, and providing the administrative framework for K–12 education and welfare and health care programs. In K–12, for example, states control curriculum standards for local districts, credentialing of teachers, and new school construction. At the other end of the scale are such local program areas as parks and recreation, libraries, and land-use regulation, in which uniform state-wide standards are less common and state fiscal support is minimal. Transportation fits in the middle, since local public works departments receive most of their street and road maintenance funds from the gas tax and other state sources yet have relative discretion over program decisions.

We can extend the comparison further to note that some states directly run certain programs that elsewhere are locally administered. For example, the State of Hawaii operates its K–12 schools, whereas a few other states directly administer welfare programs through regional offices.

Local Autonomy

Beyond the constitutional, legislative, and administrative patterns that frame the state-local relationship in American government, there is the more sketchy concept of community self-governance. Municipalities, counties, and other formal local governments are central to this process. They provide representation and political voice to their citizens, giving them a unique forum for the deliberation and resolution of issues both big and small. This is an aspect of American democracy that is usually bypassed by the state-local relationship in which local governments are considered much more as agents of state policy than as distinctly community institutions. And yet, local governments depend on their states for sufficient authority to thoroughly fulfill their community purposes.

ALVIN D. SOKOLOW

BIBLIOGRAPHY

Berman, David R., 1994. "State-Local Relations: Patterns, Politics, and Problems." In ICMA, *The Municipal Year Book, 1994.* Washington, DC: International City/County Management Association: 59–67.

Buckwalter, Doyle W., 1984. "State-Municipal Relations: Improving the Arch of Federalism." *State and Local Government Review,* vol. 16 (Winter): 27–33.

Cigler, Beverly A., 1994. "The County-State Connection: A National Study of Associations of Counties." *Public Administration Review,* vol. 54 (January-February): 3–11.

Gold, Steven D., and Sarah Ritchie, 1994. "State Actions Affecting Cities and Counties, 1990–93: De Facto Federalism." *Public Budgeting & Finance,* vol. 14 (Summer): 26–53.

U.S. Advisory Commission on Intergovernmental Relations, 1981. *Measuring Local Discretionary Authority.* Washington, DC: ACIR.

———, 1993a. *Local Government Autonomy: Needs for State Constitutional, Statutory, and Judicial Clarification.* Washington, DC: ACIR.

———, 1993b. *State Laws Governing Local Government Structure and Administration.* Washington, DC: ACIR.

Zimmerman, Jospeh F., 1987. "The State Mandate Problem." *State and Local Government Review,* vol. 19 (Spring): 78–84.

STATISTICS, HISTORY OF.

The evolution of how governments have gathered, analysed, and used aggregate numerical data. The field of statistics concerns itself with distributions of measurements that arise in observation of the external world. Its central problem is that of making meaningful statements about some segment of the world on the basis of examination of only a small part of it. The field of public administration concerns itself with the conduct of highly complex and uncertain societal systems involving multiple interactions and feedback among numerous economic, political, and emotional elements. The history of statistics in public administration is the record of administrative and bureaucratic effort to predict and control these elements. Both fields have historically developed through truly interdisciplinary efforts, and each has played an integral role in the evolution of the other.

Although the beginnings of the modern field of statistics predated contemporary public administration, both originated within the realm of statecraft. The root of the term "statistics" is the seventeenth-century Italian world *statista* (Pearson 1978). A "statista" was a man concerned with reasoning about the state. So the "state" in "statecraft" is the same as the "stat" in "statistics." Although the field of statistics eventually branched off in a characteristically mathematical direction, public administration remained centered in the conduct of the political, bureaucratic, and organizational affairs of state.

By modern statistical standards, the reasoning processes of the seventeenth-century *statista* were almost inconceivably primitive. The conceptual and philosophical foundations of modern empiricism had not been articulated. Nobody had yet discovered the concept of a distribution of measurements. Very few data were collected. Of those collected, many revealed sensitive military or economic information and so were guarded as state secrets. Moreover, had the data even been available, modern statistical techniques of analysis were not. Astronomers had not yet discovered error theory. Biologists had not yet discovered the concept of correlation. The field of agriculture had not yet produced the rudiments of experimental design. Gamblers had not yet worked out the calculus of probabilities.

The bulk of seventeenth-century statistical advancement originated with the "political arithmeticians." These men were bureaucrats and social reformers in England who believed that the wealth and strength of the state depend strongly on the number and character of its subjects. Their contributions came from their efforts to measure, classify, and evaluate key factors. To them we owe recognition for the first life tables, innovations in the collection of demographic information, and early techniques for calculating insurance and annuity rates (Porter 1986).

The responsibility for progress in statistical thinking in the eighteenth century also rested substantially with bureaucrats and reformers. Severely limited data caused difficulties in making accurate predictions about the society as a whole and frustrated their efforts to control the population, augment tax revenue, and centralize bureaucracy. Their protests over this situation led to notable progress in terms of the expansion of governmental mechanisms for collecting and acting upon population, government, and wealth data. These protests may also have given rise to the first distinctly public numbers about government wealth and demographic characteristics (Boorstin 1983).

The newly available data, in turn, stimulated conceptual and mathematical advancements. Statistical thinkers started to recognize that although the cause of each individual action in society may well be inaccessible, aggregate numbers and mean value could be used to discover and predict important large-scale regularities in demographic, disease, crime, and census data. The influential mathematician Adolphe Quetelet (1796–1874) suggested that observed social statistical regularities arose necessarily from the underlying stability of the "state of society" and so would continue into the future. This idea led to a profusion of efforts to not only describe but also to develop means to predict social characteristics from the data. Soon, conceptual and mathematical developments in statistics progressed to the point where statistics was viewed as a branch of applied mathematics for charting the course of economic and social evolution.

In the eighteenth and nineteenth centuries, the history of success in social statistical applications continued to be used as the primary justification for statistical explorations in other fields. The bulk of advancement in statistical thought started to occur beyond bureaucratic realms, however, largely in the sciences of astronomy, physics, biology, and economics. Some of the first formal consideration was given to the idea of continuous distributions (variables that may take on any value within a range). The rudiments of the calculus of probability were discovered and efforts were made to apply them to practical problems such as winning at the gambling table, describing planetary orbits, and predicting voting behaviors. The Reverend Thomas Bayes articulated his famous theorem, thus forever changing our understanding of the role of probability in inductive reasoning. The idea that probabilities are measurable constants of the external world was discovered, and the first formal linkage between statistics and the calculus of probability was established (Porter 1986).

The statistical tools used in modern public administration and policy analysis have virtually all been worked out since the birthdate of the modern field of mathematical statistics (Kendall 1978). This occurred around 1890, at about the same time as the modern field of public admin-

istration was born in the United States. One of the marking points was the beginning of formal investigation into joint distributions of two variables. These investigations soon led to the theory of statistical relationship and gave rise to measures of association and contingency. Concepts and techniques of correlation and regression analysis were then discovered. Leading statisticians began to concentrate on the problem of how to treat sampling problems with mathematical precision, and in doing so greatly advanced the derivation of sampling distributions. These advancements, in turn, allowed statisticians to start to make accurate inferences from samples.

In the 1920s and 1930s, the concepts of optimal estimators and of efficiency in estimation were introduced, greatly clarifying the ideas on estimation. In the late 1920s, the newly clarified ideas on estimation gave rise to the initial work on the related problem of gauging the reliability of an estimate by the use of confidence intervals. The beginnings of the theory and techniques of hypothesis testing were introduced. The foundations of a theory of experimental design was laid. Soon thereafter, the modern ideas of analysis of variance and covariance were conceived and articulated.

As of about World War II, data had become relatively abundant and the concepts and techniques of mathematical statistics had advanced to the point of prominence in the conduct of societal affairs. The period after the war brought a significant increase in the numbers of statisticians in all walks of societal life. The theory of hypothesis testing was soon integrated with societal decision processes. Multivariate data analytic techniques such as factor analysis, discriminant analysis, cannonical correlation and time-series analysis were conceived, developed, and applied to societal situations.

By the latter half of the 1960s, the language of statistics had emerged as the *sine qua non* of the social and policy sciences (deLeon and Overman 1989). Policy analysts and public administrators throughout society had started to assume that the rational approach to policy problems was to define them comprehensively and subject them to statistical analysis. Statistical analyses were believed to produce singularly accurate inferences about the future and consequences of government action. They became enshrined as the only reliable basis for solutions to societal problems. Statistics dominated public discussions.

The situation started to change to some extent as the experiences of the 1970s and 1980s provided broad challenges to the credibility of the objective and normative conclusions of societal applications of advanced statistics. Although modern statistical techniques continued to be widely accepted as indispensable tools for public administrators and policy analysts who wanted to learn from numbers about social observations, these challenges gave rise to considerable debate over the appropriate role for modern mathematical statistics in public administration. It was generally acknowledged that advances in mathematical statistics had reached a high degree of conceptual and mathematical elegance. But some leading public administrators perceived important gaps between the societal world of daily experience on one hand and the assumptions and abstractions required by many of the advanced modern techniques on the other. More public administrators, therefore, started to question the practicality of many of the techniques.

There currently exists wide disagreement with regard to exactly what level of statistical thinking skills should be required of public administrators. Some scholars argue that the affairs of state are, always have been, and always will be based upon power and politics rather than the logical and rational methods posited by statistical analysis. Moreover, some scholars add, recent advances in Complexity Theory bring into question the conventional assumption that there exists a fundamental underlying stability to the state of society (Arthur 1990). Others argue that rather than retreating from these gaps, it makes more sense to develop and apply further advanced statistical means of bridging them; for example, the newly discovered concepts and techniques of resampling.

While statistics will for the foreseeable future undoubtedly retain their traditional roots in public administration, the extent to which they will continue to play an integral role in the evolution of the field will likely depend upon public administrators' interpretations of the usefulness of advanced statistical analysis of the social and political world.

WILLIAM M. BOWEN

BIBLIOGRAPHY

Arthur, W. B., 1990. "Positive Feedbacks in the Economy." *Scientific American,* vol. 262, no. 2: 92–99.
Boorstin, Daniel J., 1983. *The Discoverers: A History of Man's Search to Know His World and Himself.* New York: Random House.
deLeon, Peter, and E. Sam Overman, 1989. "A History of the Policy Sciences." In Jack Rabin, W. Bartley Hildreth, and Gerald J. Miller, eds. *Handbook of Public Administration.* New York: Marcel Dekker: 398–438.
Kendall, Maurice G., 1978. "The History of Statistical Method." In William H. Kruskal and Judith M. Tanur, ed. *International Encyclopedia of Statistics,* vol. 2. New York: Free Press: 1093–1101.
Pearson, E. S., ed. 1978. *The History of Statistics in the 17th and 18th Centuries.* New York: MacMillan.
Porter, Theodore M., 1986. *The Rise of Statistical Thinking: 1820–1900.* Princeton, NJ: Princeton University Press.

STATUTORY CORPORATION.   A form of nondepartmental organization used in many countries.

The term is synonymous with public corporation (more often used in Britain), crown corporation (Canada), and government corporation (United States; see **government corporation**). A statutory corporation is frequently employed for the management of public enterprises (see **public enterprise**), but it is used for the management of other public activities as well. The Australian case is illustrative. There statutory corporations have been popular at least since 1883, when the Victorian Railways Commission was established to take over the management of the public railway system from the department that had previously had control. The model provided by this pioneering body was refined and used again and again as the Australian federal and state governments came increasingly to believe that the management of public enterprises should be "hived off" from the ministerial/departmental/public service core of government. The form then came to be used quite extensively for services other than those falling within the area of commercial public enterprise, notably in the management of public institutions like universities, research establishments, hospitals, libraries, museums, and art galleries.

A statutory corporation is established by a special statute (or sometimes a regulation under a statute), which serves as the creating charter. This charter lays down the nature of the governing body (usually a board plus executive management) and the supporting staff service and prescribes powers, functions, obligations, and relationships with the supervising minister, other stakeholders in government (such as ministers for finance and auditors general) and the legislature itself. The corporation is a body corporate at law (it is thus incorporated) and is separate from the legal personality of the state. It becomes first-instance decisionmaker, that is, decisions are made in its own right and its own name, although ministers may have reserve powers of approval and direction in specified policy areas. Its autonomy extends variously to subpolicymaking decisions applying policy, staffing, finance, and general management. In all these ways, it stands apart from the generality of government.

Advantages claimed for the statutory corporation over the public/civil service department are that it has superior ability to focus on the task at hand, to bring professional/specialist/management skills appropriate to the particular activity to bear, to develop esprit de corps within its own staff service, to stand apart from the partisan-political directions that characterize government itself and may be harmful to the successful discharge of particular functions, and to respond speedily and flexibly to commercial/market pressures. Also, as with other forms of nondepartmental organization such as noncorporate statutory authorities (with their separate legal incorporation, statutory corporations form a subcategory within the broader category of statutory authorities), executive agencies (long known in Sweden but much newer in the Anglo-Saxon countries), and state-owned companies, statutory corporations provide practical expression of the view that central ministries should determine policies but that implementation should be the responsibility of separate organizations.

By contrast, it is often urged that such organizations exacerbate problems of coordination and make it more difficult to secure the harmonization of the total operations of a governmental system. Some statutory corporations have been known to defy properly constituted governments: hence the search for compromise accountability/control formulas noted in the entry on public enterprise.

The late twentieth-century reform movement has introduced the term "corporatization." To some, this refers to the creation of, or the strengthening of the commercial character of, either kind of public-sector corporate body, the statutory corporation, or the state-owned company. Somewhat confusingly, others insist that it applies only to the companies.

ROGER WETTENHALL

BIBLIOGRAPHY

Ashley, C. A. and R. G. H. Smails, 1965. *Canadian Crown Corporations.* Toronto: Macmillan.

Kewley, T. H., 1957. "Some General Features of the Statutory Corporation in Australia." *Public Administration* (Sydney), vol. 16 (March): 3–28.

Prichard, J. R. S., ed., 1983. *Crown Corporations in Canada: The Calculus of Instrumental Choice.* Toronto: Butterworth.

Robson, W. A., 1962. "The Public Corporation in Britain." Chapter 3 of *Nationalized Industry and Public Ownership,* 2d ed. London: Allen & Unwin: 46–77.

Wettenhall, Roger, 1993. "Australia's Statutory Corporations and the American Public Authority Tradition." *Canberra Bulletin of Public Administration,* no. 75 (December): 40–50.

⟩ ⟩ ⟩, 1995. "Corporations and Corporatisation: An Administrative History Perspective." *Public Law Review* (Sydney), vol. 6 (March): 7–23.

STEIN, FREIHERR HEINRICH FREDRICH KARL vom und zum (1757-1831).

The Prussian statesman known for his ideas on self-administration and governmental administration. In 1780, Stein started his career as a jurist in the Prussian Civil Service. In 1804, he was appointed Minister for Economic Affairs. After the Tilsit Peace in 1807, he became the leading minister in Prussia and began to renew Prussia by inner reforms (Scheel 1966). Pressured by Napoleon, he resigned in 1808 and was outlawed. He was assigned as a counselor to the Russian Czar Alexander I and lived in exile in Prague and Brunn (Brno). He continued his fight against Napoleon, in writing the Kalisch Proclamation (1813). After the defeat of Napoleon, he helped to build up the freed regions, especially in Eastern Prussia, as the leader of the Central Administrative Council.

In his Nassau memorandum "On the Appropriate Design of the Superior and the Provincial, Financial, and Police Authorities in the Prussian Monarchy" of 1807, he combined liberal French ideas and democratic English-marked ideas with a reformative and yet tradition-conscious conservatism of its own nature. Much of that, but by far not all of it, was to be realized in 1810 by the government of Chancellor Karl August von Hardenberg (1750–1822). In his Riga memorandum (1807), the diplomat and liberal rationalist Hardenberg called for "democratic reforms in the monarchist state," but without putting emphasis on the self-administration of realm estates that dominated Stein's thoughts. The ideas of Stein, Hardenberg, and other contemporaries must consequently be seen in a close connection (Becker 1986); that is why we speak of the "Stein-Hardenberg Reforms" (Hubatsch 1977). Without Stein, a lot would not have been possible, but Stein would also not have been able to achieve much on his own.

Stein and Self-Administration

Self-administration as it is featured today has its historical origin in German communal law. This mainly applies to the West German territories, where a strong pressure for independence has always been prevailing (Forsthoff 1973). Thus, German communal law also originates in old German cooperative ideas such as representing a piece of medieval public law in the modern state (Scholler and Broß 1976). Stein and Hardenberg mark a type of communal constitution maintained until today's magistrate constitution. The central self-administration body is the assembly of town representatives that exercise a legal and executive power. The assembly of town representatives elects the magistrate. Doubtlessly, the example of Prussia gave impetus to self-administration in Germany. This model has continued until today.

The basic Steinian question of whether the community holds its own sovereignty or has its sovereignty "borrowed" from the government is also still on the agenda.

Development of the Administrative Organization

A feature of modern governmental organization is the principle supported by Stein that separates justice and administration. Inside the executive branch, he pleaded for a deconcentration of individual political portfolios where governmental authorities are responsible and authorized to perform the governmental functions of their portfolio (portfolio principle). In its extreme form, this model has disappeared as a coordination between portfolios can only happen through a superior instance (chancellor principle). Today, the Stein-Hardenberg Reforms are mainly honored with regard to the unity of administration idealized in Germany. The principle of unity of administration demands that "authorities of the same level are not legally or factually independent, but are under a uniform management and control, united in an administrative unity" (Püttner

1989, p. 81). Nearly all institutional administrative reforms from the days of Stein recur on this principle.

What Stein Means to the Present

It is only possible to understand the organization of public administration at present in the Federal Republic of Germany if one looks at the background of the constitutional and administrative history of the nineteenth and twentieth centuries. This applies both to the organizational separation of Reich or federal and state administration and to the organization of self-administration especially at the communal level (Rudolf 1983). A basic question of the research of German administrative history mainly in connection with the legacy of Freiherr vom Stein is whether the modern constitutional and administrative state of the nineteenth century continuously developed from the efforts of the absolute state or whether a break took place around 1800. Presumably, this question can never be completely answered as within Germany there always were and still are different routes of tradition. At least for Prussia, Freiherr vom Stein must be conceded the part of a pioneer for modern developments, regardless of whether these were initiated generally or by Stein. The self-administration initiated by Freiherr vom Stein in Prussia involved a more or less strong participation of the citizen in communal affairs and was extended to rural communities in the course of the nineteenth century. The old feudalist orders and the regional differences were thus, in fact, eliminated for the most part, but both the establishment of a unitary governmental administrative organization and the introduction of communal self-administration have been in the long-term interests of the state. Although Stein contributed little to the science of administration, he influenced the ideas on the links between governmental and administrative organizations. He therefore influenced quite a long line of administrative scientists, as for example, Lorenz von Stein (see **Stein, Lorenz von**).

MARTIN MORLOK AND MANFRED MILLER

BIBLIOGRAPHY

Becker, Bernd, 1986. *Zusammenhänge zwischen den Ideen zu den Verwaltungsreformen von Montgelas, Stein und Hardenberg. Vergleich des Ansbacher Memoire von 1796, der Nassauischen Denkschrift von 1807 und der Rigaer Denkschrift von 1807.* Bayerische Verwaltungsblätter, 705–712, 744–750.
Forsthoff, Ernst, 1973. *Lehrbuch des Verwaltungsrechts,* 10th ed. Vol. 1. Munich: Beck.
Hubatsch, Walther, 1977. *Die Stein-Hardenbergschen Reformen.* Darmstadt: Wissenschaftliche Buchgesellschaft.
Püttner, Günter, 1989. *Verwaltungslehre. Ein Studienbuch,* 2d. ed. Munich: Beck.
Rudolf, Walter, 1983. *Verwaltungsorganisation.* In Hans-Uwe Erichsen, Wolfgang Martens, eds., *Allgemeines Verwaltungsrecht,* 6th ed., Berlin/New York: De Gruyter, 533–584.
Scheel, Heinrich, ed., 1966. *Das Reformministerium Stein. Akten zur Verfassungs-und Verwaltungsgeschichte aus den Jahren 1807–08.* Berlin: Akademie-Verlag.
Scholler, Heinrich, and Siegfried Broß 1976. *Grundzüge des Kommunalrechts in der Bundesrepublik Deutschland.* Heidelberg/Karlsrune: C. F. Müller.

STEIN, LORENZ VON (1815–1890). German scholar. After an early career which included journalism and politics, he accepted the chair of government and national economy at the University of Vienna, a position he held for over 30 years. Felix Gilbert (1977) claims that Stein "is clearly one of the most interesting figures the German scholarly world produced in the nineteenth century," but that it is difficult "to say whether he belongs to the idealistic, metaphysical half of the nineteenth century or to its positivistic, realistic half" (pp. 411–412). He has been variously described as a sociologist, historian, political economist, political theorist, and social philosopher. The difficulty in placing him within any modern discipline results from his interest in every aspect of society, but all his diverse studies culminated in the development of a systematic and comprehensive theory of public administration.

Stein's Theory of Administration

Because Stein lived and wrote in that transitional period from the ancien régime to industrial society, his theory of administration has been interpreted in a number of ways. A case can be made that he was the last great writer in the cameralist tradition in Germany and that his work was not far from what was known as *Polizeiwissenschaft* (Lindenfeld 1989). This "science of the police" was intended to educate public administrators. It included not only public safety but also such governmental activities as health, education, welfare, as well as more technical fields such as public works and mining.

In his eight-volume *Verwaltungslehre* (administrative theory), Stein followed the cameralist tradition of classifying the functions of government. These included the military, foreign affairs, finance, justice, and "inner administration," or the domestic functions originally controlled by a minister of the interior. This latter function was the object of his science of administration and he treated such topics as population policy, education, transportation, agriculture, and forestry. Practical advice on the administration of these areas was developed, just as was the case with his predecessors.

However, Stein's approach to these traditional topics was energized by a spirit far removed from the pedantically applied eudaemonics of the cameralists whose mission was to advise the prince how to impose from above happiness on his subjects whether they wanted it or not. He does not, therefore, deserve the judgment that he was "rather the last great name in the earlier tradition of German administrative science, than a precursor of the modern" (Dunsire 1973, p. 77). Stein was one of the first social scientists to emphasize the administration of the state as a critical factor in the development of modern society. His theory was an attempt to promote administration as the answer to the enduring problem of political philosophy—how to reconcile the interests of the individual with the needs of the collective.

Sociologists have long regarded Stein as an original student, along with his contemporary Karl Marx, of the dynamics of capitalist society. In Stein's view, Western society had evolved from feudalism and the medieval estates, in which the social classes were rendered immobile by the dominant worldview, to the "civil society" of industrialism. In this latest stage of history, a class of restless entrepreneurs would inevitably exploit the non-property-owning class, just as Marx predicted. But Stein rejected the Marxist contention that the have-nots would eventually be driven into such a hopeless condition that revolt against the exploiters was their only alternative. His argument was that a state, separate from civil society, in the Hegelian sense, could ameliorate class warfare while preserving individual freedom.

Stein rejected republicanism since he was convinced that the bourgeoisie would follow their natural inclination and use the instruments of government to their own advantage. This would be especially true of public administration if it were an object of the class struggle within civil society. The preferred political arrangement was a state headed by a hereditary monarchy. This state could stand apart from civil society and ensure that the life opportunities for the propertyless were not at the mercy of people driven by class interest.

Stein (1887) argued that "we have essentially overcome the epoch of constitution building and that the critical area for future development lies in administration" (p. 1). The constitution is the stable, predictable part of the state, whereas "a completion of administration is impossible" (Stein 1876, p. 51). Administration is the state in action, dealing with the particulars that make up the life of a nation. Or in Stein's description of the personality of the state, the legislature represents the will whereas administration is the act. Just as those two features are integrated within the personality of the individual, so too lawmaking and administration are separate but interdependent parts of the state. Administration may be subordinate to the will of the state, but it claims an independent sphere of action.

What then is the function of administration as it exercises its discretion? For Stein, it is the protection of the freedom of the individual personalities as they pursue their interests in civil society. The self-determination of the individual was a major feature of Stein's political philosophy, but his sociological analysis informed him that this self-determination could be to the detriment of others. Therefore,

administration must prevent the lower classes from sinking into a condition of "unfreedom" which would disqualify them from equal participation in civil society. Stein's administration would not limit unnecessarily the freedom of the propertied classes, but it would maintain opportunities for the unpropertied. He therefore placed great emphasis on public education as a way for the lower classes to stay in the game. Administration, he asserted, "will be the more perfect the more it proves able to offer everybody the possibility of highest personal development" (Mengelberg 1964, p. 53).

Like Hegel, and unlike modern public choice theorists, Stein had to make a case for the administrators as being somehow above the petty strife of civil society. Their association with the selfless monarch was one element. In an early work (Stein 1850) he maintained that "in every human society, there are a number of individuals, to whom nature has given a pure interest in the welfare of the whole, who on the basis of their entire life activity, are especially qualified to work for the development of the whole and to subordinate to it any special interest" (p. 19). Only when detached from civil society, through their association with the monarch, will these "true officials" be able to fulfill their social responsibility. Obviously, Stein was heavily influenced by Hegel's vision of a "universal class" of public servants.

His mature work on *Verwaltungslehre* was dedicated to providing those selfless officials with the science necessary to make their efforts on behalf of society effective. In his eyes, *Staatswissenschaft* (science of the state) was the master science and encompassed all aspects of society. Naturally, officials should be trained in the principles of administration, but citizens as well should recognize that "in the future we may say that the true qualification for participation in public life lies at least as much in a clear awareness of administration, its principles, its duties and its law" (Stein 1876, p. 2). The study of administration, then, was intended to inform administrators and the administered in their common responsibilities to an organic whole.

Stein placed great emphasis on the participation of the citizens in administration (*Selbstverwaltung*). Through municipal governments and other autonomous public bodies, as well as societies, unions, and associations, individuals were in the best position to assist in the special function of the state, namely, the construction of a unity out of all the special interests. Within the confines of a state's laws, the citizens themselves are given great responsibility by Stein for maintaining social harmony.

Stein constructed a system of administration that would ensure the well-being of all citizens while maintaining the stability of society. Public administration was not a matter of technical details and office routines. It was the active life of the state and of society. Unlike the fussy bureaucrats of cameralism, concerned with the proper color of Easter eggs and beer brewing, Stein's administrators were charged with the greatest ethical responsibility for the preservation of civil society through their careful attention to the needs of the disadvantaged.

Stein's Impact on the Study of Administration

Lorenz von Stein founded no school and left no influential students to carry on his work. He remains largely unknown to the Anglo-Saxon world with but one work available in translation and that only in an abridged form (Mengelberg 1964). Even in his homeland, his work on administration was rendered obsolete before it was completed. By the 1860s, the German states had determined the key to responsible government was to be found in the creation of the *Rechtsstaat,* a government constrained by legal rules. For administrators, education in administrative law became the prerequisite for a career in the bureaucracy. Practical training in the work of administration could be picked up on the job, but it was critical that officials understood the narrow legal categories within which they could operate. An empirically oriented administrative science, as advocated by Stein, continued to lead "a shadowy existence" (Blank 1969, p. 373). This *Juristenmonopol* continues to dominate German public administration to the present day. In the 1950s, German students of public administration began to call for a return to Stein's approach to the subject, largely as a symbol of the reaction against the excessive emphasis on legal education.

Elsewhere, Stein may have had his greatest immediate impact in Japan, since he was one of the authorities consulted by the reformers under the Meiji Restoration of the empire (Pittau 1967). In the United States, traces of Stein can be found in the works of the founders of public administration. Woodrow Wilson's article "The Study of Administration" (1887) used Stein's argument that the age of constitutions has been replaced by administration, and Wilson followed the German in insisting that the study of administration is the crucial question of the day. Wilson also quotes Stein, without attribution, that "the idea of the state is the conscience of administration."

American writers took from Stein his distinction between "will" and the "act" (or "deed" as Wilson translated it). Originally, Americans accepted Stein's dictum that administration had a will of its own and was not simply the unthinking response to political will. Goodnow (1990) also agreed that "the organ of government whose main function is the execution of the will of the state is often, and indeed usually, entrusted with the expression of that will in its details" (p. 15). By the time of W. F. Willoughby's early textbook, the will as determined by politics left administration with little discretion (1927, p. 10). The politics-administration dichotomy had superseded Stein's far more flexible, and realistic, description of the relationship between the two spheres of government.

Conclusion

It may seem a little late in the day to revive a political thinker whose system of government rested on the principle of hereditary monarchy, even a so-called social monarchy. But if we regard his monarch as only an emblem of an impartial state administration, there is much to be learned from Stein. We are coming to appreciate the intrinsic liberalism of Hegel and his followers such as Stein. These thinkers were not advocates of a ruthlessly authoritarian system, but instead were seriously engaged in defining a system of government that allowed individuals to achieve their potential in a world increasingly dominated by organs of administration. At a time when Americans are still floundering toward a definition of the state and Europeans are moving toward the privatization of the state, there is much to be learned from Stein's analysis of the proper role of public administration. As Rutgers (1994) correctly concludes, "To be able to grasp public administration not merely as some necessary evil, we need to rethink the concept of the state. Von Stein's ideas provide an attractive starting point for doing so" (p. 409).

ROBERT D. MIEWALD

BIBLIOGRAPHY

Blank, Hans-Joachim, 1969. "Verwaltung und Verwaltungswissenschaft." In Gisela Kress and Dieter Senghaas, ed., *Politikwissenschaft.* Frankfurt: Europäische Verlangsanstalt.

Dunsire, Andrew, 1973. *Administration: The Word and the Science.* London: Martin Robinson.

Gilbert, Felix, 1977. "From Political to Social History: Lorenz von Stein and the Revolution of 1848." *History: Choice and Commitment.* Cambridge, MA: Harvard University Press.

Goodnow, Frank, 1900. *Politics and Administration: A Study in Government.* New York: Macmillan.

Lindenfeld, David F., 1989. "The Decline of Polizeiwissenschaft: Continuity and Change in the Study of Administration in German Universities in the 19th Century." In Erk Heyen, ed., *Formation und Transformation des Verwaltungswissens in Frankreich und Deutschland (18./19. Jh.).* Baden-Baden: Nomos.

Mengelberg, Kaethe, ed. and trans., 1964. *The History of the Social Movement in France, 1789–1850.* Totowa, NJ: Bedminster Press.

Mutius, Albert von, ed., 1992. *Lorenz von Stein 1890–1990.* Heidelberg: R. v. Decker's Verlag.

Pittau, Joseph, 1967. *Political Thought in Early Meiji Japan, 1868–1889.* Cambridge, MA: Harvard University Press.

Rutgers, Mark R., 1994. "Can the Study of Public Administration Do Without a Concept of the State? Reflections on the Work of Lorenz von Stein." *Administration and Society,* vol. 26: 395–412.

Schnur, Roman, ed., 1978. *Staat und Gesellschaft: Studien über Lorenz von Stein.* Berlin: Duncker and Humblot.

Stein, Lorenz von, 1850. *Geschichte der socialen Bewegung in Frankreich von 1789 bis auf unsere Tage,* vol. 3. Leipzig: Otto Wigand.

———, 1876. *Handbuch der Verwaltungslehre,* 2d ed. Stuttgart: J. G. Cotta.

———, 1866–1884. *Die Verwaltungslehre,* Stuttgart: J. G. Cotta.

Willoughby, W. F., 1927. *Principles of Public Administration.* Washington, D.C.: Brookings Institution.

Wilson, Woodrow, 1887. "The Study of Administration." *Political Science Quarterly,* vol 2: 197–222.

STEWARDSHIP. The disinterested performance of a duty by government and/or its agents on behalf of a superior.

Despite the variety of uses of the term "stewardship" in the literature and practice of public administration, it has retained a surprising consistency of meaning that reflects its etymological roots. Although the term has biblical origins, its use in government arose during the medieval period. It was associated with the work performed on behalf of a lord or, in the case of kingship, on behalf of the crown. Normally, this work involved responsibility for managing the basic financial and household activities of the estate. After the English civil wars in the 1640s, stewardship increasingly became associated with action undertaken on behalf of the "people" or their surrogates. Thus, when the term "stewardship" is found in the literature and practice of contemporary public administration, it still reflects its etymological origins of disinterested performance of householdlike duties by government and/or its agents on behalf of a superior.

There are three characteristics of the term that have been consistently reflected throughout history and are retained in their current usage in the literature and practice of public administration. First, stewardship has always entailed some kind of subordinate role to a superior on whose behalf one acts as a steward. Second, stewardship has always been associated with managing the basic, but critically important, activities of an enterprise that is too large and complicated to be performed by one person. Finally, the activities undertaken by stewards have always required a distinctive competence in managing those rudimentary financial, legal, and housekeeping functions that are critical to the well-being of the larger organizational entity. Each of these characteristics is responsible for creating a distinctive set of questions and, consequently, for the considerable debate and writing about the appropriate stewardship role of career administrators in systems of democratic governance.

1. Upon whose behalf do public administrators act as stewards?
2. What managerial functions and tasks can appropriately be delegated to administrative subordinates?
3. What kind of expertise and competence is necessary for the successful performance of one's stewardship role?

Stewardship: Who Do Career Administrators Serve?

Who do career administrators serve when they perform their stewardship responsibilities? This question is answered quite differently depending on which system of governance one uses as the basis for answering the question. The answer is somewhat clearer in France and England than it is in the United States, where career administrators carry out their work within a separation of powers system in which no one branch of government is sovereign over the other. In England, career administrators operate under a doctrine of "ministerial responsibility," which attaches their stewardship responsibility to the government ministers of the day (Rohr, in Cooper 1994, Chap. 27). In France, however, where the principle of the "general will" is embodied in the doctrine of parliamentary supremacy, career administrators hold stewardship allegiance to Parliament rather than to the individual government ministers themselves. At a practical level, this creates the possibility for career administrators in France to invoke their stewardship responsibility to Parliament as a whole in opposition to the policies or practices of a given minister.

Because of the American constitutional tradition of separation of powers, the locus of stewardship responsibility is much more problematic for career administrators in the United States. To whom do administrators owe allegiance? Is it Congress, that makes the laws? Or is it the president who executes the laws? Or is it the courts who interpret the laws? Or is it the U.S. Constitution as a whole and its encompassing web of offices, processes, and institutions? An increasing number of scholars have argued that career administrators in the United States are stewards of the constitutional enterprise as a whole (Rohr 1986, 1987; Burke 1986; Kass and Catron 1990, Chaps. 2 and 4; Morgan, in Cooper 1994, Chap. 7). In charging administrators with responsibility for the whole, the question arises as to what distinguishes the stewardship responsibility of career administrators from other public officials, such as judges and elected officeholders who also pledge their allegiance to the constitutional enterprise as a whole?

John Rohr, one of the leading advocates of a central stewardship role for career administrators in the American democratic process, answers this question by arguing that the career public service now performs a role originally intended by the founders to be played by both the U.S. House and Senate. Senatorial attributes like duration, expertise, and stability have been eroded by electoral changes. "In a word, today's Senate is not the sort of institution the Federalists wanted and the Anti-Federalists feared. The closest approximation. . . can be found in the career civil service, especially at its higher levels." Rohr also argued that with its merit system and affirmative action

policies, the American bureaucracy serves to curb the excessive filtering and refining, which the Anti-Federalists feared would undermine the representative function of the House of Representatives. In short, "the administrative state with its huge career public service, heals and repairs a defect in the Constitution of the United States" (Rohr 1987, p. 142; Rohr 1986).

A variation on Rohr's argument uses the balance wheel metaphor to emphasize the important stewardship role American career administrators play as "keepers of the central questions" that are necessary to hold the American system of constitutional governance on course: balancing concerns for efficiency and effectiveness with the need for responsiveness, balancing the protection of individual rights with majority rule, and balancing the substantive claims of liberty, property, and equality. The justification for career administrators playing this role rests on two considerations: the peculiar competence that career administrators bring to their work and the social and economic transformations that have eroded the capacity of the various social and governance institutions to participate meaningfully in helping to perform this balancing role (Morgan, in Cooper 1994, Chap. 7).

Stewardship and the Limits of Delegation

Stewardship presupposes the delegation of authority by a superior to act on the superior's behalf. This presupposition affects two central domains of administrative practice, one involving internal management systems and the other involving the relationship of administrative entities and their agents to the other institutions of democratic governance. The managerial domain is concerned with creating the most propitious conditions for delegating responsibility downward within an organization in order to achieve effectively the organization's mission. In like manner, the governance domain is concerned with creating the necessary authority for administrators to exercise their stewardship responsibility, regardless of what managerial system is in place.

The managerial side of the delegation issue has been influenced by the same kind of considerations that have dominated private-sector organizations. Much energy has been devoted to designing organizational structures, employee incentive systems, and task management mechanisms that will result in the most productive outcomes and highest levels of employee satisfaction (Likert 1961; McGregor 1967; Deming 1986). The governance side of the delegation issue has focused on various efforts to strike an appropriate balance between controlling the abuses of administrative discretion and structuring its exercise in ways that recognize the distinctive contributions of the administrative function in contrast to the legislative and judicial activities of democratic governance.

The starting point for striking this balance necessarily begins in modern day rule-of-law systems with an affirmative grant of authority by the administrator's legally constituted superior. There is a presumption that career administrators have no authority to act without legal authorization to do so. In practice, this legal authorization is frequently difficult to find, since the vast majority of action undertaken by administrative agents comes from informal action that cannot be tied directly and immediately to any formal legal process such as rulemaking, adjudication, or judicial review. In the case of the United States, where formal administrative rulemaking is more widely practiced than in any other country, one student of the administrative process has estimated that 80 to 90 percent of administrative discretion is exercised without any direct and formal connection to any legal authorization (Davis 1971). Many argue that since the practical realities of administrative life preclude this kind of direct legal authority, in order to preserve "a government of laws and not of men," administrative systems should rely much more extensively on internally initiated organizational processes that confine, structure, and check the exercise of administrative discretion (Davis 1971) and on the passage of laws with clearer administrative standards (Lowi 1979).

Despite Herculean efforts to make administrative stewardship legally safe for democracy, vast amounts of discretion continue to exist without very precise legal guidelines for its exercise. When legal controls have been pushed as far as possible, the debate over administrative discretion shifts away from a focus on the negative merit of controlling its abuse through law to a focus on the positive merit that arises from the distinctive contributions that administrative stewards can make to the democratic governance process. At this point adherence to law as the focal point of administrative stewardship gives way to discussions of administrative competence.

Stewardship and Competence

It goes without saying that one entrusts others with stewardship responsibility only to the extent that they possess the competence to carry out the functions entrusted to them. But what kind of competence do administrators need, especially in modern systems of democratic governance? Three different answers can be found to this question in the literature and writing on public administration. Each answer reflects the kind of peculiar competence that is believed necessary to preserve a healthy system of democratic governance—public accountability, efficient and effective administration of the public's business, and the protection of individual rights.

Ensuring Accountability

When legal accountability proves insufficient to guide the discretionary exercise of stewardship authority, nonlegal forms of accountability increase in importance. There are as many different versions of administrative accountability as there are democratic masters. Are these masters the elected officials? Are they the organized interest groups that attempt to influence the electoral and administrative processes? Or are they the public institutions, their organizational missions, and the collective wisdom that these institutions embody? Answers to these questions give rise to at least three types of nonlegal administrative accountability: policy accountability, facilitative accountability, and institutional accountability. A somewhat different kind of administrative competence is necessary to successfully carry out each of these models of accountability.

The most common model of administrative accountability, made famous by Woodrow Wilson, draws a distinction between policy-level questions that determine "what to do" and administrative-level questions that shape "how to" carry out these directions. Under this model, administrative competence consists of the capacity to apply one's skills in a neutral technical manner, indifferent to the ends being served.

Increasingly, the Wilsonian model of policy accountability has been undermined in the Western industrialized world by the proliferation of a multiplicity of interest groups and the simultaneous difficulty this creates for sustaining a consistent societywide policy consensus. In this kind of hyperpluralistic environment, the model of neutral administrative competence gives way to even-handed facilitation of the contested claims of various constituency interests. In the words of one student of the current administrative process in Great Britain, career administrators increasingly negotiate "the common ground of disputed value territory . . . keep the show on the road, settle disputes and make things happen" (Richards 1992, p. 17). This view is even more pervasive in the United States, where interest groups have long dominated the policy and administrative processes (Lowi 1979).

Closely aligned with the model of facilitative accountability is the role career administrators can play in structuring and facilitating an ongoing dialogue with citizens in what have been characterized as "public encounters" (Goodsell 1981). These encounters provide an opportunity for administrators to educate the citizenry by modeling the conditions for healthy public discourse between the government and its citizens. Many argue that this kind of stewardship activity plays a decisive role in building and maintaining a community of shared meaning (Fox and Miller 1994; Cooper 1991; White, in Kass and Catron 1990, Chap. 5).

A final version of accountability that is emphasized by some scholars focuses on the wisdom and prudence embodied in institutional practices and the unique qualities of the bureaucratic setting, such as the rules of evidence, burdens of proof, and decision rules. Taken together, these arm administrators with a special kind of prudence or practical wisdom that enables them to coalesce considerations of workability, acceptability, and the proper fit of a proposed administrative course of action with the circumstances and capacity of the agency (Morgan, in Kass and Catron 1990, Chap. 2; Terry 1995; Morgan, in Bowman 1991, Chap. 2). This model of institutional accountability emphasizes the importance of being guided by what has proven to be workable in the past in addition to being guided by the policy directives of elected officials and the preferences of constituency interests.

Promoting Efficiency and Effectiveness

The most widely recognized competence associated with administrative stewardship is the promotion of the efficient and effective management of the public's business. In fact, the values of efficiency and effectiveness have served as the driving force, especially in the United States, for the creation of a professional cadre of career public servants (Stever 1988). It is the framework that has guided the classical Weberian model of bureaucracy and the policy-administration dichotomy made famous by Woodrow Wilson. But even in Great Britain and France, where the principle of civil servant autonomy is not as evident, assisting the ministers (as is the case in Great Britain's system of ministerial responsibility) or assisting the Parliament (as is the case in France's system of parliamentary supremacy) is done in the name of, and for the sake of, making governmental policy initiatives more efficient and effective.

Protection of Individual Rights

The stewardship responsibility of career administrators to protect individual rights is especially evident in the United States. Lockean principles of democratic self-government, a strong separation of powers tradition, and a very active Supreme Court have actualized the commitment to individual rights by career administrators in ways that go far beyond the administrative practices found in England and France. This tradition of individual rights is so strong that some scholars have made it the primary moral responsibility of career administrators in the United States (Davis 1971).

In summary, the usage of the term "stewardship" in discussions involving public policy and public administration in modern democratic systems of governance reflect two characteristics that are part of its etymological history. First, administrators are fiduciary agents of their democratic lords and masters. At times, this lord and master is seen as the *vox populi*, but, more often, it is the elected representatives, the laws, and the constitutions that are the mediating expressions of the *vox populi*. Second, career administrators are increasingly viewed as critically important, if not equal partners, in stewarding the healthy functioning of our modern systems of constitutional democracy.

DOUGLAS F. MORGAN

BIBLIOGRAPHY

Bowman, James S., 1991. *Ethical Frontiers in Public Management.* San Francisco, CA: Jossey-Bass.

Burke, John P., 1986. *Bureaucratic Responsibility.* Baltimore, MD: Johns Hopkins.

Cooper, Terry, 1994. *Handbook of Public Administrative Ethics.* New York: Marcel Dekker.

———, 1991. *An Ethic of Citizenship for Public Administration.* Englewood Cliffs, NJ: Prentice-Hall.

Davis, Kenneth Culp., 1971. *Discretionary Justice: A Preliminary Inquiry.* Urbana: University of Illinois Press.

Deming, W. Edwards, 1986. *Out of the Crisis.* Cambridge, MA: MIT Press.

Fox, Charles, and Hugh T. Miller, 1994. *Postmodern Public Administration: Toward Discourse.* Newbury Park, CA: Sage.

Goodsell, Charles T., ed., 1981. *The Public Encounter: Where State and Citizen Meet.* Bloomington: Indiana University Press.

Kass, Henry D., and Catron, Bayard, 1990. *Images and Identities in Public Administration.* Newbury Park, CA: Sage.

Lowi, Theodore, 1979. *The End of Liberalism: The Second Republic of the U.S.*, 2d ed. New York: W. W. Norton.

Likert, Rensis, 1961. *New Patterns of Management.* New York: McGraw-Hill.

McGregor, Douglas M., 1967. *The Professional Manager.* New York: McGraw-Hill.

Richards, Sue, 1992. "Changing Patterns of Legitimation in Public Management." *Public Policy and Administration,* vol. 7 (Winter) 15–28.

Rohr, John A., 1986. *To Run a Constitution: The Legitimacy of the Administrative State.* Lawrence: University of Kansas.

———1987. *Ethics for Bureaucrats: An Essay on Law and Values,* rev. New York: Marcel Dekker.

Stever, James A., 1988. *The End of Public Administration: Problems of the Profession in the Post-Progressive Era.* New York: Transnational Publishers.

Terry, Larry, 1995. *The Administrator As Conservator: The Leadership of Public Bureaucracies.* Newbury Park, CA: Sage.

STONE, DONALD CRAWFORD (1903–1995).

A major figure in the development of public administration institutions in the 1930s and 1940s and the founding dean of the Graduate School of Public and International Affairs at the University of Pittsburgh (1957). An outspoken critic of late twentieth-century public administration education, he continued into his nineties to consult and develop courses in administration through the Coalition to Improve Management in State and Local Government at Indiana University at Indianapolis.

Don Stone grew up in Lakewood, Ohio, a suburb of Cleveland, the son of a businessman. His parents were strongly interested in public affairs, management, and self-reliance, which they passed on to Don and his older brother, Harold.

He graduated from Colgate University in 1925, where he majored in political science with a special focus on the development of democratic institutions and comparative government. After graduation, he was persuaded to try out a new graduate program in city management at Syracuse University and became a member of the second class at the Maxwell School. It being risky for a Colgate man to go to Syracuse, he persuaded his class treasurer to attend also; his older brother Harold enrolled after the semester started.

Don's management skills were evident from his early years. As a college junior, he became house manager, secretary, and treasurer of his fraternity, which had been mismanaged. He instituted budget and accounting systems, competitive purchasing and recruitment, and monthly reports. He was also an elected member of the Athletic Governing Board, business manager of the literary magazine, president of the Student Christian Association, and secretary of the Colgate Student Athletic Club. A consummate athlete for most of his life, he won six varsity letters at Colgate in basketball and track and held the Ohio state high hurdle record for about 20 years. In his seventies, he was notorious for defeating much younger opponents on the tennis court.

A review of Don Stone's professional accomplishments reads like a history of public administration. His mentors were Luther Gulick and Louis Brownlow. He was assistant to the first city manager of Cincinnati, Colonel Sherrill (1926–1928); staff member at the Institute of Public Administration in New York, where he worked with Gulick (1928–1929); and director of research for the International City Management Association (1930–1933), then a part of the Public Administration Clearing House (PACH) in Chicago, which Brownlow directed. PACH is often called "1313" after its address at 1313 East 60th Street near the University of Chicago. In 1933, he became executive director of the Public Administration Service (PAS) created as the consulting, research, and publication center of PACH. In this capacity, Stone was instrumental in founding the American Public Works Association (APWA) and the American Society for Public Administration (ASPA). He wrote the constitutions for both organizations. He served as consultant to Harry Hopkins and the Roosevelt administration's Work Projects Administration (WPA), a major New Deal initiative to provide employment through public works projects.

From 1939 to 1948, Stone was assistant director of the Bureau of the Budget (BOB). One of his first tasks was to coordinate preparation of Reorganization Plan No. 1, which created the Executive Office of the President (EOP). He helped organize BOB and recruited highly qualified people to make it an efficient and effective element of the EOP.

When the Marshall Plan (European Economic Recovery Act) was enacted in 1948, Stone was appointed director of administration, a post he served in until 1951. He had done a study of European infrastructure in the early 1930s and combined his interests in public works and democratic government in this distinctly U.S. effort to restore the social, political, and economic viability of former enemies as well as allies. Stone saw the rebuilding of infrastructure in war-torn countries as essential to fostering freedom and economic development. The programs also forced the countries to work together on restoration of transportation, electric power, and so forth, which helped to rebuild democracy and repel domination by the Soviet Union. His last post with the federal government was in the Mutual Security Agency, which he left in 1953 to become president of Springfield College in Massachusetts.

In his four years at Springfield, he revamped the administration of the college, instituted good management and budgeting techniques, streamlined the academic program, and undertook a major capital campaign. He left Springfield in 1957, at the invitation of Edward Litchfield, Chancellor of the University of Pittsburgh, to establish the Graduate School of Public and International Affairs (GSPIA).

GSPIA was designed to be a school for practitioners of government, whether administrators or academics. Its original degree programs were in Public Administration, Urban Affairs, and International Affairs. He later developed the program in Public Works Administration, which was jointly offered by the School of Engineering and the Graduate School of Public Health. The program was supported by the APWA Education Foundation and provided public management skills to public works practitioners, who were mostly engineers. Although it was a highly successful program, it was abolished by a later dean because of its practitioner orientation.

He stepped down as dean in 1969 and left Pitt in 1974 to become distinguished public service professor at Carnegie Mellon University, where he continued to teach and consult until 1992. In 1984, he established the National Coalition to Improve Management in State and Local Government, which he moved to Indianapolis in 1992.

Stone's principal contribution to the field of public administration has been in the development of efficient and effective public organizations with "clearly assigned executive responsibility and accountability" (APWA 1992, p. 55). In his writings and his leadership, he demonstrated his belief that public administrators have an active role in implementing public systems and disagreed with the strict distinction between policy and administration. "How can one better serve the public interest in a democracy than by trying to help a political executive develop vision, integrity, competence? My basic premise is that good organization, management, operations, and effective results are both in the public interest and the best political policy" (APWA 1992, p. 51).

He incorporated this philosophy into his teaching at both GSPIA and Carnegie Mellon; however, his belief in public management as a vocation clashed with traditional political science views of bureaucratic behavior. Critical of the encroachment of political science into public administration programs and its diminution of practice, his reaction, typical of his problemsolving approach throughout his life, was to demonstrate the value of public management as a pursuit in itself. In 1990, he developed a model course outline for educating executives in the principles and practice of public management that was marketed by the Coalition to Improve State and Local Government.

Don Stone committed his life to the improvement of the administration of government and every other organization he was associated with. He was president of ASPA, president of the National Association for Schools of Public Affairs and Administration (NASPAA), vice president of the American Political Science Association, president of the American Consortium for International Public Administration, and a fellow of the National Academy of Public Administration.

Don shared his career with his life partner Alice, whom he married in 1928. It was evident to all who attended their 50th wedding anniversary party that they were still very much in love. Having completed a master's degree in government and public law at Columbia University, Alice was Don's professional support as well as manager of the household, which eventually included four children. They passed on their love of democracy and good government to their children through weekly family councils where they decided by consensus such matters as the family vacation and what charities to support.

Together the Stones fostered a feeling of community wherever they went, enlarging their family to include their professional colleagues. They provided social support for the families at 1313, who were often separated because of travel requirements. At GSPIA, the Stones entertained faculty and students frequently; ever mindful of the needs of foreign students, they bought up a supply of furniture from an old hotel and parcelled it out to foreign students as needed. The enthusiasm and sense of civic responsibility generated by the Stones touches everyone who has known them.

Don Stone was the ultimate practitioner-academic, a talented problem solver who practiced the art as well as the science of administration. After 30 years of the practice of public administration, he spent the next 40 years teaching others as well as doing. Well into his eighties, his students at Carnegie Mellon rated his course as the best they had ever taken.

His impact on the field continues in the institutions he founded and the people whose lives he influenced. Moreover, Don Stone serves as the model public administrator, a true citizen of the world who took it as his civic duty to make it all run better.

MARY M. TIMNEY

BIBLIOGRAPHY

American Public Works Association (APWA), 1992. *An Interview with Donald C. Stone.* Chicago: Public Works Historical Society.

Marquis Who's Who in America (1992–1993). New Providence, NJ: Reed Reference.

STRATEGIC BUDGETING. A system of budgeting in which money is allocated to a set of strategies based on specific goals, objectives, missions, and the philosophy of an organization. Like most budgeting systems in practice today, its purpose is to provide a mechanism by which the scarce resources of a government can be judiciously allocated to meet its needs and the expectations of its citizens. Although not entirely a new idea, strategic budgeting is considered by many as an important development in the long history of budget reforms in the country.

Since the beginning of this century, public budgeting in the United States has gone through extensive reforms. Some of these reforms have been driven by the need to strengthen administrative processes and some were driven by the need to achieve effective fiscal control, to ensure legislative accountability, and more important, to improve the public's understanding of the budget. To a large extent, the course of these reforms and their success or failure reflect the economic and political environment in which budget decisions are made and the problems that are germane in transforming the strategies of reform into routine budget activities. Strategic budgeting possesses considerable merit in this regard because it combines the objectives underlying these reforms in the most effective manner.

Strategic budgeting, as the name implies, is a forward-looking system built on the position, strengths, and weaknesses of an organization. Traditional budget systems take an inward view focusing more on the internal activities of an organization, which places a limit on the extent to which an organization can effectively deal with the changes in its internal and external climate. Strategic budgeting takes a broad, open approach directed to both internal and external activities of an organization. This adds a new dimension to the traditional budget process by enlarging an organization's view of management and making it more useful as an approach to deal with the changing forces that influence its management functions.

Strategic Budgeting as an Extension of Strategic Planning

Strategic budgeting has its origin in strategic planning. Strategic planning is a process that deals with the future based on current decisions. It starts by setting up an organization's mission and philosophy, delineating its goals and objectives, defining strategies, outlining policies to achieve them, and finally, mapping out a set of detailed actions to ensure that these goals, objectives, and strategies are fully realized. Stated simply, it is a process of describing in advance what kind of planning efforts one will undertake, who is going to undertake them, and what will be done with the results. These questions are simple yet flexible, which gives strategic planning a universal appeal. They also highlight its importance as an approach consisting of a unique set of functions that must be addressed in a logical fashion to understand its dynamics and to have a full view of the tasks it is expected to accomplish.

As a process, strategic planning is continuous and feedback oriented. It is continuous because the formulation of strategies takes place in an environment that is constantly changing. It is feedback oriented because the changing environment requires constant updating of information generated at each stage of the process. Strategic planning, above all, is action oriented. As an action-oriented approach, it can transform the activities of a management process into concrete decisions by producing results that are tangible and can be measured in a meaningful fashion. It can bridge the gap between what is designed as a process and what is achieved in reality; that is, between theory and practice. In conventional terminology, this is known as "operationalization," a process that ties strategic planning to tactical or operational planning.

There is often a tendency among the students of public budgeting to confuse strategic planning with long-range planning. Strategic planning is not long-range planning, although it has a long-term bias. Long-range planning looks into the future based on past performance, whereas strategic planning focuses on reaching future targets, utilizing judgment, analysis, and measures used in operational planning. However, like long-range planning, strategic planning is conducted by upper-level management using a much longer time frame, whereas operational planning is carried out by middle- or lower-level management with a much shorter time frame, usually a year or less.

Strategic budgeting integrates both strategic and operational planning through budgetary control, reinforced by an organization's philosophy and commitment of its resources toward that end. In other words, strategic planning sets the tone for strategic budgeting so that budget details can be developed for an agency in congruence with the philosophy, goals, and objectives of an organization. In this sense, strategic budgeting is more than a process; it is the outcome of analysis of all possible planning and related decisions that affect an organization both in the short and long term.

Strategic Budgeting and Its Relationship with Other Budgeting Systems

As the latest to come into the budgeting scene, strategic budgeting can be regarded as a variant of many of the existing budgeting systems. It has some of the same features of the existing systems, yet has certain characteristics that make it unique as well as interesting. Structurally, strategic budgeting does not differ much from most of its predecessors. What makes it different is the long-term orientation that allows it to be more flexible and open to rational and behavioral methods of operation. Philosophically, strategic budgeting may be described as simply moving from function to program and from program to strategy, following traditional budgeting procedures. This transition from process to procedure is necessary to justify changes in budget requests for old, new or special programs. Technically, strategic budgeting is probably closer, to zero-based budgeting (ZBB) than any other system in the sense that it looks at a budget afresh each year without the assumption, as in incremental budgeting, that past trends will continue into the future or that the current budget must reflect this trend with marginal adjustment for inflation and other related factors.

From an operational perspective, in particular, it is easier to take corrective measures in a timely fashion with strategic budgeting than any other budgeting system because of its forward looking approach since, by definition, most planning activities are. Although zero-based budgeting allows for preventive control, it is an integral part of strategic budgeting. Organizationally, strategic budgeting is more top-down and in some sense similar to planning, programming, budgeting system (PPBS). Whereas ZBB is viewed as a bottom-up, participatory budgeting system, in strategic budgeting participation is essential for top-level management with sufficient scope for participation by middle- and lower-level managers. As in PPBS, the participation by middle- and lower-level management is necessary to ensure proper implementation of strategies, whereas the top-level management is responsible for designing the organizational philosophy, missions, and goals.

The Basic Operating Elements of Strategic Budgeting

Like most budgeting systems, strategic budgeting is simple and can be easily tailored to suit an organization's structure, needs, and circumstances. This apparent flexibility also makes it suitable for adapting to a structure similar to program budgeting by explicitly orienting it toward an organization's goals (program philosophy), objectives (targets), strategies (methods), and activities (specific tasks or actions). Understanding this relationship is critical, especially in governmental organizations where requests for appropriation are frequently justified at the program and activity level. Although the specifics may differ, the structure of a strategic budgeting system is essentially the same for all organizations. It must be precise to give a clear picture of the direction in which an organization is going, flexible to accommodate its changing needs and conditions, and rational to make certain that the elements of the structure are logically connected.

The following constitute the basic operating elements of a strategic budgeting system: organizational philosophy, agency mission, agency goals, objectives, strategies, and ac-

tions. Organizational philosophy is the global view of an organization, its mission and purpose toward which it must strive. Frequently, it represents statements concerning a set of preferences and beliefs that motivate the behavior of an organization. They are ethical in nature and serve as a socially internalized guide to decisionmaking. All other functions and activities of the decision process are extensions of this initial belief system and must follow from it. For instance, the members of a community that has a serious crime problem may value safe streets as the ideal living environment for all its residents. Assuming that this value gets translated into concrete action, then all other activities must be formulated in light of this shared concern.

As a natural extension of an initial belief system, the various components that make up a strategic budgeting system serve three important purposes in the overall management process, which are partly normative, partly management oriented, and partly tactical. As a normative process, strategic budgeting must define the mission that an agency within an organization desires to achieve. The mission establishes a linkage between the organization's philosophy and agency goals. It represents the core values and principles that provide the rationale for the existence of an agency.

As a management process, strategic budgeting must specify the goals, objectives, and strategies that an agency needs to undertake in order to realize its mission and, through it, the goals and philosophy of the organization. To be more specific, goals are general ends to which an agency must direct all its efforts, whereas objectives are targets for action by an agency. They are quantitative statements of what an agency plans to achieve within a specific time period. By contrast, strategies are methods employed by an agency to achieve the goals, objectives, and quantified results of its action. Quantification helps facilitate data collection and measurement that are necessary to justify budget requests, ensure budget allocation and, finally, evaluate the funded programs and activities for efficiency (output) and effectiveness (outcome) of an agency operation. Lastly, as a tactical process, it must determine the operational control that transforms strategies into a series of tasks, called actions, thus making it easier to implement them (Figure I). It is important to note, however, that unlike a private organization, defining goals, objectives, and strategies is probably the most difficult task facing a government. There are several reasons for this. First of all, the goods and services a government provides are characteristically different from those offered by a private organization. The frequent presence of the free-riding problem, the exclusion principle, and the indivisibleness of many of these goods and services makes it difficult for a government to determine the exact nature of demand and the quantity of services to be provided. Second, public decisions frequently are made in conflicting environments,

FIGURE I. A STRATEGIC BUDGET PROCESS

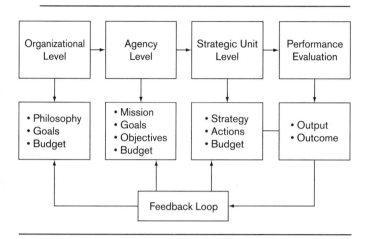

An Illustrative Example

Perhaps a simple illustration will help us understand how strategic budgeting works. Consider a hypothetical agency, which we will call strategic unit, in the process of developing its annual budget. A strategic unit could be anything—an organization, an agency, or an operational unit within an agency. Suppose our strategic unit deals with environmental quality management (EQM) and has identified a set of goals and objectives consistent with the general philosophy and goals of the organization of which it is a part. Next, the agency needs to prepare a set of strategies, called "strategic packages." In some respects, the strategic packages are similar to the decision packages of zero-based budgeting, but with a long-term focus. Developing these packages is the most crucial exercise in the entire process since much of the decision on budget allocation depends on these strategies and how well they have been put together to achieve the stated goals and objectives not only of the agency but also of the organization as a whole. As a general rule, before selecting the packages, each strategic unit must do some preliminary analysis of data for each package to justify its selection. In particular, the unit must ask how feasible and attainable are these strategies or are the problems of attainment due to lack of resources—financial, organizational, or any other?

Once the preliminary analysis has been done, the units can begin to design the strategic packages. Several things are worth noting during this stage of the process. To begin with, each package should contain some identity information such as the name of the package, its number, the name of the unit, the date and the name of the preparer. The purpose of this simple exercise is to help define the nature and responsibility of the unit and to show how it is linked, if at all, with other units of an organization. Second, and perhaps more important than any other requirement in the entire process, is the fact that the information used by a unit to select a particular strategy be valid, reliable, and consistent. They must also conform to any legal requirements, mandates, or legislative intentions. Third, the packages must be designed as flexibly as possible to accommodate any possible enhancement in the budget. There is a parallel here with zero-based budgeting where flexibility is incorporated through a rolling budget so that new fiscal years could be added as the old ones are deleted. Finally, the packages should have options for contingency plans, providing information on conceivable contingencies, possible countermeasures, establishment of triggerpoints, and any other consideration. This is where strategic budgeting differs from zero-based budgeting. The contingencies do not have to be exhaustive or prepared for every single fiscal year as long as they cover the plan period, whether it is a one-year or a five-year strategic plan.

Table I presents summary information about the strategic unit in our hypothetical example in terms of a sin-

which make it necessary for the management process to constantly sensitize the decision packages to outside political considerations, citizens, and special interest groups. Third, the decisionmakers often find it hard to agree on a set of performance criteria that could be used to measure the efficiency and effectiveness of public services in a consistent fashion. Fourth, but not least, is the widely held belief that the nature of bureaucracy itself renders public decisionmaking inefficient. In other words, as organizations become large, they tend to become more bureaucratic, i.e., they become less reflective of public wants and expectations.

These issues and concerns facing a government clearly indicate that the selection of goals, objectives, and strategies that are acceptable to all participants in a decision process is not a simple task. The last several decades of cumulative research by economists, political scientists, and social psychologists on what constitutes a rational public choice has not produced any tangible result. Efforts to empirically test it have not produced any superior result either. In a situation where reality departs from the ideals of a rational choice model, it is obvious that some compromises have to be made. It is not uncommon, therefore, for public decisionmakers to use decision rules that satisfice rather than optimize. To paraphrase a common sentiment among many public administration scholars, administrative agencies frequently make adjustments on demand rather than initiate a decision process that seeks a clear definition of goals and objectives, or they wait for tensions between established patterns and unmet needs to signal a change in policy, or they do not make any great departures from customary activities. Strategic budgeting vis-à-vis strategic planning can go a long way toward correcting this problem by setting a process in motion that is focused, dynamic, and yet operational.

TABLE I. Summary Information for a Sample Strategic Unit: Environmental Quality Management

FY XXXX
Unit Code
Prepared By   Date Prepared
Goal 1: Improve air quality.

Objective 1: Reduce air pollutants to achieve federal standards by the year XXXX.

   Strategy 1: Implement EPA's ozone policy.

      Action A: Percent of major targets met.

      Action B: Number of onsite monitors.

      Output/Outcome associated with Strategy 1 for Objective 1.

   Strategy 2: Promote and enforce local air quality.

      Action A: Number of preventive workshops held.

      Action B: Number of partnership programs executed.

      Output/Outcome associated with Strategy 2 for Objective 1.

Objective 2: Reduce air toxic emissions by 40 percent between FY xxxx and FY xxxx.

   Strategy 1: Conduct ongoing studies of toxic chemical exposure.

      Action A: Number of studies conducted.

      Action B: Number of study participants.

      Action C: Percent of potential exposure cases analyzed.

      Output/Outcome associated with Strategy 1 for Objective 2.

   Strategy 2: Implement comprehensive air toxics program.

      Action A: Number of discharges inventoried.

      Action B: Percent reduction of toxic chemical discharges from previous year.

      Output/Outcome associated with Strategy 2 for Objective 2.

NOTE: Actual numbers should be used for every item in the table, if they are available. Also, note that the numeral or letter to the right of goal, objectives, strategies, and actions represent priority.

gle goal, related objectives and corresponding strategies the agency is planning to achieve for the coming fiscal year. In reality, there is no limit as to the number of goals, objectives, strategic packages, and actions a unit could entail. The actual number should be determined by the size of the unit, the number of current and future programs it plans to offer, the history of its budget, and so on. Table I also shows the priority assigned by the decisionmakers of our strategic unit to various objectives, strategies, and actions for the goal in question. Like ZBB, prioritization is an integral part of strategic budgeting. The primary objective of prioritization is to accomplish the most out of the limited resources available to an organization. Since the sum of the resources required by all the packages usually exceeds the amount available, some rational methods of allocation should be used by the organization. Common sense suggests that the method must be equitable so that, on a long-term basis, the strategic objectives can be achieved in the most efficient and effective manner.

Once the rankings on the proposed packages have been determined and approved, the strategic budget is ready to be executed. Execution of the budget needs close monitoring to establish compliance with appropriation guidelines. The budget itself should provide information on the allocation for at least two years to allow for comparison between proposed and current allocations. It should also provide detailed information on funding in order to show the extent of contributions the various sources are making to the proposed budget. Table II presents an example of budget request for the agency goals, objectives, and strategies. Conceptually, the proposed budget could be further broken down in terms of the traditional object classification system. The object classification, or line-itemization, would allow the agency to show the costs specific to these strategies. As a matter of common sense, governments should use only the direct costs for the majority of its operations, while indirect costs should be used on a basis that is most appropriate for a strategic unit rather than for the entire government.

The example presented here is simple, but the principle and the procedure suggested can be applied to develop an actual (full-fledged) budget for an entire organization. However, as the scale of the budget gets large, it becomes critically important that the agency missions, goals, objectives, and strategies are synchronized (through regular budget meetings and other procedural activities) to minimize any potential conflict between agency interests and those of the organization. Careful attention must be given to develop strategic packages so as to minimize waste or duplication of programs and activities as well as to guarantee their achievability within a specified time. As in ZBB, problems will emerge when prioritizing

TABLE II. A Sample Budget Request for the Strategic Unit
Goal 1: Improve Air Quality FY XXXX

	Last Year's Budget	Current Year's Budget	Proposed Budget
Objective 1:			
Strategy 1	$2,000,000	$2,250,000	$2,700,000
Action A	[% of above]	[% of above]	[% of above]
Action B	[% remained]	[% remained]	[% remained]
Strategy 2	$ 150,000	$ 200,000	$ 300,000
Action A	[% of above]	[% of above]	[% of above]
Action B	[% remained]	[% remained]	[% remained]
Objective 2:			
Strategy 1	$ 750,000	$1,000,000	$1,350,000
Action A	[% of above]	[% of above]	[% of above]
Action B	[% of above]	[% of above]	[% of above]
Action C	[% remained]	[% remained]	[% remained]
Strategy 2	**$ 300,000**	**$ 350,000**	**$ 450,000**
Action A	[% of above]	[% of above]	[% of above]
Action B	[% remained	[% remained]	[% remained]
Total Goal:	$3,200,000	$3,800,000	$4,800,000
Funding Source (Percent of Total):			
GF Revenue	30.00	35.00	30.00
Fees and Charges	40.00	40.00	40.00
Federal Funds	30.00	25.00	30.00
Total Percent:	100.00	100.00	100.00

Note: Numbers are fictitious and used for illustration only, currency note necessarily U.S. dollars.

these packages, but the frustration can be minimized by isolating programs that are mandated from those which are not and leaving prioritization only for the nonmandated ones. As always, a clear statement of goals, objectives, and strategies plus a clear understanding of the constraints facing an agency or government should make it easier to decide on a set of appropriate priorities. Furthermore, attention should be given to develop measures that could improve the reliability of budget requests. Efforts should also be made to improve the quality of these data if they are to be used as effective measures by which to make budgetary decisions and evaluate the performance of programs and activities once they have been funded.

Summary and Conclusion

The fundamental principle that underlies strategic budgeting is the rational allocation of resources through systematic integration (with strategic planning) and consolidation of efforts to minimize waste and duplication. These are novel and ideal objectives, but they are not beyond the reach of any organization. The success of strategic budgeting and its future as a viable system depends on how an or-

ganization views these efforts and the kinds of measures it takes to realize them.

To be successful, at least in theory, an organization implementing a strategic budgeting system must try to focus on three things: first, it must design and develop a monitoring system to keep track of the changes in its internal as well as external environment and the effect these changes have on the system. With easy availability of database and on-line information systems today, it should not be a difficult task to achieve. Second, it must focus on personnel skills. Frequently in the past, the failure of many of the budget reforms, in particular budget management systems, has been attributed to the weaknesses inherent in the systems rather than focusing on the need to understand if adequate skills and training could have made a difference. Proper training is necessary not only to understand how a budget process works but, more specifically, to utilize one's ability to integrate the diverse components that make up a budget system. The effect of synergy must be thoroughly understood and applied here. Third, as many governments currently using ZBB, PPBS, or any other budgeting system know well, no budgeting activity could be complete without a proper evaluation system in place. Although disagreements may abound on what should be an ideal basis for evaluating performance, there should be some general agreement on the need to effectively develop a set of criteria that can effectively measure the net benefit resulting from a strategic budgeting system. Quality of information, as noted earlier, should remain the single most important concern regardless of the criteria one chooses to use.

AMAN KHAN

STRATEGIC LEADERSHIP.

The inspiration and mobilization of oneself and others to undertake disciplined efforts to produce fundamental decisions and actions that shape and guide what an organization (or other entity) is, what it does, and why it does it (Bryson 1988, p. 5; Bryson and Crosby 1992, p. 31). The definition makes it clear that strategic planning is not a substitute for effective leadership. Indeed, there is no substitute for effective leadership when it comes to strategic thinking and acting.

The following interconnected leadership tasks are important if strategic planning and implementation are to be effective:

- understanding the context
- understanding the people involved, including oneself
- sponsoring the process
- championing the process
- facilitating the process
- fostering collective leadership
- using forums to create a meaningful process, clarify mandates, articulate mission, identify strategic issues, and possibly develop a vision of success
- making and implementing decisions in arenas
- enforcing rules, settling disputes, and managing residual conflicts
- putting it all together

Understanding the Context

Leaders need an appreciation of social, political, and economic history, but at the same time, they must avoid being captured by that history (Burns 1978; Neustadt and May 1986; Hunt 1991). They must see history as the interplay of continuity, or stability, and change, and recognize how best to balance these forces in a given context. They also must have an intimate knowledge of their organization in order to make sense of the organization in relation to the broader context (Mintzberg 1994). Leaders' understanding of history and their organization is important for recognizing emergent strategies, understanding how strategic planning might help their organization, tailoring the process to the organization's circumstances, negotiating the initial agreement, framing issues effectively, developing viable strategies for addressing them, and getting those strategies adopted and implemented.

External and internal organizational assessments, stakeholder analyses, and special studies all are designed to attune strategic planning participants to important specifics of the context within which the organization exists. But those explorations typically occur after the process has started. Even before the process begins, leaders need some understanding of the context, so they can have a general idea about how to use the process to take advantage of the world as it is in order to make it better. It is therefore very important for leaders to stay in touch with the world through personal contacts and observation, broad reading, continuing education, and reflection.

Leaders should be especially attentive to the possibilities for rather dramatic strategic change. Organizational strategies typically remain stable over long periods and then suddenly change all at once in response to cumulative changes in their environments (Kingdon 1984, p. 178; Mintzberg 1994, p. 75). Leaders need to be in touch with the possibilities for significant change in order to know whether strategic planning should be used to help formulate major intended strategy changes—typically through raising the visibility and priority of given strategies already present in nascent form—or whether it will be primarily a tool to program improvements in stable strategies. Without some intuitive sense of whether big or small changes are in the cards, strategic planning might be used quite inappropriately. Hopes for big changes might be raised when they are not possible, or time might be wasted in programming strategies that ought to be changed.

Understanding the People Involved, Including Oneself

Leaders should have a reasonable understanding of the people who are or should be involved in strategic planning and implementation, including themselves. The leaders should develop an appreciation of the rich diversity as well as the commonality among these people. This is the heart of personal leadership. Understanding oneself and others is particularly important for developing the strength of character and insight that invigorates leadership and increases the chances that strategic planning and implementation will help the organization. Such strength enables people to focus on what matters to them, to balance competing demands, to develop spiritual depth, to maintain a sense of humor, and to find the courage to take risks, to explore difficult issues and new strategies, and to pursue what might be unpopular causes—activities that, in turn, reinforce strength of character.

Useful approaches to understanding oneself and others range from formal assessments to deep study and reflection to informal storytelling. Effective strategic thinking and acting seem to depend a great deal on intuition, creativity, and pattern recognition, none of which can be programmed, although they may be recognized, facilitated, and encouraged

(Mintzberg 1994). Knowing people well, relying on the nominations of trusted colleagues, and betting on the basis of past performance thus may be about the only ways of finding people who are effective strategists.

Sponsoring the Process

Process sponsors typically are top positional leaders. They have enough prestige, power, and authority to commit the organization to undertaking strategic planning and to hold people accountable for doing so. They are not necessarily involved in the day-to-day details of making strategic planning work—the champions do that—but they do set the stage for success and pay careful attention to the progress of the process. They have a vested interested in a successful outcome and do what they can to make sure it happens. They also typically are important sources of knowledge about key strategic issues and effective strategies for addressing them. The information they have about the organization and its environment is invaluable. They also are likely to be especially knowledgeable about how to fit the process to key decision points so that the work of strategic planning forums can inform decisions in the relevant arenas.

Leaders interested in sponsoring a strategic planning process should consider the following guidelines:

1. Articulate the purpose and importance of the strategic planning effort: Many participants will need some convincing about why the organization should undertake a strategic planning effort. Leaders can start by outlining their views of the organization's past, present, and future. The discussion is likely to focus on core organizational missions and competencies, key changes in the environment, significant strategic issues that the organization faces or will face, possible actions the organization will need to consider, and the likely consequences of failure to engage in strategic planning. Based on this sketch, leaders should outline in general how they want the organization to engage in strategic planning and what they hope the outcomes and benefits of doing so will be.

2. Commit necessary resources—time, money, energy, legitimacy—to the effort: A crucial way of making the process real is through allocating resources to it. Nothing will demonstrate leaders' seriousness (or lack of it) about strategic planning more than that.

3. Emphasize at the beginning and at critical points that action and change will result: This is another crucial way of making the process real for participants and getting them to take it seriously. If they see that strategic planning is real in its consequences, they will invest the necessary effort in the process.

4. Encourage and reward creative thinking, constructive debate, and multiple sources of input and insight: It is important for sponsors to emphasize the importance of creativity, constructive debate, and the value of strategically significant ideas no matter what their origin. It is also important for them to reward those who deliver what the leaders say they value. Encouraging constructive debate also means anticipating where conflicts might develop and thinking about how those conflicts might be addressed productively. In particular, leaders must think about which conflicts can be addressed within the existing rules of the game and which can be managed effectively only if the rules of the game are changed.

5. Be aware of the possible need for outside consultants: Outside consultants may be needed to help design the process, facilitate aspects of it, do various studies, or perform other tasks. It is a sign of strength to ask for help when you need it; enough money must be budgeted to pay for any consultants you may need.

6. Be willing to exercise power and authority to keep the process on track: Strategic planning is inherently prone to break down (Bryson and Roering: 1988, 1989). For one thing, effective strategic planning is a nonroutine kind of activity and, as March and Simon (1958, p. 185) have pointed out, there is a sort of "Gresham's Law of Planning" at work in organizations: "Daily routine drives out planning."

Another danger with strategic planning is that people are likely to fight or flee whenever they are asked to deal with tough issues or failing strategies, serious conflicts, or significant changes. Sponsors have a key role to play in keeping the process going through the difficult patches. How these difficulties are handled will say a lot about the leaders' and organization's characters. The challenges are an opportunity to demonstrate courage, forge strong characters, and end up with a more effective organization to boot (Selznick 1957; Czikzentmihalyi 1992; Terry 1993). Wise dispute resolution and conflict management strategies are called for, but they also may need to be backed up by sufficient power and authority to make them work well.

Championing the Process

The champions are the people who have primary responsibility for managing the strategic planning process day to day. They are the ones who keep track of progress and also pay attention to all of the details. They model the kind of behavior they hope to get from other participants: reasoned, diligent, committed, enthusiastic, and good-spirited pursuit of the common good. They are the cheerleaders who, along with the sponsors, keep the process on track and push, encourage, and cajole the strategic planning team and other key participants through any difficult spots. Sometimes the sponsors and champions are the same people, but usually they are not.

Champions should keep the following guidelines in mind:

1. Keep strategic planning high on people's agendas: Daily routine easily can drive out attention to strategic planning. Blocking out time in people's appointment books is one way to gather participants together and focus their attention. Another is calling on sponsors to periodically emphasize the importance of the process. Yet another is to publish updates on the process in special memoranda or regular newsletters. Yet another is to circulate "think pieces," special reports, relevant audio tapes, and so on, that encourage strategic thought and action. By whatever means, people will need to be reminded and shown on a regular basis that something good will come from getting together to talk about what is important and then doing something about it.

2. Attend to the process without promoting specific solutions: Champions are far more likely to gain people's participation and constructive involvement if they are seen more as advocates for the process rather than for specific solutions. If the champions are seen as committed partisans of specific solutions, then other participants may boycott or torpedo the process rather than seek to find mutually agreeable strategies to address key issues.

3. Think juncturally about what has to come together (people, tasks, information, reports) at or before key decision points: When it comes to strategy formulation and strategic planning, time is not linear; instead, it is junctural. The best champions think like theater directors, orchestrators, choreographers, or playwrights. They think about stage setting, themes, acts and scenes, actors and audiences, and how to get the right people with the right information on stage at the right time and then get them off.

4. Organize time, space, materials, and participation needed for the process to succeed: Without attention to the details of the process, its benefits simply will not be achieved. The "trivialities" of the process matter a great deal–they are not trivial at all (Huxham 1990). Effective champions therefore arrange the retreats, book the rooms, make sure any necessary supplies and equipment are handy, send out the meeting notices, distribute the briefing papers and minutes, oversee the production details of draft and final plans, and keep track of the work program.

5. Pay attention to the language used to describe strategic planning and implementation: One function of strategic planning is to provide a vocabulary and format to allow people to share views about what is fundamental for the organization (Mintzberg 1994, p. 352). At various points in the process, participants are therefore likely to wonder about the meaning of particular plan-

ning concepts and how they relate to substantive matters of concern. An introduction to strategic planning, often in a retreat setting, typically is a useful way to begin developing a common vocabulary of concepts with which to organize efforts to plan strategically. As the process proceeds further, almost invariably discussion will focus again at various points on the meaning of planning concepts and how they relate to the subjects of group discussion and specific products of group work. Champions should be prepared to discuss similarities and differences among various concepts and how they do or do not relate to substantive concerns and products. The specific vocabulary a group uses to label things does not matter as much as development of a shared understanding of what things mean.

6. Keep pushing the process along: Successful strategic planning processes can vary from a few weeks or months to two or more years (Bryson and Roering 1988, 1989). Some processes must fail one or more times before they succeed. Some never succeed. Part of the role of champions is to keep pushing until the process does succeed, or until it is clear that it will fail and there is no point to continuing. At the same time, it is important to remember that strategic planning is likely to "feel like a failure in the middle," as Kanter (1983) has said of innovations. Champions keep pushing to help the strategic planning team and organization move through the failure stage toward success. Champions also need to know when it is time to quit pushing, at least for a while, and when it is time to quit for good.

Facilitating the Process

Process facilitators are often helpful in moving a strategic planning process along because of their group process skills, the attention they can give to structuring and managing group interactions, and the likelihood that they have no stake in the substantive outcomes of the process, particularly if they are outsiders. The presence of a facilitator means that champions can be free to participate in substantive discussions without having to worry too much about managing group process.

A skilled facilitator also can help build the level of trust, interpersonal skills, and conflict management ability in a group. Building trust is important because often the members of a strategic planning team come from various parts of the organization and have never worked together before, let alone on fundamental strategic questions facing the organization.

Skilled facilitation usually depends on the establishment of a successful partnership among facilitators, sponsors, and champions. For facilitator to do their work well, they must learn a great deal very quickly about the organization, its politics, hidden issues, culture, and "secrets." They must quickly gain the trust of the sponsors and champions, learn the lay of the land, and demonstrate their ability to further the strategic planning effort. But they can do none of those things unless the sponsors and champions put a great deal into the relationship as well. The sponsors, champions, and facilitators usually form the core group that moves the process forward with the help of the strategic planning team that is usually a part of most planning efforts (Friend and Hickling 1987; Bellman 1990; Bentley 1994).

Facilitators should come to any process with a well-developed set of group process skills (Johnson and Johnson 1991; Schein 1988; Bentley 1994), along with skills especially applicable to strategic planning for public and nonprofit organizations (Friend and Hickling 1987; Bryson 1988, 1995; Nutt and Backoff 1992). Equipped with these skills, they then should consider following these guidelines:

1. Know the strategic planning process and explain how it works at the beginning and at many points along the way. Participants often will be experiencing a new process at the same time that they work on issues of real importance to the organization. The fact that so much will be new means that people can get lost easily. Facilitators play a key role in explaining to people where they are, where they can head, and how they might get there.

2. Tailor the process to the organization and the groups involved: There is general agreement that strategic planning processes must be fit to the unique circumstances in which organizations and groups find themselves (Bryson and Delbecq 1979; Christensen 1985; Bryson, Bromiley, and Jung 1990; Bryson and Bromiley 1993; Sager 1994; Mintzberg 1994). Facilitators, along with sponsors and champions, are the ones who are in the best position to design the process so that it fits the organization, its circumstances, and the participants. Facilitators must pay careful attention to both the tasks of strategic planning and the socioemotional maintenance of the groups and teams involved in the process. Both dimensions are crucial to effective group functioning and, indeed, are the basic elements of effective team leadership (Johnson and Johnson 1991).

3. Convey a sense of humor and enthusiasm for the process and help groups get unstuck: Sponsors and champions can express humor and enthusiasm for the process, but not the way a facilitator can. Strategic planning can be alternately tension ridden and tedious. Good facilitators can help manage the tensions and relieve the tedium. Facilitators also can help groups confront the difficulties that arise over the course of a strategic planning process. By helping groups reframe their situations imaginatively, invent new options, channel conflict constructively, and tap hidden sources of courage, hope, and optimism, facilitators can provide or tap important resources to help groups move forward (Von Oech 1983; Simon 1988; Seligman 1990; Buzan and Buzan 1993; Terry 1993; Morgan 1993; Bentley 1994).

4. Press groups toward action and the assignment of responsibility for specific actions: Part of keeping the process moving is making sure that action is taken in a timely way. Partly this is a matter of keeping people's interest, enthusiasm, and commitment up. If the whole process is devoted entirely to talking, with no acting, people will quickly quit participating. It is also partly a matter of recognizing that not all of the thinking has to take place before any of the acting can occur. Whenever useful and wise actions become apparent—as a result of attention to mission and mandates, stakeholder analyses, strengths, weaknesses, opportunities and threat (SWOT) analyses, strategic issue identification, and various strategizing efforts—they should be taken, as long as they do not jeopardize possible choices that decisionmakers might want to make in the future. And partly it is a matter of recognizing that there are limits to thinking out things in advance. Often people can only know what they think by acting first, and often important strategies can only emerge by taking small steps and using adaptive learning to figure things out as one goes along (Weick 1979; Mintzberg 1994).

   By pushing people toward action, there is always a danger of inducing premature closure. People may act on what is immediately at hand without thinking creatively about other options or simply waiting until the time is right. A good facilitator will have a well-developed intuitive sense about when to push for action and when to hold back. He or she will also be good at probing people and groups about the merits of options and the advisability of taking specific actions.

5. Congratulate people whenever possible: In our experience, most people in most organizations suffer from chronic—and sometimes acute—positive reinforcement deprivation. And yet people respond very favorably to kind words and praise from people who are important to them. Indeed, many excellently managed organizations are known for the praise and emotional support they provide their employees (Peters and Waterman 1982; Kanter 1983, 1989). Facilitators are in an especially good position to congratulate people and say good things about them in a genuine and natural way.

Fostering Collective Leadership

When strategic planning is successful for public organizations, it is a collective achievement. Many people contribute to its success, sometimes by leading, other times by following. Collective leadership may be fostered through the following approaches:

1. Rely on teams: The team is the basic vehicle for furthering strategic planning. Champions, in particular, will find much of their time will be focused on making sure strategic planning teams or task forces perform well and make effective contributions. There are two reasons why teams are so important. The first is that no one person can have all the relevant quantitative and qualitative information, so forming a team is one way to increase the information available for strategic planning. The second reason is political. To be viable, strategic planning and strategies will need support at many points throughout the organization and from external stakeholders. A strategic plan and intended strategies will need the support of a critical coalition when they are adopted and during implementation. A wisely constructed strategic planning team can provide the initial basis for such a coalition and team members can do much of the work leading to formation of the necessary coalition.

   Team leaders naturally must focus on the accomplishment of team goals or tasks, but they also must attend to individual team members' needs and consciously promote group cohesion (Johnson and Johnson 1991). Team leadership involves a right balance of direction, mentoring, and facilitation—what Schaef (1985) describes as enabling "others to make their contributions while simultaneously making one's own" (p. 128). Team leaders will benefit from

   - communicating effectively,
   - balancing unity and diversity,
   - defining team roles, goals, and norms,
   - establishing an atmosphere of trust,
   - fostering group creativity and sound decisionmaking,
   - obtaining necessary resources,
   - tailoring direction and support to team members to fit their competence and commitment,
   - rewarding achievement and overcoming adversity.

2. Focus on network and coalition development: Coalitions basically organize around ideas and interests that allow people to see that they can achieve together what they could not achieve separately. The way issues, goals, or visions—and strategies for achieving them—are framed will structure how stakeholders interpret their interests, how they assess the costs and benefits of joining a coalition, and the form and content of winning and losing arguments. Therefore, leaders must articulate a view of the world that lies behind the way issues, goals, visions, and strategies are framed in such a way that will draw significant support from

key stakeholders. The worldview public leaders should seek is one that will call up widely shared notions of what constitutes the public interest and the common good.

A strategic plan's or strategy's political acceptability increase, as the benefits of adopting and implementing it increase, while the costs of doing so diminish, for key stakeholders. As Light (1991) notes in relation to presidential agenda setting, it is primarily the issues with the greatest potential benefit for key stakeholders that get on the agenda whereas the ones that are the least costly for key stakeholders are the ones that receive prime consideration. Moreover, any proposal likely to be adopted and implemented will be a carefully tailored response to specific circumstances, rather than an off-the-shelf solution imported from somewhere else.

It is very important to keep in mind that, typically, every member of a winning coalition will not agree on every specific of an entire plan or set of strategies, and that is okay. It is also important to keep in mind that coalition development depends on following many of the same guidelines that help develop effective teams. In particular, coalitions are probably more likely to be formed if ways can be found to develop strategies for valuing the diversity of coalition members and their various ideas and special gifts. Acquiring the necessary resources, of which the coalition itself will be a major source, is vital. And rewarding and celebrating collective achievements and sharing credit for them broadly are also likely to help.

In a broader sense, public leaders should work to build a sense of community—that is, a sense of relationship, mutual empowerment, and common purpose—within and beyond their organization. This is desirable because so many of the problems public and nonprofit organizations are called on to address require multiorganizational, or community, responses. Community may be tied to a place or be what Heifetz and Sinder (1988) and others have called a community of interest, an interorganizational network that often transcends geographic and political boundaries and is designed to address transorganizational problems (Trist 1983). Leaders contribute to community building by facilitating communal definition and resolution of issues, fostering democratic leader-follower relations (Kahn 1982; Boyte 1980), providing resources, and using their knowledge of group process to help people work together. Most important, Palmer (1990) suggests, leaders build community by "making space for other people to act" (p. 138).

3. Establish specific mechanisms for sharing power, responsibility, and accountability: Authority is not usually shared by policymaking bodies or chief executives—and often cannot be by law—but that does not

mean power, responsibility, and accountability cannot be shared. Doing so can foster participation, trigger information and resource flows, and help build commitment to plans and strategies and their implementation. The use of strategic planning teams, strategic issue task forces, and implementation teams are typical vehicles for sharing power. Action plans should indicate any shared responsibilities. Credit is something else that should be broadly shared.

Using Forums to Create and Communicate Meaning

Forums are the basic settings we humans use to create shared meaning (Bryson and Crosby 1992). Much of the work of strategic planning takes place in forums, where fairly free-flowing consideration of ideas and views can take place before proposals are developed for adoption and action in arenas. The tasks of sponsoring, championing, and facilitating strategic planning are primarily performed in forums. Strategic planning retreats, team meetings, task force meetings, focus groups, strategic planning newsletters, and strategic plans themselves—when used as educational devices—are all examples of the use of forums. These forums can be used to help develop a shared understanding about what the organization is, what it does or should do, and why.

The "foruming" work in strategic planning involves creating a meaningful process, clarifying mandates, articulating mission, identifying and framing strategic issues, outlining viable strategies, and perhaps developing a vision of success (Bryson 1988, 1995).

Creating and communicating meaning is the work of visionary leadership. (Sometimes visionary leadership results in a vision of success for the organization, but in the present discussion visioning covers a broader range of purposes; it is meant more as a verb than a noun.) Leaders become visionary when they play a vital role in interpreting current reality, fostering a collective group mission, and shaping a collective sense—perhaps a vision—of the future (Doig and Hargrove 1987; Denhardt 1993). Furthermore, visionary leaders must understand important aspects of their own and others' internal worlds, and they must also grasp the meaning of related external worlds. As truth tellers and direction givers, they help people make sense of experience, and they offer guidance for coping with the present and the future by helping answer the questions; What's going on here? Where are we heading? And how will things look when we get there? They frame and shape the perceived context for action (Smircich and Morgan 1989), and they "manage" important stakeholders' perceptions of the organization, its strategies, and their effects (Lynn 1987; Neustadt 1990). In order to foster change, particularly major change, they become skilled in the follow-

ing methods of creating and communicating new meanings.

1. Understanding the design and use of forums: Leaders, sponsors, champions, and facilitators must be adept in designing and using formal and informal forums—that is, settings for the creation and communication of meaning. The main design elements include communicative capabilities, interpretive schemes (ways of framing and reframing "reality"), keeping people focused on the importance of strategic thinking and acting and on the process of strategic planning, communicating effectively, modes of argumentation, and rules of access to the forums.

2. Seizing opportunities to be interpreters and direction givers in areas of uncertainty and difficulty: Leadership opportunities expand in times of difficulty, confusion, and crisis, when old approaches clearly are not working and people are searching for meaningful accounts of what has happened and what can be done about it (Boal and Bryson 1987; Kouzes and Posner 1987; Schein 1992). Focusing on strategic issues or failing strategies therefore provides opportunities for exercising leadership, for inspiring and mobilizing others to figure out what might be done to improve the organization's performance in the eyes of key stakeholders. Turning dangers, threats, and crises into manageable challenges is an important task for visionary leaders (Dutton and Jackson 1987; Jackson and Dutton 1988; Dutton and Ashford 1993).

3. Revealing and naming real needs and real conditions: New meaning unfolds as leaders encourage people to see the "real" situation and its portents. They find and communicate a way to align experiences and feelings about a situation with behaviors that have consequences people care about (Boal and Bryson 1987; Neustadt 1990).

To illuminate "real" conditions, leaders may use intuition or integrative thinking (Cleveland 1985; Quinn 1988; Mintzberg 1994). They formally or informally scan their environment and discern the patterns emerging from local conditions, or they accept patterns and issues identified by other people, such as pollsters or planners. Simply articulating these patterns publicly and convincingly can be an act of revelation. However, leaders cannot just delineate emerging patterns and issues; they must also explain them (Neustadt 1990). They must relate what they see to their knowledge of societal systems (Maccoby 1983) and to people's experience (Boal and Bryson 1987). Going further, leaders alert followers to the need for action by their "uncovering and exploiting of contradictions in values and between values and practice" (Burns 1978, p. 43).

4. Helping followers frame and reframe issues and strategies: In revealing and explaining real conditions, leaders are laying the groundwork for framing and reframing issues facing the organization and strategies for addressing them (Stone 1988; Bolman and Deal 1991; Morgan 1993). The framing process consists of naming and explaining the issue, opening the door to alternative ways of addressing it, and suggesting outcomes. The reframing process involves breaking with old ways of viewing an issue or strategy and developing a new appreciation of it.

5. Offer compelling visions of the future: Leaders convey their visions through stories rooted in shared history yet focused on the future. These stories link people's experience of the present (cognitions), what they might do about the situation (behaviors), and what they might expect to happen as a result (consequences); in other words, the stories help people grasp desirable and potentially real futures (Brickman 1978; Boal and Bryson 1987). Effective stories are rich with metaphors that make sense of people's experience, are comprehensive yet open ended, and impel people toward union or common ground (Terry 1993). Finally, leaders transmit their own belief in their visionary stories through vivid, energetic, optimistic language (Kouzes and Posner 1987).

6. Championing, though not necessarily originating, new and improved ideas for dealing with strategic issues: Championing ideas for addressing issues is different from championing the process of strategic planning, but is nonetheless important. Astute leaders gather ideas from many sources (Burns 1978; Neustadt 1990; Meltsner 1990; Mintzberg 1994). Within organizations and political communities, they foster an atmosphere in which innovative approaches flourish (Kouzes and Posner 1987; Heifetz and Sinder 1988). The best political leaders, says Burns, provide intellectual leadership by sorting out large public issues and by combining analytical ideas, data, and moral reasoning to clarify needed action. Acting in the mode of Schon's (1983) "reflective practitioner," these leaders champion "improved" ideas, ones that have emerged from practice and been refined by critical reflection.

7. Detailing actions and expected consequences: Often actions and consequences are an integral part of leaders' visions, or organizational missions and strategies, and become more detailed as implementations proceed. Crises, however, can necessitate reversing this sequence. When old behaviors are not working and disaster is imminent, followers may wish leaders to prescribe new behaviors and may be willing to try those behaviors without a clear vision of the outcome for the organization as a whole or its specific strategies. To sustain a leader-follower relationship founded on crisis, however, leaders must soon link the recommended course of action to a "higher purpose" (Boal and Bryson 1987, p. 17), such as a shared sense of mission. Providing evidence of causal links between the new behaviors and desired outcomes is also critical.

Using Arenas to Make and Implement Decisions

Public leaders are also required to be political leaders—partly because all organizations have their political aspects (Mintzberg 1994; Pfeffer 1992; Fesler and Kettl 1994), and partly because public organizations are inherently involved in politicized decisionmaking much of the time. As political leaders, they ultimately fail or succeed through their impact on decisionmaking and implementation. The key to success, and the heart of political leadership, is understanding how intergroup power relationships shape decisionmaking and implementation outcomes. Particularly important is understanding how to affect outcomes by having some things never come up for a decision. Specifically, political leaders must undertake the following responsibilities.

1. Understand the design and use of arenas: Political leaders must be skilled in designing and using formal and informal arenas, the basic settings for decisionmaking (Bryson and Crosby 1992). These arenas may be legislative, executive, or administrative in the public sector. It is in arenas that the products of forums—such as strategic plans and important aspects of strategies—are adopted as is, altered, or rejected. The basic design elements of arenas are the decisionmaking and implementation capabilities of various actors (including policymaking bodies, organizations, subunits, groups, and individuals), the arenas' domains, agendas, planning, budgeting, decisionmaking, and implementation methods, and rules governing access to the arenas. These design elements can be used to shape overt and latent conflicts, and decisions and nondecisions.

A major issue in any strategic planning process is how to sequence the move from planning forums to decisionmaking arenas. A large fraction of the necessary strategic thinking will occur as part of the dialogue and discussion in forums, particularly ones that include key decisionmakers. Once viable proposals have been worked out, they then can move to arenas for any necessary revisions, adoption, and implementation—or else rejection. At a minimum, managing the transition from forums to arenas depends on figuring out when key decision points will occur and then designing the planning process to fit those points in such a way that decisions in arenas can be influenced constructively by the work done in forums.

A further issue is how to sequence any moves from arenas to courts, where underlying norms are reinforced, residual conflicts are managed, and disputes are resolved. The decisions made in arenas usually cannot–and should not try to–cover all of the details that may arise during implementation. Some advance thinking therefore is almost always in order about how these residual or subsidiary conflicts might be handled constructively, either in other arenas or through the use of formal or informal courts.

2. Mediating and shaping conflict within and among stakeholders: Conflict, or at least recognizable differences, are necessary if people are to be offered real choices in arenas (Burns 1978), and if decisionmakers are to understand the choices and their consequences (Janis 1989). Further, political leaders must possess transactional skills for dealing with followers, other leaders, and various key stakeholders who have conflicting agendas. To forge winning coalitions, they must bargain and negotiate, inventing options for mutual gain so that they can trade things of value that they control for others' support.

3. Understanding the dynamics of political influence and how to target resources appropriately: The first requirement for influencing political decisionmaking may be knowing whom to influence. Who controls the agenda of the relevant decisionmaking bodies, whether city councils, boards of directors, or some other group? Who chairs the group and any relevant committees? The next requirement is knowing how to influence. What forms of providing information, lobbying, vote trading, arm twisting, and so on are acceptable? Should change advocates try to change the composition of the decisionmaking bodies? Given the available time, energy, and resources, how might they best be spent (Coplin and O'Leary 1976; Kaufman 1986; Benveniste 1989)? Basically, political leaders manipulate the costs and benefits of actions, so supporters are more motivated to act in desired directions and opponents are less motivated to resist (Kaufman 1986; Baron 1987).

   Outcomes in arenas can be affected dramatically by influencing the agenda of what comes up for decision and what does not, thereby becoming a "nondecision." Decision outcomes also can be affected by "strategic voting" in which participants use their knowledge of voting rules and manipulation of their vote resource to steer outcomes in directions they favor. Reshaping the way issues are viewed also can have dramatic effects on how people vote (Riker 1986).

4. Build winning, sustainable coalitions: For strategic planning to be effective, a coalition of support must be built for the process and its outcomes. There must be a coalition in place that is strong enough to adopt

intended strategies and to defend them during implementation. Building winning coalitions can be pretty gritty work. As William Riker (1986) notes, "Politics is winning and losing, which depend, mostly, on how large and strong one side is relative to the other. The actions of politics consist in making agreements to join people in alliances and coalitions–hardly the stuff to release readers' adrenaline as do seductions, quarrels, or chases" (p. 52). Finding ideas (visions, goals, strategies) that people can support that further their interests is a large part of the process, but so is making deals in which something is traded in exchange for that support.

5. Avoiding bureaucratic imprisonment: Political leaders in government, particularly, may find their ability to make and implement needed decisions severely constrained by the bureaucracies in which they serve. Those bureaucracies usually have intricate institutionalized rules and procedures and entrenched personnel that hamper any kind of change. Leaders committed to change must continually challenge the rules, or else find their way around them, including appealing over the heads of resistant bureaucrats to high-level decisionmakers or to key external stakeholders (Burns 1978; Lynn 1987; Kouzes and Posner 1987).

Enforcing Rules, Settling Disputes, and Managing Residual Conflicts

Public leaders must also be ethical leaders. Acting in formal and informal courts, they must reinforce ethical principles, respect for constitutions, laws, charters, articles of incorporation, regulations, ordinances, and so on, as well as resolve conflicts about their application. Courts operate whenever two actors having a conflict rely on a third party (manager, facilitator, mediator, arbitrator, judge) to help them address it. Managing conflict and settling disputes not only takes care of the issue at hand but reinforces the important societal or organizational norms used to handle it. The following tasks are vital to exercising ethical leadership.

1. Understanding the design and use of formal and informal courts: Leaders must be skilled in the design and use of formal and informal courts, the settings for enforcing ethical principles, constitutions, and laws, and for managing residual conflicts and settling disputes (Bryson and Crosby 1992). Formal courts theoretically provide the ultimate social sanctions for conduct mandated or promoted through formal policymaking arenas, but in practice the informal "court of public opinion" can be even more powerful. The basic design elements of courts include conflict management and sanctioning capabilities, norms–broadly conceived and ranging from laws to social mores,

jurisdiction, conflict management and dispute resolution methods, and rules governing access to the courts.

2. Fostering organizational integrity and educating others about ethics, constitutions, laws, and norms: In nurturing public organizations that contribute to the common good, leaders must adopt practices and systems that Douglas Wallace and Jan White (1988) call "organizational integrity." Such leaders make a public commitment to ethical principles and then act on them. They involve the organization's stakeholders in ethical analysis and decisionmaking, inculcate a sense of personal responsibility in followers, and reward ethical behavior.

3. Applying constitutions, laws, and norms to specific cases: Constitutions, such as the U.S. Constitution, are usually broad frameworks establishing basic organizational purposes, structures, and procedures. Laws, although much more narrowly drawn, still typically apply to broad classes of people or actions; moreover, they may emerge from the legislative process containing purposeful omissions and generalities that were necessary to obtain enough votes for passage (Posner 1985). Therefore, both constitutions and laws require authoritative interpretation as they are applied to specific cases. In the U.S. judicial system, judges, jurors, and attorneys, and even interest groups filing *amicus curiae* briefs, all contribute to that authoritative interpretation. Outside the formal courts, leaders typically must apply norms rather than laws.

4. Adapting constitutions, laws, and norms to changing times: Judicial principles endure even as the conditions that prompted them and the people who created them change dramatically. Sometimes public leaders are able to reshape the law to current needs in legislative, executive, or administrative arenas; often, however, as Ralph Neely (1981) suggests, leaders must ask formal courts to mandate a change because vested interests that tend to oppose change hold sway over the executive and legislative branches.

5. Resolving conflicts among constitutions, laws, and norms: Ethical leaders working through the courts must find legitimate bases for deciding among conflicting principles. This may mean relying on judicial enforcement or on reconciliation of constitutions, laws, and norms. Conflict management and dispute resolution methods typically emphasize the desirability of finding principles or norms that all can support as legitimate bases for settling disputes (Filley 1975; Fisher and Ury 1981; Susskind and Cruikshank 1987). Obviously, these principles and norms should be applied in such a way that the public interest is served and the common good advanced.

One of the best tests for discerning the public interest or common good is respect for future generations, which as Carol Lewis (1989) points out, typically requires an understanding of the context and "accommodating rather than spurning the important values, principles, and interests at stake" (p. 47). Another test is empathy, which calls upon public and nonprofit leaders to act as stewards of the "vulnerable, dependent, and politically inarticulate, those mostly likely to be overlooked in formulations of the public interest" (Lewis 1989, p. 47; see also Block 1993).

Putting It All Together

The tasks of leadership for strategic planning are complex and many. Unless the organization is very small, no single person or group can perform them all. Effective strategic planning is a collective phenomenon, typically involving sponsors, champions, facilitators, teams, task forces, and others in various ways at various times. Over the course of a strategy change cycle, leaders must put together the elements we have described in such a way that organizational effectiveness is enhanced—thereby making some important part of the world outside the organization noticeably better.

JOHN M. BRYSON
AND BARBARA C. CROSBY
Authors' note: Adapted from Bryson (1995)

BIBLIOGRAPHY

Baron, D. P., 1987. "An Introduction to Political Analysis for Business." Graduate School of Business, Stanford University.

Bellman, G. M., 1990. *The Consultant's Calling: Bringing Who You Are to What You Do.* San Francisco, CA: Jossey-Bass.

Bentley, T., 1994. *Facilitation: Providing Opportunities for Learning.* United Kingdom: McGraw-Hill.

Benveniste, G., 1989. *Mastering the Politics of Planning.* San Francisco: Jossey-Bass.

Block, Peter, 1993. *Stewardship.* San Francisco: Berrett-Koehler.

Boal, K. B., and J. M. Bryson, 1987. "Charismatic Leadership: A Phenomenological and Structural Approach." In J. G. Hunt, B. R. Balinga, H. P. Dachler, and C. A. Schriescheim, eds., *Emerging Leadership Vistas.* New York: Pergamon Press.

Bolman, L. G., and T. E. Deal, 1991. *Reframing Organizations.* San Francisco, CA: Jossey-Bass.

Boyte, H. C., 1980. *Backyard Revolution.* Philadelphia: Temple University Press.

Brickman, P., 1978. "Is It Real?" In J. H. Harvey, W. Ickes, and R. F. Kidd, eds., *New Directions in Attribution Research,* vol. 2. Hillsdale, NJ: Lawrence Erlbaum.

Bryson, J. M., 1988. *Strategic Planning for Public and Nonprofit Organizations.* San Francisco: Jossey-Bass.

———, 1995. *Strategic Planning for Public and Nonprofit Organizations.* 2d ed. San Francisco: Jossey-Bass.

Bryson, J. M., F. Ackerman, C. Eden and C. B. Finn, 1944. "Critical Incidents and Emergent Issues in the Management of Large-Scale Change Efforts." Baltimore, MD: Johns Hopkins University Press.

Bryson, J. M., and P. Bromily, 1993. "Critical Factors Affecting the Planning and Implementation of Major Projects." *Strategic Management Journal,* vol. 14: 319–337.

Bryson, J. M., P. Bromiley and Y. S. Jung, 1990. "Influences of Context and Process on Project Planning Success." *Journal of Planning Education and Research* vol. 9, no. 3: 183–195.

Bryson, J. M., and B. C. Crosby, 1992. *Leadership for the Common Good: Tackling Public Problems in a Shared-Power World.* San Francisco, CA: Jossey-Bass.

Bryson, J. M., and A. L. Delbecq, 1979. "A Contingent Approach to Strategy and Tactics in Project Planning." *Journal of the America Planning Association,* vol. 45, no. 2: 167–179.

Bryson, J. M., and W. D. Roering, 1988. "Initiation of Strategic Planning by Governments." *Public Administration Review,* vol. 48: 99–1004.

———, 1989. "Mobilizing Innovation Efforts: The Case of Government Strategic Planning." In A. H. Van de Ven, H. Angle, and M. S. Poole, eds., *Research on the Management of Innovation.* New York: HarperCollins.

Burns, J. M., 1978. *Leadership.* New York: Harper and Row.

Buzan, T., and B. Buzan, 1993. *The Mind Map Book: Radiant Thinking: The Major Evolution in Human Thought.* London: BBC Books.

Christensen, K. S., 1985. "Coping with Uncertainty in Planning." *Journal of the American Planning Association,* vol. 51: 63–73.

Cleveland, H., 1985. *The Knowledge Executive.* New York: E. P. Dutton.

Coplin, W., and M. O'Leary, 1976. *Everyman's Prince: A Guide to Understanding Your Political Problem.* Boston: Duxbury Press.

Czikzentmihalyi, M., 1992. *Flow: The Psychology of Happiness.* New York: Harper and Row.

Denhardt, R. B., 1993. *The Pursuit of Significance: Strategies for Managerial Success in Public Organizations.* Belmont, CA: Wadsworth.

Doig, J. W., and E. C. Hargrove, eds., 1987. *Leadership and Innovation: A Biographical Perspective on Entrepreneurs in Government.* Baltimore: Johns Hopkins University Press.

Dutton, J. E., and S. J. Ashford, 1993. "Selling Issues to Top Management." *Academy of Management Review,* vol. 18 no. 3: 397–428.

Dutton, J. E., and S. E. Jackson, 1987. "Categorizing Strategic Issues: Links to Organizational Action." *Academy of Management Review,* vol. 12, no. 1: 76–90.

———, 1988. "Discerning Threats and Opportunities." *Administrative Science Quarterly,* vol. 33: 370–387.

Fesler, J., and D. Kettl, 1994. *The Politics of the Administrative Process,* 2d ed. Chatham, NJ: Chatham House.

Filley, A., 1975. *Interpersonal Conflict Resolution.* Glenview, IL: Scott, Foresman.

Fisher, R., and W. Ury, 1981. *Getting to Yes: Negotiating Agreement Without Giving In.* New York: Penguin Books.

Friend, J., and A. Hickling, 1987. *Planning Under Pressure: The Strategic Choice Approach.* Oxford: Pergamon.

Heifetz, R. A., and R. M. Sinder, 1988. "Political Leadership: Managing the Public's Problem Solving." In R. B. Reich, ed., *The Power of Public Ideas.* Cambridge, MA: Ballinger.

Hunt, H. G., 1991. *Leadership: A New Synthesis.* Newbury Park, CA: Sage.

Huxham, C., 1990. "Our Trivialities in Process." In Colin Eden and Jim Radford, *Tackling Strategic Problems: The Role of Group Decision Support.* Newbury Park, CA: Sage.

Jackson, S. E., and J. E. Dutton, 1988. "Discerning Threats and Opportunities." *Administrative Science Quarterly,* vol. 33: 370–387.

Janis, I. L., 1989. *Crucial Decisions: Leadership in Policymaking and Crisis Management.* New York: Free Press.

Johnson, D. W., and F. P. Johnson, 1991. *Joining Together,* 4th ed. Englewood Cliffs, NJ: Prentice-Hall.

Kahn, S. 1982. *Organizing.* New York: McGraw-Hill.

Kanter, R. M., 1983. *The Changemasters.* New York: Simon & Schuster.

———, 1989. *When Giants Learn to Dance. Mastering the Challenge of Strategy, Management, and Careers in the 1990s.* New York: Simon & Schuster.

Kaufman, J. L., 1986. "Making Planners More Effective Strategists." In Barry Checkoway ed., *Strategic Perspectives on Planning Practice.* Lexington, MA: Lexington Books.

Kingdon, J. R., 1984. *Agendas, Alternatives, and Public Policies.* Boston: Little, Brown.

Kouzes, J. M., and B. Z. Posner, 1987. *The Leadership Challenge: How to Get Extraordinary Things Done in Organizations.* San Francisco, CA: Jossey-Bass.

Lewis, C. W., 1989. *The Ethics Challenge in Public Service: A Problem-Solving Guide.* San Francisco, CA: Jossey-Bass.

Light, P. C., 1991. *The President's Agenda.* Baltimore, MD: Johns Hopkins University Press.

Lynn, L. E., Jr., 1987. *Managing Public Policy.* Boston: Little, Brown.

Maccoby, M., 1983. *The Leader.* New York: Ballentine.

March, J., and H. Simon, 1958. *Organizations.* New York: Wiley.

Meltsner, A. J., 1990. *Rules for Rulers: The Politics of Advice.* Philadelphia, PA: Temple University Press.

Mintzberg, H., 1994. *The Rise and Fall of Strategic Planning.* New York: Free Press.

Morgan, G., 1993. *Imaginization: The Art of Creative Management.* Newbury Park, CA: Sage.

Neely, Ralph, 1981. *How the Courts Govern America.* New Haven, CT: Yale University Press.

Neustadt, R. E., 1991. *Presidential Power and the Modern Presidents.* New York: Free Press.

Neustadt, R. E., and E. R. May, 1986. *Thinking in Time: The Uses of History for Decision Makers.* New York: Free Press.

Nutt, Paul, and Robert Backoff, 1992. *Strategic Management of Public and Third-Sector Organizations:* San Francisco, CA: Jossey-Bass.

Palmer, P. J., 1990. *The Active Life: A Spirituality of Work, Creativity, and Courage.* New York: Harper & Row.

Peters, G., 1995. *The Politics of Bureaucracy.* New York: Longman.

Peters, T. J., and R. H. Waterman, Jr., 1982. *In Search of Excellence: Lessons from America's Best-Run Companies.* New York: Harper & Row.

Pfeffer, J., 1992. *Managing with Power: Politics and Influence in Organizations.* Boston, MA: Harvard Business School Press.

Posner, R. A., 1985. *The Federal Courts: Crisis and Reform.* Cambridge, MA: Harvard University Press.

Quinn, R. E., 1988. *Beyond Rational Management: Mastering the Paradoxes and Competing Demands of High Performance.* San Francisco, CA: Jossey-Bass.

Riker, W. H., 1986. *The Art of Political Manipulation.* New Haven, CT: Yale University Press.

Sager, T., 1994. *Communicative Planning Theory.* England: Ashgate.

Schaef, A. W., 1985. *Women's Reality.* San Francisco, CA: Harper & Row.

Schein, E. H., 1988. *Process Consultation: Its Role in Organization Development.* Reading, MA: Addison-Wesley.

———, 1992. *Organizational Culture and Leadership.* San Francisco, CA: Jossey-Bass.

Schon, D. A., 1983. *The Reflective Practitioner.* New York: Basic Books.

Seligman, M. E. P., 1990. *Learned Optimism.* New York: Alfred A. Knopf.

Selznick, P., 1957. *Leadership in Administration.* Berkeley: University of California Press.

Simon, S. B., 1988. *Getting Unstuck, Breaking through Your Barriers to Change.* New York: Warner.

Smircich, L., and G. Morgan, 1989. "Leadership: The Management of Meaning." *Journal of Applied Behavioral Science,* vol. 18: 257–273.

Stone, D. A., 1988. *Policy Paradox and Political Reason.* Glenview, IL: Scott, Foresman.

Susskind, L., and J. Cruikshank, 1987. *Breaking the Impasse: Consensual Approaches to Resolving Public Disputes.* New York: Basic Books.

Terry, R., 1993. *Authentic Leadership: Courage in Action.* San Francisco, CA: Jossey-Bass.

Trist, E., 1983. "Referent Organizations and the Development of Inter-organizational Domains." *Human Relations,* vol. 36, 3: 269–284.

Von Oech, R., 1983. *A Whack on the Side of the Head: How to Unlock Your Mind for Innovation.* New York: Basic Books.

Wallace, D., and J. B. White, 1988. "Building Integrity in Organizations." *New Management* vol. 6, no. 1 (Summer): 30–35.

Weick, K., 1979. *The Social Psychology of Organizing,* 2d ed. Reading, MA: Addison-Wesley.

STRATEGIC PLANNING. A "disciplined effort to produce fundamental decisions and actions that shape and guide what an organization is, what it does, and why it does it" (Bryson 1988, p. 5). Strategic planning consists of a set of concepts, procedures, and tools developed primarily, but far from exclusively, in the private sector. This history has been amply documented by others (Ansoff 1980; Bracker 1980; Quinn 1980; Mintzberg 1994). The experience of the last fifteen years, and a growing body of literature, however, indicate that strategic planning approaches either developed in the private sector, or else strongly influenced by them, can help public organizations, as well as communities or other entities, deal in effective ways with their dramatically changing environments.

That does not mean, however, that all approaches to what might be called corporate-style strategic planning are equally applicable to the public sector. This entry, therefore, will compare and contrast six approaches to corporate strategic planning (actually eight approaches grouped into six categories), discuss their applicability to the public sector, and identify the most important contingencies governing their use.

Remember that corporate strategic planning typically focuses on an organization and what it should do to improve its performance and not on a community, or on a function, such as transportation or health care within a community, or marketing or personnel within an organization. Most of what follows focuses primarily on organizations and how they might plan to improve their performance. But applications to communities and functions will be discussed as well.

It should be noted that careful tests of corporate-style strategic planning in the public sector are few in number (Bryson 1983b; Boal and Bryson 1987; Boschken 1988, 1994; Bryson, Bromiley, and Jung 1990; Bryson and Bromiley 1993; Stone and Crittenden 1993; Mintzberg 1994). Nevertheless, there is enough experience with corporate strategic planning in the private sector, and increasingly in the public sector, to reach some tentative conclusions about what works under what conditions and why.

The remainder of this entry is divided into two sections. The first discusses the six approaches and compares and contrasts them along several dimensions, including key features, assumptions, strengths, weaknesses, and contingencies governing their use in the public sector. The second section presents conclusions about the applicability of strategic planning to public organizations and purposes. The principal conclusions are (1) that public strategic planning is well on its way to becoming part of the standard repertoire of public leaders, managers, and planners and (2) that, nevertheless, public personnel must be very careful how they engage in strategic planning, since not all approaches are equally useful and since a number of conditions govern the successful use of each approach.

Approaches to Strategic Planning

This section briefly sets forth six schools of strategic planning thought developed primarily, but by no means exclusively, in the private sector. The strategic planning process includes general policy and direction setting, situation assessments, strategic issues identification, strategy development, decisionmaking, implementation, and evaluation (Bryson 1988b, 1995, 1996). Attention will be given first to three approaches that cover more of the process and that emphasize policy and direction setting; then the discussion will move to approaches that focus more narrowly on elements in the later stages of the process.

Approaches That Cover Much of the Process and Emphasize Policy and Direction Setting

The Harvard Policy Model The Harvard policy model was developed as part of the business policy courses taught at the Harvard Business School since the 1920s (Bower et al. 1993). The approach provides the principal (though often implicit) inspiration behind the most widely cited recent models of public and nonprofit sector strategic planning, including my own (Olsen and Eadie 1982; Barry 1986; Bryson 1988b, 1995; Nutt and Backoff 1992).

The main purpose of the Harvard model is to help a firm develop the best "fit" between itself and its environment; that is, to develop the best strategy for the firm. As articulated by K. Andrews (1980), strategy is "a pattern of purposes and policies defining the company and its business." One discerns the best strategy by analyzing the internal strengths and weaknesses of the company and the values of senior management and by identifying the external threats and opportunities in the environment and the social obligations of the firm. Then one designs the appropriate organizational structure, processes, relationships, and behaviors necessary to implement the strategy and focuses on providing the leadership necessary to implement the strategy.

Effective use of the model presumes that senior management can agree on the firm's situation and the appropriate strategic response and has enough authority to enforce its decisions. A final important assumption of the model, common to all approaches to strategic planning, is that if the appropriate strategy is identified and implemented, the organization will be more effective. Attention also is paid to the need for effective implementation.

In the business world, the Harvard model appears to be best applied at the strategic business unit (SBU) level. A strategic business unit is a distinct business that has its own competitors and can be managed somewhat independently of other units within the organization (Rue and Holland 1986). The SBU, in other worlds, provides an important yet bounded and manageable focus for the model. John Montanari and Jeffrey Bracker (1986) argued that the public equivalent of the SBU is the strategic public planning unit (SPPU), which typically would be an agency or department that addresses issues fundamentally similar to one another (such as related health issues, related transportation issues, or related education issues).

The Harvard model is also applicable at the higher and broader corporate level in the private and public sectors. The model probably would have to be supplemented with other approaches, however, such as the portfolio and strategic issues management approaches, to be discussed later. A portfolio approach is needed because a principal strategic concern at the corporate level is oversight of a portfolio of businesses, in the private sector, and a portfolio of agencies or departments in the public sector. Strategic issues management is needed because much high-level work typically is quite political and articulating and addressing issues is the heart of political decisionmaking (Bryson and Crosby 1992).

The systematic assessment of strengths, weaknesses, opportunities, and threats—known as a SWOT analysis—is a primary strength of the Harvard model. This element of the model appears to be applicable in the public sector to organizations, functions, and communities. Another strength is its emphasis on the need to link strategy formulation and implementation in effective ways. The main weaknesses of the Harvard model are that it does not draw attention to strategic issues or offer specific advice on how to develop strategies, except to note that effective strategies will build on strengths, how to take advantage of opportunities, and how to overcome or minimize weaknesses and threats.

Strategic Planning Systems. Strategic planning is often viewed as a system whereby managers go about making, implementing, and controlling important decisions across functions and levels in the firm. Peter Lorange (1980), for example, has argued that any strategic planning system must address four fundamental questions:

1. Where are we going? (mission)
2. How do we get there? (strategies)
3. What is our blueprint for action? (budgets)
4. How do we know if we are on track? (control)

Strategic planning systems vary along several dimensions: The comprehensiveness of decision areas included, the formal rationality of the decision process, and the tightness of control exercised over implementation of the decisions (Armstrong 1982; Goold, Campbell, and Luchs 1993a, 1993b), as well as how the strategy process itself will be tailored to the organization and managed (Chakravarthy and Lorange 1991). The strength of these systems is their attempt to coordinate the various elements of an organization's strategy across levels and functions. Their weakness is that excessive comprehensiveness, prescription, and control can drive out attention to mission, strategy, and organizational structure (Frederickson and Mitchell 1984; Frederickson 1984; Mintzberg 1994) and can exceed the ability of participants to comprehend the system and the information it produces (Bryson, Van de Ven, and Roering 1987).

Strategic planning systems are applicable to public organizations (and to a lesser extent communities), for regardless of the nature of the particular organization, it makes sense to coordinate decisionmaking across levels and functions and to concentrate on whether the organization is implementing its strategies and accomplishing its mission (Boschken 1988, 1992, 1994). It is important to remember, however, that a strategic planning system characterized by substantial comprehensiveness, formal rationality in decisionmaking, and tight control will work only in an organization that has a clear mission, clear goals and objectives, relatively simple tasks to perform, centralized authority, clear performance indicators, and information about actual performance available at reasonable cost. While some public organizations—such as hospitals and police and fire departments—operate under such conditions, most do not. As a result, most public sector strategic planning systems typically focus on a few areas of concern, rely on a decision process in which politics play a major role, and control something other than program outcomes (e.g., budget expenditures) (Wildavsky 1979a; Barzelay 1992; Osborne and Gaebler 1992; Bryson 1995). That is changing, however. For example, the U.S. federal government is now moving toward performance-based strategic management as a result of the Government Performance and Results Act of 1993 (Public Law 103-62) and a number of states are following suit (National Governors Association 1993).

Stakeholder Management Approaches. R. Edward Freeman (1984) stated that corporate strategy can be understood as a corporation's mode of relating or building bridges to its stakeholders. A stakeholder for Freeman is any group or individual who is affected by or who can affect the future of the corporation; for example, customers, employees, suppliers, owners, governments, financial institutions, and critics. He argued that a corporate strategy will be effective only if it satisfies the needs of multiple groups. Traditional private-sector models of strategy have focused only on economic actors, but Freeman argued that changes in the current business environment require that other political and social actors be considered as well.

Because it integrates economic, political, and social concerns, the stakeholder model is one of the approaches most applicable to the public sector. Many interest groups have stakes in public organizations, functions, and communities. For example, local economic development planning typically involves government, developers, bankers, the chamber of commerce, actual or potential employers, neighborhood groups, environmentalists, and so on. Local economic development planners would be wise to identify key stakeholders, their interests, what they will support, and strategies and tactics that might work in dealing with them (Kaufman 1979; Nutt and Backoff 1992). John Bryson, R. E. Freeman, and William Roering (1986) argue in addition that an organization's mission and values ought to be formulated in stakeholder terms. That is, an organization should figure out what its mission ought to be in relation to each stakeholder group; otherwise, it will not be able to differentiate its responses well enough to satisfy its key stakeholders.

The strengths of the stakeholder model are its recognition of the many claims—both complementary and competing—placed on organizations by insiders and outsiders and its awareness of the need to satisfy at least the key stakeholders if the organization is to survive. The weaknesses of the model are the absence of criteria with which to judge competing claims and the need for more advice on developing strategies to deal with divergent stakeholder interests.

Freeman has applied the stakeholder concept primarily at the corporate and industry levels in the private sector, but it seems applicable to all levels in the public sectors. Researchers have not yet made rigorous tests of the model's usefulness in the private, public, or nonprofit sectors, but several public and nonprofit case studies indicate that stakeholder analyses are quite useful as part of the strategic planning effort (Bryson, 1988b, 1995; Nutt and Backoff 1992; Bryson and Crosby 1992; Kemp 1993; Boschken 1992, 1994). If the model is to be used successfully, there must be the possibility that key decisionmakers can achieve reasonable agreement about who the key stakeholders are and what the response to their claims should be.

A number of other encompassing approaches to strategic planning have been developed primarily in the United Kingdom in the field of operations research. These include Strategic Options Development and Analysis (SODA) (Eden and Huxham 1988; Eden 1989; Bryson and Finn 1995), soft systems methodology (Checkland 1981, 1991), and strategic choice (Friend and Hickling 1987). They are used mostly in Europe but are finding application elsewhere as well.

Content Approaches

The three approaches presented so far have more to do with managing an entire strategic planning process than with identifying specific strategy content. The process approaches do not prescribe answers, although good answers are presumed to emerge from appropriate application. In contrast, the tools to be discussed next—portfolio models and competitive analysis—primarily concern content and do yield answers. In fact, the models are antithetical to process when process concerns get in the way of developing the "right" answers. Other important content approaches not covered in this entry, due to space limitations, include "reinventing government" (Osborne and Gaebler 1992; Gore 1993; Thompson and Jones 1994), systems analysis (Churchman 1968; Senge 1990), and "reengineering the organization" (Hammer and Champy 1993; Linden 1994).

Portfolio Models. The idea of strategic planning as managing a portfolio of businesses is based on an analogy with investment practice. Just as an investor assembles a portfolio of stocks to manage risk and to realize optimum returns, a corporate manager can think of the corporation as a portfolio of businesses with diverse potentials that can be balanced to manage return and cash flow. The intellectual history of portfolio theory in corporate strategy is complex (Wind and Mahajan 1981). For our purposes, it is adequate to use as an example the portfolio model developed by the Boston Consulting Group (BCG): the famous BCG matrix (Henderson 1979; Hax and Majiluf 1984).

Bruce Henderson, founder of the Boston Consulting Group, argued that all business costs followed a well-known pattern: unit costs dropped by one-third every time volume (or turnover) doubled. Hence, he postulated a relationship, known as the experience curve, between unit costs and volume. This relationship leads to some generic strategic advice: Gain market share, for then unit costs will fall and profit potential will increase.

Henderson said that any business could be categorized into one of four types, depending on how its industry was growing and how large a share of the market it had:

1. High growth/high share businesses ("stars"), which generate substantial cash but also require large invest-

ments if their market share is to be maintained or increased.

2. Low growth/high share businesses ("cash cows"), which generate large cash flows but require low investment and therefore generate profits that can be used elsewhere.

3. Low growth/low share businesses ("dogs"), which produce little cash and offer little prospect of increased share.

4. High growth/low share businesses ("question marks"), which would require substantial investment in order to become stars or cash cows. The question is whether the investment is worth it.

Although the applications of portfolio theory to the public sector may be less obvious than those of the three approaches described earlier, they are nonetheless just as powerful (MacMillan 1983; Ring 1988; Nutt and Backoff 1992). Many public organizations consist of "multiple businesses" that are only marginally related. Often resources from various sources are committed to these unrelated businesses. That means the public and managers must make portfolio decisions, although usually without the help of portfolio models that frame those decisions strategically. The BCG approach, like most private-sector portfolio models, uses only economic criteria, not political or social criteria that might be necessary for public applications. Private-sector portfolio approaches, therefore, must be modified substantially for public and nonprofit use. (Indeed, thoughtful critics argue that because private-sector portfolio approaches ignore the missions, values, cultures, and competencies of the companies that comprise the portfolios, they can do far more harm than good. Strategic management which relies only on economically based portfolio analysis can produce disastrous results and, therefore, is itself probably bankrupt; see Hurst 1986; Mintzberg 1994).

The strength of portfolio approaches is that they provide a method of measuring entities of some sort (businesses, investment options, proposals, or problems) against dimensions that are deemed to be of strategic importance (share and growth, or position and attractiveness). Weaknesses include the difficulty of knowing what the appropriate strategic dimensions are, difficulties of classifying entities against dimensions, and the lack of clarity about how to use the tool as part of larger strategic planning process.

If modified to include political and social factors, portfolio approaches can be used in the public sector to make informed strategic decisions. They can be used in conjunction with an overall strategic planning process to provide useful information on an organization, function, or community in relation to its environment. Unlike the process models, however, portfolio approaches provide an "answer;" that is, once the dimensions for comparison and the entities to be compared are specified, the portfolio models prescribe how the organization or community should relate to its environment. Such models will work only if a dominant coalition is convinced that the answers they produce are correct.

Competitive Analysis. Another important content approach that assists strategy selection has been developed by Michael Porter (1980, 1985, 1990, 1994) and his associates. Called "competitive analysis," it assumes that by analyzing the forces that shape an industry, one can predict the general level of profits throughout the industry and the likely success of any particular strategy for a strategic business unit.

Porter (1980) hypothesized that five key competitive forces shape an industry: relative power of customers, relative power of suppliers, threat of substitute products, threat of new entrants, and the amount of rivalrous activity among the players in the industry. Katherine Harrigan (1981) has argued that "exit barriers"–that is, the barriers that would prevent a company from leaving an industry–are a sixth force influencing success in some industries. Two of the main propositions in the competitive analysis school are as follows: (1) The stronger the forces that shape an industry, the lower the general level of returns in the industry; and (2) the stronger the forces affecting a strategic business unit, the lower the profits for that unit.

Two additional concepts are crucial in Porter's view. Competitive advantage grows out of the value a firm creates for its customers that exceeds the cost of producing it. Competitive advantage grows out of the value chain, the linkage of discrete primary activities (inbound logistics, operations, outbound logistics, marketing and sales, service) and support activities (firm infrasructure, human resource management, technology development, procurement) that create value for which the customer is willing to pay. Profits are found in the margin between what things cost and what their value is to the customer. Every buyer and supplier has a value chain, which leads to an additional important proposition: The more a supplier understands a buyer's value chain, the greater the firm's ability to create value for that buyer.

For many public organizations, there are equivalents to the forces that affect private industry. For example, client or customer power is often important; suppliers of services (contractors and the organization's own labor supply) also can exercise power. There are fewer new entrants in the public sector, but recently private and nonprofit organizations have begun to compete more forcefully with public organizations. Governments and public agencies often compete with one another (public hospitals for patients; state and local governments for industrial plants).

An effective organization in the public sector, therefore, must understand the forces at work in its "industry" in order to compete effectively and must offer value to its customers that exceeds the cost of producing it. On another level, planning for a specific public function (health care, transportation, or recreation) can benefit from competitive analysis if the function can be considered an industry. In addition, economic development agencies must understand the forces at work in given industries and on specific firms if they are to understand whether and how to nurture those industries and firms. Finally, although communities do compete with one another, competitive analysis probably does not apply at this level because communities are not industries in any meaningful sense.

By contrast, Porter points out in *The Competitive Advantage of Nations* (1990) that for the foreseeable future self-reinforcing agglomerations of firms and networks are crucial aspects of successful international economic competition. U.S. Secretary of Labor Robert Reich (1992), the German Marshall Fund (Widener et al. 1992), and Neal Pierce (1991) make the same point. In effect, not just firms, but metropolitan regions (Singapore, Hong Kong, the Silicon Valley, New York, London, Paris) are key economic actors. Regions interested in competing on the world stage, therefore, should try to develop the infrastructure necessary for virtuous (rather than vicious) cycles of economic growth to unfold. In other words, wise investments in education, transportation and transit systems, water and sewer systems, parks and recreation, housing, and so on, can help firms reduce their costs—particularly the costs of acquiring an educated labor force—and thus improve firms' abilities to compete internationally.

The strength of competitive analysis is that it provides a systematic way of assessing industries and the strategic options facing SBUs within those industries. Public organizations can use competitive analysis to discover ways to help the private firms in their regions. When applied directly to public organizations, however, competitive analysis has two weaknesses: It is often difficult to know what the "industry" is and what forces affect it, and the key to organizational success in the public world is often collaboration instead of competition. Competitive analysis for the public organizations, therefore, must be coupled with a consideration of social and political forces and the possibilities for collaboration (Huxham 1993; Winer and Ray 1994).

Another Process Approach

We now leave content approaches to focus again on a process approach—strategic issues management—that is less encompassing than the previous process approaches and typically is less encompassing than the content approaches as well.

Strategic Issues Management. Strategic issues management approaches are process components, pieces of a larger strategic planning process. In the private sector,

strategic issues management is primarily associated with Igor Ansoff (1980) and focuses attention on the recognition and resolution of strategic issues—"forthcoming developments, either inside or outside the organization, which are likely to have an important impact on the ability of the enterprise to meet its objectives" (p. 133). In the public sector, strategic issue management is primarily associated with Douglas Eadie (1986, 1989), Bryson (1988, 1995), and Paul Nutt and Robert Backoff (1992).

The concept of strategic issues first emerged when practitioners of corporate strategic planning realized a step was missing between the SWOT analysis of the Harvard model and the development of strategies. That step was the identification of strategic issues. Many organizations now include a strategic issue identification step as part of full-blown strategy revision exercises and also as part of less comprehensive annual strategic reviews (Chakravarthy and Lorange 1991). Full-blown annual revision has proved impractical because strategy revision takes substantial management energy and attention, and in any case most strategies take several years to implement. Instead, most firms are undertaking comprehensive strategy revisions several years apart (typically four or five) and in the interim are focusing their annual strategic planning processes on the identification and resolution of a few key strategic issues that emerge from SWOT analyses, environmental scans, and other analyses (Hambrick 1982; Pflaum and Delmont 1987; Heath 1988).

In recent years, many organizations also have developed strategic issues management processes actually separated from their annual strategic planning processes. Many important issues emerge too quickly, with too much urgency, to be handled as part of an annual process. When confronted with such issues, top managers typically appoint temporary teams or task forces to develop responses for immediate implementation.

Strategic issue management is clearly applicable to public organizations, since the agendas of these organizations consist of issues that should be managed strategically (Nutt and Backoff 1992; Bryson and Crosby 1992). In other words, they should be managed based on a sense of mission and mandates and in the context of an environmental assessment and stakeholder analysis. The strength of the approach is its ability to recognize and analyze key issues quickly. The approach also applies to functions or communities, as long as some group, organization, or coalition is able to engage in the process and to manage the issue. The main weakness is that in general the approach offers no specific advice on exactly how to frame the issues other than to precede their identification with a situational analysis of some sort. Nutt (1992, pp. 119–145), and Nutt and Backoff (1995) have gone the furthest in remedying this defect. They argued that public organizations exist within "tension fields" comprised of often conflicting or contradictory pressures for equity, preservation of the status quo, transition to a new state, and productivity improvement. Nutt and Backoff argued that exploration of the various combinations of these tensions, as they apply in specific circumstances, can lead strategic planners to the wisest formulation of strategic issues and strategies.

Process Strategies

The final two approaches to be discussed are process strategies. They are logical incrementalism and strategic planning as a framework for innovation. Process strategies are approaches to implementing a strategy that already has been developed in very broad outline and is subject to revision based on experience with its implementation. Other important process strategies not discussed in this entry, due to space limitations, include total quality management (Coucheu 1993, pp. 173–186; Cohen and Brand 1993), strategic negotiations (Pettigrew 1977; Mintzberg 1983; Mintzberg and Waters 1985; Pettigrew, Ferlie, and McKee 1992; Susskind and Cruikshank 1987), collaboration (Gray 1989; Huxham 1991, 1993; Winer and Ray 1994), and the management of culture (Hampden-Turner 1990; Schein 1992).

Logical Incrementalism. In incremental approaches, strategy is a loosely linked group of decisions that are handled incrementally. Decisions are handled individually below the corporate level because such decentralization is politically expedient–organizational leaders should reserve their political clout for crucial decisions. Decentralization also is necessary since often only those closest to decisions have enough information to make good ones.

The incremental approach is identified principally with James Quinn (1980; Mintzberg and Quinn 1991), although the influence of Charles Lindblom (1959; Braybrook and Lindblom 1963; Lindblom 1965, 1977, 1980) is apparent. Quinn developed the concept of logical incrementalism–or incrementalism in the service of overall corporate purposes–and as a result transformed incrementalism into a strategic approach. Logical incrementalism is a process approach that, in effect, fuses strategy formulation and implementation. The strengths of the approach are its ability to handle complexity and change, its emphasis on minor as well as major decisions, its attention to informal as well as formal processes, and its political realism. A related strength is that incremental changes in degree can add up over time into changes in time (Mintzberg 1987; Bryson 1988a, 1995; Bryson and Crosby 1992). The major weakness of the approach is that it does not guarantee that the various loosely linked decisions will add up to fulfillment of corporate purposes.

Logical incrementalism would appear to be very applicable to public organizations, as it is possible to establish some overarching set of strategic objectives to be served by the approach. When applied at the community level, there is a close relationship between logical incrementalism and collaboration. Indeed, collaborative purposes and arrangements typically emerge in an incremental fashion as organizations individually and collectively explore their self-interests and possible collaborative advantages, establish collaborative relationships, and manage changes incrementally within a collaborative framework (Huxham 1993; Winer and Ray 1994).

Strategic Planning as a Framework for Innovation. The earlier discussion about strategic planning systems noted that excessive comprehensiveness, prescription, and control can drive out attention to mission, strategy, and organizational structure. The systems in other words, can become ends in themselves and drive out creativity, innovation, and new product and market development, without which most businesses would die. Many businesses, therefore, have found it necessary to emphasize innovative strategies as a counterbalance to the excessive control orientation of many strategic planning systems. In other words, while one important reason for installing a strategic planning system is the need to exercise control across functions and levels, an equally important need for organizations is to design systems that promote creativity and entrepreneurship at the local level and prevent centralization and bureaucracy from stifling the wellsprings of business growth and change (Taylor 1984; Waterman 1987).

The framework-for-innovation approach to corporate strategic planning relies on many elements of the approaches discussed earlier, such as SWOT analyses and portfolio methods. This approach differs from earlier ones in four emphases: (1) innovation as a strategy, (2) specific management practices to support the strategy (such as project teams; venture groups; diversification, acquisition, and divestment task forces; research and development operations; new product and market groups; and a variety of organizational development techniques), (3) development of a "vision of success" that provides the decentralized and entrepreneurial parts of the organization with a common set of superordinate goals toward which to work, and (4) nurture of an entrepreneurial company culture (Pinchot 1985).

Minnesota employed a framework-for-innovation approach, called Strive for Excellence in Performance (STEP), under Governor Rudy Perpich in the 1980s. The STEP steering committee, cochaired by the governor and the chair of the state's big-business association, provided legitimacy and access to resources to experiment with projects proposed by state employees. A number of useful changes in the way the state provided goods and services resulted (Hale and Williams 1989; Barzelay 1992).

The main strength of the approach is that it allows for innovation and entrepreneurship while maintaining central control. It also is quite compatible with other approaches, such as reinventing government, systems analysis, reengineering the organization, and total quality management. The weaknesses of the approach are that typically—and perhaps necessarily—a great many, often costly, mistakes are made as part of the innovation process and that there is a certain loss of accountability in very decentralized systems (Peters and Waterman 1982; Mintzberg 1994). Those weaknesses reduce the applicability to the public sector, in particular, in which mistakes are less acceptable and the pressures to be accountable for details (as opposed to results) are often greater (Barzelay 1992; Jackson and Palmer 1992).

Nonetheless, the innovation approach would appear to be applicable to public organizations when the management of innovation is necessary, as in the redesign of a public service. Innovation as a strategy also can and should be pursued for functions and communities. Too often a distressing equation has operated in the public sector: More money equals more service, less money equals less service. As public budgets have become increasingly strapped, there has not been enough innovation in public service redesign. The equation does not have to be destiny; it is possible that creative effort and innovation might actually result in more service for less money (Osborne and Gaebler 1992; Gore 1993). It is particularly interesting to note that private and nonprofit sector innovations may be the answer to many public-sector problems. For example, many governments rely on private and nonprofit organizations to produce essentially "public" services on a contract basis.

Conclusions

Several conclusions emerge from this review and analysis. First, it should be clear that strategic planning is not a single concept, procedure, or tool. In fact, it embraces a range of approaches that vary in their applicability to public purposes and in the conditions that govern their successful use. The approaches vary in the extent to which they encompass broad policy and direction setting, internal and external assessments, attention to key stakeholders, the identification of key issues, development of strategies to deal with each issue, decisionmaking, implementation, and monitoring and interpretation of results.

Second, a strategic planning process applicable to public organizations and communities will need to allow for the full range of strategic planning activities from policy and direction setting through monitoring of results. Such a process will contrast, therefore, with most private-sector approaches that tend to emphasize different parts of such a complete process. A further contrast would be that private-sector approaches typically are focused only on organiza-

tions and not on functions that cross governmental or organizational boundaries, or on communities or larger entities.

Third, while any generic strategic planning process may be a useful guide to thought and action, it will have to be applied with care in a given situation, as is true of any planning process (Bryson and Delbecq 1979; Christensen 1985; Chakravarthy and Lorange 1991; Nutt 1992; Sager 1994). Because every planning process should be tailored to fit specific situations, every process in practice will be a hybrid (Bryson 1988b, 1995).

Fourth, familiarity with strategic planning should be a standard part of the intellectual and skill repertoire of all public managers and planners. Given the dramatic changes in the environments of their organizations in recent years, we can expect key public decisionmakers and planners to seek effective strategies to deal with the changes. When applied appropriately, strategic planning provides a set of concepts, procedures, and tools for formulating and implementing such strategies. The most effective leaders, managers, and planners no doubt are now, and will be increasingly in the future, the ones who are best at strategic planning.

Fifth, asserting the increased importance of strategic planning raises the question of the appropriate role of the strategic planner. In many ways, this is an old debate in the planning literature. Should the planner be a technician, politician, or hybrid—both technician and politician (Howe and Kaufman 1979; Howe 1980)? Should the planner be a process facilitator (Schein 1988) or what Bolan (1971) calls an "expert on experts?" Or should the planner not be a planner at all, at least formally, but rather a policymaker or a line manager (Bryson, Van de Ven, and Roering 1987; Mintzberg 1994)? Clearly, the strategic planner can be solely a technician only when content approaches are used. When all other approaches are used, the strategic planner (or planning team) should be a hybrid so that there is some assurance that both political and technical concerns are addressed. (Obviously, the specific proportions of technical expertise and political or process expertise would vary depending on the situation.) Furthermore, since strategic planning tends to fuse planning and decisionmaking, it is helpful to think of decisionmakers as strategic planners and to think of strategic planners as facilitators of strategic decisionmaking across levels and functions in organizations or communities.

Finally, research must explore a number of theoretical and empirical issues in order to advance the knowledge and practice of public-sector strategic planning. In particular, strategic planning processes that are responsive to different situations must be developed and tested. These processes should specify key situational factors governing their use; provide specific advice on how to formulate and implement strategies in different situations; be explicitly political; indicate how to deal with plural, ambiguous, or conflicting goals or objectives; link context, content, process, and outcomes; indicate how collaboration as well as competition is to be handled; and specify roles for those involved in the process. Other topics in need of attention include the nature of strategic leadership; ways to promote and institutionalize strategic planning across organizational levels, functions that bridge organizational boundaries, and intra- and interorganizational networks; and the ways in which information technologies can help or hinder the process. Progress has been made on all of these fronts (Checkoway 1986; Bryson and Einsweiler 1988; Boschken 1988, 1994; Kemp 1993; Bryson 1995), but work clearly is necessary if we are to understand better when and how to use strategic planning to further public purposes.

JOHN M. BRYSON

NOTE: Adapted from Bryson (1988b, p. 22–45) and from a paper prepared for presentation at the workshop on "Strategic Approaches to Planning: Towards Shared Urban Policies," Politecnico die Milano, Facolta di Architettura, Milano, Italy, March 16–17, 1995.

BIBLIOGRAPHY

Andrews, Kenneth, 1980. *The Concept of Corporate Strategy.* Homewood, IL: R. D. Irwin.

Ansoff, I., 1980. "Strategic Issue Management." *Strategic Management Journal,* vol. 1, no. 2: 131–148.

Armstrong, J. S., 1982. The Value of Formal Planning for Strategic Decisions: Review of Empirical Research. *Strategic Management Journal,* vol. 3, no. 2: 197–211.

Backoff, Robert, and Paul Nutt, 1992. *Strategic Management for Public and Third-Sector Organizations.* San Francisco, CA: Jossey-Bass.

Barry, B., 1986. *Strategic Planning Workbook for Nonprofit Organizations.* St. Paul, MN: Amherst H. Wilder Foundation.

Barzelay, M., 1992. *Breaking Through Bureaucracy.* Berkeley: University of California Press.

Boal, K. B., and J. M. Bryson, 1987. "Representation, Testing, and Policy Implications of Planning Processes." *Strategic Management Journal,* vol. 8: 211–231.

Bolan, R. S., 1971. "Generalist With a Specialty–Still Valid? Educating the Planner: An Expert on Experts." *Planning 1971: Selected Papers from the ASPO National Conference.* Chicago: American Society of Planning Officials.

Boschken, H. L., 1988. *Strategic Design and Organizational Change,* London: The University of Alabama Press.

———, 1992. "Analyzing Performance Skewness in Public Agencies: The Case of Urban Mass Transit." *Journal of Public Administration Research and Theory,* vol. 2, no. 3: 265–288.

———, 1994. "Organizational Performance and Multiple Constituencies." *Public Administration Review,* vol. 54: 308–312.

Bower, J., C. Bartlett, C. Christensen, A. Pearson and K. Andrews, 1993. *Business Policy: Text and Cases,* 7th ed. Homewood, IL: Irwin.

Bracker, J., 1980. "The Historical Development of the Strategic Management Concept." *Academy of Management Review,* vol. 5, no. 2: 219–224.

Braybrook, D., and C. Lindblom, 1963. *A Strategy for Decision: Policy Evaluation as a Social Process.* New York: Free Press.

Bryson, J. M., 1983. "Representing and Testing Procedural Planning Methods." In I. Masser, ed., *Evaluating Urban Planning Efforts.* Aldershot, England: Gower.

———, 1988a. "Strategic Planning: Big Wins and Small Wins." *Public Money and Management,* vol. 8, no. 3: 11–15.

———, 1988b. *Strategic Planning for Public and Nonprofit Organizations.* San Francisco, CA: Jossey-Bass.

———, 1995. *Strategic Planning for Public and Nonprofit Organizations,* rev. ed. San Francisco, CA: Jossey-Bass.

———, 1996. "Understanding Options for Strategic Planning." In J. Perry, ed., *Handbook of Public Administration,* 479-598 San Francisco, CA: Jossey-Bass.

Bryson, J. M., and P. Bromiley, 1993. "Critical Factors Affecting the Planning and Implementation of Major Projects." *Strategic Management Journal,* vol. 14: 319–337.

Bryson, J., P. Bromily, and Y. S. Jung, 1990. "Influences of Context and Process on Project Planning Success." *Journal of Planning Education and Research,* vol. 9, no. 3: 183–195.

Bryson, J. M., and B. C. Crosby, 1992. *Leadership for the Common Good.* San Francisco, CA: Jossey-Bass.

Bryson, J. M., and A. L. Delbecq, 1979. "A Contingent Approach to Strategy and Tactics in Project Planning." *Journal of the American Planning Association,* vol. 45: 167–179.

Bryson, J. M., and R. C. Einsweiler, eds., 1988. *Strategic Planning for Public Purposes–Threats and Opportunities for Planners.* Chicago, IL, and Washington, DC: Planners Press of the American Planning Association.

Bryson, J. M., and C. B. Finn, 1995. "Development and Use of Strategy Maps to Enhance Organizational Performance." In A. Halachmi, and G. Bouckaert, eds., *The Challenge of Management in a Changing World,* 247-280. San Francisco, CA: Jossey-Bass.

Bryson, J. M., R. E. Freeman, and W. D. Roering, 1986. "Strategic Planning in the Public Sector: Approaches and Directions." In B. Checkoway, ed., *Strategic Perspectives on Planning Practice,* 65–85 Lexington, MA.: Lexington Books.

Bryson, J. M., A. H. Van de Ven, and W. D. Roering, 1987. "Strategic Planning and the Revitalization of the Public Service." In R. Denhardt and E. Jennings, eds., *Toward a New Public Service,* 55–75 Columbia: Extension Publications, University Of Missouri.

Chakravarthy, B., and P. Lorange, 1991. *Managing the Strategy Process: A Framework for the Multi-business Firm.* Englewood Cliffs, NJ: Prentice-Hall.

Checkland, P. B., 1981. *Systems Thinking, System Practice.* Chichester, England: Wiley.

Checkland, P. B., and J. Scholes, 1991. *Soft Systems Methodology in Action.* New York: Wiley.

Checkoway, B., ed., 1986. *Strategic Perspectives on Planning Practice.* Lexington, MA: Lexington Books.

Christensen, K. S., 1985. "Coping with Uncertainty in Planning". *Journal of the American Planning Association,* vol. 51, no. 1: 63–73.

———, 1993. "Teaching Savvy." *Journal of Planning Education and Research,* vol. 12, no. 3: 202–212.

Churchman, C. W., 1968. *The Systems Approach.* NY: Dell.

Cohen, S., and R. Brand, 1993. *Total Quality Management in Government.* San Francisco, CA: Jossey-Bass.

Coucheu, T., 1993. *Making Quality Happen.* San Francisco, CA: Jossey-Bass.

Dutton, J., and S. Ashford, 1993. "Selling Issues to Top Management." *Academy of Management Review,* vol. 18, no. 3: 397–428.

Dutton, J., and S. Jackson, 1987. "Categorizing Strategic Issues: Links to Organizational Action." *Academy of Management Review,* vol. 12, no. 1: 76–90.

Eadie, Douglas, 1986. "Strategic Issue Management: Improving the Council-Manager Relationship." *ICMA MIS Report,* vol. 18, no. 6: 2–12.

———, 1989. "Building the Capacity for Strategic Management." In J. L. Perry, ed., *Handbook of Public Administration.* San Francisco, CA: Jossey-Bass.

Eden, C., 1989. "Using Cognitive Mapping for Strategic Options Development and Analysis (SODA)." In J. Rosenhead, ed., *Rational Analysis for a Problematic World.* New York: Wiley.

Eden, Colin, and Chris Huxham, 1988. "Action-Oriented Strategic Management." *Journal of the Operational Research Society,* vol. 39, no. 10: 889–899.

Fesler, J., and D. Kettl, 1994. *The Politics of the Administrative Process,* 2d ed. Chatham, NJ: Chatham House.

Frederickson, James, 1984. "The Comprehensiveness of Strategic Decision Processes," *Academy of Management Journal.* vol. 39 (10): 445-466.

Frederickson, James, and R. R. Mitchell, 1984. "Strategic Decision Processes: Comprehensiveness and Performance in an Industry with an Unstable Environment." *Academy of Management Journal,* vol. 27, no. 2: 399–423.

Freeman, R. E., 1984. "Strategic Management: A Stakeholder Approach." Boston: Pitman.

Friend, J., and A. Hickling, 1987. *Planning Under Pressure.* Oxford: Pergamon Press.

Goold, M., A. Campbell, and K. Luchs, 1993a. "Strategies and Styles Revisited: Strategic Planning and Financial Control." *Long Range Planning,* vol. 26, no. 5: 49–60.

———, 1993b. "Strategies and Styles Revisited: Strategic Control Companies." *Long Range Planning,* vol. 26, no. 6: 150–162

Gore, A., 1993. *The Gore Report on Reinventing Government.* New York: Times Books.

Gray, B., 1989. *Collaborating: Finding Common Ground for Multiparty Problems.* San Francisco, CA: Jossey-Bass.

Hale, Sandra, and Mary Williams, eds., 1989. *Managing Change: A Guide to Producing Innovation from Within.* Washington, DC: Urban Institute Press.

Hambrick, D. C., 1982. "Environmental Scanning and Organizational Strategy." *Strategic Management Journal,* vol. 3, no. 2: 159–174.

Hammer, M., and J. Champy, 1993. *Reengineering the Corporation.* New York: Harper Business.

Hampden-Turner, C., 1990. *Corporate Culture.* Hutchinson, Great Britain: Economist Books.

Harrigan, K., 1981. "Barriers to Entry and Competitive Strategies." *Strategic Management Journal,* vol. 2: 395–412.

Hax, A. C., and N. S. Majiluf, 1984. *Strategic Management: An Integrative Approach.* Englewood Cliffs, NJ: Prentice-Hall.

Heath, R. L., 1988. *Strategic Issues Management.* San Francisco, CA: Jossey-Bass.

Henderson, B., 1979. *Henderson on Corporate Strategy.* Cambridge, MA: Abt Books.

Howe, E., 1980. "Role Choices of Urban Planners." *Journal of the American Planning Association,* vol. 46: 398–409.

Howe, E., and J. Kaufman, 1979. "The Ethics of Contemporary American Planners." *Journal of the American Planning Association,* vol. 45: 243–255.

Hurst, D. K., 1986. "Why Strategic Management Is Bankrupt." *Organizational Dynamics,* vol. 15: 4–27.

Huxham, Chris, 1991. "Facilitating Collaboration: Issues in Multi-Organizational Group Decision Support." *Journal of the Operational Research Society,* vol. 42: 1037–1046.

———, 1993. "Pursuing Collaborative Advantage." *Journal of the Operational Research Society.* vol. 44, 44: 599-611.

Jackson, S. E., and J. E. Dutton, "Discerning Threats and Opportunities." *Administrative Science Quarterly,* vol. 33: 370–387.

Jackson, P. M., and Bob Palmer, 1992. *Performance Measurement: A Management Guide.* Leicester, England: Management Center University of Leicester.

Kaufman, J. L. 1979. "The Planner as Interventionist in Public Policy Issues." In R. Burchell and G. Sternlieb, eds., *Planning Theory in the 1980s.* New Brunswick: Center for Urban Policy Research.

Kemp, R. L., 1992. *Strategic Planning in Local Government: A Casebook.* Chicago, IL: American Planning Association.

———, 1993. *Strategic Planning for Local Government.* Jefferson: Mcfarland and Company.

Lindblom, C. E., 1959. "The Science of Muddling Through." *Public Administration Review,* vol. 19: 79–88.

———, 1965. *The Intelligence of Democracy.* New York: Free Press.

———, 1977. *Politics and Markets.* New York: Free Press.

———, 1980. *The Policy-Making Process.* 2d ed. Englewood Cliffs, NJ: Prentice-Hall.

Linden, R. M., 1994. *Seamless Government: A Practical Guide to Reengineering in the Public Sector.* San Francisco, CA: Jossey-Bass.

Lorange, P., 1980. *Corporate Planning: An Executive Viewpoint.* Englewood Cliffs, NJ: Prentice-Hall.

MacMillan, I., 1983. "Competitive Strategies for Not-for-Profit Agencies." *Advances in Strategic Management,* vol. 1: 61–82.

Mintzberg, H., 1983. *Power in and around Organizations.* Englewood Cliffs, NJ: Prentice-Hall.

———, 1987. "Crafting Strategy." *Harvard Business Review,* vol. 87, no. 4: 66–75.

———, 1990. "The Design School: Reconsidering the Basic Premises of Strategic Management." *Strategic Management Journal,* vol. 11: 171–195.

———, 1994. *The Rise and Fall of Strategic Planning.* New York: Free Press.

Mintzberg, H., and James Quinn, 1991. *The Strategy Process,* 2d ed. Englewood Cliffs, NJ: Prentice-Hall.

Mintzberg, H., and J. A. Waters, 1985. "Of Strategies, Deliberate and Emergent." *Strategic Management Journal,* vol. 6: 257–272.

Montanari, J. R., and J. S. Bracker, 1986. "The Strategic Management Process." *Strategic Management Journal,* vol. 7, no. 3: 251–265.

National Governors Association, 1993. An Action Agenda to Redesign State Governement. Washington, D.C.: National Governors Association.

Nutt, Paul, 1992. *Managing Planned Change.* New York: Macmillan.

Nutt, Paul, and R. W. Backoff, 1987. "A Strategic Management Process for Public and Third-Sector Organizations." *Journal of the American Planning Association,* vol. 53 : 44–57.

———, 1993. "Organizational Publicness and Its Implications for Strategic Management." *Journal of Public Administration Research and Theory,* vol. 3, no. 2: 209–231.

Nutt, Paul, and R. W. Backoff, 1995. "Strategy for Public and Third Sector Organizations." *Journal of Public Administration Research and Theory.* vol. 5(2):189–211

Olsen, J. B., and D. C. Eadie, 1982. *The Game Plan: Governance with Foresight.* Washington, DC: Council of State Planning Agencies.

Osborne, D., and T. Gaebler, 1992. *Reinventing Government.* Reading, MA: Addison-Wesley.

O'Toole, J., 1985. *Vanguard Management.* New York: Doubleday.

Peters, G., 1995. *The Politics of Bureaucracy,* 4th ed. New York: Longman.

Peters, T. J., and R. H. Waterman, Jr., 1982. *In Search of Excellence: Lessons from America's Best-Run Companies.* New York: Harper & Row.

Pettigrew, A., 1977. "Strategy Formulation as a Political Process." *International Studies in Management and Organization,* vol. 7, no. 2: 78–87.

Pettigrew, A., E. Ferlie, and L. Mckee, 1992. *Shaping Strategic Change.* Newbury Park, CA: Sage.

Pflaum, A., and T. Delmont, 1987. "External Scanning–A Tool for Planners." *Journal of the American Planning Association,* vol. 53, no. 1: 56–67.

Pierce, Neal, 1989. *Urban Challenges: A Vision for the Future.* Phoenix, AZ: Arizonel Republic, Phoenix Gazette.

Pinchot, G., III, 1985. *Enterpreneuring.* New York: Harper & Row.

Porter, M., 1980. *Competitive Strategy: Techniques for Analyzing Industries and Competitors.* New York: Free Press.

———, 1985. *Competitive Advantage: Creating and Sustaining Superior Performance.* New York: Free Press.

———, 1990. *The Competitive Advantage of Nations.* New York: Free Press.

———, 1994. *Competitive Strategies for Changing Industries.* Boston, MA: Harvard Business School Management Productions.

Quinn, J. B., 1980. *Strategies for Change: Logical Incrementalism.* Homewood, IL: R. D. Irwin.

Reich, R. B., 1992. *The Work of Nations.* New York: Vintage.

Ring, Peter, 1988. "Strategic Issues and Where Do They Come From?" In John Bryson and Robert Einsweiler *Strategic Planning for Public Purposes–Threats and Opportunities for Planners:* 69–83. American Planning Association.

Rue, L. W., and P. G. Holland, 1986. *Strategic Management: Concepts and Experiences.* New York: McGraw-Hill.

Sager, T., 1994. *Communicative Planning Theory.* Aldershot, United Kingdom: Avebury.

Schein, E., 1988. *Process Consultation. Vol. 1: Its Role in Organization Development.* Reading, MA: Addison-Wesley.

———, 1992. *Organizational Culture and Leadership,* 2d ed. San Francisco, CA: Jossey-Bass.

Senge, P. M., 1990. *The Fifth Discipline: The Art and Practice of the Learning Organization.* New York: Doubleday.

Stone, M., and W. Crittenden, 1993. "A Guide to Journal Articles on Strategic Management in Nonprofit Organizations." *Nonprofit Management and Leadership,* vol. 4: 193–213.

Susskind, L. E., and J. Cruikshank, 1987. *Breaking the Impasse: Consensual Approaches to Resolving Public Disputes.* New York: Basic Books.

Swanstrom, T., 1987. "The Limits of Strategic Planning for Cities." *Journal of Urban Affairs,* vol. 9: 139–157.

Taylor, B., 1984. "Strategic Planning–Which Style Do You Need?" *Long Range Planning,* vol. 17: 51–62.

Thompson, F., and L. R. Jones, 1994. *Reinventing the Pentagon: How the New Public Management Can Bring Institutional Renewal.* San Francisco, CA: Jossey-Bass.

Waterman, R. H., 1987. *The Renewal Factor.* New York: Bankam.

Waterman, R. H., Jr., T. J. Peters, and J. R. Phillips, 1980. "Structure Is Not Organization." *Business Horizons,* 14–26.

Widener, R., et al., 1992. *Divided Cities in the Global Economy: Human Strategies.* Columbia, SC: PASRAS Fund.

Wildavsky, A., 1979a. *The Politics of the Budgetary Process.* Boston, MA: Little, Brown.

———, 1979b. *Speaking Truth to Power.* Boston, MA: Little, Brown.

Wind, Y., and V. Mahajan, 1981. "Designing Product and Business Portfolios." *Harvard Business Review,* vol. 59: 155–165.

Winer, M., and K. Ray, 1994. *Collaboration Handbook.* St. Paul, MN: Amherst H. Wilder Foundation.

STRATEGIC SUPPLY MANAGEMENT.

Represents a radical reengineering of a significant but usually undervalued activity of both private and government organizations: purchasing. Traditionally, purchasing or procurement involves the process of selecting and buying goods and services on behalf of a government, on the basis of some fairly well defined criteria. Purchasing policy has usually been developed through a complex mix of financial and operating rules and the process has usually been administered by a centralized purchasing group.

This process has long been a government activity. The writings of Livy, around 315 B.C.E., show evidence of substantial and essential contracting between government and the private sector to ensure Roman armies were adequately fed and clothed. Livy also described the types of deals that were struck with suppliers that gave them some opportunities for expansion of their businesses and protection from some of the exigencies of the time, such as military service, and insurance against risk, particularly the elements.

While there is very little new about the existence of government purchasing, the way in which it can be managed has the potential to greatly enhance its service to governments. These changes to the process have the potential to transform this unheralded but significant organization function into a valued government activity that provides better quality products and services to government organizations at lower overall cost. However, a fundamental change in expectations about the responsibilities of the purchasing function, and a shift away from the traditional focus upon the purchase transactions of ordering and tendering, will be essential if the process is to assume a more value-added approach. The changes have to do with rethinking the procurement process, seeing it as a strategic function rather than a transactional activity.

The process of strategic supply management represents a sophisticated and wide-ranging version of purchasing or procurement. Strategic supply management implies that an organization can gain considerable financial and operating benefits from taking a more strategic view of the procurement process. This view shows that an organization can proactively manage the supply chain from the moment a decision is made to consider buying a product or service to the time the product or service is no longer of use to the organization. This "whole of life" view of products (and services) represents a radical departure from the traditional method of purchasing, which, while claiming to provide government with " the best value for the money," often encourages the purchase of products on the principle of lowest cost.

The traditional model of procurement regards transactions as the focal point of the purchase process. The issue of a purchase order to a supplier is seen as both the capstone and conclusion of the purchase process. A great deal of effort is devoted to ensuring that the purchasing process has gained the cheapest price from the available suppliers prepared for the bid, that organizational purchasing policies have been adhered to, and that the correct procedures were applied throughout the buying process. In the past, the function of purchasing was sometimes regarded as something of a mystery by other staff, and the status of the function was quite low. However, despite this lack of status, the amount of power the procurement department had over the purchase process through its management and control of the clerical process was immense. This power was often resented because the ultimate users of the products and services being purchased through the typically centralized purchase function felt that their needs and opinions were overlooked in the purchase process and that assessment of purchase bids (tenders) on the basis of price and other criteria known only to the procurement department was very inadequate.

Despite its focus on the purchasing transaction, the amount of money processed by a procurement department is usually very substantial. Estimates of the proportion of total funds influenced by procurement in an organization vary widely depending upon the type of activity undertaken by the organization. However, there is adequate evidence to show that procurement may influence from between 10 to 70 percent of a commercial organization's expenditure, and in the case of government organizations, the proportion can also be significant (for example, some data show local government procurement can be up to 18 percent of total expenditure). An appreciation of the size of the funds managed by purchasing staff and managers helps to show why a more proactive and sophisticated procurement function can have a significant influence on the financial performance of government organizations.

The emerging view of procurement takes a supply chain perspective, which suggests that much better value for money and effort will be achieved if an organization manages the supply process rather taking a simplistic, reactive view using a simple quote or tender-based system. The supply chain model suggests that the purchasing process manages a complex chain of product development, end-user, and supplier coordination. The supply chain may commence with the broad identification of the product or service required, the development of appropriate specifications by meetings of end-users, purchasing coordinators, and representatives of suppliers. After agreement upon a final design, advertising for qualified, interested parties to submit supply proposals will occur. The evaluation of those proposals on a series of parameters including "whole-of-life" cost and potential quality and delivery standards will take place before the selection of one or more supplier(s). Once a suitable contract for the goods or services is completed, the management and monitoring of supplier and product performance will become an ongoing process until the need for the goods and services is complete, at which time the purchasing function may be involved in the selection of suitable disposal or termination strategies.

This complex chain provides the basis upon which government organizations can greatly improve the quality of goods and services they acquire to perform their functions and reduce costs. It also raises expectations about the value-added services that can be provided by a specialist procurement function in place of the simple contract assessment and clerical activities currently the basis of many public-sector procurement systems. The focus of purchasing management and their support staff needs to change rapidly from an administrative focus upon form and detail to product research, team facilitation, assessment of "whole-of-life" costs, and supplier management.

The reengineering of purchasing has been facilitated by the advent of electronic means of managing procurement transactions. Electronic Data Interchange (EDI) enables organizations to establish a database that provides details of all contracts that have been negotiated by the procurement teams. In its most sophisticated form, an EDI system enables staff of the host organization and its approved suppliers to access the database of existing suppliers and the relevant contracts. Organization staff can use the database to select and order the goods and services already available under existing contracts negotiated with suppliers. Suppliers can use the system to issue invoices, advise delivery times, bill, and be paid by the ordering organization. EDI enables a "seamless" organization system to be developed. With adequate delegations, the system frees the procurement staff from the task of order entry and their purchasing skills can be used to manage rather than process. The development of EDI or similar information-based systems means that the days of an individual with the specific responsibility for issuing purchasing orders are passing, that function being delegated to any staff member with appropriate authority who can handle the order process through the IT network.

A simplistic view of the purchase process suggests that the entire process could be delegated to any individual. However, the reality for larger organizations suggests that for control purposes and a specialist approach to procurement, employing a group of trained individuals can provide significant advantages for an organization, in either private or public sectors. One of the principal groups of skills for procurement staff lies in the ability to organize, advise, coordinate, and negotiate the acquisition of products and services. This skill amounts to an ability to manage a small procurement team of end-users and, depending upon the matter under consideration, designers, engineers, legal and financial advisers, and any other relevant specialist. Apart from managing the team process, the procurement specialist can be expected to manage the negotiation process once the procurement team reaches the point of discussing their needs with suppliers. At this point, the negotiations skills of a procurement specialist come to the fore: organizing the best deal, but not just in terms of price.

It is expected that a contract for goods will be let to the supplier(s) able to offer a number of advantages. First, the best "whole-of-life" cost for the goods will be a key issue. This approach to cost covers not just the purchase price but also includes maintenance, insurance, other operating costs, and disposal costs. Second, the procurement specialist will be in a position to advise on the ability of the supplier to deliver goods and services on time and within price and quality specifications. This service links to the environmental research that would be normally provided by the procurement specialist on the location and availability of likely suppliers. Third, the procurement specialist needs to check that end-user needs are met at all stages of the negotiations (within the cost, service delivery, and other policy requirements of the organization), this being a major criticism of traditional procurement practices. Fourth, the monitoring of suppliers, so that agreed performance levels are maintained, is important. This ensures that the needs of the organization are not being prejudiced by supplier delays or quality problems. In some organizations, this will be regarded as part of a strategic partnering process, which will commence at the time of precontract negotiations, will be incorporated into the contract that is eventually agreed upon, and will continue throughout the life of the contract. Liaison with end-users will also be maintained during the life of the contract to ensure that their expectations continue to be met, that control of the contract is maintained, and that supplier performance meets end-user satisfaction.

One of the major concerns of public sector managers is accountability. This applies not only to actual expenditure of government funds but also to the process by which contracts are let. In the past, accountability requirements were met, for example, by obtaining quotes from several suppliers before purchasing items or services of low value,

or by developing a specification and asking suppliers to lodge a tender or bid to supply items or services of high value. The difference between the value of "low-value" and "high-value" purchases varied according to government policy and regulations. One of the consequences of this system was that the cost of buying low-value items was very high because of the procedural requirements compared to the cost of the item to be supplied. A strategic supply approach suggests that for low-value purchases, the process may be better handled by having approved suppliers for products up to a certain value or to simply permit these purchases to be made by a corporate credit card. Such cards have become increasingly popular in both public- and private-sector organizations, although their issue needs to be accompanied by suitable staff training and tight control over the purchasing limit of each cardholder and the use that can be made of the card.

The management of tendering for high-value purchases is more complex. Here, government buying practices need to be ethically managed and give fair opportunity for qualified suppliers to have access to the tendering process. This can be achieved through using a well publicized list of available tenders from government, offered traditionally through the print media but now increasingly distributed through an electronic bulletin board. Where suppliers are to be involved from early design stages, a system of prequalification of suppliers may be used to involve a fairly selected group of suppliers to participate or to allow industry representatives to engage in preliminary negotiations on behalf of all potential suppliers. Successful bidders may then be invited to contract to provide their goods or services over an extended period subject to meeting continuing benchmarks on quality, delivery, and price. There are a variety of approaches to the strategic management of contracting that are beyond the scope of this entry.

The case for decentralizing the procurement function within government is not clear. Decentralization may give users a sense of greater flexibility and freedom from the controls of a purchasing function. However, it may be found that the desired flexibility can be achieved through the use of a decentralized ordering system (such as EDI) yet gain the sourcing, price, and negotiation advantages of using a centralized, professionally skilled group of purchasing practitioners handling the more difficult parts of the purchase process. The centralized supply function needs to ensure it satisfies the needs of end-users by ensuring they are engaged in the design, planning, specification, and tender assessment stages of most contracts. The centralized function can improve its worth to clients by providing market information of new developments that may assist users in performing their tasks more effectively. Centralizing purchasing also ensures that government organizations gain the greatest possible price and service advantages as a large customer yet can maintain adequate financial control over the process.

At each stage of the procurement process, the procurement specialist should be involved only to add value for the end-user and the organization. For this reason, the basic order entry presently conducted in many procurement departments should gradually be handed over to the end-user, with the necessary operating and financial controls normally found in an organization. A strategic management approach to purchasing and supply management in the public sector has the potential to save governments significant amounts of taxpayers' money and deliver better quality and value for the money. A major change in attitude toward the role and function of purchasing can assist the transformation of government purchasing to a proactive, strategic element of public-sector operations.

GUY CALLENDER

BIBLIOGRAPHY

Burt, D. N, and M. F. Doyle, 1993. *The American Keiretsu.* Homewood: Business One Irwin.

Ellram, L. M., and A. Carr, 1994. "Strategic Purchasing: A History and Review of the Literature." *International Journal of Purchasing and Materials Management,* vol. 30, no. 2 (Spring): 9–18.

Gadde, L. K., and H. Hakansson, 1993. *Professional Purchasing.* London: Routledge.

Gehani, R. R., 1993. "Quality Value-Chain: A Meta-Synthesis of Frontiers of the Quality Movement." *Academy of Management Executives,* vol. 7, no. 3: 29–42.

Gore, A., 1993. *Creating a Government That Works Better and Costs Less: The Report of the National Performance Review.* New York: Plume.

Leenders, M. R., and H. E. Fearon, 1993. *Purchasing and Materials Management,* 10th ed. Homewood: Richard D. Irwin.

Porter, M. E., 1990. *The Competitive Advantage of Nations.* London: Macmillan.

van Weele, A. J., 1994. *Purchasing Management: Analysis, Planning, and Practice.* London: Chapman and Hall.

Zenz, G. J., 1994. *Purchasing and the Management of Materials.* New York: John Wiley and Sons.

STRATEGY. A plan, usually military, for achieving political or other objectives. The word has a very loose usage in everyday language and a number of more precise meanings in a variety of disciplines ranging from decision theory to mathematics and military studies. In general usage, the term simply refers to any plan, scheme, or program for achieving an objective. Thus, one might have a strategy for winning a game, making a fortune, passing an examination, or robbing a bank. Used in this general way, the term merely indicates a degree of forethought about how a goal is to be achieved.

But the origin of both the noun "strategy" and its related adjective "strategic" has a much more precise military connotation, being connected with two Greek words— "stratos" meaning "army" and "agein" meaning "to lead," hence, the long-standing association of strategy with the art or science of generalship and the management of armed forces in war. Despite the multitude of ways in which the term "strategy" is currently used, this military meaning is still the most common. Typically, the term strategy is linked to the use of military power in the pursuit of political or military objectives. The strategists' attention is focused on the way in which the legally sanctioned instrument of violence, which is embodied in a state's armed forces, is used, either in pursuit of national interests in competition with other states or in an internal security role against subversive or revolutionary forces. Of course, since governments do not enjoy a monopoly of military capability, it is not unusual for terrorist organizations, guerrilla movements, ethnic minorities, and insurgents to involve themselves in strategic planning. No matter who controls military power, it is "strategy" that converts it into a purposive instrument.

Through the centuries, there have been many distinguished strategists. Some regard Sun Tzu as the first; others give the honor to Thucydides. But it is probably fair to say that the roots of modern strategy are mainly to be found in the nineteenth century when Carl von Clausewitz developed an impressive body of thought about land warfare and Alfred Thayer Mahan, an American naval officer, laid the foundations of modern naval strategy. The approach of most nineteenth and early twentieth century strategic thinkers was historical; they reflected on past military campaigns and tried to draw lessons from them. Over the years, various attempts were made to distill strategic wisdom down to a handful of "principles of war" that would have universal applicability. Advice to "avoid dispersion," to "concentrate force," to "press home advantages gained," to "avoid distractions," and so forth are the sort of rather trite recommendations that often emerged from quite scholarly reflection on war. In elaborating these principles, strategists emphasized the importance of maneuver, concentration, surprise, initiative, flexibility, and so on.

The object of strategy is to break or bend the enemy's will to resist, and it might be thought that the best way to do this is by direct confrontation and the application of superior force. However, various strategists have emphasized that this is not always the most fruitful approach. Sir Basil Liddell Hart (1941) made the points that "a direct approach to one's mental object, or physical objective, along the 'line of natural expectation' for the opponent, tends to produce negative results." He therefore favored an "indirect approach" that would take the enemy by surprise. "In most campaigns the dislocation of the enemy's psychological and physical balance has been the vital prelude to a successful attempt at his overthrow" (pp. 4–5). This strategy of "the indirect approach" was hinted at by Napoleon in his famous dictum "the moral is to the physical as three to one." General A. Beaufre (1965) also noted the importance of "the indirect approach." "The game of strategy can, like music, be played in two keys. The major key is di-

rect strategy in which force is the essential factor. The minor key is indirect strategy, in which force recedes into the background and its place is taken by psychology and planning" (p. 134).

In the nuclear age, the subject matter of military "strategy" has expanded enormously. Strategy is now as much concerned with the preservation of peace and international stability as it is with the conduct of war. Hence, its scope now includes the development of crisis management techniques, the pursuit of disarmament and arms control, and the implementation and preservation of deterrence policies. It is now widely appreciated that if these objectives are to be achieved, strategic policies must include elements of cooperation as well as competition with potential enemies. This implies that strategy is no longer a "zero sum game" in which a gain for one side inevitably means a loss for another. The fact that potential or actual enemies can have common interests—for instance, in a modicum of international order, in avoiding Armageddon, in preventing accidental war or unplanned escalation—means that strategies have to have collaborative as well as competitive features built into them. In the words of Thomas Schelling (1960), strategy is "concerned not just with enemies who dislike each other but with *partners* who distrust or disagree with each other. It is concerned not just with the division of gains and losses between two claimants but with the possibility that particular outcomes are worse (better) for both claimants than certain other outcomes" (p. 5).

It is worth noting that not all military planning is described as "strategic." Usually, this adjective is reserved specifically for military planning at the very highest level. In this context a distinction is usually drawn between "tactics" and "strategy." The term "tactics" refers to the kind of low-level, short-term, localized military planning that is conducted within the context of the battlefield, or even below that level in the case of minor military engagements. Plans for holding or taking a bridge, establishing a bridgehead, or destroying a minor target would be regarded as "tactical." "Strategy," by way of contrast, is high level, broad brush, and long term. Indeed, the term "grand strategy" is sometimes used to emphasize the importance of this political/strategic level of decisionmaking, which is usually the province of statesmen and very senior officers who, between them, carry the responsibility for planning the overall conduct of a war and the ultimate defeat of the enemy. Hitler's plan, code-named Barbarossa, for the conquest of Russia, and the allied invasion plan (Overlord) would fall into this category of "grand strategy." What is interesting about strategy at this level is that it is never a purely military activity and is usually much less technical than tactics. Perhaps one way of highlighting the difference between "strategy" and "tactics" is to suggest that "tactics" are essentially about how "strategy" is implemented.

After World War II, the notion that the term "strategic" conveyed special significance and importance was reinforced by a new usage. A distinction was drawn between "strategic" nuclear weapons with large yields and intercontinental ranges and "tactical" or "theater" weapons with smaller yields whose use was confined to the battlefield. A similar distinction was drawn between "strategic" bombing, characterized by deep penetration strikes into the industrial and military heartland of the enemy, and "tactical" bombing, which referred to short- or intermediate-range bombing raids designed to interdict enemy logistics and supply systems or to support ground operations by friendly forces. This distinction is not absolutely clear-cut, but it is generally accepted that "strategic" strikes, like "strategic" weapons and "strategic" plans, are more important than their counterparts at the tactical level.

Historically, strategists have tended to separate the three environments—land, sea, and air—in which military power is used, and individual strategists have made their reputations by concentrating on one of these environments. Von Clausewitz, Henri de Jomini, Foch, Liddell Hart developed theories of land warfare—sometimes called "continental strategy;" Mahan and Julian Corbett were sea power theorists; Douhet, Billy Mitchell, and Seversky were interested in air power. But, in the nuclear age, these divisions have been eroded by technological developments that enable particular weapons to be air launched, sea launched, or land based. Modern guns and missiles can be mounted on ships, tanks, or aircraft. From whatever platform they are launched, missiles, shells, and bullets all travel through the air and can be aimed at targets on land, at sea, or in the air. In other words, weapons launched in one environment are increasingly likely to be felt in another, and this suggests that the land, sea, air division is no longer appropriate. Since World War II, it has become increasingly difficult to pigeonhole strategists in the three traditional categories. The writings of nuclear strategists like Bernard Brodie, William Kaufmann, Herman Kahn, Henry Kissinger, and Thomas Schelling certainly do not fit the traditional pattern.

In his classic work *On War*, von Clausewitz (1908) defined strategy as "the employment of the battle as the means towards the attainment of the object of war" (p. 165). As Liddell Hart (1941) pointed out, this definition suffers the defect of narrowing the meaning of strategy "to the pure utilisation of battle, thus conveying the idea that battle is the only means to the strategical end" (p.184). The elder Graf Helmut von Moltke, the German general, described strategy as "the practical adaptation of the means placed at a general's disposal to the attainment of the object in view." (in Liddell Hart, 1941 p. 185). Liddell Hart arrived at a similar though shorter definition. According to him, strategy is "the art of distributing and applying military means to fulfil the ends of policy" (p. 187). In other words, strategy is concerned with applying given military resources to achieving particular political objectives. This definition has at least two advantages. First, it is equally applicable in peacetime and war; and second, it hints at the subordination of war to politics.

The reputation of von Clausewitz rests largely on his perception of this last point, namely, that if war is to be functional and not pointless violence, then the politician must be in control of it. Von Clausewitz's famous recommendation that war ought to be a continuation of political intercourse with an admixture of other means has rightly become the most famous of all strategic aphorisms. Firm political control of the professional soldier is also necessary if the worst excesses of militarism are to be avoided. Alfred Vagts (1967) defined civilian militarism as "the unquestioning embrace of military values, ethos, principles, attitudes; as ranking military institutions and considerations above all others in the state" (p. 453). Few people wish to live in a society that is controlled by a military elite and dominated by a military ethos. That is why it is important that strategists should be responsible to democratically elected political leaders.

Today, "strategy" still involves the consideration and evaluation of the various choices available to states in their use of military force for ends clearly defined by political authorities; but it also encompasses the consideration of those ends themselves. While it may be argued that politicians rather than their military servants should decide the goals of democratically controlled military policy, they should not do so without consulting those who, by virtue of specialist knowledge, are best able to think through the implications of pursuing particular policies, and who are therefore in a position to advise as to their practicability and consequences. Strategists are now government advisers as well as government executives, and, in consequence, strategy has become more than a "means-ends" relationship focused solely on how to achieve particular objectives. It now encompasses discussion of what those objectives should be.

In a changing international environment, the process of reexamining the aims of national policy should be a continuous one, and although it is agreed that in democratic societies the politicians should exercise ultimate control, the decisions they make must at least take into account the advice they receive from experts. If, as Clemenceau is reputed to have said, "war is much too serious a matter to be left to the generals," it is also much too serious to be left to the politicians. And so, in formulating strategy, dialogue is required between political and military minds. In one of the pioneering works in the field, Henry Kissinger (1957) made a convincing plea for this dialogue: "A separation of strategy and policy can be achieved only to the detriment of both. It causes military policy to become identified with the most absolute applications of power and it tempts diplomacy into an over concern with finesse. Since the difficult problems of national policy are in the area where political, economic, psychological and military factors overlap, we should give up the fiction that there is such a thing as 'purely' military advice" (p. 422).

In recent years, purely military definitions of strategy have virtually disappeared because, as mentioned before, they fail to convey either the flavor or scope of activities that straddle peace and war and that are as much concerned with statesmanship as with the conduct of war. Almost everyone agrees with Liddell Hart's view that "old concepts, and old definitions, of strategy have become *not only obsolete, but nonsensical* with the development of nuclear weapons . . . to aim at winning a war, to take victory as your object, is no more than a state of lunacy." The view that strategy is not so much concerned with the conduct of war as with the conduct of peace is reflected in the motto of the Strategic Air Command: "Peace is our profession."

Any satisfactory definition of modern strategy must take into account the peacetime applications of strategic thinking and must endeavor to locate the use of military force in the more general context of foreign policymaking. Robert Osgood (1962) suggested that "military strategy must now be understood as nothing less than the overall plan for utilizing the capacity for armed coercion—in conjunction with the economic, diplomatic, and psychological instruments of power—to support foreign policy most effectively by overt, covert, and tacit means". (p. 5) In the words of Henry Kissinger, "It is the task of strategic doctrine to translate power into policy. (p. 157)"

There is some danger that interpretations such as these may make it impossible for the student to distinguish strategy either from foreign policymaking or even from the larger subject of international politics in which it is subsumed. Certainly, the distinctions are not clear-cut. If anything, they reflect differences of emphasis and perspective rather than radical differences in subject matter. The student of strategy has chosen to focus the attention on—but not to confine it to—the way in which military force is exploited in international conflicts. The student remains interested in the more general study of international politics, but by slanting the approach, one can pursue in depth on part of the subject without losing sight of the others. In a sense, "strategy" has a sharp focus—the use of military force—but not a very well defined perimeter.

In its broadest sense, and traditionally, strategy is about the pursuit of security, in particular the military security of states. However, in recent years it has become clear that states now face threats to which a military response is quite inappropriate. The threats posed by environmental pollution, global warming, economic deprivation, population growth, and migration cannot be countered either by the threat or use of force. This has led some to favor expanding the strategists' notion of "security" to incorporate security against these new threats that now confront us. The International Institute for Strategic

Studies has recently amended its mission statement to include "study and discussion of . . . any major international security issues including without limitation those of a political, strategic, economic, social or ecological nature." The danger inherent in this approach is that the study of strategy may become indistinguishable from the study of "world issues" in general and will lose the military focus that gave it intellectual coherence.

Traditional strategy has also come under fire from critics who believe that it has been too much concerned with state security and has paid too little attention to the security needs of the individuals who live within the state and who feel more threatened by unemployment, poverty, inadequate health care, and so forth than by foreign aggression or internal subversion. The danger here is that the study of strategy may eventually become indistinguishable from the study of how to promote human contentment. "World issues" and "human happiness" may be worthy subjects in their own right, but, apart from a common concern with "security," loosely defined, it is difficult to link them intellectually with "strategy" as normally understood, and there may be no good reason for corrupting an established discipline by trying to do so.

Not everyone has defined "strategy" in terms of military affairs. Some have chosen definitions that emphasize not the subject matter that is dealt with but the patterns of thought that are associated with its analysis. They have noted that what distinguishes strategic from other kinds of thinking is a rather distinctive way of looking at conflict, which can be applied to many social situations that have nothing to do with military conflict.

All that is required for strategic thinking is a social situation in which there is a clash of will and a possibility that force or its equivalent will be used in its resolution. It does not matter at all whether the clash of will is in business, sport, marriage, or politics. This rather abstract view of strategy owes much to that branch of mathematics known as "game theory," a subject which may be defined as a theory of rational decisionmaking in situations involving conflicts of interest between independent actors. A distinction has been drawn between games of chance–where winning depends on luck, as in Ludo or Snakes and Ladders–and games of skill–where winning depends on ability, as, for instance, by reaching a standard in athletics or by being awarded a first class honors degree–and games of strategy–where winning depends on outwitting an opponent, as in poker, chess, war, and so on. Success in a strategy game depends not only on how good you are but on how good your opponent is. In the theory of games, strategy is used to denote the purely rational, artful behavior of competitors whose aim is to win and whose decisions are to some extent dependent on their opponents' decisions.

More particularly, it refers to a competitor's plan for playing the game from start to finish; and it states what one will do in every conceivable situation in which one may find oneself during the course of the game. Instead of deciding what to do at each move in the game, the player formulates in advance of the play a plan for playing the game from beginning to end. In other words, in game theory, a strategy is a complete prescription for playing the game that takes into account all the possible contingencies that may occur as result of one's opponent's moves.

Military conflict is not much like a game, but some insights into it may be derived from an approach that regards war and conflict as a kind of contest in which the "players" are trying to win. In some respects the intelligent, sophisticated behavior of the military strategist pitting his wits against an enemy is comparable to the moves of a player in a game of chess or poker. The conflicts are very different, but the thought processes of those engaged in them may be similar, and so long as one does not read too much into this fact, it is an illuminating insight. Thomas Schelling (1960), a strategist who made a formidable contribution to the thinking about nuclear strategy, is someone who has drawn our attention to the structural similarities that may lie beneath such diverse activities as war, chess, and poker.

Andre Beaufre (1965) is another military strategist who has emphasized the general applicability of strategic thinking: "Strategy is the abstract interplay which . . . springs from the clash between two opposing wills. It is the art which enables a man, no matter what the techniques employed, to master the problems set by any clash of wills and as a result to employ the techniques available with maximum efficiency. It is therefore the art of the dialectic of force, or, more precisely, *the art of the dialectic of two opposing wills using force to resolve their dispute*" (p. 22).

So long as it concerned itself with questions of military tactics and with narrow defense issues, it was inevitable that strategy should be monopolized by military men and the staff colleges containing them. The expertise that was a prerequisite of informed study was available only to professional soldiers, and for hundreds of years strategy remained a *recherche* subject taken up mainly by officers with an intellectual turn of mind. But once the subject was expanded to include broader aspects of government and national policymaking, the way was open for wider debate.

It was quickly realized that direct military experience was a much less important qualification for developing strategic ideas than a trained analytical mind grounded preferably in one of the social sciences or history. Even so, were it not for the suffering of two world wars and the invention of nuclear weapons capable of destroying the entire human race, it is doubtful whether strategy would ever have attracted the attention of more than a handful of scholars. However, the cost and destructiveness of modern war made it inevitable that more intellectual effort would be devoted to strategic questions during the first 50 years of the Atomic Age than was expended on them during the previous 200 years. It is now true to say that most of the present output of strategic writing is produced by civilians working mainly in universities or comparable research institutions. Certainly, the foundations of contemporary strategic thought–particularly nuclear thought–were laid in a handful of progressive think tanks and universities, mostly in the United States. The contribution of these academic experts has been considerable and is almost universally acknowledged.

Now that the Cold War is over and the threat of major nuclear war considerably diminished, strategists are grappling with the prospect of more independent low-level violence of the sort that has erupted in the former Yugoslavia and Soviet Union. Arguably, handling this kind of conflict may require more traditional technical military expertise than implementing the strategy of deterrence or planning strategic war. If this proves to be the case, strategy may once again become the rather recondite pursuit of the military intellectual with practical knowledge of military operations on the ground.

JOHN GARNETT

BIBLIOGRAPHY

Baylis, John, Ken Booth, John Garnett, and Phil Williams, 1987. *Contemporary Strategy*, 2d ed. London: Croom Helm.
Beaufre, Andre, 1965. *An Introduction to Strategy*. London: Faber and Faber.
Buchan, Alistair, ed., 1970. *Problems of Modern Strategy*. London: Chatto and Windus.
Clausewitz, Carl von, 1908. *On War*, trans J. J. Graham. London: Routledge.
Kissinger, Henry, A., 1957. *Nuclear Weapons and Foreign Policy*. New York: Harper and Row.
Liddell Hart, Basil, 1941. *The Strategy of the Indirect Approach*. London: Faber and Faber.
———, 1960. *Deterrent or Defence*. London: Stevens.
Osgood, Robert E., 1962. *NATO: The Entangling Alliance*. Chicago: Chicago University Press.
Schelling, Thomas C., *The Strategy of Conflict*. Cambridge, MA: Harvard University Press.
Vagts, Alfred, 1967. *History of Militarism*. New York: Free Press.

STREET-LEVEL BUREAUCRATS. Defined as those public service workers who interact directly with citizens in the course of their jobs and who have substantial discretion in the execution of their work (Lipsky 1980).

Street-level bureaucrats are people working within a system that has given them the responsibility of allocating limited resources. Michael Lipsky (1980) stated that they engender conflict because they deal with people and make decisions that have the power to affect people's lives. They are agents of social control because, as Lipsky explained, "the public sector plays a critical part in softening the impact of the economic system on those who are not its primary beneficiaries and inducing people to accept the neglect or inadequacy of primary economic and social institutions" (p. 10).

Herbert Simon (1976) realized the importance of these individuals when he wrote, "In the study of organization, the operative employee [interpreted as street-level bureaucrats in this entry] must be at the focus of attention, for the success of the structure will be judged by his performance within it. Insight into the structure and function of an organization can best be gained by analyzing the manner in which the decisions and behavior of such employees are influenced within and by the organizations" (p. 3).

Charles Goodsell (1994) defined street level bureaucrats as "ordinary people." They possess characteristics very similar to those of the general public. Their demographic characteristics, political opinions, and personal attitudes are quite similar to those of the general populace (Lewis 1990).

Street-level bureaucrats can best be described by focusing on their decisionmaking process. It is important to point out that the unit of analysis in most literature is the decisionmaker, a label that is usually attached to the manager. However, in a general sense, the theories presented in the literature can be applied to street-level bureaucrats for the reasons outlined before. I have chosen to present the different theories that apply to street-level bureaucrats' decisionmaking processes under different categories. These categories are not exhaustive or conclusive but can serve as guidance for the reader to follow the enormous literature covering decisionmaking and its application to street-level bureaucrats.

Decisionmaking at the Street Level

The Decisionmaking Process

Focusing on the decisionmaker as the unit of analysis, Simon presented his theory of bounded rationality in which he categorized the "administrative man" as a satisficer. Simon's definition of administrative man refers to those who make decisions in an organization. Therefore, this definition can be implied to include street-level bureaucrats because, as mentioned earlier, they too make decisions. Simon (1976) stated that the administrators' abilities to make decisions are limited by their skills, values, and knowledge. As a result, organizations have the responsibility to provide their employees with the information and the environment necessary to help then approach rationality.

Moreover, according to this theory, unlike the "economic man," the "administrative man" does not have the capacity to maximize by selecting the best alternative from those available to him. Instead, he satisfices by making choices using a narrow-minded approach. He "looks for a course of action that is satisfactory or 'good enough'" (p. xxix). However, there is nothing narrow-minded in satisfying. Most individuals will try to reach a decision that maximizes, but the circumstances will make them settle for a decision that satisfies because that is the best decision considering the situation. In fact, economic theory (for which Simon won a Nobel Prize in 1978) has consistently shown that the "economic man" satisfies, at least in the pursuit of profits, rather than maximizes.

Given the premises of his theory ("administrative man" is a satisfier), Simon stated that vertical specialization (division of decisionmaking duties between operative and supervisory personnel) "is essential to achieve coordination among the operative employees, permits greater expertise in the making of decisions and allows the operative personnel [street-level bureaucrat] to be held accountable for their decisions" (p. 9). This substitutes individual autonomy to make decisions with an organizational decisionmaking process (p. 8).

However, a side effect of specialization is an increase in discretion. As can be noted, it is this specialization that gives street-level bureaucrats the discretion and hence the power to apply rules as they see fit accordingly. A corollary follows: The individual's autonomy is not substituted; it is simply guided by the organizational decisionmaking process.

The Individualist Perspective

Anthony Downs (1967) defines bureaucrats (and, hence, street-level bureaucrats) as utility maximizers. These individuals are motivated to behave and make decisions by their individual motives. He identified five types of officials that fit two broadly defined categories: purely self-interested officials and mixed-motive officials.

Officials within the self-interested category include the climbers, whose most important values are attaining power, income, and prestige. This category also includes the conservers, whose actions will be geared toward maintaining the amount of power, money, and prestige that they already have. Climbers and conservers are motivated to act in a way that will produce the most benefits for themselves. Therefore, their superior, and the organization, can easily influence their decisions so long as they perceive that their interest will be actually served.

The second category includes the mixed-motive officials. These officials' motives are a combination of self-interest and altruism. This category includes the zealots, the advocates, and the statesmen. The ability of the organization to indoctrinate mixed-motive officials varies with each type. Mixed-motives officials are loyal to a larger number of values including seeking goals connected with the public interest. Each of the three types of mixed-motive offi-

cials has their own concept of what "public interest" is. Their concept, in turn, shapes the decisionmaking behavior related to their job.

The zealots, Downs explained, define public interest as "the promotion of very specific policy goals" (p. 101). They seek power for the sake of power and to promote the policies they are loyal to. They promote these policies even when colleagues and superiors disagree with them. Advocates, by contrast, are easily influenced by their colleagues, superiors, and subordinates. However, they are aggressive when pursuing policies and changes that benefit or enhance their own section in the organization or other sections. The other type of mixed-motive officials, the statesmen, are concerned with the "general welfare" and seeks power to be able to influence national policies and actions (p. 88). Specialization is a major constraint in the statesmen's pursuit for these broad goals. Downs implied that although statesmanship is verbally encouraged in bureaucracy, it is not rewarded. It can only be found at the lowest level because bureaucrats who exhibit such behavior are never promoted.

Downs concluded that most people become conservers. That is, they tend to avoid changes as they grow older and remain fixed in their positions. Downs also explained that this tendency of bureaucrats to become conservers "results from the basic personalities or expectations they bring with them" (p. 98). This view led him to develop the "'Law of Increasing Conservatism.' In every bureau, there is an inherent pressure upon the vast majority of officials to become conservers in the long run" (p. 99).

The Organization Perspective

Ralph Hummel's (1977) criticisms of bureaucracy—a system that produces bureaucrats whose only concerns are controlling and efficiently handling their cases—are perfectly justified if one accepts Robert Presthus' (1978) assertions about the level of influence that organizations have on their members. The question he addressed in *The Organizational Society* was why individuals accept such an imposition. The answer he provided is based on three typologies. First, and foremost, he contended that individuals have had to accommodate to the expectations of organizations, which has led to the growth of three personality types: the upward-mobiles, the indifferents, and the ambivalents (p. 5).

Basically, the underlying assumption of Presthus' theory is that individuals are indoctrinated by the organization, but they adapt to the organization's environment differently due to their socialization experience and, ultimately, their genetics. It follows then that individuals'—specifically street-level bureaucrats'—decisions will be a result of the interplay of organizational values, socialization experiences, and genetics.

The upward-mobiles are highly committed to their work. Their behavior results from the need to avoid anxiety producing situations. They have great respect for organizational authority, are fully committed to the organization, and will act in an impersonal manner.

The second type of personality in Presthus' typology is the indifferent. Presthus stated that the great majority of people who work in bureaucratic settings fall within this category. These people are disenchanted by the conditions in their workplace and their work. They refuse to compete for the rewards offered by the organization, have a tendency to reject majority values, have little loyalty for the organization, are white-collar workers, and focus on their leisure-time activities. Their origins are the working class or lower middle class.

Indifferents reflect the bureaucrats' characteristics described by Hummel (1977). Hummel stated that bureaucrats are not concerned with justice, freedom, violence, oppression, illness, death, victory, defeat, love, hate, salvation, and damnation, or with service delivery. Street-level bureaucrats who fall in this category will most likely be the ones to make the most impersonal decisions due to their lack of care for both the organization and their clients.

Last, the third type of personality described by Presthus is the ambivalent, or neurotic. "Creative and anxious, their values conflict with bureaucratic claims for loyalty and adaptability" (p. 228). According to Presthus, "the ambivalent's tragedy is that they care too much but can do too little " (p. 251). However, they are the organizational innovators. Presthus asserted that ambivalents have little career chances (p. 228).

The Environmentalist View

James Q. Wilson (1989) implies that street-level bureaucrats are cost minimizers. In this perspective, street-level bureaucrats' decisions are not only shaped by their attitudes (values, habits, beliefs, etc.) but also by the situation in which they operate and by their clients' attitudes. Wilson believes that workers value convenience and equity over accommodation and responsiveness. Workers try to minimize the burden of handling complicated, uncooperative, and demanding clients and the possibility that their decisions could later be considered unfair or unjustified (p. 52). Moreover, he stated that "the imperative of the situation more than the attitudes of the worker shape the way tasks are performed in welfare agencies." Thus, workers provided better services for those clients who helped them minimize their cost by cooperating, as opposed to those clients who refused to cooperate, therefore raising the workers' cost (p. 53).

In addition, Wilson stated that the conditions under which workers operate make a difference in their behavior. In instances where individuals must perform their duties under close supervision, their attitudes will have little influence on their behavior. In other instances, individual attitudes do more strongly affect behavior. Wilson further stated that organizations could change behavior without changing individuals' attitudes. This can be done by developing rules that specify how a job is to be performed and by strongly enforcing those rules.

Conclusion

Like regular people, street-level bureaucrats make decisions based on their personal beliefs and values. Notwithstanding, unlike regular people, their decisionmaking process in the context of their work is rather complicated. They must weigh their own values against those of the organization. At the same time, they have to apply their professional skills to successfully use the information provided by their clients. Finally, their decisions will be shaped by the context of the situation at hand.

PATRIA D. DE LANCER

BIBLIOGRAPHY

Downs, A., 1967. *Inside Bureaucracy.* New York: Little, Brown.
Goodsell, C., 1994. *The Case for Bureaucracy,* 3d ed. New Jersey: Chatham House.
Hummel, R., 1977. *The Bureaucratic Experience.* New York: St. Martin's.
Lewis, G. B., 1990. "In Search for the Machiavellian Milquetoasts: Comparing Attitudes of Bureaucrats and Ordinary People." *Public Administration Review,* vol. 50: 220–227.
Lipsky, M., 1980. *Street-Level Bureaucracy.* New York: Rusell Sage.
Presthus, R. V., 1978. *The Organizational Society.* New York: St. Martin's.
Preston, L. M., 1987. "Freedom and Bureaucracy." *American Journal of Political Science*: 773–795.
Simon, H. A., 1976. *Administrative Behavior: A Study of Decision-Making Processes in Administrative Organization,* 3d ed. New York: Free Press.
Wilson, J. Q., 1989. *Bureaucracy.* New York: Basic Books.

STRESS. The effect that environmental, organizational, job/role, or personal characteristics have on an individual's physical, emotional, and mental condition.

Everyone is always under some type of stress, whether positive or negative. Holidays, vacations, and outstanding personal achievements could produce positive stress, whereas divorce, death of a spouse, or losing a job could produce negative stress, or distress.

Environmental factors also cause stress. Employees in the United States, like those in Japan and Canada, seem more vulnerable to stress because they take fewer vacation days than employees in Austria, Brazil, Denmark, or Sweden. Poor lighting, uncomfortable temperatures, inadequate work space, outdated equipment, and noise create stress in work environments (Eisenberg and Goodall 1993). Efforts to satisfy customers cause frustration when there are barriers that are beyond employees' control, such as unnecessary procurement regulations or rigid procedural requirements.

Some individuals can tolerate more stress than others. Type A personalities, who are competitive, hard-driving, and continually active, are more vulnerable than Type B personalities. Individuals experiencing problems in their personal lives are more vulnerable than others.

High blood pressure, a physiological indicator of stress, is part of the "fight-or-flight response." This response was first described by Walter Cannon of the Harvard Medical School. When an animal perceives a threatening situation, much as a person's perception of a stressful situation requiring a behavioral adjustment, the hypothalamus in the brain signals release of epinephrine and norepinephrine (also called adrenalin and noradrenalin). These chemicals activate the nervous system and increase metabolism (oxygen consumption), blood pressure, heart rate, rate of breathing, amount of blood pumped by the heart, and amount of blood pumped to the skeletal muscles (Benson 1974). Suppose that an agency is "right-sizing" and many positions are being abolished and redesigned. Employees who learn that their jobs are being abolished could experience the "fight-or-flight response." Should they fight and resist the change or should they flee the agency? There is a high probability that when employees learn that their jobs are in jeopardy, they will experience stress. With the physiological reaction, increases in metabolism, blood pressure, and heart beat, they may also experience an emotional reaction, for example, anger. Because fighting and fleeing are generally unacceptable behaviors at work and lead to hypertension, managers and employees in agencies are developing skills in alternative behaviors, such as constructive confrontation and problem resolution.

According to R. Edward Bergmark (1991) in a 1990 Gallup study, 56 percent of the organizations surveyed reported emotional and mental health problems were "fairly pervasive" in their companies. Thirty-six percent reported that stress, anxiety, and depression greatly affected employees' abilities to function and that an employee suffering from stress, anxiety, or depression lost at least 16 days of work per year. The American Institute of Stress estimated that stress disorders cost US $100 billion per year in absenteeism and reduced productivity ("How Business Beats Stress" 1985).

Employees are winning lawsuits based on claims that their employers are liable for mental and emotional problems and for stress that is work related. Employers are reacting to the litigiousness by developing strategies to help employees manage their stress. Generally, their concern goes beyond a reaction to litigiousness. Employers have humanitarian motives based on the beliefs that a trained employee is a valuable asset to the organization and that, if possible, that valuable asset should be protected. Employers would also like to reduce the costs associated with employees' stress, for example, absenteeism, accidents, health claims, turnover, and low productivity.

One strategy for prevention and treatment of stress used in both private- and public-sector organizations is the employee assistance program (see **alcoholism**, **wellness programs**, and **crisis intervention**). Comparing the economic benefits the organization derived to their cost, Kennecott Copper Company in Ogden, Utah estimated a 6 to 1 benefit to cost ratio per year for an employee assistance program that assisted troubled employees. Kennecott conducted a study of 150 men referred to the program for treatment of alcoholism and stress disorders; their average treatment period was 12.7 months. Comparisons made before and after treatment showed that their absenteeism decreased 52 percent; weekly indemnity decreased 74.6 percent; and health, medical, and surgical costs decreased 55.3 percent after treatment.

Organizations can implement stress management strategies, such as the Japanese "hostility rooms," where employees may go for stress relief, or job redesign so that employees are challenged without unreasonable demands for productivity. Some public agencies provide training to help employees manage stress in their lives. For example, a facilitator of a program for managers and employees in the U.S. Internal Revenue Service (IRS) and the U.S. Small Business Administration enabled employees to assess the degree of stress they were experiencing and learn and practice various stress management techniques, such as participative management, coping skills, improvements in nutrition, and aerobic, stretching, and relaxation exercises. This process resembles the model for total stress management in the United Kingdom, where the problems associated with stress at work are acute. The IRS also provides facilitators and allows time for team-building sessions. In these sessions, employees learn to confront, discuss, and resolve issues that cause stress at work. Some stressors that are addressed in such sessions are diversity of ideas, management practices, race, gender, and expression of emotions at work.

Summary

The stress that employees continually experience, whether at home or at work, results in costs to organizations where they work. Whether it is fear of litigation, the need to reduce operating costs, or humanitarian concerns that precipitate the response, there is a need for employers to acknowledge the impact of stress, to facilitate programs to enable employees to assess the extent to which stress effects their lives, to implement stress reduction programs, to implement employee assistance programs, and to provide adequate health benefits so that employees have access to adequate treatment. In addition, stress is an issue for policymakers in the United States, who are exploring alternative health care programs and considering the viability of provisions for mental health care.

BONNIE G. MANI

BIBLIOGRAPHY

Benson, Herbert, 1974. "Your Innate Asset for Combating Stress." *Harvard Business Review,* vol. 52, no. 4 (July-August): 49–60.
Bergmark, R. Edward, Marcie Parker, Philip H. Dell, and Cynthia Polich, 1991. "EA Programs: The Challenge, the Opportunity." *Employee Assistance* (July) 9.
Eisenberg, Eric M., and H. L. Goodall, 1993. *Organizational Communication: Balancing Creativity and Constraint.* New York: St. Martin's.
"How Business Beats Stress" 1985. *The Economist* (U.K.), April 13: 83.

STRIKE. A collective action by workers to cease, slow down, or otherwise interfere with work in order to secure or resist a change in wages, benefits, or working conditions, to express a grievance, or to protest an unfair labor practice by the employer. A strike is a temporary action, with employees expecting to return to their jobs after the dispute has been resolved. It is permitted for private-sector workers in the United States by the National Labor Relations Act of 1935 and by statute or the courts for certain public-sector employees in 12 states. The right to strike is a fundamental part of the private-sector labor relations process, as is its counterpart, the management "lock out" of employees from their place of work. In the public sector, however, strikes are prohibited in most jurisdictions, and disputes are settled through other dispute resolution procedures such as mediation and arbitration.

The term "strike" originates from sailors taking down, or "striking," their sails to stop work. Strike actions evolved from protests by individual workers to collective protests and work stoppages. There were waves of strikes throughout Europe and Great Britain in the early 1800s and general uprisings among many workers. One strike in Lyon, France, in 1834 required 20,000 soldiers to restore order. General strikes, which are job actions by all or most of the workforce in a jurisdiction or industry, were conducted during these years. In some instances, groups of rural workers known as Luddites, after leader Ned Ludd in Great Britain, sabotaged machinery, railroads, and printing presses to protest the rise of technology. Another round of serious strikes led by miners occurred in Europe in the 1880s.

In the United States, strikes have been rather common, especially in industry. But there have also been a large number of strikes by government employees, as documented by David Ziskind (1971) in *One Thousand Strikes of Government Employees.* Early work stoppages include an 1835 action by civilian Navy yard workers seeking better hours and improved working conditions and an 1880 strike by Pennsylvania teachers. Early federal employee work stoppages took place in the Government Printing Office (1863) and in federal arsenals (1890s).

The first significant wave of public employee strikes in the United States occurred in the early 1900s. Watertown Arsenal workers struck over the introduction of time and motion techniques in 1911, and workers engaged in a variety of lines of work ranging from moth control to grave digging walked off their jobs as well. Firefighters struck in many jurisdictions all over the United States from 1903 to 1921, as did police, seeking shorter hours, improved conditions of work and higher pay. One such strike occurred in Boston in 1919, when police officers walked out over extremely low wages and long hours. The police organization, affiliated with the American Federation of Labor (AFL), struck after lodging multiple protests to the police commissioner. The commissioner fired them all, but law and order quickly broke down. Governor Calvin Coolidge responded with the state militia and made his famous declaration that "there is no right to strike against the public safety by anybody, anywhere, anytime." Eventually new police officers were hired and the crisis abated. Many of the dismissed officers' demands were granted to the new policemen. The AFL suffered a serious blow, however, as all 37 of its chartered police units were dechartered.

It is difficult to analyze strike data in the United States after 1980, because that was the last year that complete data were collected by the Bureau of Labor Statistics. We do know that a smaller percentage of public employees go out on strike, and when they do it is for much shorter periods of time, when comparisons are made with the private sector. The top year for strikes in government was 1979, when nearly 500 work stoppages occurred in federal, state, and local government. Since then the number has decreased dramatically, probably because of the effectiveness of other dispute resolution procedures and the increasing taxpayer resentment of government and its employees. Not to be overlooked is the importance of the 1981 strike by the Professional Air Traffic Controllers Organization (PATCO), which was countered by a very unsympathetic President Ronald Reagan, who discharged all strikers and refused to hire them back. The message was quite clear to unions at all levels of government. From 1986 to 1990, there was an average of fewer than 30 strikes per year.

An important factor in discouraging strikes in both the public and private sectors is the hiring of permanent replacement workers. A 1989 Supreme Court decision up-

held the right of employers to hire permanent replacements for workers who walk off the job and to favor workers who stay on the job when their colleagues strike. Moreover, public opinion has turned against the unions on this issue and against unions in general. The result has been less dramatic alternatives to a full-blown strike, such as slowdowns, work-to-the-rule, filing unfair labor practice charges (see **unfair labor practice**), and filing grievances (see **grievance machinery**).

Debate over whether or not public employees should have the legal right to strike has been ongoing since the early 1880s. It is perhaps the most controversial issue in public-sector labor relations. Several arguments are used in opposition to strikes. The sovereignty argument asserts that constitutionally sovereignty is vested in the American people, and the people's workers should not be permitted to strike because it directly challenges the people's will and undermines the authority of government. It is argued that public employee strikes distort the political process by giving a special interest group—a union—political and policy advantages over other interest groups. It is also said that there is an absence of constraints in the labor market to hold down public employee personnel costs if the strike is permitted, because public services are essentially monopolistic. Relatedly, public employees are said to be engaged in providing essential services for which there are no adequate substitutes in the private sector. A strike of an essential service poses unacceptable threats to public health and safety, and takes advantage of a tendency of public officials to cave in to public pressure to settle a strike on terms favorable to the union.

Those in favor of a legal right of public employees to strike point out that not all government services are essential to health and safety in any immediate sense, and strikes would not be unduly disruptive of citizens' lives. And there are private-sector alternatives for many government services, such as private schools and sanitation collection. In some cases, public- and private-sector workers are involved in identical work, yet the right to strike is denied only to the former. For instance, private and nonprofit hospital employees may legally strike, but public hospital workers cannot. It is further observed that strike bans are not particularly effective in preventing strikes. Strikes continue to take place whether or not they are forbidden by law, and in those states that permit public employee strikes, the incidence of such job actions has not been higher than in states that continue to prohibit the strike. It should also be noted that public employers are much more able to cope effectively with strikes today than they once were and public opinion tends to support a hard line by public management against strikes. There are also substantial pressures on public employees to settle a strike quickly, because they do not receive their paychecks while they are off the job and very rarely does their union have a strike fund to help employees make ends meet until the next paycheck.

As noted, strikes are legal under the National Labor Relations Act (NLRA), although some restrictions are placed on work stoppages by the Taft-Hartley amendments to the NLRA. For example, in stoppages that threaten public health and safety, the president may order hearings and issue an 80-day injunction against the strike during which the Federal Mediation and Conciliation Service may intervene.

Federal employees are flatly prohibited from engaging in work stoppages by Public Law 330 (1955) and the Civil Service Reform Act of 1978. Members of the armed forces are prohibited from striking by a Department of Defense directive. In state and local government, strikes have been prohibited by state laws, attorney general opinions, court decisions, and local ordinances. A big round of strike prohibitions came after the Boston police strike and another just after World War II. The constitutionality of these antistrike laws has been upheld consistently by the courts.

Today public employee strikes are outlawed in 37 states, and the vast majority of collective bargaining contracts contain no-strike clauses to prevent strikes during the life of a negotiated contract. But 12 states legislatively grant the right to strike for some state and local employees under certain conditions. Vermont was the first to legalize strikes in 1967 for nonessential local government services. Pennsylvania followed in 1970. Other states include Alaska, Hawaii, Montana, Minnesota, Oregon, Rhode Island, Illinois, Wisconsin, and Ohio.

These statutes generally prohibit police, correctional workers, firefighters, and hospital workers from going out on strike. Most also require that specific steps and conditions be complied with before a strike is called by the union. Among common prestrike conditions are submission of the dispute to mediation, fact-finding, or other techniques. Notice is also required. Slightly different conditions prevail in the 5 states in which judicial decisions have granted the right to strike (for example, nurses in West Virginia and teachers in Louisiana). A peculiar situation prevails in California, where the state supreme court declared that in the absence of express language forbidding strikes, local government workers can legally walk off the job. The practical impacts of this apparent intrusion on legislative domain have been negligible.

Public employees strike for any number of reasons. According to Bureau of Labor Statistics figures that were kept until the early 1980s, economic disputes fostered the largest percentage of strikes (65 percent), followed by union organization and security (14 percent), and administrative matters (13 percent). Interunion and intraunion disputes accounted for only 1 percent of government work stoppages since 1964, compared to 12 percent in the private sector, with the differential being largely because public-sector unions have avoided the destructive organizing conflicts that have been so common in the private sector. The official figures tell an incomplete story, because they rely on reasons officially reported for strikes. Often there are many hidden factors underlying work stoppages such as the prevailing relationship between union and management, or conditions specific to a jurisdiction.

The highest proportion of strikes in government has been recorded in the relatively homogeneous unions of teachers, firefighters, police, and sanitation workers, where working conditions can be dangerous and problems are relatively well defined.

Various microlevel variables are also related to strike activity. For example, research indicates that men are more likely to favor job actions than women, and the young are more militant than the old. The higher the level of formal education, the lower the propensity to strike. Job satisfaction is negatively related to strike behavior.

Another factor influencing strike behavior is the bargaining power of the respective parties. Strong unions, according to research by Burton and Krider, are less likely to strike than weak unions for two reasons: The employer tends to be more generous in collective bargaining because of the fear of a costly confrontation, and strong unions are more willing to accept less than what they could actually win through a work stoppage, because they do not want to seriously damage the employer. Relative bargaining power fluctuates with economic and labor market conditions, the strength and commitment of union members, the union's ability to control the labor market, the leadership skills and effectiveness of union and management leaders and negotiators, public opinion, and many other variables.

Strikes may also ensue from faulty negotiations, as one or both parties misjudge the other's true bargaining interests, willingness to engage in a strike, or understanding of what a reasonable settlement would resemble. Collective negotiations can collapse from inept performances by negotiators, personality conflicts, unrealistic demands, and general inability to communicate between the parties.

The tactics employed by the union in a strike situation vary. Usually a formal majority vote of the members of the bargaining unit occurs following the membership's rejection of the final contract proposal by the employer. After the strike vote, the union attempts to put maximal pressure on the employer and elected officials to settle. Media coverage is orchestrated for maximal effect. News briefings, press conferences, advertisements, and displays of solidarity for the broadcast media are all part of the script. Picket lines offer high visibility and may, if honored by nonstriking workers, cause new problems for management (see **picketing**).

Union leadership does not normally call a strike without carefully calculating the possible ramifications and the odds of winning concessions. A strike committee, composed of stewards and various other representatives, helps weigh the costs and benefits of further escalating activities or making concessions. Above all, union leaders attempt to maintain the support of the bargaining unit membership. Unlike in the private sector, unions in government seldom have a strike fund to help workers make financial ends meet while they go without a paycheck, which is not surprising, since work stoppages are illegal in most public jurisdictions. This factor helps increase pressure on union members to reach a rapid resolution of the dispute.

RICHARD C. KEARNEY

BIBLIOGRAPHY

Edwards, P. K., 1981. *Strikes in the United States, 1881–1974.* New York: St. Martin's.

Kearney, Richard C., 1992. *Labor Relations in the Public Sector.* New York: Marcel Dekker: Chapter 6.

Paterson, Lee T., and John Liebert, 1974. *Management Strike Handbook.* Chicago: International Personnel Management Association.

Saso, Carmen D., 1970. *Coping with Public Employee Strikes.* Chicago: Public Personnel Association.

Ziskind, David, 1971. *One Thousand Strikes of Government Employees.* Salem, NH: Ayer.

STRUCTURE (ORGANIZATIONAL).

The apportionment of cooperative effort of people in an organization into units, subunits, and management positions, and the arrangement of authority relationships and communication channels (both top-down and bottom-up) within and between these entities. Such structure is a framework through which the purposes, objectives, and tasks to be achieved are both separated and integrated. Through separation of duties, structure clarifies who should do what. The way these duties are integrated explains to the members of the organization how they should work together.

In defining organizational structure, at least three issues should be addressed:

1. What should the units of the organization be? Traditionally, all key activities derived from organizational goals require organizational representation. Basically all the activities in an organization belong to one of four categories (Drucker 1973):

   - top management activities (maintaining external relations, envisioning the organization's mission, making decisions during major crisis situations, and building the human aspects of the organization);
   - results-producing activities (operations directly producing revenues or services);
   - results-contributing, or staff, activities (advising, teaching, training, legal research, etc.);
   - hygiene and housekeeping activities (such as employee assistance, cleaning, etc.).

2. What should the relationships between different types of organizational units be? The types of activities listed above should be treated differently in terms of their contributions, thus determining ranking and placement of organization units. Accordingly,

- results-producing activities should never be subordinate to nonresult activities;
- support activities should never be mixed up with results-producing activities;
- top-management activities are incompatible with other activities;
- advisory staff should be few, lean, and nonoperational; advisory work should not be a lifetime career, but rather a temporary function of growing career professionals;
- hygiene and housekeeping activities should be kept separate from other work or else they will not get done.

3. Where should decisions be carried out and to whom are they addressed? Typically, managers are advised that decisions are to be made as close to the place of action as possible and by those who have detailed knowledge and greatest experience on the subject; however, decisions should be made at a high enough level so that managers who must share a decision do share it and those managers and employees who must at least know about it do know.

The design and redesign of organizational structure is a search for particular answers to these three basic questions. There are also several important basic elements to be dealt with in order to build organizational structure:

- Specialization (division of labor, functionalization) is a process of decomposition of overall tasks of the organization into smaller activities and of assigning them to particular units or members of an organization that are professionally competent to do them.
- Standardization sets definite requirements as to how different operations inside the organization should be fulfilled in a uniform and consistent manner. It provides criteria against which the performance of organization units may be assessed, that is, how members are measured in order to monitor internal operations.
- Coordination is a combination of procedures integrating the operations of different units and members of an organization. These procedures can be both formal and informal. In more bureaucratic organizations, established rules and standards are often quite enough to link the operations. In less structured organizations, coordination requires spe-

cial attention in order to funnel the activities in the direction of established goals, and it is based to a much greater extent on informal procedures.

- Authority is a characteristic of decisionmaking and activation of these decisions. It answers the question who—in what situation—has the right to decide and to act. The major issues are how authority is distributed among the levels of management and to what extent functions are centralized or decentralized. Authority represented as a chain of command flows from the first person in the organization to the bottom line manager. Information and communication from the bottom to the top of the organizational structure flows back through the same channels as the chain of command. Proper distribution of authority should meet the following requirements:

1. The occupants of managerial positions who are responsible for certain functions have to be given enough authority to exercise them.
2. Proper span of control should be established. Span of control, or span of management, refers to the number of positions that one manager can supervise. The smaller the span of control, the more levels of management exist in the organization.
3. The number of levels of management should be defined in order to maintain a proper balance between them and the span of control. Usually, it depends on the size of the organization, particularly the number of employees. Downsizing the organization through removal of middle managers' positions increases the span of control and results either in the partial loss of control or in less specialization of management.
4. Degree of centralization of authority should be properly established. The more authority that is delegated to lower-level managers, the less is the level of centralized control, and the more open and flexible is the organization.

The authority-oriented chain of command represents the vertical dimension of organizational structure. The horizontal dimension is defined by the way the basic operations of the organization are structured and assigned to organizational units. Subdividing operations of an organization and assigning them to particular units or groups of employees is called departmentalization. Departmentalization is based on specialization and standardization of work, and its major goal is to assign people and establish operations in such a way that decisions and information flow easily through the organization. The particular type of departmentalization depends upon which goals are viewed by management as most important, the size of the organization, and so forth. If the priority of goals is changing, or if the organization is growing quickly, departmentalization also is modified.

There are several traditionally recognized types of organizational structures (Heyel 1982; Nixon 1992). Some of them may be called elementary, or basic, types of organization structure. They are the simplest forms and are used to design more complex organizations.

Basic Structures

Although organizations can be structured along product (service) lines, geographic specific or demographic specifics, from an organizational perspective, there are two basic structures—line and functional—that repeat in different permutations in all organizations.

Line Structure

This is the simplest one. It assumes a direct line of responsibility and control from the general manager to intermediate "line" executives, then to lower-level managers and supervisors, and then to employees. Line and staff structure was developed to provide line executives in large and complex organizations with specific advice on particular functions (research and development, planning, distribution, public relations, etc.). In smaller organizations, these functions may be assigned just to one assistant. In bigger organizations, these are usually units that form staff departments, supplementing the line organization.

Functional Structure

This is a pure form strongly advocated by Frederick Taylor under the rubric of "functional foremanship." Under a pure functional structure, "superspecialization" assumes that one person is in charge of production, one is responsible for scheduling, one for maintenance, and so on. And all of them deal directly with the workers. This arrangement does not work because of the practical difficulties that emerge when one employee has many different bosses. Instead, the principle of functional specialization is used to group similar positions that are needed to produce and sell or deliver a product or service to execute a definite function. In this arrangement, the chain of command flows downward from the chief executive to the deputies, who are responsible for execution of specific functions. Line managers report to the deputies on these specific functions. Further down the hierarchy, tasks are also divided functionally by process.

Functional structures are typically used by smaller organizations employing a simpler technology and operating in a more stable and simple environment (Daft 1985); however, the functional principle is easily applicable to all sizes and types of organizations. The major advantages are the efficiencies and economies of scale that result from the grouping of specialists within each function. These specialists can attain in-depth skill development. People with the same orientation are grouped together, which promotes skill specialization and reduces duplication of resources. It enhances quality and professionalism.

The major disadvantage is the difficulty of achieving cross-departmental communication, cooperation, and coordination. Specialists within a functional department tend to focus on the pursuit of departmental goals rather than to cooperate with other functional departments in the pursuit of organizational goals. Under such a structure, problems between functional departments may be solved only by a high-level manager who has authority over conflicting departments. These coordination difficulties may increase the organization's response time to environmental threats and opportunities. It takes time, but even when the problem finds this "cross-over" point, the occupant of the coordinating position may be too distant from the problem to be of much help (Mintzberg 1979). Besides, a functional orientation emphasizes routine tasks, encourages narrow perspectives, and obscures accountability for outcomes.

Hybrid Structures

Depending on specific characteristics and tasks of real organizations, their organizational structure is usually a combination of the elements of basic structures. Such structures are called "hybrid structures."

Line and Functional Staff Structure

This type combines the advantages of the line and staff organization and functional specialization. Functional staff departments are given responsibility and authority over specialized operations (inspection, employment, purchasing, etc.). These functions are performed by specialized personnel, apart from the line operators, who are responsible to their own line supervisors. If there is a disagreement between a staff and line operating unit, it may be solved only by the manager who has authority over both units; that is, staff units may influence line operations only through the line manager who has the requisite level of authority.

In big organizations, staff functions may be decentralized. Separate operating units, like plants in big corporations or regional divisions of governmental agencies, have their owns staff departments responsible to the local operating manager. Central management retains staff departments serving in an advisory and resource capacity to the local staff functions. Often such hybrid organization structure incorporates both operating units and functional departments centralized and located at the top management level of organization. This kind of arrangement may often be found in connection with divisional structure.

Divisional Structure (Self-Contained Unit, Profit Center)

Divisional structure is the most widely used further modification of the line and functional staff type of organization structure for big organizations. As an organization becomes larger (more employees or participants) and more complex in terms of the number and/or types of products, services, and operations, there is a tendency to switch to a divisional structure. Divisional structure groups, under a single manager, include positions whose occupants are performing dissimilar functions but are focusing on a specific product, service, or group of them; a specific customer or customer/client group; or a particular geographical region.

Divisional structure is typically used by larger organizations that are employing a more complex technology and operating in a more unstable and complex environment. Its major advantages are better coordination between and among functions within the division or self-contained unit and a more intense focus on the product, service, or operation. This provides faster response to environmental threats and opportunities. The major disadvantages of divisional structure are the reduction of the benefits in specialization compared to functional structure, and the difficulties in achieving coordination across the divisions (Daft 1985).

In large organizations facing an uncertain external environment, a high level of centralization of management of both staff functions and divisional operations may bring an additional advantage as it combines a high level of coordination in divisional structure with the specialization of such functional areas like research and development or information processing at the top of the organization. However, although the role of functional managers at the top is to advise and provide services to divisional managers (and employees inside divisions), there is always a high probability of conflicts between them.

Line, Functional Staff, and Committee Structure

In addition to the previous model, this structure uses task committees for solving complex problems in order to facilitate coordination and cooperation. Committees are established for special duties and may be permanent or "standing" committees or set up for temporary needs only.

Depending on what power of authority is given to a committee, it may be either a pure consulting body or a decisionmaker. In the first case, a committee has limited functions inside the traditional closed model of formal organization. In the last case, when committees are given important managerial functions, the organization structure is dramatically changed. Such an arrangement is a further response to growing uncertainty and complexity of the environment, and is called ad-hocracy; the term was first used by Alvin Toffler (1970) in *Future Shock*.

The core idea of ad-hocracy is less emphasis on hierarchy and more on collaboration between participants in changing relations. Ad-hocracy is in part a synonym for the structure built after an open model of formal organization. Ad-hocracy is highly flexible and capable of going from one complex task to another with minimal delay. Ad-hocracy involves breaking the rules of traditional organizational structures: level of specialization is relatively low; the classical requirement of reporting to one's boss does not work; the number of different jobs and positions is less than in a closed bureaucratic organization; control is achieved through the commitment of the employees to the organization's mission rather than through hierarchy; and decisionmaking is by those who have professional competence to solve the problem, not merely the formal occupants of managerial positions. Ad-hocracy groups the specialists in functional units for housekeeping purposes only. To do their work, they are deployed in project teams.

Matrix Structure

The earliest example of hybrid organization structure built on the ad-hocracy principle is the matrix structure. This ad-hocracy-type of organization may be called a "superhybrid structure." It uses simultaneous arrangements of both a functional and a divisional structure. An important and unique feature of this structure is that employees may report to more than one boss. Functional units are responsible for developing and deploying, in the form of narrowly skilled specialists, a technical resource. Project (product, service) managers are responsible for project completion. The major goal of such a complicated arrangement is a balance of authority between project and functional managers. Otherwise, if the project manager dominates, the customer's needs (particular schedule requirements, costs, product features) may be met, yet the result may be immature. If the functional manager dominates, the final product may be superior, but the project may continue forever, costs may skyrocket, and the final product may have many more features than the customer requested. Basically there are three reasons why organizations may consider using matrix structure:

1. The necessity to deal with large flows of complex information. Matrix structure is most suitable for coping with information overload. It offers possibilities for both vertical and horizontal sharing of information among large numbers of individuals inside an organization. In an unstable and relatively unpredictable environment, it offers more possibilities for reasonable responses to emerging problems.

2. The possibility of more effectively sharing scarce and/or expensive resources. It allows for economy of scale because of sharing specialists and resources of functional units across divisions or projects.

3. The possibility of a dual focus on organizational technology (functional units) and product, on services or operations (divisional units, projects). This is of crucial importance in organizations, both private and public, dealing with high technologies. Design and production of complex technological systems require organizations to pay equal attention both to technical issues and requirements for every particular project.

The major disadvantages of the matrix structure result from its advantages. Dual command structure places constant stress on employees and produces power struggles for dominance between functional and project (divisional) managers. These disadvantages, however, may be overcome if formal introduction of a matrix structure is accompanied by the efforts to also change the climate of the organization and the relationships of an organization's members. Conflict in organizational structures (i.e., project versus function or line versus staff) should be continually resolved in formal organizations, especially those built on a closed model.

Line authority exists along the chain of command and is dedicated to the achievement of the organization's main goals. Functional authority is "the right that an individual or department has delegated to it over specified processes, practices, policies, or other matters relating to activities undertaken by personnel in departments other than its own" (Koontz and O'Donnell 1974 p. 175). Staff or functional positions provide information, advice, and services to line positions. In some structures, they are engaged also in control activities: monitoring how line or divisional managers follow personnel, financial, and other policies or controlling product development and the production project in a matrix structure. Degrees of such conflicts may vary due to the authority of staff or functional specialists and managers.

When staff advice is given only by request (advisory staff), line managers may accept or reject it. In other cases, line managers must obtain staff advice, but need not accept it (compulsory staff). When organizational structure includes concurring staff authority, line managers and staff specialists must mutually agree on the decision. In the case of functional authority, as in matrix structure, the project (line, divisional) manager must request and accept the opinion of the staff (functional) specialist prior to making a decision in the specialist's area of expertise. In the last two cases, the line manager may receive an "advisory" (i.e., policy memo) conflicting not only with personal judgment, but also with the orders of the immediate line boss or with the "advice" of other staff or functional specialists (Gerloff 1985).

In the case of matrix structure, one of the major managerial tasks of a project (product) manager is coordination and resolution of conflicts between functional specialists participating in the same project. Conflicts themselves are not necessarily negative. What really often causes friction is lack of clarity in understanding the line-staff concept.

Network Structure

Another type of organizational structure, which is one of the most recent, is "network." An organization with a network structure contracts out all aspects of the operations. It puts together complete packages by contracting with manufacturers, transporters, marketing companies, and retail stores/chains. Any needed function is obtained with a phone call. Products never come near the company's doors. Network organizations are mainly industrial companies that do not possess an industrial production facility. They represent organizational structure for the postindustrial era. The network organization can take advantage of new technologies and markets, as well as of cheap foreign labor. Following the divisional structure of the 1920s and the post–World War II matrix structure, the network organizational structure represents the third major organizational innovation.

Some traditional businesses, such as publishers, construction firms, and clothes manufacturers, have always contracted out work. Recent improvements in communications have made it possible for many more types of businesses to enter this type of operation through coordination of suppliers, producers, and customers worldwide. At any one time, all of the functions of a traditional organization are in place through contractual arrangements. From a structural point of view, there is a dramatic difference between network and traditional, that is, divisional, structure. In network organizations, a chain of command, or hierarchy, is replaced by a chain of purchase orders and relationships to other organizations. For people affiliated with network structure, such financial or legal skills are less important than the ability to catch trends and to develop strong outside relationships with suppliers and customers. Making contacts and networking are their basic skills.

The advantages of network structure are that it is dynamic and fast moving, it reduces overhead expenses, it needs less capital investment, it is highly innovative, and it may quickly adopt new outside technologies. Projects (or products) that become unprofitable can easily be terminated. On the negative side, network organization is very sensitive to competition from suppliers if they are selling on the same market or to the competitors. Production and quality cannot be directly controlled. Network organizations do not do research and development, so they cannot create new products themselves. Their earnings are often rather unstable.

Although contracting out is a widespread practice in public-sector organizations, there are virtually no examples of network structure inside the public sector.

More and more organizations are presently turning to new ideas. One of these is the idea of the "virtual organization" or "virtual office," first introduced by Toffler (1981). From an organizational structure perspective it means introduction of a "structureless organization." But how can an organization not have an organizational structure? What is behind these ideas? Actually, a network organization is very close to a structureless organization. Hierarchy is almost eliminated. Employees, but not organizational units, are performing major operations. But the modern world of real organizations offers examples of further advances in this direction.

In 1994, Chiat/Day Inc., an advertising agency, introduced the concept of the virtual office. It was considered as part of a corporate emphasis on continually enhancing client service, improving staff satisfaction and creativity, and boosting bottom-line results. In the "virtual office" of the Chiat/Day headquarters in Venice, California, employees are no longer bound by either the management or physical constraints of a conventional office environment. A special team architecture concept was implemented: Office space was subdivided into conference rooms and zones, compartmentalized by activities. Instead of traditional operational and functional departments, temporary strategic business units were introduced. These units focus entirely on a single client. Due to the most advanced communication system (local computer network, dial-up computer access technology), the employees can get any information they need from any place both inside and outside the office building. They are free to define their working schedule and adjust it to their client's needs in order to share their time between several strategic business units and activities. The number of such organizations will grow in the future, providing new possibilities for successful performance under conditions of uncertainty and constant change.

Public organizations have historically adopted orthodox patterns of structure. However, as a function of the continuing "tax revolt," that is, shrinking resources that generate pressures to become more productive and to contract out, the public sector has become more structurally adaptive. Matrix organization is more evident, particularly in terms of task forces and teams. Network structure will become a necessary adaptation to the extent that public agencies are forced (politically and financially) to shift services from management of in-house production (i.e., public employees) to oversight and coordination of contracted out services (i.e., employees of private-sector and not-for-profit organizations). On balance, however, the greater accountability required of the public sector acts as a countertendency, inclining public agencies to adopt conservative, low-risk patterns of behavior and, therefore, orthodox structures.

PAVEL MAKEYENKO,
VATCHE GABRIELIAN, AND
MARC HOLZER

BIBLIOGRAPHY

Daft, Richard L., 1985. *Organization Theory and Design.* New York: McGraw-Hill.
Drucker, Peter F., 1973. *Management: Tasks, Responsibilities, Practices.* New York: Harper & Row.
Gerloff, Edwin A., 1985. *Organization Theory and Design.* New York: McGraw-Hill.
Heyel, Carl, ed., 1982. *The Encyclopedia of Management.* New York: Van Nostrand Reinhold.
Koontz, H., and C. O'Donnell, 1974. *Essentials of Management.* New York: McGraw-Hill.
Mintzberg, Henry, 1979. *The Structuring of Organizations.* Englewood Cliffs, NJ: Prentice-Hall.
Nixon, Judith M., ed., 1992. *Organization Chart: Structures of More Than 200 Business and Non-Profit Organizations.* Detroit, MI: Gale Research.
Toffler, Alvin, 1970. *Future Shock.* New York: Random House.
———, 1981. *The Third Wave.* New York: Bantam Books.
"Virtual Office Runs on Telecommunications," 1994. *Managing Office Technology* (June) Bantam 57–58.

SUBSIDIARITY.

SUBSIDIARITY. The principle that states that a higher organizational unit of government assumes functions if and in so far as the lower units of which it is composed are unable to assume these functions as well or better.

Conceptual Problems

A discussion about the principle of subsidiarity inevitably runs into difficulties as a result of the lack of a generally accepted definition (which immediately relativizes the given definition). In general, the purpose of the principle is to limit the interference of the higher authority. However, there is no agreement about the questions to what extent and through what criteria this interference has to be limited.

First, it is important to point to the difference between the nonterritorial and territorial (or horizontal and vertical) concepts of subsidiarity. The first (and oldest) concept refers to the relationship between the private sector and the public sector, with the latter only intervening in order to support the private sector. The second (and now most frequently used) concept refers to the relationship between several levels of government.

Second, there are different views on whether the function of the principle of subsidiarity is to distribute powers or rather to regulate the exercise of powers and justify the use of powers in particular cases.

Third, there is a difference between the negative and the positive concepts of subsidiarity. The former refers to the limitation or even interdiction of the interference of the higher organization in relation to the lower units if certain criteria are fulfilled. The latter refers to the possibility or even obligation of interventions of the higher organization if certain criteria are fulfilled.

Fourth, there are different opinions about the degree of obligation or interdiction to interfere or not to interfere. For instance, is the higher entity "allowed" or "obliged" to interfere when certain criteria are met? Fifth, there are different views on whether the principle of subsidiarity can be used only to transfer power from the higher to the lower unit or also from the lower to the higher unit.

Finally, disagreement exists concerning the criteria to interdict or justify intervention. For instance, should the higher unit interfere when, in comparison with the lower unit, it can act "better," or more "efficiently," "effectively" or "satisfactorily"? Other possible criteria are the extent to which interference is "necessary" or to which a certain action has effects that extend beyond certain boundaries. The problem of criteria becomes even more complicated when these criteria are further qualified. For instance, is the higher entity allowed to intervene when the lower entity cannot act "efficiently," "efficiently enough," or "sufficiently efficient?"

Subsidiarity and Its Origin in Catholic Social Doctrine

The notion of subsidiarity can be traced back to Aristotle and has been used by Thomas Aquinas, Johannes Althusius, John Locke, Montesquieu, John Stuart Mill, Pierre-Joseph Proudhon, and others. It in particular gained importance through the work of nineteenth-century social Catholic thinkers in Germany, who had a considerable influence on sociopolitical ideas formulated by the Vatican. The principle of subsidiarity was explicitly mentioned for the first time as "principle of subsidiary function" in *Quadragesimo Anno* (1931), the encyclical of Pope Pius XI on reconstruction of the social order. This encyclical contains the following expression of this principle: "Just as it is gravely wrong to take from individuals what they can accomplish by their own initiative and industry and give it to the community, so also it is an injustice and at the same item a grave evil and disturbance of right order to assign to a greater and higher association what lesser and subordinate organizations can do" (paragraph 79).

The church's main intention was to restrict the state's interference, although the concept encapsulated also the idea that the state should intervene when necessary in order to supplement and help other bodies. Small social groups should be autonomous and sovereign in a pluralist society. They should be assisted in their activities, though by a state that neither substitutes for social groups nor is shackled by their demands but one that serves the public good and provides legal order.

In its Catholic origin, subsidiarity was concerned primarily with the ordering of relationships between the

public authorities and civil societies and was not related to the principle of territoriality. The principle of subsidiarity was a principle of social organization rather than a constitutional or legal concept. It was not a self-standing concept but a guideline to be applied in combination with other principles of social action. In Catholic social doctrine, the principle of subsidiarity was intrinsically linked with principles such as personalism, solidarity, pluralism, and distributive justice that have found their expression on the European continent in Christian democracy and in the Christian democratic version of the welfare state.

Subsidiarity in Federal States

Although in its Catholic origin, the principle of subsidiarity was not related to territoriality, it has increasingly been used to explain the relationship between territorial organizations: the supranational polity, the state, the region, and local communities. The focus on the relationship between territorial organizations explains why the principle of subsidiarity is most often associated with a federalist theory of the state (although, to a certain extent, it can also be applied in unitary states, such as in the relationship between local communities and the central government). The existence of a relationship between the principle of subsidiarity and federalism is clear. In a federal structure, powers or competences are shared between constituent bodies. The principle of subsidiarity can be one of the principles to guide the allocation of powers of competences and to achieve a vertical separation of powers. Its real impact is, however, less clear in view of the disagreement about both its exact definition and the possibility to operationalize this principle.

What is the role of the principle of subsidiarity in federal states? Although subsidiarity is considered as being inherently linked to the federal ideas, in most federal constitutions it has not been adopted explicitly as a general constitutional principle but has found its expression in lists of competences and "necessary and proper" clauses. The principle of subsidiarity does not rank among the main principles that were used to guide subsequent constitutional developments in federal states.

The principle of subsidiarity had a somewhat more important position in West Germany, which can be explained by the importance of subsidiarity as a sociophilosophical concept in West Germany. Although the principle is not explicitly mentioned in the German Basic Law of 1949, the idea of subsidiarity is at the foundation of Article 72 (second paragraph):

The Federation shall have the right to legislate in these matters to the extent that a need for regulation by federal legislation exists because:

1. a matter cannot be effectively regulated by the legislation of individual Länder ["states"], or

2. the regulation of a matter by a Land law might prejudice the interest of other Länder or of the people as a whole, or

3. the maintenance of legal or economic uniformity or living conditions beyond the territory of any one Land, necessitates such regulation.

Although the introduction of this principle into the Basic Law was to limit centralization, in practice there has been a shift of powers to the federal government. This reveals the weakness of the federal guarantee of subsidiary powers for the states. This weakness is also linked to the fact that, traditionally, the principle of subsidiarity has been considered as a political-philosophical concept rather than a general principle of German constitutional law. The principle of subsidiarity has never been a major subject in the political debate in Germany. This changed in the mid-1980s when the German regions emphasized this concept to protect the powers conferred upon them by the German federal constitution against a further transfer of power from the member states to the institutions of the European Union.

The notion of subsidiarity as a mechanism for reconceptualizing power sharing between regional and state governments has also been used at the beginning of the 1990s in discussions and negotiations in other federal states such as Australia and Canada—however, without major consequences. In Europe, the principle became increasingly important. First, because a growing number of states introduced multitiered governments of one sort or another. Second, because it became a major issue in the debate about the European integration process. Nevertheless, even in these cases where subsidiarity became more important, this principle seems to be used more as an ad hoc or ex post facto justification of new divisions of power than as an effective principle to divide competences between the different levels of government.

The Principle of Subsidiarity in the European Union

The Treaty on European Union of February 1992 introduced the concept of subsidiarity formally into the treaty provisions. The principle is mentioned first in the last paragraph of Article B of Title I ("Common Provisions") of the treaty: "The objectives of the Union shall be achieved as provided in this Treaty and in accordance with the conditions and the timetable set out therein while respecting the principle of subsidiarity as defined in Article 3b of the Treaty establishing the European Community."

Article 3b of Title II ("Provisions Amending the Treaty Establishing the European Economic Community with a View to Establishing the European Community") states:

The Community shall act within the limits of the powers conferred upon it by this Treaty and of the objectives assigned to it therein.

In areas which do not fall within its exclusive competence, the Community shall take action, in accordance with the principle of subsidiarity, only if and in so far as the objectives of the proposed action cannot be sufficiently achieved by the Member States and can therefore, by reason of the scale or effects of the proposed action, be better achieved by the Community. Any action by the Community shall not go beyond what is necessary to achieve the objectives of this Treaty.

After the signing of the Maastricht Treaty, discussion continued on whether the principle of subsidiarity was aimed either at regulating in a "neutral" way the exercise of the competences of the Union or at restricting European Community (EC) interference (as requested especially by the British government). The prior question, however, was whether this principle could be used at all for other than declaratory reasons. The ambiguity of the wording of Article 3b, the inclusion of criteria that are not always reconcilable, and the lack of clear guidelines for its operationalization gave rise to serious doubts about its applicability. Doubts also existed about the willingness of the Court of Justice to make judgments about this vague concept.

Despite these doubts, the principle of subsidiarity became increasingly popular in 1992–1993, as the EC leaders considered it as a politically useful instrument to answer the growing criticism against the Treaty on European Union and the shift of national sovereignty to the European Union. The European Council agreed in December 1992 in Edinburgh to the overall approach to the application of the subsidiarity principle and Article 3b. This approach implied a strengthening of the obligation to respect the principle of subsidiarity but at the same time severely restricted the possible consequences of the application of subsidiarity. In October 1993, an Interinstitutional Agreement was adopted by the European Parliament, the council, and the commission on procedures of implementing the principle of subsidiarity.

In November 1993, the commission proposed the withdrawal, revision, or simplification of commission proposals and existing legislation that were not fully justified in terms of subsidiarity. However, these proposals were more the result of a rationalization of community legislation than of a reexamination on the basis of subsidiarity considerations. The commission instructed its departments to ensure that each explanatory memorandum added to legislative proposals include detailed answers to a series of questions relating to the subsidiarity criteria (such as, What is the community dimension of the problem?, What is the most effective solution, given the means available to the community and to member states?, and What is the specific added value of the proposed community action and the cost of failing to act?).

The operational procedures accepted at the end of 1993 and in particular the questions defined by the commission can result in a certain degree of influence of the subsidiarity principle on decisionmaking in the European Union. The disagreement that remains between the member states on both the principle of subsidiarity and the aims of European integration calls into question the possible impact of this principle. The efforts to translate the subsidiarity principle into operational terms seemed indeed as much aimed at avoiding that this principle would change the existing distribution of powers and disturb the institutional balance as at assuring that the principle is transformed into a genuinely effective instrument. Day-to-day practice will have to indicate how the principle of subsidiarity will affect in reality the decisionmaking process and the union-state relationship within the European Union.

STEPHAN KEUKELEIRE

BIBLIOGRAPHY

Cass, Deborah Z., 1992. "The Word That Saves Maastricht? The Principle of Subsidiarity and the Division of Powers Within the European Community." *Common Market Law Review*, vol. 29, no. 6: 1107–1136.

Duff, Andrew, ed., 1993. *Subsidiarity within the European Community*. London: Federal Trust for Education and Research.

Emiliou, Nicholas, 1992. "Subsidiarity: An Effective Barrier against 'the Enterprises of Ambition'?" *European Law Review*, vol. 17, no. 5: 383–407.

Endo, Ken 1994. "The Principle of Subsidiarity: From Johannes Althusius to Jacques Delors." *The Hokkaido Law Review*, vol. 44, no. 6: 2064–1965.

Making Sense of Subsidiarity: How Much Centralization for Europe?, 1993. London: Centre for Economic Policy Research.

Neunreither, Karlheinz, 1993. "Subsidiarity as a Guiding Principle for European Community Activities." *Government and Opposition*, vol. 28, no. 2: 206–220.

Peterson, John, 1994. "Subsidiarity: A Definition to Suit Any Vision." *Parliamentary Affairs*, vol. 47, no. 1: 117–132.

Subsidiarity: The Challenge of Change, 1991. Maastricht: EIPA.

Weale, Albert, and Andrea Bosco, eds., 1994. *Federalism and Subsidiarity. A Definition and Comparison*. London: Lothian Foundation.

Wilke, Marc, and Helen Wallace, 1992. "Subsidiarity: Approaches to Power-Sharing in the European Community." *RIIA Discussion Papers*, vol. 27: 1–43.

SUGGESTION SYSTEMS.

"Formal, measurable processes for capturing, analyzing, implementing, and recognizing employee-generated organizational improvements" (Carnevale and Sharp 1993, p. 82).

Suggestion systems date to the human relations movement of the 1930s when organizations implemented them as a way to give employees an anonymous voice in airing complaints and identifying opportunities to improve production. The programs generally fell into disrepute as employers failed to take them seriously. Suggestion plans made a comeback in the 1960s and 1970s as various organizations restructured them to focus on cost reductions and to build morale. Employers also began to reward employees with small cash awards for the best ideas. These low-cost initiatives for eliciting employees' proposals were a precursor of modern problem solving groups in organizations (Applebaum and Batt 1994).

The principle concept behind suggestion systems is that knowledge is the key technology in organizations. Suggestion systems help organizations profit from the experience and know-how of staff. They support the notion that people closest to the point of production or service are often in the best position to improve work processes. Suggestion systems are formal methods designed to exploit the human capital assets, that is, the knowledge, skills, and abilities of people in organizations. The thought that competitive advantage resides in the knowledge base of organizations is at the heart of suggestionlike programs like quality circles, Rucker, Scanlan, and IMPROSHARE plans. Although there are variations in how each of these operate, all are forms of gain sharing or the idea of paying bonuses to employees based on improvements in operations (see Lawler 1986, pp. 144–169).

Suggestion systems are a form of employee participation. The virtues of employee participation have been known since the Hawthorne Studies. For example, participation improves decision quality, strengthens commitment to decision implementation, develops leadership skills, increases learning, and is a form of feedback in a work system (Levine and Strauss 1989). The increased use of participation to boost organizational achievement is the most common workplace reform in recent years. It is a central component in the Japanese management philosophy (Ouchi 1981), prescriptions for realizing excellence in organizations (Peters and Waterman 1982), methods to produce quality goods and services (Deming 1986), and recent initiatives to revitalize and reinvent government (Osborne and Gaebler 1992).

Suggestion systems are motivational. They appeal to both higher- and lower-order needs and provide both intrinsic and extrinsic rewards to people. They stimulate performance-to-reward expectancies, which energize employees into taking action to secure something they value. Involvement in a suggestions program also satisfies affiliation needs as well as ego concerns. Further, making suggestions on how to improve work are expressions of mastery, self-confidence, and desire to reach one's full potential. Even if a person's proposition is not accepted, it is likely that some positive notice will be forthcoming simply for making it.

Suggestion systems ease organizational communication. They help overcome the structural barriers that impede information flow in hierarchical organizations. They also provide opportunities for staff to talk about necessary improvements in work methods. The very existence of such programs transmits the symbolic message that the organization values what people know and welcomes their input.

Suggestion programs symbolize trust. Trust has major implications for organizational performance. The most important characteristic of trust is that it is a reciprocal attitude; people tend to trust those who demonstrate trust in them. Suggestion programs display trust in the motivation and competence of employees. Such faith is often self-fulfilling. This depends, of course, on the extent to which suggestion plans are credible. If the espoused theory that "we value and want your ideas" is experienced as empty rhetoric, suggestion designs will backfire and cause cynicism. Too often suggestion boxes become the focus of ridicule, monuments to management indifference to staff input.

In summary, suggestion policies are forms of employee involvement and participation that capitalize on the know-how of staff. Suggestion systems are motivational and, finally, are expressions of trust in the capacities of workers. Given the physics of trust formation, the high-trust aspects of suggestion programs are likely to be reciprocated by elevated trust in the organization.

A Typical Suggestion Process

There are various ways to structure suggestion systems. However, most share a set of common features. The first step in the process typically involves the suggestor identifying an idea and talking about it with the immediate supervisor. The recommendation is then formalized and submitted for analysis and review. The proposal is evaluated in terms of workability, alternatives, estimated savings, and implementation costs. If the idea is not accepted, the suggestor is notified of reasons for nonadoption or advice about resubmission. If the submission is sanctioned, there is customarily some public notice of the award and a presentation ceremony of some kind. The award itself can take many forms—ranging from a certificate of appreciation to the more typical sharing of some percentage of the actual savings with the suggestor(s). Public announcement of the award is important in demonstrating the kind of innova-

tive behavior that the organization is seeking from other employees and strengthens a program's credibility. Finally, the winning idea is put into practice.

Making Suggestion Systems Work

Since participation in suggestion systems is voluntary, the first problem in making them work is to find ways to get staff involved. There is a positive relationship between extent of employee involvement and the amount of cost savings realized by employers (U.S. Merit Systems Protection Board 1986; Carnevale and Sharp 1993). Therefore, it is crucial to a program's success that its existence is well advertised and that staff are encouraged to get involved.

Second, employees must be motivated to take part in the program. Suggestion systems are motivational only if sufficiently attractive rewards are available that stimulate workers to participate. The nature of the rewards should be varied since employees are interested in a wide variety of inducements. Finally, while a host of prizes are potentially motivational, the attractiveness of cash rewards should not be underestimated.

Third, organizations should consider using suggestion plans to reward teamwork. Much of the work accomplished in contemporary organizations arises out of group efforts. One of the persistent problems in human resources administration is finding a way to reward the contributions of work teams. Suggestion programs provide one answer to this predicament. In gain sharing, for instance, benefits are allotted above a certain baseline between the organization and employees at the work unit or suborganizational level. Moreover, rewarding teams, not just individuals, reinforces teamwork behaviors and reduces destructive competition that may arise in exclusively individual-based pay systems.

Fourth, suggestion program designs must decide whether employees ought to be rewarded for improvements they identify during the performance of their everyday responsibilities. Many suggestion programs subscribe to the view that employees are expected to be creative, and ideas on how to improve their jobs should not warrant additional remuneration. To realize a benefit, staff is expected to find winning proposals outside its ordinary scope of action. The wisdom of this perspective is questionable. Enhancing organizational performance is so critical in the public sector that persons who stretch themselves beyond the limits of their prescribed roles ought to be rewarded. People customarily know their own jobs best and need to be encouraged to improve them.

Fifth, suggestion programs must be integrated with other forms of workplace innovations. Too often, suggestions programs are tangential activities and, like recent organizational experiences with quality circles, will not work if they are not made part of more fundamental change strategies. It is not reasonable to expect that they will transform organizations into high performing systems by themselves.

Sixth, suggestion plans require top management support to work. Leaders show employees what is important to them not by what they talk about, but by how and where they spend their time. If suggestion programs are seen as a secondary consideration for leaders, that is the kind of priority they will get from the rest of the staff. If top leadership is serious about the potential benefits of such plans, they need to visibly and actively support them.

Seventh, cash savings should not be the only basis upon which suggestion policies are judged. In an era of resource scarcity, there is the temptation to conclude that only those ideas that save money are worthwhile. That kind of thinking limits the gains that can be realized from suggestion plans. For instance, identifying, analyzing, and submitting ideas for organizational improvement is a learning experience for everyone involved. The kind of analysis demanded by suggestion programs inevitably forces participants to better understand work processes, procedures, and objectives. Every proposal compels people, perhaps for the first time, to carefully think through what they are doing and why they are doing it. A suggestion encourages organizations to be at least mildly introspective about their purposes and the means they employ to achieve them.

An important question is whether suggestion programs are out-of-date in an age of total quality management (TQM). In a recent General Accounting Office study, it was found that a "spirit of innovation" was a key factor in achieving quality in organizations, and "creative suggestions for quality improvement were recognized and rewarded" in successful agency programs. The investigation also found that there was an average annual increase in the number of suggestions of 16.6 percent after quality plans were introduced in five of the seven organizations studied. In the remaining two organizations, the number of individual suggestions declined after the introduction of TQM, but that was attributed to the growing number of team-based proposals.

Organizations that want to identify best practices in the design and operation of suggestion plans can look to the National Association of Suggestion Systems (NASS) in Arlington, Virginia, (now called the Employee Involvement Association) that issues annual awards to firms with outstanding programs based on the percentage of employees participating, the gross number of suggestions received, the percentage adopted of those submitted, savings-to-cost ratios, and total savings realized.

Suggestion systems are depreciated when thought of as nothing more than a "suggestion box" device. Suggestion programs are valuable in improving organizational performance when taken seriously.

DAVID CARNEVALE

BIBLIOGRAPHY

Applebaum, Eileen, and Rosemary Batt, 1994. *The New American Workplace: Transforming Work Systems in the United States.* Ithaca, NY: ILR Press.
Carnevale, David, and Brett Sharp, 1993. "The Old Employee Suggestion Box: An Undervalued Force for Productivity Improvement." *Review of Public Personnel Administration,* vol. 13: 82–92.
Deming, W. Edwards, 1986. *Out of Crisis.* Massachusetts Institute of Technology: Cambridge Center for Advanced Engineering Study.
Lawler, E. Edward, III, 1986. *High Involvement Management: Participative Strategies for Improving Organizational Performance.* San Francisco, CA: Jossey-Bass.
Levine, David, and George Strauss, 1989. "Employee Participation and Involvement." In *Investing in People: A Strategy to Address America's Workforce Crisis,* Background Papers, vol. 2. Washington, DC: U.S. Department of Labor.
Osborne, David, and Ted Gaebler, 1992. *Reinventing Government.* Reading, MA: Addison-Wesley.
Ouchi, William, 1981. *Theory Z: How American Business Can Meet the Japanese Challenge.* New York: Addison-Wesley.
Peters, Tom, and Robert Waterman, 1982. *In Search of Excellence: Lessons from America's Best-Run Companies.* New York: Harper & Row.
U.S. Merit Systems Protection Board, 1986. *Getting Involved: Improving Federal Management with Employee Participation.* Washington, DC: U.S. Merit Systems Protection Board.

SUNSET LAWS. Provisions in statutes which automatically terminate a law, agency, program, and so forth, at the end of a specified time period unless reauthorized by the legislature. The concern that once created, government agencies live forever regardless of their merit or effectiveness has given rise to sunset laws. These legislative provisions attempt to change the presumption of permanent existence of agencies and programs to a presumption of termination (i.e., the "sun will set on them") unless their effectiveness is proven. Sunset laws provide for the automatic termination of agencies unless the legislature takes positive action to renew their existence. Sunset laws have often been tied to budget reforms such as zero-based budgeting (ZBB) in an attempt to reduce the size and inefficiency of government. These programs have been experimented with at all levels of government in the United States and were particularly popular in the late 1970s and early 1980s.

The enactment of sunset laws represents discontent with the process of legislative oversight and review of agency operations and the often cozy relationships between interest groups, agencies, and legislative committees. Sunset laws work by establishing a finite interval for the existence of an agency, anywhere from four to ten years. The legislature then presumably undertakes a thorough examination of the costs and benefits of the agency and decides whether to reauthorize funding. The intent of sunset laws is to remove the underlying assumption that funding will be approved year after year and, instead, requires a definitive action by the legislature if the agency is to continue. Sunset laws, in effect, provide a potential veto power to a legislature and its oversight committees. They are also intended to increase the accountability of agency officials and executive branch reviewers, who must pay more attention to documenting the performance of the agency over a fixed period.

Sunset laws were first enacted by American states and were soon after considered by Congress. Colorado is credited with being the first state to adopt this reform in 1976 but limited it to top regulatory agencies. It was followed closely by Florida, which included both agencies and substantive laws. Colorado reviewed 13 different state agencies during its first year and eliminated 3 of them. By 1985, some 35 states had enacted some form of sunset legislation, providing many variations on a theme. States specified different lengths of time for agencies or programs to exist, which legislative committee or subcommittee would perform the review, and what kinds of information would be required to document performance.

Congress also considered sunset legislation for the first time in 1976. Senator Edmund Muskie (D.–Maine) introduced legislation that would have automatically terminated funding for most federal agencies if they were not specifically reauthorized after a comprehensive review. The reform was reintroduced in 1977 as S2 (a high-priority bill) and was supported by President Jimmy Carter as consistent with his introduction of ZBB in the federal government. A bill requiring reauthorization of programs every six years was eventually reported unanimously by the Senate Government Affairs Committee but was bottled up by the Rules Committee for more than a year.

In 1978, the full Senate approved an amended version S2, requiring that all programs be reauthorized or terminated every ten years, as amended by the Rules Committee. All regulatory agencies were included but many programs, such as agencies monitoring civil rights, were exempted. The bill never became law, however, because the House of Representatives failed to act on it. Sunset legislation was reintroduced in the Senate in 1979, but a growing number of committee chairmen opposed the more stringent requirements. Although the watered down bill was still labeled "sunset" legislation, not a single program faced mandatory review or would automatically be eliminated. With dwindling congressional support, even this version failed to reach the Senate floor.

Despite the fact that the more sweeping sunset provisions originally envisioned by Muskie and Carter failed to be enacted into law, sunset provisions were increasingly included in a number of individual statutes and authorizing legislation over subsequent years. For example, a Water Resources Reform measure enacted in 1986 contained sunset provisions that had a meaningful effect on the authorizing committees by putting a time limit on when money could be appropriated. Any projects not funded within five years would automatically expire. In addition, the statute reauthorized some 300 water projects that had never been funded. Other examples of sunset provisions in congressional legislation during the 1980s include child care and medical benefits legislation, federal insurance programs, securities regulation, and the Special Prosecutor (Special Counsel) law.

In general, despite the appeal of the concept of mandatory termination of government programs after a fixed period of time, sunset laws have generally been ineffective at reducing the size of bureaucracies at both the state and national levels. For example, although Colorado eliminated three agencies in its first round of sunset review, the meager savings of US $11,000 was far less than the US $212,000 it cost to conduct the evaluations. The director of Common Cause in Colorado, a citizen's lobby, concluded that the law was ineffective because powerful interest groups were able to convince legislators that their favored programs and agencies should be retained. At the federal level, agencies, lobbyists, and committee chairmen were able to block comprehensive sunset legislation. Although some sunset provisions were included in individual measures, the concept has remained more symbolic than substantive in attempting to reduce the size of the bureaucracy. Simply calling for mandatory review or claiming that the sun will automatically set on agencies and programs does nothing to disturb the powerful array of political forces that benefit from a program and prevent its elimination.

LANCE T. LELOUP

BIBLIOGRAPHY

Congress and the Nation, vols. 5–8, 1977–1992. Washington, DC: Congressional Quarterly.

LeLoup, Lance T, 1980. *Budgetary Politics*. 2d ed. Brunswick, OH: Kings Court Communications: 275–276.

Lynch, Thomas D., 1985. *Public Budgeting in America*. Englewood Cliffs, NJ: Prentice-Hall: 65.

Warren, Kenneth, 1996. *Administrative Law in the Political System*. Englewood Cliffs, NJ: Prentice-Hall: 195–196.

SUNSHINE LAWS.

Laws that assert as public policy that meetings, records, votes, actions, and deliberations of public governmental bodies are to be open to the public. They have been passed in every state and by the federal government. The United States Congress enacted the Federal Sunshine Act (90 Stat, 1241) in 1976 as an amendment to the Administrative Procedure Act. By the time the federal government passed its Sunshine Law, every state had already passed similar laws, granting public access to governmental meetings (Fox 1979, pp. 305–306). Such laws were developed based upon a premise that in a democratic society, information and knowledge provide the basis upon which we can hold our governments accountable for their actions.

Until the early 1950s and 1960s, much of the American government legislative process was conducted in less than an open forum. It was the general feeling of those who began to frame the sunshine law statutes requiring the open meetings that the openness would discourage corruption and would result in greater responsiveness and accountability to the public. Also, such openness brings additional perspectives to topics under discussion.

The effectiveness of these statutes has varied. In some states, the exceptions were so numerous as to make the laws so porous as to be ineffective. Accordingly, there has been a trend through the late 1980s and early 1990s to reduce the number of exceptions and to reemphasize the purpose of the laws.

The general trend has been toward a commitment to openness. As an example, in Missouri, the Sate Statute 610.011 RSMo. states: "It is the public policy of this State that meetings, records, votes, actions and deliberations of public governmental bodies be open to the public unless otherwise provided by law." Wording such as that stated in the Missouri Statute indicates that the public business is open as a general matter and, therefore, may only be closed regarding (specific) matters such as personnel and litigation. Clearly, the common thread of all (state) open meetings law is to promote the democratic system of government and to ensure the free flow of information to the public.

For many years, sunshine laws did not apply to the state levels or the federal legislative branch. However, as the years have progressed and through the pressure for access to the information that affects our private lives, the legislators have come to embrace the concept that open meetings should apply to every level of government. There are of course exceptions. Reality puts certain limits on the information that is available to the public or at least as to when that information is available. Certainly at the federal level, information with regards to military actions, foreign relations, and national security would not be subject to "open meetings," at least at the time of the action. Much of this information is obtained through the Freedom of Information Act.

Provisions and Application

Most state statutes contain both procedural and substantive provisions. Typically, legislation defines what is meant by a meeting, sets forth requirements for public notice, access to public records, circumstances in which the meetings may be closed, how one can bring legal action and identify the penalties for violation of the law.

In discussing definitions as to whom these laws will apply, Kenneth Warren (1996, p. 195) addressed some problems created by the language of the federal statute. Two common challenges have arisen over what is meant in the act by the terms "agency" and "agency meetings." The act states that "an agency is one which is heading a collegial body composed of two or more individual members, a majority of whom are appointed to such position by the President with the advice and consent of the Senate, and any subdivision thereof authorized to act on behalf of the agency" (Section 552b[2] [1]). In fact, in one case regarding the Chrysler Loan Guarantee Board, the D.C. Circuit Court accepted the board's argument that it should not be subject to the Sunshine Act because members, even though appointed to certain governmental posts by the president, served in an official capacity and therefore were not appointed specifically to the board (*Simons v. Chrysler Loan Guarantee Board*, 67 Fed. 2nd FP 2nd 238, 1981).

In most states, the laws will apply initially to all levels of government except judicial proceedings. In general, public governmental bodies include institutions of higher education, departments of any political subdivision, school district, or special purpose districts. Some states, however, have exempted certain boards and entities that are engaged in quasi-judicial decisions such as bonds, industrial development authorities, and so forth. "Quasi-judicial" includes those entities that perform a public function or have as their primary purpose to enter into contracts with public governmental bodies or to engage primarily in carrying out activities pursuant to agreements with public bodies. However, if the decisions of a quasi-judicial board ultimately result in a decision of the governing bodies, the trend of new legislation will hold that these boards and commissions are to be subject to open disclosure.

In many states, questions have arisen as to what qualifies as a "meeting." In most states, this means that there must be a "quorum" present to constitute a meeting. Generally speaking, whenever a quorum gathers and their purpose is to discuss or take action on a public matter, then a public meeting is taking place and all procedural requirements ensue. Informal gatherings such as social events are not included in the public meetings definition; however, there have been rulings that would imply that when the majority party meets for lunch and the specific purpose of that meeting was to discuss public business and to formulate a policy or develop a stand on specific legislation, that meeting would be open to public scrutiny even if called a social gathering.

Other procedural questions have arisen as to what is a "public governmental body." In Missouri, for example, the law includes advisory committees, boards, and commissions as well as committees or subcommittees that are formed by the entities themselves. As long as the entity is appointed by or under the direction and authority of any of the public governmental bodies that are contained in the statutes, it will come under the open meeting law.

Another important procedural aspect involves "notice" requirements. Most states set a time limit, which sets a minimum number of hours prior to a meeting that a notice is to be made posted or available. Statutes require that the notices be posted in such a manner as to be accessible to the citizens and to identify the date, the time, and the place of the meeting. There may also be a requirement for an agenda and a statement of whether or not the meeting is to be open or closed. A closed meeting does not avoid the requirement for the notice. Exceptional circumstances that prevent the 24-hour notice may be given but should be the exception rather than the rule.

Most states require that records of the public governmental body be maintained and that the public may have access to those records. A custodian of records is identified by each governmental body, and in most instances for a nominal fee, the information is to be provided upon request to the general public.

All states provide exceptions to open sessions. Generally, the exceptions include litigation; leasing; purchase or sale of real estate (where public knowledge might adversely affect the transaction); the hiring, firing, disciplining, or promoting of an employee; welfare cases where the individual can be identified; software codes for electronic data; individually identifiable personnel records and actions; and records that are protected from disclosure by some other form of the law. Many argue that without exceptions, the result will be a "chilling effect," which inhibits participants from speaking out and possibly being embarrassed based upon a fear of ridicule or misunderstanding. Some forget that human nature really does not always fit nicely into the written law.

Obviously, some items need to be confidential. Litigation matters are often closed to maintain the lawyer-client privilege, discuss strategies, settlement options, and ways to avoid litigation. Disclosure of such information might aid the adversary. The same can be said about leasing and land purchase arrangements and the final stance that the governmental body may want to take in negotiating on such issues.

Another exception deals with the matters of personnel, hiring, firing, and discipline. There is no need in general to air problems of individual employees, although the ultimate votes on issues of personnel in most states are to be made public at the end of the action.

Most states have specific procedural rules regarding how their governmental bodies can go into closed sessions. Generally these require specific reasons for going into the closed meeting, a public vote by the members to go into a closed session (typically by roll call) and a specific statutory statement that only the topic cited as the reason for the closed meeting can be discussed during that closed session.

Remedies for Violation

The open meeting statutes provide for remedies for violations. In most states, actions that are taken in violation of the open meeting laws may be either void or voidable after a court hearing. Some statutes have placed a monetary fine against the individual members who violate the open meetings act and can include payment by the individual member of all the costs and attorneys' fees to any parties successful in establishing a violation.

The courts are mixed in their approach to the enforcement remedies for violations and perhaps have looked for ways to uphold the law but at the same time not void the action taken by the legislative bodies. The courts have fashioned theories that a closed session vote may be subsequently ratified at a later public meeting in that corrective measures can be taken specifically to address issues that were perhaps voted upon in an improper fashion so as to cure any defect. Other courts argue that if there was "substantial compliance" with the purpose and intent of the law, that is sufficient to allow the law to go into effect.

Courts and legislatures have been careful to act in overturning a law or ordinance passed by a public body because there may be adverse effects on other individuals and their rights if they have acted in reliance with the action that was passed. Each case is generally taken on a case by case basis in order to avoid harsh consequences that might result from invalidating the actions that have been taken.

MARY R. DOMAHIDY AND DOUGLAS R. BEACH

BIBLIOGRAPHY

Fox, Howard I., 1979. "Government in the Sunshine." *1978 Annual Survey of American Law.*
Office of Missouri Attorney General Jay Nixon, 1993. The Missouri Sunshine Law (August).
Warren, Kenneth, 1996. *Administrative Law in the Political System,* 3d ed. Englewood Cliffs, NJ: Prentice-Hall.

SUPPLY-SIDE ECONOMICS.

Economic policies designed to stimulate gross domestic product by increasing the nation's productive capacity. Supply-side economists believe that increasing productive capacity allows the economy to expand while reducing pressure on prices. Supply side policies emphasize reducing marginal tax rates, including income taxes, capital gains taxes, and corporate profits taxes. Reducing marginal tax rates presumably expands the supply of capital and human resources, increasing productive capacity.

Supply-side economics provides an alternative to traditional fiscal and monetary policy for stimulating gross domestic product (GDP). Supply-side economics hypothesizes that actual GDP automatically adjusts to the economy's productive capacity, called potential GDP. When the economy is producing at potential GDP, economic expansion must be supported by growth in economic capacity or it will increase prices rather than GDP. Increasing the economic capacity accommodates growth while reducing the pressure on prices.

Supply-Side Economics Versus Fiscal and Monetary Policy

Traditional fiscal and monetary policy are demand-side economic policies. They stimulate GDP by increasing the aggregate demand for goods and services (see **fiscal policy** and **monetary policy**). Aggregate demand includes consumption, investment, government, and net export demand (exports minus imports). Fiscal policy involves government expenditures and tax policy. Government expenditures directly influence government demand; tax policy (e.g., income taxes and preferential capital gains tax treatment) influences both consumption demand and investment demand. Monetary policy manipulates the money supply to influence prices and interest rates. Changes in the interest rate influence investment demand and consumption demand (indirectly through savings rates). Changes in domestic price levels affect net export demand.

The criticism of demand-side economics centers on the ease with which actual GDP adjusts to its productive capacity. Potential GDP represents the economy's output when all resources are fully employed (including labor, capital, and natural resources). (Full employment does not mean 100 percent resource utilization. Natural unemployment allows for people voluntarily seeking better jobs or transitioning from declining to expanding industries. Currently, 5 to 6 percent unemployment is considered full employment.) Supply-side economics postulates that flexible resource prices will automatically move the economy to potential GDP. If resource prices are flexible, they will adjust until all resources are fully employed. For underemployed resources, price will fall. Production becomes more profitable, encouraging firms to expand output. GDP will expand until underemployment is eliminated. For overemployed resources, prices will increase, firms' profits will decrease, production will decrease and overemployment will be eliminated.

If market adjustments automatically eliminate resource over- and underemployment, traditional demand-side economics is unnecessary and counterproductive. In the supply-side model, recessions are only temporary and automatically eliminated by resource price adjustments. If the adjustment is relatively quick, it is unnecessary to stimulate the economy by increasing aggregate demand. Furthermore, increases in aggregate demand become counterproductive over time. Because the economy automatically returns to full employment, fiscal and monetary policy do not affect long-run GDP. Instead, they simply increase prices.

Supply-Side Economic Policies

In the supply-side model, the only way to increase long-run GDP is to expand economic capacity. Increasing economic capacity creates unemployment in the resource markets. As the economy adjusts to full employment, GDP increases and prices decrease. Economic growth can be sustained in the long run if supported by an increase in economic capacity.

Economic capacity is determined by the quantity of available resources (e.g., labor, capital, and natural resources), resource quality (e.g., labor education, training, and experience; the level of technology; etc.), and the institutional structure affecting the efficiency with which resources are used (e.g., industrial infrastructure, minimum wage rates, unemployment compensation, etc.). Supply-side economics focuses on increasing economic capacity by increasing resource quantity and quality, either directly or indirectly by adjusting institutional arrangements.

For example, consider the effect of income taxes on the labor supply. The cost of leisure (forgone income) increases with the wage rate. Thus, individuals will supply more labor (consume less leisure) as the wage rate increases. Lowering income tax rates increases the effective wage rate. This increases the labor supply. People enter the labor force (particularly secondary income earners), work longer hours and retire later. In addition, reducing income tax rates increases capital market efficiency by encouraging savings and discouraging unproductive tax shelter investments. Using similar reasoning, reducing corporate profits and capital gains taxes and accelerating depreciation al-

FIGURE I. Laffer Curve

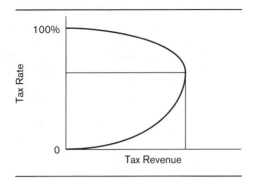

lowances encourages capital investment. Thus, lowering tax rates will increase the labor supply and the capital stock, expanding economic capacity.

Supply-Side Economics and the Federal Budget Deficit

Supply-side economics emphasizes tax rate reductions to increase economic capacity. In traditional economic models, this would increase the government budget deficit. However, the supply-side model suggests that lowering tax rates may increase the government's tax revenue. Tax revenues are determined by both tax rates and the taxable income. Tax revenues decrease with the tax rate if taxable income remains unchanged. Tax revenues increase with taxable income if tax rates remain unchanged. If reducing tax rates increases taxable income, the effect on tax revenues is ambiguous. It may increase or decrease.

This possibility is illustrated by the Laffer Curve (see Figure I). The Laffer Curve shows the relationship between tax rates and tax revenues. A zero tax rate maximizes the incentive to work, but tax revenues are zero. A 100 percent tax rate eliminates all incentive to work, so tax revenues are again zero. Thus, tax revenues must reach a maximum at some tax rate between zero and 100 percent. At low tax rates, tax revenues increase with the tax rate. At high tax rates, tax revenues decrease as tax rates increase.

The Laffer Curve's general proposition is irrefutable. Debate over the Laffer Curve centers on identifying the tax rate that maximizes tax revenues. In the early 1960s, the highest marginal income tax rate was 91 percent. By 1965, the highest marginal income tax rate had fallen to 70 percent. By 1986, the highest marginal income tax rate had fallen further to 33 percent. Unfortunately, it is impossible to determine whether tax revenue peaked with a 33 percent, 70 percent, or 91 percent marginal tax rate. Thus, the effect of supply-side economic policy on federal tax revenues and budget deficits is unclear.

Supply-Side Economics in the Short and Long Run

Both supply-side economics and traditional fiscal policy suggest tax cuts to stimulate GDP. Fiscal policy emphasizes the effect of tax cuts on aggregate demand. Supply-side economics emphasizes the effect of tax cuts on economic capacity. In actuality, both viewpoints may be correct, but the effects may occur at different times. Supply-side economics is not designed to moderate the short-run fluctuations in economic activity normally associated with business cycles. Supply-side policies need time to be effective. Individuals need time to adjust their labor/leisure choices before changes in income tax rates will affect the labor supply. In the short run, lower taxes will increase aggregate demand through the impact on household consumption demand. Similarly, accelerated depreciation and lower corporate profits and capital gains taxes will increase investment, but it takes time to translate investment into expanded production capacity. In the short run, aggregate demand increases through the impact on investment demand. Supply-side economics focuses on the long-run impacts of changes in tax rates; traditional demand-side economics focuses on their short-run impact.

WILLIAM R. GATES

BIBLIOGRAPHY

Biven, W. Carl, 1989. *Who Killed John Maynard Keynes?* Homewood, IL: Dow Jones-Irwin.

Canto, Victor A., Douglas H. Joines, and Arthur B. Laffer, 1983. *Foundations of Supply-Side Economics.* San Diego: Academic Press.

Federal Reserve Bank of Atlanta, 1982. *Supply-Side Economics in the 1980s.*

Lindsey, Lawrence, 1989. *The Growth Experience: How the New Tax Policy Is Transforming the U.S. Economy.* New York: Basic Books.

Roberts, Paul Craig, 1984. *The Supply-Side Revolution.* Cambridge, MA: Harvard University Press.

SUPRANATIONAL ORGANIZATION.

An international body that exercises authority over and above that of its member states, either for a particular functional area of activity or more generally for a number of policy areas.

Origin

The idea of an authority above that of the sovereign state had to await the development of just such states and their recognition of the need for close cooperative arrangements. During the Middle Ages in Europe, entities such as the Holy Roman Empire exercised their rule over smaller territorial domains such as kingdoms, principalities, and city-states, and the Catholic Church claimed a spiritual—and in some cases temporal—power above Catholic rulers. From about the sixteenth century, Europe became more clearly organized into recognized sovereign states whose rulers claimed the final legal jurisdiction over their territory. Relations between such sovereign states were governed by international law and eventually states in the rest of the world—first in the Americas, then in the Mideast and East Asia, and more recently in other parts of Asia and Africa—were brought into this system. During the nineteenth century, the first international agreements were made between states establishing supranational organizations. These were the various commissions set up to manage Europe's large rivers, the most important being the Danube Commission. This body of experts took over the management of the navigation of the river from the states along its banks and charged a uniform set of dues to users. Another example was the *Zollverein*, the customs union, established in parts of Germany after the Austro-Prussian War of 1866. Its Customs Council and Customs Parliament made laws on trade matters for a number of German states. The river commissions functioned at a technical level and did not have specific political aims, although the *Zollverien* could be seen as favoring greater German unity. During World War I, the Allied powers established a number of economic boards with executive committees having wide powers to organize matters such as the provision of food and transport for the benefit of the war effort rather than to suit national needs. After World War II, the Council of Europe called for the coordinated administration of economic and technical organizations on a supranational plane. The main response came in the form of the Schuman Plan, which proposed the establishment of a European Coal and Steel Community (ECSC) with a supranational High Authority overseeing those industries. France was joined by the Federal Republic of Germany, Belgium, the Netherlands, Luxembourg, and Italy in this project in 1952, but the idea of a European Defense Community and a European Political Community for the same states was turned down. Instead, a European Economic Community (EEC) and a European Atomic Energy Community (Euratom) were established in 1957, although their institutions seemed to lack the powers of the High Authority. Since then, the institutions of all three communities have been merged into one—the European Communities (EC)—and this was transformed into the European Union (EU) in November 1993. The communities' institutions of this union—especially the commission, the European Parliament, and the European Court of Justice—are generally recognized as exercising, in their areas of competence, authority above the member states.

The Theory

Ideas about supranational organizations shed light on the criteria for their existence and their position in international relations and in relation to the state. Peter Hay (1966) lists four main criteria for a supranational authority: the independence of the organization and its institutions from member states, the ability to bind member states by weighted or majority votes, the binding effect of its law on persons without the need for national legislation, and a transfer of jurisdiction from the member states to the organization (p. 34). Paul Taylor (1978) covers these points but also adds that the goals of the supranational organization should be legitimated in the national and collective systems and that there should be compliance with, and the habit of obedience to, its laws. Article 9 of the treaty founding the ECSC required both the members of the High Authority and the member states to respect its "supranational authority," but these words were not mentioned in the treaties setting up the EEC and Euratom, and it was Taylor's view in 1978 that the EC was not supranational (p. 233). However, using both his criteria and those of Hay, it does now seem that the EC element of the European Union is supranational in the areas where it has competence. A difficulty arises—both in theory and in practice—when placing a supranational authority in international law. In acting the way that it does in determining the rules and regulations for, say, the steel industry or agriculture in the member states, the supranational body can seem like a federal authority, a confusion confounded in the EC by the existence of an apparent executive (the commission), a court (the European Court of Justice), and a parliament (the European Parliament). Federalist thinkers, such as Jean Monnet and Altiero Spinelli, have hoped that the EC would develop into a United States of Europe, but supranational authority does not necessarily lead in that direction. However, its statelike activities make such a body difficult to fit into the traditional concepts of international law with the stress on the sovereignty of states. How then, it is asked, can there be an authority above states? Answers have often stressed the singular nature of the EC, with Ernst Haas (1958) placing the emphasis on the particular conditions surrounding the creation of the ECSC and the EEC in a period when nationalism was weak in the founding states (p. xvi). It remains to be seen whether the concept of supranationalism can survive a strengthening of nationalism in the states of the European Union.

Variations in States and Regions

The supranational elements in the EC have often been controversial. Although it was reduced in the EEC compared with the ECSC, there was still an important supranational contribution in the commission, the European Parliament, and the court. In the mid-1960s, the commission, in particular, was challenged by President de Gaulle of France, who considered that it was attempting to take too much power to itself. Since the end of the 1960s, the commission has developed over time, as have the powers of the European Parliament. The court has built up a corpus of community-based law. After de Gaulle, the original six members of the EC have been the most supportive of the development of the supranational element. The United Kingdom and Denmark have been most skeptical and, in some cases, hostile to this aspect. Whereas the earlier members represented countries that had suffered during World War II, that was not the case for the United Kingdom, and the wartime occupation of Denmark was limited. Both states have resisted any move to a federal-like structure by the supranational elements in the EC and were insistent that the word "federal" should be excluded from the 1992 Treaty on European Union. Both states saw popular and political resistance to the ratification of the treaty and have since declared their opposition to a further development of the supranational element.

Variations in Different Regimes

A federal system of government could be expected to admit a supranational authority above it more readily than that of a unitary state. Federal constitutions involve a division of responsibility for particular policies, with the federal authority exercising at least foreign, defense, and the major aspects of economic policy, and the individual states often being left other specific policies and residual authority. The concept of subsidiarity, introduced into the Treaty on European Union, allowed the exercise of powers at union level only if they could not be more effectively employed at a lower level of government. In the eyes of the United Kingdom, this trimmed the supranational power of the EU, but federal states such as Germany saw it as part of a more rational distribution of power between lower authorities, intermediate entities such as the member states, and the institutions of the European Union.

Attitude of the United States

In contrast with the federal states in the European Union, the United States is wary of any supranational authorities, as these may detract from the jealously guarded powers of the branches of the U.S. government and judiciary. The United States has been able to be a member of the North Atlantic Treaty Organization (NATO) as its institutions—despite their important powers—are not regarded as supranational. U.S. governments have also resisted any exercise of power by the United Nations as that could be considered above the authority of the U.S. Constitution. The United States has been reluctant to participate in any peace enforcement operations under Chapter 7 of the UN Charter, except on its own terms. U.S. action against Iraq in 1991 was undertaken using UN Security Council Chapter 7 resolutions, but a tight control was kept of the operation by the U.S. national authorities. The U.S. Senate has also reserved to itself the right to contradict the rulings of the international trade body formed in 1995, the World Trade Organization (WTO). Though the reality of trade power may be slipping away from the United States, its legislators do not want to delegate the right to take decisions on such matters to an international body. This contrasts with the member states of the European Union, who find their commercial policy being partly determined by the commission, which negotiates on their behalf in the WTO on most trade questions.

CLIVE ARCHER

BIBLIOGRAPHY

Etzioni, Amitai, 1962. "The Dialectics of Supranational Unification." *American Political Science Review*, vol. 56, no. 4: 927–935.

Gormley, W. Paul, 1966. *The Procedural Status of the Individual Before International and Supranational Tribunals*. The Hague: Martinus Nijhoff.

Haas, Ernst B., 1958. *The Uniting of Europe: Political, Social, and Economic Forces 1950–1957*. Stanford, CA: Stanford University Press.

Hay, Peter, 1966. *Federalism and Supranational Organizations*. Urbana and London: University of Illinois Press.

Rosentiel, Francis, 1963. "Reflections on the Notion of Supranationality." *Journal of Common Market Studies*, vol. 2 (November): 127–139.

Taylor, Paul, 1978. "Elements of Supranationalism: The Power and Authority of International Institutions." In Paul Taylor and A. J. R. Groom, eds., *International Organisation: A Conceptual Approach*. London: Frances Pinter: 216–235.

SURVEY METHOD.

A systematic approach to gathering facts about a neighborhood or community; a important element in the early development of the field of public administration in the United States. As practiced in the early twentieth century, the survey method, or social survey as it was sometimes known, consisted of first-hand investigation and analysis of economic, sociological, and related aspects of a designated community or group. Although some surveys during this period aimed at the kind of scientific objectivity that characterizes modern-day survey research, most social surveys were intended to yield facts on which to base policies and programs to ameliorate social, and particularly urban, ills.

As typically practiced, the social survey involved field work rather than reliance on preexisting data. Surveys attempted exhaustive and in-depth investigation of individuals, families, and households within a given local area. The approach aimed to yield quantitative information, however rudimentary, which could be used to identify and justify appropriate social interventions.

English Precursors

The roots of the survey lie in nineteenth-century England, in the efforts of a variety of well-to-do individuals concerned about the effects of poverty. As early as 1797, Sir Frederic Morton published *The State of the Poor*, a compilation of facts about poverty and the administration of the Poor Laws. In 1851, Henry Mayhew began investigations that led to a four-volume work entitled *London Labour and the London Poor*, which presented descriptive and statistical information. The real inventor of the social survey, however, was Charles Booth, whose seventeen-volume *Life and Labour of the People in London*, published between 1889 and 1903, constituted the first great empirical study in the social survey tradition.

A number of innovations separated Booth's work from previous efforts. For one thing, in focusing consciously on poverty per se, rather than on poor people, he attempted to introduce an element of precision into the concept of poverty, where previously there had been considerable vagueness. For another, Booth and his team of researchers were able to draw on the systematic observations of school attendance officers, who performed house-by-house surveillance and could be interviewed about the conditions of families in each dwelling. The results included detailed, color-coded maps of East London neighborhoods, delineating levels of poverty on each block. Booth used the findings to argue that poverty was not preordained, as was widely thought; rather government could and should take on the responsibility to help people in need. His study supported a number of reform movements, and several policies, including old-age pensions, can be traced to his work.

The Survey in America

The first full-blown social survey in the United States was conducted by residents of Hull House, founded in 1889 by Jane Addams and Ellen Gates Starr. Hull House was one of the earliest American settlement houses; like its counterparts, it was established in order that educated middle-class people might take up residence in distressed urban neighborhoods, provide services to the poor, forge linkages among people of different classes, and thereby improve social stability. From the outset, Addams, Starr, and their colleagues recognized the need for systematic fact gathering. The leader in the research effort was Hull House resident Florence Kelley, a pioneering child labor reformer, who in 1892 had been appointed a special agent of the Illinois Bureau of Labor Statistics to investigate Chicago sweatshops and was able to mobilize resources of the U.S. Department of Labor to support the settlement's study. *Hull-House Maps and Papers: A Presentation of Nationalities and Wages in a Congested District of Chicago, Together with Comments and Essays on Problems Growing out of the Social Conditions (HHM&P)* was published in 1895.

The Hull House report included articles on sweatshop labor, charities in Cook County, child labor, women's labor organizations, and various ethnic groups in Chicago's Nineteenth Ward, the geographic focus of the survey. The volume was especially notable for its large and detailed maps, which conveyed with a vividness unmatched by dry tables and graphs the concentration of ethnic groups in certain blocks, the relationship between ethnicity and weekly income, the relegation of the very poor to crowded, airless rooms in the rear of tenements while those with more resources clustered at the front. The Hull House maps matched those of the Booth study in graphic detail; they exceeded Booth's in providing household-by-household information and in delineating patterns of ethnicity. According to Kathryn Sklar (1991), *HHM&P* constituted the flagship example of social science analysis of working-class life in the first decade of the twentieth century.

Other surveys followed, notably a study of Boston's South End by Robert A. Woods and the residents of South End House; the Pittsburgh Survey of 1909, the Springfield (Illinois) Survey, and the Cleveland Survey. In the 1920s, an increasing number of surveys were conducted, many of them supported by the Russell Sage Foundation, most of them performed by social reformers and philanthropists.

The Survey Approach in
Early Public Administration

As employed by municipal reformers in the early 1900s, the survey took on somewhat different form, although the blend of systematic fact gathering and advocacy persisted. In 1900, most municipal governments were controlled by political machines, whose bosses filled administrative jobs more on the basis of party loyalty than managerial ability. Educated middle-class people, concerned about growing urban problems and excluded from working-class machine politics, turned to investigation as a way of demonstrating the need for reform.

The first such investigation was launched in 1906 by the newly formed New York Bureau of Municipal Research. Blocked by Tammany Hall from digging into municipal finance and accounting practices, the bureau decided to conduct an outdoor survey of city street cleaning and repair. Results documented the shocking state of the streets, marshaled evidence of the need for better administrative methods, and led to the forced resignation of the Manhattan borough president.

The success of the New York survey showed reformers that objectivity, science, and facts could be the key to dislodging the hold of machine bosses and their cronies on governmental processes. Reformers were able to argue that their efforts were focused on "methods rather than ... men" (Hopkins 1912, p. 235) and were therefore disinterested. Similar bureaus sprang up in a number of other cities, and municipal research remained a keystone of administrative reform until World War II. Gradually, the power of Tammany Hall and other city machines declined, and if the decline was slow, many bosses were embarrassed into launching their own campaigns to make city administrations more efficient (see **municipal research bureaus**).

As practiced by municipal government reformers in bureaus of municipal research, the survey lost much of its focus on the poor, as well as the connotation that a survey involved exhaustive study of the conditions of people's lives. Gradually, in fact, the term "survey," as used by administrative reformers, came to signify virtually any systematic information-gathering effort. According to public administration pioneer Luther Gulick, first director of the New York Institute of Public Administration, an outgrowth of the New York Bureau, "Survey ... conveyed the idea of the inclusive, objective and scientific approach which the Bureau applied to its work" (Quoted in Schiesl 1977, p. 117). Surveys included investigations of the public schools, the water department, purchasing practices, position classifications, the sanitary code, property tax assessment methods, and accrual accounting, to offer only a few examples.

According to Alice Stone's and Donald Stone's (1975) history of early public administration, "The survey reports constituted a new kind of literature about public administration" (p. 21) and in fact spurred the development of training, then formal education, as reformers realized the need for public employees to have specific managerial skills in order to implement study recommendations. As cultivated by municipal researchers, the survey method was the soil out of which public administration as an academic field germinated.

Professionalization of the Survey Method

Both the social survey as practiced by settlement house residents and other social welfare reformers, and what might be called the administrative survey of the municipal bureaus, faded out by mid-century. Social investigation moved from an amateur to a professionalized status and found its home in university social science departments and government agencies. The development of modern statistical sampling and other survey research techniques, as well as increasing emphasis on separating objective study from policy advocacy, transformed the survey, as did its increasing use for commercial purposes such as marketing and media research.

CAMILLA STIVERS

BIBLIOGRAPHY

Addams, Jane, 1981 [1910]. *Twenty Years at Hull House.* New York: Penguin/Signet.

Bulmer, Martin, Kevin Bales, and Kathryn Kish Sklar, eds., 1991. *The Social Survey in Historical Perspective 1880–1930.* Cambridge: Cambridge University Press.

Hopkins, George B., 1912. "The New York Bureau of Municipal Research." *Annals of the American Academy of Political and Social Science* (May): 235–244.

Schiesl, Murray J., 1977. *The Politics of Efficiency: Municipal Administration and Reform in America 1880–1920.* Berkeley: University of California Press.

Sklar, Kathryn Kish, 1991. "Hull-House Maps and Papers: Social Science as Women's Work in the 1890s." In Martin Bulmer, Kevin Bales, and Kathryn Kish Sklar, eds., *The Social Survey in Historical Perspective 1880–1930.* Cambridge: Cambridge University Press: 111–147.

Stone, Alice B., and Donald C. Stone, 1975. "Early Development of Education in Public Administration." In Frederick C. Mosher, ed., *American Public Administration: Past, Present, Future.* Tuscaloosa: University of Alabama Press: 11–48.

SYSTEMS ANALYSIS. Defined by Howard McCurdy as "a continuous process of reviewing objectives, designing alternative methods for achieving them, and weighing the effectiveness and costs of the alternatives, largely in economic terms." Indeed, systems analysis has been widely used to design a course of action to achieve certain specific goals and to evaluate the success or failure of an organization to accomplish those goals mostly in economic terms. This common application of systems analysis simplifies organizational response to an input-output function. Beyond this, the application of the results of systems analysis for mitigating organizational dysfunction is problematical because it is unable to explain the internal workings of an organization and, thus, is not useful in explicating overlapping functions beyond showing that they exist.

Systems analysis, as we know of it today, is an outgrowth of Ludwig von Bertalanffy's general systems theory, which attempted to organize scientific knowledge into a unified system to offset the increasing specialization of scientists. However, instead of unifying scientific disciplines, "systems" has itself become a branch of science rather than its unifying medium. Although the systems approach has failed to bring all scientific disciplines under a coherent rational scheme, used as a heuristic tool, it provides analysts with a tool to examine relationships along a unifying theme or function. Perhaps its most useful function is to assist in defining components that are central to a function or structure that is being mapped and those that are subcomponents or even outside of the area of interest.

Systems analysis has been incorporated into computer technology because they are both driven by linearly linked hierarchical components. The basic function of a computer systems analyst is to design computer applications to perform certain functions, paralleling somewhat systems analysis in the public administration context. However, not surprisingly, the general systems application to societal organizations by administrative theorists as a method for elucidating organizational systems has not met with the same success as in computer applications. The concatenated linear hierarchical structure of computer logic is a good fit for general systems theory. Human organizations, by contrast, defy neat compartmentalization because the organization chart does not include informal networks that could be as important or more important than the formal structure. The major concepts of organizational systems and their relationship to the systems approach are briefly discussed here.

Systems of organizational structures can be categorized as mechanical, homeostatic, and adaptive. Mechanical models include the works of most of the "classical" students of administrative theory, such as Max Weber and Frederick Taylor. Their notion of a sustainable organizational structure is essentially a closed system that rejects external inputs because they can negatively affect its equilibrium. The Weberian bureaucratic model was taken to new levels by Taylor by injecting the notion of pay incentives to increase assembly-line productivity. He also formalized methods of measuring production efficiency by removing the human element from factory assembly lines and instead focused on functions; for example, he timed how long it takes a worker to shovel a certain amount of coal. But his far-reaching contribution, still in use today, was the use of wages as the incentive for increasing productivity in other job sites besides factories.

The homeostatic model, according to Daniel Katz and Robert Kahn, is "a structure which imports energy from the external world, transforms it, and exports a product to the environment." This model has the characteristics of both the mechanical and adaptive model. It has a feedback system, which is absent in the mechanical model, that allows an organization to respond to changes by adjusting the input-output ratio; but one of the weaknesses of systems analysis is its inability to describe how homeostasis is achieved by an organization in responding to external inputs.

The adaptive model defines an organizational construct as an open system that uses external inputs to maintain itself. By its nature, adaptive organizations have networks of internal and external communication linkages because they require external inputs and, thus, have boundaries that are fuzzy. To understand these organizations, knowledge of how they handle the uncertainty introduced by the external information inputs, particularly when the volume of information increases, is important. But it is not known how adaptive, self-regulating, and self-directed systems have the ability to modify their structures to respond to external inputs.

Because organizational structures today are required to process large amounts of external and internally generated information, the ability of organizations to fulfill their goals and objectives lies in their capacity for processing information. In addition, societal systems are increasingly buffeted by external demands for timely responsiveness, and analysis of complex organizational structures should include the flow and sources of information and communication through the organization. Organizational information channels are as significant in understanding its operation as its functional divisions.

There are inherent difficulties in the use of systems analysis as an analytical tool for examining societal systems due to the ability to clearly define the systemic boundary. Even von Bertalanffy has expressed concerns about the utility of the systems approach for analyzing organization structures because it can never be all inclusive to enable analysts to ascribe boundaries to the analysis. The result of omitting important components within the scope of analysis is an unintended consequence.

ROSE T. PFUND

BIBLIOGRAPHY

Bertalanffy, Ludwig von, 1968. *General Systems Theory*. New York: George Braziller.
Katz, Daniel, and Robert Kahn, 1978 *The Social Psychology of Organizations*, 2d ed. New York : Wiley.
LaPorte, Todd R., 1975. *Organized Social Complexity: Challenge to Politics and Policy*. Princeton, NJ: Princeton University Press.
McCurdy, Howard E., 1977. *Public Administration: A Synthesis*. Menlo Park, CA: Benjamin Cummins.

SYSTEMS THEORY. A collection of general concepts, principles, methods, techniques, and analyses that are associated with the study of systems, also called general systems theory. Systems are those ubiquitous entities, both physical and abstract, that are defined by system theorists and analysts as having all the traits and characteristics of a system. Systems theory is not a theory in the traditional sense, but rather an approach or a transdisciplinary field of study.

Systems theory was pioneered in the discipline of biology in the early 1950s and eventually spread to many disciplines and professions. Ludwig von Bertalanffy is commonly accepted to be the founder and organizer of general systems theory (von Bertalanffy 1968). In biology, systems theory was used to reorganize relationships among the various forms and levels of life from the molecular to the social. The growth in systems thinking corresponds closely with the growth in computer technology and information theory. Systems theory was clearly influential in the intellectual development of cybernetics, which is the study of information and control processes in systems (Ashby 1958).

In the 1950s and 1960s, systems theory was a new theoretical perspective for understanding and predicting natural and artificial phenomena. It set itself apart from the existing approaches in many scientific disciplines of historical, reductionistic, and behavioral methods of scientific inquiry. General systems theory was intended to be a new paradigm for the scientific exploration of wholes and wholeness, interrelatedness and interdependence. Systems theory has become so pervasive that many of us do not even understand the strength of the influence that it has on our own thinking. The systems approach is still very influential in most disciplines and professions, even today.

A system is a set or arrangement of objects or concepts that are related so as to form a whole. All systems can be described using generic systems concepts such as input, processes, outputs, feedback and feedforward loops, equilibrium, homeostasis, and open and closed systems. All systems can be explained not only in simple causal terms, but are also said to be goal directed and purposeful, or, in systems terms, teleological. Original systems theorists made distinctions between real systems (e.g., a galaxy, a cell, an atom) and conceptual systems (e.g., logic, mathematics, music). Distinctions were also drawn in general systems theory between various forms of systems technology, systems philosophy, and systems epistemology. Systems theorists also came to view systems as being closed or open to their environment. Those more open to the environment were more dynamic and subject to change than were closed systems. Every physical and abstract entity can be described in systems terms.

More specifically, systems management is a broad approach to managing organizations that views the organization as a unitary whole composed of interrelated parts with an identifiable boundary and an external environment. C. West Churchman was an operations researcher and systems philosopher as well as an early advocate of the systems approach to management. In his 1968 book, Churchman outlines the basic input-output model of the organizational system. He identifies five steps of system description as measure of performance, environment, resources, components or subsystems, and management as the decisionmaking power. Fremont Kast and James Rosenzweig (1970) in their landmark textbook used system theory as a conceptual scheme to consider interrelationships among organizational subsystems and interactions between the system and suprasystems. They viewed the organization as consisting of several major subsystems: technical subsystem, structural subsystem, psychological subsystem, managerial subsystem. Kast and Rosenzweig also formulated the contingency view that understood organization systems to be very dynamic and complex requiring analysis and prescription of organizational problems under varying conditions and specific situations. Many of the more famous management techniques in the past 40 years, such as management-by-objectives and planning, programming, budgeting systems, have relied on systems theory as their basis. The growth of management information systems is also clearly predicated on the principles of systems theory and the application of information technology to management decisions.

The particular influence of systems theory on public administration and policy were no less than in other disciplines like economics, political science, or sociology. Among the earliest works using systems theory to conceptualize and examine government and bureaucracy was Ira Sharkansky's (1978) textbook on public administration, now in its fourth edition. More recently, one of the most explicit systems approaches to public administration was Louis Gawthrop's (1985) book, which outlined numerous principles of public organizational design and ethics based on advanced systems theoretical principles. In public policy perhaps the classic treatment and critique of general systems theory is Ida Hoos (1983). While most systems theorists saw advantages in viewing organizational and policy processes as systems, many also saw that systems thinking also produced a conservative, equilibrium-oriented attitude toward their topics.

Today, systems theory has developed beyond its initial principles to what is now known as theories of complexity, or chaos theory. In many ways, chaos theory is advanced systems theory that stresses the greater complexity and dynamic nature of all systems, often to the point that they appear chaotic. Douglas Kiel (1994) has produced a book that defines the new nonlinear methods of systems theory; he concludes that change and uncertainty are the norms, not the exceptions, in public administration. General systems theory will prove to be one of the more important historical influences on the discipline and profession of public administration in the latter half of the twentieth century. It will symbolize both the increasing rationalization of administrative practice and government, as well as the increasing scientific nature of public administration research and method.

E. SAMUEL OVERMAN

REFERENCES

Ashby, W. Roy, 1958. *An Introduction to Cybernetics.* New York: John Wiley & Sons.

Bertalanffy, Ludwig von, 1968. *General Systems Theory.* New York: George Braziller.

Churchman, C. West, 1968. *The Systems Approach.* New York: Basic Books.

Gawthrop, Louis, 1985. *Public Sector Management, Systems, and Ethics.* Bloomington: Indiana University Press.

Hoos, Ida, 1983. *Systems Analysis and Public Policy,* rev. ed. Berkeley: University of California Press.

Kast, Fremont E., and James E. Rosenzweig, 1970. *Organizations and Management: A Systems Approach.* New York: McGraw-Hill.

Kiel, L. Douglas, 1994. *Managing Chaos and Complexity in Government.* San Francisco, CA: Jossey-Bass.

Sharkansky, Ira, 1978. *Public Administration: Policy Making in Government Agencies.* 4th ed. Chicago: Rand McNally.

T

TACTICS. The techniques of deploying and directing military forces in coordinated combat activities against an enemy in order to achieve the objectives defined by strategy or operations. Twentieth-century Western military thought and practice have established tactics as those plans that are left to relatively junior officers to carry out. If strategy is the art and science of using resources in support of national objectives, converting power into policy and operational design, tactics convert military strategy into the maneuvering of aircraft, ships, and troops in actual conflict.

Tactics offers the same problem of definition that bedevils most military concepts: the line dividing tactics and other things is unclear and changes over time. What seem in theory to be clear and distinctive differences between tactics and strategy become more uncertain in practice. A senior scientific intelligence officer during World War II, R. V. Jones of the British Air Ministry put the point well in his remark that "strategy is nothing but tactics talked through a brass hat" (Jones 1978, p. 504).

Since the end of the cold war, much effort has been expended in countries of the North Atlantic Treaty Organization (NATO) and in those of the former Warsaw Pact to define the whole range of military activities rather more usefully. The consensus accepted the German General Staff's analysis during the first half of the twentieth century. The meaning of strategy was extended upward to incorporate all elements of national decisionmaking about national security, not just military instruments. The lower levels of military strategy were defined as operations—the control and direction of large forces within a single theater of war—and led to the development of operational art. Tactics overlapped the lower end of operations, being the means by which individual field force commanders within the combat theater achieved their objectives. Below that were fighting instructions and rules of engagement, covering precise matters of military detail at the unit level and its command and control. Lately, the evolution of military doctrine has sought to encompass all these elements of the spectrum, thereby accepting the areas of overlap that occur in definition.

This conceptual framework works well for total war and the cold war. It has much less applicability to the requirements of United Nations peacekeeping and peace enforcement. With operations in the 1990s, such as Somalia and Bosnia, political micromanagement of military matters in circumstances short of all-out war has been the order of the day. The operational level of war has, in practice, disappeared. And, once again, strategy and tactics have become almost indistinguishable. For those who see

command in warfare as an extension of the sciences, this is confusing and regrettable; for those who see it as something closer to art, this is no more than the latest development requiring the application of military flair and genius.

PETER FOOT

BIBLIOGRAPHY

Jones, R. V., 1978. *Most Secret War: British Scientific Intelligence 1939–1945.* London: Hamish Hamilton.
Paret, Peter, ed., 1986. *The Makers of Modern Strategy: From Machiavelli to the Nuclear Age.* Oxford: Oxford University Press.
Royal Navy, The, 1995. *The Fundamentals of British Maritime Doctrine.* London: HMSO.

TARGET-BASED BUDGETING. A budget reform that requires the budget office to give targets, or maximum amounts to the departments before they draw up their budget requests. The departmental request must be within these targets, or it will be returned to the department for revision.

Overview

In its simplest form, target-based budgeting is a budget reform that rejuggles some of the traditional functions of the budget office and the departments during the process of budget requests. Under traditional, incremental budgeting, budget requests came up from the departments based on few or no prior constraints from the budget office. The totals of the requests would normally exceed the revenue available, forcing the budget office to cut back the departmental requests. Such cutbacks would either be across the board, requiring little knowledge of the department's operations, or be targeted, under the assumption that the budget office was armed to find the fat in department budget proposals.

The traditional model led to a number of widely acknowledged problems. Perhaps the most serious of those problems was an oppositional relationship between the budget office and the departments, and a mood of mutual mistrust and game playing. Department heads often inflated their budget requests because they expected across the board cuts and still had to be able to manage their departments. Budget officers came to look on the departments as duplicitous and their requests as exaggerated. The budget office staff learned to watch out for departmental tricks and sometimes evaluated themselves in terms of their ability to find and catch those tricks.

When the budget office staff tried to find and cut the fat in the departments' budgets, they were often frustrated by their lack of understanding of departmental operations. The results were unpleasant on an interpersonal basis and damaging to management. Unrealistic departmental estimates were often cut back unwisely by the budget office, encouraging even more unrealistic departmental estimates.

Target-based budgets resolve these problems by requiring the budget office to give firm ceilings to the departments for their budget requests at the beginning of the budget process. These ceilings are framed by the budget office's estimates of the total revenue that will be available as well as specific policy guidance from the budget office, mayor, manager, and council. The departments have to keep their requests under this ceiling or target. If they fail to do so, the budget office gives their budget requests back to them for revision. The revisions are accepted only if they come in at or under the ceilings. The decisions of what to cut to get under the ceilings are made by the departments, not by the budget office. Under target-based budgeting, the departmental estimates must be realistic. The game playing and antagonism that characterized incremental budgeting are eliminated. The responsibility for ensuring that budget requests do not exceed revenue lies with the budget office, while the responsibility for making managerially responsible cuts goes to the departments.

History

The earliest reference to target-based budgeting in the budget literature is in Arthur Buck's 1929 text *Public Budgeting*. He describes a system of budgeting in Berkeley, California, in the 1920s that would today be recognized as target-based.

After several years of experimenting with commission government and experiencing the logrolling and high rates of expenditure that came to be associated with that form, a reform group advocating the adoption of the city manager form also argued for budgeting reform and ultimately included requirements for more stringent budgeting in the new Council-Manager Charter effective in 1923. The city had been running deficits in the early 1920s, just prior to the adoption of the city manager form, at least in part because of war-induced inflation and resulting salary increases combined with tax limits and a citizenry unwilling to override the limits.

While the requirement for more stringent budgeting was written into the charter, the new budget system was given life and form by the first city manager, John Edy, and his budget officer, J. H. Jamison. Their goal was to rebalance the budget within the tax limits by controlling the departmental requests while creating a little flexibility in the budget for capital projects and new or expanded services. Many of the conditions that spawned target-based budgeting in the 1920s are similar to conditions today. In 1929, budget reformer Buck (1929) described the system that Edy and Jamison had worked out:

> The manager, with the assistance of his budget officer, J. H. Jamison, makes a careful analysis of the current year's

budget in the light of the work program and in this way decides upon the total budget for the forthcoming year, definitely allocating to each spending agency the maximum amount which it may spend during the budget year. Each spending agency is then notified of the maximum amount which it may spend and asked to submit its estimates so as not to exceed this amount. In the event that a spending agency desires to submit requests in excess of the amount allowed by the manager, it must do so on supplementary estimate sheets and arrange the requests in the order of their importance. These additional requests are allowed only in the event and to the extent that revenue is found to be available to meet them at the subsequent date when the budget is formulated. Mr. Edy claims that this method has greatly reduced the work of preparing the city budget, since the estimates require very little revision and practically no redrafting. (p. 307)

Some people think that target-based budgeting is a spinoff of zero-based budgeting, because its prioritization of expenditures is like that of zero-based budgeting, even though in target-based budgeting prioritization occurs only at the margins of the budget. However, the clear existence of target-based budgeting in the 1920s suggests that target-based budgeting existed prior to zero-based budgeting and was not a derivative of it.

Implementing Target-Based Budgeting

In practice, the ceilings, or targets, in target-based budgets are often a percentage of a constant services or maintenance of effort budget. The cost for each department of providing this year's level of services next year is figured by the budget office. The maintenance of effort figure is considered by many budget officers to be the key to keeping the costs of services from growing from year to year. Maintenance of effort is usually calculated by subtracting one-time costs from the present budget, adding in one-time costs for the following year, including specific inflation estimates where appropriate, and sometimes including the estimated increases in labor costs. The targets given to the departments, which provide ceilings for their budget requests, can be more or less than the maintenance of effort figure, but the maintenance of effort figure is normally the starting point.

Departments can be given one target for all expenditures, or two, one for capital and one for operating. The ideal is to use one target, to maximize the kinds of trade-offs that departments can make and encourage department heads to innovate. For example, in meeting a target, a department head might propose to substitute a piece of equipment for several employees, reducing costs. If capital and operating targets are separate, the possibility of such trade-offs is eliminated. However, if it seems likely that a single target would be abused, the dual targets can be substituted. For example, if department heads eliminate all capital items from their requests in order to get under the target in one year, and then argue the next year that they have to have a variety of capital items because they had none the previous year, the greater control of the dual targets may be preferable.

Assuming for a moment a single consolidated target, when a department prepares its request, if its target is less than the constant services or maintenance of effort amount, some of the current year's expenditures have to be squeezed out. If those expenditures are still deemed important, the department head can put the squeezed out items on a second list, sometimes called the unfunded list. Other items can also be placed on the unfunded list, such as service expansions or requests for other items that were not in the current year's budget. Some cities require service expansion requests to be handled on a third form, with a specific justification of need. For each unfunded list, the department rank orders the unfunded items and provides the budget office with an explanation of each item and the managerial and service impacts of not funding it.

Attractions of Target-Based Budgeting

Part of what target-based budgeting is supposed to accomplish is to create some flexibility to accommodate new expenditures or priorities within severely constrained budgets. Department heads are usually given the option of putting new requests into the funded list and taking other, less important items out of the current year's budget to pay for the new items or increases. This creates the possibility of some trade-offs within departmental budgets.

When the unfunded lists are collected from each department, they are merged into a citywide list (or lists) based on citywide priorities. This aggregated list is funded in priority order as far as funding allows. The money to fund the unfunded list comes from the difference between the total of the targets to the departments and the actual amount of expected revenue. In other words, the targets can be set below expected revenue in order to create a pool of funds for both urgent addbacks and new projects. The result may be a small amount of reallocation between departments. In some years, all departments may be forced to cut out their lowest-priority items, while some of them may get their low-priority items back plus other new requests.

Politicians and city managers particularly appreciate the ability of target-based budgeting to create this pool of funds for reallocation or for new policy initiatives within highly constrained budgets. For the city manager, the pool of funds can be used to bolster the capital budget for routine expenses such as street maintenance. Politicians like the ability to fund high-visibility projects such as crime patrols or drug outreach and education.

However, in practice, the reallocation aspect of target-based budgeting may get lost. The system can deteriorate into across-the-board allocations not particularly different in impact from the across-the-board cuts that used to be performed by the budget office in the old incrementalist days. If all departments are given the same target—say 10 percent reduction—and if there are no addbacks, due to constrained revenue, then the target-based budgeting system leads to simple across-the-board reductions. If each department's unfunded priorities list is treated as requiring equal treatment, or as commonly occurs, one department gets a larger share one year balanced by a larger share for another department in another year, the potentials for reallocation are limited.

Another attraction of target-based budgeting for politicians is that it makes it both possible and easy to reduce revenues and to force cuts on departments that the departments have to implement. Some cities that have used target-based budgeting have used it not only when revenues were declining, but when politicians wanted to cut the property tax and get political credit for it. Target-based budgeting makes continual reduction in revenue sources so easy that politicians sometimes find it tempting to continue to cut revenues without much concern for how the departments are coping with effects on management and service delivery. The result can be irrational for the departments because they cannot maintain a constant level of services with continually declining revenues.

Because this temptation is more or less built into target-based budgeting, target-based budgeting is often accompanied by some kind of service-level analysis and a kind of contract between the departments and the council for a certain level of services for a certain level of funding. If the council is willing to have less service for less revenue, the departments have to go along, but the council is bound by the agreement as well as the department and is not supposed to continually reduce resources while expecting the same or higher levels of services. If this kind of agreement is to work, the elected officials have to feel bound by it and have to believe there is not much waste in the departments. These conditions do not always hold.

IRENE S. RUBIN

BIBLIOGRAPHY

Buck, A. E., 1929. *Public Budgeting*. New York: Harper.
Lewis, V., 1988. "Reflections on Budget Systems." *Public Budgeting and Finance*, vol. 8, no. 1: 4–19.
Rocca, H., 1935. *Council-Manager Government in Berkeley, California*. Berkeley, CA: James J. Gillick.
Rubin, I. S., 1991. "Budgeting for Our Times: Target-Based Budgeting." *Public Budgeting and Finance*, vol. 11, no. 3: 5–14.

Wenz, T., and A. Nolan, 1982. "Budgeting for the Future: Target Base Budgeting." *Public Budgeting and Finance,* vol. 2, no. 2: 88–91.

TAX ADMINISTRATION.
The application of tax laws for the collection of public revenue.

Most public revenue comes not from the sales proceeds of a voluntary exchange between buyer and seller but rather from the government's application of its power to collect sovereign coercive payments–taxes–that, in combination with revenue from a variety of lesser sources, finance government operations. These taxes do not purchase any specific public service; indeed, faithful payment of taxes owed buys nothing from government but serves only to keep the taxpayer out of difficulty with tax collectors and other law enforcement officers. Such payments are not free-will offerings volunteered from civic duty after individuals establish what their own "fair shares" would be. They are required liabilities that the government has established as the appropriate payment that emerges from the application of a politically determined structure of revenue laws. Payment of the amount established in that structure is compulsory. This power to tax, the governmental authority to take resources from private owners for public use, is the fundamental act of faith in government that permits provision of public services in a market economy and serves as the basis for political power of the modern state (Schumpeter 1918).

The application of these tax structures faces a natural tension in the private economy: For core government services, there is no distinction in service enjoyed according to the amount of tax paid. Those paying no tax, indeed, receive services that are not distinguishable from those available to those who do pay. Hence, individuals and business firms have considerable selfish economic interest in reducing their own tax payments while others in their taxing jurisdiction pay as much of the full amount as can be collected. So long as aggregate tax collections cover the cost of the services available to all, then any private entity is economically served by reducing its own tax payment.

Tax administrators must counteract this economic inclination if government is to have adequate resources available to provide public services. Taxes are not payments for services rendered and tax structures can be designed according to plans separate from those associated with what services will be provided. That separability gives government the ability to accomplish public goals from the revenue side, as well as from spending choices, a flexibility not available in marketplace transactions between buyer and seller. However, to preserve the productivity of the revenue system, tax administrators must ensure that these taxes will not be viewed as voluntary offerings and that honest taxpayers will not believe that their tax payments place them at an important competitive disadvantage against their neighbors.

Elements of Tax Policy

Tax policy seeks, according to George Break and Joseph Pechman (1975), "to transfer control of resources from one group in the society to another and to do so in ways that do not jeopardize, and may even facilitate, the attainment of other economic goals" (p. 4). Tax administration accomplishes this transfer, seeking to raise the public revenue envisioned in tax laws, but those laws need to be framed so that they accomplish the transfer of resources to public use with the least harm to social and economic well-being. Fiscal analysts normally evaluate tax options according to four basic criteria:

1. *Yield*: Taxes may be levied for nonrevenue purposes, that is, to regulate, discourage, or assist certain activities, but usually taxes are designed to raise money for public purposes. By that standard, a tax would normally not be desirable unless it will raise meaningful revenue at a socially and economically acceptable tax rate. Once enacted, however, not all taxes perform in the same fashion over time. In particular, taxes have different responsiveness to economic growth, inflation, interest rates, national and regional recessions, and other economic phenomena. Choices about the overall revenue portfolio for a government have to weigh these behavioral characteristics with the underlying fiscal objectives of that unit. For instance, a government with a citizenry having a demand for public services that grows more rapidly than the economy would be poorly served by taxes whose growth lags behind the economy. Similarly, a government with a strict balanced budget requirement would need to avoid taxes which are highly sensitive to economic fluctuations. Although heavy use of a single revenue source may be in the fiscal interest of some governments, for example, reliance on consumer taxes in a tourist-destination enclave, many governments seek more diversity and balance in their revenue portfolios to protect yield through a variety of economic circumstances.

2. *Equity*: Governments may choose between two logical standards for distributing the cost of government: benefits received, in which shares of that cost are distributed in proportion to the returns that taxpayers get from those services, and ability to pay, in which cost shares are allocated in relation to tax-bearing capacity. The former standard, quasi-market as it is, has attractive attributes: Because payment comes from beneficiaries, individuals cannot benefit at the expense of others, and revenue flows give important signals about which government services are desired by the public. Unfortunately, calculating the share of service benefits received by a particular taxpayer with the degree of precision necessary for preparation of an individual tax bill normally is impossible. Furthermore, the

approach breaks down completely for the finance of services that intend income redistribution: To charge the beneficiaries negates a fundamental objective of providing the service.

Ability to pay, assigning tax shares according to tax-bearing capacity, is the more typical standard for financing both pure public goods, where nonappropriable returns prevent assignment of individual benefit, and other services, where benefit-received finance might be feasible. The fairness principle has both horizontal and vertical dimensions. Horizontal equity requires, in the words of the U.S. Supreme Court, "the reasonable attainment of a rough equity in tax treatment of similarly situated" taxpayers (*Allegheny Pittsburgh Coal Company 1989*). Differences based on clear distinctions or classifications can be acceptable when the system establishes how taxpayers are not fully equal, but arbitrary or capricious differences would be inconsistent with equity. Vertical equity requires that taxpayers with greater capacity bear the cost of government–that is, pay a higher tax. Most taxes do require higher tax from those with greater tax-bearing capacity, but some taxes are such that tax payments rise less rapidly than capacity (they are regressive), some are such that payments rise just as fast as capacity (they are proportional), and some are such that payments rise faster than capacity (they are progressive). The choice among these distributional possibilities is politically volatile because it entails the possibility of using the tax system to take from some and give to others.

3. *Economic effects*: Application of the tax should distort economic decisions made by individuals and businesses as little as possible. The difference between pretax and posttax returns induces economic reaction in work choice, investment decisions, structure of business operations, location of business operations, and so on. These distortions of producer or consumer choice cause a loss to private economy producers beyond the minimum necessary from transferring resources from private to public use. In general, tax policy seeks to harm the private economy no more than what is absolutely necessary to transfer resources to public use.

4. *Collectibility*: The cost of raising a particular sum of revenue should be minimized, given the achievement of an appropriate degree of equity in administration. This cost of collection, however, extends beyond the spending of the tax collection agencies, but includes the costs that taxpayers must incur in regard to fulfilling their tax responsibilities. These costs, while often sizable and necessary for conscientious compliance with the tax law, are fundamentally no more productive than administrative costs and, again subject to concerns about distributional fairness, worth minimizing. Full collection cost, administrative plus compli-

ance, represent the appropriate target for control and reduction (Payne 1993).

Tax Policy and Administration

The fundamental concern of tax administrators must be that of producing revenue to support the operations of government. Revenue management, however, concerns more than yield. Penniman (1980) notes, "The tax official's service can be generalized only in terms of the value of the revenue he collects for the operation of all government and in the fairness with which he collects such revenue within the state's tax framework" (p. 173). Not only does the concern with fairness encompass the need to avoid hurtful, intentional discrimination, but it also produces an internal conflict in resource allocation that complicates managerial choice. Administrative resources are not free and choices have to be made between avenues for the pursuit of tax collections. Some potential quests for tax liability, although likely to produce some collections, promise to yield less than the cost of seeking them. Under a pure revenue objective, the best-returning categories for administrative enforcement–line of business, type of income received, organizational nature of the taxpayer, and so forth–would be examined first, until the administrative budget is exhausted. Some tax liability–the fundamentally more complicated or more skillfully hidden–would go unsought and unpaid. Leaving this tax unpaid, however, creates an unfair disadvantage for the honest taxpayer. The authorities can maximize net revenue from the budget without regard to enforcement equity. Most governments, however, will be concerned with equity as well and will seek enforcement fairness. That may not mean the extreme position of ensuring equal error (nonpayment) rates, but it normally means that tax error rates, including both intentional and accidental, do not systematically advantage certain taxpayers. As Surrey (1967) observed, "A tax administration which seeks compliance must protect those who comply or else compliance will not be forthcoming" (p. 506).

Taxes differ in the balance of requirements they place on tax administrators and on taxpayers in the collection process (Shoup 1969). Some taxes, like the real property tax, are taxpayer-passive. The taxpayer has minimal responsibility in the process; tax administrators, by contrast, must maintain records about the property, determine the taxable base for that property, establish the rates and other provisions appropriate for the parcel, calculate the bill for the property holder, and account for and distribute payments to the proper taxing units. For these taxes, collection cost is overwhelmingly administrative because collections processes are predominantly in the realm of the tax authorities, not the taxpayer.

Other taxes, like the individual income tax, place major requirements on the taxpayer rather than the administrator. The taxpayer must maintain income and expense records during the year and organize these records for a taxpayer–prepared return that proposes the tax liability for the year. Administrators distribute reporting materials and receive returns and payments, but they predominantly tailor their efforts to facilitate and encourage this compliance by the taxpayer, sometimes through targeted enforcement to verify appropriate compliance, but administrative return is primarily through revenue encouraged rather than revenue directly discovered. The cost of these administrative efforts is much less in aggregate than those of taxpayer compliance. For these taxpayer-active taxes, efficient administration seeks to induce voluntary compliance with the tax law, thus yielding revenue at low collection (administrative and compliance) cost.

Elements of the Collection Process

The nature of tax administration differs among the types of tax. Thus, the process for collecting a taxpayer-active tax on the value of an economic stock, like a real property tax, would not closely match that for a taxpayer-active tax on transactions in an economic flow, like a retail sales tax. Six steps—inventory preparation, base assessment, tax computation and collection, audit, appeal-protest, and enforcement—constitute the broad outline of tax administration, although the content of each differs somewhat to the specifics of the subject tax. The first step, preparation of an inventory of tax eligibles, establishes a foundation for collecting the tax, in terms both of ensuring completeness of coverage and of providing a standard against which delinquency can be ultimately checked. For taxes like those applied to retail sales and individual income, both taxpayer-active taxes, the inventory becomes a mailing list for form distribution; for real property taxes, the inventory is a tax map, sometimes from aerial photos, that establishes a physical checklist for completeness of property records kept by the government. Although these inventories may be on file cards, microforms, or machine-readable formats, almost all American governments now maintain inventories for major taxes in computer-accessible formats.

Base assessment, establishing the values upon which tax will be applied, characteristically requires an accounting tabulation of transactions that have occurred within a tax period, as with taxable sales or employee wages in a quarter or income in a year. There will be interpretational issues, but the flow of market transactions usually establishes a clear base. Much of the data may come from third-party reports, sometimes electronically submitted, by employers, financial institutions, and the like, so the flow of highly reliable information easily available to tax authorities is great and represents an important stock of data for enforcement research. Simply by electronically comparing the return data with the third-party reports, administrators generate significant enforcement findings. These data may ultimately become the basis for return-free filing, a system under which tax administrators use information on tax-

payer filing status, number of people in the taxpaying unit, and third-party-reported compensation to automatically compute returns without effort by the taxpayer. Tax authorities in Great Britain, Germany, and Japan use such "return-free" systems to some extent; the United States goes no further than electronic filing (U.S. General Accounting Office 1992).

Property taxes follow a different pattern because they apply to the estimated value, for tax purposes, of the stock value of a parcel of property at a particular date. It is not based on current transactions, but on a stock estimation. To attain valuations that yield consistent treatment of properties is both the most critical and the most difficult element of property tax administration. To treat all parcel holders equitably requires that all parcels in a taxing unit be appraised consistently according to whatever valuation standard is the law. Faithful application of the standard approaches to property appraisal—comparable sales, income capitalization, and cost or summation—can help, but achieving uniform treatment of all parcels is no easy task (Eckert 1990). Assessment uniformity will be improved when the law directs assessment at a high fraction, ideally 100 percent, of market value; when the effective property tax rate is high; when laws provide formal programs of relief targeted to the elderly and of use value assessment for agricultural property; when assessors have good technical tools (tax maps, computerized mass appraisal systems, and access to building permit data); and reassessments are done on a short, regular cycle (Bowman and Mikesell 1990). But not all states want to bear the costs of adopting such systems, and uniformity remains a problem in many jurisdictions.

Tax computation, remittance, and revenue accounting brings revenue to the Treasury, assures prompt collection and deposit of payments, and pursues missing returns. For taxpayer-passive taxes, real property taxes for example, revenue authorities apply statutory tax rates, exemptions, and other structural features to the tax base records they maintain and submit bills for payment. Revenue accounting systems then track the payment process, ultimately flagging delinquent accounts for enforcement proceedings. For taxpayer-active taxes, sales or individual income for example, the taxpayer (or someone acting as the taxpayer's representative) applies tax structures to the base previously valued through an accumulation of transaction records during the year and submits a return. These returns, often scheduled with progress payments during the year to be followed by a reconciliation at yearend, may accompany required electronic transfer of funds for larger payments to provide quick and certain availability of revenue for the recipient government. Returns are compared with the master inventory of taxpayers to determine delinquencies and to initiate procedures to elicit missing returns and any payment due. Initial contacts are normally by mail and telephone; later contacts on business taxes may be in person, although computer-controlled mailings and telephone contacts constitute the normal delinquency control strategy.

Audit seeks to maintain substantial compliance with the tax law. In a taxpayer-passive system, audit will be focused on evaluating the assessment of tax administrators. For example, in real property taxation, the concern will be the extent to which property assessors have estimated the tax base according to a consistent and uniform standard across similar properties. In a taxpayer-active system, tax audits seek to encourage voluntary compliance with the tax law by making noncompliance appear to be an uneconomic gamble because of the danger of being caught and penalized. As Norman Nowak (1970) noted, "The auditing of the taxpayer's books is the usual means whereby respect for the tax service in finding and punishing evasion is developed. On the effectiveness of this function hinges the percentage of tax evasion that each country will have" (p. 68). Although audits do bring direct recovery of revenue, the indirect effect of induced compliance should be many times greater than those findings. Only a small percentage of all accounts will be audited because of scarce administrative resources, so selection of audit assignments for impact on overall compliance, both voluntary and direct, is critical for equitable and economical collection of a tax.

Tax statutes contain many uncertainties about how certain economic arrangements are to be taxed. Protesting and appeals clarify these areas of uncertainty, thus making a valuable contribution to the process of legislation. Some costs associated with these processes can be reduced by clear administrative regulations, but it is not economical to expect that all questions will be answered in those regulations, especially when technological change is rapidly altering the nature of commerce. A smooth appeal process, often through a specialized tax court, helps ensure that laws will be applied uniformly and economically and that uncertainty about application of the law will be fairly and speedily clarified.

The final administrative step is enforcement, the application of remedies to protect the public purse when other collection avenues have been fruitless. Few accounts will enter this stage, but it is the necessary last resort to protect taxpayers from being at a competitive and an equity disadvantage against those who do not pay their taxes. Enforcement of most taxes involves attachment of individual assets or wages, but property tax enforcement often involves the sale of the property against which the tax was levied. Few enforcement actions are likely to be popular, but sale of properties because of unpaid property tax creates greater dispute than other remedies, and politicians are often reluctant to hold necessary tax sales. Such delays can create blocks of orphan properties in declining neighborhoods when accumulated delinquent taxes approximate the market value of the property parcel and no one will hold clear title to the property.

Summary

Successful application of a system of taxation is critical for government in a market system because the system achieves the transfer of resources from private ownership to government use. The transfer must yield revenue sufficient for government operation, but there are other planning concerns beyond yield. In particular, the transfer may be arranged to distribute costs equitably, structured to minimize distortion of economic activity, and designed to reduce the cost of collecting that revenue. These collection structures require varying combinations of taxpayer responsibility and government administration. Those based on significant taxpayer responsibility have administrative processes tailored to induce voluntary compliance and to ensure economic protection of honest taxpayers.

JOHN L. MIKESELL

BIBLIOGRAPHY

Allegheny Pittsburgh Coal Company v. County Commission of Webster County, West Virginia, 1989. 109 S.Ct. 633.

Bowman, John H., and John L. Mikesell, 1990. "Improving Administration of the Property Tax: A Review of Prescriptions and Their Impacts." *Public Budgeting and Financial Management*, vol. 2: 151–176.

Break, George F., and Joseph A. Pechman, 1975. *Federal Tax Reform: The Impossible Dream?* Washington, DC: Brookings Institution.

Eckert, Joseph K., ed., 1990. *Property Appraisal and Assessment Administration.* Chicago, IL: International Association of Assessing Officers.

Mikesell, John. L., 1995. *Fiscal Administration.* Belmont, CA: Wadsworth.

Nowak, Norman D., 1970. *Tax Administration in Theory and Practice.* New York: Praeger.

Payne, James L., 1993. *Costly Returns: The Burdens of the U.S. Tax System.* San Francisco, CA: Institute for Contemporary Studies.

Penniman, Clara, 1980. *State Income Tax Administration.* Baltimore: Johns Hopkins University Press.

Schumpeter, Joseph A., 1918. "The Crisis of the Tax State." In R. Swedberg, ed., *The Economics and Sociology of Capitalism*, 1991. Princeton, NJ: Princeton University Press.

Shoup, Carl S., 1969. *Public Finance.* Chicago: Aldine.

Surrey, Stanley S., 1967. "Tax Administration in Underdeveloped Countries." In R. Bird and O. Oldman, eds., *Readings in Taxation in Developing Countries*, rev. ed. Baltimore: Johns Hopkins University Press.

U.S. General Accounting Office, 1992. *Internal Revenue Service: Opportunities to Reduce Taxpayer Burden Through Return-Free Filing.* GAO/GGD-92-88BR. Washington, DC: U.S. General Accounting Office.

TAX AMNESTY. A program under which delinquent taxpayers are allowed to file returns and pay previously owed delinquent taxes without threat of civil or criminal prosecution by the taxing entity. Tax amnesties abate the delinquency but do not remove the underlying liability for the taxes owed. Tax amnesties are usually limited in time period and followed by stricter penalties upon detection of taxpayer noncompliance.

Origin

Between 1982 and 1992, 33 states and the District of Columbia conducted some type of tax amnesty program, with other states considering them. Table I contains state-by-state information about amnesty programs conducted between 1982 and 1990. Most state tax amnesty programs have been authorized by the state legislatures, although some were conducted based on previous legislation permitting the waiver of tax penalties. The programs tend to be short, anywhere from 30 to 90 days, and carry waivers of all civil and criminal penalties for amnesty participants. Most programs have applied to individual income taxes, but Florida and Texas have conducted amnesties in the absence of income taxes. Some states have waived full or partial interest on delinquent taxes or allowed payments to be made on installment plans. Some states have included current accounts receivable in the amnesty programs, but others have not included accounts receivable. Most states have increased the penalty for tax evasion subsequent to the amnesty period, and have increased the funding for post-amnesty tax code enforcement. Tax amnesty programs address two compatible tax policy goals: increased taxpayer compliance and increased tax revenues.

Current Practice

Tax amnesty programs are usually put forth as part of a tax enforcement and compliance program, not as a stand-alone program. States have tended to rely on the Internal Revenue Service (IRS) to enforce tax compliance: The IRS shares information with the states, and some states coordinate audits with the IRS. Jeffrey Dubin, Michael Graetz, and Louis Wilde (1992) find that when the IRS has been active in a state, the state is less likely to conduct a tax amnesty program. But as IRS auditing rates decreased during the 1980s, the states were less likely to "free ride" on the compliance programs of the IRS and conducted their own tax compliance strategies, including tax amnesty programs. Tax amnesty programs have been most successful when they have been conducted as one of several components of a well-publicized overarching program geared toward increasing taxpayer compliance.

Tax amnesties have occurred during a time of overall fiscal decline. During a period of sustained fiscal decline and diminishing resources due to taxpayer revolts and revenue limitation efforts, tax amnesty at the state level has provided a one-time fiscal enhancement. However, states have not conducted amnesties during times of severe fiscal stress. Perhaps the administrative costs and innovative nature of such programs make them difficult to initiate during severely constrained periods. State tax amnesty programs have generated over US $1.5 billion in revenues from over 750,000 participants, most of whom were individual income taxpayers. Discussion continues about the long-term implications of tax amnesty programs to the fiscal entity beyond the one-time revenue boost realized during the amnesty period. Critics claim that in the long term, tax amnesty programs provide a disincentive to paying taxes that will eventually decrease revenues.

Tax amnesty programs are not solely a state phenomenon. Chicago, New York, Los Angeles, and Detroit have conducted or considered tax amnesty programs. Other agencies with responsibility for the collection of particular taxes have also conducted amnesty programs. The prospect of a federal tax amnesty has been discussed, but such efforts have been unsuccessful. While the Internal Revenue Service does not support a tax amnesty program at the federal level, it does routinely exempt voluntary payments from delinquent taxpayers from civil and criminal penalties, although all interest due is collected. As a part of the IRS Compliance 2000 program, the IRS issued a written statement saying that it will not recommend criminal prosecution for voluntary disclosures, thereby codifying this previously informal tradition.

Theoretical Framework

Economic explanations for criminal behavior assume that individuals are rational, with full information about their own incomes and the probabilities of detection and incarceration. When applied to tax compliance behavior, the economic theory of criminal behavior suggests that some individuals will rationally decide to evade paying taxes. Further, these individuals will evade taxes whenever the expected benefits exceed the expected costs, given their particular attitudes about risk. As analysts consider the costs of an additional audit against the yield, the notion of "optimal" tax evasion emerges.

Some analysts have taken exception with this simplistic view, and have modeled taxpayer attitude, the effects of marginal tax rates, and other factors into the decision to cheat. In addition to tax rate, the probability of audit and severity of penalty have been cited as correlates of tax compliance. Not all occupations provide identical opportunities to evade; federal and state tax withholding systems subject many workers to third-party reporting if they work for tax-compliant employers. As a result, the proportion of workers unemployed, employed in manufacturing jobs, and self-employed also have been identified as determinants of tax evasion.

Proponents of tax amnesty rely on the claim that delinquent taxes are often attributable to nonfilers. They argue that simply getting these individuals on the tax rolls

TABLE I. CHARACTERISTICS OF STATE TAX AMNESTY PROGRAMS 1982–1990.

State	Amnesty Period	Legislative Authorization	Taxes Covered	Accounts Receivable	Interest Waived (in %)	Installment Arrangements
Alabama	1/20/84–4/01/84	no	all	no	no	no
Arizona	11/22/82–1/20/83	no	all	no	no	yes
Arkansas	9/01/87–11/30/87	yes	all	no	no	yes
California	12/10/84–3/15/85	yes	individual income	yes	no	yes
	12/10/84–3/15/85	yes	sales	no	no	yes
Colorado	9/16/85–11/15/85	yes	all	no	no	yes
Connecticut	9/01/90–11/30/90	yes	all	yes	no	yes
Florida	1/01/87–6/30/87	yes	intangibles	no	no	no
	1/01/88–8/30/83	yes	all	yes	no	yes
Idaho	10/01/84–11/30/84	no	all	no	no	no
Illinois	10/01/84–11/30/84	yes	all	yes	50	no
Iowa	9/02/86–10/31/86	yes	all	yes	50	no
Kansas	7/01/84–9/30/84	yes	all	no	no	no
Kentucky	9/15/88–12/16/88	yes	all	yes	50	yes
Louisiansa	10/01/85–12/31/85	yes	all	no	no	yes
	10/01/87–12/15/87	yes	all	no	no	yes
Maine	11/01/90–12/31/90	yes	all	yes	50	yes
Maryland	9/01/87–11/02/87	yes	all	yes	no	no
Massachusetts	10/17/83–1/17/84	yes	all	yes	no	yes
Michigan	5/12/86–6/30/86	yes	all	yes	no	no
Minnesota	8/01/84–10/31/84	yes	all	yes	no	no
Mississippi	9/01/86–11/30/86	yes	all	no	100	no
Missouri	9/01/83–10/31/83	no	all	no	no	no
New Jersey	9/10/87–12/08/87	yes	all	yes	no	yes
New Mexico	8/15/85–11/13/85	yes	all	no	100	yes
New York	11/01/85–1/31/86	yes	all	yes	no	yes
N. Carolina	9/01/89–12/01/89	yes	all	yes	no	no
N. Dakota	9/01/83–11/30/83	no	all	no	no	yes
Oklahoma	7/01/84–12/31/84	yes	income, sales	yes	no	no
Rhode Island	10/15/86–1/12/87	yes	all	no	no	yes
S. Carolina	9/01/85–11/30/85	yes	all	yes	no	yes
Texas	2/01/84–2/29/84	no	all	no	no	no
Vermont	5/15/90–6/25/90	yes	all	yes	no	no
Virginia	2/01/90–3/31/90	yes	all	yes	no	no
Washington, D.C.	7/01/87–9/30/87	yes	all	yes	50–100	yes
W. Virginia	10/01/86–12/31/86	yes	all	yes	no	yes
Wisconsin	9/15/85–11/22/85	yes	all	yes	yes	yes

gives the governmental entity a record of their existence and will facilitate future receipts. For example, studies show that nonfilers account for only 0.1 percent of collections, or US $0.77 per capita, while accounts receivable programs, which involve previously identified tax delinquents, generated US $11.09 per capita, or 1.1 percent of annual revenue collections. These underreporters are already on the tax rolls and are just "coming clean" to avoid penalty and possible criminal prosecution. Opponents of

tax amnesty argue that such taxpayers might continue to underreport in the future in order to take advantage of potential future amnesties. The experience of states that conduct multiple amnesties will have to be analyzed to see which of these claims bears up under scrutiny.

Proponents of tax amnesty programs claim that getting delinquents on the tax rolls will increase future compliance. James Alm and William Beck (1993) look at the long-run effects of amnesty programs on compliance and the implications for tax revenues. Even if proponents are correct in the assertion that tax amnesty will expand the tax rolls, the taxing entity strives to maximize revenues, not just participation. Increasing the number of filers will enhance future compliance if the audit and penalty rates are sufficient to encourage continuing voluntary compliance among these new filers. If not, then the additional filers provide only a one-time revenue increase for the taxing entity. Additionally, amnesty programs could provide a disincentive for future compliance among those who believe that another amnesty will occur.

Proponents of tax amnesty programs claim that the introduction of stiffer penalties will reduce future tax evasion through underreporting or nonreporting, and will increase revenues in the long run. Detractors claim that amnesty programs will disillusion currently compliant taxpayers who will feel unforgiving toward tax amnesty participants who have not been punished for their tax evasion. These disillusioned taxpayers are more likely to underreport in the future, as a reaction to the unfairness of the initial amnesty. Also, amnesty participants might believe that their future tax burdens will be forgiven at some future date and will continue to underreport. Daniel Nagin (1993) does not even include tax amnesty as an instrument to combat noncompliance. Reasoning that amnesty reduces the cost of noncompliance, Nagin suspects that it might have a deleterious effect on future compliance rates.

Tax amnesty programs are costly to administer, leading some to question their cost-effectiveness. Publicity, both for the amnesty program and the postamnesty enforcement program, is critical to the success of a tax amnesty program. In addition, staff hours are required for planning, implementation, management, and evaluation of the tax amnesty program. The nature of tax amnesty programs means that the workload is highly uncertain, which exacerbates the administrative difficulties.

Although the IRS has recently taken a stance opposing tax amnesty, the IRS routinely does not prosecute nonfilers and underreporters who voluntarily surrender delinquent taxes and associated interest to the IRS. Only delinquents whom the IRS identifies are subject to involuntary payment of past due taxes and subjected to any criminal penalty. This tacit amnesty lacks two features that are regarded as critical for the success of amnesty programs: limited time period of the amnesty program and increased future penalties for noncompliance.

The IRS phenomenon has led some analysts to suggest that the IRS acts as a high-interest money lender. Credit "customers" (tax evaders) include some individuals who would not qualify for credit in ordinary capital markets. Given their attitude toward risk and their willingness to pay for capital in the current period, some individuals might decide to "borrow" from the IRS. By cheating on their federal taxes, the tax cheaters are effectively paying probabilistic interest rates in the form of possible penalties and late fees. Tax amnesties afford the possibility to "borrow" for some finite period and then pay back without fear of civil or criminal prosecution.

Paula S. Kearns

BIBLIOGRAPHY

Allingham, Michael G., and Agnar Sandmo, 1972. "Income Tax Evasion: A Theoretical Analysis." *Journal of Public Economics*, vol. 1 (November) 323–338.
Alm, James, and William Beck, 1993. "Tax Amnesties and Compliance in the Long Run: A Time Series Analysis." *National Tax Journal*, vol. 46 (March) 53–60.
Dubin, Jeffrey A., Michael J. Graetz, and Louis L. Wilde, 1992. "State Tax Amnesties: Causes." *Quarterly Journal of Economics*: vol 107 No. 3, 1057–1070.
Federation of Tax Administrators, 1990. *State Tax Amnesty Programs*. Research Report No. 133 (August).
Mikesell, John L., 1986. "Amnesties for State Tax Evaders: The Nature of and Response to Recent Programs." *National Tax Journal*, vol. 39 (December) 507–525.
Nagin, Daniel S., 1993. "Policy Options for Combatting Tax Noncompliance." *Journal of Policy Analysis and Management*, vol. 9 (Fall) 7–22.

TAX-EXEMPT ORGANIZATION.

An organization exempt from income taxation because it operates to provide either broad social benefits to the public or mutual benefits to its members. Many organizations are also exempt from state and local income and property taxes, although the exemptions vary with each local jurisdiction.

Reason for Exemption

In the United States, Congress determined that two categories of nonprofit organizations qualified for exemption from income taxation: social benefit organizations and mutual benefit organizations. Social benefit organizations operate to improve the quality of life in a community. Examples include charitable organizations and social welfare organizations (see **charitable organization** and **social welfare organization**). Mutual benefit organizations operate to promote the welfare of the members of the organization rather than the public at large. Examples include labor unions, trade associations, and social clubs.

An essential feature of both types of organizations is that they must not be organized to enrich investors. For example, a music school that is owned by a few teachers and investors will not qualify as a charity, whereas a similar school that is part of a college will. A privately owned restaurant cannot qualify for tax-exemption, whereas a private social club that restricts its dining facilities to its members can. Similarly, a privately owned business that gathers statistics about industry sales and sells it to purchasers will not qualify as a tax-exempt organization, whereas a nonprofit trade association that gathers and distributes similar information to its members will. Although the purpose of many mutual benefit organizations is to improve the economic vitality of their members, that is not considered a form of private benefit that will prohibit tax-exempt status.

Despite a general exemption from income tax, a tax-exempt organization will generally be liable for income tax on profits from unrelated business activities. This can arise from fund-raising activities, such as selling holiday cards, or from certain investments, such as being a partner in a mining operation.

Economic Activity

The number of tax-exempt organizations in the United States has significantly increased in recent years, according to the Internal Revenue Service (IRS) Statistics of Income Bulletin issued August 1995. In 1990, there were 1,022,223 tax-exempt organizations, which is a 27 percent increase over the 806,375 organizations that existed in 1978. Over that time period, the assets of tax-exempt organizations increased by 150 percent to over US $1 trillion and their revenues increased by 225 percent to US $560 billion, whereas the nation's gross domestic product (GDP) increased by only 52 percent. In 1990, the revenue of tax-exempt organizations constituted nearly 10 percent of the nation's GDP, an increase from 6 percent in 1975. Charities alone accounted for more than 7 percent of GDP in 1990.

Charitable organizations comprise the largest category of tax-exempt organizations (48 percent of all tax-exempt organizations described in Section 501(c)), followed by social welfare organizations (14 percent), fraternal organizations (10 percent), labor and agricultural organizations (7 percent), business leagues (6 percent), and social clubs (6 percent). Certain segments of the tax-exempt sector are growing faster than others. Whereas the number of tax-exempt organizations grew by 27 percent from 1978 to 1990, the greatest growth was in the number of charities (67 percent), business leagues (45 percent), and social welfare organizations (14 percent). By comparison, the number of labor and agricultural organizations decreased by 18 percent.

Overview of Legal Requirements

Most state statutes specify procedures to establish a nonprofit corporation or some other form of nonprofit organization, such as a cooperative or a benevolent association. Many statutes require the organization to specify in its organization documents (e.g., articles of incorporation, bylaws) whether it is a social benefit or a mutual benefit organization. Complying with these state laws does not ensure that an organization will be tax-exempt under the federal income tax laws. Instead, each organization's governing documents must also contain specific provisions that comply with the federal laws that grant tax-exemption.

Most organizations must apply to the IRS for tax-exempt status before they will be treated as tax-exempt, although churches are a notable exception.

Section 501(c) Organizations. The most important statute that grants tax-exemption is Section 501(c) of the Internal Revenue Code. It lists 25 types of tax-exempt organizations in relatively random order. In order to obtain tax-exemption, most organizations structure their legal documents and limit their operations to comply with the appropriate exemption. Many organizations can describe their operations to outsiders by simply referring to the appropriate paragraph of the statute.

The different types of tax-exempt organizations are listed here in the order that they appear in Section 501(c). For example, number (3) on the list corresponds to Section 501(c)(3). The number in brackets represents the number of that type of organization that existed in the United States in 1991, according to IRS records. The following types of organizations are exempt from federal income tax under Section 501(c):

1. A tax-exempt corporation organized by an act of Congress that is an instrumentality of the United States. Examples include the Federal Deposit Insurance Corporation (FDIC) and the Pension Benefit Guarantee corporation (PBGC). [9]
2. A corporation organized for the exclusive purpose of holding title to property, collecting income therefrom and turning over the entire amount, less expenses, to another tax-exempt organization. [6,408]
3. A charitable organization that engages primarily in charitable activities. [516,554 plus an estimated 340,000 churches for a total of 856,554]
4. A social welfare organization that promotes the general welfare of a community by bringing about civic betterments and social improvements. The statute also exempts certain local associations of employees, such as a local police relief association. [142,811]
5. A labor union, agricultural, or horticultural organization. A labor organization is an association of workers who have combined to promote their interests by bargaining collectively with their employers to secure better working conditions, wages, and similar benefits. An example is the United Auto Workers. An agricultural or horticultural organization operates to improve the economic conditions of agriculture or horticulture workers, the grade of their products, and the efficiency of production. [72,009]
6. A trade association, business league, chamber of commerce, real-estate board, board of trade, or professional football league. Examples include the American Medical Association and a city's Chamber of Commerce. [68,442]
7. A social club organized for pleasure, recreation, and other nonprofit purposes, provided that substantially

all of its activities are restricted for such purposes. Although revenue paid by members as dues, service fees, and charges for meals will generally be tax-exempt, a social club will pay tax on its investment income. [63,922]

8. A fraternal benefit society, order, or association that operates under the lodge system or for the exclusive benefit of its members and provides for the payment of life, sickness, accident, or other benefits to its members and their dependents (compare with 10 below). [98,840]

9. A voluntary employees' beneficiary association (VEBA) that provides for the payment of life, sick, accident, or other benefits to the employee members of such association or their dependents. [14,708]

10. A fraternity, sorority, domestic fraternal society, order, or association that operates under the lodge system and devotes its net earnings exclusively to religious, charitable, scientific, literary, educational, and fraternal purposes and that does not pay life, sick, accident, or other benefits to its members and their dependents (compare with 8 above). [18,360]

11. A local teachers' retirement fund whose income consists solely of amounts received from public taxation, assessments on the teaching salaries of members, and income from investments. [10]

12. A mutual ditch or irrigation company, mutual or cooperative telephone company, or a local benevolent life insurance association; but only if 85 percent or more of the income consists of amounts collected from members for the sole purpose of meeting losses and expenses. [5,984]

13. A cemetery association or company that is owned and operated exclusively for the benefit of its members or is operated not for profit. [8,781]

14. Certain types of nonprofit credit unions that are organized and operated for mutual purposes and certain types of mutual associations (organized before 1958) that provide reserve funds and insure deposits at banks and savings and loan associations. [6,219]

15. Certain types of insurance company (other than a life insurance company) whose net premiums do not exceed US $350,000 in a year. [1,147]

16. A corporation to finance the ordinary crop operations of its members. [20]

17. A trust that provides supplemental unemployment benefits to employees. [644]

18. A trust created before June 25, 1959, that is part of a pension plan that is funded only by contributions of employees. [8]

19. A post or organization that has at least 75 percent of its members comprised of past or present members of the U.S. Armed Forces. [27,962]

20. An organization that is part of a qualified group legal services plan. [206]

21. A trust established to pay claims to miners and other victims of black lung disease. [23]

22. A trust established by sponsors of a multiemployer plan (usually a union-administered retirement plan) to pay certain pension plan withdrawal liabilities. [None]

23. An association to provide insurance and other benefits to veterans associations, but only if the association was established before 1880. [2]

24. A trust to pay certain types of retirement income obligations. [None]

25. A corporation or trust that holds title to buildings and other real property for certain retirement plans, charities, or governmental subdivisions (maximum 35 beneficiaries of each organization). [181]

Other Tax-Exempt Organizations

1. A qualified retirement, pension, profit-sharing, and stock bonus plan is tax-exempt. Such a retirement plan will not pay tax on revenue from contributions from employers or from investment income, but it will be liable for tax on unrelated business income. Sections 401(a) and 501(a). [unknown]

2. A charitable remainder trust that distributes amounts annually to a person for life, or for a fixed number of years, and then terminates and distributes its assets to a charity (see **deferred giving**). In 1995, the Tax Court concluded that a charitable remainder trust will lose its tax-exempt status in any year that it has unrelated business taxable income. [16,000]

3. A farmer's cooperative is tax-exempt (Section 521). Most cooperatives merely share costs among their members rather than operate a business for profit, and they are therefore generally exempt from taxation under Subchapter T of the Internal Revenue Code. [2,129; by comparison there were 3,219 taxable farmers' cooperatives]

4. Special rules apply to cooperative service organizations of hospitals (Section 501(e) [72 in existence]) and for a pooled investment fund of educational organizations (Section 501(f) [Only 1 in existence, "The Common Fund"]).

5. A political organization (political party, election committee, etc.) is tax-exempt with respect to the amounts it receives from contributions, member dues, and proceeds from fund-raising events. However, it must pay income tax at the highest corporate rate (currently 35 percent) on its net investment income. In addition, a political candidate will be liable for income tax if any amounts are diverted for his or her personal use (Section 527).

6. A homeowners association (an organization that manages a subdivision development or a condominium) is tax-exempt with respect to the amounts it receives as membership dues, fees, or assessments from owners of

the managed property. However, it must pay a 30 percent income tax on its net investment income (Section 528).

Many nations have adopted similar policies to those of the United States and have exempted social welfare and mutual organizations from income, sales, and property taxes. Of course, the laws vary from nation to nation.

CHRISTOPHER HOYT

BIBLIOGRAPHY

Internal Revenue Service, 1995. *IRS Statistics of Income Bulletin, Summer 1995*. Washington, DC.

TAX EXPENDITURE.

A legal reduction in effective tax rates for certain classes of taxpayers, resulting in lower taxes for the individual beneficiaries and, consequently, lower tax revenues for the government.

Tax expenditures are exceptions in the tax code, placed there because of some behavior or action a taxpayer undertakes or experiences, rather than the taxpayer's income alone. By granting legal exceptions to taxes due, tax expenditures erode the tax base. Tension exists between special interests that wish to chip away at the tax base—the items and income covered by taxes—creating special exemptions and exclusions for their clients and group members, and those concerned with revenue adequacy or fairness, who wish to keep the tax base from being eroded. Much of what passes for debate over tax reform is actually debate over the type, nature, and extent of tax expenditures that shall be inserted into the tax code.

Tax Expenditures as Benefits for Individuals and Groups

Tax expenditures used to be called "tax loopholes." The term "tax expenditure" has come into vogue in recent decades as a less biased expression for the transfer of benefits through the tax code, but one that still emphasizes shifting money from the government to special groups. From the viewpoint of recipients, benefits received as tax expenditures are no less desirable or beneficial than benefits bestowed as transfer payments through budget expenditures. Tax expenditures create effective tax rates lower than nominal tax rates for beneficiaries and differential effective rates for eligible taxpayers compared to noneligible taxpayers with similar incomes.

Critics of this newer terminology, as well as of the concept of tax expenditure, have questioned the notion that the government is bestowing a benefit by "allowing" recipients to keep private income earned through market activities. Supporters argue that collective decisions have been to purchase collective goods and to allocate the burden of paying for those goods across income classes. Recipients of tax expenditures use political clout to avoid paying their "fair share" of the tax burden.

The Federal Tax Expenditure Budget

The federal tax expenditure budget has become an important tool for federal policymakers in judging the extent to which special exemptions have eroded the tax base. The 1974 Congressional Budget Act requires the president's budget to report tax expenditures for revenue plans contained in the federal budget. In that legislation, tax expenditures are defined within the act as "revenue losses attributable to provisions of the federal tax laws which allow a special exclusion, exemption, or deduction from gross income or which provide a special credit, a preferential rate of tax, or a deferral of tax liability."

In addition to its redistributive impacts, policymakers have viewed tax expenditure as an alternative policy tool to budget expenditures, credit assistance, and regulatory instruments. At times, federal tax expenditures have encouraged such diverse activities as investment, housing, charities, municipal borrowing, and oil exploration.

Tax expenditure budgets outline the major legislative exemptions listed here, the beneficiary group, and the estimated revenue loss/size of benefit emanating from each legislative exception. Although in practice, full tax expenditure budgets have only been developed at the federal level, in theory, they could also be developed by state and local governments as well. Although some fiscal notes developed for states have used some of the same analytic techniques, they have not been expanded into full tax expenditure budgets.

Estimating Tax Expenditures

Initially, analyzing tax expenditures involved estimating revenue loss from provisions different from "normal tax structure." Analysts used the section of the president's budget message devoted to tax expenditures to guide them in identifying tax expenditures. Computing what the government does not collect from individuals and corporations proved difficult. Subsequently, tax expenditures have been estimated as outlay equivalents rather than as revenue losses, although revenue losses continue to be shown separately in the budget.

A newer technique involves estimating tax expenditures as the outlays that would be required to provide beneficiaries with an equal after-tax income—a technique that results in higher numbers than the revenue loss procedure, since taxpayers would have to pay taxes on the higher income derived from direct budget outlays. Since both outlays and receipts are raised by the amount of the outlay equivalent, however, the federal deficit is not changed by the newer methodology.

The Pervasiveness and Magnitude of Tax Expenditures

The 1986 Tax Reform Act lowered marginal tax rates considerably, from a maximum of 50 percent on individuals to a maximum of 33 percent. Simultaneously, the tax base was extended through the abolition of several tax expenditures. Among those removed from the tax code were interest on consumer debt, preferential treatment for capital gains, and deductions for state and local sales taxes. Tax deductible contributions to Individual Retirement Accounts (IRAs) were limited. Nonetheless, substantial tax expenditures remain.

Federal tax expenditures are big dollars, even after the attempt in 1986 to eliminate many of them. In 1988, federal tax expenditures were estimated by the Congressional Budget Office at one-third the size of direct budget expenditures. In that year, the dollar volume of tax expenditures exceeded the federal deficit by almost US $200 billion. Eliminating tax expenditures would have eliminated the federal deficit and generated a surplus to apply toward debt reduction. Despite the drain of tax expenditures on federal revenues, the public and many politicians consider the abolition of tax expenditures to be a tax increase rather than the elimination of some special privilege.

Categories of Tax Expenditures

Common U.S. tax expenditures may be categorized into three major groups: The first is personal deductions under the individual income tax, for such items as state and local income and property taxes, contributions to charity, medical expenses, and mortgage interest paid. The second category of tax expenditures is exclusions from taxable income, such as interest on state and local government bonds, employee benefits, and transfer payments, including Social Security, veterans' benefits, and welfare. The third category is tax credits and accelerated depreciation for investment.

Preference of High Income Groups for Tax Expenditures over Direct Budget Expenditures

The use of tax expenditures is not class neutral. More affluent income classes and corporations have been frequent recipients of government benefits granted through the tax code, whereas poorer income classes more commonly receive government benefits through transfer payments allocated by direct budget expenditures. Several reasons underlie this class preference in method of receiving government benefits. Low-income groups that do not pay tax do not benefit from tax expenditures. Lower-income classes do not pay much tax, since they are in lower marginal tax brackets. The lowest-income groups may fall below the income level that is a minimum for paying income tax. They are less likely to own property and benefit from mortgage interest deductions, a standard middle-class tax expenditure.

High-income groups have higher marginal tax rates and therefore benefit more from exclusions and deductions than do moderate or low income groups. Under progressive tax systems, high income groups receive more tax savings for every dollar shielded from taxes than do low income groups. While the 1986 tax changes significantly reduced marginal rates on high income groups, rates subsequently still ranged from 12 to 33 percent, making a tax expenditure worth almost three times as much to those in the highest bracket as to those in the lowest bracket.

Political Advantages of Tax Expenditures to Direct Budget Expenditures

Politically sophisticated groups prefer tax expenditures because they are less visible than direct budget expenditures and therefore are less subject to opposition. The visibility of direct budget expenditures sometimes causes them to become a target of political opposition. For example, welfare and social service expenditures are very visible, with recipients clearly identified along with the dollar amount individual beneficiaries receive and total expenditures made for those purposes.

By contrast, tax expenditures are much less visible to the public. Often identifying who and how many beneficiaries are receiving a particular tax expenditure is difficult and may involve making assumptions about the economic behavior of recipient groups. Higher-income groups and corporations are considerably more sophisticated politically than are less-educated, low-income groups and realize the advantages of low public visibility.

Tax codes, and the benefits transferred through it in the form of tax expenditures, continue indefinitely once enacted, since debate over existing tax expenditures is episodic and irregular. As discussed earlier, the tax and budget processes differ substantially in that the latter needs overt action to continue whereas the former continues unless there is overt action. Budget appropriations are debated annually, not only nationally, but in most states. Even states with biennial budget processes often have smaller stopgap supplemental appropriations bills in the off-budget years. Thus, every year, recipients of direct expenditures must defend their budget base.

Neither the federal nor state governments annually scrutinize their entire tax code in the same fashion. Tax codes and tax expenditures are scrutinized irregularly, with long periods sometimes existing between waves of tax reform. During the interim, few questions are directed toward the continued existence of tax expenditures.

Tax expenditures, as methods of achieving public purposes and goals, are not held to the same rigorous standards of performance as are direct budget expenditures. Direct budget expenditures are not only more visible but are often subject to performance evaluation studies by the executive agencies, federal departments, outside consultants, the Office of Management and Budget, the General Accounting Office, and the Congressional Budget Office. Program failures become the object of political ridicule and public outcry. By contrast, tax expenditures are rarely subjected to rigorous evaluation studies of the same fashion applied to direct expenditures. Ineffective tax expenditures that do not achieve their stated public purpose but that do erode the tax base and lower the effective tax rate for beneficiary groups are allowed to continue with little criticism.

Tax expenditures reduce overall funding for government and hence coincide with conservative biases toward a small government with little redistribution between income classes. While some affluent taxpayers do not hold these biases, their prevalence among higher-income groups is quite common. The decided preference of high-income groups and corporations for tax expenditures over direct expenditures does not mean that the middle class never benefits from exclusions and deductions from the tax code. In particular, the middle class, as well as upper-income groups, has benefited from the mortgage interest deduction and Social Security exclusion.

Reforming Tax Expenditures

Several reforms have been proposed to address some of these difficulties: One reform would be to require Congress to declare its intention with general tax policy and allow the Treasury Department to work out the details. Only major conflicts would be brought back to the attention of the tax committees. Proponents argue that this procedure would contribute to the simplification of tax law. Critics argue that the Treasury Department is not elected and would be just as subject to influence from special interest groups as is Congress.

A second reform would be to organize commissions of experts periodically, perhaps every five years, to reexamine the tax code and report recommendations for legislation. Supporters contend greater use of special commissions would inject regular, detached examination of the tax code into the fiscal policy process. Critics contend that special commissions would not alter the tax legislative process within Congress or diminish the power of special interests there.

Others argue to reform the tax structure through sunset legislation. With sunset provisions, the tax code would expire unless reenacted, much like appropriations within the budget process. In a modified form, only major tax expenditures would be subject to a time limit and expiration through sunset provisions unless reenacted. Supporters argue that this would force reevaluation and examination of revenues, relative to current needs. Critics contend it would create chaos.

Some critics of the use of tax expenditures argue for greater coordination of the taxing and spending committees within Congress. Supporters argue that this would increase accountability and diminish free spending. Critics contend that the federal programs with the greatest increases in spending–namely Social Security and Medicare–have been within the jurisdiction of the taxing committees where responsibility for raising program revenues and approving program spending has been combined.

Other critics contend greater emphasis should be placed on the fiscal implications of tax policy. Various procedures have been suggested to accomplish this, including binding directives from the budget committees to the taxing committees. Skeptics argue, however, that procedural reforms will not diminish the impact of special interests on tax legislation and will not require stabilization needs to take precedence over the distribution of benefits through the tax code.

Marcia Lynn Whicker

BIBLIOGRAPHY

Mikesell, John L., 1986. *Fiscal Administration: Analysis and Applications for the Public Sector*, 2d ed. Chicago, IL: Dorsey Press.

Pechman, Joseph A., 1987. *Federal Tax Policy*, 5th ed. Washington, DC: Brookings Institution.

TAX INCIDENCE.   The burden taxes place on different taxpayers.

Both the terms of tax incidence and tax burden refer to who pays taxes. Although they have sometimes been used interchangeably, they do have slightly different meanings. Tax incidence refers to the distribution of the share of taxes paid across various income groups, whereas tax burden more typically refers to the impact of taxes on the individuals. Embedded in notions of tax incidence is the assumption that taxes can be and are redistributive, shifting income from some groups to others. Also embedded is the idea of fairness–that some redistribution is fairer than others so that some groups are more deserving of tax-shifted income than others.

Growing Public Sensitivity to Income Shares

The economic shifts of the 1980s and 1990s propelled the United States into a global economy, with growing income inequality. Even before the tax cuts and income shifts of the 1980s, however, Alice Rivlin, then Director of the Congressional Budget Office, suggested three reasons why public attention to relative income shares of different groups and classes would heighten.

First, television and other forms of electronic communication have made citizens increasingly conscious of the material and economic status of other income groups with a graphic force that neither radio nor the print media could equal. Increased consciousness of relative status has led to demands by groups previously removed from the economic mainstream to be incorporated into income and benefit flows to which they lacked access in the past.

Second, groups that were previously unorganized and relatively impotent politically have learned to organize to pressure for favorable redistributive policies. Pressure politics for policies altering the current distribution of income have increased as blacks, Chicanos, the elderly, public employees, and other groups have come of political age. Under one interpretation, the 1980s with its worsening inequality, reduction in social spending, and tilt of the tax system toward the rich represented a backlash against the effectiveness of these groups in preceding decades.

The third reason advanced by Rivlin for increasing focus on income shares is changing demographic and social forces. As more women entered the labor market and became heads of single parent families, the inequality between those families and more traditional husband-wife families headed by a male increased. Consequently, by the end of the 1980s, one out of four children lived in poverty. Even in husband-wife families, the entry of women into the labor force did not diminish inequality to the extent that professionals marry other professionals while routine production and service workers are also likely to marry each other.

Additionally, Lester Thurow suggested that an episodic sluggish economy would provide a fourth reason for increased concern over income shares. With an expanding pie from increasing productivity and a rapidly rising gross national product (GNP), the income share of each group may advance absolutely without incurring relative gains. With sluggish or declining productivity such as that experienced during the recession of the late 1980s and early 1990s and a less rapidly growing or even shrinking pie, absolute and relative gains necessarily coincide. The gain of one income group can only come at the expense of others, converting nonconflictual, non-zero-sum politics into conflict-embedded, zero-sum politics.

Documenting the growth of income inequality in the late twentieth century in the United States, Kevin Phillips showed how in an increasingly class-oriented and bifurcated political arena, the middle class chose in the 1970s and 1980s to shift from its New Deal alliance with the lower classes to a new allegiance with the upper classes and the rich, to the economic detriment of the poor. Later he documented how that shift has redounded to the detriment of the middle class as well.

Principles of Tax Equity

Given the growing inequality in income and increased attention to income shares of different groups, the role of taxes in determining that distribution has received particular focus. Several vague principles of equity have emerged, although consensus around these principles remains weak. Horizontal equity involves treating individuals in similar income brackets and economic circumstances similarly in terms of tax payments and government benefits. The principle of vertical equity has often been transformed into a related one—ability to pay. This has come to represent redistribution from the more to the less affluent by charging high-income groups higher tax rates and by providing greater proportionate benefits to low income individuals.

Economists use the notions of progressivity, proportionality, and regressivity to discuss tax incidence and who pays. Taxes have been classified by economists based on their redistributive impacts:

- *Progressive taxes* place a higher burden as a proportion of personal income on the affluent than on the poor. Progressive taxes enhance income equality, since high-income individuals pay a greater proportion of their income than do poor individuals.
- *Proportional taxes* are income distribution neutral. With proportional taxes, all individuals regardless of income level pay the same proportion in taxes.
- *Regressive taxes* place a higher burden as a proportion of personal income on the poor than on the affluent. Regressive taxes promote greater income inequality, since low-income individuals pay a greater proportion of their income than do high-income individuals.

How the Level of the Taxing Government and Income Status of the Taxed Group Affect Tax Incidence

The level of government at which services are financed and provided is not neutral in its redistributive impact. Proponents of progressive redistribution often favor federal taxation and financing of public goods over state taxation for several reasons. First, the federal tax system, especially prior to the sweeping reforms of 1986, which reduced the number of tax brackets and broadened each, was more progressive than most state and local tax systems. Second, the potential for setting higher standards and higher minimum levels for benefit programs is greater at the federal level. And third, the greater the overall potential for redistributive action, the greater the diversity or heterogeneity in income levels. Income diversity is greater nationwide than in most states. Poor states, for example, have less potential for redistribution than does the federal government, where the gap between the rich and poor is greater.

Income groups also differ as to whether they prefer taxes or spending as a redistributive tool. The affluent favor redistribution through taxes, whereas the less affluent favor government benefit programs. Since the affluent are in higher marginal tax brackets, they benefit more from tax reductions than do less affluent citizens.

The Federal Income Tax

The income tax has been both the largest source of federal tax revenues and the most progressive of U.S. taxes. The tax has a progressive rate structure and is based on the notion that taxpayers have different abilities to pay. Its actual progressivity has been eroded by tax expenditures—special exemptions and exclusions—created throughout the years, as well as a significant reduction in the number of tax brackets in 1986. Ability to pay has been defined in terms of income through the differential rate schedule and family responsibilities by allowing per capita personal exemptions and having different rate schedules depending on personal status (married, unmarried, head of household, etc.). For 30 years after its enactment in 1913, the tax applied only to a relatively small proportion of the population with high incomes, further enhancing its progressivity. Since World War II, it has applied broadly, as both incomes and tax rates have risen.

Before the 1986 Tax Reform Act, the rate schedule for the personal income tax included 14 brackets. The 1986 changes dropped the number of brackets to 2—15 and 28 percent—but due to changes for high-income taxpayers in personal exemptions during the phaseout, the effective high rate for a time was 33 percent, creating a third bracket. After the phaseout, the top bracket reverted to 28 percent. The reduction in number of income tax brackets from 14 to 3 reduced income tax progressivity. For taxpayers with high incomes yet low tax liabilities due to income exclusions and other tax expenditures, an alternative minimum tax must be calculated.

Reductions in the level of income taxes in the 1980s reduced their potential and actual redistributive impacts. The Economic Recovery and Tax Act (ERTA) of 1981 was passed during the early years of the Reagan administration. ERTA cut income tax rates 25 percent across a three-year period (5 percent the first year and 10 percent of the original base in each of the second and third years). It also provided mortgage capital gain rollover, universal individual retirement account (IRA) deduction, nonitemized charitable deductions, accelerated depreciation (ACR), and tax indexing. The combined effect of these changes was reduced income tax progressivity.

Taxes on wages and salaries are collected through a withholding system, first introduced in 1943. Tax pay-ments on other sources of income must be paid in quarterly installments during the year in which the income is received. Since withholding minimizes tax cheating, some reformists have tried to apply that collection system to interest and earnings on intangible assets, as well as to earned income. These reformists argue that the absence of withholding on sources of income likely to accrue to more affluent taxpayers and the subsequent underreporting of that type of income has a regressive impact.

Across time, taxes on earned income have constituted a greater proportion of total taxes collected from the individual income tax, indicating a greater incidence of failure to pay taxes on income derived from assets and other income sources other than wages and salaries. These proposed changes in collection procedures, however, have met great political resistance by the institutions, such as banks and investment houses, that would be responsible for implementing the extended withholding system, as well as from taxpayers who have such sources of income.

The progressive nature of the income tax has resulted in stabilization effects. Because of its progressive rate structure, the personal income tax has automatic stabilizing characteristics, and its yield automatically rises and falls more than in proportion to change in income. When the economy is growing and incomes are rising, income tax receipts grow even faster, helping to thwart the possibility of inflation and an overheated economy. Conversely, when the economy is slowing down and incomes are falling, income tax receipts fall faster, leaving more disposable income and serving to prop up the economy.

Payroll Taxes

The second largest source of federal revenue, payroll taxes are used in the United States to finance the Social Security system and benefits. Citizens pay a flat rate tax that is matched by employers; by the mid-1990s, the rate paid by citizens approached 8 percent Social Security tax on personal income up to a specified income ceiling. While the income ceiling has been historically well above the median family income, the ceiling makes the tax more regressive than it would otherwise be. The scope of the system has grown greatly since its modest beginnings. By the 1990s, Social Security, also called the federal Old Age, Survivors, Disability, and Hospital Insurance program (OASDHI), covered more than 95 percent of all persons in paid jobs, with over 48 million people currently receiving some form of Social Security payment. The flat payroll tax on earnings, up to the ceiling, has been described by Joseph Pechman as progressive for the income at the bottom of the income sale, roughly proportional for a small middle group, and regressive at most income levels, especially the upper income levels.

To help reduce the burden of Social Security on low incomes, Congress has implemented limited "refundable" income tax credits for some groups. One way to reduce the system's regressivity is to remove the ceiling. Alternatively, some reformists advocate abolishing the payroll tax and financing Social Security from a progressive income tax.

The Corporate Income Tax

The history of the corporate income tax has been one of declining importance in the overall federal revenue structure. For 17 of 28 years between 1913 and 1941, corporate income tax receipts exceeded those derived from the individual income tax. Between 1941 and 1967, the corporate income tax was the second most important source of federal revenue, behind the individual income tax. Since 1968, it has been superseded by the payroll tax financing Social Security and has fallen in importance dramatically. By 1986, it accounted for only 8 percent of total federal revenues, compared to 28 percent 30 years earlier. During that time frame, corporate tax rates have been reduced from 52 to 34 percent of taxable profits.

The corporate income tax has a flat schedule but is still complicated by the myriad of special applications for various types of businesses and business situations. Corporations are taxed on capital gains as they are realized and may offset capital losses only against capital gains. Net operating losses may be carried backward against operating income for three years. The cost of capital equipment may be depreciated, and depletion allowances are allowed to write off the cost of exploration for minerals, oil, and gas. Current outlays for research and development may be deducted in the year in which they are made.

Dividends paid by one corporation to another are taxed at a low rate, and U.S. taxes must be paid on foreign as well as domestic income. Corporations with no more than 35 shareholders may choose to be treated as partnerships for tax purposes, and financial institutions such as banks, savings and loans, and insurance companies are allowed to accumulate tax-free reserves.

Critics of the corporate income tax have charged that its burden is actually shifted forward to consumers so that it is a regressive consumption tax in disguise; that dividend payments to stockholders are "doubly taxed," once as retained earnings within the corporation and again as individual stockholder income; that the tax curtails business investment and retards growth; and that it has been applied in a discriminatory manner across industries.

Supporters counter that the degree of shifting depends on how competitive markets are and that there is little shifting in competitive markets. Further, corporations are separate legal entities with many privileges, and corporate income should accordingly be taxed separately from, and in addition to, taxing stockholder income.

Excise Taxes

In addition to income and payroll taxes, the federal government levies a variety of other taxes, including excise taxes on liquor, gasoline, cigarettes, air travel, long-distance phone calls, and customs taxes. Excise taxes, in essence, are selected sales taxes. Taxes on commodities or services deemed morally or socially undesirable are sometimes called sumptuary taxes. In 1978, special automobile excise taxes were imposed to promote fuel efficiency, that varied with the fuel consumption of the vehicle to which it was applied. In 1980, a crude oil windfall profits tax was enacted. In general, sales taxes are considered regressive, but to the extent they are placed upon items used mostly by higher-income groups, regressivity is mitigated.

Estate and Gift Taxes

A very small source of federal revenue is derived from estate and gift taxes. The gross estate tax consists of all property owned by a decedent at the time of death, including stocks, bonds, real estate, mortgages, and personal property. After many allowable deductions, including a marriage deduction for spouses, the unified estate and gift tax rates are applied above a floor. Estate and gift taxes are not broad-based mass taxes, and less than 2 percent of all those who died in 1985 had estates subject to the tax. Since low-income groups are exempted and for transfers above a certain level a constant tax rate has been applied, the overall impact of estate and gift taxes has been progressive.

State-Selected Sales Taxes

State-selected sales taxes have generally preceded the development and application of the general retail sales taxes. Selected sales taxes may be divided into benefit taxes, mostly on motor fuel, where ostensibly consumers of roads and road repairs "pay" for these benefits through gasoline taxes and sumptuary, or "sin," taxes. Of these, the motor fuels taxes produce the most revenue. The tax incidence of the motor fuels tax (i.e., who pays) largely depends on whether it is assumed to fall more heavily upon the general consumer or upon businesses. Sumptuary taxes include those on liquor, tobacco, alcohol, and pari-mutuels. Demand for items subject to the "sin" taxes is inelastic, limiting the revenue growth of these sources. Sumptuary taxes are regressive.

State General Sales Taxes

The Great Depression of the 1930s forced states to adopt the general retail sales tax to collect enough revenues to fund government, since revenues from other tax sources fell to inadequate levels as the Depression deepened. In recent times, it has become the largest revenue producer for the states. Local governments sometimes "piggyback" an additional levy onto the state general sales tax. This tax is largely recognized as regressive. In the 1986 tax reforms, Congress eliminated the federal tax deduction for state and local sales taxes, increasing its overall regressivity. Some states exempt necessities such as food and drugs to diminish its regressive impact, but other states do not.

The Local Property Tax

The property tax remains the most productive tax used by local jurisdictions. It has become a mainstay of local government finance, in part, because taxable property has largely been limited to real estate and automobiles. Real estate cannot be moved to escape local taxation, making tax evasion difficult, and making it possible to enforce the tax at the local level. Other potential tax bases, such as income and intangible properties, including equities and debt instruments, are mobile and easy to hide, making enforcement of any local taxes on those bases problematic.

How regressive the local property tax is depends, in part, on the assumptions made about tax shifting. If the burden of local property taxes is assumed to be shifted forward to renters, it becomes regressive. If it is assumed to be borne by the owners of the capital, it becomes less regressive, and even mildly progressive. Some states have implemented circuit breaker and homestead exemption programs for categories of taxpayers such as the elderly and low-income home owners to reduce its regressivity and provide tax relief.

Measuring Tax Incidence with Deductive Equilibrium Analysis

Considerable disagreement exists about the appropriate way to measure tax structure incidence, and no single measurement comparable to the unemployment index or the consumer price index has been developed to aid politicians debating proposed tax changes. Two separate approaches have been used—deductive equilibrium analysis and empirically based inductive techniques.

Under the deductive equilibrium approach, supply and demand equations describing the economy are developed using an equilibrium model that assumes the economy is able to and should reach equilibrium, where supply equals demand under market competition. This model is widely accepted in economics and influences the advice economists provide policymakers.

Equilibrium implies marginal pricing so that the marginal utility (satisfaction) of the last unit of a good consumed equals the marginal price paid for it by the consumer, and the marginal price of the last unit of a good supplied by the producer equals the marginal cost of producing it. With partial equilibrium analysis, prices for goods

are examined in isolation so that a change in the price of one good does not necessarily affect the prices of other goods. With general equilibrium analysis, all prices are viewed as dependent upon one another.

Under these assumptions, analysts employing equilibrium analysis examine the impact of tax policy on commodity prices and the equilibrium conditions. Tax incidence is measured in terms of relative changes in commodity prices for the factors of production (e.g., capital and labor). Although equilibrium analyses of tax policy are widespread and common among economists, they provide little assistance to national policymakers or the public when trying to analyze and understand the redistributive effects of proposed tax changes.

One reason for this failure to address questions of interest to national policymakers and their constituencies is the reluctance of economists to specify redistributive goals. While obtaining superficial agreement over the desirability of horizontal equity, consensus is by no means universal, nor is the definition. Some economists have argued that the concept of horizontal equity should be reformulated in terms of utility (satisfaction) rather than ability to pay measured by income. Others have questioned the desirability of horizontal equity on efficiency grounds, arguing that an efficient tax system is more important than a fair one.

The economists' criterion of Pareto optimum has not been applied widely by actual policymakers. This criterion specifies that any action that can increase overall satisfaction (income) without undercutting the satisfaction of a single person should be enacted. But politicians know that tax changes rarely, if ever, meet this criterion.

Measuring Tax Incidence with Empirical Studies

In addition to equilibrium analyses to assess tax incidence, some economists have conducted empirical studies of tax incidence. These studies have also confronted problems and have been sensitive to the assumptions made. One difficulty is how to assess the impact of indirect taxes that are placed on things or transactions rather than on individuals, as are direct taxes. While it is reasonable to assume that the individual on whom the direct tax (such as an income or payroll tax) is placed bears the burden of paying it, who bears the burden of indirect taxes (corporate income taxes, gasoline taxes, excise and sales taxes, customs taxes, etc.) is less clear.

Under certain conditions, the tax burden can be shifted forward to consumers and renters, or backward to producers and suppliers, so that the individual or corporation that initially pays the tax is not the unit that ultimately bears its burden. Analysts must make assumptions about degrees of shifting and who bears these tax burdens, and the conclusions they make about the progressivity and regressivity of various taxes and proposed tax changes is highly dependent upon the assumptions they make.

A second difficulty is that tax changes do not occur in isolation but typically are accompanied by changes in spending as well. Sorting out these two impacts is difficult when using a before and after income distribution comparison to assess tax incidence. Measures have been developed of income inequality, across the distribution of income classes, especially the Gini index of inequality.

Presumably a progressive tax change will result in a decrease in income inequality, whereas a regressive tax change will result in an increase in inequality. If there is no change in the degree of inequality, the tax change would be neutral. A common assumption employed in tax incidence studies using this approach is that governmental expenditures resulting from the tax change are distributionally neutral—a highly speculative assumption at best.

This assumption also ignores distortions in the labor-leisure trade-off that may be induced by the tax change, as well as tax-generated distortions in the willingness to take risks. By focusing only on the distribution of income in a particular year, this approach also ignores the life cycle nature of income. Personal income usually increases from youth through middle age and then declines in old age. Hence the distribution of population in various age cohorts may affect the before-tax and after-tax Gini coefficients, although the age-generated affect will be attributed to tax incidence.

Further, after-tax inequality is a function of three quantities—the inequality of income before the tax, the average tax rate, and the tax progressivity. This approach fails to distinguish between reductions in inequality caused by the average tax rate and those caused by tax progressivity.

Some economists have applied measures of inequality, such as the Gini index approach, directly to taxes paid by different income classes to measure tax burden more directly rather than measuring tax incidence indirectly through shifts in the income distribution. This approach also has several problems. The biggest is that data on actual taxes paid by various income groups can be collected only after a tax change has been implemented, and hence the method has limited utility when trying to assess the impact of proposed tax changes before they are implemented. While the potential taxes paid by an average taxpayer in a particular class can be calculated beforehand, such calculations do not capture how taxpayers will behave in response to the tax and how many will alter behavior that affects taxes due as a result of the tax change.

Further, the analyst must still make assumptions about the degree to which indirect and nonpersonal taxes are shifted. Assuming competitive market conditions implies less shifting, whereas noncompetitive assumptions result in greater shifting. Finally, measures that apply the Gini coefficient directly to taxes do a poor job of the incidence of taxes that vary in impact across different income ranges so

that the tax is progressive in some ranges and regressive or proportional in others.

Using Indirect Measures of Tax Incidence

Given the above difficulties with direct measures of tax incidence, economists have also used indirect measures, especially measures of tax elasticity, or how fast tax revenues grow relative to the growth in the tax base, usually measured as income—as a substitute for a direct measure of tax progressivity. This indirect measurement approach is based on the fact that progressive taxes are also elastic, whereas regressive taxes are inelastic. Employing this relationship, some economists have used measures of tax elasticity as substitute measures for tax incidence. Yet, this approach is also plagued by the difficulty of applying it to proposed tax changes before they are implemented.

The Politics of Tax Incidence

In the absence of better measures of the redistributive impacts of taxes, policymakers continue to respond to the pressures of special interests and constituents on an ad hoc basis when formulating and voting on tax legislation. The overall federal tax system remains only very mildly progressive. Taxes at other levels are mostly viewed as regressive. Political debate over how tax reductions should be dispersed are often couched in terms of stabilization benefits to be derived rather than in terms of the redistributive benefits to income classes, which really drives much of the politics surrounding tax changes. Proponents of both progressive and regressive taxation have also used stabilization impacts of taxes to support their positions. Lower-income groups spend more of their disposable income than do upper-income groups, having what economists call a higher marginal propensity to consume (MPC) and a lower marginal propensity to invest (MPI). Accordingly, proponents of progressivity argue tax changes concentrated on lower-income groups have been assumed by economists to have a stronger impact than those focused on upper-income groups. Little empirical evidence supports this view, however, and, in fact, contrary evidence exists that the impact of a tax change on consumption is largely independent of its distribution among income groups.

Using debate over stabilization effects to divert attention from redistributive effects often assumes a partisan dimension. Democrats have sometimes argued for tax cuts for the lower- and lower-middle-income groups, primarily Democrat constituencies, on the stabilization grounds that the cut will be more stimulative, since lower-income groups will spend their tax savings, pumping the money into the economy rather than saving it. Republicans, by contrast, have more commonly argued for tax cuts for the upper-middle and upper-income groups, primarily Republican constituencies, also on stabilization grounds. Republicans contend that extra disposable income for these groups will be more stimulative than extra money for lower-income groups, because upper-income groups are more likely to spend their additional dollars on consumer durables, such as cars and appliances. These types of expenditures are more stimulative to production, according to Republican logic, than equal dollar expenditures made by lower-income groups for nondurables, such as food and rent. Thus, in the politics of tax changes, rhetoric revolves around stabilization issues while motives and decisionmaking in large part revolve around redistributive concerns.

MARCIA LYNN WHICKER

BIBLIOGRAPHY

Browning, Edgar K., 1978. "The Burden of Taxation." *Journal of Political Economy*, vol. 86 (August) 649–671.

Pechman, Joseph A., 1987. *Federal Tax Policy*, 5th ed. Washington, DC: Brookings Institution.

Phillips, Kevin, 1990. *The Politics of Rich and Poor*. New York: Random House.

———, 1993. *Boiling Point: Democrats, Republicans, and the Decline of Middle Class Prosperity*. New York: Random House.

Rivlin, Alice M., 1975. "Income Distribution–Can Economists Help?" *American Economic Review Papers and Proceedings*, vol. 65 (May) 1–15.

Suits, Daniel B., 1977. "The Measure of Tax Progressivity." *American Economic Review*, vol. 67 (September) 747–752.

Thurow, Lester C., 1980. *The Zero-Sum Society: Distribution and the Possibilities for Economic Change*. New York: Penguin Books.

TAX REVOLT. A process by which an unforeseen mass mobilization of citizens pressures government officials into abandoning their support for existing tax policy and restructuring tax appropriations in a manner and/or amount deemed more suitable to the immediate preferences of the voting majority.

Philosophical Themes

In contemporary parlance, a tax revolt is not an actual revolt in any definitional sense. Rather, it operates within the realm of law in a manner that, although undesired by the existing regime, is nevertheless considered legitimate. In most instances, the objective of the tax revolt has been to realize a reduction in property taxes. But this has not always been the case.

The legitimacy of a tax revolt has its roots in the philosophical and political thinking of the eighteenth century enlightenment. In a broad sense, two common political themes were shared by many European writers during this time: First, the legitimate purpose of government is to protect the private property created by individuals when they mix their labor with material found in nature; and second, governments should extract tax revenue sufficient to secure the common protection of the property of all individuals. It was argued that taxation in excess of this end would have the ill effect of thwarting an individual's incentive to create and acquire property, thereby diminishing industrial production and the general well-being of society.

In eighteenth-century America, "no taxation without representation" rhetorically expressed the popular infusion of these philosophical themes. During the latter half of the century, colonists organized demonstrations and boycotts to protest numerous tax initiatives imposed by the British Crown. In most cases this resulted in a lowering of taxes on various commodities and imports. Popular resistance to taxation continued under the Articles of Confederation (1777–1789). Shay's Rebellion (1786) was pivotal in that it demonstrated the extent to which thousands of Massachusetts farmers were willing to threaten violence against their own government in order to alter a taxation system that they believed was unjustly burdensome on landed interests.

By 1789, these themes became institutionalized as a result of the political influence of the constitutional founders. They were instrumental in forming a government in which no tax could be legitimately levied without the consent of the people or their representatives in the legislature. This fundamental presupposition, that the people have the right to regulate the taxing authority of government, lies at the heart of all tax revolts in the American experience. Whereas the phrase "no taxation without representation" implies the legitimacy of taxation given the appropriate representation, the debate quickly expanded to include not only criticism of the taxation process, but also the level of taxation.

Tax Revolt in America

For most of the nineteenth century, almost all of the domestic tax revenue came from property taxes. In the early twentieth century, many states developed a personal property tax to help finance the growing responsibilities of government. The federal government soon followed suit by establishing a federally mandated personal income tax. Although the nineteenth century produced some popular resistance to property taxes in some states, the Great Depression (1929–1941) helped make tax revolts in America a national phenomena. Within the context of this economic hardship, between 1930 and 1933 over 16 states and numerous localities were compelled by popular pressure to significantly reduce property taxes.

New Deal social programs resulting from Franklin D. Roosevelt's presidency (1933–1945) helped mitigate much of the public anger over taxes by providing government sponsored programs that reduced unemployment and improved the living conditions of most Americans. For the next several decades, all kinds of taxes from all levels of government steadily increased in order to finance a burgeoning host of social programs designed to promote economic growth and improve the general welfare of all citizens. The trend of rising taxation accompanied by growing government services was met with resistance in the 1970s by various politically conservative interest groups. In 1978, California voters passed Proposition 13, a referendum that constitutionally limited property taxes.

Proposition 13

Proposition 13 was the first of more than 58 separate but similar referenda in other states from 1979 to 1984 restricting the taxing authority of state and local governments. Several important events helped set the stage for Proposition 13. In 1973, California and the rest of the nation were recovering from a severe recession. The recovery was accompanied by soaring inflation and an even more rapid rise in property values resulting from a real-estate boom. In spite of the rise in incomes and property values, the progressive tax structure in California remained unchanged. As a result, the tax burden experienced by residents greatly increased relative to any improvement in their living standards. In short, by 1977–1978 total state taxes were increasing at almost twice the rate of personal income, and California property taxes were more than 50 percent above the national average. The anger felt toward government in this respect was fueled by a general public distrust of government prevalent in the aftermath of the Watergate scandal (1972–1974) and America's controversial involvement in the Vietnam war (1964–1975).

Proposition 13 contained several provisions that would have the effect of reducing property taxes by well over 50 percent. In June 1978, California voters overwhelmingly passed Proposition 13 by a 65 percent majority. This was soon followed in 1979 by the successful passage of Proposition 4, which was designed to prevent any real increases in government spending. However, in 1980 California voters rejected Proposition 9, which would have reduced personal state income tax rates by 50 percent.

Variations on the Theme

Although tax revolts are often perceived as a conservative reaction to high taxes, this is not always the case. In Great Britain, the Conservative government led by Prime Minister Margaret Thatcher (b. 1925) was confronted by intense popular resistance in 1988 when it made local tax authorities switch from collecting revenue from property taxes to taxing adults as individuals. This would discourage the majority of local residents from irresponsibly demanding that wealthy businesses finance unnecessary local services. In order to instill more popular responsibility into the tax structure, and also to help business, the Thatcher government legislated that local governments receive their revenue from individuals. Although the Thatcher government referred to this as a "community charge," it was dubbed by

opponents as a "poll tax." Popular, and sometimes violent, protest led the Thatcher government to rescind the "poll tax" in 1991. In this particular case, the tax revolt did not intend to reduce taxes in general, but was a response to a restructuring and reduction of taxes that voters perceived as unfair and regressive.

The aftermath of tax revolts has produced some unanticipated changes. In the American experience, tax revolts have been accompanied by a majority consensus that government is too big and it spends too much. Corrected for inflation, state and local residents paid less taxes than they did before. In spite of this, voters have been much less willing to relinquish the social services provided by government. In order to preserve as many programs as possible, and in an attempt to minimize the inevitable downsizing of government institutions, much of the revenues lost through the reduction in property taxes have been supplanted by increases in user fees and various other à la carte taxes. Furthermore, the property tax limitations placed on local authorities have made them more reliant on block grants from the state legislatures, thereby diminishing the autonomy of local governments and augmenting the centralization of power within states.

Although it is possible to describe tax revolts, clarify their contextual settings, and generalize about their effects, it is another matter altogether to identify the underlying causes of a tax revolt. Some scholars claim it is an economic response to high taxes and poor services or perhaps a general dissatisfaction with a government that is perceived as bloated and wasteful. Other scholars focus on political explanations that emphasize voters either expressing their displeasure for the reigning political party or perhaps being prodded into action by a political party. Still other scholars interpret the social behavior of the tax revolt as a symbolic manifestation of a general frustration and malaise prevalent in postmodern society.

CURTIS PEET

BIBLIOGRAPHY

Adams, James Ring, 1984. *Secrets of the Tax Revolt.* San Diego, CA: Harcourt Brace Jovanovich.

Eatman, Nile, and David Kieffer, 1984. "Distributive Consequences of a Property Tax Revolt." *Economic Inquiry,* vol. 22 (October) 508–528.

Lowery, David, and Lee Sigelman, 1981. "Understanding the Tax Revolt: Eight Explanations." *American Political Science Review,* vol. 75:963–974.

O'Sullivan, Arthur, Terri A. Sexton, and Steven M. Sheffrin, 1995. *Property Taxes and Tax Revolts: The Legacy of Proposition 13.* New York: Cambridge University Press.

Sears, David O., and Jack Citrin. 1985. *Tax Revolt: Something for Nothing in California,* 2d ed. Cambridge, MA: Harvard University Press.

TAXES. Mandatory payments that governments extract from citizens and other beneficiaries in order to finance government operations.

Taxes are one of two phenomena, the other being death, that popular wisdom holds are inevitable. This inevitability is linked to the need for government revenue to meet public functions, especially purchasing public goods. Government is the only institution within society with the authority to allocate values and resources comprehensively, a task that requires resources that taxes provide. Economists make a "free rider" argument that government must have compulsory authority to collect taxes to finance public goods. Without compulsory taxation, individuals would have no incentive to pay their respective shares, since any person could still enjoy the good if others decided to purchase it. If everyone decided to get a "free ride" on neighbors, there would be no public goods, and the necessary services government provides would cease.

The current U.S. tax structure has remained relatively constant since World War II, when the federal government substantially increased individual and corporate taxes, in part to fund the war. Changes since then, including lowering the tax rates, increasing exemptions and personal deductions, and raising payroll taxes, have not altered the basic structure of the system.

A Low U.S. Tax Burden Compared to Other Countries

Both politics and economics have helped to shape the United States tax system. It has several salient characteristics. Despite consistent citizen perceptions to the contrary, the United States has a low tax burden relative to other nations. U.S. taxes remain lower than those of most advanced European countries. In the mid 1980s, for example, U.S. taxes constituted 29 percent of the gross national product (GNP) compared to 27 percent for Japan, 31 percent for Australia, 32 percent for Switzerland, 33 percent for Canada, 38 percent for Germany and Britain. Austria, Belgium, Denmark, France, Italy, the Netherlands, and Norway all taxed at percentages ranging between 40 and 50 percent, and Sweden's taxes exceeded 50 percent of GNP.

Even though U.S. taxes are a comparatively smaller proportion of GNP than taxes in other countries, they constitute a large dollar volume. In 1991, federal tax revenues alone exceeded US $1 trillion. Combined state and local tax revenues were also over US $1 trillion, making total government taxes in excess of US $2 trillion. At the beginning of the Clinton presidency in 1994, the federal government remained the "rich Uncle Sam," collecting over 60 percent of all government revenues. Yet, tax revenues have been increasing at the state and local levels, partially to offset recent declines in federal grants.

The United States, in comparison to other nations, relies heavily upon individual and corporate income taxes, which constitute 42 percent of tax revenues for all levels of government combined. This percentage is somewhat higher for the federal government (55 percent) and lower for state and local government (21 percent). In recent decades, however, payroll taxes have been increasing in importance, mostly in the form of Social Security taxes. By the 1990s, payroll taxes constituted a third of revenues at the national level and a fifth at state and local levels.

Tax Sharing Across Levels of Government

In the U.S. federal system, taxes are shared across governments so that considerable tax overlap exists at all three levels of government. Both the federal and state governments have separate constitutional authority to tax, and this contributes to tax overlap, especially between the federal and state governments. Although some specialization exists, with the federal government relying most heavily upon income taxes, states upon the general sales tax, and local governments upon property tax, tax policy more closely resembles the "marble cake" model of federalism rather than the neatly categorized "layer cake" image. Despite the tax and expenditure limitation (TEL) movement of the late 1970s and early 1980s, opposition to state and local taxes has been unable to stop the spread of income tax usage to the states so that most states use both sales and income taxes.

Taxes for Allocation—Buying Public Goods

In the United States, tax policy continues to be a major instrument of social as well as economic policy, with the goals of raising money to purchase public goods (allocation), stabilizing and sometimes stimulating the economy (stabilization), and distributing tax burdens and redistributing income fairly (redistribution). Allocation, spending public money for public goods to meet public needs efficiently, is the oldest government function financed by tax revenues. Public goods include such things as national defense, diplomacy and citizen services abroad, providing a secure financial system, environmental protection, and social welfare programs. Public goods have two distinguishing characteristics. First, they are indivisible, for their very nature defies subdivision. Second, the consumption of public goods is nonexclusive. One individual's consumption of a public good does not prohibit another individual from consuming the same good. Because of this, the free rider problem mentioned above makes taxes necessary, mandatory, and inevitable.

Taxes and Keynesian Stabilization

Government also has responsibility for stabilizing the economy and redistributing wealth and may use taxes as a mechanism to achieve these functions. These functions are not mutually exclusive. A single government action or program may involve the purchase of a public good for the allocation function while simultaneously having a stabilization effect on the economy and altering the existing distribution of income and wealth. But equally important, taxes may be involved in all.

Stabilization, the second oldest of these three major government functions involves government using fiscal policy to counter business and economic cycles through countercyclical spending and taxing. Stabilization was first embraced in the United States in the 1930s and was called "Keynesian" economics after John Maynard Keynes, who first articulated how government could use tax and budget policy to prevent inflation, recessions, and depressions. Keynes argued that taxes and spending should be used like rudders are on a boat to keep the economy on "even keel."

When demand is outstripping supply, leading to inflationary pressures that cause prices to rise, the fiscal policy levers should be deployed to take money out of the economy, reducing demand and lowering prices. Taxes are raised to combat inflation, according to Keynesian stabilization policy, to reduce after-tax consumer incomes and lower demand for goods and services. When supply has outstripped demand, leading to a sluggish economy, excess inventories, and rising unemployment, then taxes should be lowered. With lower taxes, consumer income and with it demand for goods and services rise. As demand increases, the economy is restored to health.

Some experts have noted that although, in theory, fiscal policy pertaining to taxes is easy to implement in periods of recession when the Keynesian prescription is to lower taxes, it is difficult in periods of inflation when taxes are to be raised. In a democracy, citizens can inflict their anger over raised taxes on politicians who supported the fiscally correct policy at the ballot box. In the United States in the 1980s and 1990s, citizens have been especially inclined to throw out politicians who support tax increases, and, in fact, supporting tax decreases regardless of allocation and stabilization policy needs has been politically popular.

Some consensus has emerged on the stabilization goals of controlling unemployment and inflation, but typically, the two political parties have differed on which is more important. Historically, playing to their different constituencies, Republicans considered controlling inflation to be the more important goal, whereas Democrats considered lowering unemployment the more important.

Stagflation and Supply-Side Stabilization Policy

During the 1970s, stagflation—the simultaneous worsening of both inflation and unemployment—in contradistinction to what the traditional economic theory specified would happen caused both parties to make strong calls for lowering inflation. Traditional free enterprise theory contended that inflation and unemployment would be inversely related so that when one improved, the other worsened. Further the solutions for addressing each were also inversely related. Raising taxes to combat inflation would worsen a recession, whereas lowering taxes to combat a recession would worsen inflation. During the late 1970s, inflation and unemployment both rose to double-digit levels, causing theorists to assert that the trade-offs between inflation and unemployment were still occurring, but due to structural rigidities in the economy, these trade-offs were taking place at ever higher levels. The Phillips Curve, a graphic depiction of these trade-offs, was occurring at ever higher levels.

The stagflation of the late 1970s set the stage for the embrace of supply-side economics in the 1980s in the United States during the Reagan era. Indeed, supply-side policies were often dubbed "Reaganomics" after the president and his advisers, who were avid supporters. Modern-day supply-side theory grew in popularity in the face of the failure of Keynesian fiscal policy in the late 1970s to cope with "stagflation"—simultaneously rising inflation and unemployment. Reaganomics flip-flopped in its position on how taxes should be modified during inflation, a key difference, since this position was diametrically opposed to the policy prescription of Keynesian economics when prices were rising.

Underpinned by the Laffer Curve depicting trade-offs between tax rates and tax revenues, modern-day supply-side theory was propounded by Congressman Jack Kemp (R–N.Y.) and Senator William Roth (R–DL.), as well as the Reagan administration. Supply-side stabilization theorists focused upon the supply-side of the ratio between demand and supply, as well as the demand side. Proponents agreed with Keynesian philosophy that when the economy was overheating, cuts in government spending were necessary to reduce aggregate demand. Supply-siders departed from Keynesians, however, by contending that cuts in taxes, not tax increases, would help to eliminate inflation.

Supply-siders contended that cuts in taxes would result in increases in personal disposable income, which would stimulate an increase in savings. Savings, in turn, would be invested in new plants and equipment, stimulating production and increasing the quantity and quality of goods and services. As the quantity and quality of goods and services increased, prices would be prevented from rapid increases. Further, the increase in productivity would increase government tax receipts so that deficits would not grow, even though taxes were cut. The Laffer Curve captured this hypothetical ability of supply-side policy to maintain or lower deficits in the face of massive tax cuts by depicting a proposed, and not empirically verified, curvilinear relationship between tax rates and tax revenues. In theory, two tax rates, one high and one low, would yield the same total tax revenue. Supply-siders assumed the United States was operating at the high side of the curve and would not worsen deficits by substantially lowering rates. This thinking formed the justification for the 1981 tax cuts in the United States. The 1981 tax cuts were followed by tax enhancements in 1982 and further deep cuts and radical restructuring of the U.S. tax code in 1986. Collectively, these changes were the largest in the federal income tax since its adoption.

Formally titled the Economic Recovery and Tax Act of 1981, ERTA cut income tax rates 25 percent across a three-year period (5 percent the first year and 10 percent of the original base in each of the second and third years). It also provided mortgage capital gain rollover, universal individual retirement account (IRA) deduction, nonitemized charitable deductions, accelerated depreciation (ACR), and tax indexing. Under President Reagan's urging, ERTA passed both Houses of Congress. In contrast to the predictions of supply-siders, however, and in accordance with Keynesian theory, deficits rose dramatically.

In May 1982, Reagan was forced to agree with a Republican Senate budget proposal that would increase taxes US $95 billion and cut defense spending by US $22 billion. On August 19, 1982, the largest tax increase in history to that date passed as the Tax Equity and Fiscal Responsibility Act (TEFRA). TEFRA raised taxes by US $98.3 billion. The net effect of TEFRA was to recapture about 25 percent of the ERTA tax cuts, leaving through 1988 about US $215 billion of tax cuts in place. Deficits, however, continued to rise, in part from increased defense spending as well as tax changes.

Despite growing federal deficits, Congress responded to Reagan's call for tax reform, passing the Tax Reform Act of 1986. House Ways and Means Committee Chairman Dan Rostenkowski and Senate Finance Chairman Bob Packwood negotiated the final tax reform bill in relative secrecy. The progressive rate schedule for the personal income tax was reduced from 15 brackets, with a maximum rate of 50 percent, to 3 brackets: 15, 28, and 33 percent. A number of deductions were reduced or eliminated and personal exemptions were increased substantially. The corporate tax rate was reduced from 46 to 34 percent, while elimination of investment tax credits, accelerated depreciation, and other tax changes broadened the corporate tax base.

Criticisms of Supply-Side Stabilization

Critics charged the Reagan tax cuts tripled the national debt and lavished the largest benefits upon major groups in the Reagan constituency. During the 1980s, federal deficits rose, increasing national debt from less than US $1 trillion to over US $4 trillion by the mid-1990s. Critics of supply-side stabilization policy argued that the tax cuts of the 1980s and lack of fiscal discipline were largely to blame. Nevertheless, tax cut fever again stalked the Potomac after

the Republican sweep of Congress in the 1994 mid-term elections. Led by Newt Gingrich, Speaker of the House and an outspoken critic of large government, the House Republicans pushed through a tax cut bill proposing US $189 billion reduction in taxes over five years as part of the "Contract with America" policy platform Republicans promised to act on during the first 100 days of Congress.

Not only has disagreement occurred over the appropriate level of taxes, but also over whether and how taxes should be used to promote productivity and long-term economic growth. Tax incentives used in the past as inducements to capital formation have included tax credits, rapid depreciation schedules, depletion allowances, preferential capital gains tax rates, and deductions of interest payments. The impact of these tax expenditures on productivity has not been as rigorously evaluated as are typical program expenditures.

Taxation and the Size of Government

Underlying partisan differences over the appropriate role and level of taxes are differing views of how much taxes contribute to the growth of government. Plainly, taxes and spending are positively correlated so that both increase or decrease at about the same time, but economists and policymakers disagree about whether taxes drive spending or the reverse. Milton Friedman has contended that taxes drive spending so that higher taxes do not lead to lower deficits but rather to more spending.

James Buchanan, Richard Wagner, and other public choice economists argue the manner in which the government obtains the revenues, rather than the level of the revenues, is the most important element in determining government spending. They contend raising revenues from direct taxation acts as a constraint on government spending so that when high taxes result in high tax rates, government spending is slowed. By contrast, deficit spending and inflationary finance result in higher rates of government spending. With deficit spending, citizens pay "indirect" taxes through higher interest when government financing "crowds out" private financing and through inflation. The economic instability caused by the higher interest rates and inflation further expands government as it intervenes to stabilize the economy. This view holds that voters routinely underestimate their tax burdens and the cost of public services, since taxes are often hidden, either as product taxes or through withholding. The resulting fiscal illusion from the hidden nature of taxes allows governments to become bigger than they otherwise would be.

Robert Barro disagrees with both the Friedman and Buchanan-Wagner theses, that taxes either directly or indirectly drive spending, forcing government to be bigger than it should. Barro argues that higher spending forces up taxes. Using annual data for the 1946–1983 period, Anderson, Wallace, and Warner find some support for this position, concluding that increases in expenditures lead to higher taxes, but not vice versa. Other observers support this by noting that, subsquently as well, increases in taxes have appeared to follow increases in deficits and debt.

The Multiplier Effect

As a fiscal policy tool, tax legislation is passed by Congress and signed into law by the president, who must consider economic effects of taxes on fiscal policy outcomes as well as political consequences. The first economic effect is the multiplier effect, the fact that impact of a tax change is multiplied beyond its initial level so that second and third round impacts are considered. Cutting taxes may have an expansionary effect far greater than the size of the initial tax reduction. The initial amount by which disposable income is increased from the tax cut is subsequently respent minus taxes in the second round of effects. In the third round, the amount left at the end of the second round is respent, again minus taxes. The multiplier is a number that measures the size of this expansionary impact. Most economists generally assume a multiplier of 2.5 when considering the impact of taxes. A multiplier of 2.5 means that an initial increase in dollars in the economy will have an expansionary effect 2.5 times greater than the initial tax change. Similarly, a tax increase has a contractionary effect greater than the initial additional amount removed from disposable income, and that impact may also be measured by the multiplier. The value for the multiplier is determined, in large part, by the rate of turnover of dollars in the economy.

Comparing the Impacts of Tax and Spending Changes

A second economic effect is that economists contend tax changes are less powerful than the equivalent dollar government spending change. Taxation is a less precise fiscal policy tool than government spending, for policymakers set tax rates rather than the absolute amount of tax dollars to be withheld from the economy or added to it. The final impact of a tax change depends on the size of the rate change, the health of the economy, which influences how many taxpayers there are and their levels of income, and taxpayer attitudes toward the economic future. When government spending is altered, the entire amount of the change is immediately pumped into or withheld from the economy.

The impact of tax changes may be smaller and may be delayed. When taxes are increased, consumers may draw down savings to initially postpone the impact of the tax increase on their disposable income, delaying and possibly reducing the fiscal policy effects of the tax increase. When taxes are decreased, whether or not taxpayers immediately spend the entire additional disposable income depends on their attitudes toward the future. Pessimistic taxpayers who are fearful of the economic future may choose to save a portion of the additional tax dollars, whereas more optimistic taxpayers may spend the entire amount, or larger portions of it. Thus, the fiscal policy effect of a tax cut is less than that of a government spending increase, because taxpayers benefiting from the tax cut may choose to save rather than spend some of their tax-cut income. Permanent tax reductions have a stronger impact on consumption behavior than one-time windfalls. Taxpayers will alter their spending habits and behavior if they think a tax cut is permanent, but not if they anticipate that it is temporary. Further, the first-round effect of a spending change is greater than a tax change with a government spending change, where the entire amount of the change is available for second round spending. By contrast, with a tax cut, consumers save some portion, so the entire first round is not available for second-round spending.

The Automatic Stabilizing Effect of Some Taxes

A third economic effect that economists and policymakers consider is the automatic stabilizing impact of certain taxes. To the extent taxes are progressive, placing higher taxes on the rich than on the poor, they have an automatic stabilizing effect in that progressive taxes automatically act in a countercyclical fashion to take money in and out of the economy without direct intervention by policymakers. This stabilizing impact augments discretionary changes to diminish economic fluctuations induced by business cycles. With the federal individual income tax, the automatic stabilizing effect means that rising incomes that may become inflationary force citizens into higher marginal tax brackets, whereas declining income implies the reverse. The number of tax brackets in the federal income tax code and the total progressivity of the system with the adoption of the 1986 tax cuts reduced but did not eliminate the automatic stabilizing potential of the federal income tax. In inflationary periods, more citizens moving into higher marginal tax brackets automatically increases tax receipts and withdraws more money from the economy, curbing inflationary pressures. In recessionary periods, taxpayers slide into lower marginal tax brackets and more money is automatically left in citizen hands, countering declining demand. To the extent that taxes are indexed to the rate of inflation, as the federal income tax has been, the automatic stabilizing effect is reduced or eliminated.

Related to the automatic stabilizing effect of progressive tax structures are fiscal dividend and fiscal drag. These terms have been used to describe an upward creep in full-employment revenues in times of economic growth, and both refer to the same fiscal policy effect. The former, fiscal dividend, refers to the additional revenues the federal government will recoup with economic growth, while the latter, fiscal drag, refers to the depressing effect extracting a larger share of the GNP in taxes will have on personal spending and on the economy. Some policy advocates have proposed indexing the tax system as a way of reducing fiscal drag, as well as reducing the tax burden on individuals during inflationary periods. With indexing, tax brackets are expanded and exemptions and the standard deduction are increased in rough accordance with the increases in the inflation rate.

Assessing the Impact of Tax Changes on Full Employment GNP

A fourth stabilization effect considered by policymakers is not just whether a tax change would increase or decrease the current deficit, but what its impact would be on a full-employment GNP. If the proposed tax change would result in a full-employment budget surplus, it is restrictive; proposed changes that would result in full-employment budget deficits are expansionary. By this reasoning, proposed tax changes that result in actual deficits but in full-employment budget surpluses are not inflationary, whereas changes that result in both actual and full-employment budget deficits are inflationary. In recent years in the United States, fiscal policies have been adopted that produce both types of deficits.

The Redistributive Impact of Taxes

In addition to raising money for allocation so government may purchase public goods, and stabilizing the economy, taxes also redistribute income and wealth among groups of citizens. This third function of U.S. taxes is by far the most controversial and is highly politicized. Several vague principles of equity have emerged, although consensus around these principles remains weak. Horizontal equity involves taxing individuals in similar income brackets and economic circumstances similarly. The principle of vertical equity has often been transformed into a related one–ability to pay–and has come to represent redistribution from the more to the less affluent. Overall, the U.S. tax system has been only marginally redistributive.

MARCIA LYNN WHICKER

BIBLIOGRAPHY

Boskin, Michael J., 1987. *Reagan and the Economy: The Successes, Failures, and Unfinished Agenda.* San Francisco: Institute for Contemporary Studies Press.
Galbraith, John Kenneth, 1977. *The Age of Uncertainty.* Boston: Houghton Mifflin.
McConnell, Campbell R., 1975. *Economics: Principles, Problems, and Policies,* 6th ed. New York: McGraw-Hill.
Pechman, Joseph A., 1987. *Federal Tax Policy,* 5th ed. Washington, DC: Brookings Institution.
Roberts, Paul Craig, 1984. *The Supply-Side Revolution: An Insider's Account of Policymaking in Washington.* Cambridge, MA: Harvard University Press.
Rubin, Irene, 1993. *The Politics of Public Budgeting.* Chatham, NJ: Chatham House.
Samuelson, Paul A., and William D. Nordhaus, 1989. *Economics,* 13th ed. New York: McGraw-Hill.
Stiglitz, Joseph E., 1986. *Economics of the Public Sector.* New York: W. W. Norton.
Stockman, David A., 1987. *The Triumph of Politics: The Inside Story of the Reagan Revolution.* New York: Avon Books.

TAYLOR, FREDERICK WINSLOW (1856–1915).

The engineer, inventor, management consultant, and efficiency expert known as "the father of Scientific Management."

Taylor's distinguished engineering career culminated in the presidency of the American Society for Mechanical Engineers in 1906. He patented or copatented some 45 inventions, the most significant among them being the Taylor-White patents on high-speed steel. Far more important, however, was his application of the scientific method to the study of labor productivity, with emphasis on developing methods to eliminate the common pattern of evasion of work that he called "systematic soldiering." Through the "time study" of work with a stopwatch, the systematization of work through written records, standardization, the increase in the division of labor, the use of coordinative planning, and the application of a differential piecework rate, Taylor increased the efficiency of production and the control of management over labor, making possible at the same time both higher profits and higher wages.

Taylor's methods of work study and organization were adapted for use in government and other nonindustrial settings. They form the foundation of the Administrative Management School of Public Administration that reformed the operations of the executive branch of the American government, as well as being the core of reforms in such wide-ranging fields as educational administration, city management, and government-industrial planning (see **scientific management**). Many of the original Taylor techniques are still in use today, although in modernized form, and they are incorporated into the modern discipline of industrial engineering.

Taylor was born on March 20, 1856, in Germantown, Pennsylvania, then a suburb of Philadelphia. His father, Franklin Taylor, was of English Quaker descent, a lawyer with substantial property. His mother, Emily Winslow Taylor, was a strong-minded antislavery campaigner whose Quaker family originally came from New England puritan stock. She bequeathed to her son, according to his official biographer, Frank Barker Copley (1923), her love of order and "a *whale* of a New England conscience." Taylor's passion for control and his ferocious self-discipline manifested themselves in childhood, when he demanded the right to adjudicate childhood games and created for himself a machine contrived of a "harness of straps and wooden points" in which he slept, hoping to banish his "terrifying dreams." He slept "in a bolt-upright sitting posture" for the rest of his life, eschewing rich food and high living for an austere and virtuous life style.

These elements of character cast long shadows in the system of industrial management that he pioneered and to which he rightly referred as a "mental revolution." Educated at the Philips Exeter Academy, Taylor watched with fascination as his mathematics instructor timed examinations with a stopwatch, finding in this idea the later germ of his workplace innovation of "time study." When his eyesight began to fail, he was, at the age of 18, forced to forgo plans for Harvard and legal study. Although he enjoyed participating in clubs and societies for choral activities, drama, and sports (his competitiveness, love of invention, and prankish sense of humor led him to develop, at various times, a curiously bent tennis racket and a two-handled golf club designed to give him victory), he soon became bored with being idle at home and took work as an apprentice in a pump manufacturing company owned by a friend of the family.

In 1878, as a journeyman machinist, he went to work at Midvale Steel, where he remained for the next 12 years, rising to chief engineer and earning a degree in mechanical engineering from Stevens Institute of Technology in his off-hours. At Midvale, a company known for its advanced industrial practice, two great talents began to unfold in him: a gift for mechanical invention and a driving compulsion to create organizational innovations that would bring order, efficiency, and industrial peace to the often chaotic and conflict-ridden workplace of the late nineteenth century. High productivity, he believed, would lead to prosperity and happiness for all humankind.

As he moved from Midvale in 1893 through other prominent Pennsylvania firms and eventually to Bethlehem Steel in 1898, he conducted systematic experiments in metal cutting, in overhead belting, on concrete, and on labor productivity. By 1902, financially successful, he was able to retire from paid work and devote himself full-time to publicizing the Taylor System of production efficiency.

Taylor gathered around him in his work a group of like-minded innovators, such as Henry L. Gantt, Morris L. Cooke, Carl Barth, and Frank and Lillian Gilbreth, who developed important elements that added to the system as well as applications that spread it beyond the factory. In late 1910, the Taylor system received national publicity when at Interstate Commerce Commission hearings on railroad rates, efficiency experts testified that the railroads could save a million dollars a day with modern management methods. The Taylor System, redubbed "Scientific Management" during the hearings to give it more popular appeal, became the center of a national efficiency craze that has never totally abated.

The efficiency fad also set off a rising storm of criticism. Trade union representatives pointed out that Taylorism smashed crafts, replacing expensive skilled labor with cheaper unskilled labor, and that workers faced a "speedup" without adequate protection from mental or physical fatigue, despite the claims of Taylor and his followers. Opposition arose not only from organized labor, but also from traditional managers, who distrusted the expense of transition, Taylor's scheme of functional foremanship, and the necessity of giving up personal power to professional planners. After a strike at the Watertown Arsenal, Taylor was forced in 1912 to defend his system before a Special Committee of the House of Representatives. The hearings culminated in a decision to ban the stopwatch and certain other features of the Taylor System from government installations. This temporary setback did not, however, stop the progress of Scientific Management, which continued to evolve and spread. By the time of World War I, versions of Scientific Management were being adopted in industrial establishments around the world, where they became the foundation of modern mass-production efficiency.

Taylor had married in 1884, when he was made chief engineer at Midvale. Childless, his wife had adopted three distant cousins who were orphaned by a murder-suicide. As the storms of publicity and labor opposition gathered around Taylorism, his wife, in the winter of 1910–1911, began to display symptoms of clinical depression. Her growing illness drained him with worry as he fought during those same years to publicize and defend his system. The onset of World War I in 1914 horrified him; his dream of high production leading inevitably to human happiness seemed to be in ruins. At last, exhausted, he neglected an illness that turned into pneumonia and was hospitalized in 1915. On the day after his 59th birthday, he was heard winding his watch at the curious hour of 4:30 in the morning. It was his last act in life; half an hour later, he was found dead.

JUDITH A. MERKLE

BIBLIOGRAPHY

Copley, Frank Barker, 1923. *Frederick W. Taylor, Father of Scientific Management,* New York: American Society of Mechanical Engineers.

Kakar, Sudhir, 1970. *Frederick Taylor: A Study in Personality and Innovation.* Cambridge: Massachusetts Institute of Technology.

Merkle, Judith A., 1980. *Management and Ideology: The Legacy of the International Scientific Management Movement.* Berkeley and London: University of California Press.

Nelson, Daniel, 1980. *Frederick W. Taylor and the Rise of Scientific Management.* Madison: University of Wisconsin Press.

Taylor, Frederick W., 1911. *The Principles of Scientific Management.* New York: Harper and Brothers.

———, 1911. *Shop Management.* New York: Harper and Brothers.

Urwick, Lyndall F., 1956. *The Making of Scientific Management.* London: Newman, Neame.

Wrege, Charles D., and Ronald G. Greenwood, 1991. *Frederick W. Taylor: The Father of Scientific Management; Myth and Reality*. Homewood, IL: Business One Irwin.

TECHNOLOGY TRANSFER.

The process by which an innovation is transmitted from donor to recipient. In the context of world trade, technology transfer can involve restrictions imposed by the national government of the donor, usually to preserve a strategic military advantage.

Usage and History

Technology transfer (sometimes referred to as TT) has two levels of meaning. Used in its fundamental sense, the term pertains to how ideas, inventions, and goods pass from one party to another. In the narrower sense, often applied or assumed during discussions of public policy, technology transfer refers to the sale of material or designs for scientific applications, especially when the items for sale have direct or potential military application.

Much has been written about technology transfer and dissemination (also known as diffusion), examining the subject from a variety of perspectives. The most straightforward approach has been the linear or stage model, which discusses steps involved in the transfer of technology from one party to another, that is, from innovation to transfer/diffusion to adoption. Another important array of perspectives has been from various areas of expertise: historical, anthropological, sociological, economic, business/commerce, scientific/academic, military, environmental, communications, public policy, and others. Still another way of looking at technology transfer is in terms of impact: the impact of technology transfer on the recipient or on society as a whole, and the impact of a society on technology transfer. Technology transfer can also be considered in terms of the actors involved (including individuals, groups, organizations, and societies) and the environment in which it does or does not take place (group norms, raw materials, base of knowledge, etc.). This article looks at both the concepts and practices of technology transfer.

Defining Technology

The term "technology" leads to more than one definition. Taken in the broadest sense, technology includes everything civilization employs to sustain itself: applied knowledge and ideas; spoken and written languages, rites, customs and traditions; objects found in nature and put to use; crafted and manufactured goods and tools; even objects of art, prized simply for their aesthetic or symbolic value. This definition of technology forms the basis for any discussion of technology transfer and dissemination in its primary sense.

Technology in its material forms is readily recognized. Often unacknowledged are a society's intangible technologies sometimes referred to as "social technologies." Examples range from representative democracy to administrative law, from bicameral legislatures to total quality management, from cost-benefit analysis to value-added taxes, and from staggered terms of office to land-grant colleges. As with material technologies, social technologies are fully subject to both technology evolution and technology transfer. The array of social technologies involved in policy, administration, and governance is huge and may well exceed the material technologies unique to these areas of human endeavor.

A second, more restrictive, use of the word technology pertains to the fruits of sophisticated applied technology and the means to create those products. This definition is assumed in the context of a nation's military and economic security. Included here are powerful computers along with many of their hardware and software elements; offensive and defensive weapons systems, including key components thereof; space exploration technology; some metallurgical and chemical processes; as well as designs and, some cases, raw materials for creating such commodities.

A third use of the world "technology" is as a way of saying "gadgets." These are high-tech devices, usually electronic, often involving computer circuitry. Because this definition is commonly used in casual conversation, it needs to be acknowledged here; it is, however, only a narrow slice of the broader definitions of technology that are the basis for this essay.

The Process View

Technology transfer involves three stages: developing a technological innovation, communicating that innovation, and using that innovation outside of its original setting. Each stage subdivides into a series of steps. The innovation process involves idea formulation, experimenting or prototyping, and creation. The communication process, also known as marketing, involves the spread of information about the innovation and the persuasion of potential adopters. The adoption process involves the decision to adopt, preparation and implementation, use of the innovation, and results. The steps are neither evenly paced nor necessarily linear, but occur in some manner.

Generic Model

Technology transfer is a process that can take many forms, all of which involve a donor and one or more recipients. Donors and recipients can be individuals or organizations, including governments. The donor may be the originator; often, however, the donor is an earlier user of the technology who has become known to the recipient.

Transmission. Most donor-recipient situations are analogous to conversation. (see Figure I). As with conversation, there is a sending party (donor, marked [a]), a receiving party (recipient, [d]), a transmission medium or array of media ([c]), and a message (i.e., the technology being transferred, [b]). As with conversation, feedback ([e]) and extended dialogue may be involved. As with conversation, the receiving party may understand—or be interested in—only a portion of the message. And as with conversation, the recipient may apply the message in ways the sender does not expect.

With direct technology transfer, the donor and recipient are aware of one another and, typically, are in direct communication. Technology dissemination, unlike technology transfer, is a one-way transmission (see Figure II). Technology dissemination is more akin to a broadcast than to a conversation. As with a conversation, the ingredients involved are sender ([a]), receiver ([d]), medium ([c]), message ([b]). But dissemination does not involve feedback. For technology dissemination, the communications medium may be word of mouth, news reports, observation of competitors' methods, and many other means. Unlike technology transfer, technology dissemination seldom involves sustained, two-way contact between donor and recipient.

Reciprocity. Another difference between technology transfer and technology dissemination is that technology transfer can involve reciprocity (marked "[e]" in Figure I), although that need not be the case. When reciprocity is involved, it may range from direct payment to acknowledgment to two-way sharing of knowledge. Many transactions involve direct payment through which the recipient purchases the technology or technological acumen from the recipient (e.g., a bureau may hire consultants to provide organizational reengineering skills to a cadre of bureau employees). Acknowledgment may range from a simple announcement (e.g., "We wish to thank . . .") to recognizing the originator in the name of the technology (e.g., the British Thermal Unit, the Wankel engine, Roberts' Rules of Order). Knowledge sharing is a form of reciprocation likely in scientific circles, often through such transfer mechanisms as journal articles and formal conferences (e.g., International Conference on AIDS). Even technology transfer undertaken for humanitarian reasons, such as through the Peace Corps or the Agency for International Development, is likely to involve direct or indirect reciprocity. Indirect reciprocation may take the form of greater allegiance in international politics; direct reciprocation may occur in the demand that the recipient acquire the technology through a firm based in the donor country.

Impact. Whether technology is transferred between specific parties or diffused throughout a society, the measure of its success is not in how fully the technology is adopted—rather, the measure has become what level of impact the technology has had and at what cost (in every form) (see element [g] in Figures I and II). Successful technology transfer results not just in the use of the technology.

The downstream result may actually be considered in terms of outcome: saved energy, time, money, or lives; reduced worry or pollution; or greater convenience, comfort, safety, or enjoyment. That outcome must be expressed in net terms, after subtracting the costs involved. The costs are direct as well as indirect, intangible as well as tangible, and long term as well as short term. Economic costs are almost always involved—for setup, operations, and materials. Other costs may be in terms of privacy, environmental degradation, reduced freedom, or the reverse aspect of any outcome factor (e.g., energy use).

Many Perspectives

The process of technology transfer can be analyzed from a variety of perspectives: from the point of view of one of the actors (e.g., donor, recipient), the social units involved (e.g., individual, government), the technology itself, or the environment in which transfer may take place.

Actors/Social Units. One perspective by which to examine technology transfer is by social unit or level. Levels include individuals, small groups, organizations, and whole societies. Much transfer is between parallel levels, very often organizations (company A to company B). When transfers cross societal or national boundaries, which is frequently the case, point-to-point contact may still be at the organizational level (company A in country X to province government Q in country Y). But transfers also occur on nonparallel levels. A noteworthy example is the work of American quality consultant W. Edwards Deming who taught quality control methods to Japanese industries in the 1950s.

Deming, in fact, is an excellent example of what is known as a "change agent" or "boundary spanner"—that is, someone who acts as the trigger for innovation or transmitter from donor to recipient.

Pull/Push. Technology transfer can be examined from the point of view of the technology being transferred or from the point of view of the recipient. Technology transfer has a relatively low flow (i.e., rate of transfer) where users are responsible for recognizing, obtaining, and adapting a technology they need—usually, users are preoccupied with handling the existing situation and have little time to search for the best replacement technology, whether it be a new machine or a more efficient process. Technology transfer where the technology itself is the focus or where the donor is aggressively marketing the technology, by contrast, may transfer the technology inappropriately, thereby providing more than the recipient can apply. (How many buttons don't you understand on your pocket calculator or the fax machine in your office or your VCR?) Examples usually come in waves and are easy to spot, often by asking what is trendy at the moment among businesses or governmental entities. Business executives may "need" cellular phones or stress management training. Government

FIGURE I. Technology Transfer

In **Technology Transfer,** a donor [a] transmits an innovation [b] by way of a two-direction communications medium [c] to one or more recipients [d]. The recipient uses feedback communication [e] to consult the donor about adaptation and implementation concerns and, often, to provide reciprocation to the donor. Using borrowed or available resources [f], the recipient applies the technology to realize a new or augmented outcome [g].

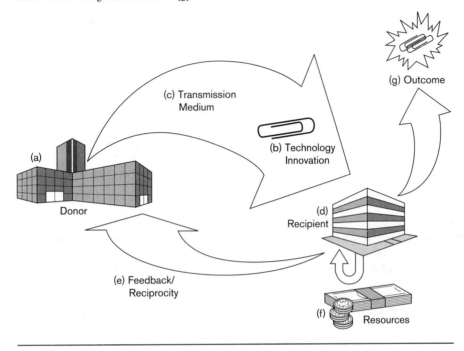

FIGURE II. Technology Dissemination

In **Technology Dissemination,** a donor [a]spreads information about an innovation [b] through one or more communications media [c]. As potential recipients [d] gain an understanding of the innovation, the outcome [g] may be to adopt the technology for their own use or to ignore it.

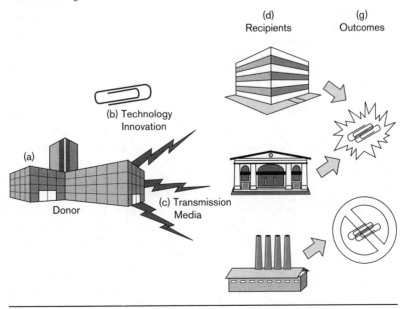

agencies, large and small, may be required to adopt a sophisticated budget or accounting technique such as zero-based budgeting or outcome-oriented budgeting.

This dilemma is sometimes discussed in terms of market pull and technology push—that is, whether technology transfer is driven more strongly by the needs of the user or by the allure (i.e., the perceived value) of the technology itself. This is easiest to visualize through example. Environmental concerns are a major force when it comes to market pull. Unhealthful, polluted natural resources such as the air we breathe and the water we drink, often underscored in developed countries by pollution control standards, "pull"—or foster—technology innovation and transfer of products and processes benign to the environment. Thus, market pull involves policy as well as economics.

That is less likely for technology "push." Some of you reading this page have marked it or other pages in this encyclopedia with a small piece of paper, probably yellow, with a reusable tacky adhesive on one edge—it is called a "Post-it" by 3M, the company that invented it. Nobody asked for Post-its; rather, potential adopters ran across them, caught on to their advantages, began using, them, and continue to apply them in creative ways.

Environment. The setting or environment in which technology transfer takes place is also a rich subject of study. Environment encompasses such factors as raw materials, technical acumen, disposition of the potential recipient, and the relationship between the recipient and donor. A recipient can take advantage of a technology innovation through materials and other resources needed to implement the technology (marked [f] in Figure I). This may mean having to substitute or adapt resources (e.g., energy sources to power a manufacturing plant). Resources, like technology itself, can be intangible, such as where the recipient population is likely to acquire the technical knowledge and skill to maintain and apply a technology innovation.

Beyond materials and skill, cultural norms incline the recipient be open to—or suspicious of—change, and technology transfer is more likely to occur between parties who already enjoy an open, comfortable relationship.

The Worldly View

The conceptual discussion, above, is useful for understanding how and where the process of technology transfer fits into the world around us today But technology transfer can also be seen in less abstract terms. This worldly view involves military concerns, business opportunities, scientific endeavors, and humanitarian objectives—interwoven in complex ways.

Preserving National Security

Two highly interdependent technology transfer entanglements are military interests and international business pursuits. Technology transfer is a sensitive element of national security. That was certainly true during the cold war period covering much of this half of the century, when the democratic governments of the West and the communist governments of the East each strove to achieve and maintain technological and military advantage over adversary nations. The arms race—both nuclear and conventional—was fought using espionage and counterintelligence, often aimed at wresting military secrets from the opposing side.

In the post–cold war era, security issues in technology transfer still abound. Although a residue of East/West cold war caution remains, today's strongest concerns pertain to international terrorism, regional domination by military means, and rogue nations—that is, countries whose leaders willfully disregard international agreements and protocols in their dealings with other nations.

No nation is willing to place in jeopardy its ability to defend its borders, its people, or its natural and economic assets. Consequently, nations with fully developed economies impose trade restrictions on what technology can be exported to other countries. Some restrictions are unequivocal—such as a ban on exporting plans, equipment, and raw materials that could supply another nation with nuclear technologies or the know-how to develop its own nuclear weapons and industries. Restrictions apply on a case-by-case basis for less sensitive technology transfer—such as the sale of conventional (i.e., nonnuclear) military weapons and aircraft to nations regarded as friendly to the source country. Information and communications technology, genetic engineering and other biology-oriented technology, and other cutting-edge technologies are also likely to be considered "sensitive" technologies (i.e., of strategic importance) and, therefore, subject to constraints on what can be sold to other nations, how much and under what conditions something may be sold, and which nations qualify.

Restrictions are imposed and monitored by national governments of the originating country. In the United States, both the Department of Commerce and the Department of Defense have components responsible for review and monitoring. Other departments and agencies within the executive branch also play enforcement and related roles including, for example, the Treasury Department's Customs Service and the Department of Justice, which prosecutes alleged violations of U.S. secrecy laws. The U.S. Congress enacts laws to control national security aspects of technology transfer, to itemize specifically proscribed technologies, and generally to set out the conditions under which transfers may and may not take place.

At times, military and commercial interests collide, which can lead to intense lobbying, news headlines, litigation, and even revisions to the law. For the most part, however, business interests are able to work within—rather than to resist—the technology transfer confines imposed by their national governments. This is often done by adapting defense technology to commercial uses (known as spinoff) and building commercial innovations into military applications (known as spinon).

Business Interests

Because businesses working on government contracts undertake technology innovation and transfer, elaborate security precautions are common wherever sensitive technologies are developed and manufactured. After all, military espionage involves technology transfer as well as knowledge about military strength and strategy. Industrial espionage is also a worry of the private sector. While industrial espionage may span national borders, it more often involves rival companies. In the case of transnational corporations, both borders and business competitors may be involved. Consequently, the control of technology transfer is, in itself, big business.

Business and government also use international trade agreements, patent laws, and copyright laws to control the transfer of technology and preserve intellectual property rights to the technology. The European Union (EU) binds an increasing number of European nations and their immediate neighbors into a single economic community. The North American Free Trade Agreement (NAFTA) substantially widened trade opportunity and cast aside economic barriers between Canada, Mexico, and the United States in 1993 and holds the potential to encompass most nations of South and North America and the Caribbean. The General Agreement on Tariffs and Trade (GATT), ratified by most participants in 1994, brings more than a 150 nations under a consolidated set of rules of trade and international commerce. GATT has also established a World Trade Organization (WTO) to monitor those rules and adjudicate disagreements between member nations.

Organizations and agreements such as these have a profound impact on technology transfer, both in terms of increased flow and increased control. Even though most trade does not involve the transfer of technologies new to the trade recipient, increased flow in technology transfer can nevertheless be sensed—and often measured—in terms of volume of trade, range of products traded, and variety of trading partners. Technology transfer activity is most likely in trade between countries with well-developed economies and in trade from developed to less-developed countries. Increased control of technology transfer is also of considerable economic importance to individuals and businesses in countries where the technology originates. This is because international agreements such as GATT provide mechanisms for encouraging licensing agreements and enforcing copyrights and patent rights and thereby, according to theories of technology innovation and transfer, encourage innovation through privately funded research and development because of the potential of downstream profitmaking.

Profit drives business enterprises and, thus, much technology transfer as well. In profit-motivated environments,

technology transfer occurs when employees change employers or leave to form companies on their own; when companies, frequently from different parts of the globe, form joint ventures, such as has happened in automobile manufacturing; when industries in one country realize they can capitalize on potential product innovations and market niches overlooked or discounted by firms where a technology has originated, such as with high-tech home electronics; and when parties in one country directly purchase new technology from private organizations based in another country, such as installing commercial telecommunications or building a major dam. Illicit technology transfer takes place when recipients ignore patents and intellectual property rights in order to capitalize on the innovations of others without securing their permission or arranging to compensate the donor.

Scientific, Political, and Humanitarian Ventures

Technology transfer also comes about through scientific activity. Although this can take many forms, two important mechanisms are through joint ventures of the science and business communities and through open exchange of research findings.

Perhaps the most famous coalition is in Japan. Called MITI, for the Ministry of International Trade and Industry, the group combines the efforts of academic scientists, business capital, and government sponsorship. Its aim is to advance Japan's position as a world leader in developing and exporting advanced electronics for consumer and business use. A similar consortium in the United States is SEMATEC, the Semiconductor Research Corporation, a research coalition of universities and of major American companies involved in aspects of computer manufacture and marketing. Although not modeled after MITI, the two alliances share similar research and development goals of promoting down-the-road competitive advantage to that nation's information technology industries; unlike MITI, however, SEMATEC has no government sponsorship. In Europe, nations have joined forces for the European Laboratory for Particle Physics (CERN) and have undertaken other research and development programs—often with colorful acronyms such as ESPRIT, which stands for the European Specific Program for Research in Information Technology.

The European Space Agency (ESA) is a commercial space venture and chief competitor to the U.S. National Aeronautics and Space Administration (NASA), which itself operates limited joint science and technology programs with other nations. Many other cooperative national and international endeavors exist—in medicine and health, environment, and other fields—funded by imaginative combinations of governments, business coalitions, academic institutions, and sometimes world bodies such as the United Nations.

International exchange of scientific information, an essential step in much technology transfer, is promoted through the open exchange of science research data and findings through publications and conferences. International conferences can be based around virtually any technology, tangible or intangible. Other examples include conferences on strategic planning, population control, species preservation, and even tax administration and compliance.

Technology transfer is also advanced through groups that broker and publish manufacturing and industrial standards. The Institute of Electrical and Electronics Engineers (IEEE) and the American National Standards Institute (ANSI) are examples. Federal research grants help underwrite academic and scientific research and include direct sponsorship of some research and dissemination organizations (e.g., the National Science Foundation, National Institute of Health, and Center for Disease Control).

Government, business, and science often share in efforts to advance humanitarian and political goals. Among ventures sponsored by the United States, the Peace Corps and the National Service Programs (AmeriCorps) share a basic goal of teaching improved self-sufficiency to less-advantaged communities—that is, basic technology transfer. Foreign aid programs sometimes involve direct shipments of emergency medicines, food, and other supplies but usually involve longer-term goals with self-sufficiency as one of the objectives. Unlike business and military ventures, these are characterized by openness rather than by secrecy and control.

Technology Transfer and Society

The interplay between technology and society is both vast and vibrant. Technology transfer is a huge force helping to shape any society. Society, in turn, determines the pace and direction of technology transfer. Moreover, when one society comes into contact with another, the dynamics between society and technology transfer can become especially stark and turbulent.

Impact of Technology Transfer on Society

British commentator James Burke has perhaps done more than anyone in the last generation to popularize an appreciation for the impact that technology transfer and dissemination have on society. Beginning in the late 1970s with a television series called Connections, Burke's television documentaries and accompanying texts have traced and illustrated the ubiquitous, quirky nature of how societies evolve through the transmission of innovations across time, borders, and populations.

Civilization can be visualized as growing in three ways. One, simple population growth, takes place when births and survival outpace the death rate in a society, as when food is in good supply and pestilence is at bay. Another, annexation, occurs when new populations are incorporated, such as the expansion of the Ancient Roman Empire. A third, evolution, occurs as a civilization adopts increasingly sophisticated sociopolitical practices and complex artifacts. All three dimensions of growth involve technology transfer. Population growth depends largely on good agriculture and other food-gathering processes along with a knowledge of good sanitary practices and benign medical treatments. Annexing less civilized populations involves direct transfer of the technologies of the more developed civilization. Evolving civilization depends on unending innovation and adoption of innovations.

The pace of that evolution accelerates over time. Primitive societies typically change only marginally, even when measured over centuries—a stability comforting to most members of the society. Innovation is rare; transfer takes place even more rarely. By contrast, the tempo of innovation and technology transfer in highly developed societies can seem overwhelming, inducing what futurists Alvin and Heidi Toffler characterize as "future shock"—that is, an inability to handle the ever changing, ever new aspects of modern society. Although many members of such a society have difficulty handling the sensory and decisionmaking overload that threatens them (and that would be unthinkable in older, slower societies), other members find the fast pace of change addictive. They seek newness—new things, ideas, experiences—as an amusement, as an escape from boredom, and as status symbols. Newness and changes are fed by innovation and technology transfer. Even "back to basics" and "return to nature" rely on technology transfer in the form of a growing array of environmental preservation and rehabilitation techniques. The speed of innovation and technology transfer closely matches and helps drive the pace of evolution of society.

Impact of Society on Technology Transfer

In a reciprocal fashion, society greatly influences the pace and nature of technology transfer. The outlook of a society—open or secretive, inquisitive or superstitious, at war or at peace with neighboring societies—is a strong determinate of how technology transfer takes place. Technology transfer can be resisted, as with the Amish and numerous other fundamentalist religious groups. Technologies can also be adopted and subsequently repudiated, as with the embrace and eventual rejection of communism in many Eastern-bloc societies and capitalist democracy in many lesser-developed nations of the world. Isolationist and totalitarian societies resist technology transfer that must cross their borders. Even nonwarring societies hostile to one another avoid certain donor-recipient relationships while engaging in transfer activities with societies considered friendly, superior, or both—arms and military technology are examples of such transactions.

Technology transfer is likely to be successful only when undertaken in a context the recipient can understand and appreciate. The 1958 novel *The Ugly American,* by William Lederer and Eugene Burdick, illustrates this situation in a passage in which an American in a southeast Asian village notices that older villagers are painfully bent over–they clean using short-handled brooms made from coconut fronds. As villagers visit the American couple's hut one day, the wife cuts some fronds, fashions them into a broom as she has learned from the villagers, but attaches a long piece of bamboo for the handle. She then sweeps while continuing to visit. Though the broom looks strange, it seems strong and comfortable. Upon finding a source of tall bamboo, some villagers begin using long-handled brooms, and, over time, the technology innovation spreads throughout the village. Would a truckload of commercially manufactured brooms have been as readily accepted? Probably not–Western brooms would have seemed alien, expensive, and even insulting.

Society both restrains and encourages technology transfer, which in turn shapes society. Each is a creature of the other. The interlocking dance of society and its technology gave civilization its beginning, made our world what it is today, and blazes our way into the future. In fact, the process of technology transfer is as fundamental to civilization as DNA is to life itself.

KENNETH L. NICHOLS

BIBLIOGRAPHY

Aguayo, Rafael, 1990. *Dr. Deming: The American Who Taught the Japanese About Quality.* New York: Fireside.

Bijker, Wiebe E., Thomas P. Hughes, and Trevor Pinch, eds., 1987. *The Social Construction of Technological Systems: New Directions in the Sociology and History of Technology.* Cambridge: MIT Press.

Burke, James, 1978. *Connections.* Boston: Little, Brown.

Ciciotti, Enrico, Neil Alderman, and Alfred Thwaites, eds., 1990. *Technological Change in a Spatial Context: Theory, Empirical Evidence, and Policy.* New York: Springer-Verlag.

Havelock, Ronald G., 1969. *Planning for Innovation Through Dissemination and Utilization of Knowledge.* Ann Arbor: Institute for Social Research.

Inkster, Ian, 1991. *Science and Technology in History: An Approach to Industrial Development.* New Brunswick, NJ: Rutgers University Press.

Jeremy, David J., ed., 1994. *Technology Transfer and Business Enterprise.* Brookfield, VT: Edward Elgar.

Kuhn, Thomas S., 1970. *The Structure of Scientific Revolutions,* 2d ed. Chicago: University of Chicago Press.

Lederer, William J., and Eugene Burdick, 1958. *The Ugly American.* New York: W. W. Norton.

Mumford, Lewis, 1967. *The Myth of the Machine: Technics and Human Development.* New York: Harcourt Brace Jovanovich.

Rogers, Everett M., 1983. *Diffusion of Innovations,* 3d ed. New York: Free Press.

Toffler, Alvin, 1970. *Future Shock.* New York: Random House.

Tornatsky, Louis G., et al., 1983. *The Process of Technological Innovation: Reviewing the Literature.* Washington, DC: National Science Foundation.

Williams, Frederick, and David. V. Gibson, eds., 1990. *Technology Transfer: A Communication Perspective.* Newbury Park, CA: Sage.

TELECOMMUNICATIONS POLICY.

The actions taken by a society to promote and regulate wireline and wireless communications, including telephony, telegraph, radio, television, computer-to-computer communication, fax, satellite communications, and other forms of communications through electronic or optical means.

Telecommunications policy has assumed a central place in the economic, political, social, and cultural activities of nearly every nation. This is due to the role of telecommunications in business, government, the formation of public opinion, and as a major medium for bringing entertainment to mass audiences.

Promotion of telecommunications is undertaken by nations because of the impetus that telecommunications advancement provides to economic development, capacity for growth, and the realization of national potential. Regulation is considered vital because telecommunications is viewed as an essential service comparable to transportation, electricity, or water. It has been regulated in many nations much like a public utility, with the regulatory agencies pledged to safeguard the public interest. In a sense, regulation complements and assists promotion. Many regulations, such as assignment of frequencies to prevent interference or requirements that a dominant carrier must allow other carriers to connect with its networks, facilitate access to and expanded use of telecommunications. By contrast, regulations that prevent competition may impede telecommunications advancement and keep prices artificially high.

Promotion of telecommunications takes many forms. These include (1) direct government investment in telecommunications infrastructure and operations, (2) incentives to private firms to build and operate telecommunications facilities and services, (3) subsidies and other funding arrangements to help reach the goal of universal service to provide, to the extent possible, access for everyone to basic telephone service, and (4) taxes on telecommunications equipment or usage to finance subsidies or special services (for example some countries impose a tax on each TV set to help finance public broadcasting; some local governments impose a tax on telephone usage to finance enhanced emergency [E911] telephone service, which shows the 911 operator on a computer screen the calling number and phone location).

Regulation may involve (1) approval of rates and charges, including imposing price ceilings, (2) measures to prevent interference to transmissions or reception (3) requirements to ensure interconnectivity and user access to various systems and services, (4) requirements on carriers to provide universal service, (5) regulations to assure that companies wishing to enter a market are not excluded due to practices of the dominant firms, such as refusing to provide access to local connections or equipment, and (6) requirements that all carriers and broadcasters adhere to technical and quality standards. Regulators issue licenses to broadcasters and assign frequencies to licensees, usually for a specific period, subject to renewal. Licenses may be available without charge, in various ways, ranging from "first come, first served," which may involve hearings to determine which applicant is better suited to serve a specific market, to lotteries. Tenders or competitive bids are used in Europe, but not in the United States. Recently, auctions have been utilized for awarding licenses. Auctions for wireless telephone, data, and other services have netted billions for the U.S. Treasury. Proposals to auction radio and TV have been made but not adopted in the U.S. Licenses for AM and FM sound broadcasting as well as for cellular telephone frequencies have been auctioned in New Zealand and some other nations.

Since many telecommunications transmissions are worldwide, international coordination is needed. This is done primarily by the International Telecommunication Union (ITU), a specialized agency of the United Nations, located in Geneva, Switzerland. Through the auspices of the ITU, which has 187 member nations, two-thirds of which are developing countries, internationally agreed rules and standards are established. The ITU does not have authority to regulate telecommunications and radiotransmissions directly, since these are the province of sovereign nations. Nevertheless, ITU recommendations and agreements are almost always followed by member nations due to practical considerations even though increased international competition has tended to weaken this level of support. The ITU's recommendations permit international switching and interconnection of telecommunication signals, establish international tariff structures, establish guidelines for radiocommunication emissions, interference levels and equipment standards (including television and sound broadcasting). ITU Regional and World Radiocommunication Conferences allot frequency bands, assign frequencies and set technical requirements and interference limits for radiocommunication emissions of all types, including satellite communications.

With respect to satellite communications, the ITU allocates frequencies and orbital positions (or "slots") in the geostationary orbit to member nations (frequencies and slots allocated by the ITU to nations are assigned by these nations to companies, government agencies or other users in these nations). Until 1992, orbital slots and frequencies were available on a "first come, first served" basis for fixed periods subject to renewal. Developing countries expressed concern that this approach favored industrialized nations who would take most of the advantageous slots. To assure future access, countries applied for slots even though they were not ready to use them. As a result many allocations of slots remained unused for long periods, creating "paper" scarcities of the geostationary orbit resource. Recently, real scarcities have developed in some popular orbital positions. The 1992 ITU World Administration Radio Confer-

ence responded to the concerns of developing countries by allocating pre-assigned blocks of frequencies and orbital slots in "expansion" bands, providing guaranteed access to the goestationary orbit both to developing and industrialized nations.

Recently, some observers have questioned whether the ITU, given its lack of enforcement powers, will be able to cope with major changes in satellite communications which could cause serious problems over claims to favorable orbital slots and in frequency interference. These changes include the large number of satellites to be launched in the near future, vigorous competition among several new private satellite networks and the rapid development of mobile services utilizing satellites in nongeostationary orbits. New approaches, including a "Global Satellite Communications Code of Conduct" with self posted bonds and the potential for stiff penalties for violators, may be needed to deal with such problems. (For a discussion of this issue, see Pelton, 1995.)

Many nations prohibit pornographic and obscene content in broadcasts and telephone transmissions. The U.S. Telecommunications Act of 1996 requires manufacturers of TV sets to include circuitry (the so-called "V" chip) which would allow a parent to block programs which have been rated by the TV networks to be excessevely violent or to contain sexually explicit material. With the intent to protect children, the U.S. Communications Decency Act of 1996 made it a crime punishable by two years in prison and a $250,000 fine to transmit "indecent" material over the Internet in a manner accessible to minors. In 1997, the U.S. Supreme Court declared this provision of the Act unconstitutional for violating the free speech guarantees of the First Amendment to the U.S. constitution. The Court found this provision of the Act to be overly broad and vague. The Act had been challenged by Internet users, civil liberties organizations, computer industry groups, publishers and the American Library Association as a form of censorship. The court gave to the Internet the highest level of First Amendment protection, comparable to books, magazines and newspapers. The Court made a distinction between the Internet and radio or TV broadcasts, observing that the Internet is not as pervasive a medium as TV or radio—where the Court has permitted greater government regulation—because computer users must spend effort to search for indecent communications. Given the nature of the Internet, the Court said, there was no way a person transmitting indecent material could be sure that a minor would not see it. Most users of the Internet, the Court noted, like chat rooms, news groups and the World Wide Web, "are open to all comers." In its opinion, the Court said that "in order to deny minors access to potentially harmful speech, the Act effectively suppresses a large amount of speech that adults have a constitutional right to receive and to address to one another." The Court let stand a provision of the Act which bars pornography and obscenity on the Internet which are outside the protection of the First Amendment.

Innovations in technology for telecommunications have permitted a rapid expansion of services for both wireline and wireless communication. Fiber optic networks, digital signaling, and related developments have accelerated broadband services (broadband refers to high speed transmissions that can carry voice, video, and data simultaneously.) These and other developments have made it possible for telephone networks to carry television signals and for cable TV networks to carry telephone calls. The computer is rapidly becoming a device for watching television, sending text, data, and video communications worldwide as well as for two-way voice communications using special software. Cellular phones, personal communications devices, and satellite signals to mobile telephones are becoming more versatile and promise to bring full communications services to even the most remote areas.

A prime example of the possibilities opened up by advanced technology is the Internet and the World Wide Web (WWW), which is accessed through the Internet. The Internet—which may be defined as a network of computer networks—has made it possible for persons to communicate on a global basis by text, voice, and video effectively and efficiently through computers of all types. The WWW connects not only networks but also permits users to access information from a tremendous range of companies, government and not-for-profit agencies as well as to purchase a wide range of services and products. Through WWW, companies and government and not-for-profit agencies can communicate directly with customers and clients and provide service and information to them in real time at nearly every location in the world. Presently, over 60 million people use the Internet with some 6 million people logging on every day. Usage is expected to grow exponentially over the next decade. Technological advances have made it possible to access the Internet through wireless as well as wireline transmissions. This promises to make connections with the most rural and remote areas feasible. One example of how rapidly access to remote and rural areas is growing is the Honolulu-based PEACESAT, which provides access to the Internet, via low-data-rate satellite communications, to hundreds of remote islands in the Pacific basin. This enables low-cost disaster communications, distance learning and other services.

The benefits of advanced telecommunications have been enjoyed disproportionately by the more affluent members of society, especially in large cities in industrialized countries. This situation has led to a communications and information gap between the rich and poor within nations and between industrialized and developing countries. Many observers believe that the rapid advance of telecommunications technology, while holding the potential of making telecommunications generally available to people who have not enjoyed its benefits, will actually result in widening the gap. This may happen because telecommunications companies may not make investments for spreading telecommunications, especially for enhanced services, to rural and remote areas, developing countries, or the inner cities, where the prospects for financial return are uncertain. Special measures, such as dedicated funds or subsidies, may have to be taken to alleviate this problem. (For a discussion of this point, see Independent Commission 1985 and Hudson 1984 and 1995.)

Origin and Subsequent History

The beginnings of communications policy may be traced to the widespread use of the telephone in the early 1900s. In the United States between 1907 and 1913, 26 states enacted laws making physical interconnection compulsory. In 1910, the U.S. Congress gave the Interstate Commerce Commission authority to regulate telephone and telegraph carriers, which were declared common carriers, whose rates were to be "just and reasonable."

The Communications Act of 1934 created the U.S. Federal Communications Commission (FCC) to regulate the U.S. communications industry. As technology advanced, the jurisdiction of the FCC expanded beyond interstate telephony and radio to include television, wireless communications such as cellular telephones and paging systems, satellite communications, and cable TV prices and business practices. States and local governments in the United States regulate intrastate telephony and award franchises to cable TV companies. In other nations, generally, national governments regulate their communications industries through special regulatory agencies.

Historically, telecommunications facilities have been owned and operated in most nations by government. The United States and some other nations have had private ownership and operation of telecommunications. Where private ownership and operation of telephone facilities and services have taken place, usually one firm has been dominant and that firm as well as any other public telephone firms have been subjected to close regulation. In the United States, the American Telegraph and Telephone Company (AT&T) exercised a virtual monopoly over long-distance and local telephone services with competition in some areas only. This situation began to change in the 1960s when rival long-distance carriers started to challenge AT&T. In 1984, as a result of a judgement in an antitrust suit brought by the U.S. Department of Justice, AT&T was broken up. AT&T continued its long-distance services but had to divest itself of local telephone operations. These were taken over by the establishment of seven regional Bell operating companies (known as RBOCs), which have had a virtual monopoly in public local telephone services in their respective regions. The 1984 judgment prohibited the RBOCs from offering long distance services.

The U.S. Telecommunications Act of 1996 was intended by Congress to "provide for a pro-competitive deregulatory national policy framework designed to accelerate rapidly private sector deployment of advanced telecommunications and information technologies and services to all Americans by opening all telecommunicaitons markets to competition." The Act permits long distance, cable and utility companies to offer local telephone services. The Act requires incumbent local telephone companies (i.e., the current local telephone monopoly companies—the RBOCs, the General Telephone and Electric Co., (GTE) and some smaller firms) to make available to new entrants (1) interconnections to their networks at reasonable costs on a non-discriminatory basis (2) access to unbundled network elements —bundling refers to the practice of combining basic with enhanced services (3) and to offer local telephone company retail services for resale to requesting telecommunications carriers at wholesale prices. These provisions allow new entrants to offer local services without building entirely new networks.

The Act also permits local telephone companies to apply for permission to offer long distance services provided that they have complied with provisions of the Act designed to open local markets to competition. Also, under the Act, telephone companies are able to offer home video services.

In many nations where the government owned and operated all telephone service, privatization has taken place, as is the case in the United Kingdom, Spain, Argentina, Chile, Mexico, Japan, and Hong Kong, among others. In some cases, competitors to the privatized firm have merged. In the United Kingdom, for example, British Telecom, the privatized dominant firm has a competitor in Mercury Communications, a wholly owned subsidiary of Cable and Wireless.

With regard to broadcasting, governments owned and operated radio and TV stations in most nations. In the United States, private companies have dominated the field of broadcasting. In nations with government ownership and operation, privatization has taken place for at least some of the broadcast facilities.

Policy Issues

The most significant issues in telecommunications policy are the following:

1. *Liberalization*—The lifting of technological, regulatory, financial, and political restrictions imposed by governments or monopolies on telecommunications facilities and services.
2. *Competition*—Government and private monopolies for long-distance and local telephone services have been broken in many countries, resulting in the beginnings of competitive markets.
3. *Interconnectivity*—Unless the services and facilities of established dominant carriers are interconnected with

other services and facilities at reasonable charges, many users, especially those who lack financial and technical capacity, will be denied access to the full range of services.
4. *Free flow of diverse information (non-censorship)*—In democratic nations, regulation of public telephone companies and broadcasters ensured that all types of views and information would be transmitted. With the emergence of extensive private telephone, cable, and computer networks not subject to such regulations, there are questions as to whether free flow will be maintained.
5. *Universal service*—Attempts to reach this goal have been aided by subsidies and other measures to keep local rates low. With the advent of deregulation, privatization, and increased competition, such aids are being cut or eliminated. Achieving universal service in this context is a major challenge.
6. *Privacy*—Wireless and computer-to-computer telecommunications are much harder to keep private than traditional wireline transmission. Steps to protect privacy while preserving freedom of expression and open communications are the subject of intense debate and scrutiny.

Analyses of Policy Issues

This section provides brief analyses of the six policy issues that were just identified.

Liberalization

There has been a strong trend toward liberalization of government or monopolistic control of telecommunications in many countries. This trend has many facets, including privatization of telephone and broadcasting services formerly owned and operated by governments, deregulation of rates and content rules for transmissions, and relaxation of barriers for entry of new firms into markets or services.

Although there is general agreement that liberalization has been overdue, there is also concern that this trend is going too far, particularly with regard to deregulation of rates and lack of protection for new entrants. Specifically, there is concern that large established firms will use their economic power through mergers and other means to isolate smaller new entrants. Those who oppose rapid and full deregulation point out that in many areas, telephone services and cable TV have been provided without real competition. They argue that there should be vibrant competition before an industry is deregulated. Otherwise, deregulation could result in unregulated monopolies, according to this view.

Competition

Competition in telephone and cable TV services had been considered inefficient by regulators in most nations. Their reasoning was that it would be wasteful for more than one carrier to wire an entire nation or a large geographic area. Thus, these services have been provided by a dominant carrier subject to close regulation of rates and other matters, as well as special requirements.

The negative views of regulators toward competition began to change for four reasons. First, private networks invested in fiber optic cables for bringing more versatile business services, forcing dominant public carriers to build fiber optic networks of their own. Second, microwave transmissions and satellite communications provided an alternative to wireline services for many applications. Third, by using fiber optic in combination with satellite and microwave, private networks could bypass local telephone companies for access to long-distance services. Fourth, computer-to-computer communication provides an alternative to long-distance conventional telephony at the price of a local call. Reflecting on these changes, regulators began to focus on the advantages of competition, including lower rates, expanded offerings, and technology advances. Although regulators in many nations now encourage competition, new entrants in many countries have yet to establish a strong foothold, especially in local telephone services and cable TV.

Interconnectivity

This issue is affected by three factors: (1) the resistance of dominant carriers to allow new entrants to interconnect with their facilities; (2) the practice of "bundling" basic with enhanced equipment or services. In effect, when this is done, only users who pay for the total "bundled" package can access the basic service; and (3) the proliferation of new telecommunications equipment and the different technical approaches or standards upon which the new equipment or transmission modes are based. Those who argue that regulators should take steps to require interconnectivity point to the long-term gains of interconnected systems for economic growth and broader user access.

Those who are against regulation to ensure interconnectivity argue that firms have the right to develop tailored systems for specialized users and should not have to go to the expense and trouble of making their systems "transparent" to all potential users. They also defend "bundling" as a way to bring the most advanced technical developments to enhanced services desired by specialized users. In addition, they argue that increased competition combined with advanced technology provides so many avenues for communication that interconnection requirements are no longer as necessary as in earlier times. They point to the unregulated Internet as an example of a service that connects all forms of computer equipment on a worldwide basis.

As noted, the Telecommunications Act of 1996 requires incumbent local telephone companies to provide interconnections to new entrants on a non-discriminatory

basis and at reasonable costs, as well as to provide nondiscriminatory access to network elements on an unbundled basis.

Free Flow of Diverse Information (Non-Censorship)

One of the reasons for regulation of telecommunications in democratic countries has been to ensure the free flow of diverse information. To facilitate reaching this objective, public telephone companies have been required to grant access to all persons on a nondiscriminatory, content-neutral basis. Laws and regulations have protected public telephone firms from libel and damage suits, which could result from the content that they are required to carry. With the emergence of new communications providers, such as contract carriers and systems integrators not subject to such regulation, the prospects for continuing free flow of diverse information are in doubt.

Systems integrators that provide "one-stop" access to all telecommunications networks—public and private, wireline and wireless—are in a position to block information that they deem objectionable. Even though the systems integrator carries content from a public network, it could block the transmission of that information by denying user access to its service.

Those who believe this situation is a threat to the free flow of diverse information recommend that government regulators impose the same requirements for access and free flow on private carriers and integrators as on the public networks. Those who oppose such regulation argue that there are now so many channels for communications—and more are developing each year—that access is no longer a problem and that all types of views can be transmitted on some of the many telecommunications services available. They note that even when views are officially prohibited by governments, such views nevertheless are transmitted through fax, computer communications, particularly on the Internet, and other means.

Universal Service

Implementation strategies have centered on providing very low rates to persons who cannot afford standard telephone charges and to extending telephone infrastructure to rural and remote areas that did not have service due to the high cost of wiring such "thin route" areas.

To enable telephone carriers to offer low rates and to invest in rural telephony, governments have followed two basic courses. One is to subsidize with taxpayer funds. The second is to permit cross-subsidies of revenues among services offered by carriers. For example, business rates or long-distance rates are set higher than needed to cover costs plus a profit, with the surplus used to subsidize local rates or to offset investment costs of extending lines. In the U.S., local telephone companies priced access charges which long distance carriers pay to reach their customers over local networks high enough to subsidize local rates, including especially low rates for people with low income.

These approaches worked in the years before adding taxes became politically unacceptable and one or two companies dominated telephone services. Currently, however, public telephone companies must lower long-distance and business rates to meet competition, making cross-subsidies less viable. In the United States, the breakup of AT&T and the creation of the regional Bell operating companies (RBOCs) have eliminated the possibility of cross-subsidies between most long-distance and local revenues.

Another important development affecting universal service is the advent of contract carriers and systems integrators not subject to universal service requirements to which public telephone companies must adhere. These firms can choose their customers, shutting out those that cannot pay their rates. In this context, should public telephone companies still be required to provide universal service?

Those who argue that universal service must be required state that one of several financing options could be utilized. These include a telecommunications sales or value-added tax levied either on telephone bills or on all telecommunications activities, including telephone bills, computer and cable services, and telecommunications products and equipment. The comprehensive tax would not fall heavily on only one part of the telecommunications business but could be politically unpopular.

Another alternative is a telecommunications value-added account system that allocates burdens on all carriers, integrates existing universal service approaches, and provides credits for universal service performance. Under this system, all carriers would receive credit for providing universal service. If a carrier did not offer universal service, it would pay into the account at a higher rate. Proportional allocation of burden could be determined by using various criteria, such as number of access lines, customers, or message units. Vouchers would be available to users who could redeem them at various competing carriers. Redeemed vouchers would be credited to the account of the carrier providing the service. (For a discussion of this system, see Noam 1994c.)

Those who question whether universal service should be mandated for the long term argue that the proliferation of technological changes and the numerous competitors will bring about market conditions in which most people will be able to find basic telephone services at affordable rates.

Recently, some analysts of telecommunications policy have sought to broaden the definition of universal service. Changes in technology and in user needs make it important, they contend, for an enhanced version of universal service to be available through libraries, schools, clinics, and community centers. This is important since to succeed economically and socially in modern society people need information and training, which they cannot access through basic

telephone service. Either individuals need state of the art computers with modems, e-mail, Internet access, and CD roms in their homes or they need access to such facilities in their communities. Since individual ownership of such equipment is too expensive for the vast majority of people, community access is the only practical alternative.

Such a broad definition will require much more than the approaches described previously for ensuring access for all to basic telephone service. Targeted subsidies from governments or special financing through communications funds receiving contributions from profitable telecommunications firms will be needed to assure community access. In addition, national policies and incentives will be needed to ensure interconnectivity and interoperability of various networks and services. This is necessary so that people living in rural or remote areas or the inner city are not excluded from access because providers have not invested in modern equipment to serve areas with weak prospects for high profits. A national policy for promoting the installation of digital switching everywhere and for ending surcharges for touchtone service (which is necessary for telephone users to access enhanced information services) would be needed to achieve interconnectivity and interoperability. (For a discussion of the broader concept, see Hudson 1995.)

The Telecommunications Act of 1996 recognized the need for universal service both for basic telephony and for expanded access, as well as the importance of establishing new ways to provide subsidies while also promoting competition. In May, 1997, acting under the authority of the Act, the Federal Communications Commission established funds to help schools and libraries pay for high speed connections to the Internet and to provide rural health care centers with telecommunications services at low rates. Schools and libraries in financially poor districts would receive greater support. In addition, low income inner city and rural residents would be assured of very low rates for telephone services. To finance these universal service arrangements, the revenue of telecommunications companies are assessed. The FCC also reduced access charges which long distance companies pay for connections to local telephone company networks. To help offset the loss of revenue to local companies, the FCC imposed increased local telephone rates for second residence and business lines.

Privacy

The new modes of transmitting messages via telecommunications have intensified the age-old issue of privacy of communications. Wireless communications and computer-to-computer communications are relatively easy to intercept. In some cases, computer "hackers" have been able to break into so-called secure computer files to steal confidential or proprietary data. They may also infect files with computer viruses, which effectively render computers useless, and even plant false information in them. Personal information, such as medical, financial, and employment records can be accessed by technologically able persons even though such files are not open to public inspection and are protected by laws and regulations.

Those who are concerned that privacy protection must be strengthened call for government action to require organizations that have confidential information to encode all data and impose electronic barriers against intrusion. This could require government supervision and registry of coding keys. Those who believe that government regulation is not needed argue that voluntary measures by such organizations will be sufficient and point out that, to a great extent, privacy is already compromised since personal information is shared by insurance companies and credit card companies whenever a person uses medical insurance or applies for credit. In these cases, persons waive their rights to privacy in order to obtain benefits. Imposing government interference could lead to the danger of a police state, they argue. In 1997, Microsoft and Netscape joined with other computer firms to develop technology to protect the privacy of Internet users.

Administrative Considerations

There is a strong need for professional administration of telecommunications operations. Administrators are concerned with the following:

1. Operations planning involves economic analysis of user needs coordinated with national and international trends in infrastructure, technology, and public policy.
2. Control assures that the operations units have an adequate management information system and that adequate statistics are collected on traffic, faults, and equipment performance.
3. Financial analysis determines whether operations generate sufficient revenues from the users and other sources to cover costs and to generate a sufficient return on capital for systems expansion and technological updating. What trends indicate that this situation will change?
4. Personnel systems are implemented for recruiting highly qualified staff for the complex equipment and transmission modes of modern telecommunications networks. This is a particular problem in developing countries, which lack trained indigenous personnel.
5. Organizational structure assures that operational units have sufficient flexibility to provide users with reliable, efficient, and quality services at reasonable rates.
6. Facilities should not only be state of the art, they should be conducted with minimum disruption and be cost effective. This, in turn, requires administration that coordinates and adjusts relationships among owners, sponsors, and users, and ensures that facilities

have adequate maintenance and supply. The optimum mix of technologies for achieving the objectives of users while minimizing costs should be determined. This is especially important due to the proliferation of technologies for transmission. Combinations of fiber optic and copper cables may be the best mix for certain user applications, especially if copper is already in place, even though the more costly fiber optic has greater versatility. Combinations of satellite and fiber optic transmissions may be the most economical and reliable option for international communications. Satellite links may be necessary to reach rural and remote areas and provide a backup for failures of underseas fiber optic cables.

7. Regulations are a potential source of great difficulty and should be thoroughly understood. Procedures for checking with regulatory authorities should be established. Even though many regulations are being abolished or relaxed, new approaches to regulation for universal service, privacy, and interconnectivity are being considered. Administrators should develop channels to participate in the formulation of new regulatory approaches.
8. Standards are especially vital due to the international nature of telecommunications and the advent of advanced wireless services and computer networks such as the World Wide Web. Standards must be clearly identified in all relevant manuals, and clear-cut instructions and procedures for their application must be developed. Obstacles to introducing new services to a nation from other nations due to differences in standards should be clearly identified, and discussions should be held to resolve issues.
9. Even though liberalization will make the marketplace the primary mechanism for stimulating provision of innovate services, it will be necessary to establish performance indicators and measures for such goals as universal service, interconnectivity, and privacy protection. Governmental or industry association committees to monitor performance will be needed. (For a discussion of this issue, see Hudson 1995.)
10. Ongoing education is needed to ensure that users learn about new telecommunications services and facilities. They will need information on applications, benefits, and pricing and how to make choices among service options. Such education will be particularly needed for public service applications, such as kiosks for access to government information and services and for interactive citizen-agency dialogues.
11. Training of telecommunications personnel in the new technologies will be important, not only for proficiency in operations and maintenance but also to sensitize personnel to the need for privacy protection and to devise ways through which equipment and facilities can be utilized to promote interconnectivity and

access. As indicated earlier, training of local personnel is of special importance in developing countries.

In view of the current trends in telecommunications policy, the most significant administrative issues are as follows:

1. What institutional arrangements would facilitate increased competition while preserving the goals of affordable rates, universal service, interconnectivity, efficiency, and reliability?
2. What measures should be taken to ensure that standards are universal and realistic?
3. What measures are most appropriate for evaluating the performance of telecommunications industries, especially with regard to meeting the goals of universal service, reliability, network efficiency, and creating opportunities for technological progress?

Future Prospects

In the new era of liberalization, greater competition, deregulation, and proliferating technologies, there is great potential for bringing the benefits of telecommunications to everyone in the world. This prospect should lead to improvements in the quality of life, not only for the more well off segments of society but also for those less fortunate. However, there is the danger that the telecommunications and information gap may be widened if the newer services are provided mainly to those able to pay high prices. Since telecommunications is a key factor in economic, political, social, and cultural development worldwide, policy and administration should ensure that the benefits of advanced telecommunications are spread to people everywhere.

ARTHUR L. LEVINE

BIBLIOGRAPHY

Brock, Gerald W., 1994. *Telecommunications Policy for the Information Age: From Monopoly to Competition.* Cambridge, MA: Harvard University Press.
Compaine, Benjamin M. and Mitchell J. Weinraub, 1995. "Universal Access to Online Services: an Examination of the Issue." *Telecommunications Policy.* vol. 21, no. 1:15-33.
Frieden, Rob, 1995. "Universal Personal Communications in the New Telecommunications World Order: Access to Wireline Networks." *Telecommunications Policy,* vol. 19, no. 1:43-49.
Gore, Albert, Jr., 1991. "Information for the Global Village: Computers, Networks, and Public Policy." *Scientific American,* vol. 265, no. 3 (September) 150.
Hudson, Heather E., 1984. *When Telephones Reach the Village.* Norwood, NJ: Ablex.
———,1995. "Converging Technologies and Changing Realities: Universal Service in the Information Age." *Proceedings of the Pacific Telecommunications Seventeenth Annual Conference,* Honolulu, Hawaii, Jan. 22-26:316-322.
Independent Commission for World Wide Telecommunications Development of the ITU (Maitland Commission Report), 1985. *The Missing Link.* Geneva, Switzerland: ITU.
Information Infrastructure Task Force, 1993. *The National Information Infrastructure: Agenda for Action.* Washington, DC: U.S. Department of Commerce, National Telecommunications and Information Administration.
Levine, Arthur L., 1985. "Teleports and the Role of Local Government." *New York Affairs,* vol. 3, no. 1: NY 4-6.
National Telecommunications and Information Administration, 1994. *20/20 Visions.* Washington, DC: U.S. Department of Commerce.
Noam, Eli M., 1994a. "Beyond Liberalization: From the Network of Networks to the System of Systems." *Telecommunications Policy,* vol. 18, no. 4:286-294.
———,1994b. "Beyond Liberalization II: The Impending Doom of Common Carriage." *Telecommunications Policy,* vol. 18, no. 6:435-452.
———,1994c. "Beyond Liberalization III: Reforming Universal Service." *Telecommunications Policy,* vol. 18, no. 9:687-704.
Organization for Economic Cooperation and Development, 1993. *The Economics of Radio Frequency Allocation.* Paris: OECD.
Parker, Edwin. B., and Heather E. Hudson, 1992. *Electronic Byways: State Policies for Rural Development Through Telecommunications.* Boulder, CO: Westview.
Pelton, Joseph N., 1995. *Wireless and Satellite Telecommunications: The Technology, the Market and the Regulations.* Upper Saddle River, New Jersey: Prentice Hall.
———, 1981. *Global Talk: Computers, World Communications, and Man.* Brighton, Sussex, England: Harvester.
Phillips, Charles F., Jr., 1994. *The Regulation of Public Utilities: Theory and Practice.* Arlington, VA: Public Utilities Reports.
Vietor, Richard H. K., 1989. "AT&T and the Public Good: Regulation and Competition in Telecommunications." In Stephen P. Bradley and Jerry A. Hausman, eds., *Future Competition in Telecommunications.* Boston: Harvard Business School Press, 27-103.

TERRORISM. Random or directed violence and intimidation for political purposes. In his book *The Anatomy of Terrorism,* David Long (1990) suggests this definition: "The threat or use of criminal violence for political purposes by individuals or groups, acting for or in opposition to established government authority, with the intention to shock or intimidate a target audience wider than the immediate victims" (p. 3). Viewed by the world as a weapon of the weak, the passionate, and the relatively powerless, terrorism is imprecise due to its nature, use, and penchant to evoke fear from the populace as well as oversimplification and sensationalization by the news media. It is a complex phenomenon ranging from the isolated actions of individuals, the organized efforts of purposeful groups, or the policies of regimes that use terrorism to sustain their own power base or to sponsor covert terrorism in other states. Terrorists are often labeled as "crusaders," "criminals," or "crazies," depending on the prevailing standards of conduct or behavior in a particular community, situation, or cultural context. Terrorism is often international or transnational in its impact due in large part to the role of the mass media in furthering its intended goal to influence world opinion and the actions of individual or groups of nation-states.

History

Although terrorism is as old as violence itself, the word as used by contemporary commentators dates back to the "reign of terror" in revolutionary France (1793–1794) when more than 17,000 citizens were officially executed and many thousands more perished under less official circumstances. Terrorism, in one form or another, has been practiced by discontents from all sides of the political, economic, or religious spectrum in every society. It has been used on occasion with severe results by governments themselves. It is associated with recrimination, criminal intent, targeting of innocent victims, and other reprehensive forms of political violence. It has evolved into a highly subjective term used by many to describe extremely abnormal, politically motivated violence.

We can trace early episodes of "political violence" to left-wing movements in mid- to late-nineteenth-century Russia, such as the revolutionary group Norodnaya Volya ("The Will of the People") that assassinated several government and police officials and eventually killed Tsar Alexander II in 1881. The Norodnaya Volya pursued a violent and organized agenda as a response by intellectual revolutionaries to the autocratic repression of the tsarist regime. Its importance in the history of terrorism, as documented by Walter Laqueur and Yonah Alexander (1987) underlies the group's systematic pursuit of its goals. This group used selective violence in pursuit of civil liberties and political rights in the face of the repressive Russian government establishment. It brought a sophistication and methodology to what once may have been random violence of a deprived few to seize power from a nonresponsive regime. At the beginning of the twentieth century, they were succeeded by an even more effective terrorist group, the Social Revolutionary Party, which used assassination and other forms of violence so productively that it was emulated by groups in Armenia, the Balkans, India, and elsewhere. At the turn of the century, with the stage set for war in Europe, organized political terrorist groups such the Irish Fenians, who attacked the English, Armenian lefists against the Turks, and other nationalist-separatist groups carried out their planned violence. Following World War I, the other end of the political spectrum arose with a vengeance in the form of severe right-wing terrorism. Fascist movements in Croatia, Italy, Germany, and Spain flourished in a reactionary abyss of vigilantism.

The belief in "propaganda by deed," striving for political, economic, and social status-quo change that would improve their lot, contempt for liberal democracy, and strong group identification with their goals became common characteristics of extreme violent groups on the left and right. The roots of modern terrorism began to take hold in the 1930s and 1940s in the colonial regimes of the Middle East, Cyprus, northern Africa, southern Africa, and Asia.

Contemporary Terrorism

The framework of modern political, economic, and social violence can best be understood in the context of its unique nature, purpose, actions, and the counterterrorism options available to nation-states and coalitions of states. Contemporary writers, political figures, and the mass media portray modern terrorist actions in what Brian Jenkins (1985) refers to as a "theater" atmosphere played more than ever on a genuinely international stage. This contributes to a further "blurring" of the topic of terrorism and what to do about it when identifying the opportunities available to democracies for counterstrategies, joint operations, state sponsorship, and collaborative alliances.

Jay Shafritz, E. F. Gibbons, Jr., and Gregory Scott (1991) offer several characteristics of modern terrorism that differentiate it from terror of the past:

- modern terrorism is left-wing to a greater degree than ever before;
- the modern print and broadcast media have brought terrorist incidents and actors to the forefront of world events;
- modern communications, transportation, and weapons technology have vastly aided the causes of terrorists and have contributed to the more international nature of modern terrorism;
- nations have become in several instances intimately involved with terrorist organizations, and terrorism has in some cases taken on the character of "war by proxy"; and
- the constitutional principles of the liberal democracies hamper military options for combatting terrorism, as well as surveillance activities, in ways that did not restrain nations of the past (p. xi).

In many ways, we are living out the legacy of the failure of the North American and European New Left, the mid-1960s student-led violence in response to U.S. anticommunist global policies, and the rekindling of a number of postcolonial nationalist/separatist movements in Ireland, Spain, the Middle East, and Asia. The worrisome emergence of a radical "far right" in the form of constitutionalist "militias," skinheads, white supremicists, and other such groups in the United States is another source of concern for contemporary leaders.

The "modern age" of terrorism in the late 1980s has taken on increased significance due to the post–cold war period. The uncertainty of international security relationships, the recent surge in multilateral "peacekeeping and humanitarian operations," and the increase in post-USSR, nationalist-inspired activities have generated new opportunities for transnational and nation-based terrorist organizations. Nation-states facing international terrorism are approaching these activities with a call for multilateral, highly collaborative solutions. There are three perspectives that modern analysts bring to their study of modern terrorism that result in viewing it in one of three ways: politically inspired, criminal, or guerilla activity. Also, there is an emerging view that terrorism includes groups that support the commercial or business objectives associated with the transport, sale, and distribution of illegal commodities such as drugs, aliens, weapons, currency, precious metals, and even nuclear materials. In order to gain a better understanding of the scope and nature of terrorism today, it may be useful to categorize these groups that often interact and overlap in what can be viewed as "marriages of convenience." This exercise in typology is often criticized as useful only to academic debate; however, many authors and practitioners view this process of definition as a way to better understand the new opportunities for terrorist organizations to comingle with criminal organizations for mutual benefit that undermines and threatens the community. The following categories should prove useful to gain a better understanding of the amorphous nature of terrorism.

Dissident or "Doctrinal"

These organizations carry on a struggle for power—political, religious, social, ethnic, and so on—by attacking the dominant system of their community. This often occurs within the boundaries of one nation, overlaps within a region, or ferments around the world. We think most often of left-wing revolutionary or disenfranchised political or religious minority groups fighting for their homeland, those striving to restore fundamental religious or social values, or factions of anarchists or nihilists. Groups that come to mind are the Irish Republican Army, the Basque ETA, Sendero Luminiso in Peru, Sikh nationalists in India, the German Red Army Faction, the Japanese Red Army, Kurdish rebels, Armenian groups, Islamic Fundamentalist Shi'ite groups such as Hamas, Hizballah, and the Fuerzas Armadas Revolucionarias de Columbia (FARC), rebels who seek political and territorial control by using militant violence against the established systems of justice, economics, religion, and culture.

The February 1993 terrorist bombing of the World Trade Center complex in New York City and subsequent revelations of plans to bomb additional sites in that area are excellent examples of the global spread of terrorist actions to bring pressure to bear on liberal democracies like the United States to cease their support for traditional governments in power such as Egypt, Algeria, Israel, Pakistan, and India, who are resisting extremely violent religious fundamentalist groups.

This category includes other groups such as right-wing extremists who use violence to preserve the status-quo such as the Ulster Defense Association, the death squads of El Salvador and Guatemala, Gush Emunim vigilantes in Israel, the Turkish Grey Wolves, the German Hoffman Sports Group, the American Ku Klux Klan, neo-Nazi groups, and other "hate" extremist organizations.

This extensive category combines the nationalistic and religious motives of deprived, frustrated, and/or alienated groups who employ the tools of violence (crime, fear, innocent victims, brutality, and media hype) to create disharmony within state boundaries and throughout the world. In today's post–cold war period this has caused such analysts as Jenkins, of RAND Corp. (1985) to refer to terrorism as "the other World War."

Establishment and State-Sponsored

This is a form of coercion by violent acts in order to preserve the dominant political, religious, or social order or further its self-interests internally or throughout its region or the world. In effect, some states have found the use of extreme violence either directly or through indirect support of violent groups an effective way to maintain control over its populace. The incumbent powers in a state use physical or psychological force to perpetuate the status quo. The use of targeted or indiscriminate violence by state-inspired or supported vigilante groups is one example of "establishment" terrorism. Sanctioned violence, through surrogates or by government law enforcement or military groups, can be a gray area manifesting itself in various forms of planned or retaliatory acts. Syrian control over the activities of the militant Hizballah groups in southern Lebanon is supportive of President Hafez al Assad's peace prospects with Israel. It also places the Palestine Liberation Organization government in the new territories, the joint negotiations of the PLO and Israel, and the remainder of the region hostage to Syrian interests. This state sponsorship of a shadowy terrorist group provides a very effective vehicle for clandestine pursuit of violent state objectives with minimal expense and high level of deniability. This takes on an insidious form of state involvement to preserve economic and political privilege with the use of "death squads" in Guatemala and El Salvador in the 1980s and more contemporary alleged law enforcement groups murdering and kidnapping "street kids" in Brazil. In particular, the Middle East and Latin American regions promise a future of fragile political, economic, and social systems that breed more authoritarian movements with high potential for increased use of military or stern law enforcement solutions. Various forms of human repression and ethnic genocide have occurred in recent times in the African Congo (formerly Zaire), Rawanda, Iraq, Turkey, Romania, Haiti, India, Cambodia, and other areas either through active state involvement or the inability of the state to control or influence such events.

State sponsorship is an unclear notion often given more credence than it deserves. During the cold war of the late 1970s and 1980s, the frequency of terrorist actions increased as a tool to achieve certain groups' goals. This was described as part of a Soviet Union–sponsored, worldwide "terror network" of left-wing organizations taking their orders from Moscow. State control of fiercely independent groups is often overstated by analysts and members of the

media who pursue a formal connection and related explanation to satisfy the appetites of readers or viewers who often subscribe to a "global conspiracy" approach to explain world events. This is particularly true when interpreting events in a complex regional scenario such as the Middle East, where nations like Iran, Iraq, Syria have provided advice, comfort, and resources to various Shi'ite fundamentalist groups for decades. This does not necessarily mean that these nations always control the plans and actions of these groups.

Commercial and New Partners Using Terror

Violence-prone groups who desire wealth, ideological reform, and territorial control have developed cooperative agreements and ventures to bring about a new form of terrorism that some writers identify as "commercial." Emerging terms such as "narcoterrorism" and "ecoterrorism" and other modern forms of criminal activity that employ violent means in a variety of ways deserve identification and further analysis. The future trend is the likelihood of more dissident, insurgent, and commercially motivated terrorist group cooperation to build more illegally acquired capacity and to gain wealth. The illegal drug trade in Latin America combines the efforts of leftist Peruvian, Colombian, and Mexican groups in commercial ventures with rightist drug "cartels" that strengthen their antigovernment programs and further their material goals. Phil Williams (1994) cites "increased interdependence between nations, the ease of international travel and communications, the permeability of national boundaries, and the globalisation of international financial networks" (p. 97) as explanation for the emergence and adaptability of these partnerships. He describes these transnational criminal organizations (TCOs) as operating in a global environment with all the characteristics of a global industry that, at least for now, gains most of its illegal profits from drug trafficking. For all partners in this activity, this provides necessary funds for the purchase of weapons, corruption of government officials, travel, propaganda, political campaigns, and other illegal and often legal revolutionary activities. This form of terrorism has provided groups such as the Nigerians, Mexicans, Brazilians, Japanese Yakuza, Asian gangs, and even Russian criminal organizations with a direct linkage to liberal democracies and their market economies. Money laundering, forgery, violence directed toward internal country justice systems, movement of illegal drugs, transport of nuclear materials, passage of illegal aliens, and many other activities are symptoms of this new form of commercial terrorism. Peter A. Lupsha (1989) finds in the Western hemisphere, "a variety of alliances, or for lack of a better term, 'marriages of convenience' between insurgents and drug trafficking organizations" (p. 65). These various forms of commercial terrorism have become a security threat to nations that host these activities and to those areas of the globe that provide the demand for their illegal products. A particularly serious commodity is the prospect of il-

legal transport of nuclear materials or biological agents to nations that seek these weapons to maintain their relative balance in a regional power competition, such as the Middle East, South Asia, or eastern Asia. With the apparent loss of accountability for nuclear materials by the former Soviet Union and related instability in Russia, this has become a very serious prospect for future world security arrangements.

Counterterrorism Policy and Practices

Developed and developing "Third World" nations alike are threatened by the scourge of terrorism. It is a menace to Western democratic society, newly forming collective trade blocs, and to less stable, emerging governments throughout the world. Political systems that foster the values of individual freedom of expression and movement, justice, and collective goods must learn how to deal with terror by finding means to counter it. Scholars and practitioners suggest that there must be a coordination of unilateral, bilateral, and collective strategies and tactics to deal with these unpredictable challenges. These violent acts have included in recent years the use of chemical agents in Japan in 1995, attacks on U.S. embassy staff in countries such as Pakistan, indiscriminate killing in the Arab world and Latin America, and recent devastating bombings in the United States. Countering such actions requires concerted effort and ultimately calls for international cooperative solutions. Highly visible actions such as acceleration of the judicial process, martial law, extradition of perpetrators, economic sanctions, surgical retaliation, restrictions on the media, refusal to give in to hostage demands, and more covert operations such as surveillance, human collection of intelligence, computerized data banks, smart systems, and various electronic communications measures must be employed to counter or prevent terrorist activities. Collaboration among governments and security forces is crucial due to the transnational nature and variety of methods used by modern terrorists.

Deterrence

Deterrence is an active form of prevention that is intended to dissuade terrorist groups or individuals from employing violence to gain their objectives. International criminal statutes to punish individuals and sanctions for state sponsorship of terrorism at a body like the United Nations would be an excellent beginning to deter international terrorist activity. This would include, for example, more liberal use of United Nations Security Council resolutions, like Number 748, passed on March 31, 1992, which provides for severe sanctions against Libya for flagrant support of international terrorists and harboring the Pan Am Flight 103 (Locherbie, Scotland) bombing suspects. In addition, more responsive extradition of suspected terrorists by states rather than the continuation of dependence on often delayed bilateral initiatives could be pursued through international agreements. Also, strong economic sanctions could be used on an international, regional, or state-to-state basis and enforced by United Nations forces if needed. Multinational countermeasures such as these are a preferred course of action due to the network of international terror organizations particularly when considering the commercial forms described earlier. These multinational deterrence measures should also include the establishment of a World Court that provides a system of justice for transnational criminals. This would provide a safety net for providing due process for international terrorists while having no limiting effect on unilateral or bilateral responses to extreme criminal behavior. Other forms of deterrence include a stated policy of no concessions for hostages, economic trading restrictions, or even blockades against state supporters of terrorist actions, and, most important, a counterterrorism policy that remains flexible and retains the initiative in dealing with terrorist organizations. Global collaboration to discourage terrorist activity must include an extensive sharing of technology generated and human collected intelligence. The establishment of an international clearinghouse for this essential information is already being planned by the United States, European powers, Russia, and others through the sponsorship of the United Nations. Tighter immigration and entry screening, boycotting of certain airports and national registered seacraft, and the improvement of physical and personal security overseas for foreign travelers are other means to deter ad hoc or even well-planned acts of terror. The media have been strongly encouraged to provide for self-regulation concerning the exercise of restraint in dealing with such violent activity by selective blackouts of coverage of these events. In some instances, there could be mandated statutory restrictions on televised or telecommunicated coverage of terrorist acts. Some of these government-imposed limits on media coverage exist today in England and Germany. The United States currently depends on market forces to regulate media coverage of violence and self-limitation by broadcast networks with law enforcement officials and in some cases the courts providing for some restrictions for ongoing investigations of such activity. Given the broad freedom of speech accorded citizens in most liberal democracies, the media have been judicious in self-regulation, and terrorist groups have been careful to plan their use of media to express their purposes. Moderate extremists often use the media for their own purposes in disassociating themselves from the more radical fringes of their respective groups. For example, the Palestine Liberation Organization (PLO) has been careful to distance itself in the public media from the radical groups associated with Islamic Fundmentalism.

The general public must come to the realization that to deter terrorism around the world and in domestic situations, there will be monetary costs, and possibly loss of human life and property. Domestic extremism in the United States and abroad have become all too frequent occurences. James Wootten (1993) highlights in his CRS Issue Brief, "The U.S. State Department offers rewards of up to $4 million to anyone providing information that would prevent or resolve an act of terrorism against U.S. citizens or U.S. property overseas under the 'Rewards Program for Terrorism Information,' established by the 1984 Act to Combat International Terrorism (P.L. 98-533)." The United States Congress and President Bill Clinton arrived at a major watershed in developing legal disincentives for terrorist acts with the passage of the Comprehensive Terrorism Prevention Act of 1995 (P.L. 104-132, April 24, 1996). This legislation provides for aggressive judicial reform of habeas corpus rules, civil and criminal remedies, victim assistance, immigration and asylum reforms, transportation of weapons and chemical materials restrictions, criminal alien procedural reforms, overseas posting of U.S. Secret Service agents, international law enforcement and judicial cooperation, and funding support for local, state, and national law enforcement improvements. This is a contemporary example of proactive anti-terrorism policy that can be emulated by other democracies. These and other positive deterrence measures are designed to prevent the disruption of order and peaceful security in democratic societies and to stimulate international counterterrorism cooperation.

Preemptive Actions and Retaliation

More aggressive preventive measures to counter terrorist activities are available to democracies in the form of covert operations in foreign areas; the use of preemptive military, law enforcement, or economic force; or retaliatory actions as authorized by the chief executive or elected representatives.

President Reagan retaliated against Libya in 1986 under the authority of National Security Directive 138 for its role in international terror conspiracies resulting in the loss of American lives overseas. Democracies have reserved the right to pursue these counterterrorism policy options primarily to bring pressure on sponsoring states but have used them sparingly because of the danger of encouraging even more radicalization of existing groups or the formation of new extreme groups. The potential use of deadly force by democracies can serve as an important deterrent since the extremist groups are unable to predict the impact of such actions on their organization and the support linkages that they have enjoyed. However, as a cautionary note, terrorism and its impact is often overstated, and democracies must be careful not to overreact. What we believe to be acts of terror may be symptomatic of some other problem altogether. Governments must not compromise the very values and principles that they stand for in responding to the scourge of terrorism. An improved understanding of what lies behind certain unexplained acts of violence and what can be done to prevent these acts by responsible governments on a multilateral basis should be the focal point of future counterterror policy.

JOHN MCALLISTER

BIBLIOGRAPHY

Alexander, Yonah, and Alan O'Day, series eds. 1994. *The International Library of Terrorism*, vols. 1–5. New York: G. K. Hall.

Collins, J. M., 1993. "Transnational Terrorism and Counterterrorism." *U.S. Library of Congress, CRS Report # 93-328S* (March 18).

Crenshaw, Martha, 1986. "The Psychology of Political Terrorism." In Margaret G. Hermann, ed., *Political Psychology: Contemporary Problems and Issues*. San Francisco, CA: Jossey-Bass, 379–413.

Godson, Roy, and William J. Olson, 1993. "International Organized Crime: Emerging Threat to U.S. Security." *Testimony, U.S. House of Representatives Committee on Foreign Affairs* (November 4).

Hoffman, Bruce, 1993. "Future Trends in Terrorist Targeting and Tactics." *RAND Corp. Report-239*. Santa Monica, CA: RAND Corp.

Jenkins, Brian M., 1985. *International Terrorism: The Other World War*. Santa Monica, CA: RAND Corp.

Kegley, Charles W., ed. 1990. *International Terrorism: Characteristics, Causes, Controls*. New York: St. Martin's.

Laqueur, Walter, and Yonah Alexander, 1987. *The Terrorism Reader: A Historical Anthology*. New York: Meridian.

Long, David E., 1990. *The Anatomy of Terrorism*. New York: Free Press.

Lupsha, Peter A., 1989. "Towards an Etiology of Drug Trafficking and Insurgent Relations: The Phenomenon of Narco-Terrorism." *International Journal of Comparative and Applied Criminal Justice*, vol. 13 (Fall) 61–75.

Metz, Steven, 1993. *The Future of Insurgency*. Carlisle, PA: Strategic Studies Institute, U.S. Army War College.

Reich, Walter, ed., 1990. *Origins of Terrorism: Psychologies, Ideologies, Theologies, and States of Mind*. Cambridge: Cambridge University Press.

Schmid, Alex, 1984. *Political Terrorism: A Research Guide*. New Brunswick, NJ: TransAction Books.

Sederberg, Peter C., 1989. *Terrorist Myths—Illusion, Rhetoric, and Reality*. Englewood Cliffs, NJ: Prentice-Hall.

Shafritz, Jay M., E. F. Gibbons, Jr., and Gregory E. J. Scott, 1991. *Almanac of Modern Terrorism*. New York: Facts-on-File.

Tilford, Earl H., Jr., ed. 1995. *World View: The 1995 Strategic Assessment from the Strategic Studies Institute*. Carlisle, PA: U.S. Army War College.

U.S. Department of State, *Annual Reports, 1987–1993*. "Patterns in Global Terrorism." Washington, DC: Government Printing Office.

Wardlaw, Grant, 1989. *Political Terrorism: Theory, Tactics, and Counter-Measures*, 2d ed. Cambridge: Cambridge University Press.

———, 1988. "Linkages Between Illegal Drugs Traffic and Terrorism." *Conflict Quarterly*, vol. 8 (Summer) 5–26.

Wilkinson, Paul, 1987. *Terrorism and the Liberal State*, 2d ed. London: Macmillan.

Williams, Phil, 1994. "Transnational Criminal Organizations and International Security." *Survival* (Spring) 96–113.

Wootten, James P., 1993. "Terrorism: U.S. Policy Options." *U.S. Library of Congress Report # IB92074* (March 25).

THATCHERISM.

A set of right-wing political ideas, associated with the premiership of Margaret Thatcher, which shaped the style of British government from 1979 and survived her fall from power in 1990. As with most political leaders in twentieth-century Britain, whether Conservative or otherwise, her enthusiasm was more for government as an instrument for change rather than for democracy itself. Democracy is something for government to enhance not for making government better. She intended to take power in order to cede power, but her eleven years gave her apparently few opportunities to deliver the second half of the remit (Jenkins 1995, p. 21).

At the heart of Thatcherism lie the moral and intellectual challenges to political and economic orthodoxy in the United Kingdom during the 1970s. The moral case was that the middle classes and the aged had come to depend on the British welfare state, creating rising national debts for later generations to finance in an economy that could not afford it. Instead of a generation looking after its successors, it was one that would bankrupt them. This perception was readily assimilated by those associated with the neoclassical and monetarist economic critique of Keynesianism. Thatcher herself believed strongly in the veracity of the economic theories of Frederich von Hayek and Milton Friedman; her political and intellectual mentor, Keith Joseph, was instrumental in converting these ideas into the political and policy context of the United Kingdom. Her supporters argue that the failure of Thatcherism was substantially the consequence of opposition within the British political establishment and the reluctance of the civil service to recast itself.

Although failing to produce a smaller state sector, as a percentage of gross national product, than she inherited, Thatcher was dedicated to the proposition that less government is better. The following list of instinctive positions embodies the main components of Thatcherism: government borrowing caused inflation; commercial management techniques were self-evidently preferable to traditions of British administration; civil service privileges inhibited progressive change; nationalization was anathema and had to be reversed by privatization; overmighty trade unions, the needless cause of unemployment, had to be neutered; individual self-reliance in a property-owning, share-owning democracy had to be facilitated by government; all corporatist instincts, Socialist or otherwise, were counterproductive.

Thatcher's period in office remains controversial. According to taste, during her period in power, "Britain was reborn either as a freer and more hopeful place, or as a crueller and more divided one" (Jenkins 1995, p. 3). However, the more helpful, less political distinction is the one between the tenets of Thatcherism and its application under her leadership. For a credo that celebrated the assertion that "there is no alternative," Thatcherism gave the appearance of validity to the more banal political truth that to hold on to office for more than a decade requires substantial policy revision and crisis management. Beginning in the early 1980s, her closest and most fervently ideological advisers became disillusioned with her caution. Arguably, only after her 1987 electoral success did she begin systematically to apply her earlier agenda. By then, the political establishment's patience was exhausted and she was dropped from office. Convictions stemming from the 1970s may have been at the heart of Thatcherism; domestic political compromises within the economic cycle were her legacy for the 1990s.

Perhaps that helps explain why, after her political demise, her successor, John Major, was to oversee a renewed impetus to those elements of Thatcherism involving the size of the state: privatization and the reform of government. Building on the developments of the previous decade, it may be Major and Tony Blair and not Thatcher, who provide an answer to the question posed by Professor Peter Hennessy: "Can the crossword puzzle mind, reared on Greats at Oxford or Mathematics at Cambridge provide the kind of skills Britain needs for the 20th century?" (Dynes and Walker 1995, p. 87).

BIBLIOGRAPHY

Dynes, Michael, and David Walker, 1995. *The Times Guide to the New British State: The Government Machine in the 1990s*. London: Times Books.
Jenkins, Simon, 1995. *Accountable to None: The Tory Nationalization of Britain*. London: Hamish Hamilton.
Riddell, Peter, 1991. *The Thatcher Era and Its Legacy*. London: Blackwell.
Young, Hugo, 1991. *One of Us*. London: Macmillan.

THIRD PARTY GOVERNMENT.

A term coined by Lester Salamon in 1981 to describe the fundamental pattern of relationships between government and the private sector in the delivery of public services in the United States: "The central characteristic of this pattern is the use of nongovernmental, or at least non-federal governmental, entities to carry out governmental purposes, and the exercise by these entities of a substantial degree of discretion over the spending of public funds and the exercise of public authority" (Salamon 1987, p. 110). The concept of third party government serves as a counterweight to theories of the private, nonprofit sector that view the nonprofit as a residual sector that fills in where government or commercial businesses fail (see **contract failure** and **government failure**). In the third party government model, private, nonprofit organizations serve as partners with government in the provision of public services rather than as substitutes or gap fillers. In this view, government

typically provides the finances and influences service policies, while nonprofits deliver the services. The precise mechanisms used to finance these arrangements vary considerably. They include governmental grants, contracts and loan guarantees, and demand-side subsidies such as consumer vouchers, reimbursements, or tax deductions (Salamon 1987).

Considerable empirical evidence exists for the third party government view of the role of nonprofit organizations. Salamon (1987) documents that the governmental nonprofit sector partnership arrangements enjoy a long history in the United States. However, the 1960s was the watershed era in which the United States emphatically embraced the third party government model by significantly expanding expenditures on social programs without commensurate enlargement of government employment. Rather than delivered through government bureaucracy, new services were implemented largely through arrangements with private, nonprofit suppliers. Not incidentally, the expansion of government social programs in the late 1960s and 1970s corresponded to the period of fastest growth for the U.S. nonprofit sector (Hodgkinson et al. 1992).

Evidence for the third party government model is also found in the finances of nonprofit organizations. In general, government funding is the second largest source of revenue for charitable, nonprofit, service-providing organizations in the United States, representing 31 percent of their revenues compared to 18 percent for charitable giving (Salamon 1992). Fees and sales revenues dominate at 51 percent. The share of revenue from government varies considerably by subsector, however, with nonprofit organizations in the social services and civic organizations more heavily dependent on government funds than nonprofits in other fields. Worldwide, government funding is also found to be the second largest source of revenue for nonprofit organizations, with France and Germany the exceptions where government is the largest source of support (Salamon and Anheier 1994).

The theory of third party government, that is, nonprofits as a partner to rather than substitute for government, is based on an assessment of the comparative advantages of government and nonprofit organizations in carrying out the tasks associated with delivering public services. Overall, government is seen as relatively more efficient in raising and distributing funds, formulating policies for the benefit of the entire society, and in redistributing resources to correct for inequities and externalities. Alternatively, nonprofits are seen to be more efficient at customizing services to local preferences and delivering them at lower cost or higher quality. Salamon (1987) also points out that third party government arrangements are effective in reconciling the American public's preference for pluralism and its ideological antagonism toward large government with its demands for public services.

Salamon (1987) developed an alternative theory of third party government to explain the role of the American nonprofit sector by directly challenging the premises of the "contract failure" and "government failure" theories of the nonprofit sector. In particular, Salamon postulates that the voluntary, nonprofit sector should be the primary point of reference and that government intervenes in the delivery of public services only to compensate for the weaknesses of the voluntary sector. In this connection, he (1987) describes four ways in which voluntary organizations can fall short:

1. *Philanthropic insufficiency* reflects the free rider problem associated with voluntary support of public goods and argues for governmental financing through taxation to provide adequate funding.

2. *Philanthropic particularism* recognizes that voluntary action depends on the efforts of cohesive groups and may miss important segments of society that are not addressed by such groups. This deficiency argues for government to ensure more complete coverage. Government may also have a role in increasing efficiency by exploiting economies of scale not achievable by smaller organizations individually and by providing coordination to avoid unnecessary duplication of services supplied by individual voluntary agencies.

3. *Philanthropic paternalism* recognizes that the allocation of voluntary resources is influenced primarily by those wealthy enough to donate them. This deficiency argues for government intervention and support to allow a wider spectrum of views to influence the allocation of nonprofit sector resources.

4. *Philanthropic amateurism* recognizes that a substantial portion of the work of nonprofit organizations is carried out by volunteers or well-meaning amateurs who may not have the time or training to provide services in the most effective way. This weakness argues for government regulation and support to allow nonprofits to become more professional in their approaches to providing the services and in the quality of their workforces.

Overall, Salamon's "voluntary failure" theory articulates how government and voluntary agencies can serve as complementary partners to one another in the delivery of public services. Although voluntary organizations can be responsive to the grassroots needs of local groups and causes that enjoy sufficient private support, they cannot be counted on to generate adequate levels of resources or coordinate those resources to achieve efficient and equitable levels of service provision. Conversely, governments cannot be relied upon to be responsive to variations in local needs and preferences, but they are able to generate and redistribute necessary resources through taxation and expenditure policies and to take a wide view of societal needs. Thus, government, according to the theory, can serve the complementary roles of financing, coordinating, and regulating the services that nonprofits can best deliver.

This ideal of the nonprofit-government partnership has been questioned on a number of grounds:

- that contracting with private agencies results in a loss of accountability for expenditure of public resources (Smith and Lipsky 1993; Bernstein 1991);
- that the government-nonprofit partnership transforms nonprofit organizations into "vendors," undermining their autonomy and independence and distorting their missions to conform with government requirements (Salamon 1987; Kramer 1980);
- that the partnership model leads to the bureaucratization and professionalization of nonprofit organizations, making them more costly and less responsive to community needs (Salamon 1987);
- that the partnership model results in the devolvement of political power and authority from government to private parties, raising fundamental questions of democratic governance (Smith and Lipsky 1993);
- that the partnership model creates series problems of managing nonprofit organizations, including constraints on cash flow and budgeting caused by governmental regulations and practices (Bernstein 1991; Grossman 1992).

The severity of these problems and their long-run implications for the viability of nonprofit organizations and their partnership arrangements with government remain important issues of debate and continuing research.

One of the main contributions of third party government theory is to provide a sobering perspective on the implications of cutbacks in governmental expenditures for public services. An inference commonly made from the alternative theory of "government failure" is that the nonprofit sector serves essentially as a substitute for government in the provision of public goods. In this view, cutbacks in government can be expected to result in compensatory growth of the nonprofit sector. However, the third party government model suggests the opposite effect—that government cutbacks may result in reductions in support of nonprofit organizations and the services they provide.

This debate is not merely of theoretical interest. The view that government and the nonprofit sector are essentially competitors in conflict with one another, rather than collaborating partners, drove the policies of the Reagan administration in its quest to pare down the federal budget (Salamon and Abramson 1982). Empirical analysis shows these policies to have been based on questionable premises. According to Salamon and Abramson's (1994) analysis of federal spending reductions in the 1980s, "The changes in federal spending . . . not only increased the demand for services from private, nonprofit organizations. . . . They simultaneously made it more difficult for nonprofits to meet this increased demand because they reduced the revenues that nonprofit organizations receive from federal programs" (p. 7). In that same report, Salamon and Abramson analyzed whether private contributions have replaced lost government funds. For selected areas of social services over the 1980–1995 period, they found only partial compensation: "Private giving has fortunately risen sufficiently to offset the direct revenue losses to nonprofit organizations during this period, but it has not grown enough to offset the cumulative overall reduction in real federal spending in these fields or to cope with the residue of unmet needs that have amassed during the decade" (p. 15).

The issue of government's relationship to nonprofits goes far beyond the borders of the United States. Analyzing studies of the nonprofit sector in nine different European countries, Benjamin Gidron, Ralph Kramer, and Lester Salamon (1992) identified a variety of ways in which government and the nonprofit sector combine to finance and deliver public services. Although the collaborative third party government model is most prominent in the United States, the questions it raises about the appropriate juxtaposition of the two sectors apply elsewhere. In particular, as governments everywhere, in their quests to become more efficient and democratic, reexamine the ways in which they provide public welfare and other services, the experience with third party government in the United States grows in interest.

In the United Kingdom, the Thatcher government, intent on reducing the role of government, adopted an ideology similar to that of the Reagan administration in the United States. However, the starting point for placing greater reliance on the nonprofit sector was considerably different (Taylor 1992). In the United Kingdom, both the finance and the delivery of social welfare services were dominated by government and the voluntary sector played an essentially residual role, assisted modestly by government grants-in-aid. The thrust of the Conservative government policy has been to contract out the delivery of services to private organizations, thus making the role of the nonprofit sector more prominent and the arrangements for service delivery more similar to those in the United States. The changes in Britain have stirred controversies familiar to those heard in the United States. First, there is concern over the degree to which government will maintain its financial support as it privatizes service delivery. Second, there is concern that the new contractual regime will undermine the integrity of voluntary organizations, reducing their diversity, innovativeness, and independence and making them more like businesses or extensions of governmental bureaucracy.

The contemporary experiences of the United States and the United Kingdom demonstrate that the third party government paradigm remains an important construct for analyzing the implications for nonprofits, as governments respond to pervasive pressures to streamline their services and respond more effectively to diverse political constituencies. The model also serves as an important beacon to governments as they seek to become more efficient without damaging the capacities of nonprofit organizations to deliver services to vulnerable populations.

DENNIS R. YOUNG

BIBLIOGRAPHY

Bernstein, Susan R., 1991. *Managing Contracted Services in the Nonprofit Agency.* Philadelphia, PA: Temple University Press.

Gidron, Benjamin, Ralph M. Kramer, and Lester M. Salamon, eds., 1992. *Government and the Third Sector.* San Francisco, CA: Jossey-Bass.

Grossman, David A., 1992. "Paying Nonprofits: Streamlining the New York State System." *Nonprofit Management and Leadership,* vol. 3, no. 1, (Fall): 81–91.

Hodgkinson, Virginia A., Murray S. Weitzman, Christopher M. Toppe, and Stephen M. Noga, eds., 1992. *Nonprofit Almanac 1992–1993.* San Francisco, CA: Jossey-Bass.

Kramer, Ralph, 1980. *Voluntary Agencies in the Welfare State.* Berkeley: University of California Press.

Salamon, Lester M., 1981. "Rethinking Public Management: Third-Party Government and the Changing Forms of Public Action." *Public Policy,* vol. 29:255–275.

———, 1987. "Partners in Public Service." Chapter 6 in Walter W. Powell, *The Nonprofit Sector: A Research Handbook.* New Haven, CT: Yale University Press, 99–117.

———, 1992. *America's Nonprofit Sector.* New York: Foundation Center.

Salamon, Lester M. and Alan J. Abramson, 1982. *The Federal Budget and the Nonprofit Sector.* Washington, D.C.: Urban Institute Press.

———, 1994. "The Federal Budget and the Nonprofit Sector: FY 1995." A Report to Independent Sector. Baltimore: Institute for Policy Studies, Johns Hopkins University.

Salamon, Lester M., and Helmut K. Anheier, 1994. *The Emerging Sector: An Overview.* Baltimore: Institute for Policy Studies, Johns Hopkins University.

Smith, Steven R., and Michael Lipsky, 1993. *Nonprofits for Hire.* Cambridge, MA: Harvard University Press.

Taylor, Marilyn, 1992. "The Changing Role of the Nonprofit Sector in Britain." Chapter 7 in Benjamin Gidron, Ralph M. Kramer, and Lester M. Salamon, eds., *Government and the Third Sector.* San Francisco, CA: Jossey-Bass, 147–175.

TIME AND MOTION STUDIES. Systematically observing, analyzing, and measuring the separate actions in performing a job to establish a standard time for each performance and to improve productivity. Time study was developed by Frederick Winslow Taylor (1856–1915) as a key part of scientific management to ascertain time standards and construct piecerates (see **Taylor, Frederick Winslow**). Frank Bunker Gilbreth (1868–1924) and his wife, Lillian Moller Gilbreth (1878–1972), developed motion study as an alternate method of determining more efficient ways of doing work. By the 1920s, efficiency consultants often combined the two methods to investigate preferred strategies for completing a given job.

Time Study

Taylor developed time study as a machine-shop supervisor at the Midvale Steel Company in the 1880s. After a fight with the machinists over raising output, he saw the problem of increasing production as stemming from the company's inability to define a fair day's standard for each task. In *Shop Management* (1903) he noted:

> The great defect, then, common to all the ordinary systems of manufacturing . . . is that their starting-point, their very foundation, rests upon . . . deceit, and that throughout their whole course in the one element which is most vital both to employer and workmen, namely the speed at which work is done, they are allowed to drift instead of being intelligently directed. (p. 45)

A more efficient system would emerge when managers used scientific fact-finding methods to determine empirically the approximate time workers needed to complete specific jobs and performed workplace experiments to see how shifts in equipment or tools affected worker times.

Taylor's time study requires deconstructing a job into elementary actions and timing each with a stopwatch under varying conditions. The number of discrete elements varies with the task. As a consultant for the Bethlehem Steel Co. between 1898 and 1901, Taylor identified five separate elements for the relatively simple job of loading pig-iron on railroad cars. These were picking up the pig from the ground, walking with it on level ground, walking with it up an incline, throwing the pig down, and walking back empty to get a new load. He identified 77 discrete elements for the more complex job of preparing to do machine work on lathes.

At a 1912 American Society of Mechanical Engineers meeting, Taylor divided time study into analytical and constructive phases. During analysis, the researchers break the job into as many simple movements as they can. A skilled worker is selected and each of the worker's movements are timed and recorded. To ascertain the time needed in actual practice, the researcher adds a certain percentage of seconds for delays, interruptions, and rest periods. In general, Taylor considered it best to explain the operation to the workers and obtain their consent. However, an associate of his, Sanford Thompson, did time people surreptitiously with a "watch book," a notebook that contained a concealed stopwatch operated by pressing a finger on the notebook cover.

The constructive phase involves building a file of movements and times and experimenting to improve times by changing tools, machines, or layout. For example, after a series of experiments, Taylor found that shovelers were most productive when they worked with a load of 21 pounds on their shovels. As a result, he got the Bethlehem Co. to stop telling workers to bring their own shovels from home and to start issuing each worker a shovel that would hold 21 pounds of whatever material was being lifted, a smaller one for coal and a larger one for ashes.

Time study was conceived as a profession much like a draftsman. Accordingly, proper shop management required that time work should be done by properly trained specialists in a separate planning department rather than by a line supervisor. This meant that time study could disturb the balance of line-staff relationships; first-line supervisors could lose some of their authority to staff researchers in the planning department. It also meant that the company had to have enough faith in scientific management to agree to hire people who would not bear direct line responsibilities and whose impact on the bottom line might come only after a significant wait.

Taylor cautioned executives not to expect time study to work instant wonders. Even learning about simple tasks could take a significant amount of effort. Timing the elements in pig-iron loading took two years with two people available to do the experiments. It took a group of researchers three years to study shoveling at the Bethlehem Co.

Although Taylor concentrated on factory work, he noted in *Shop Management* (1903) that all kinds of activities could be profitably submitted to time study, including clerical and office tasks. About a year after his death in 1915, articles in the *American Political Science Review* discussed the need to use time study to ascertain a fair day's work in public-sector tasks such as inspecting water fixtures and reading meters.

Motion Study

As Taylor mentioned in *The Principles of Scientific Management* (1911), Frank Gilbreth used time study to set effective piecerates as a building contractor in the early 1900s. Around 1912, Gilbreth developed a new technique for measuring work. Called micromotion study, it involved filming a worker against a cross-sectioned background while a clock measuring time to a millionth of an hour recorded how long it took the person to perform each motion.

In 1913 and 1914, Frank Gilbreth refined motion study techniques while consulting for the Herrmann-Aukam Company in Germany. First, he developed the cyclegraph, a finger ring with a miniature electric light to be worn by a worker. The light's movement placed a bright line on a single time-exposed photograph. A line with twists and turns was considered to show inefficient movement. Gilbreth's aim was to change the worker's tools until a short, smooth line appeared.

Next, two methodological variations were added to the cyclegraph. With the chronocyclegraph, Gilbreth interrupted the flow of current to the light to obtain, through a series of flashes, a record of the time and direction of the worker's motions. With the stereochronocyclegraph he produced a three-dimensional image of motion by using time-exposed photographs from two somewhat offset cameras, both of which could be viewed through a stereopticon, or stereoscope.

In 1915, the Gilbreths developed a basic vocabulary of work motions, which they called "therbligs." These motions were search, find, select, grasp, position, transport load, assemble, disassemble, use, inspect, preposition, release load, transport empty, wait (unavoidable delay), wait (avoidable delay), and rest. The Gilbreths examined each therblig on micromotion film as a basis for plotting a "simultaneous cycle motion," or "simo," chart showing which actions each part of a worker's body did at a given point in time. They argued that these charts allowed them to measure objectively the correct dimensions of worker motion. Researchers were supposed to use the charts to redesign operations (e.g., by decreasing the time of movements by placing tools nearer to the worker). Like Taylor, the Gilbreths opposed secret study of worker motions.

The Gilbreths insisted that micromotion techniques were superior to conventional time analysis because some work was too fast for the stopwatch to record; they also argued that motion study was superior because it eliminated unnecessary on-the-job fatigue as well as increasing output. They urged its use as a technique outside of the factory sphere to rehabilitate wounded soldiers.

During the early 1920s, some tension existed between orthodox Taylor followers, who used conventional time study, and the Gilbreths. Beginning in 1927, however, a consensus emerged in both camps that time and motion study were fundamentally complementary.

Implementing Time and Motion Studies

Time and motion studies were first installed in private-sector manufacturing organizations as part of business' push toward greater efficiency in the early twentieth century. In America, their installation often led to conflict with the International Association of Machinists (IAM) and other trade unions, which argued that the new techniques promoted speedups, fatigue, and rate cuts. Labor concerns sparked strikes at Joseph & Feiss, a men's suit manufacturer, the American Locomotive Company, Firestone Tire & Rubber, and other firms.

As time and motion studies diffused to Europe, similar controversies developed there. In France, the introduction of time study resulted in a strike at Renault in 1907; in Russia, a strike followed the introduction of time study into the Aivaz plant in 1913. Workers at the Auergesellschaft company in Germany successfully banded together to keep Frank Gilbreth from bringing motion study to the shop floor in 1914.

Many contemporary social scientists subscribe to the IAM's early condemnation of time and motion study. In *Labor and Monopoly Capitalism* Braverman (1972) argues that these techniques degrade work and alter the balance of power between manager and worker. Their use is faulted for allowing the manager access to the traditional knowledge about job skills that had been the historical province of the worker alone. Contemporary public administration textbooks endorse this interpretation in describing Taylor's work and Taylorism.

A smaller group of social scientists accepts the cogency of Taylor's own arguments for time study. In *Frederick Taylor and the Public Administration Community*, Hindy Lauer Schachter (1989) stressed the avenue for promotion afforded by the planning department as well as the ability of a genuine work science to improve productivity and help workers increase their living standards. In *Reduced Worktime and the Management of Production*, Chris Nyland (1989), showed that unions supported time study after 1920 to advance their interest in a shorter working day.

Time and motion studies had their earliest public-sector application in military installations. The United States Navy timed ship scalers, caulkers, and riveters at the Mare Island Yard off of San Francisco in 1906 and 1908. The Army Ordnance Department brought Dwight Merrick, a time study person who had worked with Taylor, to the Watertown, Massachusetts, arsenal in 1911. As part of the international diffusion of scientific management, French officers introduced time study at the Penhoet navy yard in 1914. In England, the Health of Munition Workers Committee used motion study to investigate fatigue among munitions workers during World War I.

As had occured in the private sector, time and motion studies in the government sparked controversy. The navy stopped using the practice at Mare Island because of pressure from line officers alleging that it upset the prevailing balance between line and staff. Attempts to time foundry workers at Watertown led to a week-long strike and the appointment of a House of Representatives Committee chaired by William Wilson (D.–Pa.) to investigate government agency use of stopwatches. The implementation of motion study by a government-created committee in England led to criticisms from prominent psychologists that no one best way to do labor existed; individual worker differences inevitably led to the use of variant methods.

The House of Representatives committee hearings, which began in October 1911, presented an occasion to resolve some of these issues. In particular, the hearings afforded both Taylor and the IAM a platform to present their views on time study. The union hoped that the committee would condemn the new technique as oppressive. Taylor testified for 12 hours before the committee, saying that workers should not fear time study because it required their agreement and the use of volunteers. After listening to testimony until February 1912, the committee concluded that no evidence showed that time study injured workers, and the army continued to use the method.

The end of the hearings did not end the IAM's campaign to abolish time study in federal installations. The machinists union continued to lobby legislators to eliminate time and motion studies in the public sector. In 1914, Representative Frederick Dietrick, from the Watertown arsenal district in Massachusetts, put a rider on the Army and Navy Appropriations Bill providing that no part of the appropriations should be available for the salaries of government personnel using a stopwatch or other time-measuring device to study work. The rider passed the House, but not the Senate, and the two versions of the bill were sent to the joint Congressional Legislative Conference Committee to be reconciled. The committee chose to look at the navy bill first. Since the navy had stopped using time study at Mare Island, its officers did not object to the amendment, and when the legislators examined the army bill afterward, they used the navy's approach as a precedent. The inclusion of the Dietrick amendment in the bill's final version meant that stopwatches were banned from federal armed forces production centers almost precisely at the time that some of the controversy over implementing scientific management was receding in the private sector. After Taylor's death in 1915, a partial rapprochement took place between his followers and union leaders in business. This reconciliation did not have a chance to occur in army and navy installations, where time and motion techniques were illegal. The rider continued to appear on army, navy, and post office appropriation bills until 1949.

HINDY LAUER SCHACHTER

BIBLIOGRAPHY

Aitken, Hugh, 1960. *Taylorism at Watertown Arsenal.* Cambridge, MA: Harvard University Press.
Copley, Frank, 1923. *Frederick W. Taylor.* New York: Harper and Brothers.
Gilbreth, Frank Bunker, 1912. *Primer of Scientific Management.* New York: Van Nostrand Reinhold.
Gilbreth, Frank Bunker, and Lillian Moller Gilbreth, 1920. *Motion Study for the Handicapped.* London: George Routledge and Sons.
Nelson, Daniel, 1980. *Frederick W. Taylor and the Rise of Scientific Management.* Madison: University of Wisconsin Press.
———, 1992. "Scientific Management in Retrospect." In Daniel Nelson, ed., *A Mental Revolution: Scientific Management Since Taylor.* Columbus: Ohio University Press, 5–39.
Nyland, Chris, 1989. *Reduced Worktime and the Management of Production.* Cambridge: Cambridge University Press.
Price, Brian, 1992. "Frank and Lillian Gilbreth and the Motion Study Controversy, 1907–1930." In Daniel Nelson, ed., *A Mental Revolution: Scientific Management Since Taylor.* Columbus: Ohio University Press, 58–76.
Schachter, Hindy Lauer, 1989. *Frederick Taylor and the Public Administration Community.* Albany: State University of New York Press.
Taylor, Frederick Winslow, 1903. *Shop Management.* New York: Harper and Brothers.
———, 1911. *The Principles of Scientific Management.* New York: Harper and Brothers.

TIME MANAGEMENT.

The ability to use time effectively. The measure of effective time use has changed dramatically in the past 30 years, in large part because of the changing nature of society and of work. Time management, as practiced 30 years ago, was most closely related to time and motion studies and to scientific management as defined and practiced by Frederick Winslow Taylor (1911). The purpose of time management under the premises of scientific management was to accomplish the most work in the least amount of time through the manipulation of machines, work flow, and work processes.

Peter Drucker (1966) urged managers to practice five habits of effectivity, one of which was concentration on the few major areas where superior performance would produce outstanding results. It was important to hold to priorities, deciding what not to do in order to be able to allocate time to tasks related to high priority areas. "Nothing else distinguishes an effective executive," he wrote, "as the tender loving care of time." (p. 57).

R. Alec MacKenzie (1972) began the revolution in how we think about work and time management, especially managerial work and time, in his book *The Time Trap.* "Time management," he wrote, "contains one great paradox. No one has enough time–yet everyone has all there is. This paradox drives home the point that time is not the problem; the problem is how we utilize time" (p. 2).

MacKenzie based some of his work on earlier research by Joseph Juran (1964), who identified the Pareto principle, that 20 percent of the time expended yields 80 percent of the results. he directed readers to develop "to do" lists, to prioritize those lists as "A," "B," and "C" tasks, and to work first on "A" tasks, or those tasks that would lead to the greatest results. MacKenzie emphasized the elimination of time wasters by organizing one's work space, handling each piece of paper only once, eliminating unnecessary letters and memos, increasing one's reading speed, blocking interruptions, delegating tasks effectively, and attacking large projects or problems with the "Swiss cheese" approach that tackles only one small part of a project at a time.

MacKenzie's best-seller was followed by Alan Lakein's (1973) *How to Get Control of Your Time and Your Life.* Lakein's approach to time management emphasized the clarification of life goals and values. Managers were asked to identify their professional and personal goals, and to manage the minutes of their days so as to move toward those goals. Lakein also suggested methods for overcoming procrastination, which he felt to be the major enemy of effective time management. Lakein's writing and public presentations popularized the use of time management systems, including better-known ones such as Day Timers, Day Runners, and Franklin Time Planner.

The most recent entry into the time management field is Stephen Covey, whose *Seven Habits of Highly Effective People* (1989) included Habit 3 of "Putting First Things First." Covey's approach to time management is to identify roles in an individual's life and to plan activities according to those roles. These roles are based on a set of personal principles, developed as a part of Habit 1 ("Be Proactive") and Habit 2 ("Begin with the End in Mind").

Covey identified all activities as having two dimensions: important/unimportant and urgent/not urgent. Covey described effective time managers as those who spend more time in important, not urgent activities, which he labels as "Quadrant II" activities. "Quadrant I" activities (important and urgent) and "Quadrant III" activities (not important, but urgent) are, he believes, the focus of most time management systems.

Effective time managers, Covey (1989) argued, manage their lives effectively—"from a center of sound principles, from a knowledge of (their) personal mission, with a focus on the important as well as the urgent, and within the framework of maintaining a balance between increasing . . . production and increasing . . . production capability" (p. 160). Covey moved time management beyond daily planning and planning for the "now" into focusing on a larger perspective and placing activities within the context of principles, personal mission, roles, and goals. Thus, Covey's time management system requires a manager to establish a personal mission and priorities, and to schedule time to plan for and take action on those priorities, even if the results are distant or intangible.

Covey's work is supported by field research that demonstrates that real-life bosses are not "time technicians" but, rather, flexible time users. Open, unstructured time and brief, unscheduled conversations allow top executives to stay "plugged in" (Deutschman 1992). Time management is thus moving away from structured and controlled systems to dynamic and humane approaches that emphasize roles and relationships and constant communication. Time management also may be returning to ancient advice: "For everything there is a season, and a time for every matter under heaven" (Ecclesiastes 3:1).

SUSAN C PADDOCK

BIBLIOGRAPHY

Covey, Stephen R., 1989. *Seven Habits of Highly Effective People: Powerful Lessons in Personal Change.* New York: Simon and Schuster.

Deutschman, Alan, 1992. "The CEO'S Secret of Managing Time." *Fortune* (June 1) 135–146.

Drucker, Peter F., 1966. "How to Manage Your Time." *Harper's* (December) 56–60.

Juran, Joseph M., 1964. *Managerial Breakthrough.* New York: McGraw-Hill.

Lakein, Alan, 1973. *How to Get Control of Your Time and Your Life.* New York: Signet Books.

MacKenzie, R. Alec, 1972. *The Time Trap: How to Get More Done in Less Time.* New York: AMACOM.

Taylor, Frederick W., 1911. *Principles of Scientific Management.* New York: Harper and Row.

TOOL TROPISM. In administration, denotes the tendency of managers to adopt rational-instrumental techniques for the purpose of improving organizational efficiency and accomplishing goals. It is their psychological response to new ideas that they learn outside of the organization; these ideas seem to offer practical solutions to their organizational problems. Managers want to improve organizational performance by adopting new managerial techniques and rational-instrumental solutions (Ramos 1981). Managers learn new skills by attending college programs or training workshops, reading literature on new management approaches, or interacting with organizational consultants. The common proclivity is to adopt tools that are popular and successful in the private sector. All management techniques and tools used in the public sector are the result of faddisms, egotism and quick-fixism. There are more than 120 different management techniques taught in business schools today (Armstrong 1986). Many of these techniques have been adopted by public managers. It would, of course, be impossible to list all the tools that public administrators have used throughout the years, but the most popular ones are as follows: total quality management (TQM), quality circles (QC), strategic planning (SP), management-by-objectives (MBO), zero-based budgeting (ZBB), and planning, programming, budgeting system (PPBS).

Public managers have used these tools in an attempt to deal with organizational complexity and efficiency. A manager's wish to use these tools can be called tool tropism. Tropism, as a concept in biology refers to the response that plants and animals make to an external stimulus—whether it is a sunflower turning toward the light or a manager turning to the latest administrative technique. It is the manager's conscious effort to change the organization for the better by focusing attention on organizational goals, efficiency, and productivity. There are limits, of course, on the use of rational techniques—even if we devise the most comprehensive approach imaginable—and these limits are set for the average employee. It is therefore appropriate to critique how the technical approach aims to deal with complex administrative situations. Although techniques are useful in solving routine problems that do not require much social interaction, they are generally inadequate when applied to nonroutine, complex situations that demand innovative and creative solutions. Management techniques are tools designed to coordinate (or manipulate) human activities in organizations in order to meet desired ends. For example, activities used to implement TQM, ZBB, MBO, and PPBS are largely means to ends; that is, they are used to meet established goals and objectives. Also, for many public managers and executives, the growth in administrative agencies and program functions has also led them to consider ways of simplifying the processes of control and planning and of stressing the importance of the accomplishment of goals.

Faddish Management Techniques

Tool tropism may satisfy psychological needs of managers and participants as they adopt a faddish technique in their attempt to deal with the problem of organizational inefficiency. Faddish management techniques used in the public sector are generally spread by management consultants. When a particular technique is no longer popular largely as a result of changing political power in government, they invent a different tool to attract new clients. This faddish behavior of managers as well as consultants is ephemeral. Managers develop pathological behavior when they try to emulate various techniques used by other managers in solving managerial problems similar to their own.

Commonly acknowledged managerial pathologies include a simplistic view of organizational reality and a drift toward reification of organizational processes. All managerial tools assume the objective nature of organizational reality, that is to say, there is an underlying belief that human situations can be explained and predicted through the application of concepts and procedures of a technical and functional framework. Individuals' subjective ideas are supposed to be related to the functional requirements of a model or theory. Anything that does not fit into this objective framework tends to be ignored. For example, in a cost-benefit analysis, unquantifiable elements such as values, emotions, and political factors are often deliberately ignored in order to calculate the maximum benefit for the minimum cost. This is also the case in a cost-effectiveness analysis in identifying relevant alternatives. Although the analytical techniques used in systems analysis are supposed to be value free and impartial, the personal bias of policy analysts is inevitable, because the analysis is, after all, performed by human beings (Hoos 1972).

The problem of relying on a management technique as a framework for organizational action is the tendency of a framework to reify human activities. The assumptions and methods underlying a management technique, theory, or model lead to the development of a metaphorical framework that is applied to the explanation and prediction of organizational reality. Once a metaphor is constructed and applied to the organizational processes, managers may attempt to implement a technique uncritically, metaphorically processing social reality and human thought into an objectified product. Situational and subjective elements are reduced to "things" (Tinker 1986, Berger and Luckmann 1966). Thus, a metaphor inevitably provides only an incomplete representation of organizational reality. All of the popular techniques used in public administration in the last three decades, PPBS, MBO, ZBB, TQM, and SP, are defined as "Systems." Edward Deming, known as the

founder of QC in Japanese industry, insisted that "85 percent of the problems in any operation [of TQM] are the fault of the system, not the workers" (quoted in Walters 1992, p. 42). People blame the systems as if they are living things that control human actions and consciousness. Although one may consider MBO and TQM as management metaphors that emphasize process and product, these tools tend to reify problems of social relations and human conditions by appraising them as nonproblematic.

When executives and managers are preoccupied with using a rational tool as a framework for making their decisions, they may lose their critical consciousness and uncritically adhere to tool management. When they do this, they not only reify the complex elements into an objective thing or quantifiable information, but they also obfuscate the purpose of their choice and action. When Robert McNamara was Secretary of the U.S. Defense Department, he tried to develop the military strategies used during the Vietnam conflict by heavily relying on PPBS. He was accused of being overly concerned with computer data, slide rules, and war maps. He closely inspected the military issues of the joint chiefs of staff, demanding "to know the specific reasons for their individual views, and if those reasons struck him as logically or factually unsound he rejected them" (Brodie 1965, p. 675). McNamara and his staff were the designers of PPBS in the Defense Department in the 1960s. They introduced the system in an effort to overcome the problems caused by incremental budgeting and decisionmaking. Once they came to depend on this rational system (technique), they forgot that they themselves had constructed the system in the first place and therefore could change it when it proved to be inadequate in its design.

All of the preceding examples are human constructs, created by and for humanity in order to offer solace and regularity in a rapidly changing world. Public organizations swarm with reified concepts, including management techniques, rules and regulations, performance measurement, and evaluation techniques, all of which, it is commonly supposed, have qualities that make them stand above and apart from humanity. People create techniques and systems and give them the powers of something beyond us. They tend to reify phenomena because it is easy to allow things to continue as they are, and eventually, the reified techniques and metaphors are accepted as being normal. In addition, reification appears to contribute stability to our organizations and personal expectations. In reified situations, human meanings are no longer viewed as innovation producing, but rather, as being products of the nature of things.

Jong S. Jun

BIBLIOGRAPHY

Armstrong, Michael, 1986. *A Handbook of Management Techniques*. New York: Nichols.

Berger, Peter L., and Thomas Luckmann, 1966. *The Social Con-struction of Reality: A Treatise in the Sociology of Knowledge.* New York: Anchor Books.

Brodie, Bernard, 1965. "The McNamara Phenomenon." *World Politics,* vol. 17 (July): 674–689.

Hoos, Ida, 1972. *Systems Analysis in Public Policy: A Critique.* Berkeley: University of California Press.

Ramos, Alberto Guerreiro, 1981. *The New Science of Organiza-tions: A Reconceptualization of the Wealth of Nations.* Toronto: University of Toronto Press.

Tinker, Tony, 1986. "Metaphor or Reification: Are Radical Hu-manists Really Libertarian Anarchists?" *Journal of Manage-ment Studies,* vol. 23, no. 4 (July): 363–383.

Walters, Jonathan, 1992. "The Cult of Total Quality." *Governing* (May): 38–42.

TORT CLAIMS ACT.

In essence, these sections of the United States Code eliminate the United States' blanket immunity from being sued by private individuals, granting that lawsuits against the government will be allowed in certain circumstances. Found in 28 U.S.C. section 1346(b) and 28 U.S.C. sections 2671 through 2680.

Originally, the common law doctrine of "sovereign immunity" dictated that a person could not bring suit against the United States government without its consent. This doctrine emerged from the ancient belief that the king could do no wrong and thus could not be held legally responsible for negligent acts. The Supreme Court of the United States adopted this concept in 1821, holding that no person could pursue an action against the U.S. government unless the government in some way consented.

In 1946, the Congress of the United States partially waived this sovereign immunity by enacting the Federal Tort Claims Act. It is now possible to bring suit against the U.S. government under certain conditions. It should be noted that the Federal Tort Claims Act and accompanying regulations are rather complex and bringing a claim against the United States under the Federal Tort Claims Act is much more difficult than bringing a general claim under state law. The Federal Tort Claims Act provides that

> subject to the provisions of Chapter 171 of this title, the district courts shall have exclusive jurisdiction of civil actions on claims against the United States, for money damages, accruing on and after January 1, 1945, for injury or loss of property, or personal injury or death caused by the negligent or wrongful act or omission of any employee of the government while acting within the scope of his [her] office or employment, under circum-stances where the United States, if a private person, would be liable to the claimant in accordance with the law of the place or the act or omission occurred.

Under this statutory framework, the United States govern-ment becomes legally responsible for the negligent acts of its employee, if the employee is on the job, acting in the furtherance of the government's business. If these circum-stances are proven, an individual may file suit against the U.S. government.

A government "employee" under the Federal Tort Claims Act includes officers or employees of federal agen-cies, members of the armed forces of the United States, members of the National Guard while engaged in training or duty, and persons acting on behalf of a federal agency. Federal law, rather than state law, determines whether or not somebody is considered an employee under the Fed-eral Tort Claims Act.

Under 28 U.S.C., section 2671, "federal agency" is de-fined to include the executive department, independent es-tablishments of the United States and corporations acting as instrumentalities of the United States. All of these enti-ties fall under the act.

However, these determinations are not always easy. It is important to determine for purposes of the Federal Tort Claims Act whether or not a party or entity is an indepen-dent contractor or an agent for the government. If the party or entity is deemed to be an independent contractor, the government will not be liable. This can be a difficult question, but the usual deciding factor here is whether or not the federal government has the power to control the physical performance of the agent's duties. Numerous federal cases discuss what is and what is not an agent of the United States. For example, Amtrak and the Federal Reserve Banks have been held not to be federal agencies under the act. However, the Federal Deposit Insurance Corporation (FDIC) has been held to be an agent of the government. This determination of agency is crucial in ap-plying the act.

Finally, under the Federal Tort Claims Act, it must clearly be shown that a government employee was indeed acting within the course and scope of employment for the government at the time of the action that engendered the suit. This is often a complicated legal question and is de-cided by the law of the state in which the action occurred.

In essence, under the act, the U.S. government can thus be held vicariously liable for the acts of its employees, in the same manner as a private employer might be held li-able for the acts of its employees under the legal doctrine of *respondeat superior.*

CARL CANNON POHLE

BIBLIOGRAPHY

Cohens v. Virginia, 19 U.S. 264 (1821).

Warren, Kenneth, 1988. *Administrative Law in the Political System,* 2d ed. St. Paul, MN: West Publishing.

TORT LIABILITY (IN GOVERNMENT).

Wrongs committed by government agents for which civil redress may be available to victims. Tort liability suits typically seek monetary damages payments by offenders. This entry discusses main features of the tort liability system for American government, regarding public agencies and employees as defendants, primarily as affected by two major federal statutes of broad application and by related major judicial doctrines.

Introduction

For rather unclear reasons, "sovereign immunity" is a legal norm in America, meaning that national and state governments cannot be sued without their consent. But through statutory enactments by legislatures and courts interpretations of statutes and the Constitution, governments in America have become suable for tort liability in many respects. Such developments probably have been in part a response to the growth of governmental functions and impacts on the society, especially in the last six decades.

Types of Claims

Tort liability claims can arise in connection with almost any kind of governmental activity but are especially likely in certain topical areas, because of the nature and/or scale of the activities involved–such as criminal justice administration and highway construction and maintenance. A tort claim against government and/or its employees is likely to fall into one or more of the following broad categories: personal bodily injury or death, damage to or destruction of property or other economic harm, defamation, emotional/psychological harm, denial of a constitutional or statutory right, or expense of litigation. Thus harm may be tangible or intangible. Plaintiffs may be private individuals or organizations. They may also be public employees suing their employer or former employer.

Private Bills as a Remedy

An alternative to a tort liability suit against government is a legislature's enactment of "private bills"–legislation responding to claims or other petitions concerning specific persons rather than being on general public matters. This approach to remedies was frequently used historically. It has important justifications. At the federal level, it applies one's First Amendment right "to petition the Government for a redress of grievances." It involves the legislature's power to spend money. It avoids the potential expense to a plaintiff of bringing a suit in court. It affords legislators important opportunities to render constituency service through casework and supposedly provides individualized justice, fitting the special case.

However, the private bill approach has severe limitations (Zillman 1989, pp. 691–695). Such bills drain time from legislatures. Thus, a legislature may deal with only a small percentage of cases submitted. Moreover, a legislature is likely to lack adequate means for careful and timely processing of claims cases. Consequently, outcomes can be affected by arbitrary circumstances, such as how strongly a particular legislator is interested in the case, and calendar pressures. A substantial correspondence between outcomes and justice seems doubtful. Often, success is denied to meritorious cases and granted to non- or less-meritorious ones. Legislators' casework on private tort bills adds to what critics call unfair advantages of incumbents in elections, especially in Congress, while inability of legislators to satisfy many tort claimants can create political liabilities with voters. In part because of considerations such as the foregoing, legislators have enacted tort statutes providing for adjudicatory systems in executive agencies and/or the courts. But the private bill system retains importance as a supplemental device.

Public-Sector and Private-Sector Tort Liability

Although this entry's focus is on tort liability of governments and government employees rather than private liability, some interrelationships should be noted. Where work processes in the two realms are similar or identical, liability law concerning such processes is likely to overlap. Some examples are private and public physicians and hospitals, educational activities, personnel management, and transportation. Governments that privatize certain functions, such as prison operation, may retain some tort liability. Various laws impose legal requirements on both businesses and governments, violation of which can create liability for damages, such as the Americans with Disabilities Act, and several civil rights and environmental protection statutes.

Law on private torts certainly affects case law on public-sector torts. Two recent significant examples concern punitive damages, discussed later, and sexual harassment (Robinson et al. 1993). Court interpretations in two major private tort cases on what constitutes sexual harassment are applicable to public employees (*Meritor Savings Bank v. Vinson*, 106 S.Ct. 2399 [1986]; *Harris v. Forklift Systems, Inc.*, 114 S.Ct. 367 [1993]). Private tort law impacts insurance premiums and insurance availability for governments. Some general statutes–for example, the Federal Tort Claims Act (FTCA) of 1946–concerning governmental torts hinge liability on the applicable law regarding private torts. Finally, differentiating clearly between public and private sectors is sometimes difficult, given their complex interconnections and the variety of their organizational forms.

Claims Against Federal Defendants

Over 40 different federal statutes provide remedies for particular program-area torts or certain types of broad liability problems. The most important law concerning federal defendants is the FTCA.

The Federal Tort Claims Act

Adopted in 1946, the FTCA is a general tort statute providing monetary relief for injury or loss of property, or personal injury or death caused by "the negligent or wrongful act or omission of any [federal] employee . . . acting within the scope of his [her] . . . employment, under circumstances where the United States, if a private person, would be liable to the claimant [under] . . . the law of the place where the act or omission occurred" (28 U.S.C. sec. 1346). Claims must go first to the federal agency involved. If the agency denies the claim or fails to act on it within six months, the claimant can sue in federal court (secs. 1402, 2675). The court tries the case without a jury (sec. 2402). Suit is only against government, not an employee, and government liability is barred for punitive damages and attorneys' fees. The act also prohibits attorneys from collecting fees from the successful plaintiff higher than 20 percent of the award amount in an administratively resolved case or 25 percent in a court-resolved case (secs. 2674, 2412[d][1][A], 2678). The FTCA also bars common law tort suits (suits not based on a statute or the Constitution) against federal employees (sec. 2679[b]).

The FTCA has broad coverage. However, it also contains large exceptions, listed in 28 U.S.C., sec. 2680. Thus the act is inapplicable to "any claim" based on

(a) an act or omission of an employee of the government, exercising due care, in the execution of a statute or regulation, whether or not such statute or regulation be valid, or based upon the exercise or performance [of] or the failure to exercise or perform a discretionary function or duty . . . , whether or not the discretion involved be abused;

(b) loss, miscarriage, or negligent transmission of letters or postal matter;

(c) assessment or collection of any tax or customs duty, or the detention of any goods or merchandise by any . . . law-enforcement officer;

(d) admiralty

(e) an act or omission of any employee . . . in administering . . . [the "Trading with the Enemy Act" of 1917];

(f) damages caused by . . . establishment of quarantine by the United States;

. . .

(h) assault, battery, false imprisonment, false arrest, malicious prosecution, abuse of process, libel, slander, misrepresentation, deceit, or interference with contract rights: Provided that, with regard to acts or omissions of investigative or law enforcement officers . . . , the provisions . . . shall apply to any claim arising . . . out of assault, battery, false imprisonment, false arrest, abuse of process, or malicious prosecution . . . [Such federal officer is one] empowered by law to execute searches, to seize evidence, or to make arrests for violations of federal law;

(i) damages caused by the fiscal operations of the Treasury or . . . regulation of the monetary system;

(j) combatant activities of the military or naval forces, or the Coast Guard, during time of war;

(k) [events] in a foreign country;

(l) activities of the Tennessee Valley Authority;

(m) activities of the Panama Canal Company;

(n) activities of a federal land bank, a federal intermediate credit bank or a bank for cooperatives.

Besides the foregoing statutory limitations, the FTCA has been narrowed by court interpretation. The Supreme Court has held that injured armed services personnel cannot obtain a remedy under the act against one of the military services regarding "activity incident to service," even if noncombat (*Feres v. U.S.*, 71 S.Ct. 153, 156–159 [1950]), and even if off duty (*U.S. v. Shearer*, 105 S.Ct. 3039, 3041–3044 [1985]). (Such personnel have other available remedies.)

Probably the most important controversy about the FTCA involves the difficult interpretative application of "discretionary function exception." That means the act does not cover decisions involving exercise of choice. Courts' efforts at distinguishing conceptually between discretionary and nondiscretionary action have been only partially successful, in part because even middle- and lower-level employees must exercise some policy judgment in the process of applying policy. Several Supreme Court cases have contributed guidelines of a sort, but most are unclear. Thus partial reliance was placed on the distinction between planning and operational functions in *Dalehite v. U.S.*, 73 S.Ct. 956, 967–968, 971(1953). In *U.S. v. Varig Airlines*, the Court seemed to associate regulatory action broadly with discretion, 104 S.Ct. 2755 (1984). The Court explained: "Congress wished to prevent judicial 'second-guessing' of legislative and administrative decisions grounded in social, economic, and political policy through the medium of an action in tort" (2764–2765). But in *Berkovitz v. U.S.*, the Court held that "the discretionary function exception will not apply when a federal statute, regulation, or policy specifically prescribes a course of action for an employee to follow" (108 S.Ct. 1954, 1958 [1988]). The Court in *U.S. v. Gaubert* emphasized that discretion insulated from liability may exist at the day-to-day operational level and not merely the planning level (111 S.Ct. 1267, 1274–1279 [1991]).

Various other features of the FTCA also limit its impact greatly in providing remedies. Two of these are as follows: Sec. 2680(h) excludes a large array of intentional torts from coverage (except that it does cover six of those types when committed by federal "law enforcement officers"), and its coverage is dependent on law of the individual state as applied to private persons. Most federal law places on the private persons it covers obligations that state law does not impose. Absence of state counterpart law in such instances means that in many circumstances FTCA remedies do not reach wrongful action by federal employees. Moreover, in general the U.S. Constitution limits only government, not private persons; this makes the FTCA largely inapplicable to the vast area of constitutional torts.

Although the Supreme Court remarked in the *Dalehite* case that liability under the FTCA did not apply to "acts of a governmental nature or function" (73 S.Ct. 956, 964), in later cases the Court condemned efforts to divide governmental activities into separately labeled categories of "governmental" and "nongovernmental" or "proprietary" and then to use such distinctions as a basis for tort case decisions. Such line drawing, it said, is utterly artificial, unhelpful, and incapable of rational and consistent application (*Indian Towing Company v. U.S.*, 76 S.Ct. 122, 124–126 [1955]; regarding 42 U.S.C., sec. [1983], *Owen v. City of Independence, Missouri*, 100 S.Ct. 1398, 1412–1413 [1980]).

"Bivens-Type" Cases

Most kinds of possible constitutional rights violations, by most categories of federal employees, are not covered by the FTCA. In the landmark 1971 *Bivens* decision, the Supreme Court held that Fourth Amendment violations by federal employees are redressable by victims' suits against the employees directly under the Constitution, *Bivens v. Six Unknown Named Agents of Federal Bureau of Narcotics*, 91 S.Ct. 1999, 2002–2005. Subsequent cases broadened the applicability of the *Bivens* doctrine to other constitutional rights: *Butz v. Economou*, 98 S.Ct. 2894, 2907–2910 (1978); *Davis v. Passman*, 99 S.Ct. 2264, 2271–2279 (1979); *Carlson v. Green*, 100 S.Ct. 1468, 1471–1475 (1980). Bivens-type suits involve constitutional torts, are against employees only, and are not limited by the exceptions clauses in the FTCA. Thus, they can reach discretionary actions and intentional torts. Decisions in such suits are not based on the law of the place (state), nor on a comparison with the private person, and may involve jury trials, punitive damages, and awards of attorneys' fees. Except for federal employees whose functions guarantee them absolute immunity from tort liability, defendants have only qualified (good faith) immunity.

In *Carlson*, the Court held a Bivens-type suit to be available even though in that case's circumstances an FTCA suit also could have been brought. But in various later cases the Court concluded that access to alternative remedies in certain contexts precludes resort to a Bivens-type suit; for example, *Schweiker v. Chilicky*, 108 S.Ct. 2460, 2468–2471 (1988). To ease somewhat the potential strain of Bivens-type cases on federal servants by making it easier for trial courts to dismiss frivolous cases early, the Supreme Court held in 1982: "Bare allegations of malice should not suffice to subject . . . officials either to the costs of trial or to the burdens of broad-reaching discovery. . . . Officials performing discretionary functions generally are shielded from liability for civil damages insofar as their conduct does not violate clearly established statutory or constitutional rights of which a reasonable person would have known" (*Harlow v. Fitzgerald*, 102 S.Ct. 2727, 2738–2739).

Federal Tort Law Impacting State/Local Government

All individual states have statutes on immunity and liability. But federal tort law heavily affects the state and local levels

42 U.S.C., Sec. 1983

For state employees and local governments and employees, the most important tort liability statute is the federal Civil Rights Act of 1871, 42 U.S.C., sec. 1983. Its terms are brief and broad:

> Every person who, under color of any statute, ordinance, regulation, custom, or usage, of any State or Territory or the District of Columbia, subjects, or causes to be subjected, any citizen of the United States or other person within the jurisdiction thereof to the deprivation of any rights, privileges, or immunities secured by the Constitution and laws, shall be liable to the party injured in an action at law, suit in equity, or other proper proceeding for redress.

Adopted to implement sec. 5 of the Fourteenth Amendment, it originally was aimed at protecting the newly freed blacks against the Ku Klux Klan. The Act generated few court cases until the 1960s. By the 1980s, sec. 1983 had become "the second most heavily litigated section of the United States Code; only federal habeas corpus claims are more numerous" (Schuck 1983, p. 199).

A partial turning point was *Monroe v. Pape* in 1961, which held the act applicable to redress constitutional rights violations besides those involving racial discrimination and fully independent of the availability of any state remedy. It also held that only employees could be sued under the Act, as a city was not a "person" under sec. 1983, 81 S.Ct. 473, 476, 482, 486. But in 1978, the Supreme Court interpreted sec. 1983 as including local entities as persons suable, overruling Monroe on that point (*Monell v. Department of Social Services of City of New York*, 98 S.Ct. 2018, 2035). Local entities are not automatically liable for rights violations by their employees–the doctrine of *respondeat superior* does not apply to public employers. Entity culpability depends on whether the employees involved were implementing official policy or custom (2036–2038). In 1980, the Court decided that a city that commits constitutional rights violations cannot plead good faith immunity, although employees can do so. Even if its officers acted in good faith, the city is absolutely liable (*Owen v. City of Independence*, 100 S.Ct. 1398, 1409, 1415–1419 [1980]).

Then in *Maine v. Thiboutot* (1980), the Court interpreted sec. 1983's phrase "and laws" literally to mean that sec. 1983 suits can be brought for violations of federal statutory rights and attorneys' fees are awardable therein under sec. 1988, 100 S.Ct. 2502, 2504–2505, 2507–2508. The reach of *Maine* has been limited by later holdings that a sec. 1983 proceeding cannot be brought concerning a statutory rights violation "where Congress has foreclosed such enforcement of the statute in the enactment itself and where the statute did not create enforceable rights, privileges, or immunities within the meaning of [sec.] . . . 1983" (*Wright v. City of Roanoke Redevelopment and Housing Authority*, 107 S.Ct. 766, 770 [1987]; *Suter v. Artist M*, 112 S.Ct. 1360, 1370 [1992]).

Because of the Eleventh Amendment, state entities cannot be sued in federal court under sec. 1983 for damages payable from state money, in absence of "Congressional purpose to abrogate" that immunity (*Quern v. Jordan*, 99 S.Ct. 1139, 1145–1147 [1979]) and Congressional capacity of such abrogation is very limited, *Seminole Tribe of Florida v. Florida*, 116 S.Ct. 1114, 1119, 1123-33 (1996). Sec. 1983 suits can be brought in state as well as federal courts, but state entities (in contrast to local) are not "persons" suable even in the state court thereunder, and state employees are not suable in their "official" capacities because, the Court reasoned, that would amount to suing the state (*Will v. Michigan Department of State Police*, 109 S.Ct. 2304, 2309–2312 [1989]). But state employees are suable under sec. 1983 in their "personal" capacity for actions in office (*Hafer v. Melo*, 112 S.Ct. 358, 362–365 [1991]).

Among its vast implications for government is sec. 1983's impact on public personnel management. Thus, for example, a city is liable for "failure to train" where that "amounts to deliberate indifference to the rights of persons" affected by the employees' performance (*City of Canton, Ohio, v. Harris*, 109 S.Ct. 1197, 1204 [1989]). A local entity also may be liable in tort for negligent hiring, retention, entrustment, supervision, and so forth (Walter 1992).

Some Related Major Judicial Doctrines

Tort liability in government is a highly complex subject with large subtopics. Three of the most important are immunity, attorneys' fees, and punitive damages.

Immunity

Functions of some types of government employees have been adjudged to be of such a nature that the public interest requires absolute immunity from tort liability for persons exercising such functions, even if with malice or beyond authority. These categories include legislators and, by derivation, legislative aides (*Tenney v. Brandhove*, 71 S.Ct. 783, 786–789 [1951], *Gravel v. U.S.*, 92 S.Ct. 2614, 2622–2629 [1972]); the president, regarding any "official acts" (*Nixon v. Fitzgerald*, 102 S.Ct. 2690, 2701–2705 [1982]); administrators exercising rulemaking authority (*Lake Country Estates, Inc. v. Tahoe Regional Planning Agency*, 99 S.Ct. 1171, 1178–1179 [1979]); judges (*Stump v. Sparkman*, 98 S.Ct. 1099, 1105–1108 [1978]); administrative law judges or

their counterparts (*Butz v. Economou*, 98 S.Ct. 2894, 2912–2916 [1978]); prosecutors (*Imbler v. Pachtman*, 96 S.Ct. 984, 990–995 [1976]); and witnesses in a court trial–who often are public employees (*Briscoe v. La Hue*, 103 S.Ct. 1108, 1111 [1983]).

Rationales for such special protection include historical tradition and the central concept of need for the exercise of courage in these roles to act for society's good. Particular consideration for legislators and their aides involves the reluctance of courts to evaluate legislators' motives; the "speech or debate" clause of the Constitution's Article I, Section 6; the political passion and controversy in legislative enactment struggles; and the discretionary nature of legislative policymaking. Some of these concerns also apply to the rulemaking task exercised by government administrators.

The president's "unique position" underlies the absolute immunity. The broad array of extraordinarily weighty and sensitive responsibilities, with great impact on society from their exercise, high visibility of the presidential role, separation of powers, and availability of other checks against presidential abuse of power were main reasons the Court cited.

Judges have to make decisions with often drastic implications for a party to a case, such as punishments or determination of property rights. Tort liability would jeopardize judicial independence and the finality of court decisions, it is thought. Administrative adjudicators and prosecutors in their judicially related roles likewise need to be unintimidated and undistracted by tort suits.

Employees of government held not to have absolute immunity regarding exercise of certain functions have only "qualified" or "good faith" immunity. Thus, they may still prevail as defendants if they can show they acted reasonably in good faith. The Court has denied absolute immunity under 42 U.S.C.A., sec. 1983 to, for example, governors of states, heads of public universities, and National Guard personnel (*Scheuer v. Rhodes*, 94 S.Ct. 1683, 1691–1693 [1974]); state public defenders (*Tower v. Glover*, 104 S.Ct. 2820, 2824–2826 [1984]); members of a local public school board (*Wood v. Strickland*, 95 S.Ct. 992, 999–1003 [1975]); the head of a public mental hospital (*O'Connor v. Donaldson*, 95 S.Ct. 2486, 2494–2495 [1975]); police officers (*Pierson v. Ray*, 87 S.Ct. 1213, 1218–1219 [1967]); and the head of a state prison and various officers therein (*Procunier, Corrections Director v. Navarette*, 98 S.Ct. 855, 859–862 [1978]).

Likewise, in a Bivens-type suit, only qualified (not absolute) immunity is available to heads of federal cabinet departments–except in their rulemaking (*Butz v. Economou*, 98 S.Ct. 2894, 2907–2911 [1978]) and to presidential aides in general (*Harlow v. Fitzgerald*, 102 S.Ct. 2727, 2733–2736 [1982]).

Moreover, some limits exist even on "absolute" immunity. In *Pulliam v. Allen*, 104 S.Ct. 1970 (1984), a magistrate often had required posting of bail by parties who had been arrested for "nonjailable offenses under Virginia law." Such an arrestee unable to produce bail was jailed. The federal district court enjoined the magistrate's practice in response to a sec. 1983 suit and awarded plaintiffs attorneys' fees against the magistrate under 42 U.S.C., sec. 1988. The Supreme Court upheld the award and the injunction (1981–1982). Further, judicial absolute immunity does not extend to a judge's administrative decisions demoting and firing a probation officer, *Forrester v. White*, 108 S.Ct. 538, 544–546 (1988).

A state prosecuting attorney has only qualified immunity under sec. 1983 in "giving legal advice to the police." The test of when immunity is absolute is "whether the prosecutor's actions are closely associated with the judicial process" (*Burns v. Reed*, 111 S.Ct. 1934, 1940–1944 [1991]). A prosecutor has only qualified immunity in the detective-like work of "preliminary investigation of . . . crime" and thus could be sued for allegedly creating fake evidence. The prosecutor does not become an "advocate for the state," protected by absolute immunity, "before he has probable cause to have anyone arrested." The prosecutor also has only qualified immunity in communications with the media (*Buckley v. Fitzsimmons*, 113 S.Ct. 2606, 2615–2618 [1993]).

Attorneys' Fees

A major expense component in tort cases is attorneys' fees. Sometimes statutes regulate these sharply, as in the Federal Tort Claims Act. In 1976, Congress provided (42 U.S.C., sec. 1988) that in a sec. 1983 suit, "the court, in its discretion, may allow the prevailing party, other than the United States, a reasonable attorney's fee." *Johnson v. Georgia Highway Express, Inc.* 488 F. 2d 714 (5th Cir. 1974) identifies an apparently comprehensive array of criteria for determining what is a reasonable fee, criteria heavily influential in sec. 1983 cases:

1. The time and labor required.
2. The novelty and difficulty of the questions.
3. The skill requisite to perform the legal service properly.
4. The preclusion of other employment . . . due to acceptance of the case.
5. The customary fee.
6. Whether the fee is fixed or contingent.
7. Time limitations imposed by the client or the circumstances.
8. The amount [i.e., "of damages or back pay"] involved and the results obtained.
9. The experience, reputation, and ability of the attorneys.
10. The "undesirability" of the case.
11. The nature and length of the professional relationship with the client.
12. Awards in similar cases (717–719).

The sixth item was modified by *Blanchard v. Bergeron*, 109 S.Ct. 939, 944–946 (1989), holding that a contingency fee agreement cannot limit the amount of attorney fees awardable as reasonable by the trial judge.

When is someone a "prevailing party"? Courts apply the term only to plaintiffs. Requiring losing plaintiffs to pay attorneys' fees of a government or public employee defendant would tend to defeat Congress' intention (in sec. 1988) to encourage plaintiffs to be private attorneys general, as a check against arbitrary government. If a case involves multiple issues and each side wins on some, when is a plaintiff a prevailing party? Rejecting the view that the plaintiff must win on the "central issue" to qualify, the Supreme Court has ruled the test to be whether "the plaintiff has succeeded on 'any significant issue,'" causing "the material alteration of the legal relationship of the parties" (*Texas State Teachers Association v. Garland Independent School District*, 109 S.Ct. 1486, 1492–1494 [1989]). A plaintiff winning only "nominal damages" is a prevailing party but not entitled to an award of attorneys' fees (*Farrar v. Hobby*, 113 S.Ct. 566, 573–575 [1992]).

Punitive Damages

A losing defendant in a tort liability suit may be required to pay compensatory (or "actual") damages, essentially to make the victim whole. Another kind of award is punitive (or "exemplary") damages for retribution and deterrence of future wrongdoing by the defendant or others. Punitive damages play a significant role in the tort liability system. Sometimes such awards are many times larger than compensatory damages in the same case. Punitive damages may be restricted by statute, as in the FTCA, or by court interpretation of application law.

Punitive damages cannot be imposed under 42 U.S.C., sec. 1983 against a municipality (*City of Newport v. Fact Concerts, Inc.*, 101 S.Ct. 2748, 2756–2762 [1981]) nor presumably on any local government. The Court relied upon common law and policy considerations. Punitive damages upon the entity penalize the taxpayers, not the government employee wrongdoers, and such damages constitute a "windfall" to the victim. Entity malice is only malice of individuals, who are not necessarily deterred from wrongdoing by punitive damages upon the entity. Moreover, since "evidence of a tortfeasor's wealth" has been "traditionally admissible as a measure of the amount of punitive damages that should be awarded, the . . . taxing power of a municipality may" tempt the jury into hurting that government's capacity to serve its citizens adequately (2761).

Individual public servants can be subjected to punitive damages under sec. 1983, when found to have acted either maliciously or with "reckless or callous indifference to the federally protected rights of others" (*Smith v. Wade*, 103 S.Ct. 1625, 1640 [1983]).

Use of the punitive damages device has been controversial. Issues include whether it really is needed, its consequences to parties and society, and the extent to which it lends itself to arbitrary application. Instructive herein is *Pacific Mutual Life Insurance Company v. Haslip,* 111 S.Ct. 1032 (1991), involving private torts. An insurance agent committed fraud against a customer. The Supreme Court upheld a punitive damages award against the employer company and its agent, despite such award being "more than four times the amount of compensatory damages" awarded to the customer victim and "more than 2000 times [her] . . . out-of-pocket expenses." The Court majority held that the requirements of due process were satisfied, because state law provided some decisional criteria to the jury, and appellate review of the trial court judgment was available (111 S.Ct. 1032, 1045–1046). But to dissenter Justice Sandra Day O'Connor, the case illustrated a broad problem with common law punitive damages as applied today:

> Imposed wisely and with restraint, they . . . [may] advance legitimate state interests. Imposed indiscriminately, . . . they have a devastating potential for harm. . . . States routinely authorize civil juries to impose punitive damages without providing them any meaningful instructions. . . . Such instructions are so fraught with uncertainty that they defy rational implementation. Instead, they encourage inconsistent and unpredictable results by inviting juries to rely on private beliefs and personal predilections (111 S.Ct. 1032, 1056; contrast Zwier 1991).

In a landmark 1996 private torts decision, the Supreme Court (5/4) invalidated a state court's punitive damages award, as so excessively big as to deny due process (BMW of North America, Inc. v. Gore, 11b S.Ct. 1589).

Some Implications of Tort Liability in Government

Legal developments about government and employee tort liability have several major implications.

1. Their scope and complexity are now so great, especially regarding 42 U.S.C., sec. 1983, that governments and their employees face difficult challenges in trying to keep abreast of changes potentially affecting them in this dynamic, evolving field. Reasonable "knowledge of constitutional law is considered a matter of basic *job competence* for public administrators" (Rosenbloom and Carroll 1990, p. 30).
2. The scope of vulnerability of entities and/or employees to tort liability is expanding on balance, through new statutes such as the Americans with Disabilities Act of 1990, the Civil Rights Act of 1991, and a recent series (O'Leary 1993) of far-reaching environmental laws. Vulnerability also seems to be expanding through court interpretations of particular aspects of relevant law, such as on regulatory takings, and through judicial approaches to tort law in general (Schuck 1988).
3. Overall, the tort liability system today provides government entities and employees with fairly strong economic reasons to avoid violating constitutional and other legal rights of people.
4. As elaborate as existing systems are, significant gaps remain that are productive of injustice. Categories of real victims lack adequate remedies.
5. Economic burdens borne by the public sector from negotiated or litigated outcomes in the tort system are now very substantial, especially for many local governments (Huber 1988; MacManus and Turner 1993; but contrast Lee 1987).
6. Some critics (for example, Davis and Pierce 1994, section 19.2, 19.7; Schuck 1983, pp. 100–121; Wise 1985, pp. 851–855) advocate reforms making the government entity the sole defendant in liability cases and relying on the entity to hold its own employees accountable. They fear that unrealistically high expectations of legal understanding may be placed on employees, in an often unclear, confusing, inconsistent, and evolving legal context. Supposed likely consequences are frequent injustices to employees and risk aversion—excessive concern with the potential of being sued personally. Risk aversion distracts from job accomplishment, nurtures overemphasis on self-protection, and inhibits vigorous administration. But skeptics wonder whether potential disciplinary measures by public agencies are a sufficient substitute for personal liability. "Overdeterrence may be eliminated by also eliminating beneficial deterrence" (Keeton, Dobbs, Keeton, and Owen 1984, p. 1069; and see Braveman 1989, pp. 101–134).
7. The tort system has contributed greatly to the large expansion in recent decades of the impact of courts and judicial policymaking on government administration (Rosenbloom 1983, pp. 185–203; Schuck 1988, pp. 93–109).
8. Risk management is a growing field of major importance to which government administrators are compelled by circumstances to give attention (Johnson and Ross 1989, pp. 2–11; Rynard 1991).
9. The tort system, especially in Bivens-type and sec. 1983 cases, generates a great number of opportunities for lawyers and considerable rewards to the legal profession, which, like government administration, surely needs to become more efficient and less expensive.

DALMAS H. NELSON

BIBLIOGRAPHY

Braveman, Daan, 1989. *Protecting Constitutional Freedoms: A Role for Federal Courts.* Westport, CT: Greenwood Press, 101–134.

Davis, Kenneth Culp, and Richard J. Pierce, Jr., 1994. *Administrative Law Treatise,* 3d ed., vol. 3. Boston: Little, Brown Chapter 19.

Huber, Peter W., 1988. *Liability: The Legal Revolution and Its Consequences.* New York: Basic Books.

Johnson, R. Bradley, and Bernard H. Ross, 1989. "Risk Management in the Public Sector." *The Municipal Yearbook 1989.* Washington, DC: International City Management Association.

Keeton, W. Page, Dan B. Dobbs, Robert E. Keeton, and David G. Owen, 1984. *Prosser and Keeton on the Law of Torts.* 5th ed. St. Paul, MN: West Publishing.

Lee, Yong S., 1987. "Civil Liability of State and Local Governments: Myth and Reality." *Public Administration Review,* vol. 47 (March-April): 160–170.

MacManus, Susan A., and Patricia A. Turner, 1993. "Litigation as a Budgetary Constraint: Problem Areas and Costs." *Public Administration Review,* vol. 53 (September-October): 462–472.

O'Leary, Rosemary, 1993. "Five Trends in Government Liability under Environmental Laws: Implications for Public Administration." *Public Administration Review,* vol. 53 (November-December): 542–549.

Robinson, Robert K., Billie M. Allen, Geralyn McClure Franklin, and David L. Duhon, 1993, "Sexual Harassment in the Workplace: A Review of the Legal Rights and Responsibilities of All Parties." *Public Personnel Management,* vol. 22 (Spring): 123–135.

Rosenbloom, David H., 1983. *Public Administration and Law: Bench v. Bureau in the United States.* New York: Marcel Dekker.

Rosenbloom, David H., and James D. Carroll, 1990. *Toward Constitutional Competence: A Casebook for Public Administrators.* Englewood Cliffs, NJ: Prentice-Hall.

Rynard, Thomas, 1991. *Insurance and Risk Management for State and Local Government,* vol. 1. New York: Matthew Bender.

Schuck, Peter H., 1983. *Suing Government: Citizen Remedies for Official Wrongs.* New Haven, CT: Yale University Press.

———, 1988. "The New Ideology of Tort Law." *Public Interest,* no. 92 (Summer): 93–109.

Walter, Robert J., 1992. "Public Employees' Potential Liability from Negligence in Employment Decisions." *Public Administration Review,* vol. 52 (September-October): 491–496.

Wise, Charles R., 1985. "Suits against Federal Employees for Constitutional Violations: A Search for Reasonableness." *Public Administration Review,* vol. 45 (November-December): 845–856.

Zillman, Donald N., 1989. "Congress, Courts, and Government Tort Liability: Reflections on the Discretionary Function Exception to the Federal Tort Claims Act." *Utah Law Review,* vol. 1989, no. 3: 687–740.

Zwier, Paul J., 1991. "Due Process and Punitive Damages." *Utah Law Review,* vol. 1991, no. 2: 407–443.

TOTAL QUALITY MANAGEMENT (TQM).

An overall philosophy of management and method of work reform that focuses on customer service, continuous improvement, and employee involvement in organizational functions. "Total" means applying the search for quality in every aspect of work; "quality" implies meeting and exceeding customer expectations; "management" mandates the development of an organizational capacity to constantly improve.

History

During World War II, quality standards were developed for American war material. They were based on the work of statistician Walter Stewart, who found that all kinds of repeatable activity are characterized by variation and who developed a method–control charts–to monitor and analyze variation over time. The standards enabled the production of reliable, high-quality supplies.

The U.S. economy was the only one in the world that emerged from the conflict stronger than when it began. For a population that experienced widespread shortages and rationing during the war, American industry could not make products fast enough. The quality control of the war years was abandoned for high-volume sales to meet marketplace demand.

Japan, then occupied by the United States, was one of the most devastated countries in the world. As a maritime trading nation, it realized that it could never regain self-sufficiency and become competitive on the basis of poor quality goods. Japanese companies, with the assistance of American consultants W. Edwards Deming and Joseph Juran affected the introduction of quality control systems. Led by Japanese Union of Scientists and Engineers, basic industries were reestablished in the 1950s. Japan, a beneficiary of postwar stability as well as the Korean War and later the Vietnam War, entered a period of rapid growth, which, by the 1960s, was widely referred to as the Japanese miracle. International competitiveness and relatively high growth continued under conditions of energy scarcity in the 1970s. It was not until a 1980 NBC White Paper–"If Japan Can, Why Can't We?"–that the American general public recognized the magnitude of the Japanese challenge.

There was, as a result, an immediate search for the "secret" of Japan's success. Japanese-style employee teams called quality circles were adopted and abandoned in many American organizations when quick results did not occur. By the mid to late 1980s, however, a second generation of quality initiatives took place when it was recognized that a strategic approach to quality–total quality management–may be the only way to successfully compete in a global economy of the 1990s.

Theory

Total quality management is an organizational transformation strategy that posits sustained productivity improvement can be achieved by applying a quality philosophy and statistical techniques. Many people have contributed in significant ways to the field of quality management; three major pioneers are W. Edwards Deming, Joseph Juran, and Philip Crosby.

In the Deming approach, the required transformation can occur if management's deadly diseases are eliminated and 14 points are adopted. The diseases are a lack of constancy of purpose, short-term thinking, an emphasis on easily available data (with little concern for process-improvement data), performance appraisal, mobility of management, exorbitant medical costs, and excessive legal liability costs. The 14 points are as follows: (1) Create a constancy of purpose, (2) adopt the new philosophy, (3) cease dependence on mass inspection, (4) end lowest-bid contracting, (5) improve every process, (6) institute training, (7) institute leadership, (8) drive out fear, (9) break down barriers between departments, (10) eliminate slogans, exhortations, and targets for the workforce, (11) abolish arbitrary production quotas, (12) remove barriers that rob employees of pride in work, (13) institute a program of education and self-improvement, and (14) make the quality transformation everyone's job.

The assumption is that the organization, not the employees, is the object of management; the organization is a system of interlocking processes (supplier-customer chains) designed by management. The goal is to reduce variation in these processes by involving employees in meeting customer expectations. The leader must have a theory—what Deming calls profound knowledge—for the 14 points to be effective. In fact, it is maintained that managers, not employees, are responsible for 94 percent of the problems that occur in organizations. The theory that management must use has these components: a knowledge of variation, the knowledge that increasing quality reduces costs, and a knowledge of the psychology of cooperation.

Juran ranks near Deming in the contributions that he has made to quality improvement. His approach parallels Deming's, as Juran's ten steps to quality improvement are to build quality awareness, to set improvement goals, to organize to achieve goals, to provide training, to implement problem-solving projects, to report progress, to give recognition, to communicate results, to keep score, and to build quality improvement into the organization's regular systems. The three primary managerial functions for managing change include quality planning (developing the systems necessary to meet customer expectations), quality control (assessing actual performance), and quality improvement (create the processes necessary to make improvements).

Philip Crosby has identified four absolutes of quality: a definition of quality (quality means conformance to standards), the system for achievement of quality (the prevention of defects), a performance standard (zero defects), and measurement (the price of nonconformance). A 14-step quality improvement program consists of management commitment, quality improvement teams, quality measurement, the cost of quality, quality awareness, corrective action, zero defects planning, supervisory training, an inaugural Zero Defects Day, goal setting, error cause removal, recognition, quality councils, and doing it over again.

While there are some differences in how quality goals may be accomplished, the philosophies of the three experts all share the same objective: to create an integrated total quality system with an emphasis on continuous improvement and employee involvement. They also believe that statistical tools (e.g., Pareto charts, fishbone diagrams, flowcharts) and management techniques (such as participative management, brainstorming, quality circles) do not automatically produce quality. Instead, the power of the human mind to identify problems and correct them must be guided by a complete approach to quality. Overall, TQM is a revolutionary way to manage organizations because it emphasizes a systems approach, long-time horizons, a cultural change in employer-employee relationships, and a never-ending search for excellence.

Current Practice and Variation

TQM is now employed in a wide range of public and private organizations in such functions as accounting, communication, contract management, document distribution, entitlement programs, information systems, law enforcement, loan processing, medical care, patents, personnel, public works, supply management collection, and many others. Recent studies reveal that over three-fourths of companies see quality as a major goal and 80 percent of Fortune 1000 firms have quality improvement programs. In the late 1980s, the national government created the Federal Quality Institute to promote quality initiatives and by 1992 over two-thirds of agencies were using some form of TQM.

The popularity of TQM can be explained because of its proven track record (in Japan and other countries as well as noted success stories among American firms such as Xerox, Federal Express, Corning, Motorola, and Ford), because it integrates many familiar management approaches (scientific management, group dynamics, organizational development, corporate culture), and because it is consistent with many widely admired values (e.g., humanism, service, quality). An emphasis on quality in the public sector is especially important because of competition from privatization initiatives, because business is the standard by which government is often evaluated, because citizens demand quality services, and because of the need for employees to take pride in their work.

The widespread use of quality techniques is encouraged by quality awards (e.g., the Deming Prize in Japan and the Baldrige Award in the United States), which mandate that award winners disseminate information about their success. These awards have become an important catalyst for transforming organizations by speeding up the timetable for learning and by subjecting organizations to outside evaluation. In order to create a benchmark for the large number of organizational and national quality standards, the International Standards Organization (ISO) in Geneva, Switzerland, developed a set of uniform standards, ISO 9000–9004, in 1987. Endorsed by over 50 countries, they provide a framework for quality assurance throughout the production process that can be used worldwide, an important dimension of international trade. Companies desiring to compete at this level can undergo the ISO 9000 certification process, which involves establishing a quality program that meets ISO requirements.

The promise of total quality management—to create more value so that people can have a better life—is nurtured by the success stories of award winners, the quality movement (its professional associations, local chapters, conferences, journals, and consultants), and documented changes in attitudes among managers over time. Indeed, some commentators maintain that TQM is to the post–Industrial Revolution what scientific management was to the Industrial Revolution; the development of quality systems is seen as a necessity if organizations are to prosper in the future.

Given such promise for TQM, serious problems nonetheless exist. There is a very high failure rate for quality initiatives in many organizations; this is not surprising given the fact that many are already failing due to management diseases and the difficulty in adopting a new work paradigm. In addition, dramatic environmental changes in today's business world can overtake any management initiative.

Despite the promise and because of the problems, prospects for TQM are uncertain. There are three alternative futures. The first is business as usual—disappointed by the failure of TQM to provide a quick fix, self-fulfilling prophecies of fad-to-failure cycles take over. The organization reverts to its traditional style of management—at least until the next ineffective management fad is tried.

In the second outcome—partial success—TQM is seen as a useful, if limited and oversold, innovation. Within organizations, it may be defined as quality initiatives that focus only on those processes with which organizations are most comfortable or have existing expertise. They lack, accordingly, an overall strategy and maintain organizational routines incompatible to TQM, thereby limiting its potential. Partial success at the societal level means that select companies in direct competition with foreign firms and certain government agencies with special demands for quality adopt TQM, but no general cultural transformation occurs.

In the final scenario, the depth and breadth of TQM deployment is complete: Quality is adopted by all organizations across all sectors of the economy as vestiges of traditional management are swept away, and TQM is integrated into daily management. The three scenarios are not necessarily mutually exclusive, at least in the short run; the first could lead to the second, which in turn could produce the third. And by Japanese standards, TQM elsewhere is still in its formative period—it may be too early to forecast whether quality will be rejected, partially accepted, or embraced by organizations.

Is quality a fad? Are not approaches "beyond TQM," such as reengineering, being tried? Most new techniques are derivative of TQM, and there is no reason to assume that it is a static technique since continuous improvement

is an integral component of the philosophy. The claim that TQM, or its variations, may have a faddish character does not make it unworthy of pursuing. Lasting change can take place when genuine innovations are fully implemented.

JAMES S. BOWMAN

BIBLIOGRAPHY

Aguayo, Rafael, 1990. *Dr. Deming: The American Who Taught the Japanese about Quality.* New York: Lyle Stuart.

Carr, David K., and Ian D. Littman, 1990. *Excellence in Government: Total Quality Management in the 1990s.* Rosslyn, VA: Coopers and Lybrand.

Cohen, Steven, and Ronald Brand, 1993. *Total Quality Management in Government.* San Francisco, CA: Jossey-Bass.

Crosby, Philip B., 1979. *Quality Is Free.* New York: New American Library.

Deming, W. Edwards, 1982. *Quality, Productivity, and Competitive Position.* Cambridge, MA: M.I.T. Center for Advanced Engineering Study.

———, 1986. *Out of the Crisis.* Cambridge, MA: M.I.T. Center for Advanced Engineering Study.

The Deming Library, 1983–. 20 volumes. Chicago, IL: Films, Inc.

Feigenbaum, Arthur J., 1983. *Total Quality Control.* New York: McGraw-Hill.

Hammer, Michael, and James Campy, 1993. *Reengineering the Corporation: A Manifesto for Business Revolution.* New York: HarperCollins.

Imai, Masaaki, 1986. *Kaizen: The Key to Japan's Competitive Success.* New York: Random House Business Division.

Ishikawa, Kaoru, 1982. *Guide to Quality Control,* 2d ed. White Plains, NY: UNIPUB.

Juran, Joseph M., 1979. *Quality Control Handbook,* 3d ed. New York: McGraw-Hill.

———, 1988. *Planning for Quality.* New York: Free Press.

Lawler, Edward E., III, et al., 1992. *Employee Involvement and Total Quality Management.* San Francisco, CA: Jossey-Bass.

Linden, Russell M., 1994. *Seamless Government: A Practical Guide to Re-engineering the Public Sector.* San Francisco, CA: Jossey-Bass.

Neave, Henry R., 1990. *The Deming Dimension.* Knoxville, TN: SPC Press.

Schmidt, Warren H., and Jerome P. Finnigan, 1992. *The Race Without a Finish Line: America's Quest for Total Quality.* San Francisco, CA: Jossey-Bass.

Tenner, Arthur R., and Irving J. DeToro, 1992. *Total Quality Management: Three Steps to Continuous Improvement.* Reading, MA: Addison-Wesley.

U.S. General Accounting Office, 1991. *Management Practices: U.S. Companies Improve Performance through Quality Efforts.* Washington, DC: U.S. General Accounting Office.

———, 1992. *Quality Management: A Survey of Federal Organizations.* Washington, DC: U.S. General Accounting Office.

TRADE BLOCKS.

Nations that voluntarily establish a free, or near free, economic market among themselves.

Introduction

Three major regional trading blocks are emerging in the world. Each will be described in detail, but first, an explanation is given on how the current trade blocks came into existence.

Post–World War II History

The end of World War II marked the beginning of a new era in world trade relations. A major shift took place from the closed and restrictive trade policies of the 1920s and early 1930s to a more open and freer system of trade liberalization in the post–World War II era. The United States spearheaded this policy as a result of the reconstruction of the war-ravaged economies of Europe and Japan.

Among the victors of the war, the United States and Canada were the only nations that did not sustain major infrastructure and economic devastation. This enabled the United States to assume a leadership role in the revitalization and reconstruction of the economy of Western Europe and later Japan by providing massive emergency aid and loans.

Prompted by the emerging cold war, the immediate concern was to reestablish the economies of those nations and encourage the move toward global trade and liberalization. The United States informally linked the need for free trade with their foreign aid to Europe under the Marshall Plan. This trade and foreign policy not only encouraged and restored the competitiveness of Europe, but it also removed earlier trade barriers that had prevailed prior to and during World War II. In brief, the United States policy after the World War II era sought to end trade discrimination, to gradually reduce tariffs based on the most-favored-nation principle, and to create a multilateral trade.

The emergence of the cold war complicated and changed the single international economic order of the multilateral trade system. An altered economic and political order emerged, based on the hostile relationship between the United States and its allies versus the communist nations. Both used the trade policy for strategic and military purposes. Trade was used as an aggressive foreign policy mechanism.

Consequently, two economic systems emerged. In the Western democracies, the United States shaped the future of trade in the capitalist block through the Bretton Woods institutions. These include the International Bank of Reconstruction and Development (IRBD), the International Monetary Fund (IMF), and later the General Agreement on Tariffs and Trade (GATT). In the communist East, the Soviet Union imposed a socialist-oriented economic system on its eastern neighbors based on Marxist economic principles.

In the West, the GATT became the forum for trade negotiations and a resolution of trade disputes. The GATT was given credit for most of the Western national growth and prosperity in international trade. It provided a framework for trade negotiations in areas such as tariffs, quotas, subsidies, and the diminished use of trade restrictions considered to be the main barriers to free trade. Since the 1950s when the United States owned nearly 50 percent of the world's manufacturing capacity, both Western and world economic conditions had changed. Europe and Japan have rebuilt their productive capabilities and have become strong competitors.

Three Trade Blocks

Today, three main trading blocks are emerging alongside the multilateral trade order that has existed since World War II. The main trade blocks include the European Community (EC), North America, and the Pacific Rim. The emergence of these trading blocks marks the end of the post–World War II era and the United States' dominant role in international economics. As these blocks become fully operational, they collectively will manage and dominate the world economy.

The European Community

The unification of the European Community into a single market establishes a market of more than 341.6 million people with a combined gross national product (GNP) per capita of over US $14,624. The common market removes most internal European fiscal trade barriers, including technical and physical obstacles. If the EC decides to expand and include obvious candidates, their market would be over 374. 3 million people with a combined GNP per capita of over US $15,315.

The implications of the EC and other major trade blocks raise questions about the future of multilateral trade. Pessimists believe that such blocks will erect a "Fortress Europe" to protect EC producers or a "Fortress America" to protect North American producers from external competitors. If the pessimists are right, then the future of multilateral trade negotiations may be in jeopardy. Europe, North America, and the Pacific Rim might concentrate more on bilateral or regional trade rather than multilateral arrangements.

EC and American policy statements, however, suggest that it will not be a "fortress" or a closed market but a "partnership" relationship with other blocks. These assurances are likely to hold true, especially when each community's self-interest is taken into consideration. Past trade patterns show that the EC's and North America's economies are tied closely to international or worldwide foreign trade. According to Michael Calingaert (1989) in "What Europe Means for United States Business," the EC's "ratio of exports to gross domestic product is about double that of the United States, and it is also the world's largest exporter accounting for 20 percent of the total compared to 14 percent for the United States" (pp. 30–36).

North American Trade History

A unique trade relations history exists among the United States, Mexico, and Canada. Trade relations between the

United States and Canada are not new, but an extensive trading relationship between Mexico and the United States is new. There is little trade between Canada and Mexico. Until 1886, a free trade agreement existed between Canada and the United States. Then it was replaced by the British North America Act of 1867, because the issue of national sovereignty was a major concern to most Canadians. This and other issues overshadowed desires for free trade between the two neighbor nations until the twentieth century. Historically, Mexico pursued a protectionist trade policy, and only since the 1990s has it adopted a liberalized trade policy. That policy, coupled with the anticipation that a North American Free Trade Agreement (NAFTA) might be concluded, helped the Mexican economy greatly and stimulated trade between Mexico and the United States.

The protectionist Canadian-U.S. trade policy started to reverse during the Great Depression when several bilateral trade arrangements or agreements were signed, especially in the sectorial trade. According to John Whaley and Roderick Hill (1985) in *Canada-United States Free Trade,* "these agreements in turn laid the groundwork for the evolution of the GATT as the main instrument of global and multilateral approach to trade policy by the major industrialized countries" (pp. 1–42).

Both nations differed sharply in trading patterns as they emerged from World War II. The United States, unlike Canada, was not dependent on foreign trade. In 1950, for example, exports and imports combined accounted for 8 percent of the U.S. GNP, compared to 47 percent for Canada. The heavy reliance of Canada on foreign trade was one of the driving forces that led to its desire for an open and integrated flow of goods and capital between both nations or the closer linkage of Canadian trade to the U.S. economy. The increasing dependence of the Canadian economy on the United States is reflected in the growth patterns of its exports. Over the years, Canadian exports to the United States increased from 51 percent in 1951 to 69 percent in 1972 and to 70 percent in 1987. Expressed in terms of GNP, U.S. trade with Canada accounted for 20 percent of Canada's GNP. However, Canadian exports to the United States accounted for only 2 percent of the U.S. GNP during the same year.

North American Trade

The passage of the North American Free Trade Agreement created a single North American market. On June 11, 1990, the U.S. government and the Mexican government agreed to seek a free trade agreement similar to the one already in place between the United States and Canada. This has led to a continentwide free market that extends from Canada to Mexico. U.S. companies are now encouraged to adopt continentwide or cross-border investments and trade strategies in order to use the advantages of the North American free trade policy.

With NAFTA, North America is an effective counterweight to the European Community and Pacific Rim trade blocks. With a combined population of over 365.3 million people, North America is the largest trading block in the world. Its combined market size roughly exceeds US $6 trillion compared to the European Community's US $5 trillion. Despite Mexico's low GNP and high population, North America still enjoys a higher average GNP per capita of over US $16,464.

Despite these positive developments, there still exist crucial economic and political issues related to the effective implementation of the NAFTA agreement. For example, economically, Mexico is debt ridden, but the doubts of investors in the United States were eased by NAFTA and Mexico's impressive economic success. In the 1990s, Mexico implemented austere economic measures, including devaluation of the peso and cuts in government spending. In 1992, Hilda Aburto noted in her paper "Bureaucracy and Policy in Mexico" that inflation in Mexico used to run at 300 percent but that it was cut to 20 percent. In 1982, Mexico had 1,155 government companies; in 1992, it had 222. The income from the sale of those government properties was worth US $23 billion to the Mexican government. The 1991 growth in gross domestic product (GDP) was 4.8 percent, the highest rate in ten years. The public-sector foreign debt went from 54 percent of GDP in 1987 to 37.7 percent in 1992.

The nations of the world are developing more competitive economies. NAFTA should help Mexico, the United States, and Canada in improving their economic condition. Economic success is defined not only in terms of having a favorable balance of trade but in bringing more jobs, especially higher-paying jobs, to a nation's work force. Effective economic policy will be adaptable, will focus on encouraging quality and effective products and services in its actions, and will nurture innovations that lead to practical products and living standard improvements for the nations' citizens.

Pacific Rim Trade

The other potential regional trade block is the Pacific Rim. This area is the most dynamic and fastest growing in the world. However, progress in establishing a Pacific Rim trade block is slow. As of 1991, the six countries of the Association of the Southeast Asian Nations (ASEAN)–Brunei, Malaysia, Indonesia, the Philippines, Singapore, and Thailand–have a combined population of over 323.9 million people and an average GNP per capita of US $845. Other important western Pacific nations include Russia, China, Japan, South Korea, Taiwan, Australia, and New Zealand. If the eastern Pacific nations were included, the Pacific Rim membership list would expand significantly. Japan is extremely important with a population of over 123.8 million and a remarkable per-capita GNP of over US $23,730.

In the past 30 years, the Pacific Rim has been the most dynamic and fastest-growing region in the world. The economies of the Pacific Rim countries grew at the remarkable rate of about 6 percent per year. This surpassed the growth rate in the West by a ratio of 2 to 1.

Behind this growth exists the Japanese leadership role. Japan has provided unprecedented and continued investments in many Asian countries and has increased their trade and public/private industrial development. Japan's investments in the region are therefore intertwined with the development of trade interdependence. This is partially attributed to Japan's huge demand for processed materials from the other Pacific Rim countries. Those countries in turn need technology and capital from Japan. Rachael MacCulloch (1990) noted in "The United States-Canada Free Trade Agreement," "Japan appears to be constructing a new co-prosperity zone in the Pacific Rim. The arrangement is informal, and direct investment is the key force, but emergence of the trading zone of a financial integration centered in Tokyo is a reality" (pp. 79–89).

Interestingly, Asia realizes that its continuing economic success depends on its easy access to the North American market. Also America understands that it has three times more trade with Asia than with Europe. That market for many Asian countries is about 25 percent of their annual export revenues. If the world trade process fails and a protectionist NAFTA policy emerges, Asian nations realize that they will not benefit. They would be likely to reevaluate their trade policy. American presidential leadership argues that a protectionist NAFTA will not emerge and that an economic surge in North America would enhance trade with other partners, including Asia. However, that view is doubted. For example, Malaysia attempted to create an East Asian Economic Caucus (EAEC), which excludes non-Asian Pacific Rim countries such as the United States, Canada, Australia, and New Zealand. The United States criticized the attempt, and Japan failed to endorse the EAEC. ASEAN (the six countries of the Association of Southeast Asian Nations) have the most to lose if NAFTA turns protectionist due to their member state transitional status to industrialized economies.

In a bold step in 1993, the ASEAN created the ASEAN Free Trade Area (AFTA). This Singapore-led plan's goal is to cut tariffs on 15 groups of manufactured goods and to slash intra-ASEAN tariffs on all manufactured goods to a maximum of 5 percent by January 1, 2008. Americans and Canadians support AFTA and argue NAFTA's market integration will extend across the Pacific. However, Malaysia remains concerned about the potential protectionist policies of NAFTA.

Another move to encourage trans-Pacific trade and investment is the Asia Pacific Economic Cooperation (APEC). This group includes ASEAN nations plus Japan, South Korea, China, Taiwan, Hong Kong, the United States, Canada, Australia, and New Zealand. America favors APEC, but it has a relatively minor agenda to date. It has the potential of binding the Pacific nations more closely together. Both America and Japan support APEC, but is potential is not yet realized.

Conclusion

The future consolidation of trade blocks as the main basis for conducting world trade has an impact on the multilateral trade system. The multilateral approach needs to expand market accessibility in presently restricted areas, to liberalize trade in agriculture and textile goods, and to extend world rules to nonmanufacturing service sectors, including insurance, banking, finance, and construction. Progress needs to be made against international trade restrictions, especially nontariff barriers. However, achieving international consensus is difficult given national interest group politics such as agriculture in democratic countries such as the United States, France, and Japan.

A significant long-term economic and social trend of considerable importance may be occurring. However, the apparent trend discussed here is only beginning to emerge. Its future share and consequence are difficult to predict. However, this trend is likely to be significant and largely shaped by the success or failure of attempts to expand world trade and the interrelated multinational trade agreements.

THOMAS D. LYNCH AND
NICETTE L. SHORT

BIBLIOGRAPHY

Aburto, Hilda, 1992. "Bureaucracy and Policy in Mexico." Presented at the International Conference on Bureaucracy and Policy: A Comparative Perspective in Seoul, Korea, October. Sponsored by the Association of Korean Public Administration.

Calingaert, Michael, 1989. "What Europe Means for United States Business." *Business Economics*, vol. 24 (Winter) 30–36.

Culbertson, John M., 1990. "Workable Trade Policy for Today's Economic and Political World." In Frank J. Macchiorola, ed. *International Trade: The Changing Role of the United States.* New York: Academy of Political Science, 151–164.

MacCulloch, Rachael, 1990. "The United States-Canada Free Trade Agreement." In Frank Macchiorola, ed., *International Trade: The Changing Role of the United States.* New York: Academy of Political Science, 79–89.

Méndez, Jose Luis, 1996. "The Current Challenges Facing Public Administration in North America." Special issue of *International Journal of Public Administration*, vol. 19, no. 8.

Negal, Stuart, 1991. *Global Policy Issues.* New York: St. Martin's.

Sek, Lender, 1993. *North American Free Trade Agreement.* CRS Report No. IB90140. Washington, DC: U.S. Library of Congress, Congressional Research Service.

Whaley, John, and Roderick Hill, 1985. *Canada-United States Free Trade.* Toronto: University of Toronto.

TRAGEDY OF THE COMMONS. The ruin of the commons brought about by human activity in pursuit of private gains with disregard to the overall consequences. The commons is a public good that can be shared by the masses. The commons is a part of our social institution, first established by the body of English common law that antedates the Roman conquest. This law recognized that there are some objects in our society that had never been but should be appropriated among individuals (Crowe 1977, p. 54). The word "commons" is thus generally used to refer to land, air, and water. Often the overexploitation of the commons for maximization of individual gains leads to its destruction or results in the tragedy of the commons.

Garrett Hardin has illustrated the tragedy of the commons in a simple example of a pasture land where each herdsman tries to maximize gains by addition of more cattle to the commons. Such an arrangement may work well as long as the number of herdsmen and cattle is below the carrying capacity of the land. But with the unrestricted addition of cattle to the grazing land, the carrying capacity of the pasture is soon overwhelmed, and this leads to the destruction of the commons. Thus an individual's rational decision to maximize private gains does not always lead to the maximization of social benefit but results in the tragedy of the commons.

An economic analysis of the tragedy of the commons reveals two basic components of the utility function of the herdsmen. The first one usually reckoned by any entrepreneur is the positive component of utility associated with the addition of one more animal to the herd. As the herdsman receives all the monetary profits from the sales proceed of the animal, the positive utility in such a case is nearly 1. The second is the negative component of utility, a function of overgrazing brought about by the addition of an extra animal to the herd. Since the effects of overgrazing are shared by all herdsmen, the negative utility is thus only a fraction of 1 (Hardin 1993a, pp. 131–132).

Given that positive utility outweighs the benefits of negative utility, the latter is most likely to be ignored. Each rational herdsman would most likely add another animal to the herd to reap the benefits of marginal utility. But in the long run, the consequence of such actions can only be disastrous or result in a tragedy. According to Hardin, as long as individuals continue to behave as independent, rational, and free entrepreneurs without any restrictions on their activities, the tragedy of the commons will continue to pose a serious problem in the society.

Often the tragedy of the commons offers valuable insight into the problems of free access to public property, which leads to its indiscriminate use and over exploitation. In our society, the basic assumption is that a common property is free for use by whomever feels a need for it (Hardin 1977a, p. 47). According to Hardin, under such conditions of free access, there may exist no problem for a few centuries as long as the birth and death rates level the population growth and does not lead to exceedence in the

carrying capacity of the land. But a time may be reached when the unrestricted growth of population may create excessive pressure on the commons and lead to its gradual destruction. Thus the principle of the tragedy of the commons is associated with our societal problems of overpopulation and pollution.

According to Hardin, the unrestricted growth of human population freed of its control of macro and nearly all micro predators is likely to cause great misery and scarcity of resources until we impose restraints on such growth processes. Even though rapid advancements in science and technology have made it possible to increase the carrying capacity of land by the optimum utilization of resources and by expanding the area of food supply but transgression of the carrying capacity even for a short period is a mistake. It initiates natural processes of degradation that undermine the value of resources and render them useless. For example, in the Mediterranean region, human folly in the exceedence of carrying capacity of the land has brought about serious environmental degradation on the eastern and western shores of the sea (Hardin 1993b, p. 150).

In order to justify the existence of the commons that we share and to prevent their destruction by individual profit maximizers, Hardin has pointed out the necessity for control of population (Hardin 1993a, p. 142). There exists no doubt that modern science and technology have helped us to increase life expectancy and to decrease the mortality rates from common diseases, but this has resulted in a population disequilibrium. If utter misery is to be avoided along with the universal ruin of the commons, it is important that we create and maintain countervailing forces of control on population growth (Hardin 1993b, p. 148).

Given the fact that a public good is indivisible and no potential consumers can be excluded from enjoying the benefits of it (Ostrom and Ostrom 1971, p. 206), the imposition of laws to limit its use is likely to draw much opposition from the public. The industrialization of the economy and the unrestricted access to natural resources of air, land, and water, have brought about the indiscriminate disposal of toxic and nontoxic wastes into these resources by private polluters (Hardin 1993a, p. 133). These factors have encouraged the use of a low-cost technology that emits harmful substances into the surrounding air and water. This helps the factory owner to realize the full monetary benefits while experiencing only a fraction of the risk associated with exposure to such harmful products (Goodstein 1995, p. 34). Thus, in the adoption of such a least cost approach toward the disposal of wastes and pollutants, the destruction of the commons is inevitable.

The problem of free access to the commons can be also used to explain the rapid rate of depletion of the natural resources, for example, the fishing stock in the commercial fisheries of the world. Off the coast of New

England, the unrestricted access to the marine resources of the sea has been responsible for the drastic decline in the trawler catch of flounder and haddock. But fishermen still continue to launch intensive fishing operations in these waters using expensive boats and sophisticated technology to increase their catch of the dwindling stock. Individual efforts to increase profitability are often associated with their liability of mortgage payments for expensive boats; thus, they cannot afford to limit their catch (Goodstein 1995, p. 35). As a result, an individual fisherman's decision to reap the maximum benefits from a common marine resource by increasing the number of trawlers in the water can only prove to be disastrous in terms of depletion of fishing stock along with an adverse impact on the economy.

In the overexploitation of the global commons that we share, Hardin has pointed out the seriousness of the problems of international commons of air and water (Hardin 1977a, p. 49). As these commons transcend national boundaries, the problems of global warming and depletion of stratospheric ozone pose serious threats to the existence of mankind. Since no property rights can be established in these commons, solutions to global problems are difficult. The United Nations can only issue a declaration or a charter for the protection of these commons, but compliance by individual countries is difficult to monitor.

In our society, the mere existence of public goods and the benefits derived from those goods at a minimal cost produce little or no incentives to take any initiatives to conserve or maintain the quality of the good shared in common (Ostrom and Ostrom 1971, p. 207). This is mainly due to the fact that the right to use is not matched with corresponding responsibility to manage the commons (Hardin 1977c, p. 66). As a result, the commons can only be justified under conditions of low population density (Hardin 1993a, p. 141).

In the absence of adequate voluntary action to conserve resources and in individual tendencies toward overexploitation of the commons, there exists a problem whose partial solution lies mainly in two options. The first option is the assignment of responsibility to the government for the conservation of the commons. The government can restrict its use either by regulations or in lieu of payments that may limit the overuse of commons. A good example can be seen in the conservation of the national parks and forests for public use and the use of highway tolls to restrict overuse and to pay for its maintenance. The second option lies in the abandonment of commons in favor of private property or granting of rights of use; for example, common lands have been sold off as agricultural land while mining rights have been sold to companies with exclusive rights for exploitation by the owner only.

The advocates of private property rights believe that in a system of private property the responsibility lies with the individual or group of owners to maintain their property. The incentive to conserve lies in the fear of reduced profitability from overexploitation of private lands or resources. For example, a farmer will know exactly the number of heads of cattle a piece of land can support and will therefore take adequate measures not to exceed the ideal number. This is consequent upon realization of the fact that if the land is overgrazed, weeds will take over and erosion will cause damage to the soil, which would reduce profitability in the long run (Hardin 1977b, p. 265). Thus, to avoid this mistake, the owner of the land is most likely to take the best care of it in its optimal use. But this is not possible in the commons, where the sharing ethics and selfish trends of overexploitation by the few leads to a tragedy that affects all users. Thus, one of the solutions to the tragedy of the commons lies in the appropriation of the commons and its division as a private property among the appropriators (Boulding 1977, p. 285).

There are a few commons that cannot be appropriated among the users; for example, the air and water resources are freely available for the use of everyone on this planet. Since no technical solutions or international regulations may prove to be useful in preventing the misuse, it is only education that can create an awareness about the dangers of overexploitation of the commons. The recognition of such dangers can only help to bring about a better management of such commons and make users more responsible for the consequences of misuse. Thus, a change in attitude toward the use of commons can possibly help to avert the tragedy of the commons.

SARMISTHA R. MAJUMDAR

BIBLIOGRAPHY

Boulding, Kenneth, 1977. "Commons and Community: The Idea of a Public." In G. Hardin, and J. Baden, eds. *Managing the Commons*. San Francisco, CA: W. H. Freeman, 280–294.

Crowe, Beryl L., 1977. "The Tragedy of the Commons Revisited." In G. Hardin and J. Baden, eds. *Managing the Commons*. San Francisco, CA: W. H. Freeman, 53–65.

Goodstein, Eban, 1995. *Economics and the Environment*. Englewood Cliffs, NJ: Prentice-Hall.

Hardin, Garrett, 1977a. "Denial and Disguise." In G. Hardin and J. Baden, eds. *Managing the Commons*. San Francisco, CA: W. H. Freeman, 45–64.

———, 1977b. "Living on a Lifeboat." In G. Hardin and J. Baden, eds. *Managing the Commons*. San Francisco, CA: W. H. Freeman, 261–278.

———, 1977c. "An Operational Analysis of Responsibility." In G. Hardin and J. Baden, eds. *Managing the Commons*. San Francisco, CA: W.H. Freeman, 66–75.

———, 1993a. "The Tragedy of the Commons." In Herman E. Daly and Kenneth N. Townsend, eds. *Valuing the Earth*. Cambridge, MA: MIT Press, 127–144.

———, 1993b. "Second Thoughts on 'The Tragedy of the Commons.'" In Herman E. Daly and Kenneth N. Townsend, eds. *Valuing the Earth*. Cambridge, MA: MIT Press, 145–151.

Ostrom, Vincent, and Eleanor Ostrom, 1971. "Public Choice: A Different Approach to the Study of Public Administration." *Public Administration Review* (March-April): 203–212.

TRAINING AND DEVELOPMENT.   An area of human resources management focusing primarily on the provision of organized learning experiences by the organization for the purpose of improving performance and/or enhancing individual growth. Training and development, also called human resource development, refers broadly to a developmental or growth process and the array of activities that encourage an individual to further one's knowledge and skills. In the first edition of his book *Developing Human Resources,* Leonard Nadler [1970] coined the phrase "human resource development" and presented a framework to define the field. Today the terms "training and development" and "human resource development" are generally used interchangeably, although some argue that human resource development better describes the broad scope of the field. The area of training and development is often differentiated from that of organization development, which focuses primarily on planned change at the unit or organizational level for the purpose of improving an organization's problem-solving and renewal processes (see **organization development**). Despite the distinction, in recent years these functions are increasingly being placed in the same organizational unit.

Three types of activities are included under the training and development function: training, education, and development. Training refers primarily to learning activities that are focused on the present job of the individual. Although training may include a discussion of general principles, training tends to focus on specific knowledge and skills needed to do one's job. Training activities occur primarily in classroom settings, although some types of training, such as on-the-job training, occur at the actual job site. Education refers primarily to learning activities that prepare individuals for jobs other than the one currently held. In this sense, learning that occurs in colleges and universities is placed under the heading of education since it prepares individuals for jobs other than the one currently held, that of being a student. Moreover, education tends to be principle driven and therefore focuses more broadly on a discipline than on a particular job. Development refers primarily to learning activities that are centered on the growth of the learner rather than on a particular job and therefore is less focused on learning outcomes. Although development is not job focused, development activities may be career focused; workshops or seminars on career planning or time and stress management are examples of activities that may fall in this category. Alternatively, development activities may focus more broadly on obtaining knowledge and skills purely for the sake of satisfying one's intellectual curiosity or enhancing one's quality of life; learning to play an instrument or taking a course out-side one's own discipline are examples of activities that may fall in this category.

Brief Historical Overview of Public-Sector Training and Development

Although most regard the field of training and development as one that has emerged within the past century, some argue that the field is as old as the concept of work. That is, as long as people have worked, there has been a need for someone to teach them how to perform the work. Certainly, the field dates back to early periods of history where individuals learned their work by apprenticing with an experienced worker. Interestingly, apprenticeship programs are still used today in some government organizations, although the apprentice is of course no longer indentured to the experienced worker. One example of a long-standing apprenticeship program in the U.S. federal government exists in the Government Printing Office. The program has existed since the agency was first established in 1861, when the government purchased a printing plant, as well as its apprenticeship program, from a private company. Since that time, the Government Printing Office has had an apprenticeship program in the printing trades.

The need for more formal training and development programs emerged in the United States in the late 1890s and early 1900s during the period of industrial development. During this time, the United States also experienced a large influx of immigrants, many of whom needed to be trained for their new jobs, and organizations in both the public and private sectors began setting up internal training and development units within their personnel departments. While many government agencies provided training for their employees during this time, the National Bureau of Standards Graduate School, established in 1908, is considered to be the oldest established training agency for federal employees. In 1938, President Roosevelt issued Executive Order No. 7916, which gave responsibility for training and development to the director of personnel in each department; in 1958, this executive order was superseded by the Government Employees Training Act. During those 20 years, the field of training and development in organizations experienced a period of significant growth, as organizations in the United States extended their definition of training and development beyond the traditional types of technical training and began to offer training courses for supervisors and managers as well; it should be noted that this type of training did not become well established in Europe until about a decade later. Nevertheless, by the beginning of the 1960s, training and development was a firmly established, although not always well-funded, component of human resources management. In 1961, the first textbook on training in organizations, *Training in Business and Industry,* written by William McGehee and Paul Thayer, was published.

This growth trend continued into the 1960s and 1970s as changes in office technology, as well as in the demographic composition of the workforce, created an increased need for training and development within work organizations. Government agencies that were sufficiently large, and therefore, well funded, broadened the scope of responsibility of the training and development units to include the provision of in-house programs, the provision of information about centralized government programs, and the provision of information about nongovernmental programs in the private sector and colleges and universities that would be paid by the agencies. Smaller government agencies, especially those at the state and local levels, however, were often not able to meet the increasing demand for training and development for their employees. The Intergovernmental Personnel Act of 1970 partially alleviated this problem by providing opportunities and grants to state and local government employees to participate in federal in-service training programs.

The early 1980s saw somewhat of a decline in training and development activities as many government agencies faced budget reductions and found training and development to be an easy target for cutbacks. A turnaround in this trend began, however, during the late 1980s, as organizations in both the public and private sectors in the United States, as well as in Europe and Asia, began to plan (and think) strategically. Specifically, organizations began to understand that human resources management, generally, and training and development, more specifically, had an important role to play in the planning process and to recognize that investment in training and development is an investment in the organization that benefits the employee, rather than an employee benefit that may have an impact on the organization. Moreover, organizations began to realize that decisions about investments in training and development need to be made with the same careful consideration as any other investment decision and should be made in accordance with the organization's mission.

Current Training and Development Issues

As was noted earlier, the need to view training and development within the context of strategic human resources management is true of public organizations across the globe. In the 1990s, with the advent of the global economy and high-speed telecommunications technology, many of the training and development issues faced by public-sector organizations in the United States do not differ substantially either from those of private-sector organizations in the United States or from those private- and public-sector organizations in other industrialized countries, as well as some of the developing countries. For example, it is estimated that every seven years the amount of information doubles, making it increasingly difficult for employees to stay current with new and developing practices in their fields. Thus, it is expected that half of what professionals know when they complete their formal education is obsolete within five years. This suggests that the most important training and development issues in the coming years for all organizations, public and private, in industrialized and developing countries, are in the areas of (1) continuous learning by individuals who need to routinely update their knowledge and skills and (2) helping employees become more adaptive to organizational change.

In order for public organizations to link training and development with the organization's mission, they need to take a systems view of training and development. Such a view sees training and development as a continuous cycle of needs assessment, design and delivery, and evaluation. Needs assessments can be conducted at four organizational levels: task, person, organization, and demographic. Task analyses focus on the knowledge, skills, abilities, and other personal characteristics (KSAOs) that are needed to perform the agency's tasks. This can be done at the level of the individual job, identifying how the task is performed and establishing standards of competent and expert performance. It can also be done at the unit level, examining the various work processes and work flows, identifying what KSAOs are need to perform the various components of each work process. Finally, this can be done at the organizational level, focusing on the organization's core technology and most typical work processes. In performing task analyses, organizations should be cognizant of future, as well as current, organizational tasks, thinking about how changes in office technology will change the nature of the task being performed. For example, how will computing technology change the tasks of secretarial and clerical positions?

Person analyses focus on the needs of the individual, examining the current KSAOs possessed by the particular individual, as well as discrepancies between actual behaviors and ideal or expected behaviors. When discrepancies between actual and ideal behaviors are the result of a lack of a specific KSAO, training or education may be an appropriate solution. Alternatively, if the discrepancy is not attributable to a lack of KSAOs, but rather to an unwillingness to use what the individual has, training or education is likely not appropriate. Since adults may resist being sent to training, it is important to involve employees in these analyses and to have them help identify reasons for any discrepancies.

Organizational analyses focus on the organization's ability to support training and development efforts. As was noted earlier, smaller agencies, with commensurately smaller budgets, are often unable to mount internal (in-house) training programs. They may, however, be able to tap into other available resources in other agencies, in centralized agencies that provide training and development programs, or from local educational institutions. It should be noted that European countries, as well as many developing countries, tend to rely more on centralized training and development agencies than does the United States. A second component of this analysis focuses more on the climate of the organization, asking questions about whether individuals who participate in training and development activities will be supported in using what they learned when they return to their work environments. Public managers must recognize that they are accountable for the public funds spent on training and development activities and that the use of these resources should be seen as resulting in a payoff in the work environment.

Finally, demographic analyses have recently emerged as a fourth component of needs assessments. These analyses look more globally at how the demographic characteristics may influence organizational training and development needs. For example, has the increase in the number of women in management positions changed the type of management training to be provided? Does an aging workforce result in needs for different types of training delivery mechanisms? Do changes in the demographic composition of agencies' clientele require new types of training for employees? (See **workforce diversity** and **affirmative action.**)

The second component of the training and development cycle focuses on the design and delivery of these experiences. Two related questions must be asked: First, how should the experience be delivered, and second, who should participate? As noted earlier, not all training and development activities are delivered in the classroom. On-the-job training involves developing a training protocol at the actual worksite. Programmed instruction and computer-based training may occur at a training center or at the job site of the individual. In the classroom, there are a variety of activities, including lectures, small and large group discussions, role plays, simulations, case studies, and other types of exercises that may be used to present the material in the most stimulating manner. Most important, the design and delivery of training needs to be sensitive to the principles of andragogy, the art and science of helping adults learn. For example, adults need to know why they are expected to learn something, they must see its relevance to their job or desire to learn. Second, they tend to be independent and self-directed and may have difficulty in the role of student. Adults also generally come to learning situations with a great deal of relevant knowledge and experience, which should be used rather than ignored during the training and development experience.

The third component of the training and development cycle focuses on evaluation or the question of whether the training and development accomplished what it was expected to accomplish. As indicated above, the strategic view of human resources management sees training and development as an organizational investment and, as with any other organizational investment, one must ask what is the return on investment. Moreover, because this is a cycle,

results of the evaluation phase become input to the needs assessment phase, providing information about how to enhance future training and development activities. Evaluation is often divided into four elements: reaction, learning, behavior, and results. Reaction evaluation is the most common type of evaluation and may ask about such issues as whether employees enjoyed the experience, whether the material was relevant and appropriate to their level of knowledge, whether the material was presented well by the instructor, whether the setting was conducive to learning, and so on. Learning focuses on the cognitive, rather than affective, reaction to the course. These types of evaluations tend to be used more in educational than in training situations and ask whether participants understood and absorbed the principles and concepts presented. Although this is useful information, in work organizations it is often less practical than questions about whether the participants can and will use the material in their work settings, which is the focus of behavioral evaluations. These evaluations ask whether the person is actually behaving differently on the job as a result of the training and development activity. Such evaluations generally require a carefully designed study that measures behavior before the training and development activity, as well as one or more times after the training to examine whether behavior has changed. In addition, information may be gathered from the individuals themselves, as well as from their employees, supervisors, and peers. Finally, results evaluations ask larger questions about changes in organizational performance. Such changes as increased productivity, enhanced quality of services, reduced costs, and improved morale are used as indicators of changes in organizational performance. It should be noted that while the latter two types of evaluation are much more difficult to conduct than are the first two, they are vitally important. As indicated in the discussion of organizational analyses, public managers are accountable for how public funds are spent. Managers need to know whether training and development activities are actually resulting in improved performance by the employee and in the organization in general.

The Future of Training and Development

It is expected that training and development will play an increasingly crucial role in public organizations over the next few decades. As indicated, the trend is to view training and developing as an investment in the organization's future. In addition, over the past decade, organizations in both the public and private sectors have begun changing the structure of work processes through such innovations as total quality management, employee involvement programs, and semiautonomous work teams. These innovations, designed to enhance productivity and customer satisfaction, can only work if employees have the appropriate tools to make them work. In some cases, these tools are specific techniques to examine work processes; in other cases, the tools involve such skills as dealing with change, thinking creatively, and managing interpersonal and intergroup conflict. The experiences of organizations that have adopted such innovations indicate that a major key to success has been a focus on training and development. Clearly, training and development will increasingly be an important vehicle to help organizations meet the challenges presented by continuous changes in the economic, social, and technological environments. More than ever, organizations will need to approach training and development strategically, using a systems approach.

SUE R. FAERMAN

BIBLIOGRAPHY

Carnevale, Anthony P., Leila J. Gainer, and Janice Villet, 1990. *Training in America: The Organization and Strategic Role of Training.* San Francisco, CA: Jossey-Bass.

Craig, Robert L., 1987. *Training and Development Handbook: A Guide to Human Resource Development,* 3d ed. New York: McGraw-Hill.

DeSario, Jack P., Sue R. Faerman, and James D. Slack, 1994. *Local Government Information and Training Needs in the 21st Century.* Westport, CT: Quorom Books.

Goldstein, Irwin L., et al., 1989. *Training and Development in Organizations.* San Francisco, CA: Jossey-Bass.

Kerrigan, John E., and Jeff S. Luke, 1987. *Management Training Strategies for Developing Countries.* Boulder, CO: Lynne Rienner.

Knowles, Malcolm S., 1984. *Andragogy in Action: Applying Modern Principles of Adult Learning.* San Francisco, CA: Jossey-Bass.

McGehee, William and Paul W. Thayer, 1961. *Training in Business and Industry.* New York: Wiley.

Mulder, Martin, Alexander J. Romiszowski, and Pieter C. van der Sijde, eds., 1990. *Strategic Human Resource Development.* Amsterdam, the Netherlands: Swets and Zeitlinger, B. V.

Nadler, Leonard, and Zeace Nadler, 1989. *Developing Human Resources,* 3d ed. San Francisco, CA: Jossey-Bass.

Robinson, Dana Gaines, and James C. Robinson, *Training for Impact: How to Link Training to Business Needs and Measure the Results.* San Francisco, CA: Jossey-Bass.

Van Wart, Montgomery, N. Joseph Cayer, and Steve Cook, 1993. *Handbook of Training and Development for the Public Sector.* San Francisco, CA: Jossey-Bass.

TRANSACTIONAL ANALYSIS (TA).

An approach to psychotherapy derived from Gestalt therapy that defines the basic unit of social intercourse as a transaction. It is a rational approach to understanding behavior that is based on the notion that people can learn to trust themselves and each other.

TA was first developed as a field within psychology and documented by Eric Berne (1961, 1964). It was popularized, however, by Thomas Harris' 1967 book *I'm OK—You're OK.* TA has been used as an approach to organizational improvement since early in the decade of the 1970s (James 1975; James and Jongeward 1971).

"Gestalt" is a German word that means essentially an organized whole—a whole that works well together. The aim of Gestalt therapy is to help people become aware of, admit, reclaim, and integrate the fragmented parts of their personality (Perls 1969). TA uses Gestalt therapy's focus on wholeness, emotional awareness, and moments of self-discovery. The core components of TA include ego states, transactions, life positions, life scripts, strokes, and games.

In TA terms, all humans have three "ego states" from which transactions emanate and that are distinct sources of behavior: parent, adult, and child. The parent ego state contains the attitudes and behaviors a person learns from early external influences, primarily parents. The parent is expressed toward others through prejudicial, critical, or nurturing behavior. Inwardly, it is experienced as life-long parent messages that continue to influence the inner child. The adult ego state is organized, adaptable, and analytical. It deals objectively with current reality. When the adult is activated, a person can think rationally, understand the consequences of actions, and make conscious decisions. The child ego state is the inner world of feelings and experiences which contains all of the impulses that come naturally to an infant as well as the memories of the child's early experiences and responses.

Transactions between individuals are classified as complementary, crossed, simple, or ulterior, based upon the response that the initiator receives to a transaction stimulus. A complementary transaction occurs when the initial message elicits the expected response. Crossed transactions are frequent sources of difficulties between people. The person who initiates a transaction expecting a particular response but does not receive it, is "crossed" and feels misunderstood and hurt. The purpose for an ulterior transaction is disguised.

TA identifies four "life positions": "I'm OK, you're OK," "I'm OK, you're not OK," "I'm not OK, you're OK," and "I'm not OK, you're not OK." "I'm OK, you're OK" is a mentally healthy position from which people view themselves and others constructively. The "I'm OK, you're not OK" life position is taken by people who feel victimized or persecuted. They blame others for their miseries. "I'm not OK, you're OK" is common to persons who feel powerless in comparison with others. "I'm not OK, you're not OK" is taken by people who lose interest in living.

According to TA, everyone has the biological and psychological need to be touched and to be recognized by others. These needs, or hungers, can be satisfied with strokes, that can be given by physical touching or in a symbolic form of touching, such as a look, a word, or an act that communicates recognition of a person as an individual. Infants will not grow normally without the touch of others. This need is usually met for infants through the everyday intimate transactions of diapering, feeding, powdering, fondling, and caressing that nurturing parents give to their babies. As a child grows older, the hunger for physical touching develops into a hunger for recognition. Positive strokes are complementary transactions, often expressions of affection that communicate and support the "I'm OK, you're OK" life position. Negative strokes often are critical of a person or of the person's behavior.

People play psychological games with one another, but they are not played for enjoyment. Psychological games are played to win, but a person who plays games as a way of life is not a winner. Games are programmed. Sometimes the inner child ego state sends a message to others in order to provoke them into game playing. Sending such a message is called a "sweatshirt message." For example, someone whose shoulders droop, who whines and looks anxious may be wearing a sweatshirt message that says, "I'm a victim." The sweatshirt message invites others to put them down or alternatively to rescue them. Games that are played from the "persecutor" or "rescuer" life script reinforce a negative position about others, as in the "I'm OK, you're not OK" life position. In contrast, games that are played from the "victim" life script reinforce a negative life position, most often "I'm not OK, you're OK."

TA has been used in organization development (OD) since 1970. TA training can help managers understand their relationships with people at work, causes of "irrational" employee behaviors, and reasons for unnecessary friction in contacts between employees and external publics. It provides an easily understood, nonthreatening model for changing behaviors and thus for organizational improvement. Its use, however, as a tool of OD appears to have declined in recent years.

J. Steven Ott

BIBLIOGRAPHY

Berne, Eric, 1961. *Transactional Analysis in Psychotherapy.* New York: Grove Press.
——, 1964. *Games People Play.* New York: Grove Press.
Harris, Thomas A., 1967. *I'm OK–You're OK: A Practical Guide to Transactional Analysis.* New York: Harper & Row.
James, Muriel, 1975. *The OK Boss.* Reading, MA: Addison-Wesley.
James, Muriel, and Dorothy Jongeward, 1971. *Born to Win: Transactional Analysis with Gestalt Experiments:.* Reading, MA: Addison-Wesley.
Perls, Frederick S., 1969. *Gestalt Therapy Verbatim.* Lafayette, CA: Real People Press.
Steiner, Claude, 1974. *Scripts People Live.* New York: Grove Press.

TRANSPORTATION POLICY.
Government policies concerning the provision, regulation, management, and pricing of publicly or privately owned facilities for the movement of people and goods.

Significance of Transportation to Society

Transportation is one of the glues that binds a community together, whether at a local, regional, national, or international scale. Trade and the development of an area's economic potential are only made possible through transportation links.

Transportation has been dominant historically in forming the location of cities and the pattern of settlements. Most, if not all, major world cities owe their preeminence to transportation as either modal interchanges (especially ports) like London, New York, or Hong Kong or as major transshipment nodes like Chicago or Frankfurt.

Defense and transportation have historically been inextricably linked, as witnessed by the pattern of railroads in central Europe, the U.S. interstate highway system, or former imperial outposts like Singapore.

Transportation has been at the forefront of technological development. The history of technology is reflected in and epitomized by transportation technology, whether by ship, rail, road, or air.

Similarly, transportation has been at the forefront of managerial practice, since the inevitably widespread nature of transportation enterprises has required the development of control and reporting mechanisms, which only came later to more localized enterprises. (Indeed, it has been said that in the early days of the development of American and Canadian railroads, the only prior model of management was the Roman Catholic church, such was the novelty of the spatial dimension of railway activities).

Transportation Goals

For all of these reasons, transportation is central to public policy in any developed nation. However, the corollary of this is that transport is rarely, if ever, an end in itself. People and goods do not move for the sake of moving, and the goals of transportation are inevitably means to achieving some broader economic or social purpose. For this reason, transportation policy goals are almost always expressed in terms of what they contribute to broader national goals.

These broader goals may be related to a wide range of activities. Perhaps the most common ones are as follows:

- defense (as mentioned earlier);
- economic efficiency, principally through enabling goods to be moved to customers at lower cost, thus stimulating trade;
- national development, through opening up underdeveloped regions to closer settlement, as epitomized by the nineteenth-century American railroads;
- equity, for example, in the provision of access and mobility to poorer groups within the community or in terms of regulation to prevent monopoly exploitation of users by transportation providers;

- industry policy, for example, in the development and manufacture of transportation equipment like automobiles, trucks, ships, or aircraft;
- urban and regional development, in terms of using transportation infrastructure and services to achieve a desired pattern and direction of growth; and
- more recently, the pursuit of environmental objectives, for example, in terms of air quality or energy conservation.

The common feature of all of these is that objectives developed elsewhere in the continuum of public policy have a direct influence on transportation, whereas transportation policies are typically aimed at influencing outcomes beyond the transportation sector.

Within this milieu, it is possible to identify three discernible megatrends in transportation policy over recent decades. These are deregulation, privatization, and (not surprisingly) transportation as a tool of national social and economic policy.

Deregulation

Deregulation of economic activity in the transportation sector has been actively pursued in many countries since the early 1970s.

The need for regulation was identified very early in the development of railways in the early part of the nineteenth century, in the interests first of safety and later to curtail monopoly exploitation. Over the years, in most countries with an extensive railway network, these controls became pervasive. Typically, rates were controlled, with prices set not according to cost of providing a service but according to customers' ability to pay (*ad valorem* pricing, whereby a high-value product attracted a higher rate than a low-value product). Overall, prices were set so that the industry as a whole was profitable. This led, in the long run, to inevitable consequences: first, that the rail industry had little knowledge of costs and second, that it was not in any position to compete with new challengers.

The main such challenger was, of course, motor transport. This too was heavily regulated in most developed countries from its very inception in the 1920s. In part, this reflected the political power of railway interests (railways worldwide sought to compete with road transportation by having legislators and regulators restrain the competition, and it is only in the last 20 years or so that American railroads moved to tackle motor carriers on the basis of price and service rather than regulation). However, the early regulation of the motor transportation industry also owed much to the poor state of the road networks and the not unreasonable policy goal of favoring the use of existing rail and water infrastructure.

As a result, motor transportation (whether of people or of goods) was and still is in many countries severely constrained. Typically, these regulations covered entry to the industry, rates, services, commodities carried, and so forth. In many countries, vast bureaucracies grew with the sole purpose of regulating the minutiae of activities of road transportation firms. And as with the railroads, the profitability of these firms was virtually guaranteed.

Starting in the 1970s, these cosy arrangements began to be dismantled in most countries. (Actually the first major deregulation could be said to have occurred in Australia, when in 1954 judicial interpretation of the Australian Constitution determined that governments may not regulate interstate trade. It is surely no coincidence that Australian transport companies flourished internationally once deregulation took hold elsewhere, applying the lessons learned in the deregulated Australian environment).

Governments realized that regulation benefited mainly the industries and firms being regulated and did not serve either the interests of the customers or the broader national interest. Thus, in relatively short order over the 1970s and 1980s, most countries largely dismantled their regulatory controls on road and rail transport and allowed competitive forces to prevail. In some countries, particularly the United States, a similar policy was adopted for the aviation industry.

In most cases, however, governments acknowledged that there was a need for ongoing public sector oversight of factors that, if left solely to the market, would likely not be in the public interest. These predominantly related to safety and environmental issues. The distinction was made between economic or quantity regulation (which regulates outcomes) and quality regulation (which regulates how an industry behaves).

In summary, there has been a very substantial change in the nature and intent of government policy toward transportation industries in many countries, which has seen a move away from a cosseted industry overseen by a multitude of administrators to a competitive industry whose safety and environmental impacts are watched. The effects have generally been a more competitive industry, with more niche operators, each focusing on specialist tasks that are suited to a firm's expertise or technology.

Privatization

The second major thrust on a global scale has been the privatization of key aspects of transportation. In most countries (the United States being the major exception), key transportation operations were for a long time publicly owned—railroads, airlines, ports, airports, urban transit, bus companies, and even shipping lines and trucking firms. And in all countries, roads were and still are essentially a publicly provided infrastructure, except for toll roads (which were a significant feature in only a few countries like France, Italy, and Japan).

This is now changing. Led perhaps by Britain, previously state-owned transportation enterprises are being wholly or fully privatized by their government owners worldwide. And there are numerous examples of authorization being given to the private sector to build and operate new roads, particularly in Asia, but also in America and elsewhere.

The prime reasons for this are essentially ideological; the belief that the private sector can do a better job than the public sector in managing enterprises and that the public sector should be smaller. A corollary of the latter is that there are pressures to reduce taxes and hence government spending; allowing the private sector to take responsibility for the provision of infrastructure contributes to this, while the sale of assets enables taxes to be cut, at least in the short term.

Transportation as a Tool of Broader Policy

As mentioned in the introduction to this contribution, transportation is by its very nature subservient to broader national policy goals. However, in a few instances, this is made explicit. Two examples must suffice to make the point.

First, in relation to industrial development, Europe and more recently America have embarked on massive publicly funded research programs aimed at "intelligent" transportation systems. Although in both cases the focus is transportation, the bigger agenda is achieving a technological lead in the emerging electronic and software industries, which, it is expected, will be key generators of wealth in the decades ahead; transportation is the focus, but international competitiveness is the game.

Second, in relation to environmental issues, because transportation consumes a high proportion of the world's energy (especially that which derives from liquid petroleum), it is an inevitable focus of attention. Whether at a local or a global scale, concern over emissions and other environmental impacts is increasing; sustainable transportation is likely to be the key transportation policy issue in the years ahead. But once again, although transportation is the focus, the real issue is much broader.

Conclusion

Transportation policy is only meaningful in the context of broader policy objectives, since transportation only exists to serve wider community goals. In recent decades, there has been a substantial international convergence of policy in the transportation sector which has seen a move away from economic regulation toward quality regulation, an increased private sector involvement in the ownership and operation of transportation enterprises, and a wider recognition that transportation is the focus of key strategic issues related to industrial competitiveness and environmental sustainability.

KENNETH W. OGDEN

TREATY ON EUROPEAN UNION.
Treaty on European Union (or Treaty of Maastricht). The 1992 revision of the Treaty of Paris and the Treaties of Rome (establishing the European Communities), which extended the competences of the European Community into new policy fields, which foresaw the establishment of an Economic and Monetary Union by the end of the 1990s and of a Common Foreign and Security Policy, and which strengthened the position of the European Parliament through the introduction of the codecision procedure.

Origins

Several factors are at the basis of changes that were accepted in the Treaty of Maastricht.

A first set of factors is related to the internal dynamics of the process of European integration. The new dynamism of the European Community (EC) in the second half of the 1980s, symbolized by the Single European Act and the "1992 initiative" on the completion of an internal market, resulted in pressure to adopt further institutional changes and widen the scope of community competences. First, the Single European Act of 1986, which revised the original community treaties, had formalized the objective to establish the European internal market and had introduced the cooperation procedure and the use of majority votes in decisionmaking. This, however, was considered as insufficient by several member states and by the European Parliament, who wanted more far-reaching adaptations to the treaties. Second, the implementation of the internal market project had increased the pressure to complete the internal market with a genuine economic and monetary policy and with initiatives in other policy fields.

A second set of factors is related to external pressures. The end of the communist regimes in Eastern Europe and of the East-West confrontation and division in 1989–1990 increased the pressure to strengthen the European Community and to develop its foreign and security policy in order to provide a pole of stability on the European continent. The perspective of German unification in 1990 was a second major external motivation to strengthen the European Community. Several member states considered that only a powerful European Community could "control" this enlarged and more powerful Germany at the heart of the European continent.

These pressures resulted in 1990 in the convening of two Intergovernmental Conferences, the first on the Economic and Monetary Union (EMU), the second on the European Political Union (EPU). These conferences resulted in the European Council meeting of Maastricht in December 1991. During this meeting, after rather difficult negotiations, the heads of state and government of the 12 member states accepted the Treaty on European Union, or Treaty of Maastricht. On February 7, 1992, the Treaty on European Union was solemnly signed in Maastricht.

The treaty only entered into force on November 1, 1993, as a result of the considerable problems with the ratification by the member states. In June 1992, the Danish population rejected in a referendum the treaty by a narrow majority. This was the start of a crisis in the post-Maastricht period. The Treaty of Maastricht was accepted by a large majority of the Irish population, but in the French referendum, the majority in favor of the Treaty was extremely narrow. The growing criticism against the Maastricht Treaty and against the European Community in general led the European Council in Lisbon, Birmingham, and Edinburgh in 1992 to adopt decisions intended at bringing the community closer to the citizen and at answering the fears expressed in Denmark and other countries. Only in the autumn of 1993, after a second Danish referendum had yielded a positive result and the German and British courts had delivered their rulings, was the treaty ratified in all member states and could it enter into force.

The Treaty of Maastricht foresaw in one of its final provisions that a new Intergovernmental Conference would be convened in 1996 to examine what provisions of the Maastricht Treaty should be revised. The Intergovernmental Conference of 1996–1997 resulted in the European Council Meeting in Amsterdam, the Netherlands in June 1997. This points again to the disappointment of several member states about the outcome of the Intergovernmental Conference of 1990–1991 and the compromises they had to accept.

Basic Features

Before examining the treaty provisions on the union's competences and institutional framework, an analysis of the union's objectives and of the structure of the treaty must be provided. Two other features of the treaty must be analyzed as well: the citizenship of the union and the introduction of the principle of subsidiarity.

Objectives

The first article of the treaty states that a European Union is established by this treaty, which "marks a new stage in the process of creating an ever closer union among the peoples of Europe, in which decisions are taken as closely as possible to the citizen." This sentence in Article A refers to two major points of conflict and ambiguity in the treaty and in the attitude of the member states vis-á-vis the process of European integration. First, the general objective is "an ever closer union" and not a "federation"—a con-

cept that was rejected by the United Kingdom. Second, it indicates the tension between the process of integration and the fear that the distance between the European Union and the citizen would become too large—a fear that also resulted in the inclusion of the principle of subsidiarity in the treaty.

What are the objectives of the European Union? The union sets itself the following objectives:

- to promote economic and social progress, which is balanced and sustainable, in particular through the creation of an area without internal frontiers, through the strengthening of economic and social cohesion, and through the establishment of an economic and monetary union, ultimately including a single currency;
- to assert its identity on the international scene, in particular through the implementation of a common foreign and security policy including the eventual framing of a common defense policy, which might in time lead to a common defense;
- to strengthen the protection of the rights and interests of the nationals of its member states through the introduction of a citizenship of the union;
- to develop close cooperation on justice and home affairs;
- to maintain in full the "acquis communautaire" (that means, the achievements of community integration) and build on it.

Citizenship

The Treaty on European Union establishes the "citizenship of the union," which implies that every person holding the nationality of a member state will be a citizen of the union, with rights and duties conferred by the treaty.

What are these rights as a citizen of the European Union? First, every citizen of the union has the right to move and reside freely within the territory of the member states. Second, all citizens of the union living in member states of which they are not nationals will have the right to vote and to stand as candidates at municipal elections or in elections to the European Parliament in that member state, under the same conditions as nationals of that state. Third, all citizens shall, in the territory of a third country in which the member state of which they are nationals is not represented, be entitled to protection by the diplomatic or consular authorities of any member state, on the same conditions as the nationals of that state. Finally, every citizen of the union has the right to petition the European Parliament and to apply to the ombudsman of the union.

The Principle of Subsidiarity

After enumerating the objectives of the union, Article B notes that these shall be achieved while respecting the principle of subsidiarity as defined in Article 3B of the treaty establishing the European Community. Article 3B states:

> The Community shall act within the limits of the powers conferred upon it by this Treaty and of the objectives assigned to it therein.
>
> In areas which do not fall within its exclusive competence, the Community shall take action, in accordance with the principle of subsidiarity, only if and in so far as the objectives of the proposed action cannot be sufficiently achieved by the Member States and can therefore, by reason of the scale or effects of the proposed action, be better achieved by the Community.
>
> Any action by the Community shall not go beyond what is necessary to achieve the objectives of this Treaty.

This article, aimed at the delimitation of community action, was considered a necessary counterweight to the strengthening of the institutions and competences of the community. After the signing of the Maastricht Treaty, the question remained whether the principle of subsidiarity was aimed either at regulating in a "neutral" way the exercise of the competences of the union or at restricting its interference (as wanted especially by the British government). Another point of discussion was related to the question whether this principle could be used at all for other than declaratory reasons. The ambiguity of the wording of Article 3B, the inclusion of criteria that are not always reconcilable, and the lack of clear guidelines for its operationalization gave rise to serious doubts about its applicability.

The Structure of the Treaty

The European Union is based on a "three-pillar" structure, linked together through "Common Provisions" (Title I) and "Final Provisions" (Title VII).

The first pillar, the community pillar, consists of amendments and additions to the existing Treaty of Paris and Treaties of Rome as modified by the Single European Act. This pillar consists of three titles: "Provisions amending the Treaty establishing the European Economic Community with a view to establishing the European Community" (Title II), "Provisions amending the European Coal and Steel Community" (Title III), and "Provisions amending the Treaty establishing the European Atomic Energy Community" (Title IV).

The most extensive of the three communities, the European Economic Community, was renamed "European Community." This implies, first, that the name that was already in common usage be enshrined in law. Second, it indicates that the functions of the community that are not of a purely economic nature gain in importance. In this first pillar, the three community institutions—the (European) Council, the European Parliament, and the Commission—all take full part in the decisionmaking process, with the council using majority voting in a considerable number of cases.

The second pillar consists of the "Common Foreign and Security Policy" and the third pillar consists of "Cooperation in the field of justice and home affairs." Both pillars are laid down in a framework of mainly intergovernmental cooperation. This implies that the (European) Council is the main institution in the decisionmaking process, with the commission only to some extent associated and the European Parliament consulted. It also implies that nearly all decisions in these fields are taken in the council by unanimity.

Together, these three pillars constitute the European Union, with the European Community pillar by far the most extensive in scope and the obligations for member states the most specific and wide-ranging. This "pillar" structure points to the fact that the member states were not ready to transfer full powers in all areas to the community. Hence, during the Intergovernmental Conference, they were not able to agree on the inclusion of the common foreign and security policy and of the cooperation in the field of justice and home affairs within the normal community structure.

Competences of the European Union

The Treaty of Maastricht extends the competences of the union to several new policy areas and widens the already existing competences. The policy field that is treated most extensively in the treaty is related to the economic and monetary policy of the union.

"Economic and Monetary Union"

The main new policy field included in the first pillar of the treaty is related to the objective of establishing an Economic and Monetary Union. Its main features are the close coordination of the economic policies of the member states, the creation of a European Central Bank, and the introduction of a single currency—the European Currency Unit (ECU)—which has to replace the national currencies of the participating member states.

The Treaty of Maastricht and the "protocol on the convergence criteria" defines criteria for participation in the final stage of the Economic and Monetary Union. These "convergence criteria" are as follows:

- *Price Stability*: The average rate of inflation, observed over a period of one year before the examination for the final stage, must not exceed by more than 1.5 percentage points that of the three best performing member states in terms of price stability.
- *Public Finances*: At the time of the examination, the council should not detect any excessive deficit on the part of the member states. The deficit is deemed to be excessive if the budget deficit is more than 3 percent of

the gross domestic product or if total government debt exceeds 60 percent of the gross domestic product.

- *Exchange Rates*: This criterion requires the observance of the normal fluctuation margins provided for by the Exchange Rate Mechanism of the European Monetary System, without severe tensions for at least two years before the examination and without devaluations against the currency of any other member state.
- *Interest Rates*: Observed over a period of one year before the examination, the average nominal long-term interest rate may not exceed by more than 2 percentage points that of the three member states who have the best results in terms of price stability.

This Economic and Monetary Union is to be established in three stages. The first stage, from July 1, 1990, saw the removal of most restrictions on capital movements between the member states. During the second stage, from January 1994 on, the member states enhance their efforts to try to eradicate their "weaknesses" in view of the criteria of the final stage. Multiannual programs are adopted with the aim to meet the criteria. A European Monetary Institute is created with the task to prepare the establishment of the European Central Bank.

Before the third and final stage, the council—acting by a qualified majority on a recommendation of the commission—assesses for each member state whether it fulfills the necessary conditions for the adoption of a single currency. The heads of state or government decide by qualified majority whether a majority of the member states fulfill the necessary conditions for the adoption of a single currency, whether it is appropriate for the community to enter the third stage and at what date, then, the third stage will start. Even if by the end of 1997 no date has been set for the beginning of the third stage, the final stage will in any case begin on January 1, 1999, independent of the number of member states that can participate. Special arrangements are foreseen for the "member states with a derogation," being the member states that are not able or not willing to move to the third stage of the European and Monetary Union.

Other New Competences in the First Pillar

Article 2 of the provisions on the European Community defines in general terms the task of the community: By establishing a common market and an economic and monetary union and by implementing the common policies and activities, the community shall promote throughout the community a harmonious and balanced development of economic activities, sustainable and noninflationary growth respecting the environment, a high degree of convergence of economic performance, a high level of employment and of social protection, the raising of the standard of living and quality of life, and economic and social cohesion and solidarity among member states.

In a following provision, the activities of the European Union in the different old and new policy fields are enumerated. Besides the economic and monetary policy, the main new fields are education and youth, culture, public health, consumer protection, trans-European networks and development cooperation. The competences in other policy fields, such as social policy, economic and social cohesion, and environment are extended. The European Community's competences in most of these fields, however, are much more limited than those in the field of economic and monetary policy.

Common Foreign and Security Policy

The "Common Foreign and Security Policy," established by the Treaty of Maastricht, replaces the previously existing European Political Cooperation. Article J.1(1) of Title V ("Provisions on a common foreign and security policy") states that "the Union and its member states shall define and implement a common foreign and security policy, governed by the provisions of this Title and covering all areas of foreign and security policy." This implies that the military as well as the economic and political aspects of security policy fall under the competence of the European Union. This also appears from Article J.4, which mentions that the "common foreign and security policy shall include all questions related to the security of the Union, including the eventual framing of a common defence policy, which might in time lead to a common defence." The scope of the European Union's external action is thus extended as the European Political Cooperation was only focused on political and economic aspects of security. Different provisions apply for decisions with defense implications.

It is important to emphasize that the aim of the Common Foreign and Security Policy is to define a "common" policy, not a "single" policy. The treaty provisions indicate that the council only defines a common position "whenever it deems it necessary" and that the union implements joint action "in the areas in which the member states have important interests in common." Moreover, the council has to decide explicitly that a matter should be the subject of joint action. This implies that the policy of the union is not aimed at replacing but at complementing the foreign and security policy of the member states. It also explains why the Common Foreign and Security Policy has a policy toward only some areas in the world and toward only some security issues.

Cooperation in the Fields of Justice and Home Affairs

The opening of the borders within the European Community (as a result of the internal market program) and the changes in the Eastern bloc and the end of the East-West division (which allowed for a greater movement of people between East and West) were two reasons why the EC member states wanted to include a title on the "Provisions on cooperation in the fields of justice and home affairs" in the Maastricht Treaty.

What are the areas that Title VI defines as matters of common interest and which may become the subject of joint positions, cooperation, joint action, and conventions? Article K.1 defines six areas that may be the subject of an initiative of the commission as well as of the member states:

- asylum policy;
- rules governing the crossing by persons of the external borders of the member states and the exercise of controls thereon;
- immigration policy and policy regarding nationals of third countries (conditions of entry and movement; conditions of residence, including family reunion and access to employment; combating unauthorized immigration, residence, and work);
- combating drug addiction (in so far as this is not covered by the three areas that can only be subject of an initiative of the member states);
- combating fraud on an international scale (in so far as this is not covered by the three areas that can only be subject of an initiative of the member states);
- judicial cooperation in civil matters.

Three areas can be subject of an initiative of the member states only:

- cooperation in combating criminal matters;
- customs cooperation;
- policy cooperation for the purposes of preventing and combating terrorism, unlawful drug trafficking, and other serious forms of international crime, including if necessary certain aspects of customs cooperation, in connection with the organization of a system for exchanging information within a European Police Office (Europol).

This list indicates that the purpose was to cooperate only in some policy areas and not to establish a full-fledged policy in the field of justice and home affairs. The motivations to include this title in the Maastricht Treaty (the opening of the borders and the end of the East-West division) explain why this Title VI only selects this limited number of areas as matters of common interest.

Institutional Provisions

Article C of the "Common Provisions" mentions that the union shall be served by a single institutional framework, which shall ensure the consistency and the continuity of the activities of the union. Despite this emphasis on a "single institutional framework," the institutions have different competences in the three pillars of the European Union.

This implies that only the provisions on the first pillar (the community pillar) considers the commission and the European Parliament as genuine partners to the council in the decisionmaking process.

What are the new institutional provisions of the European Union as foreseen in the Maastricht Treaty? In the community pillar, the treaty first introduces the "co-decision procedure," which further increases the impact of the European Parliament. Second, it extends the use of the existing "cooperation procedure" and "assent procedure." Third, it extends the use of majority votes in the council to more policy fields. Fourth, it establishes a new "Committee of the Regions." In the second and third pillar, it determines intergovernmental procedures for the Common Foreign and Security Policy and the cooperation in the field of justice and home affairs.

The "Co-decision Procedure"

This new procedure, which is a further elaboration of the cooperation procedure, increases the European Parliament's legislative powers to a considerable extent. Its two main features, the introduction of a right of veto in the third reading and the establishment of a "Conciliation Committee," transform the European Parliament into a genuine partner of the council in the decisionmaking of the European Union.

The first characteristic of the codecision procedure is the involvement of a Conciliation Committee composed of the members of the council or their representatives and an equal number of representatives of the European Parliament. When convened, this committee has the task of reaching agreement on a joint text, requiring approval by qualified majority of the council or their representatives and an absolute majority of Parliament's representatives. If within six weeks, the Conciliation Committee approves a joint text, this text is laid before the full council and Parliament for adoption by the same majorities. If one of the institutions rejects the text, the proposal is lost and the procedure is over.

The commission takes part in the Conciliation Committee's proceedings and takes all the necessary initiatives with a view to reconciling the positions of the European Parliament and the council. However, the commission has not the same decisive role as in the case of the cooperation procedure. The creation of the Conciliation Committee allows the European Parliament to negotiate directly with the council and to reach with it an agreement. The Parliament is thus not to the same degree dependent on the support of the commission as in the cooperation procedure.

The second characteristic of the co-decision procedure is that it introduces a third reading and gives the European Parliament the possibility, in this third reading, to reject by an absolute majority of its members the text accepted by the council. This possibility to see its text rejected by the European Parliament forces the council to take the parliamentary views more seriously. This right of veto is of a negative nature though: The Parliament can reject a text but does not have the power to get its own view accepted.

The co-decision procedure covers most decisions with regard to the internal market and the freedom of establishment, as well as a limited number of decisions on education, environment, public health, consumer protection, trans-European networks, research and technological developments, and culture. The co-decision procedure in some areas, however, requires the use of unanimity in the council, as is the case for the two last mentioned policy fields.

The Extension of the "Cooperation Procedure" and "Assent Procedure"

The codecision procedure covers several policy areas that were previously covered by the cooperation procedure (which was introduced by the Single European Act of 1986). The codecision procedure does not supersede the cooperation procedure though, which implies a further complication of the decisionmaking system of the European Union. The use of the cooperation procedure was extended to several new policy fields. Examples are certain decisions with regard to transportation, monetary policy, social policy, vocational training, trans-European networks, environment, and development cooperation.

The Treaty on European Union widens the scope of the assent procedure, which was introduced by the Single European Act. In this assent procedure, the decision of the council is only accepted if it obtains the assent of the European Parliament. This procedure is widened to cover a wider range of international agreements as well as some legislative decisions with regard to the right of the citizens to move and reside freely within the territory of the member states, the objectives of the Structural Funds, the powers of the European Central Bank, and proposals relating to the establishment of a uniform electoral procedure for the elections for the European Parliament. The influence of the European Parliament is increased as a result of the wider scope of the assent procedure but is diminished as a result of the new voting requirements. In most cases, the assent procedure requires a simple majority and no longer the absolute majority of the total number of members of the European Parliament. This new voting requirement makes it easier for the council to get the assent of the Parliament.

The Treaty on European Union extends the use of majority voting in the Council of Ministers to policy fields where unanimity was previously needed. Examples are certain decisions on monetary policy, education and vocational training, consumer protection, and trans-European networks.

The Establishment of a "Committee of the Regions"

In addition to the "Economic and Social Committee" established by the Treaty of Rome of 1957, the Treaty on European Union establishes a new "Committee of the Regions." This committee consists of representatives of regional and local bodies and has advisory status. The establishment of this committee was an indication of the growing political role of the regions in several member states of the European Union, such as Germany, Belgium, and Spain. The fact that the regions play no political role in some other member states resulted in this committee having no more than advisory powers. This different degree of power of the regions in the different member states explains also the very heterogeneous membership of this committee.

Decisionmaking in the Second and Third Pillar

Decisionmaking in the second and third pillar is characterized by its intergovernmental features: the unanimity rule, the preponderance of the (European) Council, and the marginal role of the European Parliament and the commission.

Both in the Common Foreign and Security Policy and in the cooperation in the fields of justice and home affairs is the council the only institution with power of decision. The commission is "fully associated," the European Parliament is consulted and can make recommendations, but neither has a real influence on the decisionmaking of the council. In some policy areas in the third pillar, the commission is allowed to submit proposals. In the Common Foreign and Security Policy, a special role is played by the European Council, which defines the principles of and general guidelines for this policy. The council takes the decisions necessary for defining and implementing the Common Foreign and Security Policy on the basis of the general guidelines adopted by the European Council.

In both pillars, the council in general acts unanimously, except for procedural questions and in a very limited number of cases provided for in the Treaty. In both pillars, when adopting a "joint action," the council can define by unanimity those matters on which decisions are to be taken by a qualified majority (with this qualified majority having as supplementary requirement that at least eight member states vote in favor). This implies that decisions by majority votes are indeed possible, but that any member state can block this possibility to depart from the unanimity rule, which relativizes the possibility of majority votes. Majority voting is also possible in the field of justice and home affairs for measures implementing conventions. In this case, these measures have to be adopted in the council by a majority of two-thirds.

STEPHAN KEUKELEIRE

BIBLIOGRAPHY

Cafruny, Alan W., and Glenda G. Rosenthal, eds., 1993. *The State of the European Community: The Maastricht Debates and Beyond.* Essex: Longman.

Corbett, Richard, 1993. *The Treaty of Maastricht. From Conception to Ratification: A Comprehensive Reference Guide.* Essex: Longman.

Dehousse, Renaud, ed., 1994. *Europe After Maastricht: An Ever Closer Union?* Munïch: Law Books in Europe.

Everling, Ulrich, 1992. "Reflections on the Structure of the European Union." *Common Market Law Review,* vol. 29, no. 6: 1053–1071.

Hartley, Trevor C., 1993. "Constitutional and Institutional Aspects of the Maastricht Agreement." *International and Comparative Law Quarterly,* vol. 42, no. 2: 213–237.

Laursen, Finn, and Sophie Vanhoonacker, eds., 1992. *The Intergovernmental Conference on Political Union: Institutional Reforms, New Policies, and International Identity of the European Community.* Maastricht: EIPA.

———, 1994. *The Ratification of the Maastricht Treaty: Issues, Debates, and Future Implications.* Maastricht: EIPA.

Monar, Joerg, Werner Ungerer, and Wolfgang Wessels, eds., 1993. *The Maastricht Treaty on European Union: Legal Complexity and Political Dynamic.* Brussels: European Interuniversity Press.

O' Keeffe, David, and Patrick M. Twomey, eds., 1994. *Legal Issues of the Maastricht Treaty.* London: Chancery Law Publishing.

TRINITARIAN CHANGE: ALPHA, BETA, AND GAMMA.

A tripartite model of change used in analyzing human attitudes, opinions, and feelings. Recent theory and research establish that "change" is best viewed in plural rather than singular terms, with "trinitarian change" being perhaps the most developed view of this kind. Basically, the notion distinguishes differences in degree from differences in state and uses them to construct three kinds of change—labeled alpha, beta, and gamma. The distinctions have great practical and theoretic relevance. For example, the results of any research over time with human subjects can be interpreted only in the light of the specific kind of change that has occurred.

Change is much in the air nowadays, and that exuberance attracts as well as underwhelms. For example, the mere fact of change remains unrevealing absent some credible working answers to a host of questions: Change to what? At what costs? And with which probable side effects? More basically, the dominant view in recent years proposes that several kinds of change exist and need to be distinguished for both theoretical and practical reasons.

Given continuing debate about the details of measurement (e.g., Armenakis 1988), behavioral scientists have come to a basic agreement that several kinds of change

exist. A trinitarian model encompasses alpha, beta, and gamma subtypes (Golembiewski 1990; Golembiewski, Billingsley, and Yeager 1976), and the basic distinction between them involves "degree" and "state." Thus water, or H_2O, can exist across a broad range of temperatures as well as in different states—solid, liquid, gas, and plasma. At times, two samples of H_2O may have the same temperature while they are in different states, or they may have different temperatures in the same state. Making the correct distinctions is crucial in both description and choicemaking.

Similar distinctions can be useful, even critical, in connection with human attitudes, opinions, or feelings. Considering two or more points in time, all comparisons of self-reports can involve any one of three kinds of change:

- *alpha change*: when both the psychological domain as well as the intervals for estimating degrees of difference in that state remain basically constant;
- *beta change*: when the state remains constant, but variations occur in some of the intervals used in estimating degree;
- *gamma change*: when both the state and the estimating intervals change substantially.

These distinctions involving state and degree are consequential when considering all human attitudes, opinions, and feelings. Consider a simple example: taking baby to be fitted for shoes at two points in time about 6 months apart. If we know only alpha change has occurred, a direct interpretation of the shoe salesperson's reading of the two measurements is possible. If beta occurs, however, one cannot be sure. Change has occurred in some (but not all) of the intervals used to estimate degree, and the second estimate just might fall in the intervals that have "stretched" or "shrunk" between observations, with the consequence that uncertainty exists about the meaning of the two measurements. If gamma occurs, no meaningful comparisons of the two measurements are possible. All direct comparisons between observations are meaningless and possibly harmful if not dangerous.

Of course, the measuring rod in the shoe store is pretty good at generating alpha-only estimates in Euclidean spaces. The foot-measuring tool changes a bit with humidity and temperature, but it basically permits valid and reliable estimates and hence is not subject to beta or gamma changes.

The typical measuring instruments used in behavioral research—in opinion polls, in various experiments, and so on—are subject to all three kinds of change. Consequently, for many practical and theoretical purposes, the trinitarian model has revolutionary implications, even as it leaves open such important questions in a specific comparison as the character and direction of beta and especially gamma change. To illustrate, unless we can rule out beta and especially gamma change, no clear interpretation is possible of any results of theoretical or applied research. We will not know if the patient really feels better after having taken the new medicine, although other measures of well-being exist that do not rely on self-reports. And we cannot confidently interpret the results of an experiment, interpret the before versus after effects of an intervention intended to influence human functioning, or compare responses to the "same" polling items at different items. In sum, trinitarian change refers to difficult learning, but makes some progress while leaving much to be learned.

ROBERT T. GOLEMBIEWSKI

BIBLIOGRAPHY

Armenakis, Achilles A., 1988. "A Review of Research on the Change Typology." In William A. Pasmore and Richard W. Woodman, eds., *Research in Organizational Change and Development,* vol. 2. Greenwich, CT: JAI Press.

Golembiewski, Robert T., 1990. *Ironies in Organizational Development.* New Brunswick, N.J.: Transaction Publishers.

Golembiewski, Robert T., Keith Billingsley, and Samuel Yeager, 1976. "Measuring Change and Persistence in Human Affairs." *Journal of Applied Behavioral Science,* vol. 12 (December) 133–157.

TRUST FUND. A budget account designated by law as a trust fund that has specially designated (earmarked) receipts.

Background

Currently, there are over 150 federal trust funds in existence in the United States. These funds are scattered throughout the federal government with more that 40 percent of them concentrated in five departments–Agriculture, Interior, Defense, Health and Human Services, and Transportation. There are a wide variety of purposes associated with federal trust funds, ranging from accounts containing earmarked receipts for Social Security and Medicare to accounts consisting of monies received by the federal government as gifts, bequests, and donations. The vast majority of trust funds are relatively small, with the ten largest accounting for slightly less than 99 percent of total trust fund receipts in fiscal year 1993 (Table I). In fiscal year 1993, these trust funds had a surplus of receipts over outlays that amounted to slightly more than US $100 billion and had a cumulative surplus of more than US $1 trillion.

History

Due to the large number of trust funds at the federal level, it is difficult to trace the exact history of each fund. Trust funds have come into existence over time as Congress has determined a need to place earmarked receipts in a fund where inflows and outflows can be tracked. In other words, trust funds basically serve a bookkeeping role.

TABLE I. TRUST FUND BUDGET
FISCAL YEAR 1993–1994
(BILLIONS OF DOLLARS)

	Receipts	Outlays	Annual Surplus Balance	Accumulated Balance
Social Security[1]	351.4	304.6	46.8	373.9
Medicare[2]	156.1	145.9	10.2	149.4
Federal Civilian Employees Retirement	63.3	35.3	28.0	318.6
Unemployment insurance	41.3	39.9	1.4	37.1
Military Retirement	35.3	25.7	9.6	97.7
Highway	19.6	18.5	1.1	23.0
Foreign Military Sales	13.2	13.1	0.1	6.6
Railroad Retirement	11.4	10.8	0.6	11.6
Airport and Airway	4.3	6.7	(2.4)	12.8
Veteran's Life Insurance	1.5	1.1	0.4	13.3
All Other	7.8	3.6	4.3	36.3
LESS: Adjustments for Payments between Accounts	(3.7)	(3.7)	NA	NA
TOTAL	701.5	601.5	100.1	1080.3

[1]Federal old-age, survivors, and disability insurance trust funds.
[2]Hospital insurance and supplementary medical insurance trust funds.

SOURCE: Executive Office of the President, Office of Management and Budget, 1994. *Budget of the United States Government, Analytical Perspectives, Fiscal Year 1995.* Washington, DC: Government Printing Office.

The largest trust funds generally are used for social insurance and retirement entitlements. In fiscal year 1993–1994 well over 80 percent of gross trust fund receipts were designated for these programs (Table I).

Not surprisingly, the earliest trust funds were created to help track receipts and outlays for social insurance and retirement programs. For example, the Civil Service Retirement and Disability Trust Fund was established by the Civil Service Retirement Act in 1920. The first two tax-financed trusts, the Old Age Survivors Insurance Trust Fund and the Unemployment Trust Fund were created by the Social Security Act of 1935. In 1936, the Railroad Retirement Trust Fund was created, followed by the creation of the Social Security Disability Insurance Trust Fund in 1956 and the creation of the Medicare Hospital Insurance Trust Fund in 1965. Two transportation-related trust funds—the Highway Trust Fund and the Airport and Airways Trust Fund—were created in 1956 and 1970, respectively.

Trust fund receipts come from a number of sources including Social Security payroll taxes, railroad retirement taxes, unemployment insurance taxes, employee retirement contributions, excise taxes, user charges, and contributions. The early trust funds initially were set up on an accrual basis, equating annual payments to the fund with the present value of benefits earned by beneficiaries during a particular year. It was not long before this practice was abandoned in favor of a pay-as-you-go financing scheme. Most of the largest trust funds remained on a pay-as-you-go basis until the 1980s. Under this financing approach, taxes and fees were set at levels sufficiently high to finance benefits, cover administrative expenses, and maintain reserves equal to approximately one year's expenditures.

In the 1980s, full (or partial) accrual funding came into vogue for some of the large trust funds. For example, the Social Security amendments of 1977 and 1983 increased payroll taxes above the level necessary to finance current expenditures, leading to the accumulation of a sizable fund balance of almost US $374 billion in fiscal year 1993–1994. Fund balances are projected to increase through the first decade of the twenty-first century. The change in payroll taxes was intended to prepare the Social Security trust fund for the large increase in expenditures that will occur as the "baby boomers" begin retiring around 2010. In 1985, military retirement benefits were placed on a full accrual funding basis and in 1986 federal civilian retirement benefits were placed on a full accrual funding basis.

Trends

Trust funds have become an increasingly significant portion of the U.S. federal budget over the years. In 1953, roughly 9 percent of federal receipts were earmarked for trust fund programs. This percentage grew to approximately 30 percent by 1973, and in 1993 trust fund receipts accounted for roughly 39 percent of federal receipts (Figure I). Trust fund outlays showed a similar rate of growth, accounting for 6 percent of federal outlays in 1953, constituting approximately 32 percent of federal outlays by 1973, and amounting to almost 40 percent of federal outlays in 1993. During the same period of time, annual trust fund surpluses grew from US $3.4 million in 1953 to US $10.8 million in 1973 to more than US $100 million in 1993.

FIGURE I. TRUST FUNDS AS A PERCENTAGE OF TOTAL FEDERAL RECEIPTS AND OUTLAYS

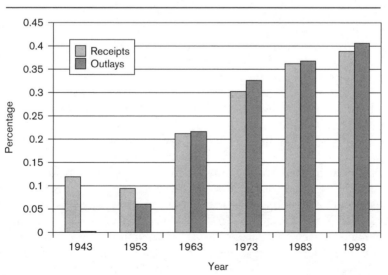

SOURCE: Executive Office of the President, Office of Management and Budget, 1994. *Budget of the United States Government, Analytical Perspectives, Fiscal year 1995*. Washington, DC: Government Printing Office.

Definitional and Conceptual Issues

Despite the appearance that trust funds are a relatively straightforward budgetary concept, further definitional and conceptual elaboration is necessary in order to develop a more robust understanding of the role trust funds play in the unified federal budget.

Definition

The federal budget is divided into two fund groups—federal funds and trust funds. Trust funds differ from the general fund, the major component of federal funds, because trust funds are financed by earmarked receipts. However, this is a necessary condition, not a sufficient condition. In other words, the earmarking of funds is not what distinguishes trust funds from other funds in the federal budget. Other funds like public enterprise funds, intragovernmental revolving funds, and special funds also receive financing from earmarked receipts. An example of a public enterprise revolving fund is the U.S. Postal Service Fund, which receives funds generated by mail services and other services it provides. These funds may be spent on postal service operations without congressional appropriation. Intragovernmental revolving funds receive monies generated by the sale of services among government agencies. Special funds are set up by statute for very specific purposes, and receipts earmarked for this purpose are available only for the purpose spelled out in the law.

The sufficient condition that distinguishes a trust fund from all other funds is its explicit designation as a trust fund in the law. The Office of Management and Budget (OMB), with the U.S. Department of the Treasury's assistance, classifies an account as a trust fund when earmarked funds are assigned by law to a program and the law identifies the account as a trust fund account. In the absence of the trust fund designation in the law, OMB would classify the account as a public enterprise, intragovernmental revolving, or special fund.

Trust funds may be either revolving or nonrevolving funds. The former fund's receipts may be spent when needed to finance operations or programs without further congressional action. The latter fund must receive authorization from Congress before it may expend funds it has collected.

No overriding guidelines exist to assist Congress in determining whether a particular program or a specific account deserves trust fund designation. Decisions are made on a case-by-case basis. As a result, there tends to be a lack of consistency with regard to the treatment of similarly situated funds. For example, OMB classifies the Department of Energy's Nuclear Waste Fund as a special fund while the Environmental Protection Agency's Hazardous Substance Superfund is classified as a trust fund. Despite close similarities between the structure and operation of both programs, Congress chose to designate the Superfund as a trust fund and not to designate the Nuclear Waste Fund as a trust fund.

Types of Trust Funds

Virtually all of the more than 150 federal trust funds can be classified as one of three general types of trust funds: user-financed programs, federal employees' retirement programs, and social insurance programs.

User-Financed Programs. The two major trust funds that fall under this category heading are the Highway and the Airport and Airways trust funds. Specific user charges such as motor fuel taxes and airline ticket taxes are levied by the government, and these revenues are earmarked for the purpose of acquiring, building, repairing, maintaining, and operating infrastructure. Designation as a trust fund account is justified on the grounds separate accounting is necessary to keep track of user charge receipts and outlays.

Federal Employees' Retirement Programs. The Federal Civilian Employees Retirement and the Military Retirement trust funds are the two largest funds in this category. Both federal agencies and federal employees make contributions to trust funds in this category. The rationale for levying charges to pay for present and future pension costs of federal employees is to get a full accounting of federal workers' compensation costs. Failure to levy charges for these costs would significantly understate the federal government's total personnel costs.

Social Insurance Programs. Social Security and Medicare, the largest trust funds in terms of receipts, are examples of this type of trust fund. Social insurance programs are unique and do not have counterparts in the private sector or at the state and local level. They essentially are redistributive programs. Despite paying taxes that build up a future entitlement to benefits, there is no direct relationship between taxes paid and benefits received.

Comparison with Private Trust Funds

Federal trust funds differ considerably from private trust funds. In the private sector, a trust is a legal document that allows one person or institution to hold title to assets owned by another individual or group of individuals. A private trust has a grantor who transfers assets to a trustee who manages the assets for the benefit of the beneficiaries of the trust. The assets in the trust are kept separate from other assets and the trustee conserves and uses the assets as directed by the trust document and related laws.

At the federal level, there is no formal, legal relationship between grantor and the trustee. The beneficiaries do not own the assets in the trust and despite the maintenance of separate accounting records, the monies in the trust fund are commingled with other government monies.

Probably the most significant difference between private trust funds and federal trust funds is the fact the latter lack the legal protections the former have. Congress can make changes to the terms and conditions associated with federal trust funds while the terms and conditions governing private trust funds cannot be changed easily without legal consequences.

Trust Funds and the Federal Deficit

In 1969, the federal government adopted a unified budget that consolidated receipts and outlays from both federal funds and trust funds. With the unified budget came a single surplus or deficit number, and this has led to a continuing debate on the role trust funds play in masking the true size of the deficit. To fully understand this debate, it first is necessary to understand how trust fund surpluses are handled.

Investment of Trust Fund Surpluses

When receipts earmarked for trust funds exceed spending from those trust funds, the surplus funds add to the balance in the fund. Since 1934, federal trust funds have amassed a cumulative surplus of more than US $1 trillion. From 1983 to 1994 alone, slightly less than US $900 billion have been added to this cumulative surplus.

The management of trust fund balances has remained virtually the same over the years. In most cases, law requires trust fund surpluses to be invested in U.S. Treasury securities. For example, the Civil Service Retirement and Disability Trust Fund was established in 1920 by the Civil Service Retirement Act. In that act, it was mandated that surpluses in the trust fund be invested in interest-bearing U.S. securities. That investment restriction remains in effect today.

When incoming receipts are earmarked for trust funds, the Treasury credits the appropriate funds with Treasury securities. These trust fund receipts may come from a variety of sources including social insurance taxes, certain excise taxes, various other charges, and intrabudget transfers. These intrabudget transfers basically constitute transfers from the federal funds ledger of the budget to the trust fund ledger. Examples of these transfers include payments by federal agencies into employee retirement funds, a transfer that covers approximately three-fourths of the cost of the Medicare Supplemental Insurance program, and interest earned on fund balances. Outlays from the trust fund are charged to the trust fund by subtracting Treasury securities that have been credited to the fund.

Trust fund balances exist on paper but do not represent cash holdings. The Treasury maintains accounting records that show treasury debt owed to the trust fund, similar to Treasury debt owed to the public. The federal government's gross debt—the amount of debt that is governed by the statutory debt ceiling—is calculated as the sum of trust fund securities and Treasury securities held by the public.

One significant difference between the two types of debt is the former does not involve private credit markets. Trust fund balances are invested in special, nonmarketable Treasury securities known as the government account series. This series uses a book-entry system; purchases are credited to accounts without physically issuing securities.

Federal Trust Funds' Impact on the Federal Budget Deficit

It has been argued that federal trust funds affect the federal budget deficit in at least two ways:

1. Limited investment options result in a reduced rate of return on trust fund balances.
2. Treatment of trust fund surpluses in the unified budget "masks" the true size of the federal budget deficit.

Limited Investment Options.   Restricting trust fund investments to U.S. Treasury securities results in less than competitive rates of return, according to some critics. Although it is conceivable that trust funds may be able to get higher rates of return in the private credit markets, therefore enhancing the overall deficit picture, the funds would also incur greater risk associated with changing interest rates and price fluctuations.

In fact, investment in private securities would not have a significant effect on the government's overall balance sheet. If the surplus funds in the trust funds were invested in the private credit markets and were not available to the Treasury, the Treasury would have to sell more bills, notes, and bonds on the open market to the public. In other words, gross federal debt would not change significantly; the composition of gross federal debt held by the public and federal agencies would change.

The Relationship Between Trust Fund Surpluses and the Deficit.   A frequent criticism of the unified federal budget, adopted in 1969, is that the deficit reported by this budgeting approach understates the true deficit problem. The inference is the federal funds deficit is the true measure of the federal government's deficit because it represents the amount current revenues are out of balance with current expenditures. Figure II shows that during the last ten years trust fund surpluses have offset federal funds deficits in amounts ranging from US $33 billion to US $123 billion.

In a sense, trust fund surpluses are being used by the Treasury to finance government programs and services other than those specifically designated by Congress. Eventually, the balances in the trust funds will be needed for the originally designated programs and services, resulting in trust fund outlays exceeding receipts. In turn, the Treasury securities credited to the trust fund accounts will

FIGURE II. TRUST AND FEDERAL FUND CONTRIBUTIONS TO THE FEDERAL BUDGET DEFICIT

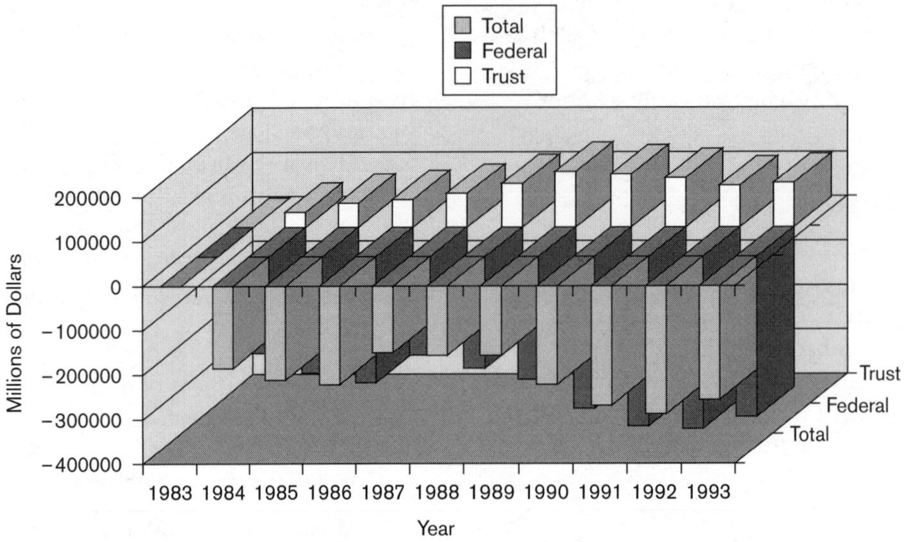

SOURCE: Executive Office of the President, Office of Management and Budget, 1994. *Budget of the United States Government, Analytical Perspectives, Fiscal year 1995.* Washington, DC: Government Printing Office.

be redeemed, forcing the federal government to increase its borrowing in the private capital markets or to raise taxes.

Another concern is that deficit pressures will result in a misuse of the trust funds. As pressure mounts to reduce the federal budget deficit, discretionary spending of trust fund receipts may be constrained. By slowing outlays from trust funds, surpluses will continue to grow, which, in turn, make the unified budget deficit look smaller.

While there is some truth to these arguments, trust funds also have a built-in mechanism that should work to mitigate the aforementioned misuse of trust fund surpluses. One of the things that distinguishes public trust funds from private trust funds is the lack of legal protections. If Congress wants to change the terms of the trust fund, it may without suffering legal ramifications. Therefore, mounting trust fund surpluses that lack justification on an actuarial basis will presumably result in pressure to either spend the accumulated funds on designated programs or reduce the revenue flow earmarked for that particular trust fund.

Other Public Trust Funds

The preceding description of federal trust funds underscores the idiosyncratic nature of public trust funds. There is a lack of consistent definition and an uneven treatment of trust funds at the federal level. One can only presume the same degree of inconsistency and variation of use exists at the state and local level in the United States and at the national and subnational levels throughout the world.

User-financed, employee retirement program, and special trust funds are fairly common at the state and local

level in the United States. Presumably, public trust funds are used in a similar fashion throughout the world.

C. KURT ZORN

BIBLIOGRAPHY

Cogan, John F., Timothy J. Muris, and Allen Schick, 1994. *The Budget Puzzle: Understanding Federal Spending.* Stanford, CA: Stanford University Press.

Executive Office of the President, Office of Management and Budget, 1994. *Budget of the United States Government, Analytical Perspectives, Fiscal Year 1995.* Washington, DC: Government Printing Office.

Havens, Harry S., 1988–89. "The Budget Dilemma: Searching for a New Consensus." *The GAO Journal* (Winter): 10–21; 24–28.

United States Congressional Budget Office, May 1993. *Federal Debt and Interest Costs.* Washington, DC: Congressional Budget Office.

United States General Accounting Office, 1988. *Budget Issues: Trust Funds and Their Relationship to the Federal Budget.* GAO/AFMD-88-55 (September). Washington, DC: Government Accounting Office.

———1993. *A Glossary of Terms Used in the Federal Budget Process: Exposure Draft.* GAO/AFMD-2.1.1. (January). Washington, DC: Government Accounting Office.

TURNOVER. The rate at which employees leave their work organization and are replaced. Employers are concerned with turnover because a high rate of turnover normally suggests some problem in the organization that causes people to want to leave. In addition, turnover affects the productivity of the organization as experienced skilled employees have to be replaced by those needing training to be able to complete the work of the organization. Constant recruiting of new employees diverts important resources from more productive activities. The training needed for new hires is also costly to the organization. In addition, employees who stay with the organization usually have to pick up the slack and morale suffers.

Pay often is cited as a major reason for high turnover. Thus, one of the justifications used for pay increases for public employees is that it will help retain good employees. Many of the pay-for-performance or merit pay experiments have been grounded in the expectation that the systems will help reduce turnover rates (see **pay-for-performance**). More broadly, high turnover rates may indicate an unhealthy organization and lack of commitment. Unemployment rates usually affect turnover rates with turnover rates declining as other opportunities decline. All capitalist nations face shifting turnover rates as economic conditions change.

Identification of the problems that lead to high turnover dictates the approach to correct the problem. Selection of the appropriate employees in the first place is important to matching the individual to the job. Once employed, a good orientation program with clear communication about the rewards will help reduce unreasonable expectations of employees and likely will improve job satisfaction. Training and development programs often address the problems and improve the organizational environment such that the organization becomes a more pleasant place to work.

Job enrichment programs and career advancement opportunities may reduce turnover if job satisfaction is the reason for high turnover. Employees tend to be more committed to the organization if they see a future with it and if they feel they are contributing to the work of the organization. Job enrichment usually provides for the employee performing a wider range of activities and having greater discretion. Through job enrichment, employees are likely to have a greater sense of how their work relates to the overall work of the organization.

N. JOSEPH CAYER

BIBLIOGRAPHY

Kessner, I. F., and D. R. Dalton, 1982. "Turnover Benefits: The Other Side of the Costs' Coin." *Personnel*, vol. 59 (September-October): 69–76.
U.S. Office of Personnel Management, 1989. "Federal Employee Turnover Study." *Supplement Federal White-Collar Pay System.* Washington, DC: U.S. Office of Personnel Management.
Winn, R., 1984. "A Comparison of Internal and External Factors Affecting Voluntary Turnover." *Review of Public Personnel Administration*, vol. 5 (Fall): 68–75.

TWIN-HEADED EXECUTIVE IN FRANCE.
The sharing of decisionmaking powers between the president and the prime minister in the French executive.

Executive Power in the Fifth Republic

The current French political regime, the Fifth Republic, was established in 1958, following the collapse of its predecessor, the Fourth Republic (1946–1958). In an attempt to counter the central weakness of the previous regime, the constitution of the Fifth Republic created a strong executive and a weak legislature. Within the executive, a constitutional dyarchy was installed. Powers were shared between the president of the republic and the prime minister, so creating a twin-headed, or bicephalous, executive. Immediately, though, the system was presidentialized and, for much of the period since 1958, the president has been the dominant force within the executive. However, this situation has endured only for so long as the president has been supported by a loyal parliamentary majority. When the majority has opposed the president, then prime ministerial leadership has occurred. This is known as "cohabitation." For these reasons, the Fifth Republic is characterized by an executive dyarchy whereby leadership responsibilities may shift from a directly elected president to a prime minister who is responsible to Parliament. As such, the Fifth Republic is itself a unique case among a small, but growing set of so-called semipresidential regimes.

A Constitutional Dyarchy
The 1958 Constitution gives considerable powers to both the president and the prime minister. For example, in terms of policymaking responsibilities, the Constitution seems to encourage a system of limited prime ministerial government. Article 20 states that the government decides and directs the policy of the nation, that it has the administration and the armed forces at its disposal, and that it is accountable to the lower house of the legislature, the national assembly. Article 21 states that the prime minister is in general charge of the government's work and is personally responsible for national defense and the implementation of laws. Article 8 states that the prime minister has the right to propose the names of government ministers to the president for approval. So, the prime minister is placed at the head of a government, the members of which he or she has chosen and which is collectively responsible for the day-to-day realization and implementation of public policy. At the same time, the president, who serves for seven years and who may not be dismissed from office, except for the crime of high treason (Article 68), also has certain policymaking powers. In times of national emergency, the president may issue decrees that have the force of law (Article 16). In normal times, the president is given particular responsibility for negotiating and ratifying international treaties (Article 52). At all times, the president is charged with seeing that the Constitution is respected, for ensuring, by his arbitration, the regular functioning of public authorities and the continuity of the state and for guaranteeing national independence and territorial integrity (Article 5).

TABLE I. PRESIDENTS AND PRIME MINISTERS IN THE FIFTH FRENCH REPUBLIC

President	Prime Minister
Charles de Gaulle (1959–1969)	Michel Debré (1959–1962)
	Georges Pompidou (1962–1968)
	Maurice Couve de Murville (1968–1969)
Georges Pompidou (1969–1974)	Jacques Chaban-Delmas (1969–1972)
	Pierre Messmer (1972–1974)
Valéry Giscard d'Estaing (1974–1981)	Jacques Chirac (1974–1976)
	Raymond Barre (1976–1981)
François Mitterrand (1981–1995)	Pierre Mauroy (1981–1984)
	Laurent Fabius (1984–1986)
	Jacques Chirac (1986–1988)
	Michel Rocard (1988–1991)
	Edith Cresson (1991–1992)
	Pierre Bérégovoy (1992–1993)
	Edouard Balladur (1993–1995)
Jacques Chirac (1995–)	Alain Juppé (1995–1997)
	Lionel Jospin (1997– . . .)

In terms of other responsibilities, the 1958 Constitution gives further powers to both the president and the prime minister. On the one hand, the president is responsible for appointing (but not dismissing) the prime minister (Article 8), for chairing meetings of government members in the council of ministers (Article 9), for heading the armed forces (Article 15), for accrediting French ambassadors abroad (Article 14), and for naming three of the nine members (including the president) of the constitutional council, the French equivalent of the U.S. Supreme Court (Article 56). In addition, the president has the right of pardon (Article 17) and the power to dissolve the national assembly, although not more than once a year (Article 12). On the other hand, the prime minister has the right to issue decrees (Article 21) in the areas in which Parliament is not permitted to legislate (Article 34), to request an extraordinary session of parliament (Article 29), to initiate legislation (Article 39), to accelerate the legislative process (Article 45), and to call for a vote of confidence in the government (Article 49). Finally, both the president and the prime minister have the right to make certain civil and military appointments (Articles 13 and 21), to submit a bill to the constitutional council for approval (Article 61), and to propose constitutional amendments (Article 89).

For one observer at least, the result of this constitutional division of labor is such that "the central question of any constitution—who rules?—is fudged" (Wright 1989, p. 12). The prime minister is charged with guiding and coordinating all matters that concern the immediate governance of the country. The president is given the general task of overseeing and protecting the long-term interests of the regime. Both are required to perform key leadership functions. In 1958, the textual ambiguities of the Constitution made it unclear as to whether a form of presidential or prime ministerial government would emerge in the new republic or whether a mixed system of government would prevail (Hoffman 1959). Soon, however, the situation was clarified. Within a short period of time, power within the twin-headed executive was skewed unequivocally toward the president. The Fifth Republic's political system underwent a process of presidentialization (Suleiman 1980).

The Presidentialization of the System

In January 1959, Charles de Gaulle (1890–1970) assumed office as the first president of the new republic. De Gaulle was a towering figure. After the Nazi occupation of France in 1940, he led the French resistance forces in exile. Following the liberation of the country, he headed a provisional government (1944–1946), which introduced many key reforms. Throughout the Fourth Republic, he opposed the regime and was untainted by its failure. As president of the Fifth Republic from 1959–1969, de Gaulle utilized the authority that he derived from his record to exercise a form of personal leadership (Hoffman and Hoffman 1968). From 1959 to 1962, he confined himself largely to foreign and defense policymaking and to the resolution of the problem that had brought down the Fourth Republic, the war in Algeria. After 1962 and the granting of Algerian independence, he also intervened in domestic policymaking. He was able to appoint loyal prime ministers who were willing to play a subordinate role. He was closely associated with all major policy decisions. In so doing, de Gaulle grafted *de facto* presidential powers onto the *de jure* ambiguities of the constitutional dyarchy. He set a precedent for presidential leadership, which his successors were expected to emulate and by which their performance was judged.

During de Gaulle's incumbency, a reform was passed that institutionalized the tendency toward presidential leadership and that formally established the semipresidential character of the Fifth Republic (see below). This reform was the November 1962 constitutional law. In the original text of the 1958 Constitution, the president was indirectly elected by an electoral college, whose members consisted mainly of local government representatives (Articles 6 and 7). Following a referendum in October 1962, these articles were amended so that, henceforth, the president would be directly elected by universal suffrage. Whereas prior to this reform the Presidency lacked legitimacy, afterward there was a direct link with the people. The Presidency gained a popular and political authority. Beginning with the first election under the new procedure in 1965, presidential elections became the focus of political activity in the system. Since then, they have provided the main opportunity for successful candidates to set the country's policy agenda, such as with François Mitterrand's "110 Proposals for Government" in 1981. They have also created a climate of expectations, upon which newly elected presidents have capitalized so as to exert their influence over the decision-making process. They have personalized the political system and provided presidents with a key leadership resource.

Nevertheless, whatever the significance of the precedent set by de Gaulle and the November 1962 constitutional law, the factor that has guaranteed presidential leadership in the Fifth Republic has been the presence of a supportive parliamentary majority in the national assembly (Duverger 1978). On the occasions when the majority has been favorable, presidents have been able to appoint loyal prime ministers, safe in the knowledge that they will not be dismissed from office. In return for their appointment, prime ministers have submitted themselves to the unwritten agreement that they will only propose the legislation that the president wants them to propose. In this way, when the majority has been supportive, prime ministers have served as the conduit between the process of presidential agenda setting and its legislative realization. The active support of prime ministers for presidents has meant that the letter of the Constitution has not been violated. Policymaking has occurred in the prime minister's name, even if its inspiration has been presidential. This has meant that the Fifth Republic has operated more along the lines of a monocratic presidential system then a presidential–prime ministerial dyarchy. Indeed, in a famous press conference in January 1964, de Gaulle confirmed that this was his vision of executive leadership in the Fifth Republic. He said: "One could not accept that a dyarchy existed at the top. But, anyway, this is not the case. The president is obviously alone in holding and delegating state authority."

This is not to say, though, that, even when the majority has supported the president, prime ministers have been insignificant political actors (Elgie and Machin 1991). On the contrary, they have been indispensable to the smooth functioning of the system. Their primary function has been to manage the business of government. The prime minister is responsible for the essential administrative services of the government. These include the general secretariat of the government, which provides administrative assistance to the government collectively, the general secretariat of national defense, which prepares defense policy meetings, and the general secretariat of the interministerial committee on European economic cooperation, which coordinates the European Union dimension of government policy. Responsibility for these services means that the prime minister is central to the governmental stages of the policy process. The prime minister is also responsible for managing the government's relations with Parliament. It is the prime minister who, if necessary, wheels and deals with parliamentarians. In this way, the prime minister is also central to the parliamentary stages of the policy process. The significance of these functions means that the only prime ministers who have sunk without trace have been the self-effacing ones, such as Maurice Couve de Murville and Pierre Messmer, or the inept ones, such as Edith Cresson. Other prime ministers, such as Michel Debré, Georges Pompidou, Jacques Chaban-Delmas, Jacques Chirac, and Michel Rocard, have been major political figures in their own right. Indeed, the ambition of some of these prime ministers has brought them into conflict with the president. Ultimately, however, it is a conflict that they are bound to lose. The presidentialization of the Fifth Republic has meant that whatever the importance of their role, prime ministers have been politically subordinate to presidents. The only exception to this rule has occurred during periods of "cohabitation."

Cohabitation

In 1986 and then again in 1993 and in 1997, the legislative election returned a majority to the national assembly which was openly hostile to the president, so ushering in a period of political cohabitation. Cohabitation is the situation where a president from one political family holds office at the same time as a prime minister from an opposing one. During cohabitation, the conditions for presidential leadership are absent. The Presidency is denuded of a large part of its popular authority, being no longer supported by a parliamentary majority and being unable to appoint a loyal prime minister or to set the legislative agenda. By contrast, the conditions for prime ministerial leadership are created. The prime minister benefits from a considerable degree of popular legitimacy and is in a position to lead the newly elected majority and to assume responsibility for realizing its manifesto proposals. In short, during cohabitation, the letter of Articles 20 and 21 of the 1958 Constitution is applied. The prime minister is responsible for policymaking and not the president.

From March 1986 to May 1988, a socialist president, Mitterrand, was forced to cohabit with a right-wing national assembly majority and with a gaullist prime minister, Chirac, who was drawn from this majority. Mitterrand again faced this situation after the March 1993 election, when another right-wing majority was returned and when another gaullist, Edouard Balladur, was appointed as prime minister. On both occasions, there was prime ministerial leadership. With the support of a parliamentary majority, both Chirac and Balladur were able to control the policy process. During the first period of cohabitation, Chirac was responsible for taking key policy decisions (Elgie 1993). For example, he decided which of the state-controlled television channels should be privatized, and he oversaw the budgetary policymaking process. During the second period, Balladur played a similar role. He was instrumental in determining France's position during the General Agreement on Tariffs and Trade (GATT) negotiations, and he also decided the manner in which the July 1993 constitutional amendment, limiting the right of political asylum, was adopted.

During cohabitation, the president's policymaking role is greatly reduced. From 1986 to 1988, Mitterrand was unable to alter the course of domestic policy. He did state his opposition to the government's privatization program, for example, but he was unable to prevent its application. Only in the realm of foreign and defense policymaking did he maintain an influence. This is consistent with the wording of Articles 5, 14, 15, and 52 (see earlier). For example, he was insistent that France's short-range nuclear arms were not "tactical," battlefield weapons, but part of a wider, "strategic" whole (Howorth 1993, p. 158). After 1993, Mitterrand's position was weaker than it had been during the first period of cohabitation. The right's victory in 1993 was much greater than in 1986, and the president's room for maneuver was reduced accordingly. He was also weakened by age (he was 76 in 1993) and illness. Consequently, even in foreign and defense policymaking, he was less influential than before. For example, Balladur assumed responsibility for sending French troops to manage the security and humanitarian problem in Rwanda. In sum, during cohabitation, the president is not a cipher. The president can remain in office and criticize, obstruct, and, in some areas, influence government policy. However, the president loses the ability to set the strategic orientation of the government and to take the most important policy decisions.

In 1997 right-wing President Chirac was forced into co-habitation with a socialist prime minister, Lionel Jospin.

France: A Semipresidential Regime

Since the constitutional law of November 1962, the Fifth Republic may be classed as a semipresidential regime (Duverger 1980). This is a regime where a directly elected president who enjoys certain powers and who is not responsible to the legislature coexists with a prime minister who also enjoys certain powers and who is responsible to the legislature. Semipresidentialism represents a hybrid form of government composed of the essential characteristic of both presidential and parliamentary regimes. There is a small set of established semipresidential regimes, which comprises Austria, Finland, France, Iceland, the Republic of Ireland, and Portugal, as well as a larger set of similar, newly formed regimes, which includes Poland, Sri Lanka, and Ukraine. In the established semipresidential regimes at least, there is no consistent distribution of power between the two elements of the executive. In Austria, Iceland, and the Republic of Ireland, presidents have been figureheads, and heads of government have been consistently responsible for policymaking. In Finland and Portugal, the powers of the two institutions have been more evenly balanced. In France, as has been shown, there has been a general tendency toward presidential government tempered by periods of prime ministerial leadership. In this way, France has been a unique case amongst a small set of regimes with a twin-headed executive.

ROBERT ELGIE

BIBLIOGRAPHY

Duverger, Maurice, 1978. *Echec au roi*. Paris: Albin Michel.
———, 1980. "A New Political System: Semi-presidential Government." *European Journal of Political Research*, vol. 8, 165–187.
Elgie, Robert, 1993. *The Role of the Prime Minister in France, 1981–91*. New York: St. Martin's .
Elgie, Robert, and Howard Machin, 1991. "France: The Limits to Prime-ministerial Government in a Semi-presidential System." In G. W. Jones, ed., *West European Prime Ministers*. Portland, OR: Frank Cass, 62–78.
Hoffman, Stanley H., 1959. "The French Constitution of 1958: The Final Text and Its Prospects." *American Political Science Review*, vol. 53, no. 2: 332–357.
Hoffman, Stanley H., and Inge Hoffman, 1968. "The Will to Grandeur: de Gaulle as Political Artist." *Daedalus*, vol. 97, no. 3: 829–887.
Howorth, Jolyon, 1993. "The President's Special Role in Foreign and Defence Policy." In Jack Hayward, ed., *De Gaulle to Mitterrand, Presidential Power in France*. London: Hurst, 150–189.
Suleiman, Ezra N., 1980. "Presidential Government in France." In Ezra N. Suleiman and Richard Rose, eds., *Presidents and Prime Ministers*. Washington, D.C.: American Enterprise Institute, 94–138.
Wright, Vincent, 1989. *The Government and Politics of France*. London: Unwin Hyman.

U

UNEMPLOYMENT INSURANCE.

A program that pays benefits to partially offset the loss of wages due to unemployment.

Background

At the height of the Great Depression, President Franklin D. Roosevelt's Committee on Economic Security recommended the establishment of two national social insurance systems. The first program would provide old-age benefits to retired workers and the second program would provide compensation for the unemployed. In 1935, the Social Security Act created both of these programs—the social security and unemployment insurance (UI) programs.

From its inception, the intent was to entice states to participate in UI so it would be a federal-state relationship. By 1937, all states had adopted unemployment insurance laws patterned after model legislation prepared by the Social Security Board. The board, whose formation had been recommended by the President's Committee on Economic Security, had the responsibility of assisting states in setting up their UI systems and monitoring changes in state UI systems.

Original Structure of the UI System

The Social Security Act of 1935 contained two titles that dealt with unemployment insurance—Title III, which provided for administrative grants, and Title IX, which provided for the financing of the system. The federal administrative grants, under Title III. were to assist in the proper administration of the federal UI law among the states and were at the discretion of the Social Security Board.

Under Title IX, employers were required to pay a federal unemployment insurance excise tax if they employed eight or more people for 20 or more weeks a year. The tax rate initially was set at 1 percent of total payroll in 1936, increasing to 2 percent in 1937 and 3 percent in 1938. Some kinds of employment were excluded from the tax, such as agricultural labor, domestic employees; individuals providing service for nonprofit organizations of a religious, charitable, scientific, literary, or educational nature; and individuals working for the federal, state, and local levels of government.

As an incentive to get states to levy their own UI excise taxes, employers making contributions to state unemployment compensation programs were eligible for credit up to 90 percent of the federal tax. The credit was contingent on the state UI law conforming to federal guidelines established by the Social Security Board.

A trust fund was created by the 1935 act (see **trustfund**). The Unemployment Trust Fund was to receive the UI excise taxes collected by the federal and state governments and to invest the funds in federal securities.

Objectives of Unemployment Insurance

The UI system was created with a number of objectives in mind. First and foremost, unemployment insurance was intended to alleviate the hardships that result from the loss of income during periods of unemployment. Unemployment insurance would provide cash to enable workers basically to maintain their living standard. Secondary objectives included allowing an unemployed worker time to locate new employment or regain old employment, providing the unemployed time to retrain for a new job and providing a degree of stabilization during difficult economic times.

Conceptual Issues

The UI system is structured to systematically accumulate funds during good economic times in order to provide benefits during periods of high unemployment. Therefore, the concepts of solvency and reserves are of utmost importance to the successful operation of a UI system.

Solvency

State unemployment insurance systems seek to balance benefit payments to recipients with contributions to the system. The traditional principle holds that the pool of reserves should be structured so it is able to finance unemployment benefits during a succession of economic cycles without going into the red. A system is considered insolvent when it lacks sufficient resources—accumulated reserves from prior periods plus employer contributions during the current period—to pay benefits earned during the period. Insolvency does not mean benefits go unpaid because the federal-state UI structure allows states to borrow from the federal unemployment trust fund to cover payments when insolvency occurs.

There are three primary approaches that can be used to maintain solvency in a state unemployment insurance system: countercyclical, replenishment, and balancing reserves. The three approaches differ in the requirements they place on reserve fund levels held in the state system and the effect they have on UI tax rate changes over time.

Countercyclical Finance. One of the stated objectives of the UI system is to provide a measure of countercyclical stabilization to counter swings in the business cycle. The system operates as an automatic stabilizer; as unemployment increases, tax contributions decline and benefit payments increase, providing a dampening effect on the decline of economic activity. In an expansion, the reverse occurs, constraining potential inflationary pressures.

In order to maximize the countercyclical potential of an unemployment insurance system, the tax rate schedule would rise when benefit payment requirements are low and fall when benefit payment requirements are high. However, this means an extraordinary fund reserve must be generated during prosperous times because revenue production is severely restricted during recessionary times.

Replenishment. A second fund solvency approach relies on a rapid replenishment of funds through increased employer contributions during periods when benefit payments are high. In general, UI taxes in a given year are set at a level sufficient to replace prior year benefit costs. The key to this UI system structure is the responsiveness and productive potential of the tax schedule, not the size of reserve fund balances. Solvency depends on the ability of the tax structure to ensure adequate reserves from year to year, not levels of accumulated reserves.

The replenishment approach is contrary to countercyclical fiscal policy because it typically requires high tax schedules during periods of substantial unemployment. The resultant tax burden may hamper the ability of the economy to recover.

Clearly, this approach does not promote tax rate stability. However, it does permit solvency in the face of small reserve balances. Therefore elements of the replenishment approach are unavoidable in most state UI system financing structures, at least to some extent.

Balancing Reserve Fund. The third fund solvency approach uses a reserve fund to balance benefit payments and contribution revenue in a manner that permits constant tax rates over an economic cycle. The balance accumulated during expansion is therefore higher than that required for replenishment, but lower than the balance required for countercyclical finance. The distinguishing characteristic of this approach is the intention that tax rates remain stable over the economic cycle; the other approaches do not presume such stability.

In practice, the balancing reserve fund solvency approach appears to be the predominant approach used by states. However, elements of the other two approaches are incorporated to some degree in various UI state systems.

Adequacy

An unemployment insurance reserve fund contributes to the solvency of the system by providing a pool of funds the system can draw from whenever benefit payments exceed contributions. Normally, the reserve fund will be drawn down in periods in which contributions fall below benefit payments and augmented in periods in which contributions exceed benefit payments.

At first glance, it seems higher reserves would be preferable to lower reserves because higher reserves provide greater protection against insolvency. However, this conclusion is wrong. Large UI fund reserves represent a diversion of capital away from productive uses in the private sec-

tor. Anything larger than an adequate reserve fund, one sufficiently large to protect against system insolvency under normal economic circumstances, can be quite costly in terms of forgone opportunities. Therefore, a sound reserve fund policy should attempt to ensure benefit payments do not exceed contributions received in addition to accumulated reserve balances during any specific period of time.

Overview of the Current Unemployment Insurance System

The UI system truly is a federal-state partnership. The federal government sets out guidelines for the state UI systems, leaving states a great degree of autonomy with regard to the specifics of carrying out their UI programs. States can determine their own eligibility requirements, level of benefits, and duration of benefits, and states can levy and collect their own taxes.

The Unemployment Trust Fund consists of 56 accounts. There are three federal accounts: one that provides for the administration of federal and state UI programs, one that handles loans to states with insolvent UI accounts (federal loan account), and one that furnishes 50 percent of the funding for an extended benefits program. These three accounts are financed through a federal tax on employer payrolls. In addition to the three federal accounts, each state has its own account, as do the District of Columbia, Puerto Rico, and the Virgin Islands. These 53 accounts finance regular UI benefits and the other 50 percent of the extended benefits program through a state UI tax on employers.

Benefits

In his book *Unemployment Insurance in the United States,* Saul Blaustein (1993) observed that in 1990 approximately 111 million jobs were covered by all state and federal UI programs, compared to the 34 million jobs covered in 1950 (p. 31). This 226-percent increase is more than twice the increase in employment during the same 40-year period. Much of this increase can be attributed to an expansion of coverage under UI programs.

Over the years, amendments have been made to federal law that have changed the coverage and scope of the federal-state system. One of the more significant changes occurred in 1956 when coverage was extended to firms with four or more employees. However, the effect of this change in the federal law was limited because many states had already extended their coverage to firms that size or smaller. Amendments in 1970 and 1976 increased coverage further. Coverage was extended to firms with one or more workers, employees of nonprofit organizations (with only employees of churches and religious organizations remaining uncovered), state and local employees (with minor exceptions), and employees of large agricultural employers (ten or more workers in at least 20 weeks of the year).

Another significant change in UI benefits occurred in 1970. Public Law 91–373 created an extended benefit program. Under this program, the duration of UI benefits was extended an additional 13 weeks past the 26 week maximum, under certain conditions. The extended benefits program is triggered when state unemployment rates exceed certain unemployment thresholds and is financed jointly by federal and state UI taxes.

Financing

The unemployment insurance tax structure is a dual system involving both the federal and state government. The federal tax may be regarded as the driving force because of the 90-percent credit allowed against federal UI tax liability for approved state UI systems. For example, at the inception of the UI program when the 3-percent federal payroll tax was instituted, the 90-percent credit meant the cost to an employer of paying a 2.7-percent state rate was zero. The 2.7-percent state tax simply represented federal tax that the employer would not have to pay. The remaining 0.3 percent of federal tax was used to administer the combined federal-state program.

The federal UI tax rate has increased over the years, but the 90-percent credit has remained in place. In 1993, the federal tax rate was 6.2 percent, and states could qualify for a credit up to 5.4 percent. The reason the maximum credit was only 5.4 percent is because 0.2 percent of the 6.2 percent federal rate is earmarked for the extended benefits program. The 0.2 percent are not covered by the credit.

Not surprisingly, as the federal tax rate has increased so have state tax rates. In 1948, 48 states had rates below 4 percent. In 1971, 24 states had rates below 4 percent while 3 states had rates of 5 percent and over. In 1983, only 3 states had rates below 4 percent and 30 states had rates 5 percent and over. In 1990, all states had tax rates equal to or exceeding 5.4 percent with 15 states setting rates at 8 percent or above.

The aforementioned tax rates are maximum rates. Employers with good experience ratings generally qualify for a lower tax rate. In other words, the tax rate paid by each employer is based in part on the firm's record with regard to layoffs. Employers with a poor experience rating (history of a high number of layoffs) usually pay a higher UI rate than firms with a better experience rating.

The base for UI taxation originally was the total payroll of a firm. In 1940, it was changed to a taxable wage base of US $3,000. The rationale for the change was to bring the tax base in line with that of the old-age insurance program–Social Security. Over the years, the taxable wage base has increased, to US $4,200 in 1972, to US $6,000 in 1978, and to US $7,000 in 1983. States, of course, have the ability to set their taxable wage bases higher than the federal standard. In 1992, 37 states had wage bases above the federal level.

Crisis in Funding

Originally, the UI system was created as a forward funding system. This means that tax rates and benefit levels were constructed so reserves accumulate during economic upswings sufficient to cover the increased unemployment benefits that occur during economic downswings. For the first three decades of the UI program, trust fund reserves were adequate to cover economic downturns. Despite the creation of the federal loan account in 1954, only three states chose this option in the period leading up to the 1970s.

Economic slowdowns in the 1970s, the stagflation of the late 1970s, and the deep recession that started in 1982 put a real strain on the UI system. These extended economic downturns forced a number of state UI funds into insolvency, compelling the states to borrow from the federal loan fund. Loans from the federal loan account increased from less than US $300 million during the 1950s and 1960s to US $5.6 billion during the 1970s and to US $24.2 billion in the 1980s. At the same time, the number of states that became insolvent and needed to borrow from the loan fund grew from a handful of states in the early 1970s to 21 states during the 1981–1982 recession.

In response to increased insolvency in state UI trust fund accounts, the federal government provided incentives to states to raise tax rates, to reduce benefits, and began to charge interest on loans from the federal loan account. Up to 1982 when interest charges were implemented, states had been able to borrow funds from the federal loan account interest free. The only restriction was the loans had to be repaid within a specified period of time or the state would suffer a reduction in the federal tax credit allowed for UI tax payments.

States also responded to the increased insolvency in the UI system. Between 1978 and 1990, 40 states either increased their tax rates or increased their taxable wage base or both. During the same period of time, 37 states reduced their benefits through a reduction in the maximum number of weeks benefits are available or by raising the minimum earnings requirement to qualify for UI benefits or by increasing their penalties for those who do not actively seek employment or who fail to accept suitable employment when available.

The European Experience

In 1989, 34 European countries had compulsory unemployment insurance. Not surprisingly, there are substantial differences between U.S. and Western European UI programs. Significant differences also exist among the various Western European programs. A brief overview of three countries' programs helps demonstrate these differences.

West Germany

West Germany relies on a three-tier system of income replacement. Unemployment insurance covers approximately 90 percent of wage and salary workers and is funded by mandatory contributions from employers and workers. Unemployment assistance is available for those who exhaust their UI benefits and for those who cannot qualify for the UI program. It is a means-tested program that is federally funded taking on characteristics of a redistributive income-maintenance program. The third part of Germany's income replacement system is public welfare. This is a program for the chronically unemployed, who need prolonged benefits, or for those who are nearing retirement age.

Great Britain

Great Britain has two major income replacement programs. The first is a flat-rate unemployment insurance benefit program that is part of the social security system. The system is financed through mandatory social insurance contributions by workers and employers.

Unemployment benefits account for about 10 percent of the disbursements from the National Insurance Fund with the remaining 90 percent going for old-age pensions, sickness and disability benefits, and payments for other social insurance programs. The second program is an extended benefits program called the Supplemental Benefit Program. This is a means-tested allowance with unlimited duration for those not working full-time and those whose total income falls below a designated amount. Along with the unemployed, the program supports elderly pensioners and single mothers.

Sweden

There are two parallel income maintenance programs in Sweden that cover different components of the labor force. Approximately 80 percent of the workforce is covered by 45 UI societies that are operated mainly by trade unions. The government regulates these societies, but they are voluntary. Funds come from worker contributions, but the government pays the lion's share of benefit costs, relying on a tax on employers' payrolls to help finance this expenditure. The second program is the cash assistance program that was introduced in 1974 to help pay daily unemployment allowances for a limited time period for those who were not members of the UI societies. Those targeted by the program are new entrants and reentrants into the workforce and those who have exhausted their other UI benefits.

C. KURT ZORN

BIBLIOGRAPHY

Blaustein, Saul J., 1993. *Unemployment Insurance in the United States*. Kalamazoo, MI: W. E. Upjohn Institute for Employment Research.

Reubens, Beatrice, 1990. "Unemployment Insurance in Western Europe: Responses to High Unemployment, 1973–1983." In W. Lee Hansen and James F. Byers, eds., *Unemployment Insurance*. Madison: University of Wisconsin Press, 173–207.

United States Department of Labor, Employment and Training Administration, Unemployment Insurance Service, assorted years. *Comparison of State Unemployment Insurance Laws*. Washington, DC: Department of Labor.

United States General Accounting Office, 1990. *Unemployment Insurance: Trust Fund Reserves Inadequate to Meet Recession Needs*. GAO/HRD-90-124 (May). Washington, DC: Government Accounting Office.

———, 1993. *Unemployment Insurance: Program's Ability to Meet Objectives Jeopardized*. GAO/HRD-93-107 (September) Washington, DC: Government Accounting Office.

Vroman, Wayne, 1990. *Unemployment Insurance Trust Fund Adequacy in the 1990s*. Kalamazoo, MI: W. E. Upjohn Institute for Employment Research.

UNFAIR LABOR PRACTICE. Conduct on the part of either management or the union that violates provisions of national or state labor relations statutes. Most state laws are modeled on the National Labor Relations Act. Typical unfair labor practices include the following:

For employers:

- interfering with, restraining, or coercing employees in the exercise of their rights granted under statute;
- dominating, interfering, or assisting in the formation or administration of an employee organization;
- encouraging or discouraging membership in any labor organization through discrimination in hiring, tenure, or other terms or conditions of employment;
- discharging or discriminating against an employee because he or she has filed charges or given testimony under the statute, or because he or she has joined an employee organization;
- refusing to meet and bargain in good faith with the recognized employee organization;
- denying rights of exclusive representation to the duly designated bargaining agent;
- refusing or avoiding statutory impasse procedures;
- violating the terms of a collective bargaining contract.

For employee organizations:

- interfering with, restraining, or coercing employees in the exercise of their rights granted under statute;
- interfering with, restraining, or coercing an employer with respect to protecting the exercise of employee rights under statute or selecting a bargaining agent;
- refusing to meet or bargain in good faith;
- refusing or avoiding statutory impasse procedures;
- engaging in or instigating a strike;
- hindering or interfering with an employee's work performance or productivity.

Administrative responsibility for determining whether or not unfair labor practices have occurred is assigned to the National Labor Relations Board (NLRB) in the private sector. Charges are heard first in 1 of the 33 regional offices of the NLRB. Judicial-type proceedings include rules of evidence and other requirements. State labor relations boards and the Federal Labor Relations Authority perform this function for the public sector. A written complaint is filed by the plaintiff and must normally be responded to within seven days. If the alleged unfair labor practice is found to have taken place, the administrative agency generally has authority to issue a cease-and-desist order against the accused and to reinstate any unjustly dismissed employees, with back pay. Compliance officers are normally responsible for ensuring that the parties respond to the administrative agency's order.

Cases may take up to two or three years to process, depending on the jurisdiction and case backlog. Appeals through the federal or state legal systems can further delay the process. In the private sector, employers have been accused and found guilty of deliberately committing unfair labor practices to discourage unionization, particularly in the southern textile industry. Violators must pay fines for contempt of NLRB orders, but some firms have accepted this as a cost of doing business without unions.

In some instances, parties to an unfair labor practice charge forgo official hearings and negotiate a voluntary settlement. Typically, the administrative agency will honor such an agreement and attempt to see that it is enforced.

RICHARD C. KEARNEY

UNIFIED BUDGET.

The budget that includes all fiscal activities of the government.

The "unified budget" is a concept from the U.S. federal government that was coined by the President's Commission on Budget Concepts. President Lyndon B. Johnson created the Commission in 1967 and appointed fiscal experts from the executive and legislative branches and from academia and business. The commission was asked to develop recommendations for improving budget presentation, which Johnson judged desirable because of widespread criticism of how his administration had manipulated budget concepts to show smaller deficits than were actually being incurred.

The commission's most important recommendation was that the government's fiscal activities be reported comprehensively in a unified budget format. This was done beginning in fiscal year 1969–1970. Before 1969, the budget was often presented in either the "administrative budget" or "consolidated cash" format. The scope of the administrative budget was limited to appropriated accounts. The scope of the consolidated cash budget was broader, including most trust funds. Having two alternative formats gave the president an opportunity to minimize the number that

was reported to the public as "the deficit." For example, when the cash flow of the trust funds was projected to be negative for the budget year, using the administrative budget format—which excluded the trust funds—reduced the reported deficit.

The commission supported the unified budget format with a sophisticated argument. It recognized that budgets are intended to serve multiple purposes, including signaling cash and debt management needs, allocating resources to different purposes, and embodying fiscal policy. It believed that different accounting practices were necessary for these alternative purposes but also recognized that a multiplicity of budget concepts could confuse the public. The commission proposed that this dilemma be resolved by adopting complementary budget concepts *within* the comprehensive structure provided by the unified budget format. Unfortunately, this argument never gained a full popular understanding—almost all members of the public and the media continue to overemphasize the cash-flow deficit figure.

Although the unified budget format was certainly much more comprehensive than its predecessor, it retained some exclusions. The most important was the Federal Reserve System. The commission observed that most of the Federal Reserve's transactions were for the conduct of monetary policy and that incorporating the Federal Reserve into the primary fiscal policy document would be analytically confusing. Doing so would also threaten the operational independence of the Federal Reserve, which the commission believed was politically undesirable. Since 1969, some other exclusions were made from the unified budget for political reasons (see **off-budget**). One deserves mention here, however: Social Security. Since the Social Security Act Amendments of 1983, Social Security revenues have exceeded outlays, and the resulting surpluses have been converted into investments in Treasury bonds. Social Security was legally removed from the unified budget by the 1985 Balanced Budget Act (informally known as the "Gramm-Rudman-Hollings Act") because of concerns that these surpluses could be raided. In practice, however, the format used by budget agencies has preserved the unified budget in fact if not in name. Summary tables typically show the "total budget," a format indistinguishable from the unified budget, and then honor the "off-budget" status of Social Security by adding memoranda lines that separate the total budget into "on-budget" and "off-budget" components.

The Unified Budget, National Income Accounting, and Gross Domestic Product Budgeting

One argument made by the Commission on Budget Concepts was that the deficit, a cash-flow measure, provided a rough guide to the course of fiscal policy. In practice, macroeconomists rely not on the budget figures to understand the federal sector of the economy, but instead on the National Income and Product Accounts, a data series compiled by the Commerce Department's Bureau of Economic Analysis. The accounting conventions used to prepare this data series differ somewhat from the unified budget, particularly with regard to the treatment of loans and voluntary transactions. Presidential and congressional budget projections usually recast budget totals into the National Income and Product Accounts framework for macroeconomic analyses.

Herbert Stein (1989), a former chairman of the Council of Economic Advisors, has argued that the unified budget measure also fails to meet the goal of rationally allocating resources to different purposes. Although the unified budget format comprehensively covers the financial transactions of the federal government, it generally ignores the financial transactions of the private sector. This has led some policymakers to ignore interdependencies between the two sectors. One of many areas that could be cited is health, where policymakers have sought to reduce costs, increase access, and improve quality. Since the unified budget counts only federal costs, one way the federal government has "reduced costs" is by shifting these costs to the private sector. Stein suggests that a solution to this kind of problem is to deemphasize the focus on the unified budget, instead broadening policymakers' perspectives so that they "budget the economy."

The Practices of U.S. State and Local Governments and Other Countries

The unified budget format is not generally used by the state and local governments of the United States. In contrast, most states use a fund structure that distinguishes between general, special, proprietary (businesslike), and fiduciary funds. Each fund type uses accounting principles that are specific to that type. For example, proprietary funds often use depreciation accounting, while general funds do not.

The focus of the operating budget process is on the operating funds, and the focus of the capital budget process is on selected special funds, especially those that finance roads and other major public works. This separation of budget processes is generally intended to place special emphasis on major investments, which are largely funded from the proceeds of borrowing. Since states and localities must compete in credit markets for access to financial capital, these governments use capital budgeting to try to avoid serious mistakes that could impair bond ratings and increase the long-run cost of borrowing. Operating and capital budgets are often integrated to a degree by analyses of the life-cycle operating costs of capital investments. In addition, many states and localities reduce debt service costs by first financing some capital projects from general revenues, a practice known as "pay-as-you-go" financing.

These practices to a degree "reunify" the formally separate operating and capital budgets. And while the differentiated fund format does deemphasize budgetary consideration of the proprietary and fiduciary funds, the Government Accounting Standards Board requires states and localities to report on these funds in conjunction with the operating and capital budgets in Comprehensive Annual Financial Reports, or "CAFRs."

Most countries develop a comprehensive measure of the government's financial transactions that is roughly comparable to the unified budget deficit–the "public sector borrowing requirement." In general, however, the budget formats used in most other developed countries are also less comprehensive. Unfortunately, there is no central information source on the actual budget structures of countries that would allow a reliable comparison of these structures. Although comparative financial databases are constructed by the United Nations, the Organization for Economic Cooperation and Development, the World Bank, and the International Monetary Fund, these databases typically convert the actual budget structural practices of countries into a "normalized" format. For example, federal, state, and local government expenditures are usually aggregated into a national account, even for nations with federal systems in which the state and local governments have sovereignty over their funds. This practice, while useful for making comparisons of different countries' financial performance, does not allow comparisons of the actual processes that they use. This is an area where there is a great need for further research.

ROY T. MEYERS

BIBLIOGRAPHY

International Monetary Fund, 1986. *A Manual on Government Finance Statistics.* Washington, DC: IMF.
Organization for Economic Cooperation and Development, 1987. *The Control and Management of Government Expenditure.* Paris: OECD.
President's Commission on Budget Concepts, 1967. *Report of the President's Commission on Budget Concepts* (October), 1–35.
Stein, Herbert, 1989. *Governing the $5 Trillion Economy.* New York: Oxford University Press.

UNION. An organization of workers formed to pursue mutual interest in wages, benefits, and working conditions (see **labor organization**). Their origins may be traced in the United States to organizations of skilled craftsmen, including shoemakers, printers, cordwainers, and cabinet makers, who began to join together during the colonial period (circa 1648–1787) to improve their economic and working conditions. These workers were organized at a local level on the basis of their craft–not across crafts or across geographical areas. During the early 1800s, there were efforts to organize across trades and at national and even international levels, but without much success. A major stumbling block to effective organizing was the absence of a facultative legal environment. Unions were often charged in the courts with being a criminal conspiracy against free trade.

The rise of unions awaited the Industrial Revolution. In Europe, labor began concentrating in mills and workshops in the mid-nineteenth century along the same sort of craft dimensions as developed some years afterward in the United States. In Great Britain, a "new model unionism" arose in the factories and railways as such workers sought collective bargaining status. The Amalgamated Society of Engineers in 1851 became the largest new model union with 12,000 members. An 1859 dispute with construction workers led to the creation of the London Trades Council, which coordinated union action in that city, and similar organizations were established in other cities, with strong internal organization including paid administrators. In 1868, a National Trades Union Congress arose to coordinate union activities in England. In France, Proudhonism sought to promote labor as the basis of all social activity. After the Revolution of 1848, worker organizations were created as cooperatives, mutual aid societies, and educational societies in France, eventually to evolve into trade unions.

By the 1860s, there were attempts at international organization of workers in Europe along the lines drawn originally by Karl Marx (1848) in *The Communist Manifesto* ("Workers of the world unite!"). A wide variety of union-style organizations were evident in Europe, including Catholic, Marxist, and anarchist, but Marxism was a dominant force among the unionists across the Continent from the 1870s into the twentieth century. Marx's ideal egalitarian society placed industrial workers at the core of its theory. In the 1870s and 1880s, Marxists helped form workers' parties to compete in the political arena.

Gradually, the labor movement in Europe and the United Kingdom transcended craft lines and spread to large factory enterprises. It was not a peaceful process, and it was punctuated by waves of strikes, some of them violent. Some governments, for example those in Germany and Russia, attempted to suppress the labor challenge presented by socialists and anarchists. Significant differences in the ideologies and membership of Marxists and anarchists did not help the cause of organized labor.

In the United States, mass production of goods following the Civil War laid the groundwork for the flowering of unions in the twentieth century. The threats of impersonalization of labor, job insecurity, and immigration of cheap labor created an unsettled workforce, especially in the cities. Unions found the ground quite fertile and began flowering across the country. This included the public sector, as government employees in skilled occupations sought the ten-hour day and eventually the eight-hour day. The ideological battles of Europe did not play nearly so great a role in the development of unions in the United States, although many different philosophies competed for the allegiance of workers during the late 1800s and early 1900s.

The Industrial Workers of the World (Wobblies) shared the European penchant for social and political action by labor, rejecting capitalism outright and aiming to use the general strike (see **strike**) to bring the system to its knees. The Wobblies did engage in several large strikes in the United States and Europe during World War I, but they were severely repressed by the national government in the United States, and many of its leaders were jailed.

In the United States, the ethos of business unionism, as originally espoused by Samuel Gompers, soon dominated the labor movement. Economic objectives and improvements in working conditions were viewed as more important than social and political change. The Marxist and anarchist perspectives never gained widespread credence.

The first major effort by a union to capture the new and rapidly growing pool of factory workers was the Knights of Labor. Established in 1869 as a craft union for custom tailors in Philadelphia, the Knights gradually folded other crafts into its tent, evolving by 1878 into the first national union in the United States. The Knights also began adding factory workers to its rolls, which numbered 700,000 members by 1886. However, its membership was divisive and its leadership weak, and a series of strikes resulted in serious setbacks and the near extinction of the organization by the turn of the century.

The American Federation of Labor (AFL) (see **AFL-CIO**), which was created in 1881 as a union of craft workers, picked up the craft union pieces of the Knights of Labor and elected Samuel Gompers the first national president. Gompers' leadership made the AFL into a powerful force within the context of pragmatic economic objectives. The union survived government and corporate repression, the death of Gompers, years of yellow-dog contracts, court injunctions, and the Great Depression. The AFL did not, however, organize nonskilled factory workers until it experienced a secession movement led by John L. Lewis of the United Mine Workers, who left the AFL to form the Congress of Industrial Organizations (CIO). The CIO successfully organized factory workers, especially in the auto and steel industries. Eventually, in 1955, after years of competition, the AFL and CIO merged into "the united house of labor." In this year, one in three of the nation's nonagricultural workers was a union member. It was the pinnacle of unionization in the private sector. By 1990, private sector union membership had fallen to about 12 percent of nonagricultural employment.

Unions in the private sector are no longer primarily blue-collar organizations. As the nation experienced a shift toward white-collar employment and service industries, unions began organizing these workers in growing numbers. Relatedly, traditionally private-sector unions have moved to organize public-sector employees in a variety of functions, often competing with all-public unions such as the American Federation of State, County, and Municipal Employees.

Unions in government experienced little sustained success in the United States during the nineteenth century. Organizing occurred in the naval shipyards and later among postal workers in federal employment, but unions were discouraged by the government. A "gag order" issued by President Theodore Roosevelt in 1902 forbade postal workers from lobbying activities, union-busting tactics also countered organizing activity. But the postal unions, led by the AFL and the national Federation of Post Office Clerks, won congressional passage of the Lloyd-LaFollette Act of 1912, guaranteeing federal employees the First Amendment right to organize and petition Congress for a redress of grievances.

Organizing efforts spread to most other federal government functions during the early 1900s. In 1917, the National Federation of Federal Employees formed a broad-based union to cover all federal civilian workers except postal workers and those previously organized by AFL affiliates. Two other general-purpose unions soon followed: the American Federation of Government Employees and the National Association of Government Employees.

In the state and local sectors organizing activity began with a craft orientation, especially with teachers, firefighters, and police officers. Early on, such organizations as the National Education Association (established 1870) were primarily intended to advance the interests of teachers and school administrators through nonbargaining and nonconfrontational activities, but a steady accumulation of grievances drove them into a more aggressive posture. Similarly, early firefighter and police organizations served as mutual aid societies. In 1918, the AFL chartered the International Association of Firefighters and in 1919 certified 37 local police organizations. Growing employee militancy resulted in strikes in all three functions, but one in particular—the Boston police strike of 1919—took on national proportions. It prompted intervention by Massachusetts Governor Calvin Coolidge and the National Guard after several days of looting and mob rule and, by the time it was resolved, had set back the union movement in police and other state and local functions.

The largest state and local government union today, the American Federation of State, County, and Municipal Employees (AFSCME) was born in 1932 as the Wisconsin State Employees Association. It merged with state and local organizations of the American Federation of Government Employees and commenced a slow period of growth in a general environment of employer hostility.

Public-employee unionization began spreading rapidly during the 1960s at all levels of government. The reasons were several, including the general growth of government,

the favorable experience of unions in the private sector, changes in the legal environment favorable to organizing, and the general climate of social change and turmoil that characterized the decade of the 1960s. The single most important event was President John F. Kennedy's Executive Order 10988 of 1962, which guaranteed unionization and collective bargaining rights for federal employees. The spillover effects of E.O. 10988 in state and local government were significant in legitimizing public-employee unionization and collective bargaining.

Between 1964 and 1968, federal-employee unionization increased to almost one-half the civilian workforce, then stabilized. Membership then began a slow erosion in 1976, which continues today. Problems federal unions confront are substantial, including the absence of union security provisions (see **union security provision**) and the inability to negotiate over pay and benefits. The free rider problem is substantial in the absence of requirements for nonmembers, whom the unions must represent as members of the bargaining unit, to pay union dues or their equivalent.

Only about one-third of federal civilian employees belong to a union today, even though a much higher proportion are represented by a union in collective bargaining and grievance procedures. The largest nonpostal federal unions are the American Federation of Government Employees, the National Federation of Federal Employees, the National Treasury Employees Union, the National Association of Government Employees, and the Metal Trades Council. For postal workers, the largest unions are the National Association of Letter Carriers, the American Postal Workers Union, the National Rural Letter Carriers Association, and the National Alliance of Postal and Federal Employees.

Prospects for future federal-employee growth is dim without significant revision of the relevant provisions of the Civil Service Reform Act of 1978 to permit the unions to bargain over pay and benefits and to compel the payment of dues by all members of the bargaining units.

About 44 percent of all state and local employees belong to unions today. Membership figures vary by type of government and by function. Townships report the highest percentage of organized employees (61.4 percent), followed by school districts, municipalities, states, counties, and special districts. By function, firefighters have the highest membership levels (64.9 percent), followed by teachers, police, sanitation, welfare, highways, and hospitals. Membership figures are highest in states with comprehensive collective bargaining legislation (see **labor law**) and permissive legal settings, such as Connecticut, Massachusetts, New York, and Michigan, and lowest in states that do not provide for collective bargaining, including North and South Carolina and Virginia. There are regional variations to public-sector union membership. Figures are highest in the industrial Northeast and Midwest and lowest in the southern and southwestern states.

Public-sector unions may be all-public, organizing only government workers, or mixed, organizing both public- and private-sector employees. AFSCME is essentially an all-public union, as is the International Association of Fire Fighters. Examples of mixed unions are the Service Employees International Union and the International Brotherhood of Teamsters. The largest individual unions in state and local government are the National Education Association (2 million), AFSCME (1.1 million), the American Federation of Teachers (780,000), the Service Employees International Union (475,000), the Fraternal Order of Police (230,000), and the International Association of Fire Fighters (142,000).

Union activities in government involve collective bargaining in jurisdictions where they enjoy bargaining rights, as well as lobbying and electoral activities. They provide membership services such as insurance plans, buying services, and social opportunities. National unions, such as AFSCME, are organized internally through a national office with a decentralized structure consisting of district councils and locals. The highest policymaking body for AFSCME is an international convention, held annually. Locals elect delegates to the convention. Otherwise, policy is developed by a national executive board. Some unions, like AFSCME, are run according to democratic principles. Others have more authoritarian structures.

Unions in government are challenged today by several factors, the most important of which are government retrenchment and "downsizing," unsympathetic public opinion, the changing nature of the workforce, and pressures for increased labor-management cooperation.

Beginning in the mid-1970s, state and local governments experienced a reverse of many years of steadily rising revenues, spending, and employment. Fiscal crises were proclaimed in many jurisdictions, with concomitant pressure for reductions-in-force and wage and benefit containment. Taxpayer resistance to government spending also picked up strength. The implications for public employee unions were negative. Unions, which once devoted their energies to gaining higher pay and a broader scope of benefits for their members, were more likely to concentrate on holding their own and limiting givebacks to employers. Job security has become problematic in the face of freezes, downsizing, and attrition policies.

For unions, such retrenchment policies have two important results. First, membership rolls have stopped growing and even declined in some jurisdictions and functions, with a corresponding loss of union bargaining power and financial resources. Second, fiscal constraints restrict the scope of what unions can do for their members in terms of wages and benefits, no matter how hard they bargain. Job security has become the most important union objective in fiscally struggling jurisdictions.

Negative public opinion concerning unions and government generally has risen greatly since the mid-1970s.

Union approval ratings, as high as 72 percent in 1957 have plummeted to less than 60 percent. As institutions in U.S. society, unions rank at or near the bottom; only 11 percent of respondents to a national survey in 1991 expressed a "great deal of confidence" in labor organizations. Similarly, union leaders do not inspire a great deal of public confidence, undoubtedly because of the scandals, corruption, and lawbreaking associated with several high-profile unions in the private sector. Also contributing to low public opinion ratings have been ill-advised actions of unions in government, including disruptions of public services, recalcitrance in adapting to the need for changes in work rules, and open resistance to the contracting out of public services. Union public relations efforts, such as those sponsored by AFSCME in newspapers and the broadcast media, have done little to lower the level of public hosility.

Unions have not yet accommodated important changes in the nature of the U.S. workforce. Demographic factors in the labor force include an aging workforce that consists increasingly of women and minorities. The culture of work and the needs of workers are changing dramatically, with concurrent challenges to public managers and unions. With some exceptions, unions have not redefined their roles for the future, which is critical if they are to remain viable organizations. Public-sector unions have been much more sensitive to the needs of women and minorities than have private-sector unions, but much remains to be done if membership is to be expanded and more collective bargaining recognitions are to be won, especially in the predominantly nonunion states of the Sunbelt.

Finally, the call for labor-management cooperation presents a special challenge to public-sector unions. The case for more cooperative relationships to replace the traditionally adversarial relationship between labor and management is being made at all levels of government. Experiments are under way with labor-management committees for dispute settlement and problem identification and resolution. Such committees typically deal with issues outside the collective bargaining process, as representatives of labor and management seek to find mutually beneficial solutions to workplace problems. There are also efforts to adopt "win-win" bargaining opportunities and relationships (see **collective bargaining**).

Other trends of critical importance to the future of public-employee unions are privatization and the campaign for making government service provision more efficient. Both trends imply smaller government workforces and fewer members in bargaining units. Such factors indicate that public employee unions' growth opportunities are limited in the years ahead. Unless unions are able to win collective bargaining rights in additional states and localities and, at the federal level, amend the Civil Service Reform Act of 1978 to incorporate union security arrangements and negotiating rights for wages and benefits, membership levels are likely to hold steady and even decline in some jurisdictions and functions.

RICHARD C. KEARNEY

BIBLIOGRAPHY

Barbash, Jack, 1967. *American Unions*. New York: Random House.
Bok, Derek, and John T. Dunlop, 1970. *Labor and the American Community*. New York: Simon and Schuster.
Commons, John R. et al., 1980. *History of Labor in the United States*. New York: Macmillan.
Kearney, Richard C., 1992. *Labor Relations in the Public Sector*. New York: Marcel Dekker, Chapter 2.
Marx, Karl and Fredrich Engels, 1967. *The Communist Manifesto*. Baltimore, MD: Penguin Books.
Nesbitt, Murray B., 1976. *Labor Relations in the Federal Government Service*. Washington, DC: Bureau of National Affairs.
Stieber, Jack, 1973. *Public Employee Unionism: Structure, Growth, Policy*. Washington, DC: Brookings Institution.

UNION SECURITY PROVISION.

Requirements that employees in a bargaining unit join a union, remain in a union, or pay a proportion of union dues as a condition of employment. Such agreements can be negotiated by an employer and a labor organization or can be mandated in collective bargaining legislation. The purpose of union security arrangements is to secure the institutional viability of a union as exclusive representative of the employees in a bargaining unit. Where no union security provisions exist, this condition is said to be an "open shop."

There are six forms of union security provisions:

1. *Closed Shop*: This is an agreement that provides that only union members in good standing may be hired by the employer. This was the usual relationship in certain trades such as printing, construction, and longshoring, in which the union located jobs for its members. The Taft-Hartley Act of 1947 prohibits all closed-shop agreements for firms involved in interstate commerce, and the closed shop is not authorized in government jurisdictions in the United States. However, "union hiring hall" practices exist de facto in some settings, such as mass transit.

2. *Union shop*: All new and continuing employees must, as a condition of employment, join the union within a specified period of time (usually 30 days) and maintain their membership throughout the duration of the collective bargaining contract. Unlike the closed shop, there is no preemployment membership requirement. The union shop is permitted in the U.S. private sector and in collective bargaining statutes for public employees in five states.

3. *Agency Shop*: Under this provision employees are not required to join the union, but they still must pay the employee organization a sum of money equivalent to union dues in order to defray union expenses incurred during contract negotiations and administration of the collective bargaining agreement. The District of Columbia and ten states permit this arrangement as a condition of employment through statute or regulation. The agency shop is legal under the National Labor Relations Act but may be outlawed by states under Section 14(b) of the Taft-Hartley Act (the right-to-work clause). The agency shop represents a compromise between the union shop and free riding (open shop).

4. *Maintenance of Membership*: Here, all union members must maintain their organizational affiliation throughout the life of the contract as a condition of employment. Nonmembers are not required to join. Three states, Alaska, California, and Wisconsin, specifically provide for this arrangement, although it is a prevalent practice throughout the states that have comprehensive bargaining legislation for public employees.

5. *Fair Share*: A variation on the agency shop in which employees must pay a certain portion of regular union dues to cover the organization's costs for collective bargaining activities. It differs from the agency shop in that other, noncollective bargaining activities are not paid for by members of the bargaining unit who choose not to join the union. The fair share is authorized in at least nine states.

6. *Dues Checkoff*: This arrangement requires that the employers automatically deduct union dues from the paychecks of employees and remit the funds to the union. The dues checkoff is typically found in conjunction with union or agency shop.

The use of union security provisions has steadily increased since the mid-1960s in the U.S. public sector. These arrangements are desirable for unions because they help increase or maintain membership in the union while ensuring a high rate of dues collection. The financially sound union is a secure and politically strong union. Importantly, union security provisions alleviate the problem of free riders—members of the bargaining unit who enjoy the benefits of union representation but who refuse to join the organization or pay dues. Union security can also be beneficial for the public employer, which gains labor peace from a stable union.

Arguments against the closed- and union-shop arrangements include the charge that these provisions violate an individual's right to freedom of association and freedom of speech under the First Amendment. Unions are private, voluntary organizations in which membership should be by the conscious choice of the individual. The employee should not be required to support the ideology or political program of a union or pay dues to it. The 20 right-to-work states that prohibit union security arrangements represent this argument.

A number of U.S. Supreme Court cases have addressed union security. A trilogy of cases in the 1950s and 1960s upheld and protected private-sector employees' First Amendment rights under the Railway Labor Act. In *Railway Employee Department, IAM v. Hanson* (1956), the Court ruled that a union security provision is constitutional so long as dues collection did not serve as a "cover for forcing ideological conformity . . . in contravention of the First Amendment." In 1961, the Court held that unions cannot use dues to support political causes if an employee objects (*International Association of Machinists v. Street*). The Court suggested in *Brotherhood of Railway Clerks v. Allen* in 1963 that unions should adopt a voluntary plan to enable dissenters to avoid having a portion of their dues applied to political purposes.

The principles developed in these three cases were applied to the public sector in *Abood v. Detroit Board of Education* (1977). Here, the Court found that an agency shop is valid so long as the union does not require its members to financially support an ideological position or political cause with which they disagree. But it is difficult to distinguish between acceptable and unacceptable use of union representation and service fees. What must be determined is which union expenditures are incurred for the purposes of exclusive representation of bargaining unit employees on labor-management issues (*Ellis v. Railway Clerks*, 1984). For example, the U.S. Supreme Court has approved national union conventions, social activities, and publications as necessary and reasonable expenses. Activities not directly related to contract negotiation or administration should not be funded with nonmembers' service fees. Further specification of a procedure for identifying acceptable and unacceptable uses of service fees came in the U.S. Supreme Court decision of *Chicago Teachers' Union v. Hudson* (1986). According to the Court, the union must give nonmembers an adequate explanation of the basis for the fee, a venue for challenging the amount of the fee before an impartial decisionmaker, and an escrow account to hold amounts in dispute while challenges are pending. Additional procedural instruction to unions was provided in *Lehnert v. Ferris Faculty Association* (1991). The Court said that expenses chargeable to nonmembers must be germane to collective bargaining activities, justified by the government's interest in labor peace and avoiding free riders, and not significantly burdensome to free speech. Specifically allowed were union convention costs and strike preparation costs. Disallowed were lobbying, electoral, and other expenses associated with political activity.

RICHARD C. KEARNEY

BIBLIOGRAPHY

Kearney, Richard C., 1992. *Labor Relations in the Public Sector,* 2d ed. New York: Marcel Dekker.

UNITED WAY. A charitable system that raises money for health and human services and supports the delivery of those services. This system provides a structure within which people can participate in helping fellow citizens in their own communities. In the United States of America, there are approximately 2,000 community-based organizations, each of which is separately incorporated as a United Way and is governed by an independent board of volunteer directors. United Ways range in scope from small-town, all-volunteer operations to large, professionally staffed, urban offices. As part of the total United Way system, these local autonomous United Ways are served by state United Way organizations as well as the United Way of America regional and national offices.

History of the United Way System

The development of the United Way system reflects an interplay of simultaneous local and national efforts. The concept dates back to 1887 when religious leaders in Denver, Colorado, founded the Charity Organizations Society to plan and coordinate local social services and conduct a single fundraising campaign for 22 agencies. The formation of this society reflected the belief that an organized effort would increase the efficiency and effectiveness of charitable giving within a community. This belief was reinforced by similar actions being taken throughout the United States. In 1895, the first independent federation of Jewish agencies was formed in Boston; in 1900, the Committee on Benevolent Associations was formed to set standards and monitor charities in Cleveland; in 1908, the first community planning program, Associated Charities, was formed in Pittsburgh; and in 1910, a council was formed to prevent overlapping services and multiple solicitations in Columbus, Ohio. By 1911, there were 129 Charity Organization Societies in cities throughout the country. Sixty of these joined together to form the National Association of Societies for Organizing Charity in order to coordinate their efforts and share information.

In addition to the purposes of unifying solicitations and monitoring and coordinating services, there arose the need to allocate donor contributions in a fair and balanced manner. In 1913, such an allocation system was incorporated into the nation's first modern Community Chest created in Cleveland. In 1919, the same name was used in Rochester, New York, and by 1929, there were 353 Community Chests in the country. At the same time these local organizations were being formed, similar efforts were being made on a national level. In 1918, the National Charities Information Bureau was established to monitor national charitable organizations, and the American Association for Community Organizations (AACO) was begun to stimulate collective community planning and develop standards for the work of community organizations. By 1927, the

AACO became the Association of Community Chests and Councils.

During the next 20 years, the Community Chest concept continued to take hold in cities throughout the country. Several national activities supported this growth. In 1931, Community Chests mobilized to respond to the needs created by the Great Depression, and President Hoover permitted the Washington, D.C., Community Chest to solicit federal employees. In 1933, Eleanor Roosevelt led the National Women's Committee in its mobilization to meet human needs. In 1935, Congress passed legislation allowing corporations to deduct up to 5 percent of taxable income for charitable donations. In 1942, the National War Fund was formed to raise and allocate funds for war-related charitable programs. In 1943, the government began withholding federal income taxes from employee pay, paving the way for payroll deduction of charitable contributions, and in 1946, the American Federation of Labor-Congress of Industrial Organizations (AFL-CIO) and the Community Chests and Councils signed an agreement to develop a cooperative relationship between Community Chests and organized labor. Each of these events contributed to the ongoing development of organized charity. By the end of the 1940s, the Community Chest movement had adopted the Red Feather as its national symbol and had become established in over 1,000 communities.

During the 1950s, communities across the country began to adopt the name United Fund, and by 1956, the national organization changed its name to United Community Funds and Councils of America. In 1963, Los Angeles became the first community to formally adopt the name United Way after merging over 30 Community Chest and United Fund organizations in the metropolitan area. Seven years later, the national organization reorganized under the name United Way of America.

During the 1970s, the United Way of America initiated a myriad of new efforts to enhance the role of the national organization. The National Academy for Voluntarism was established to provide continuing education for United Way volunteers and professionals. The first comprehensive classification system for social services, the United Way of America Services Identification System (UWASIS) was published. United Way International was formed to help nations around the world form United Way–type organizations. A national program for corporate development was established to enhance contributions from large national firms and their employees. United Ways and the National Football League began the largest public service campaign in the nation's history. The decade ended with a national agenda that called for increased involvement of donors in all aspects of the United Way and for more focused attention on issues related to public policy, relationships with funded agencies, and voluntarism.

United Ways across the country experienced record campaign growth in 1981 when they raised a total of US $1.68 billion, a 10-percent increase over the previous year and the largest single-year percentage increase in 25 years. In 1983, United Way of America became the fiscal agent for a first-of-its-kind US $50 million emergency food and shelter grant to the voluntary sector. This congressional grant was administered by a board operating within the Federal Emergency Management Agency. United Way's progress in fundraising and resource allocation was celebrated extensively in 1987 with numerous centennial events and the inauguration of the "Second Century Initiative," a collective effort to double funds and volunteers, as well as to become a more open and caring organization. By the close of the decade, the United Way of America had involved local United Ways in major community projects to advocate for welfare reform, increase diversity within volunteer leadership, and help with low-income housing and adult literacy.

In 1990, the total raised in local United Way campaigns across the country exceeded US $3 billion for the first time. However, general trends in fund-raising were slowing due to changes in the marketplace. This decline worsened in 1992 with the resignation of William Aramony following allegations of serious misconduct. He and two of his senior managers at the United Way of America were indicted by a federal grand jury and were later found guilty of multiple counts including conspiracy, fraud, and false tax returns. This scandal inspired sweeping reforms of the United Way of America's governance and structure. These included strict internal financial controls and an expanded board, which included representation from local United Ways. Former Peace Corps Director Elaine Chao was selected as the new president and chief executive officer and she took charge of the effort to restore confidence and improve the delivery of quality services to local United Ways and other key constituencies. In the meantime, within local communities, United Ways emphasized their autonomous governance and altered their relationship with the United Way of America as one in which they purchased services and resources in a manner similar to a trade association.

The United Way of America

The United Way of America, located at 701 North Fairfax Street in Alexandria, Virginia, is the national service and training center that supports member United Ways. Local United Way organizations may become members by paying a fee based on a formula related to local campaign results. Membership entitles the local group to use the United Way registered trademark name and logo, as well as to benefit from a variety of programs and services. The

United Way of America does not serve as a headquarters because local United Ways are, by law and in spirit, independent and autonomous of each other and the United Way of America.

The United Way of America is governed by a volunteer board of 45 members, including 15 local United Way representatives. Its purpose is to support, serve, and respond to local United Way member organizations by providing a range of assistance, including a national advertising and promotion program, a public relations partnership with the National Football League, training for United Way professionals and volunteers, support to national companies that want to cultivate a year-round relationship with United Ways, a national database for fund-raising and fund-distribution statistics, and a national network for the sharing of effective local programs.

The United Way of America also takes a leadership role in national health and human services issues. It undergirds local community building efforts with its own national partnerships and grant programs in areas such as child and youth development, literacy, and housing. The national organization also provides a system for creating a community needs assessment and action plan. In addition, the United Way of America works directly with the United States Congress and the administration to provide the nonprofit sector's perspective on proposed and existing legislation and regulations. It offers an early alert system designed to inform, coordinate, and activate local United Ways for grassroots advocacy efforts on time-sensitive issues and pending legislation.

Another important activity of the United Way of America is the provision of training and support for local staff and volunteers. This human resource development is delivered through the National Academy of Voluntarism as well as through national initiatives in youth service and volunteer diversity. Regional and national conferences also enhance the learning experiences available to staff and volunteers within local United Ways.

United Ways in Local Communities

United Ways in local communities operate to accomplish two major goals: raise funds through development of financial resources and support and enhance the coordinated delivery of health and human services. Each local organization's operations are overseen by a local board of directors.

Financial Resource Development (Fund-Raising)

The development of financial resources is achieved in most communities through an annual communitywide United Way campaign, usually conducted in the fall of each year. The total of all local campaigns in the United States exceeds US $3 billion. Each local fund-raising effort is overseen by community leaders who set a goal and then solicit funds to reach that goal.

The bedrock for the campaign is the workplace. Most major firms in a community donate a corporate gift and also promote the United Way by offering the opportunity for employees to give through payroll deduction. The approach to employees often includes special activities such as kickoff events, solicitation rallies involving agency speakers and videos, contests, and special recognition ceremonies. These activities help the potential donor to make an informed choice regarding giving and encourage contribution to the campaign. The United Way of America and most local United Ways have a clear policy against any form of coercion and strongly recommend peer solicitation within companies.

At the same time, the United Way campaign is being conducted in most communities, the federal government also holds a fund-raising campaign for all federal employees. This Combined Federal Campaign is overseen by the Office of Personnel Management and is implemented by a Principal Combined Fund Organization (PCFO) in each local community. In the majority of locations, United Way is designated as the PCFO. Federal employees designate their contributions directly to eligible agencies of their choice. Most states also conduct their own campaigns for state employees in accordance with state legislation and regulations.

Many local United Ways conduct specific fund-raising efforts in the area of leadership giving. Most communities have a system for recruiting and honoring members of a group of givers who contribute larger than average amounts such as US $500 or US $1,000 or more annually. Larger United Ways also participate in the Alexis deToqueville Society, whose members contribute US $10,000 or more annually. This society, established by the United Way of America in 1984, involves national corporate leaders in seeking major gifts from wealthy individuals. It encompasses nine levels of giving, including Megagifts of US $100,000 or more and the Million Dollar Roundtable. As of 1994, across the country, local United Ways have raised over US $100 million through 150 local Alexis de Tocqueville Societies.

Many local campaigns focus special efforts on such targeted markets as individual givers, professionals, nonprofit and public-sector organizations, and small businesses. Dollars raised from these sources are combined with corporate and employee donations, federal and state employee contributions, and leadership gifts to create a communitywide total gift, which is publicly announced at a culminating community event, often referred to as a "victory celebration." In larger urban areas, there are interim report meetings, which precede the final announcement.

In companies with organized labor, the United Way solicitation is generally jointly sponsored by labor and management and receives strong assistance from the labor community. Annual letters of endorsement from union presidents affiliated with the AFL-CIO add support to campaigns in local firms.

In many local communities, the United Way has a fund-raising partnership agreement with other groups. These groups may be fund-raising federations of agencies with a specific focus such as the Combined Health Appeal or Women's Way, or they may be large national agencies that are not already included in the local membership such as the American Cancer Society or the American Heart Association. In some agreements, donations to these partners are made through a system of donor choice.

More than 75 percent of local United Ways provide a program of "donor choice," which allows givers to designate their donations for use in a specific way. The actual choices vary among local communities and may include such options as a specific United Way member agency, a nonmember agency, a United Way in another community, or a field of service rather than a specific agency. Some communities also offer the choice to exclude a certain agency from receiving the donation.

The annual fundraising campaign is led and implemented by volunteers with support from the paid staff in the larger local United Way offices. Volunteers work on committees, which plan and oversee every aspect of the campaign. In the workplace, volunteer employees serve on coordinating committees and function as peer solicitors. In many communities, both firms and agencies donate "loaned executives" to carry out campaign assignments. It is due to the high level of volunteer involvement as well as the simplicity of payroll deduction that United Ways are able to raise funds with the unusually low fund-raising cost of an average of 15 percent of all funds raised.

Planned giving and endowment development are other fund-raising approaches used by local United Ways to attract long-term investments in the United Way system. Through these methods, potential donors are asked to include United Way in their wills, life insurance policies, retirement plans, and living trusts. They may also be asked to make a direct contribution to the local United Way endowment fund in communities that have such a mechanism for more far-reaching and permanent gifts.

In many local United Ways, the activity at the workplace is not confined to the period of the annual campaign. Programs with such titles as "United Way at Work," "Year Round Program," and "Workplace Presence" operate in firms throughout the year. Representative employee committees plan and implement activities to educate and involve the workforce in the United Way system. Specific approaches include lunchtime speakers, bulletin board displays, agency tours, on-site information and referral services, group and individual volunteer projects, and fund-raising events. This involvement throughout the year reinforces the donor's ownership of the local United Way, increases general understanding of community needs, promotes voluntarism and underscores United Way's role as a service provider to corporations and their employees.

Marketing efforts are an integral part of the financial resource development function of each local United Way. While communities develop their own marketing plans, speaker bureaus, materials, and media exposure, they may also turn to the United Way of America for help in this arena. They may rely on marketing research data as well as consultation and training. Local groups may purchase items or use the national film that features a well-known celebrity speaking on behalf of those in need. Community campaigns also benefit from the United Way of America's partnership with the National Football League to produce public-service announcements as part of an overall national advertising campaign.

Support for Delivery of Social Services

Alongside the United Way activities focused on financial resource development are the efforts to support the delivery of social services. Across the country, contributions are distributed to approximately 47,000 agencies that help people from all walks of life. United Ways in local communities fund a range of health and human services that are provided by their affiliated agencies. These services include such programs as disaster relief, emergency food and shelter, child care, youth development, physical rehabilitation, family counseling, employment training, substance abuse treatment, and health care.

In most communities, agencies apply for membership in the local United Way and must meet a set of organizational and programmatic criteria to be accepted. Admission is also based on community priorities and the availability of resources. In some cases, agencies receive general funding, whereas, in other cases, specific programs of those agencies actually receive the funding.

The primary method of distributing United Way funds is through an agency allocation process. This process is implemented by local citizens who review the management, programs, and finances of funded agencies on an annual basis. These volunteers represent all areas of their community and are knowledgeable about needed services. They make decisions about the distribution of funds through a careful process that provides accountability to contributors regarding the efficient use of donor dollars. They also strive to maintain a balance of service s within a community so that ongoing basic needs as well as high-priority causes are being addressed. Money given through a system of donor choice is either passed directly to the chosen agency or incorporated within the agency allocation.

In addition to the allocation of campaign dollars, local United Ways administer money granted by the Federal Emergency Management Agency and the Emergency Food and Shelter National Board, which is staffed by the United Way of America. Nationwide, the grants amount to a total of over US $130 million to provide meals, shelter, utility payments, and rent assistance to people in need.

Local United Ways also support the delivery of social services through a variety of community initiatives. Many provide staff and/or financial resources to support a coordinated approach to a specific problem area through such activities as grant writing, facilitation, and consultation. Generally, the problem chosen for special focus is one that has emerged from a communitywide needs assessment or that has garnered the support of other organizations that are working collaboratively with the United Way.

The United Way system maintains an ongoing relationship with governmental entities in order to coordinate and advocate for the support of human service delivery programs. Many local United Ways have active government relations programs that keep community advocates informed about local, state, and federal legislative issues. Local United Way boards of directors may approve an annual legislative agenda that guides the response to issues as they arise.

Information and referral (I&R) services are another major means of supporting the delivery of health and human services within a local community. Local United Ways operate or provide funding for more than 500 I&R services nationwide. Trained specialists assist callers by referring them to agencies that provide the help they are seeking. I&R programs gather data regarding needs in the community and often serve as a valuable link between citizens and United Way services. They maintain a community services data file, which may be available in both printed and electronic formats.

In addition to the information and referral services supported directly by the United Way, there is an active program of community services sponsored through a cooperative relationship between the local United Way and the AFL-CIO. United Ways and organized labor organizations work together to train union members to provide coworkers with information and referral in the workplace.

Another form of supporting social services within communities is the provision of services that enhance voluntarism. Many local United Ways operate or provide funding for volunteer centers that connect individuals and groups looking for volunteer opportunities with agencies who have needs for volunteer help. These centers also offer training and consultation in volunteer management and often help corporations develop internal volunteer service programs. In some localities, volunteer centers organize an annual "day of caring" event in which groups carry out volunteer activities in agencies throughout the community.

Operations

Local United Ways are governed by volunteer boards of directors that formulate policies that are implemented by volunteers in small communities or by a professional staff in larger areas. The size of the staff depends on the size of the community and can range from one paid director to a multidepartment organization of over 100 staff positions in major metropolitan areas. In these larger United Ways, in addition to the chief professional officer, the staff leadership team may include managers for the functions of financial resource development, agency relations and allocations, community initiatives, marketing and communications, finance, and administration. A key staff member in most urban areas is the labor community services liaison, who serves as a link between the United Way and the local and state labor organizations.

In addition to the board of directors, volunteers serve on committees within a structure that parallels the key strategies of the organization. Volunteers may work on such groups as a campaign cabinet, a citizen review fund distribution panel, a government relations committee, a community initiative task force, or a marketing committee. Volunteers also participate on campaign and year-round committees at the workplace. For each staff person, there are hundreds of volunteers implementing the various functions of the local United Way.

Local organizations are usually guided by long-range plans that are developed jointly by board, staff, volunteers, and community representatives. These plans reflect the needs in the community and set forth the key strategies that must be followed to meet those needs.

Future Directions

As the United Way system looks ahead to the twenty-first century, it faces two major tasks. The first is to adopt more donor-oriented approaches to financial resource development. These approaches need to include campaigns designed more specifically for a particular workplace, increased choices for donors, stronger marketing of the community fund concept, demonstration of high standards of integrity, and continued emphasis on reducing fund-raising costs. The second task is to add value to the community beyond that of the independent efforts of agencies in the area of health and human services. Such value can be added through an increased effort to focus funding on targeted sets of high-priority causes. In addition, local United Ways must work even more closely with member agencies as well as other community organizations to provide leadership in the solving of local community problems.

JANE S. HEIDE

BIBLIOGRAPHY

United Way of America, 1977. *People and Events: A History of the United Way.* Atlanta, GA: Case-Hoyt.

UNRELATED BUSINESS INCOME TAX.

An income tax imposed on the profits generated by a tax-exempt organization from business activities that are not related to its exempt function and on investment income from debt-financed investments and corporate subsidiaries.

Reason for the Tax in the United States

Whereas a tax-exempt organization generally pays no income tax on its investment income or on its revenue from its exempt activities (e.g., ticket sales by a symphony), it is liable for income tax on unrelated business taxable income. The unrelated business income tax (UBIT) was first enacted in 1950 in response to complaints from businesses that tax-exempt organizations were unfairly competing against them when they engaged in unrelated business activities.

For example, a symphony might raise money by operating a grocery store and applying all of the store's profits to help the symphony. Congress concluded that even though all of the net proceeds would be used for charitable purposes, the symphony should be subject to UBIT on its profits from the grocery store. The sale of grocery products is unrelated to the symphony's exempt function of performing classical music, and the symphony would have an unfair competitive advantage over similar grocery stores that pay income taxes.

Also in 1950, Congress imposed UBIT on a charity's net rental income if the rental property was acquired with borrowed money. It determined that charities were able to use borrowed funds to acquire rental property at a competitive advantage over taxable organizations that paid tax on net rental income. In 1969, Congress extended the tax on debt-financed UBIT to all categories of tax-exempt organizations, rather than just charities, and also expanded the types of investment income that are subject to the tax to virtually every form of investment income that is generated from borrowed money. It also extended the UBIT to rent, interest, and certain other payments that a tax-exempt organization receives from a corporate subsidiary.

Economic Activity

In 1991, according to the Statistical Bulletin by the Internal Revenue Service (IRS), 32,690 organizations (out of a total of over 1 million tax-exempt organizations) filed tax returns that reported unrelated business activities. Only 14,000 of these organizations reported a profit. The profitable organizations reported a total of US $431.1 million of net taxable income and paid taxes totaling US $116.9 million (US $74.9 million of this amount came from just 433 organizations).

The gross unrelated business revenue reported on these returns was over US $3.4 billion. Over 86 percent of this revenue was reported by five types of tax-exempt organizations: charities, trade associations, social welfare organizations, social clubs, and voluntary employees' beneficiary associations (VEBAs) (see **tax-exempt organization**). The principal sources of unrelated revenue were sales and services (43 percent), "other income" (20 percent), advertising revenue (17 percent), unrelated debt-financed property (7 percent), and investment income earned by the types of tax-exempt organizations that pay income tax on such income (principally social clubs and VEBAs–6 percent).

Overview of Legal Requirements. There are basically three situations that could make a tax-exempt organization liable for UBIT:

1. The organization is regularly carrying on a trade or business that is not substantially related to its reason for being tax-exempt. For example, a charity is operating a commercial movie theater as a way to raise money.
2. The organization borrows money to purchase investment property, such as stocks, bonds, or rental property. The portion of the investment income that is attributable to the debt is treated as "unrelated debt-financed income" and the exempt organization must pay tax on it.
3. The organization receives interest, rent, or certain other types of income payments from a subsidiary corporation over which it has 80 percent or more control.

If the gross revenue from such unrelated activities exceeds US $1,000 in any year, then a tax-exempt organization must file Form 990-T, "Exempt Organization Business Income Tax Return" with the IRS and pay any tax due. The tax on such income is calculated by using the normal corporate income tax rates, except that charitable trusts are required to use the trust tax rates.

The tax is assessed against the net income from the business activity rather than the gross revenue. There are often disputes with the IRS concerning the amount of an organization's expenses, such as staff and overhead costs, that can be charged to its unrelated business activities. Each dollar that can be allocated to the unrelated business activity will reduce the taxable income upon which UBIT is assessed.

Investment income, such as dividends, interest, and rent, are generally excluded from the computation of unrelated business income. The principal exceptions are that "unrelated debt-financed income" and payments from subsidiaries will be taxed.

In addition to paying income tax on its unrelated activities, an organization can lose its tax-exempt status if its unrelated business activities are so substantial that they overshadow the exempt activities (see **charitable organization**).

Regularly Carry on an Unrelated Trade or Business. An exempt organization will be liable for UBIT if it "regularly" carries on an "unrelated trade or business." Repeated unrelated business activities will likely trigger UBIT whereas isolated transactions will not. For example, a repertory theater that operates a bakery will be liable for UBIT but a church group that has an annual bake sale will not, because the sporadic bake sales do not constitute an activity that is regularly carried on.

There has been considerable hairsplitting as to the types of activities that are related to the organization's exempt activities and those that are not. The tax regulations state that a business activity is related to an organization's exempt purpose if it has a substantial "causal relationship to the achievement of an exempt purpose" and the business "contributes importantly to the accomplishment of the exempt purpose." Thus, the sale of milk and cream from an experimental dairy herd is an exempt way to dispose of surplus milk, but processing it into ice cream and pastries is not. The use of a theater in a museum for educational films is an exempt use, but after-hours use for ordinary entertainment is not. Sales by a museum gift shop of reproductions from its collection are considered exempt, but sales of other commercial products are not. The IRS generally treats all revenue from advertising as unrelated. In addition, a tax-exempt organization will usually incur UBIT if it invests in a partnership that operates a business, because it is indirectly participating in an unrelated business.

Unrelated Debt-Financed Income. Most types of tax-exempt organizations pay no income tax on their investment income (rents, interest, dividends, and capital gains). However, tax-exempt organizations must pay UBIT on investment income attributable to "debt-financed property." Debt-financed property is any income-producing asset that has any "acquisition indebtedness" (debt the organization incurred to acquire or improve the property) associated with it. Thus, rental property acquired with a mortgage and securities purchased on a margin account are debt-financed property.

The amount of income that is subject to UBIT is the portion of the property's net income that is attributable to the debt. For example, if a charity acquires rental property for US $500,000 by investing US $200,000 of its own

money and borrowing US $300,000, then 60 percent (US $300,000 divided by US $500,000) of the net rental income for the year is subject to UBIT. The fraction is adjusted each year based on the ratio of the debt to the "adjusted tax basis" (cost plus improvements minus depreciation deductions) of the property. For example, if in a future year the amount owed on the mortgage falls to US $160,000 and there has been US $100,000 of depreciation deductions, then only 40 percent (US $160,000 divided by the US $400,000 adjusted basis) of that year's net rental income would be subject to UBIT. This computation is made separately for each property that the organization owns.

There are two important exceptions. The first is if the property is used for exempt purposes. For example, if a charity operates a thrift shop as part of its exempt purposes and borrows money to purchase a building, 40 percent of which will be used for the thrift shop and 60 percent will be rented to miscellaneous tenants, then only 60 percent of the building will constitute debt-financed property. If 85 percent or more of the property is used for an exempt purpose, then none of the property will be treated as debt-financed property.

Another important exception applies if the tax-exempt organization receives mortgaged property as a bequest or as a gift. In the case of mortgaged property that is received as bequest upon a donor's death, the property will not be considered debt-financed property until ten years after the time of receipt. If mortgaged property is received as a gift from a living donor, the property will not be treated as debt-financed property for ten years following the time of receipt, but only if the donor held the property for more than five years and the mortgage was placed on the property more than five years before the date of the gift. Neither of these exceptions apply if the tax-exempt organization agrees to pay any part of the debt secured by the mortgage or if it pays for the donor's equity in the property.

Eighty Percent Control of a Corporation. Some charities conduct an unrelated business through a separate corporation that it owns, a subsidiary. As a general rule, a subsidiary of a tax-exempt organization is not also tax-exempt merely because all of its profits will eventually be paid to a tax-exempt organization. Instead, it will pay a corporate income tax like any other corporation. Furthermore, if the subsidiary pays rent, interest, annuities, or royalties to a tax-exempt organization that controls at least 80 percent of its stock, then the tax-exempt organization could be subject to UBIT on these amounts.

Congress's logic was that a taxable subsidiary, or a tax-exempt subsidiary subject to UBIT, could take tax deductions for rent, interest, and royalties paid to any landlord, lender, or royalty owner, even if that person were also a shareholder who controlled the corporation. These tax deductions would reduce the subsidiary's corporate income tax liability, but a tax-exempt shareholder might not otherwise pay any income tax on the amount that it receives. Congress therefore enacted a special rule that makes a tax-exempt organization that has at least 80 percent control of another corporation liable for UBIT for payments of rent, interest, royalties, or other items that the subsidiary could deduct on its income tax return. Dividends, however, are exempt since a corporation cannot deduct any dividends that it pays. If an exempt organization owns less than 80 percent of the stock of the corporation, then it will not incur UBIT on such payments.

CHRISTOPHER HOYT

BIBLIOGRAPHY

Internal Revenue Service, 1995. *IRS Statistical Bulletin.* Washington, D.C.

UP-OR-OUT SYSTEMS.

Personnel policies that require employees to leave if they do not qualify for promotion. Some personnel systems mandate that employees make steady progress through the promotional system. If they do not qualify to be promoted, they are separated from employment with the organization. The approach is most common in rank-in-person personnel systems where all individuals carry a particular rank regardless of the specific duties they perform. The U.S. military and the Foreign Service use the up-or-out system forcing individuals to retire if they do not earn promotion. A modified version of the system is used by most colleges and universities where individuals must qualify for promotion from assistant to associate professor in order to attain tenure. If individuals do not meet the criteria for promotion, they are not tenured and thus are separated from the institution. The British system also tends to use the up-or-out system in parts of its service.

The purpose of up-or-out systems is to ensure that the best people are retained by the organization. If people do not continue to develop and change with the changing needs of the organization, they will not meet the criteria for promotion and must leave the organization. Processes for implementing the system include sitting for examinations and extensive reviews of performance.

Up-or-out systems tend to produce great competitiveness in the organization. Additionally, employees seem to develop strong commitment to the organization as they succeed through the ranks. Because of the emphasis on moving up the hierarchy, there also tends to be a lot of focus on rank. At the same time, an exclusiveness and elit-

ism is likely to develop in the higher levels of the organization, and those lower in the hierarchy may find it difficult to have their ideas considered seriously because they are not given much credibility. As a result, organizations using up-or-out approaches usually become rigid and resistant to change.

N. JOSEPH CAYER

U.S. OFFICE OF MANAGEMENT AND BUDGET.

In the United States, the primary staff agency charged with the oversight of the budget preparation and execution processes for the president. Recent changes have enhanced its jurisdiction over managerial concerns in the executive branch and increased its role in budget negotiations with Congress.

The United States Government Manual describes the work of the Office of Management and Budget (OMB) as follows: "The Office of Management and Budget evaluates, formulates and coordinates management procedures and program objectives within and among Federal departments and agencies. It also controls the administration of the Federal budget, while routinely providing the President with recommendations regarding budget proposals and legislative enactments." The manual also lists 11 of the primary functions of OMB:

- to assist the president in developing and maintaining effective government by reviewing the organizational structure and management procedures of the executive branch to ensure that the intended results are achieved;
- to assist in developing efficient coordinating mechanisms to implement government activities and to expand interagency cooperation;
- to assist the president in preparing the budget and in formulating the government's fiscal program;
- to supervise and control the administration of the budget;
- to assist the president by clearing and coordinating departmental advice on proposed legislation and by making recommendations effecting presidential action on legislative enactments, in accordance with past practice;
- to assist in developing regulatory reform proposals and programs for paperwork reduction, especially reporting burdens of the public;
- to assist in considering, clearing, and, where necessary, preparing proposed executive orders and proclamations;

- to plan and develop information systems that provide the president with program performance data;
- to plan, conduct, and promote evaluation efforts that assist the president in assessing program objectives, performance, and efficiency;
- to keep the president informed of the progress of activities by government agencies with respect to work proposed, initiated, and completed, together with the relative timing of work between the several agencies of the government, all to the end that the work programs of the several agencies of the executive branch of the government may be coordinated and that the moneys appropriated by the congress may be expended in the most economical manner, barring overlapping and duplication of effort; and,
- to improve the economy, efficiency, and effectiveness of the procurement process by providing overall direction of procurement policies, regulations, procedures and forms.

To accomplish these functions, OMB has a staff of approximately 550 organized into five resource management offices, five staff offices, two support offices and three statutory offices. The entire organization is headed by a director and two deputy directors, appointed by the president with the advice and consent of the Senate.

Historical Background

Only 2 of the 11 current functions of OMB listed in the United States Government Manual directly concern the budget. They are, however, the original functions performed by OMB's predecessor when it was created by the Budget and Accounting Act of 1921 as the Bureau of the Budget within the Treasury Department.

The Budget Process Before the Bureau of the Budget

Prior to creation of the Bureau of the Budget, there did not exist a single, integrated U.S. budget for the entire federal government. Rather, federal agencies submitted their own budgets to the Treasury Department, where they were collected in a "Book of Estimates" and sent to Congress each year, without any review. Agency representatives justified their budget requests before Congress. The president played no role in the process.

It is not surprising that the executive branch lacked a system for review of agency budget requests when the United States was founded and for more than a century thereafter, since the role and functions of the federal government were quite limited. Thus, government spending was also limited. Large annual budget deficits were not a continuing problem, and the receipts from import duties and the tariff were more than adequate to cover all expen-

ditures in most years. This happy state of affairs, unfortunately, did not continue indefinitely.

Starting in 1894, there were federal budget deficits for six consecutive years. By the end of that six-year period, total government spending had greatly increased, due mainly to growth in government functions as well as the costs of the Spanish-American War. This spending growth continued and in itself would have been sufficient impetus for reform; coupled with the reforms taking place in American municipal financial practices during the late nineteenth and early twentieth century, it led President Taft to create the Commission on Economy and Efficiency in 1910.

The commission issued two reports: The first, "Economy and Efficiency in the Government Service," was transmitted to Congress on January 17, 1912; the second, "The Need for a National Budget," was sent on June 27, 1912. As pointed out in Jesse Burkhead's (1956) *Government Budgeting*, both of these reports were important because they represented an assumption of responsibility by the president for governmental management. Indeed, these reports set forth many of the criteria for the federal budget as it is conceived today, namely, the president is responsible for financial planning and management of the government's business; a national budget system should serve as an instrument of executive management and control; the budget should serve the multiple purposes of a basis for congressional action, a means of executive control and management, a basis for agency administration, and a means for presenting a definite, well-considered, comprehensive program to the public.

Bureau of the Budget: Creation and Early Years

These two reports of the Commission on Economy and Efficiency did not lead to immediate legislation. Yet, their influence was great in that the reforms they suggested were accepted by both major political parties and ultimately were embodied in the Budget and Accounting Act of 1921. This act, signed by President Harding on June 10, 1921, established the Bureau of the Budget in the Treasury Department, with a director and deputy director to be appointed by the president—without the usual requirement for advice and consent of the Senate. Although located within the Treasury Department, the Budget Bureau was made directly responsive to the president; and the absence of a required Senate confirmation signified that the director and deputy director were to be close personal advisers to the president. (This changed in 1973 when a requirement of Senate confirmation of future directors and deputy directors was added.)

The newly created bureau was given two major powers under the 1921 act: (1) to review the agency budget requests and assist the president in compiling and executing the budget for the federal government and (2) when directed by the president, to make administrative studies to secure greater economy and efficiency in the conduct of government business. The bureau proceeded immediately to carry out the first of these powers, especially since the 1921 act expressly prohibited federal agencies from submitting any budget requests to Congress except through the Bureau of the Budget or at the request of either house of Congress. The second major power, essentially that of administrative management, was not emphasized by the bureau during the 18 years that it remained in the Treasury Department. Although the Bureau of the Budget played a key role in the formulation stage of the budget process, the justification of the budget estimates before Congress continued to be handled by the federal agencies, as it had been before the creation of the Bureau of the Budget.

During its years in the Treasury Department, the Bureau of the Budget had five directors, all taking a narrow view of the bureau's role, conceiving it to be nonpolitical and concerned only with promoting economy and efficiency in carrying out the government's routine business. Such economy and efficiency, in their view, was to be achieved mainly by means of a budget review that reduced proposed expenditures. In keeping with this approach and with their view that parsimony should be the practice of those who imposed it on others, the size of the Bureau of the Budget remained very small—a staff of not more than 45—during this period. Such an approach to the role of the bureau was probably appropriate for the period, during which government programs were limited and remained generally static, and the presidents—Harding, Coolidge, and Hoover—could not be characterized as activists.

Executive Office of the President

With the Great Depression and the election of Franklin Roosevelt, the presidency became more activist than ever. The role of the government was greatly expanded and the proliferation of governmental activities and agencies, and the increased scope and complexity of the problems being dealt with by the government, created a need for improved management and executive control at the presidential level. To meet this need, President Roosevelt created the President's Committee on Administrative Management, which became known as the Brownlow Committee for its chairman, Louis Brownlow (see **Brownlow Committee**). The committee reported to the president on January 8, 1937, and on January 12 the president sent a special message to Congress summarizing the report's five major recommendations. The first recommendation dealt with expanding the White House staff. The second recommendation was to "strengthen and develop the managerial agencies of the government, particularly those dealing with the budget and efficiency research, with personnel and with planning, as management-arms of the Chief Ex-

ecutive." Other recommendations dealt with the merit system (recommendation number three), overhauling the many independent, newly created governmental entities and placing them within existing departments (recommendation number four), and establishment of the General Accounting Office (recommendation number five).

As noted by Larry Berman (1979) in *The Office of Management and Budget and the Presidency, 1921–1979,* the Brownlow Committee believed that the president would receive two types of assistance in doing his job: personal and institutional. His personal assistants would be few in number and would serve his immediate political interests. The institutional staff would be large in number and would provide continuity from president to president and a governmentwide perspective on issues, serving more the presidency rather than the particular president in office (p. 11). Berman went on to indicate that Brownlow conceived the Bureau of the Budget to be the agency to control and direct the executive branch for the president—serving as the institutional staff.

The report of the Brownlow Committee finally culminated in Reorganization Plan Number 1 of 1939. The plan, effective on July 1, 1939, moved the Bureau of the Budget out of the Treasury Department to ultimately become the largest single element of the newly established Executive Office of the President. On September 8, 1939, Executive Order 8248 was issued, spelling out the functions and duties of the various divisions of the Executive Office of the President, including the more sweeping role of the Bureau of the Budget as it had been conceived in the Brownlow Report. Meanwhile, on April 15, 1939, Harold Smith, a strong supporter of the Brownlow view of how the Bureau of the Budget should operate, became the new director of the bureau. By the time Smith's tenure as director was completed, just over seven years later (the longest period ever served by any director), the institutional role of the Bureau of the Budget had been well established under both Presidents Roosevelt and Truman, and its size had reached over 600—roughly the present level.

Creation of the Office of Management and Budget

Although the institutional role played by the Bureau of the Budget staff was well suited to the styles of both Roosevelt and Truman, the penchant of Budget Bureau career staff to serve the presidency rather than the president and to shy away from political considerations often appeared to later presidents to be unresponsive to their own immediate needs. In addition, by the 1960s the administrative management role of the bureau had declined. Reflecting his desire to exercise closer presidential control over policy management, President Richard Nixon, soon after his election, focused on reorganization of the Executive Office of the President. The result was Reorganization Plan Number 2,

FIGURE I. OFFICE OF MANAGEMENT AND BUDGET

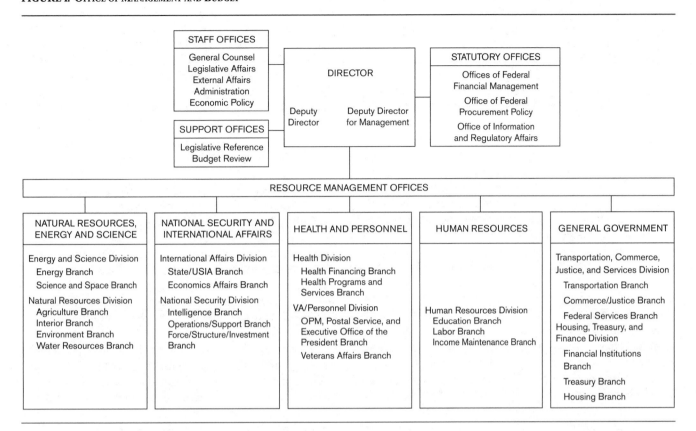

which on July 1, 1970, redesignated the Bureau of the Budget as the Office of Management and Budget.

The main objectives of the reorganization plan were to place renewed emphasis on management within the newly redesignated OMB, to remove policy control from the OMB by creation of a separate Domestic Council, and to make OMB more responsive to presidential demands by placement of a new set of political appointees, called program associate directors (PADs), in supervisory positions between the career staff of budget examiners and the budget director.

The Office of Management and Budget: Its Current Role

The current role of OMB can best be described in three main areas: the budget process, legislative reference, and administrative management.

The Budget Process

The central element of OMB as well as its main source of whatever power has been ascribed to it, has always been its budget role and its budget examiners—the career staff individuals who review agency budget requests and manage the execution of the budget. In this staff, which has traditionally maintained close day-to-day contact with the agencies whose budgets they review, resides the expertise that has enabled the organization to serve, generally with effectiveness, as the institutional staff to the presidency. The budget examiners are organized in five separate resource management offices, each of which deals with a major segment of the federal government's activities. Each resource management office is headed by a noncareer program associate director (PAD) who reports to the director and deputy director. Except for the PADs, these resource management offices consist entirely of career staff. Four of the five resource management offices include two separate divisions, the fifth consists of a single division. The divisions, in turn, include from two to four branches, each of which generally deals with one or more federal agencies and related programs (see Figure I).

As noted earlier, the budget process role of the resource management offices includes both the formulation of the president's budget, in which agency requests are reviewed and alternatives may be proposed, and the execution of the budget, in which apportionments of funds are made to the agencies to enable them to carry out their programs and to serve as a basis for agency reporting.

Consideration of the budget process makes it clear why it is so important for the president to have, in OMB, an institutional staff with a high level of neutral competence. (Neutral competence can be defined as the ability to cooperate with and give one's best analyses and judgments to a succession of partisan leaders without becoming committed to the leaders or to their political objectives.) Budget requests, as submitted by the agencies, reflect the goals and objectives of the agency heads—which often do not coincide with those of the president. Indeed, to be successful any agency head must serve as an effective representative of his/her constituency groups and thus work to foster the achievement of their goals and objectives. The sum of all the agency budget requests, in any given year, will likely not only far exceed the total that would best serve the interests of the president (and the nation), but the content of the programs included could also differ from what would be in the best presidential interests. Based upon their in-depth knowledge of the agencies and programs with which they deal, the OMB budget examiners can prepare for presidential decision, viable alternatives to the plans and budget requests offered by the agencies. Since the budget examiners have no constituency other than the presidency, the alternatives they offer generally are likely to have a more governmentwide perspective and often better serve the interests of the president. Of course, in deciding which alternative to select, the president must take into account the political dimension as well. As OMB is currently organized, with PADs directly supervising the budget review and execution process, the political dimension can be brought to bear well below the presidential level.

Legislative Reference

One of the two support offices of OMB is the Legislative Reference Division, which has the primary responsibility to coordinate the review of legislation proposed by executive branch agencies or referred by the Congress. The Legislative Reference Division "coordinates" the review largely by referring the legislative proposals to the budget examiners in the responsible divisions as well as to the PADs and other agencies that may have an interest whenever appropriate. Although not spelled out in detail in the original 1921 Budget and Accounting Act, the power to review legislative proposals was very soon determined to be implicit in that act on the basis that "recommendations for legislation, the effect of which would be to create a charge upon the public treasury or commit the Government to obligations which would later require appropriations to meet them, should first be submitted to the President before being presented to Congress" (quoted in Bureau of the Budget Circular No. 49, issued December 19, 1921). Although this early interpretation of the legislative clearance power was to limit legislation that might ultimately result

in expenditures, subsequent events and executive orders have broadened that power to include all legislative proposals. The legislative clearance process is of great importance. As noted by Bruce Johnson (1988) in "OMB and the Budget Examiner: Changes in the Reagan Era," the legislative clearance process is used by budget examiners to enforce budget decisions, and in entitlement programs legislative clearance is the primary way to make budget choices.

Administrative Management

From the very start, with the creation of the Bureau of the Budget, it has not always been clear how the administrative management function would be exercised. Initially, whatever administrative management work was performed was done by budget examiners in the course of their budget review work. The administrative management function received special emphasis after the move of the Bureau to the Executive Office of the President, and in 1939 a Division of Administrative Management was created to take the lead in dealing with these matters. Since that time, the role and organizational from of dealing with administrative management in OMB has waxed and waned and has been the object of numerous organizational changes. At present, there is a deputy director for management, appointed by the president with the advice and consent of the Senate, who supervises three statutory management offices that exist within OMB: the Office of Federal Financial Management, the Office of Federal Procurement Policy, and the Office of Information and Regulatory Affairs. The Office of Federal Financial Management seeks to improve financial management across the federal government in the areas of financial information systems, financial standards, asset management, and general agency financial management. The Office of Federal Procurement Policy is concerned with procurement ethics, lobbying practices, increasing government use of regular commercially produced "off-the-shelf" products, and sets policy for federal acquisition regulations. The Office of Information and Regulatory Affairs manages the regulatory review process and addresses problems of federal paperwork and its burdens on the public and provides policy on statistics and information management.

Before a March 1, 1994, reorganization of OMB, there had also existed a separate General Management Division, under the supervision of the deputy director for management, with responsibility for governmentwide improvement in property and personnel management, long-range planning and program evaluation, and productivity improvement. In an effort to improve coordination with the budget side of OMB (the resource management offices), this separate division was abolished and its functions and staff were merged with the resource management offices.

In the same reorganization, substantial portions of two of the three statutory management offices (excluding the Office of Information and Regulatory Affairs) were also merged with the resource management offices. This 1994 reorganization is the latest step in the effort to make the administrative management function within OMB more effective. The reorganization also redesignated OMB's budget examiners as program examiners and is based on the premise that "program review" by the resource management offices should include the full range of administrative management and budget review.

Other Functions and Organizational Units

OMB's role in dealing with executive orders and proclamations is handled by the Office of the General Counsel. Of course, as with most things that OMB does, this function normally utilizes the substantive expertise of the program examiners. The Budget Review Support Office has the major responsibility of managing and overseeing the entire budget formulation process as well as a variety of other critical functions of an OMB-wide nature, including tracking of budget-related legislation.

Changing Roles: Current Problems

As an organization so much in the public eye and exercising so powerful a role in the federal budget process, it is not surprising that OMB is the subject of some controversy. Three interrelated and partially overlapping trends have been at the root of OMB's current problems: (1) the shift in budget process emphasis from bottom-up to top-down, (2) growth in Congress's budgetary capability and power, and (3) greater politicization of OMB.

When the Bureau of the Budget was created, emphasis in the budget process was bottom-up in the sense that there was not an initial focus on budget totals; rather, the totals turned out to be whatever its parts added up to. In later times, attempts to use the budget as an instrument of fiscal policy, the growing size and importance of the deficit and the various efforts to control or reduce it, and the new congressional budget process created by the Budget and Impoundment Control Act of 1974 and the Budget Enforcement Act of 1990 as amended in 1993 all served to shift greater emphasis and importance to the totals—or to a top-down approach.

The same Budget and Impoundment Control Act of 1974 greatly increased congressional budget power and capability with the creation of the Congressional Budget Office, the budget resolution process, and the budget committees. For the first time, Congress was given its own independent capability to deal with the totals as well as the details of the budget; no longer was Congress dependent on OMB for technical support in dealing with the budget.

As described by James Pfiffner (1991) in "OMB: Professionalism, Politicization, and the Presidency," the politicization of OMB involved five separate elements: movement from an institutional to a personal staff; insertion of political appointees, the PADs, in line positions; public advocacy and visibility of the institution; loss of credibility—as a direct result of advocacy; and downgrading of the career staff.

As a result of these trends, not only has OMB become an overt advocate of the programs and policies of the current president, but it has also assumed a major role in dealing with Congress—where previously the main effort in justifying the president's budget to Congress had been left to the individual agencies. Because the congressional process deals with totals initially, in the budget resolution, no single agency can represent the administration in dealing with the budget. Only the budget director can play this role.

In order to support the budget director in dealing with Congress, a new set of tasks has been imposed on OMB: that of keeping track of and interpreting what Congress is doing: This is no small task, involving tracking and interpreting the potential budgetary impact of a host of legislative bills and resolutions at each stage of their evolution through subcommittees, committees, floor actions, and conferences. The new tasks of tracking legislation and negotiating with congressional staff, coupled with the ongoing regular tasks of reviewing the agency budget requests and preparing the president's budget, have imposed so much workload on the OMB program examiners that there is little time remaining for any of the more traditional type of budget and program analysis in reviewing details and creating viable alternatives. Potential new workload, such as supporting the new requirements of a line item veto, would even further dilute the effectiveness of an already thin staff.

In the eyes of some observers, the current situation poses serious risk for the effectiveness of OMB as a trusted institutional adviser to future presidents.

DAVID SITRIN

BIBLIOGRAPHY

Berman, Larry, 1979. *The Office of Management and Budget and the Presidency, 1921–1979*. Princeton, NJ: Princeton University Press.
———, 1987. "OMB and the Hazards of Presidential Staff Work." In Allen Schick, ed., *Perspectives on Budgeting*, 2d ed., 162–170. Washington, D.C.: American Society for Public Administration (ASPA).
Brundage, Percival F., 1970. *The Bureau of the Budget*. New York: Praeger.
Burkhead, Jesse, 1956. *Government Budgeting*. New York: John Wiley & Sons.

Helco, Hugh, 1975. "OMB and the Presidency–The Problem of Neutral Competence." *The Public Interest*, vol. 38. 80–98.

———, 1984. "Executive Budget Making." In Gregory B. Mills and John L. Palmer, eds., *Federal Budget Policy in the 1980s.* Washington, DC: Urban Institute, 225–291.

Johnson, Bruce, 1988. "OMB and the Budget Examiner: Changes in the Reagan Era." *Public Budgeting and Finance,* vol. 8 (Winter) 3–21.

———, 1989. "The OMB Budget Examiner and the Congressional Budget Process." *Public Budgeting and Finance,* vol. 9 (Spring) 5–14.

Joyce, Philip G., 1993. "The Reiterative Nature of Budget Reform: Is There Anything New in Federal Budgeting?" *Public Budgeting and Finance,* vol. 13 (Fall) 35–48.

Pearson, Norman N., 1987. "The Budget Bureau: From Routine Business to General Staff." In Allen Schick, *Perspectives on Budgeting*, 2d ed., 124–155. Washington, D.C.: ASPA.

Pfiffner, James P., 1991. "OMB: Professionalism, Politicization, and the Presidency." In S. J. Colin Campbell and Margaret Jane Wyszomirski, eds. *Executive Leadership in Anglo-American Systems.* Pittsburgh, PA: University of Pittsburgh Press 195–227.

USER FEES AND CHARGES.

Prices that governments charge for their services.

Background

In theory, user fees and charges perform the same functions that prices serve in the private market: They signal the correct allocation of resources so that the government knows how much of the service to provide and the consumer knows how much of the service to demand. If the user fees and charges are set correctly, the amount provided will equal the amount demanded.

There are some narrow differences between "charges" and "user fees" (Downing 1981). Charges represent a payment for a service and are designed to be a method of excluding individuals from enjoying that service if they do not pay. The total paid in user charges may vary by how much the service is used; for example, total water charges may increase as water consumption increases. The individual can lower total payments by reducing the use of the service. Fees, however, represent a payment to the government for expenses incurred in providing special services; for example, the expenses of police services at private events are often paid by the sponsor. Because the distinction between user fees and charges is a narrow one, the terms will be utilized interchangeably in this entry.

Fees and charges may serve a variety of purposes. In addition to their use as signals for resource allocation, they may be used as a revenue source with little regard for allocation or efficiency concerns; they may serve as a device to ensure that the service is equitably priced; or they may be used to prevent overconsumption of a service.

User charges fit under the benefit approach of financing a service, at least for those that are voluntary. The consumer of the government service should be willing to pay the user fee up to the amount at which the marginal benefits the consumer receives are equal to the fee.

Unlike the private market, a citizen does not always have the right to forego the service and avoid the fee; for example, it may be mandatory for homeowners to pay sewer connect fees. Some argue that this finance structure is not a true user charge and it may be thought of as a residential unit tax (Mikesell 1991). In many jurisdictions, however, many of these types of fees consist of more than one part. They are composed of a baseline charge that every resident must pay and an increment to cover any additional service level. In garbage collection, for example, the base fee might cover a one-container pickup whereas additional fees are charged for additional containers. In this example, the baseline charge might be the equivalent of a unit tax whereas the increment would be the charge. Others argue that since a resident has the option of moving out of the neighborhood, the entire fee can be thought of as a user fee (Downing 1992).

Two particular subtleties should be noted in any discussion of user fees and charges. First, they are not land use exactions (which are imposed on the developer and are either cash or in-kind gifts to the government to offset some of the public costs of the development). Second, there is also disagreement whether the revenues raised by special assessments are true user charges (Zorn 1991). Special assessments are the fees that residential or commercial residents pay (assessed for specific geographic areas) typically for the provision of capital services. This entry holds that these assessments are the price of living in a neighborhood and should be counted in a broad definition of fees and charges.

Theory of User Fees

There are two basic roles for prices in a market system. One role is to signal to the producers of a good how much the good would sell for in the market. The producers take this information and pay for enough resources to produce the efficient amount of the good. A second role is to signal to consumers of the good how much it will cost them to purchase the good so that they can compare the price to the marginal benefits they would receive from that purchase. Consumers who gain benefits from consumption of the good allocate their resources to purchase enough of the good so that the marginal benefit they receive is equal to the price they pay (which is the marginal cost of production). To the extent that user charges are correctly designed, they act as price signals and help the jurisdiction supply the amount of the public service that consumers demand at that price. If this occurs, public resources will be efficiently used to meet consumer preferences. To serve the allocation goal, the user charge must be correctly designed. This is a two-stage process. The first stage is a decision concerning whether the service has the particular attributes that allow the application of the market mechanism. In particular, this means that the good cannot be a pure public good and must have the characteristic of voluntary price excludability–that is consumers will voluntarily pay a price for the good and if they do not pay the price, they will not have the use of the good. For example, if a developer needs a permit to construct a building, he will voluntarily pay a user fee to the jurisdiction to obtain the permit since he cannot build without one. The city should charge the marginal cost of the city planner's time necessary to evaluate the building permit. At this point, the developer evaluates whether the benefits from receiving the permit exceed the costs of obtaining the permit.

Theoretically, for most services, user fees should be set equal to the long-run marginal costs of providing the service–that is the long-run additional costs of providing the additional amount of the good. The higher these costs, the higher the fee. This implies that the second stage–the careful measurement of these incremental costs–is necessary. These costs would include not only the production costs of the service, but also transportation costs (for example, the costs of transporting water), connection costs, and delivery costs (which may vary by population density). In some cases, user charges can also be used to finance the additional infrastructure needed for development. In these cases, the charges should have a component that is independent of the direct marginal use of the facility, since the facility itself has to be provided before it is used. This necessitates a flat charge as well as a charge that varies by use.

Four basic general principles of efficient user charge pricing have been derived (Fisher 1988):

1. The larger the proportion of marginal benefits that go to the direct users, the more efficient are user charges.
2. Unless the direct users can be easily identified and excluded from consuming the service by the price mechanism, user charges will not be efficient.
3. It is the marginal benefit-marginal cost relationship that determines the efficient amount of the service.
4. The greater the price elasticity of demand for the service, the greater the efficiency case for user charge financing.

For some governmental services, the marginal cost of including one more beneficiary of a fixed amount of the service is zero (i.e., the good is nonrival). However, user charges might still be indicated in this case if, with a zero charge, an overuse of the service occurs. This overuse could lead to congestion costs. In these cases, user charges can be utilized to ensure that the optimum amount of congestion will occur. For example, a bridge toll might be enacted to prevent bridge congestion.

Extent of Use

Nearly every basic service that local government provides garners some receipts from user fees or charges. The fees run the gamut from parking to police fingerprinting. However, even with this wide use, there is still a large amount of variation among jurisdictions in the utilization of fees and charges and also a wide variation within any jurisdiction as to the extent that the fees and charges are utilized. Because of the great variety of fees already in existence, if jurisdictions can learn from other experiences, there is a large potential for revenue growth in this area. At least one author argues that the importance of fees for local governments could triple (Downing 1992).

Table I (which uses Netzer's broad definition and includes special assessments) illustrates the extent of the use of fees and charges. During 1990–1991, they were used by all levels of government and averaged about 17 percent of revenues. However, there is a good deal of variation included in this average. For example, the national government receives about 11 percent of its revenues through fees (principally postal fees and natural resource fees) whereas local governments receive about 34 percent of their own source revenues through fees and charges. Further, there is a good deal of diversity in the source of fees: state governments receive about 12 percent of their fees and charges from utilities whereas local governments receive about 40 percent from utilities. Even after utilities are excluded, these is a heavy concentration of fees from a very few sources. Excluding utilities, states receive about 77 percent of their fee revenues from their top two sources (higher education and hospitals), whereas locals receive 46 percent from their top two (hospitals and sewerage). It can also be seen that over time, the national government is diversifying its fee structure whereas state and local governments show a slight increase in concentration of sources. Although fees received from other sources are not trivial, they are best described as a large number, scattered among a variety of services, none of which are generating a very large amount of money. Finally, it should be noted that a subcomponent of the local government category, enterprise special districts, receives a large percentage of its revenues from fees, with the figure at times approaching 90 percent (see **special district**).

Much of the increase in the use of user fees occurred during the 1970s, although the trend seems to have stabilized in the 1980s. This general increase may reflect several

TABLE I. EXTENT OF THE USE OF FEES AND CHANGES

Fees as Percent of Revenues	1960–1961	1970–1971	1980–1981	1990–1991
All Governments	12.9	13.1	14.3	17.0
National	9.2	6.1	8.3	10.7
State	8.6	9.6	12.2	13.0
Local	28.3	24.0	33.9	34.1
Utilities as Percent of Total Fees				
State	0	0	19.7	12.0
Local	48.1	41.1	43.5	40.4
Top Two Sources Not Including Utilities as Percent of Fees				
National	81.7	78.8	70.7	67.4
State	69.1	72.2	76.5	76.6
Local	40.9	38.6	46.3	46.0

Definitions: Fees include utilities and special assessment charges; revenues are own source general revenues plus utilities and special assessments.

SOURCE: Bureau of Census, 1994 *Government Finances*. Washington D.C. USGPO.

mutually reinforcing propensities:

1. An increasing dislike of broad-based taxes that often seem to fund ill-defined government programs and as such are often the subject of tax revolts, especially the property tax;
2. the ease of imposing a fee, which can often be done without a formal vote of the jurisdiction's population;
3. an increase in spending on functions that have always been user-charged financed, for example; an increase in local-government-operated utilities and airports;
4. both an increase toward the provision of services that are user fee coincident with an increase in the extent to which user charges finance that spending, for example sewerage, health care (through third party reimbursement), or public higher education;
5. an increase in the importance of user charges for particular services, for example, recreation and refuse collection; and
6. an increase in interstate tax competition, leading to more benefit types of taxation (Netzer 1992; Bailey 1994).

Some Administrative Considerations

There are five basic administrative considerations concerning the use of fees and charges:

1. the determination of the correct fee;
2. the determination of the fee for natural monopolies;
3. the difference between the statutory incidence and the economic incidence of the fee;
4. the trade-off between the fees collected and the administrative and compliance costs of collecting those fees;
5. the acceptance of the implementing jurisdiction of the inherent revenue risks of using fees and charges.

At times it can be difficult to determine the theoretically correct fee that reflects the long-run marginal cost of providing the service. Often increments of the service are lumpy, engineering cost data are not available by small increments of service, not all components of the marginal costs (such as opportunity costs) are easily obtained, and accounting rules (such as those relating to depreciation expenses) are incorrectly used from the perspective of economically accurate calculations. In these cases, jurisdictions tend to use average costs, which depending upon the extent to which scale economies are realized, may be either higher or lower than marginal costs.

A second difficulty in calculating the correct fee is accounting for any externalities associated with the provided service. To the extent that these externalities are generated because of the service, the marginal costs should include the amount necessary to internalize the externality. Unfortunately, the costs or benefits of externalities are often even more difficult to measure than those of direct service provision.

If the efficiency rule of setting price equal to marginal costs were followed for a natural monopoly, the revenues per unit would not cover average costs. A situation would then occur in which a monopolist who was forced to price efficiently would lose money and ultimately go bankrupt. In theory, the best solution to this problem would be the application of a two-part tariff, in which each consumer of the product of the natural monopoly would pay both a fixed charge and a charge that varied by output. In practice, average cost pricing or a regulated price adjusted to guarantee a fixed return is typically used.

The economic and statutory incidence of most user fees is the same. The burden is not shifted in the short run. This gives the fee a tendency to be regressive since it does not consider the income of the consumer. Any jurisdiction that moves to a large increase in use of user fees, especially those that are not completely voluntary, must be aware of this negative feature. Often, "life-line" types of programs—such as reduced rates for low income customers—are used to protect the poor in these cases. However, the voluntary element in the use of the service and therefore the total paid would tend to mitigate some of this negative aspect. It is sometimes claimed that some fees are shifted forward from the legal payer to another party. Typically, this argument concerns land use fees, in which the developer argues that the price of the development will increase, and therefore the fee is shifted to the home buyer. This is usually an incorrect argument in a competitive market in the short run—if the developer could charge a higher price before the fee, he would have. The incidence of the fee depends upon the market elasticities of supply and demand for the development. Note, though, in the long run, the developer is likely to move to a lower-cost environment, and housing prices could increase.

User fees are not costless to collect. Administration costs that the jurisdiction faces include the expenses of measuring use of the service, billing costs, and collection costs. Determining the legality of the charge could also add to administrative costs. Citizens face compliance costs that include such factors as time spent in calculating the correct payment, waiting time at toll booths, and perhaps postage and handling costs. Compliance costs will also increase if citizens are resentful of the charge. These costs must be added to determine the total costs of collection.

Finally, the jurisdiction must realize that moving to user charges increases the risk in revenue forecasts. To the extent that the demand for service is either misestimated or changes, the revenues garnered through these charges will change. For example, a recession might lead to a fall in revenues raised by construction permit charges.

An International Dimension

Although comparative analysis among countries is difficult because of definitional differences and because of differences in service responsibility (between public and private sectors and among levels of government), some attempts have been undertaken. The Organization for Economic Cooperation and Development (OECD) has generally defined user charges as required payments for noncapital goods and services, excluding any charges from state and national governments and charges for industrial services. Although this definition is incomplete (for example, it ignores infrastructure charges), it does give a basis for some analysis, although the U.S. data may be seriously biased down.

During the decade of the 1980s, the United States was about in the middle of the ten developed countries for which reliable data could be obtained in terms of increases in user charges, ranking sixth. The country with the largest increase, Australia, increased user changes by 425 percent; the country with the smallest increase, Germany, increased charges by 55 percent. The United States increased charges by 124 percent (Bailey 1994). In terms of the ratio of user charges to local taxes, the United States was again in the middle, with the charges being about 26 percent of local taxes. In comparison, in Ireland this ratio was 160 percent, whereas in Denmark the ratio was 12 percent.

The Future

The future of user charges depends upon a variety of factors. To the extent that the past explanations for the expansion of user charges, as noted above, remain viable, it is to be expected that the employment of fees will expand. There are also several additional reasons for a belief that this expansion will continue.

To the extent that the United States continues to engage in a downsizing of state aid to local governments, there is likely to be pressure on local governments to discover ways of increasing their revenues. User charges can be justified because they can be explicitly linked to particular services. Further, as long as the movement toward the various methods of contracting occurs, user charges are more likely to advance, since the contractors will be more likely to utilize these charges rather than depend on general tax revenues. Technological improvements will also lead to an increase in the ease of implementing user charges. For example, in some cases it may be possible to automatically bill for charges as a car enters an expressway. Perhaps most important, user fees and charges will be seen as legitimate tools for measuring consumer demands for government services and will act as a justification for public service provision.

Jeffrey I. Chapman

BIBLIOGRAPHY

Bailey, Stephen J., 1994. "User-Charges for Urban Services." *Urban Studies*, vol. 31, nos. 4/5: 745–765.

Bos, Dieter, 1985. "Public Sector Pricing." In A. J. Auerbach and M. Feldstein, eds., *Handbook of Public Economics,* vol. 1. New York: North-Holland, 129–212.

Downing, Paul B., 1981. *User Charges and Service Fees.* Washington, D.C.: HUD Urban Consortium.

———, 1992. "The Revenue Potential of User Charges in Municipal Finance." *Public Finance Quarterly,* vol. 20, no. 4: 512–527.

Fisher, Ronald C., 1988. *State and Local Public Finance.* Glenview, IL: Scott, Foresman.

Mikesell, John L., 1991. *Fiscal Administration,* 3d ed. Pacific Grove, CA: Brooks/Cole.

Netzer, Dick, 1992. "Differences in Reliance on User Charges by American State and Local Governments." *Public Finance Quarterly,* vol. 20, no. 4 (October): 499–511.

Zorn, C. Kurt, 1991. "User Charges and Fees." In John E. Peterson and Dennis R. Strachota, eds., *Local Government Finance.* Chicago: Government Finance Officers Association, 135–152.

V

VALUES ASSESSMENT. Also called "values clarification" and "values restructuring," it refers to the gathering, analysis, and utilization of stated, actual, and future (i.e., desired) values in order to improve alignment among individuals, organizations, and society at large. Stated values are what an individual or organization says it does; actual values can be either demonstrated or perceived performance or behavior; and future values are those that the organization and/or individual choose to adopt with the purpose of changing current and actual values over time. Values restructuring is caused by societal value shifts and organizational value adjustments.

Value shifts are substantial changes in social systems that consequently affect subsystems such as public administration (Kanter *et al.* 1993). In stable societies, major shifts only occur every few generations. In the United States it seems to result in a 50-year cycle, epochal changes having occurred in the 1930s move to activist government, the 1880s progressivism, the 1830s Jacksonian patronage-responsiveness movement, and so on (Lan and Rosenbloom 1992; Rosenbloom and Ross 1994). This infrequent level of substantial value changes is particularly important for us now because we are in the midst of a substantial value shift (Peters 1992, 1994; Ingraham and Romzek 1994).

Value adjustments are the intermittent adaptations that institutional subsystems such as churches, civic organizations, and public agencies go through as a result of value shifts. Value adjustments often do not occur in a direct linear relationship with value shifts because of internal traditions, priorities, rigidities, and critical mass issues. Value adjustments occur more like the pressure that builds up for earthquakes; sometimes pressure produces a larger number of small earthquakes, and other times, there is a big earthquake with aftershocks. In the private sector, organizations that cannot make appropriate value adjustments usually go out of business. In the public sector, many agencies are not allowed to die, but they may remain in a state of suspended malaise for decades if they are unable proactively to adjust priorities and values. Value adjustments also occur at the level of the individual.

Although individual and societal perspectives are indirectly considered in this entry, it focuses on the organizational perspective. Because organizations are complex entities, it is wise to have numerous types of assessments before trying either to better align current values or adopt new values. Seven types of value assessment strategies are discussed here: (1) mission, values, and planning and vision statement assessment, (2) ethics assessments, (3) customer and citizen assessments, (4) employee assessments, (5) performance assessments, (6) benchmarking, and (7) quality assessments.

Although most organizations have performed some of these assessments within the last four or five years, few organizations have conducted all of them and, until recently, organizations often analyzed assessment information without acting on the information. Selection of a few new or revised assessment strategies is generally preferred over use of all of them because of the resources required to administer them and analyze the results. Which assessment strategies to use is largely an executive decision based on informal criteria. In practice, public-sector executives are turning more and more to customer, employee, and quality assessments for fresh perspectives.

Mission, Values, and Planning and Vision Statement Assessments

Organizations generally have formal statements of what they do, what they value, and how they plan to achieve their goals. Organizational value adjustments usually begin with a review of these statements. In the public sector, this area is deceptively complex because, as Levin and Sanger (1994) note, "public organizations have diverse and multiple goals, defined for them by external elements; private firms have far fewer and can define their goals themselves" (p. 69).

Mission statements represent the global purpose of an organization or system. Organizational missions generally change slowly, although it is useful to revisit them from time to time for clarity and currency, even in stable times. In the public sector, mission statements can be found in the authorizing legislation. Mission statements are also found in published documents as a part of the budget process, for public education, and for internal training purposes. So profound are many of the current organizational value changes in the public sector that some organizations are seeking or experiencing changes in their authorizing legislation to fundamentally change their core purpose.

Values statements express the organization's principles by which members will operate. Such statements were relatively uncommon in the past since values had changed little for a long time but have become much more common in the last decade. Traditional values are largely implicit and may be best explored by comparing them to values that are being adopted by many contemporary organizations. Generation of a values statement have been widely hailed as a highly useful tool for those organizations changing their values set. Table I highlights some of the general values adjustments occurring in many organizations today.

As Table I indicates, the range of values shifting is startling. At the macrolevel, there is new emphasis on competition, market incentives, continuous improvement, weeding out programs, and reengineering processes. Values about structure are now emphasizing decentralization,

TABLE I. A COMPARISON OF TRADITIONAL PUBLIC SECTOR VALUES WITH THOSE COMPETING FOR EMPHASIS

Traditional	New
Macro Level Values	
Monopoly	Competition
Regulation (org. for control)	Market Incentives (org. around mission)
Reduction vs. Growth	Continuous Improvement
Adding Programs	Changing Programs
Values About Structure	
Centralized	Decentralized
Supervisor as Controller	Supervisor as Helper
Nondemocratic	Participative
Individual Work	Teamwork
Hierarchical Organization	Flat Organization
Simple Jobs	Multidimensional Jobs
Single Service	Multi Versions of Service
Values About Work	
Expert Focus (internally driven)	Customer Focus (externally driven)
Focus on Tradition (status quo)	Focus on Innovation (change)
Problem Analysis	Seeing Possibilities
Measurement Is Feared	Measurement Is an Opportunity
Protective	Productive
Performance	Ability
Inspection and Control	Prevention
Values About Employees	
System Indifference	Employee Needs
Employees as Expense	Employee as Asset
Manager Focus	Employee Focus
Appraisal/Sanction/ Ranking	Development/Learning/ Recognition

The author thanks James Flanagan, City of Phoenix for help with this table.

teamwork, flattened organizational structure, multidimensional jobs, and multiple versions of service provision. Values about work now generally emphasize customer (citizen) focus, innovation, creativity, measurement as a positive stimulus, bottom-line productivity, maximizing worker potential, and prevention of problems rather than reaction to them. Values about employees have stressed their needs, employees as assets, shifting management functions to frontline workers, and increasing employee development generally.

Planning statements are nearly as common as mission statements. They are efforts to define planned achievements. Planning and vision statements are found as a part of strategic plans, the budget process, and public relations materials. Vision statements are also future oriented but tend to be more global, less detail oriented, more inspiring, and realistic about the challenges that inevitably face achievement. Contemporary planning has tended to deemphasize and reduce inflexible, long-term strategic planning models and integrate popularly held vision elements. For example, planning models are increasingly allowing for learning and change as a natural part of the project cycle (Hamel and Prahalad 1994; Peters 1992, 1994).

Ethics Assessments

Ethics assessments, also sometimes called ethics audits (Lewis 1991), may either determine what the stated legal norms are and/or probe the gap between the stated legal values and the actual performance of the organization. The former is best done by an ethics audit structural assessment and the latter by an ethics audit perceptual assessment.

An ethics audit structural assessment is usually conducted by one or a few people. The researches determine, through document review, interviews, and expert analysis, what general ethics controls exist (such as conflict of interest), how operational areas that commonly lead to ethical breaches are controlled (such as travel), and what types of support for ethical normal exist (such as through training).

An ethics audit perceptual assessment focuses on what employees perceive rather than the controls and stated policies themselves. This is important since some organizations have few ethics policies and are nonetheless perceived to be highly ethical environments, and other organizations have many rules but are considered unethical environments. Perceptual assessments may survey overall ethical issues, select operational issues, and types of support and inspiration. Perceptual assessments should either survey a large sample or the entire agency. Although responses must be anonymous, responses can be color coded by division for better followup.

If ethical controls are already tight and commonly internalized, executives may decide to place assessment resources elsewhere.

Customer and Citizen Assessments

An explosion of interest in values related to customer and citizen values has led to an immense expansion of assessment use in this area in the public sector. Previously, there was a tendency to rely on experts to analyze and recommend from their experience. More recently, the tendency is to seek out direct input from customers and citizens and to use these direct data in problem selection and decision-making processes. Customer assessments are considered by many the single most powerful tool in assisting government organizations to make value adjustments today. Five types of customer-citizen assessments will be discussed: customer identification, citizen surveys, customer focus groups, customer complaint resolution, and community visioning.

Customer identification (similar to what was formerly called stakeholder analysis) is a popular tool in quality improvement initiatives. The assumption is that many organizations and units have become so process oriented and legalistic, and so captured by self-interests and territoriality, that they have forgotten just who their customers (stakeholders) are. Customer analyses can be powerful tools for discussion and for focusing more sophisticated assessment strategies that succeed them.

Citizen surveys are generally more expensive but reliable ways to tap into contemporary citizen values. They are more common at the local government level in which it was recently reported that 74 percent of all local governments implementing quality improvement initiatives promoted some sort of customer satisfaction survey (West, Berman, and Milakovich 1993). They can serve two functions. First, they rate perceptions of past services. Second, they rank perceptions of future expenditures.

Customer focus groups are a less expensive and ambitious assessment strategy but are nonetheless time-consuming to conduct properly. Focus groups can be selected at random but are more often selected based on prior experience. They can range from 3 to 50, but 5 to 15 is generally recommended for manageability. If focus groups precede other customer assessments, their aim is generally broad and exploratory. If they follow other customer assessments such as citizen surveys, they often concentrate on one or two issues that have been targeted as problems, but they look at those issues in great depth.

Customer complaint resolution in the public sector was generally handled by relatively legalistic dispute systems (administrative law) in the past. Several new trends are emerging. One is a trend to track complaints by type over time. This provides valuable information about systemic problems that are more efficiently handled by process changes or improvements rather than as individual problems to resolve. Another trend is to be more proactive in getting point of service evaluations (which assists in complaint tracking). Sometimes these evaluations are cards that are placed on service counters. In other cases, evaluation cards are sent periodically to every nth customer. Many police departments have begun sending every 20th ticketed speeding "customer" an evaluation form asking about the officer's courtesy, informativeness, and accuracy.

Community visioning is a process that encourages citizen input about ideal futures of their locality. By envisioning an ideal future and unifying behind it, community members contribute ideas, direction, and enthusiasm to the political process, which normally tends to be rather divisive in today's environment. Such a process simultaneously reflects and molds community values as citizens envisage ideals to achieve, rather than solely focus on problems to solve and conventional implementation issues (Peirce and Hall 1993; Chrislip and Larson 1994). The challenge is to relate these community "feelings" to tangible organizational value adjustments.

Employee Assessments

A long-time emphasis (and many would now assert imbalance) placed on the issues and values of management has recently veered toward a new focus on employee input and values as organizations become flatter and many management issues are decentralized to self-managing employee teams. Due to this trend, assessments of employee opinions and values have become much more common and more important in helping organizations make value adjustments. Three types are discussed here: employee opinion surveys, employee focus groups, and employee value sorts.

Employee opinion surveys can be administered internally or by an external consultant, whose experience and neutrality may improve confidence in the results. Employee opinion surveys tend to focus on the factors and levels of job satisfaction and evaluations of organizational effectiveness in various areas. Although a strict sense of confidentiality must be maintained, results can be identified by division so that feedback can be more specific and follow-up action can be more targeted. As with other survey data, it is useful to see results compared on a longitudinal basis.

Employee focus groups are relatively easy to assemble. They usually are used to identify the detailed aspects of an already articulated problem (such as a general problem identified in an employee opinion survey), to brainstorm alternate strategies, or to critique a revised process. Employee focus groups bring not only employee values to bear, but employee creativity as well.

One important use of employee value sorts is to gather employee perceptions of organizational values. Such a profile can be useful when new values are being considered for the organization. Because high-performing organizations tend to have similar organization value clusters, a wide range of perceptions in this type of value sorts should lead to sustained employee discussions about organizational value adjustments in order to enhance loose consensus (Katzenbach and Smith 1993; Drucker 1993). Employee value sorts can also be used to identify specific employee values about their preferred work environment. Because employees rank aspects of work differently, a profile of those values can assist management in meeting those needs better as well as enhancing employee understanding of alternate priorities. For example, those in a research unit may place a high value on a creative work environment, freedom, and support. However, the administrative and clerical elements of that same unit may place a low value on those elements and instead select structure, security, and financial rewards as the most important values.

Performance Assessments

Every organization and unit has its own performance standards. In the public sector, performance standards traditionally have suffered from at least six problems: weak comparability with other similar units, lack of unit costs, lack of rewards for efficiency, inability to measure true effectiveness, inability to measure team and system performance, and a deficiency in identifying and correcting systemic errors. Because of the tremendous importance of performance standards in a competitive environment, there has been much work in this area in the last decade (Hatry *et al.* 1990; Harris 1995), but the results are still rudimentary. Without improvement in performance assessment that remedies traditional weaknesses, organizations will have difficulty in tying their value adjustments to concrete goals. This section will look at three major areas of performance assessments: traditional, evaluation, and new.

Traditional performance standards include those that focus on individuals, organizational units, and the overall organization. Individuals have workload requirements such as the amount of work that must be produced, the size of the budget to be managed, the number of employees to supervise, and so forth. They also have performance criteria that have recently been enhanced with the new emphasis on quality such as error rates, timeliness, customer relations, service and product appearance, expertise, ease of use and access, and problem solving ability. Organizational units have similar performance standards aggregated at the next, higher level but must also consider whether customer needs are being met overall, whether the services provided are in statutory compliance, and what constitutes unit and individual success. Some other traditional performance measures include productivity per employee, safety (accidents), absenteeism, and turnover. At the highest level, the organization monitors its operating and capital costs against authorized expenditure estimates.

Evaluation and audit performance measures are internal mechanisms that monitor performance. Internal comptrollers and auditors monitor expenditure requests and fund balances. Management monitors worker compliance with statutes and policies. Cash disbursements are generally dually controlled: special units monitor inventory, vehicles, and fixed assets; and auditors pay special attention to the completeness and accuracy of data. In the past, most of the attention was devoted to stopping poor or illegal practices after they had occurred and thus adopted a legalistic inspection approach. There has been some value adjustment in many organizations with more interest in preventive and educational approaches in regulatory areas as well

as a search for market-based incentives to replace legal mandates in service provision areas. Finally, it should be noted that there has been much recent attention to improving efficiency measurement through the expansion of cost accounting and unit cost practices, and effectiveness measurement by focusing as much on outcomes as outputs.

While some of the newer trends in performance measurement have been intimated, there are others worthy of mention because they are likely to complement major value adjustments. Although team performance measures are still nearly nonexistent, there is a tremendous interest in bringing them into individual performance evaluations. Additional progress will need to be made as self-managed teams become more commonplace in the public sector. Continuous learning and continuous improvement are almost entirely unmeasured in most public-sector organizations, but this type of productivity must be captured quantitatively, much like the Japanese companies that routinely record thousands of improvements by thousands of workers. Measures of reengineering (Hammer and Champy 1993) or massive systems redesign (Fiorelli and Feller 1994) tend to be conjectural or nonexistent. Supplier and "partner" performance is currently moving from a adversarial approach to a more proactive, mutual problem-solving approach. Last, there is a new interest in system integration. This is leading toward a rethinking of rigid and impersonal personnel functions, a reworking of cumbersome and antiquated data management systems, an inclusion of more stakeholders in the administrative decisionmaking process, and a more aggressive attitude toward process and procedure streamlining and improvement.

Because performance assessment is where "the rubber meets the road," it is critical that organizational values reshaping carefully consider this complex area. The adoption of new values invariably means the deemphasis of other values that are deemed excessive in the current environment. For example, the extreme statutory and legalistic approach to performance measurement common in the past is being softened so that systems have greater flexibility to experiment, inspire rather than intimidate, and capture the synergy of collective thinking.

Benchmarking

Benchmarking is defined by Christopher Bogan and Michael English (1994) as seeking out superior performance through systematic search for and use of best practices including innovative ideas, effective operating procedures, and successful strategies. Today we tend to think of benchmarking primarily in its most sophisticated form, the analysis and use of practices adapted from world-class leaders. However, Bogan and English point out a seven-level hierarchy of benchmarking including learning from past internal successes, borrowing good ideas without regard to their origin in the organization, developing internal best practices, matching average or standard practices, establishing leadership through industry best practices, targeting national best practices without regard for industry, and matching or exceeding world-class practices. Benchmarking is the science of using internal and external comparison assessments to stimulate higher performance. Although the focus of benchmarking is on changing practices, process, and procedures, these frequently require concomitant value adjustments to implement.

Quality Assessments

There are numerous types of quality assessments today. They share a number of features: They are all relatively comprehensive and stress customer satisfaction, employee involvement and development, continuous learning and improvement, prevention over inspection, and supplier partnerships far more than was done in past organizations. Taken seriously, quality assessments inevitably cause numerous substantial values adjustments because the principles promoted are at variance with the operational values of most organizations today. Because of its renown, the Malcolm Baldrige National Quality Award will be discussed first. Other quality award systems will also be briefly mentioned.

The Malcolm Baldrige Awards have seven formal categories that are assessed: senior executive leadership, information and analysis, strategic quality planning, human resource development and management, management of process quality, quality and operational results, and customer focus and satisfaction (Malcolm Baldrige National Quality Awards 1994). The different categories receive different weights with customer focus and satisfaction being substantially more emphasized than the other categories. To score well on the Malcolm Baldrige criteria, it is assumed that the organization has conducted numerous assessments and, in fact, has institutionalized assessment as a part of organizational life. The awards do not insist on a particular assessment strategy, but they do suggest that routine assessment is the foundation of management by fact. Therefore, the types of assessment discussed in earlier sections of this chapter are consistent with Malcolm Baldrige Award criteria and implicitly expected of world-class organizations. Some of the award's outstanding strengths are their comprehensiveness and their rigor.

Malcolm Baldrige Awards are not the only relatively comprehensive quality assessments. Although they dominate, others are of note. Since 1988, the federal government has conducted the President's Award for Quality and the Quality Improvement Prototype Award (QIP). The programs currently use the same criteria, with the highest-scoring applicant receiving the Presidential Award and the

runners-up receiving the QIP Award. The award criteria have always been modeled on the Malcolm Baldrige Awards but with language more accessible to the novice quality-initiates and more consistent with the public sector. There are planes to integrate these federal awards with the Malcolm Baldrige system in the next few years (OPM 1994). Many states have initiated quality awards programs for state government agencies. Numerous states have adopted the Senate Productivity Award, which allows local government applications. Of course, the prototype for quality awards, the Deming Award, was invented in Japan. The Europeans use a system called ISO 9000, which is a quality assurance system that affects mainly the private sector at this time but is likely to have public sector ramifications by the next century.

Conclusion

The environment in which organizations exist occasionally undergoes major changes or shifts, which result in significant adjustment in values and practices in those organizations. The United States is currently responding to a major value shift in the public sector. In order to be able rationally and intelligently to adopt (or reject) "new" values, organizations must have a clear sense of what their current values are. This is much more difficult than it would seem because we take values for granted much the way we do the air we breathe, which is invisible, tasteless, and everywhere, but nonetheless critical to existence. Therefore, almost all change strategies begin with an assessment phase. If the assessment phase is too hurried or badly done, it is likely that the changes will be unsuccessful or superficial.

It is important to remember that only the rigorous investigation of values and practices leads to a genuine understanding about the need for new values. Furthermore, some of the assessment strategies discussed enhance the forward aspects of assessment, such as vision statements and visioning, customer surveys identifying future desires, employee surveys identifying strategic opportunities, benchmarking, and quality assessments. The task of distinguishing traditional and new value emphases in order to make rational decisions about what value adjustments to make can only be made after balanced assessment has been done.

MONTGOMERY VAN WART

This article is a condensed and slightly amended version of Montgomery Van Wart, 1995, "The First Step in the Reinvention Process: Assessment," *Public Administration Review* vol. 55, no. 5 (September-October) 429–438.

BIBLIOGRAPHY

Bogan, Christopher E., and Michael J. English, 1994. *Benchmarking for Best Practices*. New York: McGraw Hill.
Chrislip, David D., and Carl E. Larson, 1994. *Collaborative Leadership*. San Francisco CA: Jossey-Bass.

Drucker, Peter F., 1993. *Managing for the Future: The 1990s and Beyond.* New York: Plume.

Fiorelli, Joseph, and Richard Feller, 1994. "Re-engineering TQM and Work Redesign: An Integrative Approach to Continuous Organizational Excellence." *Public Administration Quarterly,* vol. 18, no. 1 (Spring): 54–63.

Hamel, Gary, and C. K. Prahalad, 1994. *Competing for the Future.* Boston: Harvard Business School Press.

Hammer, Michael, and James Champy, 1993. *Reengineering the Corporation: A Manifesto for Business Revolution.* New York: HarperCollins.

Harris, Jean, 1995. "Service Efforts and Accomplishments: A Primer of Current Practice and an Agenda for Future Research." *International Journal of Public Administration,* vol. 18, nos. 2–3: 253–276. See these volumes for a symposium of articles on service measures.

Hatry, Harry P., *et al.,* 1990. *Service Efforts and Accomplishments Reporting: Its Time Has Come.* Norwalk, CT: Governmental Accounting Standards Board.

Hutchins, Greg, 1993. *ISO 9000: A Comprehensive Guide to Registration, Audit Guidelines, and Successful Certification.* Essex Junction, VT: Oliver Wight.

Ingraham, Patricia W., and Barbara Romzek, eds., 1994. *New Paradigms for Government: Issues for the Changing Public Service.* San Francisco, CA: Jossey-Bass.

Kanter, Rosabeth Moss, Barry A. Stein, and Todd D. Jick, 1993. *The Challenge of Organizational Change.* New York: Free Press.

Katzenbach, Jon R., and Douglas K. Smith, 1993. *The Wisdom of Teams: Creating the High-Performance Organization.* Boston: Harvard Business School Press.

Lan, Zhigong, and David H. Rosenbloom, 1992. "Public Administration in Transition?" *Public Administration Review,* vol. 52, no. 6 (November-December): 535–537.

Levin, Martin A., and Mary Bryna Sanger, 1994. *Making Government Work: How Entrepreneurial Executives Turn Bright Ideas into Real Results.* San Francisco, CA: Jossey-Bass.

Lewis, Carol W., 1991. *The Ethics Challenge in Public Service: A Problem-Solving Guide.* San Francisco, CA: Jossey-Bass.

Malcolm Baldrige National Quality Award, 1994. *Award Criteria.*

OPM, 1994. "President's Quality Award Program Will Move to Baldrige." *Federal Quality News,* vol. 2, no. 6 (April) 1, 9.

Pierce, Neal, and John Hall, 1993. *Citistates.* Washington, DC: Seven Locks Press.

Peters, Tom, 1992. *Liberation Management.* New York: Alfred A. Knopf.

———, 1994. *The Pursuit of Wow! Every Person's Guide to Topsy-Turvy Times.* New York: Vintage.

Rosenbloom, David, and Bernard H. Ross, 1994. "Administrative Theory, Political Power, and Government Reform." In Patricia W. Ingraham and Barbara S. Romzek, eds. *New Paradigms for Government: Issues for the Changing Public Service.* San Francisco, CA: Jossey-Bass.

West, Jonathan, Evan Berman, and Mike E. Milakovich, 1993. "Total Quality Management in Local Government." *The ICMA Yearbook.* Washington, D.C.: ICMA.

VERWALTUNGSMANAGEMENT. The public administration reform movement of the Austrian government.

This contribution is a report on and discussion of a large-scale reform endeavor on the federal level based on theoretical deliberations and practical working experience in this project. It is intended to provide examples and learning opportunities concerning the approach, strengths, and weaknesses of the administrative reform. The most complex and prominent reform project on the federal level in Austria is the so-called Verwaltungsmanagement. The following pages will describe the development from 1987 to 1994, its contents, organization, methods and procedures, and the main results and further outcomes of this important and controversial project.

In 1986, a special department was installed in the Federal Chancellery that was given responsibilities in the areas of federalism and reform, developing the first ideas on the project. This constitutes a considerable change compared to former reform endeavors: no isolated, independent projects within the ministries should be undertaken but one large, complex, integrated, and interministerial project with respective subprojects.

The development of the project approach is based on the experiences in Austrian ministries and with Swiss, German, and British reform projects. The specific and strongly criticized feature of the project is that all 14 federal ministries are involved in the project simultaneously; organizational analyses are conducted in each of them and within a common overall strategic framework. Rationalization and change proposals are developed and those with high priority are implemented in a coordinated way. Based on a resolution of the ministerial council (at the end of 1989), the project was started in all ministries and was planned for a period of 5 years.

The formal framework and guidelines are laid down in an official project manual resolved and passed by the Ministerial Council. This manual also serves as an orientation basis for a competitive public tendering for consulting firms. About 70 firms submited proposals and 8 were selected based on specific evaluation criteria.

In the following, the main features of the project will be described. The description is based on the Project Manual, and open interviews with key decisionmakers.

Project Goals

- Reorganization of task and management structures, concentration on core tasks:
  adjustment of competencies and responsibilities
  contracting out
  abolishment and reduction of tasks
- Increasing productivity by 20 percent within four years:
  critical evaluation of core tasks
  improving efficiency and effectiveness
- Reducing costs of administrative processes:
  development of cost and performance ratios and indicators as management instruments

- Concentration on management tasks:
  relieving top executives of day-to-day overload and thus creating capacities for strategic tasks
  improving service functions for the citizens

One major (planned) feature of the project is that the focus should be on a stronger emphasis on results and output rather than the management by mere resource allocation (input orientation): Performance and performance responsibility are the key words. However, an important precondition is the setting of goals and objectives by the politicians and chief executives in the administration. (This being a complex and difficult task could not be reached on a broad basis until 1994–1995 and will need further efforts in order to be realized at least partially).

Strategic Project Principles

- Emphasis not on one "test-office" but on "office-tests."
- Demonstration of the federal government that there is a serious attempt to improve the public administrative performance.
- Improving close relationships with citizens–the citizen as client.
- Reform being implemented together with and not in opposition to the civil servants.
- High degree of involvement and participation of civil servants concerned into the project.
- Creating synergies and a general positive "reform climate" in order to foster the attainment of the project goals in the long run.
- Maintenance of ministerial autonomy: The project management in the Federal Chancellery is only responsible for project methods, organization, results analysis, and coordination.
- Project organization according to the principles of project management concerning planning, steering, and monitoring of progress, time, and costs and the definition and allocation of competencies and responsibilities among the participating institutions.

One of the crucial issues of the administrative reform is the way in which increased efficiency and effectiveness can be realized:

- Should the central functions and responsibilities for the federal budget administration (Ministry of Finance) and number and type of job positions (Federal Chancellery) be strengthened within these organizations? Or
- Should these functions and competencies be reduced with a simultaneous development and implementation of increased autonomy in the other ministries? This approach would require the development of appropriate planning, steering, and control instruments.

Traditionally, the first way has been emphasized until now. However, proposals from the reform project indicate a change toward decentralization and a strengthening of ministerial autonomy.

The Department of the Minister of Federalism and Administrative Reform is organized within the Federal Chancellery, and its main reform responsibility is the coordination of the relevant activities within the federal administration. Based on the Constitutional Law, the implementation of any project lies exclusively within the ministries concerned. The minister mainly plays the role of a promoter and sponsor of a service and a coordination center providing target-group-oriented services.

The reform project is oriented in two directions: (1) adaptation to changing challenges and requirements in the long range and development of respective concepts and (2) emphasis on short-term restoration in respect to economies and efficiency. Both dimensions are considered to be important. The short dimension is seen as a "therapy of symptoms" through which small-scale successes can be achieved quickly, whereas the long-term concept emphasizes the analysis and removal of the fundamental causes of the deficiencies and in this respect is a slow and laborious learning process, which has to overcome many obstacles in an incremental way.

In the areas of personnel and finance, emphasis is given primarily to long-term development and orientation. The project course consists of three phases:

Phase One: Basic administration analysis (1989)
Phase Two: In-depth and interministerial studies (1990–1994)
Phase Three: Autonomous implementation of subprojects (1994 ongoing)

Reform Project–Phase One

In Phase One, a general analysis of the strengths and weaknesses of the ministries is conducted. The primary purpose is the identification of main areas with a high potential for improvement.

Project Organization
The reform endeavor is based on a project management concept in order to coordinate all organizational units involved within the planned time and costs and to ensure the consistency of project philosophy and goal orientation in all ministries and with all external consulting firms. The project directly covers 14 ministries with about 8,700 civil servants. Indirectly–including all decentralized organizations–some 150,000 people will be affected in the long run by the project results. The description of the project organization is adapted from the official project

FIGURE I. PROJECT ORGANIZATION PHASE ONE

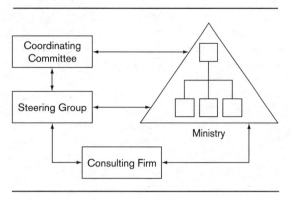

manual developed and published by the Federal Chancellery (1989).

Coordinating Committee. Chairman of the coordinating committee is the Minister of Federalism and Public Administration Reform; the committee includes representatives from all ministries and the civil servants union. The responsibilities of the committee include:

- central organizational/political institution deciding on project matters and providing the basis for governmental decisions;
- provides the organizational and financial basis for the entire project;
- monitors the project;
- applies for tendering and contracting the consulting firms and for budget allocation;
- assesses and comments on the consulting firms' reports on the ministries;
- prepares and resolves reports to the government;
- decides on motions and proposals of the steering group.

Steering Group. The responsibilities of the steering group are defined as follows:

- coordinates the overall project and the subprojects on the operational level in respect to deadlines, costs, and goals in close cooperation with the respective ministry;
- prepares the business of the coordinating committee;
- transforms the project reports about the ministries into condensed information for the government via the coordinating committee;
- coordinates all activities concerning interministerial issues.

Intraministerial Organization. The intraministerial project organization follows the principles of a matrix organization; the project coordinator has competences and re-

sponsibilities that put him into a position to control the project. The project coordinator:

- directly supports the ministerial top executives (division chiefs and/or minister) in project matters and reports to the top executives;
- is in direct contact with the steering group and is the representative of the ministry in the coordinating committee;
- is the "turntable" between the project manager of the consulting firm, the ministerial project group (civil servants on different levels of hierarchy) within the organizational units in the ministry and the steering group.

Ministerial Project Group. Appointed by the minister; for the duration of the project, the members of the project group are exempted from other duties according to project workload and priorities (approximately 25 percent of regular working time). They remain in their organizational units and work part-time on the project as required. They have sound professional knowledge of the ministry and are responsible for the support of the implementation of the subtasks, for deadlines, and for the performance of these tasks.

Personnel Representation. Union representatives are involved in all decisionmaking processes on important project steps and in the assessment of measures and recommendations.

External Consulting Firms. The external consulting firms are selected by the ministry concerned and the steering group in a joint decisionmaking process based on criteria specified in advance. A detailed differentiating profile is developed against which the firms' proposals are measured.

Analysis Area of Phase One

- Organization: goals, structure, distribution of competencies, strengths and weaknesses, relationships between central and noncentral organizations, work process analyses, interministerial issues;
- basic resource-performance relations;
- costs;
- personnel and financial capacities;
- savings potentials.

Despite a common overall framework, these areas are worked on by external firms and ministries in methodologically and conceptually different approaches and—not surprisingly—the results are manifold and diverse.

The major results are a structured representation of the organizations and tasks, the identification of those areas in which a high potential for rationalization could be expected. Important problem areas concerning the interfaces

FIGURE II. INTRAMINISTERIAL MATRIX ORGANIZATION

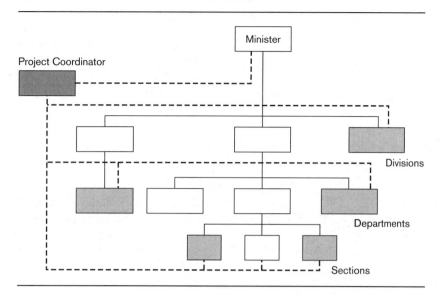

between ministries and between the center (parent ministry) and the decentralized (subordinate) organizations can be defined in detail. In particular, civil servants on all hierarchical levels are invited to develop proposals and suggestions that are systematized as one basis for the in-depth studies in Phase Two.

Major rationalization/reorganization potentials are identified as follows:

- reduction of participation rights and approval duties of ministries (ministry of finance, Federal Chancellery) concerning matters within other ministries;
- decentralization;
- organizational improvements within ministries (structure, process, technology);
- privatization.

In total about 3,700 suggestions from all ministries are structured systematically. Two-thirds of them can be realized within the ministries themselves. The rest is structured according to specific themes and forms the basis for in-depth studies concerning complex and encompassing problem areas, which promises high rationalization potentials.

The most important issues resulting from Phase One are the following:

- More than one-third of the suggestions concerned volume, effectiveness, and efficiency of task fulfilment.
- About 40 percent concerned improvements of organizational structures and processes.
- 20 percent showed room for improvement of information technology and job issues.

- 20 percent concerned leadership, motivation, pay, training.
- 10 percent concerned legal matters (change of laws) (*Verwaltungsmanagement Projektbericht* 1994, p. 11).

Reform Project—Phase Two

The analysis of Phase One resulted in nine interministerial in-depth studies, seven of which were started in 1990–1991. The most important subprojects are described below.

Reduction of Responsibility Overlapping

Overlapping of responsibilities between ministries results in considerable efficiency and effectiveness problems. The main task of this in-depth study was the analysis of multiple responsibilities in the top federal administration and the development of change proposals. Especially, the following areas were identified: task related, nonoverlapping structures, optimization of spans of control, positioning of staff units, abolishment of overlapping in the areas of budget and personnel, environmental protection, European Union and international organizations agenda, economic and cultural development, financial management, issues of youth and family, traffic, statistics.

Leadership and Personnel

Leadership and personnel are given increasing attention. Modern approaches of human resource management are to be emphasized: leadership profiles, leadership guidelines, motivation issues, personnel requirements and personnel development, growing mobility of civil servants, delegation of decisionmaking, performance orientation.

Budgeting and Management Control

Main issues are the increase in transparency of budget planning and execution, the development of management control and cost accounting systems.

Strategic Electronic Data Model

The ministries provided numerous proposals on improving information technology. This subproject focuses on the development of an integrated strategic electronic data model focusing on three major areas:

- societal conditions for the implementation of information technology (citizens' expectancies, information management in lawmaking processes);
- management aspects of technology (organization, resources, internal service fee calculation);
- technical infrastructure and international standards.

Buildings and Offices

A problematic feature of the federal administration is the permanent scarcity of office space and the fact that organizational units are scattered in many buildings resulting in logistic and work process inefficiencies. There is a high degree of scattering of ministerial units in 86 sites. This subproject aimed at

- maintenance of value and usability of federal buildings;
- efficient office allocation;
- office maintenance and logistics;
- setting of priorities based on transparent and objective requirements.

Office Management, Technical Communication, Documentation

The technical state of the art in different ministries varies to a high degree, and there is a long duration of file work processes (transport and unexplained time is almost 80 percent of the total case processing time). The project focused on the efficient completion of files under the given legal and organizational conditions, which is considered to be an important element of the legality principle and openness to scrutiny of administrative action. In order to improve the situation the emphasis is on office information systems (electronic file), rationalization, and technical workplace design.

Procurement

Federal procurement organizations and activities show a high potential of rationalization, decentralization, and standardization.

Civil Servants' Business Trips

It is interesting to note that the costs of federal business trips have increased in a way that makes it necessary to an-alyze the respective legal norms, process organization (application, approval, financial clearing), and management aspects. The taking advantage of the size of the federal administration as contract partner for services like airlines, travel agencies, railways, hotels, cars, and so forth is another important issue. The overall organization is too complicated and expensive and does not use (to a satisfactory degree) modern possibilities of travel management also because of obsolete technology and legal norms.

Project—Phase Three

The main issue of this phase (beginning in 1994) was the implementation accompaniment of intra- and interministerial projects in respect to methods, interministerial coordination, and financial and personnel support by the Federal Chancellery. One strategic idea was to initiate learning processes between organization units working on the same topics and thus to foster project developments.

Critical Assessment of Verwaltungsmanagement

Role of the Federal Chancellery

Due to the legal, historical, and organizational contingencies, the Federal Chancellery is in a rather difficult position as to reform responsibilities. In fact, it does not have formal competencies vis-à-vis the autonomy of ministries. Several functions are not clear: Concerning the reform agenda, the Federal Chancellery, on the one hand, is in a "staff position" (coordination, recommendation without direct possibilities of intervention); on the other hand, it carries responsibilities and competencies for the overall federal administration concerning decisions on personnel positions. The Chancellery is seen by the ministries as very powerful, and many conflicts concerning personnel development issues result. The permanent issue is the centralization or decentralization of personnel related competencies, and there exists a rather high degree of reluctance to accept the Federal Chancellery's influence and control functions.

Political Priorities

Another basic problem is that political interests and changing priorities on the highest levels have a tendency to reduce the status and importance of management-oriented reforms and to retard the respective projects. Accordingly, reform projects are allocated low financial and personnel resources and, therefore, the desirable momentum is lacking. Traditionally, the need and interest to really work on efficiency and effectiveness cannot be said to be highly prominent, and there are no well developed incentives to do so.

In Phase One, many single measures were developed; however, the overall success is rather limited compared to the expectations. One very positive effect is that many organizational units developed a high degree of problem awareness, and various projects promise further developments in the long range.

An Organizational-Political Perspective

A useful analysis and interpretation of the strategic and tactical reactions of individuals and organizational units to the reform project can be provided from a micropolitical perspective. Some major features of change illustrate various dimensions of individual and/or organizational policy toward or against reform endeavors.

Specific Contingencies. An important issue are the specific contingencies of the organizations concerned like the basic attitudes of management and key actors toward reform, the actual political and administrative climate and priorities, the degree of acceptance of the project coordinator, and the history of other reform projects.

Individual and Organizational Interests. Different interest groups inside and outside the administrative system (e.g., organizational units, key decisionmakers, unions, political parties, public institutions, private institutions, media) articulate very different and often conflicting requirements and subjects of change. The interest in the project (support or resistance) can depend—among other things—on

- the in-house goals that can be reached through the projects;
- the in-house goals that can be threatened by the projects;
- the possibilities to reduce external pressure through the project; main areas are resource scarcity, increasing task complexity and dynamics, critical demands of citizens for more services at no cost;
- the possibilities to improve one's own positive through specific project results.

The implementation of reforms constitute threats and pressures to the involved oganizational units and interest groups. Examples are as follows

- changes of the power structure: loss of power for units/individuals (reduction and/or loss of tasks);
- loss of personnel;
- transparency: discovery of weaknesses and slack resources;
- pressure toward more efficient and effective performance;
- sacrificing of beloved habits and behaviors;
- losing "political games" (e.g., union vs. management).

Benefits or threats of change are perceived differently in different organizational units and on different levels of hierarchy. Therefore, within organizations, the interests are not homogeneously pro or contra reform but can be different depending on the actors' subjective perception and anticipation of costs and benefits according to their interest.

External Consulting Firms. Despite the requirements to achieve unity of the firms' approaches—there are different procedures and methods of the external consulting firms—and depending on that, more or less resistance and better or worse results can be found in Phase One.

- Many external consulting firms do have problems during organizational analyses and data gathering. They lack in some respect specific knowledge of administrative norms, regulations, procedures and, therefore, are not able to ask the right questions or to assess reported situations correctly. As one consequence many of the results stated are being contended by the organizational units concerned and not accepted as "correct facts."
- External consulting firms tend to use the ministries as "a paid opportunity to learn" and only give feedback on issues that are known anyway. However, the externals' view and integration of details without wearing organizational blinkers is of great value and adds to momentum for change endeavors.

Goal Attainment

In 1994, the reform project was closed formally, but the subprojects, of course, are continuing. At any case, Verwaltungsmanagement has provided many opportunities to initiate encompassing change in the federal administration (Project Report 1994, p. 125). In general, the strengths and weaknesses as related to the goals can be summarized as follows:

Reorganization of Task and Management Structures, Concentration on Core Tasks

The main problems are the finding of now obsolete tasks and the self-definition of responsibilities and tasks by managers. In this highly sensitive area, political and organization-political strategies of resistance (micropolitics) play a particular role. The official project evaluation arrived at the conclusion that this goal has been attained in a very limited way only (Project Report 1994, p. 127).

Increasing Productivity by 20 Percent within Four Years

Officially as well as informally (on purpose or not), the term "increasing productivity" is equated with "personnel reduction." This argument, which was also published, leads to resistance by the civil servants. However, exactly this goal directs the awareness toward thinking in terms of efficiency and effectiveness and promotes the reform climate, and in several organizations modest success can be reached.

Reducing Costs of Administrative Processes

At the beginning of the project, cost awareness within the administration was practically "zero" (Project Report 1994, p. 130). The project contributes to the development (and implementation) of cost accounting approaches in several organizations and to a growing interest in the topic. As an overall result, there is an increase in cost accounting projects.

Concentration on Management Tasks

In connection with other project goals, a very important approach on leadership and personnel is developed that contributes to a climate favorable for a new way of perception of management and leadership tasks and leading away from the mere administration of organizations and personnel by chief executives. But—as holds true for most of the reform details—changes occur in homeopathic doses and in small steps.

Improving Service Functions

The idea that citizens (taxpayers) are not only "addresses of legal norms" but are clients having a right to receive services is accepted and realized to an increasing degree. This is reflected in more intensive calls for transparency of administrative costs and by an increasing focus on behavioral issues of civil servants (leadership, motivation, personnel development, performance).

Overall Assessment

The projects in Phase Two can be classified as promising. The most important topics—"leadership and personnel development" and "management control/cost accounting"—are emphasized and promoted officially. However, only little progress can be registered. A major problem in the area of management control system (in German, "Kontrolle") is the semantic closeness to "controlling" (the traditional audit and control a posteriori); therefore, it is interpreted as another very subtle instrument of a posteriori control combined with a priori elements, which has to be declined.

There is no systematic and effective promotion and marketing of successful subprojects in the diverse organizations. However, projects contribute to an improved climate, and topics that could not be approached before can be discussed now. The minister of federalism and reform

has only limited competencies in demanding the realization of resolutions taken in the Council of Ministers. He mainly has to rely on the goodwill and cooperation of the other ministers. There are also certain discrepancies between resolutions of the Council of Ministers and their realization within the ministries and subordinate organizations. The project teams in the ministries are not relieved from day-to-day business, which led to an incompatibility of tasks and responsibilities and to considerable overload that can be compensated for only by high personal committment. In this context, the problem of low (nonexisting) incentives for innovative managers and civil servants is not solved at all. From a political perspective, a reform of this dimension can be undertaken and realized in the long run only; however, politicians formulate their success criteria between election and reelection—rather short-term oriented. The overt behavior of unions is a rather constructive one. Of course, they want to score points concerning pay and quality of working life. One of the issues of the reforms concerning leadership and personnel development is the representatives' fear of a weakening of their traditional positions and influence because of improving relationships between supervisors and subordinates and the possibilities of direct and individual participation and codetermination.

Success of the reform will mainly exist on the level of interpersonal relationships between those actively and passively concerned, the increasing buildup of direct contacts, incremental step-by-step approaches and "snowball effects." Frequently it is argued that cutting back on resources represents the only possible strategy to foster reforms, and resource allocation should be undertaken on zero-based budgeting. However, exactly this type of concept presupposes specific attitudes and ways of thinking, which are assumed to be initiated and intensified by reform endeavors. In this respect, the reforms are somehow caught in a vicious circle. Another basic reform problem is the view of many concerned that innovations imply that former approaches were wrong and faults would have to be admitted. This phenomenon results in the fact that weaknesses can only be addressed and discussed in an inadequate form and openness.

Passed-on roles of civil service and traditional structures stand in the way of goal and performance discussion and reorientation. Legal norms are given as reasons for nonalterable situations, although, of course, there would exist sufficient room for maneuver. A strong internal orientation of the administration is dominating; planning and fulfillment of tasks, performance and service benefits for the clients would have to be focused on much more strongly.

Another problem represents the low quantitative and qualitative personnel capacities and the scarce budget in both the organization of the Minister of Federalism and Reform and in the ministries themselves. The question is to which extent this situation results from strategically oriented intentions against reforms based on the argument of unknown cost-benefit relations and scarce reform budget. In principle it is accepted that if reform endeavors are not supported to a high degree by top politicians and chief executives, the chances of success tend to be very low. The project Verwaltungsmanagement was not very successful in making reform a broadly accepted political topic (Project Report 1994, p. 136). The aimed at performance orientation must be seen as a goal very difficult to be attained and if at all only in the long run. The traditional principle of "resource use" still predominates administrative processes, and the issues of efficiency and effectiveness are not at all fully treated.

However, as an overall conclusion, there are various merits to the project (Project Report 1994, p. 13):

- encompassing and integrated high quality collection of proposals forming a very valuable ground for further projects;
- establishment and advancement of project management methods;
- topics, that had been declared "taboo" several years ago are now broadly discussed issues, building an important basis for ongoing work in the ministries;
- increasing the awareness concerning the necessities of implementing management know-how and promotion of a respective organizational culture toward performance, effectiveness, and efficiency.

FRANZ STREHL

BIBLIOGRAPHY

Project Report, *Verwaltungsmanagement Projektbericht,* 1994. Vienna: Federal Chancellery.
Project Manual, *"Verwaltungsmanagement,"* 1989. Vienna: Federal Chancellery.
Strehl, Franz, 1989. *Reformarbeit in der öffentlichen Verwaltung.* Frankfurt: Nomos.

VETERANS' PREFERENCE. The practice of giving special consideration to veterans in the distribution of public-sector jobs. This practice, in some form, is common in governments throughout the world. In the United States, this preference has usually taken the form of five points being added to the test scores of veterans or ten points being added to the scores of disabled veterans at the time they are considered for public-sector jobs. By awarding these veterans' preference points any public-sector jurisdiction gives them an advantage in competing with nonveterans in merit systems. The final test score determines an individual's rank on hiring registers. The more total points, the higher the rank on the hiring register; the higher the rank on a hiring register, the higher the probability of gaining employment.

Although veterans' preference as a philosophy in the United States was originally designed to help returning servicemen reenter the workforce following war, over the years veterans' preference programs have come to impact more than initial hire decisions. In addition to awarding points to veterans in initial hire decisions, some jurisdictions also make provisions in their veterans' preference statutes awarding extra points to veterans when they are competing to retain their jobs in reduction-in-force type situations, and some jurisdictions award points in promotional-type decisions.

The practice of awarding veterans' preference points has been a well-institutionalized process in the federal government since the Veterans' Preference Act of 1944; however, prior to this legislation, through individual departmental practices and customs, some federal departments were already awarding veterans' preference in some classifications. U.S. history of veterans' preference can be traced back to the administration of George Washington when he disproportionately chose military leaders for the earliest public-service positions following the Revolutionary War. Since that time, the general philosophy that the United States owes a special obligation to the defenders of liberty has become more and more institutionalized through law.

Laws similar to federal legislation providing for veterans' preference for the federal civil service also exist at the state and local levels throughout the United States. It is very common to find veterans' preference systems in place in merit systems at the state, city, and county levels.

This legislation has always been controversial. Oftentimes personnel professionals feel that awarding points based on veteran status is a violation of the spirit of the merit system wherein points are supposed to be earned by education or by experience. Women's groups have often looked at veterans' preference systems as vehicles that result in discriminatory impact against them since women have traditionally not chosen to pursue military careers. Also, traditionally the military has set quotas on the number of women that could be in the services at any one point in time.

The United States Supreme Court ruled in 1979 in *Personnel Administrator v. Feeny* that the discriminatory impact of such legislation on women was not intentional and that because women veterans were given points in the same way as male veterans, there was no violation of the Equal Protection Clause of the Fourteenth Amendment to the U.S. Constitution.

Attempts were made to eliminate veterans' preference in the federal government during the passage of the Civil Service Reform Act of 1978, but they were unsuccessful. Politically, veteran's preference legislation has been popular, and veterans groups have been quite organized and vocal in protecting their members' interests. Although they have been most controversial, it is unlikely that veterans' preference systems will disappear from merit systems of U.S. public employment in the near future.

ROBERT H. ELLIOTT

BIBLIOGRAPHY

Elliott, Robert H., 1985. "The Fairness of Veterans' Preference in a State Merit System: The Employee's View." *Public Personnel Management*, vol. 15 (Fall): 311–323.
Personnel Administrator v. Feeny, 1979. 422 U.S. 256.
Stahl, O. Glenn, 1983. *Public Personnel Administration*, 8th ed. New York: Harper and Row, 134–137.

VICKERS, SIR GEOFFREY (1894–1982).

The English solicitor, public administrator, and later, management and systems theorist, best known for his concept of appreciation and the appreciative system. Vickers wrote eight books, *The Art of Judgment* perhaps best known among them, and nearly 100 articles for journals in several different fields. Charles Geoffrey Vickers was the youngest of three children born to a lace manufacturing family in Nottingham, England. In 1913, he entered Merton College at Oxford University, where he read "Greats"–the Greek and Latin classics. A year later, with the outbreak of World War I, Vickers was made a very young officer in the Seventh Battalion of the Sherwood Foresters fighting in Belgium and later in France. His acts of heroism on the battlefield earned him the Victoria Cross and, later, the Croix de Guerre.

Vickers' Several Careers

After the war, he returned to Oxford and finished his degree in classics in 1921. A few years later, Vickers qualified as a lawyer and joined the prestigious City of London law firm of Slaughter and May. He was reputed to be, even early in his career, an "almost dangerously brilliant" attorney. In the 1930s, the gathering storm on the European continent prompted Vickers to turn his attention more to public affairs; this resulted in his involvement in the intellectual circle in London, known as "the Moot." Besides Vickers, its members included Adolph Lowe, the refugee German economist, the poet T. S. Eliot, Michael Polanyi, the scientist and later epistemologist, Karl Mannheim, the sociologist (and another refugee from Nazi Germany), and Reinhold Niebuhr, the ethicist. Although little record remains of the Moot, this was clearly in intellectually formative environment for Vickers.

World War II found Vickers back in the military, now 46 and a colonel. He was assigned to the Ministry of Economic Warfare, of which he later became director. He also became a member of the Joint Intelligence Committee of the Chief of Staff. In 1945, he was knighted for his service.

Shortly thereafter, he began a new career when he was named legal adviser to the newly created National Coal Board, the government organization that was to run the nationalized British coal mines. In 1948, Vickers was made a board member and placed in charge of manpower, training, health, education, and welfare. Upon his retirement from the coal board in 1955, he began his last and most productive career as a management and systems theorist. Still, he kept a number of positions that he then held, such as chair of the Mental Health Research Council and member of the Medical Research Council. These experiences added breadth to his already broad interdisciplinary background, and he was able to make contributions to academic discussions beyond management and systems, in medicine, psychiatry, psychology, and anthropology.

During this period of intellectual production, Vickers became what he called a "para-academic," lecturing in an unusual variety of professional programs at several universities, primarily in the United States and Canada. He was to maintain this pattern for most of the remainder of his life, until failing health curtailed his travels in the late 1970s. He spent several terms at the University of Toronto in Canada, where he led colloquia in the School of Social Work and lectured to the faculty of Applied Science and Engineering. He lectured at the School of Public Health at Harvard and contributed to their development of the concept of community medicine. In the 1970s, he spent periods of time at the city planning programs at the Massachusetts Institute of Technology and the University of California at Berkeley, as well as the public administration program at George Washington University in Washington, D.C. He also developed relationships, though fewer in number, with British academics, particularly the systems groups at the University of Lancaster and the Open University.

Systems Thinking

Even before Vickers turned to writing and scholarship during his "retirement," perhaps the single greatest influence on his own thinking was the emergence of the "systems" perspective. Beginning shortly after World War II, writers such as Norbert Wiener, Ludwig von Bertalanffy, and Ross Ashby introduced into the intellectual community a set of ideas about systems and their control that had been gestated in several, different, more technical arenas. Although their definition grew quickly problematic, systems were seen as wholes, greater than (or different from) the "sum" of their parts, as composed of interrelated parts, and as depending on some sort of "steering" mechanism to maintain those relationships over time.

For many, including Vickers, the systems metaphor seemed a promising way to resolve nagging questions about organizations and societies. Indeed, Vickers reported the advent of systems thinking as having a profound impact on him. Some systems theorists, however, became almost immediately preoccupied with the notion of a "general" systems theory, one that would apply to all systems. Unsurprisingly, given the modern, epistemological dominance of technique and rationality, this concern was captured by a general theory that fit best those systems that could be fully described, and even fully designed. Herbert Simon, for example, was to follow this path. Theorizing was thus reduced to modeling, which, construed in this explicit fashion, could not accommodate processes that are partly tacit, such as human judgment. The concomitant development of the digital computer and then of sophisticated management information systems, exacerbated this tendency in systems thinking. Beginning with *The Art of Judgment* (1965) and culminating with *Human Systems Are Different* (1983), Vickers was concerned to avoid thinking of systems in so narrow a way as to preclude an adequate account of human judgment and decisionmaking. His concept of appreciation, sufficiently expansive to describe human activity from the level of individual consciousness to the level of culture, was Vickers' means to accomplish this broadening of scope.

Appreciation

Vickers' best-known intellectual contribution is the notion of the "appreciative system." We each have an appreciative system, and these appreciative systems are what links us to one another. The twin roots of appreciation are ethics and epistemology. Our ability to make sense of contexts—to appreciate—rests on the foundation of our self and mutual expectations, themselves built by accretion through our experience. Vickers notes that the set of mutual and self expectations is the basic regulator of society. These mutual and self-expectations set the standard of what ought to be, by which deviance is defined; and they are constantly on the move under the influence of the process they mediate. The basic human experience, then, is the experience of manifold relations through time. What is uniquely human, according to Vickers, is the ability to situate oneself within a myriad of contexts simultaneously. Even at the level of individual consciousness, it is relationships, managed through time, that are central to the human experience. It was one of Vickers' most basic insights that human meaning is constituted through relationships, and the development and maintenance of relationships through time is the basis of human activity from consciousness to culture.

Vickers clearly stated his conviction that appreciation was a partly tacit process, and one which was not fully describable. It is a regrettable prejudice of modern times that those things which are fully describable are honored with the terms "scientific" and "rational," whereas those that are not are deemed unscientific or irrational. To say that something is partly tacit is not to relinquish all hope of understanding it or to relegate it to the realm of the mystical. Rationality and appreciation should not be seen as conflicting but complementary—not as dichotomous but as dialectical.

Appreciative judgment—the central theme in *The Art of Judgment* (1965)—has three components; each has the common denominator "judgment" to emphasize that the three are facets of a single process that should not be treated dichotomously:

1. Reality judgments (epistemology): judgments of what is or is not the case, including cause-effect beliefs and other complex "facts."
2. Value judgments (ethics): judgments of what should or should not be the case, including ethical oughts, wants, and desires, prudential and self-interested considerations and individual and collective goals and norms.
3. Instrumental judgments: judgments of the means available to reduce the mismatch between is and ought, including those personal resources we have available to bring to bear (time, attention, intellect, passion, money, power), and those social means that, individually or collectively, we can marshall and apply (by influence, if not by command) through communication, coalition, and various means of access to social institutions. Note that goal-seeking behavior does insufficient justice to these processes and that the notion of managing relations through time is far richer in capturing these dynamics.

Taken together, these three features—using the lens of appreciation—provide the anatomy of judging and problem solving. It is crucial to understanding Vickers' considerable contribution to note that only the third one of these is of concern to economic and rational versions of decisionmaking (the first two are taken as "given," in a kind of "hidden hand" *deus ex machina*). The ground of acting in any way whatsoever (as opposed to merely reacting in some automatic way, such as by instinct or reflex) involves some conception of the way things are and the way they might be. Purposeful action involves a perception (however dim) of a preferred state and an attempt to move toward it by selecting specific means from the indefinitely large number of possible actions. From the level of the individual manager making decisions, Vickers successively broadened his focus over time, largely in response to the continued narrowing of scope of so many other thinkers.

The Appreciative System

This same, fundamentally relational, appreciative process was then extended by Vickers to ever-more encompassing systems, from groups to organizations to political and economic relations within a society of national cultures to the most widely shared context of meaning of all—our basic humanity. The appreciative system encompasses two sets of standards or norm, which are only separable conceptually. In everybody thought and action, the two sets of norms—standards of fact and standards of value—are essentially seamless. The first set of norms, standards of fact (epistemology), represents the way we classify and characterize objects and relations, whereas the second set of norms, standards of value (ethics), represents the way in which we judge those objects and relations good or bad, welcome or unwelcome, important or unimportant, acceptable or unacceptable. Appreciation thus encompasses a variety of processes, including the ability to discriminate figure from ground, signal from noise, the ability to create and alter organized patterns with great subtlety and interaction of theme and variation, and the ability to harmonize disparate ideas—or failing that, to mute dissonance through selective inattention. These are not simply subjective processes that occur within an individual's head. Rather, they are relational, intersubjective processes that involve communicative interaction with other people. Among the features of an appreciative system are the following:

1. The ability to see patterns in complexity—and to vary those patterns according to different criteria and interests. Coupled with this is our ability to suspend the natural tendency to settle for a single pattern of reality as "the" pattern, which can close off search prematurely. This openness permits consideration of different definitions of the situation, which in turn permits consideration of a broader repertoire of response.
2. Artful selectivity in all manner of decisions about what features of the situation are "most important," given varying interests, values, and concerns. The mental pictures of reality that we construct are far more like those of the painter than of the photographer. Like the painter, we not only make many decisions about what to highlight but, at least as important, about what to omit. In management, executive attention is always among the scarcest resources; decisions on what not to pay attention to deserve careful consideration and require judgment.
3. The ability to "read the situation," which is particularly pronounced in first-rate managers. And related, how much to simplify the complexity of the environment and in what ways.
4. Appreciation is more an analogical than a logical process. It works through identifying the "fit" or "misfit" of ideas, values, experiences. This is largely an aesthetic determination.
5. Unlike the objective detachment emphasized by the "scientific" method, appreciation acknowledges the presence and indeed the investment of the self in the process. The self may be viewed as the instrument, the vehicle, or the medium through which the appreciative process works. Further, appreciation depends

on the presence of a caring bond between the self and other, subject and object. The bond may be between two people in a communicative interaction, or it may be the relation between a person and object, as between a sculptor and clay, or even between a scientist and a field inquiry.

Vickers, Barnard, and Simon

Sir Geoffrey Vickers' thought can be compared favorably in some respects with that of Chester Barnard and Herbert Simon. When Barnard (1938) wrote *The Functions of the Executive* in the 1930s, he wrote, like Vickers, as a practicing manager who saw great promise in the emerging structural-functional school of sociology, then under development by Talcott Parsons at Harvard and others. But one might say of Barnard that he was an "undisciplined" thinker, because *The Functions of the Executive* bears little resemblance to the narrower, scientific discipline of sociology as it emerged in fully developed form over the next quarter century. For example, a sociologist of management in the 1950s or 1960s simply would not have addressed the moral dimension of management, as Barnard did so eloquently in his book. Further, Barnard stated his challenge in describing managerial behavior as the difficulty of communication, "the sense of an organization, the dramatic and aesthetic feeling," and went on to lament the overly narrow, scientific approach of many, "because they are oblivious to the arts of organizing. . . . They miss the structure of the symphony, the art of its composition, and skill of its execution, because they cannot hear its tones" (Barnard 1938, p. xiv).

Simon wrote *Administrative Behavior* about a decade later, in part attacking "principles" of management that he saw as only masquerading as science. Here, he introduced the concepts of "bounded rationality" and "satisficing" as ways to ameliorate the roadblocks to explanation caused by human beings on organizations persistently acting in less than rational and less than maximizing ways. Instead of considering further the actions and behaviors behind these concepts, Simon went on to transform bounded rationality into a much narrower technical rationality in *The New Science of Management Decision* (1960), in which he extols the prospects of computerized models of decision-making, and even the potential for artificial intelligence applications for decision models, thereby completing the removal of human beings from human processes altogether.

All three authors wrote in the context of the modern age. The modern age incorporates a social, political, and economic world increasingly characterized by technical rationality, specialization, bureaucratization, and secularization. Technical rationality is a result of the combination of the Enlightenment belief in science and the subsequent succession of technological developments. At the beginning of the twentieth century, the gains of the physical sciences were so impressive to so many that they quite naturally wanted to apply the same methods in the social and political world, to achieve sciencelike precision and objectivity in these spheres as well. Technical rationality led to specialized, expert knowledge. This compartmentalization of knowledge, symbolized by the various departments and schools of the modern university, led to a contextless, a historical inquiry across the social science disciplines. Of the three authors, only Vickers' work transcends these limitations of the modern age.

The thinking of Simon and Vickers enjoyed only a brief intersection in which there were perhaps as many similarities as differences. This intersection is represented most closely by *The Art of Judgment* and *Administrative Behavior.* In his introduction to the 1983 edition of *The Art of Judgment,* the sociologist Kenneth Boulding mentions footnote 4 in Vickers' own introduction, in which the points of agreement between the two are described. Boulding observes that Vickers' concept of appreciation offers a more robust account of exercise of human judgment or decision than Simon's bounded rationality. Although both thinkers can be described as "systems" theorists in the sense that both are informed by the concept of "system," their work from that point moved in nearly opposite directions. Simon's work can be characterized as the epitome of the modern age in its scientific and overly narrow approach, whereas Vickers' work increasingly diverged from and eventually transcended the strictures of the modern age.

From Management to Culture

Vickers' interests changed and broadened over the course of his career as an author. He moved in successive stages from the sociology of management to issues of governance to a broad concern with the stability of Western culture. One of the Vickers' favorite sources was Thomas Huxley, the nineteenth-century biologist and Darwinist. He was particularly fond of citing Huxley's juxtaposition of the metaphors of the garden and the jungle. Nature, as represented by the jungle, has its own regulators; it crowds as much as possible into a given space and creates the struggle for survival. Natural selection happens as a result of a constant, daily test of the fit (or misfit) between the plant and its environment. The gardener, by contrast, prunes and weeds and thinks, using other criteria of selection–namely, appreciation.

In human culture, as in agriculture, the selection of the normative criteria by which we will govern ourselves (that is, ethics) is to some considerable extent left up to us, within the broad constraints determined by our nature. The first step is to appreciate the nature of the task and the meaning of growing in a culture. Vickers was deeply concerned that we in the West show so little understanding of community and are so disinclined to acknowledge our de-

pendence on it. Community nourishes and sustains us; it is indispensable that we remain deeply rooted in it and sustain and nourish it in return.

Our social institutions, including organizations both public and private, which are the most ubiquitous embodiment of our culture, require our most tender and our most tenacious ministrations. Vickers' vision was that, for our culture to survive in the future in anything like its present form, we will need to acquiesce to greater and greater intrusions on our individual autonomy, submit to greater exercise of authority (even though it will doubtlessly be abused), and offer up more and more attention and effort to sustaining community in opposition to the forces that threaten to disintegrate it.

GUY B. ADAMS

BIBLIOGRAPHY

Works by Sir Geoffrey Vickers:

Vickers, Geoffrey, 1965. *The Art of Judgment.* New York: Basic Books. (Reissued by Harper and Row 1983; centenary edition, Sage Publications 1995).
———, 1973. *Making Institutions Work.* New York: John Wiley and Sons.
———, 1983. *Human Systems Are Different.* New York: Harper and Row.
———, 1984. *The Vickers Papers,* ed. Open Systems Group. London: Harper and Row.
———, 1987. *Policy-Making, Communication, and Social Learning: Essays of Sir Geoffrey Vickers,* ed. Guy B. Adams, Bayard L. Catron, and John Forester. New Brunswick, NJ: Transaction Publishers.

Works on Sir Geoffrey Vickers:

Blunden, Margaret, 1984. "Geoffrey Vickers: An Intellectual Journey." In *The Vickers Papers,* ed. Open Systems Group. London: Harper and Row.
Blunden, Margaret, and Malcolm Dando, eds., 1994. "Rethinking Public Policy-Making: Questioning Assumptions, Challenging Beliefs." (Eleven Essays in Honor of Sir Geoffrey Vickers on His Centenary). *American Behavioral Scientist,* vol. 38 (September-October).

Other Works Cited:

Barnard, Chester I., 1938. *The Functions of the Executive.* Cambridge, MA: Harvard University Press.
Simon, Herbert A., 1947. *Administrative Behavior.* New York: Macmillan.
———, 1960. *The New Science of Management Decision.* New York: Harper & Row.

VIRTUAL ORGANIZATION.

Temporary organizational arrangements designed to net together various units for a defined purpose.

Introduction

These web enterprises are new approaches to thinking about how organizations should be organized. Although the tenure of these organizations is temporary, the length of the arrangement can be defined by prior agreement. Often the end date is set by a prearranged event such as the accomplishment of a project, the achievement of a mutual goal, or the decision on one part of the group to end the alliance. Virtual organizations are closely associated with popular contemporary writers, including John Naisbitt, Peter Drucker, and Robert Reich.

Why They Occur

Naisbitt in *Megatrends* (1984) discusses ten important shifts in society of which the following four are about virtual organization:

- industrial to an information society (later Drucker calls it the "knowledge society"),
- centralization to decentralization,
- hierarchies to networking, and
- either/or to multiple choice options.

Naisbitt and others attribute these important shifts to the rapid evolution of the computer and related software. They make using information in daily work activities radically different. The very nature of how we can and do accomplish our work tasks has shifted. The new jobs are increasingly information dependent. Organizations can now work better as decentralized units that connect not by hierarchies but often by information webs. Decisions that were narrow and limited with largely homogenized preferences and few choices become broader with multiple options reflecting unprecedented diversity.

A key actor in this new vision of proper organizations is what Reich (1992b) in *The Work of Nations* calls the "symbolic analysts" (p. 77). They are problem-solving, problem-identifying, and strategic-brokering professionals. These key people create ideas and jobs that not only expand the economy but raise the nation's productivity and standard of living. They function by the manipulation of symbols—data, words, and visual representations—directly related to the new information age. This type of organizations often works best as virtual, or web, enterprises.

Drucker (1992), in *Managing for the Future* (p. 157) argues large organizations have little choice but to become information based because of the vital usefulness of knowledge workers. Rapidly evolving information technology combined with competition on a world scale make the shift to knowledge-based organizations not only possible but force the shift to occur. Economic survival is at stake. Increasingly, analysis and diagnosis are more significant to organizations given their world competitive situation. The consequences of this shift to information-based organizations are flatter organizational structures and fundamental changes in the way work is done. Organizations focus not on high volume but high value. There is no need for vast

resources, armies of production workers, or rigid routines. They focus not on products but strategies centered on specialized knowledge. Today, three essential managerial skills are problem solving, problem identification, and strategic brokering.

Vertical Relationships

Effect organizations are not concerned with scale and volume but continuous discovery of new linkages that often take the shape of virtual organizations. Coordination and communication are horizontal rather than vertical. Information sharing in organizations especially among strategic brokers is essential to discover and act quickly upon new opportunities. Formal styles using scheduled meetings with fixed agendas are not as successful as frequent impromptu discussions. Mutual learning needs to take place to share insights and experiences. The strategic broker in virtual organizations helps the exchange by creating an environment for exploration and talk to take place. Instead of the classic hierarchical pyramid organizational structures, the new high-value enterprise looks more like a spider's web with the strategic broker at the center. The strategic broker orchestrates the connections between the problem solvers and the problem identifiers.

There are many connections around the web. Not all of them directly involve the strategic broker. At each contact point of the web, a new unit or team is formed involving relatively few people. Individual skills and talents are pooled so that the team's ability to look creatively for possibilities is enhanced. Over time, the members of the team are able to help one another perform better, identify individual strengths and propel the team forward. It is a marriage of technical insight with marketing know-how and strategic and financial acumen. Everything else from production to distribution is added on, as needed.

As Arie Halachmi noted (1994), a "work group" functioning as a net work can transform itself into a "workgroup." A work group is a social artifact that always evolves when individuals interact and create a social life of their own inside and outside an organizational setting. In contrast, workgroups are temporary and last only as long as the parties are aware of each other's involvement and they share a mutual interest.

Virtual Quality

A key element of a virtual organization is its ability to dissolve or redeploy when no longer needed or functional. This process must be clearly mapped out and articulated before the need arises for it to self-destruct. After the organization ends, human and physical resources are reassigned to new positions and projects on the web.

Units at the web's nexus points spring into being or dissolve based on the need for them and the function they fill. These units can be reconfigured as new leaders emerge. Points on the periphery of the web, where few threads intersect, depend on individuals who have a high value in attracting talented followers to their team. The best leadership therefore is where the most value is created, nurtured, and developed. Power within the web does not depend on formal rank or authority but on the individual's ability to add value to the unit or project.

The structure of the web eliminates much of the traditional organization middle management and the lower-level production work. Smaller jobs can be contracted out. Office space, factories, and equipment can be leased. Support personnel can be hired on short-term renewable contracts. The unit or team assumes the responsibilities for product development and sales, and it is given discretion over its own budget.

Conclusions

In the traditional public- and private-sector organization model, control is firmly lodged at the top of the pyramid. Everyone else on the organization ladder is duty bound to carry out the directives sent from above. With virtual organizations, the structure becomes almost a three-dimensional living entity. Organizational units routinely appear and disappear. They are born out of a specific identified need, grow to maturity with care and nurturing, and are laid to rest when their function is no longer required. They are designed to be fluid. Critical to the virtual organization is its ability to act, react, and interact with the entire network with speed, agility, and creativity.

Reich (1992, pp. 91–94) calls today's successful big business a collection of little virtual organizations. He calls them "enterprise webs." The center provides the "strategic insight" and binds the threads together. Contact points on the web have sufficient autonomy to create profitable connections to other webs. There is no inside or outside the organization. There are only distances from the strategic center. The list or organizations of this nature include Johnson and Johnson, Hewlett-Packard, General Electric, IBM, AT&T, and Eastman Kodak. Typically these older corporations needed to downsize and eliminate thousands of lower- and middle-level jobs to effectively restructure themselves.

THOMAS D. LYNCH AND CYNTHIA E. LYNCH

BIBLIOGRAPHY

Drucker, Peter F., 1989. *The New Realities.* New York: Harper and Row.
———, 1992. *Managing for the Future, the 1990s and Beyond.* New York: Plume Books.
Gabler, Ted, 1992. "Entrepreneurial Government Makes Good Sense." *The Public Manager,* vol. 21 (Spring): 4–6.
Gore, Al, 1993. *From Redtape to Results: Creating a Government That Works Better and Costs Less.* Report of the National Performance Review. Washington, DC: U.S. Government Printing Office.
Halachmi, Arie, 1994. "IRM: Perspectives, Issues, and Implications." *International Journal of Public Administration,* vol. 17, no. 1: 209–252.
Naisbitt, John, 1984. *Megatrends.* New York: Warner Books.
Naisbitt, John, and Patricia Aburdene, 1990. *Megatrends 2000.* New York: Avon Books.
Osborne, David, and Ted A. Gabler, 1992. "Bringing Government Back to Life." *Governing* vol. 5 (February): 46–50.
———, 1993. *Reinventing Government.* New York: Plume Books.
Reich, Robert B., 1983a. *The Next American Frontier.* New York: Penguin.
———, 1993b. *The Work of Nations.* New York: Vintage Books.
Salaman, Lester M., 1987. "Rise of Third Party Government." *The Public Manager,* vol. 16, no. 2 (Summer): 27–30.
Shafritz, Jay M., and Albert C. Hyde, eds., 1992. *Classics of Public Administration.* Pacific Grove, CA: Brooks/Cole.
Stone, Jeffrey B., 1993. "Public Entrepreneurship." A paper presented at the Southeastern Conference on Public Administration, October 7, Cocoa Beach, FL.

VOLUNTARISM.   Actions undertaken freely by individuals, groups, or organizations that are not compelled by biological need or social convention, mandated or coerced by government, or directed principally at financial or economic gain, regarded as beneficial by participants or the larger society.

As suggested by the complexity of this definition, the study of voluntarism is not for those who insist on precise terms, crisp distinctions, and tidy categories. Jon Van Til (1988) has devoted an entire book to elucidating the construct and untangling it from related concepts, such as freedom, philanthropy, volunteering, and voluntary association. Despite his commendable effort, scholars continue to struggle to explicate the field, delineate its boundaries, and remedy what Lester M. Salamon (1992, pp. 4–5) has called "the terminological tangle" (see also Salamon and Anheier 1992). Most research on the subject concentrates on either the organizational aspects of voluntarism, such as the origin, history, role, and management of not-for-profit institutions, or the voluntary behavior of individuals, particularly the motivations that lead people to donate their time and/or money to preferred causes, and the implications of such gifts for the giver and the recipient. The definition of voluntarism offered here embraces—and attempts to unify—both principal foci.

The result of this conceptualization is an emerging area of scholarly study, practical application, and public policy initiative of impressive dimension. On the one hand, voluntarism encompasses behavior as micro and seemingly insignificant (from a societal point of view) as helping a friend move, leading a church choir, contributing time to a homeless shelter, or attending a meeting of an arts club or self-help group. It includes many thousands of informal groups and grassroots associations that may meet only sporadically, have no paid personnel, rarely accumulate a respectable treasury, and struggle merely to survive, let alone pursue objectives.

On the other hand, voluntarism is concerned with the founding, operation, governance, and impacts of many of America's preeminent educational, medical, and cultural institutions, which qualify as nonprofit organizations (for example, Harvard University, Princeton University, American Cancer Society, Cedars of Lebanon Hospital, the Metropolitan Museum of Art, and the Boston Symphony Orchestra). Also included in the voluntary sector are numerous organizations that have contributed to profound changes in society, such as religious congregations and major foundations and grantmaking institutions (for example, the Rockefeller Foundation, Ford Foundation, and the Carnegie Corporation). Voluntarism is responsible for launching and sustaining vanguard social and political movements whose effects continue to reverberate in important areas, for example, civil rights, women's rights (and the women's suffrage movement that preceded it), consumer protection, environmental preservation, mental health, public health, progressive governmental reform, assistance for the needy, and numerous others (O'Neill 1989, pp. 9–122). "The accomplishments of American business and government have been awesome," acknowledges Michael O'Neill (1989), "but many of the social and moral advances in American history have come from nonprofit advocacy efforts" (p. 113).

Development of Voluntarism as a Field of Study

Although voluntarism enjoys a history as lengthy as civilization itself, so great a range is spanned by these institutions, organizations, and activities that it may have diverted attention from the field, delayed academic recognition, and prompted controversy over the meaning of the sector (Salamon 1992, p. 13; Salamon and Anheier 1992, pp. 125–128). Roger A. Lohmann (1995) illustrates the problem by trying to locate

> "the core of nonprofit organizations, voluntary action, and philanthropy . . . in the clubs, mutual aid societies, neighborhood associations, community churches, and other commons displaying uncoerced participation, shared purposes and resources, mutuality, and indigenous standards of fairness, rather than in the giant foundations, national oligarchies, and quasicommercial nonprofit firms that so often position themselves to speak in the name of the contemporary third sector" (p. 28).

Perhaps for this reason, only since the 1970s has the nonprofit sector become recognized as a distinctive academic enterprise or professional pursuit.

In 1973, philanthropist John D. Rockefeller initiated the Commission on Private Philanthropy and Public Needs, usually identified as the Filer Commission after its chairman John Filer, to heighten awareness, appreciation, and study of voluntarism. At about the same time (1972), the first professional association dedicated to scholarly inquiry in the field was organized, now known as the Association for Research on Nonprofit Organizations and Voluntary Action (ARNOVA), and began publication of a quarterly journal. In 1977, Yale University established the first academic program in the United States for study of the voluntary, nonprofit sector, the Program on Nonprofit Organizations (PONPO). In the succeeding years, interest in the field has mushroomed: At this writing, more than 30 universities worldwide have centers or other programs devoted to voluntarism, and two more journals have begun publication. Many of the schools offer a master's degree in administration, management, and/or leadership of nonprofit organizations.

Such growth notwithstanding, voluntarism has not achieved disciplinary status and remains an allied field. Scholarly inquiry in this area is decidedly interdisciplinary, attracting rich scrutiny and contributions from a great variety of academic traditions, including sociology, social work, political science, public administration, management, economics, psychology, anthropology, history, law, and numerous others. In a comprehensive review of all articles published in the leading journal in the field, *Nonprofit and Voluntary Sector Quarterly*, over the first 20 years of its existence (1972–1991), Jeffrey Brudney and Teresa Durden (1993, p. 211) found that journal authors came from 34 disciplines and that on the average each volume (four issues) contained articles by authors representing 8 different academic specializations. Given both the novelty and the heterogeneity of the scholarly research, it should not be surprising that breadth, rather than conceptual purity, is the hallmark of the voluntarism field.

Voluntarism: Between Market and State

Voluntarism can be understood as individual, group, or organizational behavior located in that sizable chasm between the marketplace and economic enterprise on the one hand (business, commerce, profitmaking, and the like) and government and the state on the other (authority, law, compulsion, and so forth), outside of the family or household. Although huge in scope and importance, this sphere is typically characterized as a "residual" category, supplementing ("following") the two predominant sectors of society: the private (the market and economic gain) and the public (government and the force of law) (Wuthnow 1991, pp. 5–8; Van Til 1988, pp. ix–x, 5–6). The sector comprises a wide variety of institutions, such as charities, research institutes, religious organizations, private colleges and universities, cooperatives, associations, foundations, hospitals, day care centers, youth organizations, advocacy groups, neighborhood organizations, and many more.

The labels used to designate the population of organizational forms falling into the residuum between the commercial and political spheres reflect the ordering of societal domains. The most common name given to this group is the "third sector." In order to ease problems of comparability in law, custom, and definition across nations, international research often incorporates this term to describe organizations that are neither profit-oriented businesses nor governmental agencies or bureaucracies (for example, Seibel and Anheier 1990, p. 7). Other titles used regularly for the same purpose include the "nonprofit" or "voluntary" and, to a lesser extent, the "independent," "charitable," "philanthropic," or even the "tax-exempt" sector.

Since by definition, organizations falling "between States and Markets," as Robert Wuthnow (1991) titles a comparative study of the voluntary sector, cannot obtain the funds necessary for survival directly from tax revenues or profits on the sale of goods or services, the question of how they remain financially viable is crucial. An examination of the sources of funding of nonprofit organizations in the United States reveals answers to this question that are at once interesting and surprising—and illustrates some of the conceptual problems involved in depicting the sector.

Sources of Nonprofit Funding

As the common labels for the sector might suggest, the traditional conception is one of a set of organizations attempting to further public purposes, financed chiefly by private, charitable contributions and philanthropy. The authoritative *Nonprofit Almanac 1992–1993: Dimensions of the Independent Sector* (Hodgkinson *et al.* 1992) paints a somewhat different picture. Although funding patterns vary by policy area, overall, private contributions accounted for just over one-quarter (27.2 percent) of total annual funds for the sector in 1989. Although the sector, too, might be considered independent of the other two sectors, its reliance on government is manifest: In 1989, government grants, contracts, and reimbursements provided a nearly equal share of sector funding, 25.8 percent. Perhaps most arresting, the single largest source of income for the nonprofit sector is, nonetheless, fees, service charges, dues payments, and other commercial income, amounting to fully 37.9 percent of funding in 1989. Under the U.S. Internal Revenue Service tax code, nonprofit organizations can realize earnings, but they are prohibited from distributing them to shareholders or individuals. The remainder of funding for the sector came from other receipts, including endowments and investments (9.1 percent). Since 1977, funding for the third sector has increased tremendously,

yet the proportion of income generated by each of these sources has remained remarkably consistent (Hodgkinson *et al.* 1992, pp. 136–137, 150–151).

Magnitude of the Voluntary, Nonprofit Sector

In a similar way, the title "third" may give a misleading impression of insignificant size and status of the voluntary, nonprofit sector. To the contrary, according to O'Neill (1989, pp. 1–2), American nonprofit organizations employ more civilians than the federal and all state governments combined, and the yearly budget of the sector exceeds the budgets of all but seven nations in the world. In the United States, for which the most accurate and comprehensive information is available, the sector encompassed an estimated 1.4 million nonprofit organizations in 1990—about 15 times the number of government agencies (Hodgkinson *et al.* 1992, p. 35). In the same year, the sector accounted for US$314.9 billion in total national income (6.8 percent of total), employed 15.8 million people (11.4 percent), and generated US$278.3 billion in total earnings from work (8.5 percent) (Hodgkinson *et al.* 1992, pp. 17–19, 33, 35).

As measured by operating expenditures of US$389.1 billion in 1990, the equivalent of 6 percent of the gross national product, Americans rely on nonprofit organizations for a great variety of services. Salamon's (1992, pp. 37–38) analysis of social welfare spending in the United States indicates that in the fields where government and the nonprofit sector are both involved (such as heath care, aid for the poor, nutritional assistance, day care, social services, housing, and related services), nonprofit expenditures exceed those of either the federal government, or state and local governments, taken separately. The scale of nonprofit activity in this domain is almost as large as government activity as a whole, more than twice as large as the state and local government role alone, and 20 percent larger than the federal role alone.

As impressive as these statistics may be, David Horton Smith (1994b) argues persuasively that they still likely underestimate the extent of voluntarism in the United States. Because standards for official reporting by nonprofit organizations are based on revenue criteria and other formal measures, the figures reported here describe the wealthiest and largest entities, but may overlook at least 70 percent, if not more, of the voluntary sector (p. 12). Smith's analysis of what he terms "the rest of the nonprofit sector"—the huge number of locally based, volunteer-run, member-benefit, largely informal, grassroots associations not tapped by these statistics—suggests an even more robust presence. By his estimates, it contains 7.5 million associations, 124 million members, 98 million active members, 264 million memberships (members can belong to several groups simultaneously), and 28 billion hours of association activity per year.

Origin of the Third Sector

Numerous scholars have speculated regarding the reasons for the origin and continued existence of a third, voluntary sector in society. Salamon (1992, pp. 7–10) summarizes five cogent explanations. The explanations are complementary, rather than mutually exclusive, and together offer a rationale for the birth and maintenance of the voluntary sector.

Historical Explanation

In an age in which citizens have routinely come to expect government to act in their interest in social and economic life, it may be difficult to recall that in most countries, society preceded the establishment of the state. In the absence of governmental institutions or agencies, individuals had to deal with common concerns and problems on their own. They often found it advantageous to join with other people to do so in voluntary groups, associations, and organizations. The result was the provision of services to meet a wide variety of community needs, such as charity, housing, culture, health, adoption, fire, and others, through a voluntary, nonprofit sector. Although desirous of help from the state, citizens nonetheless remain wary of government involvement. Thus, even after governments emerged, the nonprofit sector persisted to mobilize citizens, advocate for preferred causes, and help governments address needs through direct service activities.

Market Failure

Economists point out that the marketplace works admirably to produce goods and services that are consumed individually, such as clothing and toothpaste. For goods and services that are consumed collectively by groups of people, however, problems can arise with reliance on the market: Individuals have strong economic incentives to act as "free riders," that is, to let their fellow citizens pay for the provision of collective or public goods on the knowledge that once such goods have been created, they can share in their enjoyment whether they pay for them or not. Since all economically rational individuals will make the same calculation, however, the result will be inadequate production of collective goods, such as community safety and security, clean streets and neighborhoods, and park lands and nature preserves, to the detriment of the larger society.

The best-known mechanism for overcoming market failure is government, which through the levy of taxes compels all citizens to assume the cost of providing collective goods. Another solution is the nonprofit sector: In nonprofit organizations, groups of individuals can pool their resources to produce goods or services they mutually want but cannot convince a majority of their fellow citizens to support. Using this mechanism, groups linked by common cultural, social, or economic characteristics or interests can provide the kinds and levels of collective goods desired in the absence of majority endorsement or government involvement.

Government Failure

Despite the capability to surmount problems of market failure, democratic governments encounter difficulties in providing collective goods. In the first place, mobilizing the majority support necessary for public action can be a long and arduous process; the existence of a voluntary sector allows groups of individuals with common motives or interests to begin addressing needs that have yet to command this level of approbation or that may never succeed in doing so. Second, even when governmental action has won authorization in a particular policy domain, citizens often find fault in the size, cost, ponderousness, and unresponsiveness—in short, the "bureaucracy"—they attribute to the undertaking. Regardless of the empirical validity of such complaints, citizens may prefer that a nongovernmental mechanism, such as nonprofit organizations, actually deliver the services and respond to the needs identified, with financing provided by the public sector. Often advocated by political officials, this preference has fueled a worldwide movement for governments to contract with outside organizations for the delivery of services, one form of "privatization." The culmination has been a very complex pattern of cooperation and interdependence between the public and nonprofit sectors, especially in the United States, for the production of governmentally financed services, and a blurring of the sectors has occurred.

Pluralism/Freedom

While the first three explanations describe instrumental reasons for the existence of a nonprofit sector, such as offering an alternative means for the production of collective goods and efficiencies in the delivery of services, the last two reasons focus on expressive aspects of the sector. From this point of view, the nonprofit sector develops in a society to give voice to the great diversity of needs and preferences felt by the citizenry, for example, for gun control as well as the right to bear arms, for more open immigration policy as well as more vigorous enforcement of national borders, for ordinances banning smoking in public places as well as greater toleration of this habit, for safer automobiles and industrial equipment as well as less regulation of business, for greater freedom of choice in reproductive rights as well heightened concern for the rights of the unborn, for increased provision of child care as well as policies that encourage women to remain in the home as primary caregivers, for more tax benefits to nonprofit organizations as well as against "unfair competition" between the sector and profitmaking firms, and so forth. From civil rights to the Conservative Coalition, the nonprofit sector has spawned most of the major reform movements in the United States (O'Neill 1989). Even were gov-

ernments to possess decided instrumental advantages over nonprofit organizations in the delivery of services, a voluntary sector would remain vital to secure liberties and ensure pluralism in beliefs and their articulation.

Solidarity

The final reason for the existence of the third, voluntary sector is that it preserves a capacity for joint action among citizens. As Alexis de Toqueville observed, in democratic societies especially, equality of conditions can render individuals relatively powerless (see Salamon 1992, pp. 9–10). To overcome this tendency, they can come together to pursue common purposes in voluntary groups, associations, and organizations. Without a nonprofit sector to facilitate and activate the expression of these shared interests, much less progress would be possible across all realms of human endeavor.

Types and Purposes of Organizations in the Third Sector

As discussed previously, great diversity characterizes the voluntary, nonprofit sector with respect to both organizational form and mission. This section elaborates the types of entities and the range of purposes embraced by them.

Classifying Voluntary Organizations

Although many types of organizations inhabit the voluntary, nonprofit sector, useful commonalities exist for categorizing them and making sense of the constituent elements. The most basic classification is the distinction between "public-serving" and "member-serving" nonprofit organizations. The voluntary sector is best known for the former, or "public benefit" organizations: private nonprofit agencies founded to serve some general public, philanthropic, or charitable purpose, or to advance a like cause. This group includes schools, colleges, universities, hospitals, arts and cultural organizations, social service agencies, community development groups, legal service organizations, social action movements, research institutes, foundations, religious congregations, and others. In addition to these entities, a huge number of organizations exist primarily for the benefit of their own members rather than to advance some broader public purpose. Examples of these "mutual benefit," or "member-serving," organizations include professional associations, business associations, economic cooperatives, labor unions, member cooperatives, service organizations, fraternal organizations, veterans' organizations, pension trusts, ethnic societies, political parties, hobby groups, and sports and country clubs (O'Neill 1989, pp. 156–159).

Within the public benefit category, nonprofit organizations can be further divided into four types: funding intermediaries, religious institutions, service providers, and political action agencies (Salamon 1992, pp. 15–24). Funding intermediaries exist to generate funds and distribute them to other nonprofit organizations. This group includes both foundations and federated funders. In the United States, foundations make grants to other nonprofit organizations, usually financed through earnings on endowments, whereas federated funders collect and allocate private donations on behalf of service-providing organizations normally linked by common or allied purposes (for example, the American Cancer Society and the United Way).

A second type of public benefit, nonprofit organization consists of religious congregations, orders, and auxiliaries. These institutions engage in sacramental religious observances, and include churches, synagogues, mosques, and other places of worship. A third category of public benefit organizations are those that provide direct services. This group encompasses nonprofit agencies working in a very broad array of functional areas, such as education and library, health and personal care, culture and the arts, employment and training, counseling and rehabilitation, neighborhood and community programs, and foreign aid and development. The service providers are probably what most people have in mind when they refer to the nonprofit sector.

The final type of public benefit, nonprofit organization is the political action agencies, those that are engaged primarily in advocacy, campaigning, lobbying, and other legislative activity. Nonprofit service providers may also undertake advocacy and public education activities, but in the United States to qualify as a charitable organization under Section 501 (c)(3) of the Internal Revenue Service (IRS) tax code and receive all consequent tax advantages, advocacy must be a subsidiary function. Although all U.S. nonprofit organizations are exempt from the federal income tax, only those meeting the standards of Section 501 (c)(3) are eligible to receive tax deductible gifts from corporations and the general public (that is, contributions that can be deducted from the tax liabilities of donors). A separate provision of the IRS tax code, Section 501 (c)(4), applies to the political action agencies ("social welfare organizations"). Since the tax deductibility of gifts gives firms and organizations a powerful incentive to make them, many 501 (c)(3) service providers establish auxiliary 501 (c)(4) action agencies for lobbying and advocacy purposes so as not to jeopardize their tax status (Salamon 1992, pp. 14–15, 23–24).

Classifying Voluntary Activity

Beginning in the mid-1980s, substantial progress has been made in classifying the variety of purposes motivating organizations in the voluntary, nonprofit sector. The National Center for Charitable Statistics (NCCS) at the INDEPENDENT SECTOR organization has taken a leading role in this effort; INDEPENDENT SECTOR, a nonprofit coalition of over 850 corporate, foundation and voluntary organization members with national interest and impact in philanthropy and voluntary action, strives to encourage volunteer and non-for-profit initiative. In cooperation with the Statistics of Income Division of the United States Internal Revenue Service, NCCS has developed a comprehensive scheme for classification, entitled the "National Taxonomy of Exempt entities" (NTEE) (Hodgkinson *et al.* 1992, pp. 181–184).

Although full implementation of this helpful system (which will eventually identify organizations by primary purpose and major program as well as by type of governance, area of service, and clientele, beneficiaries, or members served) had not been achieved at this writing, information on organizational purposes and programs is available. The detailed NTEE classification of purposes lists 26 categories. For ease of presentation and statistical analysis, this large number is often collapsed into 9 major groupings. By this accounting, nonprofit organizations are active in the areas of arts, culture, and the humanities; education; environment and animals; health; human services; international and foreign affairs; public societal benefit; religion; and membership/mutual benefit (Hodgkinson *et al.* 1992, pp. 593–613).

Voluntarism and Individuals: Donating Money and Time

Treatments of voluntarism typically devote greatest attention to nonprofit organizations and to the sector as a whole. As the definition of the term emphasizes, however, a strong individual element pervades voluntarism. This element consists of the giving and volunteering behaviors that make the work of the voluntary sector possible.

As discussed earlier, charitable giving is not the only or even the largest source of funding for nonprofit organizations. Nevertheless, in 1990, total private contributions reached US$122.6 billion in the United States, or 2.77 percent of national income and 2.19 percent of personal income. Approximately 90 percent of giving came from individuals, chiefly living persons (83 percent), with a much smaller amount from personal bequests (6.4 percent); the remainder came from foundations (5.8 percent) and corporations (4.8 percent) (Hodgkinson *et al.* 1992, pp. 60). Just over half of private charitable giving (54 percent) went to religious congregations (Salamon 1992, p. 15). About three-fourths of American households make charitable contributions. Giving money and volunteering time are closely interrelated: People who make charitable contributions are much more likely to volunteer, and the incidence of volunteering increases dramatically with the percentage of income given (Hodgkinson and Weitzman 1994, pp. 27-30).

The study of volunteering behavior has stimulated considerable interest. Beginning in 1981, the INDEPENDENT SECTOR organization has commissioned a series of national surveys on volunteering in the United States,

conducted at two-year intervals since 1985. Over this period, the percentage of Americans stating that they have spent time "working in some way to help others for no monetary pay . . . over the past twelve months" has hovered at around half the population. According to the results of the most recent survey at the time of this writing, in 1993, 47.7 percent of Americans volunteered an average of 4.2 hours per week. Projected to the population, these statistics indicate that nearly 90 million people (89.2 million) volunteer, the equivalent of about 9 million full-time employees (8,839,200). If the fortunate organizations that are the recipients of this labor had to pay for it, the price tag would have been a staggering US$182.3 billion (Hodgkinson and Weitzman 1994, p. 23).

Throughout the 1980s, the reliance of all three sectors, for-profit, government, and nonprofit, on volunteer labor increased (Hodgkinson *et al.* 1992, pp. 18–19). The voluntary sector remains the prime beneficiary of this huge reservoir of time and talent. Converted to a full-time equivalent basis, of all volunteer time contributed in 1989, 69 percent went to the nonprofit sector, which also accounted for a like percentage of all volunteer work assignments (66 percent). As Jeffrey Brudney (1990) has shown, U.S. governments are markedly dependent on volunteer labor as well, in service domains such as fire and public safety, culture and the arts, health and emergency medical, education and recreation, food and homelessness. In 1989, about one-quarter of all contributed time (26 percent) and 28 percent of volunteer work assignments went to government. For-profit firms are responsible for the remainder (about 6 percent of both volunteer time and assignments). Although the number of full-time equivalent volunteers as a proportion of total employment is negligible in the for-profit sector (far less than 1 percent), volunteers constitute 40.4 percent of total employment in the U.S. nonprofit sector and 10.2 percent in government (Hodgkinson *et al.* 1992, pp. 7, 18–19, 29).

Two recent studies, the doctoral dissertation of Gabriel Berger (1991) and a review article by Smith (1994a), attempt to synthesize the results of the voluminous research on the determinants of volunteering. Based on a 1990 national survey of giving and volunteering behavior in the United States, Berger (1991) concluded that the strongest factor leading one to volunteer is to have been the target of recruitment efforts, a finding corroborated in many other surveys (e.g., Hodgkinson and Weitzman 1994). He also found that making philanthropic contributions is closely associated with volunteering to organizations (see earlier). The level of formal education received is the individual characteristic with the strongest impact on volunteering. Smith (1994a) concurred with these findings and identified other variables important volunteering, such as higher socioeconomic status and participation in other forms of social activity. Smith's research also illustrates the complexity of volunteer behavior: A complete explanation must take into account the context or environment of the individual (e.g., size of community), the individual's social background (e.g., gender), personality (e.g., sense of efficacy), attitudes (e.g., liking volunteer work), situation (e.g., receiving services from the organization), and social participation (e.g., neighborhood interaction). While Smith's (1994a, p. 256) review shows that "we know a lot about why people participate in volunteer programs and voluntary associations," because studies have not been able to incorporate such an imposing range of variables, our understanding of volunteering behavior must be limited.

Conclusion: Toward Cross-National Comparison

In his review article, Smith (1994a, p. 257) noted the need for more international research on volunteering. Aside from finding from survey research strongly suggesting that rates and amounts of charitable giving and volunteering in the United States surpass those of other nations (Hodgkinson *et al.* 1992, pp. 50–52, 81–87), little firm knowledge seems to exist cross-nationally.

With respect to international research on the broader field of voluntarism, the subject of this entry, the situation is similar. Again, although solid comparative data are elusive, estimates of the size of the nonprofit sector in other countries appear to be much lower proportionately than in the United States (Salamon, 1992, p. 28). In an insightful review of edited books presenting studies of the voluntary, nonprofit sector in various countries, Ram Cnaan and Peter Hall (1994) wrote that "even though the contributors use the same terminology, it is not clear that they are studying the same social phenomena" (p. 84). They concluded, "This field is still in its infancy and sector-level, or field-of-service level analysis may be premature. Valid generalizations will require a much broader knowledge base" (p. 85). The founding of the International Society for Third-Sector Research (ISTR) in the mid-1990s should go a long way toward ameliorating these problems and advancing knowledge of voluntarism from a global perspective.

JEFFREY L. BRUDNEY

BIBLIOGRAPHY

Berger, Gabriel, 1991. "Factors Explaining Volunteering for Organizations in General, and Social Welfare Organizations in Particular." Doctoral dissertation, Heller School of Social Welfare, Brandeis University.

Brudney, Jeffrey L., 1990. *Fostering Volunteer Programs in the Public Sector: Planning, Initiating, and Managing Voluntary Activities.* San Francisco, CA: Jossey-Bass.

Brudney, Jeffrey L., and Teresa K. Durden, 1993. "Twenty Years of the *Journal of Voluntary Action Research/Nonprofit and Voluntary Sector Quarterly:* An Assessment of Past Trends and future Directions." *Nonprofit and Voluntary Sector Quarterly,* vol. 22 (Fall) 207–218.

Cnaan, Ram A., and Peter D. Hall, 1994. "Book Reviews: *Government and the Third Sector: Emerging Relationships in Welfare States* and *The Nonprofit Sector in the Global Community: Voice from Many Nations.*" *Nonprofit and Voluntary Sector Quarterly,* vol. 23 (Spring): 79–85.

Hodgkinson, Virginia A., and Murray S. Weitzman, 1994. *Giving and Volunteering in the United States: Findings from a National Survey, 1994 Edition.* Washington, D.C.: INDEPENDENT SECTOR.

Hodgkinson, Virginia A., Murray S. Weitzman, Christopher M. Toppe, and Stephen M. Noga, 1992. *Nonprofit Almanac, 1992–1993: Dimensions of the Independent Sector.* San Francisco, CA: Jossey-Bass.

Lohmann, Roger A., 1995. "Commons: Can This Be the Name of 'Thirdness'?" *Nonprofit and Voluntary Sector Quarterly,* vol. 24 (Spring): 25–29.

O'Neill, Michael, 1989. *The Third America: The Emergence of the Nonprofit Sector in the United States.* San Francisco, CA: Jossey-Bass.

Salamon, Lester M., 1992. *America's Nonprofit Sector: A Primer.* New York: Foundation Center.

Salamon, Lester M., and Helmut K. Anheier, 1992. "In Search of the Non-Profit Sector. I: The Question of Definitions." *Voluntas,* vol. 3 (August): 125–151.

Seibel, Wolfgang, and Helmut K. Anheier, 1990. "Sociological and Political Science Approaches to the Third Sector." In Helmut K. Anheier and Wolfgang Seibel, eds. *The Third Sector: Comparative Studies of Nonprofit Organizations.* Berlin, Germany: Walter de Gruyter.

Smith, David Horton, 1994a. "Determinants of Voluntary Association Participation and Volunteering: A Literature Review. "*Nonprofit and Voluntary Sector Quarterly,* vol. 23 (Fall): 243–263.

———, 1994b. "The Rest of the Nonprofit Sector: The Nature and Magnitude of Grassroots Associations in America." Paper presented at the Annual Meeting of the Association for Research on Nonprofit Organizations and Voluntary Action, Berkeley, CA, October 20–22.

Van Til, Jon, 1988. *Mapping the Third Sector: Voluntarism in a Changing Social Economy.* New York: Foundation Center.

Wuthnow, Robert, ed. 1991. *Between States and Markets: The Voluntary Sector in Comparative Perspective.* Princeton, NJ: Princeton University Press.

VOLUNTARY ACTION. Freely chosen activity, usually directed toward the achievement of a long-term socially related goal and not merely a manifestation of biological, political, or economic drives.

Voluntary Action as the Master Concept for Understanding the Third Sector

Voluntary action is the master concept for understanding the vital institutional realm of modern societies variously identified as the third, voluntary, nonprofit, or independent sector. The standard definition was provided some decades ago by David Horton Smith and his associates

(1972): "Individual voluntary action is that which gives personal meaning to life. It is that which one freely chooses to do either for enjoyment in the short term and/or from commitment to some longer-term goal that is not merely a manifestation of bio-social man, socio-political man, or economic man" (p. 163).

Smith founded the Association for Voluntary Action Research in 1972 and served as the first editor of that association's journal, the *Journal of Voluntary Action Research*. The journal announced its intention to publish papers on the full range of human activities that might fall under the rubric of voluntary action, including voluntary associations, social movements, cause groups, voluntarism, interest groups, pluralism, citizen participation, consumer groups, participatory democracy, volunteering, altruism, helping behavior, philanthropy, social clubs, leisure behavior, political participation, religious sects, and so forth.

The implication that voluntary action has a key role to play in modern societies does not reflect the conventional scholarly assessment of its role. Its current identification as the driving force of the "third sector" seems aptly named in terms of significance customarily accorded it. It tends to be least attended in American studies. It is often confused with the other "private institutions" of the business world or dismissed as the locus of mere "do-gooding."

Voluntary action is commonly defined in residual or even negative terms. Writing from a corporate background, Theodore Levitt (1973) noted, first, that "conventional taxonomy divides society into two sectors—private and public. Private is business. Public is presumed to be 'all else.'" But "all else" is too broad a concept, Levitt asserted. It leaves an "enormous residuum," which he proceeded to call "the Third Sector." This societal arena is host to "a bewildering variety of organizations with differing degrees of visibility, power and activeness. Although they vary greatly in scope and specific purposes, their general purposes are broadly similar—to do things business and government are either not doing, not doing well, or not doing often enough" (p. 49).

Of all the terms commonly used to describe this sector, only "voluntary" and "independent" are not essentially derivative, although even they are not wholly free of derogatory implications. The "independent" sector, on the one hand, implies a judgment of putative freedom from something else, suggesting several questions for consideration: independent of what? and what of the implication of dependence? On the other hand, the term "voluntary" is clouded by the diverse uses of the term in both vernacular and scientific language—uses as diverse as "freely willed" in philosophy to "unintentionally sown" in botany—not to mention its quixotic military application and its physiological meaning as a bodily reflex under conscious control.

Clearly, it is necessary to attend to language and its many meanings if we are to make sense of this subject. Thus, it is necessary closely to examine the principal concepts used when voluntary action is studied, beginning with the individual act of volunteering that forms the basis of most concepts in this field.

Volunteering may be identified as a helping action of an individual that is valued by him or her and yet is not aimed directly at material gain nor mandated or coerced by others. Thus in the broadest sense, volunteering is any uncoerced helping activity one is engaged in not primarily for financial gain or by coercion or mandate. It is thereby different in definition from work, slavery, or conscription. It differs from employment in that it is now primarily motivated by pecuniary gain, although much paid work includes volunteering; it differs from conscription in that it is unpaid and uncoerced; and it differs from slavery in that it is not coerced.

Volunteering may be extended beyond the purely individual, and may also take the form of a group activity. Thus, the informal, spontaneous individual act of the motorist aiding an accident victim, and the formal participation of a volunteer meeting with a parolee as part of an organized program, are both acts of volunteering. Actually, there are two dimensions involved here, one varying between individual and group activity, the other varying between structured and unstructured activity. As depicted in Table I, the contexts of volunteering involve a range of activities that are all uncoerced, not primarily aimed at financial profit, and all are oriented toward helping others and possibly also oneself, as we shall see later.

Volunteering, as defined here, is similar to but somewhat less broad in definition than voluntary action as defined by David Horton Smith, Richard Reddy, and Burt Baldwin (1972, p. 163) in the quote earlier presented. By that definition, individual voluntary action may include an extramarital affair, a chess game, or the composition of a book of verse—in short, anything that feels good or meaningful and is not biologically compelled, politically coerced, or financially remunerated. Smith and his colleagues (1972) proceeded to note that a more limited concept may be desirable: "Voluntary Action directed at the long-range betterment of society and the general welfare may be the 'best' kind of voluntary action in the eyes of most people. But there are many other important kinds of voluntary action phenomena, even if not clearly aimed at the general welfare—for example, riots, wildcat strikes, fraternity hazing, shoplifting for 'kicks,' 'bingo parties,' 'social drinking,' and perhaps even watching TV" (p. 167).

With ruthless logic, Smith and his associates bring us to the precipice of a real dilemma. As founders of the Association of Voluntary Action Scholars, they recognized that a world of behavior, seemly and unseemly, public and private, is encompassed by the term "voluntary action." But from the perspective of a leader of, say, the National Center for Voluntary Action (to take the name of a prominent organization of the 1970s, now renamed), it is doubtful that such actions as "bingo parties" will generate en-

TABLE I. Basic Concepts

	INDIVIDUAL ACTION		
	Not Coerced	Deemed Beneficial	Organized
Empirical	Voluntary action	Volunteering	Voluntary associations; nonprofit organizations
Normative	Freedom	Volunteerism	Voluntarism

thusiasm, and it is nearly certain that opposition will greet such voluntary actions as shoplifting, rioting, and extramarital affairs.

Resolution of this dilemma may be achieved by two means. First, the concept of voluntary action might be defined in a narrower way, removing those actions not directed at long-range betterment and the general welfare. Simultaneously, the concept could be recognized to be broadly descriptive in nature and not referred to in value-charged ways. When speaking of voluntary action as a good thing, a term with a clear ideological content such as "volunteering" might serve better.

This usage seems conventional. Thus, it is awkward to speak of an individual "volunteering" to drink with the boys at the corner pub, or "volunteering" to spend an evening watching TV, although these are clearly forms of "voluntary action" that we celebrate among the joys of freedom. Volunteering may be seen to rest on an explicit basis of self-help, and almost all its forms contribute in some way to individual goals of career exploration and development, sociability, and other forms of personal enhancement.

A third prominent concept may now be introduced: voluntary association. This concept refers to forms of behavior that are organized and are directed at influencing broader structures of collective action and social purpose. A voluntary association is a structured group whose members have united for the purpose of advancing an interest or achieving some social purpose. Theirs is a clear aim toward a chosen form of "social betterment." Such an association is directed in its aims beyond the immediate enjoyment of fellowship and consummatory group activity; it links the group in some direct way to the larger society.

Thus, groups like neighborhood associations seeking to restrain crime or to encourage the cleaning of streets are voluntary associations by this identification; so are church-based organizations that seek to provide for school prayer, and civic organizations that aim to improve a city's economic climate; and so are groups of volunteers who hope to reduce family abuse by means of direct service and legislative advocacy. Such organizations are voluntary in a dual sense: Much of their human resources are contributed by members as volunteers, and they are nongovernmental,

nonprofit, and nonconsummatory—and thus are clearly located in the "voluntary sector" of society.

Voluntary associations are more structured and formal than voluntary action and volunteering. They are the organized vehicles of the third sector. Many voluntary associations are informal in their structure and convene to advance purposes that range from political protest to the provision of social care and service. Prominent among the contemporary ranks of voluntary associations stands a subcategory that is governmentally identified as publicly chartered, tax-free organizations. This group is called nonprofit organizations, which are certified to perform a wide range of charitable functions in society and in return for their tax-free status are required to provide public accounting of their actions. Nonprofit organizations are themselves divided into a number of categories, including philanthropies, which provide support to other nonprofits, and service-providing nonprofits.

Contemporary estimates identify well over 1 million nonprofit organizations in the United States, many of which support paid staff as well as volunteer employees and board members. Surveys also find that approximately half the U.S. population engages in regular volunteering and that 9 percent of all meaningful employment (and 7 percent of all salaries) emerge from the third sector.

These then are principal actors who inhabit the "third," "independent," or "voluntary" sector: all of us who engage in voluntary action, most of us who volunteer, and those who join with others in voluntary associations or nonprofit organizations. The behavior of these actors takes place in the broader societal milieu of organizational life and forms the empirical data for the study of voluntary action. These concepts are empirical (or positive) and reflect the concrete behavior of major actors.

Associated with each of these forms of action is a normative component—a concept that lends moral or ideological support to the phenomenon. These concepts may be identified as freedom, volunteerism, and voluntarism, respectively. Freedom is the normative concept that claims the goodness of voluntary action. Volunteerism is the normative concept that asserts the value of volunteering. And voluntarism is the normative concept that declares the worth of voluntary associations and their publicly chartered subtype, the nonprofit corporation.

As indicated in Table I, then, the third sector contains four major forms of actors, supported by three major ideological systems.

Voluntary Action Is Embedded in the Third Sector

Voluntary action's collective representation, the third sector, has been defined from the perspectives of the law, economics, organization theory, and political theory. Perri 6 and Victor Pestoff (1993) caution that "work on definitions can illuminate and can also obfuscate, depending more on how it is used than on how the definitions are framed. The danger is that definitions can be used as reasons for scholars not to look at work which falls outside the scope of the definition." In Bramson's felicitous phrase, there exists a "political context" for every social science. 6 and Pestoff observe that "academic work can easily become a prisoner of projects to 'claim' certain sorts of organizations for certain political projects."

Exhibiting elements of both the public and the private sectors, voluntary action has been seen as independent of interdependent with, and mediating to other institutional sectors of society. Voluntary action provides an important interface between the public and the private realms of society.

Although generally represented as a part of the "private" (meaning nongovernment) sector, in recent years nonprofits have been described more as "interdependent" with government. This interdependence most often has been linked to the service provider role that the sector plays with respect to government programs. Recently, some scholars have also studied the linkages created through nonprofits' roles as advocates for public policy and as representatives for special interest groups (Wolch 1990; Billis 1993).

The names used for the third sector itself are descriptive of this government/nonprofit linkage. They have been called "nonprofit private organizations" (See Salamon 1992; O'Neill 1989). This description casts nonprofits as essentially private, distinguishing them from the business sector by the caveat that they are not profit oriented. However, the name "nongovernmental public sector" has also been used to describe the sector (Etzioni 1976). In this case, the organization is considered essentially a part of the public sector, with the distinguishing characteristic being that it is not a government agency. These descriptions highlight the situation of the nonprofit sector, sitting between the public and the private.

In seeking to understand the role of voluntary action in society, an examination of the relations between institutional sectors provides a productive beginning point. This problem has occupied social theorists for many years, and among the most important work on the subject is that of several wartime Hungarian scholars and their intellectual descendants.

Writing during the dark days of World War II, Karl Polanyi and Karl Mannheim sought to understand the ways in which business, government, and social institutions related to each other. Each aimed to develop a theory of the proper relation between the sectors, hoping thereby to contribute to a world in which the maladies of fascism could be permanently banished.

To Polanyi, the key to peaceful development involved the creation of a balanced role for the three sectors of market, state, and society. The danger he saw was that the market would come to be seen as the essential institution, and its basis in contract would give rise to a misleading and incomplete vision of human freedom. There are limits to what such "free" enterprise can provide, he argued: Markets fragment human relations and render important social relations invisible. They also tend to relegate the state to a position of insignificance.

In Polanyi's (1957) view, it is only when we come to recognize that the free market alone will not solve our problems that we come face to face with the reality of society. Now we can see the dividing line between liberalism on the one hand, fascism and socialism on the other. And we also begin to see that the difference between freedom and oppression is not primarily economic. Rather, it is moral and religious (p. 258). Polanyi's work suggests a vital role for what would later be called the "third sector"—to play a leading role in the struggle for justice and freedom.

To Mannheim (1949a), the key to social reconstruction was to be found in applying knowledge to the resolution of problems and in learning how to do social planning. He introduced powerful distinctions between ideology (the interest of the status quo) and utopia (the vision of what ought to be), and between functional (what appears to work, however misguided it may be) and substantive rationality (what undergirds the resolution of genuine human needs).

Mannheim observed that modern "society is faced, not with brief unrest, but with a radical change of structure; . . . this realization is the only guarantee of preventive measures. Only if we know why Western society in the crisis zone is passing through a phase of disintegration is there any hope that the countries which still enjoy comparative peace will learn to control the future trend of events by democratic planning, and so to avoid the negative aspects of the process: dictatorship, conformity, and barbarism" (1949a p. 6).

John Friedmann, a contemporary planner, elaborated Mannheim's concern that we learn to plan for a world that will become increasingly democratic and increasingly interdependent. Friedmann (1987) identified productive roles for five sectors (p. 335–356) to play in modern society: the household, the market, the civil society (or voluntary sector), the political community (causes), and the state. The world, he observed, is best seen as a "common" (p. 383) upon which these varying institutional interests meet and contest with each other.

Also echoing themes first sounded by Polanyi and Mannheim, Harvard political scientist Robert Putnam (1993a) has studied "civic communities" in Emilia-Romagna and Tuscany (Italy). He observed that "these 'civic communities' value solidarity, civic participation, and integrity. And here democracy works." (pp. 36–37). Putnam found that the roots of these communities are deep:

> Networks of civic engagement, like . . . neighborhood associations, choral societies, cooperatives, sports clubs, mass-based parties, and the like . . . represent . . . an essential form of social capital: The denser such networks in a community, the more likely that its citizens will be able to cooperate for mutual benefit (Putnam 1993b, p. 173).

Putnam (1993a, p. 38) finds that the social capital provided by voluntary action is a public good, not provided by private agents. "This means that social capital must often be a by-product of other social activities." Echoing the work of Edgar and Jean Camper Cahn (Cahn and Rowe 1992), who developed programs utilizing "time dollars" to bank volunteered commitments into accounts from which volunteers may draw themselves, he urges that we "focus on community development, allowing space for religious organizations and choral societies and Little Leagues that may seem to have little to do with politics or economics." Putnam (1993a) concludes: "Social capital is not a substitute for effective public policy but rather a prerequisite for it and, in part, a consequence of it" (p. 42).

Voluntary Action May Be Depicted in Societal Maps

The concept of "sector" has provided the most useful way of understanding the role of voluntary action in contemporary society. Most conventional is the three-sector model, as presented, for example, in the sixth edition of Bruce Hopkins' (1992) *Law of Tax Exempt Organizations.* Business is the first sector; government is the second sector; and the voluntary nonprofit sector is the third sector. Much of the scholarship of the nonprofit field uses this model (see Van Til and Carr 1994).

Van Til (1988) offers a four-sector model of society, delineating business, government, nonprofit, and household sectors. He adds a dynamic aspect to the model by describing the interdependence of these sectors, with the household sector serving as the keystone. Households (or individual members of households) earn money and buy

products and services in the business sector, form foundations, volunteer, are members of associations in the nonprofit sector, and support government through voting and paying taxes.

Smith (1991) presents a five-sector model of society: personal (families and friendship groups), business sector, government sector, public benefit nonprofit, and private benefit nonprofit. Smith's approach divides what we traditionally think of as the nonprofit sector into smaller pieces, depending on the goals of the nonprofit organization.

A six-sector model has been developed by Rob Paton (1991), who focused on two major dimensions: the formality-informality of organization and the social or economic nature of goals sought. Paton's model identifies a range of economic styles of organization and clusters them in sectors (see Figure I).

G. F. Schuppert (1991) presents a seven-sector model (see Figure II), building on the German experience with a range of organizations that span the distance between pure voluntary action, business, and government.

FIGURE I. ROB PATON'S MAP OF THE SECTORS

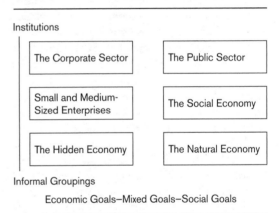

FIGURE II. SCHUPPERT'S SEVEN-SECTOR MODEL

An alternative approach tends not to begin with the identification of sectors but rather begins with a distinction between public and private action (see Dewey 1927). This dichotomous approach introduces tension between the two forms of action, implicitly introducing a relationship of power or exchange into the discussion. Franklin Gamwell (1984), for instance, uses a two-sector model, distinguishing between governmental and nongovernmental organizations and then dividing the latter into "private-regarding and public-regarding" agencies. "Public-regarding" agencies are further split on the basis of exclusivity into "less inclusive" and "more inclusive" groupings, the latter of which are then divided into "nonpolitical-regarding" and "political-regarding." Russy Sumariwalla (1983) visualizes two principal sectoral divisions also and classifies nonprofit organizations as private-sector "non-business" entities, operating either in the public interest or as part of an "all other" subcategory.

An important contribution of these simple two-sector models is that they focus less on boundaries (what fits inside) and more on relations across boundaries. As was discovered by Lord Beveridge (1948) in his pioneering study of voluntary action in Britain, the state and voluntary associations are partners in cooperation for social advance. As Susan Ostrander, Stuart Langton, and Jon Van Til (1987) would later demonstrate, the government, voluntary association, and business are more often interdependent with each other than independent of each other.

In much the same way, Ralph Kramer (1984) focused his three-sector model on relationships for the delivery of personal and social services. He added the element of power relationships, laying the foundation for a fuller understanding of nonprofits. In looking at the interrelationships among profitmaking, governmental, and voluntary organizations, he examined the activities involved and identified the five possible relationships among sectors as reprivatization, empowerment, pragmatic partnership, governmental operation, and nationalization.

Even our manner of naming the sectors (first, second, third) implies a power order. To gain perspective on this implied order, it is helpful to look at the work of Peter Dobkin Hall (1992). Hall's historical analyses invite an interesting exercise about naming the order of the sectors

(first, second, and third). The nonprofit sector is, as we have seen, most often identified as the third sector. However, at any point in history, if we were to stop and try to put order to the sectors as we viewed them from the perspective of that time and place, we might call our "first," "second," and "third" sectors differently (see also Young 1988). For example, why not call the family the first sector? It was here first. Would voluntary organizations, or government, be the "second" in order of time? The labels become very dependent on where one stands to do the labeling.

Part of the problem with understanding the "sector" issue comes from jumping into the parade in the middle of it. Lester Salamon and Helmut Anheier (1992) noted that discussion of sectors is a relatively recent academic discovery. "The emergence of the large-scale profit-making form and of public administration represented the major institutional innovations of the eighteenth and nineteenth centuries, and the results have been institutional complexes of enormous social and economic power" (p. 126). The nonprofit sector, as Hall (1992) indicated, is an even more recent invention, as it has emerged only since 1970.

Van Til's work on *Mapping the Third Sector* (1988) arrives at a model that seeks to integrate the sector approach with those focusing on action. As extended by Jacquelyn Thayer Scott (1922), who added the communitarian box to the matrix, this model identifies the essential forms of voluntary and nonprofit action and distinguishes between them. Explicit in this approach are the variety of exchanges between the third sector and the economy, politics, and family (see Figure III).

Recently, a series of interactive sectoral models have been presented. Building on the observations of earlier writers that sectoral boundaries are themselves blurred, David Billis, Pestoff, and Rudolph Bauer have presented models that combine multiple dimensions into fruitful representations.

Pestoff (1992), writing from a Swedish perspective, presents a triangular view of the sectors, setting the "voluntary nonprofit sector" in between the state, market, and community (see Figure IV). Cutting across this sector are lines of distinction between formal and informal organizations, nonprofit and for-profit groups, and public and pri-

FIGURE III. VAN TIL'S MAP OF MODELS EXTENDED BY SCOTT

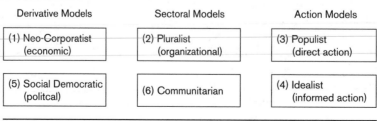

Derivative Models	Sectoral Models	Action Models
(1) Neo-Corporatist (economic)	(2) Pluralist (organizational)	(3) Populist (direct action)
(5) Social Democratic (politcal)	(6) Communitarian	(4) Idealist (informed action)

FIGURE IV. PESTOFF'S TRIANGLE

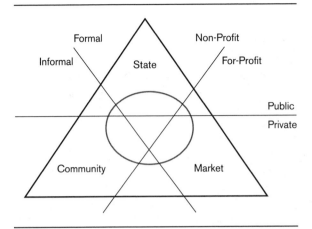

vate purposes. This triangle can be adjusted to reflect as different a structure as that of Slovenia's, by altering the size of the state and the angles of the cross-cutting lines.

Billis (1993) focused on the blurring of the sectors, noting that third-sector organizations that have both membership and paid staff and deliver operational services as well "contain structural properties of the adjacent (government and private-sector) bureaucracies and those of the associational worlds (see Figure V). Each sector, according to this view, contains a relatively pure core as well as a shared, or blurred, space. Billis also noted that the sizes of the various sectors may be adjusted to reflect different notional structures and traditions.

In an far-reaching recent presentation, historian Rudolph Bauer (1993) extended Billis' point that the voluntary sector sectors takes on major characteristics of the other sectors (see Figure VI). Bauer suggested that volunteers tend to treat voluntary organizations as though they were providers of charitable service, whereas board members tend to see them as though they were political organi-

FIGURE V. BILLIS'S VIEW OF THE BLURRING OF THE SECTORS

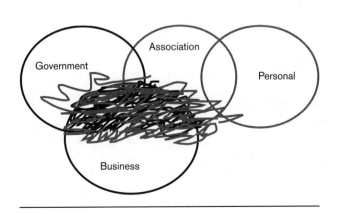

FIGURE VI. RUDOLPH BAUER'S VIEW OF THE THIRD SECTOR AS A COAT OF MANY COLORS

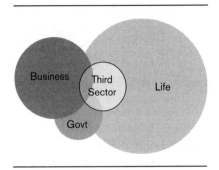

zations. Meanwhile, staff behaves as though the same organization is a business. In this way, Bauer observed, a "third-sector" organization tends to take on the coloration of business (first sector), politics (second sector), and community (fourth sector). It all depends on one's point of view, which itself is determined by one's role within the organization. Figure VI shows this representation.

Many Disciplinary Perspectives May Be Applied to the Study of Voluntary Action

Voluntary action has been described as "private action for the public good" (Payton 1988) and as "private organization serving a public purpose" (O'Neill 1989). Voluntary action fulfills a variety of societal roles: (1) supporting society's ability to act for the common good (the communitarian model, a social role), (2) partnering with government to provide collective goods and services (the shadow state model, an economic role), (3) speaking for the minorities and serving as an advocate for pluralism and diversity (the loyal opposition model, a political role).

These perspectives each give rise to their own approaches to understanding what has been called the "third-sector elephant" (recalling the old story of the manifold observations of blindfolded experts trying to identify an elephant by touch.) The economic approach argues that providing public goods that cannot be provided profitably in the market is a major task for voluntary action. The political approach argues that voluntary organizations should advocate minority opinions, argue for change, and serve as a watchdog for government. The communitarian approach argues that voluntary action provides a vehicle for individuals to join in common action for the common good.

Approaches to definition depend upon the purposes of the definer. If it is agreed that one cannot "define" the third sector in a global or all-inclusive sense, nevertheless, we can look at different perspectives from which definition has been attempted. The weight of the defining factors changes depending on one's perspective. Let us now turn to a review of some common definitional approaches that are based on disciplinary perspective.

Economic Perspective

Economic definitions of the third sector are based on the concept of exchange (see Dewey 1927). Among the most influential economic approaches are those of Mancur Olson (1965), Kenneth Boulding (1973), Henry Hansmann (1987), and Burton Weisbrod (1988). Olson defined the problem of the "free rider" as endemic to voluntary organization; Boulding posited the existence of a "grants economy", Hansmann posited market failure as a basic force behind voluntary organization development; and Weisbrod brought these elements together in an integrated theory. A weakness of the economic perspective, which lends itself well to the charting of national accounts of productivity, involves the underestimation of voluntary action. Much of what third-sector organizations do is not easily or appropriately valued in dollars (see Hodgkinson et al. 1992).

Legal Perspective

In *The Law of Exempt Organizations* (1992), Bruce Hopkins proposed a methodology for "defining" charitable organizations, which resembles the child's game "I will tell you what it is not, you guess what it is." According to Hopkins, the best way to understand is to contrast. Not surprisingly, a negative definition of nonprofits surfaces. One positive factor for inclusion in the sector is, however, provided. According to Hopkins, the "private inurement" doctrine is currently the substantial dividing line adhered to in many recent tax court decisions. Clearly a "nonprofit" is fundamentally not meant to enrich anyone.

Political Perspective

Nonprofits caught Alex de Tocqueville's eye as he looked at America because he was looking at democracy. In a sense, the third sector exists in relation to the concept of democracy in a society (see Bellah et al. 1985). More recently, Jennifer Wolch (1990) argued that one of the most significant roles of nonprofits involves advocacy, social innovation, and to "watch government." If nonprofits are perceived as intermediaries in society, then it is in their capacity as mediators that nonprofits act as advocates for the values, issues, and rights that are part of the interests of the sector. More important, they are a voice for the common good. They come to serve as a nongovernmental way of expressing the power of the people. Etzioni (1993: see also Etzioni 1976) proposed that the political role of voluntary organizations be extended to provide a forum where the community vision can develop. He sees voluntary associations functioning as agent to build a sense of "common

good" rather than as representatives of special interests in the political debate.

Organization Theory Perspective

Billis (1993) wrote that organization theory has been insufficiently applied to understanding the managerial and organizational issues in the third sector. He formulated a third sector definition from the organizational perspective. On the organizational culture of these public and private worlds, Billis reminds us that these organizations develop clearly understood rules of the game, bureaucratic structures, managerial command systems, membership and voting structures, and are based on ideas of commitment, love, and affection. In examining organizations this way Billis raises the question of how third-sector organizations represent or advocate the interests of their stakeholders and members.

Goals Perspective

Some of the definitions formulated using this perspective are the most complete ones we have. Unfortunately, they are somewhat unwieldy in both application and research. For example, Robert Anthony and David Young (1988) listed various characteristics of third-sector organizations, which include "to provide service." Who provides the services, what services are provided, and who receives the services are all important factors to understand about third-sector organizations. If a service is provided to a nonpaying client, or to the public (common goods), or if the providers are nonpaid volunteers, then we have a third-sector organization from this definitional view.

Natural Science Perspective

Van Til (1988; see also Van Til et al. 1990) has elaborated a metaphor for understanding the third sector that uses natural science images. This framework identifies forces as meteorological—climate and values, topographical (boundaries) and tectonic (underlying forces that affect the shape and nature). This three-dimensional approach provides a comprehensive framework for the exercise of definition. One can begin to "fit" other definitions of nonprofits into the three approaches. Van Til defines nonprofits much as one would the human body; who it is, what it does, what it looks like, and how it works.

Structural-Functional Perspective

We have seen some approaches based on the scholars' personal perspectives or professional background, and now we will look at an approach based on the need for a tool. Salamon and Anheier (1992) offered the structural and operational definition as a way to distinguish nonprofit organizations within a society. The defining structural-func-

TABLE II. Comparison Between Lohmann and Salamon/Anheier Definitions

Lohmann	Salamon and Anheier
Purpose is to do good	
Organized participation	Formal
	Private (nongovernmental)
	Self-governing
	Nonprofit distribution
Resources are shared	
Reciprocal relations	
	Voluntary

tional characteristics of third-sector organizations are that they are formal, private, nonprofit-distributing, self-governing, and voluntary (p. 6).

Viewed from the structural-functional perspective, the advocacy role becomes clearer. But overall, the range of characteristics and activities that one can list from the structural-functional perspective is so wide that it is possible to create definitions using this approach that define and yet touch none or very few of the same bases. Consider the comparison in Table II the Roger Lohmann (1992) and the Salamon/Anheier (1992) definitions.

In offering his definition, Lohmann focused on the human element, purpose, and organizational dynamics. In contrast, Salamon and Anheier concentrated on measurable, observable, and quantifiable characteristics. Lohmann asserted that nonprofits are organizations of "uncoerced participation, shared common goods and purpose, mutual reciprocity, and fairness" (p. 58). Salamon's position in another work (1992) moved closer to Roger Lohman's definition advanced in *The Commons* (1992). In his book, Salamon added the additional point that the purpose of a nonprofit organization must be for public good.

Lohmann concentrated on the human element, purpose and organizational dynamics; and Salamon and Anheier concentrated on measurable, observable, and quantifiable characteristics. Lohmann said nonprofits are organizations of "uncoerced participation, shared common goods and purpose, mutual reciprocity, and fairness" (p. 60). His definition provides a way of capturing a "sense of center" in the world of voluntary action.

Conclusion: Voluntary Action Is a Powerful Organizational Force In Society

Futurist Jeremy Rifkin (1995) has argued that the twenty-first century will see a continuing decline in the amount of paid work made available to individuals by both governments and corporations. This restructuring of human participation in society will provide an increasing role, he con-

tends, for the third sector. By providing shadow wages to support voluntary action and a social wage to facilitate volunteering by the underemployed, the social economy provided by the third sector may play an important role in maintaining social peace and order.

In such a time of change and challenge, it is important to recall that it is voluntary action that powers the third sector and that the third sector is relied upon by society as a crucial developer of its distinctive goals. Third-sector organizations resemble, in part, businesses, governments, and families—and interact directly with all three of these organizational forms. They receive their unique stamp, however, from their shared value of advancing the common good by means of reflective and significant voluntary group activity. What we make of the voluntary action we perform forges, in considerable part, the strength and vitality of the society we inhabit.

Jon Van Til

BIBLIOGRAPHY

Anthony, Robert, and David Young, 1988. "The Role of the Nonprofit Sector." In David Gies, J. Steven Ott, and Jay M. Shafritz, eds., *Nonprofit Organization: Essential Readings*. Pacific Grove, CA: Brooks/Cole.

Bauer, Rudolph, 1993. Plenary presentation at CIES Conference, Barcelona, June.

Bellah, Robert, N., Richard Madsen, Steven M. Tipton, William M. Sullivan, and Ann Swindler, 1985. *Habits of the Heart: Individualism and Commitment in American Life*. New York: Harper and Row.

Berger, Peter L., and Richard J. Neuhaus, 1977. *To Empower People: The Role of Mediating Structures in Public Policy*. Washington, D.C.: American Enterprise Institute for Public Policy Research.

Beveridge, Lord, 1948. *Voluntary Action: A Report on Methods of Social Advance*. London: Allen and Unwin.

Billis, David, 1993. *Organising Public and Voluntary Agencies*. London: Routledge.

Boulding, Kenneth, 1973. *The Economy of Love and Fear*. Belmont, CA: Wadsworth.

Bramson, Leon, 1961. *The Political Context of Sociology*. Princeton, NJ: Princeton University Press.

Cahn, Edgar, and Jonathan Rowe, 1992. *Time Dollars: The New Currency That Enables Americans to Turn Their Hidden Resource–Time–into Personal Security and Community Renewal.* Emmaus, PA: Rodale Press.

Dewey, John, 1927. *The Public and Its Problems.* New York: Swallow.

Etzioni, Amitai, 1968. *The Active Society.* New York: Free Press.

———, 1976. *Social Problems.* New York: Free Press.

———, 1993. *The Spirit of Community: Rights, Responsibilities, and the Communitarian Agenda.* New York: Crown.

Friedmann, John, 1987. *Planning in the Public Domain: From Knowledge to Action* Princeton, NJ: Princeton University Press.

Gamwell, Franklin I., 1984. *Beyond Preference: Liberal Theories of Independent Association.* Chicago, IL: University of Chicago Press.

Hall, Peter Dobkin, 1992. *Inventing the Nonprofit Sector and Other Essays on Philanthropy, Voluntarism, and Nonprofit Organizations.* Baltimore, MD: Johns Hopkins University Press.

Hansmann, Henry, 1987. "Economic Theories of Nonprofit Organization." In W. W. Powell, ed., *The Nonprofit Sector: A Research Handbook.* New Haven, CT: Yale University Press.

Hodgkinson, Virginia A., Murray S. Weitzman, Christopher M. Toppe, and Stephen M. Noga, 1992. *The Nonprofit Almanac 1992-1993: Dimensions of the Independent Sector.* San Francisco, CA: Jossey-Bass.

Hopkins, Bruce R., 1992. *The Law of Tax Exempt Organizations,* 6th ed. New York: Wiley.

Kramer, Ralph, 1984. *Voluntary Agencies in the Welfare State.* Berkeley: University of California Press.

Levitt, Theodore, 1973. *The Third Sector: New Tactics for a Responsive Society.* New York: Amacom.

Lohmann, Roger, 1992. *The Commons: New Perspectives on Nonprofit Organizations and Voluntary Action.* San Francisco, CA: Jossey-Bass.

Mannheim, Karl, 1949a [1929]. *Ideology and Utopia.* New York: Harcourt, Brace.

———, 1949b [1940]. *Man and Society in an Age of Transformation.* New York: Harcourt, Brace.

Olson, Mancur, 1965. *The Logic of Collective Action.* Cambridge, MA: Harvard University Press.

O'Neill, Michael, 1989. *The Third America.* San Francisco, CA: Jossey-Bass.

Ostrander, Susan, Stuart Langton, and Jon Van Til, eds., 1987. *Shifting the Debate: Public/Private Sector Relations in the Modern Welfare State.* New Brunswick, NJ: Transaction Press.

Paton, Rob, 1991. "The Social Economy; Value-Based Organizations in the Wider Society." Chapter 1 in Julian Batsleer *et al.*, eds., *Issues in Voluntary and Non-Profit Management.* Wokingham, UK: Addison-Wesley.

Payton, Robert, 1988. *Philanthropy: Voluntary Action for Public Good.* New York: American Council on Education Press.

Pestoff, Victor, 1992. Summarized in Ivan Svetlik, "The Voluntary Sector in a Post-Communist Country: The Case of Slovenia." Chapter 10 of Stein Kuhnle and Per Selle, eds., *Government and Voluntary Organizations.* Aldershot, UK: Avebury:

Polanyi, Karl, 1957 [1944]. *The Great Transformation.* Boston: Beacon Press.

Putnam, Robert D., 1993a. "The Prosperous Community: Social Capital and Public Life." *The American Prospect,* no. 13 (Spring) 35–42.

Putnam, Robert D., with Robert Leonardi and Raffaella Y. Nanetti, 1993b. *Making Democracy Work: Civic Traditions in Modern Italy.* Princeton, NJ: Princeton University Press.

Rifkin, Jeremy, 1995. *The End of Work: The Decline of the Global Labor Force and the Dawn of the Post-Market Era.* New York: Tarcher/Putnam.

Salamon, Lester M., 1992. *America's Nonprofit Sector: A Primer.* New York: Foundation Center.

Salamon, Lester M., and Helmut K. Anheier (eds.) 1997. *Defining the Nonprofit Sector–A Cross-National Analysis.* Manchester University Press.

Schuppert, G. F., 1991. "State, Market, Third Sector: Problems of Organizational Choice in the Delivery of Public Services." *Nonprofit and Voluntary Sector Quarterly,* vol. 20: 123–136.

Scott, Jacquelyn Thayer, 1992. "Voluntary Sector in Crisis: Canada's Changing Public Philosophy of the State and Its Impact on Voluntary, Charitable Organizations." Thesis submitted to the Graduate School of Public Affairs, University of Colorado, Denver.

Smith, David Horton, 1973. "The Impact of the Voluntary Sector on Society." In David Horton Smith, ed., *Voluntary Action Research: 1973.* Lexington, MA: D. C. Heath, 387–400.

———, 1991. "Four Sectors or Five? Retaining the Member-Benefit Sector." *Nonprofit and Voluntary Sector Quarterly,* vol. 20, no. 2:137–150.

Smith, David Horton, Richard Reddy, and Burt Baldwin, eds., 1972. *Voluntary Action Research 1972.* Lexington, MA: D. C. Heath.

Sumariwalla, Russy, 1983. "Preliminary Observations in Scope, Size, and Classification of the Sector." In Virginia Hodgkinson, ed., Working Papers for the Spring Research Forum; Since the Filer Commission. Washington: Independent Sector, 433–449.

Svetlik, Ivan, 1992. "The Voluntary Sector in Post-Communist Country: The Case of Slovenia." Chapter 10 of Stein Kuhnle and Per Selle, eds., *Government and Voluntary Organizations.* Aldershot, UK: Avebury.

Van Til, Jon, 1988. *Mapping the Third Sector: Voluntarism in a Changing Social Economy.* New York: Foundation Center.

Van Til, Jon, *et al.* 1990. *Critical Issues in Philanthropy.* San Francisco, CA: Jossey-Bass.

Van Til, Jon, and Joanne Carr, 1994. "Defining the Nonprofits Sector." Paper presented to the Association for Research on Nonprofit Organizations and Voluntary Action, Berkeley, October.

Weisbrod, Burton, 1988. *The Nonprofit Economy,* Cambridge, MA: Harvard University Press.

Wolch, Jennifer R., 1990. *The Shadow State: Government and Voluntary Sector in Transition.* New York: Foundation Center.

Young, Dennis R., 1988. "The Nonprofit Sector as the First Sector: Policy Implications." Part 2, no. 3 of *Looking Forward to the Year 2000: Public Policy and Philanthropy.* Research Forum Working Papers (Spring). Washington: Independent Sector.

VOLUNTARY SECTOR. A term often used to describe the nonprofit, independent, or third, sector (in addition to the government and private economic enterprise) of the social economy; the preferred usage in Canada and the United Kingdom. The term has been most closely associated with numerous publications by American sociologists David Horton Smith (1972, 1973) and Jon Van Til

(1988). Activities in this sector are usually conducted by formal organizational entities that are incorporated and governed by boards of directors and operate under a non-distribution constraint (i.e., profits or residual earnings of the organization may not be distributed to individuals who control the entity). Many of these incorporated organizations are also registered as charities and have tax-exempt status; that is, they do not pay income taxes on their earnings and donors receive some tax benefit (a deduction or a credit) for their financial contributions to the entity. When formally incorporated or registered, organizations in this sector must have clearly designated public-benefit purposes—usually related to religion, health, education, or social welfare—and partisan political activities by the entity are either prohibited or severely curtailed. However, the use of the term "voluntary sector" (as opposed to the more specific "nonprofit sector," especially in the United States) may include informal and unorganized activity by persons and groups for charitable or broadly inclusive mutual benefit purposed, so long as voluntary action is evident in governance, provision of direct services, and/or financial support.

Historical Background

Although individuals voluntary activity within and between family and clan groups likely has been characteristic of human history since the earliest times, voluntary associations appear to have been around for only about 10,000 years. Robert Anderson (1973) reports that associations arose during the Neolithic period (7,000 or 8,000 B.C.E.), with the development of villages that were not integrated into complex political and economic systems. Earliest associations were religious societies, often of a secret nature, playing important roles in conserving traditions, and building bonds and alliances across family and tribal structures. In preindustrial states, association activity expanded to include the merchant associations of Greece, China, Rome, and Egypt, and the craft guilds of medieval Europe. The rise of the industrial nation-state coincided with the spread of democracy and the growth of bureaucratic techniques in government, leading to increased formalization of electoral and bureaucratic procedures in voluntary associations—statutes of incorporation, bylaws, an executive structure—devoted to more efficiency in making decisions and taking action. Anderson (1973) added that in modern societies, voluntary associations have acquired important sociological functions, including contributing to social stability by mediating between the individual and the community, especially in support of social change, "to adapt individuals for modern participation" (p. 22).

Voluntary association and sector activity in North America had historical roots in Elizabethan England and royalist France. Charitable purposes—relief of poverty, ad-

vancement of education, advancement of religion, or other charitable purpose beneficial to the community—were first set out in the Elizabethan Poor Law (1601), although distribution of charity to the destitute was left in the hands of municipal authorities or appointed overseers. In French Canada, a state Bureau of the Poor was established in 1685, funded through a combination of crown subsidies, fines from felonies and misdemeanors, and voluntary almsgiving. Thus, in both principal North American historical traditions, public institutions (or the church) were the principal recipients of private largesse. This was echoed in the earliest English colonial charitable organizations, Harvard College and local hospital societies in both the colonial United States and Upper Canada. Peter Dobkin Hall (1987, 1994) has written extensively on the suspicion with which Americans viewed the power of individuals incorporating and holding property in order to pursue their private interests, however charitable. It was not until the latter part of the nineteenth century, in both the United States and Canada, that a clear role for private institutions in the democratic state was set out in legislation. In 1874, President Charles Eliot of Harvard successfully defended the university's tax exemption to the Massachusetts General Court on the grounds of demonstrable public benefits being derived from private charitable institutions. The Massachusetts legislature subsequently expanded the range of tax-exempt institutions, and this law was seen as a model by other states. Also in 1874, the Charity Aid Act of Ontario regularized state subsidies for religious, fraternal, and patriotic organizations operating hospitals, orphanages, and homes for unmarried mothers. This act also established government authority to inspect these private institutions and approve their management policies.

Voluntary sector associations and institutions continued to grow through the end of the nineteenth century and during the early part of the twentieth century. In the United States, this period was characterized as the "Golden Age of Philanthropy," when industrial giants like Andrew Carnegie and John D. Rockefeller parcelled out large fortunes to libraries, churches, and universities. They also established the first private grant-making foundations for charitable purposes. This period was also noted for establishment of community charitable foundations and united community fund-raising campaigns—the "Red Feather" drives, which evolved into the United Way—in both Canada and the United States.

The period of greatest growth in voluntary associations and the sector in North America, however, was after World War II. According to Hall (1994), "More than 90 percent nonprofit organizations currently in existence" (p. 3) in the United States were founded in this period. In Canada, this growth spurt peaked later, with the total number of registered charities growing by 40 percent during the 1980s (Scott 1992). These organizations are involved in a wide range of activities, including the direct delivery of services (often contracted for by the state), education of the public (including popular or moral education about public issues of the day), and advocacy for social change.

In recent years, scholars have devoted much energy to analyzing why the voluntary sector exists, what it includes (or excludes), and what factors affect its growth and structure. The theories about "why" it exists could be grouped as economic, religious, and sociopolitical. Economic theorists have been most plentiful, and a number of useful summary overviews of their work have been published. Henry Hansmann (1987) suggested economic theories of the sector can be divided into two types: theories about the role of voluntary institutions and theories about their behavior. "Role" theorists suggest that voluntary organizations serve as private producers of public goods because government or business cannot produce collective goods as well ("market failure"); or they offer a service (such as day care) where consumers may wish to "patronize a service provider in which they place more trust than they can in a proprietary firm" (p. 29) ("contract failure"); or they exist because the availability of government subsidies enables them to proliferate and compete with for-profit firms. "Behavior" theorists base their theories on the assumption that voluntary institutions cannot distribute their profits or residual earnings to those who control them. Thus, most of these theories are classical economic optimizing models: voluntary organizations will seek to maximize their budgets to enhance the importance of the organization or its managers; or they will be inherently inefficient (and fail to minimize costs) because their owners/managers do not benefit financially from efficient performance. These—and other—economic theories of the sector are important because they influence key public policies that affect it, such as tax exemption or the disallowance of for-profit firms in designated activities (such as day care or nursing homes).

Many have also written about the religious motivation for voluntary sector activity, particularly in the United States. Robert Bellah *et al.* (1985), in their landmark book *Habits of the Heart: Individualism and Commitment in American Life* wrote about the importance of the religious tradition in fostering activity that is other-oriented. A 1988 report by the Independent Sector (Hodgkinson *et al.*) supported the conclusions of a 1984 report by the Council on Foundations (Joseph *et al.*): nearly all religious congregations are actively involved in human services, especially food, nutrition, refugee aid and resettlement, day care, camps, emergency and disaster and disaster relief, schools and tutoring. The 1989 Spring Research Forum, cosponsored by Independent Sector and the United Way Institute, focused on philanthropy and the religious tradition and drew more than 20 scholarly papers dealing with the links between religious belief—Christian, Jewish, Islamic, Confucian, among others—and voluntary, charitable, and philanthropic behavior. Simplistically, these links can be summarized as flowing from the individual's belief that such behavior is (1) necessary for salvation and spiritual growth or harmony and (2) commanded by a "Higher Power."

Voluntary Sector Theories

Sociopolitical theories of the sector have emerged from the disciplines of sociology (Smith 1972, 1973; Anderson 1973; Van Til 1988) and political science (of which Douglas 1987 provides a useful summary). Smith (1973) argued that voluntary sector activity exists because of "what one does out of some kind of expectation of psychic benefits or commitment to some value, ideal, or common interest" (p. 387). The roles or functions of the sector, he added, include (1) providing society with a large variety of partially tested social innovations from which the private and public sectors can then select and institutionalize the most promising—"provid[ing] the social risk capital of human society" (p. 388), (2) providing ideologies and perspectives that challenge prevailing assumptions about social norms and activities, (3) offering novelty, beauty, and play in differing approaches to meeting human needs, and (4) assisting with social integration in society for individuals and groups. James Douglas (1987) noted political science does not offer a single measure to apply to institutions, equivalent to the economists' utility. Political scientists are concerned with the promotion of welfare and efficiency and with publicly defensible criteria for justice that balance the wishes and values of the majority against the rights of minorities. When, then, should a public service be provided by a voluntary association or organization? Douglas (1987) listed the principal replies of political science: (1) when the scale or size of the service means it is less efficient for the state to provide, (2) when an alternative, or "pilot," method of delivering the service needs to be demonstrated, and (3) when voluntary organizations present a mechanism through which conflicts of values, interests, and views can be accommodated. Conversely, the activities of voluntary associations should not be assumed by the state when (1) the service reflects the views of a small proportion of the population, (2) when the service or action is not desired by most of the population, (3) when views about the service are so diverse that no single choice or compromise is possible, or (4) when bureaucratic constraints inherent in state delivery of the service would make it less efficient or desirable.

Sectoral Boundaries

Implicitly, it would seem, voluntary sector activity is easily defined by the nature of its purpose, governance, and source or distribution of its funding. In fact, the task of "mapping" the sector has proven quite complex. Four sophisticated attempts have been undertaken to more clearly define the sectoral boundaries–by Russy Sumariwalla (1983), Ralph Kramer (1984), Franklin Gamwell (1984) and Jon Van Til (1988). Sumariwalla (1983) visualizes two principal divisions in the sector, private "nonbusiness" entities, operating either in the public interest or in an "all other" subcategory. In an alternate construct, he described the voluntary sector as "nonbusiness, nongovernmental," comprised of public interest and "all other" activities and organizations. Kramer (1984) focused his three-sector schematic on the delivery of personal and social services, and the interrelationships among profit making, governmental, and voluntary organizations. He identified the five possible relationships among sectors as reprivatization, empowerment, pragmatic partnership, governmental operation, and nationalization–a linear continuum that moves from private-sector predominance (of reprivatization) to voluntary-sector dominance (of empowerment) to increasing levels of governmental predominance (from pragmatic partnership through to nationalization). Gamwell (1984) draws on the philosophies of John Dewey and economist Milton Friedman in drawing two differing maps of the voluntary sector, before developing his own construction. The "Dewey map" defines the voluntary sector as "community-regarding," further subdividing it into "nonpublic interest" and "public interest" subsectors. The "Friedman map" subdivides the voluntary sector into "charitable" and "public service" categories. Gamwell's own map divides voluntary sector or "public-regarding" organizations on the basis of exclusively into "less inclusive" and "more inclusive" groupings. "More inclusive" groups are either "nonpolitical-regarding" or "political-regarding."

Van Til (1988) argued these maps were too simplistic and confining, because they take into account only political theory. He suggested a social science analog to natural science cartography. His topographical map, describing boundaries, closely resembles the work of Sumariwalla, Kramer, and Gamwell. The voluntary sector (which he distinguishes from the household or informal sector) is subdivided into "public-regarding or charitable" associations and membership benefit" associations. His meteorological, or climatic, map looks at the three categories of values in the voluntary sector: basic democratic values as articulated by the eighteenth century French chronicler Tocqueville, the specter of privatism (Bellah *et al.* 1985), and cultural influences that come from associational life itself (which he derives from the work of sociologist Emile Durkheim). Finally, Van Til (1988) constructed a tectonic map, seeking to understand underlying forces affecting the shape and nature of sectoral activities: bureaucratization, mass democratization, power and oligarchical control, economic concentration, and the interpenetration of sectors.

As to which organizations and activities, precisely, are in the voluntary sector, the ultimate decision is made by the state and/or by the membership of the voluntary entity itself. In the United States, the state's determination is generally made by the Internal Revenue Service (IRS), which confers tax-exempt status and classifies voluntary organizations by subsections of the Tax Code. In 1991, the IRS listed 1,055,545 tax-exempt organizations, but this number includes a wide variety of organizations with a public purpose, such as mutual insurance companies and multiemployer pension plans. Most, however, would consider the core of the voluntary sector to be those organizations that are qualified for tax-exemption under Section 501(c)(3)– those generally known as the "charitable" nonprofits, serving broad public purposes that transcend the personal the personal interests of their members or benefactors. The 501(c)(3)s in 1991 totaled less than half of all tax-exempt organizations: 516,554–of which more than 140,000 were social welfare organizations or civic leagues; about 100,000 were fraternal societies and associations; some 70,000 were labor, agricultural, and horticultural organizations; about 68,000 were business leagues and chambers of commerce; and 64,000 were social and recreational clubs. William Bowen *et al.* (1994) reported the highest rates of growth between 1975 and 1988 for associations related to science/ technology, community development, conservation/ environment, international affairs, and recreation/leisure– registering annual average increases of between 7.4 and 7.6 percent.

In Canada, Revenue Canada determines tax-exempt status, and voluntary sector "charitable" organizations are divided into categories for welfare, health, education, religion, benefit to community (libraries, museums, historical sites, community foundations and trusts, recreation, protection of animals, etc.) and other (service clubs, employees' charity trusts, amateur athletic associations, etc.). Of the 61,554 charities registered in 1991, just under half (27,886) were religious groups; 9,635 were welfare groups; 9,360 were educational organizations; 8,483 provided general benefits to the community; and 4,602 were health-related groups. During the high-growth period between 1974 and 1986, the greatest growth occurred in voluntary associations concerned broadly with public education (e.g., self-help and cultural, social, or public issues), rising from 9 to 14 percent of total charities.

A Sector Under Challenge

In both the United States and Canada, the voluntary sector is seen to be under challenge. The U.S. challenges were summarized by Hodgkinson and Lyman (1992) as including (1) identification of the sector and its members (an issue also dealt with extensively by Lohmann 1992), (2) widespread understanding and acceptance of the roles and functions, missions and practices of voluntary organizations, (3) the crisis in financing as governments restructure to meet global competitive needs, (4) lack of good research information about the sector and appropriate education about the role the sector plays in U.S. society. The challenges to the Canadian sector were set out by Jacquelyn Thayer Scott (1992), who saw issues of role acceptance and financing as associated with deeper changes in the Canadian public philosophy of the state, with which the voluntary sector is highly interactive. The proliferation of voluntary organizations during the late 1970s and 1980s was consistent with uncertainty about maintenance of the social welfare state and the rise of neocorporatism and the postindustrial global economy—but voluntary organizations were shaken as they moved to adjust from a focus on membership, constituency, and functional program direction (in a period dominated by pluralism) to concern for management efficiency (in a period increasingly dominated by neocorporatism). With indications that Canada's public philosophy of the state was moving in the 1990s toward communitarianism—a variant of democratic theory, which intentionally links individual values, needs, and aims with those of the larger community (in contrast to liberalism's historic emphasis on rights-based individualism)—Scott (1992) argued that the voluntary organization must adjust to this new reality by focusing on governance, decisionmaking processes, and values of its mission.

The interactivity of the voluntary sector with the state and its theoretical political underpinnings has been made by Kramer (1990) and Salamon (1987), as well. Lester Salamon (1987) suggested a theory of government-nonprofit partnership that recognizes the voluntary sector is limited in its ability to generate adequate resources and is vulnerable to particularism, the favoritism of the wealthy, amateurism, and self-defeating paternalism—but this corresponds well with government's strengths in generating resources, setting priorities through democratic processes, establishing quality-control standards and rights to access. Since voluntary organizations are more capable than government of personalizing service provision, operating on a smaller scale, and adjusting to the needs of clients, collaboration between government and nonprofits is more logical than replacement of one by the other, Salamon (1987) argued.

Most scholarship on the voluntary sector globally continues to be local or national case studies with few comprehensive, comparative works. The best-known of these latter are Benjamin Gidron *et al.* (1992) and Kathleen McCarthy *et al.* (1992). The former includes nine case studies, all European and mostly concerned with delivery of welfare services, illustrating their major theme that "the relationship between the third sector and the state in most countries of the world has as many elements of cooperation as it does of conflict" (p. 8). The latter study includes

20 national case studies, including some from Africa, Asia, and Latin America, and does not seek to develop a singular typology or theory. "This cultural diversity reveals a lack of consensus relating to the roles and functions of the nonprofit sector, its responsibilities, its relationship with government, and even how to define nonprofit organizations" (p. xvi). Common challenges are identified as including promoting individual participation in voluntary activity, guaranteeing freedom of association, strengthening managerial capacity, and maintaining independence and political viability for voluntary organizations. Several of these case studies note that, in many countries, voluntary organizations are seen to be in conflict with the state.

JACQUELYN THAYER SCOTT

BIBLIOGRAPHY

Anderson, Robert T., 1973. "Voluntary Associations in History: From Paleolithic to Present Times." In David Horton Smith, ed., *Voluntary Action Research: 1973*. Lexington, MA: Lexington Books, 9–28.

Bellah, Robert N., Richard Madsen, Steven M. Tipton, William M. Sullivan, and Ann Swidler, 1985. *Habits of the Heart: Individualism and Commitment in American Life*. New York: Harper and Row.

Bowen, William G., Thomas I. Nygren, Sarah E. Turner, and Elizabeth A. Duffy, 1994. *The Charitable Nonprofits*. San Francisco, CA: Jossey-Bass.

Douglas, James, 1987. "Political Theories of Nonprofit Organization." In Walter W. Powell, ed., *The Nonprofit Sector: A Research Handbook*. New Haven, CT: Yale University Press, 43–54.

Gamwell, Franklin I., 1984. *Beyond Preference: Liberal Theories of Independent Associations*. Chicago, IL: University of Chicago Press.

Gidron, Benjamin, Ralph M. Kramer, and Lester M. Salamon, eds., 1992. *Government and the Third Sector: Emerging Relationships in Welfare States*. San Francisco, CA: Jossey-Bass.

Hall, Peter Dobkin, 1987. "A Historical Overview of the Private Nonprofit Sector." In Walter W. Powell, ed., *The Nonprofit Sector: A Research Handbook*. New Haven, CT: Yale University Press, 3–26.

———, 1994. "Historical Perspectives on Nonprofit Organizations." In Robert D. Herman, ed., *The Jossey-Bass Handbook of Nonprofit Leadership and Management*. San Francisco, CA: Jossey-Bass, 3–43.

Hansmann, Henry, 1987. "Economic Theories of Nonprofit Organization." In Walter W. Powell, ed., *The Nonprofit Sector: A Research Handbook*. New Haven, CT: Yale University Press, 27–42.

Hodgkinson, Virginia A., and Richard W. Lyman, eds., 1992. *The Future of the Nonprofit Sector*. San Francisco, CA: Jossey-Bass.

Hodgkinson, Virginia A., Murray S. Weitzman, and Arthur D. Kirsch, 1988. *From Belief to Commitment: The Activities and Finances of Religious Congregations in the United States*. Washington, DC: Independent Sector.

Joseph, James A., Edgar C. Reckard, and Jean A. McDonald, 1985. *The Philanthropy of Organized Religion.* Washington, DC: Council on Foundations.

Kramer, Ralph M., 1984. *The Economic Illusion: False Choices Between Prosperity and Social Justice.* Boston: Houghton Mifflin.

———, 1990. "Voluntary Organizations in the Welfare State: On the Threshold of the '90s." *The Centre for Voluntary Organizations Working Paper 8.* London: London School of Economics and Political Science.

Lohmann, Roger A., 1992. *The Commons.* San Francisco, CA: Jossey-Bass.

McCarthy, Kathleen D., Virginia A. Hodgkinson, Russy D. Sumariwalla, eds., 1992. *The Nonprofit Sector in the Global Community: Voices from Many Nations.* San Francisco, CA: Jossey-Bass.

Salamon, Lester M., 1987. "Partners in Public Service: The Scope and Theory of Government-Nonprofit Relations." In Walter W. Powell, ed., *The Nonprofit Sector: A Research Handbook.* New Haven, CT: Yale University Press, 99–117.

Scott, Jacquelyn Thayer, 1992. "Voluntary Sector in Crisis: Canada's Changing Public Philosophy of the State and Its Impact on Voluntary Charitable Organizations." Ph.D. dissertation, University of Colorado at Denver. Ann Arbor, MI: University Microfilms.

Smith, David Horton, ed., 1972. *Voluntary Action Research: 1972.* Lexington, MA: Lexington Books.

Smith, David Horton, 1973. "The Impact of the Voluntary Sector on Society." In David Horton Smith, ed., *Voluntary Action Research: 1973.* Lexington, MA: Lexington Books, 387–400.

Sumariwalla, Russy D., 1983. "Preliminary Observations on Scope, Size, and Classification of the Sector." In Virginia A. Hodgkinson, ed., *Working Papers for the Spring Research Forum: Since the Filer Commission.* Washington, DC: Independent Sector, 433–449.

Van Til, Jon, 1988. *Mapping the Third Sector: Voluntarism in a Changing Social Economy.* New York: Foundation Center.

VOLUNTARY SOCIAL SERVICE AGENCIES.

Nonprofit social service agencies that traditionally provide services to individuals and families, job training and related services, self-help groups, social change groups, community action and neighborhood-based organizations, senior service associations, child day care, and residential care facilities (Hodgkinson and Weitzman 1984). These agencies are also referred to as public welfare or human services organizations. I distinguished these organizations from the classification of "social welfare organizations," which by IRS standards are considered 501(c)(4) "action" organizations (see **advocacy organizations**). Ralph Kramer (1987) described these organizations as providing personal social care

> to deprived, neglected, or handicapped children and youth, the needy elderly, the mentally ill—in short, all disadvantaged persons with substantial psychosocial problems. It includes such services as day care and foster care, institutional facilities, information and referral, counseling, sheltered workshops, homemakers, and vocational training and rehabilitation. . . . Typical service providers are family service agencies, community or neighborhood centers, planned parenthood federations, associations for the retarded, centers for independent living, halfway houses, visiting nurses associations, Catholic charities, and others usually included in the United Way (p. 240).

Child abuse, homelessness, feeding the hungry, alcoholism, drug addiction, mental retardation, help for AIDS victims, mental illnesses are but a few of the challenges that nonprofit social service agencies deal with daily.

Governance

Typically, these organizations are governed by a voluntary board that represents clientele and community interests, defines the mission of the agency, establishes policies, oversees programs, assures adequate resources, and utilizes professional and/or volunteer staff to provide services. Most successful agencies are characterized by an executive director who establishes a special relationship with and provides leadership to assist the board in carrying out its responsibilities. Concurrently, the executive assures services are delivered efficiently and effectively. Although most of these agencies are quite small and may lack professional management and staff, many have highly trained personnel.

The Role of Government

There is a significant ongoing public policy debate about the role of government funding of voluntary social service agencies and the shifting and complex mix of service delivery institutions. In its various forms, the role of government in social service delivery has been the dominant policy issue. After a century of debate, there is still no consensus. The fundamental questions remain. Which services should nonprofit voluntary social service agencies provide? Which should be offered by governments and at what level of government? Which should be funded by government in the form of grants, contracts, and various purchase-of-service arrangements with both nonprofit social service agencies and for-profit organizations? Which should be left strictly to the economic market place? What should be the role of charitable funding?

The Early History

Voluntary social service agencies are among the oldest nonprofit organizations in the United States and have been in the forefront responding to social needs. In early American society, communities existed to care for the common needs of their citizens. The evolutionary history of voluntary social service agencies is defined by a much more formal, distinctive, and, more recently, complex relationship to government. During the late part of the nineteenth century until the Great Depression, funds from state and local government were the primary means of support for most voluntary social service agencies providing services to children and the mentally and physically handicapped in the United States. Private philanthropy also flourished during this period and provided substantial support to voluntary social service agencies, although often motivated because public charity was frequently plagued by political abuse. With the Great Depression, both voluntary agencies and private systems were overwhelmed by the enormous social needs of the public. A new era of government responsibility for social services began. Most significantly, the federal government became much more involved in social welfare funding.

Coexisting Institutional Systems

Since the 1960s and the advent of Great Society programs, the social service economy continued to grow and become more complex and mixed. Massive sums of federal, state, and local government money flowed into social services and nonprofit organizations through grants, contracts, and various purchase-of-service arrangements. By 1975, social programs funded by government grew four times faster than those in the private sector. Social service agencies became a "third party" government in which nongovernment programs delivered by voluntary social service agencies addressed particular social needs identified and funded by government. Profit-making organizations also became contractors with government for the provision of services, particularly in such areas as day care, group homes, and residential treatment. Compounding the mix of social service institutions and delivery systems, nonprofit organizations entered the marketplace charging fees for services in competition with for-profit organizations. Kramer (1987) summarizes the relationships among these coexisting institutional systems:

> Together with governmental and profit-making organizations, voluntary agencies may relieve, replace, or reinforce the primary social systems of family, neighbors, and friends. In the public sector, voluntary agencies also may substitute for, influence, extend, and improve the work of government, or they may offer complementary services different in kind, or they can function as a public agent or vendor. Voluntary agencies also may compete with profit-making organizations in many fields of social service (p. 241).

Two Paradigms for the Provision of Service: Partnerships and Competition

Lester Salamon (1994) described the evolution of the American welfare state by the 1970s into two alternative paradigms for the provision of social services: the paradigm of competition and the paradigm of partnership. The former is guided by the economic marketplace, a conservative political ethos, and criticisms of the modern American welfare state. The Reagan administration argued that social services are provided more effectively and efficiently by state and local government and argued strongly for "privatization" of an activist federal government in all areas including social services. Despite the "Reagan revolution" (a Democratically controlled Congress slowed the pace of the "revolution"), the federal government remained a large funder of social service agencies during this period. State and local governments continued to play substantial funding roles.

The paradigm of partnership is characterized by a complex and elaborate alliance between government and the voluntary sector, which unfolded in the 1960s and 1970s with government playing a dominant role in providing financial resources. Data generated by Salamon in the early 1980s revealed the characteristics of the partnership paradigm. By 1981, 40 percent of the income of a wide variety of private, nonprofit human service agencies exclusive of hospitals and higher education institutions, came from government, as opposed to 30 percent from fees and 20 percent from private charity.

Recent Trends

Recent trends in the 1990s are characterized by the continuation of the Reagan revolution and the imposition of significant cuts and fiscal restraints by government in an attempt to reform the welfare state. Salamon (1994) reported that when we exclude the two major federal health programs, Medicare and Medicaid, nonprofit organizations ended up with about 10 percent less federal support in fiscal year 1990–1991 than in fiscal year 1980–1981. A Republican-controlled Congress that swept into office in 1994 sought to add pace to the Reagan revolution. (As a result, social service agencies are much more aggressive in fund-raising and charge higher fees to redress the loss of government dollars.)

Cuts carried out during the Reagan-Bush era were aggravated by a huge federal budget deficit. Pressures continued to build in the Republican Congress during the mid-1990s to reduce further domestic social service spending (including much speculation about Medicare and Medicaid cuts and a balanced budget promised by 2002). These promises were made despite dramatic continued growth in the number and proportion of elderly persons and a seemingly immutable cadre of hard-core, inner-city poor.

Most likely, the continued blurring and shifting of sector boundaries and pressure to reduce federal social service funding will continue. There is reason to believe there will be a greater penetration by the voluntary sector into the market economy in order to minimize the impact of loss of government funding. A concurrent commercialization of the sector will most likely include a shift from service provider subsidies to consumer subsidies (Salamon 1994).

Although new and different organizational mixes will emerge, one constant remains. The advantages of individualized and flexible approaches to human services for those who have specialized needs historically addressed by voluntary social service organizations remains unchanged. Determination of how these needs will be met and who will receive the benefits hangs in the balance of the ongoing public policy debate about costs and the extent of governmental responsibility to provide social services. As answers are forthcoming, clearly the social service safety net woven by charities and government and provided by voluntary social service agencies will differ significantly by the twenty-first century.

RICHARD D. HEIMOVICS

BIBLIOGRAPHY

Hodgkinson, V., and M. Weitzman, 1984. *Dimensions of the Independent Sector: A Statistical Profile.* Washington, DC: Independent Sector.

Kramer, Ralph M., 1987. In Walter W. Powell, eds., *The Nonprofit Sector: A Research Handbook.* New Haven, CT: Yale University Press, 240–257.

Salamon, Lester, 1994. "The Nonprofit Sector and the American Welfare State." In Robert Herman *et al.,* eds., *The Handbook of Nonprofit Leadership and Management.* San Francisco, CA: Jossey-Bass.

VOLUNTEER ADMINISTRATION.

The profession concerned with the study and practice of integrating volunteers effectively and ethically into an organization to enhance performance and results.

Each day, countless volunteers stream into the offices of a huge number of organizations. They settle into their places and begin to perform jobs that contribute substantially not only to the internal operations of the agency but also the delivery of goods and services to clients and constituents. Although these citizens are not compensated monetarily, their donations of time and talents can dramatically affect the efficiency and effectiveness of the

organization, as well as the capability to attend to needy clientele.

Such a smooth integration of volunteers into the workplace does not happen by accident or without considerable planning and preparation on the part of the sponsoring organization. As societies have grown increasingly dependent on volunteer labor to meet popular demands for goods and services, especially those provided by government and nonprofit organizations, a profession has emerged concerned with introducing unpaid citizens and sustaining their constructive participation. The field of volunteer administration is dedicated to the effective, ethical involvement of volunteers for the benefit of host organizations, their clientele, and the volunteers themselves.

Volunteer Administration as a Profession

By the mid-1980s, distinguished author, practitioner, and advocate of volunteerism Harriet Naylor (1985) could write, "We have good strategies for work analysis, job design and descriptions, recruiting, and recording" (p. 25). Naylor's (1973) *Volunteers Today—Finding, Training, and Working with Them* helped to launch the field and profession of volunteer administration, as did other major books published at about the same (for example, Wilson 1976; Stenzel and Feeney 1976). These works, and a voluminous body of research studies, reaction, and commentary, have gradually culminated in a well-accepted approach for structuring and managing volunteer programs to achieve service quality and effectiveness. Although just as in the study of private management, not all authorities concur on every particular, sufficient agreement has been attained to present requisites for a successful, organization-based volunteer effort. These components are elaborated in the following section.

Headquartered in Boulder, Colorado, the Association for Volunteer Administration (AVA) is the leading professional association in the field. AVA conducts a variety of professional development activities: The association holds an annual international conference on volunteer administration as well as numerous regional meetings, publishes a quarterly journal (*Journal of Volunteer Administration*) and newsletter (*Update*), establishes and promulgates standards of ethical conduct as well as areas of competency for practitioners in the field, and awards a performance-based "Certificate in Volunteer Administration" (CVA). At this writing, the AVA boasts 1,650 members. Although most of them live in the United States and Canada, 13 others countries are represented.

According to James Fisher and Kathleen Cole (1993), the field of volunteer administration is moving toward increased professionalization: "The emergence of volunteer administration as a profession is marked by the leadership of the AVA, by the creation of standards of practice, and by the development of a strong literature base" (p. 176). An AVA committee found that 56 institutions of higher education in the United States and Canada offer coursework in volunteer administration; 88 percent of the schools offer 18 or more hours of classroom instruction on the topic (Stringer 1993).

Findings from a major survey of AVA members further substantiate the trend toward greater professionalization (Brudney, Love and Yu, 1993–1994). completed by two-thirds of the membership, the mail survey showed that most of these officials have high levels of formal education: Over one-half have graduated college and another one-quarter have earned a master's degree or more. They profess great interest in continuing education in volunteer administration, especially advanced training; 65 percent had attended a training program in the previous year. Most hold full-time positions in volunteer administration and devote well over half their scheduled hours to this responsibility. They tend to believe that a college degree is necessary to perform their job effectively and report that they find at least some time during the week to keep up with research in the field. A solid majority claimed volunteer administration as their primary occupation and stated their intention to remain in the field.

Essential Components of Volunteer Administration

Volunteer administrators go by a variety of titles, including volunteer coordinator and director of volunteer services. In many organizations, officials in departments of personnel or human resources who also deal with paid employees are responsible for the volunteers. Regardless of job title, the volunteer administrator attends to the design, implementation, management, and evaluation of the volunteer program. These programs are intended to facilitate and coordinate the work of volunteers and paid staff members toward the attainment of agency goals. The essential components of volunteer administration are as follows (Brudney 1994):

- establishing the rationale for volunteer involvement;
- involving paid staff in volunteer program design;
- integrating the volunteer program into the organization;
- creating positions of program leadership;
- preparing job descriptions for volunteer positions;
- recruiting volunteers;
- managing volunteers;
- evaluating and recognizing the volunteer effort.

Establishing the Rationale for Volunteer Involvement

The first step in creating a volunteer program is to determine the purposes underlying citizen participation. No matter how logical such an initial move might appear, many a prospective program has succumbed to the temptation of agency leadership to "call in the volunteers" before the groundwork for their sustained involvement has been put in place. Although well-intentioned, premature efforts to enlist volunteers to "help" often turn out to be damaging instead: They raise apprehensions of paid staff members, who may question the need for volunteers, and frustrate volunteers, who may wonder precisely what jobs they are needed to perform and why. This scenario must be avoided.

The foundation for a successful volunteer program rests on a deliberate consideration by the agency of the rationale for citizen involvement and the development of explicit policy and procedures to guide this effort. Especially in times of fiscal stringency, top organizational officials may seize on economic motivations, such as "cost savings," as the principal reason for introducing volunteers. However, since a volunteer program requires expenditures of its own (for example, for recruitment, orientation, training, reimbursement, promotion, materials, and so forth), the goal is misleading. A more accurate description of the economic benefits of a volunteer program is "cost effectiveness." A well-designed program that supplements or complements the work of paid staff with that of citizens can help an agency to hold costs down in achieving a given level of service or to increase the services provided for a fixed level of expenditure (Brudney 1990; Karn 1983, 1982–1983).

A significant strength of a volunteer program is the variety of additional purposes that it might serve for an organization. For example, agency leadership may enlist volunteers to interject a more vibrant dimension of commitment and caring into its relationships with clients. Or, the goal may be to learn more about the community, nurture closer ties to the citizenry, and renew public awareness and support. Volunteers may be needed to reach clients inaccessible through normal organizational channels, that is, to engage in "outreach." They may be called upon to provide professional skills, such as computer programming, legal counsel, or accounting expertise, not readily available to an agency. The purpose may be to staff an experimental program otherwise doomed to fiscal austerity. Organizations often seek volunteers to assist with fund-raising (Hodgkinson, Weitzman, Toppe, and Noga 1992, p. 46). Enhancing responsiveness to client groups may offer yet another rationale.

Prior to recruiting volunteers, organizational leaders should decide on the appropriate goals for citizen involvement. An explicit statement of goals is useful for several reasons. First it begins to define the types of volunteer positions that will be needed and the number of individuals required to fill them. Second, it aids in delineating concrete objectives against which the program might be evaluated, once in operation. Finally, a statement of the philosophy underlying volunteer participation and the specific ends sought can help to alleviate possible anxiety on the part of paid staff members—especially if they are included in planning and development of the volunteer program.

Involving Paid Staff in Volunteer Program Design

Although the support of top organizational officials is crucial to the establishment and vitality of a volunteer program (for example, Ellis 1986; Scheier 1981), paid staff and volunteers, if they are already known to the agency or can be identified, should also be involved in defining its mission, philosophy, and procedures. Involvement adds to the knowledge base for crafting policy and inculcates a sense of ownership and commitment instrumental to gaining acceptance for innovation. Because the incorporation of volunteers into an agency can impose dramatic changes in work life, the participation of paid staff is especially important. The sharing of needs, perspectives, and information among agency leadership, employees, and prospective volunteers that ensues is crucial to determining how the volunteer program might be most effectively designed, organized, and managed to further attainment of agency goals.

Planning meetings and discussions should yield policies and procedures governing the involvement of volunteers. Agency guidelines for the program should address the central aspects of volunteer participation, including attendance and absenteeism, performance review, benefits, grievance procedures, reimbursement for expenses, confidentiality requirements, probationary acceptance period, suspension and termination, and record keeping. Steve McCurley and Rick Lynch (1989, p. 22) advised that in all areas these policies should be as comparable as possible to the respective guidelines for paid employees.

Explicit policies for the volunteer program demonstrate that the agency takes citizen participation seriously and values that contribution of volunteers. By setting the standards as high for volunteers as for paid staff, as agency builds trust and credibility, increased respect and requests for volunteers from employees, a healthy work environment, and, perhaps most important, high quality services (for example, McCurley and Lynch 1989; Wilson 1984). The guidelines should be published in a manual distributed to all volunteers and paid staff members expected

to work with them. A volunteer manual greatly facilitates managing for consistent results and handling problem situations, should they arise.

Although volunteers may not be known to the agency at the time of program formation and, thus, not involved in initial discussions concerning planning and design, once this effort is launched and in operation, they should definitely have input into major decisions affecting the program. Just as for paid employees, citizen volunteers are more likely to invest in and commit to organizational policies, and provide useful information for this purpose, if they enjoy ready access to the decisionmaking process.

Integrating the Volunteer Program into the Organization

In order to sustain citizen involvement, an organization must integrate the volunteer program into its structure and operations. A small nonprofit agency may accommodate one or several volunteers with few if any structural modifications, but larger organizations should consider alternative structural arrangements for integrating volunteers. In order of increasing comprehensiveness, these arrangements consist of ad hoc volunteer efforts, volunteer recruitment by an outside organization with the agency otherwise responsible for management (the "contract" model), decentralization of the program to operating departments, and a centralized approach.

Ad Hoc Volunteerism

Volunteer involvement may arise spontaneously to meet exigencies confronting an organization, especially on a short-term basis. Normally, citizens motivated to share their background, training, skills, and energy with organizations that could benefit by them are the catalyst. The responsiveness and alacrity with which an ad hoc volunteer effort can be mobilized are inspiring. Frequently, crisis and emergency situations provoke a spectacular response, arousing vast numbers of citizens to action in a remarkably short time.

Such spontaneous help can infuse vitality (and labor) into an agency and alert officials to the possibilities of volunteerism. Despite this advantage, only selected parts or members of the organization may be aware of an ad hoc citizen effort and, thus, be able to avail themselves of it. In addition, because energy levels and zeal wane as emergencies are tamed or fade from the limelight of publicity, the ad hoc model is quite vulnerable to the passage of time. A volunteer program requires not only an ongoing, rather than a sporadic, commitment from citizens, but also an organizational structure to sustain their contributions and make them accessible throughout the organization.

The Contract Model

A second option sometimes open to agencies is to rely on the expertise and reputation of an established organization, such as a volunteer center or clearing house, to assist in the recruitment of volunteers but to retain all other managerial responsibilities internally. Since recruitment is the most fundamental program function, professional assistance can be highly beneficial, particularly for an agency just starting a volunteer program. Some business firms seeking to develop volunteer programs in the community for their employees have extended this model: They contract with volunteer centers not only for recruitment but also other program functions, for example, placement and evaluation of volunteers (Haran, Kenney, and Vermilion 1993).

Although outside assistance may be helpful, agencies should proceed with caution. Entrusting crucial program functions to other organizations is a deterrent to developing the necessary capacity internally. By all means, organizations should nurture positive relationships with agencies in the community to attract volunteers and for other purposes. But they must avoid total dependence on external sources and work to develop appropriate mechanisms of their own.

Decentralized Program

A volunteer program can be decentralized to individual departments is an organization. The primary advantage of this approach is the flexibility to tailor programs to the needs of specific organizational units and to introduce volunteers where support for them is greatest. Unfortunately, duplication of effort across several departments, difficulties in locating sufficient expertise in volunteer management to operate multiple programs, problems in coordination across programs, and higher overall costs pose significant liabilities. Nevertheless, under the right circumstances, the decentralized approach can work admirably, for example, in starting a pilot or experimental volunteer program that might eventually be expanded to the rest of the organization. Alternatively, a lack of tasks appropriate for volunteers in some parts of the agency or, perhaps, strong opposition from various quarters may confine voluntary assistance to selected departments.

Centralized Program

The final structural arrangement is a centralized volunteer program serving the entire agency. With this approach, a single office or department is responsible for management and coordination of the program; volunteers are deployed and supervised in departments throughout the organization. The volunteer office provides guidelines, technical assistance, recruitment, screening, training, placement, and all other administration. The advantages of centralization for averting duplication of effort, assigning volunteers so as to meet their needs as well as those of the organization, and producing efficient and effective voluntary services are considerable. Yet, the approach demands broad support across the organization, especially at the top, to overcome any objections that may be raised or limitation in resources. When such backing is not forthcoming, the other structural arrangements can serve an agency quite well.

Creating Positions of Program Leadership

Regardless of the structural arrangement by which the volunteer program is integrated into the agency, the program requires a recognized leader. Just as any other manager, the volunteer coordinator (or administrator) should be a paid position. This designation sends a powerful message to other managers and employees regarding the significance and value organizational leadership places on the volunteer component. For the same reason, the position should be located as close as feasible to the apex of the agency's formal hierarchy. The volunteer administrator should enjoy prerogatives and responsibilities commensurate with positions at the same hierarchical level, including participation in relevant decision-and policymaking and access to superiors.

The volunteer coordinator has many key duties. The position bears accountability for the volunteer program, presents a focal point for contact with the program for those inside as well as outside the organization, and rewards the officeholder in relation to the success of the volunteers. As chief advocate of the program, the coordinator endeavors to express the volunteer perspective, allay any apprehensions of employees, and facilitate collaboration between paid and unpaid personnel. The incumbent represents the volunteers before the organization, promotes their interests, and builds and maintains the program.

The volunteer coordinator is responsible for recruitment and publicity, a critical function requiring active outreach in the community and highly flexible working hours. The incumbent communicates with department and organizational officials to ascertain their requirements for voluntary assistance, this task is not a one-time exercise, but an ongoing responsibility that changes with the needs and demands of the various units. The coordinator interviews and screens all applicants for volunteer positions, maintains appropriate records, places volunteers in job assignments, assists employees with supervision, and monitors, evaluates, and recognizes volunteer performance. This official must hammer the bewildering array of backgrounds, preferences, and time availabilities brought by volunteers into a workable schedule for the agency. The coordinator is responsible for orientation and training of the volunteers; since employees are often unfamiliar with the approach, the coordinator must arrange for training for them as well. Given these demands, as a volunteer program increases in size, the coordinator should plan to delegate some of these duties to volunteers and/or paid staff members.

Preparing Job Descriptions for Volunteer Positions

The essential building block of a successful volunteer program is the job description. In allocating job tasks to volunteers, the overriding consideration is that work assignments reflect the unique capabilities that citizens and employees might bring toward the realization of organizational goals.

As described above, the process of sharing the workplace begins at the program planning stage, when top agency officials and employees (and, if possible, volunteers) meet to work out explicit understandings regarding the rationale for the participation of volunteers, the nature of the jobs they are to perform, and appropriate policies and procedures governing involvement. These meetings should result in agreements concerning the types of jobs to be assigned to volunteers and those to be retained by paid staff. In conjunction with planning meetings, organizations might also conduct a survey of employees or personal interviews with them to help prepare for volunteer involvement. At a minimum, the survey should ascertain those aspects of the job that employees most enjoy performing, those that they dislike, and those for which they lack sufficient time or expertise. Organizations have enjoyed success delegating to volunteers job tasks with the following characteristics (Ellis 1986, pp. 89–90):

- tasks performed periodically, such as once a week, rather than on a daily or inflexible basis;
- tasks that do not require the specialized training or expertise of paid personnel;
- tasks that might be done more effectively by someone with special training in that skill;
- tasks for which employees feel uncomfortable or unprepared;
- tasks for which agency does not possess in-house expertise.

This process should culminate in a set of job descriptions for volunteers based on extant organizational needs and citizen talents and backgrounds. The objective is to achieve an effective deployment of paid and unpaid personnel. As changing organizational conditions warrant, and/or recruitment efforts flag, the job descriptions should be updated. To prevent conflict, organizational policy must firmly state that neither volunteers nor employees will occupy the positions reserved for the other.

Because volunteers will need the same information as paid staff to determine whether a position is of interest, the respective job descriptions should be analogous. Specifications for volunteer positions should include job title and purpose, responsibilities and activities, qualifications and time commitment, reporting relationships and supervision, and benefits and obligations. The volunteer coordinator uses the job descriptions as a basis to recruit potential volunteers, screen them for relevant competencies and interests, conduct an interview with applicants, and place them in suitable positions with the intent of matching citizen needs with those of the organization.

Recruiting Volunteers

Although job descriptions for volunteer positions greatly facilitate the recruitment process, attracting citizens for service roles may well pose the most significant challenge to organizations attempting the approach. Surveys of volunteer coordinators bear out this conclusion (Brudney 1990; Duncombe 1985). In some service domains, potential volunteers have proven sufficiently scarce or resistant to calls for assistance that it can actually prove cost-effective to hire paid personnel instead (Brudney and Duncombe 1992).

Given the centrality of recruitment to a thriving volunteer program, voluminous literature has addressed the problem and suggested potent strategies to surmount it (for example, Brudney 1995; Ellis 1994). As astute volunteer coordinators have learned, depending upon organizational needs, these techniques can be used selectively or in combination.

Job design strategies focus on meeting volunteers' needs and motivations through the content and variety of the work they are asked to perform, as well as offering greater responsibility for those volunteers who seek it. Human capital strategies place interested volunteers in positions to acquire contacts, training, and references that will increase their market value for paid employment. Ceremonial strategies present volunteers the opportunity to work with important policymaking bodies (commissions, boards, and other institutions), meet elected officials, and receive public recognition for service. Organizational change and development strategies concentrate on building an organizational culture receptive to volunteer involvement. Flexibility strategies attempt to adapt the agency to volunteer involvement, for example, by establishing volunteer jobs that can be performed outside the agency or tasks and assignments that are conducive to group-based volunteering (for example, by the family, religious congregation, or work unit or organization).

Facilitation strategies increase the pool of volunteers by such practices as allowing citizen participation during nontraditional working hours and reimbursing all out-of-pocket expenses of volunteers (for example, child care). Outreach strategies also aim to enlarge the pool by publicizing the volunteer program at the workplace, school, church, synagogue, neighborhood group, civic and other associations, and so forth.

Managing Volunteers

Managing volunteers is, perhaps, the most delicate aspect of the volunteer administrator's job. Volunteers are much less dependent on the organization than are paid employees: They can almost always leave the organization and find comparable opportunities for (donating) their labor with far less effort and inconvenience than can an employee who must have remuneration. As a result, managers do not have as much control over volunteer workers.

These differences in control help to explain some oft-noted characteristics of volunteers in the workplace. Volunteers can afford to be more selective in accepting job assignments. They may insist on substantial flexibility in work hours. They may not be as faithful in observance of agency rules and regulations, particularly those they deem burdensome or "red tape." Part of the reason may stem from the fact that nearly all who volunteer do so on a part-time basis and, thus, can be expected to have less information about organizational policy and procedures. Social interaction is part of the fun and spark of volunteering, and participants may place high value on this feature of the experience.

Given the relative autonomy of volunteers, a traditional approach to management and supervision can be expected to elicit antagonism and turnover rather than productivity and compliance. Standard organizational inducements for paid employees, such as pay, promotion, and perquisites, are not operative for volunteers. Similarly, conventional organizational sanctions are likely to prove abortive (for example, referring a problem to hierarchical superiors for resolution or disciplinary action, or threatening to do so.)

By contrast, effective management of volunteers rests on applying different techniques and incentives than commonly used for paid employees to motivate and direct work behaviors toward agency goals. Managerial investment in building trust, cooperation, teamwork, challenge, growth, achievement, values, excitement, commitment, and empowerment are much more practical strategies for this purpose than are the conventional methods. Interestingly, as contemporary management theorists have noted, the best-run commercial enterprises use these same techniques for paid personnel to yield impressive benefits and profits (Daft 1995).

To achieve success, a volunteer program must do more than promote changes in managerial style, however. It must also institute to facilitate volunteer supervision. An effective program channels talents and energies productively through such mechanisms as guidelines for volunteer involvement, formal job descriptions for volunteer positions, and interviews and careful placement of applicants. These measures help to define what volunteer service means to the agency and to citizens and to coordinate the needs and motives of both parties. Probably no factor aids more in supervising volunteers (and paid staff) than placing them in positions where they can put their strongest motivations and best skills to work.

Evaluating and Recognizing the Volunteer Effort

Organizations that rely on the assistance of volunteers may be reluctant to appear to question through evaluation the worth or impact of well-intentioned helping efforts. Nevertheless, for individual volunteers, the employees expected to work with them, and for the volunteer operation as a whole, evaluation and recognition activities are essential program functions.

Evaluation and Recognition of Volunteers

Volunteers have cogent reasons to view personnel assessment in a favorable light. A powerful motivation for volunteering is to achieve worthwhile and visible results; evaluation of performance can guide volunteers toward improvement on this dimension. No citizen contributes time to have the labor wasted in misdirected activity or to repeat easily remedied mistakes and misjudgments. Moreover, for many who contribute their time, volunteering offers an opportunity to acquire or hone desirable job skills and/or to build an attractive résumé for paid employment. To deny constructive feedback to those who give their time for organizational purposes, and who could benefit from this knowledge and hope to do so, is a disservice to the volunteer.

Normally, the volunteer coordinator will prepare the evaluation of performance; the evaluation should be conducted at regular intervals. To complement this agency-based perspective, volunteers might evaluate their own accomplishments and experience. The self-assessment should tap volunteer satisfaction with important facets of the agency work assignment, including job duties, schedule, support, training, supervision, opportunities for personal growth, and so on. Whatever the format, the goal of the evaluation is to ascertain the degree to which the needs and expectations of the volunteer and the agency have been met so that job assignments can be continued, amended, or redefined as necessary.

Agency officials might recognize and show their appreciation to volunteers through a great variety of activities: award or social events (luncheons, banquets, ceremonies), media attention (newsletters, newspapers), certificates (for tenure or special achievement), expansion of opportunities (for learning, training, management), and personal expressions of gratitude from employees or clients. A heart-felt "thank you" can be all the acknowledgment many volunteers want or need. Others require more formal recognition. The volunteer coordinator should make letters of recommendation available to all volunteers who request them. Recognition is a highly variable activity that, optimally, should be tailored to the wants and needs of individual volunteers.

Evaluation and Recognition of Employees

In general, volunteer-based services require the participation of not only citizens but also paid staff. If organizational leaders want volunteers and employees to work as partners in service delivery, program functions of evaluation and recognition should apply to both members of the team. Although frequently neglected in job analysis, employees expected to work with volunteers should have pertinent responsibilities written into their job descriptions and be held accountable for performance. Just as demonstrated talent in this dimension should be encouraged and rewarded, an employee's resistance to volunteers, or poor work record with them, should not go overlooked and, implicitly, condoned in the review. As necessary, the organization should support training activities for paid staff to develop competencies in volunteer administration.

Recognition activities for employees should follow evaluation. Like volunteers, paid staff value recognition, especially when awards ceremonies, social events, media coverage, agency publications, and the like bring their efforts and accomplishments with volunteers to the attention of organizational leadership. By taking seriously the evaluation and recognition of paid staff with regard to their collaboration with volunteers, agency officials provide incentives for an effective partnership.

Evaluation and Recognition of the Volunteer Program

The primary goals of a volunteer program are to improve agency operations, exert a positive effect on the environment, and better the circumstances of agency clients. Periodically, agencies that mobilize volunteers should undergo evaluation of the impact or progress registered by this component.

The volunteer coordinator should consider several valuable types of program evaluation. The most common is a compilation of the number of volunteers who have assisted the organization, the hours they have contributed, and the amount of client contacts or visits they have made. Many agencies go a step further by calculating the "equivalent dollar value" of the services donated by volunteers, based on the market price the organization would otherwise have to pay to employed personnel to accomplish the same tasks (for example, Karn 1983, 1982–1983).

A second type of evaluation of the volunteer program is an impact analysis. With this method, the volunteer coordinator assesses the outcomes of the program against its stated goals or mission. The analysis should review the aggregate performance and effects of the volunteers in assisting clients, addressing community problems, expediting agency operations, and meeting other objectives. Often, monetary costs are weighed against program results, as in a "cost-effectiveness" or "cost-benefit" analysis.

A third type of assessment is a process evaluation. This approach attempts to determine that procedures to meet essential program functions, such as recruitment, training, and orientation, are in place and operating effectively. Additionally, the evaluation should attempt to gauge the satisfaction of volunteers and paid staff members with the program, as well as their perceptions concerning its impact on clients and the external environment. By detecting, diagnosing, and ameliorating operational problems, a process evaluation can further the objectives of the volunteer program.

Conclusion

Volunteer administration is a profession. In the past two decades, scholars and practitioners in this field have developed and refined useful techniques for the design, implementation, management, and evaluation of volunteer programs. If volunteers are to make the kind of contribution that societies increasingly ask of them to help address pressing problems in the human and social services, effective volunteer administration holds the key.

Jeffrey L. Brudney

BIBLIOGRAPHY

Brudney, Jeffrey L., 1990. *Fostering Volunteer Programs in the Public Sector: Planning, Initiating, and Managing Voluntary Activities.* San Francisco, CA: Jossey-Bass.
———, 1994. "Designing and Managing Volunteer Programs." In Robert D. Herman, ed., *The Jossey-Bass Handbook of Nonprofit Leadership and Management.* San Francisco, CA: Jossey-Bass.

———, 1995. "The Involvement of Volunteers in the Delivery of Services: Myth and Management." In Steven W. Hays and Richard C. Kearney, eds., *Public Personnel Administration: Problems and Prospects*, 3d ed. Englewood Cliffs, NJ: Prentice-Hall.

Brudney, Jeffrey L., and William D. Duncombe, 1992. "An Economic Evaluation of Paid, Volunteer, and Mixed Staffing Options for Public Services." *Public Administration Review*, vol. 52 (September-October): 474–481.

Brudney, Jeffrey L., Teresa G. Love, and Chilik Yu, 1993–1994. "The Association for Volunteer Administration and Professionalization of the Field: Suggestions from a Survey of the Membership." *Journal of Volunteer Administration*, vol. 12 (Fall-Winter): 1–22.

Daft, Richard L., 1995. *Organization Theory and Design*, 5th ed. Minneapolis/St. Paul, MN: West Publishing.

Duncombe, Sidney, 1985. "Volunteers in City Government: Advantages, Disadvantages, and Uses." *National Civic Review*, vol. 74, no. 9: 356–364.

Ellis, Susan J., 1986. *From the Top down: The Executive Role in Volunteer Program Success*. Philadelphia, PA: Energize.

———, 1994. *The Volunteer Recruitment Book*. Philadelphia, PA: Energize.

Fisher, James C., and Kathleen M. Cole, 1993. *Leadership and Management of Volunteer Programs: A Guide for Volunteer Administrators*. San Francisco, CA: Jossey-Bass.

Haran, Lena, Sarah Kenney, and Martin Vermilion, 1993. "Contract Volunteer Services: A Model for Successful Partnership." *Leadership* (January-March) 28–30.

Hodgkinson, Virginia A., Murray S. Weitzman, Christopher M. Toppe, and Steven M. Noga, 1992. *Nonprofit Almanac, 1992–1993: Dimensions of the Independent Sector*. San Francisco, CA: Jossey-Bass.

Karn, G. Neil, 1982–1983. "Money Talks: A Guide to Establishing the True Dollar Value of Volunteer Time, Part I." *Journal of Volunteer Administration*, vol. 1 (Winter): 1–17.

———, 1983. "Money Talks: A Guide to Establishing the True Dollar Value of Volunteer Time, Part II." *Journal of Volunteer Administration*, vol. 1 (Spring): 1–19.

McCurley, Steve, and Rick Lynch, 1989. *Essential Volunteer Management*. Downers Grove, IL: VMSystems and Heritage Arts.

Naylor, Harriet H., 1973. *Volunteers Today–Finding, Training, and Working with Them*. Dryden, NY: Dryden.

———, 1985. "Beyond Managing Volunteers." *Journal of Voluntary Action Research*, vol. 14, nos. 2, 3: 25–30.

Scheier, Ivan H., 1981. "Positive Staff Attitude can Ease Volunteer Recruiting Pinch." *Hospitals*, vol. 55, no. 3: 61–63.

Stenzel, Alfred, and Helen N. Feeney, 1976. *Volunteer Training and Development: A Manual*, rev. ed. New York: Seabury.

Stringer, Gretchen E., 1993. "Report from the AVA Subcommittee on Volunteer Administration in Higher Education." *Journal of Volunteer Administration*. vol. 11, no. 3: 5–12.

Wilson, M., 1976. *The Effective Management of Volunteer Programs*. Boulder, CO: Johnson.

———, 1984. "The New Frontier: Volunteer Management Training." *Training and Development Journal*, vol. 38, no. 7: 50–52.

VOUCHER SYSTEM. Forms of noncash government transfer-subsidy payments given to eligible recipients in the form of voucher coupsons. Under a true voucher system, recipients of vouchers exchange the coupons for particular goods and services at participating suppliers or vendors of their choice. Upon receipt of the vouchers, participating suppliers can redeem the value of the vouchers for cash from the government agency that issued them.

Conditions

Research suggests that voucher systems work best under the following conditions (Bridge 1977, pp. 56–57; Savas 1987, p. 113):

1. There are widespread differences in peoples' preferences for the service, and these differences are recognized and accepted by the public as legitimate.
2. Individuals have incentives to shop aggressively for the service.
3. Individuals are well informed about market conditions, including the cost and quality of the service and where it may be obtained.
4. There are many competing suppliers of the service, or else start-up costs are low and additional suppliers can readily enter the market if the demand is there.
5. The quality of the service is easily determined by the user.
6. There is some excess capacity in the system so that people have true choices.
7. The product or service is relatively inexpensive and purchased frequently, so the user learns by experience. Furthermore, according to Lydia Manchester (1986) voucher systems that have clearly defined "goods and services" are most likely to succeed.

Type of Government Voucher Programs

There are several government-aid programs that satisfy some, if not most, of the conditions of a "true" voucher system described previously. The most notable examples in the United States include food stamps, low-income housing, Medicare and Medicaid, and G.I. Bill for higher education. Voucher programs at experimental phases are education for elementary and secondary education, culture and entertainment, privatization of state-owned assets, transportation, childcare, law, and specialized training.

Food Stamps

A widely used government-aid voucher system is the Food Stamp Program administered by the U.S. Department of Agriculture. The food stamp program meets virtually all the criteria of a true voucher system. By design, the government provides vouchers or food stamp coupons to eligible individuals who can then use the coupons to purchase a variety of edibles or food items from designated privately owned grocery stores of their choice. By allowing recipients to make purchasing decisions about what food items to buy and who to buy from, in theory the program provides incentives for them to compare the prices and quality of grocery items they desire. In other words, the program takes into account differences in individual preferences and tastes—one of the important elements of a "true" voucher system.

Since it was formally established in 1964, the food stamp program still continues to provide vouchers to eligible low-income families, which they can use to purchase food at existing grocery stores in the private market. Previously, the U.S. government used its own food distribution system to deliver food to qualified individuals. However, this approach was inefficient and restrictive in nature because it denied recipients access to the already existing "competitive and more efficient" private-sector distribution system.

The current design of the program meets most of the conditions of a true voucher system. By paying a fixed amount to recipients, it provides incentives for them to shop, that is, shop for bargains or low-cost and quality products. Moreover, in theory advertising and promotion by vendors triggered by market competition provide information to recipients about location, quality, and price of grocery items. There is no conclusive evidence suggesting that recipients use food coupons wisely and process information adequately about nutrition content, quality, and price of grocery items. Laundering of food stamp coupons by some vendors and fraudulent use or abuse of the program by some recipients are persistent problems that tend to undermine the key tenets of the voucher system.

GI Bill

The GI Bill, passed after World War II, operates almost like a true voucher system. It provides subsidy for higher education in the form of full tuition and subsistence allowance for eligible veterans admitted to private and public colleges or universities.

The GI Bill program nearly meets the criteria of a true voucher system in the sense that many colleges and universities are offering a wide selection of programs and are competing for prospective students in different locations; the voucher pays a fixed amount of the recipient's educational costs, thus providing incentives for veterans to shop for colleges and universities that offer the best deal; and veterans have access to information about institutional requirements such as admission standards, cost of education, and so forth (Bridge 1977). The GI Bill program, however, does not meet some criteria of a "true" voucher scheme. The most notable include subjectiveness involved in measuring the quality of education and the prevalence of penalties for veterans who choose transfer to another college.

Education Vouchers

The idea of using education vouchers as means to introduce competition in a service area (education) traditionally dominated by government is not new—it dates back to the early eighteenth century. Adam Smith in *The Wealth of Nations* (1776) suggested that the state should give parents money for purchasing the education they desire for their children. The premise underlying his idea was to create a competitive market for education and to allow parents to choose the school in which to enroll their children. In *The Rights of Man*, published in 1792, Thomas Paine argued that "the poor should be given special aid and that parents should be required to purchase education for their children" (Lindelow 1980, pp. 6–7). Paine believed that parental choice in education would enhance competition among schools and lead to improvement in the quality of education. In his classic essay *On Liberty* (1859 [1972]), the English philosopher and political theorist John Stuart Mill advocated the use of an educational voucher system as a means to assist families unable to defray the cost of their children's education. Mill believed that education was a societal responsibility and that a voucher system would assist low-income parents to send their children to school without creating a justification for government control of the school system. After nearly two centuries since the debate over educational vouchers began, the conservative economist Milton Friedman (1972) revived the same debate in his 1955 essay "The Role of Government in Education." Friedman proposed the use of an unrestricted, or "full," voucher system in an unregulated market system where parents have the choice to send their children to either private or public schools. He further proposed that parents should be given the option to add marginal funds of their own to a fixed voucher amount provided by the government. Under this system, "schooling would no longer be free.... Participating schools, the public ones include would charge a tuition at full cost" (West 1981, p. 103).

Attempts to implement educational voucher programs in the recent history of the United States began in the 1950s after the 1954 Supreme ruling *Brown v. Board of Education*, which effected desegregation in schools. In an attempt to avoid the desegregation ruling, some southern states established voucher programs with the intent to continue past discriminatory practices. The courts, however, declared those programs unconstitutional (Lindelow 1980). Furthermore, several ballot initiatives for adoption of voucher plans were defeated in several states including Michigan in 1978 and through Proposition 174 in California in November 1993. Critics of education vouchers content that parents are not in a better position than professionals or school administrators in judging the educational interests of their children.

During the late 1960s, the Office of Economic Opportunity (OEO), an agency of the federal government, commissioned the Center for the Study of Public Policy (CSPP) at Harvard University to prepare a report on "education vouchers." The center's report issued in 1970, entitled *Education Vouchers: A Report on Financing Elementary Education by Grants,* discussed problems that would surface in the use of vouchers. The report recommended a "regulatory compensatory voucher system." This system took into account the special needs to students—that is, provided more money for needy students (Kirkpatrick 1990).

To test the voucher theory, the report recommended the government to conduct an experiment using one particular voucher model called the "compensatory regulatory model." After an extensive national search, the Alum Rock district in San Jose, California, was selected for the pilot project. Based on the results of the Alum Rock experiment, Gary Bridge (1977) concluded that the "education vouchers stand little chance of succeeding in American elementary and secondary schools as a result of organizational and political roadblocks. . . . Parents sent their children to programs which reinforced their class social values and unionized teachers and school administrators strongly opposed introduction of competition into the delivery of precollege schooling" (p. 88). Disagreements by the opponents and proponents of education vouchers have so far made the implementation of voucher schemes at the national level impossible. Thus, voucher systems for elementary, junior high, and secondary education failed virtually all the tests of a true voucher program described earlier.

With the exception of the state of Vermont, where vouchers have been successful, workable, and noncontroversial for over a century, the history of vouchers in the United States has generally been marked by controversy and lack of progress. Beyond U.S. borders, several developed countries have established a tradition of using educational vouchers. The most notable examples include Denmark, France, Australia, Belgium, England, Canada, the Netherlands, and Ireland. In Denmark, publicly funded schools are permitted to pursue their own educational goals without state interference. Furthermore, the Danish government provides financial assistance to private schools. In light of the U.S. experience, Lindelow (1980) observed that "the Danish experience supports the view that public financing of alternative school need not be the death knell of government run public schools" (p. 18). Australia, which has a somewhat diverse population and a federal system of government like the United States, provides funds to private or parochial without controversy. The support for public and private education among Australians is broadly based (Doyle 1981; Kirkpatrick 1990).

Housing Vouchers

Provision of housing vouchers is one form of public assistance rendered by the federal government and to a limited extent by state and local governments to low-income families. Under the voucher system, instead of providing grant subsidies to private builders for construction of affordable housing, eligible low-income families are given the freedom to shop and choose the type of housing units that suit their needs and preferences without restricting where they can live and how much to spend on housing. In essence, the notion of issuing housing vouchers is rooted in the ongoing search for lesser wasteful and more efficient methods of providing low-income housing to the poor.

The administration of a housing voucher plan typically involves three parties, namely, (1) the issuer of the voucher, usually a government agency or the Department of Housing and Urban Development (HUD), (2) the recipient of the voucher, that is, an eligible low-income tenant, and (3) the housing suppliers, which include landlord, developers, and mortgage lenders (Bridge 1977). Under this kind of arrangement, the government issues a housing voucher to an eligible individual who will then shop for a unit in the marketplace, and upon finding a unit, gives the voucher to the landlord, who will then redeem it for cash from the government agency that issued the voucher. Ideally, the housing voucher system comes close to meeting the characteristics of a true voucher; namely, it takes into account differences in individual tastes and preferences; it provides consumers incentives to shop wisely; consumers can choose services from competing providers; information about cost, quality, and location of goods and services is available. According to Bridge (1977), however, "the local real estate market, the characteristics of the voucher recipients, and the rules of the voucher system" determine the "trueness" of a housing voucher plan (pp. 91–92).

During the 1970s and 1980s, the U.S. Department of Housing and Urban Development (HUD) conducted experimental voucher programs in several cities and countries across the country. The most notable and recent pilot voucher program was adopted by the Reagan administration in 1985. This program was tested for ten years and cost about US$160 million (Savas 1987). Under the experiment, tenants were given vouchers and encouraged to rent units of their choice in the marketplace. Although the pilot project demonstrated that the voucher plan is cheaper and more flexible than other low-income housing programs, it also revealed that "a significant fraction of the eligible poor were not interested to receive money to improve their housing quality" (1987, p. 200). These findings contradict a key argument advocated by housing voucher proponents— that the beneficiaries of the program are more equipped and have greater incentive to leave public housing and move to private housing if given the opportunity.

Cultural Vouchers

As an alternative to grants, vouchers have been used for promoting cultural activities most markedly in New York City and South Barwon in Australia. The objective of issuing cultural vouchers is to encourage certain individuals to attend cultural events of their choice (Bridge 1977). In New York City, culture vouchers are used to increase audience in certain cultural institutions facing a decline in attendance as well as to target low-income groups that without the voucher would not have the opportunity to seek cultural entertainment. Specifically, the culture vouchers in New York were give to low-income residents who were encouraged to seek cultural entertainment in theaters, dance programs, and other performing arts (Savas 1987, p. 220). In addition, the purpose of the vouchers program was intended to motivate cultural institutions to provide more services.

In South Barwon, Australia, the cultural voucher program targeted middle-class taxpayers. Since the mid-1970s, the city allocated about 12 percent of its recreation and parks budget to vouchers. Under the arrangement, each taxpayer is issued a voucher annually, which he/she can use in any of 150 participating organizations that perform various activities such as photography, croquet, astronomy, life saving, drama, go-cart racing, ceramics, and scouting (Savas 1987, p. 221). Critics have questioned the wisdom of taxing residents and then telling them to seek entertainment.

Medicare and Medicaid

The Medicare and Medicaid programs meet only one of the six conditions of true voucher systems examined earlier. As a voucher system, the Medicare or the Medicaid program allows eligible patients to seek medical treatment in either public or participating private health facilities. Furthermore, under both programs, patients have the freedom to choose their own physicians, clinics, hospitals, and pharmacies. However, unlike other government-run voucher systems, such as the GI Bill and the food stamp program, the Medicare and Medicaid programs lack incentives that induce recipients to shop wisely for the best available deals. There is lack of motivation for consumers to seek best prices because savings resulting from "wise"

shopping do not remain in the pockets of the consumer but go to the federal government. Moreover, patients have little information about the quality and cost of services; they face difficulties in comparing prices and quality among health providers; the services they need are expensive and less frequently purchased; and there is little competition among health care providers.

Privatization Vouchers

Beginning in 1991, several Eastern European countries and some newly independent former Soviet republics used vouchers as means to privatize state-owned enterprises. Typically, the government issues vouchers to some of its citizens; the holders of the vouchers could then use the vouchers to purchase shares in enterprises designated by the government for privatization. In 1993, for example, the Russian government distributed vouchers to 144 million citizens. Privatization voucher programs, however, have suffered a setback. The emergence of "black markets, low face value of the vouchers, trading value, and unrealistic formulas and valuations" are the unexceptional problems impeding the privatization voucher programs in Russia (Smirnoff 1994, p. 36). The Czech Republic, Mongolia, and Moldova are among other countries that have launched privatization-based voucher schemes directed at denationalizing state-owned assets. One major problem with privatization vouchers is that most voucher recipients lack understanding of the market system, coupled with limited access to information about the mechanics of better investments.

Other Vouchers

Other government-aid programs that have future potential for wider use of vouchers include transportation, childcare, drug treatment, elderly care, job training, and legal services for the poor. Some state and local governments are currently experimenting with some of these voucher systems at smaller scales.

ALEX SEKWAT

BIBLIOGRAPHY

Bridge, Gary, 1977. "Citizens Choice in Public Services: Voucher Systems." In E. S. Savas, ed., *Alternatives for Delivering Public Services: Toward Improved Performance.* New York: Diebold Institute for Public Policy Studies.

Cohen, David K., and Eleanor Farrar, 1977. "Power to the Parents—The Story of Education Vouchers." *The Public Interest,* vol. 48 (Summer) 72–97.

Doyle, Denis P., 1981. "Public Funding and Private Schooling: The State of Descriptive and Analytic Research." In Edward

M. Gaffney, Jr., ed., *Private Schools and the Public Good.* Notre Dame, IN: University of Notre Dame Press, 71–78.

Friedman, Milton, [1955] 1972. "The Role of Government in Education." In George R. La Noue, ed., *Educational Vouchers: Concepts and Controversies.* New York: Teachers College Press, 20–29.

Kirkpatrick, David W., 1990. *Choice in Schooling: A Case for Tuition Vouchers,* Chicago, IL: Loyola University Press.

Lindelow, John, 1980. *Educational Vouchers.* Reston, VA: National Association of Secondary Schools Principals.

Manchester, Lydia D., 1986. "Delivering Services with Vouchers—An Optional Approach Worth Considering." *Public Management,* vol. 68 (December): 23–24.

Mill, John S., [1859] 1972. "On Liberty." In George R. La Noue, ed., *Educational Vouchers: Concepts and Controversies.* New York: Teachers College Press.

Paine, Thomas, [1792] 1958. *The Rights of Man.* London: Dent.

Savas, Emanuel S., 1987. *Privatization: The Key to Better Government.* Chatham, NJ: Chatham House.

Smirnoff, Steve R., 1994. "Privatization in Russia." *Business Forum,* vol. 19 (Spring-Summer): 36–37.

Smith, Adam, [1776] 1937. *The Wealth of Nations.* New York: Modern Library.

West, Edwin G., 1981. "Choice or Monopoly in Education." *Policy Review,* vol. 15 (Winter): 103–117.

W

WAGE AND PRICE CONTROLS.

The fixing and regulating of wages and prices as a matter of government policy in order to create a desired economic or social condition that ostensibly would not have been produced in the absence of government intervention.

In an attempt to circumvent the perceived social and economic maladies that are sometimes associated with certain macroeconomic conditions (e.g., hyperinflation, economic recession or depression, national emergencies, etc.), policymakers have often resorted to the use of wage and price controls. One could argue that throughout history all governments have established and enforced wage and price controls at one time or another. Furthermore, one could argue that these controls did not always have the intended effect. In premodern societies, the inherent difficulties in enforcing broad regulations often necessitated that controls be limited to a single market or sector (e.g., bread). However, in both ancient and contemporary times, these types of controls were almost always detrimental over the long term in that they encouraged individuals to overconsume goods and services that were relatively cheap and find substitutes for those that were made prohibitively expensive. In order to avoid these and other types of social and economic perversions, it is necessary to regulate all wages and prices within an economy, i.e. comprehensive wage and price controls.

The twentieth century produced what is arguably the best, albeit infamous, example of a society regulated by universal wage and price controls. In the Soviet Union (1917–1989), official ideology precluded any reliance on market forces to build a modern socialist state. Wages and prices, in conjunction with employment quotas, production targets, rationing, and a host of other social and economic controls, were established by a central planning committee. In order to effectively enforce these controls, the Soviet government assumed a decidedly authoritarian, if not totalitarian, character. Until the 1970s, the Soviet Union demonstrated rapid industrial development, achieving the military status of a superpower. However, the social costs of the brutal enforcement of these controls directly resulted in the imprisonment and/or death of tens of millions of Soviet citizens. From the 1970s until its collapse in 1989, the Soviet Union faced mountain difficulty in establishing effective controls that were responsive to ever-changing domestic and international conditions. Although the comprehensive controls created by Soviet centralized planning were not by themselves a sufficient cause for the collapse of the Soviet Union, they were, nevertheless, a necessary cause.

Among Western liberal democracies, the best example of comprehensive wage and price controls can be found during World War II (1939–1945). In order to meet the production demands necessary to supply the war effort, temporary wage and price controls were implemented in Great Britain, the United States, and all countries engaged in the war. Before controls, the increase in war production was resulting in rising inflation. Efforts to control prices on selective goods was not having the desired effect. By 1943, consumer prices in the United Sates were rising at an annual rate of almost 12 percent. On April 8, 1943, President Franklin D. Roosevelt (1882–1945) issued his Hold-the-Line Order, thus fixing wages and prices at their existing levels from December 1943 to June 1946. During that period, consumer prices rose at an annual rate of 1.6 percent in spite of the fact that production was at an all-time high. However, in order to achieve these impressive results, the government had to create several new regulating institutions, adding an estimated 150,000 bureaucrats. Furthermore, in order to mitigate the detrimental effects of the black market that inevitably evolves whenever demand and supply are not in equilibrium, the government instituted an extensive rationing program. During the war years, sugar, coffee, meat, dairy products, footwear, fuels, and automobile parts were just some of the basic consumable items that had to be rationed at one time or another.

In hindsight, wage and price controls during World War II were generally successful. During the Korean War (1950–1954) wages and prices in strategic areas were controlled, but their success is more debatable. At least three factors help account for the relative success of wage and price controls during these two periods. First, they were temporary. Permanent controls would have most likely produced the type of domestic economic and social disruptions that plagued the former Soviet Union during its demise. Second, monetary and fiscal policy were adjusted to work in conjunction with wage and price controls. When, for some exogenous reason, the anticipation of inflation pushes wages and prices out of equilibrium with the money supply, controls can fix wages and prices until consumers' and producers' perceptions of the economy more accurately reflect real economic conditions. Third, patriotism helped produce widespread compliance. During a national crisis, loyal citizens are more willing to bear the hardships that often accompany wage and price controls. In later attempts at wage and price controls in the United States, one or more of these factors were missing, resulting in limited success, if not outright failure.

In August 1971, in response to public concern over inflation, President Richard Nixon (1913–1993) announced a comprehensive 90 day freeze of wages and prices. This abrupt announcement was the beginning of several phases of wage and price controls that lasted until April 1974. During this period inflation was fueled by increases in the money supply used to pay for military expenses during the Vietnam War. The excess money in circulation increased consumer demand by producing higher wages, thus making consumers willing to pay more for goods and services. Inflationary pressures increased exponentially with the shock of the first oil crisis (1973). Higher energy prices increased the cost of supplying goods and services, thereby forcing consumers to pay more. Nixon's attempt to control inflation was ultimately a failure. Although they were temporary, appeals to patriotism during the Vietnam war era did not receive the same degree of public compliance as during World War II. More important, however, monetary and fiscal spending continue. Thus, the wage and price freezes, rather than lowering inflation, merely prevented prices from rising without removing the cause of inflation. When the controls were lifted, inflation soared until both wages and prices were in equilibrium with the money supply.

Almost all economic theorists and practitioners agree that wage and price controls will not work unless monetary and fiscal spending are adjusted accordingly. There is, however, a great deal of disagreement over which should be the primary instrument for regulating the economy: monetary and fiscal policy, or wage and price controls?

CURTIS PEET

BIBLIOGRAPHY

Beckerman, Paul, 1992. *The Economics of High Inflation.* New York: St. Martin's.

Card, David, and Alan B. Krueger, 1995. *Myth and Measurement: The New Economics of the Minimum Wage.* Princeton, NJ: Princeton University Press.

Colander, David C., ed., 1979. *Solutions to Inflation.* New York: Harcourt Brace Jovanovich.

Rockoff, Hugh, 1984. *Drastic Measures: A History of Wage and Price Controls in the United States.* New York: Cambridge University Press.

Rockoff, Hugh, ed., 1992. *Price Controls.* Brookfield, VT: E. Elgar.

WALDO, DWIGHT (1913–).

The university professor who strongly influenced the intellectual development of public administration as the field redefined itself during the second half of the twentieth century. As the leading philosopher of the field, he explored the impact of ideas and political thought on public administration. No other individual had as much influence in defining the scope and values of public administration as a modern area of study.

Waldo was born in DeWitt, Nebraska, on September 28, 1913, the fourth of five children. DeWitt was an archetypical Midwestern farm town, with a population of 500. Waldo's father bred Duroc Jersey hogs, ran a horse-drawn drayage business (which became the local trucking company with the advent of the automobile), and served as the town marshal for 25 years.

Encouraged by his parents and high school teachers, Waldo left home to attend Nebraska Wesleyan University in Lincoln in the fall of 1931. It was the depth of the Great Depression, and his family could not afford a second year of tuition. Dwight transferred to the Nebraska State Teachers College at Peru in 1932 as a way of staying in school. His chief interest was English, an outgrowth of avid reading habits acquired during his youth. His enthusiasm for English fostered an elegant writing style and an interest in works of imagination that remained with him throughout his career. He intended to become a high school English teacher after his graduation from the teachers college in 1935.

In spite of the fact that Waldo accumulated the highest grade point average in his class, he could not get a job teaching. The president of the teachers college offered Waldo a small scholarship that would allow him to continue his education as a graduate student at the University of Nebraska. Waldo intended to study English, but changed majors when the political science department offered him a job reading and grading student papers. He specialized in political theory and wrote a master's thesis on the political thought of Graham Wallas, a British thinker concerned with the interaction of ideas and events. A solid academic record won Waldo a scholarship to Yale University, one of the leading institutions in political thought. In 1937, after two years at Nebraska, he received his master's degree and left for Yale.

By the spring of 1941, Waldo had passed his exams at Yale and had begun to write a dissertation on the political theory of the administrative state. He had intended to write a dissertation dealing broadly with American democratic traditions, but got caught up with the assertion then prevalent in public administration circles that experts ought to rule. This clashed with Waldo's notions of equality. What had been envisioned as a single chapter on public administration turned into the whole dissertation. Waldo occupied his fifth year at Yale writing his dissertation and teaching American government, completing his degree in the spring of 1942.

Like so many members of his generation, World War II exposed Waldo and the theories he had studied to the practical realities of public affairs. One of his professors at Yale, Harvey Mansfield, had gone to work for the U.S. Office of Price Administration. Waldo turned down an offer to teach political theory at the University of Michigan and accepted Mansfield's invitation to join him in Washington, D.C., arriving in June 1942. The Civil Service Commission initially refused to appoint Waldo when a clerk ruled that Waldo had not taken any courses that fit the orthodox definition of public administration. The incident inspired Waldo's first article in the *Public Administration Review* (Winter 1942, coauthored with Virgil Zimmermann),

"A Worm's Eye View" of the federal examination process from the perspective of newly educated applicants.

Waldo worked for the Office of Price Administration for two years, where he spent much of his time setting ceiling prices for caskets and funerals. This was followed by two years with the Government Organization Branch of the Bureau of the Budget, where he helped to plan the postwar organization of the federal establishment. Four years of practical experience allowed Waldo to sharpen the administrative insights contained in his dissertation. He took leave in 1945 to condense and revise the dissertation, which he submitted for publication at the end of that year. The work was released as *The Administrative State: A Study of the Political Theory of American Public Administration* by Ronald Press in 1948.

In stark contrast to the depression era, 1946 was a boom year for teachers as universities geared up for the growth of higher education encouraged by the GI Bill. From a number of offers, Waldo accepted an appointment as an assistant professor in the political science department at the University of California at Berkeley. Fourteen hundred students showed up for the introductory course on political science in the fall of 1946, and Waldo taught the overflow. Waldo taught in every branch of the department, as well as at other universities in the Bay Area. In 1957, after returning from a year as a technical assistance adviser at the University of Bologna, he became the acting director of the Institute of Governmental Studies at Berkeley. The Institute provided technical advice to state and local governments in California. Waldo held the position, which officially occupied one-third of his university time, until 1967.

The mid-1960s were a time of considerable turmoil on the Berkeley campus. The free speech movement erupted in the open space under Waldo's window in 1964, the first of the great student protests to end in mass arrests. The protests divided faculty and administration and helped elect conservative Governor Ronald Reagan in what had been a largely progressive state. The public administration faculty tried to break free from the political science department, which treated with disdain the idea that the liberal arts should exist to prepare students for employment. Departmental wars and painful personal relationships prompted Waldo to resign his professorship in 1966 from what was then regarded as one of the top political science programs in the world. In 1967, Waldo moved to Syracuse University, accepting the Albert Schweitzer Chair at the Maxwell School of Citizenship and Public Affairs, one of ten "super" professorships funded by the state of New York.

While still at Berkeley, Waldo was asked to take over the editorship of the *Public Administration Review (PAR)*. The disagreements between academics and practitioners that were dividing society at large had affected *PAR,* and the quality of scholarly writing had declined. Waldo used his position as editor-in-chief to redefine public adminis-

tration as a free-standing field of study that merged academics and practice. He retained the editorship for 11 years, including most of his Syracuse years.

When Waldo arrived at Syracuse University, public administration was still being taught as part of the political science department. To Waldo's relief, the establishment of public administration as an independent department in the early 1970s proceeded without acrimony. By the end of the 1970s, the public administration department at Syracuse University was rated as the top program in the nation.

Waldo relinquished the editorship of the *Public Administration Review* in 1977. In 1979, he retired from full-time teaching, taking an 18-month fellowship at the Woodrow Wilson International Center in Washington, D.C., to ease the transition. He remained in the Washington area through his retirement, writing and commenting upon the field.

Waldo's single most important intellectual contribution to the field of public administration is *The Administrative State,* first published in 1948 and reissued with some additional observations in 1984. For some 60 years, administrative scientists had argued that the prescriptions for reform were largely value free. They believed that their principles of administration would produce efficient government no matter what goals were pursued. Waldo used his knowledge of political thought to refute this notion. The administrative science movement, he argued, contained a coherent political philosophy "unmistakably related" to unique social and ideological features of American life. Administrative scientists could not escape their ideological preferences simply by claiming to be neutral.

Administrative science embraced positivism, the movement to extend the methods and spirit of science to an ever widening sphere of human affairs. It accepted the notion that experts should rule, a contentious issue in political thought ever since Plato had argued for philosopher-kings in *The Republic.* It amplified the separation of powers doctrine by creating the politics-administration dichotomy. It accepted the doctrines of utilitarianism in its elevation of efficiency to the top of the value scale. The gospel of efficiency was a by-product of the machine age, Waldo observed. It was out of step with values elevated by other societies at other times—religious faith during the Middle Ages, reason during the Enlightenment.

By exposing its philosophic roots, Waldo helped to discredit the administrative science movement. *The Administrative State* ranks as one of the three great works that sunk the early orthodoxy, along with Herbert Simon's *Administrative Behavior* (1947) and Paul Appleby's *Policy and Administration* (1949).

Waldo's denial of value neutrality collided with Simon's hope of developing a new science of administration that could separate facts from values. The two clashed in a famous exchange on the pages of the 1952 *American Political Science Review.* Waldo insisted that Simon's best ideas were unsupported by "the methodology he has asserted" (p. 97), whereas Simon accused Waldo of "loose . . . metaphorical" thinking (p. 496).

Waldo continued to comment on the development of the field into which, by his own admission, he had accidentally strayed. He published *The Study of Public Administration* in 1955 and *Perspectives on Administration* in 1956. More articles followed. He prepared the entry on "Public Administration" for the 1968 edition of the *International Encyclopedia of the Social Sciences*. Waldo articulated the vision of public administration that came to dominate the field. No longer a branch of political science, public administration depended upon a variety of fields and disciplines for the knowledge necessary to carry it out. The *Encyclopedia* article traced the evolution of the field and identified the impact of scientific management, political science, psychology and sociology, comparative studies, and operations research upon it.

By the late 1960s, the public administration field had absorbed a bewildering array of findings from other academic disciplines. The disappointment with the early administrative science movement and the early ties to political science had weakened the original core. In a 1968 article in the *Theory and Practice of Public Administration* (James Charlesworth, ed.), and again in 1975 (*American Public Administration*, edited by Frederick Mosher), Waldo lamented what he viewed as the disintegration of the field: "Public Administration is suffering from an identity crisis, having enormously expanded its periphery without retaining or creating a unifying center" (p. 185).

Seeking fresh insights on the direction of the field, Waldo promoted what became known as the "New Public Administration." Waldo used funds from his professorial chair to sponsor a 1968 conference at the Minnowbrook facility in the Adirondack Mountains of upstate New York to which he and his colleagues invited representatives from the under-30 generation. The participants responded to the turbulence of the times by embracing a proactive public administration concerned with social equity, concern for clients, and human adaptation. Conference proceedings appeared in a book assembled by Frank Marini, *Toward a New Public Administration* (1971). Waldo edited a subsequent anthology, *Public Administration in a Time of Turbulence* (1971), which grew out of papers presented at the 1969 conference of the American Political Science Association. The "New Public Administration" fizzled when calmer heads reminded its adherents that the purpose of public administration was not to make government policy but to administer it.

Public administration passed through the crises and regained its core as a sufficient number of scholars worked to apply diverse findings to the problems of governance. Again, Waldo played a key role in defining these developments. In his contribution to the *Theory and Practice of Public Administration* (Charlesworth 1968), Waldo suggested that the field should adopt a professional stance. Public administration could not become a full-fledged profession like law or medicine, which controlled entry to its ranks through licenses and exams. It could act like a profession, however, in the sense that it applied specialized bodies of knowledge to the practice of practical public administration. Seven years later, in *American Public Administration* (Mosher 1975), Waldo suggested that the field think of itself as analogous to medicine. The medical profession draws upon a number of different sciences to prepare practitioners to treat multiple ills. Likewise, public administration draws upon different disciplines to prepare practitioners for public service careers.

Waldo's eclectic interests enticed him to probe many corners of the field. Continuing his life-long interest in fiction, he published a 1968 study on *The Novelist on Organization and Administration*. He participated in the work of the comparative administration group, assembling one of the key works of that movement, *Temporal Dimensions of Development Administration* (1970). He retained an extensive interest in formal organization theory. In 1980, to mark his retirement from full-time teaching, he published *The Enterprise of Public Administration*. The book, presented in the form of 11 valedictory lectures, summed up his four decades of involvement with the field.

HOWARD E. McCURDY

BIBLIOGRAPHY

Appleby, Paul H., 1949. *Policy and Administration*. University, AL: University of Alabama Press.

Brown, Brack, and Richard Stillman, 1968. *A Search for Public Administration: The Ideas and Career of Dwight Waldo*. College Station: Texas A&M University Press.

Charlesworth, James C., ed., 1968. *Theory and Practice of Public Administration*. Philadelphia: American Academy of Political and Social Sciences.

Marini, Frank, 1993. "Leaders in the Field: Dwight Waldo." *Public Administration Review*, vol. 53 (September-October) 409–418.

Marini, Frank, ed., 1971. *Toward a New Public Administration*. Scranton, PA: Chandler.

Mosher, Frederick C., ed., 1975. *American Public Administration*. University, AL: University of Alabama Press.

Simon, Herbert A., 1947. *Administrative Behavior*. New York: Macmillan.

———, 1952. "Development of Theory of Democratic Administration: Reply." *American Political Science Review*, vol. 46 (June), 494-496.

Waldo, Dwight, 1948. *The Administrative State: A Study of the Political Theory of American Public Administration*. New York: Ronald Press. 2d ed., New York: Holmes and Meier, 1984.

———, 1952. "Development of Theory of Democratic Administration." *American Political Science Review*, vol. 46 (March), 81-103.

———, 1955. *The Study of Public Administration*. New York: Random House.

———, 1956. *Perspectives on Administration*. University, AL: University of Alabama Press.

———, 1968. *The Novelist on Organization and Administration.* Berkeley, CA: University of California Institute of Governmental Studies.

——— ed., 1970. *Temporal Dimensions of Development Administration.* Durham, NC: Duke University Press.

———, 1968. "Public Administration." *International Encyclopedia of the Social Sciences,* 17 vols., ed. David L. Sills. New York: Macmillan.

———, 1971. *Public Administration in a Time of Turbulence.* Scranton, PA: Chandler.

———, 1980. *The Enterprise of Public Administration: A Summary View.* Novato, CA: Chandler & Sharp.

WAR CABINET. A close-knit decisionmaking elite created for the attempted management of emergency situations. It is now as much a generic term as it is specific: It can equally be applied to the Israeli inner cabinet during the Six-Day War as to any group of close confidantes who are gathered around candidates in major election campaigns. It was well-described by a British former cabinet minister as a partial cabinet: "a standing or *ad hoc* committee presided over by the Prime Minister, which may—in matters of great moment or secrecy—prepare policies in detail and sometimes take decisions without prior consultation with the Cabinet as a whole" (Gordon-Walker 1970, p. 88). In most circumstances, the full cabinet is informed or consulted in due course.

In sum, war cabinets deal with, and are part of, crises. Naturally, the most obvious manifestations of a crisis are those situations that may culminate in violent conflict. If the crisis is well managed, as in the Cuban missile affair, then war is averted; if not, as with the invasion of the Falkland Islands in 1982, then war can occur. Either way, a small, ad hoc elite is assumed to be the most effective decisionmaking unit to deal with such emergencies. The purpose of reducing the size of cabinet and concentrating its work is to avoid the reference to it of all but the most important issues. The balance between direct, war-related work and the normal management of government affairs is the crucial problem for any head of government or state in times of real tension and war.

In the twentieth century, British prime ministers have faced this problem on at least six occasions—two world wars, Korea, Suez, Falklands, the Gulf. The range of British experience encompasses most of the ways in which governments have options to exercise in the management of war.

Total War

At the outbreak of World War I, Prime Minister Henry Asquith had little idea of how to lead a nation in a total war. However, he did understand quickly that concentrated attention by a few ministers was important. His war council consisted mainly of himself and ministers with relevant portfolios (foreign affairs, chancellor of the exchequor, etc.). The drawback of this arrangement was that ministers had both their respective departments to run and the war effort itself. Consequently, when Asquith was replaced by Dr. Lloyd George, the new prime minister immediately initiated a war cabinet. He was determined to set up a cabinet of five, to whom the whole control of the war could be entrusted. Of the five chosen, only one—the chancellor of the exchequer—had any departmental responsibility. This was a deliberate decision by Lloyd George in order that the members could stay in constant session. The system worked well for the duration of the war. Despite this, immediately upon the outbreak of war in 1939, British Prime Minister Neville Chamberlain ignored this example. He formed a war cabinet consisting of anything up to 15 members, utilizing the Chief of Staffs Committee in combination with a very small inner elite. He also relied heavily on subcommittees, which inevitably lead to duplication of effort, tension, and antagonism; this situation contributed, at least in part, to Chamberlain's political demise a year later.

When Winston Churchill took over as prime minister in May 1940, one of his first acts was to cut the war cabinet to eight, five Conservative Party members and three Labour. This was both functional and political given the nonpartisan war effort. However, unlike Lloyd George, Churchill left the war cabinet members with departmental responsibilities. In a cabinet reshuffle in 1942, he appointed Clement Attlee as his deputy and himself as minister of defense. Thus, in practice, the war was run by Churchill: In his roles as premier and minister of defense, he chaired the most powerful committees. The war cabinet rarely met more than twice a week, having effectively delegated the responsibility for actually running the war to Churchill. Everything other than the war effort—running the country, wealth creation, social cohesion, economic management, and the rest—was expertly delegated to highly competent subordinates. Each of these became virtual dictators in their own spheres, answerable only to that notable feature of the Churchill administration, the Lord President's Committee. The role of this committee was to ensure that the war cabinet was not distracted by issues that could not be classified as overriding importance. It consisted of a few very senior ministers, initially chaired by Neville Chamberlain, followed by Sir John Anderson and then Attlee himself, to whom was delegated complete responsibility for the home front. Churchill was thus freed from all domestic concerns.

Limited War

In June 1950, Britain, together with UN allies, was again embroiled in a war, this time in Korea. Prime Minister Attlee, as he now was, obviously with working memories of the recent war cabinet still very much in mind, decided that a limited war required a somewhat different solution to that of total war. He chose not to have a formal war cabinet but to utilize the existing committee structure. Thus the full cabinet of 17 members continued to operate while the Defense Committee, headed by Attlee and consisting of nine cabinet members, was responsible for the conduct of the war. (Reporting directly to the Defense Committee were the service chiefs.) Attlee had few party political worries to distract him in managing the British elements of this limited war. The left wing of the Party, while generally antiwar, was nevertheless pro-United Nations and the Parliamentary Opposition was still led by Churchill, a zealous declaratory anti-Communist. Also the most powerful men in the party were already members of the Defense Committee. Attlee had a relatively easy ride but should nevertheless be credited with resisting the temptation to overreact and set up a formal war cabinet.

Anthony Eden was less skillful—and, hence, less fortunate—during the Suez crisis of 1956. On the day after the nationalization of the Suez Canal by the Egyptian president, the Egypt Committee was formed. It consisted of Eden and six of his closest advisers. Traditional cabinet committee membership was eschewed in favor of the inner circle. It became Eden's personal instrument, and Suez was very much "his" war. The crucial member of the group was Lord Salisbury; his presence helped Eden carry the party. This was essential since, unlike during the Korean conflict, the Opposition opposed the basic purposes of the war and was being brilliantly led. The Egypt Committee was, in fact, an ad hoc crisis management device that failed to manage the crisis; for want of anything better, it acted as the British war cabinet for the duration of the difficulties. It was clearly an extension of the prime minister's office; it could not protect him from every aspect of the war. As a self-created consequence, he suffered enormous mental and physical stress, eventually cracking under the strain.

A quarter of a century later, the Falklands Conflict inner cabinet was essentially an ad hoc elite established the moment it became clear that crisis management had failed. In fact, the first meeting of what came to be known as the war cabinet was the day after the task force had sailed in early April 1982. The war cabinet lay somewhere between Attlee's formal utilization of the existing committee structure and Eden's rejection of it. Prime Minister Margaret Thatcher formed an official subcommittee of the Cabinet's Overseas and Defense Committee. This consisted of her plus four and represented the perfect balance of functional and political appointees. Functional were Francis Pym (Foreign Secretary) and John Nott (Defense); political were William Whitelaw (Home Secretary) and, more controversially, a relatively junior noncabinet member, Cecil Parkinson. The war cabinet met every day and sometimes twice a day. It controlled the strategic aspects of the war completely and only referred to the full cabinet on policy decisions and even then it was only for confirmation or veto and definitely not discussion. Thatcher was completely dominant in

her approach within the war cabinet and highly supportive of her military commanders. By contrast, a decade later, during the Gulf War, few demands were made on policymakers in terms of cabinet involvement. The limited nature of the level of British involvement, the low level of British control, and the briefness of the conflict meant that the existing cabinet, defense, and service chiefs could adequately handle the situation.

Conclusion

A war cabinet, or a "partial cabinet," is the cabinet system under stress. There is a crucial and massive difference of scale, in both time and threat, between "total" wars and "limited" wars. In a total war, there is an almost unwavering public support; such public acquiescence can only be available for short periods in limited wars. During the Falklands war, public support held for the duration, but one wonders if that would have been so had the war dragged on for much longer, or had the casualties been any greater. There are also the inevitable tensions between practical and political considerations that must be resolved by the prime minister, particularly in limited wars. The political priorities for prime ministers must be to carry with them first the full cabinet, then the party, then Parliament, and finally, and most importantly as time goes on, public opinion. If they can manage to do that, and stay physically and mentally healthy, they will be allowed the dubious honor of running a war cabinet free from unnecessary distractions.

CHRISTOPHER BRADY

BIBLIOGRAPHY

Franks Report, Falkland Islands Review, 1983. *Report of a Committee of Privy Councillors*, Cmnd. 8787. London: HMSO.
Gordon-Walker, P., 1970. *The Cabinet*. London: Jonathan Cape.
Janis, I. L., 1972. *Victims of Groupthink: A Psychological Study of Foreign Policy Decisions and Fiascoes*. Boston: Houghton-Mifflin.
Madgwick, P., 1991. *British Government: The Central Executive Territory*. Hemel Hempstead: Philip Allan.

WAR ON POVERTY. A set of programmatic activities undertaken in the United States in the 1960s to reduce the level of poverty in the country.

The war on poverty was part of President Lyndon Johnson's Great Society initiatives. It consisted of programs created under the Economic Opportunity Act (EOA) of 1964 but is often associated with a broader range of initiatives including Medicaid, food stamps, Model Cities, the Elementary and Secondary Education Act, and the Man-

power Development and Training Act. For many, the war on poverty was at the heart of these Great Society initiatives of the Johnson administration.

The war on poverty was initiated to deal with increasing apparent problems of need in a society of growing wealth and material abundance. It reflected optimism that the nation could solve perennial problems of inequality and disadvantage without seriously altering social structures and economic processes. Although it evoked an extraordinary amount of political thunder and lightening, it was, in many ways, quite modest in scope.

Components of the Program

The Economic Opportunity Act contained several major components: the Job Corps and a Neighborhood Youth Corps, the Community Action Program, a Rural Loan Program, a Migrant Farm Workers Program, Small Business Development Centers, a Work Experience Program, and the Volunteers in Service to America (VISTA). Reflecting the struggle over control of the program prior to its enactment, the components were assigned to various agencies. The Job Corps, administered by the Office of Economic Opportunity (OEO), was a residential training program for men and women between the ages of 16 and 21. The Neighborhood Youth Corps, assigned to the Department of Labor, provided training and work experience programs for youth who continued to live at home.

The most innovative, most distinctive, and central component of the Economic Opportunity Act was the Community Action Program, a set a activities planned and carried out by local Community Action Agencies (CAAs) that were given authority for the program under OEO. Community Action was intended as a diverse mix of social services designed to meet varied local needs, but it came to encompass a set of common elements in many communities across the country. It was also to coordinate the activities of existing agencies in a concentrated attack on poverty and to be a means of mobilizing the poor to address their own needs. As it evolved, community action typically included Head Start program to provide early childhood education for poor children, legal services to help the poor in their encounters with the legal system on matters ranging from protective orders to divorce to challenges to administrative agencies, and community health centers to make a range of health care services more accessible to the poor who lived in rural communities and central city areas inadequately served by the existing health care system.

The Rural Loan Program, administered by the Farmers Home Administration in the Department of Agriculture, made loans available to farm and nonfarm individuals and cooperatives in rural areas. Small Business Development

Centers were assigned to the Small Business Administration to provide loans to businesses developed by the poor or those who would hire the poor. The Work Experience Program, targeted at welfare recipients, was assigned to the Welfare Administration in the Department of Health, Education, and Welfare.

Finally, there was VISTA. It was to be the domestic equivalent of the Peace Corps, channeling the volunteer spirit of America into the attack on poverty. It would bring skills and enthusiasm to the task that would otherwise not be available.

Policy Formulation and Implementation

The war on poverty had its beginnings in President John F. Kennedy's administration. The president had confronted poverty during his 1960 presidential campaign and been struck by Michael Harrington's book *The Other America,* (1962) a major treatment of the "forgotten" members of American society. Kennedy initiated planning for a coordinated antipoverty effort. When Lyndon Johnson took office after the Kennedy assassination, he made the war on poverty a centerpiece of his legislative agenda, authorizing a planning group to proceed with its efforts the day after Kennedy died.

Planning for war on poverty was carried out primarily by a group of political appointees and career civil servants in the bureaucracy under the direction of the Council of Economic Advisers and the Bureau of the Budget. It was very much a presidential initiative, one that reflected a president's attempt to define his presidency. Although it was a response to real problems, it was not a response to substantial, visible public demands. And Congress was not involved in any extensive way in the formulation of the program. Congressional leaders were not consulted extensively in its development. when it went to Congress, Republican concerns were largely ignored and it was pushed through as a Democratic initiative.

Johnson announced his unconditional war on poverty in his 1964 State of the Union Address. A task force, chaired by Sargent Shriver, Director of the Peace Corps, drafted plans for legislation. Initial discussions focused on the strategy to be pursued in the poverty war. While each of the established bureaucracies had its favored approach, it was clear from the beginning that the poverty war would pursue a service strategy rather than an income strategy. Neither the president nor his staff wanted to create a program of cash benefits to lift low-income citizens out of poverty. Instead, they wanted to provide services and support that would allow the poor to take advantage of opportunities in the economic system to improve their own well-being. The program basically reflected a belief that there were deficiencies in the poor and in the system of delivering services to the poor and unemployed. Addressing those deficiencies would eliminate the barriers that kept the poor from succeeding in American life.

The major elements that were discussed as potential components of the war were education, training, and social services. As the drafters pursued the development of a policy proposal, however, they were looking for something that would be new and distinctive, something that would go beyond a simple expansion of existing programs for dealing with problems of low-income Americans. They found that unique focus in the concept of community action. Although the concept was not clearly defined and there are, even today, disputes among those who developed the legislation about what they had in mind, community action at a minimum was intended to provide a mechanism for focusing attention and effort on problems of poverty.

As critical as the service component and the unique focus was the issue of how the war would be administered. It could be turned over to the existing bureaucracy to operate under the Department of Labor or the Department of Health, Education, and Welfare, for example. Doing this, however, was inconsistent with the belief of some who were planning the program that an agency was needed that could cut across departmental boundaries. One significant element of the program was to be an effort to coordinate existing resources to address more effectively the needs of the poor. That would be difficult to do from within an existing agency. Some important actors also believed that new approaches to service delivery were needed and that was unlikely to happen at the initiative of existing agencies, which were viewed as being tied to prevailing approaches to education, training, and social service. Because the bureaucracy could be trusted at neither the federal nor the local level, new agencies would operate in both arenas.

The Economic Opportunity Act provided for an Office of Economic Opportunity to operate out of the White House and report directly to the president. This was to give it the visibility, prestige, and access to the president that would be needed to coordinate existing programs of other agencies and focus attention on a concentrated attack on poverty. In much the same way, new community action agencies at the local level would disperse funds made available under the act, involve the poor themselves in deciding how to spend those resources, coordinate local efforts, and provide a counterbalance to the local bureaucracy. This administrative framework fit well with the community action conception.

Individual program components, however, would be assigned to a variety of agencies. Labor, Health, Education, and Welfare (HEW), and Agriculture would all obtain funding and programmatic authority through the Economic Opportunity Act. This was necessary to obtain their

support for the legislation and made sense administratively and theoretically, but it led to problems for OEO. The poverty agency found it quite difficult to obtain the cooperation of these other agencies in developing a coordinated war on poverty. OEO was no general in this war, lacking the command authority and structure that any general would expect.

One of the most controversial provisions of the Economic Opportunity Act was its call for the maximum feasible participation of the poor in the development of the programs. This was not viewed by most participants the development of the legislation as a major part of the initiative; it apparently received little active discussion in the deliberations. The policy planners viewed it as a provision to ensure that the poor would receive the benefits of the program, have opportunities for employment through the program, and provide input for the program planners.

Maximum feasible participate came to be the lightening rod of the poverty program. As the program was implemented in communities across America, advocates of the poor and minority groups took advantage of this component to institute processes of political mobilization. Not only would the poor be involved in planning program activities and be hired to participate in administration of the programs, they were often mobilized to protest the actions of City Hall or other agencies. The agencies were sometimes caught in the turmoil of riots that came to dominate the urban scene in the middle and late 1960s. They had links to the civil rights movement in the South and elsewhere.

Community action frequently led to significant political advances for minorities and the poor, it sometime fostered greater responsiveness from other agencies; and it enhanced skills of many in the poor community. It also, however, led to a storm of opposition from big city mayors who resented the national government committing resources to groups that were challenging the authority of mayors and City Hall. The mayors also resented the fact that a significant bureaucracy with its many jobs had been placed outside their reach. Responding to pressures from the mayors, Congress amended the legislation in 1966 to limit the involvement of the poor and give mayors more control over the program.

The emphasis on maximum feasible participation complicated the administration of the program It opened the question of whether community action agencies would pursue a political strategy or a services strategy. Although those who pursued a political strategy received the most attention, services strategies were more prevalent. The adopted strategy had substantial implications for program administration. In addition, administrators had to set up effective administrative operations while fostering the involvement of target populations. The tension between pro-

fessional expertise and indigenous preference often led to conflict.

Intergovernmental Dimensions

The Community Action Program was one of a series of initiatives in the 1960s that continued the practice of establishing a direct relationship between the national government and America's cities. As such, it contravened traditional intergovernmental routines that saw the national government act through the states to pursue its goals. Initially, however, the program's independence from city hall threatened to break the ties between Democratic presidents and big city mayors. As authority over the program was transferred to city governments, mayors gained a new point of leverage. Although state governments were never actively involved in the program, governors were given the right to veto plans within their state. This power was seldom used.

The intergovernmental task of the community action agencies was complicated. As coordinators of diverse resources, they had to entice a multitude offered, state, and local agencies to cooperate to pursue a set of poverty reduction objectives. For many of these agencies, poverty was a secondary concern. The community action agency had no authority to command the cooperation of other agencies. Indeed, OEO itself encountered considerable difficulty getting federal departments such as Labor and Health and Human Services to consider any degree of coordination at the national level. The coordination task as originally envisioned often proved to be beyond the capability of community action agencies. The community action agencies typically came to emphasize their own set of independent programs–Head Start, legal services, community health centers, and community action. Activities such as Head Start required at least some degree of coordination with the school system, and health centers required some coordination with preexisting medical service systems. These, however, were matters of operational coordination where the various organizations were able to work out agreements. In fact, the community action agencies often contracted with the traditional agencies to provide these services.

Evaluating Success

In several ways, the war on poverty was lost almost as quickly as it began. It had modest funding to begin with and that funding never expanded to a level that would allow success in the war. It major focus, community action, became embroiled in controversy that caused the president and Congress to turn away from the poverty war as the primary vehicle for solving poverty problems or for dealing with problems of the inner city. OEO and the community action agencies were unable to take the leadership in coordinating diverse programs and agencies in a concerted effort to reduce poverty. The war did not bring an end to poverty; in fact, its various components probably had a minimal impact on poverty levels.

Despite the political turmoil of the war on poverty and the efforts of Republican administrations over the years to eliminate its vestiges, most of its program elements continue in operation today. The Office of Economic Opportunity was eliminated during the Nixon administration, and its successor, the Community Services Administration, was abolished by the Reagan administration. However, community action agencies, sometimes called that, sometimes called by other names, operate in hundreds of communities. They typically draw on a variety of grants and contracts, including the Community Services Block Grant of the Reagan administration, to offer services in low-income communities. The Head Start program, which has grown and expanded considerably over the years, is now regarded widely as the most successful of the poverty programs. The various training programs have continued through the years, although they have been written into other pieces of legislation, transferred among agencies, and modified. The Job Corps operates today under the Job Training Partnership Act as administered by the Department of Labor. Legal aid programs continue to provide important help for poor Americans. In addition, other social program initiatives were undertaken by the Republican administration of Richard Nixon, which succeeded Johnson.

Some conservative critics argue that the war on poverty was part of a larger array of initiatives in the 1960s that served to break the connections among work, responsibility, and personal well-being. They include it in their larger critique of programs that they believe have encouraged welfare dependency and a culture of poverty. This seems a poorly directed criticism of a program that did not provide cash benefits and largely sought to provide services that would help the poor become self-sufficient. It is a criticism, however, that does capture the fact that community action agencies often helped the poor pursue benefits to which they were entitled and provided legal services that allowed that poor to challenge agency rules and practices that denied them benefits.

Numerous formal evaluations of components of the war on poverty, such as Head Start and the Job Corps, have been mixed in their findings. Early evaluations of Head Start raised serious questions about its efficacy, but more recent evaluations have suggested that it makes a significant difference. Job Corps has also been found to be successful but very expensive to operate.

Success at the level of building an ongoing base of support has occurred despite the obvious fact that the war has done little to substantially reduce poverty. Although its programs have alleviated the problems of some poor Americans and offered hope to others, it never was funded at a level that would have allowed it to defeat poverty, even if it had the strategy to do that.

EDWARD T. JENNINGS, JR.

BIBLIOGRAPHY

Donovan, John, 1967. *The Politics of Poverty*. New York: Pegasus.
Harrington, Michael, 1962. *The Other America*. New York: Macmillan.
Haveman, Robert H., ed., 1977. *A Decade of Federal Antipoverty Programs: Achievements Failures, and Lessons*. New York: Academic Press
Levine, Robert A., 1970. *The Poor Ye Need Not Have with You: Lessons from the War on Poverty*. Cambridge: MIT Press.
Levitan, Sar A., 1969. *The Great Society's Poor Law: A New Approach to Poverty*. Baltimore, MD: Johns Hopkins Press.
Moynihan, Daniel P., 1970. *Maximum Feasible Misunderstanding: Community Action in the War on Poverty*. New York: Free Press.
Murray, Charles, 1984. *Losing Ground: American Social Policy, 1950–1980*. New York: Basic Books.
Sundquist, James L., ed., 1969. *On Fighting Poverty: Perspectives from Experience*. New York: Basic Books.

WATERGATE. An umbrella term that describes the scandals that led to the resignation of President Richard Nixon. It has also come to symbolize corrupt politics, abuses of presidential power, and citizen cynicism about government.

Background

Watergate itself is a hotel-office-apartment complex in Washington, D.C., where a 1972 burglary attempt to plant "bugs" in the headquarters of the Democratic National Committee was discovered and linked to the White House. This set in motion a series of events that ultimately toppled the Presidency of Richard Nixon in 1974. The national trauma that resulted has had a lasting effect upon American public administration, characterized by public distrust, disillusionment, and even contempt for governing institutions (Mosher et al. 1974).

Watergate is also a generic term that describes three distinct conspiracies: First, there was the burglary conspiracy aimed at embarrassing the Democrats. This included illegal wiretaps, plugging of leaks, and schemes to overthrow those who were seen as "enemies" of the Nixon Presidency. Second, it was a conspiracy to reelect the president that was set into motion immediately following the Nixon presidential victory. This conspiracy involved attempts to create a presidency without regard for constitutional prerogatives and institutional paranoia that took direction from the psychological make-up of the chief executive himself (Halpern 1975, pp. 3–9). It degenerated into "dirty tricks," extortion, money-laundering, spying, and connections with the international underworld. The third conspiracy was to cover up

wrong-doing and to shelter the Nixon White House from criminal culpability that arose out of the first two conspiracies. This involved perjury, defiance of the law, sabotaging of information, and obstruction of justice. These conspiracies have had lasting effects on the way that the citizenry looks upon public administration today.

Three issues arising from Watergate are especially relevant to public administration: (1) the drive for presidential power that arose from the insecurities and obsessions of Nixon himself; (2) his beliefs of executive privilege; and (3) the collapse of ethics at the highest levels of the federal government.

Power and Executive Privilege in Public Administration

Some historians have found that the most "venal and dangerous" aspect of the Nixon Presidency uncovered by Watergate was the perception of unlimited power at the highest levels of public administration—i.e., as it related to the roles and responsibilities of the chief executive and his key associates (Mosher et al. 1974). An unpleasant ambiance permeated the Nixon White House—one that was characterized by intense paranoia, an immoderate drive for power, a thirst for secret intelligence, a disregard for constitutional and legal protections, and a perceived need for expansion of the size and scope of executive staff.

Another related problem for public administration that arose in Watergate was the notion of executive privilege. This can be defined as the right of the president to make judgments to withhold important information from Congress, the courts, and the public. President Nixon argued, in clear refutation of constitutional law, that presidential actions had higher standing than the law itself. Naturally, there is much debate whether the notion of the power of executive privilege is even legitimate. As conceived by Nixon, it put many aspects of information vital to public administration into a shrouded place, gave the executive the privilege of being participant and referee in key issues, and as perceived in the White House of that time, was a privilege that appeared to have no limits (Friedman and Levantrosser 1992, pp. 163–174).

Need for Governmental Ethics

The troubling issues of presidential power and executive privilege, and other problems arising out of Watergate, generated a recognition within the public administration community itself that more of a responsible and moral government was required. Ethics at a theoretical level was seen to encompass what government ought and ought not to do under given conditions—in other words, the belief was that the ethics of public administration should reflect the values of society and had to include concepts such as justice, fairness, and equality. At the administrative level, ethics for public administrators were seen as being concerned with standards for the officials that included responsible behavior and accountability and also included, in a liberal democracy, respect for the rights of the citizenry by public servants. These values were seen as lacking in public administrators, as forcefully brought out by the scandals of Watergate.

To look at these, and related issues, a special committee, drawn from members of the National Academy of Public Administration, chaired by Frederick Mosher, was empaneled by the Senate Select Committee on Presidential Campaign Activities. A report entitled "Watergate: Its Implications for Responsible Government" ensued in 1974. The inquiry concluded that more sophisticated codes of ethics for government were needed. It also urged educational institutions, and in particular their schools of public administration, to actively focus upon the teaching of public-sector ethics. A quote from Thomas Jefferson, that the Mosher panel felt could be used as a guideline in coming to principled answers in the face of difficult public administration dilemmas, concluded the report: "Whenever you are to do a thing, though it can never be known but to yourself, ask yourself how you would act were all the world looking at you, and act accordingly" (Mosher et al. 1974, p. 126).

Watergate also gave birth to a flurry of legislation aimed at creating moral standards for the public administration—the Federal Campaign Election Act (1974), the Freedom of Information Act (1974), Government in Sunshine Act (1976), the Federal Corrupt Practices Act (1977), the Federal Corrupt Practices Act (1978), the Ethics in Government Act (1978).

Summary

The aftermath of Watergate brought about a major review of the Presidency as a public administrative institution. Much of the focus of public administration's development since the 1930s had been to concentrate power and control in the executive branch. Now that it had been accomplished, Watergate provided a dramatic lesson in what could happen if such centralized power was abused.

Watergate also raised another issue for public administration, namely, that the great bulk of administrative decisions are delegated to nonelected public officials and that these decisions then have far-reaching effects on the people. It also suggested that the kinds of decisions and actions taken by such officials depends on their personal value systems, professional ethics, and current associations (Mosher 1982), which they bring to bear on public decisions in random fashion. In Watergate, it brought forth the realization that nonelected officials will violate a variety of moral and legal provisions rather than disobey their superiors. It also surfaced scandalous breaches of the merit system. These and other issues brought to the forefront the need for standardized codes of ethics for public administration. In this regard, while Watergate raised some immediate political, legal, and ethical issues, it also surfaced disturbing questions as to whether the compromise of integrity, periodically appearing at the highest levels of public administration, is really something that is latent and widespread in the entire population (Rangel 1980, p. 9).

On a lesser note, Watergate has generated a number of new terms in the English language. The suffix "gate" now routinely connotes government cover-ups (Emery 1994, p. xii). "Dirty tricks" has moved from its more harmless meaning of "college pranking" to describe illegal power plays made by individuals in leadership positions. The word "plumbers" has developed a secondary meaning–whereby fixing leaks in the political sense means squashing detrimental information from enemy camps–a meaning whose origins come to us from the "plumbers" of Watergate.

BREENA E. COATES AND JEFFERY K. GUILER

BIBLIOGRAPHY

Emery, Fred, 1994. *Watergate: The Corruption of American Politics and the Fall of Richard Nixon.* New York: Random House.
Gutman, Amy, and Dennis Thompson, 1990. *Ethics & Politics: Cases and Comments.* Chicago, IL: Nelson-Hall.
Halpern, Paul, ed., 1975. *Why Watergate?* Pacific Palisades, CA: Palisades Publishers.
Friedman, Leon, and William F. Levantrosser, 1992. *Watergate and Afterward.* Westport, CT: Greenwood.
Mosher, Frederick C., 1982. *Democracy and the Public Service.* Oxford: Oxford University Press.
Mosher, Frederick C., et al., 1974. *Watergate: Its Implications for Responsible Government.* Washington, D.C.: National Academy of Public Administration.
Rangel, Leo, 1980. *The Mind of Watergate: An Exploration of the Compromise of Integrity.* New York: W. W. Norton.

WEBB, JAMES EDWIN (1906–1992).

Administrator of the National Aeronautics and Space Administration (NASA) in the era of Apollo; one of the truly dominant personalities in American public administration in the twentieth century. Webb served as President Truman's director of the U.S. Budget from 1946 to 1949 and undersecretary of state from 1949 to 1952. He was a lifelong student of management, served as president of the American Society for Public Administration and helped found the National Academy of Public Administration. The author of a book, *Space Age Management* (New York: McGraw Hill, 1969), Webb's name is attached to awards for excellence in public administration today. Among students and practitioners of government, he is a "Washington Legend" and has been featured in various writings on administrative achievement (Haught 1985; Doig and Hargrove 1987).

Webb was widely regarded as an imaginative, energetic, and effective administrator. He had numerous admirers, among them President Lyndon Johnson, who called Webb his best administrator. However, he was also controversial in his day, especially at NASA, and there are those who believe he exemplifies bureaucratic entrepreneurship in pursuit of government-directed technology that can be a threat to democratic accountability (McDougall 1985).

Webb was the son of a county school superintendent, a man who was a progressive reformer in his own right and who provided a model for his son of proactive administration. He was educated at the University of North Carolina at Chapel Hill and planned to be a teacher. However, circumstances and the influence of an early mentor diverted him to law. He might well have settled into becoming a small-town lawyer in Oxford, North Carolina, had the depression not disrupted his life so substantially that this ambitious and restless man looked for escape. He found it in the marine air reserve where he learned to fly and gained a new sense of self-esteem. He also made contacts that led him to a position in Washington when his service duty was over.

Thus began Webb's education as a Washington operative, working on the staff of the chairman of the House Rules Committee. Webb found himself in a pivotal position at a tumultuous time—the beginning of Roosevelt's New Deal in 1933. Then, in the mid-1930s, he gained another vantage point on Washington as right-hand man to one of the leading Washington lawyer-lobbyists. This led to Webb's being hired as an executive with the Sperry Gyroscope Company in New York City in the late 1930s and early 1940s.

Following a brief service during World War II, Webb returned to Washington as the assistant to the undersecretary of the Treasury. Before long, he was asked by President Truman to be his budget director. It was in this position that Webb gained prominence and revealed the unusual blend of political savvy and administrative skill that would mark his career.

The Bureau of the Budget (BOB), over which he took command, was losing influence with the president and stood at arms distance from the White House staff, which was small and overwhelmed by the demands of post-World War II policy development. Webb coordinated BOB's work with that of the White House staff so that "the two organizations became almost indistinguishable except on political questions, where he drew the line." He made the bureau indispensable to Truman and not only reversed its decline but enhanced its role as the central staff of the institutional Presidency (Donovan 1977, p. 269).

His reputation as an administrative leader established, Webb was asked by Truman to remain in his second term to "manage" the State Department as Dean Acheson's undersecretary. Webb went at this task with his usual confidence and enthusiasm and made substantial reforms: strengthening an existing executive secretariat to improve communication within the department and between the department and other agencies, initiating mechanisms for

linking scientific advice and recruiting technical personnel to the department, improving contacts with Congress at a time when relations between the legislature and Secretary Acheson were strained. Unfortunately, Acheson did not always appreciate his undersecretary. He was Truman's man, not Acheson's appointee. Webb felt increasingly peripheral in an agency where policy expertise, rather than administrative skill, was most valued. His morale and health suffering, Webb left the State Department before Truman's term ended.

In the mid and late 1950s, Webb worked in Oklahoma as president of the Republic Supply Company and as assistant to the president of Kerr-McGee[Oil] Industries. While there, he increasingly devoted himself to public-service activities in the state and the nation at large.

President John F. Kennedy asked Webb to head the newly formed NASA in 1961. At the time, NASA was an embattled agency whose mission was uncertain and whose competence was questioned. America was clearly behind the Soviet Union in space, and many observers questioned whether Webb, a nontechnical man, was appropriate to lead a science and technology agency.

Webb proved the perfect match for NASA and the times. Armed with Kennedy's 1961 decision to go to the moon, Webb quickly neutralized opposition within and outside his agency, built a huge constituency for NASA, and led it to Apollo's remarkable triumph eight years later in 1969. In the process, he reinvented NASA and used Apollo's momentum to accelerate progress in communication and meteorological satellites, space science, and the education of thousands of new scientists and engineers. A man who read deeply in the management literature from the time he was at Sperry, he had especially seen wisdom in the work of Mary Parker Follett, one of the pioneers in the "Human Relations School" of management and who wrote of taking individuals and creating from them a group power capable of reaching a highest common denominator of collective action (Metcalf and Urwick 1942). Now he congealed 400,000 individuals in government, industry, and universities behind an incredible goal—and actually implemented that goal. He also launched a major effort to link universities and industries to accelerate the transfer of space technology to the civilian economy. Many students of administration believe Webb's NASA was a model of excellence in public management (Sayles and Chandler 1971; Sayles 1992; Lambright 1993).

Webb's place in history is secure. However, a careful reading of his record at NASA shows he fell short in certain respects. There was the Apollo fire of 1967, which took the lives of three astronauts and which should not have happened. He left NASA without a firm post-Apollo goal. His attempt to use Apollo to reform higher education and energize an entire nation fell short.

Nevertheless, where it counted most, Apollo, Webb succeeded brilliantly and thus moved into the annals of ad-

ministrative giants. After NASA, Webb engaged in various business and public-service activities, chiefly the Smithsonian Institution. When he died in 1992, President Bush paid him a special tribute for his leadership of NASA. Buried in Arlington National Cemetery, he was survived by Patsy Webb, his wife of many years, and a son and daughter. He is subject of the biography *Powering Apollo: James E. Webb of NASA* by W. Henry Lambright (Baltimore, MD: Johns Hopkins, 1995).

W. HENRY LAMBRIGHT

BIBLIOGRAPHY

Doig, Jameson W., and Erwin C. Hargrove, 1987. *Leadership and Innovation: A Biographical Perspective on Entrepreneurs in Government.* Baltimore, MD: John Hopkins University Press.

Donovan, Robert J., 1977. *Conflict and Crisis: The Presidency of Harry S. Truman, 1945–1948.* New York: W. W. Norton.

Haught, Robert L., ed., 1985. *Giants in Management.* Washington, DC: National Academy of Public Administration.

Lambright, W. Henry, 1993. "James E. Webb: A Dominant Force in 20th Century Public Administration." *Public Administration Review,* vol. 53, no. 2 (March-April): 95–99.

McDougall, Walter, 1985. *The Heavens and the Earth: A Political History of the Space Age.* New York: Basic Books.

Metcalf, Henry C., and L. Urwick, eds., 1942. *Dynamic Administration: The Collected Papers of Mary Parker Follett.* NY: Harper and Brothers.

Sayles, Leonard R., 1992. "James Webb at NASA." *Society,* vol. 29, no. 6: 63–68.

Sayles, Leonard R., and Margaret Chandler, 1971. *Managing Large Systems: Organizations for the Future.* New York: Harper and Row.

WEBER, MAX (1864–1920).

Arguably *the* social scientist of the twentieth century. A German founder of modern sociology, Max Weber left his imprint on public administration predominantly in three substantive areas: the structure of the political and economic environments (the state, charisma, rationalization of the economy), the structure of modern organization (bureaucracy), and the motivations of modern capital enterprise. His other impact was and remains methodological. He is considered to be not only a father of empirical methodology in social science but also the originator of an interpretive adaptation of that methodology to apply to problems of history, the study of culture, and sociology, ultimately, interpretive *(verstehende)* sociology.

Perhaps nowhere in the history of social science is the relation between person and work as deeply engraved on the world as through Max Weber's life and effort. As person, teacher, researcher, and founder of a discipline, as political figure, adviser, and critic, Max Weber deeply affected his contemporaries and subsequent generations. Of continuing influence is his unyieldingly ethical though paradoxical definition of the value-related obligations of the scientist: both to admit one's own value-laden point of de-

parture and to proceed within that perspective to whatever conclusions logic, methodological rigor, and being true to the experience of one's subjects commanded.

As the concepts he shaped came into common usage—charisma, legal-rational authority, traditional authority, value rationality, instrumental rationality, bureaucracy, "Verstehen," and so forth—critics tried to hold Weber responsible for the consequences of his political ideas. For example, one author (Mommsen 1959) attempted to implicate Weber's proposal for a popularly elected president in German "Caesaristic" developments following his death. Such interpretation is un-Weberian, because deterministic, but reflects the depth to which his own and later generations have felt engaged by his intellectual and practical thought, reflecting an irony he himself observed: that fate in modern times is the consequence of Man's action contrary to his intentions. Against political hindsight, the definitive word is spoken in earthy South German dialect by Theodor Heuss, the West German President who as Max Weber's student had delivered the funeral oration at his grave: "Jetzt macht doch der Mann die Leut heut noch verrueckt" (How this man drives people crazy even today, in Baumgarten 1964, p. 613, fn. 2; for a critique of the critics, see Roth 1965).

Originally a student of law, economics, history, philosophy, and theology, Weber cofounded modern German sociology with far-reaching impact on social science as a whole. Decisive was the influence of his method, at once both value-free in analysis and interpretive in the formulation of social facts, looking for objective patterns but taking the subjective perspective of social actors as their foundation.

As teacher, he considered it is duty to scientifically unveil even "inconvenient" or discomforting facts, and he inveighed against such corruptions as "statesmanlike" compromises between different scientific findings (Weber 1958c, p. 147; see also *"Gutachten zur Werturteilsdiskussion im Ausschuss des Vereins fuer Sozialpolitik,"* in Baumgarten 1964, pp. 102–139). He nevertheless, and very likely because of his devotion to saying what had to be said, achieved the prophetic: for example, analysis of socialism as eventuating in a thoroughly bureaucratized state.

As a colleague, while prizing civility, he cast a surgically incisive light on fellow faculty, as in this question directed at aspiring academics: "Do you in all conscience believe that you can stand seeing mediocrity after mediocrity, year after year, climb beyond you, without becoming embittered and without coming to grief?" (Weber 1958c, p. 134) A merciless critic of self-interested and short-sighted faculty politics, he was always ready to take combative ethical positions, so against academic anti-Semitism: If you are a Jew seeking to enter a German academic career, *"lasciati ogni speranza."* Colleagues, now long sunk into oblivion, responded in kind though from a less than ethical position, excluding the naturally gregarious Weber from a World War I discussion group as too passionate a pessimist who would dominate (Weber 1958c, p. 134; Baumgarten 1964, pp. 610-612, 627).

As political observer and participant in deliberations preceding and following the 1918 collapse of Germany, he served as political counselor to official committees ranging from one considering a middle-European common market to another writing the new German Constitution, and was considered for minister of the interior. Unpolitick political stances were his forte, especially when his sense of national obligation and the World War I crises demanded it: against a policy of annexations, against unlimited submarine warfare, predictive of an East-West split between the United States and the Soviet Union, since 1917 for the abdication of the Kaiser, distinction between causes of the war (Russian mobilization, etc.) and German guilt: facileness and secrecy of authoritarian German politics, ultimately the impossibility of determining guilt without reference to responsibility toward the future (Baumgarten 1968, pp. xxiv–xxv).

The achievement of all this, he himself was aware (Weber's letter regarding a Freudian diagnosis of Weber's health in Baumgarten 1968, pp. 644–648), came at the cost of, and possibly on the basis of, severe disruptions of his health, both psychologically and physically, with repeated interruptions of his teaching activity. The philosopher Karl Jaspers said, "In his wide soul reverberated the fate of his times." Eventually, he found an early death—medically, of pneumonia (Baumgarten 1964; 1968, p. xii). It is impossible not to see in Weber a tragic figure precisely because his insight was unable to turn aside the tragedy of his country.

Intellectual History

The world reception has to a large degree seen Weber as a positivist scientist (partly true), through a recasting of his action concept by Talcott Parsons in the United States as a functionalist (which he was not), and with increasing recognition as an interpretivist, and in a sense, phenomenologist. The last is confirmed in American public administration through his influence on the creation of an interpretivist school (e.g., Harmon 1981; Hummel 1977, 1982, 1987, 1994) via the integration of Husserlian phenomenology and Weberian sociology by Alfred Schutz (1967).

His normative contributions have been almost totally ignored, although Weberians might question how the single most effective critic of the rise of the bureaucratic state could at the same time be considered merely a positivist, or how the person who described himself as religiously tone-deaf could write three volumes on the world's religions, co-founding the sociology of religion.

The understanding of Weber as a positivist may be attributed to a neglect of Weber's intellectual history and of his most crucial methodological writings (e.g., the critical essays contained in *Wissenschaftslehre*, 1968), with the result

that he is generally understood as epistemologically a neo-Kantian. But neo-Kantianism argues that all experience is subject to being placed into universal categories, giving positivist empiricism the justification for giving reality the choice of fitting, or not, into preconceived propositions or hypotheses. Weber, however, accomplished a unique amplification and correction of this attitude: Although the rules of logic must be applied in analysis, researchers must first find the cultural categories (values) by reference to which social actors themselves give meaning to their action (*Wertbeziehung*, or reference to values producing "meaning adequacy"); only then can any researcher treat these actions empirically (attribution of "causal adequacy") as meaningful objects. Thus, in *Ancient Judaism* (1952 [originally, 1917–1919]), prophetic events are interpreted according to the participants' own understanding of a breach in the core value of obeying God's law. This amplification of Kant, as he was then understood, could not come from the neo-Kantians; hence, whence?

Weber's antecedents and affiliations reveal a link with phenomenologists' argument that matters or states of affairs must be understood in their own terms. Specifically, Weber read and cited in one of his early methodological critiques the *Logical Investigations* of the phenomenologist Edmund Husserl ("*Roscher und Knies und die logischen Probleme der historischen Nationaloekonomie*," in *Wissenschaftslehre* 1968, pp. 77, 102, 109, 110ff).

Already in his father's house in Berlin, Weber had seen his mother play hostess to major intellectuals of his time: Theodor Mommsen, Levin Goldschmidt, Heinrich von Treitschke (under all of whom he later studied at Heidelberg [1884–1885]), Wilhelm Dilthey, and others (Baumgarten 1964, p. 621). He was therefore well acquainted with such issues as historical interpretation, concluding early on that one did not have to become Caesar to understand Caesar. Later, Weber's Heidelberg house, in 1907 for example, was the scene of a busy traffic of intellectuals of diverse orientations, including Emil Lask (a phenomenologist), the musician Mina Tobler, Friedrich Gundolf, the existential philosopher Karl Jaspers and his wife Gertrud, Werner Sombart, Robert Michels, Georg Simmel, Gertrud Baeumer, Paul Honigsheim and Karl Lowenstein (Baumgarten 1964, p. 700); at other times, Wilhelm Windelband, Georg Lukacz, Ernst Troeltsch, and, of course, his brother, Alfred (Gerth and Mills in Weber 1958c, p. 21.) Although the influence of the neo-Kantian Heinrich Rickert at Freiburg when Weber assumed his first full teaching position led to the labeling of Weber as a neo-Kantian, the association with Jaspers and Lask (the former cited on the first page of *Economy and Society*, the latter in "Roscher und Knies," 1968a, p. 16) suggests the kind of openness toward phenomenology that is reflected in Weber's amplification of the empirical method when it comes to the determination of meaning. The phenomenologist Martin Heidegger contributed to this possibility in citing Lask—*The Logic of*

Philosophy and the Doctrine of Categories: A Study of Logical Form (1911) and *The Doctrine Judgment* (1912)—as a key transitional figure leading from Edmund Husserl's *Logical Investigations* to Lask's own teacher and Weber's colleague, Rickert. Admittedly, Rickert had been Weber's colleague as early as 1895 whereas Heidegger heard Rickert praise Lask's influence in lectures following Lask's death in 1915 (Baumgarten 1968, p. 591; Heidegger in Kaufman 1975, pp. 235–236.) Yet, Weber himself cited a debt to "Husserl und Lask" in his formulation of the category of objective possibility in "On Some Categories of Interpretive Sociology" (*Wissenschaftslehre* 1968b, p. 427, fn. 1).

At issue is whether Weber gives us a mainstream positivist science in which researchers are instructed to test reality according to its fit into patterns resembling Kantian logical categories or a cultural science (Weber, *Kulturwissenschaft*) that begins with social actors' self-interpretation according to their culture's own value categories. In the latter case, Weber's concept of "*Verstehen*" (interpretive understanding) evokes the phenomenological imperative that we ought to read events in their own terms, not in ours (value neutrality).

The Structure of Politics

In politics, Max Weber established a typology of authority (domination) and its legitimation.

The modern state itself is defined as that legislatively established yet compulsory organization that holds the monopoly of legitimate physical force in a given territory (1968a, p. 54, 56). This leaves to the church (hierocracy) the monopoly of "psychological" coercion through control over salvationist goods (pp. 54, 56, 1163–1164). Mixtures are both traced and anticipated.

The definition of politics by far precedes Harold Lasswell's and midcentury political science's: Politics is social action oriented toward influencing governing, especially over appropriation, expropriation, redistribution, or allocation of its powers (1968, p. 54).

Having surveyed types of political organization and legitimation both from the beginning of Western history and universally across cultures (*The Protestant Ethic and the Spirit of Capitalism, The Religion of India, The Religion of China, Ancient Judaism*), Weber offered three major forms of political authority: charismatic, traditional, and legal-rational. He did not consider these to be exclusive, nor did he expect the typology of pure types (ideal-types) would stand up to historical change. Indeed, he expected that his concepts in general would be superseded by his successors; this expectation has been disappointed with the result that *fin de siècle* social science today works with concepts nearly a hundred years old.

Basing himself on a theory of social action that interpreted the action of human beings in terms of their own mutual self-understanding, Weber approached the problem of types of authority by asking this question: What social orientations by people toward each other contribute to the probability that commands structured in distinct ways might be obeyed?

"Chance" or probability plays a key role in laying down the patterns answering this question. An objective pattern does not have a free-standing existence apart from the likely interpretation of it by people constituting and construing the pattern. To state, for example, that people are under charismatic authority is to assert only the probability, never the certainty, that they will act according to the pattern, which defines the "ideal-type" of charismatic behavior.

The subjective origins of objective patterns of authority—not accidently, as a believer in force, does he use the term domination *(Herrschaft)*—he found in people's motives. These are to be understood not psychologically but in terms of value-orientation as the pursuit of types of values, that is, interests. In turn established authority patterns continue to keep their value as long as people believe in them (legitimation). Of the two, he considered beliefs as grounds for legitimation to be the more decisive, concluding it was useful to classify the types of domination according to the kind of claim to legitimacy typically made by each (*Economy and Society*, 1968a, p. 213). Interest motives for compliance might range all the way from enthusiasm to simple habituation to the most purely rational calculation of advantage, yet belief in authority systems' claim that one of these was compelling was decisive (p. 212). This is a consequence of Weber's understanding that what motivates people most of all is the search for meaning; in his essay on religion, it is theodicy, the sense that God or the highest values have a way of manifesting themselves in the world.

Legitimation of a system of authority exists when those obeying believe they must do so because the powerful make claims that are experienced as just and proper. Legitimacy of a system of domination could be treated sociologically "only as the probability that to a relevant degree the appropriate attitudes will exist, and the corresponding practical conduct ensues" (p. 214).

Thus, legal-rational authority is defined as resting on belief, on the part of those obeying, in the legality of enacted rules and in the right of those elevated to authority to issue commands under such rules; there is the additional assumption that, if required, reasons—either instrumental or ideal—could be given for the rules.

Traditional authority rests on the grounds of an established belief in the sanctity of immemorial traditions and the legitimacy of those exercising authority under them.

Charismatic authority rises on belief in the exceptional sanctity, heroism, or exemplary character of an individual person and in the normative patterns or order supposed to be revealed or ordained by him or her (*Economy and Society*, 1968a, p. 215).

The three ideal-types are not to be read as mutually exclusive categories but as historically overlapping so that, for example, some charismatic characteristics could show themselves toward the end of the collapse of legal-rationalism. Mixed types are eminently possible, as Weber himself suggested in advocating an institutional balance between a president (charisma) and a parliament (legal-rationalism).

Methodologically, the whole point of the distinguishing of these and other types of authority lies in their definition in terms of the social orientations of the actors involved: what meaning they see in each other's stance and what expectations therefore guide them into action. Since this central point of Weber's interpretive (*verstehende*) sociology has been by and large suppressed by rationalist American interpreters like Parsons and by those who see him as a founder of social-scientific empiricism, the possibility of ongoingly constructing new models of authority out of the changing experience of people has been largely lost. Yet, Weber himself spoke of other types, specifically citing hereditary charisma, the charisma of office, patriarchy, bureaucracy itself, the authority of status groups (*Economy and Society*, 1968a, p. 216) and describing the type of rule in the history of the city as "non-legitimate domination." This phrase serves as the usually neglected subtitle of his lengthy essay on *The City* with its exemplary probing into how people's interests brought about illegitimate rulership in the ancient *tyrannis* and the medieval *signoria* even in the exceptional absence of legitimating belief (*Economy and Society*, 1968, p. 1212–1372).

The Structure of Modern Organization (Bureaucracy)

Max Weber is best known both in business administration and public administration by his description of the ideal-typical modern organization. Yet, this contribution would have to be considered of moderate weight in the context of his entire *opus*. Weber personally and professionally had only a derivative interest and, as in his treatment of the stock market (*Die Boerse*), practical interest in organizational structures. The issue of such structure arose only because of the larger economic, cultural, and ultimately religious-civilizational question he asked in his survey of the major world religions (*Gesammelte Schriften zur Religionssoziologie* 1920, 1921): Why did the West, and only the West, become the source of cultural-historical influences "of universal importance and validity?" (prefatory remarks to vol. I, p. 1). Among these influences he counted science, highly rationalized art, the state, and, decisive for his sociological explorations of economics, capitalism (pp. 1–4ff). Only in this context of an attempt at a "universal history" (pp. 1, 10) does Weber arrive at his final focus: the reasons for the development in the West, and only in the West, of "a bourgeois (*buergerlich*) industrial capitalism with its ratio-

nal organization of free labor" (p. 10). This question leads him to search for an "occidental religious economic ethic" (vol. I: *The Protestant Ethic and the Spirit of Capitalism*) and into the exploration of the structure of bureaucracy and in the context of its purpose in the development of the modern Western economy (the essay on "Bureaucracy" in *Economy and Society*, 1968a).

Again the essay on bureaucracy is not Weber's only contribution to the subject of administration, although it may be said that his other contributions–"Patriarchalism and Patrimonialism" and "Feudalism, Staendestaat [state of estates], and Patrimonialism"–are today largely ignored, along with "Political and Hierocratic Domination" (all in *Economy and Society* 1968a).

For the most part, Weber's characterization of the structure of modern organization–bureaucracy, whether in the private or public sectors–is today recited ritualistically as a catechism. He is also facilely described in textbooks as advocating an idealized type by writers unable to distinguish a *desideratum* from Weber's methodologically crucial concept of the descriptive typification of social-orientation patterns that he called an "ideal-type" or "pure type." The concept of ideal-type had enabled Weber to point both backward to the subjective origins of a pattern of social orientations in actors themselves and forward to the resulting possibility of treating the result as an objective pattern: to be interpretive and empirical at the same time.

In this economic history, Weber is as always consistent in his attempt to describe institutions in terms of the social orientations of their members. He asks what market conditions could satisfy the needs of the early modern entrepreneurs for strict calculations of costs and profits that could lead to the decisions based on the thorough calculation of risk so definitive of reinvestment capitalism. He found the answer in their expectations of an even and predictable playing field. This was just what was lacking in countries like England, in which medieval barons divided the markets by imposing unpredictable burdens on them. As Thomas Hobbes already saw, such conditions could be remedied only by a powerful state bureaucracy, first of the king's justice and later of regulatory and administrative power.

The entire purpose of the internal structure of modern bureaucracy is defined by the role it plays in the economic markets, thus justifying even and precisely bureaucracy's rigidities: Without them the rising entrepreneurial and merchant classes of early modernity could not rely on the persistence of an institution that would make the economic playing field predictable. Weber's demonstration of the dependence of inner structure on outer function leaves open the further development of administrative structures as environmental needs change; thus, Weber's is not the final definition of the purely rational organization, and the rationality of an organization can be expected to change as

there is a change in the external values that a specific type of rationalism supports.

Weber intended his description of the modern organization to be read and understood in the context of the economics and politics within which it arose, that is in the context of his *General Economic History* (1981) and against the background of the medieval economic context presented in the descriptions of patriarchalism and patrimonialism cited previously. Today the essay "Bureaucracy" is usually read outside such contexts and in abbreviated form that not only omits its own treatment of the transition from the medieval to the modern economy but shrouds the question, Under what conditions can further developments in state administrative organization occur?

The Motivations of Capital Enterprise

Probably the most influential, not least because of Parsons's fitting English translation, substantive work of Max Weber has been his *The Protestant Ethic and the Spirit of Capitalism* (1930). Tracing late modernity's value motivations (interests) to a duty ethic (Luther) and an achievement ethic (Calvin) developed in the rise of Protestantism, Max Weber inspired a whole literature of economic development. So the sociologist Robert Bellah, in his *Tokugawa Religion* (1957) found a parallel to the Western Protestant ethic in Japan, thus anticipating the rise of the Japanese post–World War II economy. David McClelland, in his *The Achieving Society* (1961), empirically tested a version of Weber's achievement ethic cast in sociopsychological terms and found early childhood inculcation of achievement-oriented concepts leading to later business activity. McClelland's concepts of need for achievement, need for power, and need for affiliation remain classic explanations for motivation in the field of organizational behavior.

Methodology

In one form or another, as already discussed earlier, in the intellectual history, scholars and students of public administration today are using Max Weber's method. The reception of this method, unified as it might have been with Weber himself, has, however, been split between treating Weber as the first socioscientific empiricist of note ("The Condition of Farm Workers in the East-Elbian Germany," 1892), the dominant interpretation, and treating Weber as the founder of the interpretive method. Weber's own comments on this issue should have been decisive except for the dominance exercised by empirical-scientific thinking in the American academy. Weber himself said this of the relation between empirical statistics and the meaning of what is statistically aggregated:

> We [people in general] demand interpretation as to the meaning *(Sinn)* of action. Where this "meaning"–we for now leave uninvestigated what problems this concept

hides within it–can be in the individual case determined as immediately evident, there it is all the same to us whether a "rule" of what is happening allows itself to be *formulated*, which circumscribes the individual case. And, on the other hand, the formulation of such a rule, even if it could bear the character of strict lawfulness, could never lead to this: that the assignment of "meaningful" interpretation *(Deutung)* could be *replaced* by reference to it [the rule] ("Roscher und Knies" in *Wissenschaftslehre* 1924, p. 69–70).

Subjectively valid and objectively valid meanings are sharply distinguished both in this essay and in Weber's great work on theory, *Wirtschaft und Gesellschaft* (*Economy and Society* 1968a, e.g., vol. 1, p. 4).

Unexplored Contributions

Little known or unexplored in Max Weber's reception in English-language translation, among his contributions to the literature of public administration and its political environment, are his theory of revolution; his refutation of the psycho-physiological approach to the study of work (ergonomics) and, by implication, of scientific management; a coherent compilation of his individual essays and lectures toward a sociology of the state; and most of his political writings (in order in, implicitly, *Ancient Judaism*, "Zur Psycho-Physiologie der industriellen Arbeit," *Staatssoziologie*, and *Politische Schriften*).

Max Weber himself did not spell out an explicit theory of revolution, although he refers to it as forthcoming repeatedly in *Economy and Society* (1968a [1922]). Yet, an implicit theory is highly developed as is shown by the way he applies it in *Ancient Judaism* (1952). There the social, cultural, economic, and political origins of pre-Exile Judaic prophecy are explained in terms of the growing sense of meaninglessness of these realms–God, the center of meaning, has withdrawn from the world. Revolution is caused by a growing sense of meaninglessness–for which Weber on occasion uses the term *anomia*, paralleling the concept of a cofounder of modern sociology, Emile Durkheim's concept of *anomie*.

The refutation of ergonomics is contained in an untranslated methodological essay on the psycho-physiology of industrial labor ("Zur Psycho-Physik der industriellen Arbeit," 1908–1909), contained in *Gesammelte Aufsaetze zur Soziologie und Sozialpolitik* (Collected Essays in Sociology and Social Policy, 1924). There, anticipating expectancy theory, Weber critiques the existing literature, much of it French, on ergonomics and its methodology from his viewpoint that performance is as much due to how workers value a task as it is to so-called physiological and psychological conditions. The essay, if read, could have vitiated the need for the American invention of entire management schools such as those of human relations and organizational humanism, correcting scientific management. Typical, on the constructive side, is Weber's question as to "which positions at work count for them [workers] as relatively more desirable and why" (p. 53; see also, "'Energetic' Culture Theories" ["Energetische Kulturtheorien"] in *Wissenschaftslehre*, pp. 400–426).

A *Sociology of the State* (as yet untranslated from the German title *Staatssoziologie*, 2d ed., 1966, though available in large fragments in *Economy and Society* and other writings) was compiled according to Weber's own plans from published writings and lectures by Johannes Winckelmann, presenting a coherent taxonomy and theory of the modern state.

The political writings are collected in *Gesammelte Politische Schriften* (2d ed., 1958). Theodor Heuss wrote in his introduction that these essays address Weber's time even when they seem to offer the beginnings of a systematic theory and where, as in the noted essay "Politics as a Vocation," propositions reach far beyond their original context.

Finally there is a Weber literature (see Constants Seyfarth and Gert Schmidt, *Max Weber Bibliographie: Eine Dokumentation der Sekundaerliteratur,* Stuttgart: Ferdinand Enke Verlag, 1977), most of it supportive and developmental of his original achievement but some of it critical.

Reception Abroad

In the United States, long delays in the translation from the German caused a staggered reception, first in law and economics, later in history as well as economics and sociology through the *General Economic History* in 1927 and the *Protestant Ethic* in 1930, and later yet the *magnum opus Economy and Society*, not being fully available until 1968 for interpretive sociology. Major methodological essays remain untranslated.

In Germany itself, much of Weber's major work, which according to his biographer Eduard Baumgarten he had put into a drawer, was published after his death under the supervision of his wife, Marianne. The destruction of the German social sciences under the Hitler regime saw the exile of leading Weberians like Theodor Adorno and the recovery of Weberian scholarship led after the war by, among others, Juergen Habermas. Establishment of the Max Weber Archive at the University of Munich saw, under Johannes Winckelmann, to the wide distribution of Weber's ideas after the war. Italy saw the publication of Weber's dissertation as *La storia agraria romana* as early as 1907, but the *Protestant Ethic* not until 1945, *Il metodo delle scienze storico-sociali* in 1958, and *Economy and Society* in 1961. The Spanish-language reception began with the essay *La decadencia de la cultura antigua* in 1926, the general economic history as *Historia economica general* not until 1956, and *Economia y sociedad* in 1944 in Mexico and 1964 in Mexico and Buenos Aires. The *Protestant Ethic* did not see translation until 1955 in Madrid. French translations ap-

peared as *Le savant et la politique* in 1959, *The Protestant Ethic* in 1967, the *Wissenschaftslehre* as *Essais sur la theorie de la science* in 1965, followed by *Economy and Society*. Japanese translations include "Science as a Vocation" in 1936, *The Protestant Ethic*, in 1938, "Basic Concepts of Sociology" in 1953, and *Wirtschaftsgeschichte* in 1954 and 1955 (Reception publication data from Max Weber 1968c).

In the face of a Latin saying to which he himself referred—No one is obliged to attempt the impossible—it is definitive of Max Weber to have described his intentions of constituting a "universal history." This would explain to inhabitants of the modern West how they came to be what they had become and help him prophesy what might be their unenviable fate. Out of a profound and driving sense of obligation to his fellow human beings, he ended up attempting a universal social science and a universal methodology that could apply to all human beings everywhere and yet be true to their own way of seeing and living their world.

RALPH P. HUMMEL

BIBLIOGRAPHY

Baumgarten, Eduard, 1968. *"Einleitung"* (Introduction) to Max Weber, *Soziologie, Weltgeschichtliche Analysen, Politik,* 4th ed., ed. Johannes Winckelmann. Stuttgart: Alfred Kroener.

——, 1964. *Max Weber: Werk und Person.* Tuebingen: J. C. B. Mohr.

Bellah, Robert N., 1957. *Tokugawa Religion: The Values of Pre-Industrial Japan.* Glencoe, IL: Free Press.

Harmon, Michael D., 1981. *Action Theory for Public Administration.* New York: Longman.

Hummel, Ralph P., 1977, 1982, 1987, 1994. *The Bureaucratic Experience.* 4 editions. New York: St. Martin's.

Kaufman, Walter A., 1975. *Existentialism from Dostoevsky to Sartre.* New York: New American Library, 1975.

McClelland, David C., 1961. *The Achieving Society.* Princeton, N.J.: Van Nostrand.

Mommsen, Wolfgang, 1959. *Max Weber und die deutsche Politik 1890–1920.* Tuebingen: J. C. B. Mohr [Paul Siebeck].

Parsons, Talcott, 1937. *The Structure of Social Action: A Study in Social Theory with Special Reference to a Group of Recent European Writers.* New York and London: McGraw-Hill Book Company, Inc.

Parsons, Talcott, Edward Shils, Kaspar D. Naegele, Jesse R. Pitts, eds., 1961. *Theories of Society.* Glencoe, IL: Free Press.

Roth, Guenther, 1965. "Political Critiques of Max Weber." *American Sociological Review,* vol. 30 (April: 213–223).

Schutz, Alfred, 1967. *Collected Papers,* vol. 1, *The Problem of Social Reality.* The Hague: Martinus Nijhoff.

Weber, Max, 1892. *"Die Verhaeltnisse der Landarbeiter im ostelbischen Deutschland"* [The Conditions of Farm Workers in the East-Elbian Germany], *Schriften des Vereins fuer Sozialpolitik,* vol. 55. In *Gesammelte Aufsaetze zur Soziologie und Socialpolitik* [Collected Essays in Sociology and Social Policy]. Tuebingen: J. C. B. Mohr (Paul Siebeck), 1924.

——, 1920. "Vorbemerkung" [Preface] to *Gesammelte Aufsaetze zur Religionssoziologie* [Collected Essays in the Sociology of Religion], 1920, 1921, vols. 1–3. Tuebingen: J. C. B. Mohr, 1–16.

———, 1920–1921. *Gesammelte Aufsaetze zur Religionssoziologie* [Collected Essays in the Sociology of Religion], vols. 1–3. Tuebingen: J. C. B. Mohr.

———, 1923 [1958]. *Wirtschaftsgeschichte–Abriss der universalen Sozial- und Wirtschaftsgeschichte.* Aus den nachgelassenen Vorlesungen, herausgegeben von S. Hellmann and M. Palyi, ed. Johs. F. Winckelmann [*General Economic History*, trans. F. Knight. London and New York: Greenberg, 1927; reprinted, Glencoe, II: Free Press, 1950].

———, 1924a [1894]. "*Die Boerse (1894)*" [The Stock Market]. In *Gesammelte Aufsaetze zur Soziologie und Socialpolitik* [Collected Essays in Sociology and Social Policy]. Tuebingen: J. C. B. Mohr, 256–322 [Originally: Goettinger Bibliothek, ed. Fr. Naumann, Vol. 1. 17–48].

———, 1924b [1903, 1905, 1906]. "*Roscher und Knies und die logischen Probleme der historischen Nationaloekonomie*" [Roscher and Knies and the Logical Problems of Historical National Economics]. In *Gesammelte Aufsaetze zur Wissenschaftslehre,* originally 1922, 3d ed., 1968, 1–145. Tuebingen: J. C. B. Mohr [Originally: *Schmollers Jahrbuch fuer Gesetzgebung, Verwaltung und Volkswirtschaft,* vols. 27 (1903): 1181–1221, 29 (1905): 1323–1384, 30 (1906): 81–120].

———, 1924c [1908–1909]. "*Zur Psychophysik der industriellen Arbeit (1908–09)*" [On the psycho-physiology of industrial labor]. In *Gesammelte Aufsaetze zur Soziologie und Sozialpolitik* [Collected Essays in Sociology and Social Policy], ed. Marianne Weber. Tuebingen: J. C. B. Mohr (Paul Siebeck), 61–255 [Originally in *Archiv fuer Sozialwissenschaft und Sozialpolitik,* vol. 27 (1908) and vol. 28 (1909)].

———, 1930 (1952). *The Protestant Ethic and the Spirit of Capitalism.* (including "The Protestant Sects and the Spirit of Capitalism"), trans. Talcott Parsons. London: Allen & Irwin, 1930; New York: Scribner, 1952 [originally, *Die Protestantische Ethik und der Geist des Kapitalismus*]. In *Gesammelte Aufsaetze zur Religionssoziologie,* 1920. Tuebingen: J.C.B. Mohr.

———, 1951. *The Religion of China: Confucianism and Taoism,* ed. and trans. Hans H. Gerth. Glencoe, IL: Free Press.

———, 1952 [1921; 1917–1919] *Ancient Judaism,* trs. and eds. Hans H. Gerth and Don Martindale. New York: Free Press [originally in *Archiv fuer Sozialwissenschaft und Sozialforschung,* 1917–1919; later collected in *Gesammelte Aufsaetze zur Religionssoziologie,* vol. 3 Tuebingen: J. C. B. Mohr, 1921].

———, 1958a. *Gesammelte Politische Schriften,* 2d ed. Preface by Theodor Heuss. Tuebingen: J. C. B. Mohr.

———, 1958b. *The Religion of India: The Sociology of Hinduism and Buddhism,* trs. Hans H. Gerth and Don Martindale. Glencoe, IL: Free Press.

———, 1958c [1919]. "Science as a Vocation." In H. H. Gerth and C. Wright Mills, eds. and trs. *From Max Weber: Essays in Sociology* New York: Oxford University Press–Galaxy Books, 129–156 [originally, "Wissenschaft als Beruf." Berlin: Duncker & Humblot].

———, 1966. *Staatssoziologie: Soziologie zur modernen Staatsanstalt und der modernen politischen Parteien und Parlamente,* 2d, expanded edition. Ed. Johannes Winckelmann. Berlin: Duncker & Humblot [1st ed., 1956].

———, 1968a [1922]. *Economy and Society: An Outline of Interpretive Sociology,* eds. Guenther Roth and Claus Wittich; trs. Ephraim Fischoff, Hans Gerth, A. M. Henderson, Ferdinand Kolegar, C. Wright Mills, Talcott Parsons, Max Rheinstein, Guenther Roth, Edward Shils, Claus Wittich. New York: Bedminister Press.

———, 1968b [1922]. [*Wissenschaftslehre.*] *Gesammelte Aufsaetze zur Wissenschaftslehre,* ed. Johannes Winckelmann. Tuebingen: J. C. B. Mohr.

———, 1968c. *Soziologie, Weltgeschichtliche Analysen, Politik,* ed. Johannes Winckelmann. Stuttgart: Alfred Kroener.

———, 1981 [1923]. *General Economic History.* New Brunswick, NJ: Transaction Books.

WELLNESS PROGRAMS.

Formal organizational efforts on the part of employers to maintain and enhance the mental and physical health of their employees.

Health and Health Care

"Wellness is a process of being aware of and of altering behavior toward a more successful physical, mental, emotional, psychological, occupational, and spiritual existence" (Kizer 1987). The World Health Organization has defined good health as a positive balance in all four dimensions of health: physical, mental, spiritual, and social. Good health is not merely the absence of disease or infirmity, rather it is an interlocking system of well-being wherein each dimension is dependent on the other three. Using this definition, it is logical that this "good health" may be measured in levels of "wellness." The iceberg analogy of Ryan and Travis (1991) places visible signs of health on the tip of the health system iceberg while below the surface are the three layers of lifestyle behaviors, psychological properties, and philosophical transpersonal areas. Wellness implies exploring these three undersurface areas in an effort to impact the above surface area. It is based on the dual concepts of self-care and self-responsibility (Teague 1987).

Spiraling health care costs began shocking the corporate world in the 1980s. In 1982, almost 11 percent of the gross national product (GNP) was spent on health care with the expectation that it would reach 20 percent by the year 2000 if the rate of inflation did not abate. Corporations paid more than one-third of the almost US$300 billion price tag (Polakoff 1985). Several factors have contributed to the rapid rise of health care costs. The first is inflation; in 1982 the health care services component of the Consumer Price Index (CPI) rose twice as fast as the rest of the index. Advances in medical technology have costly price tags. Many of these costly treatments are being used to help our rapidly growing aging population live longer. A factor with direct impact on the industrial sector is the financing and purchasing of health care services. Consumers pay for only one-third of personal health care expenses directly; the other two-thirds are financed by a combination of third parties: private health insurers, government agencies, philanthropic organizations and industry (Chenoweth 1987). In addition, an increased propensity for litagation and increasingly larger settlements has caused the cost of medical malpractice insurance to skyrocket.

The most noteworthy finding from several major studies of populationwide health risk factors is that people can be their own worst enemies when it comes to their health (Allegrante 1984). The risk factors involved with how much we eat, drink, smoke, exercise, and manage stress are defined as controllable. These risk factors have a great deal to do with whether we achieve our maximum potential life expectancy and productivity. The average number of lost work days in 1985 for companies of 100 employees was 39 and a 1985 Harris poll estimated that 550 million workdays are lost each year due to illness, with headaches and back pain being the most heavy contributors. The U.S. Center for Disease Control has estimated that over 50 percent of all deaths under age 65 are attributable to unhealthy lifestyle choices (Sloan et. al. 1987).

Wellness Programs and Health Promotion

Wellness programs have been established in a variety of settings including the workplace, senior citizen centers, long-term care facilities, colleges and universities, and hospitals. Each program is different depending on which population is being served, what needs have been identified, and what goals have been established. The result is that efforts that in many cases began as single goal wellness programs, have developed into health promotion/disease prevention models that include three components: wellness, prevention, and holistic health care (Teague 1987).

Health promotion is any combination of health education and related organizational, political, and economic interventions that will improve or protect health. It may be defined as the science and art of helping people change their lifestyles in an effort to move toward their optimum health status (Teague 1987). Health promotion is a process of fostering awareness, influencing attitudes and identifying alternatives so that individuals can make informed choices and change their behavior in order to achieve an optimum level of physical and mental health. Much of the publicity around health promotion programs has been centered around employer-funded worksite programs. The worksite offers several advantages as a location for health promotion interventions. It has access to large numbers of people, provides social support networks to assist employees in improving their lifestyles, and offers the opportunity to track an individual's health behavior and to compare it with group norms and program objectives to evaluate success. By bringing the intervention to the employees and their family members, rather than simply providing encouragement, the organization is removing a major barrier to nonparticipation.

Companies have realized that, like their capital-intensive machinery, their employees are another capital-intensive resource and must be the target of preventive maintenance rather than after-the-breakdown repairs. As an outgrowth of the human relations organizational approach, human resource professionals have recognized that with a shrinking labor pool replacing "worn-out" employees is neither possible nor desirable. According to a survey by the U.S. Chamber of Commerce, in 1985 American companies were paying an average of US$2,560 per employee for health care, an increase of 100 percent from 1977. As a result, many organizations have decided that maintaining or improving a person's health may be the most cost-effective strategy available, and they have established worksite health promotion programs. Prior to the first health promotion activities, the traditional view of an employer's responsibility for employee health was to help employees when they were sick or injured (Jacobson et al. 1990). Studies have shown significant decreases in major medical and disability costs after implementation of a worksite fitness program. Other benefits can include improved morale, enhanced employee feelings of well-being, and reduced absenteeism rate (Elias and Murphy 1987).

In the early days of employee wellness programs, the focus of employee health was on physical examinations and treatment for sickness and injuries. These programs were often single in focus, usually targeting a single pathology, for example, high blood pressure. There were few guidelines, and early coordinators employed a hit-or-miss approach that was often based on their own or a top executive's personal interests. As these early programs showed some successes, educational materials were developed, information was shared, and guidelines were established. Wellness programs became worksite health promotion/disease prevention programs as their purpose expanded in response to growing organizational needs and interests. By 1985 66 percent of American worksites with 50 or more employees had some type of health promotion program in place. The most common activities in these programs were smoking cessation, health risk assessment, back care, stress management, exercise, off-the-job accident rehabilitation, nutrition, blood pressure control, and weight control (U.S. Department of Health and Human Services 1987).

Worksite Health Promotion/Disease Prevention programs benefit both employees and employers. For employees the benefits include increased accessibility to services, educational materials, improved coworker motivation, and better overall health. For employers, the benefits include decreased health care costs and turnover, improved employee morale and productivity, and increased employee loyalty (Jacobson et al. 1990).

In any health promotion program, it is important that physicians and other health service professionals play a major role in the establishment, implementation, and evaluation of the program. Their expertise is especially critical in the areas of needs identification, outcome evaluation, and program linkage with other organizational health-related efforts.

Components and Evaluation

A comprehensive worksite prevention program has three components: organizational health promotion, individual health promotion, and environmental modification. Richard Bellingham (1990) identified 12 essential steps in the creation and maintenance of an effective program:

- determine needs and interests, establish goals and budgets;
- involve people including providers and participants;
- select and train staff/providers;
- heighten interest and awareness with marketing and incentives;
- secure leadership commitment;
- introduce program to employees;
- offer health risk assessments;
- conduct wellness planning sessions;
- provide cost-effective, risk-reduction programs;
- create a vision of health-enhancing lifestyle possibilities;
- equip people with skills for ongoing support;
- create a healthy organization.

It is also critical that the organization's legal liability in the provision of these programs be examined at the onset to ensure that applicable standards and regulations are met.

When evaluating the effectiveness of any health promotion/disease prevention program there are three levels of evaluation that must be addressed:

1. *Process Evaluation:* measures the quality of the program and the extent to which it is implemented; this can be measured via self-surveys performed by the task force and employee satisfaction surveys;
2. *Impact Evaluation:* measures the extent to which the program has produced changes in awareness, knowledge, attitudes, beliefs, skills, intentions, and actual behaviors; this may be measured by the annual participant screenings;
3. *Outcome Evaluation:* measures the long-term effects of program participation, effects that translate into organizational benefits and improvements in the health status of the participants.

Quasi-experimental designs are more feasible than true experimental designs in an organizational setting because they do not require the random assignment of participants and nonparticipants. A Multiple Time Series Design is suitable for health promotion program evaluation because retrospective and prospective data are accessible, and observations can be made on a regularly scheduled basis. A group of nonparticipants can be designated as the control group to minimize any significant differences. The control group should be chosen so that it closely resembles the makeup of the experimental group.

PATRICE ALEXANDER

BIBLIOGRAPHY

Allegrante, John P., 1984. "Potential Uses and Misuses of Education in Health Promotion and Disease Prevention." *Teacher's College Record,* vol. 86: 359–373.

Bellingham, Richard, 1990. "Debunking the Myth of Individual Health Promotion." In Michael E. Scofield, ed., *Occupational Medicine: State of the Art Reviews,* vol. 5, no. 4 (October-December) Philadelphia, PA: Hanley & Belfus.

Chenoweth, David, 1987. *Planning Health Promotion at the Worksite.* Carmel, IN: Benchmark.

Elias, Walter S., and Robert J. Murphy, 1987. "The Case for Health Promotion Programs Containing Health Care Costs: A Review of the Literature." *American Journal of Occupational Therapy,* vol. 40 no. 11: 759–763.

Jacobson, Miriam I., Sharon L. Yenney, and Jay C. Bisgard, 1990. "An Organizational Perspective on Worksite Health Promotion." In Michael E. Scofield, ed., *Occupational Medicine: State of the Art Reviews,* vol. 5 no. 4 (October-December) Philadelphia, PA: Hanley & Belfus.

Kizer, William M., 1987. *The Healthy Workplace.* New York: John Wiley & Sons.

Polakoff, Phillip L., 1985., "Worksite Economical Settings for Preventive Health Care Programs." *Occupational Health and Safety* (June): 75–76.

Ryan, Regina Sara and John W. Travis, 1991. *Wellness: Small Change You Can Use to Make a Big Difference.* Berkeley, CA: Ten Speed Press.

Sloan, Richard P., Jessie C. Gruman, and John P. Allegrante, 1987. *Investing in Employee Health.* San Francisco, CA.: Jossey-Bass.

Teague, Michael L., 1987. *Health Promotion Programs: Achieving High-Level Wellness in the Later Years.* Indianapolis, IN: Benchmark.

US. Dept. of Health and Human Services, Office of Disease Prevention and Health Promotion, 1987. "National Survey of Worksite Health Promotion Activities." Washington, DC: U.S. Department of Health and Human Services.

WHISTLEBLOWER. "The disclosure by organizational members (former or current) of illegal, immoral, or illegitimate practices under the control of their employers, to persons or organizations that may be able to effect action" (Miceli and Near 1992). But several definitional issues remain: (1) Should the definition be expanded to include individuals who are not organizational members per se, but who are in an indirect employment relationship with the wrongdoer, such as employees of a firm doing contract work for a government agency who expose abuse within that agency? (2) Should the definition include action by individuals whose job requires that they report wrongdoing, such as auditors and inspectors general? (3) Must the disclosure be external to qualify as whistleblowing? (4) Should the term be limited to activity that is illegal or against public policy, or should it extend to breaches of codes of ethics and to behavior that is merely wasteful or otherwise incorrect? (5) Are individuals who directly benefit from exposing wrongdoing within working relationships accurately called "whistleblowers,"or should the term be reserved for those who act out of altruism? In practice, these definitional matters are addressed in the wide variety of federal and state statutes that seek to protect whistleblowing. However defined in technical terms, the fact that public policy seeks to protect whistleblowing at all is a relatively recent and remarkable development. Although much contemporary law considers whistleblowing to be a public virtue and seeks to encourage it, typical organizational cultures treat it as the sin of insubordination and attempt to stifle it. The tension between these two views is often manifested in statutes that seek to protect whistleblowers from reprisals but do not offer strong incentives to engage in whistleblowing. There are several categories of law pertaining to whistleblowers.

Federal Law Regarding Federal Employees

The federal Civil Service Reform Act of 1978 specifically sought to protect whistleblowing, which it defines substantively as disclosure of a violation of law, rule or regulation, mismanagement, gross waste of funds, abuse of authority, or substantial and specific danger to public health or safety. Since a very broad array of personnel activity is covered by law or administrative regulation, the scope of whistleblowing extends to illegal discrimination based on race, sex, national origin, age, handicap, marital status , or political affiliation; actions violating merit principles; coercion of political activity; nepotism; reprisals for appealing adverse actions; and other activity. The act placed enforcement powers in an Office of the Special Counsel (OSC), which was located within the Merit Systems Protection Board. The Whistleblower Protection Act of 1989, strengthened enforcement by making the OSC independent. Disclosure by federal employees may be internal and/or external to their organizations. External disclosure to the OSC triggers an investigation by that unit. These statutes seek to protect employees from reprisals if they reasonably believe their allegations of wrongdoing are true. In other words, an employee cannot legally be disciplined for making incorrect charges as long as he or she did not make them unreasonably, that is, with knowledge that they were false or indifference to their truth or falsity.

The Civil Service Reform Act and the Whistleblower Protection Act are based on the assumption that protection against reprisals is a key ingredient in making whistleblowing feasible. Employees who believe they have been subject to reprisals for whistleblowing can file complaints with the OSC, which can seek corrective action before the Merit Systems Protection Board (MSPB). At the OSC's initiative, federal officials can be disciplined for violations of the whistleblower protection law. If the OSC does not take the action to the MSPB, then the employee can pursue the matter in federal district court. Remedies for the employee include appropriate corrective action, costs, and attorneys' fees. Sanctions for the employer include dismissal or lesser discipline, up to five years debarment from federal employment, and fines of up to $1,000.

Other measures also seek to protect and facilitate whistleblowing by federal employees. The General Accounting Office has operated a fraud, waste, and abuse hotline, where employees and others can report misconduct. Federal inspectors general and their staffs have a specific legal duty to report wrongdoing within agencies to Congress.

Federal Contractors Under the False Claims Act

The False Claims Act of 1863, as revised in 1986, is intended to encourage whistleblowing by individuals who have knowledge of fraud or cheating against the government by federal contractors. The act seeks to protect whistleblowers from retaliation. However, unlike the acts covering federal employees, it also provides a financial incentive to disclose wrongdoing. The False Claims Act authorizes individuals to file *qui tam* actions and potentially to collect substantial sums from the company involved. *Qui tam* suites are actions brought by private individuals on behalf of the government as well. If the Department of Justice joins the action, the individual can collect up to 25 percent of the judgment; otherwise the individual is eligible for up to 30 percent. Suits can be filed within ten years of the alleged fraud and triple damages are potentially available. According to Terry Dworkin (1992), who relies on studies by the Justice Department, as much as 10 percent of the federal budget, or US$100 billion, is lost through fraud annually. Thus far, Dworkin noted the revised act seems to be working as the number of suits filed "increased twentyfold" between 1986 and 1989 (p. 247).

Other Federal Statutes

A number of federal laws specifically afford protection to individuals who report violations of their statutory provisions. Among these are laws pertaining to the environment, mining, labor relations, and equal employment opportunity. The whistleblower protections included very widely with regard to process, remedy for the employee, and sanction on the employer. For instance, violations of the Fair Labor Standards Act can potentially be punished by fines for up to US $10,000 and six months imprisonment, whereas violations of the Clean Air Act and the National Labor Relations Act require corrective action only.

State Laws

At least 34 states offer legal protection to some category of whistleblowers (Dworkin 1992, pp. 260–273). Every statute covers public employees; some cover employees working for government contractors; and others cover all employees. In terms of the substance of whistleblower allegations, all the statutes cover violations of law, but not necessarily every law. Thus, Louisiana's whistleblower protection extends only to those disclosing violations of federal, state, or local environmental laws or regulations. New York's protection for private employees pertains only to violations that involve substantial and specific dangers to the public's health or safety. In addition to violations of law, most public-sector substantive coverage extends to some form of maladministration–generally including mismanagement, gross waste or misuse of public fund, or abuse of authority. Colorado broadly protects disclosure by public employees of activities that are not in the "public interest" (Dworkin 1992, p. 261). By contrast, California, Delaware, Hawaii, Kansas, Michigan, Minnesota, New Hampshire, New Jersey, Rhode Island, and Texas protect public employees' whistleblowing only when it reports violations of law. Pennsylvania appears to be the only state that specifically extends whistleblower protection to disclosed breaches of ethical codes.

The substance of a whistleblower's charges is only one element that determines whether the disclosure is protected. The quality of the individual's belief in their truth or falsity is also important. Claims that are known by the whistleblower to be false are not protected. However, false charges are likely to be protected if they are made in good faith or with a reasonable belief that they are true. Pennsylvania, West Virginia, and Wisconsin may withhold protection from those seeking to gain personally by whistleblowing. From a practical perspective, of course, whistleblowers should make a reasonable effort to ascertain the truth of their charges; failure to do so will typically preclude protection under the various statutes.

The state statutes create an array of procedures for whistleblowers to follow in making their disclosures. Several require that the first effort to expose the wrongdoing be made internally within the employee's organization. Others allow disclosure directly to an external state agency, such as a personnel board, an auditor's office, or a law enforcement authority.

Remedies for protected employees who are harmed by their whistleblowing also vary among the states. Public employees will generally be eligible for reinstatement with backpay, benefits, and seniority as well as attorney's fees. In some states, they may receive punitive damages as well (Kentucky, Montana, New Jersey, Texas). South Carolina allows protected whistleblowers to keep 25 percent of the savings gained by disclosure, up to US$2,000 for one year (Dworkin 1992, p. 271).

Finally, the states differ with regard to the sanctions imposed on employers for actions they may take against whistleblowers, including efforts to prevent disclosure or public inquiry. Alaska allows fines of up to $10,000; Colorado notes the violation on the offender's personnel record. Other states provide for lesser fines and more severe personnel actions, including dismissal and, in Missouri, debarment from public employment for up to two years. Public employees who violate Oregon's whistleblower protection law potentially face a year in prison and debarment from the public service for five years.

Constitutional Protection

Public employees who engage in whistleblowing have also had clear constitutional protection since the U.S. Supreme Court's decision in *Pickering v. Board of Education* (1968). Under the current standard, "the determination of whether a public employer has properly discharged an employee for engaging in speech requires "a balance between the interests of the [employee] as a citizen, in commenting upon matters of public concern and the interests of the State, as an employer, in promoting the efficiency of the public services it performs through its employees" (*Rankin v. McPherson* 1986, p. 384). The Court has defined "public concern" so broadly as to include even expression of hope that if an assassination attempt is made on the president, it is successful. In *Waters v. Churchill* (1994), the Court held that the required balancing could be applied to what the public employer reasonably thought the employee remarked rather than only to what the employee actually said.

In practice, this constitutional standard gives public employees considerable protection in disclosing violations of law and specific and immediate dangers to the public's health or safety. However, unless of considerable interest to the community at large, disruptive speech or complaints about mismanagement and inefficiency may be overridden by the public employer's interest in maintaining efficiency (*Connick v. Meyers* 1983). The character of the employee's position also has a bearing on whether his or her remarks on matters of public concern are protected. Employees whose positions do not involve policymaking, confidential relationships, or public contact are likely to have wider latitude in expressing themselves.

There are several remedies for violations of public employees' constitutional right to speak out on matters of public concern. Most generally, in nonfederal jurisdictions, suits may be brought for money damages under the Civil Rights Act of 1871, now codified as 42 US Code §1983, against state employees in their personal capacities, local governments, and local employees. Remedies may also be available under state civil service regulation and whistle-blower laws (as discussed above). Federal remedies generally require actions before the MSPB.

Who Are the Whistleblowers and Why Do They Blow the Whistle?

Whistleblowing is an uncomfortable act that may expose an individual to ill treatment, emotional distress, physical threats, and substantial expenses. Despite the protective laws, whistleblowers are frequently viewed as "snitches." They often face ostracism by their employers and cowork-ers, dismissal, attacks on their credibility, probes of their personal lives, and dead-ended careers. Employers may be very reluctant to hire persons known to have blown the whistle elsewhere. Given the high personal price often paid for whistleblowing, who is inclined to do it and why?

After reviewing the limited number of studies available, Marcia Miceli and Janet Near (1992) reached the following tentative conclusions regarding the personality traits of whistleblowers. Whistleblowers are better able to recognize wrongdoing than others and have a higher level of moral judgment. They are also action oriented. There is reason, but not evidence, to suggest that whistleblowers also have higher levels of self-confidence or self-esteem than do oth-ers in their organizations. Approval is less important to them than to other employees. In terms of social character-istics, whistleblowers tend to be male, older, more senior, and better educated than other employees of the organiza-tion. Jobwise, whistleblowers do not appear to be disgrun-tled employees. They tend to be higher performers, better paid, and more satisfied than others. Socially, whistleblow-ers enjoy support from their families and friends.

Miceli and Near also offer some tentative findings re-garding the situational factors that promote whistleblow-ing. These include clear and direct evidence of wrong-doing, illegal as opposed to otherwise objectionable behavior, the ability to report through external channels, employment in a field office, organizational responsive-ness to whistleblowing, and participatory organizational cultures. By contrast, whistleblowing is less likely where wrongdoing is widely observed or when it threatens the organization's survival. It is not known whether providing cash incentives encourages whistleblowing. Surprisingly, threat of reprisal apparently has no general impact on whistleblowing.

Miceli and Near were unable to explain organizational responses to whistleblowing. Clearly, these vary dramati-cally, but it is not currently known why.

Conclusion

Whistleblowing and whistleblowers have become standard features of contemporary administrative life. Public policy protects and encourages whistleblowing, especially in the public sector and when it reveals illegality, mismanage-ment, gross waste, fraud, abuse, and/or specific dangers to the public's health or safety. There is naturally opposition to whistleblowers by those exposed in wrongdoing and by those who must respond to frivolous or potentially damag-ing false charges. Nevertheless, in developed and highly mechanized nations like the United States, ordinary indi-viduals are not always or easily able to judge the safety of the transportation, food, water, and other vital services and goods they use. Liability law may deter wrongdoing, but there are incomparable advantages to being forewarned that, say, a particular make of automobile is likely to ex-plode on impact, an elevator dangerously malfunctions, or that a type of airplane is unsafe in cold weather. School yard culture notwithstanding, there is every reason to expect that whistleblowers will increasingly be viewed as heroes.

DEBORAH D. GOLDMAN AND
DAVID H. ROSENBLOOM

BIBLIOGRAPHY

Miceli, Marcia, and Janet Near, 1992. *Blowing the Whistle: The Or-ganizational and Legal Implications for Companies and Employ-ees.* New York: Lexington Books.
Dworkin, Terry Morehead, 1992. "Legal Approaches to Whistle-Blowing." In Marcia Miceli and Janet Near, *Blowing the Whistle.* New York: Lexington Books, 232–279 .
Legal Cases:
Connick v. Meyers, 1983. 461 U.S. 138.
Pickering v. Board of Education, 1968. 391 U.S. 563.
Rankin v. McPherson, 1987. 483 U.S. 378.
Waters v. Churchill, 1994. 62 Law Week 4397.

WHITE, LEONARD D. (1891–1958).

The prolific University of Chicago scholar who wrote the first pub-lic administration text to receive wide usage (in 1926), was first editor-in-chief of *Public Administration Review,* was a member of the U.S. Civil Service Commission, and a member of a small group of men who played a significant role in the founding of public administration as an academic discipline.

On January 17, 1891, Leonard Dupee White was born in Acton, Massachusetts, to John Sidney and Bertha H. Dupee White. He completed his undergraduate work at Dartmouth College in 1914, worked for three years as an instructor in government at Clark University, and contin-ued to teach at Dartmouth for the 1918–1920 seasons. In 1920, he accepted his lifetime appointment to the Univer-sity of Chicago, where, in 1921, he completed his doctor of philosophy in political science. His dissertation was titled

"The Origin of Utility Commissions in Massachusetts." He married Una Lucille Holden in 1916. They had one daughter, Marcia (Mrs. M. Gerson Rosenthal, Jr.). He received honorary degrees from Dartmouth and Princeton Universities, in addition to numerous academic awards, principally for his series on the history of public administration, *The Federalists* (1948), *The Jeffersonians* (1951), *The Jacksonians* (1954), and *The Republican Era* (1958). (John M. Gaus, 1958, *Public Administration Review* [Summer] 231). At Chicago, he held the Ernest Dewitt Burton Distinguished Service Professorship until his retirement in 1956. At his death from cancer on February 23, 1958, he was emeritus professor. In addition to a brief analysis of his major works, this entry chronicles his life as a scholar and public servant.

For over four decades, White carved deeply into the largely untapped academic perspective that public administration, as Woodrow Wilson had implied, was worthy of a distinctive inquiry (1887). The prodigious White proved himself to the task and gave the fledgling discipline a much needed scholastic anchoring. He is best remembered for his seminal text *Introduction to the Study of Public Administration*, first published in 1926 and subject to three additional major revisions. Each revision incorporated the scholarship arising in the interims between editions. *Introduction* marks only a small portion of White's scholarship. This scholarship embraced not only his own unique involvement in the expanding inquiry, but also the debates of his day against the backdrop of the rapidly changing public administration responsibilities at the national, state, and metropolitan levels.

White's earliest academic contributions were in Illinois governance; for example "The Status of Scientific Research in Illinois" (1923) and "Evaluation of Financial Control of Research in State Governments". But he saw the need for a broader treatise on the burgeoning problems of his day: the search for "efficiency and economy" positioned against the state and municipal executive reorganization movements. This work lead naturally to *Introduction to the Study of Public Administration* (1926). In his first edition, White acknowledged his biases: Wilson's position that administration is a singular process whether it takes its form in the public or private sectors, that the study of administration begins with a study of management practices not the law, as had previously been the case, that administration is an art in need of a science, and that administration is to the heart of the problem of modern government.

Herbert Storing's critique of White's *Introduction* over its four editions underscores White's search for new principles (Storing 1965). While White never shifted dramatically from his thematic focus, he nonetheless expanded his inquiry into the issues raised in earlier editions and loosened his expectations for each of his thematic statements. White was most troubled by the proper seat of administrative power and the allocation of power among subordinates within agency. To this end, his life work involved researching personnel and management practices. He believed that the details of administration could be discovered and enumerated, but loosely acknowledged a reliance on the law, as had Frank Goodnow, to do this. Goodnow's principal works are the texts *Politics and Administration* (1900) and *The Principles of the Administrative Law of the United States* (1905). It was in the former that Goodnow delineated his famous dictum of a separation between politics and administrations. In the latter, Goodnow recommended an immersion in the law for standards of administrative practice.

In White's earliest work, he acknowledged a faith in the search for scientific principles, or Frederick Taylor's "one best way." White would cool on this approach, although not abandoning it entirely, by the fourth edition of *Introduction* (1955). By then he would find that the field was emerging, and subject to constant self-improvement. This view of administrative practice as a process denies White's earlier belief in the existence of "one best way." White appreciated later scholars such as Glenn Stahl, David Truman, Frederick Mosher, and their reliance on applied research. These scholars substantially altered White's model of administrative practice. White remained broadly flexible within his reading of the American administrative landscape, principally arising from his own deep personal involvement in the development of personnel models appropriate for large agencies.

Notwithstanding his early sympathies with Wilson and Goodnow, from the start of his important works, White regarded public administration as deeply involved in all aspects of governance. In his first edition of *Introduction* (1926), he noted that "an account of the relations of administration to the legislature and the courts will readily make clear that there is in fact no clear-cut differentiation in the kind of activity performed" (pp. 23–24). He would later solidify this view more boldly. By the fourth edition of *Introduction* (1955), he wrote, "it is now accepted that considerations of policy sweep down from the political overhead into the permanent career service, making it an agency for the refinement of policy as well as for its execution. . . . It follows that administration is inevitably bound up with policy, and through policy with politics" (pp. 6–7).

White began his intellectual life during World War I. It took him through the Great Depression of the 1930s and through World War II. He participated at center stage as a national American governance shifted from the mechanisms of fighting a global war to managing the daily lives of Americans through a plethora of public programs. White's work is best understood in the context of his own academic preparation and the turbulent age in which he lived. At Dartmouth, then at Chicago, political science embraced the historical study of governments, with the focus of these studies being the institutions of government and the notable leaders that affected them. Only at Columbia University, editorial home of Wilson's first foray into academic history, the *Political Science Quarterly,* and at the University of Wisconsin, where a unique alliance between the university and the state government was forged, was the academic community to appreciate the broader implications of governance from the administrative point of view. At the turn of the century, these perspectives had yet to take a serious foothold.

Early in his work, White began to appreciate the importance of discerning public administration as a distinctive field of inquiry. To manage this inquiry, he drew heavily from the beliefs of the Progressives that government could be used as a tool for effective change, and from the scientific management movement, which strove to achieve efficiency in administrative practice. White participated in the development of an administrative practice. He was active in Chicago affairs, served on committees outlining standards for police administration, and at the national level, completed work for the Hoover Commission. Beginning in 1934, for three years he sat on the U.S. Civil Service Commission as its minority member. From 1939 to 1941, he served on the President's Committee on Personnel Improvement; from 1948 to 1949, the Committee on Personnel Policy for the First Hoover Commission; from 1948 to 1950, the U.S. Civil Service Commission Seventh Region Loyalty Board; from 1950 to 1952, the Loyalty Review Board; and from 1953 to 1955, the Task Force on Personnel of the Second Hoover Commission.

As an academic, he was the first editor-in-chief of the journal *Public Administration Review,* which is the editorial voice and scholastic vehicle for the American Society for Public Administration. He served as its president in 1947. He edited for the *American Political Science Review* and was the parent organization's president in 1947.

Despite the obvious shift of resources to the central government, which concerned White greatly, he never lost his perspective on a pure constitutional model of federalism that deferred to the states. In his book *Trends in Public Administration* (1933), White chronicled the city manager movement, a major effort to wrest from the arms of patronage businesslike local governance practices conducted by administrators trained to manage in their selected fields, whether that be health sciences, police, budgeting, or general administration. White clearly saw that the complex problems of a modern society cannot be solved for a general good by men whose claim was a political connection rather than a specific education. White realized that the science of experts contributed significantly to the formulation of policy. All of his major works portray the public administrator as a creative, expert adviser. He grew to distrust the ability of legislative bodies to manage the affairs of the country. With the fourth edition of *Introduction,* he openly chastised Congress for its micromanagement and wished for them a minor role in the full elaboration of public policy. This bias arose naturally from his experience in dealing with complex societal problems, living with Chicago ward

politics, and the university's place in training men and women to assume responsible roles within a civic society. *Trends* recognizes that good research supplants political expediency. His goal was to shift this ideal from an undirected eclectic curiosity into a true science of administration.

Based on the founding work of the New York Bureau of Municipal Research, White solicited the input of organizations chartered toward a new public administration professionalism: the National Municipal League, the Governmental Research Association, the state Leagues of Municipalities, the American Municipal Association, the American Legislators Association, and the Public Administration Clearing House. The latter three served as disseminators and coordinators of research into public administration practice. This effort provided an overall rationale to the numerous local experiments then under way to bridge the distance between failed council forms of governance to more rationalized administrative forms.

He was a strong advocate of the efforts of the United States Chamber of Commerce to coalesce a national budget system. He saw a national communication and transportation network as the key features of a centralized administrative system, and the emergence of a national business structure as both model and inspiration to this system. Throughout his work, he viewed the "efficiency" of business as an emulative model. Yet, he never lost sight of the importance of constitutional governance and this nation's own turbulent road toward achieving a truly democratic model. He wrote in *Trends,* "If government is to fulfill its obligations in assisting to solve social problems, it must operate with the greatest attainable degree of intelligence and efficiency. The keynote of much of the development in public administration . . . is the steady search for better ways of doing public business" (1933, pp. 11–12). He called this the "new management."

In the year following the first publication of his *Introduction,* White published *The City Manager* (1927), which underscored his search for distinctive administrative principles arising from his overall desire to delineate principles of efficiency and economy. He continued to publish short research essays in national journals, although mostly within *Public Administration Review* and the *American Political Science Review.* In 1929, he wrote *The Prestige Value of Public Employment in Chicago,* again emphasizing his beliefs in a professional cadre portioned against the still widely held Jacksonian belief that public service should not be a right of expertise and that there was nothing special regarding the talents of those seeking public service. He revised this work in a study published in 1932, during his service as a member of the Civil Service Commission of the City of Chicago.

In 1930, he produced *The Civil Service in the Modern State,* a significant comparative study of administrative practices for the International Congress of the Administrative Sciences. His interest in comparative public administration continued with his volumes *Whitley Councils in the British Civil Service* (1933) and *Civil Service Abroad* (McGraw-Hill, 1935). *Civil Service Abroad* was chartered by the Commission of Inquiry on Public Service Personnel, itself established by the Social Science Research Council, headed by fellow University of Chicago colleague and chair Charles Merriam, and Columbia University's Training School for the Public Service, involving Louis Brownlow and Luther Gulick. Merriam, Brownlow, and Gulick are remembered for their joint efforts in the service of President Franklin Roosevelt to define management practices at a time when White served on the U.S. Civil Service Commission.

The marriage between Columbia University and the University of Chicago proved a fertile ground for exploring the vexing questions of a rapidly expanding administrative state. White chaired the Committee on Public Administration for the Research Council. This chairmanship lead to a comprehensive survey of public administration research. During the period 1944–1947, White continued his interests in comparative studies as vice president of the International Institute of Administrative Sciences.

White's work on the Civil Service Commission brought him into the circle with Lewis Merriam at Brookings (founded in 1927) and a former colleague, then Illinois Congressman T. V. Smith, with whom he had edited the book *Chicago–An Experiment in Social Science Research* (1929). In 1935, the lively discussions, White's insatiable appetite for research, and his commitment to the classroom led to the publication of his Louisiana State University lectures in *Government Career Service*. White integrated his Washington capitol service with his natural desire to solve public policy conundrums through the career civil servant. He saw firsthand the demands for an expertly trained, merit-based civil service, which had not as yet become a practical reality, when government leaders were routinely borrowed from the private sector. White was especially concerned about drawing newly educated college graduates into the civil service. As a minority member of the commission, he was instrumental in initiating an examination process targeted for the Junior Professional Program. The Junior Professional Program was designed to fill the newly created social science and administrative job classifications . This program served as a founding model for the Presidential Management Internship Program today. Toward the end of his life, he argued for an early formulation of a senior executive service (White 1955).

White argued that the principles of administration have guided nations since the pryamids were constructed. He turned to the archives and public papers. This interest in American history and a search for modern public administration antecedents resulted in four volumes on the subject. (White 1948; 1951; 1954; 1958). White chose not to examine the administration of the American Civil War

as he regarded it thoroughly worked. White's analysis of the departmental administrative practices throughout American history was based on his reading both primary documents and contemporary historical analyses. Although trained in the craft of historical analysis, and aiming toward being revisionary in his thesis of the central role of public administration in the shaping of American's history, his reliance on secondary sources has led some scholars to question the historical analysis (for instance, Wilmerding, 1955). Regardless, White himself acknowledged that his lifelong search was a private one.

In *Public Administration Review* (1965), Herbert Storing of the University of Chicago wrote, "Leonard D. White did not plant the seeds from which the field of public administration grew; but for four decades he tended that garden with unexcelled devotion. . . . The vast majority of students of public administration today were shaped at least in part by their exposure to White" (p. 38). White's legacy is tremendous. The circle of scholars and practitioners with whom he associated lists as the founding names of the discipline.

JOHN ALAN NICOLAY

BIBLIOGRAPHY

Works by Leonard D. White

White, Leonard D., 1926 [4th ed. 1955]. *Introduction to the Study of Public Administration*. New York: Harper & Row.
———, 1927. *The City Manager*. Chicago: University of Chicago Press.
———, 1929. *The Prestige Value of Public Employment in Chicago*. Chicago: University of Chicago Press.
———, 1933. *Trends in Public Administration*. New York: McGraw-Hill.
———, 1930. *The Civil Service in the Modern State*. Chicago: University of Chicago Press.
———, 1933. *Whitley Councils in the British Civil Service*. Chicago: University of Chicago Press.
———, 1935. *Civil Service Abroad*. New York: McGraw-Hill.
———, 1935. *Government Career Service*. Chicago: University of Chicago Press.
———, 1948. *The Federalists*. New York: Macmillan.
———, 1951. *The Jeffersonians*. New York: Macmillan.
———, 1954. *The Jacksonians*. New York: Macmillan.
———, 1958. *The Republican Era*. New York: Macmillan.
———, 1955. "The Senior Civil Service." *Public Administration Review*, vol. 15 (Fall).
White, Leonard D. and T. V. Smith, 1929 [1968]. *Chicago–An Experiment in Social Science Research*. Westport, CT: Greenwood Press.

Works about Leonard D. White

Gaus, John M., 1958. "Leonard Dupree White 1891-1958." *Public Administration Review*, vol. 18 (Summer).
Storing, Herbert J., 1965. "Leonard D. White and the Study of Public Administration." *Public Administration Review*, vol. 25 (March).
Wilmerding, Lucius, 1955. "The Jacksonians: A Study in Administrative History. " *Public Administration Review*, vol. 15 (Spring).

Other works cited

Goodnow, Frank J., 1900. *Politics and Administration.* New York: Russell and Russell.

———, 1905. *The Principles of the Adminstrative Law of the United States.* New York: G.P. Putnam.

Wilson, Woodrow, 1887. "The Study of Administration." *Political Science Quarterly*, vol. 2 (June).

WHITEHALL. A synonym for the British Civil Service—the permanent, politically neutral bureaucracy that serves central government, advising government ministers and carrying out their instructions. Ministers, by contrast, are party politicians—parliamentarians (most of them members of the elected House of Commons) holding offices in the executive branch of government, whose tenure is subject to the vagaries both of prime ministerial patronage and of the electoral process.

Whitehall and the UK Civil Service

The habit of equating the civil service and central government departments with "Whitehall," a street in southwest London, grew up in the mid-nineteenth century, when the foundations of the modern UK Civil Service were laid. In those days, government functions were few in number and limited in scope. The civil service was small, and most of it consisted of support staff—copy clerks and messengers—doing jobs that nowadays are done via allegedly labor-saving devices such as word processors, photocopiers, and telephones. Being a minister required then—and requires now—regular and easy access to the prime minister and the cabinet (both located in Downing Street, just off Whitehall) and to Parliament (at the southern end of Whitehall). Since almost all civil service work in the mid-nineteenth century involved giving advice and support to ministers, nearly all civil servants, and the offices of the ministries in which they worked, were located in and around Whitehall.

The subsequent growth of government (only partly reversed by the public-sector cuts of the 1980s and 1990s) has transformed both the structure and the spatial distribution of the civil service. Today, fewer than one in five civil servants work in London, and even fewer in Whitehall itself. Only a small and elite minority of civil service policy advisers need to work closely with ministers; the great majority of civil servants are concerned, in one way or another, with delivering public services (paying welfare benefits, collecting taxes, issuing passports, working in government laboratories, etc.), and apart from the staffs of government offices that directly serve London's population, there is no need for such civil servants to occupy expensive office space in the capital city.

The distinction between "policy advice" (the task of, at most, 5 percent of the civil service) and "service delivery" functions has been institutionalized by the transfer of most of the latter to semi-independent departmental agencies, under the Next Steps program launched in 1988 (see later).

The UK Civil Service—A Program of Definition

Britain has no codified constitution and no general Civil Service Act—and no one has ever produced a watertight legal definition of the term "civil servant." Perhaps the nearest we have got to a formal definition is that produced by the Tomlin Royal Commission on the civil service in 1931 (Drewry and Butcher 1991): "Servants of the Crown, other than holders of political or judicial offices, who are employed in a civil capacity and whose remuneration is paid wholly and directly out of moneys voted by Parliament" (p. 28). It is easier to identify who, of those employed in the public sector, is not a UK civil servant than it is to be categorical about who is. In practice, the term "civil servant" has a narrow meaning, covering the civilian, nonpolitical and nonjudicial employees of central government. Many public employees who would be called civil servants in other European countries are not so called in Britain. In 1997, local government employed nearly 2 million people (including most school teachers in state schools, social workers, public librarians, and police officers), the National Health Service employed more than 1 million people, the nationalized industries rather less than half a million (although continuing privatization exercises will reduce this total). The public sector employs almost 5 million people—only about 10 percent of whom are "civil servants," and only a tiny proportion of the latter work in Whitehall.

When Margaret Thatcher first came into office, in 1979, there were 732,000 civil servants in post. When she left office, in 1990, having promised to reduce the scale of state intervention, to cut public expenditure, and to improve the efficiency of public services, the number of civil servants had been cut to 570,000—a net reduction of about 20 percent. Policies announced in 1994–1995 promised a further reduction of the aggregate size of the civil service to less than half a million in the second half of the 1990s, mainly by further privatization and contracting out of state functions.

Civil servants work in government departments and agencies that vary greatly in size. For instance in April 1997 the Cabinet Office employed some 600 civil servants; the Treasury about 900; the Ministry of Agriculture, Fisheries, and Food, about 9,000; the Ministry of Defense, some 110,000. In many departments, most staff now work in semi-autonomous Next Steps agencies.

Apart from the important principle of political neutrality, mentioned earlier, one important distinguishing characteristic of the UK Civil Service is its reliance on "generalists." Traditionally, the top positions in the civil service have been held by people with good university de-

grees in subjects like the classics and history, and with no professional qualifications in subjects like accountancy, engineering, or law. Specialist professionals such as accountants, engineers, and lawyers are employed in the civil service, but they tend to play a secondary role in policy-making and to have a somewhat lower status than their generalist colleagues. Moreover, in contrast to other European countries, there is very little provision for in-service training. Newly appointed civil servants learn the job mainly by watching others do it. In 1970, a Civil Service College was set up, but it has a very limited role as compared with, for instance, the prestigious French École Nationale d'Administration.

The position has been changing in the last few years, and it is probably fair to say that "specialists" in some areas of government have acquired a slightly more prominent position than hitherto. Formal training has been given a somewhat higher priority. But generalism—sometimes referred to as "Oxbridge generalism," because so many top civil servants are graduates of Oxford or Cambridge Universities—is still a very prominent, and controversial, feature of the UK Civil Service.

The Theory of Ministerial Responsibility

In 1838, the British Foreign Secretary Viscount Palmerston (1784–1865) explained to the newly crowned Queen Victoria:

> The ministers who are at the head of the several departments of the state are liable any day and every day to defend themselves in Parliament; in order to do this they must be minutely acquainted with all the details of the business of their offices and the only way of being constantly armed with such information is to conduct and direct those details themselves (Parris 1969, p. 108).

Individual ministerial responsibility—whereby ministers are held, at least in theory, to be answerable to Parliament for everything that happens in their departments—remains a central element of Britain's uncodified constitution in the 1990s, though its appropriateness to modern conditions is open to question.

Individual ministerial responsibility is complemented (and to some extent diluted) by a doctrine of collective ministerial responsibility, the essence of which is that everyone holding ministerial office in a government is obliged publicly to adhere to the government's agreed policy line. Disagreements between ministers must not publicly be aired or acknowledged. Everyone holding government office must tell the same story. So must their civil servants. The rationale of this is that opponents of a divided government will quickly threaten its survival by driving wedges between its members.

Ministerial responsibility in both its individual and its collective sense is a peculiarity of the Westminster style of government, based on a "fusion of powers" (as distinct from the "separation of power," which characterizes the U.S. Constitution) whereby ministerial members of the executive are required also to be members of one of the two Houses of Parliament. This means that ministers are physically present in Parliament for purposes of accountability (e.g., via the device of parliamentary questions or by participation in debate).

Various institutional and procedural developments in the last 20 years or so have reflected long-standing concerns about Parliament's incapacity, in an age of large-scale government, effectively to control and monitor the executive and the civil service. Government departments are large; most civil servants work in semi-autonomous executive agencies a long way from London. If ministers have limited control over their civil servants, how much harder is it for Parliament to keep an effective check on the exercise of civil service functions by holding those ministers to account?

Such developments have included the establishment of a parliamentary ombudsman in the mid-1960s to investigate citizens' grievances about the administrative acts and omissions of civil servants and the recent growth of investigatory parliamentary select committees, most of them organized on a departmentally related basis, empowered to take evidence from civil servants, as well as from ministers. Ministerial responsibility is nowadays recognized by most observers (including politicians and civil servants) as an antique but often rather convenient fiction. It has become a device for avoiding rather than securing proper executive accountability. There are no modern instances of ministers resigning solely because of the misdeeds or mistakes of their civil servants. Ministerial resignations are almost always attributable either to personal misconduct or scandal or to losing the favor of the prime minister.

The practical limits of ministerial responsibility are compounded by the fact that many political and administrative episodes span a long period of time, involving several ministers and perhaps several changes of government. By the time a scandal or a major administrative error comes to light, it may have been boiling up for many years. Individual ministers stay in the same job for an average of about two years; civil servants tend to spend most of their careers in the same department, but policy advisers are usually given new jobs every two or three years. The present minister and his civil servants may be left holding the baby when most of the real blame lies with their predecessors. Sometimes the opposition will be uncomfortably aware that if they press their attack too hard, the government may retaliate by pointing out that the seeds of the present scandal were sown when they, the opposition party, were last in office.

To What Extent Are Civil Servants Accountable?

The constitutional conventions of ministerial responsibility in the 1990s remain important, despite the gulf that exists between the theory and the reality, because governments and civil servants continue to operate them. Thus the Thatcher government reaffirmed its belief in these doctrines, notably in an official memorandum on the Duties and Responsibilities of Civil Servants in Relation to Ministers (issued by the Cabinet Office in 1985, and revised several times since 1987, but not commercially published). This states:

> The Civil Service serves the Government of the day as a whole, that is to say Her Majesty's Ministers collectively, and the Prime Minister as the Minister for the Civil Service. The duty of the individual civil servant is first and foremost to the Minister of the Crown who is in charge of the department in which he or she is serving. It is the Minister who is responsible, and answerable in Parliament, for the conduct of the department's affairs and the management of its business. It is the duty of civil servants to serve their Ministers with integrity and to the best of their ability.

Thus civil servants owe their loyalty to the elected government of the day—of whatever political complexion. And the doctrine of ministerial responsibility has also been reaffirmed in the context of the Next Steps program, which is the most significant reform of the UK Civil Service in the twentieth century.

The Next Steps Program—and Beyond

We have already noted an important functional division within the civil service between those who are responsible for policy advice to ministers (no more than 5 percent of all civil servants) and service delivery (the remaining 95 percent). This distinction formed the basis of the "Next Steps" program, launched in February 1988, with Thatcher's strong support. The thinking behind this initiative is that civil service machinery for delivering public services works best if civil service managers are given freedom to manage without undue interference from above and if everyone is given a clear definition of what they are supposed to be doing, with clear performance targets.

The program has involved the progressive transfer of the service delivery functions of government departments—such as collecting taxes, processing passport applications, licensing road vehicles, providing weather forecasts, and delivering social welfare benefits—to semi-independent agencies, headed by chief executive appointed on three- or five-year contracts. The staff of agencies will (at least for the foreseeable future) continue to be civil servants, and ministers continue to be constitutionally answerable to Parliament for their activities. But chief executives, working within agreed "framework documents," defining financial and performance targets, are effectively responsible for the day-to-day running of the agency. And chief executives have become responsible to Parliament for agency budgets, and

procedures have been devised whereby they provide written answers to parliamentary questions about agency matters.

By 1997, more than 130 Next Steps agencies had been established, employing around two-thirds of all civil servants. It will be many years before the Next Steps program can fully be evaluated. But it has raised all kinds of interesting questions about where—as between ministers and chief executives—accountability for the effective and efficient delivery of these services will ultimately lie. When high explosives are found to have been smuggled into a high security prison, should the blame rest with the home secretary (the minister in charge of prison policy) or with the chief executive of the prisons service—or with the governor of the prison concerned, a middle-ranking civil servant? There seems to be no clear answer.

It should be noted that the Next Steps program does not mark the end of civil service reform in Britain. There have been moves towards "market testing" civil service functions, with a view to transferring some of them to the private sector (part of the continuing strategy of reducing civil service numbers). And some British politicians have cast envious eyes at radical reform programs in other countries—notably New Zealand, where top policy advisers are on short-term employment contracts, and ministers "buy" services from their departments.

Toward a More "Political" Civil Service?

Although civil servants owe their loyalty to the government of the day and remain in post when there is a change of government, in practice it may be difficult for an incoming administration to believe that these "neutral" official servants who so loyally served ministers of another party will be able to give equally loyal service to them. This is particularly relevant given the cumulative longevity in office of successive Conservative governments, the first of which came to power in 1979 and the last ended in 1997.

One conclusion that might be drawn from this is that the traditional idea of a politically neutral civil service may be out of date. It is certainly out of line with practice in many other West European countries. The in-coming Labour government, led by Tony Blair, was in effect posed the following question: Why do we not enhance the capacity of ministers to control events by letting them chose their own policy advisers—perhaps moving toward a variant of the Washington "spoils" system, whereby a lot of senior posts change hands whenever there is a change of Presidency?

Variations on this argument have often been heard since the late 1980s. Ministers have, from time to time, employed temporary political advisers—although in very small numbers. There has been little support for the idea of going over to a full-fledged spoils system, although it has been suggested that some variant of the German system, whereby the top two policy grades in the civil service are designated as political appointments, might be adopted in the United Kingdom. The idea of introducing something along the lines of French ministerial cabinets–a mixture of career civil servants and "outsiders"–has been mooted as a possible way of increasing ministerial control without compromising the permanent character of the core civil service.

GAVIN DREWRY

BIBLIOGRAPHY

Cabinet Office, UK, Efficiency Unit, 1988. Report to the Prime Minister, Improving Management in Government: The Next Steps. London: HMSO.

Drewry, G., ed., 1992. *The New Select Committees,* 2d ed. Oxford: Clarendon Press.

Drewry, G., and A. Butcher, 1991. *The Civil Service Today,* 2d ed. Oxford: Blackwell.

Giddings, P., ed., 1995. *Parliamentary Accountability: A Study of Parliament and Executive Agencies.* Basingstoke: Macmillan.

Greer, P., 1994. *Transforming Central Government: The Next Steps Initiative.* Philadelphia, PA: Open University Press.

Hennessy, P., 1989. *Whitehall.* London: Secker and Warburg.

Marshall, G., 1984. *Constitutional Conventions.* Oxford: Clarendon Press.

Marshall, G., ed., 1989. *Ministerial Responsibility.* Oxford: Clarendon Press.

Parris, H., 1969. *Constitutional Bureaucracy.* London: Allen and Unwin.

Pyper, R., 1995. *The British Civil Service.* Englewood Cliffs, NJ: Prentice-Hall.

Turpin, C., 1994. "Ministerial Responsibility." In Jeffrey Jowell and Dawn Oliver, eds. *The Changing Constitution,* 3d ed., Oxford: Clarendon Press.

WILDAVSKY, AARON (1930–1993).

One of the most innovative and prolific scholars of our time in the fields of political science, public policy, public administration, and public budgeting. Among his books, the classic *The Politics of the Budgetary Process* is probably his best-known contribution to the field of public administration.

Introduction

Aaron Wildavsky was a prolific contributor to the social sciences literature. Wildavsky wrote or coauthored 40 books and more than 200 published articles, essays, and book chapters. His work spanned a period of over 40 years, and its perspectives encompassed an enormous range of areas of study, issues, and topics. Among his books, the classic *The Politics of the Budgetary Process* (1964b) is probably his best known. In it, Wildavsky legitimized a behavioral and political approach to the study of budgeting, and its later editions, reflecting the changing relationships of budgeting and politics, remain essential reading. As a leading political scientist, his research also ranged into political institutions and political behavior, the Presidency and presidential elections, international and national defense policy, public policy analysis, leadership, biblical studies, community power, political culture, and much more. In each area he contributed stimulating insights, provocative

questions, and more general theory designed to encompass all of them.

Wildavsky was a graduate of Brooklyn College, served in the U.S. Army during the Korean War, was a Fulbright Scholar to Australia, received his doctorate from Yale University, taught at Oberlin College, and, from 1963 until the time of his death on September 4, 1993, at age 62, was a member of the faculty of the University of California at Berkeley and an occupant of the Class of 1940 Chair in Political Science and Public Policy. He was past chairman of the Berkeley Department of Political Science, founder and former dean of the Graduate School of Public Policy at Berkeley, past president of the American Political Science Association, and former president of the Russell Sage Foundation. Wildavsky received numerous prestigious awards and honors, including the first Charles E. Merriam Award from the American Political Science Association in recognition of career contributions applying theory to the practice of politics and government, the Paul F. Lazarsfeld Award for Research from the Evaluation Research Society, and the Harold Lasswell Award from the Policy Studies Association for his contributions to the study of public policy. In 1972, he received the American Society for Public Administration (ASPA) William E. Mosher Award, and in 1982, ASPA selected him to receive the Dwight Waldo Award, honoring his contributions to the literature of public administration and his distinguished career as a scholar and educator. He was elected as Fellow of the National Academy for Public Administration, the American Academy of Arts and Sciences, and the Center for Advanced Study in the Behavioral Sciences. He was honored by Brooklyn College with an honorary doctor of law and also was awarded honorary degrees by Yale University and the University of Bologna, one of the few non-Italians ever so honored. Wildavsky was a bold and tenacious scholar and a kind and generous colleague, teacher, and human being.

Wildavsky on Budgeting and Public Policy

Wildavsky found "opportunity from chaos" in conducting research and writing on budgeting, fiscal policy, and public policy more generally, and he seized it and worked until there was little else to say (Wildavsky 1983). From his first article on the politics of budgeting (1961) to the *The New Politics of the Budgetary Process* (1988) and subsequent articles (1992), Wildavsky provided the keys to understanding from which perspectives budgets and budgeting can best be analyzed and comprehended. Wildavsky enhanced our understanding of budgeting as a process characterized by continuous, evolutionary change and reform. Within the framework of incrementalism (1978), Wildavsky told us what should or could not be done to improve budget decision making, why and how to balance the budget (Wildavsky 1980; White and Wildavsky 1989), and how efforts to do all this should be evaluated. He lamented the dissensus so evident in the present compared to the "classical era" of budgeting, but he told us that the budget process was not the problem, but rather the victim.

The problem, he explained, was dissensus over policy in government and in our society, not budgeting. He argued in *The New Politics*, in testimony before Congress, and elsewhere that better budgeting through expenditure limits, curbing the growth, or even accepting marginal reductions in entitlements could become part of the solution—but these reforms would and could not offer "the" solutions to the many public policy dilemmas faced by Americans (Wildavsky 1988). Finding solutions to the serious problems present in the United States, alas, would be much more difficult and more a function of social and cultural change in America than mere change in the institutional mechanisms employed for resource allocation decisionmaking. He also noted at the end of his writing on budgets that budgeting under conditions of scarcity may not be incremental—sometimes cuts are not distributed equally and predicated on the base, and we should want it to be this way. He argued that in the end, we would have little choice but to accept this view.

By the early 1990s, Wildavsky and his collaborators had covered essentially everything of seminal significance about the politics and culture of budgeting. The conclusion might have been drawn by 1975, given the prodigious output and significance of the work done by Wildavsky and his collaborators including Naomi Caiden, Hugh Heclo, and others by this time. However, Wildavsky, along with Joseph White and other coauthors, demonstrated that such a conclusion would have been premature. In the study of budgeting, there remained plenty of room for future descriptive work on the emergent budgetary antics, foibles, and even successes of Congress and the president, for analysis of new proposals for budget reform, for empirical and quantitative analysis of fiscal policy decisions and their distributive consequences, and the like. However, there is not much left to be said that is new about the dynamics of the politics of budgeting except how roles and behavior previously defined are manifest. It may be granted that continued testing of hypotheses developed by Wildavsky and his collaborators should be done, but Wildavsky's work has defined the territory and it has established the standards against which future work will be judged. Aaron Wildavsky and his collaborators have explained what seems to be almost everything there is that is worth knowing about the politics of budgeting and the cultural stage upon which the annual political drama of budgeting is played.

Wildavsky's work on the politics of budgeting and more generally in the disciplines of political science and public policy reveals that he was a man of strong beliefs who was willing to buck the tide of popular opinion. He held immovable views on the necessity for stalwart protection of human freedom and the rights of the individual. He was patriotic; he believed in the efficacy of self-help; he bemoaned what he termed "the rise of radical egalitarianism" (Wildavsky 1971) and was a staunch champion of the meritocratic society. He opposed the establishment of criteria intended to broaden social and professional opportunity based solely on racial, ethnic, or any set of criteria that did not also embrace measures of accomplishment. He was critical of the costs of many government social programs and the tendency of advocates of such programs to think only about benefits rather than the relationship between benefits and costs. He believed such advocates tended to overstate the benefits and ignore many of the negative and unanticipated results of the programs they supported.

Wildavsky's Work on Risk, Health, Safety, and the Environment

The limitations inherent in trying to capture the scope of Aaron Wildavsky's work in a summary inevitably result in missing the analysis of some of his important work. In the mid-1970s, Wildavsky published an article entitled "Doing Better and Feeling Worse: The Political Pathology of Health Policy" (Wildavsky 1976). In addition to the relevance of this piece to national debate on health policy, his research on health blossomed in the latter part of the 1970s and 1980s into a full-scale assault more broadly on risk and culture, risk perception and human behavior, safety, the impact of technology, and protection of the environment. In the process of this analysis, he also addressed other issues including the safety of nuclear power, energy policy choices, and species loss. No attempt is made here to comprehensively summarize this work but reviewing some of Wildavsky's views on risk and safety is desirable if we wish to better understand how he believed people should go about dealing with complex sociotechnical issues in a democracy. This review also provides insight on how his views on risk, safety and the environment meshed with his beliefs about the threat posed by radical egalitarianism.

Wildavsky and the colleagues with whom he worked in this area, including Mary Douglas, Elizabeth Nichols (Wildavsky 1982; Douglas and Wildavsky 1982; Nichols and Wildavsky 1995), and others, staked out and thoroughly mined a territory far to the conservative end of the spectrum relative to the prevailing wisdom on risk, safety, and the environment that has stimulated passage of much government regulatory law and agency action in contemporary society. This was the problem according to Wildavsky and his colleagues and not the solution. He had found, as had other researchers, that people tend not to think probabilistically in assessing information when estimating the amount of risk they face. Research on risk has revealed that people tend to overestimate and underestimate risk probabilities under different circumstances.

Wildavsky argued that the tendency to err in risk assessment has caused the public to demand, and the government to respond with excessive statutory law, administrative rules and regulatory policies, far out of line with the actual level of risk faced by the vast majority of humans. As a consequence, government policy in the area of risk prevention—in environmental, health, and safety regulation—is much too restrictive of human freedom and far more costly than the benefits it produces. Wildavsky maintained that elected officials and government regulators had been captured by crazy environmental and safety radicals, with a giant assist from the news media. This was due in large part to their own risk aversion at not wanting to be held accountable for errors in policy should the radicals be proven right. Wildavsky also blamed scientists who had played an important role in providing the evidence to support the need for highly risk-averse and expensive government policies. He saw a leap to judgment and action by government to control the use of purportedly dangerous products and to prohibit certain kinds of individual and private sector behavior before evidence on hazard and risk was thoroughly evaluated. Essentially, he believed that as a society we were wasting huge amounts of money, time, and effort banning and controlling exposure to risks that were not proven to his satisfaction to exist.

The synopsis provided here is only a small part of the larger argument Wildavsky and his colleagues developed in four books and approximately a dozen articles, many published in highly visible newspaper and magazine articles and journals. The direction of Wildavsky's arguments against the prevailing arguments for increased government rigor in health, safety, and environmental regulation, combined with the visibility of his work due to his reputation as a scholar, brought him considerable criticism. Characteristically, in response Wildavsky did not budge or waffle. In his mind he was convinced that, for understandable but incorrect reasons, as a culture we were rushing to control before we evaluated the evidence. However, in the introduction to *But Is It True?* (Wildavsky 1994), Wildavsky responded to his critics in a moderate tone. He stated that the purpose of his long inquiry into the basis for health, safety, and environmental policy was, fundamentally, not intended to convince readers that he was right about the overestimation of and overreaction to risks. Instead, his goal was to demonstrate that average citizens, faced with a bewildering and often conflicting body of evidence and recommendations, could gather information, analyze it, and draw conclusions for themselves about what was right. As a result, they could then participate in the debate over risk and safety and attempt to influence decisions as they should in a truly democratic society. The alternative was to be dominated by special interest radicals and the politicians and scientists who served them.

Here is where his work and belief system on risk coincides with his views on the rise of radical egalitarianism. He believed that over the past two decades governments had become too responsive to the demands of radical minority opinion. He deplored the fact that government decision-makers and the citizenry in general tended to listen to only one side of arguments in which advocates of special interests, disguised as champions of the public welfare at large, tended to overstate their problems and requirements and thereby gain rewards at the expense of the welfare of the society at large. That such advocates attempted to influence the policymaking process as they did, this Wildavsky understood. After all, he was an expert on budget negotiation and he recognized strategies of advocacy and knew why they were effective in influencing public opinion and government action. What he disagreed with was the prevalence of opinion and fear that "the sky is falling." He believed the policy agenda had been captured by the "chicken littles" of the world and he deplored the consequence of this because, in his view, it contributed significantly to the decay of democracy and the democratic institutions he treasured.

Conclusion

Aaron Wildavsky was revered by his friends and colleagues and by the students fortunate enough to have worked closely with him. This love and admiration is evident in the many tributary statements made about him at the end of his life. All who knew him suffered from one thought—that he was taken from life on earth too early. Undoubtedly, had he lived longer, his personal and scholarly presence would have continued, as it had in the past, to enlighten, inspire, amuse, and, of course, to irritate those who knew him as a friend as well as those who knew him only through his writings.

Percy Tannenbaum, Professor Emeritus of Public Policy at Berkeley, recruited by Aaron as one of the founding members of the Graduate School of Public Policy, made the following observation about Wildavsky's academic and personal style:

His style was notably different from most academics in that it was clear and to the point, without ambiguity or ambivalence. One knew directly where he stood on a given issue and why. One could readily agree or disagree with his reasoning and conclusions, and he accepted both types of reaction with grace. It is a most enviable record and a rather intimidating one for others to match. . . . [These] qualities—forthrightness, honesty, integrity, responsibility, dedication very much among them—were evident in his role as a colleague. . . . His vividness sparked many a conversation or group meeting. His ideas were always provocative, his discussions always stimulating. You could always count on Aaron for a lucid and unusually quick reaction to anything you would ask him to read, often with a pithy comment or two that cut to the heart of the issue. (Institute for Governmental Studies 1993, pp. 27–28)

In assessing the breadth, quality, and creativity of his scholarship on political culture, American politics, public policy, on the many facets of the politics of budgeting and other areas, his reputation as an excellent and caring teacher and adviser to students, the nature of his relationships with his professional colleagues, and the feelings of his friends for him as a warm and giving human being, one concludes that Aaron Wildavsky was, in action and word, a real man and scholar for all seasons. As Wildavsky wrote about himself: "Every man needs a craft through which he can express himself to the extent of his abilities, and I have found mine." (Wildavsky 1971, p. 3; Polsby, 1985, p. 20). At the end of his life, Wildavsky continued to work with students and colleagues to finish up projects in progress to the extent possible and he was still formulating in his mind other ideas to explore and other pieces he wanted written.

L. R. JONES

BIBLIOGRAPHY

Douglas, A., and A. Wildavsky, 1982. *Risk and Culture: An Essay on the Selection of Technological and Environmental Dangers.* Los Angeles: University of California Press.

Institute for Governmental Studies, 1993. *Aaron Wildavsky 1930–1993.* Berkeley: Institute for Governmental Studies, 27–28, 58.

Nichols, E., and A. Wildavsky, A., 1995. *Safer Power.* Los Angeles: University of California Press.

Polsby, N., 1985. "The Contributions of President Aaron Wildavsky." *PS* 18 (Fall): 20.

White, J., and A. Wildavsky, 1989. *The Deficit and the Public Interest.* Berkeley: University of California Press.

Wildavsky, A., 1961. "Political Implications of Budgetary Reform." *Public Administration Review,* vol. 21, no. 4 (Autumn): 183–190.

———, 1964. *The Politics of the Budgetary Process.* Boston: Little, Brown.

———, 1971. *The Revolt against the Masses and Other Essays on Politics and Public Policy.* New York: Basic Books, 3.

———, 1976. "Doing Better and Feeling Worse: The Political Pathology of Heath Policy." *Daedalus.* (Winter): 105–123.

———, 1978. "A Budget for all Seasons? Why the Traditional Budget Lasts." *Public Administration Review,* vol. 38, no. 6 (November–December) 501–509.

———, 1980. *How to Limit Government Spending.* Los Angeles: University of California Press.

———, 1982. *Searching for Safety.* New Brunswick, NJ: Transaction Press.

———, 1983. "From Chaos Come Opportunity: The Movement toward Spending Limits in American and Canadian Budgeting." *Canadian Public Administration,* vol. 26, no. 2 (Summer): 163–181.

———, 1988. *The New Politics of the Budgetary Process.* Glenview, IL: Scott, Foresman.

———, 1992. "Political Implications of Budgetary Reform: A Retrospective." *Public Administration Review,* vol. 52, no. 6 (November–December): 594–603.

———, 1994, *But Is It True?* New York: Harvard University Press.

WILSON, WOODROW (1856–1924).

American political scientist, president of Princeton University, governor of New Jersey, and president of the United States. Although a leading statesman of the twentieth century, Wilson's significance for public administration rests primarily on an article. "The Study of Administration," published in 1887 in the *Political Science Quarterly.* The immediate impact of the article was not great, but later generations of scholars rediscovered it and proclaimed it to be the beginning of the discipline of public administration in the United States, as well as a seminal statement about the proper relationship of politics and administration in a democracy. After the publication of Wilson's papers, beginning in 1966, and following scholarly scrutiny at the centennial of the article, questions have been raised about Wilson's real contribution and the meaning of his distinction between politics and administration.

Wilson as a Student of Administration

Wilson graduated from Princeton in 1879. After a short and unsuccessful experience with the study and practice of law, he became a graduate student at Johns Hopkins University in 1883. There, perhaps under the influence of such German-trained professors as the economist Richard Ely, he began to inform others of his great interest in questions of administration. Wilson's attention to administrative matters may also have grown out of his admiration for British cabinet government and his disdain for the practice of American politics of the time. Henry Bragdon (1967, p. 118) suggests a more pragmatic reason: He was contemplating a career as an appointed, rather than elected, official. Whatever the case, throughout the several essays that were to culminate in his best-known book, *Congressional Government,* he stressed the complexity of the daily activity of the bureaus or businesslike side of government, which required the effort of trained specialists and not politicians.

There is no indication in the *Papers* that Wilson wrote anything on administration until after he had accepted his first teaching appointment at Bryn Mawr College in 1885 (Link 1966–1993). At that time, he produced three unpublished essays on administration, which were to form the nucleus of "The Study of Administration." In 1886, Wilson was invited to address the Historical and Political Science Association at Cornell University. As an outline for his remarks, he relied on the earlier essays, especially one entitled "The Art of Governing." Professor E.R.A. Seligman, an editor of the *Political Science Quarterly,* had already asked Wilson for a contribution to the new journal. He saw a report of the address and requested that he might see a copy for possible publication. Although Wilson protested that the essay was only "a semipopular introduction to administrative studies," he gave Seligman the manuscript of his Cornell speech, with only one minor modification. It was published in the June 1887 issue of the *Quarterly.*

"The Study of Administration" was the only work dealing specifically with the subject that Wilson was to publish. However, it was not the end of his involvement in the study of administration. Johns Hopkins University invited

Wilson to give a five-week series of lectures on administration. Beginning in 1888, he was to continue this lecture series for nine years as his academic career took him from Bryn Mawr, by way of Wesleyan, to Princeton.

From 1883, when he first began to think of himself as a student of public administration, until his final lectures at Johns Hopkins in 1897, the subject was one of Wilson's major academic concerns. "The Study of Administration" appeared fairly early in his development and, thus, the *Papers* indicate, does not represent accurately his fully mature conclusions about the subject. In the very extensive notes from his lectures, he never repudiated what has come to be seen as a basic thesis of "The Study," namely, that administration and politics can and should be separated; in fact, he never cited his earlier work. But it is clear that he moved away from his original treatment of the politics-administration question.

Richard Stillman (1973) contends that the lecture notes do not shed much light on Wilson's view of administration. Another interpretation (Rabin and Bowman 1984) of Wilson's later work is that he eventually adopted the view of politics and administration as developed by German authorities, such as Lorenz von Stein. Many of his lectures make the point that politics and administration are integrated within an organically whole state. The administration of public affairs is not mere business nor the pursuit of technical proficiency. Administrators have a political role to play and it is impossible to separate out the political component of many administrative activities. Niels Thorsen (1988) questions whether Wilson accepted the German tradition of the "science of the state" with its emphasis on organic unity.

Wilson on Politics and Administration

What Wilson really meant in his lectures on administration, at this date, is probably beside the point. "The Study of Administration" has assumed a symbolic status. For many years, the conventional wisdom in public administration held that Wilson deserved the credit or, in an increasing number of writings, the blame for establishing the "politics-administration dichotomy," that basic principle which held that politics and administration were two distinct aspects of government. Stated simply, the dichotomy said that politics would decide the purposes of government and administration would implement whatever policies had been established. The science of administration could be free of political considerations and its students could concentrate on the one best way of carrying out decisions made elsewhere.

This simplistic division of governmental functions that are, in reality, inextricably joined, caused a serious misunderstanding for scholars until it was finally acknowledged that administration is a major aspect of American politics. Textbooks from the 1930s and 1940s were based on this fundamental error, which, to be sure, allows students to concentrate on technical questions, but it prevented a clear appreciation of the political essence of administration. The harshest attack on what it is supposed that Wilson wrought was launched by Vincent Ostrom (1989). The "Wilsonian Paradigm" promoted the ideal of an apolitical, centralized bureaucracy and was the source, according to Ostrom, of "much bad medicine" in the teaching and practice of public administration. The result was a direction in administration that undermined the principles of the U.S. Constitution.

Recent scholarship suggests that Wilson should be exonerated of the charge of pushing public administration in the wrong direction. First of all, the essay is rather ambiguous on the point of politics and administration. Wilson, to be sure, made such flat statements as, "the field of administration is a field of business" and "administration lies outside the proper sphere of *politics*. Administrative questions are not political questions." The article as a whole, however, permits several interpretations of Wilson's understanding of politics. Kent Kerwin (1977) and James Carroll and Alfred Zuck (1983), in somewhat different ways, find at least three meanings attached to the word, so it is not clear that the article really supports the versions of dichotomy that were to become popular.

It should also remembered that Wilson was addressing a general audience and that, in his speaking and writing, he was sometimes accused of preferring style over substance. That is, his message was aimed not so much at scholars but rather at citizens who were nervous about the introduction of alien institutions. A large portion of the article is devoted to assuring Americans that efficient administration could be divorced from autocratic political systems. In one memorable passage, Wilson argued that, just as we can learn from a murderer to sharpen knives without intending to commit murder, so too "if I see a monarchist dyed in the wool managing a public bureau well, I can learn his business methods without changing one of my republican spots." Good administration is always the same, and democrats can learn to govern themselves without resorting to despotism. As he put it, the science of administration in the United States must study the subject in order to "distil away its foreign gases."

There is a more practical reason for absolving Wilson of the blame for the dichotomy. Later scholars did not rely on his article as the source of the idea. According to Daniel Martin's (1988) careful investigation, writers during the heyday of the politics-administration dichotomy seldom referred to the "Study of Administration" as an authoritative statement of the principle.

Wilson as the Founder of American Public Administration

Did Wilson found the American discipline of public administration? There have been many mileposts in the still incomplete construction of the administrative state in the United States. Wilson's article was only one highly visible monument. That it was produced by a man who would later become a major figure in world politics made it all the more attractive when public administration practitioners and scholars began to form the culture of their profession.

The fact is, however, that Wilson did not cause public administration to take shape out of a void. He did not inspire his contemporaries to take up the challenges posed in the article. Paul Van Riper (1983) reviewed the impact of the article on the scholarship of the time and came to the conclusion that "the 1887 work had no influence whatever on the evolution of either the theory or practice of public administration in the U.S. until well after 1950" (p. 477). "The Study of Administration" was not the seed that blossomed into the modern field of public administration.

This is not to say that Wilson should be removed from the classical canon of public administration. As Dwight Waldo (In Rabin and Bowman 1984) rightly commented, "The essay presaged the direction that thinking and action would take in years ahead: even when 'wrong' it was 'relevant'" (p. 222). If Wilson was wrong about the politics-administration dichotomy, who in later generations has come up with the perfect answer to the question of the role of administration within a democratic political system? At least he must be given credit for making an effort to resolve this enduring problem. And surely no one today can argue with Wilson's basic point: Administration is at the heart of modern politics, and public administration deserves the serious attention of all thoughtful students of American government.

ROBERT D. MIEWALD

BIBLIOGRAPHY

Bragdon, Henry W., 1967, *Woodrow Wilson: The Academic Years.* Cambridge, MA: Harvard University Press.

Carroll, James D., and Alfred M. Zuck, 1983. *"The Study of Administration" Revisited.* Washington, DC: American Society for Public Administration.

Kerwan, Kent, 1977. "The Crisis of Identity in the Study of Public Administration: Woodrow Wilson." *Polity,* vol. 9: 321–343.

Link, Arthur, 1968. "Woodrow Wilson and the Study of Administration." *Proceedings of the American Philosophical Society,* vol. 112: 431–433.

Link, Arthur, ed., 1966–1993. *The Papers of Woodrow Wilson,* 69 vols. Princeton, NJ: Princeton University Press.

Martin, Daniel W., 1988. "The Fading Legacy of Woodrow Wilson." *Public Administration Review,* vol. 48: 631–636.

Ostrom, Vincent, 1989. *The Intellectual Crisis in American Public Administration,* 2d ed. Tuscaloosa: University of Alabama Press.

Rabin, Jack, and James S. Bowman, eds., 1984. *Politics and Administration: Woodrow Wilson and American Public Administration.* New York: Marcel Dekker.

Stillman, Richard J., 1973. "Woodrow Wilson and the Study of Administration: A New Look at an Old Essay." *American Political Science Review,* vol. 67: 582–588.

Thorsen, Niels, 1988. *The Political Thought of Woodrow Wilson, 1875–1910.* Princeton, NJ: Princeton University Press.

Van Riper, Paul P., 1983. "The American Administrative State: Wilson and the Founders—An Unorthodox View." *Public Administration Review,* vol. 43: 477–490.

Walker, Larry, 1989. "Woodrow Wilson, Progressive Reform, and Public Administration." *Political Science Quarterly,* vol. 104: 509–525.

Wilson, Woodrow, 1885. *Congressional Government.* Boston: Houghton Mifflin; Reprinted, 1981, Baltimore: Johns Hopkins University Press.

———, 1887. "The Study of Administration." *Political Science Quarterly,* vol. 2: 197–222; reprinted, 1941: *Political Science Quarterly,* vol. 56: 481–506.

WISE USE MOVEMENT.

A loose coalition of interest groups in the United States that seeks to preserve multiple use of public lands. The term "wise use" is derived from nineteenth-century United States conservationist Gifford Pinchot's definition of conservation as the wise use of resources.

Interest groups often affiliated with the Wise Use Movement include farmers, miners, timber industries, property-rights groups, off-road vehicle enthusiasts and fishermen. Issues of concern to the Wise Use Movement reflect the diversity of groups affiliated with it. They include increased logging and mining on public lands, changes to or abolition of the Endangered Species Act of 1973, rollbacks of clean air and water legislation, reimbursement for property owners affected by environmental regulations, and increased access to public lands for recreational users.

Two themes characterize groups within the Wise Use Movement. First, there is a general distrust of federal land management practices in the United States. Second, there is a desire to protect local economic uses of the natural resources on public lands. Perceiving that environmentalists seek preservation of public lands that will destroy local economics dependent on resource extraction and recreational activities, the Wise Use Movement advocates multiple uses of public lands.

The Wise Use Movement is generally a rural-western phenomenon. The large percentage of federal land is western states contributes to the popularity of the Wise Use Movement in the West. The federal government owns over one-half of all the land in the 12 western states and only 4 percent of the other 37 continental states. The Wise Use Movement, however, is not entirely limited to the West. In the East, the issues are generally related to the protection of private property rights.

The Wise Use Movement is a rural phenomenon because rural communities tend to have a greater reliance on natural resource industries. These industries have historically had access to public lands at subsidized costs. The convergence of environmental concern about the impact of these industries on public lands, federal budgetary concerns about subsidizing access to these lands, and a general downturn for these industries in the economy, have placed enormous stress on rural economies. Rural areas also are naturally the location of most public land holdings. County governments with federal lands within their borders receive compensation from the federal government based upon the usage of public lands. The payments are tied to timber revenues, grazing permits, mining leases and permits, and payments-in-lieu-of-taxes paid by the federal government. Changes in resource policies can result in fewer revenues for counties. Changes in federal land management practices that hurt the local economy and/or decrease the receipts from public lands, therefore, especially impact rural western communities.

There have been several policy areas around which wise use groups have mobilized. Most are characterized by the perceived threat they represent to those who rely upon access to public lands for their economic livelihood. Enforcement of the Endangered Species Act of 1973, especially the protection of the spotted owl—a species indigenous to the valuable old growth forests in the western United States—has resulted in reductions and stoppages of timber cutting in the Pacific Northwest. As a result, conflict between wise use advocates and environmentalists has been high in communities reliant upon wood products industries.

Another policy area around which Wise Use groups have mobilized is the attempt by the federal government to change the fees that cattle ranchers pay to graze their cattle on public lands. Although historically charged fees below market cost, ranchers perceive attempts to raise fees or limit the number of cattle on public lands as a threat to their economic survival and way of life. Environmentalists and federal land managers, by contrast, express concern about the impact of cattle on stream and water quality and soil erosion. Reacting to proposed changes in federal land management, county government officials have passed ordinances in many western counties asserting that grazing fees ought to be paid to the county rather than the federal government. These ordinances are part of a County Supremacy Movement, which focuses almost exclusively on federal lands and is considered a subcategory of the Wise Use Movement.

Another example of a policy area around which Wise Use groups have moblized involves the Hardrock Mining Law of 1872. This law dedicates mining as the preferred land use in over one-half of all U.S. public lands and allows miners to obtain title to the land over the minerals. The United States Department of the Interior and environmental groups have sought to tighten restrictions in the law to decrease the number of mining claims. The mining industry and Wise Use groups opposed to further restrictions on public land useage oppose those moves.

A final example of a policy area of concern to Wise Use groups is the protection of private property rights. Federal environmental regulations on land use, especially the protection of wetlands, are often the focus on concern for Wise Use groups in this area. Wetlands are protected by the Clean Water Act of 1972, the Emergency Wetlands Resources Act of 1986, and a provision of the 1990 Food, Agriculture, Conservation, and Trade Act that establishes a Wetlands Reserve Program. Restrictions in property devel-

opment and land uses based on these laws are opposed by Wise Use groups as an unlawful "taking" of the value of their property. Wise Use groups have challenged environmental regulations restricting development using the Fifth Amendment to the U.S. Constitution, which prohibits the taking of private property without just compensation. Wise Use groups argue that property owners should be compensated for the decrease in potential property values when environmental regulation stops development. The strength of the Wise Use Movement in state legislatures is evidenced by the passage of "takings" legislation in ten states as of 1995.

There is an increasing level of conflict associated with the Wise Use Movement. Tensions run high between citizens in small communities battling over environmental issues. Vandalism and confrontational protests and counter-protests between Wise Use and environmental groups are common. Conflict between county officials and federal land managers has also risen. Recently, several western U.S. counties have threatened to arrest federal land managers who attempt to enforce environmental regulations. In one highly publicized instance in 1995, a Nye County, Nevada, commissioner bulldozed a closed forest service road to open it as forest service personnel looked on. Another example of the growing conflict is the Owyhee County, Idaho, sheriff who asserted to the press in 1995 that federal land managers must now register with him as a deputy before having legitimate right to enforce federal laws.

Estimating the size of the Wise Use Movement is difficult because of the diverse number of issues and groups lumped under this term. There are groups organized specifically around Wise Use issues and other longer-standing groups that have interests in all or part of the Wise Use agenda. Examples of Wise Use groups include the Center for the Defense of Free Enterprise, the Oregon Lands Conference, the Pennsylvania Landowners Association, and People for the West. These groups are estimated by David Helvarg in *The War against the Greens* (1994) to have less than 100,000 dues-paying members (p. 9). Groups that have an overlapping interest with the Wise Use movement include the American Farm Bureau Federation and the Cattleman's Association. Wise Use groups assert their grassroots support, although environmental groups claim that industries concerned with continued access to public lands support the groups financially.

There are some connections between the Wise Use Movement and other conservative groups in the United States. Technical support and policy analyses useful to Wise Use advocates have been provided by conservative think tanks such as the Heritage Foundation and the CATO institute. Multiple use is also appealing to some segments of the Christian Right, who reject the primacy of the environment over humanity that they perceive in environmentalism.

STEPHANIE L. WITT AND
LESLIE R. ALM

BIBLIOGRAPHY

Cawley, R. McGreggor, 1993. *Federal Land, Western Anger: The Sagebrush Rebellion and Environmental Politics.* Lawrence: University Press of Kansas.

Erm, Rene, II, 1993–1994. "The 'Wise Use' Movement: The Constitutionality of Local Action on Federal Lands Under the Preemption Doctrine." *Idaho Law Review,* vol. 30: 631–670.

Helvarg, David, 1994. *The War Against the Greens: The Wise Use Movement, the New Right, and Anti-Environmental Violence.* San Francisco, CA: Sierra Club Books.

WORK/FAMILY POLICIES.

Policies adopted by employers to accommodate the changing lifestyles of the workforce.

To meet the challenge of the dramatically increasing number of working age women in the labor force and the rise in the number of multiearner families, governments and private-sector employers in most parts of the world are adopting family-friendly policies. Although there are significant differences among countries, Western Europe has been a leader, with most developing nations slowly embracing similar benefit policies. Most such programs are government-sponsored, funded and in law, usually with universal coverage. In the United States, private-sector employers have led in instituting policies to assist employees with managing their work/family responsibilities. Joining the many companies advancing such policies, President Bill Clinton issued a presidential memorandum in July 1994, urging expansion of family-friendly work arrangements in the executive branch. The major policies and programs fall into the following categories: flexible work plans and flexible leave, dependent care, and employee assistance programs.

Flexible Work Plans

Flextime policies allow choices in days and hours of work, with employees choosing starting and stopping times within required core hours and days. Some plans allow employees to vary the number of hours they work each day and the number of days worked each week: for example, four-day weeks, usually with ten-hour days. Well over half of all U.S. private-sector employers report instituting some flexibility in work hours and days. An increasing number of state and local governments also report using such flexibilities, and the federal government, whose policies allow flexible schedules, are responding to the presidential memorandum by allowing more workers to join the program. Flextime policies vary greatly throughout the world with well-used programs in Germany, the leader in starting flextime in the late 1960s.

Flexible Workplace Policies

Flexiplace allows employees to work at home or at satellite offices for some part of the workweek. The earliest work-at-home programs, "cottage industries" employing unskilled workers, still exist in many developing countries. New flexiplace programs involve employees who "telecommute," keeping in close contact with their usual workplaces by telephone or computer. Most employers report increased productivity and happier employees with more time for families; their communities report reduced air pollution, less traffic congestion, and better energy use. U.S. federal employees in various parts of the country work in satellite work stations administered by Cooperative Administrative Support Units, an interagency structure chartered by the President's Council on Management Improvement.

Part-time and Job-sharing Policies

These programs can be for a short period in case of family emergencies or permanent for workers who want or need more personal time. "Part-time" is defined by the U.S. Bureau of Labor Statistics as working less than 35 hours a week; job sharing usually involves two workers who divide either hours or days. Sharers also divide work according to the involved individuals' skills and abilities. U.S. companies and public-sector organizations have recently started to provide benefits, often prorated, under these programs. The numbers of part-timer workers are increasing in most industrial countries.

Flexible Spending Accounts and Flexible "Cafeteria-style" Benefit Policies

Although most countries provide social insurance for their citizens, the policies and programs vary greatly in how benefits are provided, to whom, and at what level. Most Western European countries have universal coverage with uniform entitlements. Past U.S. benefit plans were designed for the "traditional" family, of which there are now many fewer. Newer plans, especially useful in two-worker families where there has been some duplicate coverage, allow benefit choices within specified cost limits. Among the choices may be medical coverage, various leave programs, wellness programs, dependent care, and occasionally financial planning and retirement options. Increasingly, private-sector companies and state and local governments have adopted these programs, often to contain benefit costs.

Leave Policies

The United States was the last of major nations to provide maternity rights and benefits. The Family and Medical Leave Act of 1993 requires public agencies, including state, local, and federal employers, schools, and private-sector employers of 50 or more people to offer covered workers 12 weeks of unpaid leave with a continuation of health benefits and the right to return to an equivalent job with the same pay and benefits. Up to 12 weeks of leave during any twelve-month period may be used for childbirth, adoption, acquisition of a foster child, care of a seriously ill child, spouse, or parent or personal illness. Both U.S. public- and private-sector employers are making changes to other leave policies to accommodate work/family concerns: for example, allowing use of personal sick leave to take care of family members, the use of leave banks to assist employees with family emergencies who have used all of their own leave, and encouraging either paid or unpaid education leave. Universally desired by employees is the ability to combine all leave and vacation programs to create individual "flexible time off" schedules.

Dependent Care Policies

Governments and private organizations often offer help with dependents. Most common are policies to assist parents with satisfactory child care arrangements. These programs may include on-site or near-site centers, community consortia, resource and referral programs, helping with child care costs, discount agreements, sick child and emergency care programs, and after-school and holiday programs. Elder care programs are expanding rapidly. Most prevalent in the United States are private-sector resource and referral services; governments sponsor activities in many countries.

Employee Assistance Policies

Both government and private sector organizations throughout the world have expanded assistance to employees through counseling, wellness programs, and training and education opportunities. Frequently in the United States, employee assistance offices are combined with work/family offices. Many have been renamed work/life offices, not only to provide a focus for both initiatives but also to recognize that employees without children may have conflicting demands that affect their worklife.

Studies show that work/family programs improve recruitment and retention of needed skilled workers and reduce employee absenteeism. When employers institute family-friendly policies, employees, particularly those who have dependent care responsibilities, report less stress, improved productivity, and better morale.

ROSSLYN S. KLEEMAN

BIBLIOGRAPHY

Information on international policies may be obtained from the Information Officer, Social Development Issues, Office of Public Information, United Nations, New York NY 10017, U.S.A.
Price, Susan Crites, and Tom Price, 1994. *The Working Parents Help Book.* Princeton, NJ: Peterson's.
U.S. General Accounting Office, 1992. *The Changing Workforce: Comparison of Federal and Nonfederal Work/Family Programs and Approaches.* Washington, DC.

Women's Bureau, 1993. *Women Workers: Trends and Issues.* Washington, DC: U.S. Department of Labor.

WORKERS' COMPENSATION.

An insurance program that provides compensation for medical expenses and a portion of lost wages to employees with work-related injuries or diseases.

Background

Workers' compensation (WC) programs provide compensation for loss due to work-related injuries or disease. Most programs share two basic characteristics. First, WC is no-fault insurance, meaning an employee does not have to prove negligence or liability on the part of the employer to collect benefits. Second, WC covers tangible losses such as medical bills and lost wages.

The cornerstone of workers' compensation programs in the United States is the no-fault arrangement. The employer and the employee enter into a compact where, in the event of a work-related injury or illness, the employer provides for medical coverage and the replacement of a significant portion of the worker's wages regardless of fault. In return, the employee gives up the right to sue the employer for damages due to the employer's negligence or to sue for pain and suffering. This no-fault arrangement is not as prevalent among other countries' programs. For example, the United Kingdom and Australia lack the no-fault arrangement.

Workers' compensation programs generally provide compensation for lost wages, payments for medical care, rehabilitation services, and compensation for survivors. In addition, state and federal WC agencies provide help in resolving disputes between employees and employers.

History

The roots of workers' compensation programs can be traced to the Industrial Revolution in England during the 1700s and in the United States in the 1800s. As manufacturing techniques changed, occupations requiring large amounts of unskilled labor were created. Working conditions also changed. As a result, the relationship between employer and employee was altered and disagreements between the two arose.

Courts in both the United States and Great Britain relied on common law to help them navigate the disputes that arose between employee and employer. Common law required employers to be reasonably diligent about employees' safety. This requirement translated into providing a safe place to work, providing an adequate number of competent fellow employees, providing safe tools and equipment, warning the employee of inherent dangers in the workplace, and making and enforcing rules to ensure the safety of employees. When the employer failed to fulfill such responsibility and injury to the employee resulted, the worker could seek damages against the employer. To defend against this claim for damages, an employer would use common law defenses. These defenses included trying to show the employee was aware of the risk and therefore voluntarily assumed the risk, trying to show the employee did not exercise a reasonable amount of care for his or her safety, therefore contributing to the negligence being claimed, and attempting to show a fellow employee really was the negligent party. The result was a legal morass that tended to favor the employer over the employee.

The workers' compensation system was a response to the problems associated with the common law approach to settling disputes. The adoption of a program that assigned liability to the employer without regard to fault in exchange for the worker giving up the right to legal action for negligent action on the employer's part was heralded as a major stride in employer-employee relations.

The first workers' compensation law in the United States was enacted by Maryland in 1902, but the law was determined to be unconstitutional. There were a few attempts by other states to enact a workers' compensation law after Maryland's, but these attempts met similar fates. It was not until 1911 that a constitutional WC system was instituted. The first state to meet success with its WC statute was Wisconsin and ten more states closely followed its lead, passing WC laws in the same year.

Not surprisingly, the early WC laws were limited in their coverage and in the benefits offered. Initially, only hazardous occupations were covered, compensation was limited to partial wage replacement for a relatively short period of time, and medical coverage was not included. Over the years, workers' compensation programs have evolved to be more expansive in their coverage and level of compensation.

Conceptual Issues

The basic objectives of workers' compensation programs include:

- prompt payment of benefits;
- adequate and equitable coverage for loss of wages due to injury or disease;
- elimination of litigation surrounding work-related injury or disease and the costs associated with legal action;
- establishment of an insurance system to guarantee benefit payments;
- promotion of health and safety in the workplace;
- payment for medical care needed as a result of work-related injury or disease;
- encouragement to employees to return to work;
- maintenance of stable and affordable costs for employers and insurers.

Obviously, the way a workers' compensation program is structured will influence how well these goals are reached.

There are a number of issues associated with the design and operation of a workers' compensation program. First, covered employment has to be defined. In other words, which employees (occupations) qualify for benefits in the event of work-related injury and disease must be specified.

Second, the injuries and diseases to be covered by workers' compensation must be identified. On the surface, this seems like an easy task—those injuries and diseases that are work-related. However, WC administrators find the determination of whether the injury or disease is work-related to be among their most daunting tasks. Especially difficult is deciding whether a disease, such as lung cancer, is due solely to work-related causes, solely to non-work-related causes, or a combination of the two.

Third, the extent and type of medical benefits must be ascertained. Questions that must be resolved include whether the WC medical benefit is separate or combined with a general medical insurance benefit program, whether the WC program should pay for medical services provided by a third party, or if the WC program should provide the medical services itself, what types of medical services should be provided, and how long the services should be provided.

Fourth, the question of disability payments must be addressed. Workers' compensation programs generally have a two-fold purpose. One purpose is to compensate workers for the temporary loss of wages due to job-related injuries or illness. The second purpose is to provide a replacement for lost wages due to a permanent disability. When dealing with both temporary and permanent disabilities, the WC program needs to decide the level of replacement of lost wages, the amount of time an employee should wait before receiving benefits, and the duration or length of the benefits.

Fifth, the extent of rehabilitation benefits has to be decided. If the injury or illness has changed a worker's ability to perform the previous job, vocational counseling and job retraining may be necessary. Finally, the level of survivor benefits and the amount of compensation of burial expenses must be determined.

Workers' Compensation in the United States

State governments control the vast majority of workers' compensation programs in the United States. They decide whether to require employers to provide WC coverage, they set the standards for WC coverage, and they provide oversight of WC programs. As a result, the extent of coverage provided, the structure of the programs, and the level of benefits provided by workers' compensation programs vary widely in the United States.

According to *Compensating Injured Railroad Workers Under the Federal Employers' Liability Act* (Transportation Research Board 1994), in 1990 approximately 90 million workers in the United States were covered by workers' compensation programs, and almost 2 percent of total payrolls in the United States were earmarked to pay for WC coverage. Approximately US $35 billion in workers' compensation benefits were paid out in 1990, and the cost of WC to employers was about US $65 billion (p. 83).

James Markham (1992) noted in *Principles of Workers Compensation Claims* that nine out of ten employees are covered by workers' compensation programs (p. 2). The major groups not covered are railroad employees, some farm workers, and some state and local government workers, including police and fire persons who generally are covered by separate programs. The vast majority of jurisdictions in the United States require employers to provide workers' compensation for their employees. Only three states do not mandate WC coverage—New Jersey, South Carolina, and Texas—but most of the employers in these states provide workers' compensation voluntarily due to concerns about exposure to negligence lawsuits.

Most workers' compensation programs are covered by private insurers or by employer self-insurance. Self-insurance means the employers do not buy insurance from a private insurer or participate in a state-run insurance pool. Instead, these employers pay WC benefits as they occur. Six states have an exclusive state workers' compensation fund and require employers to contribute to and use this fund for WC benefit payments. Thirteen other states have a state fund, but employers are not required to use the fund. Instead, the state fund is one option employers can choose to fund their WC programs. In general, state WC agencies are funded by a tax on private employers. In a few cases, some or all of the funding comes from the general fund.

When private insurance carriers are being used for the WC coverage, they deal directly with injured and ill workers with regard to WC benefits. When disputes arise, state workers' compensation boards or commissions and the courts step in to settle the disagreements.

The U.S. government has two major workers' compensation programs under its purview. Federal government employees are covered under the Federal Employees' Compensation Act of 1916. Not surprisingly, the federal government self-insures this program. The second program covers private employees in longshoring and related occupations. As a result of the Longshore and Harbor Workers' Compensation Act of 1972 (LHWCA), employers can purchase insurance or self-insure. Employees of the LHWCA help settle disputes that may arise due to this coverage.

The International Dimension

The first workers' compensation program was instituted in Germany in 1884. Poland enacted its own WC system in the same year, followed by Czechoslovakia and Austria in 1887. In 1950, 109 countries had workers' compensation programs and by 1987, 136 countries had WC programs. Of these 136 programs, only Australia, Canada, and the United States fail to have a centralized WC system. Instead, all three countries have WC programs for each state or province. The reason for this divergence from the mainstream practice may be that all three countries have a federal, not a unitary, system of government.

It is not surprising that there is a fair amount of variety in WC programs throughout the world. Eighty-nine of the 136 nations with workers' compensation laws integrate WC systems with their social security systems. Forty-one of the remaining 47 countries require WC coverage whereas the other 6 have voluntary systems.

Slightly more than 54 percent of the 136 WC systems worldwide cover all employees whereas 7 percent of the systems only cover employees in occupations specified. The remaining 39 percent of the countries fall somewhere in between these two extremes. Almost 80 percent of the 136 countries cover all medical expenses while slightly more than 2 percent cover no medical expenses. The remaining 18 percent restrict medical benefits to some extent.

In all 136 countries, employers contribute to the workers' compensation program. Employees also contribute in 21 countries whereas governments contribute in 36 countries.

Challenges to Workers' Compensation Systems

Workers' compensation programs in the United States face challenges in the years ahead. The first and foremost challenge is soaring medical costs. Overall health care costs have been rising much faster than the rate of inflation for a number of years. These increases threaten both the health care system and the WC system as ways are being sought to reduce the increases in medical costs.

A second concern is the increased use of WC systems. Studies have shown a positive relationship between increased levels of benefits and utilization rates. In other words, as benefits become more generous, people are making more claims on the WC systems. It has also been shown that economic downturns are correlated with increased utilization. Finally, a liberalization of what is considered a work-related injury or illness has increased WC system utilization. For example, mental stress claims have been allowed in some states, and the number of claims based on this illness has increased rapidly.

A third concern deals with increased litigation. While the initial purpose of workers' compensation programs was to agree on compensation without resorting to the courts, this has been changing. Difficult definitional issues have arisen with regard to what constitutes work-related injury and disease. For example, as the workforce ages, it becomes increasingly difficult to discern what injuries and diseases are associated with getting old rather than being caused by work. In the absence of easy and clear-cut definitions, increased litigation is inevitable.

C. KURT ZORN

BIBLIOGRAPHY

Machinery and Allied Products Institute, 1980. *Workers' Compensation: A System in Need of Reform.* Washington, DC: Machinery and Allied Products Institute.

Markham, James J., ed., 1992. *Principles of Workers Compensation Claims.* Malvern. PA: Insurance Institute of America.

Transportation Research Board, National Research Council, 1994. *Compensating Injured Railroad Workers Under the Federal Employers' Liability Act.* Washington, DC: National Academy Press.

Victor, Richard A., ed., 1990. *Challenges for the 1990s.* Cambridge, MA: Workers Compensation Research Institute.

Williams, C. Arthur, Jr., 1991. *An International Comparison of Workers' Compensation.* Boston. MA: Kluwer Academic Publishers. [The international section drew heavily from this source.]

WORKFORCE DIVERSITY.

The fundamental change in the composition of an organization's workforce that is now occurring in the United States and other developed countries as their cultures and populations become increasingly diverse. This demographic diversity is accompanied by economic pressures, as technological change and globalization of the economy increase public and private employers' demands for a highly trained workforce. And political pressures by women, minorities, older workers, immigrants, and persons with disabilities have resulted in legal changes in the employment rights of groups formerly excluded by law or custom from desirable professional and technical jobs (see **discrimination, age; discrimination, disability; discrimination, gender; discrimination, racial**). As a result of these changes, organizations need to design and implement workforce diversification programs. These involve subtle but sweeping changes in how they do business: changes in organizational mission, culture, policy, and practice.

Because workforce diversity is caused by the impact of societal changes on organizations, the organizational changes it causes are not isolated. Rather, they are related to other emergent trends in public personnel management such as targeted recruitment, employee development, total quality management, and nonadversarial dispute resolution. But they also conflict with other emergent human resource management trends caused by the same pressures: alternative methods of service delivery, temporary employment, and job simplification.

The changes caused by workforce diversification generate changed role expectations for all groups in public agencies: appointed and elected officials, managers and supervisors, employees, and public personnel managers. Because the objectives and underlying assumptions of diversification programs conflict with those of other prevalent management trends, workforce diversification programs generate conflicts that make effective performance by each group more difficult and demanding.

There are many examples of successful and unsuccessful work force diversification programs in a range of public- and private-sector organizations. And successful programs generally share common characteristics, as do unsuccessful ones. This entry will:

1. define workforce diversity and workforce diversification;
2. discuss its origin and history;
3. distinguish workforce diversification from equal employment opportunity and affirmative action;
4. examine its impact on organizational mission, culture, and five areas of personnel management policy and practice: recruitment and retention, job design, education and training, benefits and rewards, and performance measurement and improvement;
5. show its connection to some contemporary public management trends such as employee involvement and participation, employee development, total quality management, and nonadversarial dispute resolution; and its conflicts with other trends such as temporary employment, cost containment, and job simplification;
6. explore how workforce diversification changes role expectations and causes role conflict for elected officials and public administrators (managers, supervisors, employees, human resource managers, and affirmative action compliance specialists);
7. present successful and unsuccessful examples of work force diversification programs; and based on these examples, describe the characteristics of successful programs, and unsuccessful ones.

Definitions: Workforce Diversity and Workforce Diversification

Workforce diversity is a term that describes the range of employee characteristics that are increasingly present in the contemporary workforce of the United States and other developed countries. Although disagreement does exist over the specific definition of diversity, for our purposes it includes differences in employee and applicant characteristics (race, gender, ethnicity, national origin, language, religion, age, education, intelligence, and disabilities) that constitute the range of variation among human beings in the workforce.

Workforce diversification is a set of changes in organizational mission, culture, policies, and programs designed to enhance an organization's effectiveness by shifting its focus from tolerating diversity to embracing diversity. In public agencies, a diversification program includes a range of personnel functions: job design, recruitment and retention, pay and benefits, orientation and training, and performance evaluation and improvement.

Origin and History of Workforce Diversity

Workforce diversity has its origins in complex and interactive social, economic, political and legal changes that are taking place in Europe, the United States, and other developed nations today.

The workforce in modern industrialized nations is becoming socially more diverse. In the United States, it is comprised increasingly of immigrants whose primary language is not English and whose primary norms are not those of "mainstream" American culture. And in the United States, for example, only 15 percent of the increase in the work force between 1985 and 2000 will be white, non-Hispanic males; 64 percent of the growth will be women; and the remaining 31 percent will comprise non-white males (native-born and immigrant) (Jamieson and O'Mara 1991). It will be older. And new and current workers will require technical and professional skills increasingly in short supply because of growing deficiencies in our educational system (Johnston and Packer 1987).

Workforce diversity is not an isolated social change. It results from increasing economic pressures for organizations to remain competitive in the new global economy. Organizations strive for diversity because organization that effectively manages diversity is more effective at producing goods or services suitable for a diverse market. And a diverse organization is more effective at selling them, because consumers from diverse groups are attracted to the products or services of an organization that is attuned to their culture, language, and values.

Workforce diversity is also based on increased political power and legal protection of diverse groups, as these groups evolve through several stages of empowerment and protection. First, members of diverse groups are almost automatically excluded from the workforce, except for unskilled positions, because they are outside the "mainstream" culture. This exclusion may be based in law as well as custom. Second, as economic development and labor shortages increase, these groups are admitted into the labor market, although they face continued economic and legal discrimination and are excluded from consideration for desirable professional and technical positions. Third, as economic development and labor shortages continue, and as their political power continues to increase, group members are accepted for a range of positions, and their employment rights are protected by laws guaranteeing equal employment access (equal employment opportunity). Fourth, as these groups become increasingly powerful politically, efforts to reduce the considerable informal discrimination that continues in recruitment, promotion, pay, and benefits lead to establishment of workplace policies such as salary equality and employment proportionate with their representation in the labor market. Achievement of these goals is encouraged by voluntary affirmative action programs. If voluntary achievement efforts are unsuccessful,

conformance may be mandated by affirmative action compliance agencies or court orders. Fifth, continued social and political changes lead to the welcoming of diversity as a desirable political and social condition, and continued economic pressures lead to the development of workforce diversification programs for organizations that desire to remain competitive.

These stages in the evolution of political power and legal protection for diverse groups in the workforce are shown in Table I.

Difference Between Diversification, Equal Employment Opportunity, and Affirmative Action

Because the workforce diversification programs found in the contemporary workplace are the current stage of an evolutionary process defined by increased social participation, political power, and legal protection for minorities, it is understandable that some people consider workforce diversification programs to be simple "old wine in new bottles"–a contemporary variant on the equal employment opportunity or affirmative action programs that have characterized personnel management in the United States for the past 30 years. However, workforce diversification differs from equal employment opportunity or affirmative action programs in five important respects.

First, their purposes are different. Equal employment opportunity programs are based on organizational efforts to avoid violating employees' or applicants' legal or constitutional rights. And affirmative programs are based on organizational efforts to achieve proportional representation of selected groups. But workforce diversification programs originate from managers' objectives of increasing organizational productivity and effectiveness.

Second, diversification programs include all employees, not just employees in specified groups. Affirmative action laws protect only the employment rights of designated categories of persons (in the United States such groups as Blacks, Hispanics, Native Americans, Asian Americans,

TABLE I. POLITICAL POWER AND LEGAL PROTECTION FOR DIVERSE GROUPS IN THE WORKFORCE

Stage	Employment Status	Legal Protections
1	excluded from the workforce	none
2	admitted to the workforce, but excluded from desirable jobs	none
3	accepted into the workforce	equal employment opportunity laws and programs
4	recruited into the workforce	affirmative action laws
5	welcomed into the workforce	diversification programs

workers over 40, women, and Americans with disabilities). But workforce diversification programs are based on recognition not only of these protected groups, but also of the entire spectrum of characteristics (knowledge, skills, and abilities) that managers and personnel directors need to recognize and factor into personnel decisions in order to acquire and develop a productive workforce.

Third, workforce diversification programs affect a broader range of organizational activities. Affirmative action programs emphasize recruitment, selection, and sometimes promotion because those are the personnel functions most closely tied to proportional representation of protected groups (see **representative bureaucracy**). But workforce diversification programs include all personnel functions related to organizational effectiveness (including recruitment, promotion and retention, job design, pay and benefits, education and training, and performance measurement and improvement).

Fourth, workforce diversification programs have a different locus of control. Affirmative action and equal employment opportunity programs are based on managerial responses to outside compliance agencies' requirements. However, workforce diversification programs originate as internal organizational responses to managerial demands for enhanced productivity and effectiveness (although this response is itself a reaction to demographic changes in overall population).

Fifth, because of all of the above factors, the entire effect of diversification programs is different. Affirmative action programs tend to be viewed negatively by managers and employees, because they are based on a negative premise (What changes must we make in recruitment and selection procedures to demonstrate a "good faith effort" to achieve a representative workforce and thereby avoid sanctions by affirmative action compliance agencies or courts?). In contrast, those workforce diversification programs that are most successful tend to be viewed as positive by managers and employees, because they are based on a different question (what changes can we make in our organization's mission, culture, policies, and programs in order to become more effective and more competitive?).

Impact on Organizational Mission, Culture, Policy, and Practice

Workforce diversification has an impact on organizations that is both sweeping and subtle. It affects their mission, culture, policy, and practice in ways that are obvious and unexpected, cumulative and dramatic.

Impact on Organizational Mission

Workforce diversification encourages changes in the organization's mission, or purpose. It starts from a recognition among managers and personnel professionals that human resources are increasingly vital to organizational survival and effectiveness and that diversification programs are the best way to foster the effective use of human resources (National Performance Review 1993).

Impact on Organizational Culture

Workforce diversification requires changes in organizational culture–the values, assumptions, and communication patterns that characterize interaction among employees. These patterns are invented, discovered, or developed by members of the organization as responses to problems; they become part of the culture as they are taught to new members as the correct way to perceive, think, and feel in relation to these problems (Schein 1981). Viewed from this perspective, diversification is a change in the way organizations do business rather than just an adaptation of existing personnel policies and programs to meet the specialized needs of minorities and women. It is an effort to describe and understand the range of knowledge, skills, and abilities (KSAs) that members of diverse cultures or diverse groups can bring to the workplace. It is an effort to consciously utilize these KSAs as a key to making organizations successful and productive.

Impact on Human Resource Management Policy and Practice

A organization's decision to use workforce diversity to increase effectiveness causes changes in its human resource management policy and practice (see **human resources management**). Policy and practice are the rules and procedures that implement organizational objectives. With respect to workforce diversity, these policies and practices are management's strategic plan for accomplishing its mission through workforce diversification. And they are a message to employees, managers, and political leaders about the value the agency places on diversity in particular and on human resources in general. In an agency with effective human resource management and effective workforce diversification policies and programs, this message is explicit and positive.

Workforce diversification programs affect five specific areas of human resource management policy and practice: recruitment and retention, job design, education and training, benefits and rewards, and performance measurement and improvement (see **recruitment, job design, training and development,** and **performance appraisal**).

Recruitment and Retention. Policies and programs include strategies already commonplace in affirmative action programs: increasing the applicant pool of underrepresented groups, increasing their selection rate by developing valid alternatives for tests that have a disparate impact, and evaluating performance evaluation and mentoring systems so as to encourage retention. Yet, they differ because of the ways workforce diversification differs from affirmative action. Their purpose is productivity enhancement through a diverse workforce rather than legal compliance through recruitment or selection quotas (see **goals and quotas**); they apply to a broader spectrum of applicant and employee characteristics; they include a broader range of personnel activities; their locus of control is internal rather than external, and their tone is positive rather than negative.

Job Design. Also affected in workforce diversification efforts, job design usually leads managers to consider changes in where and how employees do work (Morgan and Tucker 1991). To attract and retain women with child- and elder-care responsibilities into the workforce, options that offer flexibility of work locations and schedules need to be considered. To attract and retain persons with disabilities, reasonable accommodation must be offered to make the workplace physically accessible and to make jobs available to persons who are otherwise qualified to perform the primary duties of the position (ADA 1990).

Education and Training. Programs influenced in two ways by diversification programs. First, employer concerns with the educational preparation of future workers have led to greater employer involvement in areas that used to be considered the domain of public school systems. Workforce training programs now include basic skills unrelated to specific job tasks (such as literacy and English as a second language). And there is increasing interest in strengthening federal and state sponsored job training programs and in sponsoring joint business-government policy initiatives such as tax incentives for costs associated with business training programs. Second, employers now routinely develop and present managerial and supervisory training courses on multicultural awareness and sensitivity.

Pay and Benefit. These policies often become more flexible and innovative as diversification progresses. Because women are the traditional family caregivers, an employer's ability to attract a diverse work force depends upon providing flexible benefits; benefits for part-time as well as full-time positions, parental leave, child- and elder-care support programs, and phased retirement policies for older workers (see **family leave and flexitime**).

Performance Measurement and Productivity Improvement. These programs often change focus because of the assumptions underlying workforce diversification programs. Managers and supervisors now need to consider the differing values and motivational perspectives of a diverse workforce (Rubaii-Barrett and Beck 1993). Workforce diversity has also brought about changing definitions of productivity based on the need for variation in managerial styles and resultant dramatic increases in organizational effectiveness (Loden and Rosener 1991). And as work teams themselves become more diverse, group evaluation techniques that recognize the importance of individual contributions to work teams also need to be encouraged.

The common threads linking these five areas of personnel policy and practice are their common objective of increased organizational effectiveness and their cumulative impact on organizational culture. Organizations that wish to attract and keep a diversified workforce must change the culture of the organization to create a climate in which persons from diverse groups feel accepted, comfortable, and productive. And this is why the tone of workforce diversification programs differs from their affirmative compliance program predecessors—affirming diversity is different from tolerating or accepting it.

Workforce Diversification and Other Management Trends

Public policy and administration is a river of theory and practice comprising many currents, some conflicting with each other. Thus, it is to be expected that workforce diversification programs are consistent with some contemporary management trends in that they share common assumptions and objectives. And these programs are inconsistent with other trends that derive from opposing assumptions and objectives.

Consistent Management Trends

Workforce diversification programs are consistent with trends such as employee involvement and participation, employee development, total quality management, and nonadversarial dispute resolution.

Employee Involvement and Participation. Considered essential for maintaining high productivity (at least among employees in key professional and technical positions). Even in the absence of significant financial rewards, employees tend to work happily and effectively when they have the necessary skills, see their work as meaningful, feel personally responsible for productivity, and have first-hand knowledge of the actual results of their labor. These psychological states are most likely to result from work designed to incorporate characteristics such as variety, significance, self-control, and feedback. They are the objective of workplace innovations such as delegation, flexible work locations and schedules, job sharing, management by objectives (MBO), and total quality management (TQM).

Employee Development. Related to diversification, at least for key professional and technical employees, because it (1) focuses planning and budget analysis on human resources, (2) facilitates cost-benefit analysis of current training and development activities, and (3) facilitates communication and commitment of organizational goals through employee participation and involvement (Rosow and Zager 1988; and Bernhard and Ingols 1988). This includes training for diversity (Solomon 1993).

Total Quality Management (TQM). An organizational change process that involves a combination of top-down and bottom-up activities: assessment of problems, identification of solutions, and designation of responsibilities for resolving them. It focuses on the connection between the quality of the work environment and the quality of individual, team, and organizational performance (Deming 1988). It is similar to team building and organizational development (French and Bell 1990). And it is congruent with workforce diversification efforts because, like diversification, it focuses on a transformation of organizational culture, policies, and programs so as to enhance productivity.

Nonadversarial Dispute Resolution. A philosophy and practice that has become more common because the challenge of channeling diversity into productivity is complicated by the breadth of expectations members of diverse cultures bring to their work, both as individuals and as members of those cultures. Without a method of settling disputes that models the organization's commitment to tolerance and respect, differences lead only to divisiveness that consumes organizational resources without positive results (Thomas 1990). And there is general recognition that traditional adversarial dispute resolution techniques are not particularly effective at resolving organizational conflicts: They build acrimony, harden bargaining positions, and delay the resolution of the original conflict. Therefore, innovative conflict resolution techniques such as "win-win" negotiation and group problem solving have become more popular. These "nonadversarial" techniques are often more effective, and they have the additional advantage of modeling the organization's commitment to respect, tolerance, and dignity.

Opposing Management Trends

Workforce diversification also conflicts with other current trends in human resource management that are caused by some of the same economic pressures: temporary employment, cost containment, and job simplification.

Temporary and Part-time Employment

An increasingly common phenomenon in the public and private workplace because it offers managers and personnel managers overwhelming advantages—flexibility, cost control, and circumvention of personnel ceilings or civil service rules. But it does have disadvantages for applicants and some employees in that it has also meant the creation of two segmented labor markets (Doeringer and Piore 1975): a primary market for skilled managerial, professional, and technical positions characterized by high pay, high status, and job security; and a secondary market for less-skilled laborer and service positions characterized by low pay, low status, and employment insecurity. While employers will increasingly utilize minorities and women because of changing workforce demographics and a labor shortage, most new jobs will be created in the service sector and filled through the secondary labor market (Hudson Institute 1988), and most employment opportunities for minorities and women will be in these new jobs rather than in more desirable professional and technical positions filled through primary labor markets. Jobs filled (coincidentally mainly by white males) through the primary labor market have relatively high qualifications, and this marked difference in qualifications creates a "glass ceiling" that hinders development or promotion of employees (particularly minorities and women) from jobs filled through the secondary market (see **glass ceiling**).

Cost Containment

Due to economic pressure, cost containment also runs counter to the pay and benefit innovations fostered by workforce diversification programs in that they lead to reduced pay and benefits for all employees. Professional and technical employees will continue to receive comparatively liberal health benefits to help ensure retention and loyalty. But their pension benefits will continue to be eroded by longer vesting periods, higher retirement ages, and a shift to defined-contribution programs. Their health care benefits will continue to be reduced through increased premiums, longer waiting periods, and benefit limitations. But it will be worse for temporary or part-time employees, who often receive no pension, health care, vacation, or sick leave benefits of any kind.

Job Simplification. Also a logical outcome of the increased use of temporary and part-time employees: Employers are forced to lower skill demands or training costs by "simplifying" rather than by "enriching" jobs. That is, employers invest little, if anything, in training temporary employees. And wherever possible, jobs filled through the secondary labor market are redesigned to minimize knowledge and skill requirements so that even untrained and unmotivated employees can perform them satisfactorily. This means designing jobs with simple and repetitive tasks, rather than giving employees control over a complete job. It makes making quality control a supervisory responsibility (as in traditional, hierarchical organizations) rather than empowering individuals or work teams to perform this function themselves. And for these temporary employees, the relationship between employees and employer is unlikely to be more than an economic transaction (pay for work). The assumptions underlying management of "permanent" professional and technical employees (such as involvement, participation, employee development, and careers) will not apply to temporary employees.

Implications for Elected Officials and Public Administrators

Workforce diversity implies changing role expectations and role conflict for elected officials, managers and supervisors, employees, personnel professionals, and affirmative action compliance specialists charged with developing or implementing personnel management policies in public agencies.

Elected Officials

For elected officials, it means making difficult choices among policy options that often conflict. These include pressures for "reinventing" government that take the form of continued pressure on public agencies to measure outputs, increase efficiency, and enhance political accountability. In public personnel administration, it means the relative ascendancy of political responsiveness and efficiency as values and the need for personnel administrators to work with other systems (besides traditional civil service and collective bargaining) to enable agencies to reach objectives and control costs (Klingner and Nalbandian 1998). And providing public services outside of traditional civil service systems controls the apparent size of the public "bureaucracy" while enhancing opportunities for contracting out. Consequently, much government growth has been through secondary labor market mechanisms and through alternative vehicles for delivering public services: purchase of service contracting, franchise agreements, subsidy arrangements, vouchers, volunteers, self-help, regulatory and tax incentives (International City Management Association 1989). Although it is possible to influence the personnel practices of contractors through minority business programs and "set-asides" (contracting quotas), the use of alternative methods of service delivery reduces the ability of the public sector to directly shape agency mission, culture, policies, and procedures so as to achieve workforce diversity.

Managers and Supervisors

Managers and supervisors are faced with the need to maintain productive organizations in the face of two contradictory truths: It is usually easier to make decisions and resolve conflicts in a homogeneous organization, at least in the short run, and organizations must be adaptable to heterogeneous and shifting environments in order to survive in the long run. This means that managers will continue to be evaluated along two criteria—short-term productivity and changes in organizational culture that enable the organization to enhance long-term effectiveness.

Employees

Employees face the need to communicate, interact, form work teams, resolve conflicts, and make decisions with other employees who may be unlike them in many charac-teristics. And they will do so in a climate of increased workplace tension due to the transformation of labor markets and increased employment opportunity for skilled and unskilled foreign workers. These changes pit workers against each other, and they pit new applicants against current employees.

Human Resource Managers

As always, human resource managers face the need to manage human resource efficiently and effectively. With respect to workforce diversity, this means the need to develop and apply two apparently contradictory human-resource strategies: policies for temporary employees designed to control costs and policies for permanent employees designed to ensure loyalty, participation, and asset development as human resources. Yet, because asset development and cost control are both valid objectives, this ambivalence will continue. And because effective human resource management depends upon the communication of clear and consistent messages, public personnel managers find it increasingly difficult when they must send different messages to different employees.

In general, therefore, workforce diversity is consistent with demands on public officials and administrators for more innovation. Human resource managers who recognize the dynamism and conflict inherent in their roles are more likely to maintain an innovative and appropriate balance between conflicting objectives. But cultivating innovation among public managers requires characteristics usually not present in the culture of contemporary organizations—reward systems that reinforce risk taking and do not penalize failure.

Affirmative Action Compliance Specialists

The transition from affirmative action compliance to workforce diversification presents affirmative action compliance specialists with a difficult dilemma. Traditionally, affirmative action specialists have relied upon their authority as interfaces between the organization and external compliance agencies. Given the five critical differences between affirmative action compliance and workforce diversification, these specialists need to redefine their own role and culture in the organization.

Examples of Workforce Diversity Programs in Practice

There are many examples of successful and unsuccessful workforce diversification programs in a range of private- and public-sector organizations. Examples include the following:

- The National Performance Review (1993) recommended a number of changes to move managers from an orientation toward personnel procedures toward creation and maintenance of a quality, diverse workforce.

- Corning Glass Works evaluates managers on their ability to "create a congenial environment" for diverse employees.
- Mobil Corporation created a special committee of executives to identify high-potential female and minority executive job candidates and to place them in line management positions viewed as critical for advancement through the "glass ceiling" (Morgan and Tucker 1991).
- Robert McCabe, President of Miami-Dade Community College, recently won a MacArthur Foundation Award for educational leadership, including a ten-year emphasis on workforce diversity as a key to community involvement and mission achievement.
- AT&T Bell Laboratories focuses its recruitment efforts on acquiring "the best and the brightest, regardless of race, lifestyle, or physical challenges." This has resulted in a comprehensive diversification program.
- Dallas, Texas, developed a diversification program that involved modifications in the delivery of city services and the formation of a development corporation for an underdeveloped minority area of the city.
- San Diego, California, developed a diversification program that involved a shift in organizational culture and consequent changes in policy and practice.

Characteristics of Effective and Ineffective Programs

In almost all cases, the effort to implement workforce diversification programs starts with both top-level support and efforts of a broad-based committee that assesses organizational culture, sets goals, and suggests policy and program alternatives. If the focus of diversification is an organization, the focus of diversification programs is internal climate, policies, and programs. In large organizations, the policy and program alternative stage may involve the work of several related task forces, each focusing on a defined area of personnel practice such as recruitment and retention. If the focus is an entire city or community, the focus may include economic and social development initiatives as well.

Effective Workforce Diversification Programs

Experts have proposed a relatively uniform set of criteria for assessing the effectiveness of workforce diversity policies and programs. These include

- a broad definition of diversity that includes a range of characteristics rather than only those used to define "protected classes" under existing affirmative action programs;

- a systematic assessment of the existing culture to determine how members at all levels view the present organization;
- top-level initiation of, commitment to, and visibility of workforce diversity as an essential organizational policy rather than as a legal compliance issue or staff function;
- establishment of specific objectives;
- integration into the managerial performance evaluation and reward structure;
- coordination with other activities such as employee development, job design, and TQM; and
- continual evaluation and improvement.

Ineffective Workforce Diversification Programs

Insufficient top-level commitment or organizational visibility generally render diversification efforts unsuccessful because the program's long-term impact on organization mission or culture is inadequate (Denison 1990).

DONALD E. KLINGNER

BIBLIOGRAPHY

ADA (Americans with Disabilities Act), 1990. P.L. 101-336, July 26, 1990.

Bernhard, H., and C. Ingols, 1988. "Six Lessons for the Corporate Classroom." *Harvard Business Review,* vol. 88 (September-October): 40–48.

Deming, W. Edwards, 1988. *Out of the Crisis.* Cambridge: MIT Center for Advanced Engineering Study.

Denison, Daniel, 1990. *Corporate Culture and Organizational Effectiveness.* New York: Wiley.

Doeringer, Peter and Michael Piore, 1975. "Unemployment and the 'Dual Labor Market.'" *The Public Interest,* vol. 38: 67–79.

French, Wendell, and C. Bell, 1990. *Organizational Development,* 4th ed. Englewood Cliffs, NJ: Prentice-Hall.

Hudson Institute, 1988. *Opportunity 2000: Creating Affirmative Action Strategies for a Changing Workforce.* Indianapolis: Hudson Institute.

International City Management Association, 1989. *Service Delivery in the 90s: Alternative Approaches for Local Governments.* Washington, DC: ICMA.

Jamieson, David, and Julie O'Mara, 1991. *Managing Workforce 2000.* San Francisco, CA: Jossey-Bass.

Johnston, W., and A. Packer, 1987. *Workforce 2000: Work and Workers for the Twenty-First Century.* Indianapolis: Hudson Institute.

Klingner, Donald, and John Nalbandian, 1998. *Public Personnel Management: Contexts and Strategies,* 4th ed. Englewood Cliffs, NJ: Prentice-Hall.

Loden, Marilyn, and Judy Rosener, 1991. *Workforce America! Managing Employee Diversity as a Vital Resource.* Homewood, IL: Business One Irwin.

Morgan, H., and K. Tucker, 1991. *Companies That Care.* New York: Fireside.

National Performance Review, 1993. *Reinventing Human Resource Management.* Washington, DC: National Performance Review, Office of the Vice President.

Rosow, J., and R. Zager, 1988. *Training—The Corporate Edge.* San Francisco, CA: Jossey-Bass.

Rubaii-Barrett, Nadia, and Ann Beck, 1993. "Minorities in the Majority: Implications for Managing Cultural Diversity." *Public Personnel Management,* vol. 22 (Winter): 503–522.

Schein, Edgar, 1981. *Organizational Culture and Leadership.* San Francisco, CA: Jossey-Bass.

Solomon, Charlene, 1993. "Managing Today's Immigrants." *Personnel Journal,* vol. 72 (February): 57–65.

Thomas, R. Roosevelt, 1990. "From Affirmative Action to Affirming Diversity." *Harvard Business Review,* vol. 68: 107–117.

WORKLOAD MEASURES.

Indicators of activity, efficiency, or volume of workload used to measure demand for services or service output for purposes of budget estimation, allocation, and evaluation.

Workload measures represent some of the earliest attempts to quantify the activities of government systematically for budget purposes. Quantitative analysis had been used successfully during World War II to determine personnel and material needs for the armed forces. In the 1950s, these techniques were applied in business and government organizations in order to make them more efficient and cost effective. Since that time budget and policy analysts, program evaluators, and performance reviewers have been employed by governments to use the techniques of quantitative analysis and qualitative evaluation to improve the performance, productivity, and success of government programs. Workload measurement is one of the quantitative techniques used in these activities.

Workload volume and service output have been an information factor in budget development and allocation since government officials and agencies first began to prepare budgets. Early budget preparers often measured workload informally, however, and did not usually include specific workload measures in the formal budget documents. Measurement of workloads began to be a significant part of the budget development and preparation process in the United States in the 1950s when performance budgeting was introduced.

Performance budgeting in the 1950s was based on the premise of cost efficiency. Performance budgets used workload measures to link expenditures to the type and amount of work to be done by a particular governmental unit and to the cost efficiency with which the work was done. In order to budget for efficient government performance, budget preparers needed to know the agency's workload, which was determined by the demand for a particular good or service. Also needed was information on the rate at which the work could be performed, the unit cost of doing the work, and where possible, the outcome of the work. For example, the workload of the garbage collection department of a particular city would be calculated from information on the number of households, businesses, and other garbage-producing entities within the city and the amount of garbage each one produced each week. Using the garbage collection workload measure, the efficiency of the garbage collectors, the frequency of collection, and the unit cost of collecting the garbage, the expenditure amount needed in the budget for garbage collection could be calculated.

In the 1960s, planning, programming, budgeting (PPB) supplanted performance budgeting in the federal government and many state and local governments. PPB included measures of program outcome, effectiveness, and impact in budget documents, as well as the more traditional workload measures. The emphasis of PPB was on the relationship between societal needs, program plans, and budget outcomes, making workload and efficiency measures less important than indicators of the impacts and results of government programs. In the 1970s, when zero-based budgeting (ZBB) replaced PPB in many governments, workload measurement, efficiency, and cost effectiveness again were emphasized in the budget process. Throughout the 1980s and 1990s, government budget processes have become more individualized, as governments have incorporated specific components of various budgetary techniques to meet their needs. Many of the elements of performance budgeting have been used in these tailor-made budget processes. Some governments have adopted a revised and updated version of performance budgeting, often tied to strategic plans. Workload measures have continued to be used by many of these governments in both the process of developing the budget, in the budget documents and presentations to decisionmakers, and in performance review and evaluation during and after the budget year.

Technically, a workload measure is an indicator of the quantifiable amount of work to be done by an individual or organization over a specific period of time. For example, a workload measure for a government organization could be the number of clients who need or demand services, the number of claims forms or other items to be processed, or the number of miles of streets or highways to be checked for potholes or for resurfacing. Workload measures are quantifiable indicators of the volume of work to be done during the period covered that either stand alone for budget and analysis purposes or are combined with other indicators to measure efficiency, productivity, or cost effectiveness. Workload measures differ from many qualitative program measures that are difficult to quantify, such as those that evaluate the quality of work completed, because workload measures must be quantifiable. Workload measures are often coupled with efficiency indicators or previously established performance standards to determine the personnel and supply needs of an organization for budget purposes.

In performance budgeting, the funds needed for a particular activity are determined in part by the level of the workload measures anticipated for the budget year and by the established standards of performance for each function. For example, one workload measure for the street repair department of a city might be the number of pot-holes that will emerge each spring and need to be repaired. This workload measure would be used to determine the budget amount needed for pothole filling in conjunction with information about the cost of filling a pothole and the performance standards for the pothole crew, including the time it takes a crew to fill a pothole, how many workers are in the crew, how much equipment they need, and how much fuel, asphalt, and other supplies are needed for each pothole. In addition to their use in budget preparation, workload measures also would be included in the performance budget documents to justify the expenditure amounts requested for a particular budget year.

As used in budgeting, the term workload measure is also used in a broader sense to include measures of unit cost, efficiency, and productivity. All of these measurements are quantifiable and relate to workload, but expand on the concept to include related factors that influence budget decisions. Unit cost is the cost per single unit of output. It can be calculated by dividing the total cost of an activity, such as pothole filling, by the output, which in this example would be the number of potholes filled. The result of that calculation would be the cost of filling one pothole, or the unit cost of pothole filling. Once unit cost is determined for a particular activity, it can be used in conjunction with workload measures to develop budgets for the activity. The basic unit cost can also be adjusted by cost differentials or inflation factors to update the projected unit costs from one year to the next or from one related activity to another. If a basic unit cost is established from actual expenditures and outputs each year and then updated as necessary to reflect any expected cost changes for a future year or years, the estimated budget for the future year can be calculated by multiplying the appropriate unit cost by the amount of the projected workload measure for that year.

Efficiency measurements usually relate the output of a government activity to its cost or to the speed with which it is done. Workload measures are often a factor in these calculations. In time-related efficiency measurements, for example, the workload volume can be measured over a particular time period and then compared to the organization's output during that time period. If output is less than workload, a backlog is being created that may indicate either inefficiency or insufficient resources to complete the workload. Efficiency is also measured by the elapsed time in completion of the workload. For example, a typical efficiency measurement for police and fire emergency calls is response time, the elapsed time between receipt of the call and arrival on the scene. In this case, the workload measure would be the volume of emergency calls, and efficiency would be measured by the speed with which emergency workers respond to the calls. Both of these types of efficiency measures can be used for budget development to determine the need for workers, equipment, and other resources. Similarly, these workload measures could be used

to help justify the need for a particular budget level to executive and legislative decisionmakers.

Cost-related efficiency calculations also use workload measures. Cost efficiency is usually measured by the amount of output in goods or services produced per dollar spent. The cost efficiency of an activity can be measured by dividing the actual output for a period of time by the full cost of producing that output, including both direct and indirect costs. In budgeting, workload measure projections can be used with cost projections to determine the cost efficiency of some activity. For example, the projected cost efficiency of filling potholes would be calculated by dividing the estimated workload, the number of potholes to be filled, by the projected cost of the pothole-filling work crew. This would determine the projected cost efficiency of the operation, that is, the number or fraction of potholes that are expected to be filled per dollar spent for that purpose. This differs from unit cost, which is the cost of filling one pothole. Cost efficiency is a useful measure to use in budget preparation for comparison through time or across activities in order to determine which activities provide the most return for the money spent.

Productivity analysis also depends on workload measures. Similar to cost efficiency, the simplest measurement of productivity is the amount or volume of output per worker in some time period. This productivity indicator can be projected for budget purposes by dividing the anticipated workload measure volume by the budgeted number of full-time equivalent workers. After a project has been completed, the actual output can be divided by the actual number of workers or worker hours to determine productivity. If the level of the workload measure of an organization increases or decreases during a budget year, this can affect productivity and may need to be reflected in the following year's budget. Workload and productivity measures also can be useful for analyzing personnel needs and determining standards for case loads or work allocation.

Workload measures are widely used in budgeting, personnel decision making, program evaluation, and performance reviews of government organizations. They are most commonly found in performance budgets, although they are also frequently used to quantify work demands in other types of budgets. Since workload measures and related measures of unit cost, efficiency, and productivity are more easily quantifiable than many other program measures, especially indicators of the quality or effectiveness of government programs, they are also used in program and performance evaluations as approximations (or "proxy measures") of less quantifiable indicators. In addition to their use in budgeting, program evaluation, and performance review, workload measures are used in the establishment of work allocation and performance standards, such as those for social worker or parole officer caseloads, customer service activities, and responses to citizen inquiries.

Glen Hahn Cope

BIBLIOGRAPHY

Aronson, J. Richard, and Eli Schwartz, eds. 1981. *Management Policies in Local Government Finance.* Washington, DC: International City Management Association.

Axelrod, Donald, 1988. *Budgeting for Modern Government.* New York: St. Martin's.

Burkhead, Jesse, 1956. *Government Budgeting.* New York: John Wiley.

Lynch, Thomas D., 1979. *Public Budgeting in America.* Englewood Cliffs, NJ: Prentice-Hall.

Mikesell, John L., 1995. *Fiscal Administration: Analysis and Applications for the Public Sector,* 4th ed. Belmont, CA: Wadsworth.

Z

ZERO-BASED BUDGETING.

A management-oriented system in which executive branch agencies develop budget requests at different funding and service levels for each activity or program and present the requests in order of decreasing benefit to the agency. It is intended to improve efficiency in allocating available resources. The most important features of the system are decision packages and the ranking process. As a budgeting reform it often has been characterized as an alternative to incrementalism, but in practice it is a refined form of incrementalism.

From Texas Instruments to Washington via Georgia

Zero-based budgeting was developed for Texas Instruments by Peter Pyhrr in 1969. Garland, Texas, was the first city to use it, followed by Wilmington, Delaware, and numerous other cities. It was adopted by Georgia for the 1973 fiscal year, by New Jersey and Texas shortly thereafter, and by the end of the decade more than half the states had adopted some version of zero-based budgeting. President Jimmy Carter, who had introduced zero-based budgeting as governor of Georgia, made it the budgeting system of the federal government during 1977–1981. In 1962, the U.S. Department of Agriculture used a variant of zero-based budgeting to prepare the 1964 fiscal year budget, but results were disappointing. Sluggish economic conditions of the 1970s made many governments receptive to a budget system that promised greater efficiency in the allocation of available resources.

Decision Packages and Ranking Process: The Core Techniques

The core techniques of zero-based budgeting are decision packages and the ranking process. Agencies begin the zero-based process by identifying cost-centers, agency subunits, or programs for which it is feasible and appropriate to assign costs for activities or services. Decision packages are prepared for each cost center. Decision packages provide to management at the next higher organization level the following kinds of information: a statement of goals, a description of the work program by which goals are to be achieved, a statement of benefits expected from activities or services in relationship to costs, an assessment of alternative methods of achieving goals, alternate levels of funding for the decision package, and a statement of the consequences of not funding the decision package. Decision packages also may contain line-items. Zero-based budget-ing is compatible with various budget formats, such as the line-item format in Georgia or the program format in Idaho.

The requirement of alternate funding levels is one of the features that distinguishes zero-based budgeting from other forms of budgeting. Decision packages typically contain at least three funding levels: minimum–below the current level of operations; continuation–maintenance of current operations; and improvement–activities of services not funded in the previous budget. Labels identifying the different funding levels may vary among governments, but meanings tend to be quite similar. Continuation level sometimes is called "current," or "maintenance," level, and improvement level sometimes is called "enhancement" level. Operational definitions may be more specific. For example, in Georgia, the minimum level was defined as a level of effort below which it would no longer be feasible or realistic to operate the program at all. The current level was defined as a level of effort that represented continuance of the previous year's objectives. Salary and price increases were to be reflected in that calculation while nonrecurring costs were to be eliminated. The improvement level was a higher level of spending for ongoing programs. More than one improvement level of funding could be prepared in a decision package. Each level of effort is expressed in terms of objectives and costs associated with achieving those objectives. Pyhrr noted that the advantage of requiring decision packages to contain different levels of effort and funding is that higher-level managers may chose from among alternate levels rather than having to arbitrarily reduce, request reworking, or reject the only funding level presented in a request. Defining the minimum level has posed a special problem for many governments. Although there is agreement that minimum is a funding level below the base (the funding level of the previous year), governments differ from each other in whether they permit agencies latitude to define the minimum or whether a fixed level such as 75 or 85 percent is specified as the minimum level for all agencies.

Perhaps the most unique feature of zero-based budgeting is the ranking process. Each decision package is ranked in order of decreasing benefit to the agency. When ranking, managers usually give higher priority to the packages that satisfy essential operating requirements and lower rankings to more discretionary packages. Minimum-level requests are placed higher than current-level requests, and current-level requests for most cost centers tend to be ranked ahead of improvement level requests. Each funding level for a decision package may be identified by a priority number for that package such as 1 of 3, 2 of 3, and 3 of 3 (for a decision package containing three funding levels). For example, if a budget request from a state agency that performs inspections of banks and thrift institutions contained only three activities–administration, inspections, and training—three decision packages each consisting of three funding levels would be entered into the ranking process. The minimum level the inspections decision package might be designated 1 of 3, the current level designated 2 of 3, and the improvement designated 3 of 3. Decision packages for administration and training would be arrayed in a similar manner. However, packages need not always be in the same relationship to each other in the ranking process. For example, if at the minimum level the packages were ranked as inspections, administration, and training, they could be ranked at the current level as inspections, training, and administration, and at the improvement level as administration, training, and inspections. It is important to note that although many governments would characterize the situation described in this example as three decision packages each consisting of three funding levels, some governments would characterize it as nine decision packages. This difference is inconsequential for the zero-based budgeting process as long as the language conventions are understood by those who need to know.

The budget format in Georgia makes available to decisionmakers a cumulative total for each decision package entered into the rank order expressed as a percentage of the previous year. When the first decision package is entered into the ranking, the cumulative total increases from 0 to perhaps 5 or 10 percent. In this sense, the budget might be considered to be zero based. As decision packages (including funding levels) are entered into the ranking, typically minimum ahead of current and both ahead of improvement, decisionmakers can observe the consequence of each additional package entered. For example, they know that if they recommend the funding of a 13th ranked package, the cumulative total will be increased from perhaps 108 percent (at the 12th ranked package) to perhaps 110 percent of the previous year's level. The consequence of recommending the 13th ranked package (which may be an improvement-level for a particular program) is thus known to be an increase of 2 percent over the next highest package. It also is known that a recommended funding at this level will constitute an increase of 10 percent over the previous year's level for the agency. The rankings depict incremental levels of effort. In practice, the effect of this process is to reduce the number of packages receiving close consideration. Budget analysis tends to focus on the lowest-ranked, current-level packages and the highest-ranked, improvement-level packages, those falling somewhere between the 90 and 110 percent levels. It is in this range that existing programs no longer in accord with organizational priorities might be reduced in order to reallocate resources to higher priority programs.

In the early days of zero-based budgeting there were instances of managers engaging in gamesmanship to thwart the intent of the system. High-priority packages were ranked low with the hope that if they were funded, all packages ranked above them also would be funded. Favorite but low priority programs were included in minimum-level packages to protect them. However, ranking rules quickly emerged to prevent such games.

The original version of zero-based budgeting, which was adapted from industry to governments, emphasized the importance of including in each decision package information about alternate ways of achieving program objectives. This feature tended not be taken seriously by government managers who often are stakeholders in existing practices and too busy during budget season to consider program alternatives.

As decision packages move to higher levels in the organization, they are consolidated with packages from other agency subunits and programs and ranked in order of decreasing benefit to the agency. Consolidation of rankings usually stops at the department level and is not attempted governmentwide where data aggregation becomes less meaningful and trade-offs among departments with different functions and responsibilities are quite difficult.

Zero-Based Budgeting: The Caricature

The initial claims made on behalf of zero-based budgeting were impressive but exaggerated. No agency would be able to assume continued funding for programs; each program would be challenged to justify its existence during each budget cycle; and every item included in a proposed budget would need to be justified.

The label was in many ways its own worst enemy. The label implies *tabula rasa* budgeting—an approach that wipes the financial slate clean at the beginning of each fiscal year by assuming that an agency has no base from the previous year upon which to build its budget request for the forthcoming year. According to such an interpretation, each agency would build its budget requests from zero without referring to the past as either guide for or constraint upon the future. Taken literally, a zero-based budget would mean no base at all. Students of public budgeting easily recognized the absurdity of such a characterization, but several statements by Jimmy Carter both as governor of Georgia and as presidential candidate gave credence to the most exaggerated caricature of zero-based budgeting. However, in actual practice it is substantially different from its caricature.

Alternative to Incrementalism? Not!

Zero-based budgeting was billed as a rational decision-making alternative to incrementalism, but in practice it is a refined form of incrementalism. In incremental budgeting, the funding level of the previous year (base) is the starting point. Agencies pursue strategies to protect, increase, and expand the base. Budget reviewers do not systematically examine activities and programs included in the base. Instead, they focus on agency requests for increments of increased funding and requests for new program initiatives. The requirement that agencies prepare minimum-level funding requests to some extent challenges incrementalist strategies, but in practice program managers tend to use the minimum decision package as an opportunity to argue against reductions in the base by citing the negative consequences of having to operate with only minimal-level funding. Similarly, the requirement that agencies prepare current-level funding requests tends to be used by program managers to argue for protection of the base. Agencies tend to use improvement-level funding requests to argue for increases in program funding. Minimum, current, and improvement decision packages amount to increments of proposed spending. When all decision packages are arrayed in rank order, it facilitates rather than discourages incremental decisionmaking. Budget reviewers are able to focus on current-level decision packages just below the base and improvement packages above the base, consider them in the context of available revenue, and decide if selected improvement requests can be funded within revenue constraints without denying current-level requests or if selected current-level requests must be denied in order to fund additional improvement requests. Because minimum-level packages tend to be ranked higher (i.e., considered more essential) than current-level packages and both tend to be ranked higher than improvement packages, the tendency to focus decisionmaking on the lowest-ranked current packages and the highest-ranked improvement packages substantially decreases the probability that most current-level packages and any minimum-level packages will be excluded. This procedure is not an alternative to incrementalism; it is a refined form of incrementalism.

Early versions of zero-based budgeting contained a feature known as the cut-off line. That line represented a level of funding decided upon by policy level officials. All decision packages ranked above the line would be recommended to the legislature for funding, whereas those falling below the line would not be recommended. In principle, the cut-off line could be moved upward or downward to include more or fewer packages depending upon the availability of resources. Ideally, the cut-off line was to be an automatic decision tool for top-level officials to adjust funding levels as resources expanded or contracted. However, it did not work well in practice. The weakness in that feature of zero-based budgeting was that it assumed that priority rankings would not change with changes in the availability of resources. However, changes in the level of resources available to agencies will generally occur somewhere in the range of lowest-ranked current packages or highest-ranked improvement packages. Faced with the possibility of not having a high-ranked

improvement package funded as the result of a negative shift in the cut-off line, agencies might prefer to reduce the cost estimate of one or more of their current packages in order to fund a high-priority improvement package. Or an agency might be willing to reduce the resource levels originally requested for some high-priority improvement packages in order to fund a greater number of improvement packages. For these reasons, the cut-off line turned out to be an unrealistic method for determining funding levels. Recosting individual decision packages works better, especially when funding levels must be adjusted downward. Experience with the cut-off line provides additional evidence that in zero-based systems, budgeting decisions continue to be incremental.

Achievements

Pyhrr recognized that in government, it is not realistic to expect from zero-based budgeting major cost savings or even major reallocations within budgets. Budget decisions are the products of political pressures and constraints exerted by actors and events outside of agencies. Constitutional or statutory requirements, public expectations that service levels will not be reduced from one year to the next, demands from interest groups concerned with the funding of new programs and the protection of existing ones, legislative support for programs that benefit the districts and constituencies of individual members, the requirements for state and local governments of intergovernmental grant-in-aid programs—especially unfunded mandates and uncontrollable spending at the federal level—particularly entitlement programs, present a formidable constraint on the ability of a budget reform technique to achieve cost savings or fund reallocations.

The most frequently cited advantage from zero-based budgeting is that it improves the quantity and quality of information available to managers about agency operations. As a bottom-up approach with greater participation in budget preparation, it presents to managers at each organizational level information through the ranking process that informs them of projected costs and expected benefits at each funding level.

THOMAS P. LAUTH

BIBLIOGRAPHY

Draper, Frank D., and Bernard T. Pitsvada, 1981. "Zero-Base Budgeting After Ten Years." *Public Administration Review*, vol. 41 (January-February): 76–83.
Hebert, F. Ted, 1977. "Zero-Based Budgeting in Historical and Political Context." *Midwest Review of Public Administration*, vol. 11 (September): 163–181.
LaFaver, John D., 1974. "Zero-Base Budgeting in New Mexico." *State Government*, vol. 47 (Spring): 108–112.

Lauth, Thomas P., 1978. "Zero-Base Budgeting in Georgia State Government: Myth and Reality." *Public Administration Review*, vol. 38 (September-October): 420–430.

Lauth, Thomas P., and Stephen C. Reick, 1979. "Modifications in Georgia Zero-Base Budgeting Procedures: 1973-1980." *Midwest Review of Public Administration*, vol. 13 (December): 225–238.

Moore, Perry, 1980. "Zero-Base Budgeting in American Cities." *Public Administration Review*, vol. 40 (May-June): 253–258.

Pyhrr, Peter A., 1970. "Zero-Base Budgeting." *Harvard Business Review*, vol. 49 (November-December): 111–121.

———, 1977. "The Zero-Base Approach to Government Budgeting." *Public Administration Review*, vol. 37 (January-February): 1–8.

Scheiring, Michael J., 1976, "Zero-Base Budgeting in New Jersey." *State Government*, vol. 49 (Summer): 174–179.

Schick, Allen, 1978. "The Road from ZBB." *Public Administration Review*, vol. 38 (March-April): 177–180.

———, 1979. *Zero-Base 80: The Status of Zero-Base Budgeting in the States.* A Report for the National Association of State Budget Officers and the Urban Institute, Washington, DC (December): 1–48.

Schick, Allen, and Harry Hatry, 1982. "Zero-Base Budgeting: The Manager's Budget." *Public Budgeting and Finance*, vol. 2 (Spring): 72–87.

Singleton, David W., Bruce A. Smith, and James R. Cleaveland, 1976. "Zero-Based Budgeting in Wilmington, Delaware." *Governmental Finance*, vol. 5 (August): 20–29.

U.S. General Accounting Office, 1979. *Streamlining Zero-Base Budgeting Will Benefit Decisionmaking.* Report to the Congress of the United States, Washington, DC (September 25): 1–56.

ZONING. The method used by municipal governments to designate areas for different forms of land use and to control the intensity of use and the bulk of the building on a particular site. A municipality's zoning ordinance includes a map and accompanying text. Zoning maps are official city documents that designate the boundaries of each zoning district, as well as where the relevant restrictions will be applied. The municipality's territory is divided into zones of different land uses, most basically between residential, industrial, commercial, and open space. Further distinctions may be made within each of these types of land uses. Zoning ordinances often include restrictions on minimum lot size, building height, setback from property lines, and the percentage of the lot that may be covered by the building. Special zoning districts may also be established to designate historic areas, economic development areas, or other special areas.

Land use is a critical determinant of many social characteristics in a community. Land uses influence and are influenced by the availability and distribution of public services, such as roads, water, and wastewater service, and other needs. Land use therefore has an enormous effect on environmental quality because of the resource and energy consumption necessary to accommodate different densi-ties of use. A particular land use may or may not be conducive to protecting important features of the natural environment, such as critical wildlife habitat, wetlands, or floodplains. Zoning ordinances are the key public control of private land use in the United States.

Origin and Subsequent History

Zoning is an extension of the state's police power into the area of land use and is valid to the extent that it advances and protects community health, safety, and welfare. Although zoning was used in Europe during the nineteenth century, the first zoning ordinance with full municipal coverage was enacted in New York City in 1916.

Zoning laws in the United States passed through three periods of development. Urbanization in the nineteenth century and very poor housing conditions in the cities, particularly in New York, led reformers to call for minimum sunlight standards and sanitary requirements. The separation of industrial, commercial, and residential and uses from each other was another Progressive era reform but was not confirmed as a legal right of municipalities (via state authority) until 1926 in the court case *Village of Euclid v. Amber Realty Company*.

From the 1920s to the 1960s, zoning expanded its reach across the states and municipalities. New York's zoning ordinance became the model for zoning laws across the country. The United States Department of Commerce distributed it to the states as the "Standard Zoning Enabling Act" in 1924, and it remains as the basic legal framework for local regulation of land use to this day. From the 1920s to the 1960s, zoning ordinances were elaborated to separate types of development in each major use category. For example, residential zones were further divided into single-family, multifamily, duplex, townhouse, and so forth.

By the 1960s, metropolitan growth and accompanying environmental and congestion problems had led to the development of the planning profession and sophisticated techniques for forecasting growth and attending to urban design issues. Courts began to evaluate zoning restrictions on their conformance to a legally sanctioned comprehensive plan. Since many zoning ordinances and maps and the land uses themselves preceded efforts at comprehensive planning, the rationality of design principles and new knowledge of environmental circumstances were often difficult to apply.

Current trends in zoning include zoning for overall density rather than type of use (within the major categories), and paying greater attention to growth management and preserving environmental and recreation amenities. Residential density is a better predictor of overall service demand than type of housing, enabling better service planning in municipalities and school districts.

Underlying Theoretical Framework

The underlying theoretical framework for zoning relates to its purpose, legitimacy and legal basis, and its strengths and weaknesses.

Basis for Zoning

The legitimacy of government's capacity to regulate private land-use decisions continues to be a controversial matter. The need for zoning arose with urbanization and industrialization. Crowded conditions foster the need to separate land uses that would otherwise impinge on each other and to introduce minimum standards of facilities and space to protect public health, safety, and welfare. As urban areas develop, additional needs and concerns arise that lead to an elaboration and expansion of zoning regulations. Land use controls begin to be seen as ways to conserve energy, reduce pollution, properly site public utility facilities, and generally shape the quality of life, including the aesthetic experience. Inadequate land-use controls can lead to serious problems such as floods or landslides, the destruction of important natural resources, and major public health hazards from toxic contamination.

Where urbanization and industrialization of land are only projected, the protection of private property rights may outweigh support for comprehensively planning and channeling the anticipated growth. Short-term private profits easily defeat longer-range public needs. Land use thus develops in a chaotic pattern. This paradox has led many authors to conclude that zoning works well in already urbanized areas, but not in undeveloped areas. As land uses fill in and incompatible uses collide, pressure increases for planning and stricter zoning.

Zoning Law

The courts have unequivocally found zoning to be a legitimate function of local government, as long as the specific decision is not unreasonable, arbitrary, or capricious. In addition, a zoning decision must not deprive a property owner of all use of the property; otherwise the courts are likely to view the act as a taking subject to the constitutional protection of the Fifth Amendment.

Strengths and Weaknesses of Zoning

Property owners are likely to seek changes in the zoning of their property whenever the value of the permitted land use is lower than what the market would pay for a more intense land use. Variances are also relatively easy to come by in many communities, where the proposed use is not opposed by neighboring property owners. Zoning alone may be a weak tool for growth management, regional planning, or for urban redevelopment. Since in almost all cases, zoning is a function of municipal government rather than any larger jurisdiction, there can be problems associated with the narrowness of focus among decisionmakers. In many cases, interested parties such as developers and realtors serve on zoning commissions. Zoning processes are also criticized because the public is usually unaware of the cumulative effect of incremental variances and revisions.

The main benefit of zoning is that it accomplishes the separation of incompatible land uses and that is one of the main tools for implementing a community's comprehensive plan. The separation of land uses may itself come under criticism for creating monotonous and sterile residential and commercial areas. Many argue that more vital communities exhibit mixed uses of shops and housing. Although the establishment of zoning districts would seem to be the rational means to predict and control development, planning for transportation and utility construction often proceeds separately and can have a greater influence on land use.

Current Practice in the United States

Application and approval of building permits are the occasion in which zoning ordinances are enforced. Generally, development proposals that conform with ordinances are approved, whereas those that feature inconsistencies may either be disapproved or directed to seek a variance from the regulation. Zoning maps are frequently changed to accommodate development. In some areas, the practice of zoning has been made more flexible and negotiable. Instead of giving away variances or revisions, communities have adopted the practice of negotiating with developers for improvements that the developer is not legally required to provide.

Zoning is used in conjunction with a number of other land use control tools, depending on the specific problem. Site plan review, architectural review, and historic preservation regulations allow communities to pursue aesthetic and cultural values in land use. Annexation can address the problem of unregulated extraterritorial growth, and limits on the pace of growth can allow a municipality to keep up with service demands. Transfer, donation, or purchase of development rights, taxation policies, preferential tax assessments, and environmental performance standards are additional growth management techniques. Public awareness and support is an element of successful zoning enforcement, which is why periodic comprehensive planning processes are so important.

There is a discrepancy between the development theoretically allowed in a jurisdiction by its zoning ordinances and the actual development that takes place. Generally, properties are not developed to near the extent permitted by zoning ordinances. Zoning does not govern land use in isolation. A variety of other public tools and private decisions combine to result in actual land use patterns. Several variations on conventional zoning have developed to improve the practice.

Types of Local Government Zoning

A variety of specialized types of zoning have developed to make the legal structure of the conventional zoning ordinance more responsive to community development needs. The names and terminology for the specialized zoning techniques vary from state to state.

Conventional Zoning Ordinances. Zoning ordinances specify the types of land uses permitted in a municipality's zoning districts, shown on an officially adopted map. Zoning ordinances are implemented when a landowner or developer seeks to construct or modify a building structure or its layout on the property.

Zoning ordinances usually specify site layout requirements, required structure characteristics, and the allowed uses for the structure, as specified for each zoning district. The ordinance also sets out the procedures by which the zoning inspector, zoning board, and general local government must make their decisions and the process by which a landowner might appeal the decision to a higher level.

Layout requirements deal with minimum lot sizes, setbacks from the public right-of-way and adjacent properties, and more specific requirements related to the type of use. For example, ordinances for residential zoning may include driveway requirements, whereas commercial zoning ordinances may include parking lot specifications. Structure characteristics that may be specified in zoning ordinances typically include height and floor to site ratios.

Occasions arise where zoning ordinances cannot be met by the property owner without an otherwise unnecessary hardship. When zoning officers and boards find this to be the case, they may grant a "variance" to the property owner, which amounts to an official forgiveness of the discrepancy between the feature on the property and the regulation. "Area variances" usually relax one of the layout or structure requirements in response to some particular characteristic of the lot. "Use variances" involve a lot-specific permit to use a site in a way other than that specified for the rest of the zoning district. Some states do not permit the granting of use variances. Zoning ordinances often anticipate classes of circumstances that would likely lead to variances. The ordinance will specify conditions that will automatically grant a "special exception," "special use permit," or "conditional use permit." The meaning of these is the same: It permits a deviant use when certain facts are found to exist. There is no legal basis for requiring property owners to change their land use simply because their property is zoned for a different land use. Such property is considered a permitted "nonconforming" use.

Planned Unit Development (PUD). Areas zoned for Planned Unit Development are large unbuilt areas of a minimum size that invite developers to construct integrated neighborhoods that will be reviewed as a single entity. Often PUDs are designed with a mix of residential and commercial uses. PUD zoning often allows relief from the conventional development standards (structure types, etc.) that would apply to single lot development in exchange for certain concessions. The system is flexible and provides vested rights to both the community and the developer. A variation to PUD zoning is a development agreement in which developers enter a contract with the municipality in which project specifications are written out. The contract bypasses the conventional zoning process.

Cluster Zoning. Cluster zoning is a variation of a PUD. Usually applied to residential developments, cluster zoning permits denser development in one part of the area in exchange for the rest of the development area being reserved for a public purpose. Cluster development is an efficient alternative to large lot or quarter zoning in that less length of streets and other utilities are needed to serve the houses. Although development is more intense, a larger block of open space is seen as a good trade-off.

Incentive Zoning. Incentive zoning is offered by communities that are seeking certain kinds of development or amenities. The offered incentive might be financial or it might allow higher densities in exchange for any number of public goods, such as low- or moderate-income housing, bike paths, or even solar access. In urban areas, compromises are developed in which height restrictions are waived if the developer provides ground-level public goods such as a small park or plaza. Communities may seek the same outcomes through exactions, in which developers are required to assume some of the specific costs that the development may create. Exactions may be closely related to the development itself, like requirements for nearby road construction or expansion, or they may be fees that the community uses to replace some amenity, such as open space, that is lost due to the development.

Impact Zoning. In impact zoning systems, developers are required to state and prove the impacts of proposed land use changes in view of performance standards. Impact zoning is used primarily in communities that are very concerned about growth management and environmental quality.

Overlay Zoning. Overlay zoning provides protection for resources, either natural or cultural, that might not otherwise be protected by zoning ordinances. They protect specific area and are also known as "special districts."

Performance Zoning. Performance zoning is relatively new, but provides more flexibility because it is based on maximum density rather than type of housing or type of commercial use. Density restrictions vary with environmental conditions. Performance zoning reduces the impulse to amend zoning district boundaries on a property-by-property basis as development fills in and the original boundaries become less meaningful.

Buffer or Transition Zoning.   Buffer zoning allows for a smooth transition of land use between disparate uses. In comprehensive planning for new developments, an effort might be made to place higher-density housing between low-density housing and commercial areas or a smaller vegetated buffer of open space.

State and Federal Zoning.   Higher-level control over private land use has grown with increasing awareness of environmental concerns, particularly the need to protect relatively fragile landscape features. Land-use problems that have led to regulatory policy include the loss of agricultural land, wetlands and coastal zones, floodplain development, surface mining, and the preservation of forest, desert, and other ecosystems for biodiversity and recreation. States have adapted various types of zoning regulations depending on their physiography and their overall political willingness to impose control on private property rights. For example, some states permit local governments to establish agricultural zoning to preserve farming as a viable economic activity. Hawaii, Vermont, Oregon, and Washington have taken the lead in establishing or requiring complete coverage of land-use zoning within the state. Federal government agencies are involved in boundary determination and regulations for wetlands and coastal zones and floodplains.

Variations in Regimes

The federal system of the United States allows for local control of land use through planning and zoning, but there are also state, regional, and federal controls. The state's greatest impact is indirect, through plans to develop infrastructure, especially roads. Regional urban organizations such as councils of government have planning responsibilities for transportation, land use, and environmental quality in metropolitan areas. Many federal policies affect land use, including but not limited to the National Environmental Policy Act, The Clean Water Act, the Clean Air Act, the Coastal Zone Management Act, the Wild and Scenic Rivers Act, and the Intermodal Surface Transportation and Energy Act. Western European land use regulations tend to be more centralized (see **comprehensive plan**).

LISA S. NELSON

BIBLIOGRAPHY

Baldwin, John H., 1985. *Environmental Planning and Management.* Boulder, CO: Westview.

Berg, Norman A. 1989. "Land Use: What You Need to Know." In Benjamin C. Dysart, III, and Marion Clawson, eds., *Public Interest in the Use of Private Lands.* New York: Praeger.

Buck, Susan J., 1991. *Understanding Environmental Administration and Law.* Washington, DC: Island Press.

Kelly, Eric Damian, 1993. *Managing Community Growth.* Westport, CT: Praeger.

Levy, John M., 1991. *Contemporary Urban Planning,* 2d ed. Englewood Cliffs, NJ: Prentice-Hall.

Wright, Robert R., And Susan W. Wright, 1985. *Land Use,* 2d ed. St. Paul: West Publishing.

Index

Boldface page numbers indicate an article title. At the bottom of each page is a key that locates pages according to volume.

A

AAFRC Trust for Philanthropy, 109
Abbasyah caliphs, 1205-6
Abbot, Carl, 397
Abbott Laboratories v. Gardner, 1988, 1999, 2000
An ABC Manager's Primer (Cokins, Stratton, and Helbling), 550
Abdulrahman-al Tawail, Mohammed, 1151
Abel v. United States, 66-68
Abel-Smith, Brian, 854
Aberbach, Joel D., 1733
Abilene Cotton Oil Co. v. Texas and Pacific R.R. Co., 1737-38
Ability to pay, **1-2**
Abney, Glenn, 96, 97, 1031, 1287
Abood v. Detroit Board of Education, 2307
Aboriginal Tent Embassy of 1972 (Australia), 1129
Abortion, 1960-63
Absenteeism, **3**
Absolute immunity, **3-6**
Absolute poverty, 1729
Abstract reasoning *(theoria)*, 63
Abu Baker, 1203
Abuse of authority, 940-41
    See also Authority
Accidental adversaries pattern, 471
Accountability
    APA provisions on, 2008
    of British civil servants, 2405-6
    corporatization and, 541-42
    in democratic systems, 9
    described, **6**
    governance problems and, 6-9
    hierarchical, 9
    insuring, 2141-42
    legal/political/professional, 9-10
    of public authorities, 1812-13
Accountability systems, 10-11
Accounting
    cost, 549-51
    described, **11-12**
    functions of, 14
    government, 998-1002
    management, 15, 1342-44
    records of, 12

structure and classification of, 12
Taylor System of, 2038
unified budget and national income, 2301-2
    See also Budgeting
Accounting bases, 13-14
Accounting, Organizations, and Society (Hofstede), 1336
Accounting processes, 14
Accounting reports, 14-15
Accounting Systems Division (GAO), 970
Accounting transactions, 12-13
Accrual accounting, 1000
Achaemenid Persian administration, 1641-44
Achebe, Chinua, 53
Acheson, Dean, 2388
Achievement, affiliation, and power needs theory, 1100
Achievement motivation culture, 110
The Achieving Society (McClelland), 2393
Acker, Joan, 451, 965, 966, 967
Ackerman, Susan Rose, 939
Ackoff, Russell, 540, 1147
Acquired immunodeficiency syndrome (AIDS), 1054
Acquired immunodeficiency syndrome (AIDS) policy, 15-17
Acronym, **17-18**
Act of Settlement of 1701 (England), 2047
Action for annulment (Court of Justice), 576-77
Action channels, 923
Action for damages (Court of Justice), 577-78
Action for default (Court of Justice), 577
Action for failure to act (Court of Justice), 577
Action learning, **18**
Action research (AR), **18-21**
Action theory, **21-23**
Action Theory for Public Administration (Harmon), 509
Active listening, **23-24**
Activist approach, 505
Activity-based costing (ABC), 550
Ad hoc balancing test, 168

Ad Hoc Commission on Descriptive Standards (1989), 126
Ad hoc volunteerism, 2367
Ad-hocracy, 2185
Adab al-Donia Wa al-Deen (al-Marwardi), 101
Adams, Elsie B., 44
Adams, Gerry, 2109
Adams, Guy B., 607, 1575, 2341
Adams, Samuel Hopkins, 1436
Adamson v. California, 196
Adaptive managers, 11
Addams, Jane, 2083, 2200
"Additional Perspectives" (Filer Commission), 886
Adenauer, Konrad, 390, 807, 1426
Adjective Check List (ACL), 340
Adjudication, **24-27**
Adjusted gross income (AGI), 1102
Administocracy, **27-29**
Administration
    American tradition of, 109-14
    arts, 128-33
    contributions of Omar ibn-äl-Khattab to, 1537-39
    corrections, 542-45
    described, **29-32**
    in developing African countries, 52-55
    environmental, 75
    financial, 887-91
    of fund-raising development, 670-74
    German tradition of, 974-79
    Indian tradition of, 1115-20
    Islamic tradition of, 1201-6
    Japanese culture of, 1207-9
    judicial, 1228-33
    Latin American tradition of, 1254-61
    Malaysian tradition of, 1327-28
    Mexican tradition of, 1386-96
    Persian/Iranian tradition of, 1640-46
    police, 1677-80
    rational model of, 1556-57
    seizure and arrest powers of, 66
    solid waste, 2089-91
    of space activities, 2100-2101
    tax, 2208-11
    of telecommunications operations, 2244-45
    user fee considerations by, 2322-23

Cahn, Edgar, 2353
Cahn, Jean Camper, 2353
Caiden, Naomi, 289, 462, 464, 548
Cain, Peter, 1088
Cairo Guidelines, 777
Caius Piso, 1037
Calder v. Bull, 402, 823, 2012
Caldera, Rafael, 391
Caldwell, Lynton Keith, 113, 778, 779, 785
California Monthly, 981
California Natural Death Act of 1976, 1995
California Savings and Loan Association v. Guerra, 695
California v. Adamson, 196
California v. Chimel, 70
California v. Hodari D, 69-70
California's Proposition 4, 622
California's Proposition 13, 226, 622-23, 1142, 1146, 1333, 1762, 2132, 2226
Calingaert, Michael, 2270
Callahan, Kathe, 186, 982, 1763
Callender, Guy, 95, 1768, 1886, 1889, 2172
Callières, François de, 679, 681
Cambridge Journal of Economics, 1799
Camp v. Association of Data Processing Organizations, 2123
Campaign management, **323-24**
Campaign for Wellesley, 2088
Campaigns
   capital, 337-38
   charitable organizations and political, 373
   media coverage/publicity of, 323
   strategic plan for, 323
Campbell, Donald T., 351, 352
Campbell, Enid, 528
Campbell, John, 463
Campbell, Joseph, 970
Campbell, Judith, 1072
Canada
   administrative reforms in, 1857
   asymmetrical federalism in, 146-47, 148
   circuit riders used in, 393
   civil law codes of, 400-401
   colonial liberalism of, 420
   community policing in, 446
   conflict of interest issue in, 484
   constitution "override" provision of, 502
   constitutional reform in, 506, 507
   contemporary policing in, 1680
   crime policy in, 599
   end-of-life treatment in, 1996
   multiculturalism in, 1445
   multiculturalism policy of, 1446
   new liberalism of, 421

political regionalism in, 1940-42
prime minister's office in, 1738-39
prostitution policy in, 1780
public service accountability in, 1253-54
state governments of, 2128
TAS and, 74-75
tax laws of, 371
women's policy machinery in, 963
Canada-United States Free Trade (Whaley and Hill), 2271
Canadian administrative law, 59
Canadian Broadcasting Corporation, 1816, 1817
Canadian Employment Equity Act of 1986, 1445
Canadian House of Commons, 1599
Canadian interest cost (CIC), 1450
Canadian International Development Agency (CIDA), 676
Canadian Journal of Economics, 1801
Canadian Journal of Political Science, 1801
Canadian Multiculturalism Act of 1989, 1444
Canadian Public Administration, 1798, 1801
Canadian White Paper of 1969, 1129
Cannon v. Davidson, 726
Cannon, Walter, 2179
Canon law, **324-29**
Canon Law Code of 1983, 326-28
Capacity building, **329-30**, 673
The Capacity to Budget (Schick), 274
The Capacity to Govern: A Report to the Club of Rome, 712, 713
Capital
   cost of borrowing, 177-78
   human v. physical, 1074-75
   postmodern forms of, 1727-28
Capital budget with geographical mapping element, 263
Capital budgeting, **330-36**, 804-6, 1343
Capital campaign, **337-38**
Capital Cities Cable, Inc. v. Crisp, 646
Capital improvement program (CIP), 1449
Capital improvement project information budget format, 265, 267
Capital investment programs (CIPs), 339-40
Capital investments, **338-40**
Capital maintenance concept, 999
Caplan, Gerald, 601
Caputo, Janette S., 314
Cárdenas, Lázaro, 1389
Cardoso, Fernando Henrique, 1258
Cardozo, Benjamin, 196-97
Career counseling, **340-42**
Career development, **342-44**
Career ladder, **344-47**
Career plateau, 347

CareerPoint, 342
Carey, Henry, 1040
Carey, John, 2051
Carey, Matthew, 1040
The Cargo of the Brig Aurora, Brunside, claimant v. United States, 658
Carlos III, Emperor, 1386
Carlos V, Emperor, 1386
Carlson v. Green, 2262, 2263
Carlyle, Thomas, 1477, 1915, 2051
Carlzon, R., 1887
Carnavale, David, 1375
Carnegie, Andrew, 930, 1501, 1663, 1665, 1666, 2359
Carnegie Commission Inquiry, 1815-16
Carnevale, David G., 1587, 2192
Carolina Environmental Study Group v. Duke Power Co., 2125
Carr v. Baker, 1226, 1235
Carrington, Keith, 2115
Carrington, Lord, 1410
Carroll, Archie, 1293
Carroll, James, 2411
Carroll, Mary Elizabeth, 1554
Carson, Rachel, 778, 787, 1017, 1491
Carter, Jimmy, 33, 310, 483, 559, 748, 827, 830, 873, 1048, 1070, 1846, 1956, 2099, 2193
Carter, Neil, 1632
Carter White House Conferences on Families, 857
Cartwright, Dorwin, 1019
Carty, Peter, 339, 340
Carvath, D. L., 22
Carver, John, 799
Case statement, **348-49,** 836
Case study, **349-52**
Casey v. Planned Parenthood, 1963, 1998
Cash accounting, 1000
Cash forecasting, 354-55
Cash management, **353-55**
Cash mobilization, 354
Cassin, René, 1179
Castles, Stephen, 1446, 1677
Catch 22 (Heller), 43
Categorical constraint, 1006
Catholic Bishop of Chicago v. NLRB, 727
Catholic social doctrine, 2188
   See also Roman Catholic Church
Catholic Social Services v. Reno, 1988, 1989
CATO Journal, 1799
CATO Policy Report, 1798
Causality, **356-57**
Cause groups, 1160
Cause-related marketing (CRM), **357-58,** 670
Cawson, Alan, 36
Cayer, N. Joseph, 3, 361, 405, 465, 764, 950, 1272, 1975, 2293, 2314

Volume Key: **1** 1-626; **2** 627-1240; **3** 1241-1900; **4** 1901-2436.

2445

Cohagan, John, 1544
Cohen, Arthur, 1063
Cohen, David, 1279
Cohen, Julius Henry, 1811
Cohen, Michael, 1907
Cohen, Raymond, 682
Coke, Edward, 2011
Coker, Richard, 1712
Cokins, Gray, 550
Cold War, 474, 498, 683
Cole, G. D. H., 853, 854
Cole, Kathleen, 2365
Cole, Margaret, 853
Cole, Michele T., 173, 1274, 1963
Coleman, James, 1314, 1668
Coleman, William D., 35
Collaborating (Gray), 1185
Collaboration
  interorganizational, 1185-89
  interpersonal trust and, 1648-49
  nonprofit interorganizational, 1189-93
Collaborative advantage, 1187
Collaborative process, 1187-88
Collaborative substance, 1188
Collective action organizations, 144
Collective bargaining
  arbitration and, 1085-86
  costing out and, 563
  labor laws on, 1242-43
  overview of, **415-18**
Collective governance pattern, 995
Collective leadership, 2153-55
Collective responsibility, 320, **418-19**
Colleens, Michelle, 225
College of Quaestors (European
  Parliament), 815, 816
Collier's, 1436
Collins, Cardiss, 776
Collins, Jim, 133
Collins, Mary E., 616
Collins, Michele, 1342
Collor de Mello, Fernando, 1258, 1259
Colonial developmentalism, 420
Colonial liberalism, **419-21**
"Colonial Socialism in Australia"
  (Butlin), 420
Colony of the Straits Settlements, 1327
Colorado v. Wolf, 69, 1226, 1682
Columbian Exposition of Chicago
  (1893), 471
Combination Acts of 1799-1800 (UK),
  1243
Combination companies, 129
Combined Federal Campaign (CFC),
  108, 880
Combined operations, **421-22**
Command, **422-24**
Command and control model (Weber),
  1314

Commanding officer, 424
"Comment on the Commentaries"
  (Bentham), 180
Commentaries (Blackstone), 193, 402
Commentaries on the Laws of England
  (Bentham), 180
Commentaries on the Laws of England
  (Blackstone), 2047
Commerce Clause (U.S. Constitution),
  784-85
Commerce and Industry Combined
  Health Appeal (CICHA), 108
Commercial Consulate of Mexico City,
  1387
Commercial Driver License (CDL), 715,
  719
Commercialization, **424-26**
"A Commission on Organization of the
  Executive Branch of Government,"
  1069
*Commission on Private Philanthropy and
  Public Needs* (Filer Commission),
  885-87, 933, 2344
Commission on Risk Assessment and
  Risk Management, 2000-2001
Commitment, employee, **426-31**
Committee on Benevolent Associations,
  2307
Committee on Government Operations
  (1988), 378
Committee of Ministers (Council of
  Europe), 568
Committee of Permanent Representatives
  (COREPER), 636
Committee on Political Education
  (COPE), 87
Committee of the Regions (EU), 2286
Commodity Credit Corporation (CCC),
  1003, 1990
Commodity substitution bias, 513
Common Assembly (European Coal and
  Steel Community), 808
Common Cause, 1160
Common Council (UK), 298
Common foreign and security policy
  (CFSP), **431-35**
Common Foreign and Security Policy
  (Treaty of Maastricht), 639, 2284
Common Law theory, 180, 2011
Common Market, 581-82
The Common People (Cole and Postgate),
  853
Common Provisions (Treaty of
  Maastricht), 432, 2283-85
Common-law alliance (U.S. and U.K.),
  2108
The Commons, 786
Commons, John R., 170
The Commons (Lohman), 2357

Communication
  interpersonal, 1194-95
  Miles's Law and, 1405
  postmodern, 1727
  social design and, 2071
  through interviewing, 350, 1198, 1214
  trust and, 1585
  using forums for, 2155-56
Communications Act of 1934, 2241
The Communist Manifesto (Marx), 615,
  2303
Communitarianism, **435-39**
Communities Organized for Public
  Services (COPS), 397
*Communities Working Collaboratively for a
  Change* (Himmelman), 1186
Community, 436-38
Community Action Agencies (CAAs),
  2383
Community Action Program (CAP), 1487,
  2383, 2384
Community Chest, 107, 108, 878, 2307-8
Community control, **439-41,** 1487
Community Development Block Grant,
  439
Community Development Journal, 1798
Community foundations, **441-22,** 930
Community (global), 437, 762-63
Community law, 581
Community Mental Health Centers Act
  of 1963, 601, 1056
Community Nutrition Institute v. Block, 1987
Community Patrol Officer Program
  (CPOP), 445-46
Community policing, **442-47**
Community power, **447-49**
Community Power Structure, 447
Community service obligation (CSO),
  1828
Community Services Administration,
  2385
Community visioning, 2327
Comparable worth, **449-56**
Comparative Administration Group
  (CAG), 457, 464, 1993
Comparative expectation standard, 880
Comparative financial analysis, 527
Comparative public administration,
  456-60
Comparative public budgeting, **461-64**
Comparative Strategy, 1798
Comparing Public Bureaucracies (Peters),
  458
Comparison budget tool, 294
Compensating Injured Railroad Workers
  Under the Federal Employers'
  Liability Act of 1994, 2416
Compensation policy, **464-65**
Compensatory damages, 627

Volume Key: **1** 1-626; **2** 627-1240; **3** 1241-1900; **4** 1901-2436.

2449

Volume Key: **1** 1-626; **2** 627-1240; **3** 1241-1900; **4** 1901-2436.

2455

Volume Key: **1** 1-626; **2** 627-1240; **3** 1241-1900; **4** 1901-2436.

2457

Volume Key: **1** 1-626; **2** 627-1240; **3** 1241-1900; **4** 1901-2436.

2461

Volume Key: **1** 1-626; **2** 627-1240; **3** 1241-1900; **4** 1901-2436.

2463

2464

Volume Key: **1** 1-626; **2** 627-1240; **3** 1241-1900; **4** 1901-2436.

Volume Key: **1** 1-626; **2** 627-1240; **3** 1241-1900; **4** 1901-2436.

2465

Volume Key: **1** 1-626; **2** 627-1240; **3** 1241-1900; **4** 1901-2436.

2467

Volume Key: **1** 1-626;   **2** 627-1240;   **3** 1241-1900;   **4** 1901-2436.

2471

2472

Volume Key: **1** 1-626; **2** 627-1240; **3** 1241-1900; **4** 1901-2436.

Volume Key: **1** 1-626; **2** 627-1240; **3** 1241-1900; **4** 1901-2436.

2475

Morrison, Herbert, 214

Morrison v. Olson, 2049

Mörsdorf, Klaus, 325-26

Mort, Paul, 742

Morton, Frederic, 2200

Mosaddegh, Dr., 1645

Moses, Robert, 1003, **1429-30,** 1862, 1863

Mosher, Frederick C., 338, 1465, 1764, 1768, 1790, 1958, 2386, 2401

Mosher, William E., 1466

Moskop, Wynne Walker, 194, 1590, 2051

Moss, Rosabeth Kanter, 1949

MOSSAD (Israel), 1153, 1155

Mossholder, Kevin, 1020

Most-Favored Nation (MFN) principle, 691

Motivation, 1427

Motivation dynamics, 1432

Motivation and Personality (Maslow), 1364

Motivation to Work study, 1431

Motivation-hygiene theory (MHT), 1221, 1430-35

Mott v. Martin, 1986

Mouton, Jane, 1550

Moxhay v. Turk, 584

Mt. Healthy City School District Board of Education v. Doyle, 757

Mua'wayah ibn abi Suffyan, 1204

Muckrakers, **1436-37**

Muddling through, **1437-41**

Mufson, Steven, 653

Muir, John, 777, 787

Muller v. Oregon, 693, 695

Mulroney, Brian, 599, 1488, 1857

Multiattribute Utility Model, 640

Multicommunity collaboration, 1936

Multicommunity partnerships, **1442-43**

Multicriteria decision models (MCDMs), 1909

Multicultural learning, 989

Multiculturalism, **1443-46**

Multiculturalism policy, **1446-47**

Multiple linkage model (MLM), 1267-68

Multiple masters dilemma, 9, 11

Multiplier effect, 2230

Mun, Thomas, 1088

Muniak, Dennis C., 1813, 1814

Municipal Accounting and Auditing, 998

Municipal Assistance Corporation (MAC) [NYC], 623, 894

Municipal bonds
  overview of, **1447-52**
  policy and strategy, **1453-58**
  security, **1458-63**

Municipal Finance Journal, 1799

Municipal Finance Officers Association
  for the Joint Economic Committee
  of Congress, 229

Municipal Finance Officers Association (MFOA), 998

Municipal government, 796, 849-52
  See also Local governments

Municipal Government Finance Officers Association, 896

Municipal housekeeping, **1463-64**

Municipal planning, 471-73

Municipal research bureaus, **1464-66**

Municipal Securities Rulemaking Board (MSRB), 1455

Municipal security rating, 585-87

The Municipal Year Book, 1177, 2131

Munro, Paul, 528

Murdoch, Charles, 216

Murdoch, Rupert, 222

Murphree, Kim L., 584

Murray, Charles, 1731

Murray, Michael A., 316

Murray, Nancy, 43

Murray, Victor, 996, 1193

Muscat, Bernadette T., 768, 1313

Musgrave, Richard, 887

Musheno, Michael, 1851

Muskie, Edmund, 2193

Muskopf v. Corning Hospital District, 5, 1875, 2092

Muslim fundamentalists, 1155

Mussolini, Benito, 1488

"Must pass" bills, 1913

Mutty, Capt. John, 276

Mutual aspirations, 133

Mutual assured destruction (MAD), 668-69

Mutual benefit organization, **1466-69,** 2083

Mutual pledge system (England), 1677

Myers, Gustavus, 1710

Myers-Briggs Type Indicator (MBTI), 341

Mysak, Joe, 1462

"Myth, Symbols and Folklore" conference (1983), 1572

N

Nader, Ralph, 1141, 1160, 1738, 1947

Nader v. Allegheny Airlines, 1738

Nadler, David A., 1561

Naff, Katherine C., 983, 1960

Nagarlok: Urban Affairs Quarterly, 1798

Nagasaki, 1360

Nagel, Stuart S., 1543, 1547, 1706

Nagin, Daniel, 2214

Naisbitt, John, 2342

Nanus, Burt, 1577

Narcoterrorism, 2248

"Narcotic effect," 1085-1186

Nash, Pat, 1713

A Nation at Risk (National Commission on Excellence in Education), 739, 740

"Nation of joiners" syndrome, 1467

Nation-centered federalism, 872

National Abortion Rights Action League (NARAL), 1963

National Academy of Public Administration, 1216-17, 1764

National Advisory Commission on Civil Disorders (Kerner Commission), 442

National Advisory Committee on Criminal Justice Standards and Goals (1973), 1681

National Aeronautics and Space Act of 1958, 2097

National Aeronautics and Space Administration (NASA), 2035, 2094, 2096-98, 2387

National Affairs Program, 919

National Association of Counties (NACs), 573-74

National Association of Legal Aid Organizations, 1274

National Association of Letter Carriers v. the Civil Service Commission, 1715

National Association of Manufacturers (NAM), 1159

National Association for the Repeal of Abortion Laws, 1963

National Association of Schools of Public Affairs and Administration (NASPAA), 1366, 1367, 1368, 1369, 1764, 1790

National Association of State Budget Officers, 225

National Association of Suggestion Systems (NASS), 2192

National Audit Office (United Kingdom), 155, 156

National Bank (1790s), 1098

National Bank of International Trade (Mexico), 1389

National Black United Federation of Charities, 881

National Bureau of Economic Research, 945, 946

National Bureau of Standards Graduate School, 2275

National Cable Assn. v. United States, 659

National capital budgeting, 496

National Center for Charitable Statistics (NCCS), 2347-48

National Center for Health Statistics, 595

National Center for Public Productivity, 183

National Center for State Court, 1229-30

National Charities Information Bureau (NCIB), **1471-72**

Volume Key: **1** 1-626; **2** 627-1240; **3** 1241-1900; **4** 1901-2436.

2481

Volume Key: **1** 1-626; **2** 627-1240; **3** 1241-1900; **4** 1901-2436.

2485

Scott, Jacquelyn Thayer, 1376, 1488, 2354, 2362
Scott, James, 545
Scott, Richard W., 925
Scott, Sir Walter, 1501
Scott, William G., 172, 607, 1502
Scotton, Richard B., 1053
Scrivener, David, 1707
Seaboard Allied Milling Corp. v. Southern Ry. Co., 1986
The Search for Collaborative Advantage (ed. by Huxham), 1187
Searle, G. R., 1089
Seasonal unemployment, 760
SEC v. Chenery Corp., 659
Second Amendment (U.S. Constitution), 197, 597
Second Civil Service Act of 1897, 1844
Second Hoover Commission, 1070
The Second Treatise on Civil Government (Locke), 402, 1865
Second Vatican Council (1962-1965), 325, 327
Secretariat Reorganization Committee of 1947 (India), 1118
Secretary (board officer), 203
Section 701 (Housing Act of 1954), 1938-39
Section 1983 (Civil Rights Act of 1871), 5, 717, 2042-43
Sections 702/703 (Administrative Procedure Act), 5
Sector blurring, 1529
Securities and Exchange Commission (SEC), 90, 900, 1455
Securities Industry Assn. v. Clarke, 2125
Security Council of the United Nations, 305
Security documents, 943
Security-motivated cultures, 110
Seeman, Melvin, 104
Segmented equality, 2074
Seidman, Harold, 547, 1826
Seitz, Raymond, 2111
Sekwat, Alex, 1010, 1161, 1295, 2375
Seldin v. Warth, 2124
Select Committee report (1921), 829
Select Committee to Investigate Tax-Exempt Foundations and Comparable Organizations, 932
Selected Acquisition Reports (SAR), 552
Self, Peter, 35, 36
Self-assessment, 340-41
Self-declared work teams, 1923
Self-determination, 1127-28
Self-government, 1127-28
Self-hatred paradigm, 616-17
Self-managed teams, 1610-11
Self-management, 1127-28

"Self-organizing" organizations, 1568
Self-organizing theory, 1728
Self-rule plus shared rule formula, 868, 869
Seller Substitution effect, 513
Selye, Hans, 314
Selznick, Philip, 34, 530, 531, 1572
SEMATEC, 2238
Sementelli, Arthur J., 884, 1504
Seminole Tribe of Florida v. Florida, 2263
Sen, Amartya, 735
Senge, Peter M., 1137, 1560, 1577, 1582
Senior Executive Service (SES), 404, 844, 1765, 1846, **2043-44**
Seniority, 697, **2044-45**
Sensitivity training groups, 1251
Separation of powers, **2045-51**
Serial method, 1353
Serle, Geoffrey, 1419
Serrano v. Priest, 742, 1819
Service clubs, 1467, 1469
Service Efforts and Accomplishments Program, 1635
Service policing style, 1679
Services
  benefit-cost analysis of, 173-80
  equitable delivery of, 793-95
  for family support, 860
Settlement conference, 104
Settlement houses, **2051-53**, 2083
Settler societies, 1127
The Seven Faces of Philanthropy (Prince and File), 708
Seven Habits of Highly Effective People (Covey), 2257
Seven Laws of 1843 (Mexico), 1387
Seventh Amendment (U.S. Constitution), 197
Sewell, G., 2114
Sexual harassment, **2053-57**
Sexual orientation discrimination, 700-701
Seymour, Harold J., 348, 2087-88
Shadow prices, 178-79
Shaffer, John S., 182, 415, 545, 1609
Shafritz, Jay M., 43, 342, 468, 1489, 1564, 2246
Shank, John, 550
Shankland v. Washington, 660
Shannon, John, 873, 2107
Shapiro, M., 776
Shapiro, S. A., 38
Shared Savings Program, 1762
Shared services, **2057-61**
Shared vision, 1582-83
Sharkansky, Ira, 156, 284, 1895, 2203
Shaughnessy v. Pedreiro, 1988
Shaw, George Bernard, 853, 1767
Shaw, Robert B., 1563

Shays, Daniel, 111
Shays's Rebellion (1786), 111, 2226
Sheehan, William, 1713
Shelley v. Kramer, 584
Shepard, Herbert, 1548
Sheppard-Towner Act of 1921, 1055, 2053
Sherman Anti-Trust Act, 117-18, 2013
Sherman, Stratford, 211
Shields v. Utah C.R. Co., 1987
Shipan, Charles, 923
Shipbuilding Labor Adjustment Board, 559
Shkurti, William J., 1982
Shön, D. A., 1569
Shop Management (Taylor), 2254, 2255
Short, Nicette L., 2272
Shoup, Carl, 889
Shreveport Grain and Elevator Co. v. United States, 658
Shrivastava, P., 1576
Shriver, Sargent, 2383
Shugart, Matthew Soberg, 2051
Sick leave, 1272
Sidgwick, Henry, 1477
Sierra Club, 774, 778, 787, 1482
Sigelman, L., 458
Silberbauer, George, 1126
Silence to violence model, 476
Silent Spring (Carson), 787, 1017, 1491
Silva, Fabio, 1819
Silverman, David, 22, 1559
Silverstein, M., 546
Simendinger, Earl A., 314
Simeon, Richard, 867
Simeone, Joseph J., 52
Simey, T. S., 1788
Simms, Marian, 421
Simon, Dorathea Pye, 2062
Simon, Herbert Alexander, 32, 119, 127, 170, 171, 182, 315, 356, 639, 643, 835, 845, 1077, 1106, 1239, 1266, 1278, 1314, 1319, 1517, 1557, 1566, 1732, 1735, 1904, 1906, **2061-63**, 2151, 2176-77, 2340-41, 2379-80
Simon, William E., 885
Simons, Robert, 1337
Simonsen, William, 1452, 1458
Sinclair, Upton, 1436
Sinder, R. M., 2154
Sindermann v. Perry, 1223
Singer, Marshall R., 1158, 1195
Singh, A., 2111
Singh, J. V., 151
Single European Act (or European Act), 431-32, 637, 814, 818, 2026, **2063-66**
Single Family Mortgage Revenue Bonds, 1460
Single-loop learning, 1560, 1576
Sink, David W., 1189, 1373

2492

Volume Key: **1** 1-626; **2** 627-1240; **3** 1241-1900; **4** 1901-2436.

Volume Key: **1** 1-626; **2** 627-1240; **3** 1241-1900; **4** 1901-2436.

2493

Soviet Constitution, 1707
Soviet imperialism, 1089
Soviet Union, 1155, 1407, 1476, 1506, 1657, 2096, 2377
  See also Russia
Soviet Union commissars, 1706-7
Space Age Management (Webb), 2034, 2387
Space policy, **2094-2102**
Space Task Group, 2097
Spain, 1930, 1931-32
Spalding v. Vilas, 5, 1532, 2092
Span of control, 926, 1346
Spanish Constitution (1978), 1931-32
Sparta, 1964-65
The Speaker of the House of Representatives (Follet), 916
Special Analysis volume, 831
Special district budgeting, 1304
Special District Government in the United States (Bollens), 2104
Special districts, **2102-7**
Special legislative session, 1009
Special Operating Agencies (SOAs) [Canada], 1860
Special relationship, **2107-12**
  See also United Kingdom; United States
Specific Purpose Financial Reports (SPFR), 14
Speed-ups and slow-downs, **2112-15**
Spelman, William, 445
Spencer, Herbert, 1488, 1915
Spencer's Case (1583), 584
Spendout rates, 488
Spicer, Michael W., 521
Spicer v. Miller, 691
Spinelli, Altiero, 2198
Spinoff effect, 1145
Spiotto, James E., 644
The Spirit of Community (Etzioni), 437
The Spirit of the Laws (Montesquieu), 2047
Spitzer, Robert J., 841
Spoils system, **2116-17**, 2119
Spring Research Forum (1989), 2360
Sprout, Harold, 779
Sprout, Margaret, 779
Sputnik, 2033, 2096
Sputnik II, 2096
Staats, Elmer B., 154, 377, 970, **2117-18**
Stacey, Ralph, 210, 364, 365
Staff-dominant situation, 995
Staffing, **2118-19**
Stagflation, 2228-29
Stahl, Glenn, 1211, 2401
Stake, Robert E., 352
Stakeholder, **2119-21**, 2157
Stalin, Joseph V., 359, 1961
Stalker, George M., 1145, 1345, 1346
Standard & Poor's Corporation, 584, 1450

Standard operating procedures (SOPs), 60
Standard and Poor's 500, 1110
Standard Zoning Enabling Act of 1924, 2432
"Standards for Charitable Solicitations" (PAS), 1653
Standards of conduct, **2122-23**
"Standards for Ethical Conduct for Employees of the Executive Branch" (*Federal Register*), 408, 414
Standing, **2123-26**
Standing Conference on Organizational Symbolism (SCOS), 1572, 1574
Stanford Research Institute (SRI), 2119-20
Stanley, Howard, 826
Stark v. Wickard, 1987
Starr, Ellen Gates, 2083, 2200
Starr, Paul, 1048
StarWars program, 2035
"The State of American Federalism in 1979" (Gordon), 1163-64
State Audit Office, 731
State and church separation, 1953
State comprehensive planning, 473
State Dept. of Env. Reg. v. Puckett Oil, 662
State doctrine act (United Kingdom), 5
State Electricity Commission of Victoria, 1863
State enterprise zone programs, 767-68
State general sales taxes, 2223
State governments
  accounting by, 1000-1001
  balanced budget requirements for, 166-67
  best practices awards of, 184-86
  biennial budgeting by, 188-93
  budget guidance used in, 269-70
  council-manager form of, 316
  differences in operating aid systems in, 745
  estoppel and, 795-96
  federal tort law impacting, 2263-64
  financial indicators used by, 897
  fiscal-year periods of, 249
  government corporation of, 1005
  health services by, 1051
  inspectors general of, 1150
  interstate compact between, 1196-97
  line-item veto of, 1285
  OSHA under, 1522-23
  overview of, **2126-28**
  procurement by, 1749
  public education funding and, 741-42
  relationship between church and, 328-29
  response to financial emergency by, 892-95
  revenue sharing and, 1982-83

  role of governor in, 1008-10
  sovereign immunity of, 2091-94
  sunshine laws of, 2194-95
  unified budget format used in, 2302
  use of off-budget by, 1531
  See also Government
State income taxes, 1105
State and Local Cost Estimate Act of 1981, 487
State and Local Fiscal Assistance Act of 1972, 1982
State and Local Government Review, 1798
State lotteries, 1312-13
State planning and development districts (SPDDs), 1384
The State of the Poor (Morton), 2200
State reinvention, **2128-29**
State Revolving Fund (SRF), 1989
State Sector Act of 1988 (New Zealand), 1411, 1498, 1500
State Services Commission (SSC) [New Zealand], 1496
State tax amnesty programs (1982-1990), 2213
State zoning practices, 2433
State-centered federalism, 872
State-local relations, **2130-33**
State-Owned Enterprises Act of 1988 (New Zealand), 1499
State-selected sales tax, 2223
"Statement of Values," 1551
Statements of Financial Accounting Concepts (SFAC), 1000
Statewide Long-Term Improved Management (SLIM) Program (State of Arizona), 186
Statham, Anne, 967-68
Statistical lying, 1320-22
Statistics, 2076, **2133-35**
Statistics of Income Bulletin (IRS), 2215
Statue of Winchester of 1285 (England), 1677
Status of Women (Canada), 963
"The Status of Women in State and Local Government" (Eyde), 882
Statutory corporation, **2135-36**
Statutory interpretation, 51
Statutory law, 725
Stayer, R., 133
Steel, Brent S., 1222
Steele, Lisa, 70
Steele v. Louisville and N.R.R., 728
Steering the Elephant (Heritage Foundation), 38
Steffens, Lincoln, 1282, 1710
Stein, Freiherr Heinrich Fredrich Karl vom und zum, **2136-37**
Stein, Herbert, 2302

Volume Key: **1** 1-626; **2** 627-1240; **3** 1241-1900; **4** 1901-2436.

2497

Volume Key: **1** 1-626; **2** 627-1240; **3** 1241-1900; **4** 1901-2436.

2499

Volume Key: **1** 1-626; **2** 627-1240; **3** 1241-1900; **4** 1901-2436.

2503

Volume Key: **1** 1-626; **2** 627-1240; **3** 1241-1900; **4** 1901-2436.

2475

Volume Key: **1** 1-626; **2** 627-1240; **3** 1241-1900; **4** 1901-2436.

2477

Volume Key: **1** 1-626; **2** 627-1240; **3** 1241-1900; **4** 1901-2436.

2479

Volume Key: **1** 1-626; **2** 627-1240; **3** 1241-1900; **4** 1901-2436.

2481

2482

Volume Key: **1** 1-626; **2** 627-1240; **3** 1241-1900; **4** 1901-2436.

Volume Key: **1** 1-626; **2** 627-1240; **3** 1241-1900; **4** 1901-2436.

2485

Volume Key: **1** 1-626; **2** 627-1240; **3** 1241-1900; **4** 1901-2436.

2487

Volume Key: **1** 1-626; **2** 627-1240; **3** 1241-1900; **4** 1901-2436.

2489

Russia, 1506, 1657, 2095
See also Post-communist budgeting;
  Soviet Union
Russia/Commonwealth of Independent
  States (CIS) space program, 2095,
  2097
Rust v. Sullivan, 838, 1963
Rustin, Bayard, 774
Rutan v. Republican Party of Illinois, 198,
  1613, 2116-17
Ryan, Carolyn, 1523
Ryan, R. M., 846
Ryan v. Panama Refining Co., 659
Rycroft, Robert, 1565

S

S. S. Pesaro v. Berizzi Bros. Co., 4
Saarbrücken Convention (1984), 2026
Sabatier, Paul, 1094, 1096
Sabato, Larry, 1008
Sabitini, Raphael, 1501
Sacks, Seymour, 587
Sadler, John, 2046
Safe Drinking Water Act of 1974, 778,
  1057
Safe Street Act, 1012
Sage, Margaret Olivia, 930
Sage Public Administration Abstracts, 1799
Sage Urban Studies Abstracts, 1799
Sagebrush Rebellion (1979-1981), 575
Sahlins, Marshall, 1123
Said, Edward, 1089
Saint-Simon, Henri Comte de, 1718
Salamon, Lester M., 145, 2251, 2252,
  2253, 2343, 2346, 2354, 2356, 2362,
  2364
Salancik, Gerald, 1970
Salant, Tanis Janes, 574
Salary compression, 2020
Salary equity, **2019-21**
Salary-setting systems, 450-51
Salerno v. United States, 68
Sales and consumption taxes, **2021-24,**
  2223
Salinas de Gortari, Carlos, 1392-93
Salisbury, Lord, 2381
Salmon v. Burgess, 823
SALT I agreements, 474
Samuelson, Paul, 947
San Antonio School District v. Rodriquez,
  742
Sanctions, 668, 1736-37
Sander, Frank E. A., 1231
Sandoval, Jonathan, 601
Sanford, Terry, 1296
Sanger, Margaret, 1962
Sapir, Edward, 616
Sapiro, Virginia, 964

SARA Model, 445
Sargentich, Thomas O., 2050
Sarney, José, 1258, 1259
Sartre, Jean-Paul, 508
SAS logistic regressions, 152
Sasanid administration, 1644
"Satisficing," 1106, 1566, 2340
Satow, Sir Ernest, 679
Saunders, Cheryl, 504, 507
Savannah-Chatham County Public
  Schools budget, 262
Savas, E. S., 37, 535, 1591, 1592, 1594,
  1950
Saward, Michael, 530
Sawer, Marian, 964
Sawhill, Isabel V., 1730
Sawyer, Charles, 839
Sawyer v. Youngstown Sheet and Tube, 839
Sawyer, W. H., 1419
Saxbe v. Williams, 2055
Say It with Figures (Zeisel), 292
Say, J. B., 772
Sayre, Wallace S., 60, 316, 548, 1843
Say's law, 1708
Scalar chain, 1350-51
Scalia, Antonin, 660, 1227, 1228, 2014,
  2125-26
Scandinavian quality awards, 1880
Scanlon, Joseph, 1374
Scapegoating theory, 615
The Scarlet Letter (Hawthorne), 44
Scavo, Carmine, 396
Scenario development planning,
  2024-25
Schachter, Hindy Lauer, 2256
Schaffer, B. B., 529
Schafran, Lynn H., 1232
Schaps, Ronald, 869
Scharpf, Fritz, 866, 1318
Schechter Poultry Corp. v. United States, 659,
  1235
Schedler, Kuno, 1638
Scheer, Admiral Rheinhard, 914
Scheffer, Walter F., 1158
Schein, Edgar, 799, 1374, 1549, 1551,
  1559, 1573-74
Schellenberg, T. R., 125
Schelling, Thomas, 2173, 2175
Schengen agreement (1985), **2026-31**
Schengen Implementing Convention
  (1990), 2027-30, 2031
Scheurer v. Rhodes, 1532, 1876
Schick, Allen, 96, 234, 242, 274, 277, 286,
  288, 289, 297, 463, 1030, 1106-7,
  1806, 1913
Schlesinger, Arthur, Jr., 2050
Schmid, Hillel, 1289
Schmitter, Philip C., 35, 1669
Schneider, Saundra K., 723, 2057

Schoenherr, Richard, 1345, 1347
Schon, D. A., 2156
Schön, Donald, 1560, 1576, 1578
*School Board of Nassau County, Fla. v.
  Airline*, 691
School district budgeting, 1304
School of München, 325-26
School of Navarra, 325, 326
The Schooner Exchange v. McFaddon, 4,
  2093
*Schor v. Union Carbide in Commodity
  Futures Trading Commission*, 661
Schott, Richard L., 73, 74
Schroeder, Larry, 785
Schultz, George P., 885
Schultz, Theodore, 1073, 1074
Schumacher, E. F., 120, 1017
Schumaker, Paul, 350
Schuman Plan (1950), 802, 807, 1426,
  2032, 2198
Schuman, Robert, 390, 807, 1426, 2032
Schumpeter, Joseph, 772, 1089, 1506-7
Schuppert, G. F., 2353
Schurz, Carl, 546
Schutz, Alfred, 22, 508, 2390
Schwartz, Bernard, 51, 65, 66, 68, 646,
  660, 661, 662, 827, 840, 1737, 1987,
  1999, 2042, 2092
Schwartz, Eli, 339
Schwartz-Shea, Peregrine, 968, 1064
Schweiker v. Chilicky, 2263
Schweitzer, Albert, 1017
Science: The Endless Frontier (Bush), 2033
Science (behavioral), 118-19
"The Science of 'Muddling Through'"
  (Lindblom), 1278
Science, Technology, and Management
  (Groves), 1359
Science, technology, and public policy,
  2032-35
Science and Technology Studies (STS),
  2032
*Scientific Foundations of Business
  Administration* (Metcalf), 917
Scientific management, 345, 980-82,
  1043-44, 1335, **2036-40**, 2113,
  2232-33
Scientific Management School, 1220
Scientific and Technological Options
  Assessment Program (STOA), 816
Scope of review, **2040-42**
See also Judicial review
"Scope of Review" (Section 706), 646
SCOPMA (Study Committee on Policy
  Management Assistance), 1163
Scorekeeping practice, 488, 491
Scorekeeping Unit (CBO), 488
Scotland Yard, 1678
Scott, Gregory, 2246

Volume Key: **1** 1-626; **2** 627-1240; **3** 1241-1900; **4** 1901-2436.

2491

Volume Key: **1** 1-626; **2** 627-1240; **3** 1241-1900; **4** 1901-2436.

2493

Volume Key: **1** 1-626; **2** 627-1240; **3** 1241-1900; **4** 1901-2436.

2495

2496

Volume Key: **1** 1-626; **2** 627-1240; **3** 1241-1900; **4** 1901-2436.

Volume Key: **1** 1-626; **2** 627-1240; **3** 1241-1900; **4** 1901-2436.

2497

Volume Key: **1** 1-626; **2** 627-1240; **3** 1241-1900; **4** 1901-2436.

2499